1965	1967	1969	1971	1973	1975	1977	1978	1979	1980	1981	1982
492.2	575.4	694.6	751.1	1,017.2	1,065.2	1,328.1	1,496.4	1,741.8	1,912.8	2,144.7	2,039.4
46.5	47.8	58.1	52.9	81.4	79.9	115.1	132.5	154.2	145.8	158.6	108.2
5.7	5.0	4.8	4.1	4.7	4.6	5.3	5.4	5.7	4.8	4.7	3.5
58.8	62.5	65.0	69.0	73.4	74.8	78.5	79.3	79.3	79.2	80.7	80.1
3.5	2.2	0.5	4.1	3.0	3.5	1.7	1.1	0.0	−0.2	2.1	−0.8
20.6	21.9	22.9	21.6	23.4	21.3	23.0	24.2	25.0	24.3	24.1	22.6
40.3	44.0	47.6	49.7	53.5	55.8	59.6	62.7	64.9	66.3	67.2	67.1
399.5	475.1	577.6	658.9	811.2	949.1	1,180.5	1,366.1	1,500.8	1,651.8	1,825.8	1,925.8
41.2	40.6	40.6	39.9	40.7	39.5	40.3	40.4	40.2	39.7	39.8	38.9
2.63	2.85	3.22	3.63	4.14	4.73	5.44	5.87	6.33	6.84	7.43	7.86
101.52	108.02	120.75	135.58	152.77	170.28	195.30	210.15	225.35	240.77	261.54	272.74
1.25	1.40	1.60	1.60	1.60	2.10	2.30	2.65	2.90	3.10	3.35	3.35
4.54	5.61	7.96	5.72	8.03	7.86	6.83	9.06	12.67	15.27	18.87	14.86
4.28	5.07	6.67	6.16	6.84	7.99	7.42	8.41	9.44	11.46	13.91	13.00
12.9	12.3	14.3	15.0	34.4	25.5	19.9	25.2	27.4	16.1	26.9	23.8
—	—	—	—	—	73	73	83	94	98	100	94
—	—	—	—	—	47	53	58	66	75	82	86
33.2	27.8	24.1	25.6	23.0	25.9	24.7	24.5	26.1	29.3	31.8	34.4
17.3	14.2	12.1	12.5	11.1	12.3	11.6	11.4	11.7	13.0	14.0	15.0
—	0.399	0.391	0.396	0.397	0.397	0.402	0.402	0.404	0.403	0.406	0.412
26.5	30.1	36.4	43.3	71.4	107.1	120.8	142.1	184.4	224.3	237.0	211.2
21.5	26.9	35.8	45.6	70.5	98.2	151.9	176.0	212.0	249.7	265.1	247.6
5.4	2.6	0.4	−1.4	7.1	18.1	−14.3	−15.1	−0.3	2.3	5.0	−5.5
13.8	16.0	17.8	17.8	20.7	23.5	28.9	32.2	37.1	43.2	43.2	57.2
3.01	3.12	3.32	3.60	4.75	12.21	14.40	14.95	25.10	37.42	35.75	31.83

(Continued in back of book)

Seventeenth Edition

Microeconomics

Principles, Problems, and Policies

Campbell R. McConnell

University of Nebraska

Stanley L. Brue

Pacific Lutheran University

McGraw-Hill Irwin

Boston Burr Ridge, IL Dubuque, IA Madison, WI New York San Francisco St. Louis
Bangkok Bogotá Caracas Kuala Lumpur Lisbon London Madrid Mexico City
Milan Montreal New Delhi Santiago Seoul Singapore Sydney Taipei Toronto

The McGraw-Hill Companies

To **Mem** and to **Terri** and **Craig**

McGraw-Hill Irwin

MICROECONOMICS: PRINCIPLES, PROBLEMS, AND POLICIES

Published by McGraw-Hill/Irwin, a business unit of The McGraw-Hill Companies, Inc., 1221 Avenue of the Americas, New York, NY, 10020.
Some ancillaries, including electronic and print components, may not be available to customers outside the United States.

This book is printed on acid-free paper.

1 2 3 4 5 6 7 8 9 0 DOW/DOW 0 9 8 7 6

ISBN 978-0-07-327309-9
MHID 0-07-327309-0

Editorial director: *Brent Gordon*
Executive editor: *Douglas Reiner*
Developmental editor II: *Rebecca Hicks*
Media producer: *Jennifer Wilson*
Lead project manager: *Lori Koetters*
Lead production supervisor: *Michael R. McCormick*
Director of design BR: *Keith J. McPherson*
Photo research coordinator: *Lori Kramer*
Photo researcher: *Keri Johnson*
Lead media project manager: *Becky Szura*
Cover design: *Sayles Graphics*
Interior design: *Maureen McCutcheon/Kay Fulton*
Cover image: *Gettyimages Paul Harris Photographer*
Typeface: *10/12 Jansen*
Compositor: *GTS – New Delhi, India Campus*
Printer: *R. R. Donnelley*

Library of Congress Cataloging-in-Publication Data

McConnell, Campbell R.
Microeconomics : principles, problems, and policies / Campbell R. McConnell, Stanley L. Brue. -- 17th ed.
p. cm.
Includes index.
ISBN-13: 978-0-07-327309-9 (alk. paper)
ISBN-10: 0-07-327309-0 (alk. paper)
1. Microeconomics. I. Brue, Stanley L., 1945- II. Title.
HB172.M3925 2008
338.5--dc22

2006029034

About the Authors

Campbell R. McConnell earned his Ph.D. from the University of Iowa after receiving degrees from Cornell College and the University of Illinois. He taught at the University of Nebraska–Lincoln from 1953 until his retirement in 1990. He is also coauthor of *Contemporary Labor Economics*, seventh edition, and *Essentials of Economics*, first edition (both The McGraw-Hill Companies), and has edited readers for the principles and labor economics courses. He is a recipient of both the University of Nebraska Distinguished Teaching Award and the James A. Lake Academic Freedom Award and is past president of the Midwest Economics Association. Professor McConnell was awarded an honorary Doctor of Laws degree from Cornell College in 1973 and received its Distinguished Achievement Award in 1994. His primary areas of interest are labor economics and economic education. He has an extensive collection of jazz recordings and enjoys reading jazz history.

Stanley L. Brue did his undergraduate work at Augustana College (South Dakota) and received its Distinguished Achievement Award in 1991. He received his Ph.D. from the University of Nebraska–Lincoln. He is a professor at Pacific Lutheran University, where he has been honored as a recipient of the Burlington Northern Faculty Achievement Award. Professor Brue has also received the national Leavey Award for excellence in economic education. He has served as national president and chair of the Board of Trustees of Omicron Delta Epsilon International Economics Honorary. He is coauthor of *Economic Scenes*, fifth edition (Prentice-Hall), *Contemporary Labor Economics*, seventh edition, *Essentials of Economics*, first edition (both The McGraw-Hill Companies), and *The Evolution of Economic Thought*, seventh edition (South-Western). For relaxation, he enjoys international travel, attending sporting events, and skiing with family and friends.

List of Key Graphs

1.2	The Production Possibilities Curve	12
2.2	The Circular Flow Diagram	39
3.6	Equilibrium Price and Quantity	54
7.1	Total and Marginal Utility	127
8.2	The Law of Diminishing Returns	149
8.5	The Relationship of the Marginal-Cost Curve to the Average-Total-Cost and Average-Variable-Cost Curves	154
8.8	The Long-Run Average-Total-Cost Curve: Unlimited Number of Plant Sizes	157
9.3	Short-Run Profit Maximization for a Purely Competitive Firm	173
9.6	The P = MC Rule and the Competitive Firm's Short-Run Supply Curve	176
9.12	Long-Run Equilibrium: A Competitive Firm and Market	183
10.4	Profit Maximization by a Pure Monopolist	196
11.1	A Monopolistically Competitive Firm: Short Run and Long Run	213
11.4	The Kinked-Demand Curve	222
14.3	Labor Supply and Labor Demand in (a) a Purely Competitive Labor Market and (b) a Single Competitive Firm	275
23.2	Trading Possibility Lines and the Gains from Trade	446
24.1	The Market for Foreign Currency (Pounds)	468

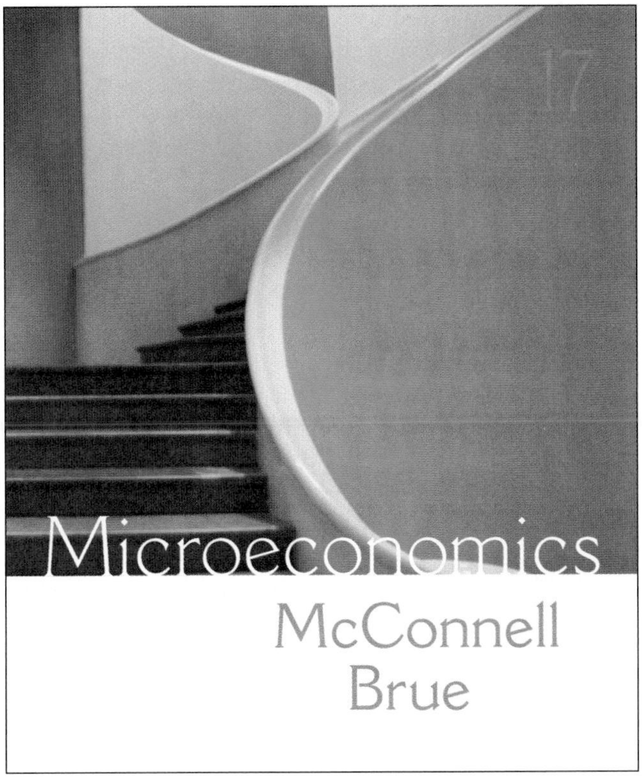

Welcome to the seventeenth edition of *Microeconomics*, the micro portion of *Economics*, the nation's best-selling economics textbook. An estimated 13 million students worldwide have now used this book. *Economics* has been adapted into Australian and Canadian editions and translated into Italian, Russian, Chinese, French, Spanish, Portuguese, and other languages. We are pleased that *Economics* continues to meet the market test: nearly one out of four U.S. students in principles courses used the sixteenth edition.

A Note about the Cover

The seventeenth edition cover includes a photograph of a staircase in the Musée des Beaux-Arts in Nancy, France. The photo is a metaphor for the step-by-step approach that we use to present basic economic principles. It also represents the simplicity, beauty, and power of basic economic models. Our goal is to entice the student to walk up the staircase. The floors above contain hundreds of years of accumulated economic knowledge, a portion of which we have captured for you here.

Preface

Fundamental Objectives

We have three main goals for *Microeconomics*:

- Help the beginning student master the principles essential for understanding the economizing problem, specific economic issues, and the policy alternatives.
- Help the student understand and apply the economic perspective and reason accurately and objectively about economic matters.
- Promote a lasting student interest in economics and the economy.

What's New and Improved?

One of the benefits of writing a successful text is the opportunity to revise—to delete the outdated and install the new, to rewrite misleading or ambiguous statements, to introduce more relevant illustrations, to improve the organizational structure, and to enhance the learning aids. A chapter-by-chapter list of changes is available at our Web site, **www.mcconnell17.com.** The more significant changes include the following.

Chapter-Level Learning Objectives

Several learning objectives have been included on the first page of each chapter. After reading a chapter, students should have mastered these core concepts. Questions in Test Banks I and II are organized according to these learning objectives, as are the narrated PowerPoint presentations.

Worked Problems

We continue to integrate the book and our Web site with in-text Web buttons that direct readers to Web site content. Specifically, we have added a third Web button consisting of a set of 50 worked problems. Written by Norris Peterson of Pacific Lutheran University, these pieces consist of side-by-side computational questions and the computational procedures used to derive the answers. In essence, they extend the textbook's explanations involving computations—for example, of the unemployment rate, the inflation rate, per-unit production costs, economic profit, and more. From a student perspective, they provide "cookbook" help for problem solving.

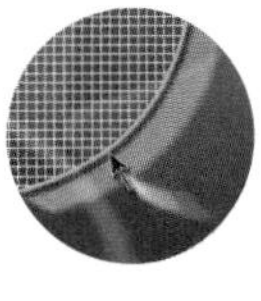

This new content joins two carryover Web buttons from the prior edition. "Interactive

Graphs" (developed under the supervision of Norris Peterson) depict more than 30 major graphs and instruct students to shift the curves, observe the outcomes, and derive relevant generalizations. "Origins of the Idea" are brief histories (written by Randy Grant of Linfield College) of 70 major ideas identified in the book. Students are interested in learning about the economists who first developed ideas such as opportunity costs, equilibrium price, the multiplier, comparative advantage, and elasticity.

New Internet Chapter

A new Internet chapter is available for free use at our Web site, **www.mcconnell17.com.** "Natural Resource and Energy Economics" (Chapter 15Web) covers topics such as the optimal rate of extraction, resource substitution, resource sustainability, oil prices, and alternative energy sources. For an outline of this chapter, see page 307 of this book.

The new Internet chapter was written by Sean Masaki Flynn. Sean is an important new member of the McConnell and Brue author team. He did his undergraduate work at USC, obtained his Ph.D. from the University of California–Berkeley (2002), and teaches at Vassar College. He is the author of the best-selling *Economics for Dummies*. We are very excited to have Sean on the authorship team, since he shares our desire to present economics in a way that is understandable to all.

The Web chapter has the same design, color, and features as regular book chapters, is readable in Adobe Acrobat format, and can be printed if desired. It is supported by the *Study Guide*, *Test Banks*, and other supplements to the book.

Consolidated Chapter

With overwhelming support of reviewers, we have consolidated the first two chapters of the prior edition into a single chapter, "Limits, Alternatives, and Choices" (Chapter 1). This new chapter quickly and directly moves the student into the subject matter of economics, demonstrating its methodology. This consolidation has the side benefit of reducing Part 1 (the common chapters in *Economics*, *Macroeconomics*, and *Microeconomics*) from six chapters to five.

Consumer Surplus, Producer Surplus, and Deadweight Loss Analysis

Our previous chapter on elasticity is now "Extensions of Demand and Supply Analysis" (Chapter 6). Along with elasticity, this chapter introduces consumer surplus, producer surplus, and deadweight loss. These topics appear again in the pure competition and pure monopoly chapters. Knowing that some instructors do not want to cover deadweight loss analysis, we have taken care to present the ideas in a way that will enable instructors to skip these insertions.

New and Relocated "Consider This" and "Last Word" Boxes

Our "Consider This" boxes are used to provide analogies, examples, or stories that help drive home central economic ideas in a student-oriented, real-world manner. For instance, the idea of trade secrets is described with the story of "cat gut" and violin strings, while McDonald's "McHits" and "McMisses" demonstrate the idea of consumer sovereignty. These brief vignettes, each accompanied by a photo, illustrate key points in a lively, colorful, and easy-to-remember way.

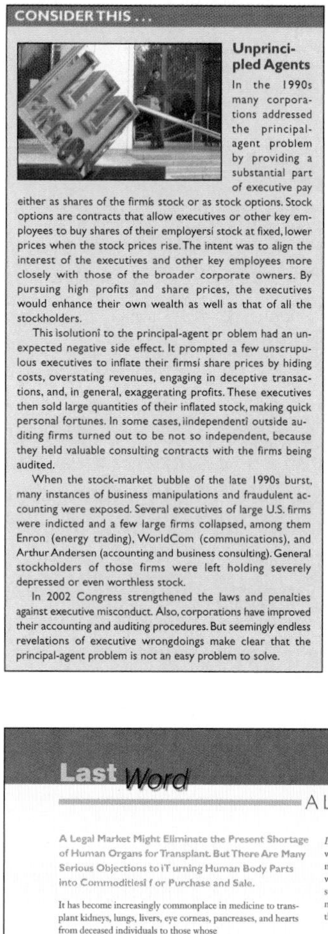

CONSIDER THIS . . .

Unprincipled Agents

In the 1990s many corporations addressed the principal-agent problem by providing a substantial part of executive pay either as shares of the firmís stock or as stock options. Stock options are contracts that allow executives or other key employees to buy shares of their employersí stock at fixed, lower prices when the stock prices rise. The intent was to align the interest of the executives and other key employees more closely with those of the broader corporate owners. By pursuing high profits and share prices, the executives would enhance their own wealth as well as that of all the stockholders.

This ìsolutionî to the principal-agent pr oblem had an unexpected negative side effect. It prompted a few unscrupulous executives to inflate their firmsí share prices by hiding costs, overstating revenues, engaging in deceptive transactions, and, in general, exaggerating profits. These executives then sold large quantities of their inflated stock, making quick personal fortunes. In some cases, ìindependentî outside auditing firms turned out to be not so independent, because they held valuable consulting contracts with the firms being audited.

When the stock-market bubble of the late 1990s burst, many instances of business manipulations and fraudulent accounting were exposed. Several executives of large U.S. firms were indicted and a few large firms collapsed, among them Enron (energy trading), WorldCom (communications), and Arthur Andersen (accounting and business consulting). General stockholders of those firms were left holding severely depressed or even worthless stock.

In 2002 Congress strengthened the laws and penalties against executive misconduct. Also, corporations have improved their accounting and auditing procedures. But seemingly endless revelations of executive wrongdoings make clear that the principal-agent problem is not an easy problem to solve.

New "Consider This" boxes include such disparate topics as fast-food lines (Chapter 1), the economics of war (Chapter 1), "buying American" (Chapter 2), ticket scalping (Chapter 3), salsa and coffee beans (Chapter 3), unprincipled agents (Chapter 4), a CPA and a house painter (Chapter 5), waste-to-oil conversion

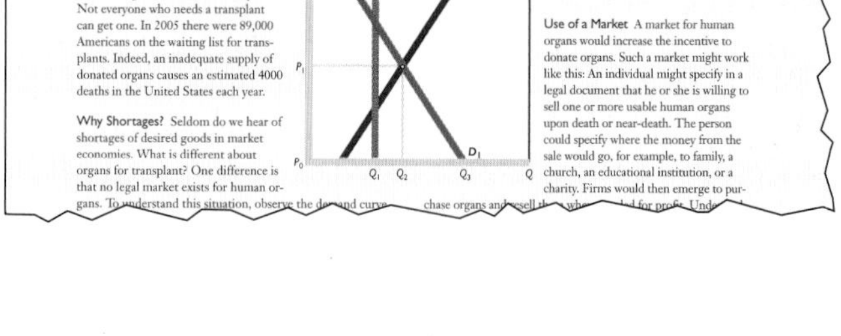

methods (Chapter 15Web), art for art's sake (Chapter 16), and the hedging of risk in agriculture (Chapter 19).

Our "Last Word" pieces are lengthier applications and case studies located toward the end of each chapter. In this edition, we included photos to pique student interest. New and relocated Last Words include those on pitfalls to sound economic reasoning (Chapter 1), a market for human organs (Chapter 3), the long-run problem of financing Social Security (Chapter 4), efficiency gains from entry (Chapter 9), the effects of economic growth of the environment (Chapter 15Web), and mandatory health insurance (Chapter 21).

Contemporary Discussions and Examples

The seventeenth edition refers to and discusses many current topics. Examples include the economics of the war in Iraq, China's rapid growth rate, the productivity acceleration, the recent profit paths of Wal-Mart and General Motors, rapidly expanding and disappearing U.S. jobs, rising oil prices, recent antitrust actions, farm subsidy programs, welfare caseloads, prescription drug coverage under Medicare, health savings accounts (HSAs), immigration impacts, large U.S. trade deficits, offshoring of American jobs, and many more.

Distinguishing Features

Comprehensive Explanations at an Appropriate Level *Microeconomics* is comprehensive, analytical, and challenging yet fully accessible to a wide range of students. The thoroughness and accessibility enable instructors to select topics for special classroom emphasis with confidence that students can read and comprehend other independently assigned material in the book. Where needed, an extra sentence of explanation is provided. Brevity at the expense of clarity is false economy.

Fundamentals of the Market System Many economies throughout the world are making difficult transitions from planning to markets. Our detailed description of the institutions and operation of the market system in Chapter 2 is even more relevant than before. We pay particular attention to property rights, entrepreneurship, freedom of enterprise and choice, competition, and the role of profits because these concepts are often misunderstood by beginning students.

Early and Full Integration of International Economics We give the principles and institutions of the global economy early treatment. Chapter 5 examines the growth of world trade and its major participants, specialization and comparative advantage, the foreign exchange market, tariffs and subsidies, and various trade agreements. This strong introduction to international economics permits "globalization" of later discussions in both the macro and the micro chapters. Then, we delve into the more difficult, graphical analysis of international trade and finance in Chapters 23 and 24.

Early and Extensive Treatment of Government Government is an integral component of modern capitalism. This book introduces the economic functions of government early and accords them systematic treatment in Chapter 4. Chapter 16 examines government and market failure in further detail, and Chapter 17 looks at salient facets of public choice theory and taxation. Part 5 of the text include issue- and policy-oriented chapters.

Stress on the Theory of the Firm and Technological Advance We have given much attention to microeconomics in general and to the theory of the firm in particular, for two reasons. First, the concepts of microeconomics are difficult for most beginning students; abbreviated expositions usually compound these difficulties by raising more questions than they answer. Second, we wanted to couple analysis of the various market structures with a discussion of the impact of each market arrangement on price, output levels, resource allocation, and the rate of technological advance. Our Chapter 12 on the microeconomics of technology is unique to principles books.

Focus on Economic Issues For many students, the chapters on antitrust, agriculture, income inequality, health care, and labor issues are where the action is centered. We guide that action along logical lines through the application of appropriate analytical tools. In this part, we favor inclusiveness; instructors can effectively choose two or three chapters from this group.

Integrated Text and Web Site *Microeconomics* and its Web site are highly integrated through in-text Web buttons, Web-based end-of-chapter questions, bonus Web chapter, multiple-choice self-tests at the Web site, online newspaper articles, math notes, and other features. Our Web site is part and parcel of our student learning package, customized to the book.

Organizational Alternatives

Although instructors generally agree on the content of principles of economics courses, they sometimes differ on how to arrange the material. *Microeconomics* includes six parts, and thus provides considerable organizational flexibility.

Some instructors will prefer to intersperse the microeconomics of Parts 2 to 4 with the problems chapters of Part 5. Chapter 19 on agriculture may follow Chapter 9 on pure competition; Chapter 18 on antitrust and regulation may follow Chapters 10 through 12 on imperfect competition models and technological advance. Chapter 22 on labor market issues (unions, discrimination, and immigration) may follow Chapter 14 on wages; and Chapter 20 on income inequality may follow Chapters 14 and 15 on distributive shares of national income.

Pedagogical Aids

Microeconomics is highly student-oriented. The "To the Student" statement at the beginning of Part 1 details the book's many pedagogical aids. The seventeenth edition is also accompanied by a variety of high-quality supplements that help students master the subject and help instructors implement customized courses.

Supplements for Students and Instructors

Study Guide One of the world's leading experts on economic education, William Walstad of the University of Nebraska–Lincoln, prepared the seventeenth edition of the *Study Guide*. Many students find the *Study Guide* indispensable. Each chapter contains an introductory statement, a checklist of behavioral objectives, an outline, a list of important terms, fill-in questions, problems and projects, objective questions, and discussion questions.

The *Guide* comprises a superb "portable tutor" for the principles student. Separate *Study Guides* are available for the macro and micro paperback editions of the text.

McGraw-Hill's Homework Manager Plus™ Homework Manager is a Web-based supplement that duplicates problem sets directly from the end-of-chapter material in your textbook. Using algorithms to provide a limitless supply of online self-graded assignments and graphing exercises, McGraw-Hill's Homework Manager™ can be used for practice, homework, and testing.

McGraw-Hill's HOMEWORK MANAGER™

All assignments can be delivered over the Web and are graded automatically. Instructors can see all of the results stored in a private grade book. Detailed results let you see at a glance how each student does on an assignment or an individual problem. Homework Manager Plus is an extension of McGraw-Hill's popular Homework Manager System. With McGraw-Hill's Homework Manager Plus™ you get all of the power of Homework Manager with an integrated online version of the text. Students receive one single access code which provides access to all of the resources available through Homework Manager Plus.

McGraw-Hill's Homework Manager Plus™ is a complete online homework solution, offering online graphing exercises, practice tests correlated with the key Learning Objectives, and full integration for Blackboard and WebCT courses.

aplia™

Aplia McGraw-Hill/Irwin and Aplia (**www.aplia.com/mhhe**) are working together to bring you high-quality content and graphing tools in economics. Aplia provides:

- High-quality problem sets.
- Detailed news analyses with exercises.
- Math tutorials with testing.
- Online synchronous experiments.

Aplia will help increase student effort and enhance greater understanding and success in the course. This new partnership enables the bundling of Aplia with McGraw-Hill economics textbooks, including the comprehensive principles

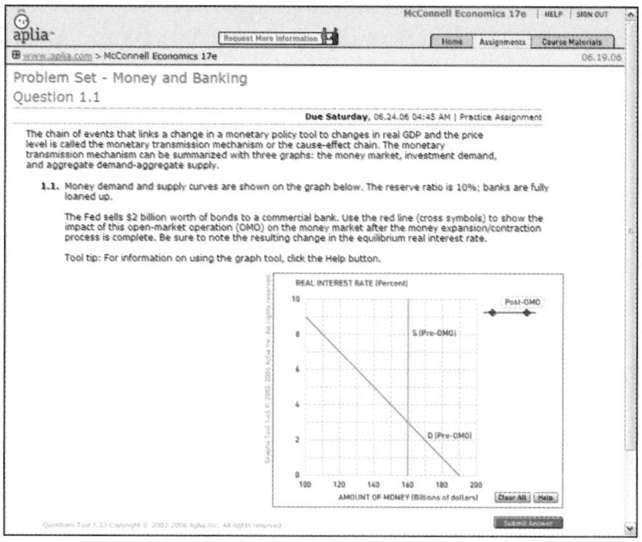

texts, one-semester splits, and the essentials books. An integrated eBook version of the text is included when access to Aplia is purchased as part of a McGraw-Hill package. New *value editions*, available directly from Aplia, include a one-color version of the complete text accompanied by full access to the Aplia application. The interactive tools and engaging materials are highly correlated to match the language and style of each McGraw-Hill book. Easy to use and set up, these new package options provide professors with even more flexibility and purchasing solutions for their students. To learn more about the McGraw-Hill/Aplia partnership, please visit **www.aplia.com.**

Online Learning Center (www.mcconnell17.com) The Web site accompanying this book contains a host of features. For example, the three kinds of highly visible "Web buttons" in the text alert the students to points in the book where they can springboard to the Web site to get more information. Students can test their knowledge of a chapter's concepts with three self-graded multiple-choice quizzes per chapter. The "See the Math" section, written by Professor Norris Peterson, enables students to explore the mathematical details of the concepts in the text. Students can also access the Solman Videos, a set of more than 250 minutes of video covering key concepts from this text. Created by Paul Solman of *The News Hour with Jim Lehrer*, the videos cover core economic concepts such as elasticity, deregulation, and perfect competition.

New to the seventeenth edition site:

- Narrated PowerPoint presentations, which students can view on the site or download to their video iPod. The PowerPoints are correlated to the key Learning Objectives for every chapter. (Premium Content)
- The Solman Videos can also be downloaded to a video iPod or mp3 player. (Premium Content)
- Standard PowerPoint Presentations, answers to Web-based questions, and self-grading tests—all specific to *Economics*.
- Optional Web chapter: "Natural Resource and Energy Economics."

Zinio eBook Experience the speed, convenience, affordability, and intelligence of Zinio eBooks (**www.textbooks.zinio.com**). Digital textbooks are exact replicas of the print version, and better. They are easy to navigate, allowing you to flip back and forth between pages, offer continual access to the Table of Contents with a toolbar button to jump directly to a chapter, topic, or page of interest. The Smart Zoom button allows you to easily zoom in and out, taking full advantage of crisp text and high-resolution diagrams and images. Rich media offer an experience beyond simply reading, with flash, video, and audio. Embedded Web links also allow you to learn more about topics of interest and, when you are finished, return to exactly where you were in the book. Find relevant information quickly and easily with the search function, which allows you to get information on specific topics, phrases, and key words. You can write electronic notes with the Zinio annotation tool as well as highlight important topics. You can also print sections in high resolution and full color. Digital textbooks will become part of your lifestyle! The Zinio reader automatically saves your textbook in your own personal library on your computer. Textbooks can be easily referenced at any time, anywhere. To learn more or to download a free sample, visit **www.textbooks.zinio.com.**

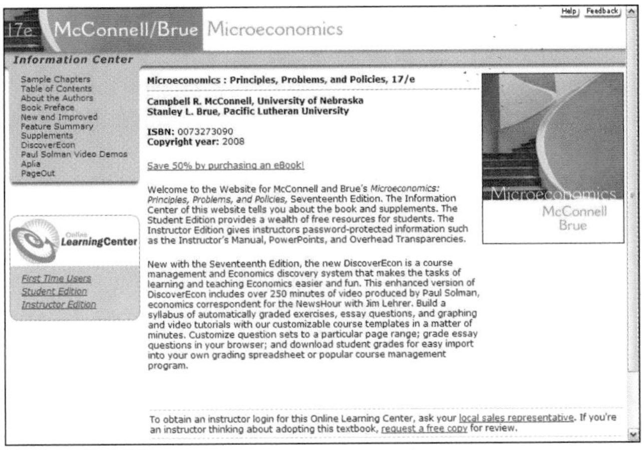

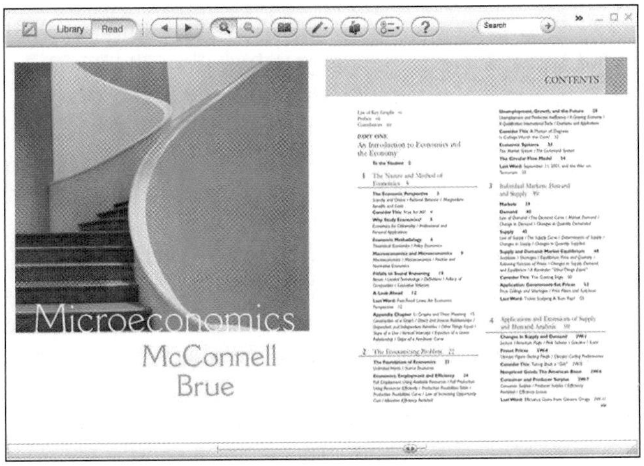

iPod Content Harness the power of one of the most popular technology tools students use today–the Apple iPod. Our innovative approach enables students to download audio and video presentations right into their iPod and take learning materials with them wherever they go. This makes review and study time as easy as putting on headphones. Visit **www.mcconnell17.com** to learn more details on available iPod content—and enhance your learning experience today. (Premium Content)

McGraw-Hill PrepCenter™ The innovative McGraw-Hill PrepCenter™ offers a dynamic Web-based solution for managing all of the digital assets that accompany this textbook. The PrepCenter serves as a digital locker for your course materials, enabling you to consolidate the resources you need into readily accessible folders that are hosted in a secure and easy-to-use online environment. To learn more about McGraw-Hill's PrepCenter™, please visit **http://prepcenter.mhhe.com/.**

Enhanced Cartridges Enhanced WebCT and Blackboard course cartridges allow instructors to manage their course and administer online examinations. Some of the new features include:

- Pretest and posttest question banks: Administer comprehensive and chapter-specific pretests and posttests to evaluate student understanding. Pre- and posttest questions are tied to the chapter learning objectives and Association to Advance Collegiate Schools of Business (AACSB) guidelines.
- Question feedback: Answer feedback directs students back to the text for concept review. Feedback comments are linked to the Narrated PowerPoint presentations by learning objective.
- Administer tests and quizzes online: You decide how students are tested. Select the questions, time limit, and feedback options.
- Narrated PowerPoint presentations: Students can view these slides on the site or download the material to their video iPod. The PowerPoints are correlated to the key learning objectives for every chapter.
- The Solman Videos can also be downloaded to a video iPod or mp3 player.
- Flashcards enhance practice and preparation.

Instructor's Manual Randy Grant of Linfield College revised and updated the *Instructor's Resource Manual.* The revised IM includes:

- Chapter summaries.
- Listings of "what's new" in each chapter.
- Teaching tips and suggestions.
- Learning objectives.
- Chapter outlines.
- Data and visual aid sources with suggestions for classroom use.
- Extra questions and problems.
- End-of-chapter correlation guides mapping content to the learning objectives and important AACSB standards.

The *Instructor's Manual* is available in hard copy or in electronic format on the Instructor's Resource CD-ROM as well as the Instructor's Side of the Online Learning Center.

Instructor's Resource CD-ROM This CD contains everything the instructor needs, including PowerPoint slides, all the charts and figures from the text, Test Banks I and III, and the *Instructor's Manual.*

Three Test Banks Test Bank I contains about 6650 multiple-choice and true-false questions, most of which were written by the text authors. *Instructor's*

Manual author Randy Grant revised Test Bank I for the seventeenth edition. Test Bank II contains around 6300 multiple-choice and true-false questions, written by William Walstad. All Test Bank I and II questions are organized by learning objective, type, level of difficulty, relevant text page number, and general AACSB classifications. Test Bank III contains more than 600 pages of short-answer questions and problems created in the style of the book's end-of-chapter questions. Test Bank III can be used to construct student assignments or design essay and problem exams. Suggested answers to the essay and problem questions are included. In all, more than 14,000 questions give instructors maximum testing flexibility while ensuring the fullest possible text correlation.

Test Banks I and II are available in computerized EZ Test versions, as well as in MS Word. EZ Test allows professors to create multiple versions of the same test by scrambling questions and answer choices. The EZ Test software will meet the various needs of the widest spectrum of computer users. Test Bank III is available in printed and MS Word formats.

Classroom Performance Systems by eInstruction This is a revolutionary system that brings ultimate interactivity to the classroom. CPS is a wireless response system that gives you immediate feedback from every student in the class. CPS units include easy-to-use software for creating and delivering questions and assessments to your class. With CPS you can ask subjective and objective questions. Then every student responds with an individual, wireless response pad, providing instant results. CPS is the perfect tool for engaging students while gathering important assessment data.

eInstruction

Instructor's can access eInstruction questions in two formats—CPS and PowerPoint. Motivate student preparation, interactivity, and active learning with these lecture-formatted questions.

Color Transparencies More than 200 new full-color transparencies were prepared for the seventeenth edition. They encompass all the figures appearing in *Economics*. Additionally, the figures and tables from the text are found on the Instructor's Resource CD-ROM.

Acknowledgments

We give special thanks to Sean Masaki Flynn of Vassar for the two new Internet chapters and Norris Peterson of Pacific Lutheran University and Randy Grant of Linfield College, who created the "button" content on our Web site. We again thank James Reese of the University of South Carolina at Spartanburg, who wrote the original Internet exercises. Although many of those questions were replaced or modified in the typical course of revision, several remain virtually unchanged. We also thank C. Norman Hollingsworth at Georgia Perimeter College for his ever-popular and creative PowerPoint slides and Terry Christesson at Clovis Community College for his Narrated Power Point slides. Finally, we thank William Walstad and Tom Barbiero (the coauthor of our Canadian edition) for their helpful ideas and insights.

We are greatly indebted to an all-star group of professionals at McGraw-Hill—in particular Gary Burke, Lucille Sutton, Rebecca Hicks, Lori Koetters, Keith McPherson, Douglas Reiner, and Brent Gordon—for their publishing and marketing expertise. To Lucille and Gary, we express our deepest gratitude for helping us keep *Economics* "number one" over the past 12 years.

We thank Keri Johnson for her selection of the Consider This and Last Word photos. Keith McPherson provided the vibrant cover.

The seventeenth edition has benefited from a number of perceptive formal reviews. The contributors, listed at the end of the Preface, were a rich source of suggestions for this revision. To each of you, and others we may have inadvertently overlooked, thank you for your considerable help in improving *Economics*.

Stanley L. Brue
Campbell R. McConnell

Reviewers

Basil Al-Hashimi, *Mesa Community College*
Ayman Amer, *Mount Mercy College*
Len Anyanwu, *Union College*
Greg Arburn, *University of Findlay*
William Ashley, *Mississippi Delta Community College*
John Atkins, *Pensacola Junior College*
Hamid Azari-Rad, *State University of New York–New Paltz*
Asatar Bair, *City College of San Francisco*
Paul Ballantyne, *University of Colorado at Colorado Springs*
Carl Bauer, *Oakton Community College*
Charles A. Bennett, *Gannon University*
Jay Bhattacharya, *Okaloosa-Walton College*
Antonio Bos, *Tusculum College*
David Bourne, *Northwest Mississippi Community College*
Douglas M. Brown, *Georgetown University*
Lara Bryant, *Florida Atlantic University*
Rebecca Cline, *Middle Georgia College Dublin Campus*
Rosa Lea Danielson, *College of DuPage*
Mahmoud R. Davoudi, *North Harris College*
Mark DeHainaut, *California University of Pennsylvania*
Kruti Dholakia, *University of Texas at Dallas*
Richard W. Dixon, *Thomas Nelson Community College*
Amrik Singh Dua, *Mt. San Antonio College*
James Dulgeroff, *San Bernardino Valley College*
Kevin C. Duncan, *Colorado State University–Pueblo*
Eugene Elander, *Plymouth State University*
Christopher A. Erickson, *New Mexico State University*
James Fallon, *Gwynedd-Mercy College*
Nikki M. Finlay, *Clayton State University*
John Francis, *Auburn University Montgomery*
S.N. Gajanan, *University of Pittsburgh*
Maria V. Gamba, *University of Findlay*
Michael G. Goode, *Central Piedmont Community College*
William D. Goodman, *Bluefield State College*
Gary Greene, *Manatee Community College–Venice*
Lisa Grobar, *California State University–Long Beach*
Phillip J. Grossman, *St. Cloud State University*
Shiv K. Gupta, *University of Findlay*
David W. Hedrick, *Central Washington University*
Elizabeth Hill, *Pennsylvania State University–Mont Alto*
Steven R. Hoagland, *Mount Union College*
Tracy Hofer, *University of Wisconsin–Stevens Point*
Jack W. Hou, *California State University–Long Beach*
Andy Howard, *Rio Hondo College*
Greg Hunter, *Cal Poly Pomona*
Tim Justice, *Columbus Technical College*
Veronica Kalich, *Baldwin-Wallace College*
Carol King, *Dana College*
Jack Kinworthy, *Concordia University*
Tori H. Knight, *Carson-Newman College*
Jacob Kurien, *Rockhurst University*
Felix B. Kwan, *Maryville University*

Contributors

James Lacey, *Hesser College*
Chris Lawrey, *Williams Baptist College*
Bozena Leven, *College of New Jersey*
Patricia Lindsey, *Butte College*
Kenneth E. Long, *New River Community College*
KT Magnusson, *Salt Lake Community College*
Monica Malanoski, *Winston Churchill High School*
Gretchen Mester, *Anne Arundel Community College*
Meghan Millea, *Mississippi State University*
Amlan Mitra, *Purdue University Calumet*
Carl B. Montano, *Lamar University*
Antoni Moskwa, *Allegheny College*
Thaddeaus Mounkurai, *Daytona Beach Community College*
Panos Mourdoukoutas, *Long Island University*
Annette Najjar, *Lindenwood University*
Louis V. Palacios-Salguero, *Rutgers University*
James E. Payne, *Illinois State University*
Wesley A. Payne, *Delgado Community College*
Joseph S. Pomykala, *Towson University*
Joe Prinzinger, *Lynchburg College*
Jeffrey Reed, *Columbia College of Missouri*
Charles A. Reichheld, *Cuyahoga Community College*
Timothy Jay Reynolds, *Alvin Community College*
Kathryn Roberts, *Chipola College*
Mike Romzy, *Waynesburg College*
Barbara Ross, *Kapi'olani Community College*
Henry Ryder, *Gloucester County College*
William C. Schaniel, *University of West Georgia*
Jerry Schwartz, *Broward Community College*
Edward M. Shaffer, *Gwynedd Mercy College*
Calvin Shipley, *Henderson State University*
Carl Simkonis, *Northern Kentucky University*
Garvin Smith, *Daytona Beach Community College*
Thomas P. Soos, *Pennsylvania State University–McKeesport*
Joanne Spitz, *University of Massachusetts–Boston*
Robert E. Tansky, *St. Clair County Community College*
Donna Thompson, *Brookdale Community College*
Lee J. Van Scyoc, *University of Wisconsin–Oshkosh*
Debra Way, *University of Cincinnati Clermont College*
Janice E. Weaver, *Drake University*
W. Parker Wheatley, *Saint John's University*
Thomas G. Wier, *Northeastern State University*
Krissa Wrigley, *University of Phoenix*

User Survey Respondents

Basil Al-Hashimi, *Mesa Community College*
Len Anyanwu, *Union College*
John Baffoe-Bonnie, *Pennsylvania State University–Delaware County*
Paul Ballantyne, *University of Colorado at Colorado Springs*
Emil Berendt, *Friends University*
John E. Bowen, *Park University*
Joyce Bremer, *Oakton Community College*
Stacey Brook, *University of Sioux Falls*
W. Todd Brotherson, *Southern Virginia University*
Douglas D. Brown, *Scottsdale Community College*
Mark Buenafe, *Mesa Community College*
Francine Butler, *Grand View College*
Chris Cusatis, *Gwynedd Mercy College*
Mahmoud R. Davoudi, *North Harris College*
Mark DeHainaut, *California University of Pennsylvania*
Richard Dempsey, *Ohio State University at Lima*
Manfred Dix, *Tulane University*
Amrik Singh Dua, *Mt. San Antonio College*
James Dulgeroff, *San Bernardino Valley College*
Erick M. Elder, *University of Arkansas at Little Rock*
Loretta Fairchild, *Nebraska Wesleyan University*
Abdollah Ferdowsi, *Ferris State University*
Lawrence Frateschi, *College of DuPage*
Arthur Friedberg, *Mohawk Valley Community College*
Yoshi Fukasawa, *Midwestern State University*
S.N. Gajanan, *University of Pittsburgh*
Maria V. Gamba, *University of Findlay*
Leticia Garcia, *Elgin Community College*
David G. Garraty, *Virginia Wesleyan College*
Philip J Grossman, *St. Cloud State University*
Lydia Harris, *Goucher College*
Charles F. Hawkins, *Lamar University*
Mark L. Healy, *William Rainey Harper College*
Michael G. Heslop, *Northern Virginia Community College*
Thomas Hiestand, *Concordia College*
Elizabeth Hill, *Pennsylvania State University–Mont Alto*
Tracy Hofer, *University of Wisconsin–Stevens Point*
Naphtali Hoffman, *Elmira College*
Andy Howard, *Rio Hondo College*
Mahshid Jalilvand, *University of Wisconsin–Stout*
R. Bruce Johnson, *Southwest Missouri State University*
Frederick M. Jungman, *Northwestern Oklahoma State University*
Veronica Kalich, *Baldwin-Wallace College*
Theodore C. Kariotis, *Towson University*
Alan Kessler, *Providence College*
Jack Kinworthy, *Concordia University*
Barry Kotlove, *Edmonds Community College*
Felix B. Kwan, *Maryville University*
Fritz Laux, *Northeastern State University*
Chris Lawrey, *Williams Baptist College*
Bozena Leven, *College of New Jersey*
KT Magnusson, *Salt Lake Community College*
Monica Malanoski, *Winston Churchill High School*
John E. Martinez, *Midwestern State University*
Jerome McElroy, *St. Mary's College*
Meghan Mille, *Mississippi State University*
Masoud Moallem, *Rockford College*
Carl B. Montano, *Lamar University*
Panos Mourdoukoutas, *Long Island University*

Joseph S. Pomykala, *Towson University*
Mitchell Redlo, *Rochester Institute of Technology*
Charles A. Reichheld, *Cuyahoga Community College*
Kathryn Roberts, *Chipola College*
Mike Romzy, *Waynesburg College*
Barbara Ross, *Kapi'olani Community College*
Henry Ryder, *Gloucester County College*
Calvin Shipley, *Henderson State University*
Carl Simkonis, *Northern Kentucky University*
Thomas P. Soos, *Pennsylvania State University–McKeesport*
Joanne Spitz, *University of Massachusetts–Boston*
Donna Thompson, *Brookdale Community College*
Michael Twomey, *University of Michigan–Dearborn*
Lee J. Van Scyoc, *University of Wisconsin–Oshkosh*
Debra Way, *University of Cincinnati Clermont College*
Janice E. Weaver, *Drake University*
Thomas G. Wier, *Northeastern State University*
Wendy Wood, *Bevill State Community College*
Krissa Wrigley, *University of Phoenix*

Brief Contents

PART ONE

Introduction to Economics and the Economy

	To the Student	*2*
1	Limits, Alternatives, and Choices	*3*
2	The Market System and the Circular Flow	*28*
3	Demand, Supply, and Market Equilibrium	*44*
4	The U.S. Economy: Private and Public Sectors	*65*
5	The United States in the Global Economy	*84*

PART TWO

Microeconomics of Product Markets

6	Extensions of Demand and Supply Analysis	*105*
7	Consumer Behavior and Utility Maximization	*125*
8	The Costs of Production	*144*
9	Pure Competition	*165*
10	Pure Monopoly	*189*
11	Monopolistic Competition and Oligopoly	*210*
12	Technology, R&D, and Efficiency	*233*

PART THREE

Microeconomics of Resource Markets

13	The Demand for Resources	*254*
14	Wage Determination	*271*
15	Rent, Interest, and Profit	*292*
15W	Natural Resource and Energy Economics (WEB CHAPTER, **www.mcconnell17.com**)	*307*

PART FOUR

Microeconomics of Government

16	Government and Market Failure	*309*
17	Public Choice Theory and the Economics of Taxation	*330*

PART FIVE

Microeconomic Issues and Policies

18	Antitrust Policy and Regulation	*348*
19	Agriculture: Economics and Policy	*364*
20	Income Inequality and Poverty	*381*
21	The Economics of Health Care	*400*
22	Labor Market Institutions and Issues: Unionism, Discrimination, Immigration	*418*

PART SIX

International Economics

23	International Trade	*441*
24	Exchange Rates, the Balance of Payments, and Trade Deficits	462
	Glossary	*G-1*
	Index	*IND-1*

List of Key Graphs *vi*
Preface *vii*
Contributors *xv*

PART ONE
Introduction to Economics and the Economy

To the Student *2*

Chapter 1
Limits, Alternatives, and Choices *3*

The Economic Perspective *4*
Scarcity and Choice / Purposeful Behavior / Marginal Analysis: Benefits and Costs
Consider This: *Free for All? 4*
Consider This: *Fast-Food Lines 5*

Theories, Principles, and Models *5*

Macroeconomics and Microeconomics *6*
Macroeconomics / Microeconomics / Positive and Normative Economics

Individuals' Economizing Problem *7*
Limited Income / Unlimited Wants / A Budget Line
Consider This: *Did Gates, Winfrey, and Rodriguez Make Bad Choices? 9*

Society's Economizing Problem *10*
Scarce Resources / Resource Categories

Production Possibilities Model *11*
Production Possibilities Table / Production Possibilities Curve / Law of Increasing Opportunity Cost / Optimal Allocation
Consider This: *The Economics of War 14*

Unemployment, Growth, and the Future *14*
A Growing Economy / Present Choices and Future Possibilities / A Qualification: International Trade
Last Word: *Pitfalls to Sound Economic Reasoning 16*

Chapter 1 Appendix: Graphs and Their Meaning *21*

Chapter 2
The Market System and the Circular Flow *28*

Economic Systems *29*
The Command System / The Market System

Characteristics of the Market System *29*
Private Property / Freedom of Enterprise and Choice / Self-Interest / Competition / Markets and Prices / Technology and Capital Goods / Specialization / Use of Money / Active, but Limited, Government
Consider This: *Buy American? 33*

Contents

Five Fundamental Questions 34
What Will Be Produced? / How Will the Goods and Services Be Produced? / Who Will Get the Output? / How Will the System Accommodate Change? / How Will the System Promote Progress?
Consider This: *McHits and McMisses* 34

The "Invisible Hand" 37

The Demise of the Command System 38
The Coordination Problem / The Incentive Problem

The Circular Flow Model 38
Resource Market / Product Market
Last Word: *Shuffling the Deck* 40

Chapter 3

Demand, Supply, and Market Equilibrium 44

Markets 45

Demand 45
Law of Demand / The Demand Curve / Market Demand / Change in Demand / Changes in Quantity Demanded

Supply 50
Law of Supply / The Supply Curve / Market Supply / Determinants of Supply / Changes in Supply / Changes in Quantity Supplied

Market Equilibrium 53
Equilibrium Price and Quantity / Rationing Function of Prices /Efficient Allocation / Changes in Supply, Demand, and Equilibrium
Consider This: *Ticket Scalping: A Bum Rap!* 55

Application: Government-Set Prices 57
Price Ceilings on Gasoline / Rent Controls / Price Floors on Wheat
Consider This: *Salsa and Coffee Beans* 58
Last Word: *A Legal Market for Human Organs?* 60

Chapter 4

The U.S. Economy: Private and Public Sectors 65

Households as Income Receivers 66
The Functional Distribution of Income / The Personal Distribution of Income

Households as Spenders 67
Personal Taxes / Personal Saving / Personal Consumption Expenditures

The Business Population 68

Legal Forms of Businesses 68
Advantages of Corporations / The Principal-Agent Problem
Consider This: *Unprincipled Agents* 70

The Public Sector: Government's Role 71
Providing the Legal Structure / Maintaining Competition / Redistributing Income Reallocating Resources / Promoting Stability / Government's Role: A Qualification
Consider This: *Street Entertainers* 74

The Circular Flow Revisited 75

Government Finance 75
Government Purchases and Transfers

Federal Finance 77
Federal Expenditures / Federal Tax Revenues

State and Local Finance 80
State Finances / Local Finances
Last Word: *Financing Social Security* 78

Chapter 5

The United States in the Global Economy 84

International Linkages 85

The United States and World Trade 85
Volume and Pattern / Rapid Trade Growth / Participants in International Trade

Specialization and Comparative Advantage 89
Comparative Advantage: Production Possibilities Analysis
Consider This: *A CPA and House Painter* 90

The Foreign Exchange Market 92
Dollar-Yen Market / Changing Rates: Depreciation and Appreciation
Consider This: *A Ticket to Ride* 93

Government and Trade 95
Trade Impediments and Subsidies / Why Government Trade Interventions? / Costs to Society

Multilateral Trade Agreements and Free-Trade Zones 96
Reciprocal Trade Agreements Act / General Agreement on Tariffs and Trade / World Trade Organization / The European Union / North American Free Trade Agreement

Global Competition 99
Last Word: *Petition of the Candlemakers, 1845* 100

PART TWO

Microeconomics of Product Markets

Chapter 6

Extensions of Demand and Supply Analysis 105

Price Elasticity of Demand 106
The Price Elasticity Coefficient and Formula / Interpretations of E_d / The Total-Revenue Test / Price Elasticity and the Total-Revenue Curve / Determinants of Price Elasticity of Demand / Applications of Price Elasticity of Demand
Consider This: *A Bit of a Stretch* 108

Price Elasticity of Supply 114
Price Elasticity of Supply: The Market Period / Price Elasticity of Supply: The Short Run / Price Elasticity of Supply: The Long Run / Applications of Price Elasticity of Supply

Cross Elasticity and Income Elasticity of Demand 116
Cross Elasticity of Demand / Income Elasticity of Demand

Consumer and Producer Surplus 118
Consumer Surplus / Producer Surplus / Efficiency Revisited / Efficiency Losses (or Deadweight Losses)
Last Word: *Elasticity and Pricing Power: Why Different Consumers Pay Different Prices* 121

Chapter 7

Consumer Behavior and Utility Maximization 125

Law of Diminishing Marginal Utility 126
Terminology / Total Utility and Marginal Utility / Marginal Utility and Demand
Consider This: *Vending Machines and Marginal Utility* 126

Theory of Consumer Behavior 128
Consumer Choice and Budget Constraint / Utility-Maximizing Rule / Numerical Example / Algebraic Restatement

Utility Maximization and the Demand Curve 131
Deriving the Demand Schedule and Curve / Income and Substitution Effects

Applications and Extensions 132
DVDs and DVD Players / The Diamond-Water Paradox / The Value of Time / Medical Care Purchases / Cash and Noncash Gifts
Last Word: *Criminal Behavior* 134

Chapter 19 Appendix: Indifference Curve Analysis 138
The Budget Line: What Is Attainable 138
Indifference Curves: What Is Preferred 139
The Indifference Map 140
Equilibrium at Tangency 140
The Measurement of Utility 141
Consider This: *Indifference Maps and Topographical Maps* 141
The Derivation of the Demand Curve 142

Chapter 8

The Costs of Production 144

Economic Costs 145
Explicit and Implicit Costs / Normal Profit as a Cost / Economic Profit (or Pure Profit) / Short Run and Long Run

Short-Run Production Relationships 147
Law of Diminishing Returns
Consider This: *Diminishing Returns from Study* 147

Short-Run Production Costs 150
Fixed, Variable, and Total Costs / Per-Unit, or Average, Costs / Marginal Cost / Shifts of the Cost Curves

Long-Run Production Costs 155
Firm Size and Costs / The Long-Run Cost Curve / Economies and Diseconomies of Scale / Minimum Efficient Scale and Industry Structure

Applications and Illustrations 160
Rising Cost of Insurance and Security / Successful Start-Up Firms / The Verson Stamping Machine / The Daily Newspaper / Aircraft and Concrete Plants
Last Word: *Don't Cry over Sunk Costs* 161

Chapter 9

Pure Competition 165

Four Market Models 166

Pure Competition: Characteristics and Occurrence 166

Demand as Seen by a Purely Competitive Seller 167
Perfectly Elastic Demand / Average, Total, and Marginal Revenue

Profit Maximization in the Short Run: Total-Revenue–Total-Cost Approach 168

Profit Maximization in the Short Run: Marginal-Revenue–Marginal Cost Approach 170
Profit-Maximizing Case / Loss-Minimizing Case / Shutdown Case
Consider This: *The Still There Motel* 174

Marginal Cost and Short-Run Supply 175
Generalized Depiction / Diminishing Returns, Production Costs, and Product Supply / Changes in Supply / Firm and Industry: Equilibrium Price

Profit Maximization in the Long Run 178
Assumptions / Goal of Our Analysis / Long-Run Equilibrium / Long-Run Supply for a Constant-Cost Industry / Long-Run Supply for an Increasing-Cost Industry / Long-Run Supply for a Decreasing-Cost Industry

Pure Competition and Efficiency 182
Productive Efficiency: P = Minimum ATC / Allocative / Efficiency: P = MC / Maximum Consumer and Producer Surplus / Dynamic Adjustments / "Invisible Hand" Revisited
Last Word: *Efficiency Gains from Entry: The Case of Generic Drugs* 185

Chapter 10

Pure Monopoly 189

An Introduction to Pure Monopoly 190
Examples of Monopoly / Dual Objectives of the Study of Monopoly

Barriers to Entry 190
Economies of Scale / Legal Barriers to Entry: Patents and Licenses / Ownership or Control of Essential Resources / Pricing and Other Strategic Barriers to Entry

Monopoly Demand 192
Marginal Revenue Is Less Than Price / The Monopolist Is a Price Maker / The Monopolist Sets Prices in the Elastic Region of Demand

Output and Price Determination 195
Cost Data / MR = MC Rule / No Monopoly Supply Curve / Misconceptions Concerning Monopoly Pricing / Possibility of Losses by Monopolist

Economic Effects of Monopoly 198
Price, Output, and Efficiency / Income Transfer / Cost Complications / Assessment and Policy Options

Price Discrimination 202
Conditions / Examples of Price Discrimination / Graphical Analysis
Consider This: *Price Discrimination at the Ballpark* 203

Regulated Monopoly 204
Socially Optimal Price: P = MC / Fair-Return Price: P = ATC / Dilemma of Regulation

Last Word: *De Beers' Diamonds: Are Monopolies Forever?* 206

Chapter 11

Monopolistic Competition and Oligopoly 210

Monopolistic Competition 211
Relatively Large Number of Sellers / Differentiated Products / Easy Entry and Exit / Advertising / Monopolistically Competitive Industries

Price and Output in Monopolistic Competition 212
The Firm's Demand Curve / The Short Run: Profit or Loss / The Long Run: Only a Normal Profit

Monopolistic Competition and Efficiency 215
Neither Productive nor Allocative Efficiency / Excess Capacity

Product Variety 216
Benefits of Product Variety / Further Complexity

Oligopoly 217
A Few Large Producers / Homogeneous or Differentiated Products Control over Price, but Mutual Interdependence / Entry Barriers / Mergers / Measures of Industry Concentration

Oligopoly Behavior: A Game-Theory Overview 219
Mutual Interdependence Revisited / Collusive Tendencies / Incentive to Cheat
Consider This: *Creative Strategic Behavior* 220

Three Oligopoly Models 221
Kinked-Demand Theory: Noncollusive Oligopoly / Cartels and Other Collusion / Price Leadership Model

Oligopoly and Advertising 227
Positive Effects of Advertising / Potential Negative Effects of Advertising

Oligopoly and Efficiency 229
Productive and Allocative Efficiency / Qualifications
Last Word: *Oligopoly in the Beer Industry* 228

Chapter 12

Technology, R&D, and Efficiency 233

Invention, Innovation, and Diffusion 234
Invention / Innovation / Diffusion / R&D Expenditures / Modern View of Technological Advance

Role of Entrepreneurs and Other Innovators 236
Forming Start-Ups / Innovating within Existing Firms / Anticipating the Future / Exploiting University and Government Scientific Research

A Firm's Optimal Amount of R&D 237
Interest-Rate Cost of Funds / Expected Rate of Return / Optimal R&D Expenditures

Increased Profit via Innovation 240
Increased Revenue via Product Innovation / Reduced Cost via Process Innovation

Imitation and R&D Incentives 242
Benefits of Being First
Consider This: *Trade Secrets* 244

Role of Market Structure 244
Market Structure and Technological Advance / Inverted-U Theory / Market Structure and Technological Advance: The Evidence

Technological Advance and Efficiency 247
Productive Efficiency / Allocative Efficiency / Creative Destruction
Last Word: *On the Path to the Personal Computer and Internet* 248

PART THREE
Microeconomics of Resource Markets

Chapter 13

The Demand for Resources 254

Significance of Resource Pricing 255
Marginal Productivity Theory of Resource Demand 255
Resource Demand as a Derived Demand / Marginal Revenue Product / Rule for Employing Resources: MRP = MRC / MRP as Resource Demand Schedule / Resource Demand under Imperfect Product Market Competition Market Demand for a Resource
Consider This: *She's The One* 259

Determinants of Resource Demand 259
Changes in Product Demand / Changes in Productivity / Changes in the Prices of Other Resources / Occupational Employment Trends

Elasticity of Resource Demand 262
Optimal Combination of Resources 264
The Least-Cost Rule / The Profit-Maximizing Rule / Numerical Illustration

Marginal Productivity Theory of Income Distribution 266
Last Word: *Input Substitution: The Case of ATMs* 267

Chapter 14

Wage Determination 271

Labor, Wages, and Earnings 272
General Level of Wages 272
Role of Productivity / Real Wages and Productivity / Secular Growth of Real Wages /

A Purely Competitive Labor Market 274
Market Demand for Labor / Market Supply of Labor / Labor Market Equilibrium

Monopsony Model 276
Upward-Sloping Labor Supply to Firm / MRC Higher than the Wage Rate / Equilibrium Wage and Employment / Examples of Monopsony Power /

Three Union Models 278
Demand-Enhancement Model / Exclusive or Craft Union Model / Inclusive or Industrial Union Model / Wage Increases and Unemployment

Bilateral Monopoly Model 281
Indeterminate Outcome of Bilateral Monopoly / Desirability of Bilateral / Monopoly

The Minimum-Wage Controversy 282
Case against the Minimum Wage / Case for the Minimum Wage / Evidence and Conclusions /

Wage Differentials 282
Marginal Revenue Productivity / Noncompeting Groups/ Compensating Differences / Market Imperfections/
Consider This: *My Entire Life* 285

Pay for Performance 286
The Principal-Agent Problem Revisited / Addenda: Negative Side Effects of Pay for Performance /
Last Word: *Are Chief Executive Officers (CEOs) Overpaid?* 288

Chapter 15

Rent, Interest, and Profit 292

Economic Rent 293
Perfectly Inelastic Supply / Changes in Demand / Land Rent: A Surplus Payment / Application: A Single Tax on Land / Productivity Differences and Rent Differences / Alternative Uses of Land

Interest 295
Loanable Funds Theory of Interest / Extending the Model / Range of Interest Rates / Pure Rate of Interest / Role of the Interest Rate / Application: Usury Laws
Consider This: *That Is Interest* 297

Economic Profit 301
Role of the Entrepreneur / Sources of Economic Profit / Functions of Profit

Income Shares 304
Last Word: *Determining the Price of Credit* 302

WEB Chapter 15 www.mcconnell17.com

Natural Resource and Energy Economics 307

Resource Supplies: Doom or Boom? 15W-2
Population Growth / Resource Consumption per Person
Consider This: *Can Governments Raise Birthrates?* 15W-3

Energy Economics 15W-7
Efficient Energy Use / Running Out of Energy?
Consider This: *Turning Entrails (and Nearly Anything Else) into Oil* 15W-9

Natural Resource Economics 15W-10

Using Present Values to Evaluate Future Possibilities 15W-10

Nonrenewable Resources 15W-11
Present Use versus Future Use / Market Failures Lead to Excessive Present Use / Applications

Renewable Resources 15W-15
Forest Management / Optimal Forest Harvesting / Optimal Fisheries Management / Policies to Limit Catch Sizes
Last Word: *Is Economic Growth Bad for the Environment?* 15W-18

PART FOUR
Microeconomics of Government

Chapter 16

Government and Market Failure 309

Public Goods 310
Private Goods Characteristics / Public Goods Characteristics / Optimal Quantity of a Public Good / Demand for Public Goods / Comparing MB and MC / Cost-Benefit Analysis /
Consider This: *Art for Art's Sake* 311

Externalities 314
Negative Externalities / Positive Externalities / Individual Bargaining: Coase Theorem / Liability Rules and Lawsuits / Government Intervention / A Market-Based Approach to Negative Externalities / Society's Optimal Amount of Externality Reduction / Global Warming

Information Failures 322
Inadequate Information Involving Sellers / Inadequate Information Involving Buyers / Qualification
Consider This: *"Lemons"* 322
Last Word: *Lojack: A Case of Positive Externalities* 326

Chapter 17

Public Choice Theory and the Economics of Taxation 330

Revealing Preferences through Majority Voting 331
Inefficient Voting Outcomes / Paradox of Voting / Median-Voter Model

Government Failure 334
Special Interests and Rent Seeking / Clear Benefits, Hidden Costs / Limited and Bundled Choice / Bureaucracy and Inefficiency / Imperfect Institutions

Apportioning the Tax Burden 336
Benefits Received versus Ability to Pay / Progressive, Proportional, and Regressive Taxes

Tax Incidence and Efficiency Loss 339
Elasticity and Tax Incidence / Efficiency Loss of a Tax / Probable Incidence of U.S. Taxes / The U.S Tax Structure
Last Word: *"Government Failure" in the News* 344

PART FIVE
Microeconomic Issues and Policies

Chapter 18

Antitrust Policy and Regulation 348

The Antitrust Laws 349
Historical Background / Sherman Act of 1890 / Clayton Act of 1914 / Federal Trade Commission Act of 1914 / Cellar-Kefauver Act of 1950

Antitrust Policy: Issues and Impacts 350
Issues of Interpretation / Issues of Enforcement / Effectiveness of Antitrust Laws
Consider This: *Of Catfish and Art (and Other Things in Common)* 354
Industrial Regulation 355
Natural Monopoly / Problems with Industrial Regulation / Legal Cartel Theory
Deregulation 357
Social Regulation 358
Distinguishing Features / The Optimal Level of Social Regulation / Two Reminders
Last Word: United States v. Microsoft 360

Chapter 19

Agriculture: Economics and Policy 364
Economics of Agriculture 365
The Short Run: Price and Income Instability / The Long Run: A Declining Industry / Farm-Household Income
Consider This: *Risky Business* 368
Economics of Farm Policy 371
Rationale for Farm Subsidies / Background: The Parity Concept / Economics of Price Supports / Reduction of Surpluses
Criticisms and Politics 374
Criticisms of the Parity Concept / Criticisms of the Price-Support System / The Politics of Farm Policy
Recent Reform 377
Freedom to Farm Act of 1996 / The Farm Act of 2002
Last Word: *The Sugar Program: A Sweet Deal* 376

Chapter 20

Income Inequality and Poverty 381
Facts about Income Inequality 382
Distribution by Income Category / Distribution by Quintiles (Fifths) / The Lorenz Curve and Gini Ratio / Income Mobility: The Time Dimension / Effect of Government Redistribution
Causes of Income Inequality 384
Ability / Education and Training / Discrimination / Preferences and Risks / Unequal Distribution of Wealth / Market Power / Luck, Connections, and Misfortune
Income Inequality over Time 386
Rising Income Inequality since 1970 / Causes of Growing Inequality
Equality versus Efficiency 388
The Case for Equality: Maximizing Total Utility / The Case for Inequality: Incentives and Efficiency / The Equality-Efficiency Tradeoff
Consider This: *Slicing the Pizza* 389
The Economics of Poverty 389
Definition of Poverty / Incidence of Poverty / Poverty Trends / Measurement Issues
The U.S. Income-Maintenance System 391
Social Insurance Programs / Public Assistance Programs
Welfare: Goals and Conflicts 394
Common Features / Conflicts among Goals
Welfare Reform 395
Last Word: *U.S. Family Wealth and Its Distribution* 396

Chapter 21

The Economics of Health Care 400
The Health Care Industry 401
Twin Problems: Costs and Access 401
High and Rising Health Care Costs 401
Health Care Spending / Quality of Care: Are We Healthier? / Economic Implications of Rising Costs / Too Much Spending?
Limited Access 404
Why the Rapid Rise in Costs? 405
Peculiarities of the Health Care Market / The Increasing Demand for Health Care / Role of Health Insurance / Supply Factors in Rising Health Care Prices / Relative Importance
Consider This: *What's Cold, Clammy, and Possibly Endangered?* 410
Reform of the Health Care System 411
Universal Access / Cost Containment: Altering Incentives / Recent Laws and Proposals
Last Word: *Mandatory Health Insurance: Play to Stay* 415

Chapter 22

Labor Market Institutions and Issues: Unionism, Discrimination, Immigration 418
Unionism in America 419
Business Unionism / Union Membership / The Decline of Unionism
Collective Bargaining 420
The Work Agreement / The Bargaining Process
Economic Effects of Unions 422
The Union Wage Advantage / Efficiency and Productivity
Labor Market Discrimination 425
Types of Discrimination / Costs of Discrimination
Economic Analysis of Discrimination 427
Taste-for-Discrimination Model / Statistical Discrimination / Occupational Segregation: The Crowding Model
Antidiscrimination Policies and Issues 431
The Affirmative Action Controversy / Recent Developments
Immigration 433
Number of Immigrants / Economics of Immigration / Complications and Modifications / Immigration: Two Views
Last Word: *Orchestrating Impartiality* 436

PART SIX
International Economics

Chapter 23

International Trade 441

Some Key Facts 442

The Economic Basis for Trade 442

Comparative Advantage: Graphical Analysis 443

Two Isolated Nations / Specializing Based on Comparative Advantage / Terms of Trade / Gains from Trade / Trade with Increasing Costs / The Case for Free Trade

Supply and Demand Analysis of Exports and Imports 448

Supply and Demand in the United States / Supply and Demand in Canada / Equilibrium World Price, Exports, and Imports

Trade Barriers 451

Economic Impact of Tariffs / Economic Impact of Quotas / Net Costs of Tariffs and Quotas

The Case for Protection: A Critical Review 454

Military Self-Sufficiency Argument / Diversification-for-Stability Argument / Infant Industry Argument / Protection-against-Dumping Argument / Increased Domestic Employment Argument / Cheap Foreign Labor Argument / Trade Adjustment Assistance

Consider This: *Shooting Yourself in the Foot* 454

Offshoring 457

The World Trade Organization 458

Last Word: *The WTO Protests* 458

Chapter 24

Exchange Rates, the Balance of Payments, and Trade Deficits 462

Financing International Trade 463

U.S. Export Transaction / U.S. Import Transaction

The Balance of Payments 463

Current Account / Capital and Financial Account / Payments, Deficits, and Surpluses

Flexible Exchange Rates 466

Depreciation and Appreciation / Determinants of Exchange Rates / Flexible Rates and the Balance of Payments / Disadvantages of Flexible Exchange Rates

Consider This: *The Big Mac Index* 469

Fixed Exchange Rates 471

Use of Reserves / Trade Policies / Exchange Controls and Rationing / Domestic Macroeconomic Adjustments

International Exchange-Rate Systems 473

The Gold Standard: Fixed Exchange Rates / The Bretton Woods System / The Current System: The Managed Float

Recent U.S. Trade Deficits 477

Causes of the Trade Deficits / Implications of U.S. Trade Deficits

Last Word: *Speculation in Currency Markets* 478

Glossary G-1

Index IND-1

PART ONE

Introduction to Economics and the Economy

1 LIMITS, ALTERNATIVES, AND CHOICES
2 THE MARKET SYSTEM AND THE CIRCULAR FLOW
3 DEMAND, SUPPLY, AND MARKET EQUILIBRIUM
4 THE U.S. ECONOMY: PRIVATE AND PUBLIC SECTORS
5 THE UNITED STATES IN THE GLOBAL ECONOMY

To the Student

This book and its ancillaries contain several features designed to help you learn economics:

- ***Web buttons*** A glance through the book reveals many pages with symbols in the margins. These "buttons" alert you to helpful learning aids available with the book. The graph button denotes "Interactive Graphs" found at the text's Web site, **www.mcconnell17.com.** Brief exercises have you interact with the graphs, for example, by clicking on a specific curve and dragging it to a new location. These exercises will enhance your understanding of the underlying concepts. The light-bulb button symbolizes "Worked Problems." Numeric problems are presented and then solved, side-by-side, step-by-step. Seeing how the problems are worked will help you solve similar problems on quizzes and exams. The egg button stands for "Origin of the Idea." Each of these pieces traces a particular idea to the person or persons who first developed it.

Interactive Graphs

Worked Problems

Origin of the Idea

After reading a chapter, thumb back through it to note the Web buttons and the number that follows them. On the home page of our Internet site select Student Edition and use the pull-down list under "Choose one" to find the Web button content for each chapter.

- ***Other Internet aids*** Our Internet site contains many other aids. In the Student Edition you will find self-testing multiple-choice quizzes, links to relevant news articles, and much more. For those of you with very strong mathematics background, be sure to note the "See the Math" section on the Web site. There you will find nearly 50 notes that develop the algebra and, in a few cases, the calculus that underlie the economic concepts.
- ***Appendix on graphs*** Be assured, however, that you will need only basic math skills to do well in the principles course. In particular, you will need to be comfortable with basic graphical analysis and a few quantitative concepts. The appendix at the end of Chapter 1 reviews graphs and slopes of curves. You may want to read it before starting Chapter 1.
- ***Reviews*** Each chapter contains two or three Quick Reviews and an end-of-chapter summary. These reviews will help you focus on essential ideas and study for exams.
- ***Key terms and Key Graphs*** Key terms are set in boldface type within the chapters, listed at the end of each chapter, and again defined in the glossary at the end of the book. Graphs with special relevance are labeled Key Graphs, and each includes a multiple-choice Quick Quiz. Your instructor may or may not emphasize all of these figures, but you should pay special attention to those that are discussed in class; you can be certain there will be exam questions on them.
- ***Consider This and Last Word boxes*** Many chapters include a Consider This box. These brief pieces provide commonplace analogies, examples, and stories that help you understand and remember central economic ideas. Each chapter concludes with a Last Word box. Some of them are revealing applications of economic ideas; others are short case studies. While it is tempting to ignore in-text boxes, don't. Most are fun to read, and all will improve your grasp of economics.
- ***Questions*** A comprehensive list of study questions is located at the end of each chapter. Several of the questions are designated Key Questions and are answered in the *Study Guide* and also at our Internet site. Also at the Internet site are three multiple-choice quizzes for each chapter.
- ***Study Guide*** We enthusiastically recommend the *Study Guide* accompanying this text. This "portable tutor" contains not only a broad sampling of various kinds of questions but a host of useful learning aids. Software-driven tutorials (Aplia, for example) are also available with the text.

Our two main goals are to help you understand and apply economics and help you improve your analytical skills. An understanding of economics will enable you to comprehend a whole range of economic, social, and political problems that otherwise would seem puzzling and perplexing. Also, your study will enhance reasoning skills that are highly prized in the workplace.

Good luck with your study. We think it will be well worth your effort.

IN THIS CHAPTER YOU WILL LEARN:

- The definition of economics and the features of the economic perspective.
- The role of economic theory in economics.
- The distinction between microeconomics and macroeconomics.
- The categories of scarce resources and the nature of the economizing problem.
- About production possibilities analysis, increasing opportunity costs, and economic growth.

1

Limits, Alternatives, and Choices

(An appendix on understanding graphs follows this chapter. If you need a quick review of this mathematical tool, you might benefit by reading the appendix first.) People's wants are numerous and varied. Biologically, people need only air, water, food, clothing, and shelter. But in modern society people also desire goods and services that provide a more comfortable or affluent standard of living. We want bottled water, soft drinks, and fruit juices, not just water from the creek. We want salads, burgers, and pizzas, not just berries and nuts. We want jeans, suits, and coats, not just woven reeds. We want apartments, condominiums, or houses, not just mud huts. And, as the saying goes, "that is not the half of it." We also want DVD players, Internet service, education, homeland security, cell phones, health care, and much more.

Fortunately, society possesses productive resources, such as labor and managerial talent, tools and machinery, and land and mineral deposits. These resources, employed in the economic system (or simply the economy), help us produce goods and services that satisfy many of our economic wants. But the blunt reality is that our economic wants far exceed the productive capacity of our scarce (limited) resources. We are forced to make choices. This unyielding truth underlies the definition of **economics,** which is the social science concerned with how individuals, institutions, and society make optimal (best) choices under conditions of scarcity.

O 1.1
Origin of the term "Economics"

The Economic Perspective

Economists view things from a unique perspective. This **economic perspective,** or economic way of thinking, has several critical and closely interrelated features.

Scarcity and Choice

From our definition of economics, we can easily see why economists view the world through the lens of scarcity. Scarce economic resources mean limited goods and services. Scarcity restricts options and demands choices. Because we "can't have it all," we must decide what we will have and what we must forgo.

At the core of economics is the idea that "there is no free lunch." You may be treated to lunch, making it "free" from your perspective, but someone bears a cost—ultimately, society. Scarce inputs of land, equipment, farm labor, the labor of cooks and waiters, and managerial talent are required. Because society could have used these resources to produce something else, it sacrifices those other goods and services in making the lunch available. Economists call such sacrifices **opportunity costs:** To obtain more of one thing, society forgoes the opportunity of getting the next best thing. That sacrifice is the opportunity cost of the choice.

CONSIDER THIS . . .

Free for All?

Free products are seemingly everywhere. Sellers offer free software, free cell phones, and free checking accounts. Dentists give out free toothbrushes. At state visitor centers, there are free brochures and maps.

Does the presence of so many free products contradict the economist's assertion "There is no free lunch"? No! Resources are used to produce each of these products, and because those resources have alternative uses, society gives up something else to get the "free" good. Where resources are used to produce goods or services, there is no free lunch.

So why are these goods offered for free? In a word: marketing! Firms sometimes offer free products to entice people to try them, hoping they will then purchase those goods later. The free software may eventually entice you to buy the producer's upgraded software. In other instances, the free brochures contain advertising for shops and restaurants, and that free e-mail program is filled with ads. In still other cases, the product is free only in conjunction with a larger purchase. To get the free bottle of soda, you must buy the large pizza. To get the free cell phone, you need to sign up for a year's worth of cell phone service.

So "free" products may or may not be truly free to individuals. They are never free to society.

Purposeful Behavior

Economics assumes that human behavior reflects "rational self-interest." Individuals look for and pursue opportunities to increase their **utility**—the pleasure, happiness, or satisfaction obtained from consuming a good or service. They allocate their time, energy, and money to maximize their satisfaction. Because they weigh costs and benefits, their economic decisions are "purposeful" or "rational," not "random" or "chaotic."

O 1.2
Utility

Consumers are purposeful in deciding what goods and services to buy. Business firms are purposeful in deciding what products to produce and how to produce them. Government entities are purposeful in deciding what public services to provide and how to finance them.

"Purposeful behavior" does not assume that people and institutions are immune from faulty logic and therefore are perfect decision makers. They sometimes make mistakes. Nor does it mean that people's decisions are unaffected by emotion or the decisions of those around them. "Purposeful behavior" simply means that people make decisions with some desired outcome in mind.

Rational self-interest is not the same as selfishness. In the economy, increasing one's own wage, rent, interest, or profit normally requires identifying and satisfying *somebody else's* wants! Also, people make personal sacrifices to others. They contribute time and money to charities because they derive pleasure from doing so. Parents help pay for their children's education for the same reason. These self-interested, but unselfish, acts help maximize the givers' satisfaction as much as any personal purchase of goods or services. Self-interested behavior is simply behavior designed to increase personal satisfaction, however it may be derived.

CONSIDER THIS . . .

Fast-Food Lines

The economic perspective is useful in analyzing all sorts of behaviors. Consider an everyday example: the behavior of fast-food customers. When customers enter the restaurant, they go to the shortest line, believing that line will minimize their time cost of obtaining food. They are acting purposefully; time is limited, and people prefer using it in some way other than standing in line.

If one fast-food line is temporarily shorter than other lines, some people will move to that line. These movers apparently view the time saving from the shorter line (marginal benefit) as exceeding the cost of moving from their present line (marginal cost). The line switching tends to equalize line lengths. No further movement of customers between lines occurs once all lines are about equal.

Fast-food customers face another cost-benefit decision when a clerk opens a new station at the counter. Should they move to the new station or stay put? Those who shift to the new line decide that the time saving from the move exceeds the extra cost of physically moving. In so deciding, customers must also consider just how quickly they can get to the new station compared with others who may be contemplating the same move. (Those who hesitate in this situation are lost!)

Customers at the fast-food establishment do not have perfect information when they select lines. Thus, not all decisions turn out as expected. For example, you might enter a short line and find someone in front of you is ordering hamburgers and fries for 40 people in the Greyhound bus parked out back (and the employee is a trainee)! Nevertheless, at the time you made your decision, you thought it was optimal.

Finally, customers must decide what food to order when they arrive at the counter. In making their choices, they again compare marginal costs and marginal benefits in attempting to obtain the greatest personal satisfaction for their expenditure.

Economists believe that what is true for the behavior of customers at fast-food restaurants is true for economic behavior in general. Faced with an array of choices, consumers, workers, and businesses rationally compare marginal costs and marginal benefits in making decisions.

Marginal Analysis: Benefits and Costs

The economic perspective focuses largely on **marginal analysis**—comparisons of marginal benefits and marginal costs, usually for decision making. To economists, "marginal" means "extra," "additional," or "a change in." Most choices or decisions involve changes in the status quo, meaning the existing state of affairs.

Should you attend school for another year? Should you study an extra hour for an exam? Should you supersize your fries? Similarly, should a business expand or reduce its output? Should government increase or decrease its funding for a missile defense system?

Each option involves marginal benefits and, because of scarce resources, marginal costs. In making choices rationally, the decision maker must compare those two amounts. Example: You and your fiancée are shopping for an engagement ring. Should you buy a $\frac{1}{2}$-carat diamond, a $\frac{5}{8}$-carat diamond, a $\frac{3}{4}$-carat diamond, a 1-carat diamond, or something even larger? The marginal cost of a larger-size diamond is the added expense beyond the cost of the smaller-size diamond. The marginal benefit is the perceived lifetime pleasure (utility) from the larger-size stone. If the marginal benefit of the larger diamond exceeds its marginal cost (and you can afford it), buy the larger stone. But if the marginal cost is more than the marginal benefit, buy the smaller diamond instead, even if you can afford the larger stone!

O 1.3
Marginal analysis

In a world of scarcity, the decision to obtain the marginal benefit associated with some specific option always includes the marginal cost of forgoing something else. The money spent on the larger-size diamond means forgoing some other product. Opportunity costs are present whenever a decision is made. **(Key Question 3)**

Theories, Principles, and Models

Like the physical and life sciences, as well as other social sciences, economics relies on the **scientific method.** That procedure consists of several elements:

- The observation of real-world behavior and outcomes.
- Based on those observations, the formulation of a possible explanation of cause and effect (hypothesis).

- The testing of this explanation by comparing the outcomes of specific events to the outcome predicted by the hypothesis.
- The acceptance, rejection, or modification of the hypothesis, based on these comparisons.
- The continued testing of the hypothesis against the facts. As favorable results accumulate, the hypothesis evolves into a theory. A very well-tested and widely accepted theory is referred to as an economic law or an **economic principle**—a statement about economic behavior or the economy that enables prediction of the probable effects of certain actions. Combinations of such laws or principles are incorporated into models, which are simplified representations of how something works, such as a market or segment of the economy.

Economists develop theories of the behavior of individuals (consumers, workers) and institutions (businesses, governments) engaged in the production, exchange, and consumption of goods and services. Theories, principles, and models are "purposeful simplifications." The full scope of economic reality itself is too complex and bewildering to be understood as a whole. In developing theories, principles, and models economists remove the clutter and simplify.

Economic principles and models are highly useful in analyzing economic behavior and understanding how the economy operates. They are the tools for ascertaining cause and effect (or action and outcome) within the economic system. Good theories do a good job of explaining and predicting. They are supported by facts concerning how individuals and institutions actually behave in producing, exchanging, and consuming goods and services.

There are some other things you should know about economic principles.

- ***Generalizations*** Economic principles are generalizations relating to economic behavior or to the economy itself. Economic principles are expressed as the tendencies of typical or average consumers, workers, or business firms. For example, economists say that consumers buy more of a particular product when its price falls. Economists recognize that some consumers may increase their purchases by a large amount, others by a small amount, and a few not at all. This "price-quantity" principle, however, holds for the typical consumer and for consumers as a group.
- ***Other-Things-Equal Assumption*** In constructing their theories, economists use the *ceteris paribus* or **other-things-equal assumption**—the assumption that factors other than those being considered do not change. They assume that all variables except those under immediate consideration are held constant for a particular analysis. For example, consider the relationship between the price of Pepsi and the amount of it purchased. Assume that of all the factors that might influence the amount of Pepsi purchased (for example, the price of Pepsi, the price of Coca-Cola, and consumer incomes and preferences), only the price of Pepsi varies. This is helpful because the economist can then focus on the "price of Pepsi–purchases of Pepsi" relationship without being confused by changes in other variables.

O 1.4
Ceteris paribus

- ***Graphical Expression*** Many economic models are expressed graphically. Be sure to read the special appendix at the end of this chapter as a review of graphs.

Macroeconomics and Microeconomics

Economists develop economic principles and models at two levels.

Macroeconomics

Macroeconomics examines either the economy as a whole or its basic subdivisions or aggregates, such as the government, household, and business sectors. An **aggregate** is a collection of specific economic units treated as if they were one unit. Therefore, we might lump together the millions of consumers in the U.S. economy and treat them as if they were one huge unit called "consumers."

In using aggregates, macroeconomics seeks to obtain an overview, or general outline, of the structure of the economy and the relationships of its major aggregates. Macroeconomics speaks of such economic measures as total output, total employment, total income, aggregate expenditures, and the general level of prices in analyzing various economic problems. No or very little attention is given to specific units making up the various aggregates.

Figuratively, macroeconomics looks at the beach, not the pieces of sand, the rocks, and the shells.

Microeconomics

Microeconomics is the part of economics concerned with individual units such as a person, a household, a firm, or an industry. At this level of analysis, the economist observes the details of an economic unit, or very small segment of the economy, under a figurative microscope. In microeconomics we look at decision making by individual customers, workers, households, and business firms. We measure the price of a specific product, the number of workers employed by a single firm, the revenue or income of a particular firm or household, or the expenditures of a specific firm, government entity, or family. In microeconomics, we examine the sand, rock, and shells, not the beach.

The macro–micro distinction does not mean that economics is so highly compartmentalized that every topic can be readily labeled as either macro or micro; many topics and subdivisions of economics are rooted in both. Example: While the problem of unemployment is usually treated as a macroeconomic topic (because unemployment relates to aggregate production), economists recognize that the decisions made by *individual* workers on how long to search for jobs and the way *specific* labor markets encourage or impede hiring are also critical in determining the unemployment rate. **(Key Question 5)**

Positive and Normative Economics

Both macroeconomics and microeconomics contain elements of positive economics and normative economics. **Positive economics** focuses on facts and cause-and-effect relationships. It includes description, theory development, and theory testing (theoretical economics). Positive economics avoids value judgments, tries to establish scientific statements about economic behavior, and deals with what the economy is actually like. Such scientific-based analysis is critical to good policy analysis.

Economic policy, on the other hand, involves **normative economics,** which incorporates value judgments about what the economy should be like or what particular policy actions should be recommended to achieve a desirable goal (policy economics). Normative economics looks at the desirability of certain aspects of the economy. It underlies expressions of support for particular economic policies.

Positive economics concerns *what is*, whereas normative economics embodies subjective feelings about *what ought to be*. Examples: Positive statement: "The unemployment rate in France is higher than that in the United States." Normative statement: "France ought to undertake policies to make its labor market more flexible to reduce unemployment rates." Whenever words such as "ought" or "should" appear in a sentence, you are very likely encountering a normative statement.

Most of the disagreement among economists involves normative, value-based policy questions. Of course, economists sometime disagree about which theories or models best represent the economy and its parts; but they agree on a full range of economic principles. Most economic controversy thus reflects differing opinions or value judgments about what society should be like.

QUICK REVIEW 1.1

- Economics examines how individuals, institutions, and society make choices under conditions of scarcity.
- The economic perspective stresses (a) resource scarcity and the necessity of making choices, (b) the assumption of rational behavior, and (c) comparisons of marginal benefit and marginal cost.
- Economists use the scientific method to establish economic theories—cause-effect generalizations about the economic behavior of individuals and institutions.
- Macroeconomics examines the economy as a whole; microeconomics focuses on specific units of the economy.
- Positive economics deals with factual statements ("what is"); normative economics involves value judgments ("what ought to be").

Individuals' Economizing Problem

A close examination of the **economizing problem**—the need to make choices because economic wants exceed economic means—will enhance your understanding of economic models and the difference between microeconomic and macroeconomic analysis. Let's first build a microeconomic model of the economizing problem faced by an individual.

Limited Income

We all have a finite amount of income, even the wealthiest among us. Even Donald Trump must decide how to spend his money! And the majority of us have much more limited means. Our income comes to us in the form of wages, interest, rent, and profit, although we may also receive money from government programs or family members. As Global Perspective 1.1 shows, the average income of Americans in 2004 was $41,400. In the poorest nations, it was less than $500.

Unlimited Wants

For better or worse, most people have virtually unlimited wants. We desire various goods and services that provide utility. Our wants extend over a wide range of products, from *necessities* (for example, food, shelter, and clothing) to *luxuries* (for example, perfumes, yachts, and sports cars).

GLOBAL PERSPECTIVE 1.1

Average Income, Selected Nations

Average income (total income/population) and therefore typical individual budget constraints vary greatly among nations.

Country	**Per Capita Income, 2004** (U.S. dollars, based on exchange rates)
Switzerland	$48,230
United States	41,400
Japan	37,180
France	30,090
South Korea	13,980
Mexico	6,770
Brazil	3,090
China	1,290
Pakistan	600
Nigeria	390
Rwanda	220
Liberia	110

Source: World Bank, **www.worldbank.org.**

Some wants such as basic food, clothing, and shelter have biological roots. Other wants, for example, specific kinds of food, clothing, and shelter, arise from the conventions and customs of society.

Over time, as new products are introduced, economic wants tend to change and multiply. Only recently have people wanted MP3 players, Internet service, digital cameras, or camera phones because those products did not exist a few decades ago. Also, the satisfaction of certain wants may trigger others: the acquisition of a Ford Focus or a Honda Civic has been known to whet the appetite for a Lexus or a Mercedes.

Services, as well as goods, satisfy our wants. Car repair work, the removal of an inflamed appendix, legal and accounting advice, and haircuts all satisfy human wants. Actually, we buy many goods, such as automobiles and washing machines, for the services they render. The differences between goods and services are often smaller than they appear to be.

For most people, the desires for goods and services cannot be fully satisfied. Bill Gates may have all that he wants for himself, but his massive charitable giving suggests that he keenly wants better health care for the world's poor. Our desires for a particular good or service can be satisfied; over a short period of time we can surely get enough toothpaste or pasta. And one appendectomy is plenty. But our desire for goods and services in general seem to be another story.

Because we have only limited income (usually through our work) but seemingly insatiable wants, it is in our self-interest to economize: to pick and choose goods and services that create maximum utility.

A Budget Line

We can clarify the economizing problem facing consumers by visualizing a **budget line** (or, more technically, a *budget constraint*). It is a schedule or curve that shows various combinations of two products a consumer can purchase with a specific money income. Although we assume two products, the analysis generalizes to the full range of products available to an individual consumer.

To understand the idea of a budget line, suppose that you received a Barnes & Noble (or Borders) gift card as a birthday present. The $120 card is soon to expire. You take the card to the store and confine your purchase decisions to two alternatives: DVDs and paperback books. DVDs are $20 each and paperback books are $10 each. Your purchase options are shown in the table in Figure 1.1.

At one extreme, you might spend all of your $120 "income" on 6 DVDs at $20 each and have nothing left to spend on books. Or, by giving up 2 DVDs and thereby gaining $40, you can have 4 DVDs at $20 each and 4 books at $10 each. And so on to the other extreme, at which you could buy 12 books at $10 each, spending your entire gift card on books with nothing left to spend on DVDs.

The graph in Figure 1.1 shows the budget line. Note that the graph is not restricted to whole units of DVDs and books as is the table. Every point on the graph represents a possible combination of DVDs and books, including fractional quantities. The slope of the graphed budget line measures the ratio of the price of books (P_b) to the price of DVDs (P_{dvd}); more precisely, the slope is $P_b/P_{dvd} = \$ - 10/\$ + 20 = -\frac{1}{2}$, or $-.5$. So you must forgo 1 DVD (measured on the vertical axis) to buy 2 books (measured on the horizontal axis). This yields a slope of $-\frac{1}{2}$ or $-.5$.

The budget line illustrates several ideas.

Attainable and Unattainable Combinations

All the combinations of DVDs and books on or inside the budget line are *attainable* from the $120 of money income. You can afford to buy, for example, 3 DVDs at $20 each

FIGURE 1.1 A consumer's budget line. The budget line (or budget constraint) shows all the combinations of any two products that can be purchased, given the prices of the products and the consumer's money income.

The Budget Line: Whole-Unit Combinations of DVDs and Paperback Books Attainable with an Income of $120

Units of DVDs (Price = $20)	Units of Books (Price = $10)	Total Expenditure
6	0	($120 = $120 + $0)
5	2	($120 = $100 + $20)
4	4	($120 = $80 + $40)
3	6	($120 = $60 + $60)
2	8	($120 = $40 + $80)
1	10	($120 = $20 + $100)
0	12	($120 = $0 + $120)

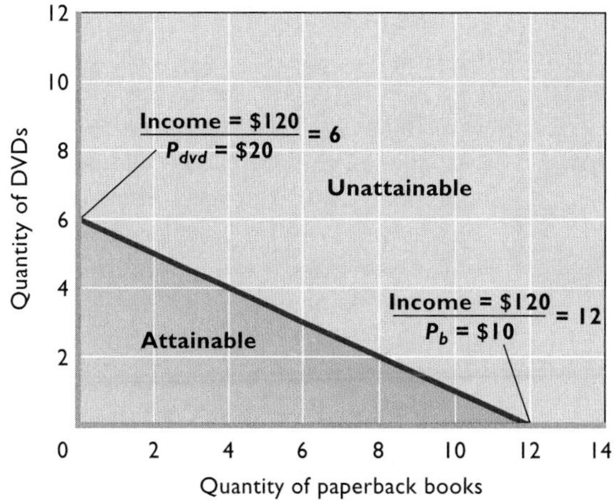

and 6 books at $10 each. You also can obviously afford to buy 2 DVDs and 5 books, if so desired, and not use up the value on the gift card. But to achieve maximum utility you will want to spend the full $120.

In contrast, all combinations beyond the budget line are *unattainable*. The $120 limit simply does not allow you to purchase, for example, 5 DVDs at $20 each and 5 books at $10 each. That $150 expenditure would clearly exceed the $120 limit. In Figure 1.1 the attainable combinations are on and within the budget line; the unattainable combinations are beyond the budget line.

Tradeoffs and Opportunity Costs The budget line in Figure 1.1 illustrates the idea of tradeoffs arising from limited income. To obtain more DVDs, you have to give up some books. For example, to obtain the first DVD, you trade off 2 books. So the opportunity cost of the first DVD is 2 books. To obtain the second DVD the opportunity cost is also 2 books. The straight-line budget constraint, with its constant slope, indicates constant opportunity cost. That is, the opportunity cost of 1 extra DVD remains the same (= 2 books) as more DVDs are purchased. And, in reverse, the opportunity cost of 1 extra book does not change (= $\frac{1}{2}$ DVD) as more books are bought.

O 1.5
Opportunity costs

Choice Limited income forces people to choose what to buy and what to forgo to fulfill wants. You will select the combination of DVDs and paperback books that you think is "best." That is, you will evaluate your marginal benefits and marginal costs (here, product price) to make choices that maximize your satisfaction. Other people, with the same $120 gift card, would undoubtedly make different choices.

CONSIDER THIS . . .

Did Gates, Winfrey, and Rodriguez Make Bad Choices?

Opportunity costs come into play in decisions well beyond simple buying decisions. Consider the different choices people make with respect to college. College graduates usually earn about 50 percent more during their lifetimes than persons with just high school diplomas. For most capable students, "Go to college, stay in college, and earn a degree" is very sound advice.

Yet Microsoft cofounder Bill Gates and talk show host Oprah Winfrey* both dropped out of college, and baseball star Alex Rodriguez ("A-Rod") never even bothered to start classes. What were they thinking? Unlike most students, Gates faced enormous opportunity costs for staying in college. He had a vision for his company, and his starting work young helped ensure Microsoft's success. Similarly, Winfrey landed a spot in local television news when she was a teenager, eventually producing and starring in the *Oprah Winfrey Show* when she was 32 years old. Getting a degree in her twenties might have interrupted the string of successes that made her famous talk show possible. And Rodriguez knew that professional athletes have short careers. Therefore, going to college directly after high school would have taken away 4 years of his peak earning potential.

So Gates, Winfrey, and Rodriguez understood opportunity costs and made their choices accordingly. The size of opportunity costs greatly matters in making individual decisions.

*Winfrey eventually went back to school and earned a degree from Tennessee State University when she was in her thirties.

Income Changes The location of the budget line varies with money income. An increase in money income shifts the budget line to the right; a decrease in money income shifts it to the left. To verify this, recalculate the table in Figure 1.1, assuming the card value (income) is (a) \$240 and (b) \$60, and plot the new budget lines in the graph. No wonder people like to have more income: That shifts their budget lines outward and enables them to buy more goods and services. But even with more income, people will still face spending tradeoffs, choices, and opportunity costs. **(Key Question 7)**

W 1.1
Budget lines

QUICK REVIEW 1.2

- Because wants exceed incomes, individuals face an economizing problem; they must decide what to buy and what to forgo.
- A budget line (budget constraint) shows the various combinations of two goods that a consumer can purchase with a specific money income.
- Straight-line budget constraints imply constant opportunity costs associated with obtaining more of either of the two goods.

Society's Economizing Problem

Society must also make choices under conditions of scarcity. It, too, faces an economizing problem. Should it devote more of its limited resources to the criminal justice system (police, courts, and prisons) or to education (teachers, books, and schools)? If it decides to devote more resources to both, what other goods and services does it forgo? Health care? Energy development?

Scarce Resources

Society has limited or scarce **economic resources,** meaning all natural, human, and manufactured resources that go into the production of goods and services. This includes the entire set of factory and farm buildings and all the equipment, tools, and machinery used to produce manufactured goods and agricultural products; all transportation and communication facilities; all types of labor; and land and mineral resources.

Resource Categories

Economists classify economic resources into four general categories.

Land Land means much more to the economist than it does to most people. To the economist **land** includes all natural resources ("gifts of nature") used in the production process, such as arable land, forests, mineral and oil deposits, and water resources.

Labor The resource **labor** consists of the physical and mental talents of individuals used in producing goods and services. The services of a logger, retail clerk, machinist, teacher, professional football player, and nuclear physicist all fall under the general heading "labor."

Capital For economists, **capital** (or capital goods) includes all manufactured aids used in producing consumer goods and services. Included are all factory, storage, transportation, and distribution facilities, as well as tools and machinery. Economists refer to the purchase of capital goods as **investment.**

Capital goods differ from consumer goods because consumer goods satisfy wants directly, whereas capital goods do so indirectly by aiding the production of consumer goods. Note that the term "capital" as used by economists refers not to money but to tools, machinery, and other productive equipment. Because money produces nothing, economists do not include it as an economic resource. Money (or money capital or financial capital) is simply a means for purchasing capital goods.

Entrepreneurial Ability Finally, there is the special human resource, distinct from labor, called **entrepreneurial ability.** The entrepreneur performs several functions:

- The entrepreneur takes the initiative in combining the resources of land, labor, and capital to produce a good or a service. Both a sparkplug and a catalyst, the entrepreneur is the driving force behind production and the agent who combines the other resources in what is hoped will be a successful business venture.
- The entrepreneur makes the strategic business decisions that set the course of an enterprise.
- The entrepreneur is an innovator. He or she commercializes new products, new production techniques, or even new forms of business organization.
- The entrepreneur is a risk bearer. The entrepreneur has no guarantee of profit. The reward for the entrepreneur's time, efforts, and abilities may be profits or losses. The entrepreneur risks not only his or her invested funds but those of associates and stockholders as well.

Because land, labor, capital, and entrepreneurial ability are combined to produce goods and services, they are called the **factors of production,** or simply "inputs."

Production Possibilities Model

Society uses its scarce resources to produce goods and services. The alternatives and choices it faces can best be understood through a macroeconomic model of production possibilities. To keep things simple, let's initially assume:

- ***Full employment*** The economy is employing all its available resources.
- ***Fixed resources*** The quantity and quality of the factors of production are fixed.
- ***Fixed technology*** The state of technology (the methods used to produce output) is constant.
- ***Two goods*** The economy is producing only two goods: pizzas and industrial robots. Pizzas symbolize **consumer goods,** products that satisfy our wants directly; industrial robots (for example, the kind used to weld automobile frames) symbolize **capital goods,** products that satisfy our wants indirectly by making possible more efficient production of consumer goods.

Production Possibilities Table

A production possibilities table lists the different combinations of two products that can be produced with a specific set of resources, assuming full employment. Table 1.1 presents a simple, hypothetical economy that is producing pizzas and industrial robots; the data are, of course, hypothetical. At alternative A, this economy would be devoting all its available resources to the production of industrial robots (capital goods); at alternative E, all resources would go to pizza production (consumer goods). Those alternatives are unrealistic extremes; an economy typically produces both capital goods and consumer goods, as in B, C, and D. As we move from alternative A to E, we increase the production of pizzas at the expense of the production of industrial robots.

TABLE 1.1 Production Possibilities of Pizzas and Industrial Robots

	Production Alternatives				
Type of Product	**A**	**B**	**C**	**D**	**E**
Pizzas (in hundred thousands)	0	1	2	3	4
Robots (in thousands)	10	9	7	4	0

Because consumer goods satisfy our wants directly, any movement toward E looks tempting. In producing more pizzas, society increases the current satisfaction of its wants. But there is a cost: More pizzas means fewer industrial robots. This shift of resources to consumer goods catches up with society over time because the stock of capital goods does not expand at the current rate, with the result that some potential for greater future production is lost. By moving toward alternative E, society chooses "more now" at the expense of "much more later."

By moving toward A, society chooses to forgo current consumption, thereby freeing up resources that can be used to increase the production of capital goods. By building up its stock of capital this way, society will have greater future production and, therefore, greater future consumption. By moving toward A, society is choosing "more later" at the cost of "less now."

Generalization: At any point in time, a fully employed economy must sacrifice some of one good to obtain more of another good. Scarce resources prohibit such an economy from having more of both goods. Society must choose among alternatives. There is no such thing as a free pizza, or a free industrial robot.

Production Possibilities Curve

The data presented in a production possibilities table are shown graphically as a **production possibilities curve.** Such a curve displays the different combinations of goods and services that society can produce in a fully employed economy, assuming a fixed availability of supplies of resources and constant technology. We arbitrarily represent the economy's output of capital goods (here, industrial robots) on the vertical axis and the output of consumer goods (here, pizzas) on the horizontal axis, as shown in **Figure 1.2 (Key Graph).**

G 1.1
Production possibilities curve

Each point on the production possibilities curve represents some maximum output of the two products. The curve is a "constraint" because it shows the limit of attainable outputs. Points on the curve are attainable as long as the economy uses all its available resources. Points lying inside the curve are also attainable, but they reflect less total output and therefore are not as desirable as points on the curve. Points inside the curve imply that the economy could have more of both industrial robots and pizzas if it achieved full employment of its resources. Points lying beyond the production possibilities curve, like *W*, would represent a greater output than the output

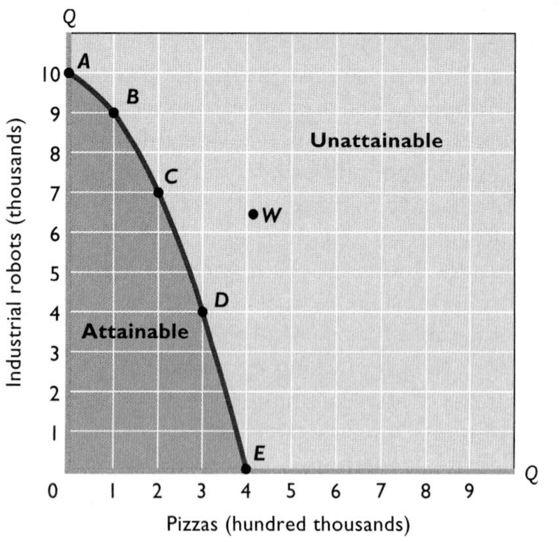

FIGURE 1.2 The production possibilities curve. Each point on the production possibilities curve represents some maximum combination of two products that can be produced if resources are fully employed. When an economy is operating on the curve, more industrial robots means less pizzas, and vice versa. Limited resources and a fixed technology make any combination of industrial robots and pizzas lying outside the curve (such as at *W*) unattainable. Points inside the curve are attainable, but they indicate that full employment is not being realized.

QUICK QUIZ 1.2

1. Production possibilities curve *ABCDE* is bowed out from the origin because:
   - **a.** the marginal benefit of pizzas declines as more pizzas are consumed.
   - **b.** the curve gets steeper as we move from *E* to *A*.
   - **c.** it reflects the law of increasing opportunity costs.
   - **d.** resources are scarce.
2. The marginal opportunity cost of the second unit of pizza is:
   - **a.** 2 units of robots.
   - **b.** 3 units of robots.
   - **c.** 7 units of robots.
   - **d.** 9 units of robots.
3. The total opportunity cost of 7 units of robots is:
   - **a.** 1 unit of pizza.
   - **b.** 2 units of pizza.
   - **c.** 3 units of pizza.
   - **d.** 4 units of pizza.
4. All points on this production possibilities curve necessarily represent:
   - **a.** society's optimal choice.
   - **b.** less than full use of resources.
   - **c.** unattainable levels of output.
   - **d.** full employment.

Answers: 1. c; 2. a; 3. b; 4. d

at any point on the curve. Such points, however, are unattainable with the current availability of resources and technology.

Law of Increasing Opportunity Cost

Figure 1.2 clearly shows that more pizzas means fewer industrial robots. The number of units of industrial robots that must be given up to obtain another unit of pizzas, of course, is the opportunity cost of that unit of pizzas.

In moving from alternative A to alternative B in Table 1.1, the cost of 1 additional unit of pizzas is 1 fewer unit of industrial robots. But when additional units are considered—B to C, C to D, and D to E—an important economic principle is revealed: For society, the opportunity cost of each additional unit of pizzas is greater than the opportunity cost of the preceding one. When we move from A to B, just 1 unit of industrial robots is sacrificed for 1 more unit of pizzas; but in going from B to C we sacrifice 2 additional units of industrial robots for 1 more unit of pizzas; then 3 more of industrial robots for 1 more of pizzas; and finally 4 for 1. Conversely, confirm that as we move from E to A, the cost of an additional unit of industrial robots (on average) is $\frac{1}{4}$, $\frac{1}{3}$, $\frac{1}{2}$, and 1 unit of pizzas, respectively, for the four successive moves.

Our example illustrates the **law of increasing opportunity costs.** As the production of a particular good increases, the opportunity cost of producing an additional unit rises.

Shape of the Curve The law of increasing opportunity costs is reflected in the shape of the production possibilities curve: The curve is bowed out from the origin of the graph. Figure 1.2 shows that when the economy moves from *A* to *E*, it must give up successively larger amounts of industrial robots (1, 2, 3, and 4) to acquire equal increments of pizzas (1, 1, 1, and 1). This is shown in the slope of the production possibilities curve, which becomes steeper as we move from *A* to *E*.

Economic Rationale The economic rationale for the law of increasing opportunity costs is that economic resources are not completely adaptable to alternative uses. Many resources are better at producing one type of good than at producing others. Some land is highly suited to growing the ingredients necessary for pizza production, but as pizza production expands society has to start using land that is less bountiful for farming. Other land is rich in mineral deposits and therefore well-suited to producing the materials needed to make industrial robots. As society steps up the production of robots, it must use land that is less and less adaptable to making their components.

If we start at *A* and move to *B* in Figure 1.2, we can shift resources whose productivity is relatively high in pizza production and low in industrial robots. But as we move from *B* to *C*, *C* to *D*, and so on, resources highly productive of pizzas become increasingly scarce. To get more pizzas, resources whose productivity in industrial robots is relatively great will be needed. Increasingly more of such resources, and hence greater sacrifices of industrial robots, will be needed to achieve each 1-unit increase in pizzas. This lack of perfect flexibility, or interchangeability, on the part of resources is the cause of increasing opportunity costs for society. **(Key Question 10)**

W 1.2
Production possibilities

Optimal Allocation

Of all the attainable combinations of pizzas and industrial robots on the curve in Figure 1.2, which is optimal (best)? That is, what specific quantities of resources should be allocated to pizzas and what specific quantities should be allocated to industrial robots in order to maximize satisfaction?

Recall that economic decisions center on comparisons of marginal benefit (MB) and marginal cost (MC). Any economic activity should be expanded as long as marginal benefit exceeds marginal cost and should be reduced if marginal cost exceeds marginal benefit. The optimal amount of the activity occurs where MB = MC. Society needs to make a similar assessment about its production decision.

Consider pizzas. We already know from the law of increasing opportunity costs that the marginal costs of additional units of pizzas will rise as more units are produced. We also know that we obtain extra or marginal benefits from additional units of pizzas. However, although economic wants in the aggregate are insatiable, the assumption that successive units of a particular product yield fewer additional benefits to society than prior units is reasonable.

The optimal quantity of pizza production is indicated by point *e* at the intersection of the MB and MC curves: 200,000 units in Figure 1.3. Why is this amount the optimal quantity? If only 100,000 units of pizzas were produced, the marginal benefit of an extra unit of them (point *a*) would exceed its marginal cost (point *b*). In money terms, MB is \$15, while MC is only \$5. When society gains something worth \$15 at a marginal cost of only \$5, it is better off. In Figure 1.3, net gains can continue to be realized until pizza-product production has been increased to 200,000.

In contrast, the production of 300,000 units of pizzas is excessive. There the MC of an added unit is \$15 (point *c*) and its MB is only \$5 (point *d*). This means that 1 unit of pizzas is worth only \$5 to society but costs it \$15 to obtain. This is a losing proposition for society!

FIGURE 1.3 Optimal output: MB = MC. Achieving the optimal output requires the expansion of a good's output until its marginal benefit (MB) and marginal cost (MC) are equal. No resources beyond that point should be allocated to the product. Here, optimal output occurs at point e, where 200,000 units of pizzas are produced.

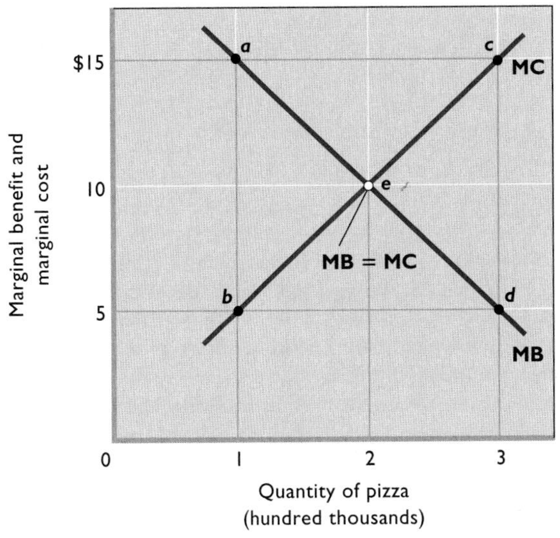

So resources are being efficiently allocated to any product when the marginal benefit and marginal cost of its output are equal (MB = MC). Suppose that by applying the same analysis to industrial robots, we find that the optimal (MB = MC) output of robots is 7000. This would mean that alternative *C* (200,000 units of pizzas and 7000 units of industrial robots) on the production possibilities curve in Figure 1.2 would be optimal for this economy. **(Key Question 11)**

CONSIDER THIS . . .

The Economics of War

Production possibilities analysis is helpful in assessing the costs and benefits of waging the broad war on terrorism, including the wars in Afghanistan and Iraq. An October 2005 estimate places the total cost of these efforts, including rebuilding expenses, at $350 billion.

If we categorize all U.S. production as either "defense goods" or "civilian goods," we can measure them on the axes of a production possibilities diagram such as that shown in Figure 1.2. The opportunity cost of using more resources for defense goods is the civilian goods sacrificed. In a fully employed economy, more defense goods are achieved at the opportunity cost of fewer civilian goods—health care, education, pollution control, personal computers, houses, and so on. The cost of war and defense is the other goods forgone. The benefits are numerous and diverse but clearly include the gains from protecting against future loss of American lives, assets, income, and well-being.

Society must assess the marginal benefit (MB) and marginal cost (MC) of additional defense goods to determine their optimal amounts—where to locate on the defense goods–civilian goods production possibilities curve. Although estimating marginal benefits and marginal costs is an imprecise art, the MB-MC framework is a useful way of approaching choices. An optimal allocation of resources requires that society expand production of defense goods until MB = MC.

The events of September 11, 2001, and the future threats they foreshadowed increased the marginal benefits of defense goods, as perceived by Americans. If we label the horizontal axis in Figure 1.3 "defense goods" and draw in a rightward shift of the MB curve, you will see that the optimal quantity of defense goods rises. In view of the concerns relating to September 11, the United States allocated more of its resources to defense. But the MB-MC analysis also reminds us we can spend too much on defense, as well as too little. The United States should not expand defense goods beyond the point where MB = MC. If it does, it will be sacrificing civilian goods of greater value than the defense goods obtained.

QUICK REVIEW 1.3

- Economists categorize economic resources as land, labor, capital, and entrepreneurial ability.
- The production possibilities curve illustrates several ideas: (a) scarcity of resources is implied by the area of unattainable combinations of output lying outside the production possibilities curve; (b) choice among outputs is reflected in the variety of attainable combinations of goods lying along the curve; (c) opportunity cost is illustrated by the downward slope of the curve; (d) the law of increasing opportunity costs is implied by the bowed-outward shape of the curve.
- A comparison of marginal benefits and marginal costs is needed to determine the best or optimal output mix on a production possibilities curve.

Unemployment, Growth, and the Future

In the depths of the Great Depression of the 1930s, one-quarter of U.S. workers were unemployed and one-third of U.S. production capacity was idle. The United States has suffered a number of considerably milder downturns since then, the latest occurring in 2001. In that year total production fell one-half a percentage point and unemployment increased by about 2 million workers.

Almost all nations have experienced widespread unemployment and unused production capacity from business downturns at one time or another. Since 1995, for example, several nations—including Argentina, Japan, Mexico, Germany, and South Korea—have had economic downturns and unemployment.

How do these realities relate to the production possibilities model? Our analysis and conclusions change if we relax the assumption that all available resources are fully employed. The five alternatives in Table 1.1 represent maximum outputs; they illustrate the combinations of pizzas and industrial robots that can be produced when the economy is operating at full employment. With unemployment, this economy would produce less than each alternative shown in the table.

Graphically, we represent situations of unemployment by points inside the original production possibilities curve (reproduced here in Figure 1.4). Point *U* is one such point. Here the economy is falling short of the various maximum combinations of pizzas and industrial robots represented

FIGURE 1.4 Unemployment and the production possibilities curve. Any point inside the production possibilities curve, such as *U*, represents unemployment or a failure to achieve full employment. The arrows indicate that by realizing full employment, the economy could operate on the curve. This means it could produce more of one or both products than it is producing at point *U*.

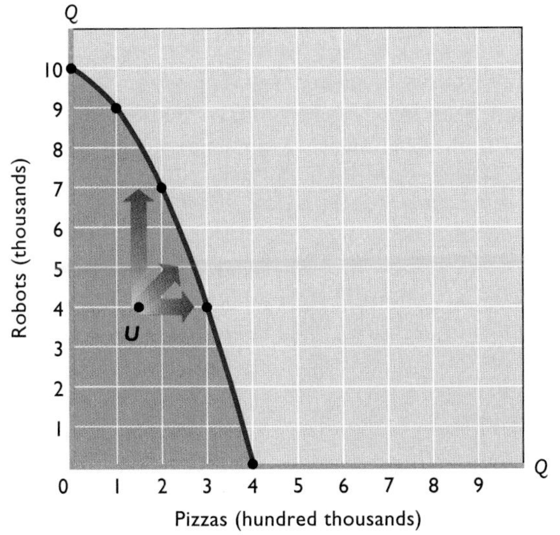

by the points on the production possibilities curve. The arrows in Figure 1.4 indicate three possible paths back to full employment. A move toward full employment would yield a greater output of one or both products.

A Growing Economy

When we drop the assumptions that the quantity and quality of resources and technology are fixed, the production possibilities curve shifts positions and the potential maximum output of the economy changes.

Increases in Resource Supplies

Although resource supplies are fixed at any specific moment, they change over time. For example, a nation's growing population brings about increases in the supplies of labor and entrepreneurial ability. Also, labor quality usually improves over time. Historically, the economy's stock of capital has increased at a significant, though unsteady, rate. And although some of our energy and mineral resources are being depleted, new sources are also being discovered. The development of irrigation programs, for example, adds to the supply of arable land.

The net result of these increased supplies of the factors of production is the ability to produce more of both consumer goods and capital goods. Thus 20 years from now, the production possibilities may supersede those shown in Table 1.1. The new production possibilities might look like those in the table in Figure 1.5. The greater abundance of resources will result in a greater potential output of one or both products at each alternative. The economy will have achieved economic growth in the form of expanded potential output. Thus, when an increase in the quantity or quality of resources occurs, the production possibilities curve shifts outward and to the right, as illustrated by the move from the inner curve to curve *A′B′C′D′E′* in Figure 1.5. This sort of shift represents growth of economic capacity, which, when used, means **economic growth:** a larger total output.

Advances in Technology

An advancing technology brings both new and better goods and improved ways of producing them. For now, let's think of technological advance as being only improvements in the methods of production, for example, the introduction of computerized systems to manage inventories and schedule production. These advances alter our previous discussion of the economizing problem by allowing society to produce more goods with available resources. As with increases in

FIGURE 1.5 Economic growth and the production possibilities curve. The increase in supplies of resources, improvements in resource quality, and technological advances that occur in a dynamic economy move the production possibilities curve outward and to the right, allowing the economy to have larger quantities of both types of goods.

	Production Alternatives				
Type of Product	**A′**	**B′**	**C′**	**D′**	**E′**
Pizzas (in hundred thousands)	0	2	4	6	8
Robots (in thousands)	14	12	9	5	0

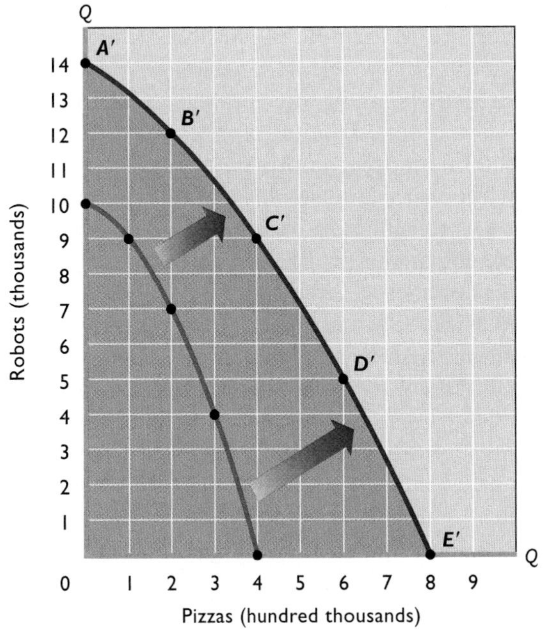

Last Word

Pitfalls to Sound Economic Reasoning

Because they affect us so personally, we often have difficulty thinking accurately and objectively about economic issues.

Here are some common pitfalls to avoid in successfully applying the economic perspective.

Biases Most people bring a bundle of biases and preconceptions to the field of economics. For example, some might think that corporate profits are excessive or that lending money is always superior to borrowing money. Others might believe that government is necessarily less efficient than businesses or that more government regulation is always better than less. Biases cloud thinking and interfere with objective analysis. All of us must be willing to shed biases and preconceptions that are not supported by facts.

Loaded Terminology The economic terminology used in newspapers and broadcast media is sometimes emotionally biased, or loaded. The writer or spokesperson may have a cause to promote or an ax to grind and may slant comments accordingly. High profits may be labeled "obscene," low wages may be called "exploitive," or self-interested behavior may be "greed." Government workers may be referred to as "mindless bureaucrats" and those favoring stronger government regulations may be called "socialists." To objectively analyze economic issues, you must be prepared to reject or discount such terminology.

Fallacy of Composition Another pitfall in economic thinking is the assumption that what is true for one individual or part of a whole is necessarily true for a group of individuals or the whole. This is a logical fallacy called the *fallacy of composition*; the assumption is not correct. A statement that is valid for an individual or part is not necessarily valid for the larger group or whole. You may see the action better if you leap to your feet to see an

resource supplies, technological advances make possible the production of more industrial robots and more pizzas.

A real-world example of improved technology is the recent surge of new technologies relating to computers, communications, and biotechnology. Technological advances have dropped the prices of computers and greatly increased their speed. Improved software has greatly increased the everyday usefulness of computers. Cellular phones and the Internet have increased communications capacity, enhancing production and improving the efficiency of markets. Advances in biotechnology have resulted in important agricultural and medical discoveries. The sum of these new technologies is so significant that they may be contributing to greater-than-normal U.S. economic growth (larger rightward shifts of the nation's production possibilities curve).

Conclusion: Economic growth is the result of (1) increases in supplies of resources, (2) improvements in resource quality, and (3) technological advances. The consequence of growth is that a full-employment economy can enjoy a greater output of both consumption goods and capital goods. Whereas static, no-growth economies must sacrifice some of one good to obtain more of another, dynamic, growing economies can have larger quantities of both goods. **(Key Question 13)**

Present Choices and Future Possibilities

An economy's current choice of positions on its production possibilities curve helps determine the future location of that curve. Let's designate the two axes of the production possibilities curve as "goods for the future" and "goods for the present," as in Figure 1.6. Goods for the future are such things as capital goods, research and education, and preventive medicine. They increase the quantity and quality of property resources, enlarge the stock of technological information, and improve the quality of human resources. As we have already seen, goods for the future, such as capital goods, are the ingredients of economic growth. Goods for the present are consumer goods, such as food, clothing, and entertainment.

outstanding play at a football game. But if all the spectators leap to their feet at the same time, nobody—including you—will have a better view than when all remained seated.

Here is an economic example: An individual farmer who reaps a particularly large crop is likely to realize a sharp gain in income. But this statement cannot be generalized to farmers as a group. The individual farmer's large "bumper" crop will not noticeably reduce crop prices because each farmer produces a negligible fraction of the total farm output. But for all farmers as a group, prices decline when total output increases. Thus, if all farmers reap bumper crops, the total output of farm products will increase, depressing crop prices. If the price declines are relatively large, total farm income might actually fall.

Post Hoc Fallacy You must think very carefully before concluding that because event A precedes event B, A is the cause of B. This kind of faulty reasoning is known as the *post hoc, ergo propter hoc*, or "after this, therefore because of this," fallacy. Noneconomic example: A professional football team hires a new coach and the team's record improves. Is the new coach the cause? Maybe. Perhaps the presence of more experienced and talented players or an easier schedule is the true cause. The rooster crows before dawn, but does not cause the sunrise.

Economic example: Many people blamed the Great Depression of the 1930s on the stock market crash of 1929. But the crash did not cause the Great Depression. The same severe weaknesses in the economy that caused the crash caused the Great Depression. The depression would have occurred even without the preceding stock market crash.

Correlation but not Causation Do not confuse correlation, or connection, with causation. Correlation between two events or two sets of data indicates only that they are associated in some systematic and dependable way. For example, we may find that when variable X increases, Y also increases. But this correlation does not necessarily mean that there is causation—that an increase in X is the cause of an increase in Y. The relationship could be purely coincidental or dependent on some other factor, Z, not included in the analysis.

Here is an example: Economists have found a positive correlation between education and income. In general, people with more education earn higher incomes than those with less education. Common sense suggests education is the cause and higher incomes are the effect; more education implies a more knowledgeable and productive worker, and such workers receive larger salaries.

But might the relationship be explainable in other ways? Are education and income correlated because the characteristics required for succeeding in education—ability and motivation— are the same ones required to be a productive and highly paid worker? If so, then people with those traits will probably both obtain more education and earn higher incomes. But greater education will not be the sole cause of the higher income.

FIGURE 1.6 Present choices and future locations of production possibilities curves. A nation's current choice favoring "present goods," as made by Presentville in (a), will cause a modest outward shift of the production possibilities curve in the future. A nation's current choice favoring "future goods," as made by Futureville in (b), will result in a greater outward shift of the curve in the future.

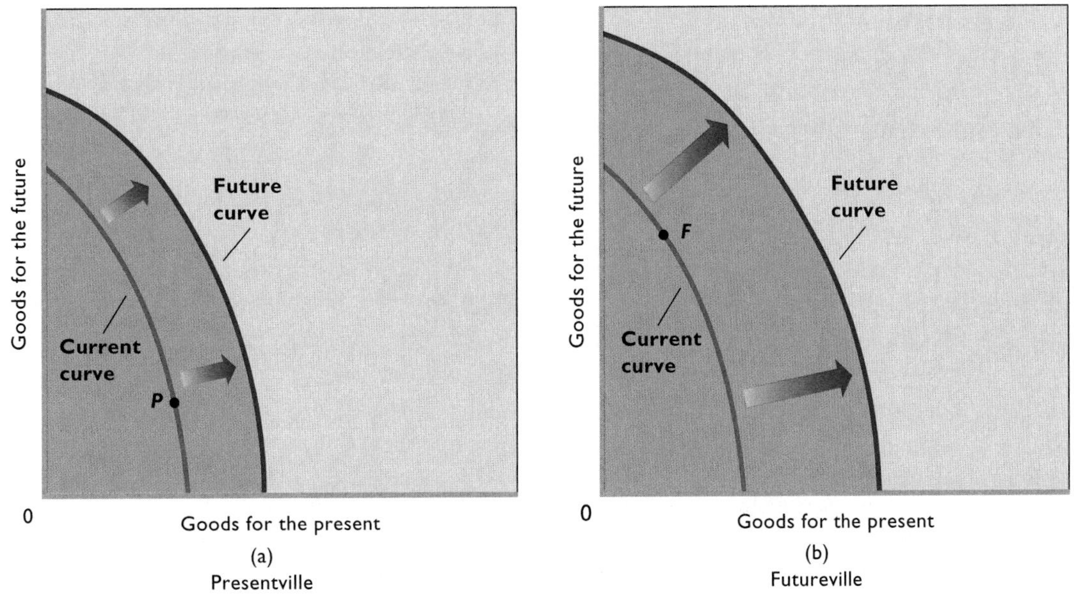

Now suppose there are two hypothetical economies, Presentville and Futureville, which are initially identical in every respect except one: Presentville's current choice of positions on its production possibilities curve strongly favors present goods over future goods. Point *P* in Figure 1.6a indicates that choice. It is located quite far down the curve to the right, indicating a high priority for goods for the present, at the expense of fewer goods for the future. Futureville, in contrast, makes a current choice that stresses larger amounts of future goods and smaller amounts of present goods, as shown by point *F* in Figure 1.6b.

G 1.2
Present choices and future possibilities

Now, other things equal, we can expect the future production possibilities curve of Futureville to be farther to the right than Presentville's curve. By currently choosing an output more favorable to technological advances and to increases in the quantity and quality of resources, Futureville will achieve greater economic growth than Presentville. In terms of capital goods, Futureville is choosing to make larger current additions to its "national factory" by devoting more of its current output to capital than Presentville. The payoff from this choice for Futureville is greater future production capacity and economic growth. The opportunity cost is fewer consumer goods in the present for Futureville to enjoy.

Is Futureville's choice thus necessarily "better" than Presentville's? That, we cannot say. The different outcomes simply reflect different preferences and priorities in the two countries. But each country will have to live with the economic consequences of its choice. **(Key Question 14)**

A Qualification: International Trade

Production possibilities analysis implies that an individual nation is limited to the combinations of output indicated by its production possibilities curve. But we must modify this principle when international specialization and trade exist.

You will see in later chapters that an economy can circumvent, through international specialization and trade, the output limits imposed by its domestic production possibilities curve. International specialization means directing domestic resources to output that a nation is highly efficient at producing. International trade involves the exchange of these goods for goods produced abroad. Specialization and trade enable a nation to get more of a desired good at less sacrifice of some other good. Rather than sacrifice 3 units of robots to get a third unit of pizza, as in Table 1.1, a nation might be able to obtain the third unit of pizza by trading only 2 units of robots for it. Specialization and trade have the same effect as having more and better resources or discovering improved production techniques; both increase the quantities of capital and consumer goods available to society. Expansion of domestic production possibilities and international trade are two separate routes for obtaining greater output.

QUICK REVIEW 1.4

- Unemployment causes an economy to operate at a point inside its production possibilities curve.
- Increases in resource supplies, improvements in resource quality, and technological advance cause economic growth, which is depicted as an outward shift of the production possibilities curve.
- An economy's present choice of capital and consumer goods helps determine the future location of its production possibilities curve.
- International specialization and trade enable a nation to obtain more goods than its production possibilities curve indicates.

Summary

1. Economics is the social science that examines how individuals, institutions, and society make optimal choices under conditions of scarcity.
2. The economic perspective includes three elements: scarcity and choice, purposeful behavior, and marginal analysis. It sees individuals and institutions making rational decisions based on comparisons of marginal costs and marginal benefits.
3. Economists employ the scientific method, in which they form and test hypotheses of cause-and-effect relationships to generate theories, laws, and principles. Economists often combine theories into representations called models.
4. Macroeconomics looks at the economy as a whole or its major aggregates. Microeconomics examines specific economic units or institutions.
5. Positive economic analysis deals with facts; normative economics reflects value judgments.
6. Individuals face an economizing problem. Because their wants exceed their income, they must decide what to purchase and what to forgo. Society also faces an economizing problem. Societal wants exceed the available resources necessary to fulfill them. Society therefore must decide what to produce and what to forgo.

7. Graphically, a budget line (or budget constraint) illustrates the economizing problem for individuals. The line shows the various combinations of two products that a consumer can purchase with a specific money income, given the prices of the two products.
8. Economic resources are inputs into the production process and can be classified as land, labor, capital, and entrepreneurial ability. Economics resources are also known as factors of production or inputs.
9. Economists illustrate society's economizing problem through production possibilities analysis. Production possibilities tables and curves show the different combinations of goods and services that can be produced in a fully employed economy, assuming that resource quantity, resource quality, and technology are fixed.
10. An economy that is fully employed and thus operating on its production possibilities curve must sacrifice the output of some types of goods and services to increase the production of others. The gain of one type of good or service is always accompanied by an opportunity cost in the form of the loss of some of the other type.
11. Because resources are not equally productive in all possible uses, shifting resources from one use to another creates increasing opportunity costs. The production of additional units of one product requires the sacrifice of increasing amounts of the other product.
12. The optimal (best) point on the production possibilities curve represents the most desirable mix of goods and is determined by expanding the production of each good until its marginal benefit (MB) equals its marginal cost (MC).
13. Over time, technological advances and increases in the quantity and quality of resources enable the economy to produce more of all goods and services, that is, to experience economic growth. Society's choice as to the mix of consumer goods and capital goods in current output is a major determinant of the future location of the production possibilities curve and thus of the extent of economic growth.

Terms and Concepts

economics
economic perspective
opportunity cost
utility
marginal analysis
scientific method
economic principle
other-things-equal assumption
macroeconomics
aggregate
microeconomics
positive economics
normative economics
economizing problem
budget line
economic resources
land
labor
capital
investment
entrepreneurial ability
factors of production
consumer goods
capital goods
production possibilities curve
law of increasing opportunity costs
economic growth

Study Questions

1. What is an opportunity cost? How does the idea relate to the definition of economics? Which of the following decisions would entail the greatest opportunity cost: Allocating a square block in the heart of New York City for a surface parking lot or allocating a square block at the edge of a typical suburb for such a lot? Explain.
2. What is meant by the term "utility" and how does the idea relate to purposeful behavior?
3. **KEY QUESTION** Cite three examples of recent decisions that you made in which you, at least implicitly, weighed marginal cost and marginal benefit.
4. What are the key elements of the scientific method and how does this method relate to economic principles and laws?
5. **KEY QUESTION** Indicate whether each of the following statements applies to microeconomics or macroeconomics:
   a. The unemployment rate in the United States was 5.2 percent in January 2005.
   b. A U.S. software firm discharged 15 workers last month and transferred the work to India.
   c. An unexpected freeze in central Florida reduced the citrus crop and caused the price of oranges to rise.
   d. U.S. output, adjusted for inflation, grew by 3.5 percent in 2005.
   e. Last week Wells Fargo Bank lowered its interest rate on business loans by one-half of 1 percentage point.
   f. The consumer price index rose by 3.4 percent in 2005.
6. State (a) a positive economic statement of your choice, and then (b) a normative economic statement relating to your first statement.
7. **KEY QUESTION** Suppose you won $15 on a lotto ticket at the local 7-Eleven and decided to spend all the winnings on candy bars and bags of peanuts. The price of candy bars is $.75 and the price of peanuts is $1.50.
   a. Construct a table showing the alternative combinations of the two products that are available.
   b. Plot the data in your table as a budget line in a graph. What is the slope of the budget line? What is the opportunity cost of one more candy bar? Of one more bag

of peanuts? Do these opportunity costs rise, fall, or remain constant as each additional unit of the product is purchased?

c. How, in general, would you decide which of the available combinations of candy bars and bags of peanuts to buy?

d. Suppose that you had won $30 on your ticket, not $15. Show the $30 budget line in your diagram. Why would this budget line be preferable to the old one?

8. What are economic resources? What categories do economists use to classify them? Why are resources also called factors of production? Why are they called inputs?

9. Why is money not considered to be a capital resource in economics? Why is entrepreneurial ability considered a category of economic resource, distinct from labor? What are the major functions of the entrepreneur?

10. **KEY QUESTION** Below is a production possibilities table for consumer goods (automobiles) and capital goods (forklifts):

	Production Alternatives				
Type of Production	**A**	**B**	**C**	**D**	**E**
Automobiles	0	2	4	6	8
Forklifts	30	27	21	12	0

a. Show these data graphically. Upon what specific assumptions is this production possibilities curve based?

b. If the economy is at point *C*, what is the cost of one more automobile? Of one more forklift? Explain how the production possibilities curve reflects the law of increasing opportunity costs.

c. If the economy characterized by this production possibilities table and curve were producing 3 automobiles and 20 fork lifts, what could you conclude about its use of its available resources?

d. What would production at a point outside the production possibilities curve indicate? What must occur before the economy can attain such a level of production?

11. **KEY QUESTION** Specify and explain the typical shapes of marginal-benefit and marginal-cost curves. How are these curves used to determine the optimal allocation of resources to a particular product? If current output is such that marginal cost exceeds marginal benefit, should more or fewer resources be allocated to this product? Explain.

12. Explain how (if at all) each of the following events affects the location of a country's production possibilities curve:
a. The quality of education increases.
b. The number of unemployed workers increases.
c. A new technique improves the efficiency of extracting copper from ore.
d. A devastating earthquake destroys numerous production facilities.

13. **KEY QUESTION** Referring to the table in question 10, suppose improvement occurs in the technology of producing forklifts but not in the technology of producing automobiles. Draw the new production possibilities curve. Now assume that a technological advance occurs in producing automobiles but not in producing forklifts. Draw the new production possibilities curve. Now draw a production possibilities curve that reflects technological improvement in the production of both goods.

14. **KEY QUESTION** On average, households in China save 40 percent of their annual income each year, whereas households in the United States save less than 5 percent. Production possibilities are growing at roughly 9 percent annually in China and 3.5 percent in the United States. Use graphical analysis of "present goods" versus "future goods" to explain the differences in growth rates.

15. Suppose that, on the basis of a nation's production possibilities curve, an economy must sacrifice 10,000 pizzas domestically to get the 1 additional industrial robot it desires but that it can get the robot from another country in exchange for 9000 pizzas. Relate this information to the following statement: "Through international specialization and trade, a nation can reduce its opportunity cost of obtaining goods and thus 'move outside its production possibilities curve.'"

16. **LAST WORD** Studies indicate that married men on average earn more income than unmarried men of the same age and education level. Why must we be cautious in concluding that marriage is the cause and higher income is the effect?

Web-Based Questions

1. **NORMATIVE ECONOMICS—REPUBLICANS VERSUS DEMOCRATS** Visit both the Republicans' **www.rnc.org/** and the Democrats' **www.democrats.org/** Web sites. Identify an economic issue that both parties address, and compare and contrast their views on that issue. Generally speaking, how much of the disagreement is based on normative economics compared to positive economics? Give an example of loaded terminology from each site.

2. **MORE LABOR RESOURCES—WHAT IS THE EVIDENCE FOR THE UNITED STATES AND JAPAN?** Go to the Bureau of Labor Statistics' Web site at **www.bls.gov/** and select Get Detailed Statistics. Look for Labor Force Statistics from the CPS and click the Most Requested Statistics icon. Find U.S. civilian employment data for the last 10 years. How many more workers were there at the end of the 10-year period than at the beginning? Next, return to the Detailed Statistics page. Use the Most Requested Statistics icon next to Foreign Labor Statistics (it's under Productivity and Technology) to find total employment growth in Japan over the last 10 years. In which of the two countries did "more labor resources" have the greatest impact in shifting the nation's production possibilities curve outward over the 10-year period?

Graphs and Their Meaning

If you glance quickly through this text, you will find many graphs. Some seem simple, while others seem more formidable. All are included to help you visualize and understand economic relationships. Physicists and chemists sometimes illustrate their theories by building arrangements of multicolored wooden balls, representing protons, neutrons, and electrons, which are held in proper relation to one another by wires or sticks. Economists most often use graphs to illustrate their models. By understanding these "pictures," you can more readily comprehend economic relationships. Most of our principles or models explain relationships between just two sets of economic facts, which can be conveniently represented with two-dimensional graphs.

Construction of a Graph

A *graph* is a visual representation of the relationship between two variables. The table in Figure 1 is a hypothetical illustration showing the relationship between income and consumption for the economy as a whole. Without even studying economics, we would expect intuitively that people would buy more goods and services when their incomes go up. Thus we are not surprised to find in the table that total consumption in the economy increases as total income increases.

The information in the table is expressed graphically in Figure 1. Here is how it is done: We want to show visually or graphically how consumption changes as income changes. Since income is the determining factor, we represent it on the **horizontal axis** of the graph, as is customary. And because consumption depends on income, we represent it on the **vertical axis** of the graph, as is also customary. Actually, what we are doing is representing the *independent variable* on the horizontal axis and the *dependent variable* on the vertical axis.

Now we arrange the vertical and horizontal scales of the graph to reflect the ranges of values of consumption and income, and we mark the scales in convenient increments. As you can see, the values marked on the scales cover all the values in the table. The increments on both scales are $100.

Because the graph has two dimensions, each point within it represents an income value and its associated consumption value. To find a point that represents one of the five income-consumption combinations in the table in Figure 1, we draw perpendiculars from the appropriate values on the vertical and horizontal axes. For example, to plot point *c* (the $200 income–$150 consumption point), we draw perpendiculars up from the horizontal (income) axis at $200 and across from the vertical (consumption) axis at $150. These perpendiculars intersect at point *c*, which represents this particular income-consumption combination. You should verify that the other income-consumption combinations shown in the table are properly located in the graph in Figure 1. Finally, by assuming that the same general relationship between income and

FIGURE 1 Graphing the direct relationship between consumption and income. Two sets of data that are positively or directly related, such as consumption and income, graph as an upsloping line.

Income per Week	Consumption per Week	Point
$ 0	$ 50	*a*
100	100	*b*
200	150	*c*
300	200	*d*
400	250	*e*

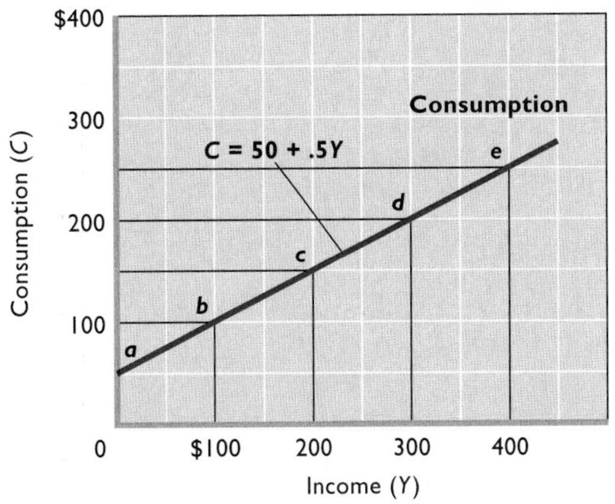

consumption prevails for all other incomes, we draw a line or smooth curve to connect these points. That line or curve represents the income-consumption relationship.

If the graph is a straight line, as in Figure 1, we say the relationship is *linear*.

Direct and Inverse Relationships

The line in Figure 1 slopes upward to the right, so it depicts a direct relationship between income and consumption. By a **direct relationship** (or positive relationship) we mean that two variables—in this case, consumption and income—change in the *same* direction. An increase in consumption is associated with an increase in income; a decrease in consumption accompanies a decrease in income. When two sets of data are positively or directly related, they always graph as an *upsloping* line, as in Figure 1.

In contrast, two sets of data may be inversely related. Consider the table in Figure 2, which shows the relationship between the price of basketball tickets and game attendance at Gigantic State University (GSU). Here we have an **inverse relationship** (or negative relationship) because the two variables change in *opposite* directions. When ticket prices decrease, attendance increases. When ticket prices increase, attendance decreases. The six data points in the table in Figure 2 are plotted in the graph. Observe that an inverse relationship always graphs as a *downsloping* line.

Dependent and Independent Variables

Although it is not always easy, economists seek to determine which variable is the "cause" and which is the "effect." Or, more formally, they seek the independent variable and the dependent variable. The **independent variable** is the cause or source; it is the variable that changes first. The **dependent variable** is the effect or outcome; it is the variable that changes because of the change in the independent variable. As noted in our income-consumption example, income generally is the independent variable and consumption the dependent variable. Income causes consumption to be what it is rather than the other way around. Similarly, ticket prices (set in advance of the season) determine attendance at GSU basketball games; attendance at games does not determine the ticket prices for those games. Ticket price is the independent variable, and the quantity of tickets purchased is the dependent variable.

You may recall from your high school courses that mathematicians always put the independent variable (cause) on the horizontal axis and the dependent variable (effect) on the vertical axis. Economists are less tidy; their graphing of independent and dependent variables is more arbitrary. Their conventional graphing of the income-consumption relationship is consistent with mathematical presentation, but economists put price and cost data on

FIGURE 2 Graphing the inverse relationship between ticket prices and game attendance. Two sets of data that are negatively or inversely related, such as ticket price and the attendance at basketball games, graph as a downsloping line.

Ticket Price	Attendance, Thousands	Point
$50	0	*a*
40	4	*b*
30	8	*c*
20	12	*d*
10	16	*e*
0	20	*f*

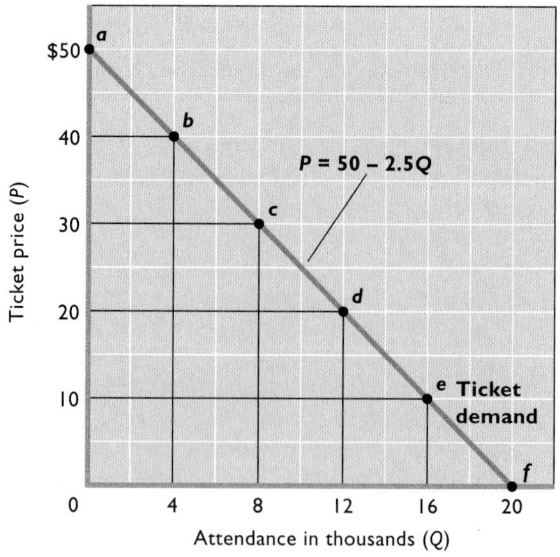

the vertical axis. Hence, economists' graphing of GSU's ticket price–attendance data conflicts with normal mathematical procedure.

Other Things Equal

Our simple two-variable graphs purposely ignore many other factors that might affect the amount of consumption occurring at each income level or the number of people who attend GSU basketball games at each possible ticket price. When economists plot the relationship between any two variables, they employ the *ceteris paribus* (other-things-equal) assumption. Thus, in Figure 1 all factors other than income that might affect the amount of consumption are presumed to be constant or unchanged. Similarly, in Figure 2 all factors other than ticket price that might influence attendance at GSU basketball games are assumed constant. In reality, "other things" are not equal; they often change, and when they do, the relationship represented in our two tables and graphs will change. Specifically, the lines we have plotted would shift to new locations.

Consider a stock market "crash." The dramatic drop in the value of stocks might cause people to feel less wealthy and therefore less willing to consume at each level of income. The result might be a downward shift of the consumption line. To see this, you should plot a new consumption line in Figure 1, assuming that consumption is, say, $20 less at each income level. Note that the relationship remains direct; the line merely shifts downward to reflect less consumption spending at each income level.

Similarly, factors other than ticket prices might affect GSU game attendance. If GSU loses most of its games, attendance at GSU games might be less at each ticket price. To see this, redraw Figure 2, assuming that 2000 fewer fans attend GSU games at each ticket price. **(Key Appendix Question 2)**

Slope of a Line

Lines can be described in terms of their slopes. The **slope of a straight line** is the ratio of the vertical change (the rise or drop) to the horizontal change (the run) between any two points of the line.

Positive Slope

Between point *b* and point *c* in Figure 1 the rise or vertical change (the change in consumption) is +$50 and the run or horizontal change (the change in income) is +$100. Therefore:

$$\text{Slope} = \frac{\text{vertical change}}{\text{horizontal change}} = \frac{+50}{+100} = \frac{1}{2} = .5$$

Note that our slope of $\frac{1}{2}$ or .5 is positive because consumption and income change in the same direction; that is, consumption and income are directly or positively related.

The slope of .5 tells us there will be a $1 increase in consumption for every $2 increase in income. Similarly, it indicates that for every $2 decrease in income there will be a $1 decrease in consumption.

Negative Slope

Between any two of the identified points in Figure 2, say, point *c* and point *d*, the vertical change is −10 (the drop) and the horizontal change is +4 (the run). Therefore:

$$\text{Slope} = \frac{\text{vertical change}}{\text{horizontal change}} = \frac{-10}{+4}$$

$$= -2\frac{1}{2} = -2.5$$

This slope is negative because ticket price and attendance have an inverse relationship.

Note that on the horizontal axis attendance is stated in thousands of people. So the slope of −10/+4 or −2.5 means that lowering the price by $10 will increase attendance by 4000 people. This is the same as saying that a $2.50 price reduction will increase attendance by 1000 persons.

Slopes and Measurement Units

The slope of a line will be affected by the choice of units for either variable. If, in our ticket price illustration, we had chosen to measure attendance in individual people, our horizontal change would have been 4000 and the slope would have been

$$\text{Slope} = \frac{-10}{+4000} = \frac{-1}{+400} = -.0025$$

The slope depends on the way the relevant variables are measured.

Slopes and Marginal Analysis

Recall that economics is largely concerned with changes from the status quo. The concept of slope is important in economics because it reflects marginal changes—those involving 1 more (or 1 less) unit. For example, in Figure 1 the .5 slope shows that $.50 of extra or marginal consumption is associated with each $1 change in income. In this example, people collectively will consume $.50 of any $1 increase in their incomes and reduce their consumption by $.50 for each $1 decline in income.

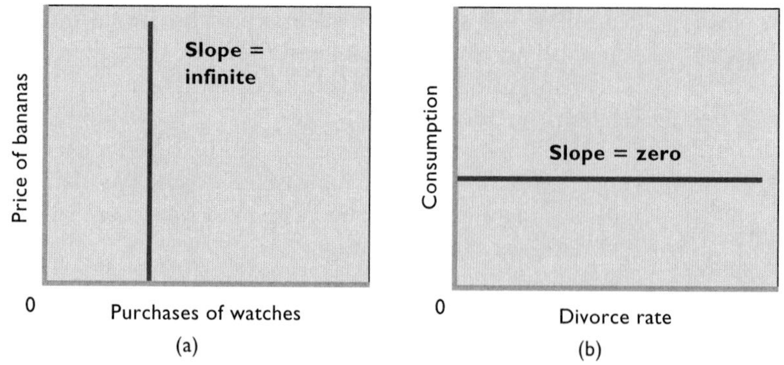

FIGURE 3 Infinite and zero slopes. (a) A line parallel to the vertical axis has an infinite slope. Here, purchases of watches remain the same no matter what happens to the price of bananas. (b) A line parallel to the horizontal axis has a slope of zero. Here, consumption remains the same no matter what happens to the divorce rate. In both (a) and (b), the two variables are totally unrelated to one another.

Infinite and Zero Slopes Many variables are unrelated or independent of one another. For example, the quantity of wristwatches purchased is not related to the price of bananas. In Figure 3a we represent the price of bananas on the vertical axis and the quantity of watches demanded on the horizontal axis. The graph of their relationship is the line parallel to the vertical axis, indicating that the same quantity of watches is purchased no matter what the price of bananas. The slope of such a line is *infinite.*

Similarly, aggregate consumption is completely unrelated to the nation's divorce rate. In Figure 3b we put consumption on the vertical axis and the divorce rate on the horizontal axis. The line parallel to the horizontal axis represents this lack of relatedness. This line has a slope of *zero.*

Vertical Intercept

A line can be located on a graph (without plotting points) if we know its slope and its vertical intercept. The **vertical intercept** of a line is the point where the line meets the vertical axis. In Figure 1 the intercept is \$50. This intercept means that if current income were zero, consumers would still spend \$50. They might do this through borrowing or by selling some of their assets. Similarly, the \$50 vertical intercept in Figure 2 shows that at a \$50 ticket price, GSU's basketball team would be playing in an empty arena.

Equation of a Linear Relationship

If we know the vertical intercept and slope, we can describe a line succinctly in equation form. In its general form, the equation of a straight line is

$$y = a + bx$$

where y = dependent variable
a = vertical intercept
b = slope of line
x = independent variable

For our income-consumption example, if C represents consumption (the dependent variable) and Y represents income (the independent variable), we can write $C = a + bY$. By substituting the known values of the intercept and the slope, we get

$$C = 50 + .5Y$$

This equation also allows us to determine the amount of consumption C at any specific level of income. You should use it to confirm that at the \$250 income level, consumption is \$175.

When economists reverse mathematical convention by putting the independent variable on the vertical axis and the dependent variable on the horizontal axis, then y stands for the independent variable, rather than the dependent variable in the general form. We noted previously that this case is relevant for our GSU ticket price–attendance data. If P represents the ticket price (independent variable) and Q represents attendance (dependent variable), their relationship is given by

$$P = 50 - 2.5Q$$

where the vertical intercept is 50 and the negative slope is $-2\frac{1}{2}$, or -2.5. Knowing the value of P lets us solve for Q, our dependent variable. You should use this equation to predict GSU ticket sales when the ticket price is \$15. **(Key Appendix Question 3)**

Slope of a Nonlinear Curve

We now move from the simple world of linear relationships (straight lines) to the more complex world of nonlinear relationships. The slope of a straight line is the same at all its points. The slope of a line representing a nonlinear relationship changes from one point to another. Such lines are referred to as *curves.* (It is also permissible to refer to a straight line as a "curve.")

Consider the downsloping curve in Figure 4. Its slope is negative throughout, but the curve flattens as we move down along it. Thus, its slope constantly changes; the curve has a different slope at each point.

To measure the slope at a specific point, we draw a straight line tangent to the curve at that point. A line is *tangent* at a point if it touches, but does not intersect, the curve at that point. Thus line *aa* is tangent to the curve in Figure 4 at point *A*. The slope of the curve at that point is equal to the slope of the tangent line. Specifically, the total vertical change (drop) in the tangent line *aa* is −20 and the total horizontal change (run) is +5. Because the slope of the tangent line *aa* is −20/+5, or −4, the slope of the curve at point *A* is also −4.

G 1.3

Curves and slopes

Line *bb* in Figure 4 is tangent to the curve at point *B*. Following the same procedure, we find the slope at *B* to be −5/+15, or $-\frac{1}{3}$. Thus, in this flatter part of the curve, the slope is less negative. **(Key Appendix Question 7)**

FIGURE 4 Determining the slopes of curves. The slope of a nonlinear curve changes from point to point on the curve. The slope at any point (say, *B*) can be determined by drawing a straight line that is tangent to that point (line *bb*) and calculating the slope of that line.

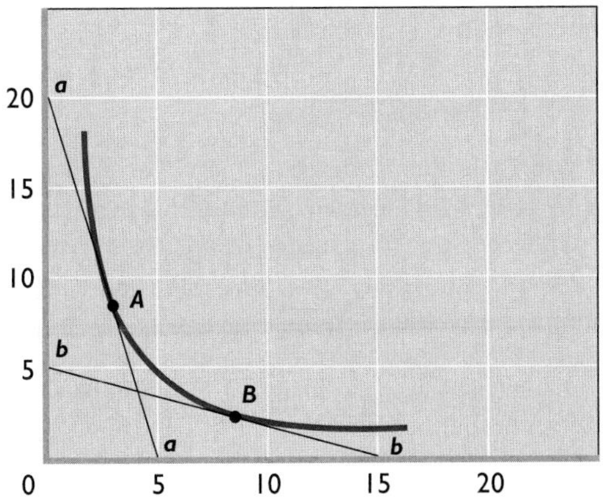

Appendix Summary

1. Graphs are a convenient and revealing way to represent economic relationships.
2. Two variables are positively or directly related when their values change in the same direction. The line (curve) representing two directly related variables slopes upward.
3. Two variables are negatively or inversely related when their values change in opposite directions. The curve representing two inversely related variables slopes downward.
4. The value of the dependent variable (the "effect") is determined by the value of the independent variable (the "cause").
5. When the "other factors" that might affect a two-variable relationship are allowed to change, the graph of the relationship will likely shift to a new location.
6. The slope of a straight line is the ratio of the vertical change to the horizontal change between any two points. The slope of an upsloping line is positive; the slope of a downsloping line is negative.
7. The slope of a line or curve depends on the units used in measuring the variables. It is especially relevant for economics because it measures marginal changes.
8. The slope of a horizontal line is zero; the slope of a vertical line is infinite.
9. The vertical intercept and slope of a line determine its location; they are used in expressing the line—and the relationship between the two variables—as an equation.
10. The slope of a curve at any point is determined by calculating the slope of a straight line tangent to the curve at that point.

Appendix Terms and Concepts

horizontal axis
vertical axis
direct relationship
inverse relationship
independent variable
dependent variable
slope of a straight line
vertical intercept

Appendix Study Questions

1. Briefly explain the use of graphs as a way to represent economic relationships. What is an inverse relationship? How does it graph? What is a direct relationship? How does it graph? Graph and explain the relationships you would expect to find between (*a*) the number of inches of rainfall per month and the sale of umbrellas, (*b*) the amount of tuition and the level of enrollment at a university, and (*c*) the popularity of an entertainer and the price of her concert tickets.

In each case cite and explain how variables other than those specifically mentioned might upset the expected relationship. Is your graph in previous part *b* consistent with the fact that, historically, enrollments and tuition have both increased? If not, explain any difference.

2. **KEY APPENDIX QUESTION** Indicate how each of the following might affect the data shown in the table and graph in Figure 2 of this appendix:
   a. GSU's athletic director schedules higher-quality opponents.
   b. An NBA team locates in the city where GSU plays.
   c. GSU contracts to have all its home games televised.

3. **KEY APPENDIX QUESTION** The following table contains data on the relationship between saving and income. Rearrange these data into a meaningful order and graph them on the accompanying grid. What is the slope of the line? The vertical intercept? Interpret the meaning of both the slope and the intercept. Write the equation that represents this line. What would you predict saving to be at the $12,500 level of income?

Income per Year	Saving per Year
$15,000	$1,000
0	−500
10,000	500
5,000	0
20,000	1,500

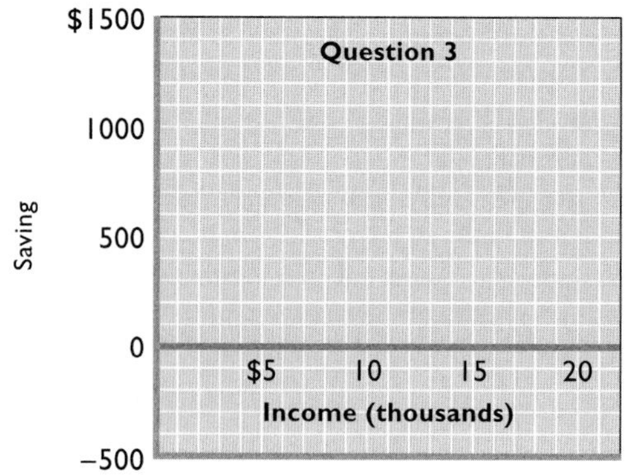

4. Construct a table from the data shown on the graph below. Which is the dependent variable and which the independent variable? Summarize the data in equation form.

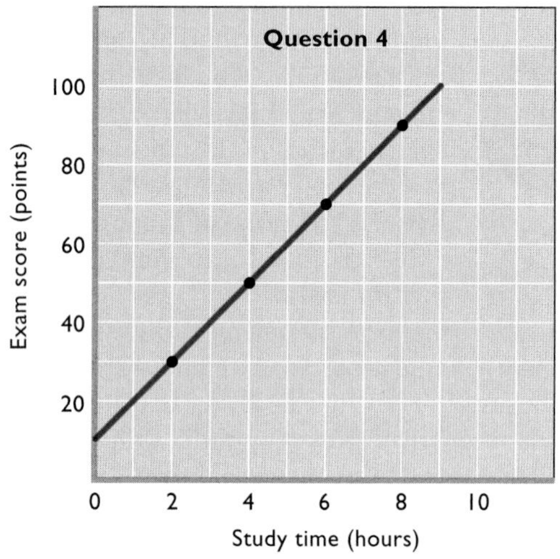

5. Suppose that when the interest rate on loans is 16 percent, businesses find it unprofitable to invest in machinery and equipment. However, when the interest rate is 14 percent, $5 billion worth of investment is profitable. At 12 percent interest, a total of $10 billion of investment is profitable. Similarly, total investment increases by $5 billion for each successive 2-percentage-point decline in the interest rate. Describe the relevant relationship between the interest rate and investment in words, in a table, on a graph, and as an equation. Put the interest rate on the vertical axis and investment on the horizontal axis. In your equation use the form $i = a + bI$, where i is the interest rate, a is the vertical intercept, b is the slope of the line (which is negative), and I is the level of investment. Comment on the advantages and disadvantages of the verbal, tabular, graphical, and equation forms of description.

6. Suppose that $C = a + bY$, where C = consumption, a = consumption at zero income, b = slope, and Y = income.
   a. Are C and Y positively related or are they negatively related?
   b. If graphed, would the curve for this equation slope upward or slope downward?
   c. Are the variables C and Y inversely related or directly related?
   d. What is the value of C if $a = 10$, $b = .50$, and $Y = 200$?
   e. What is the value of Y if $C = 100$, $a = 10$, and $b = .25$?

7. **KEY APPENDIX QUESTION** The accompanying graph shows curve *XX'* and tangents at points *A*, *B*, and *C*. Calculate the slope of the curve at these three points.

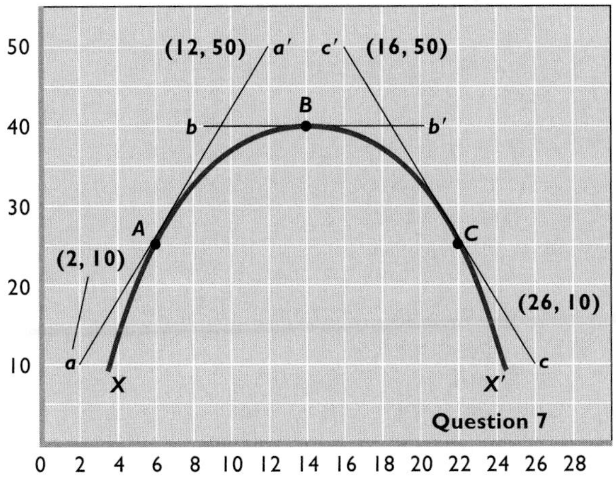

Question 7

8. In the accompanying graph, is the slope of curve *AA'* positive or negative? Does the slope increase or decrease as we move along the curve from *A* to *A'*? Answer the same two questions for curve *BB'*.

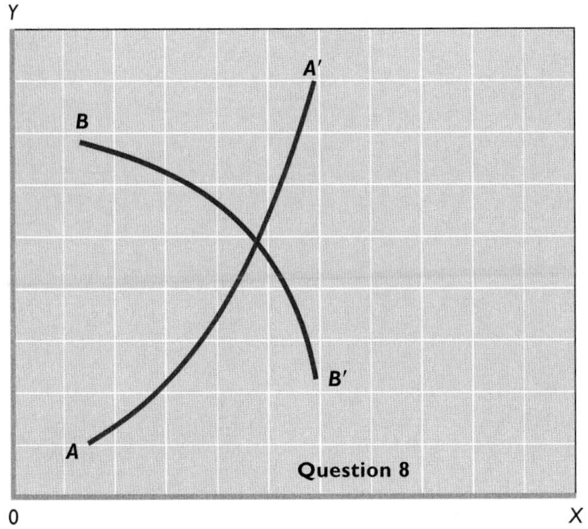

Question 8

2

IN THIS CHAPTER YOU WILL LEARN:

- The difference between a command system and a market system.
- The main characteristics of the market system.
- How the market system decides what to produce, how to produce it, and who obtains it.
- How the market system adjusts to change and promotes progress.
- The mechanics of the circular flow model.

The Market System and the Circular Flow

You are at the mall. Suppose you were assigned to compile a list of all the individual goods and services there, including the different brands and variations of each type of product. That task would be daunting and the list would be long! And even though a single shopping mall contains a remarkable quantity and variety of goods, it is only a tiny part of the national economy.

Who decided that the particular goods and services available at the mall and in the broader economy should be produced? How did the producers determine which technology and types of resources to use in producing these particular goods? Who will obtain these products? What accounts for the new and improved products among these goods? This chapter will answer these and related questions.

Economic Systems

Every society needs to develop an **economic system**—a particular set of institutional arrangements and a coordinating mechanism—to respond to the economizing problem. The economic system has to determine what goods are produced, how they are produced, who gets them, how to accommodate change, and how to promote technological progress.

Economic systems differ as to (1) who owns the factors of production and (2) the method used to motivate, coordinate, and direct economic activity. Economic systems have two polar extremes: the command system and the market system.

The Command System

The **command system** is also known as *socialism* or *communism*. In that system, government owns most property resources and economic decision making occurs through a central economic plan. A central planning board appointed by the government makes nearly all the major decisions concerning the use of resources, the composition and distribution of output, and the organization of production. The government owns most of the business firms, which produce according to government directives. The central planning board determines production goals for each enterprise and specifies the amount of resources to be allocated to each enterprise so that it can reach its production goals. The division of output between capital and consumer goods is centrally decided, and capital goods are allocated among industries on the basis of the central planning board's long-term priorities.

A pure command economy would rely exclusively on a central plan to allocate the government-owned property resources. But, in reality, even the preeminent command economy—the Soviet Union—tolerated some private ownership and incorporated some markets before its collapse in 1992. Recent reforms in Russia and most of the eastern European nations have to one degree or another transformed their command economies to capitalistic, market-oriented systems. China's reforms have not gone as far, but they have greatly reduced the reliance on central planning. Although government ownership of resources and capital in China is still extensive, the nation has increasingly relied on free markets to organize and coordinate its economy. North Korea and Cuba are the last prominent remaining examples of largely centrally planned economies. Other countries using mainly the command system include Turkmenistan, Laos, Belarus, Libya, Myanmar, and Iran. Later in this chapter, we will explore the main reasons for the general demise of the command systems.

The Market System

The polar alternative to the command system is the **market system**, or *capitalism*. The system is characterized by the private ownership of resources and the use of markets and prices to coordinate and direct economic activity. Participants act in their own self-interest. Individuals and businesses seek to achieve their economic goals through their own decisions regarding work, consumption, or production. The system allows for the private ownership of capital, communicates through prices, and coordinates economic activity through *markets*—places where buyers and sellers come together. Goods and services are produced and resources are supplied by whoever is willing and able to do so. The result is competition among independently acting buyers and sellers of each product and resource. Thus, economic decision making is widely dispersed. Also, the high potential monetary rewards create powerful incentives for existing firms to innovate and entrepreneurs to pioneer new products and processes.

In *pure* capitalism—or *laissez-faire* capitalism—government's role would be limited to protecting private property and establishing an environment appropriate to the operation of the market system. The term "laissez-faire" means "let it be," that is, keep government from interfering with the economy. The idea is that such interference will disturb the efficient working of the market system.

O 2.1
Laissez-faire

But in the capitalism practiced in the United States and most other countries, government plays a substantial role in the economy. It not only provides the rules for economic activity but also promotes economic stability and growth, provides certain goods and services that would otherwise be underproduced or not produced at all, and modifies the distribution of income. The government, however, is not the dominant economic force in deciding what to produce, how to produce it, and who will get it. That force is the market.

Characteristics of the Market System

An examination of some of the key features of the market system in detail will be very instructive.

Private Property

In a market system, private individuals and firms, not the government, own most of the property resources (land and capital). It is this extensive private ownership of capital that gives capitalism its name. This right of **private property,** coupled with the freedom to negotiate binding legal contracts, enables individuals and businesses to obtain, use, and dispose of property resources as they see fit. The right of property owners to designate who will receive their property when they die helps sustain the institution of private property.

Property rights encourage investment, innovation, exchange, maintenance of property, and economic growth. Nobody would stock a store, build a factory, or clear land for farming if someone else, or the government itself, could take that property for his or her own benefit.

Property rights also extend to intellectual property through patents, copyrights, and trademarks. Such long-term protection encourages people to write books, music, and computer programs and to invent new products and production processes without fear that others will steal them and the rewards they may bring.

Moreover, property rights facilitate exchange. The title to an automobile or the deed to a cattle ranch assures the buyer that the seller is the legitimate owner. Also, property rights encourage owners to maintain or improve their property so as to preserve or increase its value. Finally, property rights enable people to use their time and resources to produce more goods and services, rather than using them to protect and retain the property they have already produced or acquired.

Freedom of Enterprise and Choice

Closely related to private ownership of property is freedom of enterprise and choice. The market system requires that various economic units make certain choices, which are expressed and implemented in the economy's markets:

- **Freedom of enterprise** ensures that entrepreneurs and private businesses are free to obtain and use economic resources to produce their choice of goods and services and to sell them in their chosen markets.
- **Freedom of choice** enables owners to employ or dispose of their property and money as they see fit. It also allows workers to try to enter any line of work for which they are qualified. Finally, it ensures that consumers are free to buy the goods and services that best satisfy their wants and that their budgets allow.

These choices are free only within broad legal limitations, of course. Illegal choices such as selling human organs or buying illicit drugs are punished through fines and imprisonment. (Global Perspective 2.1 reveals that the degree of economic freedom varies greatly from economy to economy.)

Self-Interest

In the market system, **self-interest** is the motivating force of the various economic units as they express their free choices. Self-interest simply means that each economic unit tries to achieve its own particular goal, which usually requires delivering something of value to others. Entrepreneurs try to maximize profit or minimize loss. Property owners try to get the highest price for the sale or rent of their resources. Workers try to maximize their utility (satisfaction) by finding jobs that offer the best combination of wages, hours, fringe benefits, and working conditions. Consumers try to obtain the products they want at the lowest possible price and apportion their

O 2.2
Self-interest

GLOBAL PERSPECTIVE 2.1

Index of Economic Freedom, Selected Economies

The Index of Economic Freedom measures economic freedom using 10 broad categories such as trade policy, property rights, and government intervention, with each category containing more than 50 specific criteria. The index then ranks 157 economies according to their degree of economic freedom. A few selected rankings for 2006 are listed below.

FREE
- 1 Hong Kong
- 3 Ireland
- 9 United States

MOSTLY FREE
- 22 Belgium
- 33 Spain
- 44 France

MOSTLY UNFREE
- 81 Brazil
- 111 China
- 122 Russia

REPRESSED
- 150 Cuba
- 152 Venezuela
- 157 North Korea

Source: Heritage Foundation **(www.heritage.org)** and *The Wall Street Journal.*

expenditures to maximize their utility. The motive of self-interest gives direction and consistency to what might otherwise be a chaotic economy.

Competition

The market system depends on **competition** among economic units. The basis of this competition is freedom of choice exercised in pursuit of a monetary return. Very broadly defined, competition requires:

- Two or more buyers and two or more sellers acting independently in a particular product or resource market. (Usually there are many more than two buyers or sellers.)
- Freedom of sellers and buyers to enter or leave markets, on the basis of their economic self-interest.

Competition among buyers and sellers diffuses economic power within the businesses and households that make up the economy. When there are many buyers and sellers acting independently in a market, no single buyer or seller can dictate the price of the product or resource because others can undercut that price.

Competition also implies that producers can enter or leave an industry; no insurmountable barriers prevent an industry's expanding or contracting. This freedom of an industry to expand or contract provides the economy with the flexibility needed to remain efficient over time. Freedom of entry and exit enables the economy to adjust to changes in consumer tastes, technology, and resource availability.

The diffusion of economic power inherent in competition limits the potential abuse of that power. A producer that charges more than the competitive market price will lose sales to other producers. An employer who pays less than the competitive market wage rate will lose workers to other employers. A firm that fails to exploit new technology will lose profits to firms that do. Competition is the basic regulatory force in the market system.

Markets and Prices

We may wonder why an economy based on self-interest does not collapse in chaos. If consumers want breakfast cereal but businesses choose to produce running shoes and resource suppliers decide to make computer software, production would seem to be deadlocked by the apparent inconsistencies of free choices.

In reality, the millions of decisions made by households and businesses are highly coordinated with one another by markets and prices, which are key components of the market system. They give the system its ability to coordinate millions of daily economic decisions. A **market** is an institution or mechanism that brings buyers ("demanders") and sellers ("suppliers") into contact. A market system conveys the decisions made by buyers and sellers of products and resources. The decisions made on each side of the market determine a set of product and resource prices that guide resource owners, entrepreneurs, and consumers as they make and revise their choices and pursue their self-interest.

Just as competition is the regulatory mechanism of the market system, the market system itself is the organizing and coordinating mechanism. It is an elaborate communication network through which innumerable individual free choices are recorded, summarized, and balanced. Those who respond to market signals and heed market dictates are rewarded with greater profit and income; those who do not respond to those signals and choose to ignore market dictates are penalized. Through this mechanism society decides what the economy should produce, how production can be organized efficiently, and how the fruits of production are to be distributed among the various units that make up the economy.

QUICK REVIEW 2.1

- The market system rests on the private ownership of property and on freedom of enterprise and freedom of choice.
- The market system permits consumers, resource suppliers, and businesses to pursue and further their self-interest.
- Competition diffuses economic power and limits the actions of any single seller or buyer.
- The coordinating mechanism of capitalism is a system of markets and prices.

Technology and Capital Goods

In the market system, competition, freedom of choice, self-interest, and personal reward provide the opportunity and motivation for technological advance. The monetary rewards for new products or production techniques accrue directly to the innovator. The market system therefore encourages extensive use and rapid development of complex capital goods: tools, machinery, large-scale factories, and facilities for storage, communication, transportation, and marketing.

Advanced technology and capital goods are important because the most direct methods of production are often the least efficient. The only way to avoid that inefficiency is to rely on capital goods. It would be ridiculous for a farmer to go at production with bare hands. There are huge benefits to be derived from creating and using such capital equipment as plows, tractors, and storage bins. The more efficient production means much more abundant outputs.

Specialization

The extent to which market economies rely on **specialization** is extraordinary. Specialization is the use of resources of an individual, firm, region, or nation to produce one or a few goods or services rather than the entire range of goods and services. Those goods and services are then exchanged for a full range of desired products. The majority of consumers produce virtually none of the goods and services they consume, and they consume little or nothing of the items they produce. The person working nine to five installing windows in Lincolns may own a Ford. Many farmers sell their milk to the local dairy and then buy butter at the local grocery store. Society learned long ago that self-sufficiency breeds inefficiency. The jack-of-all-trades may be a very colorful individual but is certainly not an efficient producer.

Division of Labor Human specialization—called the **division of labor**—contributes to a society's output in several ways:

- ***Specialization makes use of differences in ability.*** Specialization enables individuals to take advantage of existing differences in their abilities and skills. If Peyton is strong, athletic, and good at throwing a football and Beyonce is beautiful, agile, and can sing, their distribution of talents can be most efficiently used if Peyton plays professional football and Beyonce records songs and gives concerts.

O 2.3
Specialization division of labor

- ***Specialization fosters learning by doing.*** Even if the abilities of two people are identical, specialization may still be advantageous. By devoting time to a single task, a person is more likely to develop the skills required and to improve techniques than by working at a number of different tasks. You learn to be a good lawyer by studying and practicing law.
- ***Specialization saves time.*** By devoting time to a single task, a person avoids the loss of time incurred in shifting from one job to another. Also, time is saved by not "fumbling around" with a task that one is not trained to do.

For all these reasons, specialization increases the total output society derives from limited resources.

Geographic Specialization Specialization also works on a regional and international basis. It is conceivable that oranges could be grown in Nebraska, but because of the unsuitability of the land, rainfall, and temperature, the costs would be very high. And it is conceivable that wheat could be grown in Florida, but such production would be costly for similar geographical reasons. So Nebraskans produce products—wheat in particular—for which their resources are best suited, and Floridians do the same, producing oranges and other citrus fruits. By specializing, both economies produce more than is needed locally. Then, very sensibly, Nebraskans and Floridians swap some of their surpluses—wheat for oranges, oranges for wheat.

Similarly, on an international scale, the United States specializes in producing such items as commercial aircraft and computers, which it sells abroad in exchange for video recorders from Japan, bananas from Honduras, and woven baskets from Thailand. Both human specialization and geographic specialization are needed to achieve efficiency in the use of limited resources.

Use of Money

A rather obvious characteristic of any economic system is the extensive use of money. Money performs several functions, but first and foremost it is a **medium of exchange.** It makes trade easier.

Specialization requires exchange. Exchange can, and sometimes does, occur through **barter**—swapping goods for goods, say, wheat for oranges. But barter poses serious problems because it requires a *coincidence of wants* between the buyer and the seller. In our example, we assumed that Nebraskans had excess wheat to trade and wanted oranges. And we assumed that Floridians had excess oranges to trade and wanted wheat. So an exchange occurred. But if such a coincidence of wants is missing, trade is stymied.

Suppose that Nebraska has no interest in Florida's oranges but wants potatoes from Idaho. And suppose that Idaho wants Florida's oranges but not Nebraska's wheat. And, to complicate matters, suppose that Florida wants some of Nebraska's wheat but none of Idaho's potatoes. We summarize the situation in Figure 2.1

In none of the cases shown in the figure is there a coincidence of wants. Trade by barter clearly would be difficult. Instead, people in each state use **money,** which is simply a convenient social invention to facilitate exchanges of goods and services. Historically, people have used cattle, cigarettes, shells, stones, pieces of metal, and many other commodities, with varying degrees of success, as a medium of exchange. But to serve as money, an item needs to pass only one test: It must be generally acceptable to sellers in exchange for their

FIGURE 2.1 Money facilitates trade when wants do not coincide. The use of money as a medium of exchange permits trade to be accomplished despite a noncoincidence of wants. (1) Nebraska trades the wheat that Florida wants for money from Floridians; (2) Nebraska trades the money it receives from Florida for the potatoes it wants from Idaho; (3) Idaho trades the money it receives from Nebraska for the oranges it wants from Florida.

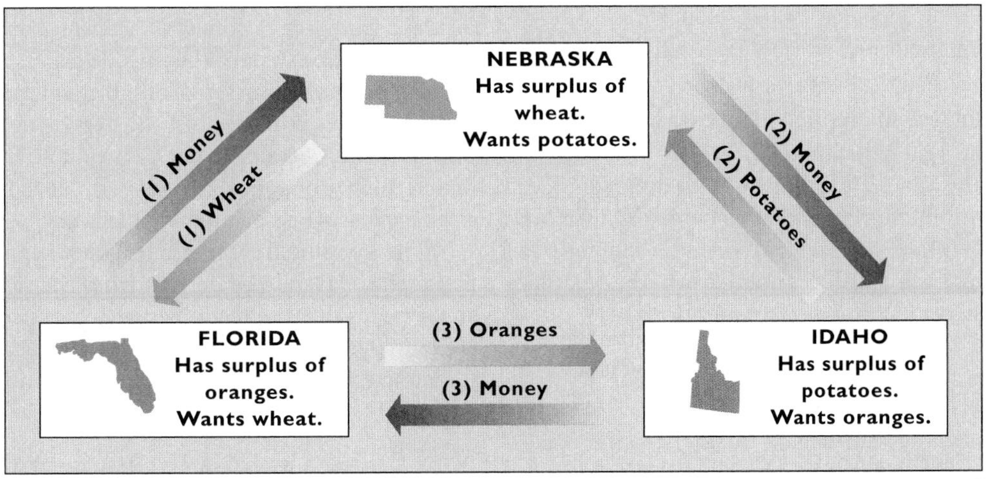

goods and services. Money is socially defined; whatever society accepts as a medium of exchange *is* money.

Most economies use pieces of paper as money. The use of paper dollars (currency) as a medium of exchange is what enables Nebraska, Florida, and Idaho to overcome their trade stalemate, as demonstrated in Figure 2.1.

On a global basis different nations have different currencies, and that complicates specialization and exchange. But markets in which currencies are bought and sold make it possible for U.S. residents, Japanese, Germans, Britons, and Mexicans, through the swapping of dollars, yen, euros, pounds, and pesos, one for another, to exchange goods and services.

CONSIDER THIS . . .

Buy American?

Will "buying American" make Americans better off? No, says Dallas Federal Reserve economist W. Michael Cox:

A common myth is that it is better for Americans to spend their money at home than abroad. The best way to expose the fallacy of this argument is to take it to its logical extreme. If it is better for me to spend my money here than abroad, then it is even better yet to buy in Texas than in New York, better yet to buy in Dallas than in Houston . . . in my own neighborhood . . . within my own family . . . to consume only what I can produce. Alone and poor.*

*"The Fruits of Free Trade," Federal Reserve Bank of Dallas, Annual Report 2002, p. 16.

Active, but Limited, Government

An active, but limited, government is the final characteristic of market systems in modern advanced industrial economies. Although a market system promotes a high degree of efficiency in the use of its resources, it has certain inherent shortcomings, called "market failures." We will discover in subsequent chapters that government can increase the overall effectiveness of the economic system in several ways.

QUICK REVIEW 2.2

- The market systems of modern industrial economies are characterized by extensive use of technologically advanced capital goods. Such goods help these economies achieve greater efficiency in production.
- Specialization is extensive in market systems; it enhances efficiency and output by enabling individuals, regions, and nations to produce the goods and services for which their resources are best suited.
- The use of money in market systems facilitates the exchange of goods and services that specialization requires.

Five Fundamental Questions

The key features of the market system help explain how market economies respond to five fundamental questions:

- What goods and services will be produced?
- How will the goods and services be produced?
- Who will get the goods and services?
- How will the system accommodate change?
- How will the system promote progress?

These five questions highlight the economic choices underlying the production possibilities curve discussed in Chapter 1. They reflect the reality of scarce resources in a world of unlimited wants. All economies, whether market or command, must address these five questions.

What Will Be Produced?

How will a market system decide on the specific types and quantities of goods to be produced? The simple answer is this: The goods and services produced at a continuing profit will be produced, and those produced at a continuing loss will not. Profits and losses are the difference between the total revenue (TR) a firm receives from the sale of its products and the total opportunity cost (TC) of producing those products. (For economists, economic costs include not only wage and salary payments to labor, and interest and rental payments for capital and land, but also payments to the entrepreneur for organizing and combining the other resources to produce a commodity.)

Continuing economic profit (TR > TC) in an industry results in expanded production and the movement of resources toward that industry. Existing firms grow and new firms enter. The industry expands. Continuing losses (TC > TR) in an industry leads to reduced production and the exit of resources from that industry. Some existing firms shrink in size; others go out of business. The industry contracts. In the market system, consumers are sovereign (in command). **Consumer sovereignty** is crucial in determining the types and quantities of goods produced. Consumers spend their income on the goods they are most willing and able to buy. Through these "**dollar votes**" they register their wants in the market. If the dollar votes for a certain product are great enough to create a profit, businesses will produce that product and offer it for sale. In contrast, if the dollar votes do not create sufficient revenues to cover costs, businesses will not produce the product. So the consumers are sovereign. They collectively direct resources to industries that are meeting consumer wants and away from industries that are not meeting consumer wants.

The dollar votes of consumers determine not only which industries will continue to exist but also which products will survive or fail. Only profitable industries, firms, and products survive. So firms are not as free to produce whatever products they wish as one might otherwise think. Consumers' buying decisions make the production of some products profitable and the production of other products unprofitable, thus restricting the choice of businesses in deciding what to produce. Businesses must match their production choices with consumer choices or else face losses and eventual bankruptcy.

The same holds true for resource suppliers. The employment of resources derives from the sale of the goods and services that the resources help produce. Autoworkers are employed because automobiles are sold. There are few remaining professors of early Latin because there are few

CONSIDER THIS . . .

McHits and McMisses

McDonald's has introduced several new menu items over the decades. Some have been profitable "hits," while others have been "misses." Ultimately, consumers decide whether a menu item is profitable and therefore whether it stays on the McDonald's menu.

- Hulaburger (1962)—McMiss
- Filet-O-Fish (1963)—McHit
- Strawberry shortcake (1966)—McMiss
- Big Mac (1968)—McHit
- Hot apple pie (1968)—McHit
- Egg McMuffin (1975)—McHit
- Drive-thru (1975)—McHit
- Chicken McNuggets (1983)—McHit
- Extra Value Meal (1991)—McHit
- McLean Deluxe (1991)—McMiss
- Arch Deluxe (1996)—McMiss
- 55-cent special (1997)—McMiss
- Big Xtra (1999)—McHit

Source: "Polishing the Golden Arches," *Forbes*, June 15, 1998, pp. 42–43, updated.

people desiring to learn the Latin language. Resource suppliers, desiring to earn income, are not truly free to allocate their resources to the production of goods that consumers do not value highly. Consumers register their preferences in the market; producers and resource suppliers, prompted by their own self-interest, respond appropriately. **(Key Question 8)**

How Will the Goods and Services Be Produced?

What combinations of resources and technologies will be used to produce goods and services? How will the production be organized? The answer: In combinations and ways that minimize the cost per unit of output. Because competition eliminates high-cost producers, profitability requires that firms produce their output at minimum cost per unit. Achieving this least-cost production necessitates, for example, that firms use the right mix of labor and capital, given the prices and productivity of those resources. It also means locating production facilities optimally to hold down production and transportation expenses.

Least-cost production also means that firms must employ the most economically efficient technique of production in producing their output. The most efficient production technique depends on:

- The available technology, that is, the various combinations of resources that will produce the desired results.
- The prices of the needed resources.

A technique that requires just a few inputs of resources to produce a specific output may be highly inefficient economically if those resources are valued very highly in the market. Economic efficiency means obtaining a particular output of product with the least input of scarce resources, when both output and resource inputs are measured in dollars and cents. The combination of resources that will produce, say, $15 worth of bathroom soap at the lowest possible cost is the most efficient.

Suppose there are three possible techniques for producing the desired $15 worth of bars of soap. Suppose also that the quantity of each resource required by each production technique and the prices of the required resources are as shown in Table 2.1. By multiplying the required quantities of each resource by its price in each of the three techniques, we can determine the total cost of producing $15 worth of soap by means of each technique.

Technique 2 is economically the most efficient, because it is the least costly. It enables society to obtain $15 worth of output by using a smaller amount of resources—$13 worth—than the $15 worth required by the two other techniques. Competition will dictate that producers use technique 2. Thus, the question of how goods will be produced is answered. They will be produced in a least-cost way.

W 2.1
Least-cost production

A change in either technology or resource prices, however, may cause a firm to shift from the technology it is using. If the price of labor falls to $.50, technique 1 becomes more desirable than technique 2. Firms will find they can lower their costs by shifting to a technology that uses more of the resource whose price has fallen. Exercise: Would a new technique involving 1 unit of labor, 4 of land, 1 of capital, and 1 of entrepreneurial ability be preferable to the techniques listed in Table 2.1, assuming the resource prices shown there? **(Key Question 9)**

Who Will Get the Output?

The market system enters the picture in two ways when determining the distribution of total output. Generally, any product will be distributed to consumers on the basis of their ability and willingness to pay its existing market price. If the price of some product, say, a small sailboat, is $3000, then buyers who are willing and able to pay that price will "sail, sail away." Consumers who are unwilling or unable to pay the price will be "sitting on the dock of the bay."

TABLE 2.1 Three Techniques for Producing $15 Worth of Bar Soap

		Units of Resource					
		Technique 1		Technique 2		Technique 3	
Resource	**Price per Unit of Resource**	**Units**	**Cost**	**Units**	**Cost**	**Units**	**Cost**
Labor	$2	4	$ 8	2	$ 4	1	$ 2
Land	1	1	1	3	3	4	4
Capital	3	1	3	1	3	2	6
Entrepreneurial ability	3	1	3	1	3	1	3
Total cost of $15 worth of bar soap			$15		$13		$15

The ability to pay the prices for sailboats and other products depends on the amount of income that consumers have, along with the prices of, and preferences for, various goods. If consumers have sufficient income and want to spend their money on a particular good, they can have it. And the amount of income they have depends on (1) the quantities of the property and human resources they supply and (2) the prices those resources command in the resource market. Resource prices (wages, interest, rent, profit) are crucial in determining the size of each person's income and therefore each person's ability to buy part of the economy's output. If a lawyer earning $200 an hour and a recreational worker earning $10 an hour both work the same number of hours each year, the lawyer will be able to take possession of 20 times as much of society's output as the recreational worker that year.

How Will the System Accommodate Change?

Market systems are dynamic: Consumer preferences, technology, and supplies of resources all change. This means that the particular allocation of resources that is now the most efficient for a specific pattern of consumer tastes, range of technological alternatives, and amount of available resources will become obsolete and inefficient as consumer preferences change, new techniques of production are discovered, and resource supplies change over time. Can the market economy adjust to such changes?

Suppose consumer tastes change. For instance, assume that consumers decide they want more fruit juice and less milk than the economy currently provides. Those changes in consumer tastes will be communicated to producers through an increase in spending on fruit and a decline in spending on milk. Other things equal, prices and profits in the fruit juice industry will rise and those in the milk industry will fall. Self-interest will induce existing competitors to expand output and entice new competitors to enter the prosperous fruit industry and will in time force firms to scale down—or even exit—the depressed milk industry.

The higher prices and greater economic profit in the fruit-juice industry will not only induce that industry to expand but will also give it the revenue needed to obtain the resources essential to its growth. Higher prices and profits will permit fruit producers to attract more resources from less urgent alternative uses. The reverse occurs in the milk industry, where fewer workers and other resources are employed. These adjustments in the economy are appropriate responses to the changes in consumer tastes. This is consumer sovereignty at work.

The market system is a gigantic communications system. Through changes in prices and profits it communicates changes in such basic matters as consumer tastes and elicits appropriate responses from businesses and resource suppliers. By affecting price and profits, changes in consumer tastes direct the expansion of some industries and the contraction of others. Those adjustments are conveyed to the resource market. As expanding industries employ more resources and contracting industries employ fewer; the resulting changes in resource prices (wages and salaries, for example) and income flows guide resources from the contracting industries to the expanding industries.

This directing or guiding function of prices and profits is a core element of the market system. Without such a system, some administrative agency such as a government planning board would have to direct businesses and resources into the appropriate industries. A similar analysis shows that the system can and does adjust to other fundamental changes—for example, to changes in technology and in the prices of various resources.

How Will the System Promote Progress?

Society desires economic growth (greater output) and higher standards of living (greater income per person). How does the market system promote technological improvements and capital accumulation, both of which contribute to a higher standard of living for society?

Technological Advance

The market system provides a strong incentive for technological advance and enables better products and processes to supplant inferior ones. An entrepreneur or firm that introduces a popular new product will gain revenue and economic profit at the expense of rivals. Firms that are highly profitable one year may find they are in financial trouble just a few years later.

Technological advance also includes new and improved methods that reduce production or distribution costs. By passing part of its cost reduction on to the consumer through a lower product price, the firm can increase sales and obtain economic profit at the expense of rival firms.

Moreover, the market system promotes the *rapid spread* of technological advance throughout an industry. Rival firms must follow the lead of the most innovative firm or else suffer immediate losses and eventual failure. In some cases, the result is **creative destruction:** The creation of new products and production methods completely destroys the market positions of firms that are wedded to existing products and older ways of doing business. Example: The advent of compact discs largely demolished long-play vinyl records, and MP3 and other digital technologies are now supplanting CDs.

Capital Accumulation Most technological advances require additional capital goods. The market system provides the resources necessary to produce those goods through increased dollar votes for capital goods. That is, the market system acknowledges dollar voting for capital goods as well as for consumer goods.

But who will register votes for capital goods? Answer: Entrepreneurs and owners of businesses. As receivers of profit income, they often use part of that income to purchase capital goods. Doing so yields even greater profit income in the future if the technological innovation is successful. Also, by paying interest or selling ownership shares, the entrepreneur and firm can attract some of the income of households as saving to increase their dollar votes for the production of more capital goods. **(Key Question 10)**

QUICK REVIEW 2.3

- The output mix of the market system is determined by profits, which in turn depend heavily on consumer preferences. Economic profits cause industries to expand; losses cause industries to contract.
- Competition forces industries to use the least costly production methods.
- Competitive markets reallocate resources in response to changes in consumer tastes, technological advances, and changes in availability of resources.
- In a market economy, consumer income and product prices determine how output will be distributed.
- Competitive markets create incentives for technological advance and capital accumulation, both of which contribute to increases in standards of living.

The "Invisible Hand"

In his 1776 book *The Wealth of Nations*, Adam Smith first noted that the operation of a market system creates a curious unity between private interests and social interests. Firms and resource suppliers, seeking to further their own self-interest and operating within the framework of a highly competitive market system, will simultaneously, as though guided by an **"invisible hand,"** promote the public or social interest. For example, we have seen that in a competitive environment, businesses seek to build new and improved products to increase profits. Those enhanced products increase society's well-being. Businesses also use the least costly combination of resources to produce a specific output because doing so is in their self-interest. To act otherwise would be to forgo profit or even to risk business failure. But, at the same time, to use scarce resources in the least costly way is clearly in the social interest as well. It "frees up" resources to produce something else that society desires.

Self-interest, awakened and guided by the competitive market system, is what induces responses appropriate to the changes in society's wants. Businesses seeking to make higher profits and to avoid losses, and resource suppliers pursuing greater monetary rewards, negotiate changes in the allocation of resources and end up with the output that society wants. Competition controls or guides self-interest such that self-interest automatically and quite unintentionally furthers the best interest of society. The invisible hand ensures that when firms maximize their profits and resource suppliers maximize their incomes, these groups also help maximize society's output and income.

Of the various virtues of the market system, three merit reemphasis:

- ***Efficiency*** The market system promotes the efficient use of resources by guiding them into the production of the goods and services most wanted by society. It forces the use of the most efficient techniques in organizing resources for production, and it encourages the development and adoption of new and more efficient production techniques.
- ***Incentives*** The market system encourages skill acquisition, hard work, and innovation. Greater work skills and effort mean greater production and higher incomes, which usually translate into a higher standard of living. Similarly, the assuming of risks by entrepreneurs can result in substantial profit incomes. Successful innovations generate economic rewards.
- ***Freedom*** The major noneconomic argument for the market system is its emphasis on personal freedom. In contrast to central planning, the market system coordinates economic activity without coercion. The market system permits—indeed, it thrives on—freedom of enterprise and choice. Entrepreneurs and workers are free to further their own self-interest, subject to the rewards and penalties imposed by the market system itself.

The Demise of the Command Systems

Our discussion of how a market system answers the five fundamental questions provides insights on why command systems of the Soviet Union, eastern Europe, and China (prior to its market reforms) failed. Those systems encountered two insurmountable problems.

The Coordination Problem

The first difficulty was the coordination problem. The central planners had to coordinate the millions of individual decisions by consumers, resource suppliers, and businesses. Consider the setting up of a factory to produce tractors. The central planners had to establish a realistic annual production target, for example, 1000 tractors. They then had to make available all the necessary inputs—labor, machinery, electric power, steel, tires, glass, paint, transportation—for the production and delivery of those 1000 tractors.

Because the outputs of many industries serve as inputs to other industries, the failure of any single industry to achieve its output target caused a chain reaction of repercussions. For example, if iron mines, for want of machinery or labor or transportation, did not supply the steel industry with the required inputs of iron ore, the steel mills were unable to fulfill the input needs of the many industries that depended on steel. Those steel-using industries (such as tractor, automobile, and transportation) were unable to fulfill their planned production goals. Eventually the chain reaction spread to all firms that used steel as an input and from there to other input buyers or final consumers.

The coordination problem became more difficult as the economies expanded. Products and production processes grew more sophisticated, and the number of industries requiring planning increased. Planning techniques that worked for the simpler economy proved highly inadequate and inefficient for the larger economy. Bottlenecks and production stoppages became the norm, not the exception. In trying to cope, planners further suppressed product variety, focusing on one or two products in each product category.

A lack of a reliable success indicator added to the coordination problem in the Soviet Union and China (prior to its market reforms). We have seen that market economies rely on profit as a success indicator. Profit depends on consumer demand, production efficiency, and product quality. In contrast, the major success indicator for the command economies usually was a quantitative production target that the central planners assigned. Production costs, product quality, and product mix were secondary considerations. Managers and workers often sacrificed product quality and variety because they were being awarded bonuses for meeting quantitative, not qualitative, targets. If meeting production goals meant sloppy assembly work and little product variety, so be it.

It was difficult at best for planners to assign quantitative production targets without unintentionally producing distortions in output. If the plan specified a production target for producing nails in terms of *weight* (tons of nails), the enterprise made only large nails. But if it specified the target as a *quantity* (thousands of nails), the firm made all small nails, and lots of them! That is precisely what happened in the centrally planned economies.

The Incentive Problem

The command economies also faced an incentive problem. Central planners determined the output mix. When they misjudged how many automobiles, shoes, shirts, and chickens were wanted at the government-determined prices, persistent shortages and surpluses of those products arose. But as long as the managers who oversaw the production of those goods were rewarded for meeting their assigned production goals, they had no incentive to adjust production in response to the shortages and surpluses. And there were no fluctuations in prices and profitability to signal that more or less of certain products was desired. Thus, many products were unavailable or in short supply, while other products were overproduced and sat for months or years in warehouses.

The command systems of the Soviet Union and China before its market reforms also lacked entrepreneurship. Central planning did not trigger the profit motive, nor did it reward innovation and enterprise. The route for getting ahead was through participation in the political hierarchy of the Communist Party. Moving up the hierarchy meant better housing, better access to health care, and the right to shop in special stores. Meeting production targets and maneuvering through the minefields of party politics were measures of success in "business." But a definition of business success based solely on political savvy was not conducive to technological advance, which is often disruptive to existing products, production methods, and organizational structures.

The Circular Flow Model

O 2.4
Circular flow diagram

The dynamic market economy creates continuous, repetitive flows of goods and services, resources, and money. The **circular flow diagram,** shown in **Figure 2.2 (Key**

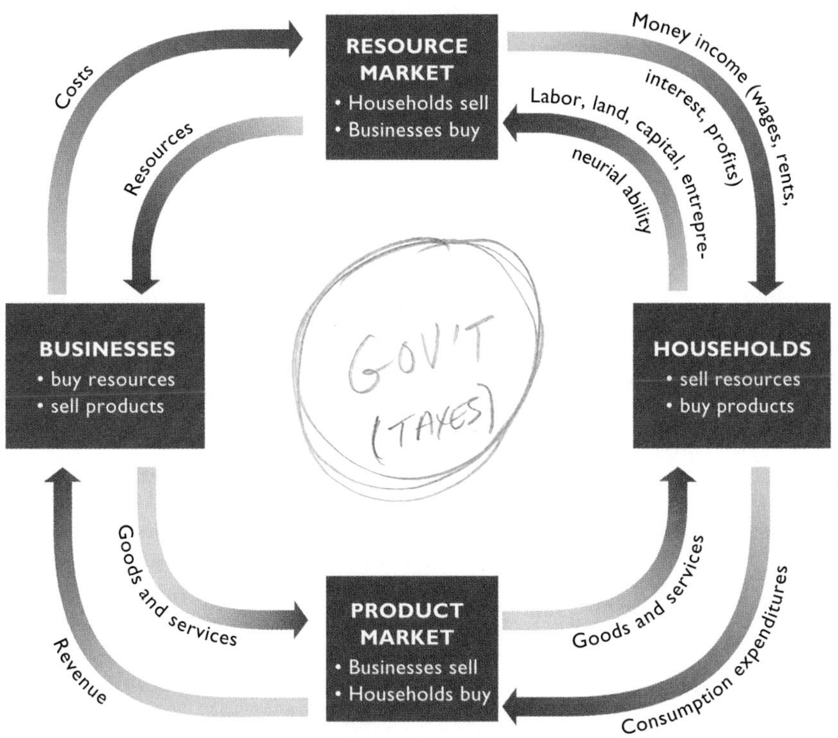

FIGURE 2.2 The circular flow diagram. Resources flow from households to businesses through the resource market, and products flow from businesses to households through the product market. Opposite these real flows are monetary flows. Households receive income from businesses (their costs) through the resource market, and businesses receive revenue from households (their expenditures) through the product market.

R.O.W. → IMPORT MARKET

QUICK QUIZ 2.2

1. The resource market is the place where:
   - **a.** households sell products and businesses buy products.
   - **b.** businesses sell resources and households sell products.
   - **c.** households sell resources and businesses buy resources (or the services of resources).
   - **d.** businesses sell resources and households buy resources (or the services of resources).
2. Which of the following would be determined in the product market?
   - **a.** a manager's salary.
   - **b.** the price of equipment used in a bottling plant.
   - **c.** the price of 80 acres of farmland.
   - **d.** the price of a new pair of athletic shoes.
3. In this circular flow diagram:
   - **a.** money flows counterclockwise.
   - **b.** resources flow counterclockwise.
   - **c.** goods and services flow clockwise.
   - **d.** households are on the selling side of the product market.
4. In this circular flow diagram:
   - **a.** households spend income in the product market.
   - **b.** firms sell resources to households.
   - **c.** households receive income through the product market.
   - **d.** households produce goods.

Answers: 1. c; 2. d; 3. b; 4. a

Graph), illustrates those flows. Observe that in the diagram we group private decision makers into *businesses* and *households* and group markets into the *resource market* and the *product market.*

Resource Market

The upper half of the circular flow diagram represents the **resource market:** the place where resources or the services of resource suppliers are bought and sold. In the resource market, households sell resources and businesses buy them. Households (that is, people) own all economic resources either directly as workers or entrepreneurs or indirectly through their ownership of business corporations. They sell their resources to businesses, which buy them because they are necessary for producing goods and services. The funds that businesses pay for resources are costs to businesses but are flows of wage, rent, interest, and profit income to the households. Productive resources

Shuffling the Deck

Economist Donald Boudreaux Marvels at the Way the Market System Systematically and Purposefully Arranges the World's Tens of Billions of Individual Resources.

In *The Future and Its Enemies*, Virginia Postrel notes the astonishing fact that if you thoroughly shuffle an ordinary deck of 52 playing cards, chances are practically 100 percent that the resulting arrangement of cards has never before existed. *Never.* Every time you shuffle a deck, you produce an arrangement of cards that exists for the first time in history.

The arithmetic works out that way. For a very small number of items, the number of possible arrangements is small. Three items, for example, can be arranged only six different ways. But the number of possible arrangements grows very large very quickly. The number of different ways to arrange five items is 120 . . . for ten items it's 3,628,800 . . . for fifteen items it's 1,307,674,368,000.

The number of different ways to arrange 52 items is 8.066×10^{67}. This is a *big* number. No human can comprehend its enormousness. By way of comparison, the number of possible ways to arrange a mere 20 items is 2,432,902,008,176,640,000—a number larger than the total number of seconds that have elapsed since the beginning of time ten billion years ago—and this number is Lilliputian compared to 8.066×10^{67}.

What's the significance of these facts about numbers? Consider the number of different resources available in the world—my labor, your labor, your land, oil, tungsten, cedar, coffee beans, chickens, rivers, the Empire State Building, [Microsoft] Windows, the wharves at Houston, the classrooms at Oxford, the airport at Miami, and on and on and on. No one can possibly count all of the different productive resources available for our use. But we can be sure that this number is at least in the tens of billions.

When you reflect on how incomprehensibly large is the number of ways to arrange a deck containing a mere 52 cards, the mind boggles at the number of different ways to arrange all the world's resources.

If our world were random—if resources combined together haphazardly, as if a giant took them all into his hands and tossed them down like so many [cards]—it's a virtual certainty that the resulting combination of resources would be useless. Unless this chance arrangement were quickly rearranged according to some productive logic, nothing worthwhile would be produced. We would all starve to death. Because only a tiny fraction of possible arrangements serves human ends, any arrangement will be useless if it is chosen randomly or with inadequate knowledge of how each and every resource might be productively combined with each other.

And yet, we witness all around us an arrangement of resources that's productive and serves human goals. Today's arrangement of resources might not be perfect, but it is vastly superior to most of the trillions upon trillions of other possible arrangements.

How have we managed to get one of the minuscule number of arrangements that works? The answer is private property—a social institution that encourages mutual accommodation.

Private property eliminates the possibility that resource arrangements will be random, for each resource owner chooses a course of action only if it promises rewards to the owner that exceed the rewards promised by all other available courses.

[The result] is a breathtakingly complex and productive arrangement of countless resources. This arrangement emerged over time (and is still emerging) as the result of billions upon billions of individual, daily, small decisions made by people seeking to better employ their resources and labor in ways that other people find helpful.

Source: Abridged from Donald J. Boudreaux, "Mutual Accommodation," *Ideas on Liberty*, May 2000, pp. 4–5. Reprinted with permission.

therefore flow from households to businesses, and money flows from businesses to households.

Product Market

Next consider the lower part of the diagram, which represents the **product market:** the place where goods and services produced by businesses are bought and sold. In the product market, businesses combine resources to produce and sell goods and services. Households use the (limited) income they have received from the sale of resources to buy goods and services. The monetary flow of consumer spending on goods and services yields sales revenues for businesses. Businesses compare those revenues to their costs in determining profitability and whether or not a particular good or service should continue to be produced.

The circular flow model depicts a complex, interrelated web of decision making and economic activity involving businesses and households. For the economy, it is the circle of life. Businesses and households are both buyers and sellers. Businesses buy resources and sell products. Households buy products and sell resources. As shown in Figure 2.2, there is a counterclockwise *real flow* of economic resources and finished goods and services and a clockwise *money flow* of income and consumption expenditures.

Summary

1. The market system and the command system are the two broad types of economic systems used to address the economizing problem. In the market system (or capitalism), private individuals own most resources, and markets coordinate most economic activity. In the command system (or socialism or communism), government owns most resources, and central planners coordinate most economic activity.
2. The market system is characterized by the private ownership of resources, including capital, and the freedom of individuals to engage in economic activities of their choice to advance their material well-being. Self-interest is the driving force of such an economy, and competition functions as a regulatory or control mechanism.
3. In the market system, markets, prices, and profits organize and make effective the many millions of individual economic decisions that occur daily.
4. Specialization, use of advanced technology, and the extensive use of capital goods are common features of market systems. Functioning as a medium of exchange, money eliminates the problems of bartering and permits easy trade and greater specialization, both domestically and internationally.
5. Every economy faces five fundamental questions: (a) What goods and services will be produced? (b) How will the goods and services be produced? (c) Who will get the goods and services? (d) How will the system accommodate change? (e) How will the system promote progress?
6. The market system produces products whose production and sale yield total revenue sufficient to cover total cost. It does not produce products for which total revenue continuously falls short of total cost. Competition forces firms to use the lowest-cost production techniques.
7. Economic profit (total revenue minus total cost) indicates that an industry is prosperous and promotes its expansion. Losses signify that an industry is not prosperous and hasten its contraction.
8. Consumer sovereignty means that both businesses and resource suppliers are subject to the wants of consumers. Through their dollar votes, consumers decide on the composition of output.
9. The prices that a household receives for the resources it supplies to the economy determine that household's income. This income determines the household's claim on the economy's output. Those who have income to spend get the products produced in the market system.
10. By communicating changes in consumer tastes to entrepreneurs and resource suppliers, the market system prompts appropriate adjustments in the allocation of the economy's resources. The market system also encourages technological advance and capital accumulation, both of which raise a nation's standard of living.
11. Competition, the primary mechanism of control in the market economy, promotes a unity of self-interest and social interests. As directed by an invisible hand, competition harnesses the self-interest motives of businesses and resource supplier to further the social interest.
12. The command systems of the Soviet Union and prereform China met their demise because of coordination difficulties under central planning and the lack of a profit incentive. The coordination problem resulted in bottlenecks, inefficiencies, and a focus on a limited number of products. The incentive problem discouraged product improvement, new product development, and entrepreneurship.
13. The circular flow model illustrates the flows of resources and products from households to businesses and from businesses to households, along with the corresponding monetary flows. Businesses are on the buying side of the resource market and the selling side of the product market. Households are on the selling side of the resource market and the buying side of the product market.

Terms and Concepts

economic system	competition	consumer sovereignty
command system	market	dollar votes
market system	specialization	creative destruction
private property	division of labor	"invisible hand"
freedom of enterprise	medium of exchange	circular flow diagram
freedom of choice	barter	resource market
self-interest	money	product market

Study Questions

1. Contrast how a market system and a command economy try to cope with economic scarcity.
2. How does self-interest help achieve society's economic goals? Why is there such a wide variety of desired goods and services in a market system? In what way are entrepreneurs and businesses at the helm of the economy but commanded by consumers?
3. Why is private property, and the protection of property rights, so critical to the success of the market system?
4. What are the advantages of using capital in the production process? What is meant by the term "division of labor"? What are the advantages of specialization in the use of human and material resources? Explain why exchange is the necessary consequence of specialization.
5. What problem does barter entail? Indicate the economic significance of money as a medium of exchange. What is meant by the statement "We want money only to part with it"?
6. Evaluate and explain the following statements:
   a. The market system is a profit-and-loss system.
   b. Competition is the disciplinarian of the market economy.
7. In the 1990s thousands of "dot-com" companies emerged with great fanfare to take advantage of the Internet and new information technologies. A few, like Yahoo, eBay, and Amazon, have generally thrived and prospered, but many others struggled and eventually failed. Explain these varied outcomes in terms of how the market system answers the question "What goods and services will be produced?"
8. **KEY QUESTION** With current technology, suppose a firm is producing 400 loaves of banana bread daily. Also assume that the least-cost combination of resources in producing those loaves is 5 units of labor, 7 units of land, 2 units of capital, and 1 unit of entrepreneurial ability, selling at prices of $40, $60, $60, and $20, respectively. If the firm can sell these 400 loaves at $2 per unit, will it continue to produce banana bread? If this firm's situation is typical for the other makers of banana bread, will resources flow to or away from this bakery good?
9. **KEY QUESTION** Assume that a business firm finds that its profit is greatest when it produces $40 worth of product A. Suppose also that each of the three techniques shown in the table below will produce the desired output:
   a. With the resource prices shown, which technique will the firm choose? Why? Will production using that technique entail profit or losses? What will be the amount of that profit or loss? Will the industry expand or contract? When will that expansion end?
   b. Assume now that a new technique, technique 4, is developed. It combines 2 units of labor, 2 of land, 6 of capital, and 3 of entrepreneurial ability. In view of the resource prices in the table, will the firm adopt the new technique? Explain your answer.
   c. Suppose that an increase in the labor supply causes the price of labor to fall to $1.50 per unit, all other resource prices remaining unchanged. Which technique will the producer now choose? Explain.
   d. "The market system causes the economy to conserve most in the use of resources that are particularly scarce in supply. Resources that are scarcest relative to the demand for them have the highest prices. As a result, producers use these resources as sparingly as is possible." Evaluate this statement. Does your answer to part c, above, bear out this contention? Explain.

		Resource Units Required		
Resource	**Price per Unit of Resource**	**Technique 1**	**Technique 2**	**Technique 3**
Labor	$3	5	2	3
Land	4	2	4	2
Capital	2	2	4	5
Entrepreneurial ability	2	4	2	4

10. **KEY QUESTION** Some large hardware stores such as Home Depot boast of carrying as many as 20,000 different products in each store. What motivated the producers of those

individual products to make them and offer them for sale? How did the producers decide on the best combinations of resources to use? Who made those resources available, and why? Who decides whether these particular hardware products should continue to be produced and offered for sale?

11. What is meant by the term "creative destruction"? How does the emergence of MP3 (iPod) technology relate to this idea?

12. In a sentence, describe the meaning of the phrase "invisible hand."

13. In market economies, firms rarely worry about the availability of inputs to produce their products, whereas in command economies input availability is a constant concern. Why the difference?

14. Distinguish between the resource market and the product market in the circular flow model. In what way are businesses and households both sellers and buyers in this model? What are the flows in the circular flow model?

15. **LAST WORD** What explains why millions of economic resources tend to get arranged logically and productively rather than haphazardly and unproductively?

Web-Based Questions

1. **DIAMONDS—INTERESTED IN BUYING ONE?** Go to the Internet auction site eBay at **www.ebay.com** and select the category Jewelry and Watches and then Loose Diamonds and Gemstones. How many loose diamonds are for sale at the moment? Note the wide array of sizes and prices of the diamonds. In what sense is there competition among the sellers in these markets? How does that competition influence prices? In what sense is there competition among buyers? How does that competition influence prices?

2. **BARTER AND THE IRS** Bartering occurs when goods or services are exchanged without the exchange of money. For some, barter's popularity is that it enables them to avoid paying taxes to the government. How might such avoidance occur? Does the Internet Revenue Service (IRS), **www.irs.ustreas.gov/**, treat barter as taxable or nontaxable income? (Type "barter" in the site's search tool.) How is the value of a barter transaction determined? What are some IRS barter examples? What does the IRS require of the members of so-called barter exchanges?

IN THIS CHAPTER YOU WILL LEARN:

- **What demand is and what affects it.**
- **What supply is and what affects it.**
- **How supply and demand together determine market equilibrium.**
- **How changes in supply and demand affect equilibrium prices and quantities.**
- **What government-set prices are and how they can cause product surpluses and shortages.**

emand, Supply, and larket Equilibrium

O 3.1
Demand and supply

According to an old joke, if you teach a parrot to say "demand and supply," you have an economist. There is an element of truth in this quip. The tools of demand and supply can take us far in understanding how individual markets work.

FIGURE 3.1 An individual buyer's demand for corn. Because price and quantity demanded are inversely related, an individual's demand schedule graphs as a downsloping curve such as *D*. Other things equal, consumers will buy more of a product as its price declines and less of the product as its price rises. (Here and in later figures, *P* stands for price and *Q* stands for quantity demanded or supplied.)

Demand for Corn	
Price per Bushel	Quantity Demanded per Week
$5	10
4	20
3	35
2	55
1	80

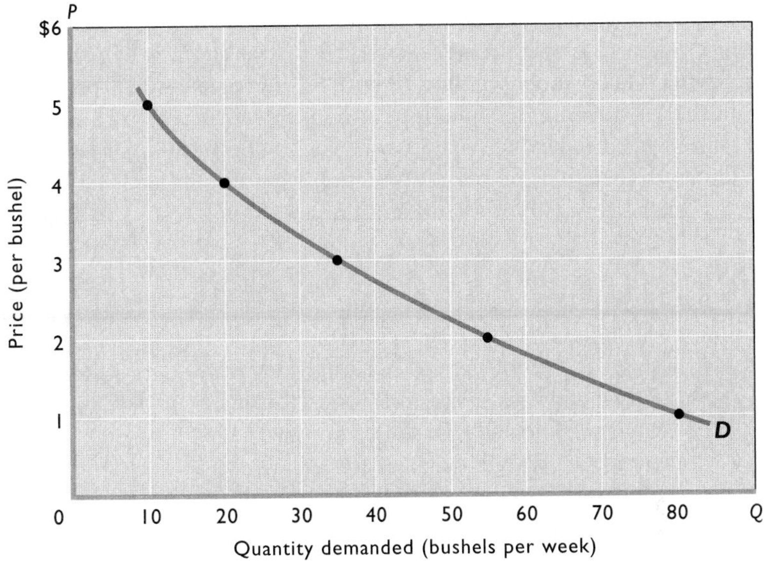

Markets

Markets bring together buyers ("demanders") and sellers ("suppliers"), and they exist in many forms. The corner gas station, an e-commerce site, the local music store, a farmer's roadside stand—all are familiar markets. The New York Stock Exchange and the Chicago Board of Trade are markets where buyers and sellers of stocks and bonds and farm commodities from all over the world communicate with one another to buy and sell. Auctioneers bring together potential buyers and sellers of art, livestock, used farm equipment, and, sometimes, real estate. In labor markets, new college graduates "sell" and employers "buy" specific labor services.

Some markets are local; others are national or international. Some are highly personal, involving face-to-face contact between demander and supplier; others are faceless, with buyer and seller never seeing or knowing each other.

To keep things simple, we will focus in this chapter on markets consisting of large numbers of independently acting buyers and sellers of standardized products. These are the highly competitive markets such as a central grain exchange, a stock market, or a market for foreign currencies in which the price is "discovered" through the interacting decisions of buyers and sellers. All such markets involve demand, supply, price, and quantity.

Demand

Demand is a schedule or a curve that shows the various amounts of a product that consumers are willing and able to purchase at each of a series of possible prices during a specified period of time.[1] Demand shows the quantities of a product that will be purchased at various possible prices, *other things equal*. Demand can easily be shown in table form. The table in Figure 3.1 is a hypothetical **demand schedule** for a *single consumer* purchasing bushels of corn.

The table reveals the relationship between the various prices of corn and the quantity of corn a particular consumer would be willing and able to purchase at each of these prices. We say "willing and able" because willingness alone is not effective in the market. You may be willing to buy a plasma television set, but if that willingness is not backed by the necessary dollars, it will not be effective and, therefore, will not be reflected in the market. In the table in Figure 3.1, if the price of corn were $5 per bushel, our consumer would be willing and able to buy 10 bushels per week; if it were $4, the consumer would be willing and able to buy 20 bushels per week; and so forth.

The table does not tell us which of the five possible prices will actually exist in the corn market. That depends

[1]This definition obviously is worded to apply to product markets. To adjust it to apply to resource markets, substitute the word "resource" for "product" and the word "businesses" for "consumers."

on demand and supply. Demand is simply a statement of a buyer's plans, or intentions, with respect to the purchase of a product.

To be meaningful, the quantities demanded at each price must relate to a specific period—a day, a week, a month. Saying "A consumer will buy 10 bushels of corn at $5 per bushel" is meaningless. Saying "A consumer will buy 10 bushels of corn per week at $5 per bushel" is meaningful. Unless a specific time period is stated, we do not know whether the demand for a product is large or small.

Law of Demand

O 3.2
Law of demand

A fundamental characteristic of demand is this: All else equal, as price falls, the quantity demanded rises, and as price rises, the quantity demanded falls. In short, there is a negative or *inverse* relationship between price and quantity demanded. Economists call this inverse relationship the **law of demand.**

The other-things-equal assumption is critical here. Many factors other than the price of the product being considered affect the amount purchased. For example, the quantity of Nikes purchased will depend not only on the price of Nikes but also on the prices of such substitutes as Reeboks, Adidas, and New Balances. The law of demand in this case says that fewer Nikes will be purchased if the price of Nikes rises and if the prices of Reeboks, Adidas, and New Balances all remain constant. In short, if the *relative price* of Nikes rises, fewer Nikes will be bought. However, if the price of Nikes and the prices of all other competing shoes increase by some amount—say, $5—consumers might buy more, less, or the same amount of Nikes.

Why the inverse relationship between price and quantity demanded? Let's look at three explanations, beginning with the simplest one:

- The law of demand is consistent with common sense. People ordinarily *do* buy more of a product at a low price than at a high price. Price is an obstacle that deters consumers from buying. The higher that obstacle, the less of a product they will buy; the lower the price obstacle, the more they will buy. The fact that businesses have "sales" is evidence of their belief in the law of demand.

O 3.3
Diminishing marginal utility

- In any specific time period, each buyer of a product will derive less satisfaction (or benefit, or utility) from each successive unit of the product consumed. The second Big Mac will yield less satisfaction to the consumer than the first, and the third still less than the second. That is, consumption is subject to **diminishing marginal utility.** And because successive units of a particular product yield less and less marginal utility, consumers will buy additional units only if the price of those units is progressively reduced.
- We can also explain the law of demand in terms of income and substitution effects. The **income effect** indicates that a lower price increases the purchasing power of a buyer's money income, enabling the buyer to purchase more of the product than before. A higher price has the opposite effect. The **substitution effect** suggests that at a lower price buyers have the incentive to substitute what is now a less expensive product for similar products that are now *relatively* more expensive. The product whose price has fallen is now "a better deal" relative to the other products.

O 3.4
Income and substitution effects

For example, a decline in the price of chicken will increase the purchasing power of consumer incomes, enabling people to buy more chicken (the income effect). At a lower price, chicken is relatively more attractive and consumers tend to substitute it for pork, lamb, beef, and fish (the substitution effect). The income and substitution effects combine to make consumers able and willing to buy more of a product at a low price than at a high price.

The Demand Curve

The inverse relationship between price and quantity demanded for any product can be represented on a simple graph, in which, by convention, we measure *quantity demanded* on the horizontal axis and *price* on the vertical axis. In the graph in Figure 3.1 we have plotted the five price-quantity data points listed in the accompanying table and connected the points with a smooth curve, labeled *D*. Such a curve is called a **demand curve.** Its downward slope reflects the law of demand—people buy more of a product, service, or resource as its price falls. The relationship between price and quantity demanded is inverse (or negative).

The table and graph in Figure 3.1 on the previous page contain exactly the same data and reflect the same relationship between price and quantity demanded. But the graph shows that relationship more simply and clearly than a table or a description in words.

Market Demand

So far, we have concentrated on just one consumer. But competition requires that more than one buyer be present in each market. By adding the quantities demanded by all

TABLE 3.1 Market Demand for Corn, Three Buyers

Price per Bushel	Quantity Demanded							Total Quantity Demanded per Week
	Joe		Jen		Jay			
$5	10	+	12	+	8	=		30
4	20	+	23	+	17	=		60
3	35	+	39	+	26	=		100
2	55	+	60	+	39	=		154
1	80	+	87	+	54	=		221

consumers at each of the various possible prices, we can get from *individual* demand to *market* demand. If there are just three buyers in the market, as represented in Table 3.1, it is relatively easy to determine the total quantity demanded at each price. Figure 3.2 shows the graphical summing procedure: At each price we add the individual quantities demanded to obtain the total quantity demanded at that price; we then plot the price and the total quantity demanded as one point on the market demand curve.

Competition, of course, ordinarily entails many more than three buyers of a product. To avoid hundreds or thousands or millions of additions, we suppose that all the buyers in a market are willing and able to buy the same amounts at each of the possible prices. Then we just multiply those amounts by the number of buyers to obtain the market demand. That is how we arrived at curve D_1 in Figure 3.3 for a market of 200 corn buyers, each with a demand as shown in the table in Figure 3.1. Table 3.2 shows the calculations.

In constructing a demand curve such as D_1 in Figure 3.3, economists assume that price is the most important influence on the amount of any product purchased. But economists know that other factors can and do affect purchases. These factors, called **determinants of demand,** are assumed to be constant when a demand curve like D_1 is drawn. They are the "other things equal" in the relationship between price and quantity demanded. When any of these determinants changes, the demand curve will shift to the right or left. For this reason, determinants of demand are sometimes referred to as *demand shifters.*

The basic determinants of demand are (1) consumers' tastes (preferences), (2) the number of buyers in the market, (3) consumers' incomes, (4) the prices of related goods, and (5) consumer expectations.

Change in Demand

A change in one or more of the determinants of demand will change the demand data (the demand schedule) in Table 3.2 and therefore the location of the demand curve in Figure 3.3. A change in the demand schedule or, graphically, a shift in the demand curve is called a *change in demand.*

If consumers desire to buy more corn at each possible price than is reflected in column 4 in Table 3.2, that *increase in demand* is shown as a shift of the demand curve to the right, say, from D_1 to D_2. Conversely, a *decrease in demand* occurs when consumers buy less corn at each possible price than is indicated in column 4, Table 3.2. The leftward shift of the demand curve from D_1 to D_3 in Figure 3.3 shows that situation.

Now let's see how changes in each determinant affect demand.

Tastes A favorable change in consumer tastes (preferences) for a product—a change that makes the product more desirable—means that more of it will be demanded at each price. Demand will increase; the demand curve will shift rightward. An unfavorable change in consumer preferences will decrease demand, shifting the demand curve to the left.

New products may affect consumer tastes; for example, the introduction of digital cameras greatly decreased the demand for film cameras. Consumers' concern over the health hazards of cholesterol and obesity have increased

FIGURE 3.2 Market demand for corn, three buyers. We establish the market demand curve D by adding horizontally the individual demand curves (D_1, D_2, and D_3) of all the consumers in the market. At the price of $3, for example, the three individual curves yield a total quantity demanded of 100 bushels.

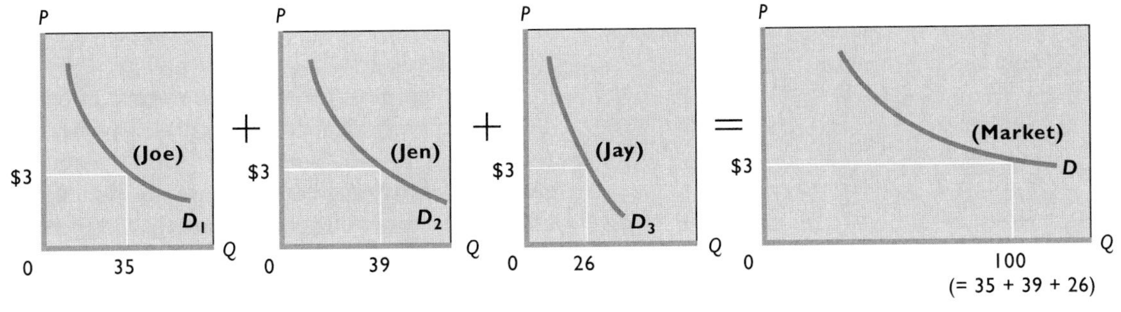

FIGURE 3.3 Changes in the demand for corn. A change in one or more of the determinants of demand causes a change in demand. An increase in demand is shown as a shift of the demand curve to the right, as from D_1 to D_2. A decrease in demand is shown as a shift of the demand curve to the left, as from D_1 to D_3. These changes in demand are to be distinguished from a change in quantity demanded, which is caused by a change in the price of the product, as shown by a movement from, say, point *a* to point *b* on fixed demand curve D_1.

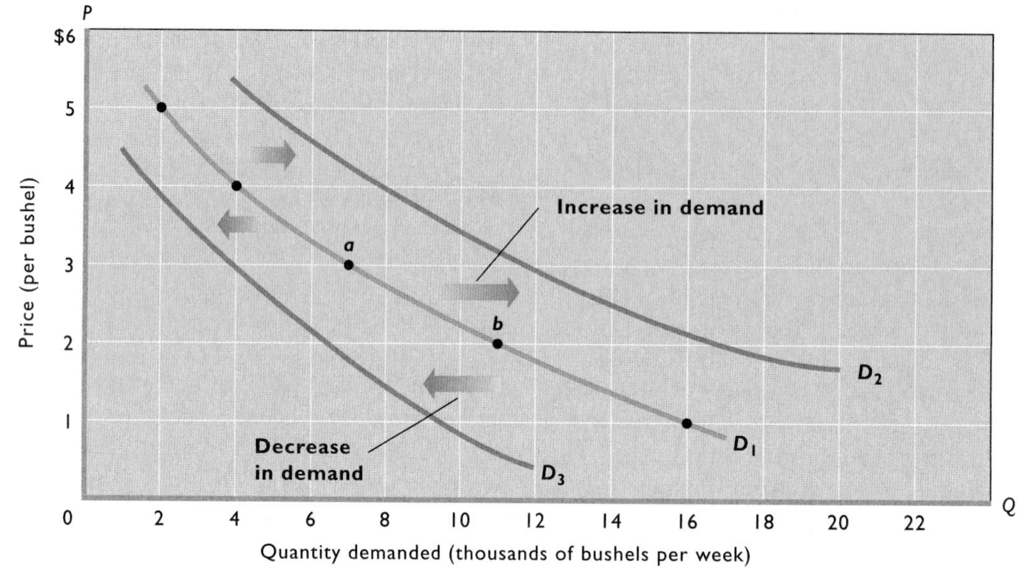

the demand for broccoli, low-calorie beverages, and fresh fruit while decreasing the demand for beef, veal, eggs, and whole milk. Over the past several years, the demand for coffee drinks and bottled water has greatly increased, driven by a change in tastes. So, too, has the demand for DVDs and MP3 players.

Number of Buyers An increase in the number of buyers in a market is likely to increase product demand; a decrease in the number of buyers will probably decrease demand. For example, the rising number of older persons in the United States in recent years has increased the demand for motor homes, medical care, and retirement communities. Large-scale immigration from Mexico has greatly increased the demand for a range of goods and services in the Southwest, including Mexican food products in local grocery stores. Improvements in communications have given financial markets international range and have thus increased the demand for stocks and bonds. International trade agreements have reduced foreign trade barriers to American farm commodities, increasing the number of buyers and therefore the demand for those products.

In contrast, the out-migration from many small rural communities has reduced the population and thus the demand for housing, home appliances, and auto repair in those towns.

TABLE 3.2 Market Demand for Corn, 200 Buyers

(1) Price per Bushel	(2) Quantity Demanded per Week, Single Buyer		(3) Number of Buyers in the Market		(4) Total Quantity Demanded per Week
$5	10	×	200	=	2,000
4	20	×	200	=	4,000
3	35	×	200	=	7,000
2	55	×	200	=	11,000
1	80	×	200	=	16,000

Income How changes in income affect demand is a more complex matter. For most products, a rise in income causes an increase in demand. Consumers typically buy more steaks, furniture, and electronic equipment as their incomes increase. Conversely, the demand for such products declines as their incomes fall. Products whose demand varies *directly* with money income are called *superior goods*, or **normal goods.**

Although most products are normal goods, there are some exceptions. As incomes increase beyond some point, the demand for used clothing, retread tires, and third-hand automobiles may decrease, because the higher incomes enable consumers to buy new versions of those products. Rising incomes may also decrease the demand for soy-enhanced hamburger. Similarly, rising incomes may cause the demand for charcoal grills to decline as wealthier consumers switch to gas grills. Goods whose demand varies *inversely* with money income are called **inferior goods.**

Prices of Related Goods A change in the price of a related good may either increase or decrease the demand for a product, depending on whether the related good is a substitute or a complement:

- A **substitute good** is one that can be used in place of another good.
- A **complementary good** is one that is used together with another good.

Substitutes Leather jackets and fleece jackets are substitute goods or, simply, *substitutes.* When two products are substitutes, an increase in the price of one will increase the demand for the other. Conversely, a decrease in the price of one will decrease the demand for the other. For example, when the prices of leather jackets rise, consumers will buy fewer leather jackets and increase their demand for fleece jackets. When the price of Colgate toothpaste declines, the demand for Crest decreases. So it is with other product pairs such as Nikes and Reeboks, Budweiser and Miller beer, or Chevrolets and Fords. They are *substitutes in consumption.*

Complements Because complementary goods (or, simply, *complements*) are used together, they are typically demanded jointly. Examples include computers and software, cell phones and cellular service, and snowboards and lift tickets. If the price of a complement (for example, lettuce) goes up, the demand for the related good (salad dressing) will decline. Conversely, if the price of a complement (for example, tuition) falls, the demand for a related good (textbooks) will increase.

Unrelated Goods The vast majority of goods are not related to one another and are called *independent goods.* Examples are butter and golf balls, potatoes and automobiles, and bananas and wristwatches. A change in the price of one has little or no effect on the demand for the other.

Consumer Expectations Changes in consumer expectations may shift demand. A newly formed expectation of higher future prices may cause consumers to buy now in order to "beat" the anticipated price rises, thus increasing current demand. That is often what happens in so-called hot real estate markets. Buyers rush in because they think the price of new homes will continue to escalate rapidly. Some buyers fear being "priced out of the market" and therefore not obtaining the home they desire. Other buyers—speculators—believe they will be able to sell the houses later at a higher price. Whichever their motivation, these buyers increase the demand for houses.

Similarly, a change in expectations concerning future income may prompt consumers to change their current spending. For example, first-round NFL draft choices may splurge on new luxury cars in anticipation of a lucrative professional football contract. Or workers who become fearful of losing their jobs may reduce their demand for, say, vacation travel.

In summary, an *increase* in demand—the decision by consumers to buy larger quantities of a product at each possible price—may be caused by:

- A favorable change in consumer tastes.
- An increase in the number of buyers.
- Rising incomes if the product is a normal good.
- Falling incomes if the product is an inferior good.
- An increase in the price of a substitute good.
- A decrease in the price of a complementary good.
- A new consumer expectation that either prices or income will be higher in the future.

You should "reverse" these generalizations to explain a *decrease* in demand. Table 3.3 provides additional illustrations of the determinants of demand. **(Key Question 3)**

Changes in Quantity Demanded

A *change in demand* must not be confused with a *change in quantity demanded.* A **change in demand** is a shift of the demand curve to the right (an increase in demand) or to the left (a decrease in demand). It occurs because the consumer's state of mind about purchasing the product has been altered in response to a change in one or more of

TABLE 3.3 Determinants of Demand: Factors That Shift the Demand Curve

Determinant	Examples
Change in buyer tastes	Physical fitness rises in popularity, increasing the demand for jogging shoes and bicycles; patriotism rises, increasing the demand for flags.
Change in number of buyers	A decline in the birthrate reduces the demand for children's toys.
Change in income	A rise in incomes increases the demand for normal goods such as restaurant meals, sports tickets, and necklaces while reducing the demand for inferior goods such as cabbage, turnips, and inexpensive wine.
Change in the prices of related goods	A reduction in airfares reduces the demand for bus transportation (substitute goods); a decline in the price of DVD players increases the demand for DVD movies (complementary goods).
Change in consumer expectations	Inclement weather in South America creates an expectation of higher future prices of coffee beans, thereby increasing today's demand for coffee beans.

the determinants of demand. Recall that "demand" is a schedule or a curve; therefore, a "change in demand" means a change in the schedule and a shift of the curve.

In contrast, a **change in quantity demanded** is a movement from one point to another point—from one price-quantity combination to another—on a fixed demand schedule or demand curve. The cause of such a change is an increase or decrease in the price of the product under consideration. In Table 3.2, for example, a decline in the price of corn from \$5 to \$4 will increase the quantity of corn demanded from 2000 to 4000 bushels.

In Figure 3.3 the shift of the demand curve D_1 to either D_2 or D_3 is a change in demand. But the movement from point *a* to point *b* on curve D_1 represents a change in quantity demanded: Demand has not changed; it is the entire curve, and it remains fixed in place.

QUICK REVIEW 3.1

- Demand is a schedule or a curve showing the amount of a product that buyers are willing and able to purchase, in a particular time period, at each possible price in a series of prices.
- The law of demand states that, other things equal, the quantity of a good purchased varies inversely with its price.
- The demand curve shifts because of changes in (a) consumer tastes, (b) the number of buyers in the market, (c) consumer income, (d) the prices of substitute or complementary goods, and (e) consumer expectations.
- A change in demand is a shift of the demand curve; a change in quantity demanded is a movement from one point to another on a fixed demand curve.

Supply

Supply is a schedule or curve showing the various amounts of a product that producers are willing and able to make available for sale at each of a series of possible prices during a specific period.[2] The table in Figure 3.4 is a hypothetical **supply schedule** for a single producer of corn. It shows the quantities of corn that will be supplied at various prices, other things equal.

Law of Supply

The table in Figure 3.4 shows a positive or direct relationship that prevails between price and quantity supplied. As price rises, the quantity supplied rises; as price falls, the quantity supplied falls. This relationship is called the **law of supply.** A supply schedule tells us that firms will produce and offer for sale more of their product at a high price than at a low price. This, again, is basically common sense.

Price is an obstacle from the standpoint of the consumer, who is on the paying end. The higher the price, the less the consumer will buy. But the supplier is on the receiving end of the product's price. To a supplier, price represents *revenue*, which serves as an incentive to produce and sell a product. The higher the price, the greater this incentive and the greater the quantity supplied.

Consider a farmer who can shift resources among alternative products. As price moves up, as shown in the table in Figure 3.4, the farmer finds it profitable to take land out of wheat, oats, and soybean production and put it into corn. And the higher corn prices enable the farmer to cover the increased costs associated with more intensive cultivation and the use of more seed, fertilizer, and pesticides. The overall result is more corn.

Now consider a manufacturer. Beyond some quantity of production, manufacturers usually encounter increasing *marginal cost*—the added cost of producing one more unit of output. Certain productive resources—in particular, the firm's plant and machinery—cannot be expanded quickly, so the firm uses more of other resources, such as labor, to produce more output. But as labor becomes more abundant relative to the fixed plant and equipment, the additional workers have relatively less space and access to equipment. For example, the added workers may have to wait to gain access to machines. As a result, each added worker produces less added output, and the marginal cost of successive units of output rises accordingly. The firm will not produce the more costly units unless it receives a higher price for them. Again, price and quantity supplied are directly related.

The Supply Curve

As with demand, it is convenient to represent individual supply graphically. In Figure 3.4, curve S is the **supply curve** that corresponds with the price-quantity supplied data in the accompanying table. The upward slope of the curve reflects the law of supply—producers offer more of a good, service, or resource for sale as its price rises. The relationship between price and quantity supplied is positive, or direct.

Market Supply

Market supply is derived from individual supply in exactly the same way that market demand is derived from individual demand. We sum the quantities supplied by each producer at each price. That is, we obtain the market supply curve by "horizontally adding" the supply curves of the individual producers. The price-quantity supplied data

[2]This definition is worded to apply to product markets. To adjust it to apply to resource markets, substitute "resource" for "product" and "owners" for "producers."

FIGURE 3.4 An individual producer's supply of corn. Because price and quantity supplied are directly related, the supply curve for an individual producer graphs as an upsloping curve. Other things equal, producers will offer more of a product for sale as its price rises and less of the product for sale as its price falls.

Supply of Corn	
Price per Bushel	Quantity Supplied per Week
$5	60
4	50
3	35
2	20
1	5

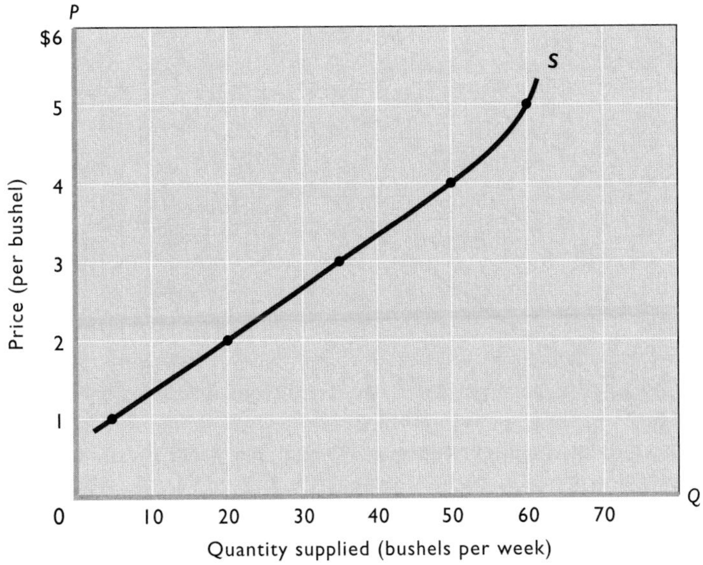

in Table 3.4 are for the many suppliers in the market, each willing to supply corn. Curve S_1 in Figure 3.5 is a graph of the market supply data. Note that the values of the axes in Figure 3.5 are the same as those used in our graph of market demand (Figure 3.3), except the change from "quantity demanded" to "quantity supplied" on the horizontal axis.

Determinants of Supply

In constructing a supply curve, we assume that price is the most significant influence on the quantity supplied of any product. But other factors (the "other things equal") can and do affect supply. The supply curve is drawn on the assumption that these other things are fixed and do not change. If one of them does change, a *change in supply* will occur, meaning that the entire supply curve will shift.

The basic **determinants of supply** are (1) resource prices, (2) technology, (3) taxes and subsidies, (4) prices of other goods, (5) producer expectations, and (6) the number of sellers in the market. A change in any one or more of these determinants of supply, or *supply shifters*, will move the supply curve for a product either right or left. A shift to the *right*, as from S_1 to S_2 in Figure 3.5, signifies an *increase* in supply: Producers supply larger quantities of the product at each possible price. A shift to the *left*, as from S_1 to S_3, indicates a *decrease* in supply: Producers offer less output at each price.

TABLE 3.4 Market Supply of Corn, 200 Producers

(1) Price per Bushel	(2) Quantity Supplied per Week, Single Producer		(3) Number of Sellers in the Market		(4) Total Quantity Supplied per Week
$5	60	×	200	=	12,000
4	50	×	200	=	10,000
3	35	×	200	=	7,000
2	20	×	200	=	4,000
1	5	×	200	=	1,000

Changes in Supply

Let's consider how changes in each of the determinants affect supply. The key idea is that costs are a major factor underlying supply curves; anything that affects costs (other than changes in output itself) usually shifts the supply curve.

Resource Prices The prices of the resources used in the production process help determine the costs of production incurred by firms. Higher *resource* prices raise production costs and, assuming a particular *product* price, squeeze profits. That reduction in profits reduces the incentive for firms to supply output at each product price. For example, an increase in the prices of sand, crushed rock, and Portland cement will increase the cost of producing concrete and reduce its supply.

In contrast, lower *resource* prices reduce production costs and increase profits. So when resource prices fall, firms supply greater output at each product price. For example, a decrease in the price of flat-panel glass will increase the supply of big-screen television sets.

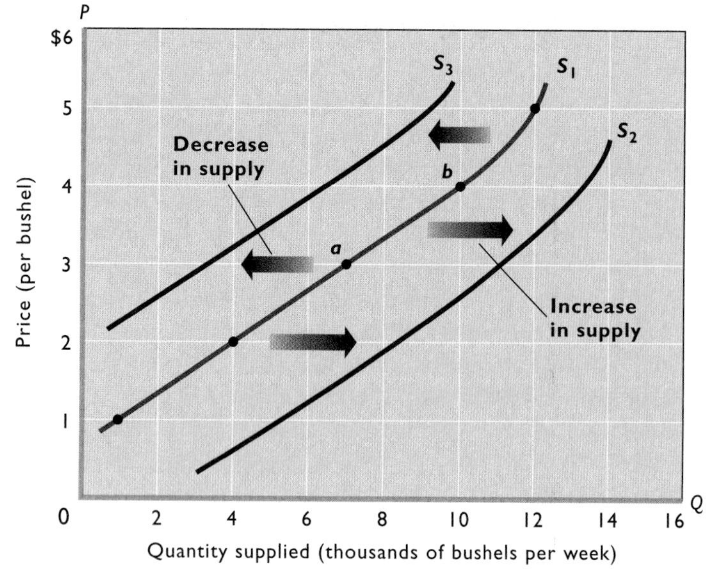

FIGURE 3.5 Changes in the supply of corn. A change in one or more of the determinants of supply causes a change in supply. An increase in supply is shown as a rightward shift of the supply curve, as from S_1 to S_2. A decrease in supply is depicted as a leftward shift of the curve, as from S_1 to S_3. In contrast, a change in the *quantity supplied* is caused by a change in the product's price and is shown by a movement from one point to another, as from *b* to *a* on fixed supply curve S_1.

Technology Improvements in technology (techniques of production) enable firms to produce units of output with fewer resources. Because resources are costly, using fewer of them lowers production costs and increases supply. Example: Technological advances in producing flat-panel computer monitors have greatly reduced their cost. Thus, manufacturers will now offer more such monitors than previously at the various prices; the supply of flat-panel monitors has increased.

Taxes and Subsidies Businesses treat most taxes as costs. An increase in sales or property taxes will increase production costs and reduce supply. In contrast, subsidies are "taxes in reverse." If the government subsidizes the production of a good, it in effect lowers the producers' costs and increases supply.

Prices of Other Goods Firms that produce a particular product, say, soccer balls, can sometimes use their plant and equipment to produce alternative goods, say, basketballs and volleyballs. The higher prices of these "other goods" may entice soccer ball producers to switch production to those other goods in order to increase profits. This *substitution in production* results in a decline in the supply of soccer balls. Alternatively, when the prices of basketballs and volleyballs decline relative to the price of soccer balls, producers of those goods may decide to produce more soccer balls instead, increasing their supply.

Producer Expectations Changes in expectations about the future price of a product may affect the producer's current willingness to supply that product. It is difficult, however, to generalize about how a new expectation of higher prices affects the present supply of a product. Farmers anticipating a higher wheat price in the future might withhold some of their current wheat harvest from the market, thereby causing a decrease in the current supply of wheat. In contrast, in many types of manufacturing industries, newly formed expectations that price will increase may induce firms to add another shift of workers or to expand their production facilities, causing current supply to increase.

Number of Sellers Other things equal, the larger the number of suppliers, the greater the market supply. As more firms enter an industry, the supply curve shifts to the right. Conversely, the smaller the number of firms in the industry, the less the market supply. This means that as firms leave an industry, the supply curve shifts to the left. Example: The United States and Canada have imposed restrictions on haddock fishing to replenish dwindling stocks. As part of that policy, the Federal government has bought the boats of some of the haddock fishers as a way of putting them out of business and decreasing the catch. The result has been a decline in the market supply of haddock.

Table 3.5 is a checklist of the determinants of supply, along with further illustrations. **(Key Question 6)**

Changes in Quantity Supplied

The distinction between a *change in supply* and a *change in quantity supplied* parallels the distinction between a change in demand and a change in quantity demanded.

TABLE 3.5 Determinants of Supply: Factors That Shift the Supply Curve

Determinant	Examples
Change in resource prices	A decrease in the price of microchips increases the supply of computers; an increase in the price of crude oil reduces the supply of gasoline.
Change in technology	The development of more effective wireless technology increases the supply of cell phones.
Changes in taxes and subsidies	An increase in the excise tax on cigarettes reduces the supply of cigarettes; a decline in subsidies to state universities reduces the supply of higher education.
Change in prices of other goods	An increase in the price of cucumbers decreases the supply of watermelons.
Change in producer expectations	An expectation of a substantial rise in future log prices decreases the supply of logs today.
Change in number of suppliers	An increase in the number of tatoo parlors increases the supply of tatoos; the formation of women's professional basketball leagues increases the supply of women's professional basketball games.

Because supply is a schedule or curve, a **change in supply** means a change in the schedule and a shift of the curve. An increase in supply shifts the curve to the right; a decrease in supply shifts it to the left. The cause of a change in supply is a change in one or more of the determinants of supply.

In contrast, a **change in quantity supplied** is a movement from one point to another on a fixed supply curve. The cause of such a movement is a change in the price of the specific product being considered.

Consider supply curve S_1 in Figure 3.5. A decline in the price of corn from \$4 to \$3 decreases the quantity of corn supplied per week from 10,000 to 7000 bushels. This movement from point *b* to point *a* along S_1 is a change in quantity supplied, not a change in supply. Supply is the full schedule of prices and quantities shown, and this schedule does not change when the price of corn changes.

QUICK REVIEW 3.2

- A supply schedule or curve shows that, other things equal, the quantity of a good supplied varies directly with its price.
- The supply curve shifts because of changes in (a) resource prices, (b) technology, (c) taxes or subsidies, (d) prices of other goods, (e) expectations of future prices, and (f) the number of suppliers.
- A change in supply is a shift of the supply curve; a change in quantity supplied is a movement from one point to another on a fixed supply curve.

Market Equilibrium

With our understanding of demand and supply, we can now show how the decisions of buyers of corn interact with the decisions of sellers to determine the equilibrium price and quantity of corn. In Table 3.6, columns 1 and 2 repeat the market supply of corn (from Table 3.4), and columns 2 and 3 repeat the market demand for corn (from Table 3.2). We assume this is a competitive market so that neither buyers nor sellers can set the price.

Equilibrium Price and Quantity

We are looking for the equilibrium price and equilibrium quantity. The **equilibrium price** (or *market-clearing price*) is the price where the intentions of buyers and sellers match. It is the price where quantity demanded equals quantity supplied. Table 3.6 reveals that at \$3, *and only at that price*, the number of bushels of corn that sellers wish to sell (7000) is identical to the number consumers want to buy (also 7000). At \$3 and 7000 bushels of corn, there is neither a shortage nor a surplus of corn. So 7000 bushels of corn in the **equilibrium quantity:** the quantity demanded and quantity supplied at the equilibrium price in a competitive market.

G 3.1
Supply and demand

Graphically, the equilibrium price is indicated by the intersection of the supply curve and the demand curve in **Figure 3.6 (Key Graph).** (The horizontal axis now measures both quantity demanded and quantity supplied.) With neither a shortage nor a surplus at \$3, the market is in equilibrium, meaning "in balance" or "at rest."

Competition among buyers and among sellers drives the price to the equilibrium price; once there, it remains unless it is subsequently disturbed by changes in demand or supply (shifts of the curves). To better understand the

TABLE 3.6 Market Supply of and Demand for Corn

(1) Total Quantity Supplied per Week	(2) Price per Bushel	(3) Total Quantity Demanded per Week	(4) Surplus (+) or Shortage (−)*
12,000	\$5	2,000	+10,000 ↓
10,000	4	4,000	+6,000 ↓
7,000	***3***	***7,000***	***0***
4,000	2	11,000	−7,000 ↑
1,000	1	16,000	−15,000 ↑

*Arrows indicate the effect on price.

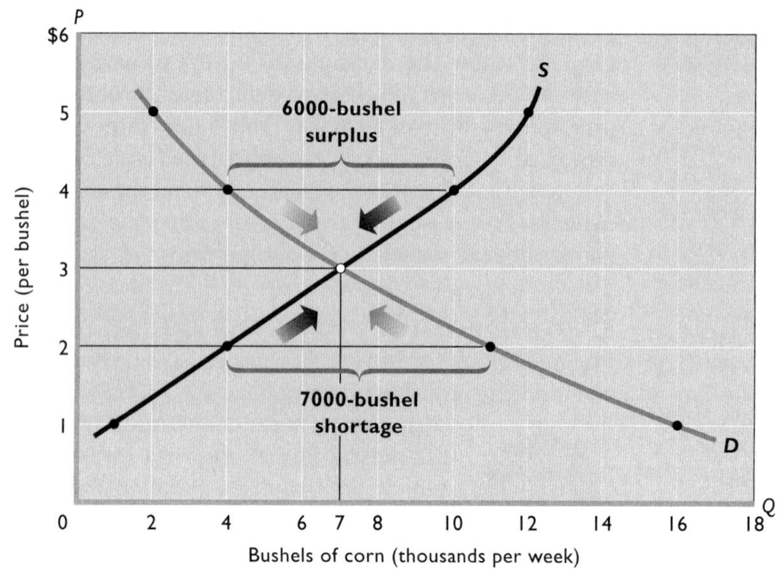

FIGURE 3.6 Equilibrium price and quantity. The intersection of the downsloping demand curve *D* and the upsloping supply curve *S* indicates the equilibrium price and quantity, here $3 and 7000 bushels of corn. The shortages of corn at below-equilibrium prices (for example, 7000 bushels at $2) drive up price. The higher prices increase the quantity supplied and reduce the quantity demanded until equilibrium is achieved. The surpluses caused by above-equilibrium prices (for example, 6000 bushels at $4) push price down. As price drops, the quantity demanded rises and the quantity supplied falls until equilibrium is established. At the equilibrium price and quantity, there are neither shortages nor surpluses of corn.

QUICK QUIZ 3.6

1. Demand curve *D* is downsloping because:
   a. producers offer less of a product for sale as the price of the product falls.
   b. lower prices of a product create income and substitution effects that lead consumers to purchase more of it.
   c. the larger the number of buyers in a market, the lower the product price.
   d. price and quantity demanded are directly (positively) related.
2. Supply curve *S*:
   a. reflects an inverse (negative) relationship between price and quantity supplied.
   b. reflects a direct (positive) relationship between price and quantity supplied.
   c. depicts the collective behavior of buyers in this market.
   d. shows that producers will offer more of a product for sale at a low product price than at a high product price.
3. At the $3 price:
   a. quantity supplied exceeds quantity demanded.
   b. quantity demanded exceeds quantity supplied.
   c. the product is abundant and a surplus exists.
   d. there is no pressure on price to rise or fall.
4. At price $5 in this market:
   a. there will be a shortage of 10,000 units.
   b. there will be a surplus of 10,000 units.
   c. quantity demanded will be 12,000 units.
   d. quantity demanded will equal quantity supplied.

Answers: 1. b; 2. b; 3. d; 4. b

uniqueness of the equilibrium price, let's consider other prices. At any above-equilibrium price, quantity supplied exceeds quantity demanded. For example, at the $4 price, sellers will offer 10,000 bushels of corn, but buyers will purchase only 4000. The $4 price encourages sellers to offer lots of corn but discourages many consumers from buying it. The result is a **surplus** (or *excess supply*) of 6000 bushels. If corn sellers produced them all, they would find themselves with 6000 unsold bushels of corn.

Surpluses drive prices down. Even if the $4 price existed temporarily, it could not persist. The large surplus would prompt competing sellers to lower the price to encourage buyers to take the surplus off their hands. As the price fell, the incentive to produce corn would decline and the incentive for consumers to buy corn would increase. As shown in Figure 3.6, the market would move to its equilibrium at $3.

Any price below the $3 equilibrium price would create a shortage; quantity demanded would exceed quantity supplied. Consider a $2 price, for example. We see in column 4 of Table 3.6 and in Figure 3.6 that quantity demanded exceeds quantity supplied at that price. The result is a **shortage** (or *excess demand*) of 7000 bushels of corn. The $2 price discourages sellers from devoting resources to corn and encourages consumers to desire more bushels than are available. The $2 price cannot persist as the equilibrium price. Many consumers who want to buy corn at this price will not obtain it. They will express a willingness to pay more than $2 to get corn. Competition among these buyers will drive up the price, eventually to the $3 equilibrium level. Unless disrupted by changes of supply or demand, this $3 price of corn will continue to prevail.

CONSIDER THIS . . .

Ticket Scalping: A Bum Rap!

Ticket prices for athletic events and musical concerts are usually set far in advance of the events. Sometimes the original ticket price is too low to be the equilibrium price. Lines form at the ticket window, and a severe shortage of tickets occurs at the printed price. What happens next? Buyers who are willing to pay more than the original price bid up the equilibrium price in resale ticket markets. The price rockets upward.

Tickets sometimes get resold for much greater amounts than the original price—market transactions known as "scalping." For example, an original buyer may resell a $75 ticket to a concert for $200, $250, or more. Reporters sometimes denounce scalpers for "ripping off" buyers by charging "exorbitant" prices.

But is scalping really a rip-off? We must first recognize that such ticket resales are voluntary transactions. If both buyer and seller did not expect to gain from the exchange, it would not occur! The seller must value the $200 more than seeing the event, and the buyer must value seeing the event at $200 or more. So there are no losers or victims here: Both buyer and seller benefit from the transaction. The scalping market simply redistributes assets (game or concert tickets) from those who would rather have the money (the other things money can buy) to those who would rather have the tickets.

Does scalping impose losses or injury on the sponsors of the event? If the sponsors are injured, it is because they initially priced tickets below the equilibrium level. Perhaps they did this to create a long waiting line and the attendant news media publicity. Alternatively, they may have had a genuine desire to keep tickets affordable for lower-income, ardent fans. In either case, the event sponsors suffer an opportunity cost in the form of less ticket revenue than they might have otherwise received. But such losses are self-inflicted and separate and distinct from the fact that some tickets are later resold at a higher price.

So is ticket scalping undesirable? Not on economic grounds! It is an entirely voluntary activity that benefits both sellers and buyers.

Rationing Function of Prices

The ability of the competitive forces of supply and demand to establish a price at which selling and buying decisions are consistent is called the rationing function of prices. In our case, the equilibrium price of $3 clears the market, leaving no burdensome surplus for sellers and no inconvenient shortage for potential buyers. And it is the combination of freely made individual decisions that sets this market-clearing price. In effect, the market outcome says that all buyers who are willing and able to pay $3 for a bushel of corn will obtain it; all buyers who cannot or will not pay $3 will go without corn. Similarly, all producers who are willing and able to offer corn for sale at $3 a bushel will sell it; all producers who cannot or will not sell for $3 per bushel will not sell their product. **(Key Question 8)**

Efficient Allocation

A competitive market such as that we have described not only rations goods to consumers but also allocates society's resources efficiently to the particular product. Competition among corn producers forces them to use the best technology and right mix of productive resources. Otherwise, their costs will be too high relative to the market price and they will be unprofitable. The result is **productive efficiency:** the production of any particular good in the least costly way. When society produces corn at the lowest achievable per-unit cost, it is expending the least-valued combination of resources to produce that product and therefore is making available more-valued resources to produce other desired goods. Suppose society has only $100 worth of resources available. If it can produce a bushel of corn using $3 of those resources, then it will have available $97 of resources remaining to produce other goods. This is clearly better than producing the corn for $5 and having only $95 of resources available for the alternative uses.

Competitive markets also produce **allocative efficiency:** the *particular mix* of goods and services most highly valued by society (minimum-cost production assumed). For example, society wants land suitable for growing corn used for that purpose, not to grow dandelions. It wants high-quality mineral water to be used for bottled water, not for gigantic blocks of refrigeration ice. It wants MP3 players (such as iPods), not cassette players and tapes. Moreover, society does not want to devote all its resources to corn, bottled water, and MP3 players. It wants to assign some resources to wheat, gasoline, and cell phones. Competitive markets make those allocatively efficient assignments.

The equilibrium price and quantity in competitive markets usually produce an assignment of resources that is "right" from an economic perspective. Demand essentially reflects the marginal benefit (MB) of the good, based on the utility received. Supply reflects the marginal cost (MC) of producing the good. The market ensures that firms produce all units of goods for which MB exceeds MC and no units for which MC exceeds MB. At the intersection of the demand and supply curves, MB equals MC and allocative efficiency results. As economists say, there is neither an "underallocaton of resources" nor an "overallocation of resources" to the product.

Changes in Supply, Demand, and Equilibrium

We know that demand might change because of fluctuations in consumer tastes or incomes, changes in consumer expectations, or variations in the prices of related goods. Supply might change in response to changes in resource prices, technology, or taxes. What effects will such changes in supply and demand have on equilibrium price and quantity?

Changes in Demand

Suppose that the supply of some good (for example, potatoes) is constant and demand increases, as shown in Figure 3.7a. As a result, the new intersection of the supply and demand curves is at higher values on both the price and the quantity axes. Clearly, an increase in demand raises both equilibrium price and equilibrium quantity. Conversely, a decrease in demand, such as that shown in Figure 3.7b, reduces both equilibrium price and equilibrium quantity. (The value of graphical analysis is now apparent: We need not fumble with columns of figures to determine the outcomes; we need only compare the new and the old points of intersection on the graph.)

Changes in Supply

What happens if the demand for some good (for example, lettuce) is constant but supply increases, as in Figure 3.7c? The new intersection of supply and demand is located at a lower equilibrium price but at a higher equilibrium quantity. An increase in supply reduces equilibrium price but increases equilibrium quantity. In contrast, if supply decreases, as in Figure 3.7d, the equilibrium price rises while the equilibrium quantity declines.

Complex Cases

When both supply and demand change, the effect is a combination of the individual effects.

Supply Increase; Demand Decrease

What effect will a supply increase and a demand decrease for some good (for example, apples) have on equilibrium price? Both changes decrease price, so the net result is a price drop greater than that resulting from either change alone.

What about equilibrium quantity? Here the effects of the changes in supply and demand are opposed: the increase in supply increases equilibrium quantity, but the decrease in demand reduces it. The direction of the change in quantity depends on the relative sizes of the changes in supply and demand. If the increase in supply is larger than the decrease in demand, the equilibrium quantity will increase. But if the decrease in demand is greater than the increase in supply, the equilibrium quantity will decrease.

Supply Decrease; Demand Increase

A decrease in supply and an increase in demand for some good (for example, gasoline) both increase price. Their combined effect is an increase in equilibrium price greater than that caused by either change separately. But their effect on equilibrium quantity is again indeterminate, depending on the relative sizes of the changes in supply and demand. If the decrease in supply is larger than the increase in demand, the equilibrium quantity will decrease. In contrast, if the increase in demand is greater than the decrease in supply, the equilibrium quantity will increase.

Supply Increase; Demand Increase

What if supply and demand both increase for some good (for example, cell phones)? A supply increase drops equilibrium price, while a demand increase boosts it. If the increase in supply is greater than the increase in demand, the equilibrium price will fall. If the opposite holds, the equilibrium price will rise.

The effect on equilibrium quantity is certain: The increases in supply and in demand each raise equilibrium quantity. Therefore, the equilibrium quantity will increase by an amount greater than that caused by either change alone.

Supply Decrease; Demand Decrease

What about decreases in both supply and demand for some good (for example, fur coats)? If the decrease in supply is greater than the decrease in demand, equilibrium price will rise. If the reverse is true, equilibrium price will fall. Because decreases in supply and in demand each reduce equilibrium quantity, we can be sure that equilibrium quantity will fall.

FIGURE 3.7 Changes in demand and supply and the effects on price and quantity. The increase in demand from D_1 to D_2 in (a) increases both equilibrium price and equilibrium quantity. The decrease in demand from D_1 to D_2 in (b) decreases both equilibrium price and equilibrium quantity. The increase in supply from S_1 to S_2 in (c) decreases equilibrium price and increases equilibrium quantity. The decline in supply from S_1 to S_2 in (d) increases equilibrium price and decreases equilibrium quantity. The boxes in the top right corners summarize the respective changes and outcomes. The upward arrows in the boxes signify increases in demand (*D*), supply (*S*), equilibrium price (*P*), and equilibrium quantity (*Q*); the downward arrows signify decreases in these items.

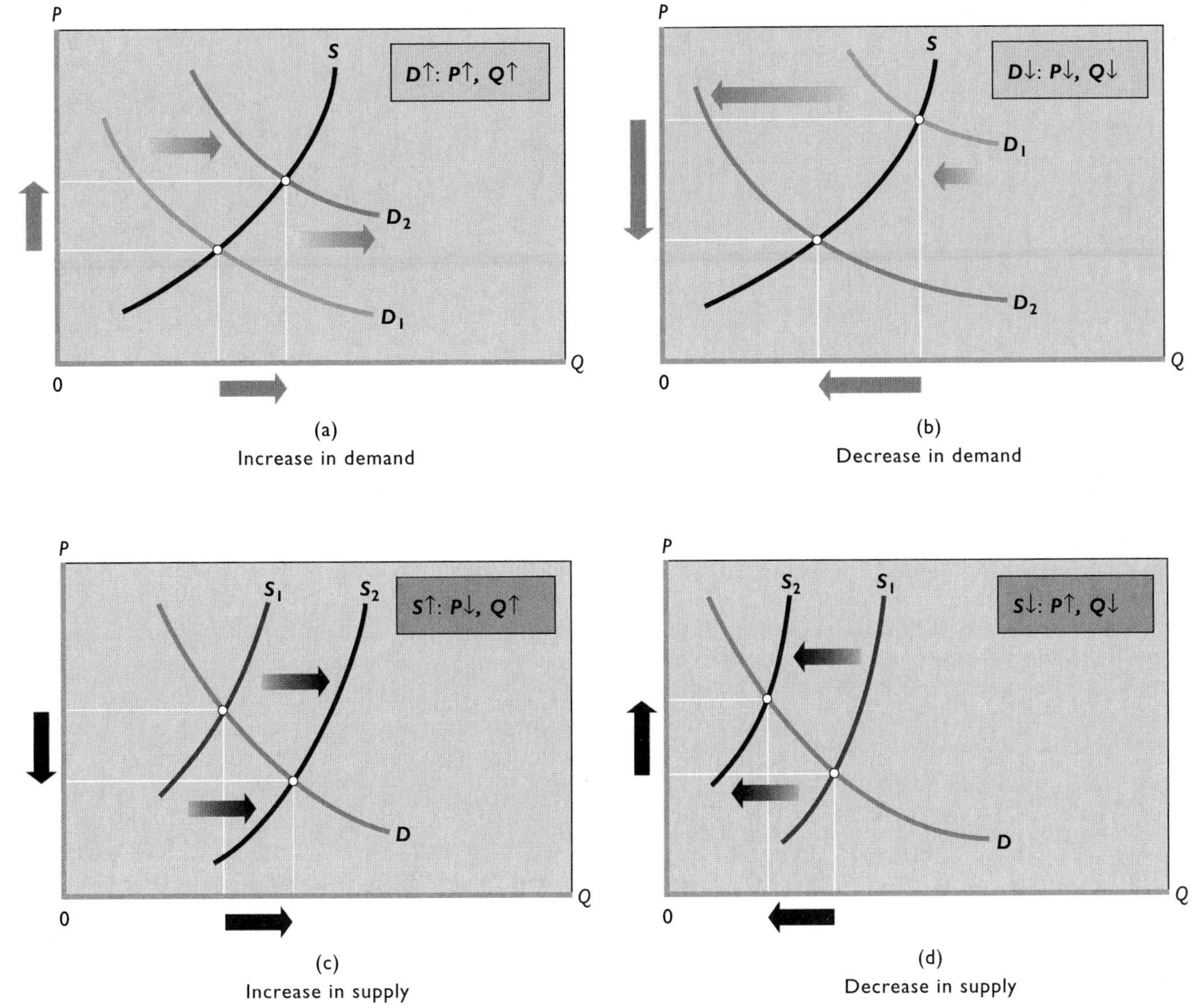

Table 3.7 summarizes these four cases. To understand them fully, you should draw supply and demand diagrams for each case to confirm the effects listed in this table.

TABLE 3.7 Effects of Changes in Both Supply and Demand

Change in Supply	Change in Demand	Effect on Equilibrium Price	Effect on Equilibrium Quantity
1. Increase	Decrease	Decrease	Indeterminate
2. Decrease	Increase	Increase	Indeterminate
3. Increase	Increase	Indeterminate	Increase
4. Decrease	Decrease	Indeterminate	Decrease

Special cases arise when a decrease in demand and a decrease in supply, or an increase in demand and an increase in supply, exactly cancel out. In both cases, the net effect on equilibrium price will be zero; price will not change. **(Key Question 9)**

Application: Government-Set Prices

Prices in most markets are free to rise or fall to their equilibrium levels, no matter how high or low those levels might be. However, government sometimes concludes that supply and demand will produce prices that are

CONSIDER THIS . . .

Salsa and Coffee Beans

If you forget the other-things-equal assumption, you can encounter situations that *seem* to be in conflict with the laws of demand and supply. For example, suppose salsa manufacturers sell 1 million bottles of salsa at $4 a bottle in 1 year; 2 million bottles at $5 in the next year; and 3 million at $6 in the year thereafter. Price and quantity purchased vary directly, and these data seem to be at odds with the law of demand. But there is no conflict here; the data do not refute the law of demand. The catch is that the law of demand's other-things-equal assumption has been violated over the 3 years in the example. Specifically, because of changing tastes and rising incomes, the demand for salsa has increased sharply, as in Figure 3.7a. The result is higher prices *and* larger quantities purchased.

Another example: The price of coffee beans occasionally shoots upward at the same time that the quantity of coffee beans harvested declines. These events seemingly contradict the direct relationship between price and quantity denoted by supply. The catch again is that the other-things-equal assumption underlying the upsloping supply curve is violated. Poor coffee harvests decrease supply, as in Figure 3.7d, increasing the equilibrium price of coffee and reducing the equilibrium quantity.

The laws of demand and supply are not refuted by observations of price and quantity made over periods of time in which either demand or supply changes.

unfairly high for buyers or unfairly low for sellers. So government may place legal limits on how high or low a price or prices may go. Is that a good idea?

Price Ceilings on Gasoline

A **price ceiling** sets the maximum legal price a seller may charge for a product or service. A price at or below the ceiling is legal; a price above it is not. The rationale for establishing price ceilings (or ceiling prices) on specific products is that they purportedly enable consumers to obtain some "essential" good or service that they could not afford at the equilibrium price. Examples are rent controls and usury laws, which specify maximum "prices" in the forms of rent and interest that can be charged to borrowers.

FIGURE 3.8 A price ceiling. A price ceiling is a maximum legal price such as P_c. When the ceiling price is below the equilibrium price, a persistent product shortage results. Here that shortage is shown by the horizontal distance between Q_d and Q_s.

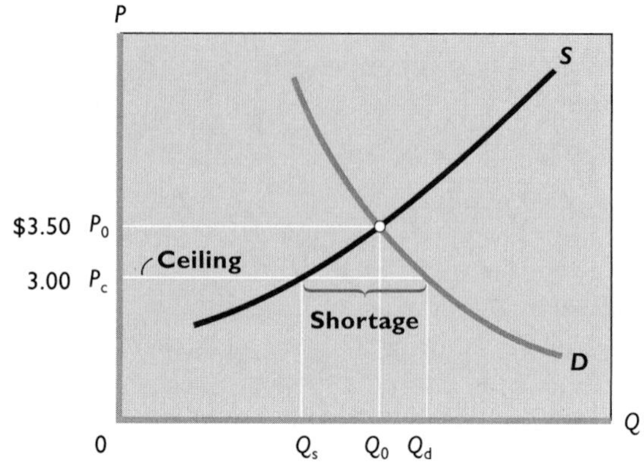

Graphical Analysis We can easily show the effects of price ceilings graphically. Suppose that rapidly rising world income boosts the purchase of automobiles and shifts the demand for gasoline to the right so that the equilibrium or market price reaches $3.50 per gallon, shown as P_0 in Figure 3.8. The rapidly rising price of gasoline greatly burdens low- and moderate-income households, which pressure government to "do something." To keep gasoline affordable for these households, the government imposes a ceiling price P_c of $3 per gallon. To impact the market, a price ceiling must be below the equilibrium price. A ceiling price of $4, for example, would have had no immediate effect on the gasoline market.

What are the effects of this $3 ceiling price? The rationing ability of the free market is rendered ineffective. Because the ceiling price P_c is below the market-clearing price P_0, there is a lasting shortage of gasoline. The quantity of gasoline demanded at P_c is Q_d and the quantity supplied is only Q_s; a persistent excess demand or shortage of amount $Q_d - Q_s$ occurs.

The price ceiling P_c prevents the usual market adjustment in which competition among buyers bids up price, inducing more production and rationing some buyers out of the market. That process would continue until the shortage disappeared at the equilibrium price and quantity, P_0 and Q_0.

By preventing these market adjustments from occurring, the price ceiling poses problems born of the market disequilibrium.

Rationing Problem How will the available supply Q_s be apportioned among buyers who want the greater amount Q_d? Should gasoline be distributed on a first-come, first-served basis, that is, to those willing and able to get in line the soonest and stay in line? Or should gas stations distribute it on the basis of favoritism? Since an unregulated shortage does not lead to an equitable distribution of gasoline, the government must establish some formal system for rationing it to consumers. One option is to issue ration coupons, which authorize bearers to purchase a fixed amount of gasoline per month. The rationing system would entail first the printing of coupons for Q_s gallons of gasoline and then the equitable distribution of the coupons among consumers so that the wealthy family of four and the poor family of four both receive the same number of coupons.

Black Markets

But ration coupons would not prevent a second problem from arising. The demand curve in Figure 3.8 reveals that many buyers are willing to pay more than the ceiling price P_c. And, of course, it is more profitable for gasoline stations to sell at prices above the ceiling. Thus, despite a sizable enforcement bureaucracy that would have to accompany the price controls, *black markets* in which gasoline is illegally bought and sold at prices above the legal limits will flourish. Counterfeiting of ration coupons will also be a problem. And since the price of gasoline is now "set by government," government might face political pressure to set the price even lower.

Rent Controls

About 200 cities in the United States, including New York City, Boston, and San Francisco, have at one time or another enacted rent controls: maximum rents established by law (or, more recently, have set maximum rent increases for existing tenants). Such laws are well intended. Their goals are to protect low-income families from escalating rents caused by perceived housing shortages and to make housing more affordable to the poor.

What have been the actual economic effects? On the demand side, it is true that as long as rents are below equilibrium, more families are willing to consume rental housing; the quantity of rental housing demanded increases at the lower price. But a large problem occurs on the supply side. Price controls make it less attractive for landlords to offer housing on the rental market. In the short run, owners may sell their rental units or convert them to condominiums. In the long run, low rents make it unprofitable for owners to repair or renovate their rental units. (Rent controls are one cause of the many abandoned apartment buildings found in larger cities.) Also, insurance companies, pension funds, and other potential new investors in housing will find it more profitable to invest in office buildings, shopping malls, or motels, where rents are not controlled.

In brief, rent controls distort market signals and thus resources are misallocated: Too few resources are allocated to rental housing, and too many to alternative uses. Ironically, although rent controls are often legislated to lessen the effects of perceived housing shortages, controls in fact are a primary cause of such shortages. For that reason, most American cities either have abandoned or are in the process of dismantling rent controls.

Price Floors on Wheat

A **price floor** is a minimum price fixed by the government. A price at or above the price floor is legal; a price below it is not. Price floors above equilibrium prices are usually invoked when society feels that the free functioning of the market system has not provided a sufficient income for certain groups of resource suppliers or producers. Supported prices for agricultural products and current minimum wages are two examples of price (or wage) floors. Let's look at the former.

Suppose the equilibrium price for wheat is $2 per bushel and, because of that low price, many farmers have extremely low incomes. The government decides to help out by establishing a legal price floor or price support of $3 per bushel.

What will be the effects? At any price above the equilibrium price, quantity supplied will exceed quantity demanded—that is, there will be a persistent excess supply or surplus of the product. Farmers will be willing to produce and offer for sale more than private buyers are willing to purchase at the price floor. As we saw with a price ceiling, an imposed legal price disrupts the rationing ability of the free market.

Graphical Analysis

Figure 3.9 illustrates the effect of a price floor graphically. Suppose that S and D are the supply and demand curves for wheat. Equilibrium price and quantity are P_0 and Q_0, respectively. If the government imposes a price floor of P_f, farmers will produce Q_s but private buyers will purchase only Q_d. The surplus is the excess of Q_s over Q_d.

The government may cope with the surplus resulting from a price floor in two ways:

- It can restrict supply (for example, by instituting acreage allotments by which farmers agree to take a certain amount of land out of production) or increase demand (for example, by researching new uses for the product involved). These actions may reduce the difference between the equilibrium price and the price floor and that way reduce the size of the resulting surplus.
- If these efforts are not wholly successful, then the government must purchase the surplus output at the $3 price (thereby subsidizing farmers) and store or otherwise dispose of it.

Last Word

A Legal Market for Human Organs?

A Legal Market Might Eliminate the Present Shortage of Human Organs for Transplant. But There Are Many Serious Objections to "Turning Human Body Parts into Commodities" for Purchase and Sale.

It has become increasingly commonplace in medicine to transplant kidneys, lungs, livers, eye corneas, pancreases, and hearts from deceased individuals to those whose organs have failed or are failing. But surgeons and many of their patients face a growing problem: There are shortages of donated organs available for transplant. Not everyone who needs a transplant can get one. In 2005 there were 89,000 Americans on the waiting list for transplants. Indeed, an inadequate supply of donated organs causes an estimated 4000 deaths in the United States each year.

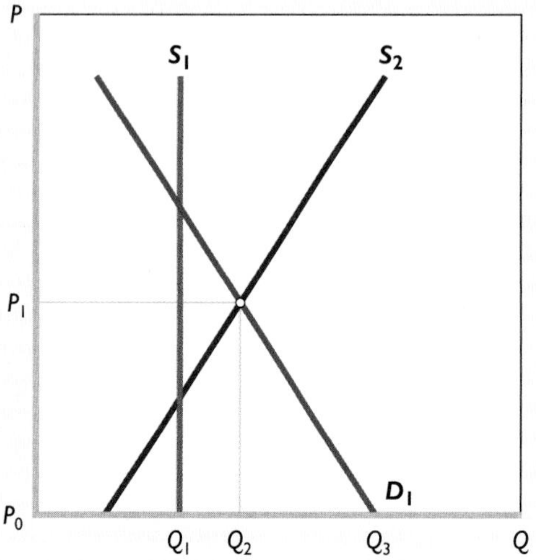

Why Shortages? Seldom do we hear of shortages of desired goods in market economies. What is different about organs for transplant? One difference is that no legal market exists for human organs. To understand this situation, observe the demand curve D_1 and supply curve S_1 in the accompanying figure. The downward slope of the demand curve tells us that if there were a market for human organs, the quantity of organs demanded would be greater at lower prices than at higher prices. Vertical supply curve S_1 represents the fixed quantity of human organs now donated via consent before death. Because the price of these donated organs is in effect zero, quantity demanded Q_3 exceeds quantity supplied Q_1. The shortage of $Q_3 - Q_1$ is rationed through a waiting list of those in medical need of transplants. Many people die while still on the waiting list.

Use of a Market A market for human organs would increase the incentive to donate organs. Such a market might work like this: An individual might specify in a legal document that he or she is willing to sell one or more usable human organs upon death or near-death. The person could specify where the money from the sale would go, for example, to family, a church, an educational institution, or a charity. Firms would then emerge to purchase organs and resell them where needed for profit. Under such

FIGURE 3.9 A price floor. A price floor is a minimum legal price such as P_f. When the price floor is above the equilibrium price, a persistent product surplus results. Here that shortage is shown by the horizontal distance between Q_s and Q_d.

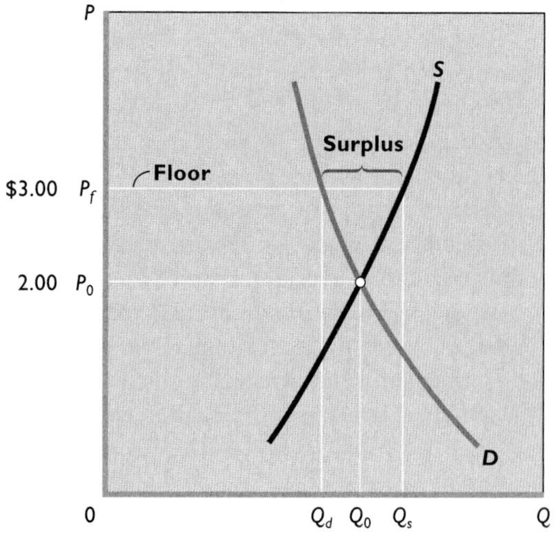

Additional Consequences

Price floors such as P_f in Figure 3.9 not only disrupt the rationing ability of prices but distort resource allocation. Without the price floor, the $2 equilibrium price of wheat would cause financial losses and force high-cost wheat producers to plant other crops or abandon farming altogether. But the $3 price floor allows them to continue to grow wheat and remain farmers. So society devotes too many of its scarce resources to wheat production and too few to producing other, more valuable, goods and services. It fails to achieve allocative efficiency.

That's not all. Consumers of wheat-based products pay higher prices because of the price floor. Taxpayers pay higher taxes to finance the government's purchase of the surplus. Also, the price floor causes potential environmental damage by encouraging wheat farmers to bring hilly, erosion-prone "marginal land" into production. The higher price also prompts imports of wheat. But, since such imports would increase the quantity of wheat supa system, the supply curve of usable organs would take on the normal upward slope of typical supply curves. The higher the expected price of an organ, the greater the number of people who would be willing to have their organs sold at death. Suppose that the supply curve is S_2 in the figure. At the equilibrium price P_1, the number of organs made available for transplant (Q_2) would equal the number purchased for transplant (also Q_2). In this generalized case, the shortage of organs would be eliminated and, of particular importance, the number of organs available for transplanting would rise from Q_1 to Q_2. This means more lives would be saved and enhanced than under the present donor system.

Objections In view of this positive outcome, why is there no such market for human organs? Critics of market-based solutions have two main objections. The first is a moral objection: Critics feel that turning human organs into commodities commercializes human beings and diminishes the special nature of human life. They say there is something unseemly about selling and buying body organs as if they were bushels of wheat or ounces of gold. (There is, however, a market for blood!) Moreover, critics note that the market would ration the available organs (as represented by Q_2 in the figure) to people who either can afford them (at P_1) or have health insurance for transplants. The poor and uninsured would be left out.

Second, a health-cost objection suggests that a market for body organs would greatly increase the cost of health care. Rather than obtaining freely donated (although "too few") body organs, patients or their insurance companies would have to pay market prices for them, further increasing the cost of medical care.

Rebuttal Supporters of market-based solutions to organ shortages point out that the laws against selling organs are simply driving the market underground. Worldwide, an estimated $1 billion-per-year illegal market in human organs has emerged. As in other illegal markets, the unscrupulous tend to thrive. This fact is dramatized by the accompanying photo, in which four Pakistani villagers show off their scars after they each sold a kidney to pay off debt. Supporters say that legalization of the market for human organs would increase organ supply from legal sources, drive down the price of organs, and reduce the abuses such as those now taking place in illegal markets.

plied and thus undermine the price floor, the government needs to erect tariffs (taxes on imports) to keep the foreign wheat out. Such tariffs usually prompt other countries to retaliate with their own tariffs against U.S. agricultural or manufacturing exports.

G 3.2

Price floors and ceilings

So it is easy to see why economists "sound the alarm" when politicians advocate imposing price ceilings or price floors such as price controls, rent controls, interest-rate lids, or agricultural price supports. In all these cases, good intentions lead to bad economic outcomes. Government-controlled prices cause shortages or surpluses, distort resource allocation, and produce negative side effects. **(Key Question 14)**

QUICK REVIEW 3.3

- In competitive markets, prices adjust to the equilibrium level at which quantity demanded equals quantity supplied.
- The equilibrium price and quantity are those indicated by the intersection of the supply and demand curves for any product or resource.
- An increase in demand increases equilibrium price and quantity; a decrease in demand decreases equilibrium price and quantity.
- An increase in supply reduces equilibrium price but increases equilibrium quantity; a decrease in supply increases equilibrium price but reduces equilibrium quantity.
- Over time, equilibrium price and quantity may change in directions that seem at odds with the laws of demand and supply because the other-things-equal assumption is violated.
- Government-controlled prices in the form of ceilings and floors stifle the rationing function of prices, distort resource allocations, and cause negative side effects.

Summary

1. Demand is a schedule or curve representing the willingness of buyers in a specific period to purchase a particular product at each of various prices. The law of demand implies that consumers will buy more of a product at a low price than at a high price. So, other things equal, the relationship between price and quantity demanded is negative or inverse and is graphed as a downsloping curve.
2. Market demand curves are found by adding horizontally the demand curves of the many individual consumers in the market.
3. Changes in one or more of the determinants of demand (consumer tastes, the number of buyers in the market, the money incomes of consumers, the prices of related goods, and consumer expectations) shift the market demand curve. A shift to the right is an increase in demand; a shift to the left is a decrease in demand. A change in demand is different from a change in the quantity demanded, the latter being a movement from one point to another point on a fixed demand curve because of a change in the product's price.
4. Supply is a schedule or curve showing the amounts of a product that producers are willing to offer in the market at each possible price during a specific period. The law of supply states that, other things equal, producers will offer more of a product at a high price than at a low price. Thus, the relationship between price and quantity supplied is positive or direct, and supply is graphed as an upsloping curve.
5. The market supply curve is the horizontal summation of the supply curves of the individual producers of the product.
6. Changes in one or more of the determinants of supply (resource prices, production techniques, taxes or subsidies, the prices of other goods, producer expectations, or the number of sellers in the market) shift the supply curve of a product. A shift to the right is an increase in supply; a shift to the left is a decrease in supply. In contrast, a change in the price of the product being considered causes a change in the quantity supplied, which is shown as a movement from one point to another point on a fixed supply curve.
7. The equilibrium price and quantity are established at the intersection of the supply and demand curves. The interaction of market demand and market supply adjusts the price to the point at which the quantities demanded and supplied are equal. This is the equilibrium price. The corresponding quantity is the equilibrium quantity.
8. The ability of market forces to synchronize selling and buying decisions to eliminate potential surpluses and shortages is known as the rationing function of prices. The equilibrium quantity in competitive markets reflects both productive efficiency (least-cost production) and allocative efficiency (the right amount of the product relative to other products).
9. A change in either demand or supply changes the equilibrium price and quantity. Increases in demand raise both equilibrium price and equilibrium quantity; decreases in demand lower both equilibrium price and equilibrium quantity. Increases in supply lower equilibrium price and raise equilibrium quantity; decreases in supply raise equilibrium price and lower equilibrium quantity.
10. Simultaneous changes in demand and supply affect equilibrium price and quantity in various ways, depending on their direction and relative magnitudes (see Table 3.7).
11. A price ceiling is a maximum price set by government and is designed to help consumers. Effective price ceilings produce persistent product shortages, and if an equitable distribution of the product is sought, government must ration the product to consumers.
12. A price floor is a minimum price set by government and is designed to aid producers. Effective price floors lead to persistent product surpluses; the government must either purchase the product or eliminate the surplus by imposing restrictions on production or increasing private demand.
13. Legally fixed prices stifle the rationing function of prices and distort the allocation of resources.

Terms and Concepts

demand	substitute good	change in quantity supplied
demand schedule	complementary good	equilibrium price
law of demand	change in demand	equilibrium quantity
diminishing marginal utility	change in quantity demanded	surplus
income effect	supply	shortage
substitution effect	supply schedule	productive efficiency
demand curve	law of supply	allocative efficiency
determinants of demand	supply curve	price ceiling
normal goods	determinants of supply	price floor
inferior goods	change in supply	

Study Questions

1. Explain the law of demand. Why does a demand curve slope downward? How is a market demand curve derived from individual demand curves?
2. What are the determinants of demand? What happens to the demand curve when any of these determinants change? Distinguish between a change in demand and a change in the quantity demanded, noting the cause(s) of each.
3. **KEY QUESTION** What effect will each of the following have on the demand for small automobiles such as the Mini Cooper and Smart car?
   a. Small automobiles become more fashionable.
   b. The price of large automobiles rises (with the price of small autos remaining the same).
   c. Income declines and small autos are an inferior good.
   d. Consumers anticipate that the price of small autos will greatly come down in the near future.
   e. The price of gasoline substantially drops.
4. Explain the law of supply. Why does the supply curve slope upward? How is the market supply curve derived from the supply curves of individual producers?
5. What are the determinants of supply? What happens to the supply curve when any of these determinants changes? Distinguish between a change in supply and a change in the quantity supplied, noting the cause(s) of each.
6. **KEY QUESTION** What effect will each of the following have on the supply of *auto* tires?
   a. A technological advance in the methods of producing tires.
   b. A decline in the number of firms in the tire industry.
   c. An increase in the prices of rubber used in the production of tires.
   d. The expectation that the equilibrium price of auto tires will be lower in the future than currently.
   e. A decline in the price of the large tires used for semi trucks and earth-hauling rigs (with no change in the price of auto tires).
   f. The levying of a per-unit tax on each auto tire sold.
   g. The granting of a 50-cent-per-unit subsidy for each auto tire produced.
7. "In the corn market, demand often exceeds supply and supply sometimes exceeds demand." "The price of corn rises and falls in response to changes in supply and demand." In which of these two statements are the terms "supply" and "demand" used correctly? Explain.
8. **KEY QUESTION** Suppose the total demand for wheat and the total supply of wheat per month in the Kansas City grain market are as shown in the accompanying table.
   a. What is the equilibrium price? What is the equilibrium quantity? Fill in the surplus-shortage column and use it to explain why your answers are correct.
   b. Graph the demand for wheat and the supply of wheat. Be sure to label the axes of your graph correctly. Label equilibrium price *P* and equilibrium quantity *Q*.

Thousands of Bushels Demanded	Price per Bushel	Thousands of Bushels Supplied	Surplus (+) or Shortage (−)
85	$3.40	72	______
80	3.70	73	______
75	4.00	75	______
70	4.30	77	______
65	4.60	79	______
60	4.90	81	______

   c. Why will $3.40 not be the equilibrium price in this market? Why not $4.90? "Surpluses drive prices up; shortages drive them down." Do you agree?
9. **KEY QUESTION** How will each of the following changes in demand and/or supply affect equilibrium price and equilibrium quantity in a competitive market; that is, do price and quantity rise, fall, or remain unchanged, or are the answers indeterminate because they depend on the magnitudes of the shifts? Use supply and demand diagrams to verify your answers.
   a. Supply decreases and demand is constant.
   b. Demand decreases and supply is constant.
   c. Supply increases and demand is constant.
   d. Demand increases and supply increases.
   e. Demand increases and supply is constant.
   f. Supply increases and demand decreases.
   g. Demand increases and supply decreases.
   h. Demand decreases and supply decreases.
10. In 2001 an outbreak of foot-and-mouth disease in Europe led to the burning of millions of cattle carcasses. What impact do you think this had on the supply of cattle hides, hide prices, the supply of leather goods, and the price of leather goods?
11. Use two market diagrams to explain how an increase in state subsidies to public colleges might affect tuition and enrollments in both public and private colleges.
12. Critically evaluate: "In comparing the two equilibrium positions in Figure 3.7b, I note that a smaller amount is actually demanded at a lower price. This refutes the law of demand."
13. For each stock in the stock market, the number of shares sold daily equals the number of shares purchased. That is, the quantity of each firm's shares demanded equals the quantity supplied. So, if this equality always occurs, why do the prices of stock shares ever change?
14. **KEY QUESTION** Refer to the table in question 8. Suppose that the government establishes a price ceiling of $3.70 for wheat. What might prompt the government to establish this price ceiling? Explain carefully the main effects. Demonstrate your answer graphically. Next, suppose that the government establishes a price floor of $4.60 for wheat. What

will be the main effects of this price floor? Demonstrate your answer graphically.

15. What do economists mean when they say that "price floors and ceilings stifle the rationing function of prices and distort resource allocation"?

16. **ADVANCED ANALYSIS** Assume that demand for a commodity is represented by the equation $P = 10 - .2Q_d$ and supply by the equation $P = 2 + .2Q_s$, where Q_d and Q_s are quantity demanded and quantity supplied, respectively, and P is price. Using the equilibrium condition $Q_s = Q_d$, solve the equations to determine equilibrium price. Now determine equilibrium quantity. Graph the two equations to substantiate your answers.

17. **LAST WORD** What is the current overall number of American candidates waiting for an organ transplant? (For the answer, visit the United Network for Organ Sharing Web site, **www.unos.org.**) For what transplant organ is the waiting list the longest? (Select "Data" and "At a glance.") Do you favor the establishment of a legal market for transplant organs? Why or why not?

Web-Based Questions

1. **FARM COMMODITY PRICES—SUPPLY AND DEMAND IN ACTION** The U.S. Department of Agriculture, **www.nass.usda.gov/,** publishes charts on the prices of farm products. Go to the USDA home page and select "Find charts and maps" and then "Agricultural Prices." Choose three farm products and determine whether their prices (as measured by "prices received by farmers") have generally increased, decreased, or stayed the same over the past 3 years. In which of the three cases, if any, do you think that supply has increased more rapidly than demand? In which of the three cases, if any, do you think that demand has increased more rapidly than supply? Explain your reasoning.

2. **CHANGES IN DEMAND—BABY DIAPERS AND RETIREMENT VILLAGES** Other things equal, an increase in the number of buyers for a product or service will increase demand. Baby diapers and retirement villages are two products designed for different population groups. The U.S. Census Bureau Web site, **www.census.gov/ipc/www/idbpyr.html,** provides population pyramids (graphs that show the distribution of population by age and sex) for countries for 2000, 2025, and 2050. View the population pyramids for Mexico, Japan, and the United States. Which country do you think will have the greatest percentage increase in demand for baby diapers between 2000 and 2050? For retirement villages? Which country do you think will have the greatest absolute increase in demand for baby diapers? For retirement villages?

IN THIS CHAPTER YOU WILL LEARN:

- Important facts about U.S. households and U.S. businesses.
- Why the corporate form of business organization dominates sales and profits.
- The problem that arises when corporate owners (principals) and their managers (agents) have different interests.
- About the economic role of government in the economy.
- The categories of government spending and the sources of government revenues.

4

The U.S. Economy: Private and Public Sectors

We now move from the general characteristics of the market economy, including the role of supply and demand, to specific information about the world's largest economy. Each year, the value of U.S. output exceeds that of Japan, Germany, the United Kingdom, and France—combined! For descriptive convenience, we will divide the economy into two sectors: the *private sector,* which includes *households* and *businesses,* and the *public sector,* or simply *government.*

Households as Income Receivers

The U.S. economy currently has about 113 million households. These households consist of one or more persons occupying a housing unit and are both the ultimate suppliers of all economic resources *and* the major spenders in the economy. We can categorize the income received by households by how it was earned and by how it was divided among households.

The Functional Distribution of Income

The **functional distribution of income** indicates how the nation's earned income is apportioned among wages, rents, interest, and profits, that is, according to the function performed by the income receiver. Wages are paid to labor; rents and interest are paid to owners of property resources; and profits are paid to the owners of corporations and unincorporated businesses.

Figure 4.1 shows the functional distribution of U.S. income earned in 2005. The largest source of income for households is the wages and salaries paid to workers. Notice that the bulk of total U.S. income (71 percent) goes to labor, not to capital. Proprietors' income—the income of doctors, lawyers, small-business owners, farmers, and owners of other unincorporated enterprises—also has a "wage" element. Some of this income is payment for one's own labor, and some of it is profit from one's own business.

The other three types of income are self-evident: Some households own corporate stock and receive dividend incomes on their holdings. Many households also own bonds and savings accounts that yield interest income. And some households receive rental income by providing buildings and natural resources (including land) to businesses and other individuals.

The Personal Distribution of Income

The **personal distribution of income** indicates how the nation's money income is divided among individual households. In Figure 4.2 households are divided into five numerically equal groups or quintiles; the heights of the bars show the percentage of total income received by each group. In 2004 the poorest 20 percent of all households received 3.4 percent of total personal income, and the richest 20 percent received 50.1 percent. Clearly there is considerable inequality in the personal distribution of U.S. income. **(Key Question 2)**

FIGURE 4.1 The functional distribution of U.S. income, 2005. Seventy-one percent of U.S. income is received as wages and salaries. Income to property owners—corporate profit, interest, and rents—accounts for about 20 percent of total income.

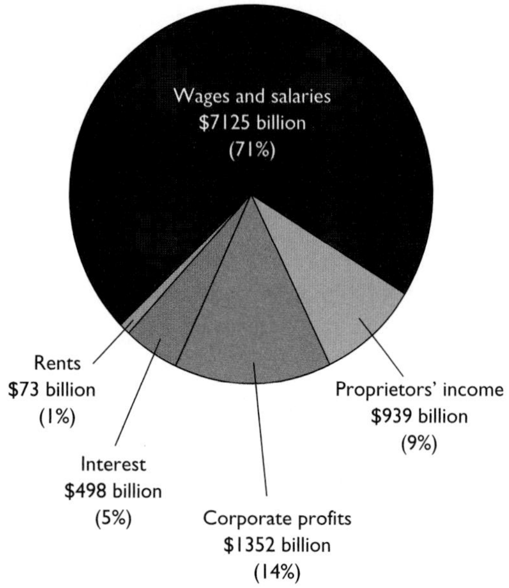

Source: Bureau of Economic Analysis.

FIGURE 4.2 The personal distribution of income among U.S. households, 2004. Personal income is unequally distributed in the United States, with the top 20 percent of households receiving about one-half of the total income. In an equal distribution, all five vertical bars would be as high as the horizontal line drawn at 20 percent; then each 20 percent of families would receive 20 percent of the nation's total income.

Numbers do not add to 100 percent due to rounding.

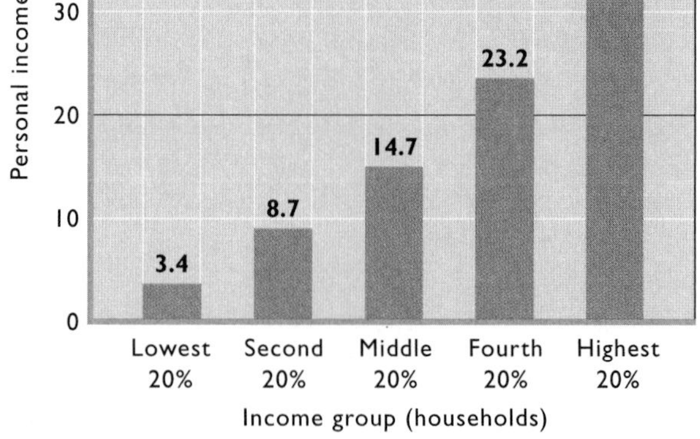

Source: Bureau of the Census.

FIGURE 4.3 The disposition of household income, 2005. Households apportion their income among taxes, saving, and consumption, with most going to consumption. (The way income is defined in this figure differs slightly from that used in Figure 4.1, accounting for the quantitative discrepancies between the "total income" amounts in the two figures.)

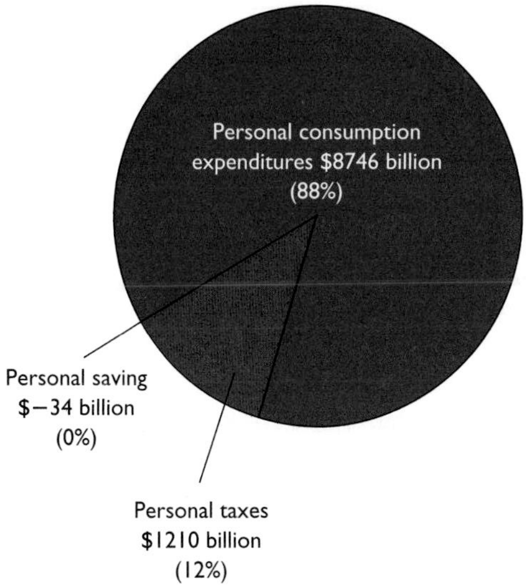

Source: Bureau of Economic Analysis.

Households as Spenders

How do households dispose of their income? Part of it flows to government as taxes, and the rest is divided between personal savings and personal consumption expenditures. In 2005, households disposed of their total personal income as shown in Figure 4.3.

Personal Taxes

U.S. households paid $1210 billion in personal taxes in 2005, or 12 percent of their $9922 billion of income. Personal taxes, of which the personal income tax is the major component, have risen in relative terms since the Second World War. In 1941, households paid just 3 percent of their total income in personal taxes.

Personal Saving

Economists define "saving" as that part of after-tax income that is not spent; hence, households have just two choices about what to do with their income after taxes—use it to consume, or save it. Saving is the portion of income that is not paid in taxes or used to purchase consumer goods but instead flows into bank accounts, insurance policies, bonds and stocks, mutual funds, and other financial assets.

U.S. households typically save about 3 percent of their income each year. Reasons for saving center on *security* and *speculation.* Households save to provide a nest egg for coping with unforeseen contingencies (sickness, accident, and unemployment), for retirement from the workforce, to finance the education of children, or simply for financial security. They may also channel part of their income to purchase stocks, speculating that their investments will increase in value.

The desire to save is not enough in itself, however. You must be able to save, and that depends on the size of your income. If your income is low, you may not be able to save any money at all. If your income is very, very low you may *dissave*—that is, spend more than your after-tax income. You do this by borrowing or by digging into savings you may have accumulated in years when your income was higher.

Both saving and consumption vary directly with income; as households garner more income, they usually save more and consume more. In fact, the top 10 percent of income receivers account for most of the personal saving in the U.S. economy.

As Figure 4.3 implies, 2005 was a highly unusual year for personal saving. It was a negative $34 billion. The sum of personal consumption and personal taxes exceeded household income in 2005. This atypical situation resulted from heavy borrowing by Americans to buy houses, to "tap" equity in their homes, and to finance purchases of imported goods.

Personal Consumption Expenditures

As Figure 4.3 shows, more than 88 percent of the total income of households flows back into the business sector as personal consumption expenditures—money spent on consumer goods.

Figure 4.4 shows how consumers divide their expenditures among durable goods, nondurable goods, and services.

FIGURE 4.4 The composition of consumer expenditures, 2005. Consumers divide their spending among durable goods (goods that have expected lives of 3 years or more), nondurable goods, and services. About 59 percent of consumer spending is for services.

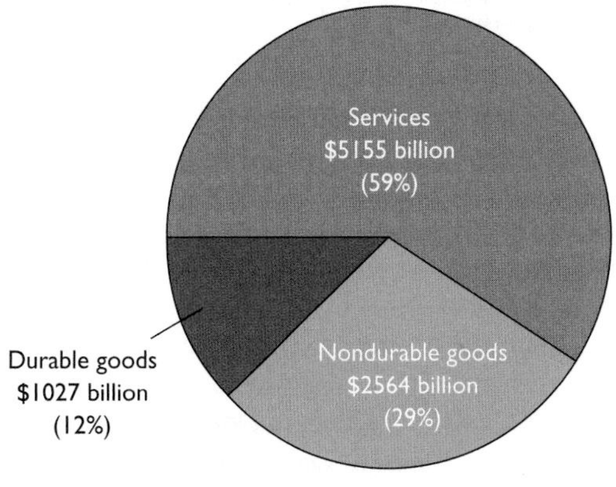

Source: Bureau of Economic Analysis.

Twelve percent of consumer expenditures are on **durable goods**—products that have expected lives of 3 years or more. Such goods include automobiles, furniture, and personal computers. Another 29 percent of consumer expenditures are on **nondurable goods**—products that have lives of less than 3 years. Included are such goods as food, clothing, and gasoline. About 59 percent of consumer expenditures are on **services**—the work done for consumers by lawyers, barbers, doctors, lodging personnel, and so on. This high percentage is the reason that the United States is often referred to as a *service-oriented economy.*

QUICK REVIEW 4.1

- The functional distribution of income indicates how income is apportioned among wages, rents, interest, and profits; the personal distribution of income indicates how income is divided among families.
- Wages and salaries are the major component of the functional distribution of income. The personal distribution of income reveals considerable inequality.
- Nearly 90 percent of household income is consumed; the rest is saved or paid in taxes.
- Consumer spending is directed to durable goods, nondurable goods, and services, with nearly 60 percent going to services.

The Business Population

Businesses constitute the second major part of the private sector. It will be useful to distinguish among a plant, a firm, and an industry:

- A **plant** is a physical establishment—a factory, farm, mine, store, or warehouse—that performs one or more functions in fabricating and distributing goods and services.
- A **firm** is a business organization that owns and operates plants. Some firms operate only one plant, but many own and operate several.
- An **industry** is a group of firms that produce the same, or similar, products.

The organizational structures of firms are often complex and varied. *Multiplant firms* may be organized horizontally, with several plants performing much the same function. Examples are the multiple bottling plants of Coca-Cola and the many individual Wal-Mart stores. Firms also may be *vertically integrated,* meaning they own plants that perform different functions in the various stages of the production process. For example, oil companies such as Shell own oil fields, refineries, and retail gasoline stations. Some firms are *conglomerates,* so named because they have plants that produce products in several industries. For example, Pfizer makes not only prescription medicines (Lipitor, Viagra) but also chewing gum (Trident, Dentyne), razors (Schick), cough drops (Halls), breath mints (Clorets, Certs), and antacids (Rolaids).

Legal Forms of Businesses

The business population is extremely diverse, ranging from giant corporations such as ExxonMobil, with 2005 sales of $328 billion and thousands of employees, to neighborhood specialty shops with one or two employees and sales of only $200 to $300 per day. There are three major legal forms of businesses:

- A **sole proprietorship** is a business owned and operated by one person. Usually, the proprietor (the owner) personally supervises its operation.
- The **partnership** form of business organization is a natural outgrowth of the sole proprietorship. In a partnership, two or more individuals (the partners) agree to own and operate a business together. Usually they pool their financial resources and business skills. Consequently, they share the risks and the profits or losses.
- A **corporation** is a legal creation that can acquire resources, own assets, produce and sell products, incur debts, extend credit, sue and be sued, and perform the functions of any other type of enterprise. A corporation is distinct and separate from the individual stockholders who own it. Hired managers run most corporations.

Figure 4.5a shows how the business population is distributed among the three major forms. About 72 percent of U.S. firms are sole proprietorships. These firms are so numerous mainly because they are easy to set up and organize. The proprietor is one's own boss and has substantial freedom of action. Partnerships constitute 8 percent of all U.S. business enterprises. The other 20 percent are corporations.

But as Figure 4.5b shows, sole proprietorships account for only 5 percent of total sales (output value) and partnerships only 11 percent. The remainder—an amazing 84 percent—accrues to corporations.

Advantages of Corporations

Certain advantages of the corporate form of business enterprise have catapulted it into a dominant sales and profit position in the United States. The corporation is by far the most effective form of business organization for raising money to finance the expansion of its facilities and capabilities. The corporation employs unique methods of finance—the selling of stocks (equity financing) and bonds

FIGURE 4.5 The business population and shares of domestic output. (a) Sole proprietorships dominate the business population numerically, but (b) corporations account for about 84 percent of total sales (output).

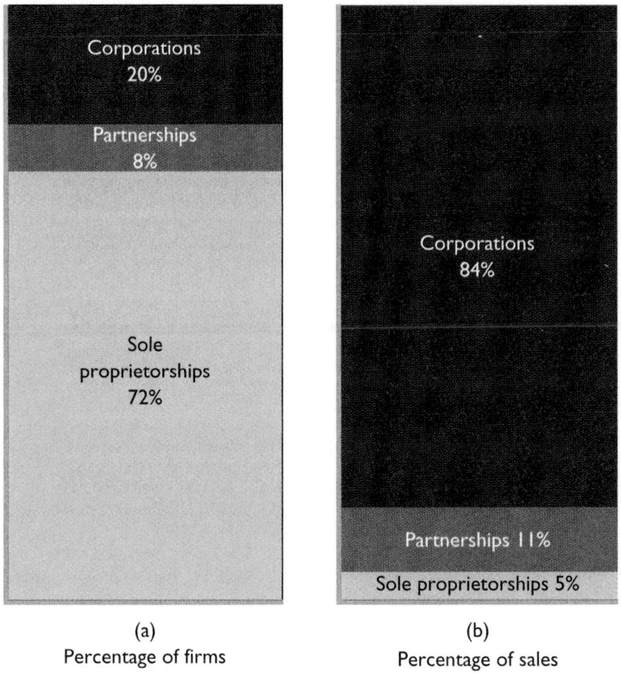

Source: U.S. Census Bureau, **www.census.gov.** Latest data.

(debt financing)—that enable it to pool the financial resources of large numbers of people.

A common **stock** represents a share in the ownership of a corporation. The purchaser of a stock certificate has the right to vote for corporate officers and to share in dividends. If you buy 1000 of the 100,000 shares issued by OutTell, Inc., then you own 1 percent of the company, are entitled to 1 percent of any dividends declared by the board of directors, and control 1 percent of the votes in the annual election of corporate officials.

In contrast, a corporate **bond** does not bestow any corporate ownership on the purchaser. A bond purchaser is simply lending money to a corporation. A bond is an IOU, in acknowledgment of a loan, whereby the corporation promises to pay the holder a fixed amount set forth on the bond at some specified future date and other fixed amounts (interest payments) every year up to the bond's maturity date. For example, you might purchase a 10-year OutTell bond with a face value of $1000 and a 5 percent rate of interest. This means that in exchange for your $1000, OT promises you a $50 interest payment for each of the next 10 years and then repays your $1000 principal at the end of that period.

Financing through sales of stocks and bonds also provides other advantages to those who purchase these *corporate securities.* An individual investor can spread risks by buying the securities of several corporations. And it is usually easy for holders of corporate securities to sell their holdings. Organized stock exchanges and bond markets simplify the transfer of securities from sellers to buyers. This "ease of sale" increases the willingness of savers to make financial investments in corporate securities. Besides, corporations have easier access to bank credit than do other types of business organizations. Corporations are better risks and are more likely to become profitable clients of banks.

Corporations provide **limited liability** to owners (stockholders), who risk only what they paid for their stock. Their personal assets are not at stake if the corporation defaults on its debts. Creditors can sue the corporation as a legal entity but cannot sue the owners of the corporation as individuals.

Because of their ability to attract financial capital, successful corporations can easily expand the scope of their operations and realize the benefits of expansion. For example, they can take advantage of mass-production technologies and division of labor. A corporation can hire specialists in production, accounting, and marketing functions and thus improve efficiency.

Unlike sole proprietorships and partnerships, the corporation has a life independent of its owners and its officers. As a legal entity, corporations are immortal. The transfer of corporate ownership through inheritance or the sale of stock does not disrupt the continuity of the corporation. Corporations have permanence that lends itself to long-range planning and growth. This permanence and growth explains why virtually all the nation's largest business enterprises are corporations.

The Principal-Agent Problem

Many of the world's corporations are extremely large. In 2005, 273 of the world's largest corporations had annual sales of more than $20 billion, and 593 firms had sales of more than $10 billion. U.S.-based ExxonMobil alone sold $328 billion of goods in 2005. Global Perspective 4.1 lists the world's 10 largest corporations, by annual sales.

But large size creates a potential problem. In sole proprietorships and partnerships, the owners of the real and financial assets of the firm enjoy direct control of those assets. But ownership of large corporations is spread over tens or hundreds of thousands of stockholders. The owners of a corporation usually do not manage it—they hire others to do so.

O 4.1
Principal-agent problem

CONSIDER THIS . . .

Unprincipled Agents

In the 1990s many corporations addressed the principal-agent problem by providing a substantial part of executive pay either as shares of the firm's stock or as stock options. Stock options are contracts that allow executives or other key employees to buy shares of their employers' stock at fixed, lower prices when the stock prices rise. The intent was to align the interest of the executives and other key employees more closely with those of the broader corporate owners. By pursuing high profits and share prices, the executives would enhance their own wealth as well as that of all the stockholders.

This "solution" to the principal-agent problem had an unexpected negative side effect. It prompted a few unscrupulous executives to inflate their firms' share prices by hiding costs, overstating revenues, engaging in deceptive transactions, and, in general, exaggerating profits. These executives then sold large quantities of their inflated stock, making quick personal fortunes. In some cases, "independent" outside auditing firms turned out to be not so independent, because they held valuable consulting contracts with the firms being audited.

When the stock-market bubble of the late 1990s burst, many instances of business manipulations and fraudulent accounting were exposed. Several executives of large U.S. firms were indicted and a few large firms collapsed, among them Enron (energy trading), WorldCom (communications), and Arthur Andersen (accounting and business consulting). General stockholders of those firms were left holding severely depressed or even worthless stock.

In 2002 Congress strengthened the laws and penalties against executive misconduct. Also, corporations have improved their accounting and auditing procedures. But seemingly endless revelations of executive wrongdoings make clear that the principal-agent problem is not an easy problem to solve.

That practice can create a **principal-agent problem.** The *principals* are the stockholders who own the corporation and who hire executives as their *agents* to run the business on their behalf. But the interests of these managers (the agents) and the wishes of the owners (the principals) do not always coincide. The owners typically want maximum company profit and stock price. However, the agent may want the power, prestige, and pay that often accompany control over a large enterprise, independent of its profitability and stock price.

So a conflict of interest may develop. For example, executives may build expensive office buildings, enjoy excessive perks such as corporate jets, and pay too much to acquire other corporations. Consequently, the firm's costs will be excessive, and the firm will fail to maximize profit and the stock price for the owners. **(Key Question 4)**

GLOBAL PERSPECTIVE 4.1

The World's 10 Largest Corporations

Five of the world's ten largest corporations, based on dollar revenue in 2005, were headquartered in the United States.

- ExxonMobil (U.S.) $328 billion
- Wal-Mart (U.S.) $312 billion
- Shell (U.K./Netherlands) $307 billion
- BP (U.K.) $249 billion
- General Motors (U.S.) $193 billion
- Chevron (U.S.) $185 billion
- Ford Motor (U.S.) $178 billion
- DaimlerChrysler (Germany) $177 billion
- Toyota (Japan) $173 billion
- ConocoPhillips (U.S.) $162 billion

Source: Fortune, **www.forbes.com.**

QUICK REVIEW 4.2

- A plant is a physical establishment that contributes to the production of goods and services; a firm is a business organization that owns and operates plants; plants may be arranged horizontally, be vertically integrated, and/or take on a conglomerate form.
- The three basic legal forms of business are the sole proprietorship, the partnership, and the corporation. While sole proprietorships make up 72 percent of all firms, corporations account for 84 percent of total sales.
- The major advantages of corporations are their ability to raise financial capital, the limited liability they bestow on owners, and their continuing life beyond the life of their owners and managers.
- The principal-agent problem is the conflict of interest that may occur when agents (executives) pursue their own objectives to the detriment of the principals' (stockholders') goals.

The Public Sector: Government's Role

The economic activities of the *public sector*—Federal, state, and local government—are extensive. We begin by discussing the economic functions of governments. What is government's role in the economy?

Providing the Legal Structure

Government provides the legal framework and the services needed for a market economy to operate effectively. The legal framework sets the legal status of business enterprises, ensures the rights of private ownership, and allows the making and enforcement of contracts. Government also establishes the legal "rules of the game" that control relationships among businesses, resource suppliers, and consumers. Discrete units of government referee economic relationships, seek out foul play, and impose penalties.

Government intervention is presumed to improve the allocation of resources. By supplying a medium of exchange, ensuring product quality, defining ownership rights, and enforcing contracts, the government increases the volume and safety of exchange. This widens the market and fosters greater specialization in the use of property and human resources. Such specialization promotes a more efficient allocation of resources.

Like the optimal amount of any "good," the optimal amount of regulation is that at which the marginal benefit and marginal cost are equal. Thus, there can be either too little regulation (MB exceeds MC) or too much regulation (MB is less than MC). The task is deciding on the right amount.

Maintaining Competition

Competition is the basic regulatory mechanism in the market system. It is the force that subjects producers and resource suppliers to the dictates of consumer sovereignty. With competition, buyers are the boss, the market is their agent, and businesses are their servants.

It is a different story where a single seller—a **monopoly**—controls an industry. By controlling supply, a monopolist can charge a higher-than-competitive price. Producer sovereignty then supplants consumer sovereignty. In the United States, government has attempted to control monopoly through *regulation* and through *antitrust.*

A few industries are natural monopolies—industries in which technology is such that only a single seller can achieve the lowest possible costs. In some cases government has allowed these monopolies to exist but has also created public commissions to regulate their prices and set their service standards. Examples of *regulated monopolies* are some firms that provide local electricity, telephone, and transportation services.

In nearly all markets, however, efficient production can best be attained with a high degree of competition. The Federal government has therefore enacted a series of antitrust (antimonopoly) laws, beginning with the Sherman Act of 1890, to prohibit certain monopoly abuses and, if necessary, break monopolists up into competing firms. Under these laws, for example, in 2000 Microsoft was found guilty of monopolizing the market for operating systems for personal computers. Rather than breaking up Microsoft, however, the government imposed a series of prohibitions and requirements that collectively limited Microsoft's ability to engage in anticompetitive actions.

Redistributing Income

The market system is impersonal and may distribute income more inequitably than society desires. It yields very large incomes to those whose labor, by virtue of inherent ability and acquired education and skills, command high wages. Similarly, those who, through hard work or inheritance, possess valuable capital and land, receive large property incomes.

But many other members of society have less productive ability, have received only modest amounts of education and training, and have accumulated or inherited no property resources. Moreover, some of the aged, the physically and mentally disabled, and the poorly educated earn small incomes or, like the unemployed, no income at all. Thus society chooses to redistribute a part of total income through a variety of government policies and programs. They are:

- ***Transfer payments*** *Transfer payments*, for example, in the form of welfare checks and food stamps, provide relief to the destitute, the dependent, the disabled, and older citizens; unemployment compensation payments provide aid to the unemployed.
- ***Market intervention*** Government also alters the distribution of income through *market intervention*, that is, by acting to modify the prices that are or would be established by market forces. Providing farmers with above-market prices for their output and requiring that firms pay minimum wages are illustrations of government interventions designed to raise the income of specific groups.
- ***Taxation*** Since the 1930s, government has used the personal income tax to take a larger proportion of the income of the rich than of the poor, thus narrowing the after-tax income difference between high-income and low-income earners.

The *extent* to which government should redistribute income is subject to lively debate. Redistribution involves both benefits and costs. The alleged benefits are greater "fairness," or "economic justice"; the alleged costs are reduced incentives to work, save, invest, and produce, and therefore a loss of total output and income.

Reallocating Resources

Market failure occurs when the competitive market system (1) produces the "wrong" amounts of certain goods and services or (2) fails to allocate any resources whatsoever to the production of certain goods and services whose output is economically justified. The first type of failure results from what economists call *externalities* or *spillovers*, and the second type involves *public goods*. Both kinds of market failure can be corrected by government action.

Externalities

When we say that competitive markets automatically bring about the efficient use of resources, we assume that all the benefits and costs for each product are fully reflected in the market demand and supply curves. That is not always the case. In some markets certain benefits or costs may escape the buyer or seller.

O 4.2
Externalities

An **externality** occurs when some of the costs or the benefits of a good are passed on to or "spill over to" someone other than the immediate buyer or seller. Such spillovers are called externalities, because they are benefits or costs that accrue to some third party that is *external* to the market transaction.

Negative Externalities

Production or consumption costs inflicted on a third party without compensation are called **negative externalities.** Environmental pollution is an example. When a chemical manufacturer or a meatpacking plant dumps its wastes into a lake or river, swimmers, fishers, and boaters—and perhaps those who drink the water—suffer external costs. When a petroleum refinery pollutes the air with smoke or a paper mill creates obnoxious odors, the community experiences external costs for which it is not compensated.

What are the economic effects? Recall that costs determine the position of the firm's supply curve. When a firm avoids some costs by polluting, its supply curve lies farther to the right than it does when the firm bears the full costs of production. As a result, the price of the product is too low and the output of the product is too large to achieve allocative efficiency. A market failure occurs in the form of an overallocation of resources to the production of the good.

Correcting for Negative Externalities

Government can do two things to correct the overallocation of resources. Both solutions are designed to internalize external costs, that is, to make the offending firm pay the costs rather than shift them to others:

- ***Legislation*** In cases of air and water pollution, the most direct action is legislation prohibiting or limiting the pollution. Such legislation forces potential polluters to pay for the proper disposal of industrial wastes—here, by installing smoke-abatement equipment or water-purification facilities. The idea is to force potential offenders, under the threat of legal action, to bear *all* the costs associated with production.
- ***Specific taxes*** A less direct action is based on the fact that taxes are a cost and therefore a determinant of a firm's supply curve. Government might levy a *specific tax*—that is, a tax confined to a particular product—on each unit of the polluting firm's output. The amount of this tax would roughly equal the estimated amount of the negative externality arising from the production of each unit of output. Through this tax, government would pass back to the offending firm a cost equivalent to the spillover cost the firm is avoiding. This would shift the firm's supply curve to the left, reducing equilibrium output and eliminating the overallocation of resources.

Positive Externalities

Sometimes externalities appear as benefits to other producers or consumers. These uncompensated spillovers accruing to third parties or the community at large are called **positive externalities.** Immunization against measles and polio results in direct benefits to the immediate consumer of those vaccines. But it also results in widespread substantial external benefits to the entire community.

Education is another example of positive externalities. Education benefits individual consumers: Better-educated people generally achieve higher incomes than less well educated people. But education also provides benefits to society, in the form of a more versatile and more productive labor force, on the one hand, and smaller outlays for crime prevention, law enforcement, and welfare programs, on the other.

External benefits mean that the market demand curve, which reflects only private benefits, understates total benefits. The demand curve for the product lies farther to the left than it would if the market took all benefits into account. As a result, a smaller amount of the product will be produced, or, alternatively, there will be an *underallocation* of resources to the product—again a market failure.

Correcting for Positive Externalities How might the underallocation of resources associated with spillover benefits be corrected? The answer is either to subsidize consumers (to increase demand), to subsidize producers (to increase supply), or, in the extreme, to have government produce the product:

- ***Subsidize consumers*** To correct the underallocation of resources to higher education, the U.S. government provides low-interest loans to students so that they can afford more education. Those loans increase the demand for higher education.
- ***Subsidize suppliers*** In some cases government finds it more convenient and administratively simpler to correct an underallocation by subsidizing suppliers. For example, in higher education, state governments provide substantial portions of the budgets of public colleges and universities. Such subsidies lower the costs of producing higher education and increase its supply. Publicly subsidized immunization programs, hospitals, and medical research are other examples.
- ***Provide goods via government*** A third policy option may be appropriate where positive externalities are extremely large: Government may finance or, in the extreme, own and operate the industry that is involved. Examples are the U.S. Postal Service and Federal aircraft control systems.

Public Goods and Services Certain goods called *private goods* are produced through the competitive market system. Examples are the wide variety of items sold in stores. Private goods have two characteristics—*rivalry* and *excludability*. "Rivalry" means that when one person buys and consumes a product, it is not available for purchase and consumption by another person. What Joan gets, Jane cannot have. *Excludability* means that buyers who are willing and able to pay the market price for the product obtain its benefits, but those unable or unwilling to pay that price do not. This characteristic enables profitable production by a private firm.

Certain other goods and services called **public goods** have the opposite characteristics—*nonrivalry* and *nonexcludability*. Everyone can simultaneously obtain the benefit from a public good such as a global positioning system, national defense, street lighting, and environmental protection. One person's benefit does not reduce the benefit available to others. More important, there is no effective way of excluding individuals from the benefit of the good once it comes into existence. The inability to exclude creates a **free-rider problem,** in which people can receive benefits from a public good without contributing to its costs. The free-rider problem makes the good unprofitable to provide by a private firm.

An example of a public good is the war on terrorism (which includes homeland defense and recent military actions abroad). This public good is thought to be economically justified by the majority of Americans because the benefits are perceived as exceeding the costs. Once the war efforts are undertaken, however, the benefits accrue to all Americans (nonrivalry). And there is no practical way to exclude any American from receiving those benefits (nonexcluability).

No private firm will undertake the war on terrorism because the benefits cannot be profitably sold (due to the free-rider problem). So here we have a service that yields substantial benefits but to which the market system will not allocate sufficient resources. Like national defense in general, the pursuit of the war on terrorism is a public good. Society signals its desire for such goods by voting for particular political candidates who support their provision. Because of the free-rider problem, the public sector provides these goods and finances them through compulsory charges in the form of taxes.

Quasi-Public Goods Government provides many goods that fit the economist's definition of a public good. However, it also provides other goods and services that could be produced and delivered in such a way that exclusion would be possible. Such goods, called **quasi-public goods,** include education, streets and highways, police and fire protection, libraries and museums, preventive medicine, and sewage disposal. They could all be priced and provided by private firms through the market system. But, as we noted earlier, because they all have substantial positive externalities, they would be underproduced by the market system. Therefore, government often provides them to avoid the underallocation of resources that would otherwise occur.

The Reallocation Process How are resources reallocated from the production of private goods to the production of public and quasi-public goods? If the resources of the economy are fully employed, government must free up resources from the production of private goods and make them available for producing public and quasi-public goods. It does so by reducing private demand for them. And it does that by levying taxes on households and businesses, taking some of their income out of the circular flow. With lower incomes and hence less purchasing power, households and businesses must curtail their consumption and investment spending. As a result, the private

CONSIDER THIS . . .

Street Entertainers

Street entertainers are often found in tourist areas of major cities. Some entertainers are highly creative and talented; others "need more practice." But, regardless of talent level, these entertainers illuminate the concepts of free riders and public goods.

Most street entertainers have a hard time earning a living from their activities (unless event organizers pay them) because they have no way of excluding nonpayers from the benefits of their entertainment. They essentially are providing public, not private, goods and must rely on voluntary payments.

The result is a significant free-rider problem. Only a few in the audience put money in the container or instrument case, and many who do so contribute only token amounts. The rest are free riders who obtain the benefits of the street entertainment and retain their money for purchases that *they* initiate.

Street entertainers are acutely aware of the free-rider problem, and some have found creative ways to lessen it. For example, some entertainers involve the audience directly in the act. This usually creates a greater sense of audience willingness (or obligation) to contribute money at the end of the performance.

"Pay for performance" is another creative approach to lessening the free-rider problem. A good example is the street entertainer painted up to look like a statue. When people drop coins into the container, the "statue" makes a slight movement. The greater the contributions, the greater the movement. But these human "statues" still face a free-rider problem: Nonpayers also get to enjoy the acts.

Finally, because talented street entertainers create a festive street environment, cities or retailers sometimes hire them to perform. The "free entertainment" attracts crowds of shoppers, who buy goods from nearby retailers. In these instances the cities or retailers use tax revenue or commercial funds to pay the entertainers, in the former case validating them as public goods.

demand for goods and services declines, as does the private demand for resources. So by diverting purchasing power from private spenders to government, taxes remove resources from private use.

Government then spends the tax proceeds to provide public and quasi-public goods and services. Taxation releases resources from the production of private consumer goods (food, clothing, television sets) and private investment goods (printing presses, boxcars, warehouses). Government shifts those resources to the production of public and quasi-public goods (post offices, submarines, parks), changing the composition of the economy's total output. **(Key Questions 9 and 10)**

Promoting Stability

An economy's level of output depends on its level of total spending relative to its production capacity. When the level of total spending matches the economy's production capacity, human and property resources are fully employed and prices in general are stable. But sometimes total spending is either inadequate or excessive and the result is either unemployment or inflation. Government promotes stability by addressing these two problems:

- **Unemployment** When private sector spending is too low, government may try to augment it so that total spending—private plus public—is sufficient to achieve full employment. It does this by increasing government spending or by lowering taxes to stimulate private spending. Also, the nation's central bank (Federal Reserve in the United States) often takes actions to lower interest rates, thereby stimulating private borrowing and spending.
- **Inflation** Inflation is a general increase in the level of prices. Prices of goods and services rise when spenders try to buy more than the economy's capacity to produce. When total spending is excessive and becomes inflationary, government may try to reduce total spending by cutting its own expenditures or by raising taxes to curtail private spending. The nation's central bank may also take actions to increase interest rates to reduce private borrowing and spending.

Government's Role: A Qualification

Government does not have an easy task in performing the aforementioned economic functions. In a democracy, government undertakes its economic role in the context of politics. To serve the public, politicians need to get elected. To stay elected, officials (presidents, senators, representatives, mayors, council members, school board members) need to satisfy their particular constituencies. At best the political realities complicate government's role in the economy; at worst, they produce undesirable economic outcomes.

In the political context, overregulation can occur in some cases; underregulation, in others. Income can be redistributed to such an extent that incentives to work, save, and invest suffer. Some public goods and quasi-public goods can be produced not because their benefits exceed their costs but because their benefits accrue to firms located in states served by powerful elected officials. Inefficiency can easily creep into government activities because of the lack of a profit incentive to hold down costs. Policies to correct negative externalities can be politically blocked by the very parties that are producing the spillovers. In short, the economic role of government, although critical to a well-functioning economy, is not always perfectly carried out.

QUICK REVIEW 4.3

- Government enhances the operation of the market system by providing an appropriate legal foundation and promoting competition.
- Transfer payments, direct market intervention, and taxation are among the ways in which government can lessen income inequality.
- Government can correct for the overallocation of resources associated with negative externalities through legislation or taxes; it can offset the underallocation of resources associated with positive externalities by granting government subsidies.
- Government provides certain public goods for which there is nonrivalry in consumption and nonexcludability of benefits; government also provides many quasi-public goods because of their large external benefits.
- To try to stabilize the economy, the government can adjust its spending and tax revenues and the nation's central bank can take monetary actions that lower or increase interest rates.

The Circular Flow Revisited

In Figure 4.6 we integrate government into the circular flow model first shown in Figure 2.2. Here flows (1) through (4) are the same as the corresponding flows in that figure. Flows (1) and (2) show business expenditures for the resources provided by households. These expenditures are costs to businesses but represent wage, rent, interest, and profit income to households. Flows (3) and (4) show household expenditures for the goods and services produced by businesses.

Now consider what happens when we add government. Flows (5) through (8) illustrate that government makes purchases in both product and resource markets. Flows (5) and (6) represent government purchases of such products as paper, computers, and military hardware from private businesses. Flows (7) and (8) represent government purchases of resources. The Federal government employs and pays salaries to members of Congress, the armed forces, Justice Department lawyers, meat inspectors, and so on. State and local governments hire and pay teachers, bus drivers, police, and firefighters. The Federal government might also lease or purchase land to expand a military base, and a city might buy land on which to build a new elementary school.

Government then provides public goods and services to both households and businesses, as shown by flows (9) and (10). To finance those public goods and services, businesses and households are required to pay taxes, as shown by flows (11) and (12). These flows are labeled as *net* taxes to indicate that they also include "taxes in reverse" in the form of transfer payments to households and subsidies to businesses. Thus, flow (11) entails various subsidies to farmers, shipbuilders, and airlines as well as income, sales, and excise taxes paid by businesses to government. Most subsidies to business are "concealed" in the form of low-interest loans, loan guarantees, tax concessions, or public facilities provided at prices below their cost. Similarly, flow (12) includes both taxes (personal income taxes, payroll taxes) collected by government directly from households and transfer payments such as welfare payments and Social Security benefits paid by government.

Government Finance

How large is the U.S. public sector? What are the main expenditure categories of Federal, state, and local governments? How are these expenditures financed?

Government Purchases and Transfers

We can get an idea of the size of government's economic role by examining government purchases of goods and services and government transfer payments. There is a significant difference between these two kinds of outlays:

- **Government purchases** are *exhaustive;* the products purchased directly absorb (require the use of) resources and are part of the domestic output. For example, the purchase of a missile absorbs the labor of physicists and engineers along with steel, explosives, and a host of other inputs.
- **Transfer payments** are *nonexhaustive;* they do not directly absorb resources or create output. Social Security benefits, welfare payments, veterans' benefits, and unemployment compensation are examples of transfer payments. Their key characteristic is that recipients make no current contribution to domestic output in return for them.

FIGURE 4.6 The circular flow and the public sector. Government buys products from the product market and employs resources from the resource market to provide public goods and services to households and businesses. Government finances its expenditures through the net taxes (taxes minus transfer payments) it receives from households and businesses.

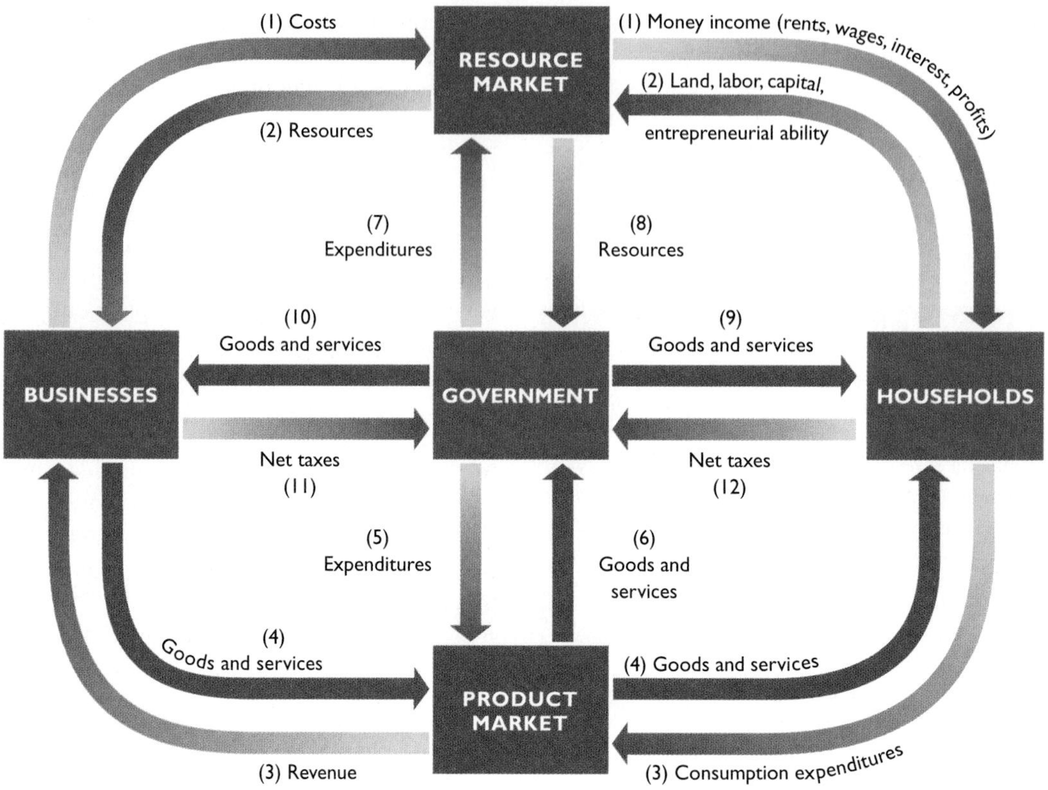

Federal, state, and local governments spent $3876 billion in 2005. Of that total, government purchases were $2360 billion and government transfers were $1516 billion. Figure 4.7 shows these amounts as percentages of U.S. domestic output for 2005 and compares them to percentages for 1960. Government purchases have declined from about 22 to 19 percent of output since 1960. But transfer payments have more than doubled as a percentage of output—from 5 percent in 1960 to 12 percent in 2005. Relative to U.S. output, total government spending is thus higher today than it was 45 years ago. This means that the tax revenues required to finance government expenditures are also higher. Today, government spending and the tax revenues needed to finance it are about 31 percent of U.S. output.

In 2006 the so-called Tax Freedom Day in the United States was April 26. On that day the average worker had earned enough (from the start of the year) to pay his or her share of the taxes required to finance government spending for the year. Tax Freedom Day arrives even

FIGURE 4.7 Government purchases, transfers, and total spending as percentages of U.S. output, 1960 and 2005. Government purchases have declined as a percentage of U.S. output since 1960. Transfer payments, however, have increased, so total government spending (purchases plus transfers) is now 31 percent of U.S. output.

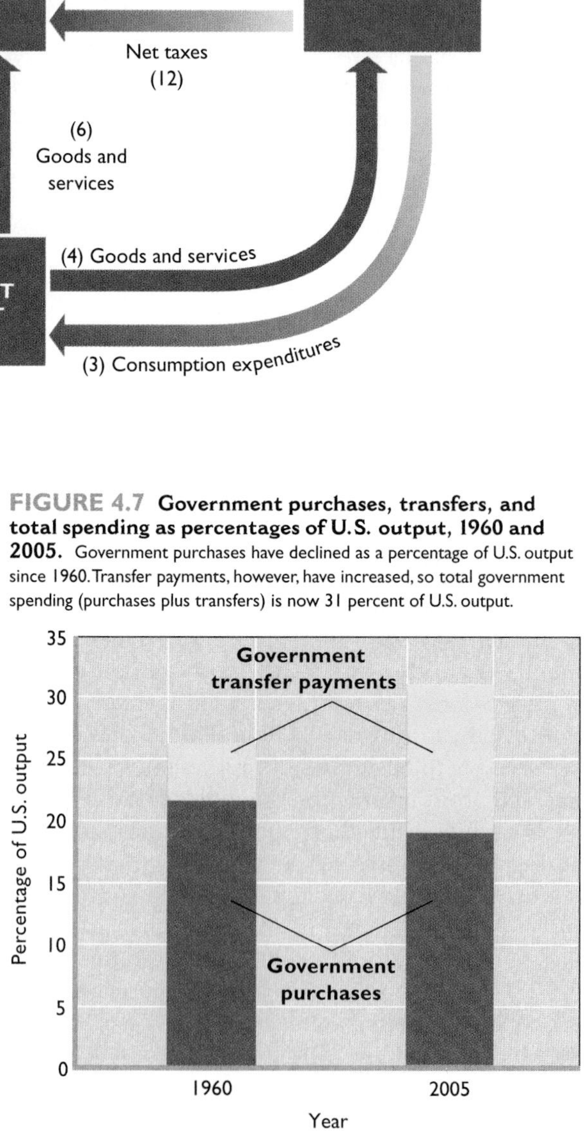

GLOBAL PERSPECTIVE 4.2

Total Tax Revenue as a Percentage of Total Output, Selected Nations

The percentage of tax revenues to total output is one measure of a country's tax burden. Among the world's industrialized nations, South Korea, Japan, the United States, and Australia have the lowest tax burdens.

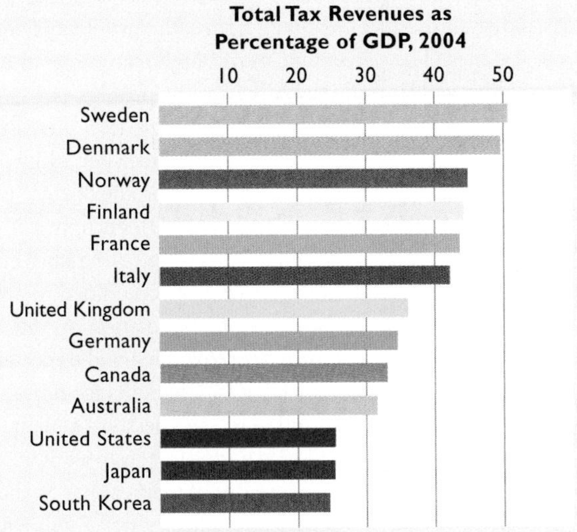

Source: Organization for Economic Cooperation and Development, **www.oecd.org.**

later in several other countries, as implied in Global Perspective 4.2.

Federal Finance

Now let's look separately at each of the Federal, state, and local units of government in the United States and compare their expenditures and taxes. Figure 4.8 tells the story for the Federal government.

Federal Expenditures

Four areas of Federal spending stand out: (1) pensions and income security, (2) national defense, (3) health, and (4) interest on the public debt. The *pensions and income security* category includes the many income-maintenance programs for the aged, persons with disabilities or handicaps, the unemployed, the retired, and families with no breadwinner. This category—dominated by the $432 billion annual Social Security program—accounts for 35 percent of total Federal expenditures. (This chapter's Last Word examines the impact of the aging U.S. population on the future financing of this area of Federal spending.) *National defense* accounts for about 20 percent of the Federal budget, underscoring the high cost of military preparedness. *Health* reflects the cost of government health programs for the retired (Medicare) and poor (Medicaid). *Interest on the public debt* is high because the public debt itself is large.

Federal Tax Revenues

The revenue side of Figure 4.8 shows that the personal income tax, payroll taxes, and the corporate income tax are the basic revenue sources, accounting respectively for 43, 37, and 13 cents of each dollar collected.

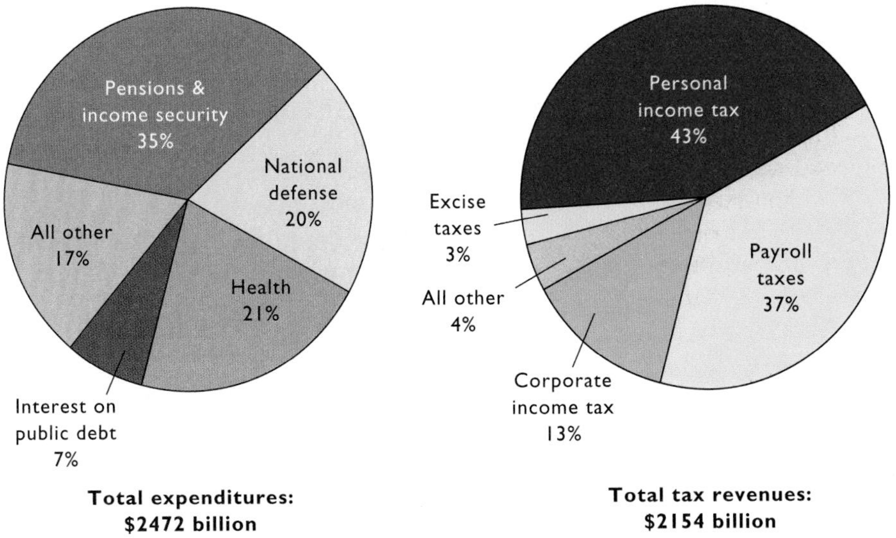

Source: U.S. Office of Management and Budget.

FIGURE 4.8 Federal expenditures and tax revenues, 2005. Federal expenditures are dominated by spending for pensions and income security, health, and national defense. A full 84 percent of Federal tax revenue is derived from just two sources: the personal income tax and payroll taxes. The $318 billion difference between expenditures and revenues reflects a budget deficit.

Last Word

Financing Social Security

There Is a Severe Long-Run Shortfall in Social Security Funding because of Growing Payments to Retiring Baby Boomers.

The Social Security program (excluding Medicare) has grown from less than one-half of 1 percent of U.S. GDP in 1950 to 4.2 percent of GDP today. That percentage is projected to grow to 6.2 percent of GDP in 2030 and slightly higher thereafter.

The $432 billion Social Security program is largely an annual "pay-as-you-go" plan, meaning that most of the current revenues from the 12.4 percent Social Security tax (the rate when the 2.9 percent Medicare tax is excluded) are paid out to current Social Security retirees. In anticipation of the large benefits owed to the baby boomers when they retire, however, the Social Security Administration has been placing an excess of current revenues over current payouts into a trust fund consisting of U.S. Treasury securities. But the accumulation of money in the Social Security trust fund will be greatly inadequate for paying the retirement benefits promised to all future retirees.

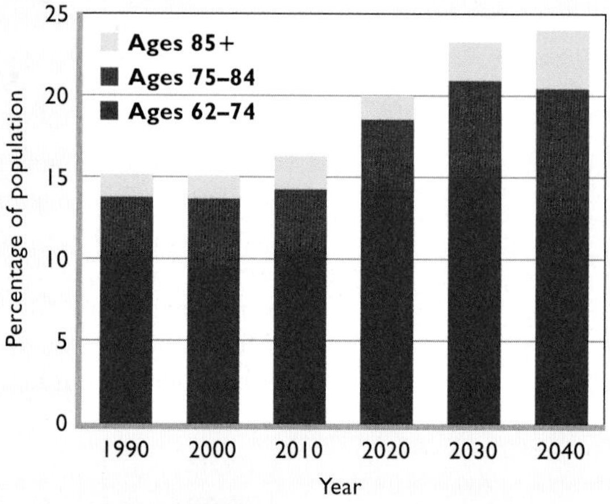

In 2017 Social Security retirement revenues will fall below Social Security retirement benefits and the system will begin dipping into the trust fund to make up the difference. The trust fund will be exhausted in 2040, after which the promised retirement benefits will immediately exceed the Social Security tax revenues by an estimated 35 percent annually, rising to 43 percent annually in 2080. The Federal government faces a several-trillion-dollar shortfall of long-run revenues for funding Social Security.

As shown in the accompanying figure, the problem is one of demographics. The percentage of the American population age 62 or older will rise substantially over the next several decades, with the greatest increases for those age 75 and older. High fertility rates during the "baby boom" (1946–1964), declining birthrates thereafter, and rising life expectancies have combined to produce an aging population. In the future, more people will be receiving Social Security benefits for longer periods and each person's benefits will be paid for by fewer workers. The number of workers per Social Security beneficiary was 5:1 in 1960. Today it is 3:1, and by 2040 it will be only 2:1.

There is no easy way to restore long-run balance to Social Security funding. Either benefits must be reduced or revenues must be increased. The Social Security Administration concludes that bringing projected Social Security revenues and

Personal Income Tax The **personal income tax** is the kingpin of the Federal tax system and merits special comment. This tax is levied on *taxable income,* that is, on the incomes of households and unincorporated businesses after certain exemptions ($3300 for each household member) and deductions (business expenses, charitable contributions, home mortgage interest payments, certain state and local taxes) are taken into account.

The Federal personal income tax is a *progressive tax,* meaning that people with higher incomes pay a larger percentage of their incomes as taxes than do people with lower incomes. The progressivity is achieved by applying higher tax rates to successive layers or brackets of income.

Columns 1 and 2 in Table 4.1 show the mechanics of the income tax for a married couple filing a joint return in

TABLE 4.1 Federal Personal Income Tax Rates, 2006*

(1) Total Taxable Income	(2) Marginal Tax Rate, %	(3) Total Tax on Highest Income In Bracket	(4) Average Tax Rate on Highest Income in Bracket, % (3) ÷ (1)
$1–$15,100	10.0	$ 1510	10.0
$15,101–$61,300	15.0	8440	13.8
$61,301–$123,700	25.0	24,040	19.4
$123,701–$188,450	28.0	42,170	22.4
$188,451–$336,550	33.0	91,043	27.1
Over $336,550	35.0		

*For a married couple filing a joint return.

payments into balance over the next 75 years would require a 13 percent permanent reduction in Social Security benefits, a 16 percent permanent increase in tax revenues, or some combination of the two.*

Several ideas have been offered to improve the financial outlook of Social Security. One idea is to boost the trust fund by investing all or part of it in corporate stocks and bonds. The Federal government would own the stock investments, and an appointed panel would oversee the direction of those investments. The presumed higher returns on the investments relative to the lower returns on U.S. securities would stretch out the life of the trust fund. Nevertheless, a substantial increase in the payroll tax would still be needed to cover the shortfalls after the trust fund is exhausted.

Another option is to increase the payroll tax immediately—perhaps by as much as 1.5 percentage points—and allocate the new revenues to individual accounts. Government would own the accumulations in the accounts, but individuals could direct their investments to a restricted list of broad stock or bond funds. When they retire, recipients could convert these individual account balances to annuities—securities paying monthly payments for life. That annuity income would supplement reduced monthly benefits from the pay-as-you-go system when the trust fund is exhausted.

A different route is to place half the payroll tax into accounts that individuals, not the government, would own, maintain, and bequeath. Individuals could invest these funds in bank certificates of deposit or in approved stock and bond funds and draw upon the accounts when they reach retirement age. A flat monthly benefit would supplement the accumulations in the private accounts. The personal security accounts would be phased in over time, so those individuals now receiving or about to receive Social Security benefits would continue to receive benefits.

These general ideas do not exhaust the possible reforms since the variations on each plan are nearly endless. Reaching consensus on Social Security reform will be difficult because every citizen has a direct economic stake in the outcome. Nevertheless, society will eventually need to confront the problem of trillions of dollars of unfunded Social Security liabilities.

*Social Security Board of Trustees. "Status of the Social Security and Medicare Programs: A Summary of the 2006 Annual Reports." **www.ssa.gov.**

†Medicare (the health insurance that accompanies Social Security) is also severely underfunded. To bring projected Medicare revenues and expenditures into long-run balance would require an immediate increase in the Medicare payroll tax by 121 percent, a 51 percent reduction of Medicare payments from their projected levels, or some combination of each. The total unfunded liabilities of Social Security and Medicare were $10 trillion in 2005.

2006. Note that a 10 percent tax rate applies to all taxable income up to $15,100 and a 15 percent rate applies to additional income up to $61,300. The rates on additional layers of income then go up to 25, 28, 33, and 35 percent.

The tax rates shown in column 2 in Table 4.1 are marginal tax rates. A **marginal tax rate** is the rate at which the tax is paid on each *additional* unit of taxable income. Thus, if a couple's taxable income is $80,000, they will pay the marginal rate of 10 percent on each dollar from $1 to $15,100, 15 percent on each dollar from $15,101 to $61,300, and 25 percent on each dollar from $61,301 to $80,000. You should confirm that their total income tax is $13,115.

The marginal tax rates in column 2 overstate the personal income tax bite because the rising rates in that column apply only to the income within each successive tax bracket. To get a better idea of the tax burden, we must consider average tax rates. The **average tax rate** is the total tax paid divided by total taxable income. The couple in our previous example is in the 25 percent tax bracket because they pay a top marginal tax rate of 25 percent on the highest dollar of their income. But their *average* tax rate is 16.4 percent (= $13,115/$80,000).

W 4.1
Taxes and progressivity

A tax whose average rate rises as income increases is a progressive tax. Such a tax claims both a larger absolute amount and a larger proportion of income as income rises. Thus we can say that the Federal personal income tax is progressive. **(Key Question 15)**

Payroll Taxes Social Security contributions are **payroll taxes**—taxes based on wages and salaries—used to finance two compulsory Federal programs for retired workers: Social Security (an income-enhancement program) and Medicare (which pays for medical services). Employers and employees pay these taxes equally. Improvements in, and extensions of, the Social Security programs, plus growth of the labor force, have resulted in significant increases in these payroll taxes in recent years. In 2006, employees and employers each paid 7.65 percent on the first $94,200 of an employee's annual earnings and 1.45 percent on all additional earnings.

Corporate Income Tax The Federal government also taxes corporate income. The **corporate income tax** is levied on a corporation's profit—the difference between its total revenue and its total expenses. For almost all corporations, the tax rate is 35 percent.

Excise Taxes Taxes on commodities or on purchases take the form of **sales and excise taxes.** The difference between the two is mainly one of coverage. Sales taxes fall on a wide range of products, whereas excises are levied individually on a small, select list of commodities. As Figure 4.8 suggests, the Federal government collects excise taxes (on the sale of such commodities as alcoholic beverages, tobacco, and gasoline) but does not levy a general sales tax; sales taxes are the primary revenue source of most state governments.

State and Local Finance

State and local governments have different mixes of revenues and expenditures than the Federal government has.

State Finances

The primary source of tax revenue for state governments is sales and excise taxes, which account for about 48 percent of all their tax revenue. State personal income taxes, which have much lower rates than the Federal income tax, are the second most important source of state tax revenue. They bring in about 34 percent of total state tax revenue. Corporate income taxes and license fees account for most of the remainder of state tax revenue.

Education expenditures account for about 35 percent of all state spending. State expenditures on public welfare are next in relative weight, at about 28 percent of the total. States also spend heavily on health and hospitals (7 percent), highway maintenance and construction (7 percent), and public safety (4 percent). That leaves about 19 percent of all state spending for a variety of other purposes.

These tax and expenditure percentages combine data from all the states, so they reveal little about the finances of individual states. States vary significantly in the taxes levied. Thus, although personal income taxes are a major source of revenue for all state governments combined, seven states do not levy a personal income tax. Also, there are great variations in the sizes of tax revenues and disbursements among the states, both in the aggregate and as percentages of personal income.

Thirty-nine states augment their tax revenues with state-run lotteries to help close the gap between their tax receipts and expenditures. Individual states also receive large intergovernmental grants from the Federal government. In fact, about 28 percent of their total revenue is in that form. States also take in revenue from miscellaneous sources such as state-owned utilities and liquor stores.

Local Finances

The local levels of government include counties, municipalities, townships, and school districts as well as cities and towns. Local governments obtain about 73 percent of their tax revenue from **property taxes.** Sales and excise taxes contribute about 17 percent of all local government tax revenue.

About 44 percent of local government expenditures go to education. Welfare, health, and hospitals (12 percent); public safety (11 percent); housing, parks, and sewerage (8 percent); and streets and highways (5 percent) are also major spending categories.

The tax revenues of local government cover less than one-half of their expenditures. The remaining revenue comes from intergovernmental grants from the Federal and state governments. Also, local governments receive considerable amounts of proprietary income, for example, revenue from government-owned utilities providing water, electricity, natural gas, and transportation.

QUICK REVIEW 4.4

- Government purchases account for about 19 percent of U.S. output; the addition of transfers increases government spending to about 31 percent of domestic output.
- Income security and national defense are the main categories of Federal spending; personal income, payroll, and corporate income taxes are the primary sources of Federal revenue.
- States rely on sales and excise taxes for revenue; their spending is largely for education and public welfare.
- Education is the main expenditure for local governments, most of whose revenue comes from property taxes.

Summary

1. The functional distribution of income shows how society's total income is divided among wages, rents, interest, and profit; the personal distribution of income shows how total income is divided among individual households.
2. Households use all their income to pay personal taxes, for saving, and to buy consumer goods. Nearly 60 percent of their consumption expenditures are for services.
3. Sole proprietorships are firms owned and usually operated by single individuals. Partnerships are firms owned and usually operated by just a handful of individuals. Corporations—the dominant form of business organization—are legal entities, distinct and separate from the individuals who own them. They often have thousands, or even millions, of owners—the stockholders.
4. Corporations finance their operations and purchases of new plant and equipment partly through the issuance of stocks and bonds. Stocks are ownership shares of a corporation, and bonds are promises to repay a loan, usually at a set rate of interest.
5. A principal-agent problem may occur in corporations when the agents (managers) hired to represent the interest of the principals (stockholders) pursue their own objectives to the detriment of the objectives of the principals.
6. Government improves the operation of the market system by (a) providing an appropriate legal and social framework and (b) acting to maintain competition.
7. Government alters the distribution of income through the tax-transfer system and through market intervention.
8. Externalities, or spillovers, cause the equilibrium output of certain goods to vary from the socially efficient output. Negative externalities result in an overallocation of resources, which can be corrected by legislation or by specific taxes. Positive externalities are accompanied by an underallocation of resources, which can be corrected by government subsidies to consumers or producers.
9. Only government is willing to provide public goods, which can be consumed by all simultaneously (nonrivalry) and entail benefits from which nonpaying consumers (free riders) cannot be excluded (nonexcludability). Because doing so is not profitable, private firms will not produce public goods. Quasi-public goods have some of the characteristics of public goods and some of the characteristics of private goods; government provides them because the private sector would underallocate resources to their production.
10. To try to stabilize the economy, the government adjusts its spending and taxes, and the nation's central bank (the Federal Reserve in the United States) uses monetary actions to alter interest rates.
11. Government purchases exhaust (use up or absorb) resources; transfer payments do not. Government purchases have declined from about 22 percent of domestic output in 1960 to 19 percent today. Transfer payments, however, have grown significantly. Total government spending now amounts to about 31 percent of domestic output.
12. The main categories of Federal spending are pensions and income security, national defense, health, and interest on the public debt; Federal revenues come primarily from personal income taxes, payroll taxes, and corporate income taxes.
13. States derive their revenue primarily from sales and excise taxes and personal income taxes; major state expenditures go to education, public welfare, health and hospitals, and highways. Local communities derive most of their revenue from property taxes; education is their most important expenditure.
14. State and local tax revenues are supplemented by sizable revenue grants from the Federal government.

Terms and Concepts

functional distribution of income
personal distribution of income
durable goods
nondurable goods
services
plant
firm
industry
sole proprietorship
partnership
corporation
stock
bond
limited liability
principal-agent problem
monopoly
externality
negative externalities
positive externalities
public goods
free-rider problem
quasi-public goods
government purchases
transfer payments
personal income tax
marginal tax rate
average tax rate
payroll taxes
corporate income tax
sales and excise taxes
property taxes

Study Questions

1. Distinguish between the functional distribution and personal distribution of income. Which is being referred to in each of the following statements? "The combined share of wage income and proprietary income has remained remarkably stable at about 80 percent since the Second World War." "The relative income of the richest households is higher today than in 1970."
2. **KEY QUESTION** Assume that the five residents of Econoville receive incomes of $50, $75, $125, $250, and $500. Present the resulting distribution of income as a graph similar to Figure 4.2. Compare the incomes of the lowest fifth and the highest fifth of the income receivers.
3. Distinguish between a plant, a firm, and an industry. Contrast a vertically integrated firm, a horizontally integrated firm, and a conglomerate. Cite an example of a horizontally integrated firm from which you have recently made a purchase.
4. **KEY QUESTION** What are the three major legal forms of business organization? Which form is the most prevalent in terms of numbers? Why do you think that is so? Which form is dominant in terms of total sales? What major advantages of this form of business organization gave rise to its dominance?
5. What is the principal-agent problem as it relates to managers and stockholders? How did firms try to solve it in the 1990s? In what way did the "solution" backfire on some firms?
6. Identify and briefly describe the main economic functions of government. What function do you think is the most controversial? Explain why.
7. What divergences arise between equilibrium output and efficient output when (*a*) negative externalities and (*b*) positive externalities are present? How might government correct these divergences? Cite an example (other than the text examples) of an external cost and an external benefit.
8. Explain why zoning laws, which allow certain land uses only in specific locations, might be justified in dealing with a problem of negative externalities. Explain why tax breaks to businesses that set up in areas of high unemployment might be justified in view of positive externalities. Explain why excise taxes on beer might be justified in dealing with a problem of external costs.
9. **KEY QUESTION** What are the two characteristics of public goods? Explain the significance of each for public provision as opposed to private provision. What is the free-rider problem as it relates to public goods? Is U.S. border patrol a public good or a private good? Why? How about satellite TV? Explain.
10. **KEY QUESTION** Draw a production possibilities curve with public goods on the vertical axis and private goods on the horizontal axis. Assuming the economy is initially operating *on the curve*, indicate how the production of public goods might be increased. How might the output of public goods be increased if the economy is initially operating at a point *inside the curve?*
11. Use the distinction between the characteristics of private and public goods to determine whether the following should be produced through the market system or provided by government: (*a*) French fries, (*b*) airport screening, (*c*) court systems, (*d*) mail delivery, and (*e*) medical care. State why you answered as you did in each case.
12. Use the circular flow diagram to show how each of the following government actions simultaneously affects the allocation of resources and the distribution of income:
    - **a.** The construction of a new high school.
    - **b.** A 2-percentage-point reduction of the corporate income tax.
    - **c.** An expansion of preschool programs for disadvantaged children.
    - **d.** The levying of an excise tax on polluters.
13. What do economists mean when they say government purchases are "exhaustive" expenditures whereas government transfer payments are "nonexhaustive" expenditures? Cite an example of a government purchase and a government transfer payment.
14. What is the most important source of revenue and the major type of expenditure at the Federal level? At the state level? At the local level?
15. **KEY QUESTION** Suppose in Fiscalville there is no tax on the first $10,000 of income, but a 20 percent tax on earnings between $10,000 and $20,000 and a 30 percent tax on income between $20,000 and $30,000. Any income above $30,000 is taxed at 40 percent. If your income is $50,000, how much will you pay in taxes? Determine your marginal and average tax rates. Is this a progressive tax? Explain.
16. **LAST WORD** What do economists mean when they refer to Social Security as a pay-as-you-go plan? What is the Social Security trust fund? What is the nature of the long-run fiscal imbalance in the Social Security retirement system? What are the broad options for addressing this problem?

Web-Based Questions

1. **PERSONAL DISTRIBUTION OF INCOME—WHAT IS THE TREND?** Visit the U.S. Census Bureau Web site at **www.census.gov/hhes/income/midclass/index.html** and select Data Highlights. Since 1970, how has the share of aggregate household income received by the lowest and highest income quintiles (fifths) changed?
2. **STATE TAXES AND EXPENDITURES PER CAPITA—WHERE DOES YOUR STATE RANK?** Go to the Census Bureau site, **www.census.gov/govs/www/state.html,** and find the table that ranks the states by tax revenue and expenditures per capita for the latest year. Where does your home state rank in each category? Where does the state in which you are attending college, if different, rank? Speculate as to why a large gap separates the high-ranking and low-ranking states.

5

IN THIS CHAPTER YOU WILL LEARN:

- **Some key facts about U.S. international trade.**
- **About comparative advantage, specialization, and international trade.**
- **How exchange rates are determined in currency markets.**
- **How and why government sometimes interferes with free international trade.**
- **The role played by free-trade zones and the World Trade Organization (WTO) in promoting international trade.**

The United States in the Global Economy

Backpackers in the wilderness like to think they are "leaving the world behind," but, like Atlas, they carry the world on their shoulders. Much of their equipment is imported—knives from Switzerland, rain gear from South Korea, cameras from Japan, aluminum pots from England, sleeping bags from China, and compasses from Finland. Moreover, they may have driven to the trailheads in Japanese-made Toyotas or German-made BMWs, sipping coffee from Brazil or snacking on bananas from Honduras.

International trade and the global economy affect all of us daily, whether we are hiking in the wilderness, driving our cars, listening to music, or working at our jobs. We cannot "leave the world behind." We are enmeshed in a global web of economic relationships—trading of goods and services, multinational corporations, cooperative ventures among the world's firms, and ties among the world's financial markets. That web is so complex that it is difficult to determine just what is—or isn't—an American product. A Finnish company owns Wilson sporting goods; a Swiss company owns Gerber baby food; and a South African corporation owns Miller Brewing. The Chrysler PT Cruiser is assembled in Mexico. Many "U.S." products such as Boeing aircraft contain numerous components from abroad, and, conversely, many "foreign" products such as Airbus planes contain numerous U.S.-produced parts.

International Linkages

Several economic flows link the U.S. economy and the economies of other nations. As identified in Figure 5.1, these flows are:

- ***Goods and services flows*** or simply ***trade flows*** The United States exports goods and services to other nations and imports goods and services from them.
- ***Capital and labor flows*** or simply ***resource flows*** U.S. firms establish production facilities—new capital—in foreign countries, and foreign firms establish production facilities in the United States. Labor also moves between nations. Each year many foreigners immigrate to the United States and some Americans move to other nations.
- ***Information and technology flows*** The United States transmits information to other nations about U.S. products, prices, interest rates, and investment opportunities and receives such information from abroad. Firms in other countries use technology created in the United States, and U.S. businesses incorporate technology developed abroad.
- ***Financial flows*** Money is transferred between the United States and other countries for several purposes, for example, paying for imports, buying foreign assets, paying interest on debt, and providing foreign aid.

The United States and World Trade

Our main goal in this chapter is to examine trade flows and the financial flows that pay for them. What is the extent and pattern of international trade, and how much has that trade grown? Who are the major participants?

Volume and Pattern

Table 5.1 suggests the importance of world trade for selected countries. Many countries, with restricted resources and limited domestic markets, cannot efficiently produce the variety of goods their citizens want. So they must import goods from other nations. That, in turn, means that they must export, or sell abroad, some of their own products. For such countries, exports may run from 25 to 50 percent or more of their gross domestic product (GDP)—the market value of all goods and services produced in an economy. Other countries, the United States, for example, have rich and diversified resource bases and large internal markets. Although the total volume of trade is huge in the United States, it constitutes a smaller percentage of GDP than it does in a number of other nations.

Volume For the United States and for the world as a whole the volume of international trade has been increasing

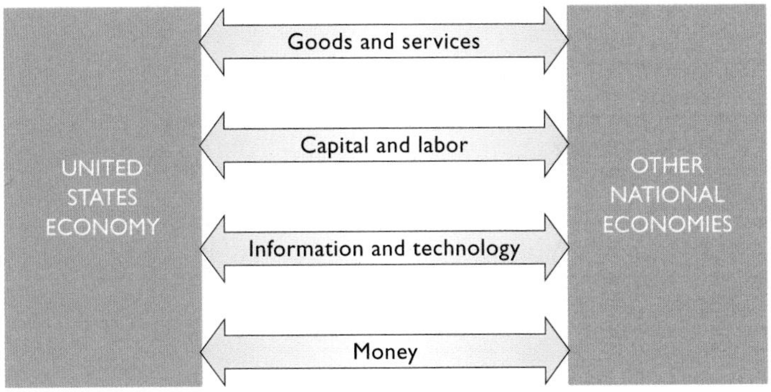

FIGURE 5.1 International linkages. The U.S. economy is intertwined with other national economies through goods and services flows (trade flows), capital and labor flows (resource flows), information and technology flows, and financial flows.

TABLE 5.1 Exports of Goods and Services as a Percentage of GDP, Selected Countries, 2005

Country	Exports as Percentage of GDP
Belgium	87
Netherlands	71
South Korea	44
Germany	40
Canada	38
New Zealand	28
Italy	27
France	26
United Kingdom	26
Spain	25
Japan	13
United States	11

Source: Derived by authors from IMF, *International Financial Statistics*, 2006.

both absolutely and relative to their GDPs. A comparison of the boxed data in Figure 5.2 reveals substantial growth in the dollar amount of U.S. exports and imports over the past several decades. The graph shows the rapid growth of U.S. exports and imports of goods and services as percentages of GDP. On a national income account basis, U.S. exports and imports were 11 and 16 percent of GDP, respectively, in 2005.

Even so, the United States now accounts for a diminished percentage of total world trade. In 1950, it supplied about one-third of the world's total exports, compared with about one-eighth today. World trade has increased more rapidly for other nations than it has for the United States. But in terms of absolute volumes of imports and exports, the United States is still the world's leading trading nation.

Dependence The United States is almost entirely dependent on other countries for bananas, cocoa, coffee, spices, tea, raw silk, nickel, tin, natural rubber, and diamonds. Imported goods compete with U.S. goods in many of our domestic markets: Japanese cameras and cars, French and Italian wines, and Swiss and Austrian snow skis are a few examples. Even the "great American pastime" of baseball relies heavily on imported gloves and baseballs.

Of course, world trade is a two-way street. Many U.S. industries rely on foreign markets. Almost all segments of U.S. agriculture rely on sales abroad; for example, exports of rice, wheat, cotton, and tobacco vary from one-fourth to more than one-half of the total output of those crops. The U.S. computer, chemical, semiconductor, aircraft,

FIGURE 5.2 U.S. trade as percentage of GDP. U.S. imports and exports have increased in volume and have greatly increased as a percentage of GDP since 1975.

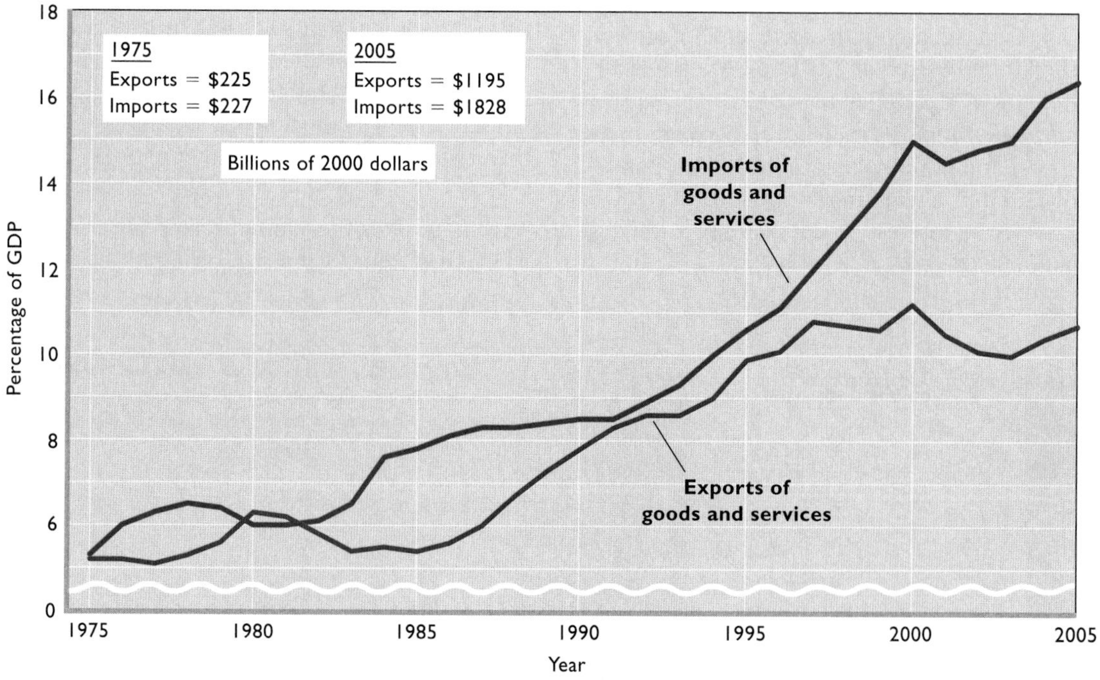

Source: Bureau of Economic Analysis. Data are compiled by the authors from the national income accounts and are adjusted for inflation (2000 dollars).

TABLE 5.2 Principal U.S. Exports and Imports of Goods, 2005 (in Billions of Dollars)

Exports	Amount	Imports	Amount
Chemicals	$68.6	Petroleum	$251.6
Consumer durables	53.5	Automobiles	123.7
Agricultural products	52.9	Household appliances	97.1
Semiconductors	47.2	Computers	93.3
Computers	45.5	Metals	83.8
Generating equipment	33.2	Clothing	79.1
Automobiles	30.4	Consumer electronics	47.3
Aircraft	29.1	Generating equipment	43.1
Medical	27.6	Semiconductors	37.1
Telecommunications	25.6	Telecommunications	25.8

Source: Consolidated by authors from Department of Commerce data.

automobile, machine tool, and coal industries, among many others, sell significant portions of their output in international markets. Table 5.2 shows some of the major commodity exports and imports of the United States.

Trade Patterns The following facts will give you an overview of U.S. international trade:

- A *trade deficit* occurs when imports exceed exports. The United States has a trade deficit in goods. In 2005, U.S. imports of goods exceeded U.S. exports of goods by $782 billion.
- A *trade surplus* occurs when exports exceed imports. The United States has a trade surplus in services (such as transportation services and financial services). In 2005, U.S. exports of services exceeded U.S. imports of services by $58 billion.
- The United States imports some of the same categories of goods that it exports, specifically, automobiles, computers, semiconductors, and telecommunications equipment (see Table 5.2).
- As Table 5.3 shows, about half of U.S. export and import trade is with other industrially advanced countries. The remainder is with developing countries, including members of the Organization of Petroleum Exporting Countries (OPEC).
- Canada is the United States' most important trading partner quantitatively. In 2005, 24 percent of U.S. exported goods were sold to Canadians, who in turn provided 17 percent of the U.S. imports of goods (see Table 5.3).
- The United States has sizable trade deficits with China and Japan. In 2005, U.S. imported goods from

TABLE 5.3 U.S. Exports and Imports of Goods by Area, 2005*

Exports to	Value, Billions of Dollars		Percentage of Total		Imports from	Value Billions of Dollars		Percentage of Total	
Industrial countries	$483		54		Industrial countries	$ 770		46	
Canada		$212		24	Canada		$291		17
Japan		53		6	Japan		138		8
European Union		183		20	Western Europe		308		18
Australia		15		2	Australia		7		1
Other		20		2	Other		26		2
Developing countries	410		46		Developing countries	904		54	
Mexico		120		13	Mexico		171		10
China		42		5	China		244		15
OPEC countries		31		4	OPEC countries		125		7
Other		217		24	Other		364		22
Total	$893		100		Total	$1674		100	

*Data are on an international transactions (balance of payments) basis and exclude military shipments.
Source: Survey of Current Business, April 2006.

China exceeded exported goods to China by $202 billion, and U.S. imported goods from Japan exceeded U.S. exported goods to Japan by $85 billion (see Table 5.3).

- The U.S. dependence on foreign oil is reflected in its trade with members of OPEC. In 2005, the United States imported $125 billion of goods (mainly oil) from OPEC members, while exporting $31 billion of goods to those countries (see Table 5.3).
- In terms of volume, the most significant U.S. export of *services* is airline transportation provided by U.S. carriers for foreign passengers.

Financial Linkages International trade requires complex financial linkages among nations. How does a nation such as the United States obtain more goods from others than it provides to them? How does the United States finance its trade deficits, such as its 2005 goods and services deficit of $724 billion (= + $58 billion in services − $782 billion in goods) in 2005? The answer is by either borrowing from foreigners or selling real assets (for example, factories, real estate) to them. The United States is the world's largest borrower of foreign funds. Moreover, nations with which the United States has large trade deficits, such as Japan, often "recycle their excess dollars" by buying U.S. real assets.

GLOBAL PERSPECTIVE 5.1

Comparative Exports

Germany, the United States, and China are the world's largest exporters.

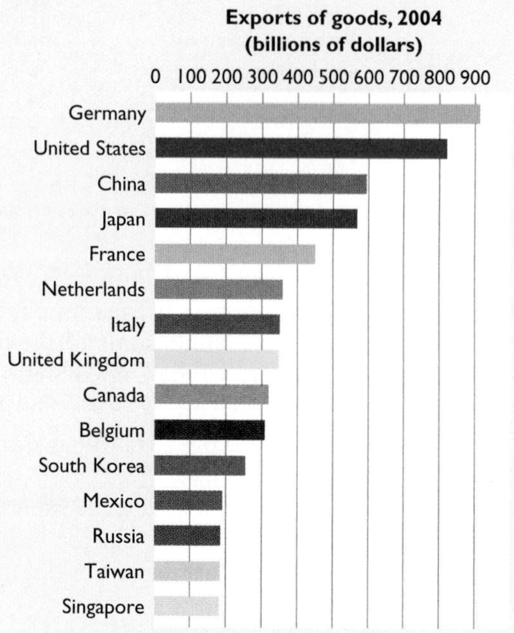

Source: World Trade Organization, **www.wto.org.**

Rapid Trade Growth

Several factors have propelled the rapid growth of international trade since the Second World War.

Transportation Technology High transportation costs are a barrier to any type of trade, particularly among traders who are distant from one another. But improvements in transportation have shrunk the globe and have fostered world trade. Airplanes now transport low-weight, high-value items such as diamonds and semiconductors swiftly from one nation to another. We now routinely transport oil in massive tankers, significantly lowering the cost of transportation per barrel. Grain is loaded onto oceangoing ships at modern, efficient grain silos at Great Lakes and coastal ports. Natural gas flows through large-diameter pipelines from exporting to importing countries—for instance, from Russia to Germany and from Canada to the United States.

Communications Technology Dramatic improvements in communications technology have also advanced world trade. Computers, the Internet, telephones, and fax (facsimile) machines now directly link traders around the world, enabling exporters to access overseas markets and to carry out trade deals. A distributor in New York can get a price quote on 1000 woven baskets in Thailand as quickly as a quotation on 1000 laptop computers in Texas. Money moves around the world in the blink of an eye. Exchange rates, stock prices, and interest rates flash onto computer screens nearly simultaneously in Los Angeles, London, and Lisbon.

General Decline in Tariffs *Tariffs* are excise taxes (duties) on imported products. They have had their ups and downs over the years, but since 1940 they have generally fallen. A glance ahead to Figure 5.5, page 96, shows that U.S. tariffs as a percentage of imports (on which duties are levied) are now about 5 percent, down from 37 percent in 1940. Many nations still maintain barriers to free trade, but, on average, tariffs have fallen significantly, thus increasing international trade.

Participants in International Trade

All the nations of the world participate to some extent in international trade.

United States, Japan, and Western Europe As Global Perspective 5.1 indicates, the top participants in world trade by total volume are Germany, the United States, China, and Japan. In 2004 those four nations had combined exports of $2.9 trillion. Along with Germany, other western European nations such as France, Britain, and Italy are major exporters and importers. The United States, Japan, and the western European nations also form the heart of the world's financial system and provide headquarters for most of the world's large **multinational corporations**—firms that have sizable production and distribution activities in other countries. Examples of such firms are Unilever (Netherlands), Nestlé (Switzerland), Coca-Cola (United States), Bayer Chemicals (Germany), and Mitsubishi (Japan).

New Participants Important new participants have arrived on the world trade scene. China, with its increased reliance on the market system and its reintegration of Hong Kong, is a major trader. Since China initiated reforms in 1978, its annual growth of output has averaged 9 percent (compared with about 3 percent in the United States). At this remarkable rate, China's total output nearly doubles every 8 years! An upsurge of exports and imports has accompanied that economic growth. In 1990 Chinese exports were about $60 billion. In 2005 they were nearly $762 billion, with about one-fifth of China's exports going to the United States. Also, China has been attracting substantial foreign investment ($60 billion in 2005 and more than $1 trillion since 1990). In fact, China has become the number-one destination of foreign investment in the world.

Other Asian economies are also active traders. In particular, Singapore, South Korea, and Taiwan are major exporters and importers. Although these three economies experienced economic difficulties in the 1990s, their combined exports exceed those of France, Britain, or Italy. Other economies of southeast Asia, particularly Malaysia and Indonesia, also have expanded their international trade.

Other changes in world trade patterns have resulted from the collapse of communism in eastern Europe and the former Soviet Union. Before that collapse, the eastern European nations of Poland, Hungary, Czechoslovakia, and East Germany traded mainly with the Soviet Union and such political allies as North Korea and Cuba. Today, East Germany is reunited with West Germany, and Poland, Hungary, and the Czech Republic have established new trade relationships with western Europe and the United States.

Russia itself has initiated far-reaching market reforms, including widespread privatization of industry, and has made major trade deals with firms around the globe. Although its transition to capitalism has been far from smooth, Russia may one day be a major trading nation. Other former Soviet republics—now independent nations—such as Estonia and Azerbaijan also have opened their economies to international trade and finance.

QUICK REVIEW 5.1

- Four main categories of economic flows link nations: goods and services flows, capital and labor flows, information and technology flows, and financial flows.
- World trade has increased globally and nationally. In terms of volume, the United States is the world's leading international trader. But with exports and imports of only about 11 to 16 percent of GDP, the United States is not as dependent on international trade as some other nations.
- Advances in transportation and communications technology and declines in tariffs have all helped expand world trade.
- The United States, China, Japan, and the western European nations dominate world trade. Recent new traders are the Asian economies of Singapore, South Korea, and Taiwan; the eastern European nations; and the former Soviet states.

Specialization and Comparative Advantage

Given the presence of an *open economy*—one that includes the international sector—the United States produces more of certain goods (exports) and fewer of other goods (imports) than it would otherwise. Thus U.S. labor and other resources are shifted toward export industries and away from import industries. For example, the United States uses more resources to make commercial aircraft and to grow wheat and less to make autos and clothing. So we ask: "Do shifts of resources like these make economic sense? Do they enhance U.S. total output and thus the U.S. standard of living?"

The answers are affirmative. Specialization and international trade increase the productivity of a nation's resources and allow for greater total output than would otherwise be possible. This idea is not new. Adam Smith had this to say in 1776:

> It is the maxim of every prudent master of a family, never to attempt to make at home what it will cost him more to make than to buy. The taylor does not attempt to make his own shoes, but buys them of the shoemaker. The shoemaker does not attempt to make his own clothes, but employs a taylor. The farmer attempts to make neither the one nor the other, but employs those different artificers....
>
> What is prudence in the conduct of every private family, can scarce be folly in that of a great kingdom. If a foreign

TABLE 5.4 Mexico's Production Possibilities Table (in Tons)

	Production Alternatives				
Product	**A**	**B**	**C**	**D**	**E**
Avocados	0	20	24	40	60
Soybeans	15	10	9	5	0

TABLE 5.5 U.S. Production Possibilities Table (in Tons)

	Production Alternatives				
Product	**R**	**S**	**T**	**U**	**V**
Avocados	0	30	33	60	90
Soybeans	30	20	19	10	0

> country can supply us with a commodity cheaper than we can make it, better buy it of them with some part of the produce of our own industry, employed in a way in which we have some advantage.[1]

Nations specialize and trade for the same reasons as individuals: Specialization and exchange result in greater overall output and income.

In the early 1800s British economist David Ricardo expanded on Smith's idea by observing that it pays for a person or a country to specialize and trade even if some potential trading partner is more productive in *all* economic activities. We demonstrate Ricardo's basic principle in the Consider This box to the right. You should read it before plunging into the more elaborate analysis of comparative advantage.

Comparative Advantage: Production Possibilities Analysis

The simple example in the Consider This box shows that specialization is economically desirable because it results in more efficient production. Now let's put specialization into the context of trading nations and use the familiar concept of the production possibilities table for our analysis.

Assumptions and Comparative Costs Suppose the production possibilities for one product in Mexico and for one product in the United States are as shown in Tables 5.4 and 5.5. Both tables reflect constant costs. Each country must give up a constant amount of one product to secure a certain increment of the other product. (This assumption simplifies our discussion without impairing the validity of our conclusions. Later we will allow for increasing costs.)

Also for simplicity, suppose that the labor forces in the United States and Mexico are of equal size. If the United States and Mexico use their entire (equal-size) labor forces to produce avocados, the United States can produce 90 tons compared with Mexico's 60 tons. Similarly, the United States can produce 30 tons of soybeans compared to Mexico's 15 tons. So output per worker in the United States exceeds that in Mexico in producing both goods, perhaps because of better technology. The United States has an *absolute advantage* (relative to Mexico) in producing either soybeans or avocados.

But gains from specialization and trade between the United States and Mexico are possible even under these

CONSIDER THIS . . .

A CPA and House Painter

Suppose that Madison, a certified public accountant (CPA), is a swifter painter than Mason, the professional painter she is thinking of hiring. Also assume that Madison can earn $50 per hour as an accountant but would have to pay Mason $15 per hour. And suppose that Madison would need 30 hours to paint her house but Mason would need 40 hours.

Should Madison take time from her accounting to paint her own house, or should she hire the painter? Madison's opportunity cost of painting her house is $1500 (= 30 hours of sacrificed CPA time × $50 per CPA hour). The cost of hiring Mason is only $600 (= 40 hours of painting × $15 per hour of painting). Although Madison is better at both accounting and painting, she will get her house painted at lower cost by specializing in accounting and using some of her earnings from accounting to hire a house painter.

Similarly, Mason can reduce his cost of obtaining accounting services by specializing in painting and using some of his income to hire Madison to prepare his income tax forms. Suppose Mason would need 10 hours to prepare his tax return, while Madison could handle the task in 2 hours. Mason would sacrifice $150 of income (= 10 hours of painting time × $15 per hour) to do something he could hire Madison to do for $100 (= 2 hours of CPA time × $50 per CPA hour). By using Madison to prepare his tax return, Mason lowers the cost of getting his tax return prepared.

What is true for our CPA and house painter is also true for nations. Specializing enables nations to reduce the cost of obtaining the goods and services they desire.

[1] Adam Smith, *The Wealth of Nations* (New York: Modern Library, 1937), p. 424. (Originally published in 1776.)

TABLE 5.6 Comparative-Advantage Example: A Summary

Soybeans	Avocados
Mexico: Must give up 4 tons of avocados to get 1 ton of soybeans	***Mexico:*** Must give up $\frac{1}{4}$ ton of soybeans to get 1 ton of avocados
United States: Must give up 3 tons of avocados to get 1 ton of soybeans	***United States:*** Must give up $\frac{1}{3}$ ton of soybeans to get 1 ton of avocados
Comparative advantage: United States	***Comparative advantage:*** Mexico

circumstances. Specialization and trade are mutually "profitable" to the two nations if the comparative costs of producing the two products *within* the two nations differ. What are the comparative costs of avocados and soybeans in Mexico? By comparing production alternatives A and B in Table 5.4, we see that 5 tons of soybeans (= 15 − 10) must be sacrificed to produce 20 tons of avocados (= 20 − 0). Or, more simply, in Mexico it costs 1 ton of soybeans (S) to produce 4 tons of avocados (A); that is, 1S ≡ 4A. (The "≡" sign simply signifies "equivalent to.") Because we assumed constant costs, this domestic opportunity cost will not change as Mexico expands the output of either product. This is evident from production possibilities B and C, where we see that 4 more tons of avocados (= 24 − 20) cost 1 unit of soybeans (= 10 − 9).

Similarly, in Table 5.5, comparing U.S. production alternatives R and S reveals that in the United States it costs 10 tons of soybeans (= 30 − 20) to obtain 30 tons of avocados (= 30 − 0). That is, the domestic comparative-cost ratio for the two products in the United States is 1S ≡ 3A. Comparing production alternatives S and T reinforces this conclusion: an extra 3 tons of avocados (= 33 − 30) comes at the sacrifice of 1 ton of soybeans (= 20 − 19).

The comparative costs of the two products within the two nations are obviously different. Economists say that the United States has a domestic comparative advantage or, simply, a **comparative advantage** over Mexico in soybeans. The United States must forgo only 3 tons of avocados to get 1 ton of soybeans, but Mexico must forgo 4 tons of avocados to get 1 ton of soybeans. In terms of domestic opportunity costs, soybeans are relatively cheaper in the United States. A nation has a comparative advantage in some product when it can produce that product at a lower domestic opportunity cost than can a potential trading partner. Mexico, in contrast, has a comparative advantage in avocados. While 1 ton of avocados costs $\frac{1}{3}$ ton of soybeans in the United States, it costs only $\frac{1}{4}$ ton of soybeans in Mexico. Comparatively speaking, avocados are cheaper in Mexico. We summarize the situation in Table 5.6. Be sure to give it a close look.

O 5.1
Absolute and comparative advantage

Because of these differences in domestic opportunity costs, if both nations specialize, each according to its comparative advantage, each can achieve a larger total output with the same total input of resources. Together they will be using their scarce resources more efficiently.

Terms of Trade The United States can shift production between soybeans and avocados at the rate of 1S for 3A. Thus, the United States would specialize in soybeans only if it could obtain *more than* 3 tons of avocados for 1 ton of soybeans by trading with Mexico. Similarly, Mexico can shift production at the rate of 4A for 1S. So it would be advantageous to Mexico to specialize in avocados if it could get 1 ton of soybeans for *less than* 4 tons of avocados.

Suppose that through negotiation the two nations agree on an exchange rate of 1 ton of soybeans for $3\frac{1}{2}$ tons of avocados. These **terms of trade** are mutually beneficial to both countries, since each can "do better" through such trade than through domestic production alone. The United States can get $3\frac{1}{2}$ tons of avocados by sending 1 ton of soybeans to Mexico, while it can get only 3 tons of avocados by shifting its own resources domestically from soybeans to avocados. Mexico can obtain 1 ton of soybeans at a lower cost of $3\frac{1}{2}$ tons of avocados through trade with the United States, compared to the cost of 4 tons if Mexico produced the ton of soybeans itself.

Gains from Specialization and Trade Let's pinpoint the gains in total output from specialization and trade. Suppose that, before specialization and trade, production alternative C in Table 5.4 and alternative T in 5.5 were the optimal product mixes for the two countries. That is, Mexico preferred 24 tons of avocados and 9 tons of soybeans (Table 5.4) and the United States preferred 33 tons of avocados and 19 tons of soybeans (Table 5.5) to all other available domestic alternatives. These outputs are shown in column 1 in Table 5.7.

Now assume that both nations specialize according to their comparative advantage, with Mexico producing 60 tons of avocados and no soybeans (alternative E) and the United States producing no avocados and 30 tons of soybeans (alternative R). These outputs are shown in column 2 in Table 5.7. Using our 1S ≡ $3\frac{1}{2}$A terms of trade, assume that Mexico exchanges 35 tons of avocados for 10 tons of U.S. soybeans. Column 3 in Table 5.7 shows the quantities exchanged in this trade, with a minus sign indicating exports and a plus sign indicating imports. As shown in column 4, after the trade Mexico has 25 tons of avocados and

TABLE 5.7 Specialization According to Comparative Advantage and the Gains from Trade (in Tons)

Country	(1) Outputs before Specialization	(2) Outputs after Specialization	(3) Amounts Traded	(4) Outputs Available after Trade	(5) Gains from Specialization and Trade (4) − (1)
Mexico	24 avocados	60 avocados	−35 avocados	25 avocados	1 avocados
	9 soybeans	0 soybeans	+10 soybeans	10 soybeans	1 soybeans
United States	33 avocados	0 avocados	+35 avocados	35 avocados	2 avocados
	19 soybeans	30 soybeans	−10 soybeans	20 soybeans	1 soybeans

10 tons of soybeans, while the United States has 35 tons of avocados and 20 tons of soybeans. Compared with their optimum product mixes before specialization and trade (column 1), *both* nations now enjoy more avocados and more soybeans! Specifically, Mexico has gained 1 ton of avocados and 1 ton of soybeans. The United States has gained 2 tons of avocados and 1 ton of soybeans. These gains are shown in column 5.

Specialization based on comparative advantage improves global resource allocation. The same total inputs of world resources and technology result in a larger global output. If Mexico and the United States allocate all their resources to avocados and soybeans, respectively, the same total inputs of resources can produce more output between them, indicating that resources are being allocated more efficiently.

Through specialization and international trade a nation can overcome the production constraints imposed by its domestic production possibilities table and curve. Our discussion of Tables 5.4, 5.5, and 5.7 has shown just how this is done. The domestic production possibilities data (Tables 5.4 and 5.5) of the two countries have not changed, meaning that neither nation's production possibilities curve has shifted. But specialization and trade mean that citizens of both countries can enjoy increased consumption (column 5 of Table 5.7). **(Key Question 4)**

W 5.1

Gains from specialization

The Foreign Exchange Market

Buyers and sellers, whether individuals, firms, or nations, use money to buy products or to pay for the use of resources. Within the domestic economy, prices are stated in terms of the domestic currency and buyers use that currency to purchase domestic products. In Mexico, for example, buyers have pesos, and that is what sellers want.

International markets are different. Sellers set their prices in terms of their domestic currencies, but buyers often possess entirely different currencies. How many dollars does it take to buy a truckload of Mexican avocados selling for 3000 pesos, a German automobile selling for 50,000 euros, or a Japanese motorcycle priced at 300,000 yen? Producers in Mexico, Germany, and Japan want payment in pesos, euros, and yen, respectively, so that they can pay their wages, rent, interest, dividends, and taxes.

A **foreign exchange market,** a market in which various national currencies are exchanged for one another, serves this need. The equilibrium prices in such currency markets are called **exchange rates.** An exchange rate is the rate at which the currency of one nation can be exchanged for the currency of another nation. (See Global Perspective 5.2.)

The market price or exchange rate of a nation's currency is an unusual price; it links all domestic prices with all foreign prices. Exchange rates enable consumers in one

GLOBAL PERSPECTIVE 5.2

Exchange Rates: Foreign Currency per U.S. Dollar

The amount of foreign currency that a dollar will buy varies greatly from nation to nation and fluctuates in response to supply and demand changes in the foreign exchange market. The amounts shown here are for March 2006.

country to translate prices of foreign goods into units of their own currency: They need only multiply the foreign product price by the exchange rate. If the U.S. dollar–yen exchange rate is \$.01 (1 cent) per yen, a Sony television set priced at ¥20,000 will cost \$200 (= 20,000 × \$.01) in the United States. If the exchange rate rises to \$.02 (2 cents) per yen, the television will cost \$400 (= 20,000 × \$.02) in the United States. Similarly, all other Japanese products would double in price to U.S. buyers in response to the altered exchange rate.

Dollar-Yen Market

How does the foreign exchange market work? Let's look briefly at the market for dollars and yen. U.S. firms exporting goods to Japan want payment in dollars, not yen; but the Japanese importers of those U.S. goods possess yen, not dollars. So the Japanese importers supply their yen in exchange for dollars in the foreign exchange market. At the same time, there are U.S. importers of Japanese goods who need to pay the Japanese exporters in yen, not dollars. These importers go to the foreign exchange market as demanders of yen. We then have a market in which the "price" is in dollars and the "product" is yen.

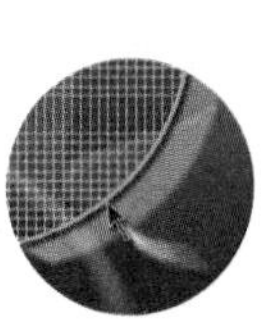

G 5.1
Exchange rates

Figure 5.3 shows the supply of yen (by Japanese importers) and the demand for yen (by U.S. importers). The intersection of demand curve D_y and supply curve S_y establishes the equilibrium dollar price of yen.

FIGURE 5.3 The market for yen. U.S. imports from Japan create a demand D_y for yen, while U.S. exports to Japan (Japan's imports) create a supply S_y of yen. The dollar price of 1 yen—the exchange rate—is determined at the intersection of the supply and demand curves. In this case the equilibrium price is \$.01, meaning that 1 cent will buy 1 yen.

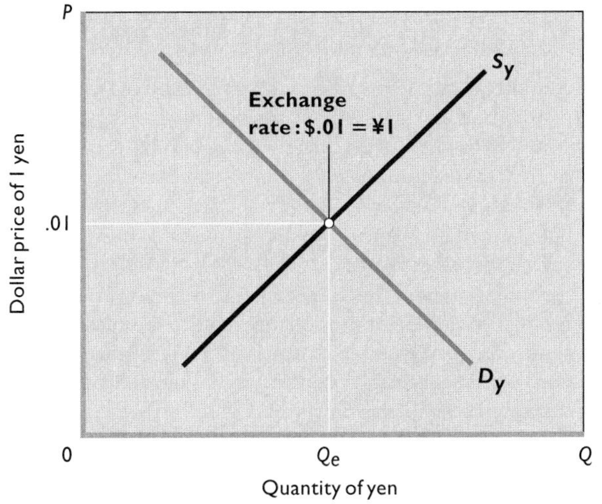

Here the equilibrium price of 1 yen—the dollar-yen exchange rate—is 1 cent per yen, or \$.01 = ¥1. At this price, the market for yen clears; there is neither a shortage nor a surplus of yen. The equilibrium \$.01 price of 1 yen means

CONSIDER THIS . . .

A Ticket to Ride

Have you ever attended a county or state fair and spent time on the rides? If so, you are aware of the dual "currencies" often used there. One currency is the *dollar;* the other is the *ride ticket.* Rides are priced in number of ride tickets, but dollars are needed to buy tickets at the kiosks. Alternative rides require different numbers of tickets. For example, the roller-coaster may require 8 tickets; the twister, 6 tickets; and the merry-go-round, 2 tickets.

Exchange rates between dollars and other currencies are analogous to the exchange rate between dollars and ride tickets.* Such tickets are a "currency" used to buy rides, and dollars and tickets are exchanged.

Initially suppose that the dollar price of each ticket is \$.25. If you were to exchange tickets for dollars on the midway, you would find that the ticket price of a dollar is 4; that is, 4 tickets will exchange for \$1. The ticket-dollar exchange rate is 1 ticket = \$.25, and the dollar-ticket exchange rate is \$1 = 4 tickets.

Although the rides are priced in tickets, not dollars, the exchange rate permits quick conversion of ticket prices into dollars. For example, the 8-ticket price of the roller-coaster ride converts to \$2 (= 8 tickets × \$.25). *Exchange rates enable buyers to convert goods priced in another currency to prices in their own currency.*

Next suppose that in some year the fair increases the price of ride tickets from \$.25 to \$.50. The dollar has *depreciated* in value, because more dollars (one-half rather than one-fourth) are needed to buy each ticket. Ride tickets have *appreciated* in value, because fewer tickets (two rather than four) are needed to obtain a dollar. Specifically, the exchange rate has changed from 1 ticket = \$.25 to 1 ticket = \$.50 or, alternatively, from \$1 = 4 tickets to \$1 = 2 tickets.

If the fair charges the same number of tickets per ride as before, the dollar price of the roller-coaster ride increases from \$2 (= 8 tickets × \$.25) to \$4 (= 8 tickets × \$.50). *Other things equal, depreciation of the dollar relative to another currency increases the dollar price of goods and services that are priced in the other currency.*

*One difference, however, is that many exchange rates are free to fluctuate depending on currency supply and demand. The fair operators fix the dollar–ride ticket exchange rate. Another difference is that the fair operators offer an unlimited quantity of tickets at that price.

that $1 will buy 100 yen or ¥100 worth of Japanese goods. Conversely, 100 yen will buy $1 worth of U.S. goods.

Changing Rates: Depreciation and Appreciation

What might cause the exchange rate to change? The determinants of the demand for and supply of yen are similar to the determinants of demand and supply for almost any product. In the United States, several things might increase the demand for—and therefore the dollar price of—yen. Incomes might rise in the United States, enabling residents to buy not only more domestic goods but also more Sony televisions, Nikon cameras, and Nissan automobiles from Japan. So people in the United States would need more yen, and the demand for yen would increase. Or a change in people's tastes might enhance their preferences for Japanese goods. When gas prices soared in the 1970s, many auto buyers in the United States shifted their demand from gas-guzzling domestic cars to gas-efficient Japanese compact cars. The result was an increased demand for yen.

The point is that an increase in the U.S. demand for Japanese goods will increase the demand for yen and raise the dollar price of yen. Suppose the dollar price of yen rises from $.01 = ¥1 to $.02 = ¥1. When the dollar price of yen increases, we say a **depreciation** of the dollar relative to the yen has occurred. It then takes more dollars (pennies in this case) to buy a single yen. Alternatively stated, the *international value of the dollar* has declined. A depreciated dollar buys fewer yen and therefore fewer Japanese goods; the yen and all Japanese goods have become more expensive to U.S. buyers. Result: Consumers in the United States shift their expenditures from Japanese goods to now less expensive American goods. The Ford Taurus becomes relatively more attractive than the Honda Accord to U.S. consumers. Conversely, because each yen buys more dollars—that is, because the international value of the yen has increased—U.S. goods become cheaper to people in Japan and U.S. exports to Japan rise.

If the opposite event occurred—if the Japanese demanded more U.S. goods—then they would supply more yen to pay for these goods. The increase in the supply of yen relative to the demand for yen would decrease the equilibrium price of yen in the foreign exchange market. For example, the dollar price of yen might decline from $.01 = ¥1 to $.005 = ¥1. A decrease in the dollar price of yen is called an **appreciation** of the dollar relative to the yen. It means that the international value of the dollar has increased. It then takes fewer dollars (or pennies) to buy a single yen; the dollar is worth more because it can purchase more yen and therefore more Japanese goods. Each Sony PlayStation becomes less expensive in terms of dollars, so people in the United States purchase more of them. In general, U.S. imports rise. Meanwhile, because it takes more yen to get a dollar, U.S. exports to Japan fall.

FIGURE 5.4 Currency appreciation and depreciation. Suppose the dollar price of a certain foreign currency rises (as illustrated by the upper left arrow). That means the international value of the dollar depreciates (upper right arrow). It also means that the foreign currency price of the dollar has declined (lower left arrow) and that the international value of the foreign currency has appreciated (lower right arrow).

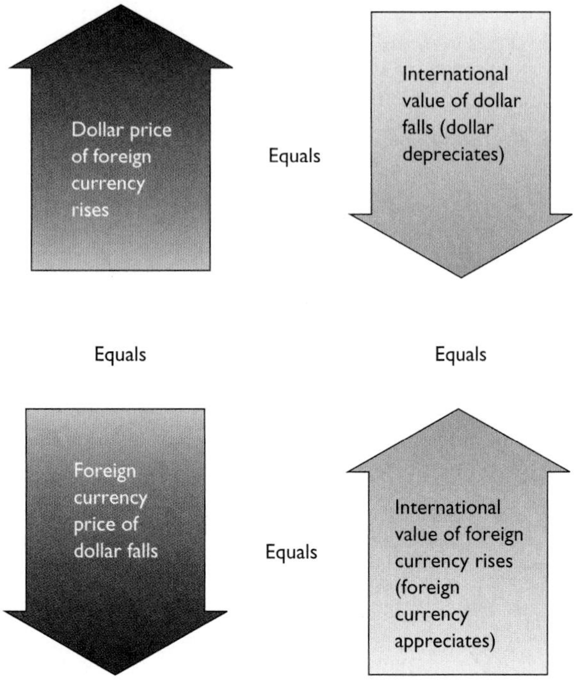

Figure 5.4 summarizes these currency relationships. **(Key Question 6)**

QUICK REVIEW 5.2

- A country has a comparative advantage when it can produce a product at a lower domestic opportunity cost than a potential trading partner can.
- Specialization based on comparative advantage increases the total output available for nations that trade with one another.
- The foreign exchange market is a market in which national currencies are exchanged.
- An appreciation of the dollar is an increase in the international value of the dollar relative to the currency of some other nation; after appreciation a dollar buys more units of that currency. A depreciation of the dollar is a decrease in the international value of the dollar relative to some other currency; after depreciation a dollar buys fewer units of that currency.

Government and Trade

If people and nations benefit from specialization and international exchange, why do governments sometimes try to restrict the free flow of imports or encourage exports? What kinds of world trade barriers can governments erect, and why would they do so?

Trade Impediments and Subsidies

There are four means by which governments commonly interfere with free trade:

- **Protective tariffs** are excise taxes or duties placed on imported goods. Protective tariffs are designed to shield domestic producers from foreign competition. They impede free trade by causing a rise in the prices of imported goods, thereby shifting demand toward domestic products. An excise tax on imported shoes, for example, would make domestically produced shoes more attractive to consumers.
- **Import quotas** are limits on the quantities or total value of specific items that may be imported. Once a quota is "filled," further imports of that product are choked off. Import quotas are more effective than tariffs in retarding international commerce. With a tariff, a product can go on being imported in large quantities; with an import quota, however, all imports are prohibited once the quota is filled.
- **Nontariff barriers** (and, implicitly, *nonquota* barriers) include onerous licensing requirements, unreasonable standards pertaining to product quality, or simply bureaucratic red tape in customs procedures. Some nations require that importers of foreign goods obtain licenses and then restrict the number of licenses issued. Although many nations carefully inspect imported agricultural products to prevent the introduction of potentially harmful insects, some countries use lengthy inspections to impede imports.
- **Export subsidies** consist of government payments to domestic producers of export goods. By reducing production costs, the subsidies enable producers to charge lower prices and thus to sell more exports in world markets. Two examples: Some European governments have heavily subsidized Airbus Industries, a European firm that produces commercial aircraft, to help Airbus compete against the American firm Boeing. The United States and other nations have subsidized domestic farmers to boost the domestic food supply. Such subsidies have lowered the market price of food and have artificially lowered export prices on agricultural produce.

Why Government Trade Interventions?

In view of the benefits of free trade, what accounts for the impulse to impede imports and boost exports through government policy? There are several reasons—some legitimate, most not.

Misunderstanding the Gains from Trade It is a commonly accepted myth that the greatest benefit to be derived from international trade is greater domestic employment in the export sector. This suggests that exports are "good" because they increase domestic employment, whereas imports are "bad" because they deprive people of jobs at home. Actually, the true benefit created by international trade is the overall increase in output obtained through specialization and exchange. A nation can fully employ its resources, including labor, with or without international trade. International trade, however, enables society to use its resources in ways that increase its total output and therefore its overall well-being.

A nation does not need international trade to operate *on* its production possibilities curve. A closed (nontrading) national economy can have full employment without international trade. However, through world trade an economy can reach a point of consumption *beyond* its domestic production possibilities curve. The gain from trade is the extra output obtained from abroad—the imports obtained for less cost than the cost if they were produced at home.

Political Considerations While a nation as a whole gains from trade, trade may harm particular domestic industries and particular groups of resource suppliers. In our earlier comparative-advantage example, specialization and trade adversely affected the U.S. avocado industry and the Mexican soybean industry. Those industries might seek to preserve their economic positions by persuading their respective governments to protect them from imports—perhaps through tariffs or import quotas.

Those who directly benefit from import protection are few in number but have much at stake. Thus, they have a strong incentive to pursue political activity to achieve their aims. However, the overall cost of tariffs and quotas typically greatly exceeds the benefits. It is not uncommon to find that it costs the public $200,000 or more a year to protect a domestic job that pays less than one-fourth that amount. Moreover, because these costs are buried in the price of goods and spread out over millions of citizens, the cost born by each individual citizen is quite small. In the political arena, the voice of the relatively few producers demanding *protectionism* is loud and constant, whereas the voice of those footing the bill is soft or nonexistent.

Indeed, the public may be won over by the apparent plausibility ("Cut imports and prevent domestic unemployment") and the patriotic ring ("Buy American!") of the protectionist arguments. The alleged benefits of tariffs are immediate and clear-cut to the public, but the adverse effects cited by economists are obscure and dispersed over the entire economy. When political deal making is added in—"You back tariffs for the apparel industry in my state, and I'll back tariffs on the auto industry in your state"—the outcome can be a network of protective tariffs, import quotas, and export subsidies.

Costs to Society

Tariffs and quotas benefit domestic producers of the protected products, but they harm domestic consumers, who must pay higher than world prices for the protected goods. They also hurt domestic firms that use the protected goods as inputs in their production processes. For example, a tariff on imported steel would boost the price of steel girders, thus hurting firms that construct large buildings. Also, tariffs and quotas reduce competition in the protected industries. With less competition from foreign producers, domestic firms may be slow to design and implement cost-saving production methods and introduce new or improved products.

Multilateral Trade Agreements and Free-Trade Zones

When one nation enacts barriers against imports, the nations whose exports suffer may retaliate with trade barriers of their own. In such a *trade war,* escalating tariffs choke world trade and reduce everyone's economic well-being. The **Smoot-Hawley Tariff Act** of 1930 is a classic example. Although that act was meant to reduce imports and stimulate U.S. production, the high tariffs it authorized prompted adversely affected nations to retaliate with tariffs equally high. International trade fell, lowering the output and income of all nations. Economic historians generally agree that the Smoot-Hawley Tariff Act was a contributing cause of the Great Depression. Aware of that fact, nations have worked to lower tariffs worldwide. Their pursuit of free trade has been aided by powerful domestic interest groups: Exporters of goods and services, importers of foreign components used in "domestic" products, and domestic sellers of imported products all strongly support lower tariffs.

Figure 5.5 makes clear that while the United States has been a high-tariff nation over much of its history, U.S. tariffs have generally declined during the past half-century.

FIGURE 5.5 U.S. tariff rates, 1860–2005. Historically, U.S. tariff rates have fluctuated. But beginning with the Reciprocal Trade Agreements Act of 1934, the trend has been downward.

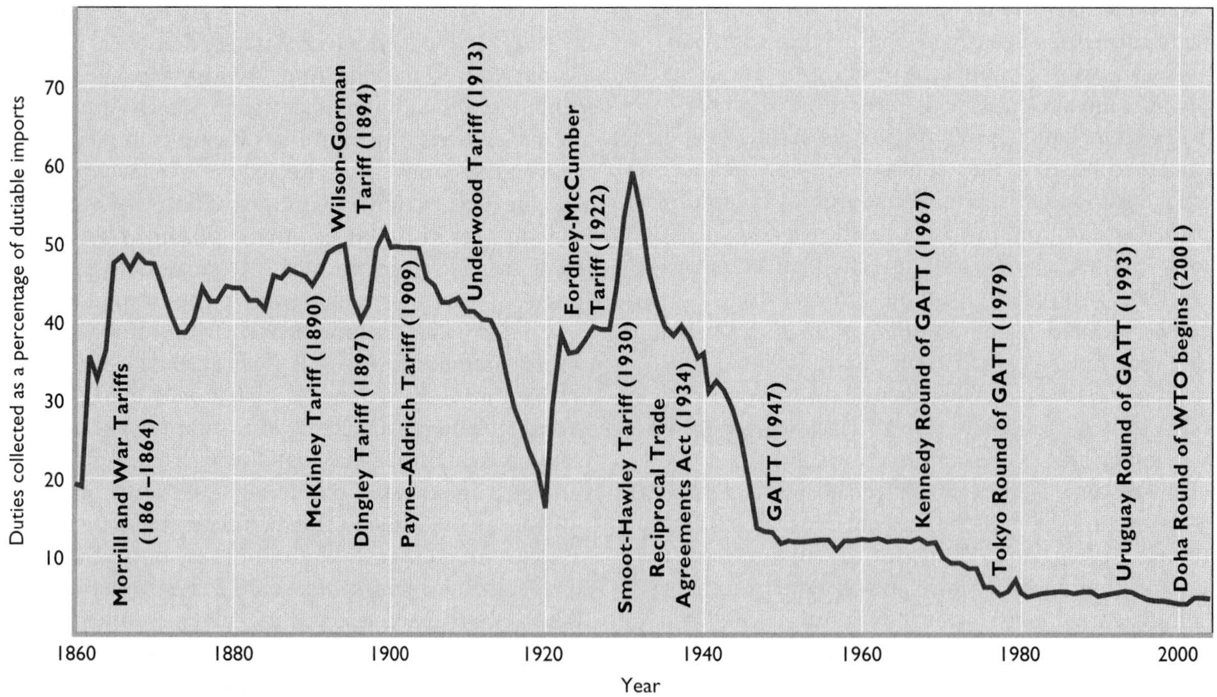

Source: U.S. Department of Commerce data.

Reciprocal Trade Agreements Act

The **Reciprocal Trade Agreements Act** of 1934 started the downward trend of tariffs. Aimed at reducing tariffs, this act had two main features:

- ***Negotiating authority*** It authorized the president to negotiate with foreign nations agreements that would reduce existing U.S. tariffs by up to 50 percent. Those reductions were contingent on the actions other nations took to lower tariffs on U.S. exports.
- ***Generalized reductions*** The specific tariff reductions negotiated between the United States and any particular nation were generalized through **most-favored-nation clauses**, which often accompany such agreements. These clauses stipulate that any subsequently reduced U.S. tariffs, resulting from negotiation with any other nation, would apply equally to any nation that signed the original agreement. So if the United States negotiates a reduction in tariffs on wristwatches with, say, France, the lower U.S. tariffs on imported French watches also apply to the imports of the other nations having most-favored-nation status, say, Japan and Switzerland. This way, the reductions in U.S. tariffs automatically apply to many nations.

General Agreement on Tariffs and Trade

The Reciprocal Trade Agreements Act provided only bilateral (between two nations) negotiations. Its approach was broadened in 1947 when 23 nations, including the United States, signed the **General Agreement on Tariffs and Trade (GATT).** GATT was based on three principles: (1) equal, nondiscriminatory trade treatment for all member nations, (2) the reduction of tariffs by multilateral negotiation, and (3) the elimination of import quotas. Basically, GATT provided a forum for the negotiation of reduced trade barriers on a multilateral basis among nations.

Since the Second World War, member nations have completed eight "rounds" of GATT negotiations to reduce trade barriers. The eighth round of negotiations began in Uruguay in 1986. After 7 years of complex discussions, in 1993 the 128 member nations reached a new agreement. The *Uruguay Round* agreement took effect on January 1, 1995, and its provisions were phased in through 2005.

Under this agreement, tariffs on thousands of products were eliminated or reduced, with overall tariffs dropping by 33 percent. The agreement also liberalized government rules that in the past impeded the global market for such services as advertising, legal services, tourist services, and financial services. Quotas on imported textiles and apparel were phased out and replaced with tariffs. Other provisions reduced agricultural subsidies paid to farmers and protected intellectual property (patents, trademarks, copyrights) against piracy.

World Trade Organization

The Uruguay Round agreement established the **World Trade Organization (WTO)** as GATT's successor. Some 149 nations belong to the WTO, with China being one of the latest entrants. The WTO oversees trade agreements reached by the member nations and rules on trade disputes among them. It also provides forums for further rounds of trade negotiations. The ninth and latest round of negotiations—the **Doha Round**—was launched in Doha, Qatar, in late 2001. (The trade rounds occur over several years in several venues but are named after the city or country of origination.) The negotiations are aimed at further reducing tariffs and quotas, as well as agricultural subsidies that distort trade. One of this chapter's Web-based questions asks you to update the progress of the Doha Round.

GATT and the WTO have been positive forces in the trend toward liberalized world trade. The trade rules agreed upon by the member nations provide a strong and necessary bulwark against the protectionism called for by the special-interest groups in the various nations.

For that reason and others, the WTO is controversial. Critics are concerned that rules crafted to expand international trade and investment enable firms to circumvent national laws that protect workers and the environment. What good are minimum-wage laws, worker safety laws, collective bargaining rights, and environmental laws if firms can easily shift their production to nations that have weaker laws or consumers can buy goods produced in those countries?

Proponents of the WTO respond that labor and environmental protections should be pursued directly in nations that have low standards and via international organizations other than the WTO. These issues should not be linked to the process of trade liberalization, which confers widespread economic benefits across nations. Moreover, say proponents of the WTO, many environmental and labor concerns are greatly overblown. Most world trade is among advanced industrial countries, not between them and countries that have lower environmental and labor standards. Moreover, the free flow of goods and resources raises output and income in the developing nations. Historically, such increases in living standards have eventually resulted in stronger, not weaker, protections for the environment and for workers.

The European Union

Countries have also sought to reduce tariffs by creating regional *free-trade zones*—also called *trade blocs*. The most dramatic example is the **European Union (EU),** formerly called the European Economic Community. Initiated in 1958 as the Common Market, in 2003 the EU comprised 15 European nations—France, Germany, United Kingdom, Italy, Belgium, the Netherlands, Luxembourg, Denmark, Ireland, Greece, Spain, Portugal, Austria, Finland, and Sweden. In 2004, the EU expanded by 10 additional European countries—Poland, Hungary, Czech Republic, Slovakia, Lithuania, Latvia, Estonia, Slovenia, Malta, and Cyprus.

The EU Trade Bloc

The EU has abolished tariffs and import quotas on nearly all products traded among the participating nations and established a common system of tariffs applicable to all goods received from nations outside the EU. It has also liberalized the movement of capital and labor within the EU and has created common policies in other economic matters of joint concern, such as agriculture, transportation, and business practices. The EU is now a strong **trade bloc:** a group of countries having common identity, economic interests, and trade rules.

EU integration has achieved for Europe what the U.S. constitutional prohibition on tariffs by individual states has achieved for the United States: increased regional specialization, greater productivity, greater output, and faster economic growth. The free flow of goods and services has created large markets for EU industries. The resulting economies of large-scale production have enabled these industries to achieve much lower costs than they could have achieved in their small, single-nation markets.

The effects of EU success on nonmember nations, such as the United States, have been mixed. A peaceful and increasingly prosperous EU makes its members better customers for U.S. exports. But U.S. firms and other nonmember firms have been faced with tariffs and other barriers that make it difficult for them to compete against firms within the EU trade bloc. For example, autos produced in Germany and sold in Spain or France face no tariffs, whereas U.S. and Japanese autos exported to EU countries do. This puts U.S. and Japanese firms at a serious disadvantage.

By giving preferences to countries within their free-trade zone, trade blocs such as the EU tend to reduce their members' trade with non-bloc members. Thus, the world loses some of the benefits of a completely open global trading system. Eliminating that disadvantage has been one of the motivations for liberalizing global trade through the World Trade Organization. Those liberalizations apply equally to all nations that belong to the WTO.

The Euro

One of the most significant accomplishments of the EU was the establishment of the so-called Euro Zone in the early 2000s. In 2006, 12 members of the EU used the **euro** as a common currency. Great Britain, Denmark, and Sweden have opted out of the common currency, at least for now. But gone are French francs, German marks, Italian liras, and other national currencies within the Euro Zone.

Economists expect the euro to raise the standard of living of the Euro Zone members over time. By ending the inconvenience and expense of exchanging currencies, the euro will enhance the free flow of goods, services, and resources among the Euro Zone members. It will also enable consumers and businesses to comparison shop for outputs and inputs, and this will increase competition, reduce prices, and lower costs.

North American Free Trade Agreement

In 1993 Canada, Mexico, and the United States formed a major trade bloc. The **North American Free Trade Agreement (NAFTA)** established a free-trade zone that has about the same combined output as the EU but encompasses a much larger geographic area. NAFTA has greatly reduced tariffs and other trade barriers between Canada, Mexico, and the United States and will eliminate them entirely by 2008.

Critics of NAFTA feared that it would cause a massive loss of U.S. jobs as firms moved to Mexico to take advantage of lower wages and weaker regulations on pollution and workplace safety. Also, there was concern that Japan and South Korea would build plants in Mexico and transport goods tariff-free to the United States, further hurting U.S. firms and workers.

In retrospect, critics were much too pessimistic. Since the passage of NAFTA in 1993, employment in the United States has increased by 21 million workers and the unemployment rate has declined from 6.9 to 5.1 percent. Increased trade among Canada, Mexico, and the United States has enhanced the standard of living in all three countries. **(Key Question 10)**

QUICK REVIEW 5.3

- Governments curtail imports and promote exports through protective tariffs, import quotas, nontariff barriers, and export subsidies.
- The General Agreement on Tariffs and Trade (GATT) established multinational reductions in tariffs and import quotas. The Uruguay Round of GATT (1993) reduced tariffs worldwide, liberalized international trade in services, strengthened protections for intellectual property, and reduced agricultural subsidies.
- The World Trade Organization (WTO)—GATT's successor—rules on trade disputes and provides forums for negotiations on further rounds of trade liberalization. The current round is called the Doha Round.
- The European Union (EU) and the North American Free Trade Agreement (NAFTA) have reduced internal trade barriers among their members by establishing large free-trade zones. Of the 25 EU members (as of 2006), 12 now have a common currency—the euro.

GLOBAL PERSPECTIVE 5.3

The Top 12 Globalized Nations, 2005

Foreign Policy magazine publishes an annual list of the worlds' most globalized nations, based on 13 key indicators such as foreign trade, cross-border travel, Internet use, and international investment flows. Here is the magazine's list, in descending order, for 2005.

1. Singapore
2. Ireland
3. Switzerland
4. United States
5. Netherlands
6. Canada
7. Denmark
8. Sweden
9. Austria
10. Finland
11. New Zealand
12. United Kingdom

Source: A. T. Kearney, *Foreign Policy,* **www.foreignpolicy.com** and **www.atkearney.com.**

Global Competition

Globalization—the integration of industry, commerce, communication, travel, and culture among the world's nations—is one of the major trends of our time. (See Global Perspective 5.3 for a list of the top 12 globalized nations, according to one set of criteria.) There is a lively debate internationally as to whether globalization is a positive or negative force. Those who support globalization focus on the improvements to general standards of living that it brings. Those who oppose it express concerns about its impacts on the environment, unionized workers, and the poor. (We discuss this issue in detail in a later Last Word.)

One thing about globalization is certain and relevant to our present discussion: It has brought intense competition both within the United States and across the globe. In the United States, imports have gained major shares of many markets, including those for cars, steel, lumber, car tires, clothing, sporting goods, electronics, and toys. Nevertheless, hundreds of U.S. firms have prospered in the global marketplace. Such firms as Boeing, McDonald's, Intel, Coca-Cola, Microsoft, Monsanto, Procter & Gamble, and Caterpillar have continued to retain high market shares at home and have dramatically expanded their sales abroad. Of course, not all firms have been successful. Some have not been able to compete, because their international competitors make higher-quality products, have lower production costs, or both.

Is the heightened competition that accompanies the global economy a good thing? Although some domestic producers *do* get hurt and their workers must find employment elsewhere, foreign competition clearly benefits consumers and society in general. Imports break down the monopoly power of existing firms, thereby lowering product prices and providing consumers with a greater variety of goods. Foreign competition also forces domestic producers to become more efficient and to improve product quality; that has already happened in several U.S. industries, including steel and autos. Most U.S. firms can and do compete quite successfully in the global marketplace.

What about the U.S. firms that cannot compete successfully in open markets? The unfortunate reality is that they must sell off production facilities, scale back their operations, and try to develop new products. If they remain unprofitable despite their best efforts, they will need to go out of business. Persistent economic losses mean that scarce resources are not being used efficiently. Shifting those resources to alternative, profitable uses will increase total U.S. output. It will be far less expensive for the United States to provide training and, if necessary, relocation assistance to laid-off workers than to try to protect these jobs from foreign competition.

Petition of the Candlemakers, 1845

French Economist Frédéric Bastiat (1801–1850) Devastated the Proponents of Protectionism by Satirically Extending Their Reasoning to Its Logical and Absurd Conclusions.

Petition of the Manufacturers of Candles, Waxlights, Lamps, Candlesticks, Street Lamps, Snuffers, Extinguishers, and of the Producers of Oil Tallow, Rosin, Alcohol, and, Generally, of Everything Connected with Lighting.

TO MESSIEURS THE MEMBERS OF THE CHAMBER OF DEPUTIES.

Gentlemen—You are on the right road. You reject abstract theories, and have little consideration for cheapness and plenty. Your chief care is the interest of the producer. You desire to emancipate him from external competition, and reserve the national market for national industry.

We are about to offer you an admirable opportunity of applying your—what shall we call it? your theory? No; nothing is more deceptive than theory; your doctrine? your system? your principle? but you dislike doctrines, you abhor systems, and as for principles, you deny that there are any in social economy: we shall say, then, your practice, your practice without theory and without principle.

We are suffering from the intolerable competition of a foreign rival, placed, it would seem, in a condition so far superior to ours for the production of light, that he absolutely inundates our national market with it at a price fabulously reduced. The moment he shows himself, our trade leaves us—all consumers apply to him; and a branch of native industry, having countless ramifications, is all at once rendered completely stagnant. This rival . . . is no other than the Sun.

What we pray for is, that it may please you to pass a law ordering the shutting up of all windows, skylights, dormer windows, outside and inside shutters, curtains, blinds, bull's-eyes; in a word, of all openings, holes, chinks, clefts, and fissures, by or through which the light of the sun has been in use to enter houses, to the prejudice of the meritorious manufacturers with which we flatter ourselves we have accommodated our country,—a country which, in gratitude, ought not to abandon us now to a strife so unequal.

If you shut up as much as possible all access to natural light, and create a demand for artificial light, which of our French manufacturers will not be encouraged by it?

If more tallow is consumed, then there must be more oxen and sheep; and, consequently, we shall behold the multiplication of artificial meadows, meat, wool, hides, and, above all, manure, which is the basis and foundation of all agricultural wealth.

The same remark applies to navigation. Thousands of vessels will proceed to the whale fishery; and, in a short time, we shall possess a navy capable of maintaining the honor of France, and gratifying the patriotic aspirations of your petitioners, the undersigned candlemakers and others.

Only have the goodness to reflect, Gentlemen, and you will be convinced that there is, perhaps, no Frenchman, from the wealthy coalmaster to the humblest vender of lucifer matches, whose lot will not be ameliorated by the success of this our petition.

Source: Frédéric Bastiat, *Economic Sophisms* (Edinburgh: Oliver and Boyd, Tweeddale Court, 1873), pp. 49–53, abridged.

Summary

1. Goods and services flows, capital and labor flows, information and technology flows, and financial flows link the United States and other countries.
2. International trade is growing in importance globally and for the United States. World trade is significant to the United States in two respects: (a) The absolute volumes of U.S. imports and exports exceed those of any other single nation. (b) The United States is completely dependent on trade for certain commodities and materials that cannot be obtained domestically.
3. Principal U.S. exports include chemicals, consumer durables, agricultural products, semiconductors, and computers. Principal imports include oil, automobiles, household appliances, computers, and metals. Quantitatively, Canada is the United States' most important trading partner.
4. Global trade has been greatly facilitated by (a) improvements in transportation technology, (b) improvements in communications technology, and (c) general declines in tariffs. Although the United States, Japan, and the western European nations dominate the global economy, the total volume of trade has been increased by the contributions of several new trade participants. They include the Asian economies of Singapore, South Korea, Taiwan, and China (including Hong Kong), the eastern European countries (such as the Czech Republic, Hungary, and Poland), and the newly independent countries of the former Soviet Union (such as Estonia, Ukraine, and Azerbaijan).
5. Specialization based on comparative advantage enables nations to achieve higher standards of living through trade with other countries. A trading partner should specialize in products and services for which its domestic opportunity costs are lowest. The terms of trade must be such that both nations can obtain more of some product via trade than they could obtain by producing it at home.
6. The foreign exchange market sets exchange rates between currencies. Each nation's imports create a supply of its own currency and a demand for foreign currencies. The resulting supply-demand equilibrium sets the exchange rate that links the currencies of all nations. Depreciation of a nation's currency reduces its imports and increases its exports; appreciation increases its imports and reduces its exports.
7. Governments influence trade flows through (a) protective tariffs, (b) quotas, (c) nontariff barriers, and (d) export subsidies. Such impediments to free trade result from misunderstandings about the advantages of free trade and from political considerations. By artificially increasing product prices, trade barriers cost U.S. consumers billions of dollars annually.
8. The Reciprocal Trade Agreements Act of 1934 marked the beginning of a trend toward lower U.S. tariffs. Most-favored-nation status allows a nation to export goods into the United States at the United States' lowest tariff level, then or at any later time.
9. In 1947 the General Agreement on Tariffs and Trade (GATT) was formed to encourage nondiscriminatory treatment for all member nations, to reduce tariffs, and to eliminate import quotas. The Uruguay Round of GATT negotiations (1993) reduced tariffs and quotas, liberalized trade in services, reduced agricultural subsidies, reduced pirating of intellectual property, and phased out quotas on textiles.
10. GATT's successor, the World Trade Organization (WTO), has 149 member nations. It implements WTO agreements, rules on trade disputes between members, and provides forums for continued discussions on trade liberalization. The latest round of trade negotiations—the Doha Round—began in late 2001 and as of mid-2006 was still in progress.
11. Free-trade zones (trade blocs) liberalize trade within regions but may at the same time impede trade with non-bloc members. Two examples of free-trade arrangements are the 25-member European Union (EU) and the North American Free Trade Agreement (NAFTA), comprising Canada, Mexico, and the United States. Twelve of the EU nations have abandoned their national currencies for a common currency called the euro.
12. The global economy has created intense foreign competition in many U.S. product markets, but most U.S. firms are able to compete well both at home and globally.

Terms and Concepts

multinational corporations
comparative advantage
terms of trade
foreign exchange market
exchange rates
depreciation
appreciation
protective tariffs
import quotas
nontariff barriers
export subsidies
Smoot-Hawley Tariff Act
Reciprocal Trade Agreements Act
most-favored-nation clauses
General Agreement on Tariffs and Trade (GATT)
World Trade Organization (WTO)
Doha Round
European Union (EU)
trade bloc
euro
North American Free Trade Agreement (NAFTA)

Study Questions

1. Describe the four major economic flows that link the United States with other nations. Provide a specific example to illustrate each flow. Explain the relationships between the top and bottom flows in Figure 5.1.
2. How important is international trade to the U.S. economy? In terms of volume, does the United States trade more with the industrially advanced economies or with developing economies? What country is the United States' most important trading partner, quantitatively?
3. What factors account for the rapid growth of world trade since the Second World War? Who are the major players in international trade today? Besides Japan, what other Asian nations play significant roles in international trade?
4. **KEY QUESTION** The following are production possibilities tables for China and the United States. Assume that before specialization and trade the optimal product mix for China is alternative B and for the United States is alternative U.

	China Production Possibilities					
Product	**A**	**B**	**C**	**D**	**E**	**F**
Apparel (in thousands)	30	24	18	12	6	0
Chemicals (in tons)	0	6	12	18	24	30

	U.S. Production Possibilities					
Product	**R**	**S**	**T**	**U**	**V**	**W**
Apparel (in thousands)	10	8	6	4	2	0
Chemicals (in tons)	0	4	8	12	16	20

   a. Are comparative-cost conditions such that the two areas should specialize? If so, what product should each produce?
   b. What is the total gain in apparel and chemical output that would result from such specialization?
   c. What are the limits of the terms of trade? Suppose actual terms of trade are 1 unit of apparel for $1\frac{1}{2}$ units of chemicals and that 4 units of apparel are exchanged for 6 units of chemicals. What are the gains from specialization and trade for each nation?
   d. Explain why this illustration allows you to conclude that specialization according to comparative advantage results in more efficient use of world resources.
5. Suppose that the comparative-cost ratios of two products—baby formula and tuna fish—are as follows in the hypothetical nations of Canswicki and Tunata:

   Canswicki: 1 can baby formula ≡ 2 cans tuna fish
   Tunata: 1 can baby formula ≡ 4 cans tuna fish

   In what product should each nation specialize? Explain why terms of trade of 1 can baby formula ≡ $2\frac{1}{2}$ cans tuna fish would be acceptable to both nations.
6. **KEY QUESTION** True or False? "U.S. exports create a demand for foreign currencies; foreign imports of U.S. goods create a supply of foreign currencies." Explain. Would a decline in U.S. consumer income or a weakening of U.S. preferences for foreign products cause the dollar to depreciate or to appreciate? Other things equal, what would be the effects of that depreciation or appreciation on U.S. exports and imports?
7. If the European euro were to decline in value (depreciate) in the foreign exchange market, would it be easier or harder for the French to sell their wine in the United States? Suppose you were planning a trip to Paris. How would depreciation of the euro change the dollar cost of your trip?
8. True or False? "An increase in the American dollar price of the South Korean won implies that the South Korean won has depreciated in value." Explain.
9. What measures do governments take to promote exports and restrict imports? Who benefits and who loses from protectionist policies? What is the net outcome for society?
10. **KEY QUESTION** Identify and state the significance of each of the following: (*a*) WTO; (*b*) EU; (*c*) euro; (*d*) NAFTA. What commonality do they share?
11. Explain: "Free-trade zones such as the EU and NAFTA lead a double life: They can promote free trade among members, but they pose serious trade obstacles for nonmembers." Do you think the net effects of trade blocs are good or bad for world trade? Why? How do the efforts of the WTO relate to these trade blocs?
12. Speculate as to why some U.S. firms strongly support trade liberalization while other U.S. firms favor protectionism. Speculate as to why some U.S. labor unions strongly support trade liberalization while other U.S. labor unions strongly oppose it.
13. What is the Doha Round and why is it so-named? How does it relate to the WTO? How does it relate to the Uruguay Round?
14. **LAST WORD** What point is Bastiat trying to make in his imaginary petition of the candlemakers?

Web-Based Questions

1. **TRADE BALANCES WITH PARTNER COUNTRIES** The U.S. Census Bureau, at **www.census.gov/foreign-trade/statistics,** lists the top trading partners of the United States (imports and exports added together) as well as the top 10 countries with which the United States has a trade surplus and a trade deficit. Using the current year-to-date data, compare the top 10 deficit and surplus countries with the top 10 trading partners. Are deficit and surplus countries equally represented in the top 10 trading partners list, or does one group dominate the list? The top 10 trading partners represent what percent of U.S. imports and what percent of U.S. exports?

2. **FOREIGN EXCHANGE RATES—THE YEN FOR DOLLARS** The Federal Reserve System Web site, **www.federalreserve.gov/releases/H10/hist/,** provides historical foreign-exchange-rate data for a wide variety of currencies. Look at the data for the Japanese yen from 1995 to the present. Assume that you were in Tokyo every New Year's from January 1, 2000, to this year and bought a *bento* (box lunch) for 1000 yen each year. Convert this amount to dollars using the yen-dollar exchange rate for each January since 2000, and plot the dollar price of the *bento* over time. Has the dollar appreciated or depreciated against the yen? What was the least amount in dollars that your box lunch cost? The most?

3. **THE DOHA ROUND—WHAT IS THE CURRENT STATUS?** Determine and briefly summarize the current status of the Doha Round of trade negotiations by accessing the World Trade Organization site, **www.wto.org.** Is the round still in progress or has it been concluded with an agreement? If the former, when and where was the latest ministerial meeting? If the latter, what are the main features of the agreement?

PART TWO

Microeconomics of Product Markets

6 EXTENSIONS OF DEMAND AND SUPPLY ANALYSIS
7 CONSUMER BEHAVIOR AND UTILITY MAXIMIZATION
8 THE COSTS OF PRODUCTION
9 PURE COMPETITION
10 PURE MONOPOLY
11 MONOPOLISTIC COMPETITION AND OLIGOPOLY
12 TECHNOLOGY, R&D, AND EFFICIENCY

IN THIS CHAPTER YOU WILL LEARN:

- About price elasticity of demand and how it can be applied.
- The usefulness of the total revenue test for price elasticity of demand.
- About price elasticity of supply and how it can be applied.
- About cross elasticity of demand and income elasticity of demand.
- About consumer surplus, producer surplus, and efficiency losses.

6

Extensions of Demand and Supply Analysis

Today's market economies rely mainly on the activities of consumers, businesses, and resource suppliers to allocate resources efficiently. Those activities and their outcomes are the subject of microeconomics, to which we now turn.

In this chapter we extend our previous discussion of demand and supply by explaining significant ideas that help us answer such questions as: Why do buyers of some products (for example, ocean cruises) respond to price increases by substantially reducing their purchases while buyers of other products (say, gasoline) respond by only slightly cutting back their purchases? Why do higher market prices for some products (for example, chicken) cause producers to greatly increase their output while price rises for other products (say, gold) cause only limited increases in output? Why does the demand for some products (for example, books) rise a great deal when household income increases while the demand for other products (say, milk) rises just a little? How is it that most consumers obtain products at prices below the prices they actually would have been willing to pay? How is it that most producers obtain higher prices for their products than the prices they actually would have been willing to accept?

The ideas of *elasticity, consumer surplus*, and *producer surplus* help answer these questions. Let's begin by looking at elasticity.

Price Elasticity of Demand

The law of demand tells us that consumers will buy more of a product when its price declines and less when its price increases. But how much more or less will they buy? The amount varies from product to product and over different price ranges for the same product. It also may vary over time. And such variations matter. For example, a firm contemplating a price hike will want to know how consumers will respond. If they remain highly loyal and continue to buy, the firm's revenue will rise. But if consumers defect en masse to other sellers or other products, its revenue will tumble.

The responsiveness (or sensitivity) of consumers to a price change is measured by a product's **price elasticity of demand.** For some products—for example, restaurant meals—consumers are highly responsive to price changes. Modest price changes cause very large changes in the quantity purchased. Economists say that the demand for such products is *relatively elastic* or simply *elastic.*

O 6.1

Price elasticity of demand

For other products—for example, toothpaste—consumers pay much less attention to price changes. Substantial price changes cause only small changes in the amount purchased. The demand for such products is *relatively inelastic* or simply *inelastic.*

The Price-Elasticity Coefficient and Formula

Economists measure the degree of price elasticity or inelasticity of demand with the coefficient E_d, defined as

$$E_d = \frac{\text{percentage change in quantity demanded of product X}}{\text{percentage change in price of product X}}$$

The percentage changes in the equation are calculated by dividing the *change* in quantity demanded by the original quantity demanded and by dividing the *change* in price by the original price. So we can restate the formula as

$$E_d = \frac{\text{change in quantity demanded of X}}{\text{original quantity demanded of X}} \div \frac{\text{change in price of X}}{\text{original price of X}}$$

Using Averages Unfortunately, an annoying problem arises in computing the price-elasticity coefficient. A price change from, say, \$4 to \$5 along a demand curve is a 25 percent (= \$1/\$4) increase, but the opposite price change from \$5 to \$4 along the same curve is a 20 percent (= \$1/\$5) decrease. Which percentage change in price should we use in the denominator to compute the price-elasticity coefficient? And when quantity changes, for example, from 10 to 20, it is a 100 percent (= 10/10) increase. But when quantity falls from 20 to 10 along the identical demand curve, it is a 50 percent (= 10/20) decrease. Should we use 100 percent or 50 percent in the numerator of the elasticity formula? Elasticity should be the same whether price rises or falls!

The simplest solution to the problem is to use the **midpoint formula** for calculating elasticity. This formula simply averages the two prices and the two quantities as the reference points for computing the percentages. That is,

$$E_d = \frac{\text{change in quantity}}{\text{sum of quantities}/2} \div \frac{\text{change in price}}{\text{sum of prices}/2}$$

For the same \$5 − \$4 price range, the price reference is \$4.50 [= (\$5 + \$4)/2], and for the same 10–20 quantity range, the quantity reference is 15 units [= (10 + 20)/2]. The percentage change in price is now \$1/\$4.50, or about 22 percent, and the percentage change in quantity is $\frac{10}{15}$, or about 67 percent. So E_d is about 3. This solution eliminates the "up versus down" problem. All the price-elasticity coefficients that follow are calculated using this midpoint formula.

W 6.1

Elasticity of demand

Using Percentages Why use percentages rather than absolute amounts in measuring consumer responsiveness? There are two reasons.

First, if we use absolute changes, the choice of units will arbitrarily affect our impression of buyer responsiveness. To illustrate: If the price of a bag of popcorn at the local softball game is reduced from $3 to $2 and consumers increase their purchases from 60 to 100 bags, it will seem that consumers are quite sensitive to price changes and therefore that demand is elastic. After all, a price change of 1 unit has caused a change in the amount demanded of 40 units. But by changing the monetary unit from dollars to pennies (why not?), we find that a price change of 100 units (pennies) causes a quantity change of 40 units. This may falsely lead us to believe that demand is inelastic. We avoid this problem by using percentage changes. This particular price decline is the same whether we measure it in dollars or pennies.

Second, by using percentages, we can correctly compare consumer responsiveness to changes in the prices of different products. It makes little sense to compare the effects on quantity demanded of (1) a $1 increase in the price of a $10,000 used car with (2) a $1 increase in the price of a $1 soft drink. Here the price of the used car has increased by .01 percent while the price of the soft drink is up by 100 percent. We can more sensibly compare the consumer responsiveness to price increases by using some common percentage increase in price for both.

Elimination of Minus Sign

We know from the downsloping demand curve that price and quantity demanded are inversely related. Thus, the price-elasticity coefficient of demand E_d will always be a negative number. As an example, if price declines, then quantity demanded will increase. This means that the numerator in our formula will be positive and the denominator negative, yielding a negative E_d. For an increase in price, the numerator will be negative but the denominator positive, again yielding a negative E_d.

Economists usually ignore the minus sign and simply present the absolute value of the elasticity coefficient to avoid an ambiguity that might otherwise arise. It can be confusing to say that an E_d of -4 is greater than one of -2. This possible confusion is avoided when we say an E_d of 4 reveals greater elasticity than one of 2. So, in what follows, we ignore the minus sign in the coefficient of price elasticity of demand and show only the absolute value. Incidentally, the ambiguity does not arise with supply because price and quantity supplied are positively related. All elasticity of supply coefficients therefore are positive numbers.

Interpretations of E_d

We can interpret the coefficient of price elasticity of demand as follows.

Elastic Demand

Demand is **elastic** if a specific percentage change in price results in a larger percentage change in quantity demanded. Then E_d will be greater than 1. Example: Suppose that a 2 percent decline in the price of cut flowers results in a 4 percent increase in quantity demanded. Then demand for cut flowers is elastic and

$$E_d = \frac{.04}{.02} = 2$$

Inelastic Demand

If a specific percentage change in price produces a smaller percentage change in quantity demanded, demand is **inelastic.** Then E_d will be less than 1. Example: Suppose that a 2 percent decline in the price of coffee leads to only a 1 percent increase in quantity demanded. Then demand is inelastic and

$$E_d = \frac{.01}{.02} = .5$$

Unit Elasticity

The case separating elastic and inelastic demands occurs where a percentage change in price and the resulting percentage change in quantity demanded are the same. Example: Suppose that a 2 percent drop in the price of chocolate causes a 2 percent increase in quantity demanded. This special case is termed **unit elasticity** because E_d is exactly 1, or unity. In this example,

$$E_d = \frac{.02}{.02} = 1$$

Extreme Cases

When we say demand is "inelastic," we do not mean that consumers are completely unresponsive to a price change. In that extreme situation, where a price change results in no change whatsoever in the quantity demanded, economists say that demand is **perfectly inelastic.** The price-elasticity coefficient is zero because there is no response to a change in price. Approximate examples include an acute diabetic's demand for insulin or an addict's demand for heroin. A line parallel to the vertical axis, such as D_1 in Figure 6.1a, shows perfectly inelastic demand graphically.

Conversely, when we say demand is "elastic," we do not mean that consumers are completely responsive to a price change. In that extreme situation, where a small price reduction causes buyers to increase their purchases from zero to all they can obtain, the elasticity coefficient is infinite ($= \infty$) and economists say demand is **perfectly elastic.** A line parallel to the horizontal axis, such as D_2 in Figure 6.1b, shows perfectly elastic demand. You will see in Chapter 9 that such a demand applies to a firm—say, a raspberry grower—that is selling its product in a purely competitive market.

FIGURE 6.1 Perfectly inelastic and elastic demands. Demand curve D_1 in (a) represents perfectly inelastic demand ($E_d = 0$). A price increase will result in no change in quantity demanded. Demand curve D_2 in (b) represents perfectly elastic demand. A price increase will cause quantity demanded to decline from an infinite amount to zero ($E_d = \infty$).

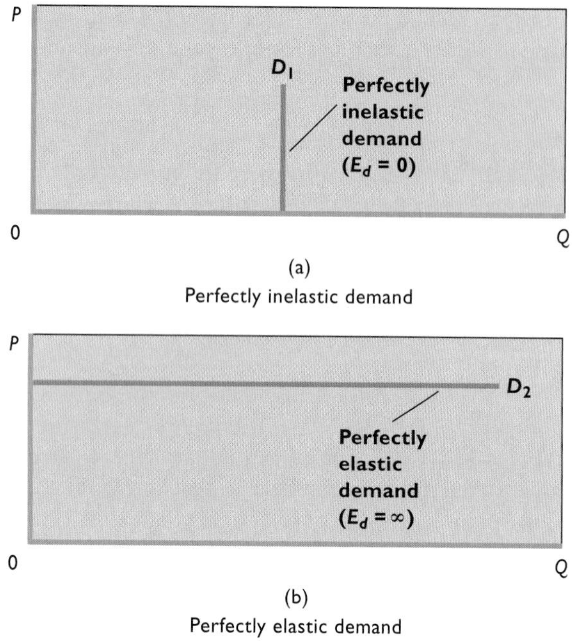

The Total-Revenue Test

The importance of elasticity for firms relates to the effect of price changes on total revenue and thus on profits (total revenue minus total costs).

Total revenue (TR) is the total amount the seller receives from the sale of a product in a particular time period; it is calculated by multiplying the product price (*P*) by the quantity demanded and sold (*Q*). In equation form:

$$\text{TR} = P \times Q$$

Graphically, total revenue is represented by the $P \times Q$ rectangle lying below a point on a demand curve. At point *a* in Figure 6.2a, for example, price is \$2 and quantity demanded is 10 units. So total revenue is \$20 (= \$2 × 10), shown by the rectangle composed of the gold and orange areas under the demand curve. We know from basic geometry that the area of a rectangle is found by multiplying one side by the other. Here, one side is "price" (\$2) and the other is "quantity demanded" (10 units).

Total revenue and the price elasticity of demand are related. In fact, the easiest way to infer whether demand is elastic or inelastic is to employ the **total-revenue test.** Here is the test: Note what happens to total revenue when price changes. If total revenue changes in the opposite direction from price, demand is elastic. If total revenue changes in the same direction as price, demand is inelastic. If total revenue does not change when price changes, demand is unit-elastic.

CONSIDER THIS . . .

A Bit of a Stretch

The following analogy might help you remember the distinction between "elastic" and "inelastic." Imagine two objects—one an Ace elastic bandage used to wrap injured joints and the other a relatively firm rubber tie-down (rubber strap) used for securing items for transport. The Ace bandage stretches a great deal when pulled with a particular force; the rubber tie-down stretches some, but not a lot.

Similar differences occur for the quantity demanded of various products when their prices change. For some products, a price change causes a substantial "stretch" of quantity demanded. When this stretch in percentage terms exceeds the percentage change in price, demand is elastic. For other products, quantity demanded stretches very little in response to the price change. When this stretch in percentage terms is less than the percentage change in price, demand is inelastic.

In summary:

- Elastic demand displays considerable "quantity stretch" (as with the Ace bandage).
- Inelastic demand displays relatively little "quantity stretch" (as with the rubber tie-down).

And through extension:

- Perfectly elastic demand has infinite quantity stretch.
- Perfectly inelastic demand has zero quantity stretch.

Elastic Demand If demand is elastic, a decrease in price will increase total revenue. Even though a lesser price is received per unit, enough additional units are sold to more than make up for the lower price. For an example, look at demand curve D_1 in Figure 6.2a. We have already established that at point *a*, total revenue is \$20 (= \$2 × 10), shown as the gold plus orange area. If the price declines from \$2 to \$1 (point *b*), the quantity demanded becomes 40 units and total revenue is \$40 (= \$1 × 40). As a result of the price decline, total revenue has increased from \$20

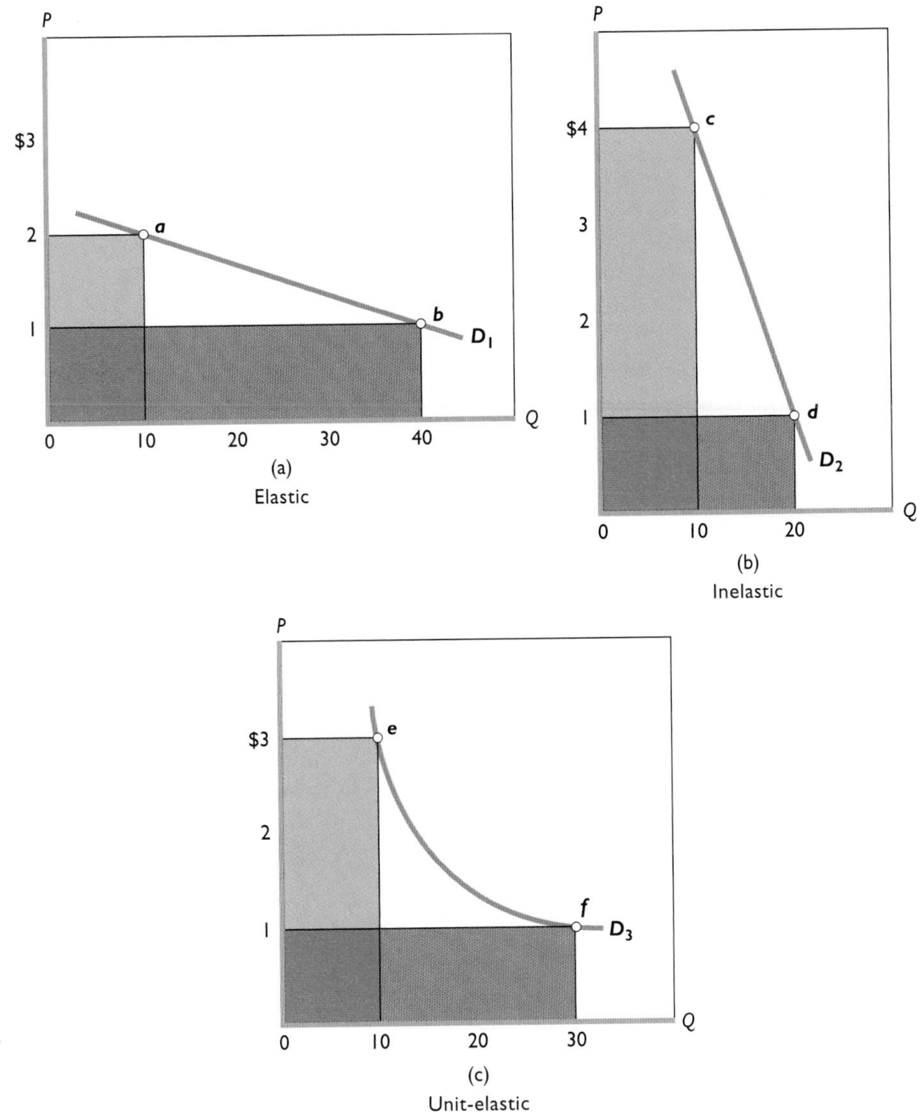

FIGURE 6.2 The total-revenue test for price elasticity. (a) Price declines from \$2 to \$1, and total revenue increases from \$20 to \$40. So demand is elastic. The gain in revenue (brown area) exceeds the loss of revenue (gold area). (b) Price declines from \$4 to \$1, and total revenue falls from \$40 to \$20. So, demand is inelastic. The gain in revenue (brown area) is less than the loss of revenue (gold area). (c) Price declines from \$3 to \$1, and total revenue does not change. Demand is unit-elastic. The gain in revenue (brown area) equals the loss of revenue (gold area).

to \$40. Total revenue has increased in this case because the \$1 decline in price applies to 10 units, with a consequent revenue loss of \$10 (the gold area). But 30 more units are sold at \$1 each, resulting in a revenue gain of \$30 (the brown area). Visually, the gain of the brown area clearly exceeds the loss of the gold area. As indicated, the overall result is a net increase in total revenue of \$20 (= \$30 − \$10).

The analysis is reversible: If demand is elastic, a price increase will reduce total revenue. The revenue gained on the higher-priced units will be more than offset by the revenue lost from the lower quantity sold. Bottom line: Other things equal, when price and total revenue move in opposite directions, demand is elastic. E_d is greater than 1, meaning the percentage change in quantity demanded is greater than the percentage change in price.

Inelastic Demand If demand is inelastic, a price decrease will reduce total revenue. The increase in sales will not fully offset the decline in revenue per unit, and total revenue will decline. To see this, look at demand curve D_2 in Figure 6.2b. At point *c* on the curve, price is \$4 and quantity demanded is 10. Thus total revenue is \$40, shown by the combined gold and orange rectangle. If the price drops to \$1 (point *d*), total revenue declines to \$20, which obviously is less than \$40. Total revenue has declined because the loss of revenue (the gold area) from the lower unit price is larger than the gain in revenue (the brown area) from the accompanying increase in sales. Price has fallen, and total revenue has also declined.

W 6.2

Total-revenue test

Our analysis is again reversible: If demand is inelastic, a price increase will increase total revenue. So, other things equal, when price and total revenue move in the same direction, demand is inelastic. E_d is less than 1, meaning the percentage change in quantity demanded is less than the percentage change in price.

Unit Elasticity In the special case of unit elasticity, an increase or a decrease in price leaves total revenue unchanged. The loss in revenue from a lower unit price is exactly offset by the gain in revenue from the accompanying increase in sales. Conversely, the gain in revenue from a higher unit price is exactly offset by the revenue loss associated with the accompanying decline in the amount demanded.

In Figure 6.2c (demand curve D_3) we find that at the price of \$3, 10 units will be sold, yielding total revenue of \$30. At the lower \$1 price, a total of 30 units will be sold, again resulting in \$30 of total revenue. The \$2 price reduction causes the loss of revenue shown by the gold area, but this is exactly offset by the revenue gain shown by the brown area. Total revenue does not change. In fact, that would be true for all price changes along this particular curve.

Other things equal, when price changes and total revenue remains constant, demand is unit-elastic (or unitary). E_d is 1, meaning the percentage change in quantity equals the percentage change in price.

Price Elasticity along a Linear Demand Curve Now a major confession! Although the demand curves depicted in Figure 6.2 nicely illustrate the total-revenue test for elasticity, two of the graphs involve specific movements along linear (straight-line) demand curves. That presents no problem for explaining the total-revenue test. However, you need to know that elasticity typically varies over the different price ranges of the same demand curve. (The exception is the curve in Figure 6.2c. Elasticity is 1 along the entire curve.)

Table 6.1 and Figure 6.3 demonstrate that elasticity typically varies over the different price ranges of the same demand schedule or curve. We use the hypothetical data for movie tickets in columns 1 and 2 of Table 6.1 to plot the demand curve D in Figure 6.3a. For all downsloping straight-line and most other demand curves, demand is more price-elastic toward the upper left (the \$5–\$8 price range of D) than toward the lower right (the \$4–\$1 price range of D).

This is the consequence of the arithmetic properties of the elasticity measure. Specifically, in the upper left segment of the demand curve, the percentage change in quantity is large because the original reference quantity is small. Similarly, the percentage change in price is small in that segment because the original reference price is large. The relatively large percentage change in quantity divided by the relatively small change in price yields a large E_d—an elastic demand.

G 6.1

Elasticity and revenue

The reverse holds true for the lower right segment of the demand curve. Here the percentage change in quantity is small because the original reference quantity is large; similarly, the percentage change in price is large because the original reference price is small. The relatively small percentage change in quantity divided by the relatively large percentage change in price results in a small E_d—an inelastic demand.

TABLE 6.1 Price Elasticity of Demand for Movie Tickets as Measured by the Elasticity Coefficient and the Total-Revenue Test

(1) Total Quantity of Tickets Demanded per Week, Thousands	(2) Price per Ticket	(3) Elasticity Coefficient (E_d)	(4) Total Revenue, (1) × (2)	(5) Total-Revenue Test
1	\$8		\$ 8000	
		5.00		Elastic
2	7		14,000	
		2.60		Elastic
3	6		18,000	
		1.57		Elastic
4	5		20,000	
		1.00		Unit elastic
5	4		20,000	
		0.64		Inelastic
6	3		18,000	
		0.38		Inelastic
7	2		14,000	
		0.20		Inelastic
8	1		8000	

FIGURE 6.3 The relation between price elasticity of demand for movie tickets and total revenue. Demand curve *D* in (a) is based on Table 6.1 and is marked to show that the hypothetical weekly demand for movie tickets is elastic at higher price ranges and inelastic at lower price ranges. The total-revenue curve TR in (b) is derived from demand curve *D*. When price falls and TR increases, demand is elastic; when price falls and TR is unchanged, demand is unit-elastic; and when price falls and TR declines, demand is inelastic.

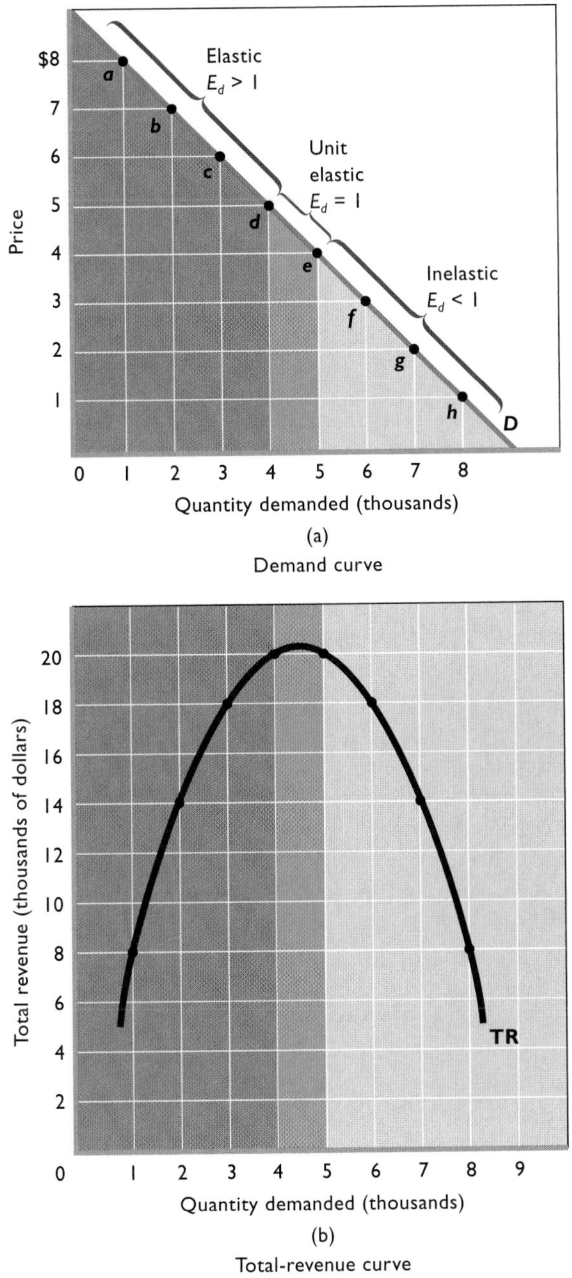

The demand curve in Figure 6.3a also illustrates that the slope of a demand curve—its flatness or steepness—is not a sound basis for judging elasticity. The catch is that the slope of the curve is computed from *absolute* changes in price and quantity, while elasticity involves *relative* or *percentage* changes in price and quantity. The demand curve in Figure 6.3a is linear, which by definition means that the slope is constant throughout. But we have demonstrated that such a curve is elastic in its high-price ($8–$5) range and inelastic in its low-price ($4–$1) range. **(Key Question 2)**

Price Elasticity and the Total-Revenue Curve

In Figure 6.3b we graphed the total revenue per week to the theater owner that corresponds to each price-quantity combination indicated along demand curve *D* in Figure 6.3a. The price–quantity-demanded combination represented by point *a* on the demand curve yields total revenue of $8000 (= $8×1000 tickets). In Figure 6.3b, we graphed this $8000 amount vertically at 1 unit (1000 tickets) demanded. Similarly, the price–quantity-demanded combination represented by point *b* in the upper panel yields total revenue of $14,000 (= $7×2000 tickets). This amount is graphed vertically at 2 units (2000 tickets) demanded in the lower panel. The ultimate result of such graphing is total-revenue curve TR, which first slopes upward, then reaches a maximum, and finally turns downward.

Comparison of curves *D* and TR sharply focuses the relationship between elasticity and total revenue. Lowering the ticket price in the elastic range of demand—for example, from $8 to $5—increases total revenue. Conversely, increasing the ticket price in that range reduces total revenue. In both cases, price and total revenue change in opposite directions, confirming that demand is elastic.

The $5 – $4 price range of demand curve *D* reflects unit elasticity. When price either decreases from $5 to $4 or increases from $4 to $5, total revenue remains $20,000. In both cases, price has changed and total revenue has remained constant, confirming that demand is unit-elastic when we consider these particular price changes.

In the inelastic range of demand curve *D*, lowering the price—for example, from $4 to $1—decreases total revenue, as shown in Figure 6.3b. Raising the price boosts total revenue. In both cases, price and total revenue move in the same direction, confirming that demand is inelastic.

Table 6.2 summarizes the characteristics of price elasticity of demand. You should review it carefully. **(Key Question 4)**

Determinants of Price Elasticity of Demand

We cannot say just what will determine the price elasticity of demand in each individual situation. However, the following generalizations are often helpful.

TABLE 6.2 Price Elasticity of Demand: A Summary

Absolute Value of Elasticity Coefficient	Demand Is:	Description	Impact on Total Revenue of a: Price Increase	Price Decrease
Greater than 1 ($E_d > 1$)	Elastic or relatively elastic	Quantity demanded changes by a larger percentage than does price	Total revenue decreases	Total revenue increases
Equal to 1 ($E_d = 1$)	Unit or unitary elastic	Quantity demanded changes by the same percentage as does price	Total revenue is unchanged	Total revenue is unchanged
Less than 1 ($E_d < 1$)	Inelastic or relatively inelastic	Quantity demanded changes by a smaller percentage than does price	Total revenue increases	Total revenue decreases

Substitutability Generally, the larger the number of substitute goods that are available, the greater the price elasticity of demand. Various brands of candy bars are generally substitutable for one another, making the demand for one brand of candy bar, say Snickers, highly elastic. Toward the other extreme, the demand for tooth repair (or tooth pulling) is quite inelastic because there simply are no close substitutes when those procedures are required.

The elasticity of demand for a product depends on how narrowly the product is defined. Demand for Reebok sneakers is more elastic than is the overall demand for shoes. Many other brands are readily substitutable for Reebok sneakers, but there are few, if any, good substitutes for shoes.

Proportion of Income Other things equal, the higher the price of a good relative to consumers' incomes, the greater the price elasticity of demand. A 10 percent increase in the price of low-priced pencils or chewing gum amounts to a few more pennies relative to one's income, and quantity demanded will probably decline only slightly. Thus, price elasticity for such low-priced items tends to be low. But a 10 percent increase in the price of relatively high-priced automobiles or housing means additional expenditures of perhaps \$3000 or \$20,000, respectively. These price increases are significant fractions of the annual incomes and budgets of most families, and quantities demanded will likely diminish significantly. Price elasticity for such items tends to be high.

Luxuries versus Necessities In general, the more that a good is considered to be a "luxury" rather than a "necessity," the greater is the price elasticity of demand. Electricity is generally regarded as a necessity; it is difficult to get along without it. A price increase will not significantly reduce the amount of lighting and power used in a household. (Note the very low price-elasticity coefficient of this good in Table 6.3.) An extreme case: A person does not decline an operation for acute appendicitis because the physician's fee has just gone up.

On the other hand, vacation travel and jewelry are luxuries, which, by definition, can easily be forgone. If the prices of vacation travel and jewelry rise, a consumer need not buy them and will suffer no great hardship without them.

What about the demand for a common product like salt? It is highly inelastic on three counts: Few good substitutes are available; salt is a negligible item in the family budget; and it is a "necessity" rather than a luxury.

Time Generally, product demand is more elastic the longer the time period under consideration. Consumers often need time to adjust to changes in prices. For example, when the price of a product rises, time is needed to find and experiment with other products to see if they are acceptable. Consumers may not immediately reduce their purchases very much when the price of beef rises by 10 percent, but in time they may shift to chicken, pork, or fish.

Another consideration is product durability. Studies show that "short-run" demand for gasoline is more inelastic ($E_d = .2$) than is "long-run" demand ($E_d = .7$). In the short run, people are "stuck" with their present cars and trucks, but with rising gasoline prices they eventually replace them with smaller, more fuel-efficient vehicles. They also switch to mass transit where it is available.

Table 6.3 shows estimated price-elasticity coefficients for a number of products. Each reflects some combination of the elasticity determinants just discussed. **(Key Question 5)** LEAD TIME

Applications of Price Elasticity of Demand

The concept of price elasticity of demand has great practical significance, as the following examples suggest.

Large Crop Yields The demand for most farm products is highly inelastic; E_d is perhaps .20 or .25. As a result, increases in the output of farm products arising from a good growing season or from increased productivity tend to depress both the prices of farm products and

TABLE 6.3 Selected Price Elasticities of Demand

Product or Service	Coefficient of Price Elasticity of Demand (E_d)	Product or Service	Coefficient of Price Elasticity of Demand (E_d)
Newspapers	.10	Milk	.63
Electricity (household)	.13	Household appliances	.63
Bread	.15	Movies	.87
Major league baseball tickets	.23	Beer	.90
Telephone service	.26	Shoes	.91
Sugar	.30	Motor vehicles	1.14
Medical care	.31	Beef	1.27
Eggs	.32	China, glassware, tableware	1.54
Legal services	.37	Residential land	1.60
Automobile repair	.40	Restaurant meals	2.27
Clothing	.49	Lamb and mutton	2.65
Gasoline	.60	Fresh peas	2.83

Source: Compiled from numerous studies and sources reporting price elasticity of demand.

the total revenues (incomes) of farmers. For farmers as a group, the inelastic demand for their products means that large crop yields may be undesirable. For policymakers it means that achieving the goal of higher total farm income requires that farm output be restricted.

Excise Taxes The government pays attention to elasticity of demand when it selects goods and services on which to levy excise taxes. If a $1 tax is levied on a product and 10,000 units are sold, tax revenue will be $10,000 (= $1 × 10,000 units sold). If the government raises the tax to $1.50 but the higher price that results reduces sales to 4000 because of elastic demand, tax revenue will decline to $6000 (= $1.50 × 4000 units sold). Because a higher tax on a product with elastic demand will bring in less tax revenue, legislatures tend to seek out products that have inelastic demand—such as liquor, gasoline, and cigarettes—when levying excises. In fact, the Federal government, in its effort to reduce the budget deficit, increased taxes on those very categories of goods in 1991.

Decriminalization of Illegal Drugs In recent years proposals to legalize drugs have been widely debated. Proponents contend that drugs should be treated like alcohol; they should be made legal for adults and regulated for purity and potency. The current war on drugs, it is argued, has been unsuccessful, and the associated costs—including enlarged police forces, the construction of more prisons, an overburdened court system, and untold human costs—have increased markedly. Legalization would allegedly reduce drug trafficking significantly by taking the profit out of it. Crack cocaine and heroin, for example, are cheap to produce and could be sold at low prices in legal markets. Because the demand of addicts is highly inelastic, the amounts consumed at the lower prices would increase only modestly. Addicts' total expenditures for cocaine and heroin would decline, and so would the street crime that finances those expenditures.

Opponents of legalization say that the overall demand for cocaine and heroin is far more elastic than proponents think. In addition to the inelastic demand of addicts, there is another market segment whose demand is relatively elastic. This segment consists of the occasional users or "dabblers," who use hard drugs when their prices are low but who abstain or substitute, say, alcohol when their prices are high. Thus, the lower prices associated with the legalization of hard drugs would increase consumption by dabblers. Also, removal of the legal prohibitions against using drugs might make drug use more socially acceptable, increasing the demand for cocaine and heroin.

Many economists predict that the legalization of cocaine and heroin would reduce street prices by up to 60 percent, depending on if and how much they were taxed. According to an important study, price declines of that size would increase the number of occasional users of heroin by 54 percent and the number of occasional users of cocaine by 33 percent. The total quantity of heroin demanded would rise by an estimated 100 percent, and the quantity of cocaine demanded would rise by 50 percent.[1] Moreover, many existing and first-time dabblers might in

[1]Henry Saffer and Frank Chaloupka, "The Demand for Illegal Drugs," *Economic Inquiry*, July 1999, pp. 401–411.

time become addicts. The overall result, say the opponents of legalization, would be higher social costs, possibly including an increase in street crime.

QUICK REVIEW 6.1

- The price elasticity of demand coefficient E_d is the ratio of the percentage change in quantity demanded to the percentage change in price. The *averages* of the two prices and two quantities are used as the base references in calculating the percentage changes.
- When E_d is greater than 1, demand is elastic; when E_d is less than 1, demand is inelastic; when E_d is equal to 1, demand is of unit elasticity.
- When price changes, total revenue will change in the opposite direction if demand is price-elastic, in the same direction if demand is price-inelastic, and not at all if demand is unit-elastic.
- Demand is typically elastic in the high-price (low-quantity) range of the demand curve and inelastic in the low-price (high-quantity) range of the curve.
- Price elasticity of demand is greater (a) the larger the number of substitutes available; (b) the higher the price of a product relative to one's budget; (c) the greater the extent to which the product is a luxury; and (d) the longer the time period involved.

Price Elasticity of Supply

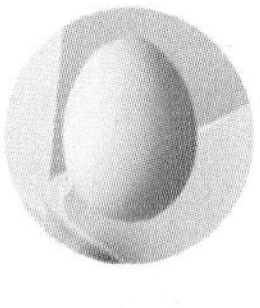

O 6.2
Price elasticity of supply

The concept of price elasticity also applies to supply. If producers are relatively responsive to price changes, supply is elastic. If they are relatively insensitive to price changes, supply is inelastic.

We measure the degree of price elasticity or inelasticity of supply with the coefficient E_s, defined almost like E_d except that we substitute "percentage change in quantity supplied" for "percentage change in quantity demanded":

$$E_s = \frac{\text{percentage change in quantity supplied of product X}}{\text{percentage change in price of product X}}$$

For reasons explained earlier, the averages, or midpoints, of the before and after quantities supplied and the before and after prices are used as reference points for the percentage changes. Suppose an increase in the price of a good from \$4 to \$6 increases the quantity supplied from 10 units to 14 units. The percentage change in price would be $\frac{2}{5}$, or 40 percent, and the percentage change in quantity would be $\frac{4}{12}$, or 33 percent:

$$E_s = \frac{.33}{.40} = .83$$

In this case, supply is inelastic, since the price-elasticity coefficient is less than 1. If E_s is greater than 1, supply is elastic. If it is equal to 1, supply is unit-elastic. Also, E_s is never negative, since price and quantity supplied are directly related. Thus, there are no minus signs to drop, as was necessary with elasticity of demand.

The degree of **price elasticity of supply** depends on how easily—and therefore quickly—producers can shift resources between alternative uses. The easier and more rapidly producers can shift resources between alternative uses, the greater the price elasticity of supply. Take the case of Christmas trees. A firm's response to, say, an increase in the price of trees depends on its ability to shift resources from the production of other products (whose prices we assume remain constant) to the production of trees. And shifting resources takes time: The longer the time, the greater the resource "shiftability." So we can expect a greater response, and therefore greater elasticity of supply, the longer a firm has to adjust to a price change.

In analyzing the impact of time on elasticity, economists distinguish among the immediate market period, the short run, and the long run.

Price Elasticity of Supply: The Market Period

The **market period** is the period that occurs when the time immediately after a change in market price is too short for producers to respond with a change in quantity supplied. Suppose the owner of a small farm brings to market one truckload of tomatoes that is the entire season's output. The supply curve for the tomatoes is perfectly inelastic (vertical); the farmer will sell the truckload whether the price is high or low. Why? Because the farmer can offer only one truckload of tomatoes even if the price of tomatoes is much higher than anticipated. He or she might like to offer more tomatoes, but tomatoes cannot be produced overnight. Another full growing season is needed to respond to a higher-than-expected price by producing more than one truckload. Similarly, because the product is perishable, the farmer cannot withhold it from the market. If the price is lower than anticipated, he or she will still sell the entire truckload.

The farmer's costs of production, incidentally, will not enter into this decision to sell. Though the price of tomatoes may fall far short of production costs, the farmer will nevertheless sell out to avoid a total loss through spoilage. During the market period, our farmer's supply of tomatoes

FIGURE 6.4 Time and the elasticity of supply. The greater the amount of time producers have to adjust to a change in demand, here from D_1 to D_2, the greater will be their output response. In the immediate market period (a) there is insufficient time to change output, and so supply is perfectly inelastic. In the short run (b) plant capacity is fixed, but changing the intensity of its use can alter output; supply is therefore more elastic. In the long run (c) all desired adjustments, including changes in plant capacity, can be made, and supply becomes still more elastic.

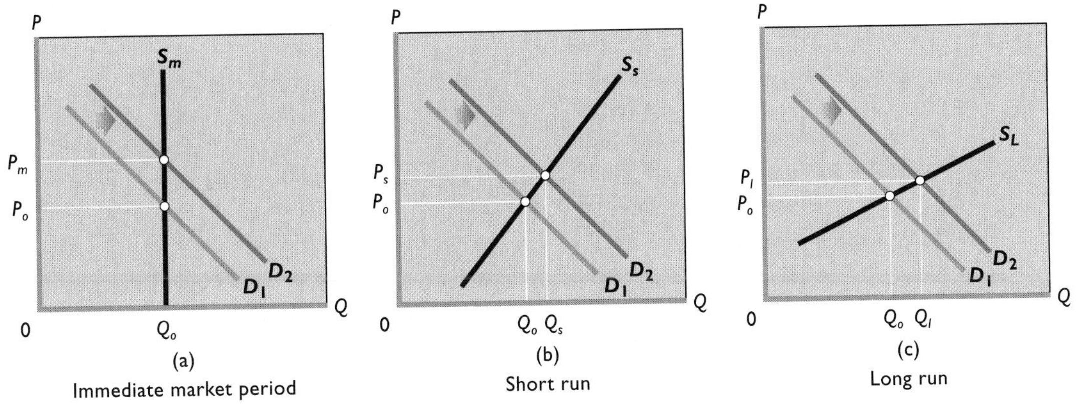

is fixed: Only one truckload is offered no matter how high or low the price.

Figure 6.4a shows the farmer's vertical supply curve during the market period. Supply is perfectly inelastic because the farmer does not have time to respond to a change in demand, say, from D_1 to D_2. The resulting price increase from P_0 to P_m simply determines which buyers get the fixed quantity supplied; it elicits no increase in output.

However, not all supply curves need be perfectly inelastic immediately after a price change. If the product is not perishable and the price rises, producers may choose to increase quantity supplied by drawing down their inventories of unsold, stored goods. This will cause the market supply curve to attain some positive slope. For our tomato farmer, the market period may be a full growing season; for producers of goods that can be inexpensively stored, there may be no market period at all.

Price Elasticity of Supply: The Short Run

The **short run** in microeconomics is a period of time too short to change plant capacity but long enough to use fixed plant more or less intensively. In the short run, our farmer's plant (land and farm machinery) is fixed. But he does have time in the short run to cultivate tomatoes more intensively by applying more labor and more fertilizer and pesticides to the crop. The result is a somewhat greater output in response to a presumed increase in demand; this greater output is reflected in a more elastic supply of tomatoes, as shown by S_s in Figure 6.4b. Note now that the increase in demand from D_1 to D_2 is met by an increase in quantity (from Q_0 to Q_s), so there is a smaller price adjustment (from P_0 to P_s) than would be the case in the market period. The equilibrium price is therefore lower in the short run than in the market period.

Price Elasticity of Supply: The Long Run

The **long run** in microeconomics is a time period long enough for firms to adjust their plant sizes and for new firms to enter (or existing firms to leave) the industry. In the "tomato industry," for example, our farmer has time to acquire additional land and buy more machinery and equipment. Furthermore, other farmers may, over time, be attracted to tomato farming by the increased demand and higher price. Such adjustments create a larger supply response, as represented by the more elastic supply curve S_L in Figure 6.4c. The outcome is a smaller price rise (P_0 to P_1) and a larger output increase (Q_0 to Q_1) in response to the increase in demand from D_1 to D_2.

There is no total-revenue test for elasticity of supply. Supply shows a positive or direct relationship between price and amount supplied; the supply curve is upsloping. Regardless of the degree of elasticity or inelasticity, price and total revenue always move together. **(Key Question 8)**

Applications of Price Elasticity of Supply

The idea of price elasticity of supply has widespread applicability, as suggested by the following examples.

Antiques and Reproductions The *Antiques Road Show* is a popular PBS television program in which people bring antiques to a central location for appraisal by experts. Some people are pleased to learn that their old piece of furniture or funky folk art is worth a large amount, say, $30,000 or more.

The high price of an antique results from strong demand and limited, highly inelastic supply. Because a genuine antique can no longer be reproduced, its quantity supplied either does not rise or rises only slightly as its price goes up. The higher price might prompt the discovery of a few more of the remaining originals and thus add to the quantity available for sale, but this quantity response is usually quite small. So the supply of antiques and other collectibles tends to be inelastic. For one-of-a-kind antiques, the supply is perfectly inelastic.

Factors such as increased population, higher income, and greater enthusiasm for collecting antiques have increased the demand for antiques over time. Because the supply of antiques is limited and inelastic, those increases in demand have greatly boosted the prices of antiques.

Contrast the inelastic supply of original antiques with the elastic supply of modern "made-to-look-old" reproductions. Such faux antiques are quite popular and widely available at furniture stores and knickknack shops. When the demand for reproductions increases, the firms making them simply boost production. Because the supply of reproductions is highly elastic, increased demand raises their prices only slightly.

Volatile Gold Prices The price of gold is quite volatile, sometimes shooting upward one period and plummeting downward the next. The main sources of these fluctuations are shifts in demand and highly inelastic supply. Gold production is a costly and time-consuming process of exploration, mining, and refining. Moreover, the physical availability of gold is highly limited. For both reasons, increases in gold prices do not elicit substantial increases in quantity supplied. Conversely, gold mining is costly to shut down and existing gold bars are expensive to store. Price decreases therefore do not produce large drops in the quantity of gold supplied. In short, the supply of gold is inelastic.

The demand for gold is partly derived from the demand for its uses, such as for jewelry, dental fillings, and coins. But people also demand gold as a speculative financial investment. They increase their demand for gold when they fear general inflation or domestic or international turmoil that might undermine the value of currency and more traditional investments. They reduce their demand when events settle down. Because of the inelastic supply of gold, even relatively small changes in demand produce relatively large changes in price. (Web-based question 1 at the end of the chapter provides you with a route for finding the current price of gold.)

Cross Elasticity and Income Elasticity of Demand

Price elasticities measure the responsiveness of the quantity of a product demanded or supplied when its price changes. The consumption of a good also is affected by a change in the price of a related product or by a change in income.

Cross Elasticity of Demand

The **cross elasticity of demand** measures how sensitive consumer purchases of one product (say, X) are to a change in the price of some other product (say, Y). We calculate the coefficient of cross elasticity of demand E_{xy} just as we do the coefficient of simple price elasticity, except that we relate the percentage change in the consumption of X to the percentage change in the price of Y:

$$E_{xy} = \frac{\text{percentage change in quantity demanded of product X}}{\text{percentage change in price of product Y}}$$

This cross-elasticity (or cross-price-elasticity) concept allows us to quantify and more fully understand substitute and complementary goods, introduced in Chapter 3.

Substitute Goods If cross elasticity of demand is positive, meaning that sales of X move in the same direction as a change in the price of Y, then X and Y are substitute goods. An example is Evian water (X) and Dasani (Y). An increase in the price of Evian causes consumers to buy more Dasani, resulting in a positive cross elasticity. The larger the positive cross-elasticity coefficient, the greater is the substitutability between the two products.

Complementary Goods When cross elasticity is negative, we know that X and Y "go together"; an increase in the price of one decreases the demand for the other. So the two are complementary goods. For example, an increase in the price of digital cameras will decrease the amount of memory sticks purchased. The larger the negative cross-elasticity coefficient, the greater is the complementarity between the two goods.

Independent Goods A zero or near-zero cross elasticity suggests that the two products being considered are unrelated or independent goods. An example is walnuts and plums: We would not expect a change in the price of walnuts to have any effect on purchases of plums, and vice versa.

Application The degree of substitutability of products, measured by the cross-elasticity coefficient, is important to businesses and government. For example, suppose that Coca-Cola is considering whether or not to lower the price of its Sprite brand. Not only will it want to know something about the price elasticity of demand for Sprite (will the price cut increase or decrease total revenue?), but it will also be interested in knowing if the increased sales of Sprite will come at the expense of its Coke brand. How sensitive are the sales of one of its products (Coke) to a change in the price of another of its products (Sprite)? By how much will the increased sales of Sprite "cannibalize" the sales of Coke? A low cross elasticity would indicate that Coke and Sprite are weak substitutes for each other and that a lower price for Sprite would have little effect on Coke sales.

Government also implicitly uses the idea of cross elasticity of demand in assessing whether a proposed merger between two large firms will substantially reduce competition and therefore violate the antitrust laws. For example, the cross elasticity between Coke and Pepsi is high, making them strong substitutes for each other. Consequently, the government would likely block a merger between them because the merger would lessen competition. In contrast, the cross elasticity between cola and gasoline is low or zero. A merger between Coke and Shell would have a minimal effect on competition. So government would let that merger happen. **(Key Question 9)**

Income Elasticity of Demand

Income elasticity of demand measures the degree to which consumers respond to a change in their incomes by buying more or less of a particular good. The coefficient of income elasticity of demand E_i is determined with the formula

$$E_i = \frac{\text{percentage change in quantity demanded}}{\text{percentage change in income}}$$

Normal Goods For most goods, the income-elasticity coefficient E_i is positive, meaning that more of them are demanded as incomes rise. Such goods are called normal or superior goods, which we first described in Chapter 3. But the value of E_i varies greatly among normal goods. For example, income elasticity of demand for automobiles is about +3, while income elasticity for most farm products is only about +.20.

Inferior Goods A negative income-elasticity coefficient designates an inferior good. Retread tires, cabbage, long-distance bus tickets, used clothing, and muscatel wine are likely candidates. Consumers decrease their purchases of inferior goods as incomes rise.

Insights Coefficients of income elasticity of demand provide insights into the economy. For example, income elasticity helps explain the expansion and contraction of industries in the United States. On average, total income in the economy has grown 2 to 3 percent annually. As income has expanded, industries producing products for which demand is quite income-elastic have expanded their outputs. Thus automobiles (E_i = +3), housing (E_i = +1.5), books (E_i = +1.4), and restaurant meals (E_i = +1.4) have all experienced strong growth of output. Meanwhile, industries producing products for which income elasticity is low or negative have tended to grow less rapidly or to decline. For example, agriculture (E_i = +.20) has grown far more slowly than has the economy's total output. We do not eat twice as much when our income doubles.

As another example, when recessions occur and people's incomes decline, grocery stores fare relatively better than stores selling electronic equipment. People do not substantially cut back on their purchases of food when their incomes fall; income elasticity of demand for food is relatively low. But they do substantially cut back on their purchases of electronic equipment; income elasticity on such equipment is relatively high. **(Key Question 10)**

In Table 6.4 we provide a convenient synopsis of the cross-elasticity and income-elasticity concepts.

TABLE 6.4 Cross and Income Elasticities of Demand

Value of Coefficient	Description	Type of Good(s)
Cross elasticity:		
Positive ($E_{wz} > 0$)	Quantity demanded of W changes in same direction as change in price of Z	Substitutes
Negative ($E_{xy} < 0$)	Quantity demanded of X changes in opposite direction from change in price of Y	Complements
Income elasticity:		
Positive ($E_i > 0$)	Quantity demanded of the product changes in same direction as change in income	Normal or superior
Negative ($E_i < 0$)	Quantity demanded of the product changes in opposite direction from change in income	Inferior

QUICK REVIEW 6.2

- Price elasticity of supply measures the sensitivity of suppliers to changes in the price of a product. The price-elasticity-of-supply coefficient E_s is the ratio of the percentage change in quantity supplied to the percentage change in price. The elasticity of supply varies directly with the amount of time producers have to respond to the price change.
- The cross-elasticity-of-demand coefficient E_{xy} is computed as the percentage change in the quantity demanded of product X divided by the percentage change in the price of product Y. If the cross-elasticity coefficient is positive, the two products are substitutes; if negative, they are complements.
- The income-elasticity coefficient E_i is computed as the percentage change in quantity demanded divided by the percentage change in income. A positive coefficient indicates a normal or superior good. The coefficient is negative for an inferior good.

Consumer and Producer Surplus

Our final goal for this chapter is to examine the following reality: Consumers and producers obtain "benefit surpluses" through market transactions. These surpluses vary in size among the separate buyers and sellers.

Consumer Surplus

The benefit surplus received by a consumer or consumers in a market is called **consumer surplus**—the difference between the maximum price a consumer is (or consumers are) willing to pay for a product and the actual price. In nearly all markets, consumers individually and collectively gain greater total utility in dollar terms (total satisfaction) from their purchases than the amount of their expenditures (= product price × quantity). This utility surplus arises because all consumers pay the equilibrium price even though many would be willing to pay more than that price to obtain the product.

Consider Figure 6.5, where we assume the equilibrium price, P_1, of oranges is \$8 per bag. The portion of the demand curve *D* lying above the \$8 equilibrium price shows that many consumers of oranges would be willing to pay more than \$8 per bag rather than go without oranges.

See Table 6.5, for example, where column 2 reveals that Bob is willing to pay a maximum of \$13 for a bag of oranges; Barb, \$12; Bill, \$11; Bart, \$10; and Brent, \$9. Betty, in contrast, is willing to pay only the \$8 equilibrium price. Because all six buyers listed obtain the oranges for the \$8 equilibrium price (column 3), five of them obtain a consumer surplus. Column 4 shows that Bob receives a consumer surplus of \$5 (= \$13 − \$8); Barb, \$4 (= \$12 − \$8); Bill, \$3 (= \$11 − \$8); Bart, \$2 (= \$10 − \$8); and Brent, \$1 (= \$9 − \$8). Only Betty receives no consumer surplus because her maximum willingness to pay \$8 matches the \$8 equilibrium price.

FIGURE 6.5 Consumer surplus. Consumer surplus—shown as the green triangle—reflects the differences between the maximum prices consumers are willing to pay for a product and the lower equilibrium price, here assumed to be \$8. For quantity Q_1, consumers are willing to pay the sum of the amounts represented by the green triangle and the tan rectangle. Because they need only the amount shown as the tan rectangle, the green triangle reflects consumer surplus.

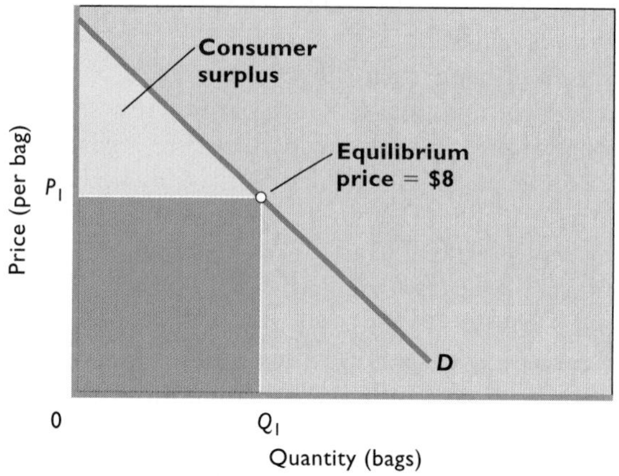

Obviously, most markets have more than six people. Suppose there are many other consumers besides Bob, Barb, Bill, Bart, Brent, and Betty in the market represented by Figure 6.5. It is reasonable to assume that many of these additional people are willing to pay more than \$8 for a bag of oranges. By adding together the individual consumer surpluses obtained by our named and unnamed buyers, we obtain the collective consumer surplus in this specific market. To obtain the Q_1 bags of oranges represented, consumers collectively are willing to pay the total amount shown by the sum of the green triangle and tan rectangle under the demand curve and to the left of Q_1. But consumers need pay only the amount represented by the tan rectangle (= $P_1 \times Q_1$). So the green triangle is the

TABLE 6.5 Consumer Surplus

(1) Person	(2) Maximum Price Willing to Pay	(3) Actual Price (Equilibrium Price)	(4) Consumer Surplus
Bob	\$13	\$8	\$5 (= \$13 − \$8)
Barb	12	8	4 (= \$12 − \$8)
Bill	11	8	3 (= \$11 − \$8)
Bart	10	8	2 (= \$10 − \$8)
Brent	9	8	1 (= \$9 − \$8)
Betty	8	8	0 (= \$8 − \$8)

consumer surplus in this market. It is the sum of the vertical distances between the demand curve and the $8 equilibrium price at each quantity up to Q_1. Alternatively, it is the sum of the gaps between maximum willingness to pay and actual price, such as those we calculated in Table 6.5.

Consumer surplus and price are inversely (negatively) related. Given the demand curve, higher prices reduce consumer surplus; lower prices increase it. To test this, draw in an equilibrium price above $8 in Figure 6.5 and observe the reduced size of the triangle representing consumer surplus. When price rises, the gap narrows between the maximum willingness to pay and the actual price. Next, draw in an equilibrium price below $8 and see that consumer surplus increases. When price falls, the gap widens between maximum willingness to pay and actual price.

O 6.3
Consumer surplus

Producer Surplus

Like consumers, producers also receive a benefit surplus in markets. This **producer surplus** is the difference between the actual price a producer receives (or producers receive) and the minimum acceptable price. Sellers collectively receive a producer surplus in most markets because most sellers are willing to accept a lower-than-equilibrium price if that is required in order to sell the product. That lower acceptable price is shown by the portion of the supply curve in Figure 6.6 lying to the left of and below the assumed $8 equilibrium price.

FIGURE 6.6 Producer surplus. Producer surplus—shown as the orange triangle—reflects the differences between the minimum payments producers are willing to accept for a product and the higher equilibrium price they receive, here assumed to be $8. For quantity Q_1, producers receive the sum of the amounts represented by the orange triangle plus the tan triangle. Because they need receive only the amount shown by the tan triangle, the orange triangle reflects producer surplus.

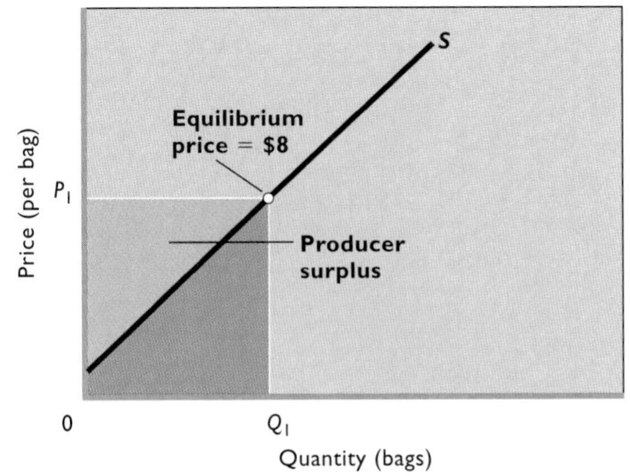

TABLE 6.6 Producer Surplus

(1) Person	(2) Minimum Acceptable Price	(3) Actual Price (Equilibrium Price)	(4) Producer Surplus
Carlos	$3	$8	$5 (= $8 − $3)
Courtney	4	8	4 (= $8 − $4)
Chuck	5	8	3 (= $8 − $5)
Cindy	6	8	2 (= $8 − $6)
Craig	7	8	1 (= $8 − $7)
Chad	8	8	0 (= $8 − $8)

Suppose that Carlos, Courtney, Chuck, Cindy, Craig, and Chad are six of the many sellers of oranges in the market. Due to differences in production costs, suppose that Carlos' minimum acceptable payment for a bag of oranges is $3, as shown in column 2 of Table 6.6, whereas Courtney's minimum acceptable payment is $4, Chuck's is $5, Cindy's is $6, Craig's is $7, and Chad's is $8. But each seller receives as payment the equilibrium price of $8. As shown in column 4, Carlos thus obtains a producer surplus of $5 (= $8 − $3); Courtney, $4 (= $8 − $4); Chuck, $3 (= $8 − $5); Cindy, $2 (= $8 − $6); Craig, $1 (= $8 − $7); and Chad, zero (= $8 − $8).

By summing the producer surpluses of these sellers along with those of other sellers, we obtain the producer surplus for the entire market for oranges. In Figure 6.6, producers collect revenues of $P_1 \times Q_1$, which is the sum of the orange triangle and the tan triangle. As shown by the supply curve, however, revenues of only those illustrated by the tan triangle would be required to entice producers to offer Q_1 bags of oranges for sale. The sellers therefore receive a producer surplus shown by the orange triangle. That surplus is the sum of the vertical distances between the supply curve and the $8 equilibrium price at each of the quantities to the left of Q_1.

There is a direct (positive) relationship between equilibrium price and the amount of producer surplus. Given the supply curve, lower prices reduce producer surplus; higher prices increase it. If you pencil in a lower equilibrium price than $8, you will see that the producer surplus triangle gets smaller. The gaps between the minimum acceptable payments and the actual prices narrow when the price falls. If you pencil in an equilibrium price above $8, the size of the producer surplus triangle increases. The gaps between minimum acceptable payments and actual prices widen when the price increases.

W 6.3
Consumer and producer surplus

FIGURE 6.7 Efficiency: maximum combined consumer and producer surplus. At quantity Q_1 the combined amount of consumer surplus, shown as the green triangle, and producer surplus, shown as the orange triangle, is maximized. Efficiency occurs because, at Q_1, maximum willingness to pay, reflected by the points on the demand curve, equals minimum acceptable price, reflected by the points on the supply curve.

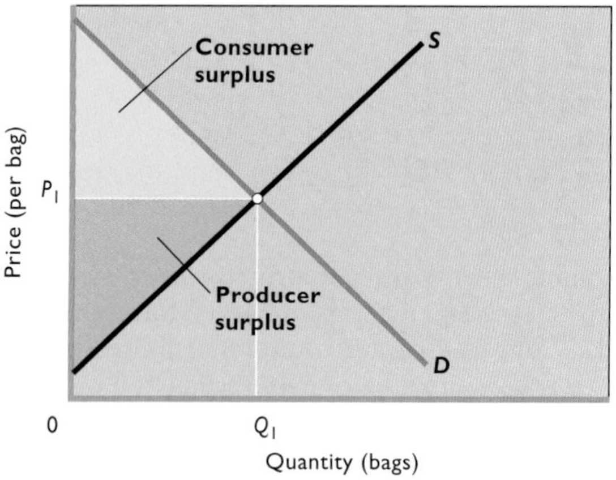

Efficiency Revisited

In Figure 6.7 we bring together the demand and supply curves of Figures 6.5 and 6.6 to show the equilibrium price and quantity and the previously described regions of consumer and producer surplus. All markets that have downward-sloping demand curves and upward-sloping supply curves yield consumer and producer surplus.

The equilibrium quantity in Figure 6.7 reflects economic efficiency. *Productive efficiency* is achieved because competition forces producers to use the best techniques and combinations of resources in growing and selling oranges. Production costs of each level of output are minimized. *Allocative efficiency* is achieved because the correct quantity of output—Q_1—is produced relative to other goods and services. Points on the demand curve in Figure 6.7 measure the marginal benefit (MB) of oranges at each level of output. Points on the supply curve measure the marginal cost (MC) of oranges at each output level. The demand and supply curves intersect at the equilibrium output Q_1, indicating that MB = MC. (For the significance of the MB = MC equality for efficiency, review the discussion relating to Figure 1.3).

Our analysis of consumer and producer surplus provides another way of thinking about efficiency. Each point on a demand curve identifies not only the marginal benefit of the corresponding unit of output but also the *maximum willingness to pay* for it. Willingness to pay derives from the benefit that a product provides. Similarly, each point on the supply curve identifies not only the marginal cost of a good but also the *minimum acceptable price* for the good. To stay profitable, sellers must receive minimum prices that "cover" their marginal costs.

In Figure 6.7 the maximum willingness to pay for each bag of oranges up to Q_1 exceeds the corresponding minimum acceptable price. So each of these bags adds a positive amount (= maximum willingness to pay *minus* minimum acceptable price) to the *total* of consumer and producer surplus. Only at the equilibrium price Q_1, where maximum willingness to pay for the last unit equals minimum acceptable price for that unit, does society exhaust all the opportunities to add to combined consumer and producer surplus. So allocative efficiency occurs where the triangle representing "consumer surplus + producer surplus" is at its maximum size.

Other things equal, competitive markets produce equilibrium prices and quantities that maximize the sum of consumer and producer surplus. Allocative efficiency occurs at quantity levels where three conditions exist:

- MB = MC (Figure 1.3).
- Maximum willingness to pay = minimum acceptable price.
- Combined consumer and producer surplus is at a maximum.

Efficiency Losses (or Deadweight Losses)

Figure 6.8 demonstrates **efficiency losses**—reductions of combined consumer and producer surplus—associated with underproduction or overproduction of a product. Suppose that output is Q_2 rather than the efficient level Q_1. The sum of consumer and producer surplus, previously *abc*, falls to *adec*. So the combined consumer and producer surplus declines by the amount of the brown

FIGURE 6.8 Efficiency losses (or deadweight losses). Quantity levels less than or greater than the efficient quantity, Q_1, create efficiency losses. The brown triangle shows the efficiency loss associated with underproduction Q_2, whereas the tan triangle illustrates the efficiency loss associated with overproduction Q_3.

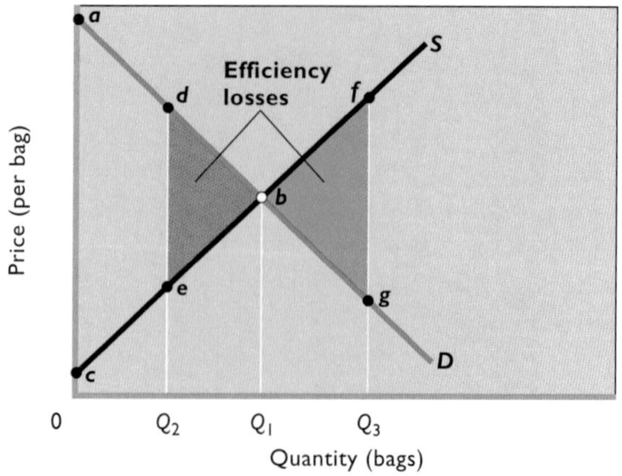

Last Word

Elasticity and Pricing Power: Why Different Consumers Pay Different Prices

Firms and Nonprofit Institutions Often Recognize and Exploit Differences in Price Elasticity of Demand.

All buyers in a highly competitive market pay the same market price for the product, regardless of their individual demand elasticities. If the price rises, Jones may have an elastic demand and greatly reduce her purchases. Green may have a unit-elastic demand and reduce his purchases less than Jones. Lopez may have an inelastic demand and hardly curtail his purchases at all. But all three consumers will pay the single higher price regardless of their demand elasticities.

In later chapters we will find that not all sellers must passively accept a "one-for-all" price. Some firms have "market power" or "pricing power" that allows them to set their product prices in their best interests. For some goods and services, firms may find it advantageous to determine differences in price elasticity of demand and then charge different prices to different buyers.

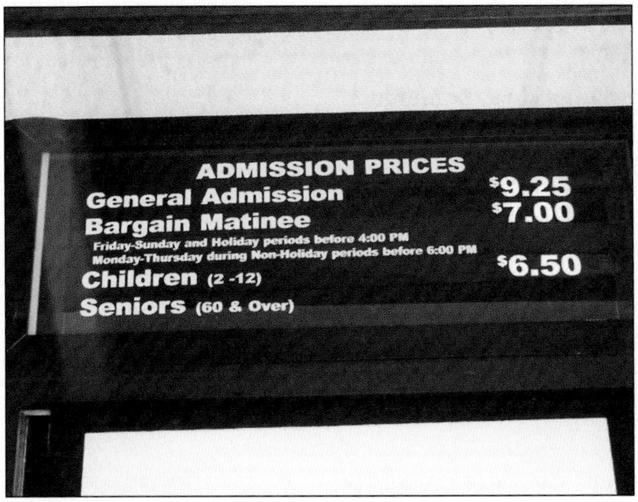

It is extremely difficult to tailor prices for each customer on the basis of price elasticity of demand, but it is relatively easy to observe differences in group elasticities. Consider airline tickets. Business travelers generally have inelastic demand for air travel. Because their time is highly valuable, they do not see slower modes of transportation as realistic substitutes. Also, their employers pay for their tickets as part of their business expenses. In contrast, leisure travelers tend to have elastic demand. They have the option to drive rather than fly or to simply not travel at all. They also pay for their tickets out of their own pockets and thus are more sensitive to price.

Airlines recognize this group difference in price elasticity of demand and charge business travelers more than leisure travelers. To accomplish that, they have to dissuade business travelers from buying the less expensive round-trip tickets aimed at leisure travelers. So they place restrictions on the lower-priced tickets. For example, they make the tickets nonrefundable, require at least 2-week advance purchase, and require Saturday-night stays. These restrictions chase off most business travelers who engage in last-minute travel and want to be home for the weekend. As a result, a business traveler often pays hundreds of dollars more for a ticket than a leisure traveler on the same plane.

Discounts for children are another example of pricing based on group differences in price elasticity of demand. For many products, children have more elastic demands than adults because children have low budgets, often financed by their parents. Sellers recognize the elasticity difference and price accordingly. The barber spends as much time cutting a child's hair as an adult's but charges the child much less. A child takes up a full seat at the baseball game but pays a lower price than an adult. A child snowboarder occupies the same space on a chairlift as an adult snowboarder but qualifies for a discounted lift ticket.

Finally, consider pricing by colleges and universities. Prospective students from low-income families generally have more elastic demands for higher education than similar students from high-income families. This makes sense because tuition is a much larger proportion of household income for a low-income student or family than for his or her high-income counterpart. Desiring a diverse student body, colleges charge different *net* prices (= tuition *minus* financial aid) to the two groups on the basis of price elasticity of demand. High-income students pay full tuition, unless they receive merit-based scholarships. Low-income students receive considerable financial aid in addition to merit-based scholarships and, in effect, pay a lower *net* price.

It is common for colleges to announce a large tuition increase and immediately cushion the news by emphasizing that they also are increasing financial aid. In effect, the college is increasing the tuition for students who have inelastic demand by the full amount and raising the *net* tuition of those with elastic demand by some lesser amount or not at all. Through this strategy, colleges boost revenue to cover rising costs while maintaining affordability for a wide range of students.

There are a number of other examples of dual or multiple pricing. All relate directly to price elasticity of demand. We will revisit this topic again in Chapter 10 when we analyze *price discrimination*—charging different prices to different customers for the same product.

triangle to the left of Q_1. That triangle represents an efficiency loss to buyers and sellers. And since buyers and sellers are members of society, it represents an efficiency loss (or a so-called **deadweight loss**) to society.

For output levels from Q_2 to Q_1, the maximum willingness to pay by consumers (as reflected by points on the demand curve) exceeds the minimum acceptable price of sellers (as reflected by points on the supply curve). By failing to produce a product for which a consumer is willing to pay, say, \$10, and for which a producer is willing to accept \$6, society suffers a \$4 loss of net benefits. The brown triangle in Figure 6.8 shows the total loss of such net benefits due to the underproduction at Q_2.

In contrast, suppose that the amount of oranges produced is Q_3 rather than the efficient level of Q_1. In Figure 6.8 the combined consumer and producer surplus therefore declines by *bfg*—the tan triangle to the right of Q_1. This triangle subtracts from the total consumer and producer surplus of *abc* that would occur if the quantity had been Q_1.

For all units beyond Q_1, the consumer's maximum willingness to pay is less than the producer's minimum acceptable price. Producing an item for which the maximum willingness to pay is, say, \$7 and the minimum acceptable price is \$10 subtracts \$3 from society's net benefits. Such production is uneconomical and creates an efficiency loss (or deadweight loss) for society. The tan triangle *bfg* to the right of Q_1 in Figure 6.8 shows the total efficiency loss from overproduction at Q_3. We are again reminded that there can be too much as well as too little of a good thing. Under most conditions, however, a competitive market ensures that the "right amount" of a particular good gets produced. **(Key Question 15)**

QUICK REVIEW 6.3

- Consumer surplus is the difference between the maximum price that a consumer is willing to pay for a product and the lower price actually paid.
- Producer surplus is the difference between the minimum price that a producer is willing to accept for a product and the higher price actually received.
- At the equilibrium price and quantity in competitive markets, marginal benefit equals marginal cost, maximum willingness to pay equals minimum acceptable price, and the total of consumer surplus and producer surplus is maximized. These individual conditions each define allocative efficiency.
- Quantities less than or greater than the allocatively efficient level of output create efficiency losses, often called deadweight losses.

Summary

1. Price elasticity of demand measures consumer response to price changes. If consumers are relatively sensitive to price changes, demand is elastic. If they are relatively unresponsive to price changes, demand is inelastic.
2. The price-elasticity coefficient E_d measures the degree of elasticity or inelasticity of demand. The coefficient is found by the formula

$$E_d = \frac{\text{percentage change in quantity demanded of X}}{\text{percentage change in price of X}}$$

   Economists use the averages of prices and quantities under consideration as reference points in determining percentage changes in price and quantity. If E_d is greater than 1, demand is elastic. If E_d is less than 1, demand is inelastic. Unit elasticity is the special case in which E_d equals 1.
3. Perfectly inelastic demand is graphed as a line parallel to the vertical axis; perfectly elastic demand is shown by a line above and parallel to the horizontal axis.
4. Elasticity varies at different price ranges on a demand curve, tending to be elastic in the upper left segment and inelastic in the lower right segment. Elasticity cannot be judged by the steepness or flatness of a demand curve.
5. If total revenue changes in the opposite direction from prices, demand is elastic. If price and total revenue change in the same direction, demand is inelastic. Where demand is of unit elasticity, a change in price leaves total revenue unchanged.
6. The number of available substitutes, the size of an item's price relative to one's budget, whether the product is a luxury or a necessity, and length of time to adjust are all determinants of elasticity of demand.
7. The elasticity concept also applies to supply. The coefficient of price elasticity of supply is found by the formula

$$E_s = \frac{\text{percentage change in quantity supplied of X}}{\text{percentage change in price of X}}$$

The averages of the prices and quantities under consideration are used as reference points for computing percentage changes. Elasticity of supply depends on the ease of shifting resources between alternative uses, which varies directly with the time producers have to adjust to a price change.

8. Cross elasticity of demand indicates how sensitive the purchase of one product is to changes in the price of another product. The coefficient of cross elasticity of demand is found by the formula

$$E_{xy} = \frac{\text{percentage change in quantity demanded of X}}{\text{percentage change in price of Y}}$$

Positive cross elasticity of demand identifies substitute goods; negative cross elasticity identifies complementary goods.

9. Income elasticity of demand indicates the responsiveness of consumer purchases to a change in income. The coefficient of income elasticity of demand is found by the formula

$$E_i = \frac{\text{percentage change in quantity demanded of X}}{\text{percentage change in income}}$$

The coefficient is positive for normal goods and negative for inferior goods.

10. Consumer surplus is the difference between the maximum price that a consumer is willing to pay for a product and the lower price actually paid; producer surplus is the difference between the minimum price that a producer is willing to accept for a product and the higher price actually received. Collectively, consumer surplus is represented by the triangle under the demand curve and above the actual price, whereas producer surplus is shown by the triangle above the supply curve and below the actual price.

11. Graphically, the combined amount of producer and consumer surplus is represented by the triangle to the left of the intersection of the supply and demand curves that is below the demand curve and above the supply curve. At the equilibrium price and quantity in competitive markets, marginal benefit equals marginal cost, maximum willingness to pay equals minimum acceptable price, and the combined amount of consumer surplus and producer surplus is maximized.

12. Output levels that are either less than or greater than the equilibrium output create efficiency losses, also called deadweight losses. These losses are reductions in the combined amount of consumer surplus and producer surplus. Underproduction creates efficiency losses because output is not being produced for which maximum willingness to pay exceeds minimum acceptable price. Overproduction creates efficiency losses because output is being produced for which minimum acceptable price exceeds maximum willingness to pay.

Terms and Concepts

price elasticity of demand
midpoint formula
elastic demand
inelastic demand
unit elasticity
perfectly inelastic demand
perfectly elastic demand
total revenue (TR)
total-revenue test
price elasticity of supply
market period
short run
long run
cross elasticity of demand
income elasticity of demand
consumer surplus
producer surplus
efficiency losses (or deadweight losses)

Study Questions

1. Explain why the choice between 1, 2, 3, 4, 5, 6, 7, and 8 "units," or 1000, 2000, 3000, 4000, 5000, 6000, 7000, and 8000 movie tickets, makes no difference in determining elasticity in Table 6.1.

2. **KEY QUESTION** Graph the accompanying demand data, and then use the midpoint formula for E_d to determine price elasticity of demand for each of the four possible \$1 price changes. What can you conclude about the relationship between the slope of a curve and its elasticity? Explain in a nontechnical way why demand is elastic in the northwest segment of the demand curve and inelastic in the southeast segment.

Product Price	Quantity Demanded
$5	1
4	2
3	3
2	4
1	5

3. **KEY QUESTION** Calculate total-revenue data from the demand schedule in question 2. Graph total revenue below your demand curve. Generalize about the relationship between price elasticity and total revenue.

4. **KEY QUESTION** How would the following changes in price affect total revenue? That is, would total revenue increase, decline, or remain unchanged?
   a. Price falls and demand is inelastic.
   b. Price rises and demand is elastic.
   c. Price rises and supply is elastic.
   d. Price rises and supply is inelastic.
   e. Price rises and demand is inelastic.
   f. Price falls and demand is elastic.
   g. Price falls and demand is of unit elasticity.
5. **KEY QUESTION** What are the major determinants of price elasticity of demand? Use those determinants and your own reasoning in judging whether demand for each of the following products is probably elastic or inelastic: (*a*) bottled water; (*b*) toothpaste; (*c*) Crest toothpaste; (*d*) ketchup; (*e*) diamond bracelets; (*f*) Microsoft Windows operating system.
6. What effect would a rule stating that university students must live in university dormitories have on the price elasticity of demand for dormitory space? What impact might this in turn have on room rates?
7. In November 1998 Vincent van Gogh's self-portrait sold at auction for \$71.5 million. Portray this sale in a demand and supply diagram, and comment on the elasticity of supply. Comedian George Carlin once mused, "If a painting can be forged well enough to fool some experts, why is the original so valuable?" Provide an answer.
8. **KEY QUESTION** What is the formula for measuring the price elasticity of supply? Suppose the price of apples goes up from \$20 to \$22 a box. In direct response, Goldsboro Farms supplies 1200 boxes of apples instead of 1000 boxes. Compute the coefficient of price elasticity (midpoints approach) for Goldsboro's supply. Is its supply elastic, or is it inelastic?
9. **KEY QUESTION** Suppose the cross elasticity of demand for products A and B is +3.6 and for products C and D is −5.4. What can you conclude about how products A and B are related? Products C and D?
10. **KEY QUESTION** The income elasticities of demand for movies, dental services, and clothing have been estimated to be +3.4, +1, and +.5, respectively. Interpret these coefficients. What does it mean if an income elasticity coefficient is negative?
11. Research has found that an increase in the price of beer would reduce the amount of marijuana consumed. Is cross elasticity of demand between the two products positive or negative? Are these products substitutes or complements? What might be the logic behind this relationship?
12. Refer to Table 6.5. If the six people listed in the table are the only consumers in the market and the equilibrium price is \$11 (not the \$8 shown), how much consumer surplus will the market generate?
13. Refer to Table 6.6. If the six people listed in the table are the only producers in the market and the equilibrium price is \$6 (not the \$8 shown), how much producer surplus will the market generate?
14. Draw a supply and demand graph and identify the areas of consumer surplus and producer surplus. Given the demand curve, what impact will an increase in supply have on the amount of consumer surplus shown in your diagram? Explain why.
15. **KEY QUESTION** Use the ideas of consumer surplus and producer surplus to explain why economists say competitive markets are efficient. Why are below- or above-equilibrium levels of output inefficient, according to these two sets of ideas?
16. **LAST WORD** What is the purpose of charging different groups of customers different prices? Supplement the three broad examples in the Last Word with two additional examples of your own. Hint: Think of price discounts based on group characteristic or time of purchase.

Web-Based Questions

1. **THE PRICE OF GOLD—TODAY, YESTERDAY, AND THROUGHOUT THE YEAR** Visit **www.goldprices.com** to find the very latest price of gold. Compare that price to the price at the beginning of the day. What was the highest price during the last 12 months? The lowest price? Assume the price fluctuations observed resulted exclusively from changes in demand. Would the observed price changes have been greater or less if the gold supply had been elastic rather than inelastic? Explain.
2. **PRICE, CROSS, AND INCOME ELASTICITIES—HOW DO THEY RELATE TO ALCOHOL AND CIGARETTES?** Go to the National Bureau of Economic Research (NBER) Web site, **www.nber.org,** and select New Working Papers. In the Google search space, type "alcohol." Use the titles and summaries of the papers to answer the following questions relating to elasticity: (*a*) Do the mentally ill have perfectly inelastic demands for cigarettes and alcohol? (*b*) Does alcohol consumption increase in bad times? (*c*) What is the effect of cigarette taxes (and smuggling) on the consumption of alcohol? What does that imply about the cross elasticity of demand between the two? (*d*) Is binge drinking among college students sensitive to the price of alcohol?

IN THIS CHAPTER YOU WILL LEARN:

- **About total utility, marginal utility, and the law of diminishing marginal utility.**
- **How rational consumers compare marginal utility-to-price ratios for products in purchasing combinations of products that maximize their utility.**
- **How a demand curve can be derived by observing the outcomes of price changes in the utility-maximization model.**
- **How the utility-maximization model helps highlight the income and substitution effects of a price change.**
- **About budget lines, indifference curves, utility maximization, and demand derivation in the indifference curve model of consumer behavior. (Appendix)**

7

Consumer Behavior and Utility Maximization

If you were to compare the shopping carts of almost any two consumers, you would observe striking differences. Why does Paula have potatoes, peaches, and Pepsi in her cart while Sam has sugar, saltines, and 7-Up in his? Why didn't Paula also buy pasta and plums? Why didn't Sam have soup and spaghetti on his grocery list?

In this chapter, you will see how individual consumers allocate their incomes among the various goods and services available to them. Given a certain budget, how does a consumer decide which goods and services to buy? As we answer this question, you will also strengthen your understanding of the law of demand.

Law of Diminishing Marginal Utility

The simplest theory of consumer behavior rests squarely on the **law of diminishing marginal utility.** This principle, first discussed in Chapter 3, is that added satisfaction declines as a consumer acquires additional units of a given product. Although consumer wants in general may be insatiable, wants for particular items can be satisfied. In a specific span of time over which consumers' tastes remain unchanged, consumers can obtain as much of a particular good or service as they can afford. But the more of that product they obtain, the less they want still more of it.

Consider durable goods, for example. A consumer's desire for an automobile, when he or she has none, may be very strong. But the desire for a second car is less intense; and for a third or fourth, weaker and weaker. Unless they are collectors, even the wealthiest families rarely have more than a half-dozen cars, although their incomes would allow them to purchase a whole fleet of vehicles.

Terminology

Evidence indicates that consumers can fulfill specific wants with succeeding units of a product but that each added unit provides less utility than the last unit purchased. Recall that a product has utility if it can satisfy a want: **Utility** is want-satisfying power. The utility of a good or service is the satisfaction or pleasure one gets from consuming it. Keep in mind three characteristics of this concept:

- "Utility" and "usefulness" are not synonymous. Paintings by Picasso may offer great utility to art connoisseurs but are useless functionally (other than for hiding a crack on a wall).
- Utility is subjective. The utility of a specific product may vary widely from person to person. A "jacked-up" truck may have great utility to someone who drives off-road but little utility to someone unable or unwilling to climb into the rig. Eyeglasses have tremendous utility to someone who has poor eyesight but no utility to a person with 20-20 vision.
- Utility is difficult to quantify. But for purposes of illustration we assume that people can measure satisfaction with units called *utils* (units of utility). For example, a particular consumer may get 100 utils of satisfaction from a smoothie, 10 utils of satisfaction from a candy bar, and 1 util of satisfaction from a stick of gum. These imaginary units of satisfaction are convenient for quantifying consumer behavior for explanatory purposes.

Total Utility and Marginal Utility

Total utility and marginal utility are related, but different, ideas. **Total utility** is the total amount of satisfaction or pleasure a person derives from consuming some specific quantity—for example, 10 units—of a good or service. **Marginal utility** is the *extra* satisfaction a consumer realizes from an additional unit of that product—for example, from the eleventh unit. Alternatively, marginal utility is the change in total utility that results from the consumption of 1 more unit of a product.

Figure 7.1 (Key Graph) and the accompanying table demonstrate the relation between total utility and

CONSIDER THIS . . .

Vending Machines and Marginal Utility

Newspaper dispensing devices and soft-drink vending machines are similar in their basic operations. Both enable consumers to buy a product by inserting coins. But there is an important difference in the two devices. The newspaper dispenser opens to the full stack of papers and seemingly "trusts" the customer to take only a single copy, whereas the vending machine displays no such "trust," requiring the consumer to buy one can at a time. Why the difference?

The idea of diminishing marginal utility is key to solving this puzzle. Most consumers take only single copies from the newspaper box because the marginal utility of a second newspaper is nearly zero. They could grab a few extra papers and try to sell them on the street, but the revenue obtained would be small relative to their time and effort. So, in selling their product, newspaper publishers rely on "zero marginal utility of the second unit," not on "consumer honesty." Also, newspapers have little "shelf life"; they are obsolete the next day. In contrast, soft-drink sellers do not allow buyers to make a single payment and then take as many cans as they want. If they did, consumers would clean out the machine because the marginal utility of successive cans of soda diminishes slowly and buyers could take extra sodas and consume them later. Soft-drink firms thus vend their products on a pay-per-can basis.

In summary, newspaper publishers and soft-drink firms use alternative vending techniques because of the highly different rates of decline in marginal utility for their products. The newspaper seller uses inexpensive dispensers that open to the full stack of papers. The soft-drink seller uses expensive vending machines that limit the consumer to a single can at a time. Each vending technique is optimal under the particular economic circumstance.

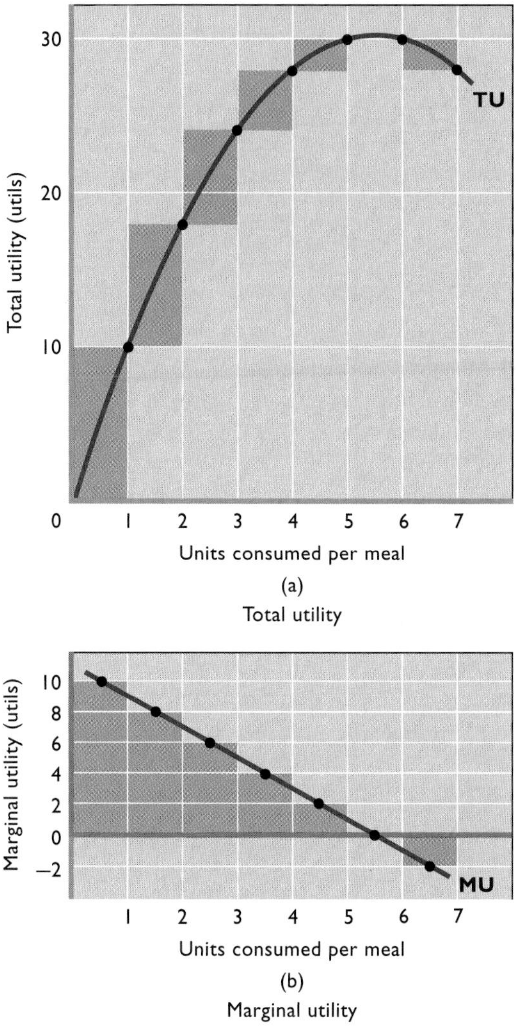

FIGURE 7.1 Total and marginal utility. Curves TU and MU are graphed from the data in the table. (a) As more of a product is consumed, total utility increases at a diminishing rate, reaches a maximum, and then declines. (b) Marginal utility, by definition, reflects the changes in total utility. Thus marginal utility diminishes with increased consumption, becomes zero when total utility is at a maximum, and is negative when total utility declines. As shown by the shaded rectangles in (a) and (b), marginal utility is the change in total utility associated with each additional taco. Or, alternatively, each new level of total utility is found by adding marginal utility to the preceding level of total utility.

(1) Tacos Consumed per Meal	(2) Total Utility, Utils	(3) Marginal Utility, Utils
0	0	
1	10	10
2	18	8
3	24	6
4	28	4
5	30	2
6	30	0
7	28	−2

QUICK QUIZ 7.1

1. Marginal utility:
   a. is the extra output a firm obtains when it adds another unit of labor.
   b. explains why product supply curves slope upward.
   c. typically rises as successive units of a good are consumed.
   d. is the extra satisfaction from the consumption of 1 more unit of some good or service.
2. Marginal utility in Figure 7.1b is positive, but declining, when total utility in Figure 7.1a is positive and:
   a. rising at an increasing rate.
   b. falling at an increasing rate.
   c. rising at a decreasing rate.
   d. falling at a decreasing rate.
3. When marginal utility is zero in graph (b), total utility in graph (a) is:
   a. also zero.
   b. neither rising nor falling.
   c. negative.
   d. rising, but at a declining rate.
4. Suppose the person represented by these graphs experienced a diminished taste for tacos. As a result the:
   a. TU curve would get steeper.
   b. MU curve would get flatter.
   c. TU and MU curves would shift downward.
   d. MU curve, but not the TU curve, would collapse to the horizontal axis.

Answers: 1. d; 2. c; 3. b; 4. c

marginal utility. The curves reflect the data in the table. Column 2 shows the total utility associated with each level of consumption of tacos. Column 3 shows the marginal utility—the change in total utility—that results from the consumption of each successive taco. Starting at the origin in Figure 7.1a, observe that each of the first 5 units increases total utility (TU), but by a diminishing amount. Total utility reaches a maximum with the addition of the sixth unit and then declines.

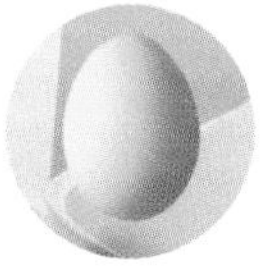

O 7.1
Diminishing marginal utility

G 7.1
Total and marginal utility

So in Figure 7.1b marginal utility (MU) remains positive but diminishes through the first 5 units (because total utility increases at a declining rate). Marginal utility is zero for the sixth unit (because that unit doesn't change total utility). Marginal utility then becomes negative with the seventh unit and beyond (because total utility is falling). Figure 7.1b and table column 3 reveal that each successive taco yields less extra utility, meaning fewer utils, than the preceding taco as the consumer's want for tacos comes closer and closer to fulfillment.[1] That is, the table and graph illustrate the law of diminishing marginal utility. **(Key Question 1)**

Marginal Utility and Demand

The law of diminishing marginal utility explains why the demand curve for a given product slopes downward. If successive units of a good yield smaller and smaller amounts of marginal, or extra, utility, then the consumer will buy additional units of a product only if its price falls. The consumer for whom Figure 7.1 is relevant may buy two tacos at a price of $1 each. But because he or she obtains less marginal utility from additional tacos, the consumer will choose not to buy more at that price. The consumer would rather spend additional dollars on products that provide more (or equal) utility, not less utility. Therefore, additional tacos with less utility are not worth buying unless the price declines. (When marginal utility becomes negative, Taco Bell would have to pay you to consume another taco!) Thus, diminishing marginal utility supports the idea that price must decrease in order for quantity demanded to increase. In other words, consumers behave in ways that make demand curves downward-sloping.

[1]Technical footnote: In Figure 7.1b we graphed marginal utility at half-units. For example, we graphed the marginal utility of 4 utils at $3\frac{1}{2}$ units because "4 utils" refers neither to the third nor the fourth unit per se but to the *addition* or *subtraction* of the fourth unit.

QUICK REVIEW 7.1

- Utility is the benefit or satisfaction a person receives from consuming a good or a service.
- The law of diminishing marginal utility indicates that gains in satisfaction become smaller as successive units of a specific product are consumed.
- Diminishing marginal utility provides a simple rationale for the law of demand.

Theory of Consumer Behavior

In addition to explaining the law of demand, the idea of diminishing marginal utility explains how consumers allocate their money incomes among the many goods and services available for purchase.

Consumer Choice and Budget Constraint

For simplicity, we will assume that the situation for the typical consumer has the following dimensions.

- ***Rational behavior*** The consumer is a rational person, who tries to use his or her money income to derive the greatest amount of satisfaction, or utility, from it. Consumers want to get "the most for their money" or, technically, to maximize their total utility. They engage in **rational behavior.**
- ***Preferences*** Each consumer has clear-cut preferences for certain of the goods and services that are available in the market. Buyers also have a good idea of how much marginal utility they will get from successive units of the various products they might purchase.
- ***Budget constraint*** At any point in time the consumer has a fixed, limited amount of money income. Since each consumer supplies a finite amount of human and property resources to society, he or she earns only limited income. Thus, as noted in Chapter 1, every consumer faces a **budget constraint,** even consumers who earn millions of dollars a year. Of course, this budget limitation is more severe for a consumer with an average income than for a consumer with an extraordinarily high income.
- ***Prices*** Goods are scarce relative to the demand for them, so every good carries a price tag. We assume that the price tags are not affected by the amounts of specific goods each person buys. After all, each person's purchase is a tiny part of total demand. Also, because the consumer has a limited number of dollars, he or she cannot buy everything wanted. This point drives home the reality of scarcity to each consumer.

So the consumer must compromise; he or she must choose the most satisfying mix of goods and services. Different individuals will choose different mixes.

Utility-Maximizing Rule

Of all the different combinations of goods and services a consumer can obtain within his or her budget, which specific combination will yield the maximum utility or satisfaction? To maximize satisfaction, the consumer should allocate his or her money income so that the last dollar spent on each product yields the same amount of extra (marginal) utility. We call this the **utility-maximizing rule.** When the consumer has "balanced his or her margins" using this rule, there is no incentive to alter the expenditure pattern. The consumer is in equilibrium and would be worse off—total utility would decline—if there were any alteration in the bundle of goods purchased, providing there is no change in taste, income, products, or prices.

Numerical Example

An illustration will help explain the utility-maximizing rule. For simplicity we limit our example to two products, but the analysis also applies if there are more. Suppose consumer Holly is analyzing which combination of two products she should purchase with her fixed daily income of $10. These products might be asparagus and breadsticks, apricots and bananas, or apples and broccoli. Let's just call them A and B.

Holly's preferences for products A and B and their prices are the basic data determining the combination that will maximize her satisfaction. Table 7.1 summarizes those data, with column 2a showing the amount of marginal utility she will derive from each successive unit of A and with column 3a showing the same thing for product B. Both columns reflect the law of diminishing marginal utility, which is assumed to begin with the second unit of each product purchased.

Marginal Utility per Dollar

To see how the utility-maximizing rule works, we must put the marginal-utility information in columns 2a and 3a on a per-dollar-spent basis. A consumer's choices are influenced not only by the extra utility that successive units of product A will yield but also by how many dollars (and therefore how many units of alternative product B) she must give up to obtain those added units of A.

The rational consumer must compare the extra utility from each product with its added cost (that is, its price).

TABLE 7.1 The Utility-Maximizing Combination of Products A and B Obtainable with an Income of $10*

(1) Unit of Product	(2) Product A: Price = $1		(3) Product B: Price = $2	
	(a) Marginal Utility, Utils	(b) Marginal Utility per Dollar (MU/Price)	(a) Marginal Utility, Utils	(b) Marginal Utility per Dollar (MU/Price)
First	10	10	24	12
Second	8	***8***	20	10
Third	7	7	18	9
Fourth	6	6	16	***8***
Fifth	5	5	12	6
Sixth	4	4	6	3
Seventh	3	3	4	2

*It is assumed in this table that the amount of marginal utility received from additional units of each of the two products is independent of the quantity of the other product. For example, the marginal-utility schedule for product A is independent of the amount of B obtained by the consumer.

Suppose you prefer a pizza whose marginal utility is, say, 36 utils to a movie whose marginal utility is 24 utils. But if the pizza's price is $12 and the movie costs only $6, you would choose the movie rather than the pizza! Why? Because the marginal utility per dollar spent would be 4 utils for the movie (= 24 utils/$6) compared to only 3 utils for the pizza (= 36 utils/$12). You could see two movies for $12 and, assuming that the marginal utility of the second movie is, say, 16 utils, your total utility would be 40 utils. Clearly, 40 units of satisfaction (= 24 utils + 16 utils) from two movies are superior to 36 utils from the same $12 expenditure on one pizza.

To make the amounts of extra utility derived from differently priced goods comparable, marginal utilities must be put on a per-dollar-spent basis. We do this in columns 2b and 3b by dividing the marginal-utility data of columns 2a and 3a by the prices of A and B—$1 and $2, respectively.

Decision-Making Process

Table 7.1 shows Holly's preferences on a unit basis and a per-dollar basis as well as the price tags of A and B. With $10 to spend, in what order should Holly allocate her dollars on units of A and B to achieve the highest degree of utility within the $10 limit imposed by her income? And what specific combination of A and B will she have obtained at the time she uses up her $10?

Concentrating on columns 2b and 3b in Table 7.1, we find that Holly should first spend $2 on the first unit of B, because its marginal utility per dollar of 12 utils is higher than A's 10 utils. But now Holly finds herself indifferent about whether she should buy a second unit of B or the first unit of A because the marginal utility per dollar of both is 10 utils. So she buys both of them. Holly now has 1 unit of A and 2 units of B. Also, the last dollar she spent on each good yielded the same marginal utility per dollar (10 utils). But this combination of A and B does not represent the maximum amount of utility that Holly can obtain. It cost her only \$5 [= (1 × \$1) + (2 × \$2)], so she has \$5 remaining, which she can spend to achieve a still higher level of total utility.

Examining columns 2b and 3b again, we find that Holly should spend the next \$2 on a third unit of B because marginal utility per dollar for the third unit of B is 9 compared with 8 for the second unit of A. But now, with 1 unit of A and 3 units of B, she is again indifferent between a second unit of A and a fourth unit of B because both provide 8 utils per dollar. So Holly purchases 1 more unit of each. Now the last dollar spent on each product provides the same marginal utility per dollar (8 utils), and Holly's money income of \$10 is exhausted.

The utility-maximizing combination of goods attainable by Holly is 2 units of A and 4 of B. By summing marginal-utility information from columns 2a and 3a, we find that Holly is obtaining 18 (= 10 + 8) utils of satisfaction from the 2 units of A and 78 (= 24 + 20 + 18 + 16) utils of satisfaction from the 4 units of B. Her \$10, optimally spent, yields 96 (= 18 + 78) utils of satisfaction.

Table 7.2 summarizes our step-by-step process for maximizing Holly's utility. Note that we have implicitly assumed that Holly spends her entire income. She neither borrows nor saves. However, saving can be regarded as a "commodity" that yields utility and can be incorporated into our analysis. In fact, we treat it that way in question 3 at the end of this chapter. **(Key Question 3)**

Inferior Options Holly can obtain other combinations of A and B with \$10, but none will yield as great a total utility as do 2 units of A and 4 of B. As an example, she can obtain 4 units of A and 3 of B for \$10. But this combination yields only 93 utils, clearly inferior to the 96 utils provided by 2 of A and 4 of B. True, there are other combinations of A and B (such as 4 of A and 5 of B or 1 of A and 2 of B) in which the marginal utility of the last dollar spent is the same for both A and B. But all such combinations either are unobtainable with Holly's limited money income (as 4 of A and 5 of B) or do not exhaust her money income (as 1 of A and 2 of B) and therefore do not yield the maximum utility attainable.

W 7.1
Consumer choice

Algebraic Restatement

Our allocation rule says that a consumer will maximize her satisfaction when she allocates her money income so that the last dollar spent on product A, the last on product B, and so forth, yield equal amounts of additional, or marginal, utility. The marginal utility per dollar spent on A is indicated by the MU of product A divided by the price of A (column 2b in Table 7.1), and the marginal utility per dollar spent on B by the MU of product B divided by the price of B (column 3b in Table 7.1). Our utility-maximizing rule merely requires that these ratios be equal. Algebraically,

$$\frac{\text{MU of product A}}{\text{Price of A}} = \frac{\text{MU of product B}}{\text{Price of B}}$$

And, of course, the consumer must exhaust her available income. Table 7.1 shows us that the combination of 2 units of A and 4 of B fulfills these conditions in that

$$\frac{8 \text{ utils}}{\$1} = \frac{16 \text{ utils}}{\$2}$$

and the consumer's \$10 income is spent.

If the equation is not fulfilled, then some reallocation of the consumer's expenditures between A and B (from the

TABLE 7.2 Sequence of Purchases to Achieve Consumer Equilibrium, Given the Data in Table 7.1

Choice Number	Potential Choices	Marginal Utility per Dollar	Purchase Decision	Income Remaining
1	First unit of A	10	First unit of B for \$2	\$8 = \$10 − \$2
	First unit of B	12		
2	First unit of A	10	First unit of A for \$1	\$5 = \$8 − \$3
	Second unit of B	10	and second unit of B for \$2	
3	Second unit of A	8	Third unit of B for \$2	\$3 = \$5 − \$2
	Third unit of B	9		
4	Second unit of A	8	Second unit of A for \$1	\$0 = \$3 − \$3
	Fourth unit of B	8	and fourth unit of B for \$2	

low to the high marginal-utility-per-dollar product) will increase the consumer's total utility. For example, if the consumer spent $10 on 4 of A and 3 of B, we would find that

$$\frac{\text{MU of A: 6 utils}}{\text{Price of A: \$1}} < \frac{\text{MU of B: 18 utils}}{\text{Price of B: \$2}}$$

Here the last dollar spent on A provides only 6 utils of satisfaction, and the last dollar spent on B provides 9 (= 18/$2). So the consumer can increase total satisfaction by purchasing more of B and less of A. As dollars are reallocated from A to B, the marginal utility per dollar of A will increase while the marginal utility per dollar of B will decrease. At some new combination of A and B the two will be equal and consumer equilibrium will be achieved. Here that combination is 2 of A and 4 of B.

Utility Maximization and the Demand Curve

Once you understand the utility-maximizing rule, you can easily see why product price and quantity demanded are inversely related. Recall that the basic determinants of an individual's demand for a specific product are (1) preferences or tastes, (2) money income, and (3) the prices of other goods. The utility data in Table 7.1 reflect our consumer's preferences. We continue to suppose that her money income is $10. And, concentrating on the construction of a simple demand curve for product B, we assume that the price of A, representing "other goods," is still $1.

Deriving the Demand Schedule and Curve

We can derive a single consumer's demand schedule for product B by considering alternative prices at which B might be sold and then determining the quantity the consumer will purchase. We already know one such price-quantity combination in the utility-maximizing example: Given tastes, income, and prices of other goods, Holly will purchase 4 units of B at $2.

Now let's assume the price of B falls to $1. The marginal-utility-per-dollar data of column 3b in Table 7.1 will double, because the price of B has been halved; the new data for column 3b are in fact identical to those in column 3a. But the purchase of 2 units of A and 4 of B is no longer an equilibrium combination. By applying the same reasoning we used previously, we now find that Holly's utility-maximizing combination is 4 units of A and 6 units of B. As summarized in the table in Figure 7.2, Holly will purchase 6 units of B when the price of B is $1. Using the data in this table, we can sketch the downward-sloping demand curve D_B shown in Figure 7.2. This exercise, then, clearly links the utility-maximizing behavior of a consumer and that person's demand curve for a particular product.

FIGURE 7.2 Deriving an individual demand curve. At a price of $2 for product B, the consumer represented by the data in the table maximizes utility by purchasing 4 units of product B. The decline in the price of product B to $1 upsets the consumer's initial utility-maximizing equilibrium. The consumer restores equilibrium by purchasing 6 rather than 4 units of product B. Thus, a simple price-quantity schedule emerges, which locates two points on a downsloping demand curve.

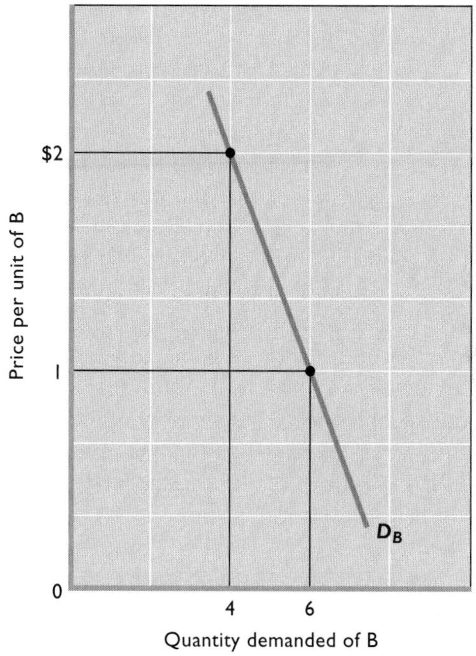

Price per Unit of B	Quantity Demanded
$2	4
1	6

Income and Substitution Effects

Recall from Chapter 3 that the **income effect** is the impact that a change in the price of a product has on a consumer's real income and consequently on the quantity demanded of that good. In contrast, the **substitution effect** is the impact that a change in a product's price has on its relative expensiveness and consequently on the quantity demanded. Both effects help explain why a demand curve such as that in Figure 7.2 is downsloping.

Our analysis of utility maximization does not allow us to sort out the income effect and substitution effect of a change in price on quantity demanded. But utility maximization does allow us to understand why the quantity demanded of product B rises when the price of B falls (the price of A being constant). Let's first look at the substitution effect. Recall that before the price of B declined, Holly was in equilibrium when purchasing 2 units of A and 4 units of B in that $MU_A(8)/P_A(\$1) = MU_B(16)/P_B(\$2)$. But after B's price decreases from \$2 to \$1, $MU_A(8)/P_A(\$1) < MU_B(16)/P_B(\$1)$. More simply stated, the last dollar spent on B now yields more utility (16 utils) than does the last dollar spent on A (8 utils). A switching of purchases from A to B is needed to restore equilibrium; that is, a *substitution* of now cheaper B for A will occur when the price of B drops.

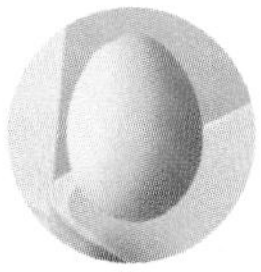

O 7.2

Income and substitution effects

What about the *income effect?* The decline in the price of B from \$2 to \$1 increases Holly's real income. Before the price decline, she was buying 2 of A and 4 of B. But at the lower \$1 price for B, Holly would have to spend only \$6 rather than \$10 on the same combination of goods. She has \$4 left over to spend on more of A, more of B, or more of both. This rise in *real income* enables her to obtain more of A and B with the same \$10 of *money income*. The income effect is the extra amount of B she decides to purchase because the decline in the price of B raised her real income. **(Key Question 4)**

QUICK REVIEW 7.2

- The theory of consumer behavior assumes that, with limited income and a set of product prices, consumers make rational choices on the basis of well-defined preferences.
- A consumer maximizes utility by allocating income so that the marginal utility per dollar spent is the same for every good purchased.
- A downward-sloping demand curve can be derived by changing the price of one product in the consumer-behavior model and noting the change in the utility-maximizing quantity of that product demanded.
- By providing insights on the income effect and substitution effects of a price decline, the utility-maximization model helps explain why demand curves are downsloping.

Applications and Extensions

Many real-world phenomena can be explained by applying the theory of consumer behavior.

DVDs and DVD Players

Every now and then a new product captures consumers' imagination. One such product is the digital versatile disk (DVD) and the DVD player. DVDs and DVD players made their debut in 1997 in the United States and about 320,000 DVD players were sold that year. In 2005 annual U.S. sales of DVD players reached 35 million and the number of DVD households reached 82 million. Nearly \$23 billion was spent buying and renting DVD movies in 2005.

This swift ascendancy of the DVD and DVD player has resulted from both price and quality considerations. Although the price of DVDs has declined only slightly, the price of DVD players has nosedived. Priced at \$1000 or more when first introduced, most players currently sell for under \$100. DVDs and DVD players are *complementary goods.* The lower price for DVD players has expanded their sales and greatly increased the demand for DVD movies.

Moreover, DVDs provide higher-quality audio and video than videocassettes (VCs) and are much easier to store. For playing movies, DVDs and VCs are *substitute goods.* The improved audio and video experience of DVDs—the greater consumer satisfaction—has produced a substitution away from VCs and toward DVDs.

In terms of our analysis, many consumers have concluded that DVDs have higher ratios of marginal utility to price (= MU/*P*) than the ratios for VCs. Those consumers have increased their total utility by purchasing DVDs rather than VCs.

The Diamond-Water Paradox

Early economists such as Adam Smith were puzzled by the fact that some "essential" goods had much lower prices than some "unimportant" goods. Why would water, essential to life, be priced below diamonds, which have much less usefulness? The paradox is resolved when we acknowledge that water is in great supply relative to demand and thus has a very low price per gallon. Diamonds, in contrast, are rare and are costly to mine, cut, and polish. Because their supply is small relative to demand, their price is very high per carat.

Moreover, the marginal utility of the last unit of water consumed is very low. The reason follows from our utility-maximizing rule. Consumers (and producers) respond to the very low price of water by using a great deal of it—for generating electricity, irrigating crops, heating buildings, watering lawns, quenching thirst, and so on. Consumption is expanded until marginal utility, which declines as more water is consumed, equals its low price. On the other hand, relatively few diamonds are purchased because of their prohibitively high price, meaning that their marginal utility remains high. In equilibrium:

$$\frac{\text{MU of water (low)}}{\text{Price of water (low)}} = \frac{\text{MU of diamonds (high)}}{\text{Price of diamonds (high)}}$$

Although the marginal utility of the last unit of water consumed is low and the marginal utility of the last diamond purchased is high, the total utility of water is very high and the total utility of diamonds quite low. The total utility derived from the consumption of water is large because of the enormous amounts of water consumed. Total utility is the sum of the marginal utilities of all the gallons of water consumed, including the trillions of gallons that have far higher marginal utilities than the last unit consumed. In contrast, the total utility derived from diamonds is low since their high price means that relatively few of them are bought. Thus the water-diamond "paradox" is solved: Water has much more total utility (roughly, usefulness) than diamonds even though the price of diamonds greatly exceeds the price of water. These relative prices relate to marginal utility, not total utility.

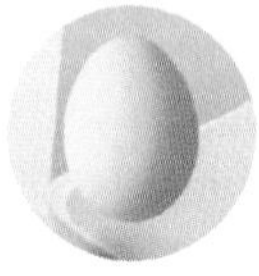

O 7.3
Diamond-water paradox

The Value of Time

The theory of consumer behavior has been generalized to account for the economic value of *time*. Both consumption and production take time. Time is a valuable economic commodity; by using an hour in productive work a person can earn $6, $10, $50, or more, depending on her or his education and skills. By using that hour for leisure or in consumption activities, the individual incurs the opportunity cost of forgone income; she or he sacrifices the $6, $10, or $50 that could have been earned by working.

Imagine a self-employed consumer named Linden who is considering buying a round of golf, on the one hand, and a concert, on the other. The market price of the golf game is $30 and that of the concert is $40. But the golf game takes more time than the concert. Suppose Linden spends 4 hours on the golf course but only 2 hours at the concert. If her time is worth $10 per hour, as evidenced by the $10 wage she can obtain by working, then the "full price" of the golf game is $70 (the $30 market price plus $40 worth of time). Similarly, the full price of the concert is $60 (the $40 market price plus $20 worth of time). We find that, contrary to what market prices alone indicate, the full price of the concert is really less than the full price of the golf game.

If we now assume that the marginal utilities derived from successive golf games and concerts are identical, traditional theory would indicate that Linden should consume more golf games than concerts because the market price of the former ($30) is lower than that of the latter ($40). But when time is taken into account, the situation is reversed and golf games ($70) are more expensive than concerts ($60). So it is rational for Linden to consume more concerts than golf games.

By accounting for time, we can explain certain observable phenomena that traditional theory does not explain. It may be rational for the unskilled worker or retiree whose time has little market value to ride a bus from Chicago to Pittsburgh. But the corporate executive, whose time is very valuable, will find it cheaper to fly, even though bus fare is only a fraction of plane fare. It is sensible for the retiree, living on a modest company pension and a Social Security check, to spend many hours shopping for bargains at the mall or taking long trips in a motor home. It is equally intelligent for the highly paid physician, working 55 hours per week, to buy a new personal computer over the Internet and take short vacations at expensive resorts.

People in other nations often feel affluent Americans are "wasteful" of food and other material goods but "overly economical" in their use of time. Americans who visit developing countries find that time is used casually or "squandered," while material goods are very highly prized and carefully used. These differences are not a paradox or a case of radically different temperaments. The differences are primarily a rational reflection of the fact that the high productivity of labor in an industrially advanced society gives time a high market value, whereas the opposite is true in a low-income, developing country.

Medical Care Purchases

The method of payment for certain goods and services affects their prices at the time we buy them and significantly changes the amount purchased. Let's go back to Table 7.1. Suppose the $1 price for A is its "true" unit value or opportunity cost. But now, for some reason, its price is only, say, $.20. A rational consumer clearly would buy more units at $.20 than at the $1 price.

That is what happens with medical care. People in the United States who have health insurance pay a fixed premium once a month that covers, say, 80 percent of all incurred health care costs. This means that when they actually need health care, its price to them will be only 20 percent of the actual market price. How would you act in such a situation? When you are ill, you would likely purchase a great deal more medical care than you would if you were confronted with the full price. As a result, financing health care through insurance is an important factor in explaining today's high expenditures on health care and the historical growth of such spending as a percentage of domestic output.

Last *Word*

Criminal Behavior

Although Economic Analysis Is Not Particularly Relevant in Explaining Some Crimes of Passion and Violence (for Example, Murder and Rape), It Does Provide Interesting Insights on Such Property Crimes as Robbery, Burglary, and Auto Theft.

Through extension, the theory of rational consumer behavior provides some useful insights on criminal behavior. Both the lawful consumer and the criminal try to maximize their total utility (or net benefit). For example, you can remove a textbook from the campus bookstore by either purchasing it or stealing it. If you *buy* the book, your action is legal; you have fully compensated the bookstore for the product. (The bookstore would rather have your money than the book.) If you *steal* the book, you have broken the law. Theft is outlawed because it imposes uncompensated costs on others. In this case, your action reduces the bookstore's revenue and profit and also may impose costs on other buyers who now must pay higher prices for their textbooks.

Why might someone engage in criminal activity such as stealing? Just like the consumer who compares the marginal utility of a good with its price, the potential criminal compares the marginal benefit from his or her action with the "price" or cost. If the marginal benefit (to the criminal) exceeds the price or marginal cost (also to the criminal), the individual undertakes the criminal activity.

Most people, however, do not engage in theft, burglary, or fraud. Why not? The answer is that they perceive the personal price of engaging in these illegal

Similar reasoning applies to purchases of buffet meals. If you buy a meal at an all-you-can-eat buffet, you will tend to eat more than if you purchased it item by item. Why not eat that second dessert? Its marginal utility is positive and its "price" is zero!

Cash and Noncash Gifts

Marginal-utility analysis also helps us understand why people generally prefer cash gifts to noncash gifts costing the same amount. The reason is simply that the noncash gifts may not match the recipient's preferences and thus may not add as much as cash to total utility. Thought of differently, consumers know their own preferences better than the gift giver does, and the $100 cash gift provides more choices.

Look back at Table 7.1. Suppose Holly has zero earned income but is given the choice of a $2 cash gift or a noncash gift of 2 units of A. Because 2 units of A can be bought with $2, these two gifts are of equal monetary value. But by spending the $2 cash gift on the first unit of B, Holly could obtain 24 utils. The noncash gift of the first 2 units of A would yield only 18 (= 10 + 8) units of utility. Conclusion: The noncash gift yields less utility to the beneficiary than does the cash gift.

Since giving noncash gifts is common, a considerable value of those gifts is potentially lost because they do not match their recipients' tastes. For example, Uncle Fred may have paid $15 for the Frank Sinatra CD he gave you for Christmas, but you would pay only $7.50 for it. Thus, a $7.50, or 50 percent, value loss is involved. Multiplied by billions spent on gifts each year, the potential loss of value is large.

But some of that loss is avoided by the creative ways individuals handle the problem. For example, newlyweds set up gift registries for their weddings to help match up their wants to the noncash gifts received. Also, people obtain cash refunds or exchanges for gifts, so they can buy goods that provide more utility. And people have even been known to "recycle gifts" by giving them to someone else at a later time. All three actions support the proposition that individuals take actions to maximize their total utility.

activities to be too high relative to the marginal benefit. That price or marginal cost to the potential criminal has several facets. First, there are the "guilt costs," which for many people are substantial. Such individuals would not steal from others even if there were no penalties for doing so. Their moral sense of right and wrong would entail too great a guilt cost relative to the benefit from the stolen good. Other types of costs include the direct costs of the criminal activity (supplies and tools) and the forgone income from legitimate activities (the opportunity cost to the criminal).

Unfortunately, guilt costs, direct costs, and forgone income are not sufficient to deter some people from stealing. So society imposes other costs, mainly fines and imprisonment, on lawbreakers. The potential of being fined increases the marginal cost to the criminal. The potential of being imprisoned boosts marginal cost still further. Most people highly value their personal freedom and lose considerable legitimate earnings while incarcerated.

Given these types of costs, the potential criminal estimates the marginal cost and benefit of committing the crime. As a simple example, suppose that the direct cost and opportunity cost of stealing an \$80 textbook both are zero. The probability of getting caught is 10 percent and, if apprehended, there will be a \$500 fine. The potential criminal will estimate the marginal cost of stealing the book as \$50 (= \$500 fine × .10 chance of apprehension). Someone who has a guilt cost of zero will choose to steal the book because the marginal benefit of \$80 will exceed the marginal cost of \$50. In contrast, someone having a guilt cost of, say, \$40, will not steal the book. The marginal benefit of \$80 will not be as great as the marginal cost of \$90 (= \$50 of penalty cost + \$40 of guilt cost).

This perspective on illegal behavior has some interesting implications. For example, other things equal, crime will rise (more of it will be "bought") when its price falls. This explains, for instance, why some people who do not steal from stores under normal circumstances participate in looting stores during riots, when the marginal cost of being apprehended has substantially declined.

Another implication is that society can reduce unlawful behavior by increasing the "price of crime." It can nourish and increase guilt costs through family, educational, and religious efforts. It can increase the direct costs of crime by using more sophisticated security systems (locks, alarms, video surveillance) so that criminals will have to buy and use more sophisticated tools. It can undertake education and training initiatives to enhance the legitimate earnings of people who might otherwise engage in illegal activity. It can increase policing to raise the probability of being apprehended for crime. And it can impose greater penalties for those who are caught and convicted.

Summary

1. The law of diminishing marginal utility states that beyond a certain quantity, additional units of a specific good will yield declining amounts of extra satisfaction to a consumer.
2. The utility-maximization model assumes that the typical consumer is rational and acts on the basis of well-defined preferences. Because income is limited and goods have prices, the consumer cannot purchase all the goods and services he or she might want. The consumer therefore selects the attainable combination of goods that maximizes his or her utility or satisfaction.
3. A consumer's utility is maximized when income is allocated so that the last dollar spent on each product purchased yields the same amount of extra satisfaction. Algebraically, the utility-maximizing rule is fulfilled when

$$\frac{\text{MU of product A}}{\text{Price of A}} = \frac{\text{MU of product B}}{\text{Price of B}}$$

   and the consumer's total income is spent.
4. The utility-maximizing rule and the demand curve are logically consistent. Because marginal utility declines, a lower price is needed to induce the consumer to buy more of a particular product.
5. The utility-maximization model illuminates the income and substitution effects of a price change. The income effect implies that a decline in the price of a product increases the consumer's real income and enables the consumer to buy more of that product with a fixed money income. The substitution effect implies that a lower price makes a product relatively more attractive and therefore increases the consumer's willingness to substitute it for other products.

Terms and Concepts

law of diminishing marginal utility
utility
total utility
marginal utility
rational behavior
budget constraint
utility-maximizing rule
income effect
substitution effect

Study Questions

1. **KEY QUESTION** Complete the following table and answer the questions below:

Units Consumed	Total Utility	Marginal Utility
0	0	
1	10	10
2	—	8
3	25	—
4	30	—
5	—	3
6	34	—

   a. At which rate is total utility increasing: a constant rate, a decreasing rate, or an increasing rate? How do you know?
   b. "A rational consumer will purchase only 1 unit of the product represented by these data, since that amount maximizes marginal utility." Do you agree? Explain why or why not.
   c. "It is possible that a rational consumer will not purchase any units of the product represented by these data." Do you agree? Explain why or why not.

2. Mrs. Wilson buys loaves of bread and quarts of milk each week at prices of $1 and 80 cents, respectively. At present she is buying these products in amounts such that the marginal utilities from the last units purchased of the two products are 80 and 70 utils, respectively. Is she buying the utility-maximizing combination of bread and milk? If not, how should she reallocate her expenditures between the two goods?

3. **KEY QUESTION** Columns 1 through 4 in the table below show the marginal utility, measured in utils, that Ricardo would get by purchasing various amounts of products A, B, C, and D. Column 5 shows the marginal utility Ricardo gets from saving. Assume that the prices of A, B, C, and D are $18, $6, $4, and $24, respectively, and that Ricardo has an income of $106.
   a. What quantities of A, B, C, and D will Ricardo purchase in maximizing his utility?
   b. How many dollars will Ricardo choose to save?
   c. Check your answers by substituting them into the algebraic statement of the utility-maximizing rule.

4. **KEY QUESTION** You are choosing between two goods, X and Y, and your marginal utility from each is as shown on the next page. If your income is $9 and the prices of X and Y are $2 and $1, respectively, what quantities of each will you purchase to maximize utility? What total utility will you realize? Assume that, other things remaining unchanged, the price of X falls to $1. What quantities of X and Y will you now purchase? Using the two prices and quantities for X, derive a demand schedule (price–quantity-demanded table) for X.

Column 1		Column 2		Column 3		Column 4		Column 5	
Units of A	MU	Units of B	MU	Units of C	MU	Units of D	MU	Number of Dollars Saved	MU
1	72	1	24	1	15	1	36	1	5
2	54	2	15	2	12	2	30	2	4
3	45	3	12	3	8	3	24	3	3
4	36	4	9	4	7	4	18	4	2
5	27	5	7	5	5	5	13	5	1
6	18	6	5	6	4	6	7	6	$\frac{1}{2}$
7	15	7	2	7	$3\frac{1}{2}$	7	4	7	$\frac{1}{4}$
8	12	8	1	8	3	8	2	8	$\frac{1}{8}$

Units of X	MUx	Units of Y	MUy
1	10	1	8
2	8	2	7
3	6	3	6
4	4	4	5
5	3	5	4
6	2	6	3

5. How can time be incorporated into the theory of consumer behavior? Explain the following comment: "Want to make millions of dollars? Devise a product that saves Americans lots of time."
6. Explain:
   a. Before economic growth, there were too few goods; after growth, there is too little time.
   b. It is irrational for an individual to take the time to be completely rational in economic decision making.
   c. Telling Santa what you want for Christmas makes sense in terms of utility maximization.
7. In the last decade or so there has been a dramatic expansion of small retail convenience stores (such as Kwik Shops, 7 Elevens, Gas 'N Shops), although their prices are generally much higher than prices in large supermarkets. What explains the success of the convenience stores?
8. Many apartment-complex owners are installing water meters for each apartment and billing the occupants according to the amount of water they use. This is in contrast to the former procedure of having a central meter for the entire complex and dividing up the water expense as part of the rent. Where individual meters have been installed, water usage has declined 10 to 40 percent. Explain that drop, referring to price and marginal utility.
9. Using the utility-maximization rule as your point of reference, explain the income and substitution effects of an increases in the price of product B, with no change in the price of product A.
10. **ADVANCED ANALYSIS** A mathematically "fair bet" is one in which a gambler bets, say, \$100, for a 10 percent chance to win \$1000 dollars (\$100 = .10 × \$1000). Assuming diminishing marginal utility of dollars, explain why this is *not* a fair bet in terms of utility. Why is it even a less fair bet when the "house" takes a cut of each dollar bet? So is gambling irrational?
11. **ADVANCED ANALYSIS** Let $MU_A = z = 10 - x$ and $MU_B = z = 21 - 2y$, where z is marginal utility per dollar measured in utils, x is the amount spent on product A, and y is the amount spent on product B. Assume that the consumer has \$10 to spend on A and B—that is, $x + y = 10$. How is the \$10 best allocated between A and B? How much utility will the marginal dollar yield?
12. **LAST WORD** In what way is criminal behavior similar to consumer behavior? Why do most people obtain goods via legal behavior as opposed to illegal behavior? What are society's main options for reducing illegal behavior?

Web-Based Questions

1. **THE ESPN SPORTSZONE—TO FEE OR NOT TO FEE?** The ESPN Sportszone, at **espn.go.com/**, is a major sports information site. Most of the content is free, but ESPN has a premium membership (see its "Insider") available for a monthly or an annual fee. Similar, but fee-free, sports content can be found at the Web sites of CNN/Sports Illustrated, **www.cnnsi.com/**, and CBS Sports Line, **cbs.sportsline.com/**. Since ESPN has put a price tag on some of its sports content, it implies that the utility of a premium membership cannot be found at a no-fee site and is therefore worth the price. Is this the case? Use the utility-maximization rule to justify your subscribing or not subscribing to the premium membership.
2. **HERE IS \$500—GO SPEND IT AT WAL-MART** Assume that you and several classmates each receive a \$500 credit voucher (good for today only) from Wal-Mart Online. Go to **www.wal-mart.com/** and select \$500 worth of merchandise. Use Add to Cart to keep a running total, and use Review Cart to print your final selection. Compare your list with your classmates' lists. What explains the differences? Would you have purchased your items if you had received \$500 in cash to be spent whenever and wherever you pleased?

Indifference Curve Analysis

The utility-maximization rule previously discussed requires individuals to measure and compare utility, much as a business would measure and compare costs or revenues. Recognizing the difficulty of measuring utility, economists have developed an explanation of consumer behavior and equilibrium in which such measurement is not required. In this more-advanced analysis, the consumer must simply rank various combinations of two goods in terms of preference. The model has two main elements: budget lines and indifference curves.

The Budget Line: What Is Attainable

We know from Chapter 1 that a **budget line** (or, more technically, the *budget constraint*) is a schedule or curve showing various combinations of two products a consumer can purchase with a specific money income. If the price of product A is $1.50 and the price of product B is $1, a consumer could purchase all the combinations of A and B shown in the table in Figure 1 with $12 of money income. At one extreme, the consumer might spend all of his or her income on 8 units of A and have nothing left to spend on B. Or, by giving up 2 units of A and thereby "freeing" $3, the consumer could have 6 units of A and 3 of B. And so on to the other extreme, at which the consumer could buy 12 units of B at $1 each, spending his or her entire money income on B with nothing left to spend on A.

Figure 1 also shows the budget line graphically. Note that the graph is not restricted to whole units of A and B as is the table. Every point on the graph represents a possible combination of A and B, including fractional quantities. The slope of the graphed budget line measures the ratio of the price of B to the price of A; more precisely, the absolute value of the slope is $P_B/P_A = \$1.00/\$1.50 = \frac{2}{3}$. This is the mathematical way of saying that the consumer must forgo 2 units of A (measured on the vertical axis) to buy 3 units of B (measured on the horizontal axis). In moving down the budget or price line, 2 units of A (at $1.50 each) must be given up to obtain 3 more units of B (at $1 each). This yields a slope of $\frac{2}{3}$.

The budget line has two other significant characteristics:

- ***Income changes*** The location of the budget line varies with money income. An increase in money income shifts the budget line to the right; a decrease in money income shifts it to the left. To verify this, recalculate the table in Figure 1, assuming that money income is (a) $24 and (b) $6, and plot the new budget lines in Figure 1.
- ***Price changes*** A change in product prices also shifts the budget line. A decline in the prices of both products—the equivalent of an increase in real income—shifts the curve to the right. (You can verify this by recalculating the table in Figure 1 and replotting Figure 1 assuming that $P_A = \$.75$ and $P_B = \$.50$.) Conversely, an increase in the prices of A and

FIGURE 1 A consumer's budget line. The budget line shows all the combinations of any two products that can be purchased, given the prices of the products and the consumer's money income.

Units of A (Price = $1.50)	Units of B (Price = $1)	Total Expenditure
8	0	$12 (= $12 + $0)
6	3	$12 (= $9 + $3)
4	6	$12 (= $6 + $6)
2	9	$12 (= $3 + $9)
0	12	$12 (= $0 + $12)

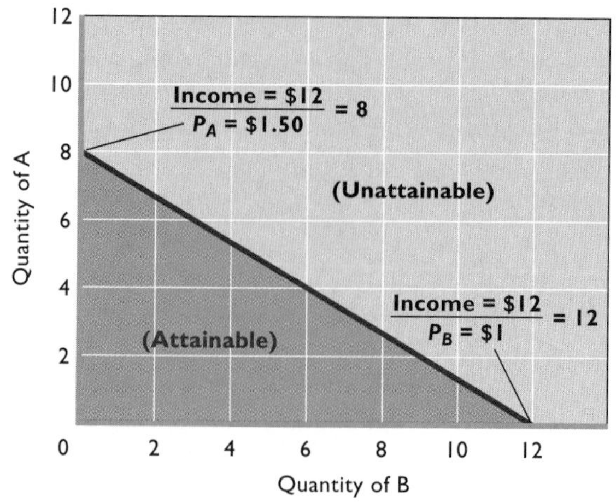

FIGURE 2 A consumer's indifference curve. Every point on indifference curve *I* represents some combination of products A and B, and all those combinations are equally satisfactory to the consumer. That is, each combination of A and B on the curve yields the same total utility.

Combination	Units of A	Units of B
j	12	2
k	6	4
l	4	6
m	3	8

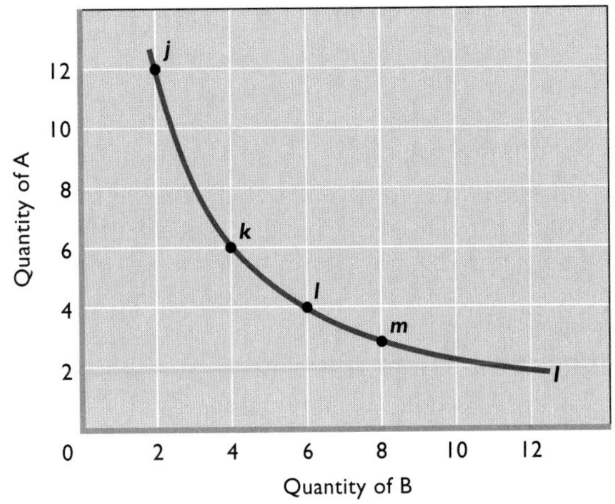

B shifts the curve to the left. (Assume $P_A = \$3$ and $P_B = \$2$, and rework the table and Figure 1 to substantiate this statement.)

Note what happens if P_B changes while P_A and money income remain constant. In particular, if P_B drops, say, from \$1 to \$.50, the lower end of the budget line fans outward to the right. Conversely, if P_B increases, say, from \$1 to \$1.50, the lower end of the line fans inward to the left. In both instances the line remains "anchored" at 8 units on the vertical axis because P_A has not changed.

Indifference Curves: What Is Preferred

Budget lines reflect "objective" market data, specifically income and prices. They reveal combinations of products A and B that can be purchased, given current money income and prices.

Indifference curves, on the other hand, reflect "subjective" information about consumer preferences for A and B. An **indifference curve** shows all the combinations of two products A and B that will yield the same total satisfaction or total utility to a consumer. The table and graph in Figure 2 present a hypothetical indifference curve for products A and B. The consumer's subjective preferences are such that he or she will realize the same total utility from each combination of A and B shown in the table or on the curve. So the consumer will be indifferent (will not care) as to which combination is actually obtained.

O 7.4
Indifference curves

Indifference curves have several important characteristics.

Indifference Curves Are Downsloping

An indifference curve slopes downward because more of one product means less of the other if total utility is to remain unchanged. Suppose the consumer moves from one combination of A and B to another, say, from *j* to *k* in Figure 2. In so doing, the consumer obtains more of product B, increasing his or her total utility. But because total utility is the same everywhere on the curve, the consumer must give up some of the other product, A, to reduce total utility by a precisely offsetting amount. Thus "more of B" necessitates "less of A," and the quantities of A and B are inversely related. A curve that reflects inversely related variables is downward-sloping.

Indifference Curves Are Convex to the Origin

Recall from the appendix to Chapter 1 that the slope of a curve at a particular point is measured by drawing a straight line that is tangent to that point and then measuring the "rise over run" of the straight line. If you drew such straight lines for several points on the curve in Figure 2, you would find that their slopes decline (in absolute terms) as you move down the curve. An indifference curve is therefore convex (bowed inward) to the origin of the graph. Its slope diminishes or becomes flatter as we move down the curve from *j* to *k* to *l*, and so on. Technically, the slope of an indifference curve at each point measures the **marginal rate of substitution (MRS)** of the combination of two goods represented by that point. The slope or MRS shows the rate at which the consumer who possesses the combination will substitute one good for the other (say, B for A) to remain equally satisfied. The diminishing slope of the indifference curve means that the willingness to substitute B for A diminishes as more of B is obtained.

The rationale for this convexity—that is, for a diminishing MRS—is that a consumer's subjective willingness to substitute B for A (or A for B) will depend on the amounts of B and A he or she has to begin with. Consider the table and graph in Figure 2 again, beginning at point *j*. Here, in relative terms, the consumer has a substantial amount of A and very little of B. Within this combination, a unit of B is very valuable (that is, its marginal utility is high), while a unit of A is less valuable (its marginal utility is low). The consumer will then be willing to give up a substantial amount of A to get, say, 2 more units of B. In this case, the consumer is willing to forgo 6 units of A to get 2 more units of B; the MRS is $\frac{6}{2}$, or 3, for the *jk* segment of the curve.

But at point *k* the consumer has less A and more B. Here A is somewhat more valuable, and B less valuable, "at the margin." In a move from point *k* to point *l*, the consumer is willing to give up only 2 units of A to get 2 more units of B, so the MRS is only $\frac{2}{2}$, or 1. Having still less of A and more of B at point *l*, the consumer is willing to give up only 1 unit of A in return for 2 more units of B and the MRS falls to $\frac{1}{2}$ between *l* and *m*.[1]

In general, as the amount of B *increases*, the marginal utility of additional units of B *decreases*. Similarly, as the quantity of A *decreases*, its marginal utility *increases*. In Figure 2 we see that in moving down the curve, the consumer will be willing to give up smaller and smaller amounts of A to offset acquiring each additional unit of B. The result is a curve with a diminishing slope, a curve that is convex to the origin. The MRS declines as one moves southeast along the indifference curve.

The Indifference Map

The single indifference curve of Figure 2 reflects some constant (but unspecified) level of total utility or satisfaction. It is possible and useful to sketch a whole series of indifference curves or an **indifference map,** as shown in Figure 3. Each curve reflects a different level of total utility and therefore never crosses another indifference curve. Specifically, each curve to the right of our original curve (labeled I_3 in Figure 3) reflects combinations of A and B that yield more utility than I_3. Each curve to the left of I_3 reflects less total utility than I_3. As we move out from the origin, each successive indifference curve represents a higher level of utility. To demonstrate this fact, draw a line in a northeasterly direction from the origin; note that its points of intersection with successive curves entail larger amounts of both A and B and therefore higher levels of total utility.

FIGURE 3 An indifference map. An indifference map is a set of indifference curves. Curves farther from the origin indicate higher levels of total utility. Thus any combination of products A and B represented by a point on I_4 has greater total utility than any combination of A and B represented by a point on I_3, I_2, or I_1.

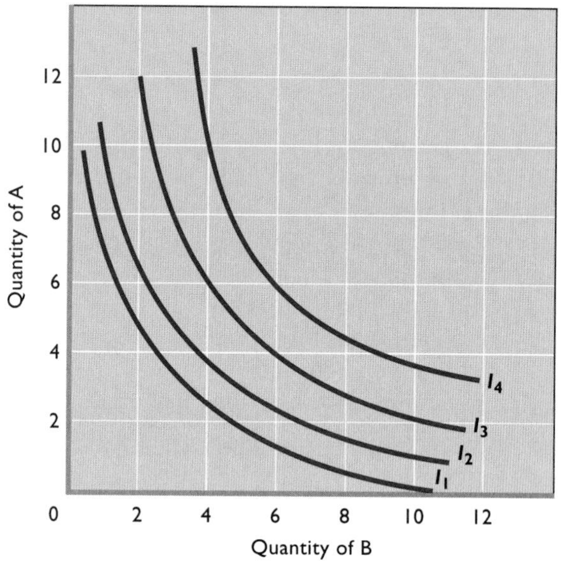

Equilibrium at Tangency

Since the axes in Figures 1 and 3 are identical, we can superimpose a budget line on the consumer's indifference map, as shown in Figure 4. By definition, the budget line indicates all the combinations of A and B that the consumer can attain with his or her money income, given the prices of A and B. Of these attainable combinations, the consumer will prefer the combination that yields the greatest satisfaction or utility. Specifically, the utility-maximizing combination will be the combination lying on the highest attainable indifference curve. It is called the consumer's **equilibrium position.**

In Figure 4 the consumer's equilibrium position is at point *X*, where the budget line is *tangent* to I_3. Why not point *Y*? Because *Y* is on a lower indifference curve, I_2. By moving "down" the budget line—by shifting dollars from purchases of A to purchases of B—the consumer can attain

[1]MRS declines continuously between *j* and *k*, *k* and *l*, and *l* and *m*. Our numerical values for MRS relate to the curve segments between points and are not the actual values of the MRS at each point. For example, the MRS *at* point *l* is $\frac{2}{3}$.

FIGURE 4 The consumer's equilibrium position. The consumer's equilibrium position is represented by point X, where the black budget line is tangent to indifference curve I_3. The consumer buys 4 units of A at $1.50 per unit and 6 of B at $1 per unit with a $12 money income. Points Z and Y represent attainable combinations of A and B but yield less total utility, as is evidenced by the fact that they are on lower indifference curves. Point W would entail more utility than X, but it requires a greater income than the $12 represented by the budget line.

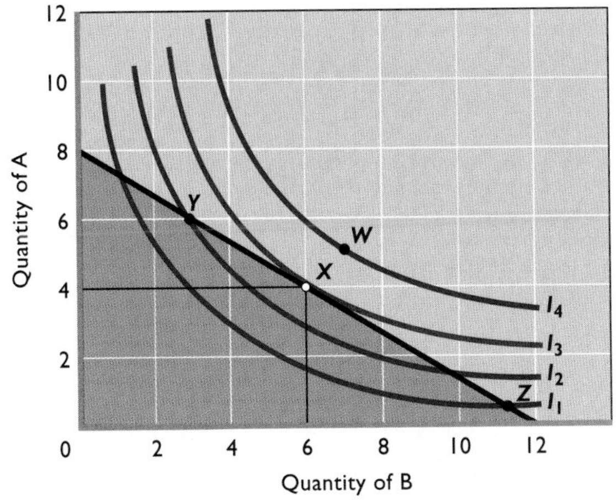

an indifference curve farther from the origin and thereby increase the total utility derived from the same income. Why not point *Z*? For the same reason: Point *Z* is on a lower indifference curve, I_1. By moving "up" the budget line—by reallocating dollars from B to A—the consumer can get on higher indifference curve I_3 and increase total utility.

How about point *W* on indifference curve I_4? While it is true that *W* would yield a greater total utility than *X*, point *W* is beyond (outside) the budget line and hence is *not* attainable by the consumer. Point *X* represents the optimal *attainable* combination of products A and B. Note that, according to the definition of tangency, the slope of the highest attainable indifference curve equals the slope of the budget line. Because the slope of the indifference curve reflects the MRS (marginal rate of substitution) and the slope of the budget line is P_B/P_A, the consumer's optimal or equilibrium position is the point where

$$\text{MRS} = \frac{P_B}{P_A}$$

(You may benefit by trying **Appendix Key Question 3** at this time.)

The Measurement of Utility

As indicated at the beginning of this appendix, an important difference exists between the marginal-utility theory of consumer demand and the indifference curve theory. The marginal-utility theory assumes that utility is *numerically* measurable, that is, that the consumer can say how much extra utility he or she derives from each extra unit of A or B. The consumer needs that information to realize the utility-maximizing (equilibrium) position, as indicated by

$$\frac{\text{Marginal utility of A}}{\text{Price of A}} = \frac{\text{Marginal utility of B}}{\text{Price of B}}$$

The indifference curve approach imposes a less stringent requirement on the consumer. He or she need only specify whether a particular combination of A and B will yield more than, less than, or the same amount of utility as some other combination of A and B will yield. The consumer need only say, for example, that 6 of A and 7 of B will yield more (or less) satisfaction than will 4 of A and 9 of B. Indifference

CONSIDER THIS . . .

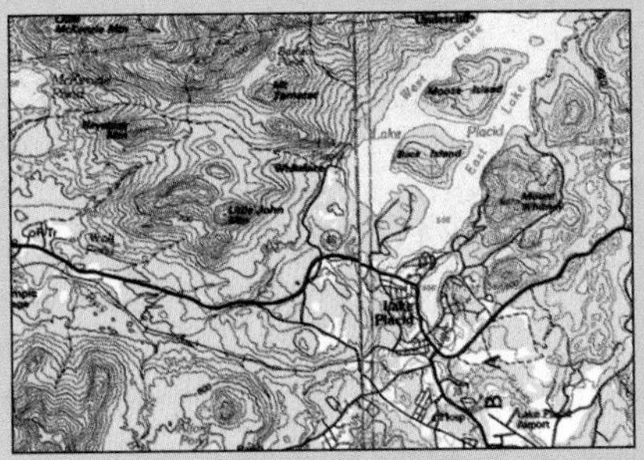

Indifference Maps and Topographical Maps

The familiar topographical map may help you understand the idea of indifference curves and indifference maps. Each line on a topographical map represents a particular elevation above sea level, say, 4000 feet. Similarly, an indifference curve represents a particular level of total utility. When you move from one point on a specific elevation line to another, the elevation remains the same. So it is with an indifference curve. A move from one position to another on the curve leaves total utility unchanged. Neither elevation lines nor indifference curves can intersect. If they did, the meaning of each line or curve would be violated. An elevation line is "an equal-elevation line"; an indifference curve is "an equal-total-utility curve."

Like the topographical map, an indifference map contains not just one line but a series of lines. That is, the topographical map may have elevation lines representing successively higher elevations of 1000, 2000, 3000, 4000, and 5000 feet. Similarly, the indifference curves on the indifference map represent successively higher levels of total utility. The climber whose goal is to maximize elevation wants to get to the highest attainable elevation line; the consumer desiring to maximize total utility wants to get to the highest attainable indifference curve.

Finally, both topographical maps and indifference maps show only a few of the many such lines that could be drawn. The topographical map, for example, leaves out the elevation lines for 1001 feet, 1002, 1003, and so on. The indifference map leaves out all the indifference curves that could be drawn between those illustrated.

curve theory does not require that the consumer specify *how much* more (or less) satisfaction will be realized.

When we compare the equilibrium situations in the two theories, we find that in the indifference curve analysis the MRS equals P_B/P_A at equilibrium; however, in the marginal-utility approach the ratio of marginal utilities equals P_B/P_A. We therefore deduce that at equilibrium the MRS is equivalent in the marginal-utility approach to the ratio of the marginal utilities of the last purchased units of the two products.[2]

The Derivation of the Demand Curve

We noted earlier that with a fixed price for A, an increase in the price of B will cause the bottom of the budget line to fan inward to the left. We can use that fact to derive a demand curve for product B. In Figure 5a we reproduce the part of Figure 4 that shows our initial consumer equilibrium at point *X*. The budget line determining this equilibrium position assumes that money income is $12 and that $P_A = \$1.50$ and $P_B = \$1$. Let's see what happens to the equilibrium position when we increase P_B to $1.50 and hold both money income and the price of A constant.

The result is shown in Figure 5a. The budget line fans to the left, yielding a new equilibrium point *X′* where it is tangent to lower indifference curve I_2. At *X′* the consumer buys 3 units of B and 5 of A, compared with 4 of A and 6 of B at *X*. Our interest is in B, and we now have sufficient information to locate two points on the demand curve for product B. We know that at equilibrium point *X* the price of B is $1 and 6 units are purchased; at equilibrium point *X′* the price of B is $1.50 and 3 units are purchased.

These data are shown graphically in Figure 5b as points on the consumer's demand curve for B. Note that the horizontal axes of Figure 5a and 5b are identical; both measure the quantity demanded of B. We can therefore drop vertical reference lines from Figure 5a down to the horizontal axis of Figure 5b. On the vertical axis of Figure 5b we locate the two chosen prices of B. Knowing that these prices yield the relevant quantities demanded, we locate two points on the demand curve for B. By simple manipulation of the price of B in an indifference curve–budget line context, we have obtained a downward-sloping demand curve for B. We have thus again derived the law of demand assuming "other things equal," since only the price of B was changed (the price of A and the consumer's money income and tastes remained constant). But, in this case, we have derived the demand curve without resorting to the questionable assumption that consumers can measure utility in units called "utils." In this indifference curve approach, consumers simply compare combinations of products A and B and determine which combination they prefer, given their incomes and the prices of the two products.

FIGURE 5 Deriving the demand curve. (a) When the price of product B is increased from $1 to $1.50, the equilibrium position moves from X to X′, decreasing the quantity of product B demanded from 6 to 3 units. (b) The demand curve for product B is determined by plotting the $1–6-unit and the $1.50–3-unit price-quantity combinations for product B.

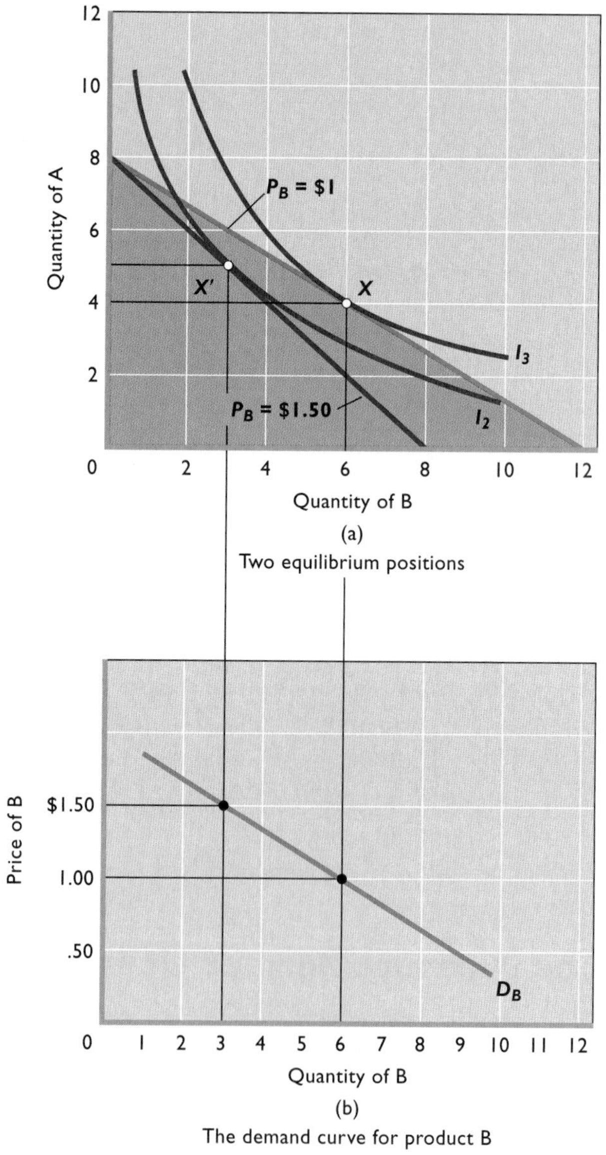

[2]Technical footnote: If we begin with the utility-maximizing rule, $MU_A/P_A = MU_B/P_B$, and then multiply through by P_B and divide through by MU_A, we obtain $P_B/P_A = MU_B/MU_A$. In indifference curve analysis we know that at the equilibrium position MRS $= P_B/P_A$. Hence, at equilibrium, MRS also equals MU_B/MU_A.

Appendix Summary

1. The indifference curve approach to consumer behavior is based on the consumer's budget line and indifference curves.
2. The budget line shows all combinations of two products that the consumer can purchase, given product prices and his or her money income.
3. A change in either product prices or money income moves the budget line.
4. An indifference curve shows all combinations of two products that will yield the same total utility to a consumer. Indifference curves are downward-sloping and convex to the origin.
5. An indifference map consists of a number of indifference curves; the farther from the origin, the higher the total utility associated with a curve.
6. The consumer is in equilibrium (utility is maximized) at the point on the budget line that lies on the highest attainable indifference curve. At that point the budget line and indifference curve are tangent.
7. Changing the price of one product shifts the budget line and determines a new equilibrium point. A downsloping demand curve can be determined by plotting the price-quantity combinations associated with two or more equilibrium points.

Appendix Terms and Concepts

budget line

indifference curve

marginal rate of substitution (MRS)

indifference map

equilibrium position

Appendix Study Questions

1. What information is embodied in a budget line? What shifts occur in the budget line when money income (*a*) increases and (*b*) decreases? What shifts occur in the budget line when the price of the product shown on the vertical axis (*a*) increases and (*b*) decreases?
2. What information is contained in an indifference curve? Why are such curves (*a*) downward-sloping and (*b*) convex to the origin? Why does total utility increase as the consumer moves to indifference curves farther from the origin? Why can't indifference curves intersect?
3. **APPENDIX KEY QUESTION** Using Figure 4, explain why the point of tangency of the budget line with an indifference curve is the consumer's equilibrium position. Explain why any point where the budget line intersects an indifference curve is not equilibrium. Explain: "The consumer is in equilibrium where MRS = P_B/P_A."
4. Assume that the data in the accompanying table give an indifference curve for Mr. Chen. Graph this curve, putting A on the vertical axis and B on the horizontal axis. Assuming that the prices of A and B are \$1.50 and \$1, respectively, and that Mr. Chen has \$24 to spend, add his budget line to your graph. What combination of A and B will Mr. Chen purchase? Does your answer meet the MRS = P_B/P_A rule for equilibrium?

Units of A	Units of B
16	6
12	8
8	12
4	24

5. Explain graphically how indifference analysis can be used to derive a demand curve.
6. **ADVANCED ANALYSIS** Demonstrate mathematically that the equilibrium condition MRS = P_B/P_A is the equivalent of the utility-maximizing rule $MU_A/P_A = MU_B/P_B$.

8

IN THIS CHAPTER YOU WILL LEARN:

- **Why economic costs include both explicit (revealed and expressed) costs and implicit (present but not obvious) costs.**
- **How the law of diminishing returns relates to a firm's short-run production costs.**
- **The distinctions between fixed and variable costs and among total, average, and marginal costs.**
- **The link between a firm's size and its average costs in the long run.**

The Costs of Production

Our attention now turns from the behavior of consumers to the behavior of producers. In market economies, a wide variety of businesses produce an even wider variety of goods and services. Each of those businesses requires economic resources in order to produce its products. In obtaining and using resources, a firm makes monetary payments to resource owners (for example, workers) and incurs opportunity costs when using resources it already owns (for example, entrepreneurial talent). Those payments and opportunity costs together make up the firm's *costs of production,* which we discuss in this chapter.

Then, in the next several chapters, we bring product demand, product prices, and revenue back into the analysis and explain how firms compare revenues and costs in determining how much to produce. Our ultimate purpose is to show how those comparisons relate to economic efficiency.

Economic Costs

Costs exist because resources are scarce, productive, and have alternative uses. When society uses a combination of resources to produce a particular product, it forgoes all alternative opportunities to use those resources for other purposes. The measure of the **economic cost,** or **opportunity cost,** of any resource used to produce a good is the value or worth the resource would have in its best alternative use.

We stressed this view of costs in our analysis of production possibilities in Chapter 1, where we found that the opportunity cost of producing more pizzas is the industrial robots that must be forgone. Similarly, the opportunity cost of the steel used in constructing office buildings is the value it would have in manufacturing automobiles or refrigerators. The paper used for printing economics textbooks is not available for printing encyclopedias or romance novels. And if an assembly-line worker is capable of assembling either personal computers or washing machines, then the cost to society of employing that worker in a computer plant is the contribution he or she would otherwise have made in producing washing machines.

Explicit and Implicit Costs

Now let's consider costs from the firm's viewpoint. Keeping opportunity costs in mind, we can say that economic costs are the payments a firm must make, or the incomes it must provide, to attract the resources it needs away from alternative production opportunities. Those payments to resource suppliers are explicit (revealed and expressed) or implicit (present but not obvious). So in producing products firms incur *explicit costs* and *implicit costs.*

- A firm's **explicit costs** are the monetary payments (or cash expenditures) it makes to those who supply labor services, materials, fuel, transportation services, and the like. Such money payments are for the use of resources owned by others.
- A firm's **implicit costs** are the opportunity costs of using its self-owned, self-employed resources. To the firm, implicit costs are the money payments that self-employed resources could have earned in their best alternative use.

Example: Suppose you are earning $22,000 a year as a sales representative for a T-shirt manufacturer. At some point you decide to open a retail store of your own to sell T-shirts. You invest $20,000 of savings that have been earning you $1000 per year. And you decide that your new firm will occupy a small store that you own and have been renting out for $5000 per year. You hire one clerk to help you in the store, paying her $18,000 annually.

A year after you open the store, you total up your accounts and find the following:

Total sales revenue		$120,000
Cost of T-shirts	$40,000	
Clerk's salary	18,000	
Utilities	5000	
Total (explicit) costs		63,000
Accounting profit		57,000

Looks good. But unfortunately your accounting profit of $57,000 ignores your implicit costs and thus overstates the economic success of your venture. By providing your own financial capital, building, and labor, you incur implicit costs (forgone incomes) of $1000 of interest, $5000 of rent, and $22,000 of wages. If your entrepreneurial talent is worth, say, $5000 annually in other business endeavors of similar scope, you have also ignored that implicit cost. So:

Accounting profit		$57,000
Forgone interest	$ 1000	
Forgone rent	5000	
Forgone wages	22,000	
Forgone entrepreneurial income	5000	
Total implicit costs		33,000
Economic profit		24,000

Normal Profit as a Cost

The $5000 implicit cost of your entrepreneurial talent in the above example is a **normal profit**. As is true of the forgone rent and forgone wages, the payment you could otherwise receive for performing entrepreneurial functions is indeed an implicit cost. If you did not realize at least this minimum, or normal, payment for your effort, you could withdraw from this line of business and shift to a more attractive endeavor. So a normal profit is a cost of doing business.

The economist includes as costs of production all the costs—explicit and implicit, including a normal profit—required to attract and retain resources in a specific line of production. For economists, a firm's economic costs are the opportunity costs of the resources used, whether those resources are owned by others or by the firm. In our example, economic costs are $96,000 (= $63,000 of explicit costs + $33,000 of implicit costs).

Economic Profit (or Pure Profit)

Obviously, then, economists use the term "profit" differently from the way accountants use it. To the accountant, profit is the firm's total revenue less its explicit costs (or accounting costs). To the economist, **economic profit** is total revenue less economic costs (explicit and implicit costs, the latter including a normal profit to the entrepreneur). So when an economist says a certain firm is earning only enough revenue to cover its costs, this means it is meeting all explicit and implicit costs and the entrepreneur is receiving a payment just large enough to retain his or her talents in the present line of production.

If a firm's total revenue exceeds all its economic costs (explicit + implicit), any residual goes to the entrepreneur. That residual is called an *economic,* or *pure, profit.* In short:

$$\text{Economic profit} = \text{total revenue} - \text{economic cost}$$

In our example, economic profit is $24,000, found by subtracting the $96,000 of economic cost from the $120,000 of revenue. An *economic* profit is not a cost, because it is a return in excess of the normal profit that is required to retain the entrepreneur in this particular line of production. Even if the economic profit is zero, the entrepreneur is still covering all explicit and implicit costs, including a normal profit. In our example, as long as accounting profit is $33,000 or more (so economic profit is zero or more), you will be earning a $5000 normal profit and will therefore continue to operate your T-shirt store.

W 8.1
Economic profit

Figure 8.1 shows the relationship among the various cost and profit concepts that we have just discussed. To test yourself, you might want to enter cost data from our example in the appropriate blocks. **(Key Question 2)**

Short Run and Long Run

When the demand for a firm's product changes, the firm's profitability may depend on how quickly it can adjust the amounts of the various resources it employs. It can easily and quickly adjust the quantities employed of many resources such as hourly labor, raw materials, fuel, and power. It needs much more time, however, to adjust its *plant capacity*—the size of the factory building, the amount of machinery and equipment, and other capital resources. In some heavy industries such as aircraft manufacturing, a firm may need several years to alter plant capacity. Because of these differences in adjustment time, economists find it useful to distinguish between two conceptual periods: the short run and the long run. We will discover that costs differ in these two time periods.

FIGURE 8.1 Economic profit versus accounting profit. Economic profit is equal to total revenue less economic costs. Economic costs are the sum of explicit and implicit costs and include a normal profit to the entrepreneur. Accounting profit is equal to total revenue less accounting (explicit) costs.

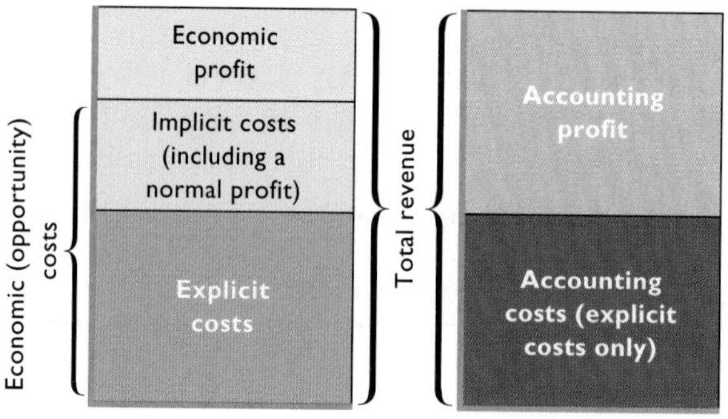

Short Run: Fixed Plant

The **short run** is a period too brief for a firm to alter its plant capacity, yet long enough to permit a change in the degree to which the fixed plant is used. The firm's plant capacity is fixed in the short run. However, the firm can vary its output by applying larger or smaller amounts of labor, materials, and other resources to that plant. It can use its existing plant capacity more or less intensively in the short run.

Long Run: Variable Plant

From the viewpoint of an existing firm, the **long run** is a period long enough for it to adjust the quantities of all the resources that it employs, including plant capacity. From the industry's viewpoint, the long run also includes enough time for existing firms to dissolve and leave the industry or for new firms to be created and enter the industry. While the short run is a "fixed-plant" period, the long run is a "variable-plant" period.

Illustrations

If Boeing hires 100 extra workers for one of its commercial airline plants or adds an entire shift of workers, we are speaking of the short run. If it adds a new production facility and installs more equipment, we are referring to the long run. The first situation is a *short-run adjustment;* the second is a *long-run adjustment.*

The short run and the long run are conceptual periods rather than calendar time periods. In light-manufacturing industries, changes in plant capacity may be accomplished almost overnight. A small T-shirt manufacturer can increase its plant capacity in a matter of days by ordering and installing two or three new cutting tables and several extra sewing machines. But for heavy industry the long run is a different matter. Shell Oil may require several years to construct a new gasoline refinery.

QUICK REVIEW 8.1

- Explicit costs are money payments a firm makes to outside suppliers of resources; implicit costs are the opportunity costs associated with a firm's use of resources it owns.
- Normal profit is the implicit cost of entrepreneurship. Economic profit is total revenue less all explicit and implicit costs, including normal profit.
- In the short run, a firm's plant capacity is fixed; in the long run, a firm can vary its plant size and firms can enter or leave the industry.

Short-Run Production Relationships

A firm's costs of producing a specific output depend on the prices of the needed resources and the quantities of resources (inputs) needed to produce that output. Resource supply and demand determine resource prices. The technological aspects of production, specifically the relationships between inputs and output, determine the quantities of resources needed. Our focus will be on the *labor*-output relationship, given a fixed plant capacity. But before examining that relationship, we need to define three terms:

- **Total product (TP)** is the total quantity, or total output, of a particular good or service produced.
- **Marginal product (MP)** is the extra output or added product associated with adding a unit of a variable resource, in this case labor, to the production process. Thus,

$$\text{Marginal product} = \frac{\text{change in total product}}{\text{change in labor input}}$$

- **Average product (AP)**, also called labor productivity, is output per unit of labor input:

$$\text{Average product} = \frac{\text{total product}}{\text{units of labor}}$$

In the short run, a firm can for a time increase its output by adding units of labor to its fixed plant. But by how much will output rise when it adds the labor? Why do we say "for a time"?

Law of Diminishing Returns

The answers are provided in general terms by the **law of diminishing returns.** This law assumes that technology is fixed and thus the techniques of production do not change. It states that as successive units of a variable resource (say, labor) are added to a fixed resource (say, capital or land), beyond some point the extra, or marginal, product that can be attributed to each additional unit of the variable resource will decline. For example, if additional workers are hired to work with a constant amount of capital equipment, output will eventually rise by smaller and smaller amounts as more workers are hired.

O 8.1
Law of diminishing returns

Rationale Suppose a farmer has a fixed resource of 80 acres planted in corn. If the farmer does not cultivate the cornfields (clear the weeds) at all, the yield will be 40 bushels per acre. If he cultivates the land once, output may rise to 50 bushels per acre. A second cultivation may increase output to 57 bushels per acre, a third to 61, and a fourth to 63. Succeeding cultivations will add less and less to the land's yield. If this were not so, the world's needs for corn could be fulfilled by extremely intense cultivation of this single 80- acre plot of land. Indeed, if diminishing returns did not occur, the world could be fed out of a flowerpot. Why not? Just keep adding more seed, fertilizer, and harvesters!

CONSIDER THIS . . .

Diminishing Returns from Study

Here is a noneconomic example of a relationship between "inputs" and "output" that may help you better understand the idea of diminishing returns. Suppose for an individual that

Total course learning = *f* (intelligence, quality of course materials, instructor effectiveness, class time, and study time)

where *f* means "function of" or "depends on." So this relationship supposes that total course learning depends on intelligence (however defined), quality of course materials such as the textbook, the effectiveness of the instructor, the amount of class time, and the amount of personal study time outside the class.

For analytical purposes, let's assume that one's intelligence, the quality of course materials, the effectiveness of the instructor, and the amount of class time are *fixed*—meaning they do not change over the length of the course. Now let's add units of study time per day over the length of the course to "produce" greater course learning. The first hour of study time per day increases total course learning. Will the second hour enhance course learning by as much as the first? By how much will the third, fourth, fifth, . . . fifteenth hour of study per day contribute to total course learning relative to the *immediate previous hour?*

We think you will agree that eventually diminishing returns to course learning will set in as successive hours of study are added each day. At some point the marginal product of an extra hour of study time will decline and, at some further point, become zero.

This is also true of production relationships within firms. As successive units of a variable input (say, labor) are added to a fixed input (say, capital), the marginal product of the variable input eventually declines. In short, diminishing returns will occur sooner or later. Total product eventually will rise at a diminishing rate, reach a maximum, and then decline.

The law of diminishing returns also holds true in nonagricultural industries. Assume a wood shop is manufacturing furniture frames. It has a specific amount of equipment such as lathes, planes, saws, and sanders. If this shop hired just one or two workers, total output and productivity (output per worker) would be very low. The workers would have to perform many different jobs, and the advantages of specialization would not be realized. Time would be lost in switching from one job to another, and machines would stand idle much of the time. In short, the plant would be understaffed, and production would be inefficient because there would be too much capital relative to the amount of labor.

The shop could eliminate those difficulties by hiring more workers. Then the equipment would be more fully used, and workers could specialize on doing a single job. Time would no longer be lost switching from job to job. As more workers were added, production would become more efficient and the marginal product of each succeeding worker would rise.

But the rise could not go on indefinitely. If still more workers were added, beyond a certain point, overcrowding would set in. Since workers would then have to wait in line to use the machinery, they would be underused. Total output would increase at a diminishing rate, because, given the fixed size of the plant, each worker would have less capital equipment to work with as more and more labor was hired. The marginal product of additional workers would decline, because there would be more labor in proportion to the fixed amount of capital. Eventually, adding still more workers would cause so much congestion that marginal product would become negative and total product would decline. At the extreme, the addition of more and more labor would exhaust all the standing room, and total product would fall to zero.

Note that the law of diminishing returns assumes that all units of labor are of equal quality. Each successive worker is presumed to have the same innate ability, motor coordination, education, training, and work experience. Marginal product ultimately diminishes, not because successive workers are less skilled or less energetic but because more workers are being used relative to the amount of plant and equipment available.

Tabular Example Table 8.1 is a numerical illustration of the law of diminishing returns. Column 2 shows the total product, or total output, resulting from combining each level of a variable input (labor) in column 1 with a fixed amount of capital.

Column 3 shows the marginal product (MP), the change in total product associated with each additional unit of labor. Note that with no labor input, total product is zero; a plant with no workers will produce no output. The first 3 units of labor reflect increasing marginal returns, with marginal products of 10, 15, and 20 units, respectively. But beginning with the fourth unit of labor, marginal product diminishes continuously, becoming zero with the seventh unit of labor and negative with the eighth.

W 8.2
Total, marginal, and average product

Average product, or output per labor unit, is shown in column 4. It is calculated by dividing total product (column 2) by the number of labor units needed to produce it (column 1). At 5 units of labor, for example, AP is 14 (= 70/5).

Graphical Portrayal **Figure 8.2 (Key Graph)** shows the diminishing-returns data in Table 8.1 graphically and further clarifies the relationships between total, marginal, and average products. (Marginal product in

TABLE 8.1 Total, Marginal, and Average Product: The Law of Diminishing Returns

(1) Units of the Variable Resource (Labor)	(2) Total Product (TP)	(3) Marginal Product (MP), Change in (2)/Change in (1)		(4) Average Product (AP), (2)/(1)
0	0			—
1	10	10	Increasing marginal returns	10.00
2	25	15		12.50
3	45	20		15.00
4	60	15	Diminishing marginal returns	15.00
5	70	10		14.00
6	75	5		12.50
7	75	0	Negative marginal returns	10.71
8	70	−5		8.75

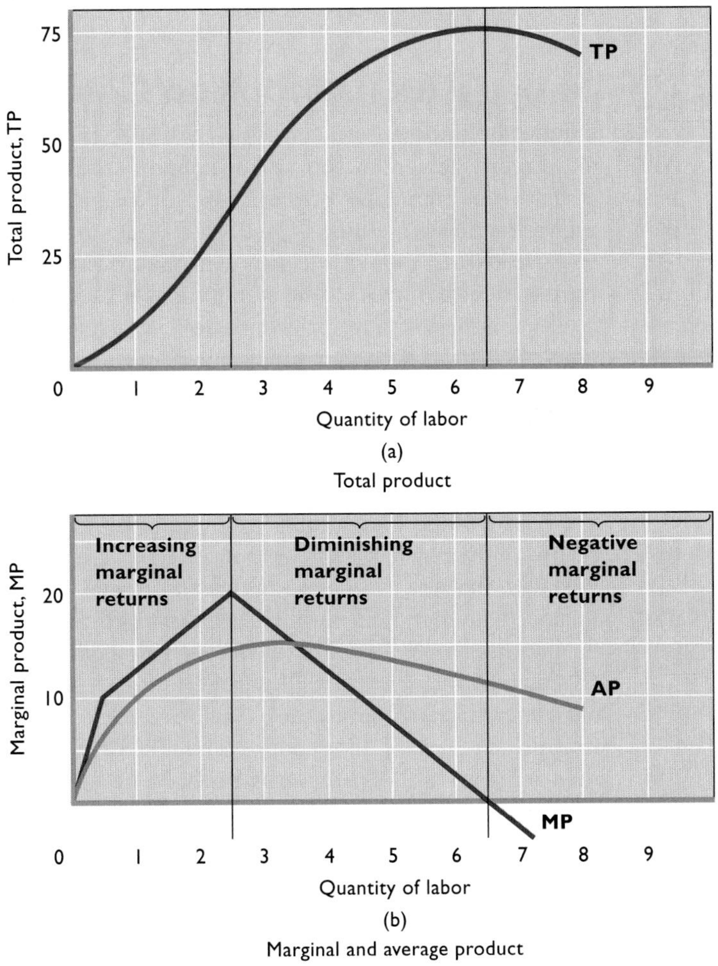

FIGURE 8.2 The law of diminishing returns. (a) As a variable resource (labor) is added to fixed amounts of other resources (land or capital), the total product that results will eventually increase by diminishing amounts, reach a maximum, and then decline. (b) Marginal product is the change in total product associated with each new unit of labor. Average product is simply output per labor unit. Note that marginal product intersects average product at the maximum average product.

QUICK QUIZ 8.2

1. Which of the following is an assumption underlying these figures?
   - **a.** Firms first hire "better" workers and then hire "poorer" workers.
   - **b.** Capital and labor are both variable, but labor increases more rapidly than capital.
   - **c.** Consumers will buy all the output (total product) produced.
   - **d.** Workers are of equal quality.
2. Marginal product is:
   - **a.** the change in total product divided by the change in the quantity of labor.
   - **b.** total product divided by the quantity of labor.
   - **c.** always positive.
   - **d.** unrelated to total product.
3. Marginal product in graph (b) is zero when:
   - **a.** average product in graph (b) stops rising.
   - **b.** the slope of the marginal-product curve in graph (b) is zero.
   - **c.** total product in graph (a) begins to rise at a diminishing rate.
   - **d.** the slope of the total-product curve in graph (a) is zero.
4. Average product in graph (b):
   - **a.** rises when it is less than marginal product.
   - **b.** is the change in total product divided by the change in the quantity of labor.
   - **c.** can never exceed marginal product.
   - **d.** falls whenever total product in graph (a) rises at a diminishing rate.

Answers: 1. d; 2. a; 3. d; 4. a

Figure 8.2b is plotted halfway between the units of labor, since it applies to the addition of each labor unit.)

Note first in Figure 8.2a that total product, TP, goes through three phases: It rises initially at an increasing rate; then it increases, but at a diminishing rate; finally, after reaching a maximum, it declines.

Geometrically, marginal product—shown by the MP curve in Figure 8.2b—is the slope of the total-product curve. Marginal product measures the change in total product associated with each succeeding unit of labor. Thus, the three phases of total product are also reflected in marginal product. Where total product is increasing at an increasing rate, marginal product is rising. Here, extra units of labor are adding larger and larger amounts to total product. Similarly, where total product is increasing but at a decreasing rate, marginal product is positive but falling. Each additional unit of labor adds less to total product than did the previous unit. When total product is at a maximum, marginal product is zero. When total product declines, marginal product becomes negative.

Average product, AP (Figure 8.2b), displays the same tendencies as marginal product. It increases, reaches a maximum, and then decreases as more and more units of labor are added to the fixed plant. But note the relationship between marginal product and average product: Where marginal product exceeds average product, average product rises. And where marginal product is less than average product, average product declines. It follows that marginal product intersects average product where average product is at a maximum.

This relationship is a mathematical necessity. If you add a larger number to a total than the current average of that total, the average must rise. And if you add a smaller number to a total than the current average of that total, the average must fall. You raise your average examination grade only when your score on an additional (marginal) examination is greater than the average of all your past scores. You lower your average when your grade on an additional exam is below your current average. In our production example, when the amount an extra worker adds to total product exceeds the average product of all workers currently employed, average product will rise. Conversely, when an extra worker adds to total product an amount that is less than the current average product, then average product will decrease.

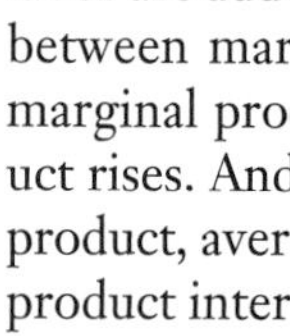

O 8.2
Production relationship

The law of diminishing returns is embodied in the shapes of all three curves. But, as our definition of the law of diminishing returns indicates, economists are most concerned with its effects on marginal product. The regions of increasing, diminishing, and negative marginal product (returns) are shown in Figure 8.2b. **(Key Question 4)**

Short-Run Production Costs

Production information such as that provided in Table 8.1 and Figure 8.2a and 8.2b must be coupled with resource prices to determine the total and per-unit costs of producing various levels of output. We know that in the short run some resources, those associated with the firm's plant, are fixed. Other resources, however, are variable. So short-run costs are either fixed or variable.

Fixed, Variable, and Total Costs

Let's see what distinguishes fixed costs, variable costs, and total costs from one another.

Fixed Costs **Fixed costs** are those costs that in total do not vary with changes in output. Fixed costs are associated with the very existence of a firm's plant and therefore must be paid even if its output is zero. Such costs as rental payments, interest on a firm's debts, a portion of depreciation on equipment and buildings, and insurance premiums are generally fixed costs; they do not increase even if a firm produces more. In column 2 of Table 8.2 we assume that the firm's total fixed cost is $100. By definition, this fixed cost is incurred at all levels of output, including zero. The firm cannot avoid paying fixed costs in the short run.

Variable Costs **Variable costs** are those costs that change with the level of output. They include payments for materials, fuel, power, transportation services, most labor, and similar variable resources. In column 3 of Table 8.2 we find that the total of variable costs changes directly with output. But note that the increases in variable cost associated with succeeding 1-unit increases in output are not equal. As production begins, variable cost will for a time increase by a decreasing amount; this is true through the fourth unit of output in Table 8.2. Beyond the fourth unit, however, variable cost rises by increasing amounts for succeeding units of output.

The reason lies in the shape of the marginal-product curve. At first, as in Figure 8.2b, marginal product is increasing, so smaller and smaller increases in the amounts of variable resources are needed to produce successive units of output. Hence the variable cost of successive units of output decreases. But when, as diminishing returns are encountered, marginal product begins to decline, larger and larger additional amounts of variable resources are needed to produce successive units of output. Total variable cost therefore increases by increasing amounts.

TABLE 8.2 Total-, Average-, and Marginal-Cost Schedules for an Individual Firm in the Short Run

Total-Cost Data				Average-Cost Data			Marginal Cost
(1) Total Product (Q)	(2) Total Fixed Cost (TFC)	(3) Total Variable Cost (TVC)	(4) Total Cost (TC) TC = TFC + TVC	(5) Average Fixed Cost (AFC) $AFC = \frac{TFC}{Q}$	(6) Average Variable Cost (AVC) $AVC = \frac{TVC}{Q}$	(7) Average Total Cost (ATC) $ATC = \frac{TC}{Q}$	(8) Marginal Cost (MC) $MC = \frac{\text{change in TC}}{\text{change in Q}}$
0	$100	$ 0	$ 100				
1	100	90	190	$100.00	$90.00	$190.00	$ 90
2	100	170	270	50.00	85.00	135.00	80
3	100	240	340	33.33	80.00	113.33	70
4	100	300	400	25.00	75.00	100.00	60
5	100	370	470	20.00	74.00	94.00	70
6	100	450	550	16.67	75.00	91.67	80
7	100	540	640	14.29	77.14	91.43	90
8	100	650	750	12.50	81.25	93.75	110
9	100	780	880	11.11	86.67	97.78	130
10	100	930	1030	10.00	93.00	103.00	150

Total Cost **Total Cost** is the sum of fixed cost and variable cost at each level of output:

$$TC = TFC + TVC$$

TC is shown in column 4 of Table 8.2. At zero units of output, total cost is equal to the firm's fixed cost. Then for each unit of the 10 units of production, total cost increases by the same amount as variable cost.

Figure 8.3 shows graphically the fixed-, variable-, and total-cost data given in Table 8.2. Observe that total variable cost, TVC, is measured vertically from the horizontal axis at each level of output. The amount of fixed cost, shown as TFC, is added vertically to the total-variable-cost curve to obtain the points on the total-cost curve TC.

The distinction between fixed and variable costs is significant to the business manager. Variable costs can be controlled or altered in the short run by changing production levels. Fixed costs are beyond the business manager's current control; they are incurred in the short run and must be paid regardless of output level.

Per-Unit, or Average, Costs

Producers are certainly interested in their total costs, but they are equally concerned with per-unit, or average, costs. In particular, average-cost data are more meaningful for making comparisons with product price, which is always stated on a per-unit basis. Average fixed cost, average variable cost, and average total cost are shown in columns 5 to 7, Table 8.2.

AFC **Average fixed cost (AFC)** for any output level is found by dividing total fixed cost (TFC) by that output (Q). That is,

$$AFC = \frac{TFC}{Q}$$

Because the total fixed cost is, by definition, the same regardless of output, AFC must decline as output increases.

FIGURE 8.3 Total cost is the sum of fixed cost and variable cost. Total variable cost (TVC) changes with output. Total fixed cost (TFC) is independent of the level of output. The total cost (TC) at any output is the vertical sum of the fixed cost and variable cost at that output.

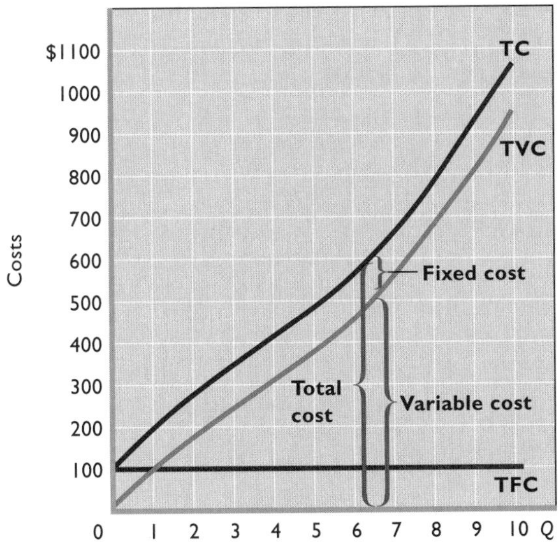

As output rises, the total fixed cost is spread over a larger and larger output. When output is just 1 unit in Table 8.2, TFC and AFC are the same at $100. But at 2 units of output, the total fixed cost of $100 becomes $50 of AFC or fixed cost per unit; then it becomes $33.33 per unit as $100 is spread over 3 units, and $25 per unit when spread over 4 units. This process is sometimes referred to as "spreading the overhead." Figure 8.4 shows that AFC graphs as a continuously declining curve as total output is increased.

AVC **Average variable cost (AVC)** for any output level is calculated by dividing total variable cost (TVC) by that output (*Q*):

$$\text{AVC} = \frac{\text{TVC}}{Q}$$

As added variable resources increase output, AVC declines initially, reaches a minimum, and then increases again. A graph of AVC is a U-shaped or saucer-shaped curve, as shown in Figure 8.4.

Because total variable cost reflects the law of diminishing returns, so must AVC, which is derived from total variable cost. Because marginal returns increase initially, fewer and fewer additional variable resources are needed to produce each of the first 4 units of output. As a result, variable cost per unit declines. AVC hits a minimum with the fifth unit of output, and beyond that point AVC rises as diminishing returns require more and more variable resources to produce each additional unit of output.

In simpler terms, at very low levels of output production is relatively inefficient and costly. Because the firm's fixed plant is understaffed, average variable cost is relatively high. As output expands, however, greater specialization and better use of the firm's capital equipment yield more efficiency, and variable cost per unit of output declines. As still more variable resources are added, a point is reached where diminishing returns are incurred. The firm's capital equipment is now staffed more intensively, and therefore each added input unit does not increase output by as much as preceding inputs. This means that AVC eventually increases.

You can verify the U or saucer shape of the AVC curve by returning to Table 8.1. Assume the price of labor is $10 per unit. By dividing average product (output per labor unit) into $10 (price per labor unit), we determine the labor cost per unit of output. Because we have assumed labor to be the only variable input, the labor cost per unit of output is the variable cost per unit of output, or AVC. When average product is initially low, AVC is high. As workers are added, average product rises and AVC falls. When average product is at its maximum, AVC is at its minimum. Then, as still more workers are added and average product declines, AVC rises. The "hump" of the average-product curve is reflected in the saucer or U shape of the AVC curve. As you will soon see, the two are mirror images of each other.

FIGURE 8.4 The average-cost curves. AFC falls as a given amount of fixed costs is apportioned over a larger and larger output. AVC initially falls because of increasing marginal returns but then rises because of diminishing marginal returns. Average total cost (ATC) is the vertical sum of average variable cost (AVC) and average fixed cost (AFC).

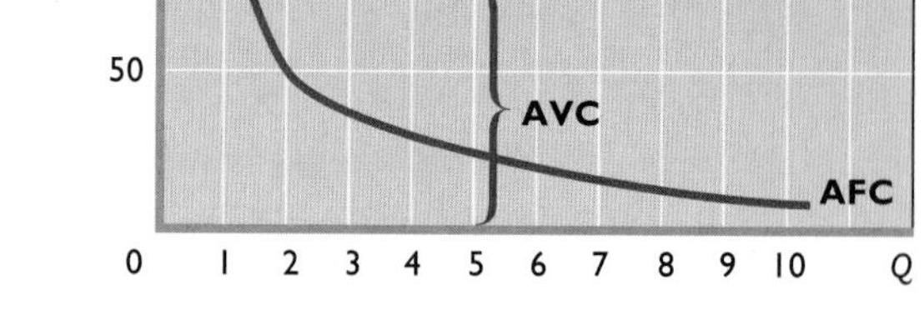

ATC **Average total cost (ATC)** for any output level is found by dividing total cost (TC) by that output (*Q*) or by adding AFC and AVC at that output:

$$\text{ATC} = \frac{\text{TC}}{Q} = \frac{\text{TFC}}{Q} + \frac{\text{TVC}}{Q} = \text{AFC} + \text{AVC}$$

Graphically, ATC can be found by adding vertically the AFC and AVC curves, as in Figure 8.4. Thus the vertical distance between the ATC and AVC curves measures AFC at any level of output.

Marginal Cost

One final and very crucial cost concept remains: **Marginal cost (MC)** is the extra, or additional, cost of producing 1 more unit of output. MC can be determined for each added unit of output by noting the change in total cost which that unit's production entails:

$$\text{MC} = \frac{\text{change in TC}}{\text{change in } Q}$$

Calculations In column 4, Table 8.2, production of the first unit of output increases total cost from $100 to $190. Therefore, the additional, or marginal, cost of that first unit is $90 (column 8). The marginal cost of the second unit is $80 (= $270 − $190); the MC of the third is

\$70 (= \$340 − \$270); and so forth. The MC for each of the 10 units of output is shown in column 8.

MC can also be calculated from the total-variable-cost column, because the only difference between total cost and total variable cost is the constant amount of fixed costs (\$100). Thus, the change in total cost and the change in total variable cost associated with each additional unit of output are always the same.

Marginal Decisions

Marginal costs are costs the firm can control directly and immediately. Specifically, MC designates all the cost incurred in producing the last unit of output. Thus, it also designates the cost that can be "saved" by not producing that last unit. Average-cost figures do not provide this information. For example, suppose the firm is undecided whether to produce 3 or 4 units of output. At 4 units Table 8.2 indicates that ATC is \$100. But the firm does not increase its total costs by \$100 by producing the fourth unit, nor does it save \$100 by not producing that unit. Rather, the change in costs involved here is only \$60, as the MC column in Table 8.2 reveals.

W 8.3
Per-unit cost

A firm's decisions as to what output level to produce are typically marginal decisions, that is, decisions to produce a few more or a few less units. Marginal cost is the change in costs when 1 more or 1 less unit of output is produced. When coupled with marginal revenue (which, as you will see in Chapter 9, indicates the change in revenue from 1 more or 1 less unit of output), marginal cost allows a firm to determine if it is profitable to expand or contract its production. The analysis in the next three chapters focuses on those marginal calculations.

Graphical Portrayal

Marginal cost is shown graphically in **Figure 8.5 (Key Graph).** Marginal cost at first declines sharply, reaches a minimum, and then rises rather abruptly. This reflects the fact that variable costs, and therefore total cost, increase first by decreasing amounts and then by increasing amounts (see columns 3 and 4, Table 8.2).

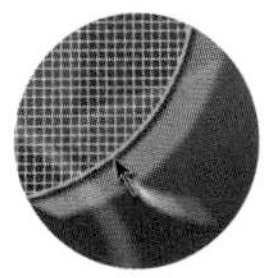

G 8.1
Production and costs

MC and Marginal Product

The marginal-cost curve's shape is a consequence of the law of diminishing returns. Looking back at Table 8.1, we can see the relationship between marginal product and marginal cost. If all units of a variable resource (here labor) are hired at the same price, the marginal cost of each extra unit of output will fall as long as the marginal product of each additional worker is rising. This is true because marginal cost is the (constant) cost of an extra worker divided by his or her marginal product. Therefore, in Table 8.1, suppose that each worker can be hired for \$10. Because the first worker's marginal product is 10 units of output, and hiring this worker increases the firm's costs by \$10, the marginal cost of each of these 10 extra units of output is \$1 (= \$10/10 units). The second worker also increases costs by \$10, but the marginal product is 15, so the marginal cost of each of these 15 extra units of output is \$.67 (= \$10/15 units). Similarly, the MC of each of the 20 extra units of output contributed by the third worker is \$.50 (= \$10/20 units). To generalize, as long as marginal product is rising, marginal cost will fall.

But with the fourth worker diminishing returns set in and marginal cost begins to rise. For the fourth worker, marginal cost is \$.67 (= \$10/15 units); for the fifth worker, MC is \$1 (\$10/10 units); for the sixth, MC is \$2 (= \$10/5 units); and so on. If the price (cost) of the variable resource remains constant, increasing marginal returns will be reflected in a declining marginal cost, and diminishing marginal returns in a rising marginal cost. The MC curve is a mirror reflection of the marginal-product curve. As you can see in Figure 8.6, when marginal product is rising, marginal cost is necessarily falling. When marginal product is at its maximum, marginal cost is at its minimum. And when marginal product is falling, marginal cost is rising.

Relation of MC to AVC and ATC

Figure 8.5 shows that the marginal-cost curve MC intersects both the AVC and the ATC curves at their minimum points. As noted earlier, this marginal-average relationship is a mathematical necessity, which a simple illustration will reveal. Suppose a baseball pitcher has allowed his opponents an average of 3 runs per game in the first three games he has pitched. Now, whether his average falls or rises as a result of pitching a fourth (marginal) game will depend on whether the additional runs he allows in that extra game are fewer or more than his current 3-run average. If in the fourth game he allows fewer than 3 runs, for example, 1, his total runs will rise from 9 to 10 and his average will fall from 3 to $2\frac{1}{2}$ (=10/4). Conversely, if in the fourth game he allows more than 3 runs, say, 7, his total will increase from 9 to 16 and his average will rise from 3 to 4 (= 16/4).

So it is with costs. When the amount (the marginal cost) added to total cost is less than the current average total cost, ATC will fall. Conversely, when the marginal

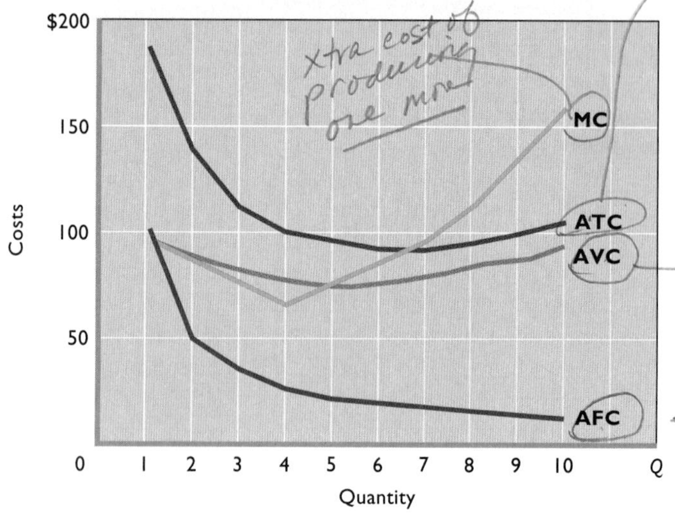

FIGURE 8.5 The relationship of the marginal-cost curve to the average-total-cost and average-variable-cost curves. The marginal-cost (MC) curve cuts through the average-total-cost (ATC) curve and the average-variable-cost (AVC) curve at their minimum points. When MC is below average total cost, ATC falls; when MC is above average total cost, ATC rises. Similarly, when MC is below average variable cost, AVC falls; when MC is above average variable cost AVC rises.

QUICK QUIZ 8.5

1. The marginal-cost curve first declines and then increases because of:
   a. increasing, then diminishing, marginal utility.
   b. the decline in the gap between ATC and AVC as output expands.
   c. increasing, then diminishing, marginal returns.
   d. constant marginal revenue.
2. The vertical distance between ATC and AVC measures:
   a. marginal cost.
   b. total fixed cost.
   c. average fixed cost.
   d. economic profit per unit.
3. ATC is:
   a. AVC − AFC.
   b. MC + AVC.
   c. AFC + AVC.
   d. (AFC + AVC) × *Q*.
4. When the marginal-cost curve lies:
   a. above the ATC curve, ATC rises.
   b. above the AVC curve, ATC rises.
   c. below the AVC curve, total fixed cost increases.
   d. below the ATC curve, total fixed cost falls.

Answers: 1. c; 2. c; 3. c; 4. a

cost exceeds ATC, ATC will rise. This means in Figure 8.5 that as long as MC lies below ATC, ATC will fall, and whenever MC lies above ATC, ATC will rise. Therefore, at the point of intersection where MC equals ATC, ATC has just ceased to fall but has not yet begun to rise. This, by definition, is the minimum point on the ATC curve. The marginal-cost curve intersects the average-total-cost curve at the ATC curve's minimum point.

Marginal cost can be defined as the addition either to total cost or to total variable cost resulting from 1 more unit of output; thus this same rationale explains why the MC curve also crosses the AVC curve at the AVC curve's minimum point. No such relationship exists between the MC curve and the average-fixed-cost curve, because the two are not related; marginal cost includes only those costs that change with output, and fixed costs by definition are those that are independent of output. **(Key Question 7)**

Shifts of the Cost Curves

Changes in either resource prices or technology will cause costs to change and therefore the cost curves to shift. If fixed costs double from $100 to $200, the AFC curve in Figure 8.5 would be shifted upward. At each level of output, fixed costs are higher. The ATC curve would also move upward, because AFC is a component of ATC. But the positions of the AVC and MC curves would be unaltered, because their locations are based on the prices of variable rather than fixed resources. However, if the price (wage) of labor or some other variable

FIGURE 8.6 The relationship between productivity curves and cost curves. The marginal-cost (MC) curve and the average-variable-cost (AVC) curve in (b) are mirror images of the marginal-product (MP) and average-product (AP) curves in (a). Assuming that labor is the only variable input and that its price (the wage rate) is constant, then when MP is rising, MC is falling, and when MP is falling, MC is rising. Under the same assumptions, when AP is rising, AVC is falling, and when AP is falling, AVC is rising.

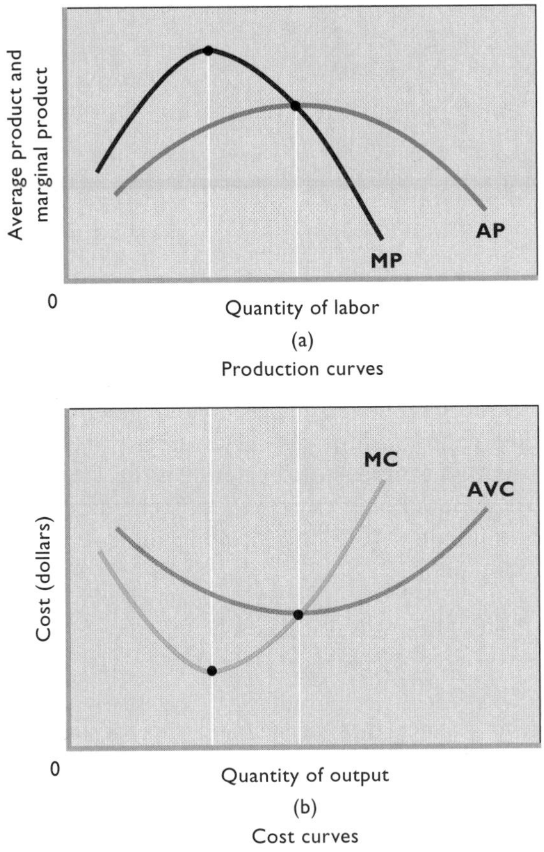

input rose, AVC, ATC, and MC would rise and those cost curves would all shift upward. The AFC curve would remain in place because fixed costs have not changed. And, of course, reductions in the prices of fixed or variable resources would reduce costs and produce shifts of the cost curves exactly opposite to those just described.

The discovery of a more efficient technology would increase the productivity of all inputs. The cost figures in Table 8.2 would all be lower. To illustrate, if labor is the only variable input, if wages are $10 per hour, and if average product is 10 units, then AVC would be $1. But if a technological improvement increases the average product of labor to 20 units, then AVC will decline to $.50. More generally, an upward shift in the productivity curves shown in Figure 8.6a means a downward shift in the cost curves portrayed in Figure 8.6b.

QUICK REVIEW 8.2

- The law of diminishing returns indicates that, beyond some point, output will increase by diminishing amounts as more units of a variable resource (labor) are added to a fixed resource (capital).
- In the short run, the total cost of any level of output is the sum of fixed and variable costs (TC = TFC + TVC).
- Average fixed, average variable, and average total costs are fixed, variable, and total costs per unit of output; marginal cost is the extra cost of producing 1 more unit of output.
- Average fixed cost declines continuously as output increases; average-variable-cost and average-total-cost curves are U- shaped, reflecting increasing and then diminishing returns; the marginal-cost curve falls but then rises, intersecting both the average-variable-cost curve and the average-total-cost curve at their minimum points.

Long-Run Production Costs

In the long run an industry and the individual firms it comprises can undertake all desired resource adjustments. That is, they can change the amount of all inputs used. The firm can alter its plant capacity; it can build a larger plant or revert to a smaller plant than that assumed in Table 8.2. The industry also can change its plant size; the long run allows sufficient time for new firms to enter or for existing firms to leave an industry. We will discuss the impact of the entry and exit of firms to and from an industry in the next chapter; here we are concerned only with changes in plant capacity made by a single firm. Let's couch our analysis in terms of average total cost (ATC), making no distinction between fixed and variable costs because all resources, and therefore all costs, are variable in the long run.

Firm Size and Costs

Suppose a single-plant manufacturer begins on a small scale and, as the result of successful operations, expands to successively larger plant sizes with larger output capacities. What happens to average total cost as this occurs? For a time, successively larger plants will lower average total cost. However, eventually the building of a still larger plant may cause ATC to rise.

Figure 8.7 illustrates this situation for five possible plant sizes. ATC-1 is the short-run average-total-cost curve for the smallest of the five plants, and ATC-5 the curve for the largest. Constructing larger plants will lower the minimum average total costs through plant size 3. But then larger plants will mean higher minimum average total costs.

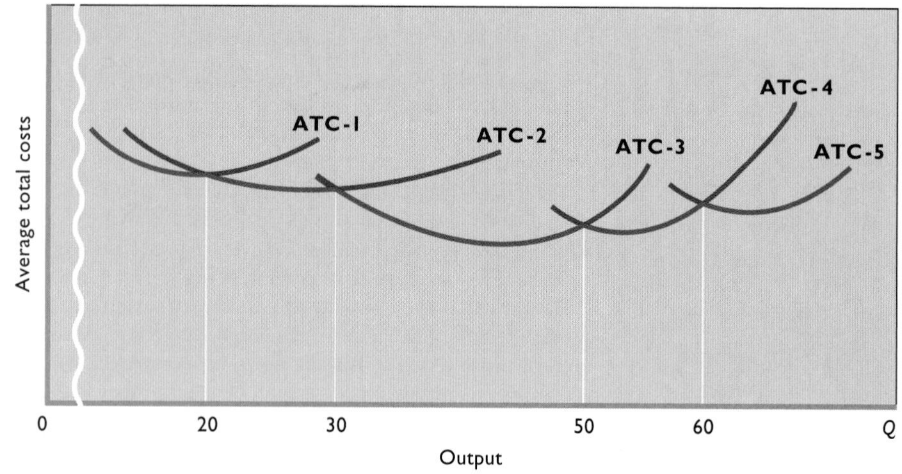

FIGURE 8.7 The long-run average-total-cost curve: five possible plant sizes. The long-run average-total-cost curve is made up of segments of the short-run cost curves (ATC-1, ATC-2, etc.) of the various-size plants from which the firm might choose. Each point on the bumpy planning curve shows the lowest unit cost attainable for any output when the firm has had time to make all desired changes in its plant size.

The Long-Run Cost Curve

The vertical lines perpendicular to the output axis in Figure 8.7 indicate the outputs at which the firm should change plant size to realize the lowest attainable average total costs of production. These are the outputs at which the per-unit costs for a larger plant drop below those for the current, smaller plant. For all outputs up to 20 units, the lowest average total costs are attainable with plant size 1. However, if the firm's volume of sales expands beyond 20 units but less than 30, it can achieve lower per-unit costs by constructing a larger plant, size 2. Although total cost will be higher at the expanded levels of production, the cost per unit of output will be less. For any output between 30 and 50 units, plant size 3 will yield the lowest average total costs. From 50 to 60 units of output, the firm must build the size-4 plant to achieve the lowest unit costs. Lowest average total costs for any output over 60 units require construction of the still larger plant, size 5.

Tracing these adjustments, we find that the long-run ATC curve for the enterprise is made up of segments of the short-run ATC curves for the various plant sizes that can be constructed. The long-run ATC curve shows the lowest average total cost at which *any output level* can be produced after the firm has had time to make all appropriate adjustments in its plant size. In Figure 8.7 the blue, bumpy curve is the firm's long-run ATC curve or, as it is often called, the firm's *planning curve.*

In most lines of production the choice of plant size is much wider than in our illustration. In many industries the number of possible plant sizes is virtually unlimited, and in time quite small changes in the volume of output will lead to changes in plant size. Graphically, this implies an unlimited number of short-run ATC curves, one for each output level, as suggested by **Figure 8.8 (Key Graph).** Then, rather than being made up of segments of short-run ATC curves as in Figure 8.7, the long-run ATC curve is made up of all the points of tangency of the unlimited number of short-run ATC curves from which the long-run ATC curve is derived. Therefore, the planning curve is smooth rather than bumpy. Each point on it tells us the minimum ATC of producing the corresponding level of output.

Economies and Diseconomies of Scale

We have assumed that for a time larger and larger plant sizes will lead to lower unit costs but that beyond some point successively larger plants will mean higher average total costs. That is, we have assumed the long-run ATC curve is U-shaped. But why should this be? Note, first, that the law of diminishing returns does not apply in the long run. That's because diminishing returns presume one resource is fixed in supply while the long run means all resources are variable. Also, our discussion assumes resource prices are constant. We can explain the U-shaped long-run average-total-cost curve in terms of economies and diseconomies of large-scale production.

Economies of Scale

Economies of scale, or economies of mass production, explain the downsloping part of the long-run ATC curve, as indicated in Figure 8.9, graphs (a), (b), and (c). As plant size increases, a number of factors will for a time lead to lower average costs of production.

Labor Specialization Increased specialization in the use of labor becomes more achievable as a plant increases in

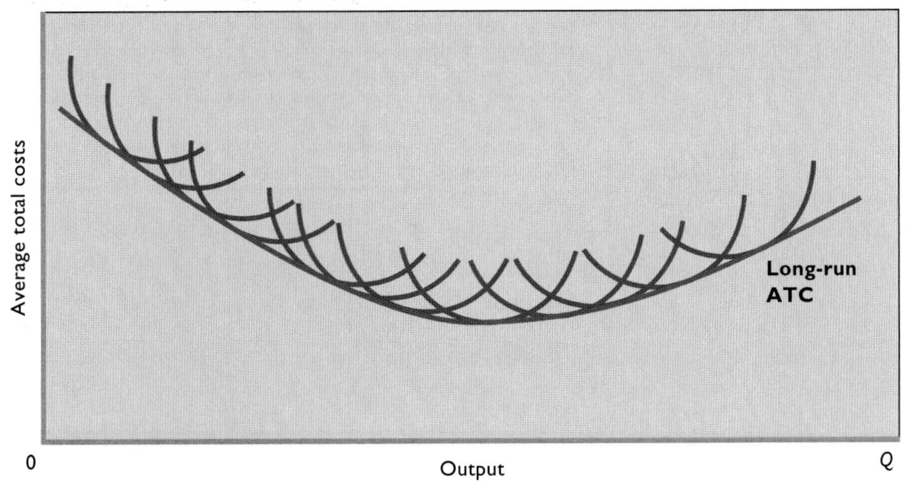

FIGURE 8.8 **The long-run average-total-cost curve: unlimited number of plant sizes.** If the number of possible plant sizes is very large, the long-run average-total-cost curve approximates a smooth curve. Economies of scale, followed by diseconomies of scale, cause the curve to be U-shaped.

QUICK QUIZ 8.8

1. The unlabeled red curves in this figure illustrate the:
   a. long-run average-total-cost curves of various firms constituting the industry.
   b. short-run average-total-cost curves of various firms constituting the industry.
   c. short-run average-total-cost curves of various plant sizes available to a particular firm.
   d. short-run marginal-cost curves of various plant sizes available to a particular firm.
2. The unlabeled red curves in this figure derive their shapes from:
   a. decreasing, then increasing, short-run returns.
   b. increasing, then decreasing, short-run returns.
   c. economies, then diseconomies, of scale.
   d. diseconomies, then economies, of scale.
3. The long-run ATC curve in this figure derives its shape from:
   a. decreasing, then increasing, short-run returns.
   b. increasing, then decreasing, short-run returns.
   c. economies, then diseconomies, of scale.
   d. diseconomies, then economies, of scale..
4. The long-run ATC curve is often called the firm's:
   a. planning curve.
   b. capital-expansion path.
   c. total-product curve.
   d. production possibilities curve.

Answers: 1. c; 2. b; 3. c; 4. a

size. Hiring more workers means jobs can be divided and subdivided. Each worker may now have just one task to perform instead of five or six. Workers can work full-time on the tasks for which they have special skills. In a small plant, skilled machinists may spend half their time performing unskilled tasks, leading to higher production costs.

Further, by working at fewer tasks, workers become even more proficient at those tasks. The jack-of-all-trades doing five or six jobs is not likely to be efficient in any of them. Concentrating on one task, the same worker may become highly efficient.

Finally, greater labor specialization eliminates the loss of time that accompanies each shift of a worker from one task to another.

Managerial Specialization Large-scale production also means better use of, and greater specialization in, management. A supervisor who can handle 20 workers is underused in a small plant that employs only 10 people. The production staff could be doubled with no increase in supervisory costs.

Small firms cannot use management specialists to best advantage. In a small plant a sales specialist may have to divide his or her time between several executive functions, for example, marketing, personnel, and finance. A larger scale of operations means that the marketing expert can supervise marketing full-time, while specialists perform other managerial functions. Greater efficiency and lower unit costs are the net result.

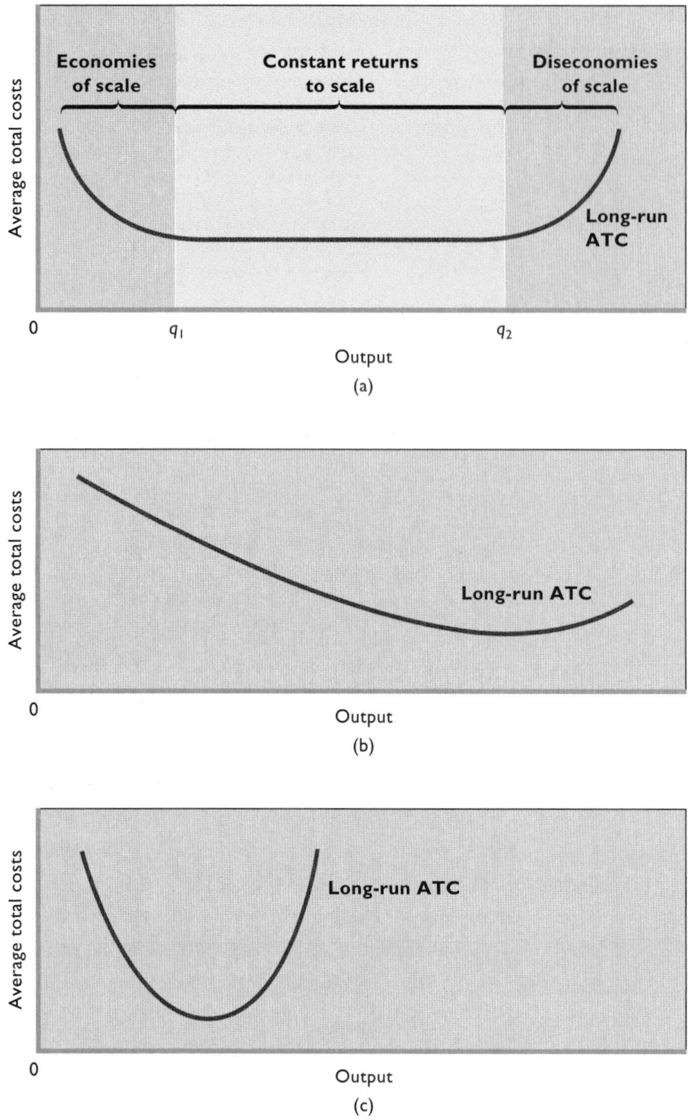

FIGURE 8.9 Various possible long-run average-total-cost curves. In (a), economies of scale are rather rapidly obtained as plant size rises, and diseconomies of scale are not encountered until a considerably large scale of output has been achieved. Thus, long-run average total cost is constant over a wide range of output. In (b), economies of scale are extensive, and diseconomies of scale occur only at very large outputs. Average total cost therefore declines over a broad range of output. In (c), economies of scale are exhausted quickly, followed immediately by diseconomies of scale. Minimum ATC thus occurs at a relatively low output.

Efficient Capital Small firms often cannot afford the most efficient equipment. In many lines of production such machinery is available only in very large and extremely expensive units. Furthermore, effective use of the equipment demands a high volume of production, and that again requires large-scale producers.

In the automobile industry the most efficient fabrication method employs robotics and elaborate assembly-line equipment. Effective use of this equipment demands an annual output of several hundred thousand automobiles. Only very large-scale producers can afford to purchase and use this equipment efficiently. The small-scale producer is faced with a dilemma. To fabricate automobiles using other equipment is inefficient and therefore more costly per unit. The alternative of purchasing the efficient equipment and underusing it at low levels of output is also inefficient and costly.

Other Factors Many products entail design and development costs, as well as other "start-up" costs, which must be incurred regardless of projected sales. These costs decline per unit as output is increased. Similarly, advertising costs decline per auto, per computer, per stereo system, and per box of detergent as more units are produced and sold. Also, the firm's production and marketing expertise usually rises as it produces and sells more output. This *learning by doing* is a further source of economies of scale.

All these factors contribute to lower average total costs for the firm that is able to expand its scale of operations. Where economies of scale are possible, an increase in all resources of, say, 10 percent will cause a more-than-proportionate increase in output of, say, 20 percent. The result will be a decline in ATC.

In many U.S. manufacturing industries economies of scale have been of great significance. Firms that have expanded their scale of operations to obtain economies of mass production have survived and flourished. Those unable to expand have become relatively high-cost producers, doomed to a struggle to survive.

Diseconomies of Scale In time the expansion of a firm may lead to diseconomies and therefore higher average total costs.

The main factor causing **diseconomies of scale** is the difficulty of efficiently controlling and coordinating a firm's operations as it becomes a large-scale producer. In a small plant a single key executive may make all the basic decisions for the plant's operation. Because of the firm's small size, the executive is close to the production line, understands the firm's operations, and can digest information and make efficient decisions.

This neat picture changes as a firm grows. There are now many management levels between the executive suite and the assembly line; top management is far removed from the actual production operations of the plant. One person cannot assemble, digest, and understand all the information essential to decision making on a large scale. Authority must be delegated to many vice-presidents, second vice-presidents, and so forth. This expansion of the management hierarchy leads to problems of communication and cooperation, bureaucratic red tape, and the possibility that decisions will not be coordinated. Similarly, decision making may be slowed down to the point that decisions fail to reflect changes in consumer tastes or technology quickly enough. The result is impaired efficiency and rising average total costs.

Also, in massive production facilities workers may feel alienated from their employers and care little about working efficiently. Opportunities to shirk, by avoiding work in favor of on-the-job leisure, may be greater in large plants than in small ones. Countering worker alienation and shirking may require additional worker supervision, which increases costs.

Where diseconomies of scale are operative, an increase in all inputs of, say, 10 percent will cause a less-than-proportionate increase in output of, say, 5 percent. As a consequence, ATC will increase. The rising portion of the long-run cost curves in Figure 8.9 illustrates diseconomies of scale.

Constant Returns to Scale In some industries a rather wide range of output may exist between the output at which economies of scale end and the output at which diseconomies of scale begin. That is, there may be a range of **constant returns to scale** over which long-run average cost does not change. The q_1q_2 output range of Figure 8.9a is an example. Here a given percentage increase in all inputs of, say, 10 percent will cause a proportionate 10 percent increase in output. Thus, in this range ATC is constant.

Minimum Efficient Scale and Industry Structure

Economies and diseconomies of scale are an important determinant of an industry's structure. Here we introduce the concept of **minimum efficient scale (MES),** which is the lowest level of output at which a firm can minimize long-run average costs. In Figure 8.9a that level occurs at q_1 units of output. Because of the extended range of constant returns to scale, firms producing substantially greater outputs could also realize the minimum attainable average costs. Specifically, firms within the q_1 to q_2 range would be equally efficient. So we would not be surprised to find an industry with such cost conditions to be populated by firms of quite different sizes. The apparel, food processing, furniture, wood products, snowboard, and small-appliance industries are examples. With an extended range of constant returns to scale, relatively large and relatively small firms can coexist in an industry and be equally successful. Another example appears to be banking.

Compare this with Figure 8.9b, where economies of scale continue over a wide range of outputs and diseconomies of scale appear only at very high levels of output. This pattern of declining long-run average total cost occurs in the automobile, aluminum, steel, and other heavy industries. The same pattern holds in several of the new industries related to information technology, for example, computer microchips, operating system software, and Internet service provision.

Given consumer demand, efficient production will be achieved with a few large-scale producers. Small firms cannot realize the minimum efficient scale and will not be able to compete. In the extreme, economies of scale might extend beyond the market's size, resulting in what is termed **natural monopoly,** a relatively rare market situation in which average total cost is minimized when only one firm produces the particular good or service.

Where economies of scale are few and diseconomies come into play quickly, the minimum efficient size occurs at a low level of output, as shown in Figure 8.9c. In such industries a particular level of consumer demand will support a large number of relatively small producers. Many retail trades and some types of farming fall into this category. So do certain kinds of light manufacturing, such as the baking, clothing, and shoe industries. Fairly small firms are more efficient than larger-scale producers in such industries.

Our point here is that the shape of the long-run average-total-cost curve is determined by technology and the economies and diseconomies of scale that result. The shape of the long-run ATC curve, in turn, can be significant in determining whether an industry is populated by a relatively large number of small firms or is dominated by a few large producers, or lies somewhere in between.

O 8.3
Minimum efficient scale and natural monopoly

But we must be cautious in our assessment because industry structure does not depend on cost conditions alone. Government policies, the geographic size of markets, managerial strategy and skill, and other factors must be considered in explaining the structure of a particular industry. **(Key Question 10)**

QUICK REVIEW 8.3

- Most firms have U-shaped long-run average-total-cost curves, reflecting economies and then diseconomies of scale.
- Economies of scale are the consequence of greater specialization of labor and management, more efficient capital equipment, and the spreading of start-up costs among more units of output.
- Diseconomies of scale are caused by the problems of coordination and communication that arise in large firms.
- Minimum efficient scale is the lowest level of output at which a firm's long-run average total cost is at a minimum.

Applications and Illustrations

The business world offers many examples relating to short-run costs, economies of scale, and minimum efficient scale (MES). Here are just a few.

Rising Cost of Insurance and Security

Following the terrorist attacks of September 11, 2001, and the threat of additional attacks, insurance premiums rose for many American businesses. In the short run, insurance premiums are fixed costs because they are independent of the level of production. The terrorist attacks also increased security costs, some of which are fixed (for example, video cameras) and others of which are variable (security workers). Together, higher insurance premiums and added security costs shifted short-run ATC curves upward for many firms.

Successful Start-Up Firms

The U.S. economy has greatly benefited over the past several decades by explosive growth of scores of highly successful start-up firms. These firms typically reduce their costs by moving from higher to lower points on their short-run cost curves and by downward and to-the-right shifts of their short-run cost curves via economies of scale. That has certainly been the case for such former start-up firms as Intel (microchips), Starbucks (coffee), Microsoft (software), Dell (personal computers), Google (Internet search engine), and Cisco Systems (Internet switching).

A major source of cost savings for rapidly growing firms is the ability to spread huge product development and advertising costs over a larger number of units of output. These firms also achieve economies of scale from learning by doing and through increased specialization of labor, management, and equipment. Many successful start-up firms experience declining average total costs over the years or even decades it takes them to reach MES.

The Verson Stamping Machine

In 1996 Verson (a U.S. firm located in Chicago) introduced a 49-foot-tall metal-stamping machine that is the size of a house and weighs as much as 12 locomotives. This $30 million machine, which cuts and sculpts raw sheets of steel into automobile hoods and fenders, enables automakers to make new parts in just 5 minutes compared with 8 hours for older stamping presses. A single machine is designed to make 5 million auto parts per year. So, to achieve the cost saving from the machine, an auto manufacturer must have sufficient auto production to use all these parts. By allowing the use of this cost-saving piece of equipment, large firm size achieves economies of scale.

The Daily Newspaper

The daily newspaper is undoubtedly one of the economy's great bargains. Think of all the resources that combine to produce it: reporters, delivery people, photographers, editors, management, printing presses, pulp mills, pulp mill workers, ink makers, loggers, logging truck drivers, and so on. Yet for 50 cents you can buy a high-quality newspaper in major cities.

The main reason for such low prices is the low average total costs that result from the spreading of fixed costs and the achieving of economies of scale. If only 100 or 200 people bought the paper each day, the average cost of each paper would be exceedingly high because the overhead costs would be spread over so few buyers. But when publishers sell thousands or hundreds of thousands of

Last *Word*

Don't Cry over Sunk Costs

Sunk Costs Are Irrelevant in Decision Making.

There is an old saying: Don't cry over spilt milk. The message is that once you have spilled a glass of milk, there is nothing you can do to recover it, so you should forget about it and "move on from there." This saying has great relevance to what economists call sunk costs. Such costs are like sunken ships on the ocean floor: Once these costs are incurred, they cannot be recovered.

Let's gain an understanding of this idea by applying it first to consumers and then to businesses. Suppose you buy an expensive ticket to an upcoming football game, but the morning of the game you wake up with a bad case of the flu. Feeling miserable, you step outside to find that the wind chill is about −10 degrees. You absolutely do not want to go to the game, but you remind yourself that you paid a steep price for the ticket. You call several people to try to sell the ticket, but you soon discover that no one is interested in it, even at a discounted price. You conclude that everyone who wants a ticket has one.

Should you go to the game? Economic analysis says that you should not take actions for which marginal cost exceeds marginal benefit. And, in this situation, the price you paid for the ticket is irrelevant to the decision. Both marginal or additional cost and marginal or additional benefit are forward-looking. If the marginal cost of going to the game is greater than the marginal benefit, the best decision is to go back to bed. This decision should be the same whether you paid \$2, \$20, or \$200 for the game ticket, because the price that you pay for something does not affect its marginal benefit. Once the ticket has been purchased and cannot be resold, its cost is irrelevant to the decision to attend the game. Since "you absolutely do not want to go," clearly the marginal cost exceeds the marginal benefit of the game.

Here is a second consumer example: Suppose a family is on vacation and stops at a roadside stand to buy some apples. The kids get back into the car and bite into their apples, immediately pronouncing them "totally mushy" and unworthy of another bite. Both parents agree that the apples are "terrible," but the father continues to eat his, because, as he says, "We paid a premium price for them." One of the older children replies, "Dad, that is irrelevant. " Although not stated very diplomatically, the child is exactly right. In making a new decision, you should ignore all costs that are not affected by the decision. The prior bad decision (in retrospect) to buy the apples should not dictate a second decision for which marginal benefit is less than marginal cost.

Now let's apply the idea of sunk costs to firms. Some of a firm's costs are not only fixed (recurring, but unrelated to the level of output) but sunk (unrecoverable). For example, a nonrefundable annual lease payment for the use of a store cannot be recouped once it has been paid. A firm's decision about whether to move from the store to a more profitable location does not depend on the amount of time remaining on the lease. If moving means greater profit, it makes sense to move whether there are 300 days, 30 days, or 3 days left on the lease.

Or, as another example, suppose a firm spends \$1 million on R&D to bring out a new product, only to discover that the product sells very poorly. Should the firm continue to produce the product at a loss even when there is no realistic hope for future success? Obviously, it should not. In making this decision, the firm realizes that the amount it has spent in developing the product is irrelevant; it should stop production of the product and cut its losses. In fact, many firms have dropped products after spending millions of dollars on their development. Examples are the quick decision by Coca-Cola to drop its New Coke and the eventual decision by McDonald's to drop its McLean Burger.

In short, if a cost has been incurred and cannot be partly or fully recouped by some other choice, a rational consumer or firm should ignore it. Sunk costs are irrelevant. Don't cry over sunk costs.

newspapers each day, they spread the overhead costs very widely. The large volume of sales also enables them to use specialized labor and large, highly efficient printing presses. Given sufficient scale and volume, the average total cost of a paper sinks to a few dimes. Moreover, the greater the number of readers, the greater is the amount of money that advertisers are willing to pay for advertising space. That added revenue helps keep the price of the newspaper low.

Aircraft and Concrete Plants

Why are there only two plants in the United States (both operated by Boeing) that produce large commercial aircraft and thousands of plants (owned by hundreds of firms) that produce ready-mixed concrete? The simple answer is that MES is radically different in the two industries. Why is that? First, economies of scale are extensive in assembling large commercial aircraft and very modest in mixing concrete. Manufacturing airplanes is a complex process that requires huge facilities, thousands of workers, and very expensive, specialized machinery. Economies of scale extend to huge plant sizes. But mixing Portland cement, sand, gravel, and water efficiently to produce concrete requires only a handful of workers and relatively inexpensive equipment. Economies of scale are exhausted at relatively small size.

The differing MESs also derive from the vastly different sizes of the geographic markets. The market for commercial airplanes is global, and aircraft manufacturers can deliver new airplanes anywhere in the world by flying them there. In contrast, the geographic market for a concrete plant is roughly the 50-mile radius that enables the concrete to be delivered before it "sets up." So thousands of small concrete plants locate close to their customers in hundreds of small and large cities in the United States.

Summary

1. Economic costs include all payments that must be received by resource owners to ensure a continued supply of needed resources to a particular line of production. Economic costs include explicit costs, which flow to resources owned and supplied by others, and implicit costs, which are payments for the use of self-owned and self-employed resources. One implicit cost is a normal profit to the entrepreneur. Economic profit occurs when total revenue exceeds total cost (= explicit costs + implicit costs, including a normal profit).
2. In the short run a firm's plant capacity is fixed. The firm can use its plant more or less intensively by adding or subtracting units of variable resources, but it does not have sufficient time in the short run to alter plant size.
3. The law of diminishing returns describes what happens to output as a fixed plant is used more intensively. As successive units of a variable resource, such as labor are added to a fixed plant, beyond some point the marginal product associated with each additional unit of a resource declines.
4. Because some resources are variable and others are fixed, costs can be classified as variable or fixed in the short run. Fixed costs are independent of the level of output; variable costs vary with output. The total cost of any output is the sum of fixed and variable costs at that output.
5. Average fixed, average variable, and average total costs are fixed, variable, and total costs per unit of output. Average fixed cost declines continuously as output increases because a fixed sum is being spread over a larger and larger number of units of production. A graph of average variable cost is U-shaped, reflecting the law of diminishing returns. Average total cost is the sum of average fixed and average variable costs; its graph is also U-shaped.
6. Marginal cost is the extra, or additional, cost of producing 1 more unit of output. It is the amount by which total cost and total variable cost change when 1 more or 1 less unit of output is produced. Graphically, the marginal-cost curve intersects the ATC and AVC curves at their minimum points.
7. Lower resource prices shift cost curves downward, as does technological progress. Higher input prices shift cost curves upward.
8. The long run is a period of time sufficiently long for a firm to vary the amounts of all resources used, including plant size. In the long run all costs are variable. The long-run ATC, or planning, curve is composed of segments of the short-run ATC curves, and it represents the various plant sizes a firm can construct in the long run.
9. The long-run ATC curve is generally U-shaped. Economies of scale are first encountered as a small firm expands. Greater specialization in the use of labor and management, the ability to use the most efficient equipment, and the spreading of start-up costs among more units of output all contribute to economies of scale. As the firm continues to grow, it will encounter diseconomies of scale stemming from the managerial complexities that accompany large-scale production. The output ranges over which economies and diseconomies of scale occur in an industry are often an important determinant of the structure of that industry.

Terms and Concepts

economic (opportunity) cost
explicit costs
implicit costs
normal profit
economic profit
short run
long run
total product (TP)
marginal product (MP)
average product (AP)
law of diminishing returns
fixed costs
variable costs
total cost
average fixed cost (AFC)
average variable cost (AVC)
average total cost (ATC)
marginal cost (MC)
economies of scale
diseconomies of scale
constant returns to scale
minimum efficient scale (MES)
natural monopoly

Study Questions

1. Distinguish between explicit and implicit costs, giving examples of each. What are some explicit and implicit costs of attending college? Why does the economist classify normal profit as a cost? Is economic profit a cost of production?
2. **KEY QUESTION** Gomez runs a small pottery firm. He hires one helper at $12,000 per year, pays annual rent of $5000 for his shop, and spends $20,000 per year on materials. He has $40,000 of his own funds invested in equipment (pottery wheels, kilns, and so forth) that could earn him $4000 per year if alternatively invested. He has been offered $15,000 per year to work as a potter for a competitor. He estimates his entrepreneurial talents are worth $3000 per year. Total annual revenue from pottery sales is $72,000. Calculate the accounting profit and the economic profit for Gomez's pottery firm.
3. Which of the following are short-run and which are long-run adjustments?
   a. Wendy's builds a new restaurant.
   b. Harley-Davidson Corporation hires 200 more production workers.
   c. A farmer increases the amount of fertilizer used on his corn crop.
   d. An Alcoa aluminum plant adds a third shift of workers.
4. **KEY QUESTION** Complete the following table by calculating marginal product and average product from the data given:

Inputs of Labor	Total Product	Marginal Product	Average Product
0	0		
1	15	______	______
2	34	______	______
3	51	______	______
4	65	______	______
5	74	______	______
6	80	______	______
7	83	______	______
8	82	______	______

Plot the total, marginal, and average products and explain in detail the relationship between each pair of curves. Explain why marginal product first rises, then declines, and ultimately becomes negative. What bearing does the law of diminishing returns have on short-run costs? Be specific. "When marginal product is rising, marginal cost is falling. And when marginal product is diminishing, marginal cost is rising." Illustrate and explain graphically.

5. Why can the distinction between fixed costs and variable costs be made in the short run? Classify the following as fixed or variable costs: advertising expenditures, fuel, interest on company-issued bonds, shipping charges, payments for raw materials, real estate taxes, executive salaries, insurance premiums, wage payments, depreciation and obsolescence charges, sales taxes, and rental payments on leased office machinery. "There are no fixed costs in the long run; all costs are variable." Explain.
6. List several fixed and variable costs associated with owning and operating an automobile. Suppose you are considering whether to drive your car or fly 1000 miles to Florida for spring break. Which costs—fixed, variable, or both—would you take into account in making your decision? Would any implicit costs be relevant? Explain.
7. **KEY QUESTION** A firm has fixed costs of $60 and variable costs as indicated in the table on the next page. Complete the table and check your calculations by referring to question 4 at the end of Chapter 9.
   a. Graph total fixed cost, total variable cost, and total cost. Explain how the law of diminishing returns influences the shapes of the variable-cost and total-cost curves.
   b. Graph AFC, AVC, ATC, and MC. Explain the derivation and shape of each of these four curves and their relationships to one another. Specifically, explain in nontechnical terms why the MC curve intersects both the AVC and the ATC curves at their minimum points.
   c. Explain how the location of each curve graphed in question 7b would be altered if (1) total fixed cost had been $100 rather than $60 and (2) total variable cost had been $10 less at each level of output.

Total Product	Total Fixed Cost	Total Variable Cost	Total Cost	Average Fixed Cost	Average Variable Cost	Average Total Cost	Marginal Cost
0	$____	$ 0	$____			$____	
1	____	45	____	$____	$____	____	$____
2	____	85	____	____	____	____	____
3	____	120	____	____	____	____	____
4	____	150	____	____	____	____	____
5	____	185	____	____	____	____	____
6	____	225	____	____	____	____	____
7	____	270	____	____	____	____	____
8	____	325	____	____	____	____	____
9	____	390	____	____	____	____	____
10	____	465	____	____	____	____	____

8. Indicate how each of the following would shift the (1) marginal-cost curve, (2) average-variable-cost curve, (3) average-fixed-cost curve, and (4) average-total-cost curve of a manufacturing firm. In each case specify the direction of the shift.
a. A reduction in business property taxes.
b. An increase in the nominal wages of production workers.
c. A decrease in the price of electricity.
d. An increase in insurance rates on plant and equipment.
e. An increase in transportation costs.

9. Suppose a firm has only three possible plant-size options, represented by the ATC curves shown in the accompanying figure. What plant size will the firm choose in producing (*a*) 50, (*b*) 130, (*c*) 160, and (*d*) 250 units of output? Draw the firm's long-run average-cost curve on the diagram and describe this curve.

10. **KEY QUESTION** Use the concepts of economies and diseconomies of scale to explain the shape of a firm's long-run ATC curve. What is the concept of minimum efficient scale? What bearing can the shape of the long-run ATC curve have on the structure of an industry?

11. **LAST WORD** What is a sunk cost? Provide an example of a sunk cost other than one from this book. Why are such costs irrelevant in making decisions about future actions?

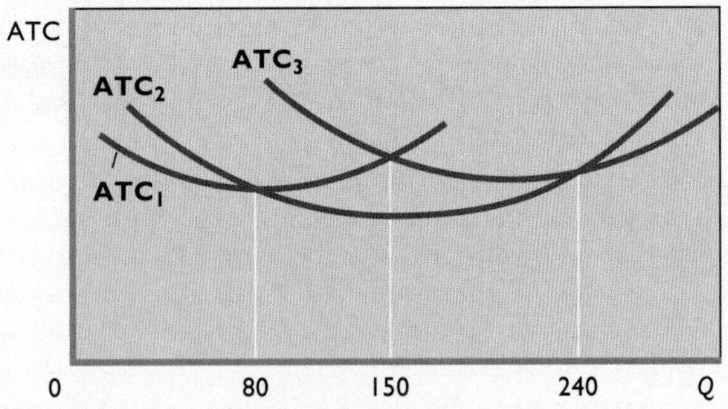

Web-Based Questions

1. **THE 10 LARGEST U.S. FIRMS—WHAT ARE THEIR SOURCES OF ECONOMIES OF SCALE?** Find the Forbes 2000 list of the world's largest firms at **www.forbes.com/lists/**. From the top 10 list, select three firms from three different industries and discuss the likely sources of the economies of scale that underlie their large size.

2. **CORPORATE ANNUAL REPORTS—IDENTIFY FIXED AND VARIABLE COSTS** Use the Google search engine at **www.google.com** to locate the home page of a company of your choice. Find and review the company's income statement in its annual report, and classify the nonrevenue items as either fixed or variable costs. Are all costs clearly identifiable as either fixed or variable? What item would be considered accounting profit? Would economic profit be higher or lower than this accounting profit?

IN THIS CHAPTER YOU WILL LEARN:

- **The names and main characteristics of the four basic market models.**
- **The conditions required for purely competitive markets.**
- **How purely competitive firms maximize profits or minimize losses.**
- **Why the marginal-cost curve and supply curve of competitive firms are identical.**
- **How industry entry and exit produce economic efficiency.**
- **The differences between constant-cost, increasing-cost, and decreasing-cost industries.**
- **How long-run competitive equilibrium results in economic efficiency.**

9

Pure Competition

In Chapter 7 we examined the relationship between product demand and total revenue, and in Chapter 8 we discussed costs of production. Now we want to put revenues and costs together to see how a business decides what price to charge and how much output to produce. But a firm's decisions concerning price and production depend greatly on the character of the industry in which it is operating. There is no "average" or "typical" industry. At one extreme is a single producer that dominates the market; at the other extreme are industries in which thousands of firms each produce a tiny fraction of market supply. Between these extremes are many other industries.

Since we cannot examine each industry individually, we will focus on several basic *models* of market structure. Together, these models will help you understand how price and output are determined in the many product markets in the economy. They will also help you evaluate the efficiency or inefficiency of those markets.

TABLE 9.1 Characteristics of the Four Basic Market Models

	Market Model			
Characteristic	**Pure Competition**	**Monopolistic Competition**	**Oligopoly**	**Pure Monopoly**
Number of firms	A very large number	Many	Few	One
Type of product	Standardized	Differentiated	Standardized or differentiated	Unique; no close substitutes
Control over price	None	Some, but within rather narrow limits	Limited by mutual interdependence; considerable with collusion	Considerable
Conditions of entry	Very easy, no obstacles	Relatively easy	Significant obstacles	Blocked
Nonprice competition	None	Considerable emphasis on advertising, brand names, trademarks	Typically a great deal, particularly with product differentiation	Mostly public relations advertising
Examples	Agriculture	Retail trade, dresses, shoes	Steel, automobiles, farm implements, many household appliances	Local utilities

Four Market Models

Economists group industries into four distinct market structures: pure competition, pure monopoly, monopolistic competition, and oligopoly. These four market models differ in several respects: the number of firms in the industry, whether those firms produce a standardized product or try to differentiate their products from those of other firms, and how easy or how difficult it is for firms to enter the industry.

Very briefly the four models are as follows:

- **Pure competition** involves a very large number of firms producing a standardized product (that is, a product identical to that of other producers, such as corn or cucumbers). New firms can enter or exit the industry very easily.
- **Pure monopoly** is a market structure in which one firm is the sole seller of a product or service (for example, a local electric utility). Since the entry of additional firms is blocked, one firm constitutes the entire industry. Because the monopolist produces a unique product, it makes no effort to differentiate its product.
- **Monopolistic competition** is characterized by a relatively large number of sellers producing differentiated products (clothing, furniture, books). There is widespread *nonprice competition*, a selling strategy in which one firm tries to distinguish its product or service from all competing products on the basis of attributes like design and workmanship (an approach called *product differentiation*). Either entry to or exit from monopolistically competitive industries is quite easy.
- **Oligopoly** involves only a few sellers of a standardized or differentiated product; so each firm is affected by the decisions of its rivals and must take those decisions into account in determining its own price and output.

Table 9.1 summarizes the characteristics of the four models for easy comparison. In discussing these market models, we will occasionally distinguish the characteristics of *pure competition* from those of the three other basic market structures, which together we will designate as **imperfect competition.**

Pure Competition: Characteristics and Occurrence

Although pure competition is relatively rare in the real world, this market model is highly relevant. A few industries more closely approximate pure competition than any other market structure. In particular, we can learn much about markets for agricultural goods, fish products, foreign exchange, basic metals, and stock shares by studying the pure-competition model. Also, pure competition is a meaningful starting point for any discussion of price and output determination. Moreover, the operation of a purely competitive economy provides a standard, or norm, for evaluating the efficiency of the real-world economy.

Let's take a fuller look at pure competition, the focus of the remainder of this chapter:

- ***Very large numbers*** A basic feature of a purely competitive market is the presence of a large number of independently acting sellers, often offering their products in large national or international markets. Examples: markets for farm commodities, the stock market, and the foreign exchange market.
- ***Standardized product*** Purely competitive firms produce a standardized (identical or homogeneous)

product. As long as the price is the same, consumers will be indifferent about which seller to buy the product from. Buyers view the products of firms B, C, D, and E as perfect substitutes for the product of firm A. Because purely competitive firms sell standardized products, they make no attempt to differentiate their products and do not engage in other forms of nonprice competition.

- ***"Price takers"*** In a purely competitive market, individual firms exert no significant control over product price. Each firm produces such a small fraction of total output that increasing or decreasing its output will not perceptibly influence total supply or, therefore, product price. In short, the competitive firm is a **price taker:** It cannot change market price; it can only adjust to it. That means that the individual competitive producer is at the mercy of the market. Asking a price higher than the market price would be futile. Consumers will not buy from firm A at \$2.05 when its 9999 competitors are selling an identical product, and therefore a perfect substitute, at \$2 per unit. Conversely, because firm A can sell as much as it chooses at \$2 per unit, there is no reason for it to charge a lower price, say, \$1.95, for to do so would shrink its profit.
- ***Free entry and exit*** New firms can freely enter and existing firms can freely leave purely competitive industries. No significant legal, technological, financial, or other obstacles prohibit new firms from selling their output in any competitive market.

Demand as Seen by a Purely Competitive Seller

We begin by examining demand from a competitive seller's viewpoint to see how it affects revenue. This seller might be a wheat farmer, a strawberry grower, a sheep rancher, a catfish raiser, or the like. Because each purely competitive firm offers only a negligible fraction of total market supply, it must accept the price predetermined by the market; it is a price taker, not a price maker.

Perfectly Elastic Demand

The demand schedule faced by the *individual firm* in a purely competitive industry is perfectly elastic at the market price, as demonstrated in Figure 9.1. As shown in column 1 of the table in Figure 9.1, the market price is \$131. The firm represented cannot obtain a higher price by restricting its output, nor does it need to lower its price to increase its sales volume. Columns 1 and 2 show that the firm can produce as little or as much as it wants and sell all the units at \$131 each.

We are *not* saying that *market* demand is perfectly elastic in a competitive market. Rather, market demand graphs as a downsloping curve. An entire industry (all firms producing a particular product) can affect price by changing industry output. For example, all firms, acting independently but simultaneously, can increase price by reducing output. But the individual competitive firm cannot do that. Its demand curve will plot as a straight, horizontal line such as *D* in Figure 9.1

Average, Total, and Marginal Revenue

The firm's demand schedule is also its average-revenue schedule. Price per unit to the purchaser is also revenue per unit, or average revenue, to the seller. To say that all buyers must pay \$131 per unit is to say that the revenue per unit, or **average revenue** received by the seller, is \$131. Price and average revenue is the same thing from different viewpoints.

The **total revenue** for each sales level is found by multiplying price by the corresponding quantity the firm can sell. (Column 1 multiplied by column 2 in the table in Figure 9.1 yields column 3.) In this case, total revenue increases by a constant amount, \$131, for each additional unit of sales. Each unit sold adds exactly its constant price to total revenue.

When a firm is pondering a change in its output, it will consider how its total revenue will change as a result. **Marginal revenue** is the change in total revenue (or the extra revenue) that results from selling 1 more unit of output. In column 3 of the table in Figure 9.1, total revenue is zero when zero units are sold. The first unit of output sold increases total revenue from zero to \$131, so marginal revenue for that unit is \$131. The second unit sold increases total revenue from \$131 to \$262, and marginal revenue is again \$131. Note in column 4 that marginal revenue is a constant \$131, as is price. In pure competition, marginal revenue and price are equal. **(Key Question 3)**

Figure 9.1 shows the purely competitive firm's total-revenue, demand, marginal-revenue, and average-revenue curves. Total revenue (TR) is a straight line that slopes upward to the right. Its slope is constant because each extra unit of sales increases TR by \$131. The demand curve (*D*) is horizontal, indicating perfect price elasticity. The marginal-revenue (MR) curve coincides with the demand curve because the product price (and hence MR) is constant. The average revenue (AR) curve equals price and therefore also coincides with the demand curve.

FIGURE 9.1 A purely competitive firm's demand and revenue curves. The demand curve (*D*) of a purely competitive firm is a horizontal line (perfectly elastic) because the firm can sell as much output as it wants at the market price (here, $131). Because each additional unit sold increases total revenue by the amount of the price, the firm's total-revenue (TR) curve is a straight upward-sloping line and its marginal-revenue (MR) curve coincides with the firm's demand curve. The average-revenue (AR) curve also coincides with the demand curve.

Firm's Demand Schedule		Firm's Revenue Data	
(1) Product Price (*P*) (Average Revenue)	(2) Quantity Demanded (*Q*)	(3) Total Revenue (TR), (1) × (2)	(4) Marginal Revenue (MR)
$131	0	$ 0	
			$131
131	1	131	
			131
131	2	262	
			131
131	3	393	
			131
131	4	524	
			131
131	5	655	
			131
131	6	786	
			131
131	7	917	
			131
131	8	1048	
			131
131	9	1179	
			131
131	10	1310	

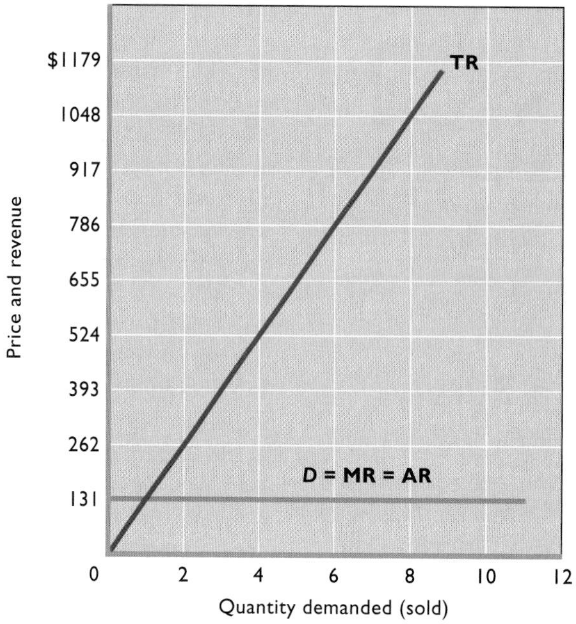

QUICK REVIEW 9.1

- In a purely competitive industry a large number of firms produce a standardized product and there are no significant barriers to entry.
- The demand seen by a purely competitive firm is perfectly elastic—horizontal on a graph—at the market price.
- Marginal revenue and average revenue for a purely competitive firm coincide with the firm's demand curve; total revenue rises by the product price for each additional unit sold.

Profit Maximization in the Short Run: Total-Revenue–Total-Cost Approach

Because the purely competitive firm is a price taker, it can maximize its economic profit (or minimize its loss) only by adjusting its *output*. And, in the short run, the firm has a fixed plant. Thus it can adjust its output only through changes in the amount of variable resources (materials, labor) it uses. It adjusts its variable

TABLE 9.2 The Profit-Maximizing Output for a Purely Competitive Firm: Total-Revenue–Total-Cost Approach (Price = $131)

				PRICE: $131	
(1) Total Product (Output) (Q)	(2) Total Fixed Cost (TFC)	(3) Total Variable Cost (TVC)	(4) Total Cost (TC)	(5) Total Revenue (TR)	(6) Profit (+) or Loss (−)
0	$100	$ 0	$ 100	$ 0	$−100
1	100	90	190	131	−59
2	100	170	270	262	−8
3	100	240	340	393	+53
4	100	300	400	524	+124
5	100	370	470	655	+185
6	100	450	550	786	+236
7	100	540	640	917	+277
8	100	650	750	1048	+298
9	100	780	***880***	***1179***	***+299***
10	100	930	1030	1310	+280

resources to achieve the output level that maximizes its profit.

There are two ways to determine the level of output at which a competitive firm will realize maximum profit or minimum loss. One method is to compare total revenue and total cost; the other is to compare marginal revenue and marginal cost. Both approaches apply to all firms, whether they are pure competitors, pure monopolists, monopolistic competitors, or oligopolists.[1]

We begin by examining profit maximization using the total-revenue–total-cost approach. Confronted with the market price of its product, the competitive producer will ask: (1) Should we produce this product? (2) If so, in what amount? (3) What economic profit (or loss) will we realize?

Let's demonstrate how a pure competitor answers these questions, given certain cost data and a specific market price. Our cost data are already familiar because they are the fixed-cost, variable-cost, and total-cost data in Table 8.2, repeated in columns 1 to 4 in Table 9.2. (Recall that these data reflect explicit and implicit costs, including a normal profit.) Assuming that the market price is $131, the total revenue for each output level is found by multiplying output (total product) by price. Total-revenue data are in column 5. Then in column 6 we find the profit or loss at each output level by subtracting total cost, TC (column 4), from total revenue, TR (column 5).

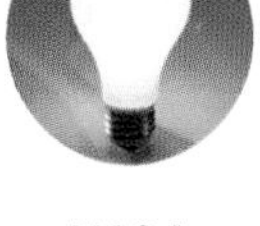

W 9.1

Profit maximization: TR − TC approach

Should the firm produce? Definitely. It can realize a profit by doing so. How much should it produce? Nine units. Column 6 tells us that this is the output at which total economic profit is at a maximum. What economic profit (or loss) will it realize? A $299 economic profit—the difference between total revenue ($1179) and total cost ($880).

Figure 9.2a compares total revenue and total cost graphically for this profit-maximizing case. Observe again that the total-revenue curve for a purely competitive firm is a straight line (Figure 9.1). Total cost increases with output in that more production requires more resources. But the rate of increase in total cost varies with the relative efficiency of the firm. Specifically, the cost data reflect Chapter 8's law of diminishing marginal returns. From zero to 4 units of output, total cost increases at a decreasing rate as the firm uses its fixed resources more efficiently. With additional output, total cost begins to rise by ever-increasing amounts because of the diminishing returns accompanying more intensive use of the plant.

Total revenue and total cost are equal where the two curves in Figure 9.2a intersect (at roughly 2 units of output). Total revenue covers all costs (including a normal profit, which is included in the cost curve), but there is no economic profit. For this reason economists call this output a **break-even point:** an output at which a firm makes a *normal profit* but not an economic profit. If we extended the data beyond 10 units of output, another break-even point would occur where total cost catches up with total revenue, somewhere between 13 and 14 units of output in Figure 9.2a. Any output within the two break-even points identified in the figure will produce an economic profit.

[1]To make sure you understand these two approaches, we will apply both of them to output determination under pure competition. But since we want to emphasize the marginal approach, we will limit our graphical application of the total-revenue approach to a situation where the firm maximizes profits. We will then use the marginal approach to examine three cases: profit maximization, loss minimization, and shutdown.

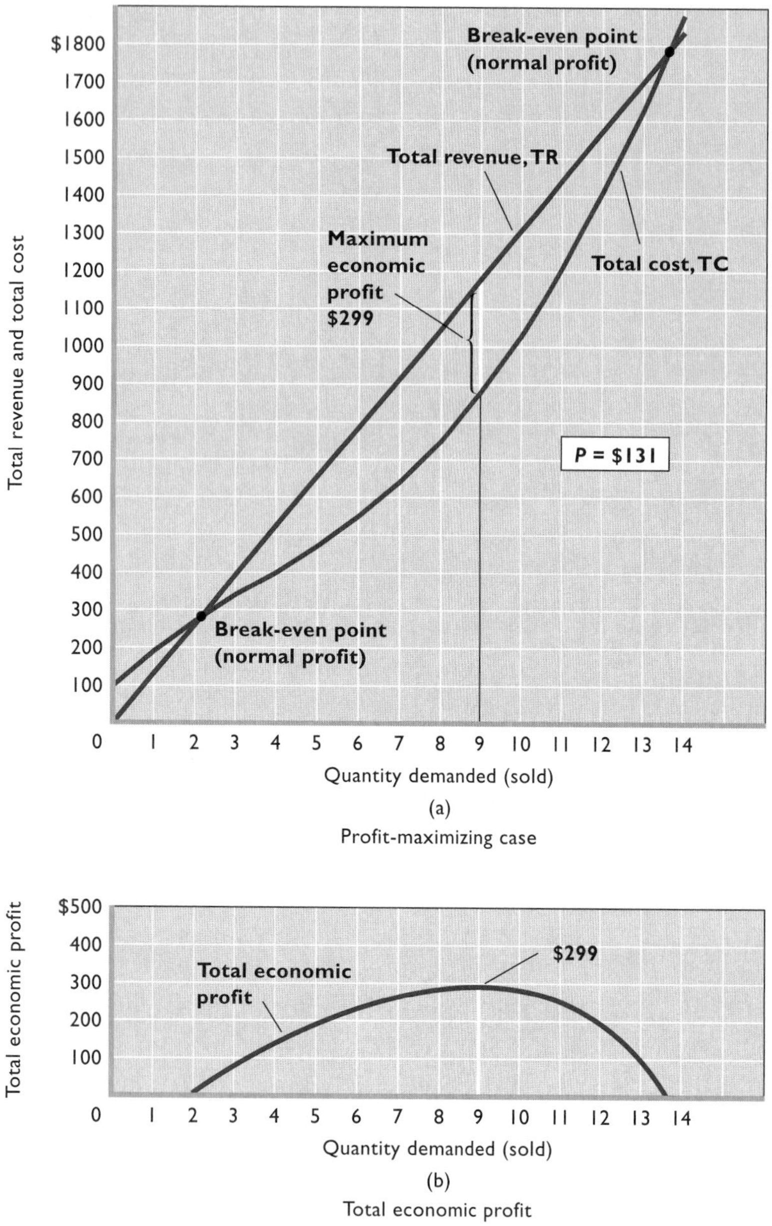

FIGURE 9.2 Total-revenue–total-cost approach to profit maximization for a purely competitive firm. (a) The firm's profit is maximized at that output (9 units) where total revenue, TR, exceeds total cost, TC, by the maximum amount. (b) The vertical distance between TR and TC in (a) is plotted as a total-economic-profit curve. Maximum economic profit is $299 at 9 units of output.

The firm achieves maximum profit, however, where the vertical distance between the total-revenue and total-cost curves is greatest. For our particular data, this is at 9 units of output, where maximum profit is $299.

The profit-maximizing output is easier to see in Figure 9.2b, where total profit is graphed for each level of output. Where the total-revenue and total-cost curves intersect in Figure 9.2a, economic profit is zero, as shown by the total-profit line in Figure 9.2b. Where the vertical distance between TR and TC is greatest in the upper graph, economic profit is at its peak ($299), as shown in the lower graph. This firm will choose to produce 9 units, since that output maximizes its profit.

Profit Maximization in the Short Run: Marginal-Revenue–Marginal-Cost Approach

In the second approach, the firm compares the amounts that each *additional* unit of output would add to total revenue and to total cost. In other words, the firm compares the *marginal revenue* (MR) and the *marginal cost* (MC) of each successive unit of output. Assuming that producing is preferable to shutting down, the firm should produce any unit of output whose marginal revenue exceeds its marginal cost because the firm would gain more in revenue from selling that unit than it would add to its costs by producing it. Conversely, if the marginal cost of a unit of output exceeds its marginal revenue, the firm should not produce that unit. Producing it would add more to costs than to revenue, and profit would decline or loss would increase.

In the initial stages of production, where output is relatively low, marginal revenue will usually (but not always) exceed marginal cost. So it is profitable to produce through this range of output. But at later stages of production, where output is relatively high, rising marginal costs will exceed marginal revenue. Obviously, a profit-maximizing firm will want to avoid output levels in that range. Separating these two production ranges is a unique point at which marginal revenue equals marginal cost. This point is the key to the output-determining rule: In the short run, the firm will maximize profit or minimize loss by producing the output at which marginal revenue equals marginal cost (as long as producing is preferable to shutting down). This profit-maximizing guide is known as the **MR = MC rule.**

Keep in mind these features of the MR = MC rule:

- For most sets of MR and MC data, MR and MC will be precisely equal at a fractional level of output. In such instances the firm should produce the last complete unit of output for which MR exceeds MC.
- As noted, the rule applies only if producing is preferable to shutting down. We will show shortly that if marginal revenue does not equal or exceed average variable cost, the firm will shut down rather than produce the MR = MC output.
- The rule is an accurate guide to profit maximization for all firms whether they are purely competitive, monopolistic, monopolistically competitive, or oligopolistic.
- The rule can be restated as P = MC when applied to a purely competitive firm. Because the demand schedule faced by a competitive seller is perfectly elastic at the going market price, product price and marginal revenue are equal. So under pure competition (and only under pure competition) we may substitute P for MR in the rule: When producing is preferable to shutting down, the competitive firm that wants to maximize its profit or minimize its loss should produce at that point where price equals marginal cost (P = MC).

Now let's apply the MR = MC rule or, because we are considering pure competition, the P = MC rule, first using the same price as used in our total-revenue–total-cost approach to profit maximization. Then, by considering other prices, we will demonstrate two additional cases: loss minimization and shutdown. It is crucial that you understand the MR = MC analysis that follows since it reappears in Chapters 10 and 11.

Profit-Maximizing Case

The first five columns in Table 9.3 reproduce the AFC, AVC, ATC, and MC data derived for our product in Table 8.2. It is the marginal-cost data of column 5 that we will compare with price (equals marginal revenue) for

TABLE 9.3 The Profit-Maximizing Output for a Purely Competitive Firm: Marginal-Revenue–Marginal-Cost Approach (Price = $131)

(1) Total Product (Output)	(2) Average Fixed Cost (AFC)	(3) Average Variable Cost (AVC)	(4) Average Total Cost (ATC)	(5) Marginal Cost (MC)	(6) Price = Marginal Revenue (MR)	(7) Total Economic Profit (+) or Loss (−)
0						$−100
1	$100.00	$90.00	$190.00	$ 90	$131	−59
2	50.00	85.00	135.00	80	131	−8
3	33.33	80.00	113.33	70	131	+53
4	25.00	75.00	100.00	60	131	+124
5	20.00	74.00	94.00	70	131	+185
6	16.67	75.00	91.67	80	131	+236
7	14.29	77.14	91.43	90	131	+277
8	12.50	81.25	93.75	110	131	+298
9	***11.11***	***86.67***	***97.78***	***130***	***131***	**+299**
10	10.00	93.00	103.00	150	131	+280

TABLE 9.4 The Loss-Minimizing Outputs for a Purely Competitive Firm: Marginal-Revenue–Marginal-Cost Approach (Prices = $81 and $71)

(1) Total Product (Output)	(2) Average Fixed Cost (AFC)	(3) Average Variable Cost (AVC)	(4) Average Total Cost (ATC)	(5) Marginal Cost (MC)	(6) $81 Price = Marginal Revenue (MR)	(7) Profit (+) or Loss (−), $81 Price	(8) $71 Price = Marginal Revenue (MR)	(9) Profit (+) or Loss (−), $71 Price
0						$−100		***$−100***
1	$100.00	$90.00	$190.00	$90	$81	−109	$71	−119
2	50.00	85.00	135.00	80	81	−108	71	−128
3	33.33	80.00	113.33	70	81	−97	71	−127
4	25.00	75.00	100.00	60	81	−76	71	−116
5	20.00	74.00	94.00	70	81	−65	71	−115
6	***16.67***	***75.00***	***91.67***	***80***	***81***	***−64***	71	−124
7	14.29	77.14	91.43	90	81	−73	71	−143
8	12.50	81.25	93.75	110	81	−102	71	−182
9	11.11	86.67	97.78	130	81	−151	71	−241
10	10.00	93.00	103.00	150	81	−220	71	−320

each unit of output. Suppose first that the market price, and therefore marginal revenue, is $131, as shown in column 6 of Table 9.3 on the previous page.

What is the profit-maximizing output? Every unit of output up to and including the ninth unit represents greater marginal revenue than marginal cost of output. Each of the first 9 units therefore adds to the firm's profit and should be produced. The tenth unit, however, should not be produced. It would add more to cost ($150) than to revenue ($131). So 9 units is the profit-maximizing output.

The economic profit realized by producing 9 units can be calculated by subtracting total cost from total revenue. Multiplying price ($131) by output (9), we find that total revenue is $1179. From the average-total-cost data in Table 9.3, we see that ATC is $97.78 at 9 units of output. Multiplying $97.78 by 9 gives us total cost of $880.[2] The difference of $299 (= $1179 − $880) is the economic profit. Clearly, this firm will prefer to operate rather than shut down.

Perhaps an easier way to calculate the economic profit is to use this simple equation, in which A is average total cost:

$$\text{Profit} = (P - A) \times Q$$

So by subtracting the average total cost ($97.78) from the product price ($131), we obtain a per-unit profit of $33.22. Multiplying that amount by 9 units of output, we determine that the profit is $299. Take some time now to verify the numbers in column 7 in Table 9.3. You will find that any output other than that which adheres to the MR = MC rule will mean either profits below $299 or losses.

W 9.2

Profit maximization: MR = MC approach

Figure 9.3 (Key Graph) shows price (= MR) and marginal cost graphically. Price equals marginal cost at the profit-maximizing output of 9 units. There the per-unit economic profit is $P - A$, where P is the market price and A is the average total cost for an output of 9 units. The total economic profit is $9 \times (P - A)$, shown by the green rectangular area.

Note that the firm wants to maximize its total profit, not its per-unit profit. Per-unit profit is greatest at 7 units of output, where price exceeds average total cost by $39.57 (= $131 − $91.43). But by producing only 7 units, the firm would be forgoing the production of 2 additional units of output that would clearly contribute to total profit. The firm is happy to accept lower per-unit profits for additional units of output because they nonetheless add to total profit.

G 9.1

Short-run profit maximization

Loss-Minimizing Case

Now let's assume that the market price is $81 rather than $131. Should the firm still produce? If so, how much? And what will be the resulting profit or loss? The answers, respectively, are "Yes," "Six units," and "A loss of $64."

The first five columns in Table 9.4 are the same as those in Table 9.3. Column 6 shows the new price (equal

[2]Most of the unit-cost data are rounded figures. Therefore, economic profits calculated from them will typically vary by a few cents from the profits determined in the total-revenue–total-cost approach. Here we simply ignore the few-cents differentials to make our answers consistent with the results of the total-revenue–total-cost approach.

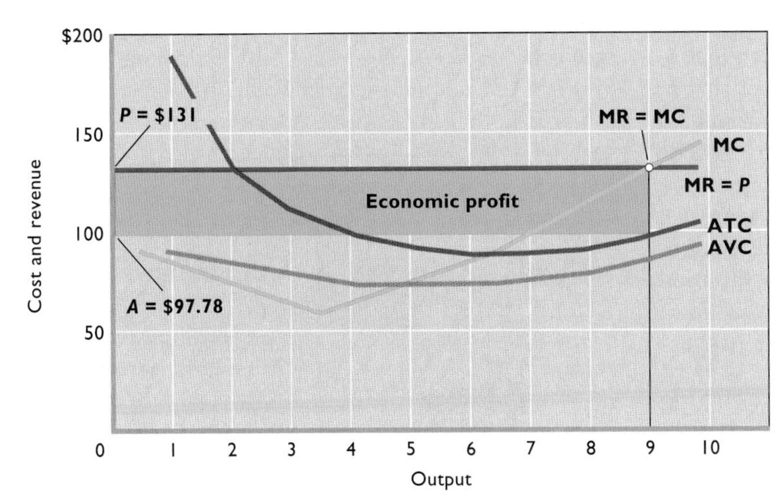

FIGURE 9.3 Short-run profit maximization for a purely competitive firm. The MR = MC output enables the purely competitive firm to maximize profits or to minimize losses. In this case MR (= *P* in pure competition) and MC are equal at an output *Q* of 9 units. There *P* exceeds the average total cost *A* = $97.78, so the firm realizes an economic profit of *P* − *A* per unit. The total economic profit is represented by the green rectangle and is 9 × (*P* − *A*).

QUICK QUIZ 9.3

1. Curve MR is horizontal because:
   a. product price falls as output increases.
   b. the law of diminishing marginal utility is at work.
   c. the market demand for this product is perfectly elastic.
   d. the firm is a price taker.
2. At a price of $131 and 7 units of output:
   a. MR exceeds MC, and the firm should expand its output.
   b. total revenue is less than total cost.
   c. AVC exceeds ATC.
   d. the firm would earn only a normal profit.
3. In maximizing profits at 9 units of output, this firm is adhering to which of the following decision rules?
   a. Produce where MR exceeds MC by the greatest amount.
   b. Produce where *P* exceeds ATC by the greatest amount.
   c. Produce where total revenue exceeds total cost by the greatest amount.
   d. Produce where average fixed costs are zero.
4. Suppose price declined from $131 to $100. This firm's:
   a. marginal-cost curve would shift downward.
   b. economic profit would fall to zero.
   c. profit-maximizing output would decline.
   d. total cost would fall by more than its total revenue.

Answers: 1. d; 2. a; 3. c; 4. c

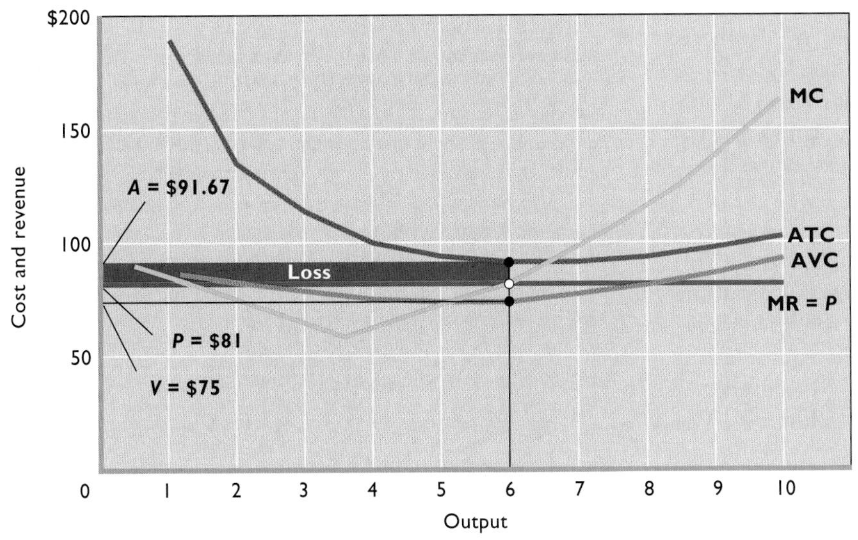

FIGURE 9.4 Short-run loss minimization for a purely competitive firm. If price *P* exceeds the minimum AVC (here $74 at *Q* = 5) but is less than ATC, the MR = MC output (here 6 units) will permit the firm to minimize its losses. In this instance the loss is *A* − *P* per unit, where *A* is the average total cost at 6 units of output. The total loss is shown by the red area and is equal to 6 × (*A* − *P*).

to MR), $81. Comparing columns 5 and 6, we find that the first unit of output adds $90 to total cost but only $81 to total revenue. One might conclude: "Don't produce—close down!" But that would be hasty. Remember that in the very early stages of production, marginal product is low, making marginal cost unusually high. The price–marginal cost relationship improves with increased production. For units 2 through 6, price exceeds marginal cost. Each of these 5 units adds more to revenue than to cost, and as shown in column 7, they decrease the total loss. Together they more than compensate for the "loss" taken on the first unit. Beyond 6 units, however, MC exceeds MR (= *P*). The firm should therefore produce 6 units. In general, the profit-seeking producer should always compare marginal revenue (or price under pure competition) with the rising portion of the marginal-cost schedule or curve.

Will production be profitable? No, because at 6 units of output the average total cost of $91.67 exceeds the price of $81 by $10.67 per unit. If we multiply that by the 6 units of output, we find the firm's total loss is $64. Alternatively, comparing the total revenue of $486 (= 6 × $81) with the total cost of $550 (= 6 × $91.67), we see again that the firm's loss is $64.

Then why produce? Because this loss is less than the firm's $100 of fixed costs, which is the $100 loss the firm would incur in the short run by closing down. The firm receives enough revenue per unit ($81) to cover its average variable costs of $75 and also provide $6 per unit, or a total of $36, to apply against fixed costs. Therefore, the firm's loss is only $64 (= $100 − $36), not $100.

This loss-minimizing case is shown graphically in Figure 9.4. Wherever price *P* exceeds average variable cost AVC but is less than ATC, the firm can pay part, but not all, of its fixed costs by producing. The loss is minimized by producing the output at which MC = MR (here, 6 units). At that output, each unit contributes $P - V$ to covering fixed cost, where V is the AVC at 6 units of output. The per-unit loss is $A - P = \$10.67$, and the total loss is $6 \times (A - P)$, or $64, as shown by the red area.

Shutdown Case

Suppose now that the market yields a price of only $71. Should the firm produce? No, because at every output the firm's average variable cost is greater than the price (compare columns 3 and 8 in Table 9.4). The smallest loss it can incur by producing is greater than the $100 fixed cost it will lose by shutting down (as shown by column 9). The best action is to shut down.

You can see this shutdown situation in Figure 9.5. Price comes closest to covering average variable costs at the MR (= *P*) = MC output of 5 units. But even here, price or revenue per unit would fall short of average variable cost by $3 (= $74 − $71). By producing at the MR (= *P*) = MC output, the firm would lose its $100 worth of

CONSIDER THIS ...

The Still There Motel

Have you ever driven by a poorly maintained business facility and wondered why the owner does not either fix up the property or go out of business? The somewhat surprising reason is that it may be unprofitable to improve the facility yet profitable to continue to operate the business as it deteriorates. Seeing why will aid your understanding of the "stay open or shut down" decision facing firms experiencing declining demand.

Consider the story of the Still There Motel on Old Highway North, Anytown, USA. The owner built the motel on the basis of traffic patterns and competition existing several decades ago. But as interstate highways were built, the motel found itself located on a relatively vacant stretch of road. Also, it faced severe competition from "chain" motels located much closer to the interstate highway.

As demand and revenue fell, Still There moved from profitability to loss. But at first its room rates and annual revenue were sufficient to cover its total variable costs and contribute some to the payment of fixed costs such as insurance and property taxes (or $P >$ AVC; $P <$ ATC). By staying open, Still There lost less than it would have if it shut down. But since its total revenue did not cover its total costs (or $P <$ ATC), the owner realized that something must be done in the long run. The owner decided to lower costs by reducing annual maintenance. In effect, the owner decided to allow the motel to deteriorate as a way of regaining temporary profitability.

This renewed profitability of Still There cannot last because in time no further reduction of maintenance costs will be possible. The deterioration of the motel structure will produce even lower room rates, and therefore even less total revenue. The owner of Still There knows that sooner or later total revenue will again fall below total cost (or *P* will again fall below ATC), even with an annual maintenance expense of zero. When that occurs, the owner will close down the business, tear down the structure, and sell the vacant property. But, in the meantime, the motel is still there—open, deteriorating, and profitable.

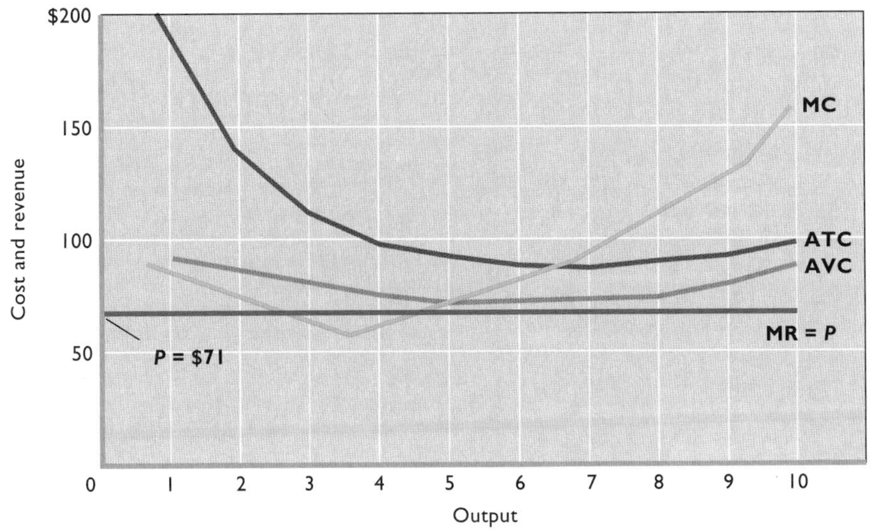

FIGURE 9.5 The short-run shutdown case for a purely competitive firm. If price *P* falls below the minimum AVC (here $74 at *Q* = 5), the competitive firm will minimize its losses in the short run by shutting down. There is no level of output at which the firm can produce and realize a loss smaller than its total fixed cost.

fixed cost plus $15 ($3 of variable cost on each of the 5 units), for a total loss of $115. This compares unfavorably with the $100 fixed-cost loss the firm would incur by shutting down and producing no output. So it will make sense for the firm to shut down rather than produce at a $71 price—or at any price less than the minimum average variable cost of $74.

The shutdown case reminds us of the qualifier to our MR (= *P*) = MC rule. A competitive firm will maximize profit or minimize loss in the short run by producing that output at which MR (= *P*) = MC, provided that market price exceeds minimum average variable cost.

Marginal Cost and Short-Run Supply

In the preceding section we simply selected three different prices and asked what quantity the profit-seeking competitive firm, faced with certain costs, would choose to offer in the market at each price. This set of product prices and corresponding quantities supplied constitutes part of the supply schedule for the competitive firm.

Table 9.5 summarizes the supply schedule data for those three prices ($131, $81, and $71) and four others. This table confirms the direct relationship between product price and quantity supplied that we identified in Chapter 3. Note first that the firm will not produce at price $61 or $71, because both are less than the $74 minimum AVC. Then note that quantity supplied increases as price increases. Observe finally that economic profit is higher at higher prices.

Generalized Depiction

Figure 9.6 (Key Graph) generalizes the MR = MC rule and the relationship between short-run production costs and the firm's supply behavior. The ATC, AVC, and MC curves are shown, along with several marginal-revenue lines drawn at possible market prices. Let's observe quantity supplied at each of these prices:

- Price P_1 is below the firm's minimum average variable cost, so at this price the firm won't operate at all. Quantity supplied will be zero, as it will be at all other prices below P_2.
- Price P_2 is just equal to the minimum average variable cost. The firm will supply Q_2 units of output (where MR_2 = MC) and just cover its total variable cost. Its loss will equal its total fixed cost. (Actually, the firm would be indifferent as to shutting down or supplying Q_2 units of output, but we assume it produces.)

TABLE 9.5 The Supply Schedule of a Competitive Firm Confronted with the Cost Data in Table 9.3

Price	Quantity Supplied	Maximum Profit (+) or Minimum Loss (−)
$151	10	$+480
131	9	+299
111	8	+138
91	7	−3
81	6	−64
71	0	−100
61	0	−100

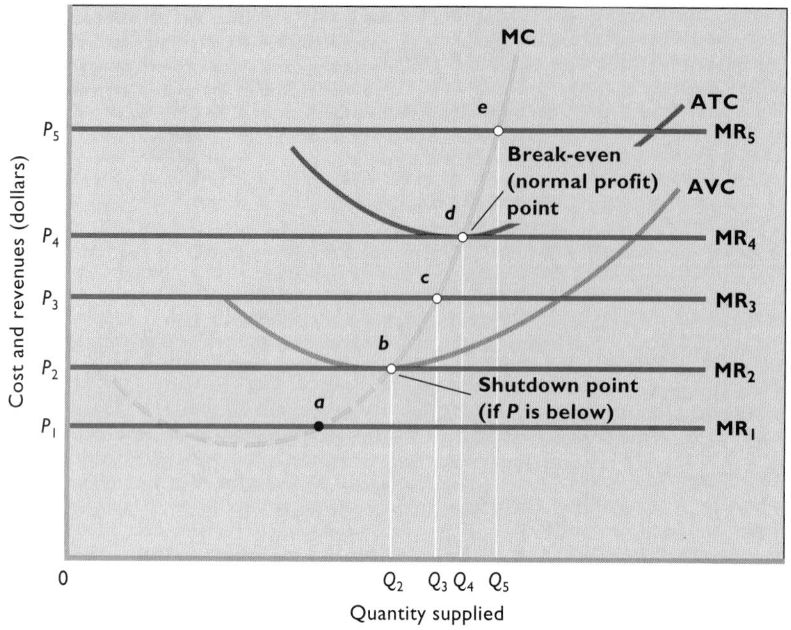

FIGURE 9.6 The $P = MC$ rule and the competitive firm's short-run supply curve. Application of the $P = MC$ rule, as modified by the shutdown case, reveals that the (solid) segment of the firm's MC curve that lies above AVC is the firm's short-run supply curve. More specifically, at price P_1, $P = MC$ at point *a*, but the firm will produce no output because P_1 is less than minimum AVC. At price P_2 the firm will operate at point *b*, where it produces Q_2 units and incurs a loss equal to its total fixed cost. At P_3 it operates at point *c*, where output is Q_3 and the loss is less than total fixed cost. With the price of P_4, the firm operates at point *d*; in this case the firm earns a normal profit because at output Q_4 price equals ATC. At price P_5 the firm operates at point e and maximizes its economic profit by producing Q_5 units.

QUICK QUIZ 9.6

1. Which of the following might increase product price from P_3 to P_5?
   a. An improvement in production technology.
   b. A decline in the price of a substitute good.
   c. An increase in the price of a complementary good.
   d. Rising incomes if the product is a normal good.
2. An increase in price from P_3 to P_5 would:
   a. shift this firm's MC curve to the right.
   b. mean that MR_5 exceeds MC at Q_3 units, inducing the firm to expand output to Q_5.
   c. decrease this firm's average variable costs.
   d. enable this firm to obtain a normal, but not an economic, profit.
3. At P_4:
   a. this firm has no economic profit.
   b. this firm will earn only a normal profit and thus will shut down.
   c. MR_4 will be less than MC at the profit-maximizing output.
   d. the profit-maximizing output will be Q_5.
4. Suppose P_4 is \$10, P_5 is \$15, Q_4 is 8 units, and Q_5 is 10 units. This firm's:
   a. supply curve is elastic over the Q_4–Q_5 range of output.
   b. supply curve is inelastic over the Q_4–Q_5 range of output.
   c. total revenue will decline if price rises from P_4 to P_5.
   d. marginal-cost curve will shift downward if price falls from P_5 to P_4.

Answers: 1. d; 2. b; 3. a; 4. b

- At price P_3 the firm will supply Q_3 units of output to minimize its short-run losses. At any other price between P_2 and P_4 the firm will minimize its losses by producing and supplying the quantity at which MR (= *P*) = MC.
- The firm will just break even at price P_4. There it will supply Q_4 units of output (where $MR_4 = MC$), earning a normal profit but not an economic profit. Total revenue will just cover total cost, including a normal profit, because the revenue per unit ($MR_4 = P_4$) and the total cost per unit (ATC) are the same.
- At price P_5 the firm will realize an economic profit by producing and supplying Q_5 units of output. In fact, at any price above P_4 the firm will obtain economic profit by producing to the point where MR (= *P*) = MC.

Note that each of the MR (= *P*) = MC intersection points labeled *b*, *c*, *d* and *e* in Figure 9.6 indicates a possible product price (on the vertical axis) and the corresponding quantity that the firm would supply at that price (on the horizontal axis). Thus, points such as these are on the upsloping supply curve of the competitive firm. Note too that quantity supplied would be zero at any price below the minimum average variable cost (AVC). We can conclude that the portion of the firm's marginal-cost curve lying above its average-variable-cost curve is its short-run supply curve. In Figure 9.6, the solid segment of the marginal-cost curve MC is this firm's **short-run supply curve.** It tells us the amount of output the firm will supply at each price in a series of prices.

Diminishing Returns, Production Costs, and Product Supply

We have now identified the links between the law of diminishing returns (Chapter 8), production costs, and product supply in the short run. Because of the law of diminishing returns, marginal costs eventually rise as more units of output are produced. And because marginal costs rise with output, a purely competitive firm must get successively higher prices to motivate it to produce additional units of output.

Viewed alternatively, higher product prices and marginal revenue encourage a purely competitive firm to expand output. As its output increases, the firm's marginal costs rise as a result of the law of diminishing returns. At some now greater output, the higher MC equals the new product price and MR. Profit once again is maximized, but at a greater total amount. Quantity supplied has increased in direct response to an increase in product price and the desire to maximize profit.

Changes in Supply

In Chapter 8 we saw that changes in such factors as the prices of variable inputs or in technology will alter costs and shift the marginal-cost or short-run supply curve to a new location. All else equal, for example, a wage increase would increase marginal cost and shift the supply curve in Figure 9.6 upward as viewed from the horizontal axis (leftward as viewed from the vertical axis). That is, supply would decrease. Similarly, technological progress that increases the productivity of labor would reduce marginal cost and shift the marginal-cost or supply curve downward as viewed from the horizontal axis (rightward as viewed from the vertical axis). This represents an increase in supply.

Firm and Industry: Equilibrium Price

In the preceding section we developed the competitive firm's short-run supply curve by applying the MR (= P) = MC rule. We now determine which of the various possible prices will actually be the market equilibrium price.

From Chapter 3 we know that in a purely competitive market, equilibrium price is determined by total, or market, supply and total demand. To derive total supply, the supply schedules or curves of the individual competitive sellers must be summed. Columns 1 and 3 in Table 9.6 repeat the supply schedule for the individual competitive firm, as derived in Table 9.5. We now assume that there are 1000 competitive firms in this industry, all having the same total and unit costs as the single firm we discussed. This lets us calculate the market supply schedule (columns 2 and 3) by multiplying the quantity-supplied figures of the single firm (column 1) by 1000.

TABLE 9.6 Firm and Market Supply and Market Demand

(1) Quantity Supplied, Single Firm	(2) Total Quantity Supplied, 1000 Firms	(3) Product Price	(4) Total Quantity Demanded
10	10,000	$151	4000
9	9000	131	6000
8	***8000***	***111***	***8000***
7	7000	91	9000
6	6000	81	11,000
0	0	71	13,000
0	0	61	16,000

Market Price and Profits

To determine the equilibrium price and output, these total-supply data must be compared with total-demand data. Let's assume that total demand is as shown in columns 3 and 4 in Table 9.6. By comparing the total quantity supplied and the total quantity demanded at the seven possible prices, we determine that the equilibrium price is $111 and the equilibrium quantity is 8000 units for the industry—8 units for each of the 1000 identical firms.

Will these conditions of market supply and demand make this a profitable or unprofitable industry? Multiplying product price ($111) by output (8 units), we find that the total revenue of each firm is $888. The total cost is $750, found by looking at column 4 in Table 9.2. The $138 difference is the economic profit of each firm. For the industry, total economic profit is $138,000. This, then, is a profitable industry.

Another way of calculating economic profit is to determine per-unit profit by subtracting average total cost ($93.75) from product price ($111) and multiplying the difference (per-unit profit of $17.25) by the firm's equilibrium level of output (8). Again we obtain an economic profit of $138 per firm and $138,000 for the industry.

Figure 9.7 shows this analysis graphically. The individual supply curves of each of the 1000 identical firms—one of which is shown as s = MC in Figure 9.7a—are summed horizontally to get the total-supply curve S =

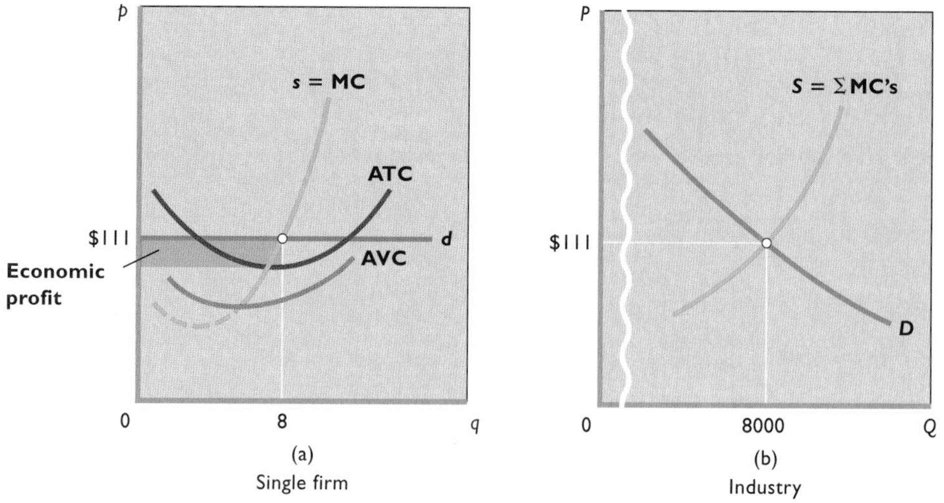

FIGURE 9.7 Short-run competitive equilibrium for (a) a firm and (b) the industry. The horizontal sum of the 1000 firms' individual supply curves (*s*) determines the industry supply curve (*S*). Given industry demand (*D*), the short-run equilibrium price and output for the industry are $111 and 8000 units. Taking the equilibrium price as given, the individual firm establishes its profit-maximizing output at 8 units and, in this case, realizes the economic profit represented by the green area.

ΣMC of Figure 9.7b. With total-demand curve *D*, it yields the equilibrium price $111 and equilibrium quantity (for the industry) 8000 units. This equilibrium price is given and unalterable to the individual firm; that is, each firm's demand curve is perfectly elastic at the equilibrium price, as indicated by *d* in Figure 9.7a. Because the individual firm is a price taker, the marginal-revenue curve coincides with the firm's demand curve *d*. This $111 price exceeds the average total cost at the firm's equilibrium MR = MC output of 8 units, so the firm earns an economic profit represented by the green area in Figure 9.7a.

Assuming no changes in costs or market demand, these diagrams reveal a genuine equilibrium in the short run. There are no shortages or surpluses in the market to cause price or total quantity to change. Nor can any firm in the industry increase its profit by altering its output. Note, too, that higher unit and marginal costs, on the one hand, or weaker market demand, on the other, could change the situation so that Figure 9.7a resembles Figure 9.4 or Figure 9.5.

Firm versus Industry Figure 9.7 underscores a point made earlier: Product price is a given fact to the *individual* competitive firm, but the supply plans of all competitive producers *as a group* are a basic determinant of product price. If we recall the fallacy of composition (Last Word, Chapter 1), we find there is no inconsistency here. Although one firm, supplying a negligible fraction of total supply, cannot affect price, the sum of the supply curves of all the firms in the industry constitutes the industry supply curve, and that curve does have an important bearing on price. **(Key Question 4)**

W 9.3
Short-run competitive equilibrium

QUICK REVIEW 9.2

- Profit is maximized, or loss minimized, at the output at which marginal revenue (or price in pure competition) equals marginal cost, provided that price exceeds average variable cost.
- If the market price is below the minimum average variable cost, the firm will minimize its losses by shutting down.
- The segment of the firm's marginal-cost curve that lies above the average-variable-cost curve is its short-run supply curve.
- Table 9.7 summarizes the MR = MC approach to determining the competitive firm's profit-maximizing output. It also shows the equivalent analysis in terms of total revenue and total cost.
- Under competition, equilibrium price is a given to the individual firm and simultaneously is the result of the production (supply) decisions of all firms as a group.

Profit Maximization in the Long Run

In the short run the industry is composed of a specific number of firms, each with a fixed, unalterable plant. Firms may shut down in the sense that they can produce zero units of output in the short run, but they do not have sufficient time to liquidate their assets and go out of business. By contrast, in the long run firms already in an industry have sufficient time either to expand or to contract their plant capacities. More important, the number of firms in the industry may either increase or decrease as new firms enter or existing firms leave. We now examine how these long-run adjustments modify our conclusions concerning short-run output and price determination.

TABLE 9.7 Output Determination in Pure Competition in the Short Run

Question	Answer
Should this firm produce?	Yes, if price is equal to, or greater than, minimum average variable cost. This means that the firm is profitable or that its losses are less than its fixed cost.
What quantity should this firm produce?	Produce where MR (= *P*) = MC; there, profit is maximized (TR exceeds TC by a maximum amount) or loss is minimized.
Will production result in economic profit?	Yes, if price exceeds average total cost (TR will exceed TC). No, if average total cost exceeds price (TC will exceed TR).

Assumptions

We make three simplifying assumptions, none of which alters our conclusions:

- ***Entry and exit only*** The only long-run adjustment is the entry or exit of firms. Moreover, we ignore all short-run adjustments in order to concentrate on the effects of the long-run adjustments.
- ***Identical costs*** All firms in the industry have identical cost curves. This assumption lets us discuss an "average," or "representative," firm, knowing that all other firms in the industry are similarly affected by any long-run adjustments that occur.
- ***Constant-cost industry*** The industry is a constant-cost industry. This means that the entry and exit of firms does not affect resource prices or, consequently, the locations of the average-total-cost curves of individual firms.

Goal of Our Analysis

The basic conclusion we seek to explain is this: After all long-run adjustments are completed, product price will be exactly equal to, and production will occur at, each firm's minimum average total cost.

This conclusion follows from two basic facts: (1) Firms seek profits and shun losses, and (2) under pure competition, firms are free to enter and leave an industry. If market price initially exceeds average total costs, the resulting economic profits will attract new firms to the industry. But this industry expansion will increase supply until price is brought back down to equality with minimum average total cost. Conversely, if price is initially less than average total cost, resulting losses will cause firms to leave the industry. As they leave, total supply will decline, bringing the price back up to equality with minimum average total cost.

Long-Run Equilibrium

Consider the average firm in a purely competitive industry that is initially in long-run equilibrium. This firm is represented in Figure 9.8a, where MR = MC and price and minimum average total cost are equal at \$50. Economic profit here is zero; the industry is in equilibrium or "at rest" because there is no tendency for firms to enter or to leave. The existing firms are earning normal profits, which, recall, are included in their cost curves. The \$50 market price is determined in Figure 9.8b by market or industry demand D_1 and supply S_1. (S_1 is a short-run sup-

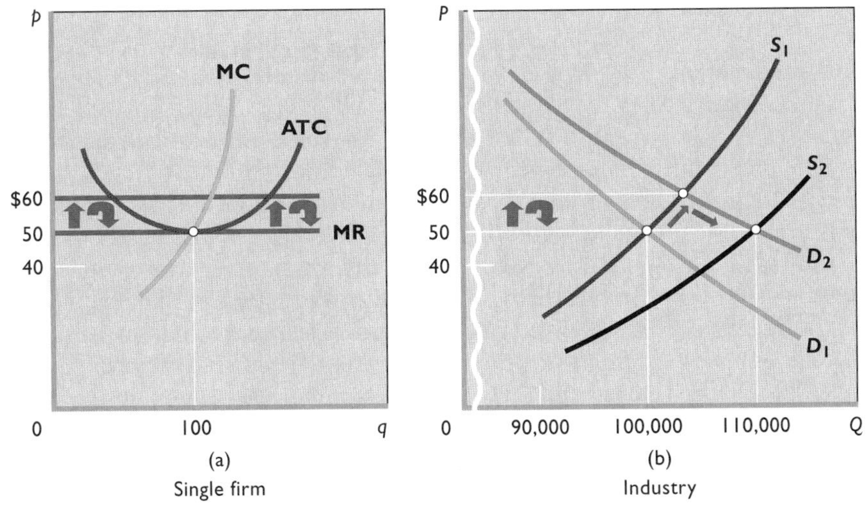

FIGURE 9.8 Temporary profits and the reestablishment of long-run equilibrium in (a) a representative firm and (b) the industry. A favorable shift in demand (D_1 to D_2) will upset the original industry equilibrium and produce economic profits. But those profits will cause new firms to enter the industry, increasing supply (S_1 to S_2) and lowering product price until economic profits are once again zero.

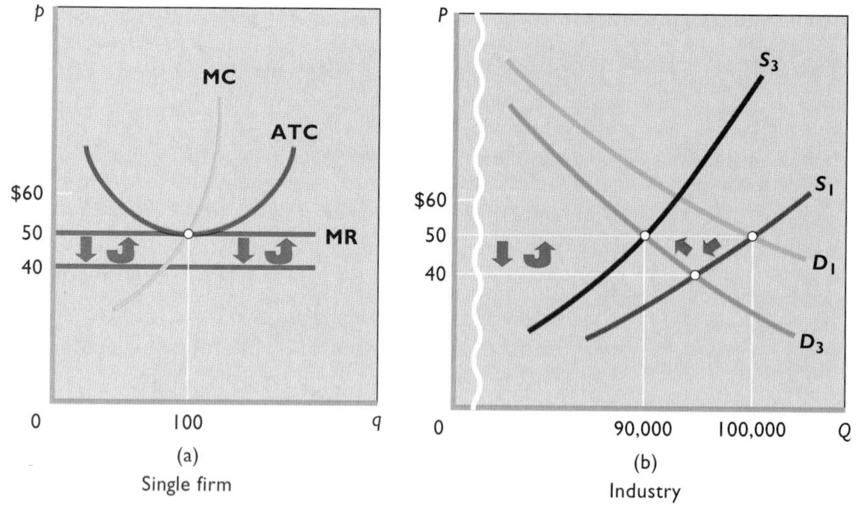

FIGURE 9.9 Temporary losses and the reestablishment of long-run equilibrium in (a) a representative firm and (b) the industry. An unfavorable shift in demand (D_1 to D_3) will upset the original industry equilibrium and produce losses. But those losses will cause firms to leave the industry, decreasing supply (S_1 to S_3) and increasing product price until all losses have disappeared.

ply curve; we will develop the long-run industry supply curve in our discussion.)

As shown on the quantity axes of the two graphs, equilibrium output in the industry is 100,000 while equilibrium output for the single firm is 100. If all firms in the industry are identical, there must be 1000 firms (= 100,000/100).

Entry Eliminates Economic Profits Let's upset the long-run equilibrium in Figure 9.8 and see what happens. Suppose a change in consumer tastes increases product demand from D_1 to D_2. Price will rise to \$60, as determined at the intersection of D_2 and S_1, and the firm's marginal-revenue curve will shift upward to \$60. This \$60 price exceeds the firm's average total cost of \$50 at output 100, creating an economic profit of \$10 per unit. This economic profit will lure new firms into the industry. Some entrants will be newly created firms; others will shift from less prosperous industries.

As firms enter, the market supply of the product increases, pushing the product price below \$60. Economic profits persist, and entry continues until short-run supply increases to S_2. Market price falls to \$50, as does marginal revenue for the firm. Price and minimum average total cost are again equal at \$50. The economic profits caused by the boost in demand have been eliminated, and, as a result, the previous incentive for more firms to enter the industry has disappeared. Long-run equilibrium has been restored.

Observe in Figure 9.8a and 9.8b that total quantity supplied is now 110,000 units and each firm is producing 100 units. Now 1100 firms rather than the original 1000 populate the industry. Economic profits have attracted 100 more firms.

Exit Eliminates Losses Now let's consider a shift in the opposite direction. We begin in Figure 9.9b with curves S_1 and D_1 setting the same initial long-run equilibrium situation as in our previous analysis, including the \$50 price.

Suppose consumer demand declines from D_1 to D_3. This forces the market price and marginal revenue down to \$40, making production unprofitable at the minimum ATC of \$50. In time the resulting losses will induce firms to leave the industry. Their owners will seek a normal profit elsewhere rather than accept the below-normal profits (loss) now confronting them. And as capital equipment wears out, some firms will simply go out of business. As this exodus of firms proceeds, however, industry supply decreases, pushing the price up from \$40 toward \$50. Losses continue and more firms leave the industry until the supply curve shifts to S_3. Once this happens, price is again \$50, just equal to the minimum average total cost. Losses have been eliminated and long-run equilibrium is restored.

In Figure 9.9a and 9.9b, total quantity supplied is now 90,000 units and each firm is producing 100 units. Only 900 firms, not the original 1000, populate the industry. Losses have forced 100 firms out.

You may have noted that we have sidestepped the question of which firms will leave the industry when losses occur by assuming that all firms have identical cost curves. In the "real world," of course, entrepreneurial talents differ. Even if resource prices and technology are the same for all firms, inferior entrepreneurs tend to incur higher costs and therefore are the first to leave an industry when demand declines. Similarly, firms with less productive labor forces will be higher-cost producers and likely candidates to quit an industry when demand decreases.

We have now reached an intermediate goal: Our analysis verifies that competition, reflected in the entry and exit of firms, eliminates economic profits or losses by adjusting price to equal minimum long-run average total cost. In addition, this competition forces firms to select output levels at which average total cost is minimized.

Long-Run Supply for a Constant-Cost Industry

Although our analysis has dealt with the long run, we have noted that the market supply curves in Figures 9.8b and 9.9b are short-run curves. What then is the character of the **long-run supply curve** of a competitive industry? The analysis points us toward an answer. The crucial factor here is the effect, if any, that changes in the number of firms in the industry will have on costs of the individual firms in the industry.

In our analysis of long-run competitive equilibrium we assumed that the industry under discussion was a **constant-cost industry.** This means that industry expansion or contraction will not affect resource prices and therefore production costs. Graphically, it means that the entry or exit of firms does not shift the long-run ATC curves of individual firms. This is the case when the industry's demand for resources is small in relation to the total demand for those resources. Then the industry can expand or contract without significantly affecting resource prices and costs.

What does the long-run supply curve of a constant-cost industry look like? The answer is contained in our previous analysis. There we saw that the entry and exit of firms changes industry output but always brings the product price back to its original level, where it is just equal to the constant minimum ATC. Specifically, we discovered that the industry would supply 90,000, 100,000, or 110,000 units of output, all at a price of $50 per unit. In other words, the long-run supply curve of a constant-cost industry is perfectly elastic.

This is demonstrated graphically in Figure 9.10, which uses data from Figures 9.8 and 9.9. Suppose industry demand is originally D_1, industry output is Q_1 (100,000 units), and product price is P_1 ($50). This situation, from Figure 9.8, is one of long-run equilibrium. We saw that when demand increases to D_2, upsetting this equilibrium, the resulting economic profits attract new firms. Because this is a constant-cost industry, entry continues and industry output expands until the price is driven back down to the level of the unchanged minimum ATC. This is at price P_2 ($50) and output Q_2 (110,000).

From Figure 9.9, we saw that a decline in market demand from D_1 to D_3 causes an exit of firms and ultimately restores equilibrium at price P_3 ($50) and output Q_3 (90,000 units). The points Z_1, Z_2, and Z_3 in Figure 9.10 represent these three price-quantity combinations. A line or curve connecting all such points shows the various price-quantity combinations that firms would produce if they had enough time to make all desired adjustments to changes in demand. This line or curve is the industry's long-run supply curve. In a constant-cost industry this curve (straight line) is horizontal, as in Figure 9.10, thus representing perfectly elastic supply.

FIGURE 9.10 The long-run supply curve for a constant-cost industry is horizontal. Because the entry or exodus of firms does not affect resource prices or, therefore, unit costs, an increase in demand (D_1 to D_2) causes an expansion in industry output (Q_1 to Q_2) but no alteration in price ($50). Similarly, a decrease in demand (D_1 to D_3) causes a contraction of output (Q_1 to Q_3) but no change in price. This means that the long-run industry supply curve (S) is horizontal through points Z_1, Z_2 and Z_3.

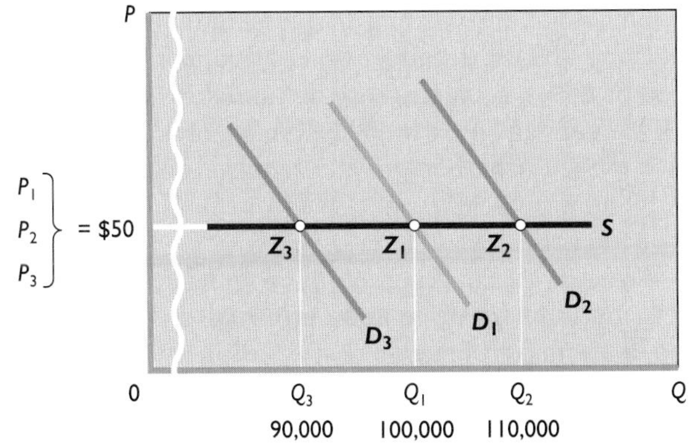

Long-Run Supply for an Increasing-Cost Industry

Constant-cost industries are a special case. Most industries are **increasing-cost industries,** in which firms' ATC curves shift upward as the industry expands and downward as the industry contracts. Usually, the entry of new firms will increase resource prices, particularly in industries using specialized resources whose supplies are not readily increased in response to an increase in resource demand. Higher resource prices result in higher long-run average total costs for all firms in the industry. These higher costs cause upward shifts in each firm's long-run ATC curve.

Thus, when an increase in product demand results in economic profits and attracts new firms to an increasing-cost industry, a two-way squeeze works to eliminate those profits. As before, the entry of new firms increases market supply and lowers the market price. But now the entire ATC curve shifts upward. The overall result is a higher-than-original equilibrium price. The industry produces a larger output at a higher product price because the industry expansion has increased resource prices and the minimum average total cost. We know that, in the long run, the product price must cover ATC.

Since greater output will be supplied at a higher price, the long-run industry supply curve is upsloping. Instead of supplying 90,000, 100,000, or 110,000 units at the same price of \$50, an increasing-cost industry might supply 90,000 units at \$45, 100,000 units at \$50, and 110,000 units at \$55. A higher price is required to induce more production, because costs per unit of output increase as production rises.

We show this in Figure 9.11. Original market demand is D_1 and industry price and output are P_1 (\$50) and Q_1 (100,000 units), respectively, at equilibrium point Y_1. An increase in demand to D_2 upsets this equilibrium and leads to economic profits. New firms enter the industry, increasing both market supply and production costs of individual firms. A new price is established at point Y_2, where P_2 is \$55 and Q_2 is 110,000 units.

Conversely, a decline in demand from D_1 to D_3 makes production unprofitable and causes firms to leave the industry. The resulting decline in resource prices reduces the minimum average total cost of production for firms that stay. A new equilibrium price is established at some level below the original price, say, at point Y_3, where P_3 is \$45 and Q_3 is 90,000 units. Connecting these three equilibrium positions, we derive the upsloping long-run supply curve S in Figure 9.11.

FIGURE 9.11 The long-run supply curve for an increasing-cost industry is upsloping. In an increasing-cost industry the entry of new firms in response to an increase in demand (D_3 to D_1 to D_2) will bid up resource prices and thereby increase unit costs. As a result, an increased industry output (Q_3 to Q_1 to Q_2) will be forthcoming only at higher prices (\$55 > \$50 > \$45). The long-run industry supply curve (S) therefore slopes upward through points Y_3, Y_1, and, Y_2.

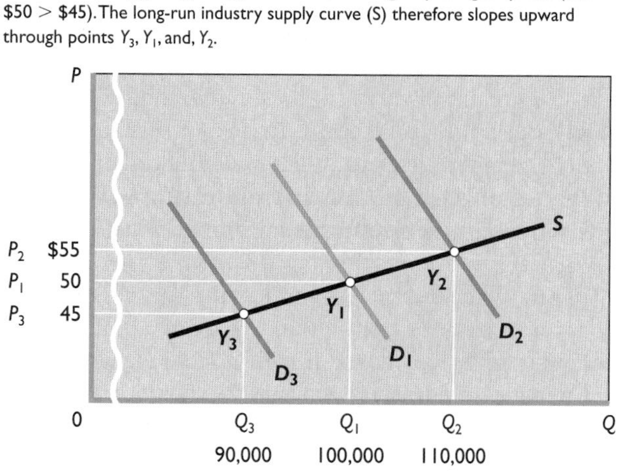

Long-Run Supply for a Decreasing-Cost Industry

In **decreasing-cost industries,** firms experience lower costs as the industry expands. The personal computer industry is an example. As demand for personal computers increased, new manufacturers of computers entered the industry and greatly increased the resource demand for the components used to build them (for example, memory chips, hard drives, monitors, and operating software). The expanded production of the components enabled the producers of those items to achieve substantial economies of scale. The decreased production costs of the components reduced their prices, which greatly lowered the computer manufacturers' average costs of production. The supply of personal computers increased by more than demand, and the price of personal computers declined.

G 9.2

Long-run competitive supply

You should rework the analysis underlying Figure 9.11 to show that the long-run supply curve of a decreasing-cost industry is *downsloping*. **(Key Question 6)**

Pure Competition and Efficiency

Figure 9.12 (Key Graph) demonstrates the efficiency characteristics of the individual firms (Figure 9.12a) and the market (Figure 9.12.b) after long-run adjustments in pure competition in a straightforward manner. Whether a purely competitive industry is a constant-cost industry or an increasing-cost industry, the final long-run equilibrium positions of all firms have the same basic efficiency characteristics. As shown in Figure 9.12a, price (and marginal revenue) will settle where it is equal to minimum average total cost: P (and MR) = minimum ATC. Moreover, since the marginal-cost curve intersects the average-total-cost curve at its minimum point, marginal cost and average total cost are equal: MC = minimum ATC. So in long-run equilibrium a triple equality occurs: P (and MR) = MC = minimum ATC. Output for each firm is Q_f.

This triple equality tells us that although a competitive firm may realize economic profit or loss in the short run, it will earn only a normal profit by producing in accordance with the MR (= P) = MC rule in the long run. Also, this triple equality suggests certain conclusions of great social significance concerning the efficiency of a purely competitive economy.

Economists agree that, subject to Chapter 4's qualifications relating to public goods and externalities, an ideal-

FIGURE 9.12 Long-run equilibrium: a competitive firm and market. (a) The equality of price (*P*), marginal cost (MC), and minimum average total cost (ATC) at output Q_f indicates that the firm is achieving productive efficiency and allocative efficiency. It is using the most efficient technology, charging the lowest price, and producing the greatest output consistent with its costs. It is receiving only a normal profit, which is incorporated into the ATC curve. The equality of price and marginal cost indicates that society allocated its scarce resources in accordance with consumer preferences. (b) In the purely competitive market, allocative efficiency occurs at the market equilibrium output Q_e. The sum of consumer surplus (green area) and producer surplus (orange area) is maximized.

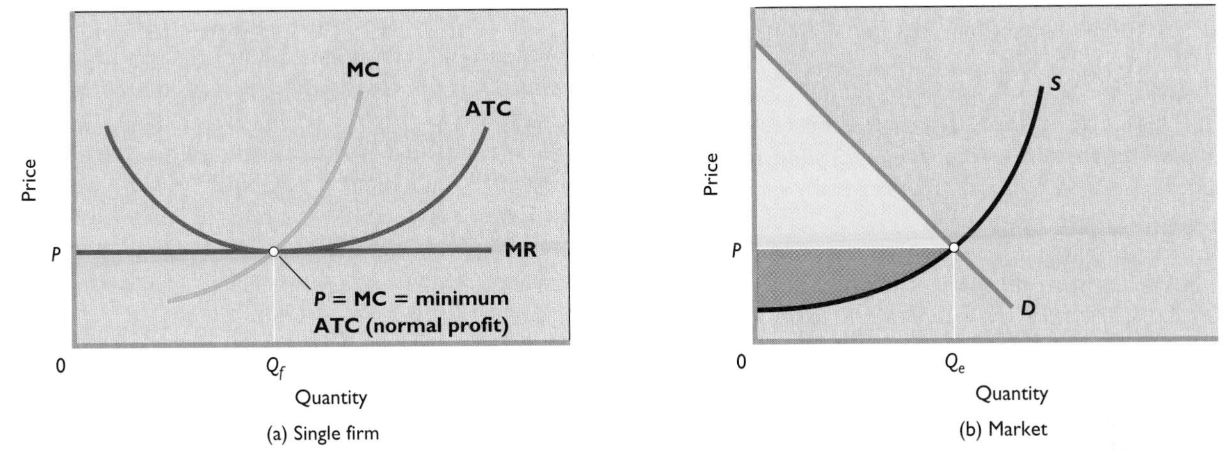

QUICK QUIZ 9.12

1. We know the firm is a price taker because:
   a. its MC curve slopes upward.
   b. its ATC curve is U-shaped.
   c. its MR curve is horizontal.
   d. MC and ATC are equal at the profit-maximizing output.
2. At this firm's profit-maximizing output:
   a. total revenue equals total cost.
   b. it is earning an economic profit.
   c. allocative, but not necessarily productive, efficiency is achieved.
   d. productive, but not necessarily allocative, efficiency is achieved.
3. The equality of *P*, MC, and minimum ATC:
   a. occurs only in constant-cost industries.
   b. encourages entry of new firms.
   c. means that the "right goods" are being produced in the "right ways."
   d. results in a zero accounting profit.
4. When *P* = MC = lowest ATC for individual firms, in the market:
   a. consumer surplus necessarily exceeds producer surplus.
   b. consumer surplus plus producer surplus is at a maximum.
   c. producer surplus necessarily exceeds consumer surplus.
   d. supply and demand are identical.

Answers: 1. c; 2. a; 3. c; 4. b

ized purely competitive economy leads to an efficient use of society's scarce resources. A competitive market economy uses the limited amounts of resources available to society in a way that maximizes the satisfaction of consumers. Efficient use of limited resources necessitates both productive efficiency and allocative efficiency.

Productive Efficiency: *P* = Minimum ATC

Productive efficiency requires that goods be produced in the least costly way. In the long run, pure competition forces firms to produce at the minimum average total cost of production and to charge a price that is just consistent with that cost. That is a highly favorable situation from the consumer's point of view. It means that unless firms use the best-available (least-cost) production methods and combinations of inputs, they will not survive. Stated differently, it means that the minimum amount of resources will be used to produce any particular output. Let's suppose that output in Figure 9.12a is cucumbers.

In the final equilibrium position shown in Figure 9.12a suppose each firm in the cucumber industry is producing 120 units (say, pickup truckloads) of output by using \$5000 (equal to average total cost of \$50 × 120 units) worth of resources. If one firm produced that same output at a total cost of, say, \$7000, its resources would be used inefficiently. Society would be faced with a net loss of \$2000 worth of alternative products. But this cannot happen in pure competition; this firm would incur a loss of

$2000, requiring it either to reduce its costs or to go out of business.

Note, too, that consumers benefit from productive efficiency by paying the lowest product price possible under the prevailing technology and cost conditions. And the firm receives only a normal profit, which is part of its economic costs and thus incorporated in its ATC curve.

Allocative Efficiency: $P = MC$

Allocative efficiency requires that resources be apportioned among firms and industries to yield the mix of products and services that is most wanted by society (least-cost production at each level of output assumed). Allocative efficiency has been realized when achieving a net gain for society by altering the combination of goods produced is impossible. Productive efficiency alone does not ensure the efficient allocation of resources. Least-cost production must be used to provide society with the "right goods"—the goods that consumers want most. Before we can show that the competitive market system does just that, we must discuss the social meaning of product prices. Two elements here are critical:

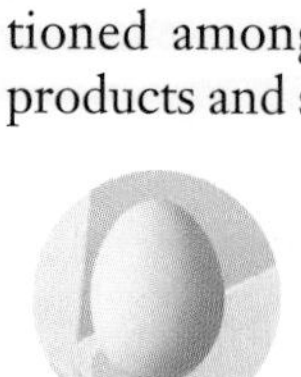

O 9.1
Allocative efficiency

- The money price of any product is society's measure of the relative worth of an additional unit of that product—for example, cucumbers. So the price of a unit of cucumbers is the marginal benefit derived from that unit of the product.
- Similarly, recalling the idea of opportunity cost, we see that the marginal cost of an additional unit of a product measures the value, or relative worth, of the other goods sacrificed to obtain it. In producing cucumbers, resources are drawn away from producing other goods. The marginal cost of producing a unit of cucumbers measures society's sacrifice of those other products.

In pure competition, when profit-motivated firms produce each good or service to the point where price (marginal benefit) and marginal cost are equal, society's resources are being allocated efficiently. Each item is being produced to the point at which the value of the last unit is equal to the value of the alternative goods sacrificed by its production. Altering the production of cucumbers would reduce consumer satisfaction. Producing cucumbers beyond the $P = MC$ point in Figure 9.12a would sacrifice alternative goods whose value to society exceeds that of the extra cucumbers. Producing cucumbers short of the $P = MC$ point would sacrifice cucumbers that society values more than the alternative goods its resources could produce. **(Key Question 7)**

Maximum Consumer and Producer Surplus

We confirm the existence of allocative efficiency in Figure 9.12b, where we see that pure competition maximizes the sum of the "benefit surpluses" to consumers and producers. Recall from Chapter 6 that **consumer surplus** is the difference between the maximum prices that consumers are willing to pay for a product and the market price of that product. In Figure 9.12b, consumer surplus is the green triangle, which is the sum of the vertical distances between the demand curve and equilibrium price. In contrast, **producer surplus** is the difference between the minimum prices that producers are willing to accept for a product and the market price of the product; it is the vertical distances between the equilibrium price and supply curve. Here producer surplus is the orange area.

At the equilibrium quantity Q_e, the combined amount of consumer surplus and producer surplus is maximized. Allocative efficiency occurs because, at Q_e, marginal benefit, reflected by points on the demand curve, equals marginal cost, reflected by the points on the supply curve. Alternatively, the maximum willingness of consumers to pay for unit Q_e equals the minimum acceptable price of that unit to producers. At any output less than Q_e, the sum of consumer and producer surplus—the combined size of the green and orange area—would be less than that shown. At any output greater than Q_e, an efficiency loss (deadweight loss) would subtract from the combined consumer and producer surplus shown by the green and orange area.

After long-run adjustments, pure competition produces allocative efficiency: A level of output at which $P = MC =$ lowest ATC, marginal benefit $=$ marginal cost, maximum willingness to pay $=$ minimum acceptable price, and combined consumer and producer surplus are maximized.

Dynamic Adjustments

A further attribute of purely competitive markets is their ability to restore the efficiency just described when disrupted by changes in the economy. A change in consumer tastes, resource supplies, or technology will automatically set in motion the appropriate realignments of resources. For example, suppose that cucumbers and pickles become dramatically more popular. First, the demand for cucumbers will increase in the market, increasing the price of cucumbers. So, at current output, the price of cucumbers will exceed their marginal cost. At this point efficiency will be lost, but the higher price will create economic profits in the cucumber industry and stimulate its expansion. The profitability of cucumbers will permit the industry to bid resources away from now less pressing uses, say, watermelons.

Last *Word*

Efficiency Gains from Entry: The Case of Generic Drugs

When a Generic Drug Becomes Available, the Price of the Drug Falls, Consumer Surplus Rises, and Society Experiences an Efficiency Gain.

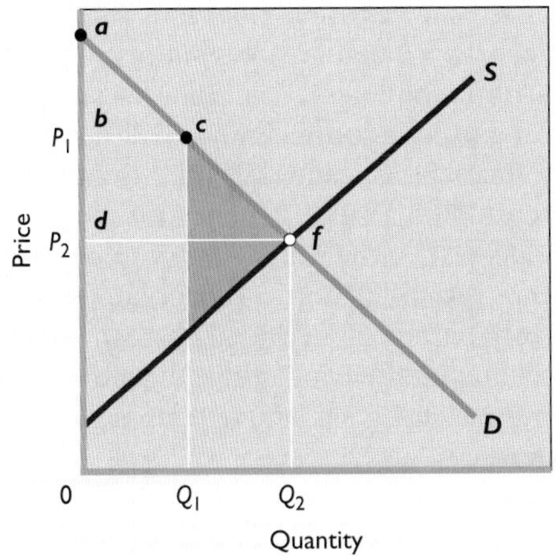

The competitive model predicts that entry will lower price, expand output, and increase efficiency. A good real-world test of this prediction occurs where entry of new producers occurs in a formerly monopolized market. Such a situation occurs when prescription drugs lose their patent protection. A patent on a prescription drug gives the pharmaceutical company that developed it an exclusive right to produce and sell the medication for 20 years from the time of patent application. Because the FDA approval process averages 8 years, the exclusive right may last for as few as 12 years. The purpose of drug patents is to encourage research and development (R&D) leading to new medications and the increased well-being they enable. With patent protection, a firm can charge prices that exceed marginal cost and average total cost and thus earn economic profits on its popular brand-name medicines. Those economic profits provide a return on past development costs and help fund more R&D.

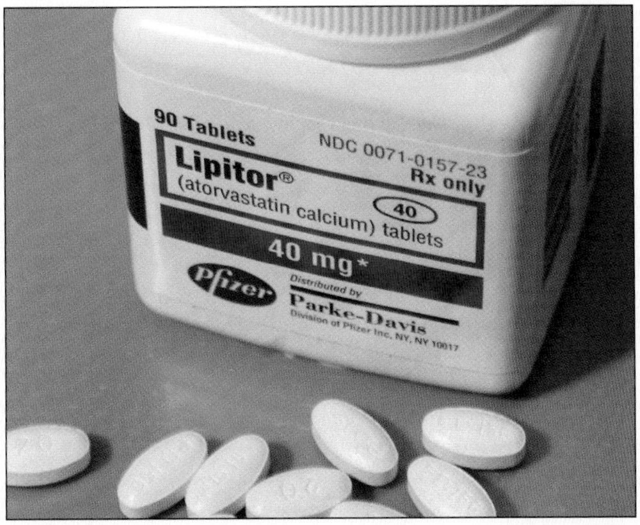

Although competitors can and often do develop similar drugs, they cannot copy and sell the patented medication. Such drugs as Lipitor (for high cholesterol), Zoloft (for depression), and Nexium (for gastrointestinal disorders) are examples of best-selling brand-name, patented drugs.

When a patent expires, any pharmaceutical company can produce and sell the drug under the generic name for the medication. An example of a generic is metroprolol (a substitute for the brand-name drug Lopressor), a beta-blocker used to treat high blood pressure. Because such generic drugs have the same chemical composition as the branded drug, they directly compete against it. The generic price is lower than the branded price, so the price of the drug (at least on average) drops as generics claim a share of the market. Studies indicate that price drop is typically 30–40 percent. Medical insurance plans often provide incentives for patients to buy generic drugs when they become available. Today, generics make up about 42 percent of all prescription drugs sold.

Seeing how patent expiration and the competition from generic drugs relate to consumer surplus and efficiency gains is useful. Consider the accompanying figure, which is similar to Figure 9.12b. The patent gives the firm monopoly power that allows it to charge a higher-than-competitive price. Suppose that the sole seller's profit-maximizing price is P_1. (We will examine how a monopolist would choose this price in the following chapter.)

The expiration of the patent creates competition from generics, which reduces the price of the medication from P_1 to, say, P_2. If you compare the consumer surplus triangles above the price lines, you can see that consumer surplus rises from *bac* to *daf* when the price falls. As the price of the medication drops from P_1 to P_2, output increases from Q_1 to Q_2. In this case, the efficiency gain from competition is shown by the addition of the gray triangle. At price P_2 and quantity Q_2, the combined amounts of consumer surplus and producer surplus are at a maximum. (In reality, the price might not drop all the way to P_2 because of continued loyalty to the branded drug by prescribing physicians.)

Patents aid consumers and society by encouraging the development of new medicines that might otherwise not be available. Entry of the generics at the time of patent expiration further helps consumers by lowering prices, increasing consumer surplus, and enhancing efficiency—just like the competitive model predicts.

Expansion of the industry will end only when the supply of cucumbers has expanded such that the price of cucumbers and their marginal cost are equal—that is, when allocative efficiency has been restored.

Similarly, a change in the supply of a particular resource—for example, the field laborers who pick cucumbers—or in a production technique will upset an existing price–marginal-cost equality by either raising or lowering marginal cost. The resulting inequality of MC and *P* will cause producers, in either pursuing profit or avoiding loss, to reallocate resources until product supply is such that price once again equals marginal cost. In so doing, they will correct any inefficiency in the allocation of resources that the original change may have temporarily imposed on the economy.

"Invisible Hand" Revisited

Finally, the highly efficient allocation of resources that a purely competitive economy promotes comes about because businesses and resource suppliers seek to further their self-interest. For private goods with no externalities (Chapter 4), the "invisible hand" (Chapter 2) is at work. The competitive system not only maximizes profits for individual producers but also, at the same time, creates a pattern of resource allocation that maximizes consumer satisfaction. The invisible hand thus organizes the private interests of producers in a way that is fully in sync with society's interest in using scarce resources efficiently. Striving for profit (and avoiding losses) produces highly desirable economic outcomes.

QUICK REVIEW 9.3

- In the long run, the entry of firms into an industry will compete away any economic profits, and the exit of firms will eliminate losses, so price and minimum average total cost are equal.
- The long-run supply curves of constant-, increasing-, and decreasing-cost industries are horizontal, upsloping, and downsloping, respectively.
- In purely competitive markets both productive efficiency (price equals minimum average total cost) and allocative efficiency (price equals marginal cost) are achieved in the long run.
- After long-run adjustments, purely competitive markets maximize the combined amounts of consumer surplus and producer surplus.

Summary

1. Economists group industries into four models based on their market structures: (a) pure competition, (b) pure monopoly, (c) monopolistic competition, and (d) oligopoly.
2. A purely competitive industry consists of a large number of independent firms producing a standardized product. Pure competition assumes that firms and resources are mobile among different industries.
3. In a competitive industry, no single firm can influence market price. This means that the firm's demand curve is perfectly elastic and price equals marginal revenue.
4. We can analyze short-run profit maximization by a competitive firm by comparing total revenue and total cost or by applying marginal analysis. A firm maximizes its short-run profit by producing the output at which total revenue exceeds total cost by the greatest amount.
5. Provided price exceeds minimum average variable cost, a competitive firm maximizes profit or minimizes loss in the short run by producing the output at which price or marginal revenue equals marginal cost. If price is less than average variable cost, the firm minimizes its loss by shutting down. If price is greater than average variable cost but is less than average total cost, the firm minimizes its loss by producing the $P = \text{MC}$ output. If price also exceeds average total cost, the firm maximizes its economic profit at the $P = \text{MC}$ output.
6. Applying the MR $(= P) = \text{MC}$ rule at various possible market prices leads to the conclusion that the segment of the firm's short-run marginal-cost curve that lies above the firm's average-variable-cost curve is its short-run supply curve.
7. In the long run, the market price of a product will equal the minimum average total cost of production. At a higher price, economic profits would cause firms to enter the industry until those profits had been competed away. At a lower price, losses would force the exit of firms from the industry until the product price rose to equal average total cost.
8. The long-run supply curve is horizontal for a constant-cost industry, upsloping for an increasing-cost industry, and downsloping for a decreasing-cost industry.
9. The long-run equality of price and minimum average total cost means that competitive firms will use the most efficient known technology and charge the lowest price consistent with their production costs. That is, the firms will achieve productive efficiency.
10. The long-run equality of price and marginal cost implies that resources will be allocated in accordance with consumer tastes. Allocative efficiency will occur. In the market, the combined amount of consumer surplus and producer surplus will be at a maximum.
11. The competitive price system will reallocate resources in response to a change in consumer tastes, in technology, or in resource supplies and will thereby maintain allocative efficiency over time.

Terms and Concepts

pure competition
pure monopoly
monopolistic competition
oligopoly
imperfect competition
price taker
average revenue
total revenue
marginal revenue
break-even point
MR = MC rule
short-run supply curve
long-run supply curve
constant-cost industry
increasing-cost industry
decreasing-cost industry
productive efficiency
allocative efficiency
consumer surplus
producer surplus

Study Questions

1. Briefly state the basic characteristics of pure competition, pure monopoly, monopolistic competition, and oligopoly. Under which of these market classifications does each of the following most accurately fit? (*a*) a supermarket in your hometown; (b) the steel industry; (c) a Kansas wheat farm; (d) the commercial bank in which you or your family has an account; (e) the automobile industry. In each case justify your classification.
2. Strictly speaking, pure competition has never existed and probably never will. Then why study it?
3. **KEY QUESTION** Use the following demand schedule to determine total revenue and marginal revenue for each possible level of sales:

Product Price	Quantity Demanded	Total Revenue	Marginal Revenue
$2	0	$_____	
			$_____
2	1	_____	
			_____
2	2	_____	
			_____
2	3	_____	
			_____
2	4	_____	
			_____
2	5	_____	

a. What can you conclude about the structure of the industry in which this firm is operating? Explain.
b. Graph the demand, total-revenue, and marginal-revenue curves for this firm.
c. Why do the demand and marginal-revenue curves coincide?
d. "Marginal revenue is the change in total revenue associated with additional units of output." Explain verbally and graphically, using the data in the table.

4. **KEY QUESTION** Assume the following cost data are for a purely competitive producer:

Total Product	Average Fixed Cost	Average Variable Cost	Average Total Cost	Marginal Cost
0				
				$45
1	$60.00	$45.00	$105.00	
				40
2	30.00	42.50	72.50	
				35
3	20.00	40.00	60.00	
				30
4	15.00	37.50	52.50	
				35
5	12.00	37.00	49.00	
				40
6	10.00	37.50	47.50	
				45
7	8.57	38.57	47.14	
				55
8	7.50	40.63	48.13	
				65
9	6.67	43.33	50.00	
				75
10	6.00	46.50	52.50	

a. At a product price of $56, will this firm produce in the short run? Why or why not? If it is preferable to produce, what will be the profit-maximizing or loss-minimizing output? Explain. What economic profit or loss will the firm realize per unit of output?
b. Answer the relevant questions of 4a assuming product price is $41.
c. Answer the relevant questions of 4a assuming product price is $32.
d. In the table below, complete the short-run supply schedule for the firm (columns 1 and 2) and indicate the profit or loss incurred at each output (column 3).

(1) Price	(2) Quantity Supplied, Single Firm	(3) Profit (+) or Loss (−)	(4) Quantity Supplied 1500 Firms
$26	_____	$_____	_____
32	_____	_____	_____
38	_____	_____	_____
41	_____	_____	_____
46	_____	_____	_____
56	_____	_____	_____
66	_____	_____	_____

e. Explain: "That segment of a competitive firm's marginal-cost curve that lies above its average-variable-cost curve constitutes the short-run supply curve for the firm." Illustrate graphically.
f. Now assume that there are 1500 identical firms in this competitive industry; that is, there are 1500 firms, each of which has the cost data shown in the table. Complete the industry supply schedule (column 4).
g. Suppose the market demand data for the product are as follows:

Price	Total Quantity Demanded
$26	17,000
32	15,000
38	13,500
41	12,000
46	10,500
56	9500
66	8000

What will be the equilibrium price? What will be the equilibrium output for the industry? For each firm? What will profit or loss be per unit? Per firm? Will this industry expand or contract in the long run?

5. Why is the equality of marginal revenue and marginal cost essential for profit maximization in all market structures? Explain why price can be substituted for marginal revenue in the MR = MC rule when an industry is purely competitive.
6. **KEY QUESTION** Using diagrams for both the industry and a representative firm, illustrate competitive long-run equilibrium. Assuming constant costs, employ these diagrams to show how (*a*) an increase and (*b*) a decrease in market demand will upset that long-run equilibrium. Trace graphically and describe verbally the adjustment processes by which long-run equilibrium is restored. Now rework your analysis for increasing- and decreasing-cost industries and compare the three long-run supply curves.
7. **KEY QUESTION** In long-run equilibrium, *P* = minimum ATC = MC. Of what significance for economic efficiency is the equality of *P* and minimum ATC? The equality of *P* and MC? Distinguish between productive efficiency and allocative efficiency in your answer.
8. Suppose that purely competitive firms producing cashews discover that *P* exceeds MC. Will their combined output of cashews be too little, too much, or just right to achieve allocative efficiency? In the long run, what will happen to the supply of cashews and the price of cashews? Use a supply and demand diagram to show how that response will change the combined amount of consumer surplus and producer surplus in the market for cashews.
9. **LAST WORD** How does a generic drug differ from its brand-name, previously patented equivalent? Explain why the price of a brand-name drug typically declines when an equivalent generic drug becomes available? Explain how that drop in price affects allocative efficiency.

Web-Based Questions

1. **YOU ARE A PURE COMPETITOR—WHAT WAS YOUR REVENUE YESTERDAY?** Suppose that you operate a purely competitive firm that buys and sells foreign currencies. Also suppose that yesterday your business activity consisted of buying 100,000 Swiss francs at the market exchange rate and selling them for a 3 percent commission. Go to the Federal Reserve Web site at **federalreserve.gov** and select, in order, Economic Research and Data, Statistics, and Foreign Exchange Rates. What was your total revenue in dollars yesterday (be sure to include your commission)? Why would your profit for the day be considerably less than this total revenue?
2. **ENTRY AND EXIT OF FIRMS—WHERE HAVE THEY OCCURRED?** Go to the Census Bureau Web site at **www.census.gov** and select Economic Census, then Comparative Statistics, and then Manufacturing. Identify three manufacturing industries that experienced large percentage increases in the number of firms between 1997 and 2002. Identify three manufacturing industries that experienced large percentage decreases. What single factor is the most likely cause of the entry and exit differences between your two groups? Explain.

IN THIS CHAPTER YOU WILL LEARN:

- **The characteristics of pure monopoly.**
- **How a pure monopoly sets its profit-maximizing output and price.**
- **About the economic effects of monopoly.**
- **Why a monopolist might prefer to charge different prices in different markets.**

10

Pure Monopoly

We turn now from pure competition to pure monopoly, which is at the opposite end of the spectrum of industry structures listed in Table 9.1. You deal with monopolies more often than you might think. When you see the logo for Microsoft's Windows on your computer, you are dealing with a monopoly (or, at least, a near-monopoly). When you purchase certain prescription drugs, you are buying monopolized products. When you make a local telephone call, turn on your lights, or subscribe to cable TV, you may be patronizing a monopoly, depending on your location.

What precisely do we mean by pure monopoly, and what conditions enable it to arise and survive? How does a pure monopolist determine its profit-maximizing price and output quantity? Does a pure monopolist achieve the efficiency associated with pure competition? If not, what should the government do about it? A simplified model of pure monopoly will help us answer these questions. This will be the first of three models of imperfect competition.

An Introduction to Pure Monopoly

Pure monopoly exists when a single firm is the sole producer of a product for which there are no close substitutes. Here are the main characteristics of pure monopoly:

- ***Single seller*** A pure, or absolute, monopoly is an industry in which a single firm is the sole producer of a specific good or the sole supplier of a service; the firm and the industry are synonymous.
- ***No close substitutes*** A pure monopoly's product is unique in that there are no close substitutes. The consumer who chooses not to buy the monopolized product must do without it.
- ***Price maker*** The pure monopolist controls the total quantity supplied and thus has considerable control over price; it is a *price maker* (unlike a pure competitor, which has no such control and therefore is a *price taker*). The pure monopolist confronts the usual downward-sloping product demand curve. It can change its product price by changing the quantity of the product it supplies. The monopolist will use this power whenever it is advantageous to do so.
- ***Blocked entry*** A pure monopolist has no immediate competitors because certain barriers keep potential competitors from entering the industry. Those barriers may be economic, technological, legal, or of some other type. But entry is totally blocked in pure monopoly.
- ***Nonprice competition*** The product produced by a pure monopolist may be either standardized (as with natural gas and electricity) or differentiated (as with Windows or Frisbees). Monopolists that have standardized products engage mainly in public relations advertising, whereas those with differentiated products sometimes advertise their products' attributes.

O 10.1
Monopoly

Examples of Monopoly

Examples of *pure* monopoly are relatively rare, but there are many examples of less pure forms. In most cities, government-owned or government-regulated public utilities—natural gas and electric companies, the water company, the cable TV company, and the local telephone company—are all monopolies or virtually so.

There are also many "near-monopolies" in which a single firm has the bulk of sales in a specific market. Intel, for example, provides 80 percent of the central microprocessors used in personal computers. First Data Corporation, via its Western Union subsidiary, accounts for 80 percent of the market for money order transfers. Brannock Device Company has an 80 percent market share of the shoe sizing devices found in shoe stores. Wham-O, through its Frisbee brand, sells 90 percent of plastic throwing disks. The De Beers diamond syndicate effectively controls 55 percent of the world's supply of rough-cut diamonds (see this chapter's Last Word).

Professional sports teams are, in a sense, monopolies because they are the sole suppliers of specific services in large geographic areas. With a few exceptions, a single major-league team in each sport serves each large American city. If you want to see a live major-league baseball game in St. Louis or Seattle, you must patronize the Cardinals or the Mariners, respectively. Other geographic monopolies exist. For example, a small town may be served by only one airline or railroad. In a small, isolated community, the local bank, movie theater, or grocery store may approximate a monopoly.

Of course, there is almost always some competition. Satellite television is a substitute for cable, and amateur softball is a substitute for professional baseball. The Linux operating system can substitute for Windows, and so on. But such substitutes are typically either more costly or in some way less appealing.

Dual Objectives of the Study of Monopoly

We want to examine pure monopoly not only for its own sake but also because such a study will help you understand the more common market structures of monopolistic competition and oligopoly, to be discussed in Chapter 11. These two market structures combine, in differing degrees, characteristics of pure competition and pure monopoly.

Barriers to Entry

The factors that prohibit firms from entering an industry are called **barriers to entry.** In pure monopoly, strong barriers to entry effectively block all potential competition. Somewhat weaker barriers may permit oligopoly, a market structure dominated by a few firms. Still weaker barriers may permit the entry of a fairly large number of competing firms giving rise to monopolistic competition. And the absence of any effective entry barriers permits the entry of a very large number of firms, which provide the basis of pure competition. So barriers to entry are pertinent not only to the extreme case of pure monopoly but also to other market structures in which there is some degree of monopolistic conditions and behavior.

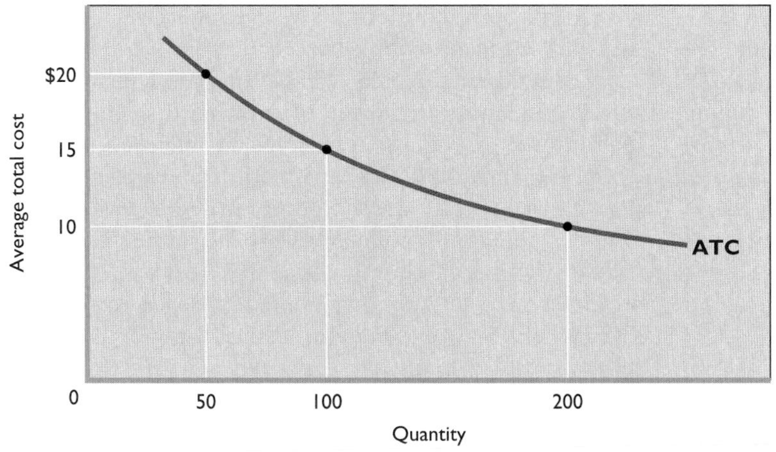

FIGURE 10.1 Economies of scale: the natural monopoly case. A declining long-run average-total-cost curve over a wide range of output quantities indicates extensive economies of scale. A single monopoly firm can produce, say, 200 units of output at lower cost ($10 each) than could two or more firms that had a combined output of 200 units.

Economies of Scale

Modern technology in some industries is such that economies of scale—declining average total cost with added firm size—are extensive. So a firm's long-run average-cost schedule will decline over a wide range of output. Given market demand, only a few large firms or, in the extreme, only a single large firm can achieve low average total costs.

Figure 10.1 indicates economies of scale over a wide range of outputs. If total consumer demand is within that output range, then only a single producer can satisfy demand at least cost. Note, for example, that a monopolist can produce 200 units at a per-unit cost of $10 and a total cost of $2000. If the industry has two firms and each produces 100 units, the unit cost is $15 and total cost rises to $3000 (= 200 units × $15). A still more competitive situation with four firms each producing 50 units would boost unit and total cost to $20 and $4000, respectively. Conclusion: When long-run ATC is declining, only a single producer, a monopolist, can produce any particular output at minimum total cost.

If a pure monopoly exists in such an industry, economies of scale will serve as an entry barrier and will protect the monopolist from competition. New firms that try to enter the industry as small-scale producers cannot realize the cost economies of the monopolist and therefore cannot obtain the normal profits necessary for survival or growth. A new firm might try to start out big, that is, to enter the industry as a large-scale producer so as to achieve the necessary economies of scale. But the massive plant facilities required would necessitate huge amounts of financing, which a new and untried enterprise would find difficult to secure. In most cases the financial obstacles and risks to "starting big" are prohibitive. This explains why efforts to enter such industries as automobiles, computer operating software, commercial aircraft, and basic steel are so rare.

In the extreme circumstance, in which the market demand curve cuts the long-run ATC curve where average total costs are still declining, the single firm is called a *natural monopoly*. It might seem that a natural monopolist's lower unit cost would enable it to charge a lower price than if the industry were more competitive. But that won't necessarily happen. A pure monopolist may, instead, set its price far above ATC and obtain substantial economic profit. In that event, the lowest-unit-cost advantage of a natural monopolist would accrue to the monopolist as profit and not as lower prices to consumers. That is why the government regulates some natural monopolies, specifying the price they may charge. We will say more about that later.

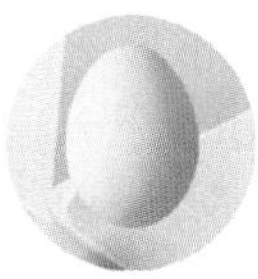

O 10.2
Minimum efficient scale

Legal Barriers to Entry: Patents and Licenses

Government also creates legal barriers to entry by awarding patents and licenses.

Patents A *patent* is the exclusive right of an inventor to use, or to allow another to use, her or his invention. Patents and patent laws aim to protect the inventor from rivals who would use the invention without having shared in the effort and expense of developing it. At the same time, patents provide the inventor with a monopoly position for the life of the patent. The world's nations have agreed on a uniform patent length of 20 years from the time of application. Patents have figured prominently in the growth of modern-day giants such as IBM, Pfizer, Intel, Xerox, General Electric, and DuPont.

Research and development (R&D) is what leads to most patentable inventions and products. Firms that gain monopoly power through their own research or by purchasing the patents of others can use patents to strengthen their market position. The profit from one patent can finance the research required to develop new patentable products. In the pharmaceutical industry, patents on prescription drugs have produced large monopoly profits that have helped finance the discovery of new patentable medicines. So monopoly power achieved through patents may well be self-sustaining, even though patents eventually expire and generic drugs then compete with the original brand.

Licenses Government may also limit entry into an industry or occupation through *licensing*. At the national level, the Federal Communications Commission licenses only so many radio and television stations in each geographic area. In many large cities one of a limited number of municipal licenses is required to drive a taxicab. The consequent restriction of the supply of cabs creates economic profit for cab owners and drivers. New cabs cannot enter the industry to drive down prices and profits. In a few instances the government might "license" itself to provide some product and thereby create a public monopoly. For example, in some states only state-owned retail outlets can sell liquor. Similarly, many states have "licensed" themselves to run lotteries.

Ownership or Control of Essential Resources

A monopolist can use private property as an obstacle to potential rivals. For example, a firm that owns or controls a resource essential to the production process can prohibit the entry of rival firms. At one time the International Nickel Company of Canada (now called Inco) controlled 90 percent of the world's known nickel reserves. A local firm may own all the nearby deposits of sand and gravel. And it is very difficult for new sports leagues to be created because existing professional sports leagues have contracts with the best players and have long-term leases on the major stadiums and arenas.

Pricing and Other Strategic Barriers to Entry

Even if a firm is not protected from entry by, say, extensive economies of scale or ownership of essential resources, entry may effectively be blocked by the way the monopolist responds to attempts by rivals to enter the industry. Confronted with a new entrant, the monopolist may "create an entry barrier" by slashing its price, stepping up its advertising, or taking other strategic actions to make it difficult for the entrant to succeed.

Examples of entry deterrence: In 2005 Dentsply, the dominant American maker of false teeth (70 percent market share) was found to have unlawfully precluded independent distributors of false teeth from carrying competing brands. The lack of access to the distributors deterred potential foreign competitors from entering the U.S. market. As another example, in 2001 a U.S. court of appeals upheld a lower court's finding that Microsoft used a series of illegal actions to maintain its monopoly in Intel-compatible PC operating systems (95 percent market share). One such action was charging higher prices for its Windows operating system to computer manufacturers that featured Netscape's Navigator rather than Microsoft's Internet Explorer.

Monopoly Demand

Now that we have explained the sources of monopoly, we want to build a model of pure monopoly so that we can analyze its price and output decisions. Let's start by making three assumptions:

- Patents, economies of scale, or resource ownership secure our monopolist's status.
- No unit of government regulates the firm.
- The firm is a single-price monopolist; it charges the same price for all units of output.

The crucial difference between a pure monopolist and a purely competitive seller lies on the demand side of the market. The purely competitive seller faces a perfectly elastic demand at the price determined by market supply and demand. It is a price taker that can sell as much or as little as it wants at the going market price. Each additional unit sold will add the amount of the constant product price to the firm's total revenue. That means that marginal revenue for the competitive seller is constant and equal to product price. (Refer to Table 9.2 and Figure 9.1 for price, marginal-revenue, and total-revenue relationships for the purely competitive firm.)

The demand curve for the monopolist (and for any imperfectly competitive seller) is very different from that of the pure competitor. Because the pure monopolist *is* the industry, its demand curve is *the market demand curve*. And because market demand is not perfectly elastic, the monopolist's demand curve is downsloping. Columns 1 and 2 in Table 10.1 illustrate this concept. Note that quantity demanded increases as price decreases.

In Chapter 9 we drew separate demand curves for the purely competitive industry and for a single firm in such an industry. But only a single demand curve is needed

TABLE 10.1 Revenue and Cost Data of a Pure Monopolist

Revenue Data				Cost Data			
(1) Quantity of Output	(2) Price (Average Revenue)	(3) Total Revenue, (1) × (2)	(4) Marginal Revenue	(5) Average Total Cost	(6) Total Cost, (1) × (5)	(7) Marginal Cost	(8) Profit [+] or Loss [−]
0	$172	$ 0			$ 100		$−100
1	162	162	$162	$190.00	190	$ 90	−28
2	152	304	142	135.00	270	80	+34
3	142	426	122	113.33	340	70	+86
4	132	528	102	100.00	400	60	+128
5	***122***	***610***	***82***	***94.00***	***470***	***70***	***+140***
6	112	672	62	91.67	550	80	+122
7	102	714	42	91.43	640	90	+74
8	92	736	22	93.75	750	110	−14
9	82	738	2	97.78	880	130	−142
10	72	720	−18	103.00	1030	150	−310

in pure monopoly. The firm and the industry are one and the same. We have graphed part of the demand data in Table 10.1 as demand curve *D* in Figure 10.2. This is the monopolist's demand curve *and* the market demand curve. The downward-sloping demand curve has three implications that are essential to understanding the monopoly model.

FIGURE 10.2 Price and marginal revenue in pure monopoly. A pure monopolist, or any other imperfect competitor with a downsloping demand curve such as *D*, must set a lower price in order to sell more output. Here, by charging $132 rather than $142, the monopolist sells an extra unit (the fourth unit) and gains $132 from that sale. But from this gain must be subtracted $30, which reflects the $10 less the monopolist charged for each of the first 3 units. Thus, the marginal revenue of the fourth unit is $102 (= $132 − $30), considerably less than its $132 price.

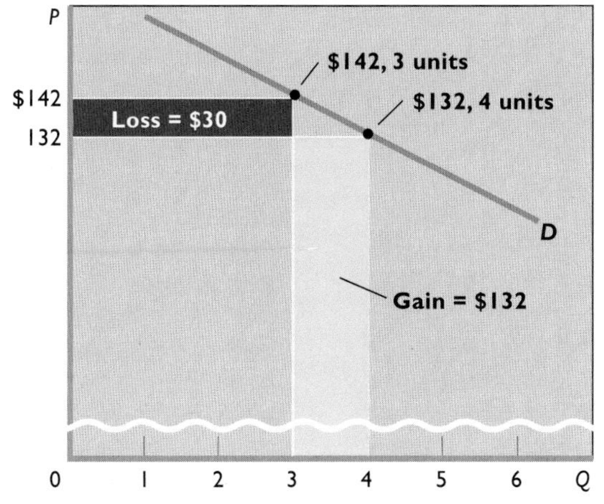

Marginal Revenue Is Less Than Price

The monopolist's downward-sloping demand curve means that it can increase sales only by charging a lower price. Consequently, marginal revenue—the change in total revenue associated with a 1 unit change in output—is less than price (average revenue) for every level of output except the first. Why so? The reason is that the lower price applies not only to the extra unit of output sold but also to all prior units of output. The monopolist could have sold these prior units at a higher price if it had not produced and sold the extra output. Each additional unit of output sold increases total revenue by an amount equal to its own price less the sum of the price cuts that apply to all prior units of output.

Figure 10.2 confirms this point. There, we have highlighted two price-quantity combinations from the monopolist's demand curve. The monopolist can sell 1 more unit at $132 than it can at $142 and that way obtain $132 (the blue area) of extra revenue. But to sell that fourth unit for $132, the monopolist must also sell the first 3 units at $132 rather than $142. The $10 reduction in revenue on 3 units results in a $30 revenue loss (the red area). The net difference in total revenue from selling a fourth unit is $102: the $132 gain from the fourth unit minus the $30 forgone on the first 3 units. This net gain (marginal revenue) of $102 from the fourth unit is clearly less than the $132 price of the fourth unit.

Column 4 in Table 10.1 shows that marginal revenue is always less than the corresponding product price in column 2, except for the first unit of output. Because marginal revenue is the change in total revenue associated with each additional unit of output, the declining amounts of marginal revenue in column 4 mean that total revenue increases at a diminishing rate (as shown in column 3).

We show the relationship between the monopolist's marginal-revenue curve and total-revenue curve in Figure 10.3. For this figure, we extended the demand and revenue data of columns 1 through 4 in Table 10.1, assuming that successive $10 price cuts each elicit 1 additional unit of sales. That is, the monopolist can sell 11 units at $62, 12 units at $52, and so on.

Note that the monopolist's MR curve lies below the demand curve, indicating that marginal revenue is less than price at every output quantity but the very first unit. Observe also the special relationship between total revenue and marginal revenue. Because marginal revenue is the change in total revenue, marginal revenue is positive while total revenue is increasing. When total revenue reaches its maximum, marginal revenue is zero. When total revenue is diminishing, marginal revenue is negative.

The Monopolist Is a Price Maker

All imperfect competitors, whether pure monopoly, oligopoly, or monopolistic competition, face downward-sloping demand curves. So firms in those industries can to one degree or another influence total supply through their own output decisions. In changing market supply, they can also influence product price. Firms with downward-sloping demand curves are *price makers.*

This is most evident in pure monopoly, where one firm controls total output. The monopolist faces a downsloping demand curve in which each output is associated with some unique price. Thus, in deciding on what volume of output to produce, the monopolist is also indirectly determining the price it will charge. Through control of output, it can "make the price." From columns 1 and 2 in Table 10.1 we find that the monopolist can charge a price of $72 if it produces and offers for sale 10 units, a price of $82 if it produces and offers for sale 9 units, and so forth.

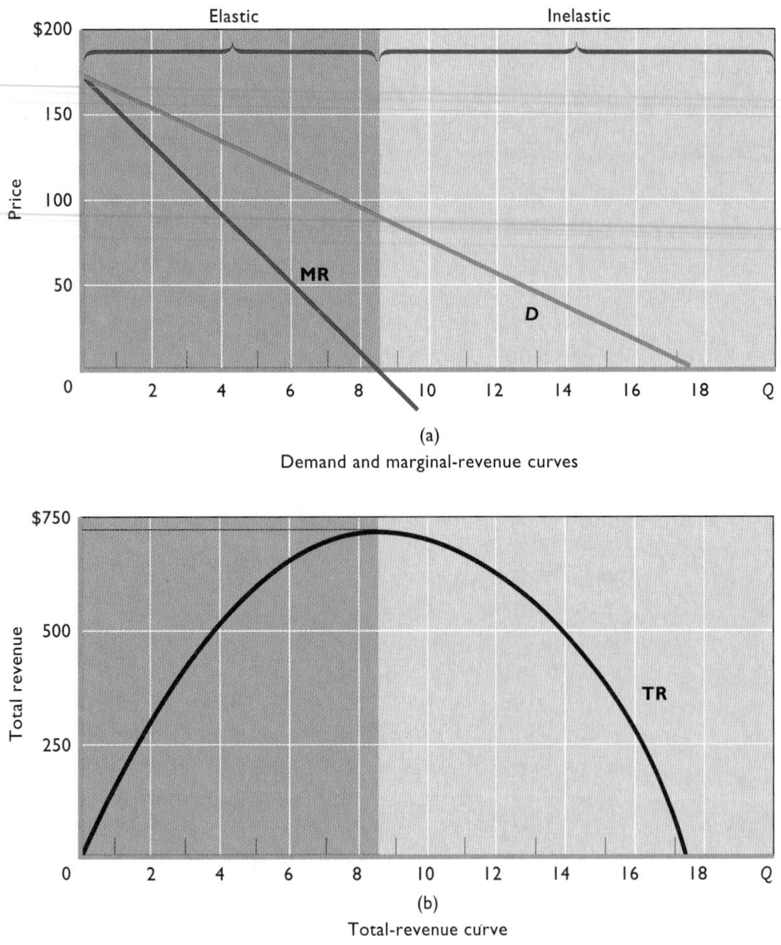

FIGURE 10.3 Demand, marginal revenue, and total revenue for a pure monopolist. (a) Because it must lower price on all units sold in order to increase its sales, an imperfectly competitive firm's marginal-revenue curve (MR) lies below its downsloping demand curve (*D*). The elastic and inelastic regions of demand are highlighted. (b) Total revenue (TR) increases at a decreasing rate, reaches a maximum, and then declines. Note that in the elastic region, TR is increasing and hence MR is positive. When TR reaches its maximum, MR is zero. In the inelastic region of demand, TR is declining, so MR is negative.

The Monopolist Sets Prices in the Elastic Region of Demand

The total-revenue test for price elasticity of demand is the basis for our third implication. Recall from Chapter 18 that the total-revenue test reveals that when demand is elastic, a decline in price will increase total revenue. Similarly, when demand is inelastic, a decline in price will reduce total revenue. Beginning at the top of demand curve *D* in Figure 10.3a, observe that as the price declines from \$172 to approximately \$82, total revenue increases (and marginal revenue therefore is positive). This means that demand is elastic in this price range. Conversely, for price declines below \$82, total revenue decreases (marginal revenue is negative), indicating that demand is inelastic there.

The implication is that a monopolist will never choose a price-quantity combination where price reductions cause total revenue to decrease (marginal revenue to be negative). The profit-maximizing monopolist will always want to avoid the inelastic segment of its demand curve in favor of some price-quantity combination in the elastic region. Here's why: To get into the inelastic region, the monopolist must lower price and increase output. In the inelastic region a lower price means less total revenue. And increased output always means increased total cost. Less total revenue and higher total cost yield lower profit. **(Key Question 4)**

QUICK REVIEW 10.1

- A pure monopolist is the sole supplier of a product or service for which there are no close substitutes.
- A monopoly survives because of entry barriers such as economies of scale, patents and licenses, the ownership of essential resources, and strategic actions to exclude rivals.
- The monopolist's demand curve is downsloping, and its marginal-revenue curve lies below its demand curve.
- The downsloping demand curve means that the monopolist is a price maker.
- The monopolist will operate in the elastic region of demand since in the inelastic region it can increase total revenue and reduce total cost by reducing output.

Output and Price Determination

At what specific price-quantity combination will a profit-maximizing monopolist choose to operate? To answer this question, we must add production costs to our analysis.

Cost Data

On the cost side, we will assume that although the firm is a monopolist in the product market, it hires resources competitively and employs the same technology as Chapter 9's competitive firm does. This lets us use the cost data we developed in Chapter 8 and applied in Chapter 9, so we can compare the price-output decisions of a pure monopoly with those of a pure competitor. Columns 5 through 7 in Table 10.1 restate the pertinent cost data from Table 8.2.

MR = MC Rule

A monopolist seeking to maximize total profit will employ the same rationale as a profit-seeking firm in a competitive industry. If producing is preferable to shutting down, it will produce up to the output at which marginal revenue equals marginal cost (MR = MC).

A comparison of columns 4 and 7 in Table 10.1 indicates that the profit-maximizing output is 5 units, because the fifth unit is the last unit of output whose marginal revenue exceeds its marginal cost. What price will the monopolist charge? The demand schedule shown as columns 1 and 2 in Table 10.1 indicates there is only one price at which 5 units can be sold: \$122.

This analysis is shown in **Figure 10.4 (Key Graph),** where we have graphed the demand, marginal-revenue, average-total-cost, and marginal-cost data of Table 10.1. The profit-maximizing output occurs at 5 units of output (Q_m), where the marginal-revenue (MR) and marginal-cost (MC) curves intersect. There, MR = MC.

To find the price the monopolist will charge, we extend a vertical line from Q_m up to the demand curve *D*. The unique price P_m at which Q_m units can be sold is \$122. In this case, it is the profit-maximizing price. The monopolist sets the quantity at Q_m to charge its profit-maximizing price of \$122.

In columns 2 and 5 in Table 10.1 we see that at 5 units of output, the product price (\$122) exceeds the average total cost (\$94). The monopolist thus earns an economic profit of \$28 per unit, and the total economic profit is then \$140 (= 5 units × \$28). In Figure 10.4, per-unit profit is $P_m - A$, where *A* is the average total cost of producing Q_m units. We find total economic profit by multiplying this per-unit profit by the profit-maximizing output Q_m.

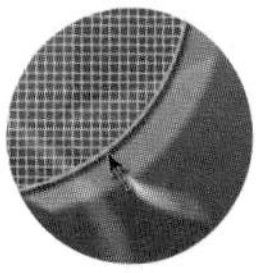

G 10.1
Monopoly

Another way we can determine the profit-maximizing output is by comparing total revenue and total cost at each possible level of production and choosing the output with the greatest positive difference. Use

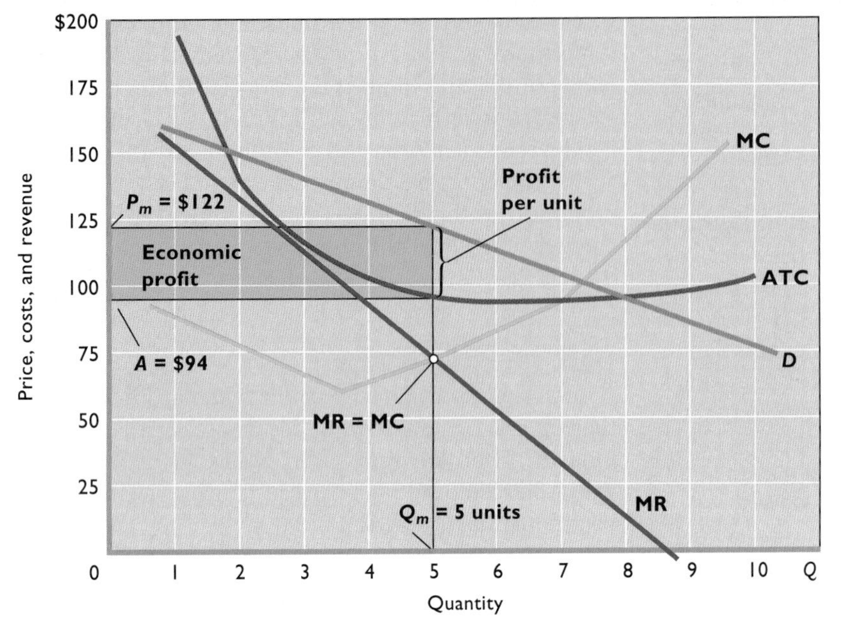

FIGURE 10.4 Profit maximization by a pure monopolist. The pure monopolist maximizes profit by producing at the MR = MC output, here Q_m = 5 units. Then, as seen from the demand curve, it will charge price P_m = \$122. Average total cost will be A = \$94, meaning that per-unit profit is $P_m - A$ and total profit is $5 \times (P_m - A)$. Total economic profit is thus represented by the green rectangle.

QUICK QUIZ 10.4

1. The MR curve lies below the demand curve in this figure because the:
   a. demand curve is linear (a straight line).
   b. demand curve is highly inelastic throughout its full length.
   c. demand curve is highly elastic throughout its full length.
   d. gain in revenue from an extra unit of output is less than the price charged for that unit of output.
2. The area labeled "Economic profit" can be found by multiplying the difference between *P* and ATC by quantity. It also can be found by:
   a. dividing profit per unit by quantity.
   b. subtracting total cost from total revenue.
   c. multiplying the coefficient of demand elasticity by quantity.
   d. multiplying the difference between *P* and MC by quantity.
3. This pure monopolist:
   a. charges the highest price that it could achieve.
   b. earns only a normal profit in the long run.
   c. restricts output to create an insurmountable entry barrier.
   d. restricts output to increase its price and total economic profit.
4. At this monopolist's profit-maximizing output:
   a. price equals marginal revenue.
   b. price equals marginal cost.
   c. price exceeds marginal cost.
   d. profit per unit is maximized.

Answers: 1. d; 2. b; 3. d; 4. c

columns 3 and 6 in Table 10.1 to verify our conclusion that 5 units is the profit-maximizing output. An accurate graphing of total revenue and total cost against output would also show the greatest difference (the maximum profit) at 5 units of output. Table 10.2 is a step-by-step summary of the process for determining the profit-maximizing output, profit-maximizing price, and economic profit in pure monopoly. **(Key Question 5)**

W 10.1

Monopoly price and output

No Monopoly Supply Curve

Recall that MR equals *P* in pure competition and that the supply curve of a purely competitive firm is determined by applying the MR (= *P*) = MC profit-maximizing rule. At any specific market-determined price the purely competitive seller will maximize profit by supplying the quantity at which MC is equal to that price. When the market price increases or decreases, the competitive firm produces more or less output. Each market price is thus associated with a specific output, and all such price-output pairs

TABLE 10.2 Steps for Graphically Determining the Profit-Maximizing Output, Profit-Maximizing Price, and Economic Profit (if Any) in Pure Monopoly

Step 1. Determine the profit-maximizing output by finding where MR = MC.

Step 2. Determine the profit-maximizing price by extending a vertical line upward from the output determined in step 1 to the pure monopolist's demand curve.

Step 3. Determine the pure monopolist's economic profit using one of two methods:

Method 1. Find profit per unit by substracting the average total cost of the profit-maximizing output from the profit-maximizing price. Then multiply the difference by the profit-maximizing output to determine economic profit (if any).

Method 2. Find total cost by multiplying the average total cost of the profit-maximizing output by that output. Find total revenue by multiplying the profit-maximizing output by the profit-maximizing price. Then subtract total cost from total revenue to determine economic profit (if any).

define the supply curve. This supply curve turns out to be the portion of the firm's MC curve that lies above the average-variable-cost curve (see Figure 9.6).

At first glance we would suspect that the pure monopolist's marginal-cost curve would also be its supply curve. But that is *not* the case. *The pure monopolist has no supply curve.* There is no unique relationship between price and quantity supplied for a monopolist. Like the competitive firm, the monopolist equates marginal revenue and marginal cost to determine output, but for the monopolist marginal revenue is less than price. Because the monopolist does not equate marginal cost to price, it is possible for different demand conditions to bring about different prices for the same output. To convince yourself of this, refer to Figure 10.4 and pencil in a new, steeper marginal-revenue curve that intersects the marginal-cost curve at the same point as does the present marginal-revenue curve. Then draw in a new demand curve that roughly corresponds with your new marginal-revenue curve. With the new curves, the same MR = MC output of 5 units now corresponds with a higher profit-maximizing price. Conclusion: There is no single, unique price associated with each output level Q_m, and so there is no supply curve for the pure monopolist.

Misconceptions Concerning Monopoly Pricing

Our analysis exposes two fallacies concerning monopoly behavior.

Not Highest Price Because a monopolist can manipulate output and price, people often believe it "will charge the highest price possible." That is incorrect. There are many prices above P_m in Figure 10.4, but the monopolist shuns them because they yield a smaller-than-maximum total profit. The monopolist seeks maximum total profit, not maximum price. Some high prices that could be charged would reduce sales and total revenue too severely to offset any decrease in total cost.

Total, Not Unit, Profit The monopolist seeks maximum *total* profit, not maximum *unit* profit. In Figure 10.4 a careful comparison of the vertical distance between average total cost and price at various possible outputs indicates that per-unit profit is greater at a point slightly to the left of the profit-maximizing output Q_m. This is seen in Table 10.1, where unit profit at 4 units of output is $32 (= $132 − $100) compared with $28 (= $122 − $94) at the profit-maximizing output of 5 units. Here the monopolist accepts a lower-than-maximum per-unit profit because additional sales more than compensate for the lower unit profit. A profit-seeking monopolist would rather sell 5 units at a profit of $28 per unit (for a total profit of $140) than 4 units at a profit of $32 per unit (for a total profit of only $128).

Possibility of Losses by Monopolist

The likelihood of economic profit is greater for a pure monopolist than for a pure competitor. In the long run the pure competitor is destined to have only a normal profit, whereas barriers to entry mean that any economic profit realized by the monopolist can persist. In pure monopoly there are no new entrants to increase supply, drive down price, and eliminate economic profit.

But pure monopoly does not guarantee profit. The monopolist is not immune from changes in tastes that reduce the demand for its product. Nor is it immune from upward-shifting cost curves caused by escalating resource prices. If the demand and cost situation faced by the monopolist is far less favorable than that in Figure 10.4, the monopolist will incur losses in the short run. Despite its dominance in the market (as, say, a seller of home

FIGURE 10.5 The loss-minimizing position of a pure monopolist. If demand D is weak and costs are high, the pure monopolist may be unable to make a profit. Because P_m exceeds V, the average variable cost at the MR = MC output Q_m, the monopolist will minimize losses in the short run by producing at that output. The loss per unit is $A - P_m$, and the total loss is indicated by the red rectangle.

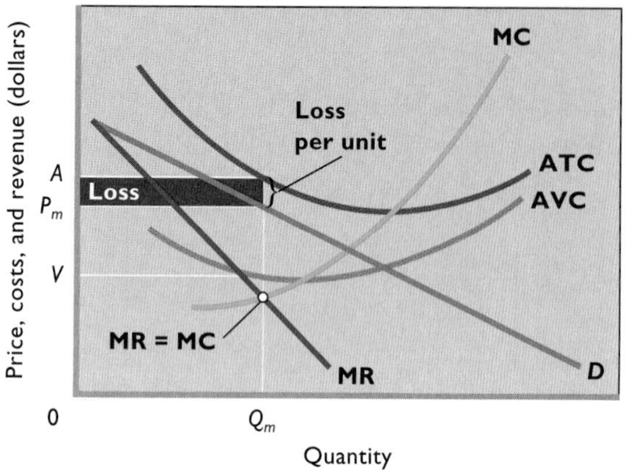

sewing machines), the monopoly enterprise in Figure 10.5 suffers a loss, as shown, because of weak demand and relatively high costs. Yet it continues to operate for the time being because its total loss is less than its fixed cost. More precisely, at output Q_m the monopolist's price P_m exceeds its average variable cost V. Its loss per unit is $A - P_m$, and the total loss is shown by the red rectangle.

Like the pure competitor, the monopolist will not persist in operating at a loss. Faced with continuing losses, in the long run the firm's owners will move their resources to alternative industries that offer better profit opportunities. Thus we can expect the monopolist to realize a normal profit or better in the long run.

Economic Effects of Monopoly

Let's now evaluate pure monopoly from the standpoint of society as a whole. Our reference for this evaluation will be the outcome of long-run efficiency in a purely competitive market, identified by the triple equality P = MC = minimum ATC.

Price, Output, and Efficiency

Figure 10.6 graphically contrasts the price, output, and efficiency outcomes of pure monopoly and a purely competitive *industry*. Starting with Figure 10.6a, we are reminded that the purely competitive industry's market supply curve S is the horizontal sum of the marginal-cost curves of all the firms in the industry. Let's suppose there are 1000 such firms. Comparing their combined supply curves S with market demand D, we get the purely competitive price and output of P_c and Q_c.

Recall that this price-output combination results in both productive efficiency and allocative efficiency. *Productive efficiency* is achieved because free entry and exit force firms to operate where average total cost is at a minimum.

FIGURE 10.6 Inefficiency of pure monopoly relative to a purely competitive industry. (a) In a purely competitive industry, entry and exit of firms ensures that price (P_c) equals marginal cost (MC) and that the minimum average-total-cost output (Q_c) is produced. Both productive efficiency (P = minimum ATC) and allocative efficiency (P = MC) are obtained. (b) In pure monopoly, the MR curve lies below the demand curve. The monopolist maximizes profit at output Q_m, where MR = MC, and charges price P_m. Thus, output is lower (Q_m rather than Q_c) and price is higher (P_m rather than P_c) than they would be in a purely competitive industry. Monopoly is inefficient, since output is less than that required for achieving minimum ATC (here at Q_c) and because the monopolist's price exceeds MC. Monopoly creates a deadweight loss (here of area *abc*).

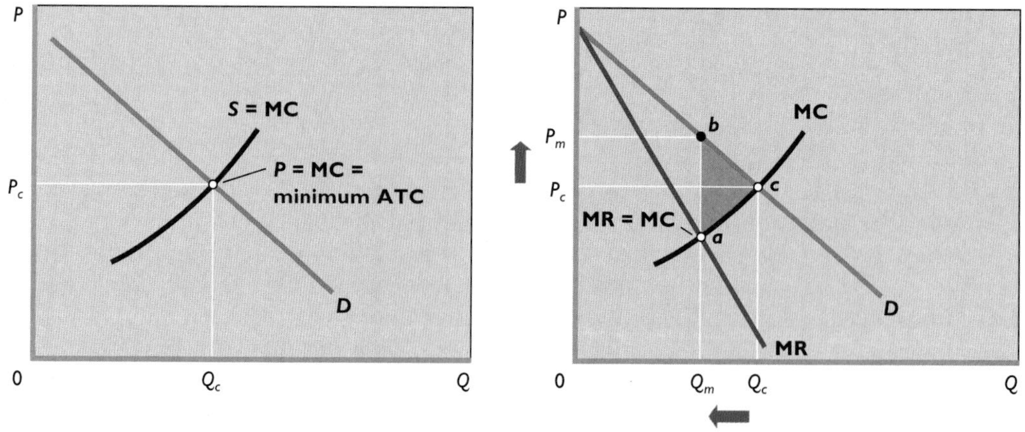

(a)
Purely competitive industry

(b)
Pure monopoly

The sum of the minimum-ATC outputs of the 1000 pure competitors is the industry output, here, Q_c. Product price is at the lowest level consistent with minimum average total cost. The *allocative efficiency* of pure competition results because production occurs up to that output at which price (the measure of a product's value or marginal benefit to society) equals marginal cost (the worth of the alternative products forgone by society in producing any given commodity). In short: P = MC = minimum ATC.

Now let's suppose that this industry becomes a pure monopoly (Figure 10.6b) as a result of one firm buying out all its competitors. We also assume that no changes in costs or market demand result from this dramatic change in the industry structure. What formerly were 1000 competing firms is now a single pure monopolist consisting of 1000 noncompeting branches.

The competitive market supply curve S has become the marginal-cost curve (MC) of the monopolist, the summation of the MC curves of its many branch plants. (Since the monopolist does not have a supply curve, as such, we have removed the S label.) The important change, however, is on the demand side. From the viewpoint of each of the 1000 individual competitive firms, demand was perfectly elastic, and marginal revenue was therefore equal to price. Each firm equated MR (= price) and MC in maximizing profits. But market demand and individual demand are the same to the pure monopolist. The firm *is* the industry, and thus the monopolist sees the downsloping demand curve D shown in Figure 10.6b.

This means that marginal revenue is less than price, that graphically the MR curve lies below demand curve D. In using the MR = MC rule, the monopolist selects output Q_m and price P_m. A comparison of both graphs in Figure 10.6 reveals that the monopolist finds it profitable to sell a smaller output at a higher price than do the competitive producers. Monopoly yields neither productive nor allocative efficiency. The monopolist's output is less than Q_c, the output at which average total cost is lowest. And price is higher than the competitive price P_c, which in long-run equilibrium in pure competition equals minimum average total cost. Thus the monopoly price *exceeds* minimum average total cost. Also, at the monopolist's Q_m output, product price is considerably higher than marginal cost, meaning that society values additional units of this monopolized product more highly than it values the alternative products the resources could otherwise produce. So the monopolist's profit-maximizing output results in an underallocation of resources. The monopolist finds it profitable to restrict output and therefore employ fewer resources than is justified from society's standpoint. So the monopolist does not achieve allocative efficiency. As confirmed by the gray triangle labeled *abc* in Figure 10.6, monopoly creates an efficiency loss (or deadweight loss) for society. The sum of consumer surplus and producer surplus is not maximized. In monopoly, then:

- P exceeds MC.
- P exceeds lowest ATC.
- an efficiency loss occurs (the sum of consumer surplus + producer surplus is less than maximum).

Income Transfer

In general, monopoly transfers income from consumers to the stockholders who own the monopoly. By virtue of their market power, monopolists charge a higher price than would a purely competitive firm with the same costs. So monopolists in effect levy a "private tax" on consumers and obtain substantial economic profits. These monopolistic profits are not equally distributed, because corporate stock is largely owned by high-income groups. The owners of monopolistic enterprises thus tend to benefit at the expense of the consumers, who "overpay" for the product. Because, on average, these owners have more income than the buyers, monopoly increases income inequality.

Exception: If the buyers of a monopoly product are wealthier than the owners of the monopoly, the income transfer from consumers to owners may reduce income inequality. But, in general, this is not the case, and we thus conclude that monopoly contributes to income inequality.

Cost Complications

Our evaluation of pure monopoly has led us to conclude that, given identical costs, a purely monopolistic industry will charge a higher price, produce a smaller output, and allocate economic resources less efficiently than a purely competitive industry. These inferior results are rooted in the entry barriers characterizing monopoly.

Now we must recognize that costs may not be the same for purely competitive and monopolistic producers. The unit cost incurred by a monopolist may be either larger or smaller than that incurred by a purely competitive firm. There are four reasons why costs may differ: (1) economies of scale, (2) a factor called "X-inefficiency," (3) the need for monopoly-preserving expenditures, and (4) the "very long run" perspective, which allows for technological advance.

Economies of Scale Once Again

Where there are extensive economies of scale, market demand may not be sufficient to support a large number of competing firms, each producing at minimum efficient scale. In such cases, an industry of one or two firms would have a lower average total cost than would the same industry made up of numerous competitive firms. At the extreme, only a single firm—a natural monopoly—might be able to achieve the lowest long-run average total cost.

Some firms relating to new information technologies—for example, computer software, Internet service, and wireless communications—have displayed extensive economies of scale. As these firms have grown, their long-run average total costs have declined because of greater use of specialized inputs, the spreading of product development costs, and learning by doing. Also, *simultaneous consumption* and *network effects* have reduced costs.

A product's ability to satisfy a large number of consumers at the same time is called **simultaneous consumption** (or *nonrivalous consumption*). Dell Computers needs to produce a personal computer for each customer, but Microsoft needs to produce its Windows program only once. Then, at very low marginal cost, Microsoft delivers its program by disk or Internet to millions of consumers. The same is true for Internet service providers, music producers, and wireless communication firms. Because marginal costs are so low, the average total cost of output declines as more customers are added.

Network effects are increases in the value of a product to each user, including existing users, as the total number of users rises. Good examples are computer software, cell phones, pagers, palm computers, and other products related to the Internet. When other people have Internet service and devices to access it, a person can conveniently send e-mail messages to them. And when they have similar software, documents, spreadsheets, and photos can be attached to the e-mail messages. The greater the number of persons connected to the system, the more the benefits of the product to each person are magnified.

Such network effects may drive a market toward monopoly because consumers tend to choose standard products that everyone else is using. The focused demand for these products permits their producers to grow rapidly and thus achieve economies of scale. Smaller firms, which have higher-cost "right" products or the "wrong" products, get acquired or go out of business.

Economists generally agree that some new information firms have not yet exhausted their economies of scale. But most economists question whether such firms are truly natural monopolies. Most firms eventually achieve their minimum efficient scale at less than the full size of the market.

Even if natural monopoly develops, the monopolist is unlikely to pass cost reductions along to consumers as price reductions. So, with perhaps a handful of exceptions, economies of scale do not change the general conclusion that monopolies are inefficient relative to more competitive industries.

X-Inefficiency

In constructing all the average-total-cost curves used in this book, we have assumed that the firm uses the most efficient existing technology. In other words, it uses the technology that permits it to achieve the lowest average total cost of whatever level of output it chooses to produce. **X-inefficiency** occurs when a firm produces output, whatever its level, at higher than the lowest possible cost of producing it. In Figure 10.7 X-inefficiency is represented by operation at points *X* and *X′* above the lowest-cost ATC curve. At these points, per-unit costs are ATC_x (as opposed to ATC_1) for output Q_1 and $ATC_{x'}$ (as opposed to ATC_2) for output Q_2. Any point above the average-total-cost curve in Figure 10.7 is possible but reflects inefficiency or "bad management" by the firm.

O 10.3
X-inefficiency

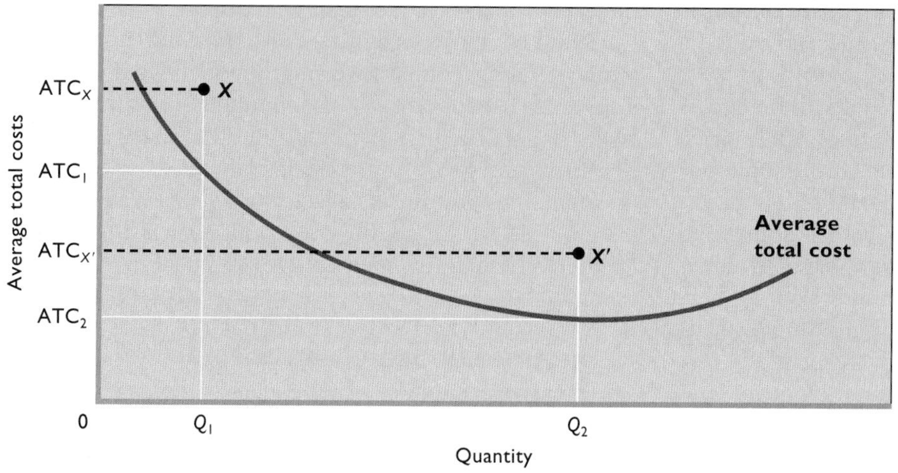

FIGURE 10.7 X-inefficiency. The average-total-cost curve (ATC) is assumed to reflect the minimum cost of producing each particular level of output. Any point above this "lowest-cost" ATC curve, such as *X* or *X′*, implies X-inefficiency: operation at greater than lowest cost for a particular level of output.

Why is X-inefficiency allowed to occur if it reduces profits? The answer is that managers may have goals, such as expanding power, an easier work life, avoiding business risk, or giving jobs to incompetent relatives, that conflict with cost minimization. Or X-inefficiency may arise because a firm's workers are poorly motivated or ineffectively supervised. Or a firm may simply become lethargic and inert, relying on rules of thumb in decision making as opposed to relevant calculations of costs and revenues.

For our purposes the relevant question is whether monopolistic firms tend more toward X-inefficiency than competitive producers do. Presumably they do. Firms in competitive industries are continually under pressure from rivals, forcing them to be internally efficient to survive. But monopolists are sheltered from such competitive forces by entry barriers, and that lack of pressure may lead to X-inefficiency.

There is no indisputable evidence regarding X-inefficiency, but what evidence we have suggests that it increases as competition decreases. A reasonable estimate is that X-inefficiency may be 10 percent or more of costs for monopolists but only 5 percent for an "average" oligopolistic industry in which the four largest firms produce 60 percent of total output.[1] In the words of one authority: "The evidence is fragmentary, but it points in the same direction. X-inefficiency exists, and it is more apt to be reduced when competitive pressures are strong than when firms enjoy insulated market positions."[2]

Rent-Seeking Expenditures

Rent-seeking behavior is any activity designed to transfer income or wealth to a particular firm or resource supplier at someone else's, or even society's, expense. We have seen that a monopolist can obtain an economic profit even in the long run. Therefore, it is no surprise that a firm may go to great expense to acquire or maintain a monopoly granted by government through legislation or an exclusive license. Such rent-seeking expenditures add nothing to the firm's output, but they clearly increase its costs. They imply that monopoly involves higher costs and less efficiency than suggested in Figure 10.6b.

Technological Advance

In the very long run, firms can reduce their costs through the discovery and implementation of new technology. If monopolists are more likely than competitive producers to develop more efficient production techniques over time, then the inefficiency of monopoly might be overstated. Since research and development (R&D) is the topic of Chapter 12, we will provide only a brief assessment here.

The general view of economists is that a pure monopolist will not be technologically progressive. Although its economic profit provides ample means to finance research and development, it has little incentive to implement new techniques (or products). The absence of competitors means that there is no external pressure for technological advance in a monopolized market. Because of its sheltered market position, the pure monopolist can afford to be inefficient and lethargic; there simply is no major penalty for being so.

One caveat: Research and technological advance may be one of the monopolist's barriers to entry. Thus, the monopolist may continue to seek technological advance to avoid falling prey to new rivals. In this case technological advance is essential to the maintenance of monopoly. But then it is potential competition, not the monopoly market structure, that is driving the technological advance. By assumption, no such competition exists in the pure monopoly model; entry is completely blocked.

Assessment and Policy Options

For reasons we have discussed, monopoly is a legitimate concern to an economy. Monopolists can charge higher-than-competitive prices that result in an underallocation of resources to the monopolized product. They can stifle innovation, engage in rent-seeking behavior, and foster X-inefficiency. Even when their costs are low because of economies of scale, there is no guarantee that the price they charge will reflect those low costs. The cost savings may simply accrue to the monopoly as greater economic profit.

Fortunately, however, monopoly is not widespread in the economy. Barriers to entry are seldom completely successful. Although research and technological advance may strengthen the market position of a monopoly, technology may also undermine monopoly power. Over time, the creation of new technologies may work to destroy monopoly positions. For example, the development of courier delivery, fax machines, and e-mail has eroded the monopoly power of the U.S. Postal Service. Cable television monopolies are now challenged by satellite TV and by new technologies that permit the transmission of audio and visual signals over the Internet.

Similarly, patents eventually expire; and even before they do, the development of new and distinct substitutable products often circumvents existing patent advantages.

---

[1]William G. Shepherd, *The Economics of Industrial Organization*, 4th ed. (Englewood Cliffs, N.J.: Prentice Hall, 1997), p. 107.

[2]F. M. Scherer and David Ross, *Industrial Market Structure and Economic Performance*, 3d ed. (Chicago: Rand McNally College Publishing, 1990), p. 672.

New sources of monopolized resources sometimes are found and competition from foreign firms may emerge. (See Global Perspective 10.1.) Finally, if a monopoly is sufficiently fearful of future competition from new products, it may keep its prices relatively low so as to discourage rivals from developing such products. If so, consumers may pay nearly competitive prices even though competition is currently lacking.

So what should government do about monopoly when it arises in the real world? Economists agree that government needs to look carefully at monopoly on a case-by-case basis. Three general policy options are available:

- If the monopoly is achieved and sustained through anticompetitive actions, creates substantial economic inefficiency, and appears to be long-lasting, the government can file charges against the monopoly under the antitrust laws. If found guilty of monopoly abuse, the firm can either be expressly prohibited from engaging in certain business activities or be broken into two or more competing firms. An example of the breakup approach was the dissolution of Standard Oil into several competing firms in 1911. In contrast, in 2001 an appeals court overruled a lower-court decision to divide Microsoft into two firms. Instead, Microsoft was prohibited from engaging in a number of specific anticompetitive business activities. (We discuss the antitrust laws and the Microsoft case in Chapter 18.)
- If the monopoly is a natural monopoly, society can allow it to continue to expand. If no competition emerges from new products, government may then decide to regulate its prices and operations. (We discuss this option later in this chapter and in Chapter 18.)
- If the monopoly appears to be unsustainable over a long period of time, say, because of emerging new technology, society can simply choose to ignore it. (In Chapter 12 we discuss the potential for real-world monopoly to collapse in the very long run.)

GLOBAL PERSPECTIVE 10.1

Competition from Foreign Multinational Corporations

Competition from foreign multinational corporations diminishes the market power of firms in the United States. Here are just a few of the hundreds of foreign multinational corporations that compete strongly with U.S. firms in certain American markets.

Company (Country)	Main Products
Bayer (Germany)	chemicals
BP Amoco (United Kingdom)	gasoline
Michelin (France)	tires
NEC (Japan)	computers
Nestlé (Switzerland)	food products
Nokia (Finland)	wireless phones
Royal Dutch/Shell (Netherlands)	gasoline
Royal Philips (Netherlands)	electronics
Sony (Japan)	electronics
Toyota (Japan)	automobiles
Unilever (Netherlands)	food products

Source: Compiled from the Fortune 500 listing of the world's largest firms, **www.fortune.com.**

QUICK REVIEW 10.2

- The monopolist maximizes profit (or minimizes loss) at the output where MR = MC and charges the price that corresponds to that output on its demand curve.
- The monopolist has no supply curve, since any of several prices can be associated with a specific quantity of output supplied.
- Assuming identical costs, a monopolist will be less efficient than a purely competitive industry because the monopolist produces less output and charges a higher price.
- The inefficiencies of monopoly may be offset or lessened by economies of scale and, less likely, by technological progress, but they may be intensified by the presence of X-inefficiency and rent-seeking expenditures.

Price Discrimination

We have assumed in this chapter that the monopolist charges a single price to all buyers. But under certain conditions the monopolist can increase its profit by charging different prices to different buyers. In so doing, the monopolist is engaging in **price discrimination,** the practice of selling a specific product at more than one price when the price differences are not justified by cost differences. Price discrimination can take three forms:

O 10.4
Price discrimination

- Charging each customer in a single market the maximum price she or he is willing to pay.

- Charging each customer one price for the first set of units purchased and a lower price for subsequent units purchased.
- Charging some customers one price and other customers another price.

Conditions

The opportunity to engage in price discrimination is not readily available to all sellers. Price discrimination is possible when the following conditions are realized:

- ***Monopoly power*** The seller must be a monopolist or, at least, must possess some degree of monopoly power, that is, some ability to control output and price.
- ***Market segregation*** At relatively low cost to itself, the seller must be able to segregate buyers into distinct classes, each of which has a different willingness or ability to pay for the product. This separation of buyers is usually based on different elasticities of demand, as the examples below will make clear.
- ***No resale*** The original purchaser cannot resell the product or service. If buyers in the low-price segment of the market could easily resell in the high-price segment, the monopolist's price-discrimination strategy would create competition in the high-price segment. This competition would reduce the price in the high-price segment and undermine the monopolist's price-discrimination policy. This condition suggests that service industries such as the transportation industry or legal and medical services, where resale is impossible, are candidates for price discrimination.

CONSIDER THIS ...

Price Discrimination at the Ballpark

Take me out to the ball game ...

Buy me some peanuts and Cracker Jack ...

Professional baseball teams earn substantial revenues through ticket sales. To maximize profit, they offer significantly lower ticket prices for children (whose demand is elastic) than those for adults (whose demand is inelastic). This discount may be as much as 50 percent.

If this type of price discrimination increases revenue and profit, why don't teams also price discriminate at the concession stands? Why don't they offer half-price hot dogs, soft drinks, peanuts, and Cracker Jack to children?

The answer involves the three requirements for successful price discrimination. All three requirements are met for game tickets: (1) The team has monopoly power; (2) it can segregate ticket buyers by age group, each group having a different elasticity of demand; and (3) children cannot resell their discounted tickets to adults.

It's a different situation at the concession stands. Specifically, the third condition is *not* met. If the team had dual prices, it could not prevent the exchange or "resale" of the concession goods from children to adults. Many adults would send children to buy food and soft drinks for them: "Here's some money, Billy. Go buy *six* hot dogs." In this case, price discrimination would reduce, not increase, team profit. Thus, children and adults are charged the same high prices at the concession stands. (These prices are high relative to those for the same goods at the local convenience store because the stadium sellers have a captured audience and thus considerable monopoly power.)

Examples of Price Discrimination

Price discrimination is widely practiced in the U.S. economy. For example, we noted in Chapter 6's Last Word that airlines charge high fares to business travelers, whose demand for travel is inelastic, and offer lower "Saturday night stay-over rates" and "7-day advance purchase fares" to attract vacationers and others whose demands are more elastic.

Electric utilities frequently segment their markets by end uses, such as lighting and heating. The absence of reasonable lighting substitutes means that the demand for electricity for illumination is inelastic and that the price per kilowatt-hour for such use is high. But the availability of natural gas and petroleum for heating makes the demand for electricity for this purpose less inelastic and the price lower.

Movie theaters and golf courses vary their charges on the basis of time (for example, higher evening and weekend rates) and age (for example, lower rates for children, senior discounts). Railroads vary the rate charged per ton-mile of freight according to the market value of the product being shipped. The shipper of 10 tons of television sets or refrigerators is charged more than the shipper of 10 tons of gravel or coal.

The issuance of discount coupons, redeemable at purchase, is a form of price discrimination. It permits firms to give price discounts to their most price-sensitive customers who have elastic demand. Less price-sensitive consumers who have less elastic demand are not as likely to undertake the clipping and redeeming of coupons. The firm thus makes a larger profit than if it had used a single-price, no-coupon strategy.

FIGURE 10.8 Price discrimination to different groups of buyers. The price-discriminating monopolist represented here maximizes its total profit by dividing the market into two segments based on differences in elasticity of demand. It then produces and sells the MR = MC output in each market segment. (For visual clarity, average total cost (ATC) is assumed to be constant. Therefore MC equals ATC at all output levels.) (a) The firm charges a higher price (here, P_b) to customers who have a less elastic demand curve and (b) a lower price (here, P_s) to customers with a more elastic demand. The price discriminator's total profit is larger than it would be with no discrimination and therefore a single price.

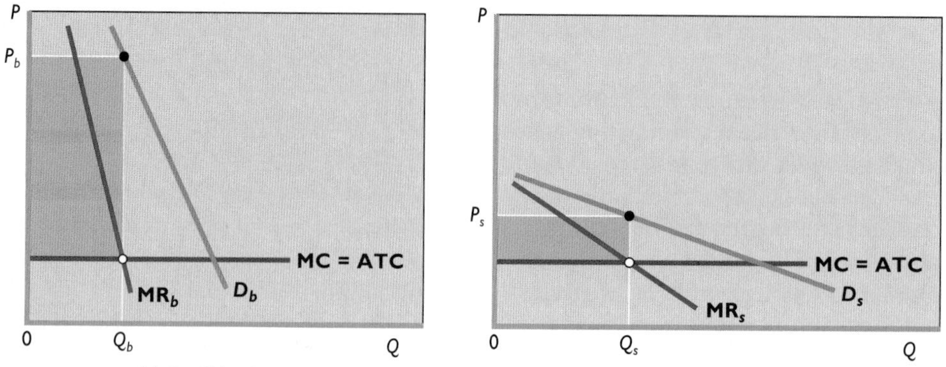

(a) Small businesses

(b) Students

Finally, price discrimination often occurs in international trade. A Russian aluminum producer, for example, might sell aluminum for less in the United States than in Russia. In the United States, this seller faces an elastic demand because several substitute suppliers are available. But in Russia, where the manufacturer dominates the market and trade barriers impede imports, consumers have fewer choices and thus demand is less elastic.

Graphical Analysis

Figure 10.8 demonstrates graphically the most frequently seen form or price discrimination. The two side-to-side graphs are for a single pure monopolist selling its product, say, software, in two segregated parts of the market. Figure 10.8a illustrates demand for software by small-business customers; Figure 10.8b, the demand for software by students. Student versions of the software are identical to the versions sold to businesses but are available (1 per person) only to customers with a student ID. Presumably, students have lower ability to pay for the software and are charged a discounted price.

The demand curve D_b in the graph to the left indicates a relatively inelastic demand for the product on the part of business customers. The demand curve D_s in the righthand graph reflects the more elastic demand of students. The marginal revenue curves (MR_b and MR_s) lie below their respective demand curves, reflecting the demand–marginal revenue relationship previously described. For visual clarity we have assumed that average total cost (ATC) is constant. Therefore marginal cost (MC) equals average total cost (ATC) at all quantities of output. These costs are the same for both versions of the software and therefore appear as the identical straight lines labeled "MC = ATC."

What price will the pure monopolist charge to each set of customers? Using the MR = MC rule for profit maximization, the firm will offer Q_b units of the software for sale to small businesses. It can sell that profit-maximizing output by charging price P_b. Again using the MR = MC rule, the monopolist will offer Q_s units of software to students. To sell those Q_s units, the firm will charge students the lower price P_s.

W 10.2
Price discrimination

Firms engage in price discrimination because it enhances their profit. The numbers (not shown) behind the curves in Figure 10.8 would clearly reveal that the sum of the two profit rectangles shown in green exceeds the single profit rectangle the firm would obtain from a single monopoly price. How do consumers fare? In this case, students clearly benefit by paying a lower price than they would if the firm charged a single monopoly price; in contrast, the price discrimination results in a higher price for business customers. Therefore, compared to the single-price situation, students buy more of the software and small businesses buy less.

Such price discrimination is common in the economy and becomes illegal only when it is part of a firm's strategy to lessen or eliminate competition. We will pick up on that topic in Chapter 18 on antitrust policy. **(Key Question 6)**

Regulated Monopoly

Natural monopolies traditionally have been subject to *rate regulation* (price regulation), although the recent trend has been to deregulate the parts of the industries where competition seems possible. For example, long-distance telephone, natural gas at the wellhead, wireless communications, cable television, and long-distance electricity transmission have been, to one degree or another, deregulated over the past several decades. And regulators in some states are beginning to allow new entrants to compete with existing local telephone and electricity providers. Nevertheless, state and local regulatory commissions still regulate the prices that most local natural gas distributors, regional telephone companies, and local electricity suppliers can charge.

Let's consider the regulation of a local natural monopoly, for example, a natural gas provider. Figure 10.9 shows the demand and the long-run cost curves facing our firm. Because of extensive economies of scale, the demand curve cuts the natural monopolist's long-run average-total-cost curve at a point where that curve is still falling. It would be inefficient to have several firms in this industry because each would produce a much smaller output, operating well to the left on the long-run average-total-cost curve. In short, each firm's lowest average total cost would be substantially higher than that of a single firm. So efficient, low-cost production requires a single seller.

We know by application of the MR = MC rule that Q_m and P_m are the profit-maximizing output and price that an unregulated monopolist would choose. Because price exceeds average total cost at output Q_m, the monopolist enjoys a substantial economic profit. Furthermore, price exceeds marginal cost, indicating an underallocation of resources to this product or service. Can government regulation bring about better results from society's point of view?

FIGURE 10.9 Regulated monopoly. The socially optimal price P_r, found where *D* and MC intersect, will result in an efficient allocation of resources but may entail losses to the monopoly. The fair-return price P_f will allow the monopolist to break even but will not fully correct the underallocation of resources.

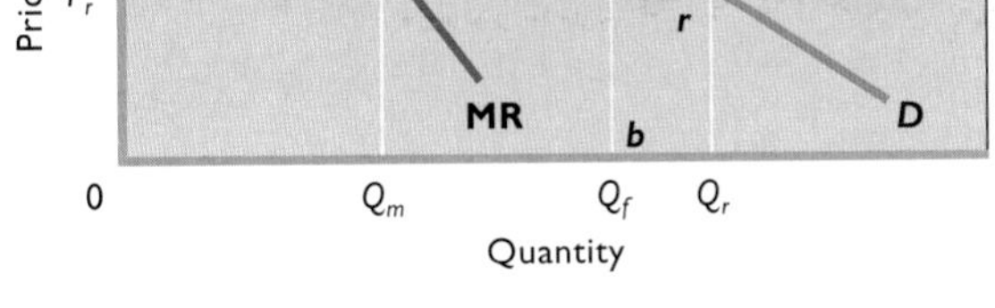

Socially Optimal Price: *P* = MC

If the objective of a regulatory commission is to achieve allocative efficiency, it should attempt to establish a legal (ceiling) price for the monopolist that is equal to marginal cost. Remembering that each point on the market demand curve designates a price-quantity combination, and noting that the marginal-cost curve cuts the demand curve only at point *r*, we see that P_r is the only price on the demand curve equal to marginal cost. The maximum or ceiling price effectively causes the monopolist's demand curve to become horizontal (indicating perfectly elastic demand) from zero out to point *r*, where the regulated price ceases to be effective. Also, out to point *r* we have MR = P_r.

Confronted with the legal price P_r, the monopolist will maximize profit or minimize loss by producing Q_r units of output, because at this output MR (= P_r) = MC. By making it illegal to charge more than P_r per unit, the regulatory agency has removed the monopolist's incentive to restrict output to Q_m to obtain a higher price and greater profit.

In short, the regulatory commission can simulate the allocative forces of pure competition by imposing the legal price P_r and letting the monopolist choose its profit-maximizing or loss-minimizing output. Production takes place where P_r = MC, and this equality indicates an efficient allocation of resources to this product or service. The price that achieves allocative efficiency is called the **socially optimal price.**

Fair-Return Price: *P* = ATC

But the socially optimal price P_r that equals marginal cost may be so low that average total costs are not covered, as is the case in Figure 10.9. The result is a loss for the firm. The reason lies in the basic character of our firm. Because it is required to meet the heaviest "peak" demands (both daily and seasonally) for natural gas, it has substantial excess production capacity when demand is relatively "normal." Its high level of investment in production facilities and economies of scale mean that its average total cost is likely to be greater than its marginal cost over a very wide range of outputs. In particular, as in Figure 10.9, average total cost is likely to be greater than the price P_r at the intersection of the demand curve and marginal-cost curve. Therefore, forcing the socially optimal price P_r on the regulated monopolist would result in short-run losses and long-run bankruptcy for the utility.

What to do? One option is to provide a public subsidy to cover the loss that marginal-cost pricing would entail. Another possibility is to condone price discrimination and hope that the additional revenue gained will permit the firm to cover costs.

Last Word

De Beers' Diamonds: Are Monopolies Forever?

De Beers Was One of the World's Strongest and Most Enduring Monopolies. But in Mid-2000 It Announced That It Could No Longer Control the Supply of Diamonds and Thus Would Abandon Its 66-Year Policy of Monopolizing the Diamond Trade.

De Beers, a Swiss-based company controlled by a South African corporation, produces about 45 percent of the world's rough-cut diamonds and purchases for resale a sizable number of the rough-cut diamonds produced by other mines worldwide. As a result, De Beers markets about 55 percent of the world's diamonds to a select group of diamond cutters and dealers. But that percentage has declined from 80 percent in the mid-1980s. Therein lies the company's problem.

Classic Monopoly Behavior De Beers' past monopoly behavior and results are a classic example of the unregulated monopoly model illustrated in Figure 10.4. No matter how many diamonds it mined or purchased, it sold only the quantity of diamonds that would yield an "appropriate" (monopoly) price. That price was well above production costs, and De Beers and its partners earned monopoly profits.

When demand fell, De Beers reduced its sales to maintain price. The excess of production over sales was then reflected in growing diamond stockpiles held by De Beers. It also attempted to bolster demand through advertising ("Diamonds are forever"). When demand was strong, it increased sales by reducing its diamond inventories.

De Beers used several methods to control the production of many mines it did not own. First, it convinced a number of independent producers that "single-channel" or monopoly marketing through De Beers would maximize their profit. Second, mines that circumvented De Beers often found their market suddenly flooded with similar diamonds from De Beers' vast stockpiles. The resulting price decline and loss of profit often would encourage a "rogue" mine into the De Beers fold. Finally, De Beers simply purchased and stockpiled diamonds produced by independent mines so that their added supplies would not "undercut" the market.

An End of an Era? Several factors have come together to unravel the monopoly. New diamond discoveries resulted in a growing leakage of diamonds into world markets outside De Beers' control. For example, significant prospecting and trading in Angola occurred. Recent diamond discoveries in Canada's Northwest Territories pose another threat. Although De Beers is a participant in that region, a large uncontrolled supply of diamonds is expected to emerge. Similarly, Russia's diamond monopoly Alrosa recently agreed with European antitrust authorities to sell progressively larger quantities of diamonds directly to the international diamond market rather than continuing to market them through De Beers.

If that was not enough, Australian diamond producer Argyle opted to withdraw from the De Beers monopoly. Its annual production of mostly low-grade industrial diamonds accounts for about 6 percent of the global $8 billion diamond market. Moreover, the international media began to focus heavily on the role that diamonds play in financing the bloody civil wars in Africa. Fearing a consumer boycott of diamonds, De Beers pledged not to buy these "conflict" diamonds or do business with any firms that did. These diamonds, however, continue to find their way into the marketplace, eluding De Beers' control.

In mid-2000 De Beers abandoned its attempt to control the supply of diamonds. It announced that it planned to transform itself from a diamond cartel to a modern firm selling "premium" diamonds and other luxury goods under the De Beers label. It therefore would gradually reduce its $4 billion stockpile of diamonds and turn its efforts to increasing the overall demand for diamonds through advertising. De Beers proclaimed that it was changing its strategy to being "the diamond supplier of choice."

With its high market share and ability to control its own production levels, De Beers will still wield considerable influence over the price of rough-cut diamonds. But it turns out that the De Beers monopoly was not forever.

In practice, regulatory commissions have pursued a third option: They modify the objective of allocative efficiency and $P = MC$ pricing. Most regulatory agencies in the United States establish a **fair-return price.** They do so because the courts have ruled that a socially optimal price leading to losses and bankruptcy deprives the monopoly's owners of their private property without due process of law. The Supreme Court has held that regulatory agencies must permit a "fair return" to utility owners.

Remembering that total cost includes a normal or "fair" profit, we see in Figure 10.9 that a fair-return price should be on the average-total-cost curve. Because the demand curve cuts average total cost only at point *f*, clearly P_f is the only price on the demand curve that permits a fair return. The corresponding output at regulated price P_f will be Q_f. Total revenue of 0*afb* will equal the utility's total cost of the same amount, and the firm will realize a normal profit.

Dilemma of Regulation

Comparing results of the socially optimal price ($P = MC$) and the fair-return price ($P = ATC$) suggests a policy dilemma, sometimes termed the *dilemma of regulation.* When its price is set to achieve the most efficient allocation of resources ($P = MC$), the regulated monopoly is likely to suffer losses. Survival of the firm would presumably depend on permanent public subsidies out of tax revenues. On the other hand, although a fair-return price ($P = ATC$) allows the monopolist to cover costs, it only partially resolves the underallocation of resources that the unregulated monopoly price would foster. That is, the fair-return price would increase output only from Q_m to Q_f in Figure 10.9, while the socially optimal output is Q_r. Despite this dilemma, regulation can improve on the results of monopoly from the social point of view. Price regulation (even at the fair-return price) can simultaneously reduce price, increase output, and reduce the economic profits of monopolies. **(Key Question 12)**

QUICK REVIEW 10.3

- Price discrimination occurs when a firm sells a product at different prices that are not based on cost differences.
- The conditions necessary for price discrimination are (a) monopoly power, (b) the ability to segregate buyers on the basis of demand elasticities, and (c) the inability of buyers to resell the product.
- Compared with single pricing by a monopolist, perfect price discrimination results in greater profit and greater output. Many consumers pay higher prices, but other buyers pay prices below the single price.
- Monopoly price can be reduced and output increased through government regulation.
- The socially optimal price ($P = MC$) achieves allocative efficiency but may result in losses; the fair-return price ($P = ATC$) yields a normal profit but fails to achieve allocative efficiency.

Summary

1. A pure monopolist is the sole producer of a commodity for which there are no close substitutes.
2. The existence of pure monopoly and other imperfectly competitive market structures is explained by barriers to entry in the form of (a) economies of scale, (b) patent ownership and research, (c) ownership or control of essential resources, and (d) pricing and other strategic behavior.
3. The pure monopolist's market situation differs from that of a competitive firm in that the monopolist's demand curve is downsloping, causing the marginal-revenue curve to lie below the demand curve. Like the competitive seller, the pure monopolist will maximize profit by equating marginal revenue and marginal cost. Barriers to entry may permit a monopolist to acquire economic profit even in the long run. However, (a) the monopolist does not charge "the highest price possible"; (b) the price that yields maximum total profit to the monopolist rarely coincides with the price that yields maximum unit profit; (c) high costs and a weak demand may prevent the monopolist from realizing any profit at all; and (d) the monopolist avoids the inelastic region of its demand curve.
4. With the same costs, the pure monopolist will find it profitable to restrict output and charge a higher price than would sellers in a purely competitive industry. This restriction of output causes resources to be misallocated, as is evidenced by the fact that price exceeds marginal cost in monopolized markets. Monopoly creates an efficiency loss (or deadweight loss) for society.
5. In general, monopoly transfers income from consumers to the owners of the monopoly. Because, on average, consumers of monopolized products have less income than the corporate owners, monopoly increases income inequality.
6. The costs monopolists and competitive producers face may not be the same. On the one hand, economies of scale may make lower unit costs available to monopolists but not to competitors. Also, pure monopoly may be more likely than pure competition to reduce costs via technological advance because of the monopolist's ability to realize economic

profit, which can be used to finance research. On the other hand, X-inefficiency—the failure to produce with the least costly combination of inputs—is more common among monopolists than among competitive firms. Also, monopolists may make costly expenditures to maintain monopoly privileges that are conferred by government. Finally, the blocked entry of rival firms weakens the monopolist's incentive to be technologically progressive.

7. A monopolist can increase its profit by practicing price discrimination, provided (a) it can segregate buyers on the basis of elasticities of demand and (b) its product or service cannot be readily transferred between the segregated markets.
8. Price regulation can be invoked to eliminate wholly or partially the tendency of monopolists to underallocate resources and to earn economic profits. The socially optimal price is determined where the demand and marginal-cost curves intersect; the fair-return price is determined where the demand and average-total-cost curves intersect.

Terms and Concepts

pure monopoly
barriers to entry
simultaneous consumption
network effects
X-inefficiency
rent-seeking behavior
price discrimination
socially optimal price
fair-return price

Study Questions

1. "No firm is completely sheltered from rivals; all firms compete for consumer dollars. If that is so, then pure monopoly does not exist." Do you agree? Explain. How might you use Chapter 6's concept of cross elasticity of demand to judge whether monopoly exists?
2. Discuss the major barriers to entry into an industry. Explain how each barrier can foster either monopoly or oligopoly. Which barriers, if any, do you feel give rise to monopoly that is socially justifiable?
3. How does the demand curve faced by a purely monopolistic seller differ from that confronting a purely competitive firm? Why does it differ? Of what significance is the difference? Why is the pure monopolist's demand curve not perfectly inelastic?
4. **KEY QUESTION** Use the demand schedule to the upper right to calculate total revenue and marginal revenue at each quantity. Plot the demand, total-revenue, and marginal-revenue curves and explain the relationships between them. Explain why the marginal revenue of the fourth unit of output is $3.50, even though its price is $5. Use Chapter 18's total-revenue test for price elasticity to designate the elastic and inelastic segments of your graphed demand curve. What generalization can you make as to the relationship between marginal revenue and elasticity of demand? Suppose the marginal cost of successive units of output was zero. What output would the profit-seeking firm produce? Finally, use your analysis to explain why a monopolist would never produce in the inelastic region of demand.

Price (*P*)	Quantity Demanded (*Q*)	Price (*P*)	Quantity Demanded (*Q*)
$7.00	0	$4.50	5
6.50	1	4.00	6
6.00	2	3.50	7
5.50	3	3.00	8
5.00	4	2.50	9

5. **KEY QUESTION** Suppose a pure monopolist is faced with the demand schedule shown below and the same cost data as the competitive producer discussed in question 4 at the end of Chapter 9. Calculate the missing total-revenue and marginal-revenue amounts, and determine the profit-maximizing price and profit-earning output for this monopolist. What is the monopolist's profit? Verify your answer graphically and by comparing total revenue and total cost.

Price	Quantity Demanded	Total Revenue	Marginal Revenue
$115	0	$_____	
100	1	_____	$_____
83	2	_____	_____
71	3	_____	_____
63	4	_____	_____
55	5	_____	_____
48	6	_____	_____
42	7	_____	_____
37	8	_____	_____
33	9	_____	_____
29	10	_____	_____

6. **KEY QUESTION** Suppose that a price-discriminating monopolist has segregated its market into two groups of buyers, the first group described by the demand and revenue data that you developed for question 5. The demand and revenue data for the second group of buyers is shown in the accompanying table. Assume that MC is $13 in both markets and MC = ATC at all output levels. What price will the firm charge in each market? Based solely on these two prices, what can you conclude about the relative elasticities of demand in the two markets? What will be this monopolist's total economic profit?

Price	Quantity Demanded	Total Revenue	Marginal Revenue
$71	0	$ 0	
			$63
63	1	63	
			47
55	2	110	
			34
48	3	144	
			24
42	4	168	
			17
37	5	185	
			13
33	6	198	
			5
29	7	203	

7. Assume that a pure monopolist and a purely competitive firm have the same unit costs. Contrast the two with respect to (*a*) price, (*b*) output, (*c*) profits, (*d*) allocation of resources, and (*e*) impact on the distribution of income. Since both monopolists and competitive firms follow the MC = MR rule in maximizing profits, how do you account for the different results? Why might the costs of a purely competitive firm and those of a monopolist be different? What are the implications of such a cost difference?

8. Critically evaluate and explain each statement:
   a. Because they can control product price, monopolists are always assured of profitable production by simply charging the highest price consumers will pay.
   b. The pure monopolist seeks the output that will yield the greatest per-unit profit.
   c. An excess of price over marginal cost is the market's way of signaling the need for more production of a good.
   d. The more profitable a firm, the greater its monopoly power.
   e. The monopolist has a pricing policy; the competitive producer does not.
   f. With respect to resource allocation, the interests of the seller and of society coincide in a purely competitive market but conflict in a monopolized market.
   g. In a sense the monopolist makes a profit for not producing; the monopolist produces profit more than it does goods.

9. Assume a monopolistic publisher has agreed to pay an author 15 percent of the total revenue from the sales of a text. Will the author and the publisher want to charge the same price for the text? Explain.

10. U.S. pharmaceutical companies charge different prices for prescription drugs to buyers in different nations, depending on elasticity of demand and government-imposed price ceilings. Explain why these companies, for profit reasons, oppose laws allowing reimportation of drugs to the United States.

11. Explain verbally and graphically how price (rate) regulation may improve the performance of monopolies. In your answer distinguish between (*a*) socially optimal (marginal-cost) pricing and (*b*) fair-return (average-total-cost) pricing. What is the "dilemma of regulation"?

12. **KEY QUESTION** It has been proposed that natural monopolists should be allowed to determine their profit-maximizing outputs and prices and then government should tax their profits away and distribute them to consumers in proportion to their purchases from the monopoly. Is this proposal as socially desirable as requiring monopolists to equate price with marginal cost or average total cost?

13. **LAST WORD** How was De Beers able to control the world price of diamonds over the past several decades even though it produced only 45 percent of the diamonds? What factors ended its monopoly? What is its new strategy for earning economic profit, rather than just normal profit?

Web-Based Questions

1. **IS MICROSOFT A MONOPOLY—WHAT DID THE COURTS CONCLUDE?** In 2002 a U.S. court of appeals imposed remedies relating to a lower court's findings that Microsoft had a monopoly in personal computer (PC) operating systems and had maintained its monopoly through illegal actions. At the U.S. Justice Department's Web site, **www.usdoj.gov**, use the DOJ Agencies listing to find Antitrust Division and then Antitrust Case Filings. Locate *U.S. v. Microsoft* and select District Court filings and then Court's Findings of Fact (11/5/99). On what basis did the court conclude that Microsoft was a monopoly (see "Market Share")? What was Microsoft's market share of Intel-compatible PC operating systems? Of all operating systems, including those of Apple computers? What evidence did the court cite in claiming that Microsoft charged above-competitive prices (see "Microsoft's Pricing Behavior")?

2. **GETTING TO KNOW YOUR STATE REGULATORY COMMISSION** Go to **www.yahoo.com** or some other standard search engine and type "public utility commissions" in the search box. Find the utilities commission for the state where you reside (or another state if you cannot find the Web site for your state commission). What industries does the state commission regulate? How many specific firms are registered or regulated? List the names of 10 such specific firms. Why are these and the other firms regulated?

IN THIS CHAPTER YOU WILL LEARN:

- **The characteristics of monopolistic competition.**
- **Why monopolistic competitors earn only a normal profit in the long run.**
- **The characteristics of oligopoly.**
- **How game theory relates to oligopoly.**
- **Why the demand curve of an oligopolist may be kinked.**
- **The incentives and obstacles to collusion among oligopolists.**
- **The potential positive and negative effects of advertising.**

Monopolistic Competition and Oligopoly

Most markets in the U.S. economy fall between the two poles of pure competition and pure monopoly. Real-world industries usually have fewer than the hundreds of producers required for pure competition and more than the single producer that defines pure monopoly. Most firms have distinguishable rather than standardized products and have some discretion over the prices they charge. Competition often occurs on the basis of price, quality, location, service, and advertising. Entry to most real-world industries ranges from easy to very difficult but is rarely completely blocked.

This chapter examines two models that more closely approximate these widespread markets. You will discover that *monopolistic competition* mixes a small amount of monopoly power with a large amount of competition. *Oligopoly,* in contrast, blends a large amount of monopoly power, a small amount of competition through entry, and considerable rivalry among industry firms.

Monopolistic Competition

Let's begin by examining **monopolistic competition,** which is characterized by (1) a relatively large number of sellers, (2) differentiated products (often promoted by heavy advertising), and (3) easy entry to, and exit from, the industry. The first and third characteristics provide the "competitive" aspect of monopolistic competition; the second characteristic provides the "monopolistic" aspect. In general, however, monopolistically competitive industries are much more competitive than they are monopolistic.

O 11.1
Monopolistic competition

Relatively Large Number of Sellers

Monopolistic competition is characterized by a fairly large number of firms, say, 25, 35, 60, or 70, not by the hundreds or thousands of firms in pure competition. Consequently, monopolistic competition involves:

- ***Small market shares*** Each firm has a comparatively small percentage of the total market and consequently has limited control over market price.
- ***No collusion*** The presence of a relatively large number of firms ensures that collusion by a group of firms to restrict output and set prices is unlikely.
- ***Independent action*** With numerous firms in an industry, there is no feeling of interdependence among them; each firm can determine its own pricing policy without considering the possible reactions of rival firms. A single firm may realize a modest increase in sales by cutting its price, but the effect of that action on competitors' sales will be nearly imperceptible and will probably trigger no response.

Differentiated Products

In contrast to pure competition, in which there is a standardized product, monopolistic competition is distinguished by **product differentiation.** Monopolistically competitive firms turn out variations of a particular product. They produce products with slightly different physical characteristics, offer varying degrees of customer service, provide varying amounts of locational convenience, or proclaim special qualities, real or imagined, for their products.

Let's examine these aspects of product differentiation in more detail.

Product Attributes Product differentiation may entail physical or qualitative differences in the products themselves. Real differences in functional features, materials, design, and workmanship are vital aspects of product differentiation. Personal computers, for example, differ in terms of storage capacity, speed, graphic displays, and included software. There are dozens of competing principles of economics textbooks that differ in content, organization, presentation and readability, pedagogical aids, and graphics and design. Most cities have a variety of retail stores selling men's and women's clothes that differ greatly in styling, materials, and quality of work. Similarly, one furniture manufacturer may feature its solid oak furniture, while a competitor stresses its solid maple furniture.

Service Service and the conditions surrounding the sale of a product are forms of product differentiation too. One grocery store may stress the helpfulness of its clerks who bag your groceries and carry them to your car. A warehouse competitor may leave bagging and carrying to its customers but feature lower prices. Customers may prefer 1-day over 3-day dry cleaning of equal quality. The prestige appeal of a store, the courteousness and helpfulness of clerks, the firm's reputation for servicing or exchanging its products, and the credit it makes available are all service aspects of product differentiation.

Location Products may also be differentiated through the location and accessibility of the stores that sell them. Small convenience stores manage to compete with large supermarkets, even though these minimarts have a more limited range of products and charge higher prices. They compete mainly on the basis of location—being close to customers and situated on busy streets. A motel's proximity to an interstate highway gives it a locational advantage that may enable it to charge a higher room rate than nearby motels in less convenient locations.

Brand Names and Packaging Product differentiation may also be created through the use of brand names and trademarks, packaging, and celebrity connections. Most aspirin tablets are very much alike, but many headache sufferers believe that one brand—for example, Bayer, Anacin, or Bufferin—is superior and worth a higher price than a generic substitute. A celebrity's name associated with jeans, perfume, or athletic equipment may enhance the appeal of those products for some buyers. Many customers prefer one style of ballpoint pen to another. Packaging that touts "natural spring" bottled water may attract additional customers.

Some Control over Price Despite the relatively large number of firms, monopolistic competitors do have some control over their product prices because of product differentiation. If consumers prefer the products of specific sellers, then within limits they will pay more to satisfy their preferences. Sellers and buyers are not linked randomly, as in a purely competitive market. But the monopolistic competitor's control over price is quite limited, since there are numerous potential substitutes for its product.

Easy Entry and Exit

Entry into monopolistically competitive industries is relatively easy compared to oligopoly or pure monopoly. Because monopolistic competitors are typically small firms, both absolutely and relatively, economies of scale are few and capital requirements are low. On the other hand, compared with pure competition, financial barriers may result from the need to develop and advertise a product that differs from rivals' products. Some firms have trade secrets relating to their products or hold trademarks on their brand names, making it difficult and costly for other firms to imitate them.

Exit from monopolistically competitive industries is relatively easy. Nothing prevents an unprofitable monopolistic competitor from holding a going-out-of-business sale and shutting down.

Advertising

The expense and effort involved in product differentiation would be wasted if consumers were not made aware of product differences. Thus, monopolistic competitors advertise their products, often heavily. The goal of product differentiation and advertising—so-called **nonprice competition**—is to make price less of a factor in consumer purchases and make product differences a greater factor. If successful, the firm's demand curve will shift to the right and will become less elastic.

Monopolistically Competitive Industries

Table 11.1 lists several manufacturing industries that approximate monopolistic competition. (The data in column 2 are self-explanatory. We will explain the data in column 3 later in this chapter.) In addition, many retail establishments in metropolitan areas are monopolistically competitive, including grocery stores, gasoline stations, barbershops, dry cleaners, clothing stores, and restaurants. Also, many providers of professional services such as medical care, legal assistance, real estate sales, and basic bookkeeping are monopolistic competitors.

Price and Output in Monopolistic Competition

We now analyze the price and output decisions of a monopolistically competitive firm. Initially, we assume that each firm in the industry is producing a specific differentiated product and engaging in a particular amount of advertising. Later we'll see how changes in the product and in the amount of advertising modify our conclusions.

The Firm's Demand Curve

Our explanation is based on **Figure 11.1 (Key Graph)**. The basic feature of that diagram is the elasticity of demand, as shown by the individual firm's demand curve. The demand curve faced by a monopolistically competitive seller is

TABLE 11.1 Percentage of Output Produced by Firms in Selected Low-Concentration U.S. Manufacturing Industries

(1) Industry	(2) Percentage of Industry Output* Produced by the Four Largest Firms	(3) Herfindahl Index for the Top 50 Firms	(1) Industry	(2) Percentage of Industry Output* Produced by the Four Largest Firms	(3) Herfindahl Index for the Top 50 Firms
Asphalt paving	25	207	Metal windows and doors	14	114
Plastic pipe	24	262	Women's dresses	13	84
Textile bags	24	263	Ready mix concrete	11	63
Bolts, nuts, and rivets	24	205	Wood trusses	10	50
Plastic bags	23	240	Stone products	10	59
Quick printing	22	319	Metal stamping	8	31
Textile machinery	20	206	Wood pallets	7	24
Sawmills	18	117	Sheet metal work	6	25
Jewelry	16	117	Signs	5	19
Curtains and draperies	16	111	Retail bakeries	4	7

*As measured by value of shipments. Data are for 2002. See **www.census.gov/epcd/www/concentration.html.**

Source: Bureau of Census, *Census of Manufacturers, 2002.*

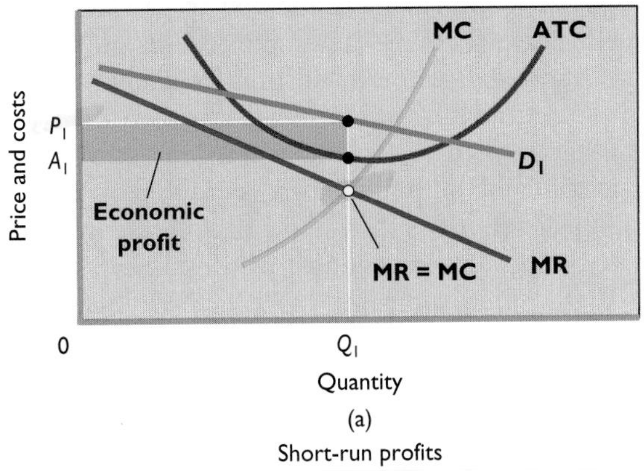

FIGURE 11.1 A monopolistically competitive firm: short run and long run. The monopolistic competitor maximizes profit or minimizes loss by producing the output at which MR = MC. The economic profit shown in (a) will induce new firms to enter, eventually eliminating economic profit. The loss shown in (b) will cause an exit of firms until normal profit is restored. After such entry and exit, the price will settle in (c) to where it just equals average total cost at the MR = MC output. At this price P_3 and output Q_3, the monopolistic competitor earns only a normal profit, and the industry is in long-run equilibrium.

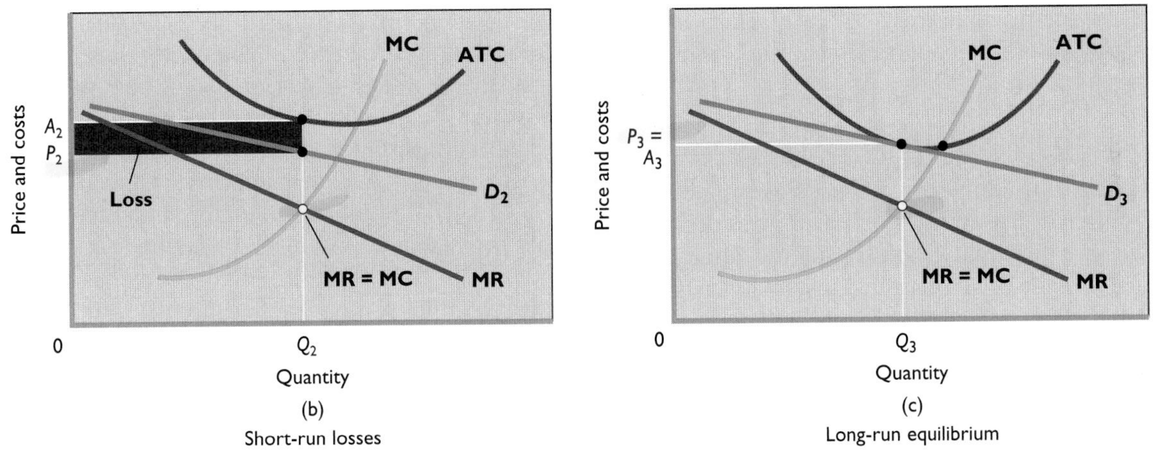

QUICK QUIZ 11.1

1. Price exceeds MC in:
   - **a.** graph (a) only.
   - **b.** graph (b) only.
   - **c.** graphs (a) and (b) only.
   - **d.** graphs (a), (b), and (c).
2. Price exceeds ATC in:
   - **a.** graph (a) only.
   - **b.** graph (b) only.
   - **c.** graphs (a) and (b) only.
   - **d.** graphs (a), (b), and (c).
3. The firm represented by Figure 11.1c is:
   - **a.** making a normal profit.
   - **b.** incurring a loss.
   - **c.** producing at the same level of output as a purely competitive firm.
   - **d.** producing a standardized product.
4. Which of the following pairs are both "competitionlike elements" in monopolistic competition?
   - **a.** Price exceeds MR; standardized product.
   - **b.** Entry is relatively easy; only a normal profit in the long run.
   - **c.** Price equals MC at the profit-maximizing output; economic profits are likely in the long run.
   - **d.** The firms' demand curve is downsloping; differentiated products.

Answers: 1. d; 2. a; 3. a; 4. b

highly, but not perfectly, elastic. It is precisely this feature that distinguishes monopolistic competition from pure monopoly and pure competition. The monopolistic competitor's demand is more elastic than the demand faced by a pure monopolist because the monopolistically competitive seller has many competitors producing closely substitutable goods. The pure monopolist has no rivals at all. Yet, for two reasons, the monopolistic competitor's demand is not perfectly elastic like that of the pure competitor. First, the monopolistic competitor has fewer rivals; second, its products are differentiated, so they are not perfect substitutes.

The price elasticity of demand faced by the monopolistically competitive firm depends on the number of rivals and the degree of product differentiation. The larger the number of rivals and the weaker the product differentiation, the greater the price elasticity of each seller's demand, that is, the closer monopolistic competition will be to pure competition.

The Short Run: Profit or Loss

The monopolistically competitive firm maximizes its profit or minimizes its loss in the short run just as do the other firms we have discussed: by producing the output at which marginal revenue equals marginal cost (MR = MC). In Figure 11.1a the firm produces output Q_1, where MR = MC. As shown by demand curve D_1, it then can charge price P_1. It realizes an economic profit, shown by the green area $[= (P_1 - A_1) \times Q_1]$.

But with less favorable demand or costs, the firm may incur a loss in the short run. We show this possibility in Figure 11.1b, where the firm's best strategy is to minimize its loss. It does so by producing output Q_2 (where MR = MC) and, as determined by demand curve D_2, by charging price P_2. Because price P_2 is less than average total cost A_2, the firm incurs a per-unit loss of $A_2 - P_2$ and a total loss represented as the red area $[= (A_2 - P_2) \times Q_2]$.

The Long Run: Only a Normal Profit

In the long run, firms will enter a profitable monopolistically competitive industry and leave an unprofitable one. So a monopolistic competitor will earn only a normal profit in the long run or, in other words, will only break even. (Remember that the cost curves include both explicit and implicit costs, including a normal profit.)

Profits: Firms Enter In the case of short-run profit (Figure 11.1a), economic profits attract new rivals, because entry to the industry is relatively easy. As new firms enter, the demand curve faced by the typical firm shifts to the left (falls). Why? Because each firm has a smaller share of total demand and now faces a larger number of close-substitute products. This decline in the firm's demand reduces its economic profit. When entry of new firms has reduced demand to the extent that the demand curve is tangent to the average-total-cost curve at the profit-maximizing output, the firm is just making a normal profit. This situation is shown in Figure 11.1c, where demand is D_3 and the firm's long-run equilibrium output is Q_3. As Figure 11.1c indicates, any greater or lesser output will entail an average total cost that exceeds product price P_3, meaning a loss for the firm. At the tangency point between the demand curve and ATC, total revenue equals total costs. With the economic profit gone, there is no further incentive for additional firms to enter.

Losses: Firms Leave When the industry suffers short-run losses, as in Figure 11.1b, some firms will exit in the long run. Faced with fewer substitute products and blessed with an expanded share of total demand, the surviving firms will see their demand curves shift to the right (rise), as to D_3. Their losses will disappear and give way to normal profits (Figure 11.1c). (For simplicity we have assumed constant costs; shifts in the cost curves as firms enter or leave would complicate our discussion slightly but would not alter our conclusions.)

Complications The representative firm in the monopolistic competition model earns only a normal profit in the long run. That outcome may not always occur, however, in the real world of small firms as opposed to the theoretical model.

- Some firms may achieve sufficient product differentiation such that other firms cannot duplicate them, even over time. One hotel in a major city may have the best location relative to business and tourist activities. Or a firm may have developed a well-known brand name that gives it a slight but very long-lasting advantage over imitators. Such firms may have sufficient monopoly power to realize modest economic profits even in the long run.
- Entry to some industries populated by small firms is not as free in reality as it is in theory. Because of product differentiation, financial barriers to entry are likely to be greater than they would be if the product were standardized. This suggests some monopoly power, with small economic profits continuing even in the long run.

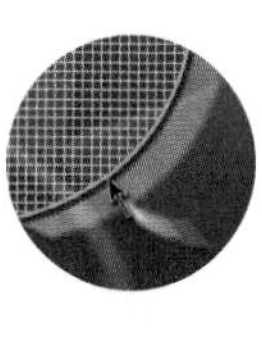

G 11.1
Monopolistic competition

With all things considered, however, the normal profit outcome—the long-run equilibrium shown in Figure 11.1c—is a reasonable portrayal of reality.

Monopolistic Competition and Efficiency

We know from Chapter 9 that economic efficiency requires the triple equality P = MC = minimum ATC. The equality of price and minimum average total cost yields *productive efficiency.* The good is being produced in the least costly way, and the price is just sufficient to cover average total cost, including a normal profit. The equality of price and marginal cost yields *allocative efficiency.* The right amount of output is being produced, and thus the right amount of society's scarce resources is being devoted to this specific use.

How efficient is monopolistic competition, as measured against this triple equality?

Neither Productive nor Allocative Efficiency

In monopolistic competition, neither productive nor allocative efficiency occurs in long-run equilibrium. We show this in Figure 11.2, which includes an enlargement of part of Figure 11.1c. First note that the profit-maximizing price P_3 slightly exceeds the lowest average total cost, A_4. Therefore, in producing the profit-maximizing output Q_3, the firm's average total cost is slightly higher than optimal from society's perspective—productive efficiency is not achieved. Also note that the profit-maximizing price P_3 exceeds marginal cost (here M_3), meaning that monopolistic competition causes an underallocation of resources. Society values each unit of output between Q_3 and Q_4 more highly than the goods it would have to forgo to produce those units. Thus, to a modest extent, monopolistic competition also fails the allocative-efficiency test. Consumers pay a higher-than-competitive price and obtain a less-than-optimal output. Indeed, monopolistic competitors must charge a higher-than-competitive price in the long run in order to achieve a normal profit. The price–marginal cost gap experienced by each monopolistic firm creates an industrywide efficiency loss (or deadweight loss).

Excess Capacity

In monopolistic competition, the gap between the minimum-ATC output and the profit-maximizing output identifies **excess capacity:** plant and equipment that are underused because firms are producing less than the

FIGURE 11.2 The inefficiency of monopolistic competition. In long-run equilibrium a monopolistic competitor achieves neither productive nor allocative efficiency. Productive efficiency is not realized because production occurs where the average total cost A_3 exceeds the minimum average total cost A_4. Allocative efficiency is not realized because the product price P_3 exceeds the marginal cost M_3. The result is an underallocation of resources and excess production capacity of $Q_4 - Q_3$.

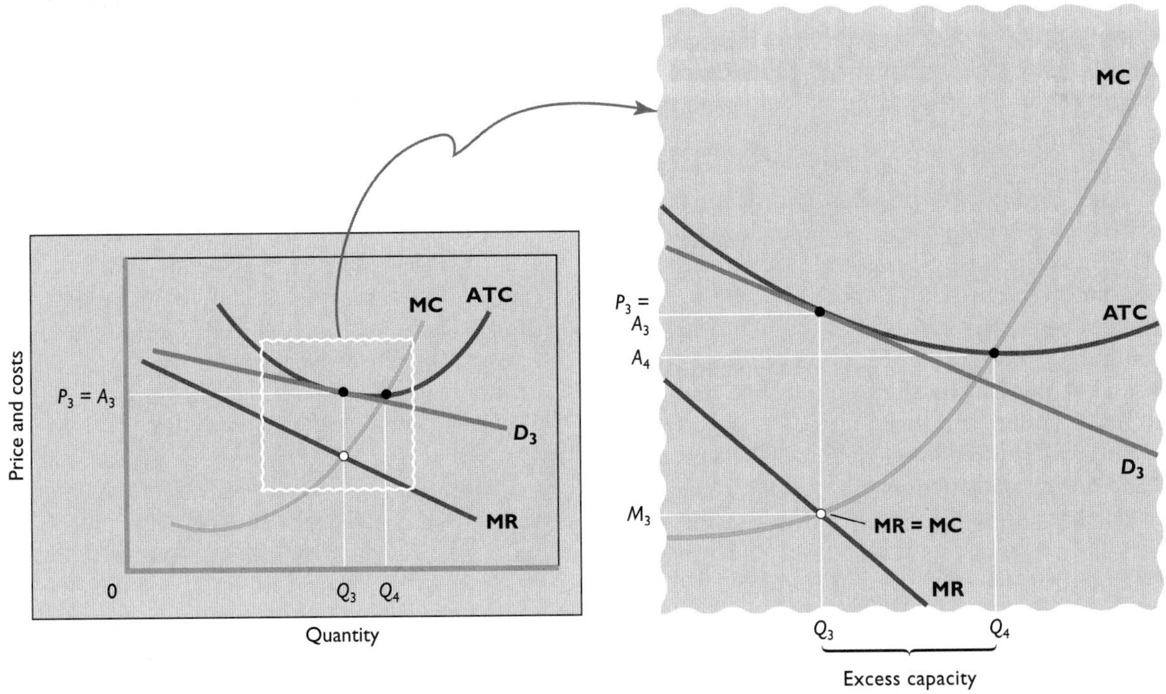

minimum-ATC output. We show this gap as the distance between Q_4 and Q_3 in Figure 11.2. If each monopolistic competitor could profitably produce at the minimum-ATC output, fewer firms could produce the same total output, and the product could be sold at a lower price. Monopolistically competitive industries thus are overcrowded with firms, each operating below its optimal capacity. This situation is typified by many kinds of retail establishments. For example, in most cities there is an abundance of small motels and restaurants that operate well below half capacity. **(Key Question 2)**

Product Variety

The situation portrayed in Figures 11.1c and 11.2 is not very satisfying to monopolistic competitors, since it foretells only a normal profit. But the profit-realizing firm of Figure 11.1a need not stand by and watch new competitors eliminate its profit by imitating its product, matching its customer service, and copying its advertising. Each firm has a product that is distinguishable in some way from those of the other producers. So the firm can attempt to stay ahead of competitors and sustain its profit through further product differentiation and better advertising. By developing or improving its product, it may be able to postpone, at least for a while, the outcome of Figure 11.1c.

Although product differentiation and advertising will add to the firm's costs, they can also increase the demand for its product. If demand increases by more than enough to compensate for the added costs, the firm will have improved its profit position. As Figure 11.2 suggests, the firm has little or no prospect of increasing profit by price cutting. So why not engage in nonprice competition?

Benefits of Product Variety

The product variety and product improvement that accompany the drive to maintain economic profit in monopolistic competition are a benefit for society—one that may offset the cost of the inefficiency associated with monopolistic competition. Consumers have a wide diversity of tastes: Some like regular fries, others like curly fries; some like contemporary furniture, others like traditional furniture. If a product is differentiated, then at any time the consumer will be offered a wide range of types, styles, brands, and quality gradations of that product. Compared with pure competition, this provides an advantage to the consumer. The range of choice is widened, and producers more fully meet the wide variation in consumer tastes.

The product improvement promoted by monopolistic competition further differentiates products and expands choices. And a successful product improvement by one firm obligates rivals to imitate or improve on that firm's temporary market advantage or else lose business. So society benefits from better products.

In fact, product differentiation creates a tradeoff between consumer choice and productive efficiency. The stronger the product differentiation, the greater is the excess capacity and, hence, the greater is the productive inefficiency. But the greater the product differentiation, the more likely the firms will satisfy the great diversity of consumer tastes. The greater is the excess-capacity problem, the wider the range of consumer choice.

Further Complexity

Finally, the ability to engage in nonprice competition makes the market situation of a monopolistic competitor more complex than Figure 11.1 indicates. That figure assumes a given (unchanging) product and a given level of advertising expenditures. But we know that, in practice, product attributes and advertising are not fixed. The monopolistically competitive firm juggles three factors—price, product, and advertising—in seeking maximum profit. It must determine what variety of product, selling at what price, and supplemented by what level of advertising will result in the greatest profit. This complex situation is not easily expressed in a simple, meaningful economic model. At best, we can say that each possible combination of price, product, and advertising poses a different demand and cost (production cost plus advertising cost) situation for the firm and that one combination yields the maximum profit. In practice, this optimal combination cannot be readily forecast but must be found by trial and error.

QUICK REVIEW 11.1

- Monopolistic competition involves a relatively large number of firms operating in a noncollusive way and producing differentiated products with easy industry entry and exit.
- In the short run, a monopolistic competitor will maximize profit or minimize loss by producing that output at which marginal revenue equals marginal cost.
- In the long run, easy entry and exit of firms cause monopolistic competitors to earn only a normal profit.
- A monopolistic competitor's long-run equilibrium output is such that price exceeds the minimum average total cost (implying that consumers do not get the product at the lowest price attainable) and price exceeds marginal cost (indicating that resources are underallocated to the product).
- The efficiency loss (or deadweight loss) associated with monopolistic competition is greatly muted by the benefits consumers receive from product variety.

Oligopoly

In terms of competitiveness, the spectrum of market structures reaches from pure competition, to monopolistic competition, to oligopoly, to pure monopoly (review Table 9.1). We now direct our attention to **oligopoly,** a market dominated by a few large producers of a homogeneous or differentiated product. Because of their "fewness," oligopolists have considerable control over their prices, but each must consider the possible reaction of rivals to its own pricing, output, and advertising decisions.

A Few Large Producers

The phrase "a few large producers" is necessarily vague because the market model of oligopoly covers much ground, ranging between pure monopoly, on the one hand, and monopolistic competition, on the other. Oligopoly encompasses the U.S. aluminum industry, in which three huge firms dominate an entire national market, and the situation in which four or five much smaller auto-parts stores enjoy roughly equal shares of the market in a medium-size town. Generally, however, when you hear a term such as "Big Three," "Big Four," or "Big Six," you can be sure it refers to an oligopolistic industry.

Homogeneous or Differentiated Products

An oligopoly may be either a **homogeneous oligopoly** or a **differentiated oligopoly,** depending on whether the firms in the oligopoly produce standardized or differentiated products. Many industrial products (steel, zinc, copper, aluminum, lead, cement, industrial alcohol) are virtually standardized products that are produced in oligopolies. Alternatively, many consumer goods industries (automobiles, tires, household appliances, electronics equipment, breakfast cereals, cigarettes, and many sporting goods) are differentiated oligopolies. These differentiated oligopolies typically engage in considerable nonprice competition supported by heavy advertising.

Control over Price, but Mutual Interdependence

Because firms are few in oligopolistic industries, each firm is a "price maker"; like the monopolist, it can set its price and output levels to maximize its profit. But unlike the monopolist, which has no rivals, the oligopolist must consider how its rivals will react to any change in its price, output, product characteristics, or advertising. Oligopoly is thus characterized by *strategic behavior* and *mutual interdependence.* By **strategic behavior,** we simply mean self-interested behavior that takes into account the reactions of others. Firms develop and implement price, quality, location, service, and advertising strategies to "grow their business" and expand their profits. But because rivals are few, there is **mutual interdependence:** a situation in which each firm's profit depends not entirely on its own price and sales strategies but also on those of the other firms. So oligopolistic firms base their decisions on how they think rivals will react. Example: In deciding whether to increase the price of its baseball gloves, Rawlings will try to predict the response of the other major producers, such as Wilson. Second example: In deciding on its advertising strategy, Burger King will take into consideration how McDonald's might react.

Entry Barriers

The same barriers to entry that create pure monopoly also contribute to the creation of oligopoly. Economies of scale are important entry barriers in a number of oligopolistic industries, such as the aircraft, rubber, and copper industries. In those industries, three or four firms might each have sufficient sales to achieve economies of scale, but new firms would have such a small market share that they could not do so. They would then be high-cost producers, and as such they could not survive. A closely related barrier is the large expenditure for capital—the cost of obtaining necessary plant and equipment—required for entering certain industries. The jet engine, automobile, commercial aircraft, and petroleum-refining industries, for example, are all characterized by very high capital requirements.

The ownership and control of raw materials help explain why oligopoly exists in many mining industries, including gold, silver, and copper. In the electronics, chemicals, photographic equipment, office equipment, and pharmaceutical industries, patents have served as entry barriers. Moreover, oligopolists can preclude the entry of new competitors through preemptive and retaliatory pricing and advertising strategies.

Mergers

Some oligopolies have emerged mainly through the growth of the dominant firms in a given industry (examples: breakfast cereals, chewing gum, candy bars). But for other industries the route to oligopoly has been through mergers (examples: steel, in its early history, and, more recently, airlines, banking, and entertainment). The merging, or combining, of two or more competing firms may substantially increase their market share, and this in turn may allow the new firm to achieve greater economies of scale.

Another motive underlying the "urge to merge" is the desire for monopoly power. The larger firm that results from a merger has greater control over market supply and thus the price of its product. Also, since it is a larger buyer of inputs, it will probably be able to demand and obtain lower prices (costs) on its production inputs.

Measures of Industry Concentration

Several means are used to measure the degree to which oligopolistic industries are concentrated in the "hands" of their largest firms. The most-often-used measures are *concentration ratios* and the *Herfindahl index.*

Concentration Ratio

A **concentration ratio** reveals the percentage of total output produced and sold by an industry's largest firms. Previously, we listed the four-firm concentration ratio—the percentage of total industry sales accounted for by the four largest firms—for a number of monopolistically competitive industries (see Table 11.1). Column 2 of Table 11.2 shows the four-firm concentration ratios for 21 oligopolistic industries. For example, the four largest U.S. producers of breakfast cereals make 78 percent of all breakfast cereals produced in the United States.

When the largest four firms in an industry control 40 percent or more of the market (as in Table 11.2), that industry is considered oligopolistic. Using this benchmark, about one-half of all U.S. manufacturing industries are oligopolies.

Although concentration ratios provide useful insights into the competitiveness or monopoly power of various industries, they have three shortcomings.

Localized Markets Concentration ratios pertain to the nation as a whole, whereas the markets for some products are highly localized because of high transportation costs. For example, the four-firm concentration ratio for ready-mix concrete is only 11 percent, suggesting a highly competitive industry. But the sheer bulk of this product limits the relevant market to a specific town or metropolitan area, and in such localized markets we often find oligopolistic concrete producers.

Interindustry Competition Since definitions of industries are somewhat arbitrary, we must be aware of **interindustry competition**—that is, competition between two products associated with different industries. The high concentration ratio for the copper industry shown in Table 11.2 understates the competition in that industry, because aluminum competes with copper in many applications (for example, in the market for electric transmission lines).

World Trade The data in Table 11.2 are only for products produced in the United States and may overstate concentration because they do not account for the **import competition** of foreign suppliers. The truck and auto tire industry is a good example. Although Table 11.2 shows that four U.S. firms produce 77 percent of the

TABLE 11.2 Percentage of Output Produced by Firms in Selected High-Concentration U.S. Manufacturing Industries

(1) Industry	(2) Percentage of Industry Output* Produced by the Four Largest Firms	(3) Herfindahl Index for the Top 50 Firms	(1) Industry	(2) Percentage of Industry Output* Produced by the Four Largest Firms	(3) Herfindahl Index for the Top 50 Firms
Primary copper	99	ND†	Petrochemicals	85	2662
Cane sugar refining	99	ND	Electronic computers	85	2662
Cigarettes	95	ND	Small-arms ammunition	83	1901
Household laundry equipment	93	ND	Motor vehicles	81	2321
Beer	91	ND	Men's slacks and jeans	80	2515
Electric light bulbs	89	2582	Aircraft	81	ND
Glass containers	88	2582	Breakfast cereals	78	2521
Turbines and generators	88	ND	Household vacuum cleaners	78	2096
Household refrigerators and freezers	85	1986	Phosphate fertilizers	78	1853
Primary aluminum	85	ND	Tires	77	1807
			Electronic computers	76	2662

*As measured by value of shipments. Data are for 2002. See **www.census.gov/epcd/www/concentration.html.**
†ND = not disclosed.

Source: Bureau of Census, *Census of Manufacturers, 2002.*

domestic output of tires, it ignores the fact that a very large portion of the truck and auto tires bought in the United States are imports. Many of the world's largest corporations are foreign, and many of them do business in the United States.

Herfindahl Index The concentration-ratio shortcomings listed above actually apply to many measures of concentration, but one of those shortcomings can be eliminated: Suppose that in industry X one firm produces all the market output. In a second industry, Y, there are four firms, each of which has 25 percent of the market. The concentration ratio is 100 percent for both these industries. But industry X is a pure monopoly, while industry Y is an oligopoly that may be facing significant economic rivalry. Most economists would agree that monopoly power (or market power) is substantially greater in industry X than in industry Y, a fact disguised by their identical 100 percent concentration ratios.

The **Herfindahl index** addresses this problem. This index is the sum of the squared percentage market shares of all firms in the industry. In equation form:

$$\text{Herfindahl index} = (\%S_1)^2 + (\%S_2)^2 + (\%S_3)^2 + \cdots + (\%S_n)^2$$

where $\%S_1$ is the percentage market share of firm 1, $\%S_2$ is the percentage market share of firm 2, and so on for each firm in the industry. By squaring the percentage market shares of all firms in the industry, the Herfindahl index gives much greater weight to larger, and thus more powerful, firms than to smaller ones. In the case of the single-firm industry X, the index would be at its maximum of 100^2, or 10,000, indicating an industry with complete monopoly power. For our supposed four-firm industry Y, the index would be $25^2 + 25^2 + 25^2 + 25^2$, or 2500, indicating much less market power. (For a purely competitive industry, the index would approach zero, since each firm's market share—$\%S$ in the equation—is extremely small.)

W 11.1
Measures of industry competition

To generalize, the larger the Herfindahl index, the greater the market power within an industry. Note in Table 11.2 that the four-firm concentration ratios for the electronic computer industry and the tire industry are similar: 78 and 77 percent. But the Herfindahl index of 2662 for the electronic computer industry suggests greater market power than the 1807 index for the tire industry. Also, contrast the much larger Herfindahl indexes in Table 11.2 with those for the low-concentration industries in Table 11.1. **(Key Question 7)**

Oligopoly Behavior: A Game-Theory Overview

Oligopoly pricing behavior has the characteristics of certain games of strategy, such as poker, chess, and bridge. The best way to play such a game depends on the way one's opponent plays. Players (and oligopolists) must pattern their actions according to the actions and expected reactions of rivals. The study of how people behave in strategic situations is called *game theory*. And we will use a simple **game-theory model** to analyze the pricing behavior of oligopolists. We assume that a duopoly, or two-firm oligopoly, is producing athletic shoes. Each of the two firms—let's call them RareAir and Uptown—has a choice of two pricing strategies: price high or price low. The profit each firm earns will depend on the strategy it chooses and the strategy its rival chooses.

O 11.2
Game theory

There are four possible combinations of strategies for the two firms, and a lettered cell in Figure 11.3 represents each combination. For example, cell C represents a low-price strategy for Uptown along with a high-price strategy for RareAir. Figure 11.3 is called a *payoff matrix*, because each cell shows the payoff (profit) to each firm that would result from each combination of strategies. Cell C shows that if Uptown adopts a low-price strategy and RareAir a high-price strategy, then Uptown will earn

FIGURE 11.3 Profit payoff (in millions) for a two-firm oligopoly. Each firm has two possible pricing strategies. RareAir's strategies are shown in the top margin, and Uptown's in the left margin. Each lettered cell of this four-cell payoff matrix represents one combination of a RareAir strategy and an Uptown strategy and shows the profit that combination would earn for each firm.

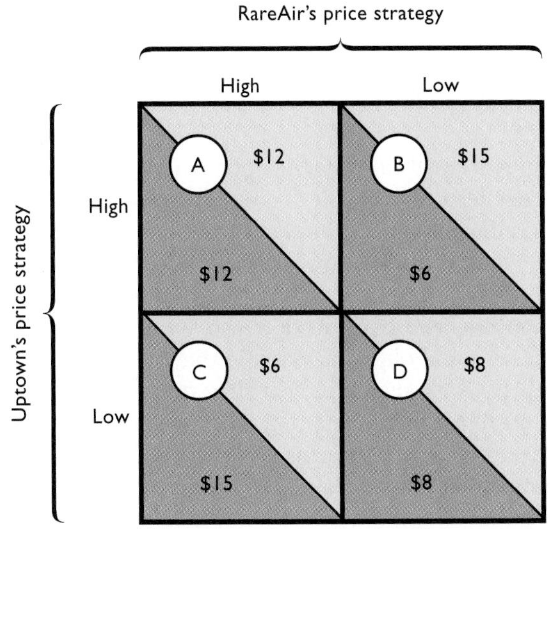

$15 million (tan portion) and RareAir will earn $6 million (green portion).

Mutual Interdependence Revisited

The data in Figure 11.3 are hypothetical, but their relationships are typical of real situations. Recall that oligopolistic firms can increase their profits, and influence their rivals' profits, by changing their pricing strategies. Each firm's profit depends on its own pricing strategy and that of its rivals. This mutual interdependence of oligopolists is the most obvious point demonstrated by Figure 11.3. If Uptown adopts a high-price strategy, its profit will be $12 million provided that RareAir also employs a high-price strategy (cell A). But if RareAir uses a low-price strategy against Uptown's high-price strategy (cell B), RareAir will increase its market share and boost its profit from $12 to $15 million. RareAir's higher profit will come at the expense of Uptown, whose profit will fall from $12 million to $6 million. Uptown's high-price strategy is a good strategy only if RareAir also employs a high-price strategy.

Collusive Tendencies

Figure 11.3 also suggests that oligopolists often can benefit from **collusion**—that is, cooperation with rivals. To see the benefits of collusion, first suppose that both firms in Figure 11.3 are acting independently and following high-price strategies. Each realizes a $12 million profit (cell A).

Note that either RareAir or Uptown could increase its profit by switching to a low-price strategy (cell B or C). The low-price firm would increase its profit to $15 million, and the high-price firm's profit would fall to $6 million. The high-price firm would be better off if it, too, adopted a low-price policy. Doing so would increase its profit from $6 million to $8 million (cell D). The effect of all this independent strategy shifting would be the reduction of both firms' profits from $12 million (cell A) to $8 million (cell D).

In real situations, too, independent action by oligopolists may lead to mutually "competitive" low-price strategies: Independent oligopolists compete with respect to price, and this leads to lower prices and lower profits. This outcome is clearly beneficial to consumers but not to the oligopolists, whose profits decrease.

How could oligopolists avoid the low-profit outcome of cell D? The answer is that they could collude, rather than establish prices competitively or independently. In our example, the two firms could agree to establish and maintain a high-price policy. So each firm will increase its profit from $8 million (cell D) to $12 million (cell A).

CONSIDER THIS . . .

Creative Strategic Behavior

The following story, offered with tongue in cheek, illustrates a localized market that exhibits some characteristics of oligopoly, including strategic behavior.

Tracy Martinez's Native American Arts and Crafts store is located in the center of a small tourist town that borders on a national park. In its early days, Tracy had a minimonopoly. Business was brisk, and prices and profits were high.

To Tracy's annoyance, two "copycat" shops opened adjacent to her store, one on either side of her shop. Worse yet, the competitors named their shops to take advantage of Tracy's advertising. One was "Native Arts and Crafts"; the other, "Indian Arts and Crafts"; These new sellers drew business away from Tracy's store, forcing her to lower her prices. The three side-by-side stores in the small, isolated town constituted a localized oligopoly for Native American arts and crafts.

Tracy began to think strategically about ways to boost profit. She decided to distinguish her shop from those on either side by offering a greater mix of high-quality, expensive products and a lesser mix of inexpensive souvenir items. The tactic worked for a while, but the other stores eventually imitated her product mix.

Then, one of the competitors next door escalated the rivalry by hanging up a large sign proclaiming "We Sell for Less!" Shortly thereafter, the other shop put up a large sign stating "We Won't Be Undersold!"

Not to be outdone, Tracy painted a colorful sign of her own and hung it above her door. It read "Main Entrance."

Incentive to Cheat

The payoff matrix also explains why an oligopolist might be strongly tempted to cheat on a collusive agreement. Suppose Uptown and RareAir agree to maintain high-price policies, with each earning $12 million in profit (cell A). Both are tempted to cheat on this collusive pricing agreement, because either firm can increase its profit to $15 million by lowering its price. If Uptown secretly cheats on the agreement by charging low prices, the payoff moves from cell A to cell C. Uptown's profit rises to $15 million, and RareAir's falls to $6 million. If RareAir cheats, the

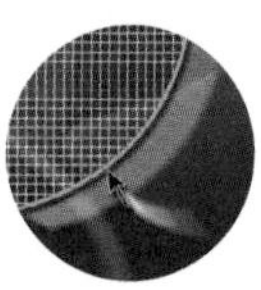

G 11.2
Game theory

payoff moves from cell A to cell B, and RareAir gets the $15 million. **(Key Question 8)**

QUICK REVIEW 11.2

- An oligopoly is made up of relatively few firms producing either homogeneous or differentiated products; these firms are mutually interdependent.
- Barriers to entry such as scale economies, control of patents or strategic resources, or the ability to engage in retaliatory pricing characterize oligopolies. Oligopolies may result from internal growth of firms, mergers, or both.
- The four-firm concentration ratio shows the percentage of an industry's sales accounted for by its four largest firms; the Herfindahl index measures the degree of market power in an industry by summing the squares of the percentage market shares held by the individual firms in the industry.
- Game theory reveals that (a) oligopolies are mutually interdependent in their pricing policies; (b) collusion enhances oligopoly profits; and (c) there is a temptation for oligopolists to cheat on a collusive agreement.

Three Oligopoly Models

To gain further insight into oligopolistic pricing and output behavior, we will examine three distinct pricing models: (1) the kinked-demand curve, (2) collusive pricing, and (3) price leadership.

Why not a single model, as in our discussions of the other market structures? There are two reasons:

- ***Diversity of oligopolies*** Oligopoly encompasses a greater range and diversity of market situations than do other market structures. It includes the *tight* oligopoly, in which two or three firms dominate an entire market, and the *loose* oligopoly, in which six or seven firms share, say, 70 or 80 percent of a market while a "competitive fringe" of firms shares the remainder. It includes both differentiated and standardized products. It includes cases in which firms act in collusion and those in which they act independently. It embodies situations in which barriers to entry are very strong and situations in which they are not quite so strong. In short, the diversity of oligopoly does not allow us to explain all oligopolistic behaviors with a single market model.
- ***Complications of interdependence*** The mutual interdependence of oligopolistic firms complicates matters significantly. Because firms cannot predict the reactions of their rivals with certainty, they cannot estimate their own demand and marginal-revenue data. Without such data, firms cannot determine their profit-maximizing price and output, even in theory, as we will see.

Despite these analytical difficulties, two interrelated characteristics of oligopolistic pricing have been observed. First, if the macroeconomy is generally stable, oligopolistic prices are typically inflexible (or "rigid" or "sticky"). Prices change less frequently under oligopoly than under pure competition, monopolistic competition, and, in some instances, pure monopoly. Second, when oligopolistic prices do change, firms are likely to change their prices together, suggesting that there is a tendency to act in concert, or collusively, in setting and changing prices (as we mentioned in the preceding section). The diversity of oligopolies and the presence of mutual interdependence are reflected in the models that follow.

Kinked-Demand Theory: Noncollusive Oligopoly

Imagine an oligopolistic industry made up of three hypothetical firms (Arch, King, and Dave's), each having about one-third of the total market for a differentiated product. Assume that the firms are "independent," meaning that they do not engage in collusive price practices. Assume, too, that the going price for Arch's product is P_0 and its current sales are Q_0, as shown in **Figure 11.4a (Key Graph).**

Now the question is, "What does the firm's demand curve look like?" Mutual interdependence and the uncertainty about rivals' reactions make this question hard to answer. The location and shape of an oligopolist's demand curve depend on how the firm's rivals will react to a price change introduced by Arch. There are two plausible assumptions about the reactions of Arch's rivals:

- ***Match price changes*** One possibility is that King and Dave's will exactly match any price change initiated by Arch. In this case, Arch's demand and marginal-revenue curves will look like the straight lines labeled D_1 and MR_1 in Figure 11.4a. Why are they so steep? Reason: If Arch cuts its price, its sales will increase only modestly because its two rivals will also cut their prices to prevent Arch from gaining an advantage over them. The small increase in sales that Arch (and its two rivals) will realize is at the expense of other industries; Arch will gain no sales from King and Dave's. If Arch raises its price, its sales will fall only modestly, because King and Dave's will match its price increase. The industry will lose sales to other industries, but Arch will lose no customers to King and Dave's.
- ***Ignore price changes*** The other possibility is that King and Dave's will ignore any price change by Arch.

FIGURE 11.4 The kinked-demand curve. (a) The slope of a noncollusive oligopolist's demand and marginal-revenue curves depends on whether its rivals match (straight lines D_1 and MR_1) or ignore (straight lines D_2 and MR_2) any price changes that it may initiate from the current price P_0. (b) In all likelihood an oligopolist's rivals will ignore a price increase but follow a price cut. This causes the oligopolist's demand curve to be kinked (D_2eD_1) and the marginal-revenue curve to have a vertical break, or gap (*fg*). Because any shift in marginal costs between MC_1 and MC_2 will cut the vertical (dashed) segment of the marginal-revenue curve, no change in either price P_0 or output Q_0 will result from such a shift.

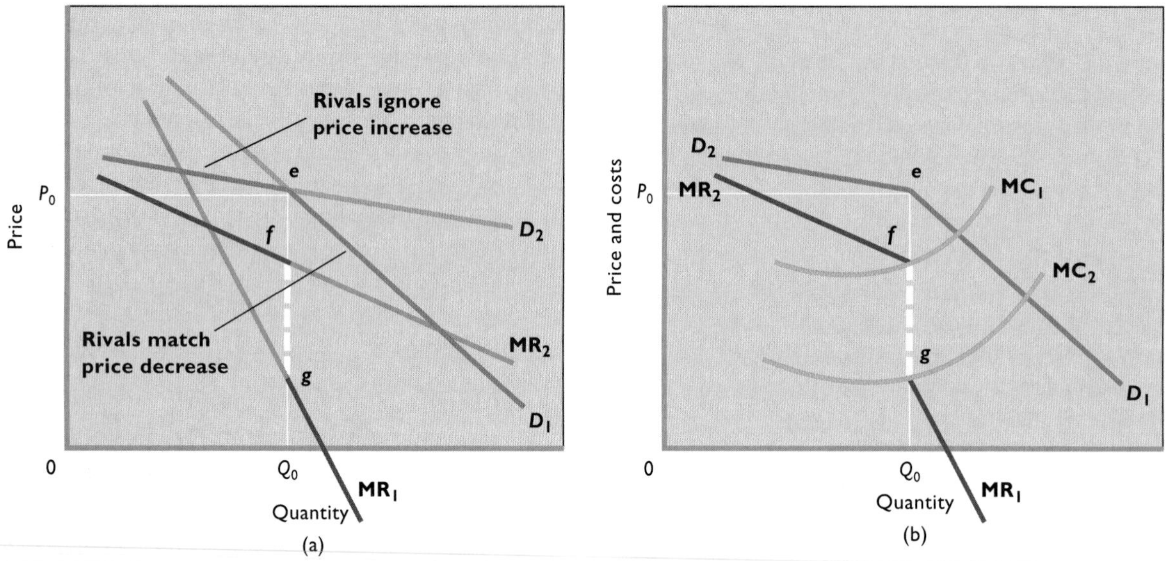

QUICK QUIZ 11.4

1. Suppose Q_0 in this figure represents annual sales of 5 million units for this firm. The other two firms in this three-firm industry sell 3 million and 2 million units, respectively. The Herfindahl index for this industry is:
   - **a.** 100 percent.
   - **b.** 400.
   - **c.** 10.
   - **d.** 3800.
2. The D_2e segment of the demand curve D_2eD_1 in graph (b) implies that:
   - **a.** this firm's total revenue will fall if it increases its price above P_0.
   - **b.** other firms will match a price increase above P_0.
   - **c.** the firm's relevant marginal-revenue curve will be MR_1 for price increases above P_0.
   - **d.** the product in this industry is necessarily standardized.
3. By matching a price cut, this firm's rivals can:
   - **a.** increase their market shares.
   - **b.** increase their marginal revenues.
   - **c.** maintain their market shares.
   - **d.** lower their total costs.
4. A shift of the marginal-cost curve from MC_2 to MC_1 in graph (b) would:
   - **a.** increase the "going price" above P_0.
   - **b.** leave price at P_0, but reduce this firm's total profit.
   - **c.** leave price at P_0, but reduce this firm's total revenue.
   - **d.** make this firm's demand curve more elastic.

Answers: 1. d; 2. a; 3. c; 4. b

In this case, the demand and marginal-revenue curves faced by Arch will resemble the straight lines D_2 and MR_2 in Figure 11.4a. Demand in this case is considerably more elastic than it was under the previous assumption. The reasons are clear: If Arch lowers its price and its rivals do not, Arch will gain sales significantly at the expense of its two rivals because it will be underselling them. Conversely, if Arch raises its price and its rivals do not, Arch will lose many customers to King and Dave's, which will be underselling it. Because of product differentiation, however, Arch's sales will not fall to zero when it raises its price; some of Arch's customers will pay the higher price because they have a strong preference for Arch's product.

A Combined Strategy Now, which is the most logical assumption for Arch to make about how its rivals will react to any price change it might initiate? The answer is, "It depends on the direction of price." Common sense and observation of oligopolistic industries suggest that a firm's rivals will match price declines below P_0 as they act to prevent the price cutter from taking their customers. But they will ignore price increases above P_0, because the rivals of the price-increasing firm stand to gain the business lost by the price booster. In other words, the dark-green left-hand segment of the "rivals ignore" demand curve D_2 seems relevant for price increases, and the dark-green right-hand segment of the "rivals match" demand curve D_1 seems relevant for price cuts. It is logical, then, or at least a reasonable assumption, that the noncollusive oligopolist faces the **kinked-demand curve** D_2eD_1, as shown in Figure 11.4b. Demand is highly elastic above the going price P_0 but much less elastic or even inelastic below that price.

Note also that if rivals match a price cut but ignore an increase, the marginal-revenue curve of the oligopolist will also have an odd shape. It, too, will be made up of two segments: the dark gray left-hand part of marginal-revenue curve MR_2 in Figure 11.4a and the dark gray right-hand part of marginal-revenue curve MR_1. Because of the sharp difference in elasticity of demand above and below the going price, there is a gap, or what we can simply treat as a vertical segment, in the marginal-revenue curve. We show this gap as the dashed segment in the combined marginal-revenue curve MR_2fgMR_1 in Figure 11.4b.

Price Inflexibility This analysis helps explain why prices are generally stable in noncollusive oligopolistic industries. There are both demand and cost reasons.

On the demand side, the kinked-demand curve gives each oligopolist reason to believe that any change in price will be for the worse. If it raises its price, many of its customers will desert it. If it lowers its price, its sales at best will increase very modestly, since rivals will match the lower price. Even if a price cut increases the oligopolist's total revenue somewhat, its costs may increase by a greater amount. And if its demand is inelastic to the right of Q_0, as it may well be, then the firm's profit will surely fall. A price decrease in the inelastic region lowers the firm's total revenue, and the production of a larger output increases its total costs.

On the cost side, the broken marginal-revenue curve suggests that even if an oligopolist's costs change substantially, the firm may have no reason to change its price. In particular, all positions of the marginal-cost curve between MC_1 and MC_2 in Figure 11.4b will result in the firm's deciding on exactly the same price and output. For all those positions, MR equals MC at output Q_0; at that output, it will charge price P_0.

Criticisms of the Model The kinked-demand analysis has two shortcomings. First, it does not explain how the going price gets to be at P_0 in Figure 11.4 in the first place. It only helps explain why oligopolists tend to stick with an existing price. The kinked-demand curve explains price inflexibility but not price itself.

Second, when the macroeconomy is unstable, oligopoly prices are not as rigid as the kinked-demand theory implies. During inflationary periods, many oligopolists have raised their prices often and substantially. And during downturns (recessions), some oligopolists have cut prices. In some instances these price reductions have set off a **price war:** successive and continuous rounds of price cuts by rivals as they attempt to maintain their market shares. **(Key Question 9)**

Cartels and Other Collusion

Our game-theory model demonstrated that oligopolists might benefit from collusion. We can say that collusion occurs whenever firms in an industry reach an agreement to fix prices, divide up the market, or otherwise restrict competition among themselves. The disadvantages and uncertainties of noncollusive, kinked-demand oligopolies are obvious. There is always the danger of a price war breaking out, especially during a general business recession. Then each firm finds that, because of unsold goods and excess capacity, it can reduce per-unit costs by increasing market share. Then, too, a new firm may surmount entry barriers and initiate aggressive price cutting to gain a foothold in the market. In addition, the kinked-demand curve's tendency toward rigid prices may adversely affect profits if general inflationary pressures increase costs. However, by controlling price through collusion, oligopolists may be able to reduce uncertainty, increase profits, and perhaps even prohibit the entry of new rivals.

Price and Output Assume once again that there are three hypothetical oligopolistic firms (Gypsum, Sheetrock, and GSR) producing, in this instance, gypsum drywall panels for finishing interior walls. All three firms produce a homogeneous product and have identical cost curves. Each firm's demand curve is indeterminate unless we know how its rivals will react to any price change. Therefore, we suppose each firm assumes that its two rivals will match either a price cut or a price increase. In other words, each firm has a demand curve like the straight line D_1 in Figure 11.4a. And since they have identical cost data, and the same demand and thus marginal-revenue

FIGURE 11.5 Collusion and the tendency toward joint-profit maximization. If oligopolistic firms face identical or highly similar demand and cost conditions, they may collude to limit their joint output and to set a single, common price. Thus each firm acts as if it were a pure monopolist, setting output at Q_0 and charging price P_0. This price and output combination maximizes each oligopolist's profit (green area) and thus the combined or joint profit of both.

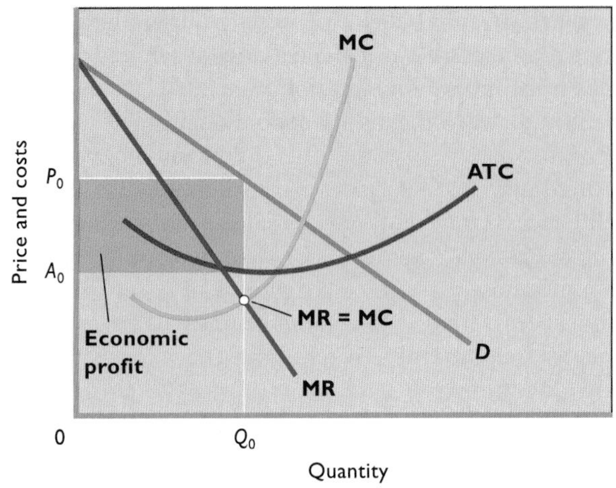

data, we can say that Figure 11.5 represents the position of each of our three oligopolistic firms.

What price and output combination should, say, Gypsum select? If Gypsum were a pure monopolist, the answer would be clear: Establish output at Q_0, where marginal revenue equals marginal cost, charge the corresponding price P_0, and enjoy the maximum profit attainable. However, Gypsum does have two rivals selling identical products, and if Gypsum's assumption that its rivals will match its price of P_0 proves to be incorrect, the consequences could be disastrous for Gypsum. Specifically, if Sheetrock and GSR actually charge prices below P_0, then Gypsum's demand curve *D* will shift sharply to the left as its potential customers turn to its rivals, which are now selling the same product at a lower price. Of course, Gypsum can retaliate by cutting its price too, but this will move all three firms down their demand curves, lowering their profits. It may even drive them to a point where average total cost exceeds price and losses are incurred.

So the question becomes, "Will Sheetrock and GSR want to charge a price below P_0?" Under our assumptions, and recognizing that Gypsum has little choice except to match any price they may set below P_0, the answer is no. Faced with the same demand and cost circumstances, Sheetrock and GSR will find it in their interest to produce Q_0 and charge P_0. This is a curious situation; each firm finds it most profitable to charge the same price, P_0, but only if its rivals actually do so! How can the three firms ensure the price P_0 and quantity Q_0 solution in which each is keenly interested? How can they avoid the less profitable outcomes associated with either higher or lower prices?

The answer is evident: They can collude. They can get together, talk it over, and agree to charge the same price, P_0. In addition to reducing the possibility of price wars, this will give each firm the maximum profit. (But it will also subject them to antitrust prosecution if they are caught!) For society, the result will be the same as would occur if the industry were a pure monopoly composed of three identical plants.

Overt Collusion: The OPEC Cartel Collusion may assume a variety of forms. The most comprehensive form of collusion is the **cartel**, a group of producers that typically creates a formal written agreement specifying how much each member will produce and charge. Output must be controlled—the market must be divided up—in order to maintain the agreed-upon price. The collusion is overt, or open to view.

Undoubtedly the most significant international cartel is the Organization of Petroleum Exporting Countries (OPEC), comprising 11 oil-producing nations (see Global Perspective 11.1). OPEC produces 40 percent of the world's oil and supplies 60 percent of all oil traded internationally. In the late 1990s it reacted vigorously to very low oil prices by greatly restricting supply. Some non-OPEC producers supported the cutback in production, and within a 15-month period the price of oil shot up from $11 a barrel to $34 a barrel. Gasoline prices in the United States rose by as much as $1 a gallon in some markets. Fearing a global political and economic backlash from the major industrial nations, OPEC upped the production quotas for its members in mid-2000. The increases in oil supply that resulted reduced the price of oil to about $25, where it remained through 2002.

OPEC supply restrictions were less of a factor in the rising oil prices in 2005 and 2006. In those years, rapidly rising demand for oil in China and supply uncertainties related to armed conflict in Iraq, Nigeria, and Lebanon drove the price of oil to $72 a barrel. In fact, even the loosening of OPEC quotas was insufficient to prevent this price hike. Should circumstances change, however, OPEC clearly has the market power to hold the price of oil substantially above its marginal cost of production.

Covert Collusion: Examples Cartels are illegal in the United States, and hence any collusion that exists is covert or secret. Yet there are numerous examples, as shown by evidence from antitrust (antimonopoly) cases. In 1993 the Borden, Pet, and Dean food companies, among others, either pleaded guilty to or were convicted of rigging bids on the prices of milk products sold to schools

GLOBAL PERSPECTIVE 11.1

The 11 OPEC Nations, Daily Oil Production, May 1, 2006

The OPEC nations produce about 40 percent of the world's oil and 60 percent of the oil sold in world markets.

OPEC Country	Barrels of Oil
Saudi Arabia	9,099,000
Iran	4,110,000
Venezuela	3,233,000
UAE	2,444,000
Nigeria	2,306,000
Kuwait	2,247,000
Iraq	1,903,000
Libya	1,500,000
Indonesia	1,451,000
Algeria	894,000
Qatar	726,000

Source: OPEC, **www.opec.org/**.

and military bases. By phone or at luncheons, company executives agreed in advance on which firm would submit the low bid for each school district or military base. In 1996 American agribusiness Archer Daniels Midland and three Japanese and South Korean firms were found to have conspired to fix the worldwide price and sales volume of a livestock feed additive. Executives for the firms secretly met in Hong Kong, Paris, Mexico City, Vancouver, and Zurich to discuss their plans.

In many other instances collusion is much subtler. **Tacit understandings** (historically called "gentlemen's agreements") are frequently made at cocktail parties, on golf courses, through phone calls, or at trade association meetings. In such agreements, competing firms reach a verbal understanding on product price, leaving market shares to be decided by nonprice competition. Although these agreements, too, violate antitrust laws—and can result in severe personal and corporate penalties—the elusive character of tacit understandings makes them more difficult to detect.

Obstacles to Collusion Normally, cartels and similar collusive arrangements are difficult to establish and maintain. Here are several barriers to collusion:

Demand and Cost Differences When oligopolists face different costs and demand curves, it is difficult for them to agree on a price. This is particularly the case in industries where products are differentiated and change frequently. Even with highly standardized products, firms usually have somewhat different market shares and operate with differing degrees of productive efficiency. Thus it is unlikely that even homogeneous oligopolists would have the same demand and cost curves.

In either case, differences in costs and demand mean that the profit-maximizing price will differ among firms; no single price will be readily acceptable to all, as we assumed was true in Figure 11.5. So price collusion depends on compromises and concessions that are not always easy to obtain and hence act as an obstacle to collusion.

Number of Firms Other things equal, the larger the number of firms, the more difficult it is to create a cartel or some other form of price collusion. Agreement on price by three or four producers that control an entire market may be relatively easy to accomplish. But such agreement is more difficult to achieve where there are, say, 10 firms, each with roughly 10 percent of the market, or where the Big Three have 70 percent of the market while a competitive fringe of 8 or 10 smaller firms battles for the remainder.

Cheating As the game-theory model makes clear, collusive oligopolists are tempted to engage in secret price cutting to increase sales and profit. The difficulty with such cheating is that buyers who are paying a high price for a product may become aware of the lower-priced sales and demand similar treatment. Or buyers receiving a price concession from one producer may use the concession as a wedge to get even larger price concessions from a rival producer. Buyers' attempts to play producers against one another may precipitate price wars among the producers. Although secret price concessions are potentially profitable, they threaten collusive oligopolies over time. Collusion is more likely to succeed when cheating is easy to detect and punish. Then the conspirators are less likely to cheat on the price agreement.

Recession Long-lasting recession usually serves as an enemy of collusion because slumping markets increase average total cost. In technical terms, as the oligopolists' demand and marginal-revenue curves shift to the left in Figure 11.5 in response to a recession, each firm moves leftward and upward to a higher operating point on its average-total-cost curve. Firms find they have substantial excess production capacity, sales are down, unit costs are up, and profits are being squeezed. Under such conditions, businesses may feel they can avoid serious profit reductions (or even losses) by cutting price and thus gaining sales at the expense of rivals.

Potential Entry The greater prices and profits that result from collusion may attract new entrants, including foreign firms. Since that would increase market supply and reduce prices and profits, successful collusion requires that colluding oligopolists block the entry of new producers.

Legal Obstacles: Antitrust Law U.S. antitrust laws prohibit cartels and price-fixing collusion. So less obvious means of price control have evolved in this country.

Price Leadership Model

Price leadership entails a type of implicit understanding by which oligopolists can coordinate prices without engaging in outright collusion based on formal agreements and secret meetings. Rather, a practice evolves whereby the "dominant firm"—usually the largest or most efficient in the industry—initiates price changes and all other firms more or less automatically follow the leader. Many industries, including farm machinery, cement, copper, newsprint, glass containers, steel, beer, fertilizer, cigarettes, and tin, are practicing, or have in the recent past practiced, price leadership.

Leadership Tactics An examination of price leadership in a variety of industries suggests that the price leader is likely to observe the following tactics.

Infrequent Price Changes Because price changes always carry the risk that rivals will not follow the lead, price adjustments are made only infrequently. The price leader does not respond to minuscule day-to-day changes in costs and demand. Price is changed only when cost and demand conditions have been altered significantly and on an industrywide basis as the result of, for example, industrywide wage increases, an increase in excise taxes, or an increase in the price of some basic input such as energy. In the automobile industry, price adjustments traditionally have been made when new models are introduced each fall.

Communications The price leader often communicates impending price adjustments to the industry through speeches by major executives, trade publication interviews, or press releases. By publicizing "the need to raise prices," the price leader seeks agreement among its competitors regarding the actual increase.

Limit Pricing The price leader does not always choose the price that maximizes short-run profits for the industry because the industry may want to discourage new firms from entering. If the cost advantages (economies of scale) of existing firms are a major barrier to entry, new entrants could surmount that barrier if the price leader and the other firms set product price high enough. New firms that are relatively inefficient because of their small size might survive and grow if the industry sets price very high. So, in order to discourage new competitors and to maintain the current oligopolistic structure of the industry, the price leader may keep price below the short-run profit-maximizing level. The strategy of establishing a price that blocks the entry of new firms is called *limit pricing.*

Breakdowns in Price Leadership: Price Wars Price leadership in oligopoly occasionally breaks down, at least temporarily, and sometimes results in a price war. An example of disruption of price leadership occurred in the breakfast cereal industry, in which Kellogg traditionally had been the price leader. General Mills countered Kellogg's leadership in 1995 by reducing the prices of its cereals by 11 percent. In 1996 Post responded with a 20 percent price cut, which Kellogg then followed. Not to be outdone, Post reduced its prices by another 11 percent.

As another example, in late 2002 Burger King set off a price war by offering its bacon cheeseburger for 99¢. McDonald's countered by placing a price tag of $1 on its Big "N" Tasty burger, which competes directly against Burger King's popular Whopper. Burger King then offered a "limited-time special" of 99¢ for Whoppers.

Most price wars eventually run their course. When all firms recognize that low prices are severely reducing their profits, they again yield price leadership to one of the industry's leading firms. That firm then begins to raise prices, and the other firms willingly follow suit.

QUICK REVIEW 11.3

- In the kinked-demand theory of oligopoly, price is relatively inflexible because a firm contemplating a price change assumes that its rivals will follow a price cut and ignore a price increase.
- Cartels agree on production limits and set a common price to maximize the joint profit of their members as if each were a unit of a single pure monopoly.
- Collusion among oligopolists is difficult because of (a) demand and cost differences among sellers, (b) the complexity of output coordination among producers, (c) the potential for cheating, (d) a tendency for agreements to break down during recessions, (e) the potential entry of new firms, and (f) antitrust laws.
- Price leadership involves an informal understanding among oligopolists to match any price change initiated by a designated firm (often the industry's dominant firm).

Oligopoly and Advertising

We have noted that oligopolists would rather not compete on the basis of price and may become involved in price collusion. Nonetheless, each firm's share of the total market is typically determined through product development and advertising, for two reasons:

- Product development and advertising campaigns are less easily duplicated than price cuts. Price cuts can be quickly and easily matched by a firm's rivals to cancel any potential gain in sales derived from that strategy. Product improvements and successful advertising, however, can produce more permanent gains in market share because they cannot be duplicated as quickly and completely as price reductions.
- Oligopolists have sufficient financial resources to engage in product development and advertising. For most oligopolists, the economic profits earned in the past can help finance current advertising and product development.

Product development (or, more broadly, "research and development") is the subject of the next chapter, so we will confine our present discussion to advertising. In 2005, firms spent an estimated $271 billion on advertising in the United States and $570 billion worldwide. Advertising is prevalent in both monopolistic competition and oligopoly. Table 11.3 lists the 10 leading U.S. advertisers in 2005.

Advertising may affect prices, competition, and efficiency both positively and negatively, depending on the circumstances. While our focus here is on advertising by oligopolists, the analysis is equally applicable to advertising by monopolistic competitors.

Positive Effects of Advertising

In order to make rational (efficient) decisions, consumers need information about product characteristics and prices. Media advertising may be a low-cost means for consumers to obtain that information. Suppose you are in the market for a high-quality camera that is not advertised or promoted in newspapers, magazines, or on the Internet. To make a rational choice, you may have to spend several days visiting stores to determine the availability, prices, and features of various brands. This search entails both direct costs (gasoline, parking fees) and indirect costs (the value of your time). By providing information about the available options, advertising and Internet promotion reduces your search time and minimizes these direct and indirect costs.

By providing information about the various competing goods that are available, advertising diminishes monopoly power. In fact, advertising is frequently associated with the introduction of new products designed to compete with existing brands. Could Toyota and Honda have so strongly challenged U.S. auto producers without advertising? Could Federal Express have sliced market share away from UPS and the U.S. Postal Service without advertising?

Viewed this way, advertising is an efficiency-enhancing activity. It is a relatively inexpensive means of providing useful information to consumers and thus lowering their search costs. By enhancing competition, advertising results in greater economic efficiency. By facilitating the introduction of new products, advertising speeds up technological

TABLE 11.3 The Largest U.S. Advertisers, 2005

Company	Advertising Spending Millions of $
Procter & Gamble	$4609
General Motors	4353
Time Warner	3494
Verizon	2484
AT&T	2471
Ford Motor	2398
Walt Disney	2279
Johnson & Johnson	2209
GlaxoSmithKline	2194
DaimlerChrysler	2179

Source: Advertising Age, **www.adage.com/.**

GLOBAL PERSPECTIVE 11.2

The World's Top 10 Brand Names

Here are the world's top 10 brands, based on four criteria: the brand's market share within its category, the brand's world appeal across age groups and nationalities, the loyalty of customers to the brand, and the ability of the brand to "stretch" to products beyond the original product.

World's Top 10 Brands

Coca-Cola
Microsoft
IBM
General Electric
Intel
Nokia
Toyota
Disney
McDonald's
Mercedes-Benz

Source: Interbrand, **www.brandchannel.com/.** Data are for 2006.

Last *Word*

Oligopoly in the Beer Industry

The Beer Industry Was Once Populated by Hundreds of Firms and an Even Larger Number of Brands. But It Now Is an Oligopoly Dominated by a Handful of Producers.

The brewing industry has undergone profound changes since the Second World War that have increased the degree of concentration in the industry. In 1947 more than 400 independent brewing companies existed in the United States. By 1967 there were 124, and by 1980 only 33. While the five largest brewers sold only 19 percent of the nation's beer in 1947, the Big Four brewers (Anheuser-Busch, SABMiller, Coors, and Pabst) currently sell 84 percent of the nation's beer. The Big Two—Anheuser-Busch (at 49 percent) and Miller (at 20 percent) —produce 69 percent. The industry is clearly an oligopoly.

Changes on the demand side of the market have contributed to the "shakeout" of small brewers from the industry. First, consumer tastes have generally shifted from the stronger-flavored beers of the small brewers to the light products of the larger brewers. Second, there has been a shift from the consumption of beer in taverns to consumption of it in the home. The beer consumed in taverns was mainly "draft" or "tap" beer from kegs, supplied by local and regional brewers that could deliver the kegs in a timely fashion at relatively low transportation cost. But the large increase in the demand for beer consumed at home opened the door for large brewers that sold their beer in bottles and aluminum cans. The large brewers could ship their beer by truck or rail over long distances and compete directly with the local brewers.

Developments on the supply side of the market have been even more profound. Technological advances speeded up the bottling and canning lines. Today, large brewers can fill and close 2000 cans per line per minute. Large plants are also able to reduce labor costs through the automating of brewing and warehousing. Furthermore, plant construction costs per barrel are about one-third less for a 4.5-million-barrel plant than for a 1.5-million-barrel plant. As a consequence of these and other factors, the minimum efficient scale in brewing is a plant size of about 4.5 million barrels, with multiple plants. Because the construction cost of a modern brewery of that size averages about $300 million, economies of scale may now constitute a significant barrier to entry.

"Blindfold" taste tests confirm that most mass-produced American beers taste alike. So brewers greatly emphasize advertising. And here Anheuser-Busch, SABMiller, and Coors, which sell national brands, enjoy major cost advantages over producers such as Pabst that have many regional brands (for example, Lonestar, Rainer, Schaefer, and Schmidts). The reason is that national television advertising is less costly *per viewer* than local spot TV advertising.

Although mergers have occurred in the brewing industry, they have not been a fundamental cause of the rising concentration. Rather, they largely have been the result of failing smaller breweries' (such as Heileman's) selling out. Dominant firms have expanded by heavily advertising their main brands and by creating new brands such as Lite, Bud Light, Genuine Draft, Keystone, and Icehouse rather than acquiring other brewers. This has sustained significant product differentiation, despite the declining number of major brewers.

progress. By increasing output, advertising can reduce long-run average total cost by enabling firms to obtain economies of scale.

Potential Negative Effects of Advertising

Not all the effects of advertising are positive, of course. Much advertising is designed simply to manipulate or persuade consumers—that is, to alter their preferences in favor of the advertiser's product. A television commercial that indicates that a popular personality drinks a particular brand of soft drink—and therefore that you should too—conveys little or no information to consumers about price or quality. In addition, advertising is sometimes based on misleading and extravagant claims that confuse consumers rather than enlighten them. Indeed, in some cases advertising may well persuade consumers to pay high prices for much-acclaimed but inferior products, forgoing better but unadvertised products selling at lower prices. Example: *Consumer Reports* has found that heavily advertised premium motor oils and fancy additives provide no better engine performance and longevity than do cheaper brands.

Firms often establish substantial brand-name loyalty and thus achieve monopoly power via their advertising (see Global Perspective 11.2). As a consequence, they are able to increase their sales, expand their market shares, and enjoy greater profits. Larger profit permits still more advertising and further enlargement of the firm's market share and profit. In time, consumers may lose the

The rise of the Miller Brewing Company from the seventh- to the second-largest producer in the 1970s was due in large measure to advertising and product differentiation. When the Philip Morris Company acquired Miller in 1970, the new management made two big changes. First, it "repositioned" Miller High Life beer into that segment of the market where potential sales were the greatest. Sold previously as the "champagne of beers," High Life had appealed heavily to upper-income consumers and to occasional women beer drinkers. Miller's new television ads featured young blue-collar workers, who were inclined to be greater beer consumers. Second, Miller then developed its low-calorie Lite beer, which was extensively promoted with Philip Morris advertising dollars. Lite proved to be the most popular new product in the history of the beer industry. Miller later introduced its Genuine Draft beer, which found its place within the top 10 brands.

But the story of the last two decades has been not Miller but, rather, Anheuser-Busch (A-B), which has greatly expanded its market share. A-B now makes the nation's top two brands: Bud Light and Budweiser account for nearly half the beer sold in the United States. Part of A-B's success owes to the demise of regional competitors. But part also is the result of A-B's strategic prowess. It has constructed state-of-the-art breweries, created effective advertising campaigns, and forged strong relationships with regional distributors. Meanwhile, Miller's market share has declined slightly in recent years. In 2002 Philip Morris sold Miller to South African Breweries (SAB). SABMiller, as the firm is now called, has significantly redesigned Miller's labeling and marketing to enhance its appeal and to expand its presence overseas.

Imported beers such as Beck, Corona, and Guinness constitute about 9 percent of the market, with individual brands seeming to wax and wane in popularity. Some local or regional microbreweries such as Samuel Adams and Pyramid, which brew "craft" or specialty beers and charge super-premium prices, have slightly whittled into the sales of the major brewers. A-B and Miller have taken notice, responding with specialty brands of their own (for example, Red Wolf, Red Dog, Killarney's, and Icehouse) and bought stakes in microbrewers Redhook Ale and Celis. But despite their local success, microbreweries account for only about 3 percent of the beer consumed in the United States and pose less of a threat to the majors than do "trendy" imported beers.

Sources: Based on Kenneth G. Elzinga, "Beer," in Walter Adams and James Brock (eds.), *The Structure of American Industry*, 10th ed. (Upper Saddle River, N.J.: Prentice Hall, 2001), pp. 85–113; and Douglas F. Greer, "Beer: Causes of Structural Change," in Larry Duetsch (ed.), *Industry Studies*, 2d ed. (New York: M. E. Sharpe, 1998), pp. 28–64. Updated data and information are mainly from *Beer Marketer's Insights*, **www.beerinsights.com,** and the Association of Brewers, **www.beertown.com.**

advantages of competitive markets and face the disadvantages of monopolized markets. Moreover, new entrants to the industry need to incur large advertising costs in order to establish their products in the marketplace; thus, advertising costs may be a barrier to entry. **(Key Question 11)**

Advertising can also be self-canceling. The advertising campaign of one fast-food hamburger chain may be offset by equally costly campaigns waged by rivals, so each firm's demand actually remains unchanged. Few, if any, extra burgers will be purchased, and each firm's market share will stay the same. But because of the advertising, the cost and hence the price of hamburgers will be higher.

When advertising either leads to increased monopoly power or is self-canceling, economic inefficiency results.

Oligopoly and Efficiency

Is oligopoly, then, an efficient market structure from society's standpoint? How do the price and output decisions of the oligopolist measure up to the triple equality P = MC = minimum ATC that occurs in pure competition?

Productive and Allocative Efficiency

Many economists believe that the outcome of some oligopolistic markets is approximately as shown in Figure 11.5. This view is bolstered by evidence that many oligopolists sustain sizable economic profits year after year. In that case, the oligopolist's production occurs where price exceeds marginal cost and average total cost. Moreover, production is below the output at which average total cost is minimized. In this view, neither productive efficiency (P = minimum ATC) nor allocative efficiency (P = MC) is likely to occur under oligopoly.

A few observers assert that oligopoly is actually less desirable than pure monopoly, because government usually regulates pure monopoly in the United States to guard against abuses of monopoly power. Informal collusion among oligopolists may yield price and output results similar to those under pure monopoly yet give the outward appearance of competition involving independent firms.

Qualifications

We should note, however, three qualifications to this view:

- ***Increased foreign competition*** In recent decades foreign competition has increased rivalry in a number of oligopolistic industries—steel, automobiles, photographic film, electric shavers, outboard motors, and copy machines, for example. This has helped to break down such cozy arrangements as price leadership and to stimulate much more competitive pricing.
- ***Limit pricing*** Recall that some oligopolists may purposely keep prices below the short-run profit-maximizing level in order to bolster entry barriers. In essence, consumers and society may get some of the benefits of competition—prices closer to marginal cost and minimum average total cost—even without the competition that free entry would provide.
- ***Technological advance*** Over time, oligopolistic industries may foster more rapid product development and greater improvement of production techniques than would be possible if they were purely competitive. Oligopolists have large economic profits from which they can fund expensive research and development (R&D). Moreover, the existence of barriers to entry may give the oligopolist some assurance that it will reap the rewards of successful R&D. Thus, the short-run economic inefficiencies of oligopolists may be partly or wholly offset by the oligopolists' contributions to better products, lower prices, and lower costs over time. We will have more to say about these more dynamic aspects of rivalry in Chapter 12.

Summary

1. The distinguishing features of monopolistic competition are (a) there are enough firms in the industry to ensure that each firm has only limited control over price, mutual interdependence is absent, and collusion is nearly impossible; (b) products are characterized by real or perceived differences so that economic rivalry entails both price and nonprice competition; and (c) entry to the industry is relatively easy. Many aspects of retailing, and some manufacturing industries in which economies of scale are few, approximate monopolistic competition.
2. Monopolistically competitive firms may earn economic profits or incur losses in the short run. The easy entry and exit of firms result in only normal profits in the long run.
3. The long-run equilibrium position of the monopolistically competitive producer is less efficient than that of the pure competitor. Under monopolistic competition, price exceeds marginal cost, suggesting an underallocation of resources to the product, and price exceeds minimum average total cost, indicating that consumers do not get the product at the lowest price that cost conditions might allow.
4. Nonprice competition provides a way that monopolistically competitive firms can offset the long-run tendency for economic profit to fall to zero. Through product differentiation, product development, and advertising, a firm may strive to increase the demand for its product more than enough to cover the added cost of such nonprice competition. Consumers benefit from the wide diversity of product choice that monopolistic competition provides.
5. In practice, the monopolistic competitor seeks the specific combination of price, product, and advertising that will maximize profit.
6. Oligopolistic industries are characterized by the presence of few firms, each having a significant fraction of the market. Firms thus situated engage in strategic behavior and are mutually interdependent: The behavior of any one firm directly affects, and is affected by, the actions of rivals. Products may be either virtually uniform or significantly differentiated. Various barriers to entry, including economies of scale, underlie and maintain oligopoly.
7. High concentration ratios are an indication of oligopoly (monopoly) power. By giving more weight to larger firms, the Herfindahl index is designed to measure market dominance in an industry.
8. Game theory (a) shows the interdependence of oligopolists' pricing policies, (b) reveals the tendency of oligopolists to collude, and (c) explains the temptation of oligopolists to cheat on collusive arrangements.

9. Noncollusive oligopolists may face a kinked-demand curve. This curve and the accompanying marginal-revenue curve help explain the price rigidity that often characterizes oligopolies; they do not, however, explain how the actual prices of products were first established.
10. The uncertainties inherent in oligopoly promote collusion. Collusive oligopolists such as cartels maximize joint profits—that is, they behave like pure monopolists. Demand and cost differences, a "large" number of firms, cheating through secret price concessions, recessions, and the antitrust laws are all obstacles to collusive oligopoly.
11. Price leadership is an informal means of collusion whereby one firm, usually the largest or most efficient, initiates price changes and the other firms in the industry follow the leader.
12. Market shares in oligopolistic industries are usually determined on the basis of product development and advertising. Oligopolists emphasize nonprice competition because (a) advertising and product variations are less easy for rivals to match and (b) oligopolists frequently have ample resources to finance nonprice competition.
13. Advertising may affect prices, competition, and efficiency either positively or negatively. Positive: It can provide consumers with low-cost information about competing products, help introduce new competing products into concentrated industries, and generally reduce monopoly power and its attendant inefficiencies. Negative: It can promote monopoly power via persuasion and the creation of entry barriers. Moreover, it can be self-canceling when engaged in by rivals; then it boosts costs and creates inefficiency while accomplishing little else.
14. Neither productive nor allocative efficiency is realized in oligopolistic markets, but oligopoly may be superior to pure competition in promoting research and development and technological progress.
15. Table 9.1, page 166, provides a concise review of the characteristics of monopolistic competition and oligopoly as they compare to those of pure competition and pure monopoly.

Terms and Concepts

monopolistic competition
product differentiation
nonprice competition
excess capacity
oligopoly
homogeneous oligopoly
differentiated oligopoly
strategic behavior
mutual interdependence
concentration ratio
interindustry competition
import competition
Herfindahl index
game-theory model
collusion
kinked-demand curve
price war
cartel
tacit understandings
price leadership

Study Questions

1. How does monopolistic competition differ from pure competition in its basic characteristics? From pure monopoly? Explain fully what product differentiation may involve. Explain how the entry of firms into its industry affects the demand curve facing a monopolistic competitor and how that, in turn, affects its economic profit.
2. **KEY QUESTION** Compare the elasticity of the monopolistic competitor's demand with that of a pure competitor and a pure monopolist. Assuming identical long-run costs, compare graphically the prices and outputs that would result in the long run under pure competition and under monopolistic competition. Contrast the two market structures in terms of productive and allocative efficiency. Explain: "Monopolistically competitive industries are characterized by too many firms, each of which produces too little."
3. "Monopolistic competition is monopolistic up to the point at which consumers become willing to buy close-substitute products and competitive beyond that point." Explain.
4. "Competition in quality and service may be just as effective as price competition in giving buyers more for their money." Do you agree? Why? Explain why monopolistically competitive firms frequently prefer nonprice competition to price competition.
5. Critically evaluate and explain:
   a. In monopolistically competitive industries economic profits are competed away in the long run; hence, there is no valid reason to criticize the performance and efficiency of such industries.
   b. In the long run, monopolistic competition leads to a monopolistic price but not to monopolistic profits.
6. Why do oligopolies exist? List five or six oligopolists whose products you own or regularly purchase. What distinguishes oligopoly from monopolistic competition?
7. **KEY QUESTION** Answer the following questions, which relate to measures of concentration:
   a. What is the meaning of a four-firm concentration ratio of 60 percent? 90 percent? What are the shortcomings of concentration ratios as measures of monopoly power?
   b. Suppose that the five firms in industry A have annual sales of 30, 30, 20, 10, and 10 percent of total industry

sales. For the five firms in industry B the figures are 60, 25, 5, 5, and 5 percent. Calculate the Herfindahl index for each industry and compare their likely competitiveness.

8. **KEY QUESTION** Explain the general meaning of the following profit payoff matrix for oligopolists C and D. All profit figures are in thousands.

D's possible prices \ C's possible prices	$40	$35
$40	$57 / $60	$59 / $55
$35	$50 / $69	$55 / $58

   a. Use the payoff matrix to explain the mutual interdependence that characterizes oligopolistic industries.
   b. Assuming no collusion between C and D, what is the likely pricing outcome?
   c. In view of your answer to 8*b*, explain why price collusion is mutually profitable. Why might there be a temptation to cheat on the collusive agreement?

9. **KEY QUESTION** What assumptions about a rival's response to price changes underlie the kinked-demand curve for oligopolists? Why is there a gap in the oligopolist's marginal-revenue curve? How does the kinked-demand curve explain price rigidity in oligopoly? What are the shortcomings of the kinked-demand model?

10. Why might price collusion occur in oligopolistic industries? Assess the economic desirability of collusive pricing. What are the main obstacles to collusion? Speculate as to why price leadership is legal in the United States, whereas price fixing is not.

11. **KEY QUESTION** Why is there so much advertising in monopolistic competition and oligopoly? How does such advertising help consumers and promote efficiency? Why might it be excessive at times?

12. **ADVANCED ANALYSIS** Construct a game-theory matrix involving two firms and their decisions on high versus low advertising budgets and the effects of each on profits. Show a circumstance in which both firms select high advertising budgets even though both would be more profitable with low advertising budgets. Why won't they unilaterally cut their advertising budgets?

13. **LAST WORD** What firm dominates the U.S. beer industry? What demand and supply factors have contributed to "fewness" in this industry?

Web-Based Questions:

1. **BOOKSELLING ON THE INTERNET—HOW DO SELLERS DIFFERENTIATE IDENTICAL BOOKS?** Use a search engine to find the current listings on the *New York Times* best-seller lists. Choose one hardbound book of fiction and one hardbound book of nonfiction from the top-five lists. Next, find the price, including shipping to your address, of your two books at both Amazon, **www.amazon.com,** and Barnes and Noble, **www.barnesandnoble.com.** Is one company less expensive? Identify the nonprice competition that might lead you to order from one company rather than the other.

2. **MARKET SHARES—TOP-10 LISTS** *Advertising Age*, at **www.adage.com,** compiles statistics on the market shares of some familiar products. Go to "Data Center" and then download the latest Fact Pack. Select the top-5, top-7, or top-10 lists for five separate nonmedia products. In general, do the very top sellers in your lists advertise more or less than the sellers toward the bottom of the lists? Are there exceptions? Do you think the top-10 lists would get turned upside down if the pattern of advertising were turned upside down? Why or why not?

IN THIS CHAPTER YOU WILL LEARN:

- The differences between an invention, an innovation, and technological diffusion.
- How entrepreneurs and other innovators further technological advance.
- How a firm determines its optimal amount of research and development (R&D).
- Why firms can benefit from their innovation even though rivals have an incentive to imitate it.
- About the role of market structure in promoting technological advance.
- How technological advance enhances productive and allocative efficiency.

12

Technology, R&D, and Efficiency

- "Just do it!" In 1968 two entrepreneurs from Oregon developed a lightweight sport shoe and formed a new company called Nike, incorporating a "swoosh" logo (designed by a graduate student for $35). Today, Nike sells more than $14 billion worth of goods annually.
- "Intel inside." In 1967 neither Intel nor its product existed. Today it is the world's largest producer of microprocessors for personal computers, with about $39 billion of annual sales.
- "Always low prices. Always." Expanding from a single store in 1962 to more than 6000 stores worldwide today, Wal-Mart's annual revenue ($316 billion) exceeds that of General Motors or IBM.

Nike, Intel, and Wal-Mart owe much of their success to **technological advance,** broadly defined as new and better goods and services or new and better ways of producing or distributing them. Nike and Intel pioneered innovative new products, and Wal-Mart developed creative ways to manage inventories and distribute goods.

Multiply these examples—perhaps on a smaller scale—by thousands in the economy! The pursuit of technological advance is a major competitive activity among firms. In this chapter, we examine some of the microeconomics of that activity.

Invention, Innovation, and Diffusion

For economists, technological advance occurs over a theoretical time period called the *very long run*, which can be as short as a few months or as long as many years. Recall that in our four market models (pure competition, monopolistic competition, oligopoly, and pure monopoly), the short run is a period in which technology and plant and equipment are fixed. In the long run, technology is constant but firms can change their plant sizes and are free to enter or exit industries. In contrast, the **very long run** is a period in which technology can change and in which firms can develop and offer entirely new products.

In Chapter 1 we saw that technological advance shifts an economy's production possibilities curve outward, enabling the economy to obtain more goods and services. Technological advance is a three-step process of invention, innovation, and diffusion.

Invention

The basis of technological advance is **invention:** the discovery of a product or process through the use of imagination, ingenious thinking, and experimentation and the first proof that it will work. Invention is a process, and the result of the process is also called an invention. The prototypes (basic working model) of the telephone, the automobile, and the microchip are inventions. Invention usually is based on scientific knowledge and is the product of individuals, either working on their own or as members of corporate R&D staffs. Later on you will see how governments encourage invention by providing the inventor with a **patent,** an exclusive right to sell any new and useful process, machine, or product for a set period of time. In 2005 the seven firms that secured the most U.S. patents were IBM (2941), Canon (1828), Hewlett-Packard (1797), Matsushita (1688), Samsung (1641), Micron (1561), and Intel (1549). Patents have a worldwide duration of 20 years from the time of application for the patent.

Innovation

Innovation draws directly on invention. While invention is the "discovery and first proof of workability," **innovation** is the first successful commercial introduction of a new product, the first use of a new method, or the creation of a new form of business enterprise. Innovation is of two types: **product innovation,** which refers to new and improved products or services; and **process innovation,** which refers to new and improved methods of production or distribution.

Unlike inventions, innovations cannot be patented. Nevertheless, innovation is a major factor in competition, since it sometimes enables a firm to "leapfrog" competitors by rendering their products or processes obsolete. For example, personal computers coupled with software for word processing pushed some major typewriter manufacturers into obscurity. More recently, innovations in hardware retailing (large warehouse stores such as Home Depot) have threatened the existence of smaller, more traditional hardware stores.

But innovation need not weaken or destroy existing firms. Aware that new products and processes may threaten their survival, existing firms have a powerful incentive to engage continuously in R&D of their own. Innovative products and processes often enable such firms to maintain or increase their profit. The aluminum cans introduced by Reynolds, disposable contact lenses by Johnson & Johnson, and scientific calculators by Hewlett-Packard are good examples. Thus, innovation can either diminish or strengthen market power.

Diffusion

Diffusion is the spread of an innovation through imitation or copying. To take advantage of new profit opportunities or to slow the erosion of profit, both new and existing firms emulate the successful innovations of others. Years ago, Alamo greatly increased its auto rentals by offering customers unlimited mileage, and Hertz, Avis, Budget, and others eventually followed. DaimlerChrysler profitably introduced a luxury version of its Jeep Grand Cherokee; other manufacturers, including Acura, Mercedes, and Lexus, countered with luxury sport-utility vehicles of their own. In 1996 Palm introduced its Palm Pilot, a palm-size personal computer. Microsoft, Handspring, OmniSky, and other firms soon brought out similar products. In each of these cases, innovation led eventually to widespread imitation—that is, to diffusion.

R&D Expenditures

As related to *businesses*, the term "research and development" is used loosely to include direct efforts toward invention, innovation, and diffusion. However, *government* also engages in R&D, particularly R&D having to do with national defense. In 2004 *total* U.S. R&D expenditures (business *plus* government) were $312 billion. Relative to GDP that amount was 2.66 percent, which is a reasonable measure of the emphasis the U.S. economy puts on technological advance. As shown in Global Perspective 12.1, this is a high percentage of GDP compared to several other nations.

American businesses spent $200 billion on R&D in 2004. Figure 12.1 shows how these R&D expenditures were allocated. Observe that U.S. firms collectively channeled 77 percent of their R&D expenditures to "development" (innovation and imitation, the route to diffusion). They spent another 19 percent on applied research, or on pursuing invention. For reasons we will mention later, only 4 percent of business R&D expenditures went for basic research, the search for general scientific principles. Of course, industries, and firms within industries, vary greatly in the amount of emphasis they place on these three processes.

FIGURE 12.1 The composition of business R&D outlays in the United States, 2004. Firms channel the bulk of their R&D spending to innovation and imitation, because both have direct commercial value; less to applied research, that is, invention; and a relatively small amount to basic scientific research.

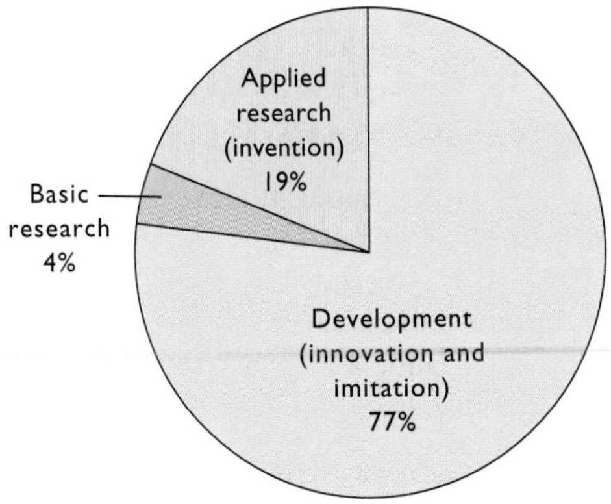

Source: National Science Foundation, **www.nsf.gov/.**

GLOBAL PERSPECTIVE 12.1

Total R&D Expenditures as a Percentage of GDP, Selected Nations

Relative R&D spending varies among leading industrial nations. From a microeconomic perspective, R&D helps promote economic efficiency; from a macroeconomic perspective, R&D helps promote economic growth.

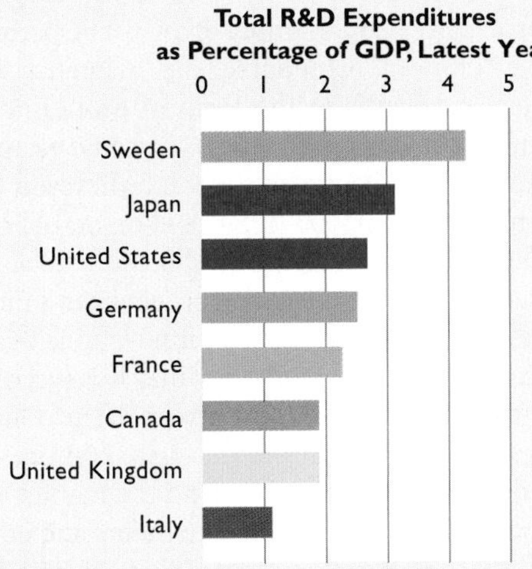

Source: National Science Foundation, **www.nsf.gov/.**

Modern View of Technological Advance

For decades most economists regarded technological advance as being external to the economy—a random outside force to which the economy adjusted. From time to time fortuitous advances in scientific and technological knowledge occurred, paving the way for major new products (automobiles, airplanes) and new production processes (assembly lines). Firms and industries, each at its own pace, then incorporated the new technology into their products or processes to enhance or maintain their profit. Then, after making the appropriate adjustments, they settled back into new long-run equilibrium positions. Although technological advance has been vitally important to the economy, economists believed it was rooted in the independent advance of science, which is largely external to the market system.

Most contemporary economists have a different view. They see capitalism itself as the driving force of technological advance. In their view, invention, innovation, and diffusion occur in response to incentives within the economy, meaning that technological advance is *internal* to capitalism. Specifically, technological advance arises from intense rivalry among individuals and firms that motivates them to seek and exploit new profit opportunities or to expand existing opportunities. That rivalry occurs both among existing firms and between existing firms and new firms. Moreover, many advances in "pure" scientific knowledge are motivated, at least in part, by the prospect of commercial applicability and eventual profit. In the modern view, entrepreneurs and other innovators are at the heart of technological advance.

Role of Entrepreneurs and Other Innovators

It will be helpful to distinguish between "entrepreneurs" and "other innovators":

- ***Entrepreneurs*** Recall that the entrepreneur is an initiator, innovator, and risk bearer—the resource that combines land, labor, and capital resources in new and unique ways to produce new goods and services. In the past a single individual, for example, Andrew Carnegie in steel, Henry Ford in automobiles, or Levi Strauss in blue jeans, carried out the entrepreneurial role. Such advances as air conditioning, the ballpoint pen, cellophane, the jet engine, insulin, xerography, and the helicopter all have an individualistic heritage. But in today's more technologically complex economy, entrepreneurship is just as likely to be carried out by entrepreneurial teams. Such teams may include only two or three people working "as their own bosses" on some new product idea or it may consist of larger groups of entrepreneurs who have pooled their financial resources.
- ***Other innovators*** This designation includes other key people involved in the pursuit of innovation who do not bear personal financial risk. Among them are key executives, scientists, and other salaried employees engaged in commercial R&D activities. (They are sometimes referred to as *intrapreneurs*, since they provide the spirit of entrepreneurship within existing firms.)

Forming Start-Ups

Entrepreneurs often form small new companies called **start-ups** that focus on creating and introducing a new product or employing a new production or distribution technique. Two people, working out of their garages, formed such a start-up in the mid-1970s. Since neither of their employers—Hewlett-Packard and Atari, the developer of Pong (the first video game)—was interested in their prototype personal computer, they founded their own company: Apple Computers. Other examples of successful start-ups are Amgen, a biotechnology firm specializing in new medical treatments; Starbucks, a seller of gourmet coffee; and Amazon, an Internet retailer.

Innovating within Existing Firms

Innovators are also at work within existing corporations, large and small. Such innovators are salaried workers, although many firms have pay systems that provide them with substantial bonuses or shares of the profit. Examples of firms known for their skillful internal innovators are 3M Corporation, the U.S. developer of Scotch tape, Post-it Note Pads, and Thinsulate insulation; and Canon, the Japanese developer of the "laser engine" for personal copiers and printers. R&D work in major corporations has produced significant technological improvements in such products as television sets, telephones, home appliances, automobiles, automobile tires, and sporting equipment.

Some large firms, aware that excessive bureaucracy can stifle creative thinking and technological advance, have separated part of their R&D and manufacturing divisions to form new, more flexible, innovative firms. Three significant examples of such "spin-off firms" are Lucent Technologies, a telephone equipment and R&D firm created by AT&T; Imation, a high-technology firm spun off by the 3M Corporation; and Palm, a maker of handheld computers, spun off by 3Com.

Anticipating the Future

Some 50 years ago a writer for *Popular Mechanics* magazine boldly predicted, "Computers in the future may weigh no more than 1.5 tons." Today's notebook computers weigh less than 3 pounds.

It is difficult to anticipate the future, but that is what innovators try to do. Those with strong anticipatory ability and determination have a knack for introducing new and improved products or services at just the right time.

The rewards for success are both monetary and nonmonetary. Product innovation and development are creative endeavors, with such intangible rewards as personal satisfaction. Also, many people simply enjoy participating in the competitive "contest." Of course, the "winners" can reap huge monetary rewards in the form of economic profits, stock appreciation, or large bonuses. Extreme examples are Bill Gates and Paul Allen, who founded Microsoft in 1975, and had a net worth in 2005 of $51 billion and $23 billion, respectively, mainly in the form of Microsoft stock.

Past successes often give entrepreneurs and innovative firms access to resources for further innovations that anticipate consumer wants. Although they may not succeed a second time, the market tends to entrust the production of goods and services to businesses that have consistently succeeded in filling consumer wants. And the market does not care whether these "winning" entrepreneurs and innovative firms are American, Brazilian, Japanese, German, or Swiss. Entrepreneurship and innovation are global in scope.

Exploiting University and Government Scientific Research

In Figure 12.1 we saw that only 4 percent of business R&D spending in the United States goes to basic scientific research. The reason the percentage is so small is that scientific principles, as such, cannot be patented, nor do they usually have immediate commercial uses. Yet new scientific knowledge is highly important to technological advance. For that reason, entrepreneurs study the scientific output of university and government laboratories to identify discoveries with commercial applicability.

Government and university labs have been the scene of many technological breakthroughs, including hybrid seed corn, nuclear energy, satellite communications, the computer "mouse," genetic engineering, and the Internet. Entire high-tech industries such as computers and biotechnology have their roots in major research universities and government laboratories. And nations with strong scientific communities tend to have the most technologically progressive firms and industries.

Also, firms increasingly help fund university research that relates to their products. Business funding of R&D at universities has grown rapidly, rising to more than $2.2 billion in 2005. Today, the separation between university scientists and innovators is narrowing; scientists and universities increasingly realize that their work may have commercial value and are teaming up with innovators to share in the potential profit.

A few firms, of course, find it profitable to conduct basic scientific research on their own. New scientific knowledge can give them a head start in creating an invention or a new product. This is particularly true in the pharmaceutical industry, where it is not uncommon for firms to parlay new scientific knowledge generated in their corporate labs into new, patentable drugs.

QUICK REVIEW 12.1

- Broadly defined, technological advance means new or improved products and services and new or improved production and distribution processes.
- Invention is the *discovery* of a new product or method; innovation is the *successful commercial application* of some invention; and diffusion is the *widespread adoption* of the innovation.
- Many economists view technological advance as mainly a response to profit opportunities arising within a capitalist economy.
- Technological advance is fostered by entrepreneurs and other innovators and is supported by the scientific research of universities and government-sponsored laboratories.

A Firm's Optimal Amount of R&D

How does a firm decide on its optimal amount of research and development? That amount depends on the firm's perception of the marginal benefit and marginal cost of R&D activity. The decision rule here flows from basic economics: to earn the greatest profit, expand a particular activity until its marginal benefit (MB) equals its marginal cost (MC). A firm that sees the marginal benefit of a particular R&D activity, say, innovation, as exceeding the marginal cost should expand that activity. In contrast, an activity whose marginal benefit promises to be less than its marginal cost should be cut back. But the R&D spending decision is complex, since it involves a present sacrifice for a future expected gain. While the cost of R&D is immediate, the expected benefits occur at some future time and are highly uncertain. So estimating those benefits is often more art than science. Nevertheless, the MB = MC way of thinking remains relevant for analyzing R&D decisions.

Interest-Rate Cost of Funds

Firms have several ways of obtaining the funds they need to finance R&D activities:

- ***Bank loans*** Some firms are able to obtain a loan from a bank or other financial institution. Then the cost of using the funds is the interest paid to the lender. The marginal cost is the cost per extra dollar borrowed, which is simply the market interest rate for borrowed funds.
- ***Bonds*** Established, profitable firms may be able to borrow funds for R&D by issuing bonds and selling them in the bond market. In this case, the cost is the interest paid to the lenders—the bondholders. Again the marginal cost of using the funds is the interest rate. (We discussed corporate bonds in Chapter 4.)
- ***Retained earnings*** A large, well-established firm may be able to draw on its own corporate savings to finance R&D. Typically, such a firm retains part of its profit rather than paying it all out as dividends to corporate owners. Some of the undistributed corporate profit, called *retained earnings*, can be used to finance R&D activity. The marginal cost is the rate at which those funds could have earned interest as deposits in a financial institution.
- ***Venture capital*** A smaller start-up firm might be able to attract venture capital to finance its R&D projects. Venture capital is financial capital, or simply

money, not real capital. **Venture capital** consists of that part of household saving used to finance high-risk business ventures in exchange for shares of the profit if the ventures succeed. The marginal cost of venture capital is the share of expected profit that the firm will have to pay to those who provided the money. This can be stated as a percentage of the venture capital, so it is essentially an interest rate.

- ***Personal savings*** Finally, individual entrepreneurs might draw on their own savings to finance the R&D for a new venture. The marginal cost of the financing is again the forgone interest rate.

Thus, whatever the source of the R&D funds, we can state the marginal cost of these funds as an interest rate *i*. For simplicity, let's assume that this interest rate is the same no matter how much financing is required. Further, we assume that a certain firm called MedTech must pay an interest rate of 8 percent, the least expensive funding available to it. Then a graph of the marginal cost of each funding amount for this firm is a horizontal line at the 8 percent interest rate, as shown in Figure 12.2. Such a graph is called an **interest-rate cost-of-funds curve.** This one tells us that MedTech can borrow $10, $10,000, $10,000,000, or more at the 8 percent interest rate. The table accompanying the graph contains the data used to construct the graph and tells us much the same thing.

With these data in hand, MedTech wants to determine how much R&D to finance in the coming year.

FIGURE 12.2 The interest-rate cost-of-funds schedule and curve. As it relates to R&D, a firm's interest-rate cost-of-funds schedule (the table) and curve (the graph) show the interest rate the firm must pay to obtain any particular amount of funds to finance R&D. Curve *i* indicates the firm can finance as little or as much R&D as it wants at a constant 8 percent rate of interest.

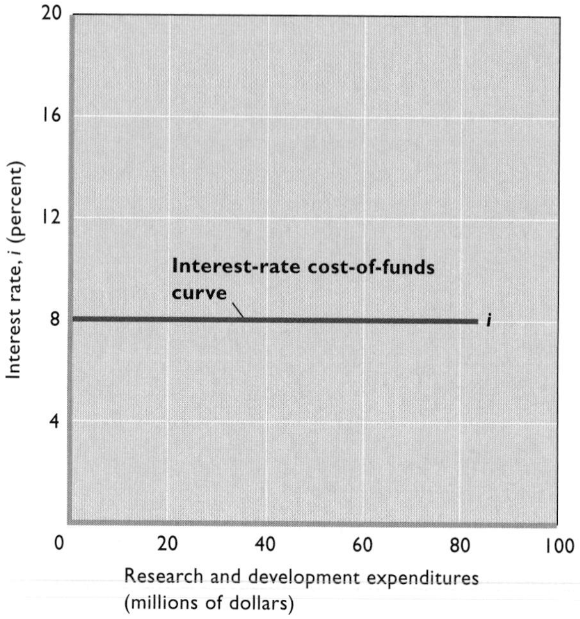

R&D, Millions	Interest-Rate Cost of Funds, %
$10	8
20	8
30	8
40	8
50	8
60	8
70	8
80	8

Expected Rate of Return

A firm's marginal benefit from R&D is its expected profit (or return) from the last (marginal) dollar spent on R&D. That is, the R&D is expected to result in a new product or production method that will increase revenue, reduce production costs, or both (in ways we will soon explain). This return is expected, not certain—there is risk in R&D decisions. Let's suppose that after considering such risks, MedTech anticipates that an R&D expenditure of $1 million will result in a new product that will yield a one-time added profit of $1.2 million a year later. The expected rate of return *r* on the $1 million R&D expenditure (after the $1 million has been repaid) is 20 percent (= $200,000/$1,000,000). This is the marginal benefit of the first $1 million of R&D. (Stretching the return over several years complicates the computation of *r*, but it does not alter the basic analysis.)

MedTech can use this same method to estimate the expected rates of return for R&D expenditures of $2 million, $3 million, $4 million, and so on. Suppose those marginal rates of return are the ones indicated in the table in Figure 12.3, where they are also graphed as the **expected-rate-of-return curve.** This curve shows the expected rate of return, which is the marginal benefit of each dollar of expenditure on R&D. The curve slopes downward because of diminishing returns to R&D expenditures. A firm will direct its initial R&D expenditures to the highest expected-rate-of-return activities and then use additional funding for activities with successively lower expected rates of return. That is, as the firm increases R&D spending, it uses it to finance R&D activities with lower and lower expected rates of return.

FIGURE 12.3 The expected-rate-of-return schedule and curve. As they relate to R&D, a firm's expected-rate-of-return schedule (the table) and curve (the graph) show the firm's expected gain in profit, as a percentage of R&D spending, for each level of R&D spending. Curve *r* slopes downward because the firm assesses its potential R&D projects in descending order of expected rates of return.

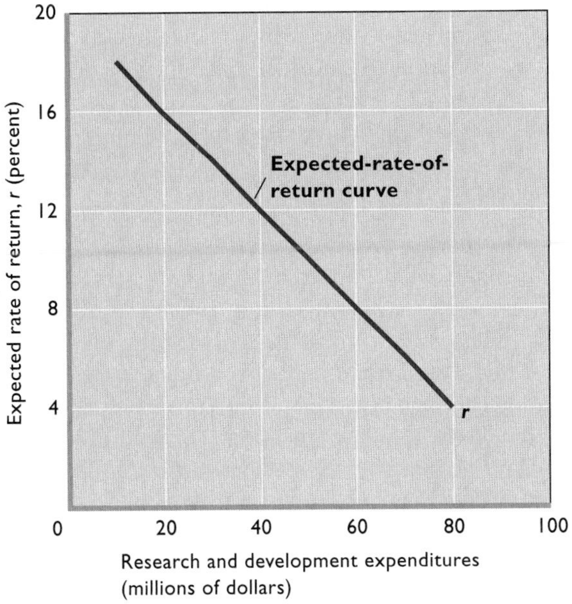

R&D, Millions	Expected Rate of Return, %
$10	18
20	16
30	14
40	12
50	10
60	8
70	6
80	4

FIGURE 12.4 A firm's optimal level of R&D expenditures. The firm's optimal level of R&D expenditures ($60 million) occurs where its expected rate of return equals the interest-rate cost of funds, as shown in both the table and the graph. At $60 million of R&D spending, the firm has taken advantage of all R&D opportunities for which the expected rate of return, *r*, exceeds or equals the 8 percent interest cost of borrowing, *i*.

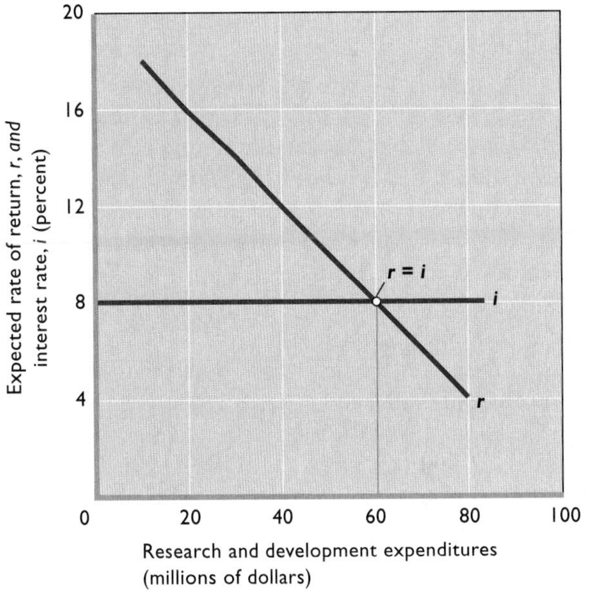

Expected Rate of Return, %	R&D, Millions	Interest-Rate Cost of Funds, %
18	$10	8
16	20	8
14	30	8
12	40	8
10	50	8
8	***60***	***8***
6	70	8
4	80	8

Optimal R&D Expenditures

Figure 12.4 combines the interest-rate cost-of-funds curve (Figure 12.2) and the expected-rate-of-return curve (Figure 12.3). The curves intersect at MedTech's **optimal amount of R&D**, which is $60 million. This amount can also be determined from the table as the amount of funding for which the expected rate of return and the interest cost of borrowing are equal (here, 8 percent).

Both the curve and the table in Figure 12.4 tell us that at $60 million of R&D expenditures, the marginal benefit and marginal cost of the last dollar spent on R&D are equal. MedTech should undertake all R&D expenditures up to $60 million, since those outlays yield a higher marginal benefit or expected rate of return, *r*, than the 8 percent marginal cost or interest-rate cost of borrowing, *i*. But it should not undertake R&D expenditures beyond $60 million; for these outlays, *r* (marginal benefit) is less than *i* (marginal cost). Only at $60 million do we have $r = i$, telling us that MedTech will spend $60 million on R&D.

W 12.1
Optimal R&D expenditures

Our analysis reinforces three important points:

- ***Optimal versus affordable R&D*** From earlier discussions we know there can be too much, as well as too little, of a "good thing." So it is with R&D and technological advance. Figure 12.4 shows that R&D expenditures make sense to a firm only as long as the expected return from the outlay equals or exceeds the cost of obtaining the funds needed to finance it. Many R&D expenditures may be affordable but not worthwhile because their marginal benefit is likely to be less than their marginal cost.

- ***Expected, not guaranteed, returns*** The outcomes from R&D are expected, not guaranteed. With 20-20 hindsight, a firm can always look back and decide whether a particular expenditure for R&D was worthwhile. But that assessment is irrelevant to the original decision. At the time of the decision, the expenditure was thought to be worthwhile on the basis of existing information and expectations. Some R&D decisions may be more like an informed gamble than the typical business decision. Invention and innovation, in particular, carry with them a great deal of risk. For every successful outcome, there are scores of costly disappointments.
- ***Adjustments*** Firms adjust their R&D expenditures when expected rates of return on various projects change (when curves such as *r* in Figure 12.4 shift). The U.S. war on terrorism, for example, increased the expected rate of return on R&D for improved security devices used at airports, train stations, harbors, and other public places. It also increased the expected return on new methods of detecting and responding to potential bioterrorism. The revised realities prompted many firms to increase their R&D expenditures for these purposes. **(Key Questions 4 and 5)**

Increased Profit via Innovation

In discussing how a firm determines its optimal amount of R&D spending, we sidestepped the question of how technological change can increase a firm's profit. Although the answer may seem obvious—by increasing revenue or reducing production costs—insights can be gained by exploring these two potential outcomes in some detail.

Increased Revenue via Product Innovation

Firms here and abroad have profitably introduced hundreds of new products in the past two or three decades. Examples include roller blades, microwave popcorn, cordless drills, digital cameras, camcorders, and projection TVs. Other new products are snowboards, cellular phones, telephone pagers, and automobile air bags. All these items reflect technological advance in the form of product innovation.

How do such new products gain consumer acceptance? As you know from Chapter 7, to maximize their satisfaction, consumers purchase products that have the highest marginal utility per dollar. They determine which products to buy in view of their limited money incomes by comparing the ratios of MU/price for the various goods. They first select the unit of the good with the highest MU/price ratio, then the one with the next highest, and so on, until their incomes are used up.

The first five columns of Table 12.1 repeat some of the information in Table 7.1. Before the introduction of new product C, the consumer maximized total utility from $10 of income by buying 2 units of A at $1 per unit and 4 units of B at $2 per unit. The total $10 budget was thus expended, with $2 spent on A and $8 on B. As shown in columns 2b and 3b, the marginal utility per dollar spent on

TABLE 12.1 Utility Maximization with the Introduction of a New Product (Income = $10)*

	(2) Product A: Price = $1		(3) Product B: Price = $2		(4) New Product C: Price = $4	
(1) Unit of Product	(a) Marginal Utility, Utils	(b) Marginal Utility per Dollar (MU/Price)	(a) Marginal Utility, Utils	(b) Marginal Utility per Dollar (MU/Price)	(a) Marginal Utility, Utils	(b) Marginal Utility per Dollar (MU/Price)
First	10	10	24	<u>*12*</u>	52	13
Second	8	***8***	20	10	48	<u>*12*</u>
Third	7	7	18	9	44	11
Fourth	6	6	16	***8***	36	9
Fifth	5	5	12	6	32	8

*It is assumed in this table that the amount of marginal utility received from additional units of each of the three products is independent of the quantity purchased of the other products. For example, the marginal-utility schedule for product C is independent of the amount of A and B purchased by the consumer.

the last unit of each product was 8 (= 8/\$1 = 16/\$2). The total utility, derived from columns 2a and 3a, was 96 utils (= 10 + 8 from the first 2 units of A plus 24 + 20 + 18 + 16 from the first 4 units of B). (If you are uncertain about this outcome, please review the discussion of Table 7.1.)

Now suppose an innovative firm offers new product C (columns 4a and 4b in Table 12.1), priced at \$4 per unit. Note that the first unit of C has a higher marginal utility per dollar (13) than any unit of A and B and that the second unit of C and the first unit of B have equal MU/price ratios of 12. To maximize satisfaction, the consumer now buys 2 units of C at \$4 per unit, 1 unit of B at \$2 per unit, and zero units of A. Our consumer has spent the entire \$10 of income (\$8 on C and \$2 on B), and the MU/price ratios of the last units of B and C are equal at 12. But as determined via columns 3a and 4a, the consumer's total utility is now 124 utils (= 24 from the first unit of B plus 52 + 48 from the first 2 units of C).

Total utility has increased by 28 utils (= 124 utils − 96 utils), and that is why product C was purchased. Consumers will buy a new product only if it increases the total utility they obtain from their limited incomes.

From the innovating firm's perspective, these "dollar votes" represent new product demand that yields increased revenue. When per-unit revenue exceeds per-unit cost, the product innovation creates per-unit profit. Total profit rises by the per-unit profit multiplied by the number of units sold. As a percentage of the original R&D expenditure, the rise in total profit is the return on that R&D expenditure. It was the basis for the expected-rate-of-return curve r in Figure 12.4.

Other related points:

- ***Importance of price*** Consumer acceptance of a new product depends on both its marginal utility and its price. (Confirm that the consumer represented in Table 12.1 would buy zero units of new product C if its price were \$8 rather than \$4.) To be successful, a new product must not only deliver utility to consumers but do so at an acceptable price.
- ***Unsuccessful new products*** For every successful new product, hundreds do not succeed; the expected return that motivates product innovation is not always realized. Examples of colossal product flops are Ford's Edsel automobile, 3-D movies, quadraphonic stereo, New Coke by Coca-Cola, Kodak disc cameras, and XFL football. Less dramatic failures include the hundreds of "dot-com" firms that have recently gone out of business. In each case, millions of dollars of R&D and promotion expense ultimately resulted in loss, not profit.
- ***Product improvements*** Most product innovation consists of incremental improvements to existing products rather than radical inventions. Examples: more fuel-efficient automobile engines, new varieties of pizza, lighter-weight shafts for golf clubs, more flavorful bubble-gum, "rock shocks" for mountain bikes, and clothing made of wrinkle-free fabrics. **(Key Question 6)**

Reduced Cost via Process Innovation

The introduction of better methods of producing products—process innovation—is also a path toward enhanced profit and a positive return on R&D expenditures. Suppose a firm introduces a new and better production process, say, assembling its product by teams rather than by a standard assembly line. Alternatively, suppose this firm replaces old equipment with more productive equipment embodying technological advance. In either case, the innovation yields an upward shift in the firm's total-product curve from TP_1 to TP_2 in Figure 12.5a. Now more units of output can be produced at each level of resource usage. Note from the figure, for example, that this firm can now produce 2500 units of output, rather than 2000 units, when using 1000 units of labor. So its average product has increased from 2 (= 2000 units of output/1000 units of labor) to 2.5 (= 2500 units of output/1000 units of labor).

The result is a downward shift in the firm's average-total-cost curve, from ATC_1 to ATC_2 in Figure 12.5b. To understand why, let's assume this firm pays \$1000 for the use of its capital and \$9 for each unit of labor. Since it uses 1000 units of labor, its labor cost is \$9000 (= \$9 × 1000); its capital cost is \$1000; and thus its total cost is \$10,000. When its output increases from 2000 to 2500 units as a result of the process innovation, its total cost remains \$10,000. So its average total cost declines from \$5 (= \$10,000/2000) to \$4 (= \$10,000/2500). Alternatively, the firm could produce the original 2000 units of output with fewer units of labor at an even lower average total cost.

This reduction in average total cost enhances the firm's profit. As a percentage of the R&D expenditure that fostered it, this extra profit is the expected return r, the basis for the rate-of-return curve in Figure 12.3. In this case, the expected rate of return arose from the prospect of lower production costs through process innovation.

W 12.2
Process innovation

Example: Computer-based inventory control systems, such as those pioneered by Wal-Mart, enabled innovators to reduce the number of people keeping track of inventories and placing reorders of sold goods. They also enabled firms to keep

FIGURE 12.5 Process innovation, total product, and average total cost. (a) Process innovation shifts a firm's total-product curve upward from TP_1 to TP_2, meaning that with a given amount of capital the firm can produce more output at each level of labor input. As shown, with 1000 units of labor it can produce 2500 rather than 2000 units of output. (b) The upward shift in the total-product curve results in a downward shift in the firm's average-total-cost curve, from ATC_1 to ATC_2. This means the firm can produce any particular unit of output at a lower average total cost than it could previously. For example, the original 2000 units can be produced at less than \$4 per unit, versus \$5 per unit originally. Or 2500 units can now be produced at \$4 per unit.

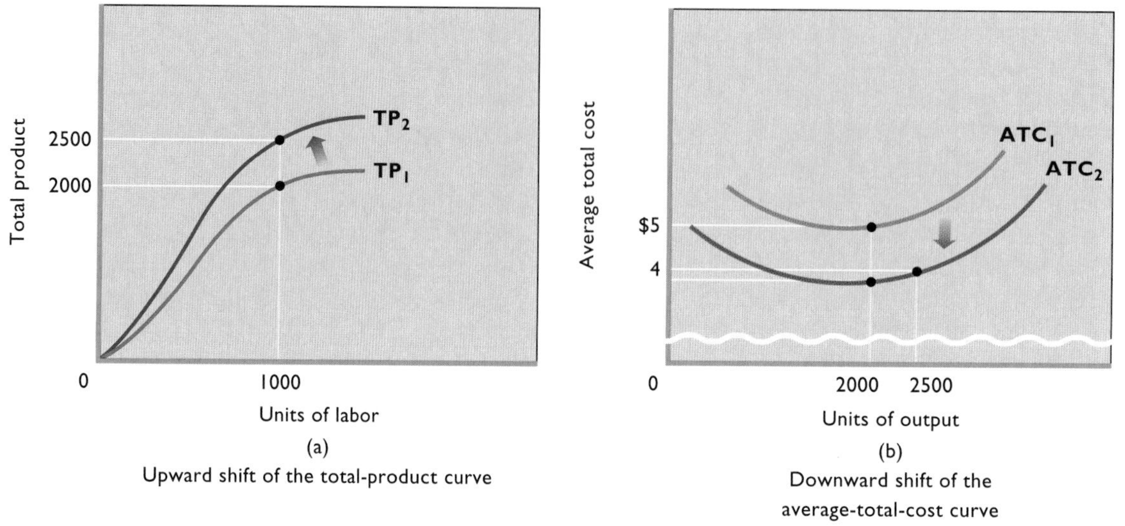

goods arriving "just in time," reducing the cost of storing inventories. The consequence? Significant increases in sales per worker, declines in average total cost, and increased profit. **(Key Question 8)**

Imitation and R&D Incentives

Our analysis of product and process innovation explains how technological advance enhances a firm's profit. But it also hints at a potential **imitation problem:** A firm's rivals may be able to imitate its new product or process, greatly reducing the originator's profit from its R&D effort. As just one example, in the 1980s U.S. auto firms took apart Japanese Honda Accords, piece by piece, to discover the secrets of their high quality. This reverse engineering—which ironically was perfected earlier by the Japanese—helped the U.S. firms incorporate innovative features into their own cars. This type of imitation is perfectly legitimate and fully anticipated; it is often the main path to widespread diffusion of an innovation.

In fact, a dominant firm that is making large profits from its existing products may let smaller firms in the industry incur the high costs of product innovation while it closely monitors their successes and failures. The dominant firm then moves quickly to imitate any successful new product; its goal is to become the second firm to embrace the innovation. In using this so-called **fast-second strategy,** the dominant firm counts on its own product-improvement abilities, marketing prowess, or economies of scale to prevail.

Examples abound: Royal Crown introduced the first diet cola, but Diet Coke and Diet Pepsi dominate diet-cola sales today. Meister-Brau introduced the first low-calorie beer, but Miller popularized the product with its Miller Lite. Gillette moved quickly with its own stainless-steel razor blade only after a smaller firm, Wilkinson, introduced this product innovation. Creative Technology (the maker of Sound Blaster audio cards for personal computers) introduced the first miniature MP3 player, but Apple Computer popularized the product with its iPod.

Benefits of Being First

Imitation and the fast-second strategy raise an important question: What incentive is there for any firm to bear the expenses and risks of innovation if competitors can imitate its new or improved product? Why not let others bear the costs and risks of product development and then just imitate the successful innovations? Although we have seen that this may be a plausible strategy in some situations, there are several protections for, and potential advantages to, taking the lead.

Patents Some technological breakthroughs, specifically inventions, can be patented. Once patented, they cannot be legally imitated for two decades from time of patent application. The purpose of patents is, in fact, to reduce imitation and its negative effect on the incentive for engaging in R&D. Example: Polaroid's patent of its instant camera enabled it to earn high economic profits for many years. When Kodak "cloned" the camera, Polaroid won a patent-infringement lawsuit against its rival. Kodak not only had to stop producing its version of the camera but had to buy back the Kodak instant cameras it had sold and pay millions of dollars in damages to Polaroid.

There are hundreds of other examples of long-run profits based on U.S. patents; they involve products from prescription drugs to pop-top cans to weed trimmers. As shown in Global Perspective 12.2, foreign citizens and firms hold U.S. patents along with American citizens and firms.

Copyrights and Trademarks *Copyrights* protect publishers of books, computer software, movies, videos, and musical compositions from having their works copied. *Trademarks* give the original innovators of products the exclusive right to use a particular product name ("M&Ms," "Barbie Doll," "Wheaties"). By reducing the problem of direct copying, these legal protections increase the incentive for product innovation. They have been strengthened worldwide through recent international trade agreements.

Brand-Name Recognition Along with trademark protection, brand-name recognition may give the original innovator a major marketing advantage for years or even decades. Consumers often identify a new product with the firm that first introduced and popularized it in the mass market. Examples: Levi's blue jeans, Kleenex soft tissues, Johnson and Johnson's Band-Aids, Sony's Walkman, and Kellogg's Corn Flakes.

Trade Secrets and Learning by Doing Some innovations involve trade secrets, without which competitors cannot imitate the product or process. Example: Coca-Cola has successfully kept its formula for Coke a secret from potential rivals. Many other firms have perfected special production techniques known only to them. In a related advantage, a firm's head start with a new product often allows it to achieve substantial cost reductions through learning by doing. The innovator's lower cost may enable it to continue to profit even after imitators have entered the market.

Time Lags Time lags between innovation and diffusion often enable innovating firms to realize a substantial economic profit. It takes time for an imitator to gain knowledge of the properties of a new innovation. And once it has that knowledge, the imitator must design a substitute product, gear up a factory for its production, and conduct a marketing campaign. Various entry barriers, such as large financial requirements, economies of scale, and price-cutting, may extend the time lag between innovation and imitation. In practice, it may take years or even decades before rival firms can successfully imitate a profitable new product and cut into the market share of the innovator. In the meantime, the innovator continues to profit.

Profitable Buyouts A final advantage of being first arises from the possibility of a buyout (outright purchase) of the innovating firm by a larger firm. Here, the innovative entrepreneurs take their rewards immediately, as cash or as shares in the purchasing firm, rather than waiting for perhaps uncertain long-run profits from their own production and marketing efforts.

Examples: Once the popularity of cellular communications became evident, AT&T bought out McCaw Communications, an early leader in this new technology. When Minnetonka's Softsoap became a huge success, it sold its product to Colgate-Palmolive. More recently, Swiss conglomerate Nestlé bought out Chef America, the highly successful maker of Hot Pockets frozen meat-and-cheese sandwiches. Such buyouts are legal under current antitrust laws as long as they do not substantially lessen competition in the affected industry. For this to be the case, there must be other strong competitors in the market. That was not true, for example, when Microsoft tried to buy out Intuit (maker of Quicken, the best-selling financial software). That buyout was disallowed because Intuit and Microsoft

GLOBAL PERSPECTIVE 12.2

Distribution of U.S. Patents, by Foreign Nation

Foreign citizens, corporations, and governments hold 45 percent of U.S. patents. The top 10 foreign countries in terms of U.S. patent holdings are listed below, with the number of U.S. patents (through 2004) in parentheses.

Top 10 Foreign Countries

Japan (574,865)
Germany (221,120)
France (84,902)
U. K. (83,991)
Canada (63,944)
Taiwan (57,605)
Italy (36,883)
Switzerland (36,802)
South Korea (35,673)
Sweden (29,696)

Source: U.S. Patent and Trademark Office, **www.uspto.gov.**

CONSIDER THIS . . .

Trade Secrets

Trade secrets have long played an important role in maintaining returns from research and development (R&D). Long before Coca-Cola's secret formula or Colonel Sanders' secret herbs and spices, the Roman citizen Erasmo (c. A.D. 130) had a secret ingredient for violin strings.* As the demand for his new product grew, he falsely identified his strings as *catgut*, when they were actually made of sheep intestines. Why the deception? At the time, it was considered to be extremely bad luck to kill a cat. By identifying his strings as catgut, he hoped that nobody would imitate his product and reduce his monopoly profit. Moreover, his product name would help him preserve his valuable trade secret.

*We discovered this anecdote in Dennis W. Carleton and Jeffrey Perloff, *Modern Industrial Organization,* 2d ed. (New York: HarperCollins, 1994), p. 139. Their source, in turn, was L. Boyd, *San Francisco Chronicle,* October 27, 1984, p. 35.

were the two main suppliers of financial software for personal computers.

In short, despite the imitation problem, significant protections and advantages enable most innovating firms to profit from their R&D efforts, as implied by the continuing high levels of R&D spending by firms year after year. As shown in Figure 12.6, business R&D spending in the United States not only remains substantial but has grown over the past quarter-century. The high levels of spending simply would not continue if imitation consistently and severely depressed rates of return on R&D expenditures.

QUICK REVIEW 12.2

- A firm's optimal R&D expenditure is the amount at which the expected rate of return (marginal benefit) from the R&D expenditure just equals the interest-rate cost of borrowing (marginal cost) required to finance it.
- Product innovation can entice consumers to substitute a new product for existing products to increase their total utility, thereby increasing the innovating firm's revenue and profit.
- Process innovation can lower a firm's production costs and increase its profit by increasing total product and decreasing average total cost.
- A firm faces reduced profitability from R&D if competitors can successfully imitate its new product or process. Nevertheless, there are significant potential protections and benefits to being first, including patents, copyrights, and trademarks; brand-name recognition; trade secrets; cost reductions from learning by doing; and major time lags between innovation and imitation.

Role of Market Structure

In view of our discussion of market structures in the last three chapters, asking whether some particular market structure or firm size is best suited to technological progress is logical. Is a highly competitive industry

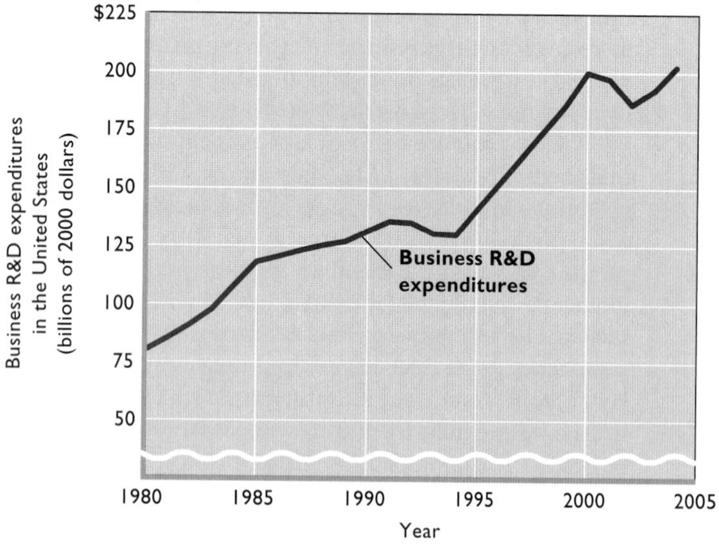

FIGURE 12.6 The growth of business R&D expenditures in the United States, 1980–2005. Inflation-adjusted R&D expenditures by firms are substantial and growing, suggesting that R&D continues to be profitable for firms, even in the face of possible imitation.

Source: National Science Foundation, **www.nsf.gov/.**

consisting of thousands of relatively small firms preferable to an industry comprising only two or three large firms? Or is some intermediate structure best?

Market Structure and Technological Advance

As a first step toward answering these questions, we survey the strengths and shortcomings of our four market models as related to technological advance.

Pure Competition Does a pure competitor have a strong incentive and strong ability to undertake R&D? On the positive side, strong competition provides a reason for such firms to innovate; competitive firms tend to be less complacent than monopolists. If a pure competitor does not seize the initiative, one or more rivals may introduce a new product or cost-reducing production technique that could drive it from the market. As a matter of short-term profit and long-term survival, the pure competitor is under continual pressure to improve products and lower costs through innovation. Also, where there are many competing firms, there is less chance that an idea for improving a product or process will be overlooked by a single firm.

On the negative side, the expected rate of return on R&D may be low or even negative for a pure competitor. Because of easy entry, its profit rewards from innovation may quickly be competed away by existing or entering firms that also produce the new product or adopt the new technology. Also, the small size of competitive firms and the fact that they earn only a normal profit in the long run lead to serious questions as to whether they can finance substantial R&D programs. Observers have noted that the high rate of technological advance in the purely competitive agricultural industry, for example, has come not from the R&D of individual farmers but from government-sponsored research and from the development of fertilizers, hybrid seed, and farm implements by oligopolistic firms.

Monopolistic Competition Like pure competitors, monopolistic competitors cannot afford to be complacent. But unlike pure competitors, which sell standardized products, monopolistic competitors have a strong profit incentive to engage in product innovation. This incentive to differentiate products from those of competitors stems from the fact that sufficiently novel products may create monopoly power and thus economic profit. There are many examples of innovative firms (McDonald's, Blockbuster Video, Starbuck's Coffee Company) that started out as monopolistic competitors in localized markets but soon gained considerable national market power, with the attendant economic profit.

For the typical firm, however, the shortcomings of monopolistic competition in relation to technological advance are the same as those of pure competition. Most monopolistic competitors remain small, which limits their ability to secure inexpensive financing for R&D. In addition, monopolistic competitors find it difficult to extract large profits from technological advances. Any economic profits from innovation are usually temporary, because entry to monopolistically competitive industries is relatively easy. In the long run, new entrants with similar goods reduce the demand for the innovator's product, leaving the innovator with only a normal profit. Monopolistic competitors therefore usually have relatively low expected rates of return on R&D expenditures.

Oligopoly Many of the characteristics of oligopoly are conducive to technological advance. First, the large size of oligopolists enables them to finance the often large R&D costs associated with major product or process innovation. In particular, the typical oligopolist realizes ongoing economic profits, a part of which is retained. This undistributed profit serves as a major source of readily available, relatively low-cost funding for R&D. Moreover, the existence of barriers to entry gives the oligopolist some assurance that it can maintain any economic profit it gains from innovation. Then, too, the large sales volume of the oligopolist enables it to spread the cost of specialized R&D equipment and teams of specialized researchers over a great many units of output. Finally, the broad scope of R&D activity within oligopolistic firms helps them offset the inevitable R&D "misses" with more-than-compensating R&D "hits." Thus, oligopolists clearly have the means and incentive to innovate.

But there is also a negative side to R&D in oligopoly. In many instances, the oligopolist's incentive to innovate may be far less than we have implied above, because oligopoly tends to breed complacency. An oligopolist may reason that introducing costly new technology and producing new products makes little sense when it currently is earning a sizable economic profit without them. The oligopolist wants to maximize its profit by exploiting fully all its capital assets. Why rush to develop a new product (say, batteries for electric automobiles) when that product's success will render obsolete much of the firm's current equipment designed to produce its existing product (say, gasoline engines)? It is not difficult to cite oligopolistic industries in which the largest firms' interest in R&D has been quite modest. Examples: the steel, cigarette, and aluminum industries.

Pure Monopoly In general, the pure monopolist has little incentive to engage in R&D; it maintains its high profit through entry barriers that, in theory, are complete. The only incentive for the pure monopolist to engage in R&D is defensive: to reduce the risk of being blindsided by some new product or production process that destroys its monopoly. If such a product is out there to be discovered, the monopolist may have an incentive to find it. By so doing, it can either exploit the new product or process for continued monopoly profit or suppress the product until the monopolist has extracted the maximum profit from its current capital assets. But, in general, economists agree that pure monopoly is the market structure least conducive to innovation.

Inverted-U Theory

Analysis like this has led some experts on technological progress to postulate a so-called **inverted-U theory** of the relationship between market structure and technological advance. This theory is illustrated in Figure 12.7, which relates R&D spending as a percentage of a firm's sales (vertical axis) to the industry's four-firm concentration ratio (horizontal axis). The "inverted-U" shape of the curve suggests that R&D effort is at best weak in both very low concentration industries (pure competition) and very high concentration industries (pure monopoly). Starting from the lowest concentrations, R&D spending as a percentage of sales rises with concentration until a concentration ratio of 50 percent or so is reached, meaning that the four largest firms account for about one-half the total industry output. Beyond that, relative R&D spending decreases as concentration rises.

The logic of the inverted-U theory follows from our discussion. Firms in industries with very low concentration ratios are mainly competitive firms. They are small, and this makes it difficult for them to finance R&D. Moreover, entry to these industries is easy, making it difficult to sustain economic profit from innovations that are not supported by patents. As a result, firms in these industries spend little on R&D relative to their sales. At the other end (far right) of the curve, where concentration is exceptionally high, monopoly profit is already high and innovation will not add much more profit. Furthermore, innovation typically requires costly retooling of very large factories, which will cut into whatever additional profit is realized. As a result, the expected rate of return from R&D is quite low, as are expenditures for R&D relative to sales. Finally, the lack of rivals makes the monopolist quite complacent about R&D.

The optimal industry structure for R&D is one in which expected returns on R&D spending are high and funds to finance it are readily available and inexpensive. From our discussion, those factors seem to occur in industries where a few firms are absolutely and relatively large but where the concentration ratio is not so high as to prohibit vigorous competition by smaller rivals. Rivalry among the larger oligopolistic firms and competition between the larger and the smaller firms then provide a strong incentive for R&D. The inverted-U theory, as represented by Figure 12.7, also points toward this "loose" oligopoly as the optimal structure for R&D spending.

FIGURE 12.7 The inverted-U theory of R&D expenditures. The inverted-U theory suggests that R&D expenditures as a percentage of sales rise with industry concentration until the four-firm concentration ratio reaches about 50 percent. Further increases in industry concentration are associated with lower relative R&D expenditures.

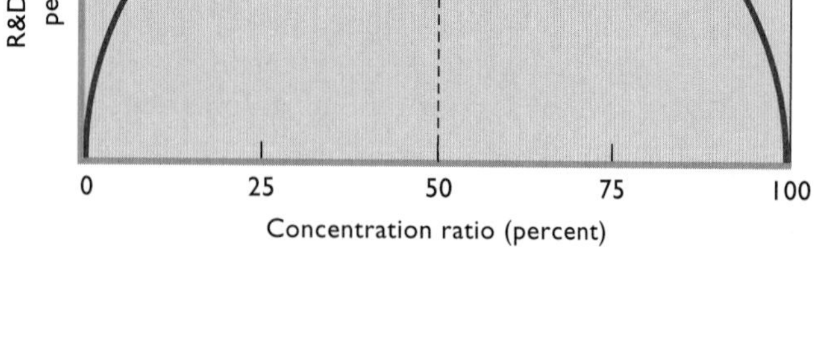

Market Structure and Technological Advance: The Evidence

Dozens of industry studies have tried to pin down the relationship between market structure and technological advance. Because those studies dealt with different industries and time periods, and used different methodologies, they are not easy to compare and summarize. Nevertheless, they provide general support for the inverted-U theory.[1] Other things equal, the optimal market structure for technological advance seems to be an industry in which there is a mix of large oligopolistic firms (a 40 to 60 percent concentration ratio), with several highly innovative smaller firms.

But our "other-things-equal" qualification is quite important here. Whether or not a particular industry is

[1]Douglas F. Greer, *Industrial Organization and Public Policy*, 3d ed. (New York: Macmillan, 1992), pp. 680–687.

highly technical may well be a more important determinant of R&D than its structure. While some concentrated industries (electronics, aircraft, and petroleum) devote large quantities of resources to R&D and are very innovative, others (cigarettes, aluminum, gypsum products) are not. The level of R&D spending within an industry seems to depend as much on its technical character and "technological opportunities" as on its market structure. There simply may be more opportunities to innovate in the computer and pharmaceutical industries, for example, than in the brick-making and coal-mining industries.

Conclusion: The inverted-U curve shown in Figure 12.7 is a useful depiction of the general relationship between R&D spending and market structure, other things equal.

Technological Advance and Efficiency

Technological advance contributes significantly to economic efficiency. New and better processes and products enable society to produce more output, as well as a higher-valued mix of output.

Productive Efficiency

Technological advance as embodied in process innovation improves *productive efficiency* by increasing the productivity of inputs (as indicated in Figure 12.5a) and by reducing average total costs (as in Figure 12.5b). In other words, it enables society to produce the same amount of a particular good or service while using fewer scarce resources, thereby freeing the unused resources to produce other goods and services. Or if society desires more of the now less expensive good, process innovation enables it to have that greater quantity without sacrificing other goods. Viewed either way, process innovation enhances productive efficiency: It reduces society's per-unit cost of whatever mix of goods and services it chooses. It thus is an important means of shifting an economy's production possibilities curve rightward.

Allocative Efficiency

Technological advance as embodied in *product* (or service) innovation enhances allocative efficiency by giving society a more preferred mix of goods and services. Recall from our earlier discussion that consumers buy a new product rather than an old product only when buying the new one increases the total utility obtained from their limited incomes. Obviously, then, the new product—and the new mix of products it implies—creates a higher level of total utility for society.

In terms of markets, the demand for the new product rises and the demand for the old product declines. The high economic profit engendered by the new product attracts resources away from less valued uses and to the production of the new product. In theory, such shifting of resources continues until the price of the new product equals its marginal cost.

There is a caveat here, however. Innovation (either product or process) can create monopoly power through patents or through the many advantages of being first. When new monopoly power results from an innovation, society may lose part of the improved efficiency it otherwise would have gained from that innovation. The reason is that the profit-maximizing monopolist restricts output to keep its product price above marginal cost. For example, Microsoft's innovative Windows product has resulted in dominance in the market for Intel-compatible operating systems for personal computers. Microsoft's substantial monopoly power permits it to charge prices that are well above marginal cost and minimum average total cost.

Creative Destruction

Although innovation can create monopoly power, it also can reduce or eliminate it. By creating competition where it previously was weak, innovation can push prices down toward marginal cost. For example, Intel's microprocessor enabled personal computers, and their ease of production eventually diminished IBM's monopoly power in the sale of computer hardware. More recently, Linux's new computer operating system has provided some promising competition for Microsoft Windows.

At the extreme, innovation may cause **creative destruction,** where the creation of new products and new production methods simultaneously destroys the monopoly market positions of firms committed to existing products and old ways of doing business. As stated many years ago by Joseph Schumpeter, who championed this view:

> In capitalist reality . . . it is . . . competition from the new commodity, the new technology, the new source of supply, the new type of business organization—competition which commands a decisive cost or quality advantage and which strikes not at the margins of profits of the existing firms but at their foundation and their very lives. This kind of competition is . . . so . . . important that it becomes a matter of comparative indifference whether competition in the ordinary sense functions more or less promptly; the powerful lever that in the [very] long run expands output and brings down prices is in any case made of other stuff.[2]

[2]Joseph A. Schumpeter, *Capitalism, Socialism, and Democracy*, 3d ed. (New York: Harper & Row, 1950), pp. 84–85.

Last Word

On the Path to the Personal Computer and Internet

Technological Advance Is Clearly Evident in the Development of the Modern Personal Computer and the Emergence of the Internet. Here Is a Brief History of Those Events.

1945 Grace Murray Hopper finds a dead moth between relay contacts in the experimental Mark II computer at Harvard University. Whenever the computer subsequently malfunctions, workers set out to "debug" the device.

1946 ENIAC is revealed. A precursor to the modern-day computer, it relies on 18,000 vacuum tubes and fills 3000 cubic feet of space.

1947 AT&T scientists invent the "transfer resistance device," later known as the transistor. It replaces the less reliable vacuum tubes in computers.

1961 Bob Noyce (who later founded Intel Corporation) and Jack Kilby invent the first integrated circuit, which miniaturizes electronic circuitry onto a single silicon chip.

1964 IBM introduces the System/360 computer. Configured as a system, it takes up nearly the same space as two tennis courts.

1965 Digital Equipment Corporation unveils its PDP-8, the first relatively small-size computer (a "minicomputer").

1969 A networking system called ARPANET is born; it is the beginning of the Internet.

1971 Intel introduces its 4004 processor (a "microprocessor"). The $200 chip is the size of a thumbnail and has as much computing capability as the earlier ENIAC.

1975 Xerox markets Alto, the first personal computer (a "microcomputer"). Bill Gates and Paul Allen found Microsoft. MITS Corporation's Altair 8800 arrives on the scene. It contains Intel's 8080 microprocessor that Intel developed a year earlier to control traffic lights.

1977 Apple II, Commodore's PET, and Tandy Radio Shack TRS-80 go on sale, setting the stage for the personal computer revolution.

1981 IBM enters the market with its personal computer powered by the Intel 8800 chip and operated by the Microsoft Disc Operating System (MS-DOS). Osborne Computer markets the Osborne 1, the first self-contained microcomputer, but within 2 years the firm declares bankruptcy. Logitech commercializes the "X-Y Position Indicator for a Display System," invented earlier by Douglas Engelbart in a government-funded research lab. Someone dubs it a "computer mouse" because it appears to have a tail.

1982 Compaq Computer "clones" the IBM machines; others do the same. Eventually Compaq becomes one of the leading sellers of personal computers.

1984 Apple introduces its Macintosh computer, with its "user-friendly" icons, attached mouse, and preloaded software. College student Michael Dell founds Dell Computers, which builds personal computers and sells them through mail order. IBM, Sears Roebuck, and

There are many examples of creative destruction: In the 1800s wagons, ships, and barges were the only means of transporting freight until the railroads broke up their monopoly; the dominant market position of the railroads was, in turn, undermined by trucks and, later, by airplanes. Movies brought new competition to live theater, at one time the "only show in town," but movies were later challenged by television. Vinyl long-playing records supplanted acetate 78-rpm phonograph records; cassettes then challenged LP records; and compact discs undermined cassettes. Now Internet music-recording technology such as MP3 threaten sales of traditional CDs. Aluminum cans and plastic bottles have displaced glass bottles in many uses. E-mail has challenged the postal service. Mass discounters such as Wal-Mart and Costco have gained market share at the expense of Sears and Montgomery Ward.

O 12.1
Creative destruction

According to Schumpeter, an innovator will automatically displace any monopolist that no longer delivers superior performance. But many contemporary economists think this notion reflects more wishful thinking than fact. In this view, the idea that creative destruction is automatic

> . . . neglects the ability of powerful established firms to erect private storm shelters—or lobby government to build public storm shelters for them—in order to shield themselves from the Schumpeterian gales of creative destruction. It

CBS team up to launch Prodigy Services, the first online computer business.

1985 Microsoft releases its Windows graphical interface operating system that improves upon MS-DOS. Ted Waitt starts a mail-order personal computer business (Gateway 2000) out of his South Dakota barn.

1990 Microsoft introduces Windows 3.0, which, like Macintosh, features windows, icons, and pull-down menus. Apple sues Microsoft for copyright infringement.

1991 The World Wide Web (an Internet system) is invented.

1993 Intel introduces its first of several Pentium chips, which greatly speed up computing. The courts reject Apple's claim that Microsoft violated its copyrights on its Macintosh operating system.

1994 Marc Andreessen starts up Netscape Communications and markets Netscape Navigator, which quickly becomes the leading software browser for the emerging Internet. David Filo and Jerry Yang develop Yahoo, a system for locating material stored on the Internet.

1995 Microsoft releases the Windows 95 operating system, which becomes the dominant operating system of personal computers (90 percent market share). Microsoft is now well established as the world's leading software producer. Sun Microsystems introduces Java, an Internet programming language.

1996 Playing catch-up with Netscape, Microsoft develops Microsoft Internet Explorer and gives it away free.

1999 Netscape's market share plunges and it merges with America Online. More than 100 million personal computers are manufactured worldwide this year alone.

2000 Sixty percent of American households have access to the Internet either at home or at work, and the Internet spreads worldwide. Internet commerce in the United States reaches $300 billion, and an estimated 1.2 million U.S. jobs are Internet-related.

2002 A Federal court of appeals finds that Microsoft has a monopoly in operating system software for Intel-compatible personal computers and has maintained its monopoly through illegal actions aimed at thwarting threats from rivals. The court imposes a set of specific restrictions on Microsoft's anticompetitive business practices.

2005 Google, the innovative Internet search company, becomes the "darling" of Wall Street as its share price rises from $85 at its initial public offering (IPO) in August 2004 to more than $400 at the end of 2005.

Source: Based partly on Diedtra Henderson, "Moore's Law Still Reigns," *Seattle Times*, Nov. 24, 1996, augmented and updated.

ignores the difference between the legal freedom of entry and the economic reality deterring the entry of potential newcomers into concentrated industries.[3]

That is, some dominant firms may be able to use strategies such as selective price cutting, buyouts, and massive advertising to block entry and competition from even the most innovative new firms and existing rivals. Moreover, rent-seeking dominant firms have been known to persuade government to give them tax breaks, subsidies, and tariff protection that strengthen their market power.

In short, while innovation in general enhances economic efficiency, in some cases it may lead to entrenched monopoly power. Further innovation may eventually destroy that monopoly power, but the process of creative destruction is neither automatic nor inevitable. On the other hand, rapid technological change, innovation, and efficiency clearly are not necessarily inconsistent with possession of monopoly power.

[3]Walter Adams and James Brock, *The Structure of American Industry*, 10th ed. (Upper Saddle River, N.J.: Prentice Hall, 2001), pp. 363–364.

Summary

1. Technological advance is evidenced by new and improved goods and services and new and improved production or distribution processes. In economists' models, technological advance occurs only in the *very long run*.
2. Invention is the discovery of a product or process through the use of imagination, ingenuity, and experimentation. Innovation is the first successful commercial introduction of a new product, the first use of a new method, or the creation of a new form of business enterprise. Diffusion is the spread of an earlier innovation among competing firms. Firms channel a majority of their R&D expenditures to innovation and imitation, rather than to basic scientific research and invention.
3. Historically, most economists viewed technological advance as a random, external force to which the economy adjusted. Many contemporary economists see technological advance as occurring in response to profit incentives within the economy and thus as an integral part of capitalism.
4. Entrepreneurs and other innovators try to anticipate the future. They play a central role in technological advance by initiating changes in products and processes. Entrepreneurs often form start-up firms that focus on creating and introducing new products. Sometimes, innovators work in the R&D labs of major corporations. Entrepreneurs and innovative firms often rely heavily on the basic research done by university and government scientists.
5. A firm's optimal amount of R&D spending occurs where its expected return (marginal benefit) from the R&D equals its interest-rate cost of funds (marginal cost) to finance the R&D. Entrepreneurs and firms use several sources to finance R&D, including (a) bank loans, (b) bonds, (c) venture capital (funds lent in return for a share of the profits if the business succeeds), (d) undistributed corporate profits (retained earnings), and (e) personal savings.
6. Product innovation, the introduction of new products, succeeds when it provides consumers with higher marginal utility per dollar spent than do existing products. The new product enables consumers to obtain greater total utility from a given income. From the firm's perspective, product innovation increases net revenue sufficiently to yield a positive rate of return on the R&D spending that produced the innovation.
7. Process innovation can lower a firm's production costs by improving its internal production techniques. Such improvement increases the firm's total product, thereby lowering its average total cost and increasing its profit. The added profit provides a positive rate of return on the R&D spending that produced the process innovation.
8. Imitation poses a potential problem for innovators, since it threatens their returns on R&D expenditures. Some dominant firms use a fast-second strategy, letting smaller firms initiate new products and then quickly imitating the successes. Nevertheless, there are significant protections and potential benefits for firms that take the lead with R&D and innovation, including (a) patent protection, (b) copyrights and trademarks, (c) lasting brand-name recognition, (d) benefits from trade secrets and learning by doing, (e) high economic profits during the time lag between a product's introduction and its imitation, and (f) the possibility of lucrative buyout offers from larger firms.
9. Each of the four basic market structures has potential strengths and weaknesses regarding the likelihood of R&D and innovation. The inverted-U theory holds that a firm's R&D spending as a percentage of its sales rises with its industry four-firm concentration ratio, reaches a peak at a 50 percent concentration ratio, and then declines as concentration increases further. Empirical evidence is not clear-cut but lends general support to this theory. For any specific industry, however, the technological opportunities that are available may count more than market structure in determining R&D spending and innovation.
10. In general, technological advance enhances both productive and allocative efficiency. But in some situations patents and the advantages of being first with an innovation can increase monopoly power. While in some cases creative destruction eventually destroys monopoly, most economists doubt that this process is either automatic or inevitable.

Terms and Concepts

technological advance
very long run
invention
patent
innovation
product innovation
process innovation
diffusion
start-ups
venture capital
interest-rate cost-of-funds curve
expected-rate-of-return curve
optimal amount of R&D
imitation problem
fast-second strategy
inverted-U theory of R&D
creative destruction

Study Questions

1. What is meant by technological advance, as broadly defined? How does technological advance enter into the definition of the very long run? Which of the following are examples of technological advance, and which are not: an improved production process; entry of a firm into a profitable purely competitive industry; the imitation of a new production process by another firm; an increase in a firm's advertising expenditures?
2. Listed below are several possible actions by firms. Write "INV" beside those that reflect invention, "INN" beside those that reflect innovation, and "DIF" beside those that reflect diffusion.
   a. An auto manufacturer adds "heated seats" as a standard feature in its luxury cars to keep pace with a rival firm whose luxury cars already have this feature.
   b. A television production company pioneers the first music video channel.
   c. A firm develops and patents a working model of a self-erasing whiteboard for classrooms.
   d. A lightbulb firm is the first to produce and market lighting fixtures with halogen lamps.
   e. A rival toy maker introduces a new Jenny doll to compete with Mattel's Barbie doll.
3. Contrast the older and the modern views of technological advance as they relate to the economy. What is the role of entrepreneurs and other innovators in technological advance? How does research by universities and government affect innovators and technological advance? Why do you think some university researchers are becoming more like entrepreneurs and less like "pure scientists"?
4. **KEY QUESTION** Suppose a firm expects that a $20 million expenditure on R&D will result in a new product that will increase its revenue by a total of $30 million 1 year from now. The firm estimates that the production cost of the new product will be $29 million.
   a. What is the expected rate of return on this R&D expenditure?
   b. Suppose the firm can get a bank loan at 6 percent interest to finance its $20 million R&D project. Will the firm undertake the project? Explain why or why not.
   c. Now suppose the interest-rate cost of borrowing, in effect, falls to 4 percent because the firm decides to use its own retained earnings to finance the R&D. Will this lower interest rate change the firm's R&D decision? Explain.
5. **KEY QUESTION** Answer the following lettered questions on the basis of the information in this table:

Amount of R&D, Millions	Expected Rate of Return on R&D, %
$10	16
20	14
30	12
40	10
50	8
60	6

   a. If the interest-rate cost of funds is 8 percent, what will be the optimal amount of R&D spending for this firm?
   b. Explain why $20 million of R&D spending will not be optimal.
   c. Why won't $60 million be optimal either?
6. **KEY QUESTION** Refer to Table 12.1 and suppose the price of new product C is $2 instead of $4. How does this affect the optimal combination of products A, B, and C for the person represented by the data? Explain: "The success of a new product depends not only on its marginal utility but also on its price."
7. Learning how to use software takes time. So once customers have learned to use a particular software package, it is easier to sell them software upgrades than to convince them to switch to new software. What implications does this have for expected rates of return on R&D spending for software firms developing upgrades versus firms developing imitative products?
8. **KEY QUESTION** Answer the following questions on the basis of this information for a single firm: total cost of capital = $1000; price paid for labor = $12 per labor unit; price paid for raw materials = $4 per raw-material unit.
   a. Suppose the firm can produce 5000 units of output by combining its fixed capital with 100 units of labor and 450 units of raw materials. What are the total cost and average total cost of producing the 5000 units of output?
   b. Now assume the firm improves its production process so that it can produce 6000 units of output by combining its fixed capital with 100 units of labor and 450 units of raw materials. What are the total cost and average cost of producing the 6000 units of output?
   c. Refer to your answers to 8*a* and 8*b* and explain how process innovation can improve economic efficiency.
9. Why might a firm making a large economic profit from its existing product employ a fast-second strategy in relationship to new or improved products? What risks does it run in pursuing this strategy? What incentive does a firm have to engage in R&D when rivals can imitate its new product?

10. Do you think the overall level of R&D would increase or decrease over the next 20 to 30 years if the lengths of new patents were extended from 20 years to, say, "forever"? What if the duration were reduced from 20 years to, say, 3 years?
11. Make a case that neither pure competition nor pure monopoly is conducive to a great deal of R&D spending and innovation. Why might oligopoly be more favorable to R&D spending and innovation than either pure competition or pure monopoly? What is the inverse-U theory, and how does it relate to your answers to these questions?
12. Evaluate: "Society does not need laws outlawing monopolization and monopoly. Inevitably, monopoly causes its own self-destruction, since its high profit is the lure for other firms or entrepreneurs to develop substitute products."
13. **LAST WORD** Identify a specific example of each of the following in this chapter's Last Word: (*a*) entrepreneurship, (*b*) invention, (*c*) innovation, and (*d*) diffusion.

Web-Based Questions

1. **THE NATIONAL SCIENCE FOUNDATION R&D STATISTICS—WHAT'S HAPPENING?** Go to the Division of Science Resource Statistics Web site, **www.nsf.gov/statisties,** to find the listing for Research & Development. Select Industry and then the most recent InfoBrief on National Patterns of R&D Resources. Use the historical charts and tables to determine whether the following R&D numbers increased, remained constant, or decreased over the last 5 years listed: (*a*) Total U.S. R&D expenditures in constant dollars, (*b*) Federal support for R&D in constant dollars, (*c*) R&D as a percentage of U.S. GDP, and (*d*) Federal support of R&D as a percentage of GDP. What are the technological implications of these figures for the United States?
2. **NASA—ARE THERE COMMERCIAL SPIN-OFFS?** Visit the Web site of NASA's Technology Transfer Office, at **www.sti.nasa.gov/tto,** to identify significant commercial benefits from secondary use of NASA technology. Search the database to find and describe five such spin-offs. How does the NASA Commercial Technology Network (**nctn.hq.nasa.gov/**) move technology from the lab to the marketplace?

PART THREE

Microeconomics of Resource Markets

13 THE DEMAND FOR RESOURCES
14 WAGE DETERMINATION
15 RENT, INTEREST, AND PROFIT
15W NATURAL RESOURCE AND ENERGY ECONOMICS

13

IN THIS CHAPTER YOU WILL LEARN:

- The significance of resource pricing.
- How the marginal revenue productivity of a resource relates to a firm's demand for that resource.
- The factors that increase or decrease resource demand.
- The determinants of elasticity of resource demand.
- How a competitive firm selects its optimal combination of resources.

The Demand for Resources

When you finish your education, you probably will be looking for a new job. But why would someone want to hire you? The answer, of course, is that you have much to offer. Employers have a demand for educated, productive workers like you.

We need to learn more about the demand for labor and other resources. So, we now turn from the pricing and production of *goods and services* to the pricing and employment of *resources*. Although firms come in various sizes and operate under highly different market conditions, each has a demand for productive resources. Firms obtain needed resources from households—the direct or indirect owners of land, labor, capital, and entrepreneurial resources. So, referring to the circular flow model (Figure 2.4, page 39), we shift our attention from the bottom loop of the diagram (where businesses supply products that households demand) to the top loop (where businesses demand resources that households supply).

This chapter looks at the *demand* for economic resources. Although the discussion is couched in terms of labor, the principles developed also apply to land, capital, and entrepreneurial ability. In Chapter 14 we will combine resource (labor) demand with labor *supply* to analyze wage rates. In Chapter 15 we will use resource demand and resource supply to examine the prices of, and returns to, other productive resources. Issues relating to the use of natural resources are the subject of Chapter 15 Web.

Significance of Resource Pricing

There are several good reasons to study resource pricing:

- ***Money-income determination*** Resource prices are a major factor in determining the income of households. The expenditures that firms make in acquiring economic resources flow as wage, rent, interest, and profit incomes to the households that supply those resources.
- ***Cost minimization*** To the firm, resource prices are costs. And to obtain the greatest profit, the firm must produce the profit-maximizing output with the most efficient (least costly) combination of resources. Resource prices play the main role in determining the quantities of land, labor, capital, and entrepreneurial ability that will be combined in producing each good or service (see Table 2.1).
- ***Resource allocation*** Just as product prices allocate finished goods and services to consumers, resource prices allocate resources among industries and firms. In a dynamic economy, where technology and product demand often change, the efficient allocation of resources over time calls for the continuing shift of resources from one use to another. Resource pricing is a major factor in producing those shifts.
- ***Policy issues*** Many policy issues surround the resource market. Examples: To what extent should government redistribute income through taxes and transfers? Should government do anything to discourage "excess" pay to corporate executives? Should it increase the legal minimum wage? Is the provision of subsidies to farmers efficient? Should government encourage or restrict labor unions? The facts and debates relating to these policy questions are grounded on resource pricing.

Marginal Productivity Theory of Resource Demand

To make things simple, let's first assume that a firm hires a certain resource in a purely competitive resource market and sells its output in a purely competitive product market. The simplicity of this situation is twofold: In a competitive product market the firm is a "price taker" and can dispose of as little or as much output as it chooses at the market price. The firm is selling such a negligible fraction of total output that its output decisions exert no influence on product price. Similarly, in the competitive resource market, the firm is a "wage taker." It hires such a negligible fraction of the total supply of the resource that its hiring decisions do not influence the resource price.

Resource Demand as a Derived Demand

Resource demand is the starting point for any discussion of resource prices. The demand for a resource is an inverse relationship between the price of the resource and the quantity of the resource demanded. This demand is a **derived demand:** It is derived from the products that the resources help produce. Resources usually do not directly satisfy customer wants but do so indirectly through their use in producing goods and services. No one wants to consume an acre of land, a John Deere tractor, or the labor services of a farmer, but households do want to consume the food and fiber products that these resources help produce. Similarly, the demand for airplanes generates a demand for assemblers, and the demands for such services as income-tax preparation, haircuts, and child care create derived demands for accountants, barbers, and child care workers.

Marginal Revenue Product

The derived nature of resource demand means that the strength of the demand for any resource will depend on:

- The productivity of the resource in helping to create a good or service.
- The market value or price of the good or service it helps produce.

A resource that is highly productive in turning out a highly valued commodity will be in great demand. On the other hand, a relatively unproductive resource that is capable of producing only a minimally valued commodity will be in little demand. And there will be no demand at all for a resource that is phenomenally efficient in producing something that no one wants to buy.

Productivity Table 13.1 shows the roles of productivity and product price in determining resource demand. Here we assume that a firm adds one variable resource, labor, to its fixed plant. Columns 1 and 2 give the number

TABLE 13.1 The Demand for Labor: Pure Competition in the Sale of the Product

(1) Units of Resource	(2) Total Product (Output)	(3) Marginal Product (MP)	(4) Product Price	(5) Total Revenue, (2) × (4)	(6) Marginal Revenue Product (MRP)
0	0		$2	$ 0	
		7			$14
1	7		2	14	
		6			12
2	13		2	26	
		5			10
3	18		2	36	
		4			8
4	22		2	44	
		3			6
5	25		2	50	
		2			4
6	27		2	54	
		1			2
7	28		2	56	

of units of the resource applied to production and the resulting total product (output). Column 3 provides the **marginal product (MP),** or additional output, resulting from using each additional unit of labor. Columns 1 through 3 remind us that the law of diminishing returns applies here, causing the marginal product of labor to fall beyond some point. For simplicity, we assume that those diminishing marginal returns—those declines in marginal product—begin with the first worker hired.

Product Price But the derived demand for a resource depends also on the price of the product it produces. Column 4 in Table 13.1 adds this price information. Product price is constant, in this case at $2, because we are assuming a competitive product market. The firm is a price taker and will sell units of output only at this market price.

Multiplying column 2 by column 4 gives us the total-revenue data of column 5. These are the amounts of revenue the firm realizes from the various levels of resource usage. From these total-revenue data we can compute **marginal revenue product (MRP)**—the change in total revenue resulting from the use of each additional unit of a resource (labor, in this case). In equation form,

$$\text{Marginal revenue product} = \frac{\text{change in total revenue}}{\text{unit change in resource quantity}}$$

The MRPs are listed in column 6 in Table 13.1.

Rule for Employing Resources: MRP = MRC

The MRP schedule, shown as columns 1 and 6, is the firm's demand schedule for labor. To explain why, we must first discuss the rule that guides a profit-seeking firm in hiring any resource: To maximize profit, a firm should hire additional units of a specific resource as long as each successive unit adds more to the firm's total revenue than it adds to total cost.

Economists use special terms to designate what each additional unit of labor or other variable resource adds to total cost and what it adds to total revenue. We have seen that MRP measures how much each successive unit of a resource adds to total revenue. The amount that each additional unit of a resource adds to the firm's total (resource) cost is called its **marginal resource cost (MRC).**

In equation form,

$$\text{Marginal resource cost} = \frac{\text{change in total (resource) cost}}{\text{unit change in resource quantity}}$$

So we can restate our rule for hiring resources as follows: It will be profitable for a firm to hire additional units of a resource up to the point at which that resource's MRP is equal to its MRC. If the number of workers a firm is currently hiring is such that the MRP of the last worker exceeds his or her MRC, the firm can profit by hiring more workers. But if the number being hired is such that the MRC of the last worker exceeds his or her MRP, the firm is hiring workers who are not "paying their way" and it can increase its profit by discharging some workers. You may have recognized that this **MRP = MRC rule** is similar to the MR = MC profit-maximizing rule employed throughout our discussion of price and output determination. The rationale of the two rules is the same, but the point of reference is now *inputs* of a resource, not *outputs* of a product.

MRP as Resource Demand Schedule

In a purely competitive labor market, market supply and market demand establish the wage rate. Because each firm hires such a small fraction of market supply, it cannot influence the market wage rate; it is a wage taker, not a wage maker. This means that for each additional unit of labor hired, total resource cost increases by exactly the amount of the constant market wage rate. The MRC of labor exactly equals the market wage rate. Thus, resource "price" (the market wage rate) and resource "cost" (marginal resource cost) are equal for a firm that hires a resource in a competitive labor market. Then the MRP = MRC rule tells us that, in pure competition, the firm will hire workers up to the point at which the market *wage rate* (its MRC) is equal to its MRP.

In terms of the data in columns 1 and 6 in Table 13.1, if the market wage rate is, say, $13.95, the firm will hire only one worker. This is so because the first worker adds $14 to total revenue and slightly less—$13.95—to total cost. In other words, because MRP exceeds MRC for the first worker, it is profitable to hire that worker. For each successive worker, however, MRC (= $13.95) exceeds MRP (= $12 or less), indicating that it will not be profitable to hire any of those workers. If the wage rate is $11.95, by the same reasoning we discover that it will pay the firm to hire both the first and second workers. Similarly, if the wage rate is $9.95, three workers will be hired. If it is $7.95, four. If it is $5.95, five. And so forth. So here is the key generalization: The MRP schedule constitutes the firm's demand for labor, because each point on this schedule (or curve) indicates the number of workers the firm would hire at each possible wage rate.

In Figure 13.1, we show the *D* = MRP curve based on the data in Table 13.1.[1] The competitive firm's resource demand curve reflects an inverse relationship between the wage rate and the quantity of labor demanded. The curve slopes downward because of diminishing returns.

FIGURE 13.1 The purely competitive seller's demand for a resource. The MRP curve is the resource demand curve; each of its points relates a particular resource price (= MRP when profit is maximized) with a corresponding quantity of the resource demanded. Under pure competition, product price is constant; therefore, the downward slope of the D = MRP curve is due solely to the decline in the resource's marginal product (law of diminishing marginal returns).

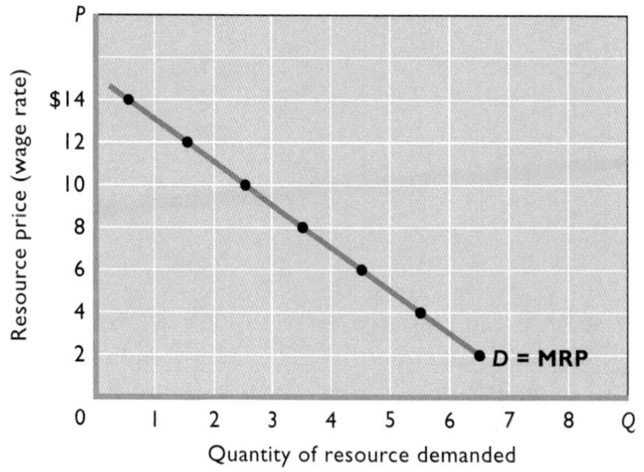

Resource Demand under Imperfect Product Market Competition

Our analysis of labor demand becomes more complex when the firm is selling its product in an imperfectly competitive market, one in which the firm is a price maker. Pure monopoly, oligopoly, and monopolistic competition in the product market all mean that the firm's product demand curve is downsloping; the firm must set a lower price to increase its sales.

The productivity data in Table 13.1 are retained in columns 1 to 3 in Table 13.2. But here we show in column 4 that product price must be lowered to sell the marginal product of each successive worker. The MRP of the purely competitive seller of Table 13.1 falls for a single reason: Marginal product diminishes. But the MRP of the imperfectly competitive seller of Table 13.2 falls for two reasons: Marginal product diminishes *and* product price falls as output increases.

We emphasize that the lower price accompanying each increase in output (total product) applies not only to the marginal product of each successive worker but also to all prior output units that otherwise could have been sold at a higher price. Observe that the marginal product of the second worker is 6 units of output. These 6 units can be sold for $2.40 each, or, as a group, for $14.40. But this is not the MRP of the second worker. To sell these 6 units, the firm must take a 20-cent price cut on the 7 units produced by the first worker—units that otherwise could have been sold for $2.60 each. Thus, the MRP of the second worker is only $13 [= $14.40 − (7 × 20 cents)], as shown.

Similarly, the third worker adds 5 units to total product, and these units are worth $2.20 each, or $11 total. But to sell these 5 units, the firm must take a 20-cent price cut on the 13 units produced by the first two workers. So the third worker's MRP is only $8.40 [= $11 − (13 × 20 cents)]. The other figures in column 6 are derived similarly.

In Figure 13.2 we graph the MRP data from Table 13.2 and label it "*D* = MRP (imperfect competition)."

[1]Note that we plot the points in Figure 13.1 halfway between succeeding numbers of resource units, because MRP is associated with the addition of 1 more unit. Thus, in Figure 13.1, for example, we plot the MRP of the second unit ($12) not at 1 or 2 but at $1\frac{1}{2}$. This "smoothing" enables us to sketch a continuously downsloping curve rather than one that moves downward in discrete steps as each new unit of labor is hired.

TABLE 13.2 The Demand for Labor: Imperfect Competition in the Sale of the Product

(1) Units of Resource	(2) Total Product (Output)	(3) Marginal Product (MP)	(4) Product Price	(5) Total Revenue, (2) × (4)	(6) Marginal Revenue Product (MRP)
0	0		$2.80	$ 0	
		7			$18.20
1	7		2.60	18.20	
		6			13.00
2	13		2.40	31.20	
		5			8.40
3	18		2.20	39.60	
		4			4.40
4	22		2.00	44.00	
		3			2.25
5	25		1.85	46.25	
		2			1.00
6	27		1.75	47.25	
		1			−1.05
7	28		1.65	46.20	

The broken-line resource demand curve, in contrast, is that of the purely competitive seller represented in Figure 13.1. A comparison of the two curves demonstrates that, other things equal, the resource demand curve of an imperfectly competitive seller is less elastic than that of a purely competitive seller. Consider the effects of an identical percentage decline in the wage rate (resource price) from $11 to $6 in Figure 13.2. Comparison of the two curves reveals that the imperfectly competitive seller (solid curve) does not expand the quantity of labor by as large a percentage as does the purely competitive seller (broken curve).

FIGURE 13.2 The imperfectly competitive seller's demand curve for a resource. An imperfectly competitive seller's resource demand curve *D* (solid) slopes downward because both marginal product and product price fall as resource employment and output rise. This downward slope is greater than that for a purely competitive seller (dashed resource demand curve) because the pure competitor can sell the added output at a constant price.

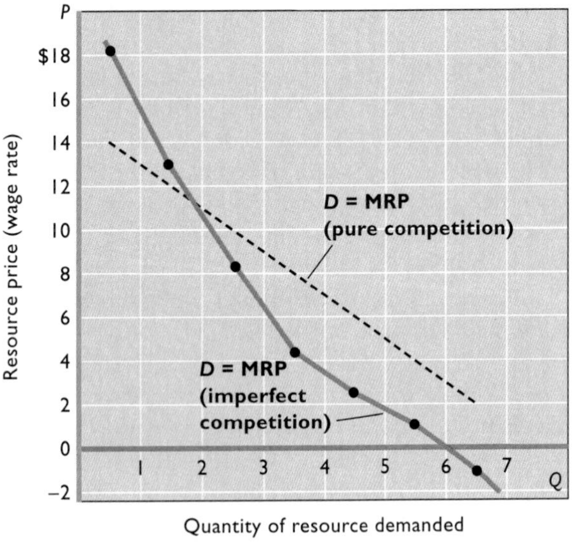

It is not surprising that the imperfectly competitive producer is less responsive to resource price cuts than the purely competitive producer. The imperfect competitor's relative reluctance to employ more resources, and produce more output, when resource prices fall reflects the imperfect competitor's tendency to restrict output in the product market. Other things equal, the imperfectly competitive seller produces less of a product than a purely competitive seller. In producing that smaller output, it demands fewer resources. **(Key Question 2)**

W 13.1
Resource demand

Market Demand for a Resource

We have now explained the individual firm's demand curve for a resource. Recall that the total, or market, demand curve for a *product* is found by summing horizontally the demand curves of all individual buyers in the market. The market demand curve for a particular *resource* is derived in essentially the same way—by summing the individual demand or MRP curves for all firms hiring that resource.

QUICK REVIEW 13.1

- To maximize profit, a firm will use a resource in an amount at which the resource's marginal revenue product equals its marginal resource cost (MRP = MRC).
- Application of the MRP = MRC rule to a firm's MRP curve demonstrates that the MRP curve is the firm's resource demand curve. In a purely competitive resource market, resource price (the wage rate) equals MRC.
- The resource demand curve of a purely competitive seller is downsloping solely because the marginal product of the resource diminishes; the resource demand curve of an imperfectly competitive seller is downsloping because marginal product diminishes and product price falls as output is increased.

CONSIDER THIS . . .

She's The One

In what economist Robert Frank calls "winner-take-all-markets," a few highly talented performers have huge earnings relative to the average performers in the market. Because consumers and firms seek out "top" performers, small differences in talent or popularity get magnified into huge differences in pay.

In these markets, consumer spending gets channeled toward a few performers. The media then "hypes" these individuals, which further increases the public's awareness of their talents. Many more consumers then buy the stars' products. Although it is not easy to stay on top, several superstars emerge.

The high earnings of superstars results from the high revenues they generate from their work. Consider Shania Twain. If she sold only a few thousand CDs and attracted only a few hundred fans to each concert, the revenue she would produce—her marginal revenue product—would be quite modest. So, too, would be her earnings.

But consumers have anointed Shania as queen of country/pop. "*She's* the one" and thus the demand for her CDs and concerts is extraordinarily high. She sells *millions* of CDs (nearly 50 million thus far), not thousands, and draws *thousands* to her concerts, not hundreds. Her extraordinarily high net earnings derive from her extraordinarily high MRP.

So it is for the other superstars in the "winner-take-all markets." Influenced by the media, but coerced by no one, consumers direct their spending toward a select few. The resulting strong demand for these stars' services reflects their high MRP. And because top talent (by definition) is very limited, superstars receive amazingly high earnings.

Determinants of Resource Demand

What will alter the demand for a resource—that is, shift the resource demand curve? The fact that resource demand is derived from *product demand* and depends on *resource productivity* suggests two "resource demand shifters." Also, our analysis of how changes in the prices of other products can shift a product's demand curve (Chapter 3) suggests another factor: changes in the prices of other *resources*.

Changes in Product Demand

Other things equal, an increase in the demand for a product will increase the demand for a resource used in its production, whereas a decrease in product demand will decrease the resource demand.

Let's see how this works. The first thing to recall is that a change in the demand for a product will change its price. In Table 13.1, let's assume that an increase in product demand boosts product price from \$2 to \$3. You should calculate the new resource demand schedule (columns 1 and 6) that would result, and plot it in Figure 13.1 to verify that the new resource demand curve lies to the right of the old demand curve. Similarly, a decline in the product demand (and price) will shift the resource demand curve to the left. This effect—resource demand changing along with product demand—demonstrates that resource demand is derived from product demand.

Example: Assuming no offsetting change in supply, an increase in the demand for new houses will drive up house prices. Those higher prices will increase the MRP of construction workers, and therefore the demand for construction workers will rise. The resource demand curve such as in Figure 13.1 or Figure 13.2 will shift to the right.

Changes in Productivity

Other things equal, an increase in the productivity of a resource will increase the demand for the resource and a decrease in productivity will reduce the resource demand. If we doubled the MP data of column 3 in Table 13.1, the MRP data of column 6 would also double, indicating a rightward shift of the resource demand curve.

The productivity of any resource may be altered in several ways:

- ***Quantities of other resources*** The marginal productivity of any resource will vary with the quantities of the other resources used with it. The greater the amount of capital and land resources used with, say, labor, the greater will be labor's marginal productivity and, thus, labor demand.
- ***Technological advance*** Technological improvements that increase the quality of other resources, such as capital, have the same effect. The better the *quality* of capital, the greater the productivity of labor used with it. Dockworkers employed with a specific amount of real capital in the form of unloading cranes are more productive than dockworkers with the same amount of real capital embodied in older conveyor-belt systems.
- ***Quality of the variable resource*** Improvements in the quality of the variable resource, such as labor, will

increase its marginal productivity and therefore its demand. In effect, there will be a new demand curve for a different, more skilled, kind of labor.

All these considerations help explain why the average level of (real) wages is higher in industrially advanced nations (for example, the United States, Germany, Japan, and France) than in developing nations (for example, India, Ethiopia, Angola, and Cambodia). Workers in industrially advanced nations are generally healthier, better educated, and better trained than are workers in developing countries. Also, in most industries they work with a larger and more efficient stock of capital goods and more abundant natural resources. This creates a strong demand for labor. On the supply side of the market, labor is *relatively* scarce compared with that in most developing nations. A strong demand and a relatively scarce supply of labor result in high wage rates in the industrially advanced nations.

Changes in the Prices of Other Resources

Changes in the prices of other resources may change the demand for a specific resource. For example, a change in the price of capital may change the demand for labor. The direction of the change in labor demand will depend on whether labor and capital are substitutes or complements in production.

Substitute Resources

Suppose the technology in a certain production process is such that labor and capital are substitutable. A firm can produce some specific amount of output using a relatively small amount of labor and a relatively large amount of capital, or vice versa. Now assume that the price of machinery (capital) falls. The effect on the demand for labor will be the net result of two opposed effects: the substitution effect and the output effect.

- ***Substitution effect*** The decline in the price of machinery prompts the firm to substitute machinery for labor. This allows the firm to produce its output at lower cost. So at the fixed wage rate, smaller quantities of labor are now employed. This **substitution effect** decreases the demand for labor. More generally, the substitution effect indicates that a firm will purchase more of an input whose relative price has declined and, conversely, use less of an input whose relative price has increased.
- ***Output effect*** Because the price of machinery has fallen, the costs of producing various outputs must also decline. With lower costs, the firm finds it profitable to produce and sell a greater output. The greater output increases the demand for all resources, including labor. So this **output effect** increases the demand for labor. More generally, the output effect means that the firm will purchase more of one particular input when the price of the other input falls and less of that particular input when the price of the other input rises.
- ***Net effect*** The substitution and output effects are both present when the price of an input changes, but they work in opposite directions. For a decline in the price of capital, the substitution effect decreases the demand for labor and the output effect increases it. The net change in labor demand depends on the relative sizes of the two effects: If the substitution effect outweighs the output effect, a decrease in the price of capital decreases the demand for labor. If the output effect exceeds the substitution effect, a decrease in the price of capital increases the demand for labor.

Complementary Resources

Recall from Chapter 3 that certain products, such as computers and software, are complementary goods; they "go together" and are jointly demanded. Resources may also be complementary; an increase in the quantity of one of them used in the production process requires an increase in the amount used of the other as well, and vice versa. Suppose a small design firm does computer-assisted design (CAD) with relatively expensive personal computers as its basic piece of capital equipment. Each computer requires a single design engineer to operate it; the machine is not automated—it will not run itself—and a second engineer would have nothing to do.

Now assume that a technological advance in the production of these computers substantially reduces their price. There can be no substitution effect, because labor and capital must be used in *fixed proportions*, one person for one machine. Capital cannot be substituted for labor. But there *is* an output effect. Other things equal, the reduction in the price of capital goods means lower production costs. Producing a larger output will therefore be profitable. In doing so, the firm will use both more capital and more labor. When labor and capital are complementary, a decline in the price of capital increases the demand for labor through the output effect.

We have cast our analysis of substitute resources and complementary resources mainly in terms of a decline in the price of capital. Table 13.3 summarizes the effects of an *increase* in the price of capital on the demand for labor. Please study it carefully.

Now that we have discussed the full list of the determinants of labor demand, let's again review their effects. Stated in terms of the labor resource, the demand for

TABLE 13.3 The Effect of an Increase in the Price of Capital on the Demand for Labor, D_L

(1) Relationship of Inputs	(2) Increase in the Price of Capital (a) Substitution Effect	(b) Output Effect	(c) Combined Effect
Substitutes in production	Labor substituted for capital	Production costs up, output down, and less of both capital and labor used	D_L increases if the substitution effect exceeds the output effect; D_L decreases if the output effect exceeds the substitution effect
Complements in production	No substitution of labor for capital	Production costs up, output down, and less of both capital and labor used	D_L decreases

labor will increase (the labor demand curve will shift rightward) when:

- The demand for (and therefore the price of) the product produced by that labor *increases*.
- The productivity (MP) of labor *increases*.
- The price of a substitute input *decreases*, provided the output effect exceeds the substitution effect.
- The price of a substitute input *increases*, provided the substitution effect exceeds the output effect.
- The price of a complementary input *decreases*.

Be sure that you can "reverse" these effects to explain a *decrease* in labor demand.

Table 13.4 provides several illustrations of the determinants of labor demand, listed by the categories of determinants we have discussed. You will benefit by giving them a close look.

Occupational Employment Trends

Changes in labor demand have considerable significance since they affect wage rates and employment in specific occupations. Increases in labor demand for certain occupational groups result in increases in their employment; decreases in labor demand result in decreases in their employment. For illustration, let's look at occupations that are growing and declining in demand. (Wage rates are the subject of the next chapter.)

The Fastest-Growing Occupations

Table 13.5 lists the 10 fastest-growing U.S. occupations for 2004 to 2014, as measured by percentage changes and projected by the Bureau of Labor Statistics. It is no coincidence that the service occupations dominate the list. In general, the demand for service workers in the United States is rapidly outpacing the demand for manufacturing, construction, and mining workers.

Of the 10 fastest-growing occupations in percentage terms, several are related to health care. The rising demands for these types of labor are derived from the growing demand for health services, caused by several factors. The aging of the U.S. population has brought with it more medical problems, the rising standard of income has led to greater expenditures on health care, and the continued

TABLE 13.4 Determinants of Labor Demand: Factors That Shift the Labor Demand Curve

Determinant	Examples
Change in product demand	Gambling increases in popularity, increasing the demand for workers at casinos. Consumers decrease their demand for leather coats, decreasing the demand for tanners. The Federal government increases spending on homeland security, increasing the demand for security personnel.
Change in productivity	An increase in the skill levels of physicians increases the demand for their services. Computer-assisted graphic design increases the productivity of, and demand for, graphic artists.
Change in the price of another resource	An increase in the price of electricity increases the cost of producing aluminum and reduces the demand for aluminum workers. The price of security equipment used by businesses to protect against illegal entry falls, decreasing the demand for night guards. The price of cell phone equipment decreases, reducing the cost of cell phone service; this in turn increases the demand for cell phone assemblers. Health-insurance premiums rise, and firms substitute part-time workers who are not covered by insurance for full-time workers who are.

TABLE 13.5 The 10 Fastest-Growing U.S. Occupations in Percentage Terms, 2004–2014

	Employment, Thousands of Jobs		
Occupation	2004	2014	Percentage Increase*
Home health aides	624	974	56%
Data communication analysts	231	357	55
Medical assistants	387	589	52
Physician assistants	62	93	50
Software engineers, applications	460	682	48
Physical therapist assistants	59	85	44
Dental hygienists	158	226	43
Software engineers, systems	340	486	43
Dental assistants	267	382	43
Personal home care aides	701	988	41

*Percentages and employment numbers may not reconcile due to rounding.

Source: Bureau of Labor Statistics, "Employment Projections," **www.bls.gov.**

TABLE 13.6 The 10 Most Rapidly Declining U.S. Occupations in Percentage Terms, 2004–2014

	Employment, Thousands of Jobs		
Occupation	2004	2014	Percentage Increase*
Meter readers, utilities	50	27	−45%
Textile machine operators	148	81	−45
Credit authorizers, checkers, and clerks	67	39	−41
Railroad brake, signal, and switch operators	17	11	−39
Mailing clerks	160	101	−37
Sewing machine operators	256	163	−37
Telephone operators	39	25	−36
File clerks	255	163	−36
Computer operators	149	101	−33
Photographic processing machine operators	54	38	−31

*Percentages and employment numbers may not reconcile due to rounding.

Source: Bureau of Labor Statistics, "Employment Projections," **www.bls.gov.**

presence of private and public insurance has allowed people to buy more health care than most could afford individually.

Three of the fastest-growing occupations are directly related to computers. The increase in the demand for data communication analysts and computer software engineers arises from the rapid rise in the demand for computers, computer services, and Internet use. It also results from the rising marginal revenue productivity of these particular workers, given the vastly improved quality of the computer and communications equipment they work with. Moreover, price declines on such equipment have had stronger output effects than substitution effects, increasing the demand for these kinds of labor.

In contrast, Table 13.6 lists the 10 U.S. occupations with the greatest projected job loss (in percentage terms) between 2004 and 2014. Eight of the occupations owe their declines mainly to "labor-saving" technological change. For example, automated or computerized equipment has greatly reduced the need for meter readers, telephone operators, credit personnel, railroad workers, mailroom clerks, and filing clerks. The advent of digital photography explains the projected decline in the employment of people operating photographic processing equipment. The significant decline in the number of traditional computer operators relates to the rapid expansion of networked personal computers.

The remaining two occupations in the declining employment list are related to textiles and apparel. The U.S. demand for these goods is increasingly being filled through imports. Those jobs are therefore rapidly disappearing in the United States.

As we indicated, the "top-10" lists shown in Tables 13.5 and 13.6 are based on percentage changes. In terms of absolute job growth and loss, the greatest projected employment growth between 2004 and 2014 is for retail salespersons (+736,000 jobs). The main sources of this growth are rising incomes and rising population. The greatest projected absolute decline in employment is for farmers and ranchers (−155,000 jobs). This decline reflects the income-inelastic demand for food, enhanced physical productivity of farm equipment, and the consolidation of smaller farms into agribusinesses.

Elasticity of Resource Demand

The employment changes we have just discussed have resulted from shifts in the locations of resource demand curves. Such changes in demand must be distinguished from changes in the quantity of a resource demanded caused by a change in the price of the specific resource under consideration. Such a change is caused not by a shift of the demand curve but, rather, by a movement from one point to another on a fixed resource demand curve. Example: In Figure 13.1 we note that an increase in the wage rate from $5 to $7 will reduce the quantity of labor demanded from 5 to 4 units. This is a change in the *quantity of labor demanded* as distinct from a *change in demand*.

The sensitivity of producers to changes in resource prices is measured by the **elasticity of resource demand.** In coefficient form,

$$E_{rd} = \frac{\text{percentage change in resource quantity}}{\text{percentage change in resource price}}$$

O 13.1

Elasticity of resource demand

When E_{rd} is greater than 1, resource demand is elastic; when E_{rd} is less than 1, resource demand is inelastic; and when E_{rd} equals 1, resource demand is unit-elastic. What determines the elasticity of resource demand? Several factors are at work.

Ease of Resource Substitutability

The degree to which resources are substitutable is a fundamental determinant of elasticity. The greater the substitutability of other resources, the more elastic is the demand for a particular resource. Because automated voice-mail systems are highly substitutable for telephone receptionists, the demand for receptionists is quite elastic. In contrast, good substitutes for physicians are rare, so demand for them is less elastic or even inelastic. If a furniture manufacturer finds that several types of wood are equally satisfactory in making coffee tables, a rise in the price of any one type of wood may cause a sharp drop in the amount demanded as the producer substitutes one of the other woods. At the other extreme, there may be no reasonable substitutes; bauxite is absolutely essential in the production of aluminum ingots. Thus, the demand for bauxite by aluminum producers is inelastic.

Time can play a role in the ease of input substitution. For example, a firm's truck drivers may obtain a substantial wage increase with little or no immediate decline in employment. But over time, as the firm's trucks wear out and are replaced, that wage increase may motivate the company to purchase larger trucks and in that way deliver the same total output with fewer drivers.

Elasticity of Product Demand

Because the demand for labor is a derived demand, the elasticity of the demand for the output that the labor is producing will influence the elasticity of the demand for labor. Other things equal, the greater the price elasticity of product demand, the greater the elasticity of resource demand. For example, suppose that the wage rate falls. This means a decline in the cost of producing the product and a drop in the product's price. If the elasticity of product demand is great, the resulting increase in the quantity of the product demanded will be large and thus necessitate a large increase in the quantity of labor to produce the additional output. This implies an elastic demand for labor. But if the demand for the product is inelastic, the increase in the amount of the product demanded will be small, as will be the increases in the quantity of labor demanded. This suggests an inelastic demand for labor.

Remember that the resource demand curve in Figure 13.1 is more elastic than the resource demand curve shown in Figure 13.2. The difference arises because in Figure 13.1 we assume a perfectly elastic product demand curve, whereas Figure 13.2 is based on a downsloping or less than perfectly elastic product demand curve.

Ratio of Resource Cost to Total Cost

The larger the proportion of total production costs accounted for by a resource, the greater the elasticity of demand for that resource. In the extreme, if labor cost is the only production cost, then a 20 percent increase in wage rates will shift all the firm's cost curves upward by 20 percent. If product demand is elastic, this substantial increase in costs will cause a relatively large decline in sales and a sharp decline in the amount of labor demanded. So labor demand is highly elastic. But if labor cost is only 50 percent of production cost, then a 20 percent increase in wage rates will increase costs by only 10 percent. With the same elasticity of product demand, this will cause a relatively small decline in sales and therefore in the amount of labor demanded. In this case the demand for labor is much less elastic. **(Key Question 5)**

QUICK REVIEW 13.2

- A resource demand curve will shift because of changes in product demand, changes in the productivity of the resource, and changes in the prices of other inputs.
- If resources A and B are substitutable, a decline in the price of A will decrease the demand for B provided the substitution effect exceeds the output effect. But if the output effect exceeds the substitution effect, the demand for B will increase.
- If resources C and D are complements, a decline in the price of C will increase the demand for D.
- Elasticity of resource demand measures the extent to which producers change the quantity of a resource they hire when its price changes.
- The elasticity of resource demand will be less the greater the difficulty of substituting other resources for the resource, the smaller the elasticity of product demand, and the smaller the proportion of total cost accounted for by the resource.

Optimal Combination of Resources

So far, our main focus has been on one variable input, labor. But in the long run firms can vary the amounts of all the resources they use. That's why we need to consider what combination of resources a firm will choose when *all* its inputs are variable. While our analysis is based on two resources, it can be extended to any number of inputs.

We will consider two interrelated questions:

- What combination of resources will minimize costs at a specific level of output?
- What combination of resources will maximize profit?

The Least-Cost Rule

A firm is producing a specific output with the **least-cost combination of resources** when the last dollar spent on each resource yields the same marginal product. That is, the cost of any output is minimized when the ratios of marginal product to price of the last units of resources used are the same for each resource. In competitive resource markets, recall, marginal resource cost is the market resource price; the firm can hire as many or as few units of the resource as it wants at that price. Then, with just two resources, labor and capital, a competitive firm minimizes its total cost of a specific output when

$$\frac{\text{Marginal product of labor } (\text{MP}_L)}{\text{Price of labor } (P_L)} = \frac{\text{Marginal product of capital } (\text{MP}_C)}{\text{Price of capital } (P_C)} \qquad (1)$$

Throughout, we will refer to the marginal products of labor and capital as MP_L and MP_C, respectively, and symbolize the price of labor by P_L and the price of capital by P_C.

A concrete example will show why fulfilling the condition in equation 1 leads to least-cost production. Assume that the price of both capital and labor is $1 per unit but that Siam Soups currently employs them in such amounts that the marginal product of labor is 10 and the marginal product of capital is 5. Our equation immediately tells us that this is not the least costly combination of resources:

$$\frac{\text{MP}_L = 10}{P_L = \$1} > \frac{\text{MP}_C = 5}{P_C = \$1}$$

Suppose Siam spends $1 less on capital and shifts that dollar to labor. It loses 5 units of output produced by the last dollar's worth of capital, but it gains 10 units of output from the extra dollar's worth of labor. Net output increases by 5 (= 10 − 5) units for the same total cost. More such shifting of dollars from capital to labor will push the firm *down* along its MP curve for labor and *up* along its MP curve for capital, increasing output and moving the firm toward a position of equilibrium where equation 1 is fulfilled. At that equilibrium position, the MP per dollar for the last unit of both labor and capital might be, for example, 7. And Siam will be producing a greater output for the same (original) cost.

Whenever the same total-resource cost can result in a greater total output, the cost per unit—and therefore the total cost of any specific level of output—can be reduced. Being able to produce a *larger* output with a *specific* total cost is the same as being able to produce a *specific* output with a *smaller* total cost. If Siam buys $1 less of capital, its output will fall by 5 units. If it spends only $.50 of that dollar on labor, the firm will increase its output by a compensating 5 units (= $\frac{1}{2}$ of the MP per dollar). Then the firm will realize the same total output at a $.50 lower total cost.

The cost of producing any specific output can be reduced as long as equation 1 does not hold. But when dollars have been shifted between capital and labor to the point where equation 1 holds, no additional changes in the use of capital and labor will reduce costs further. Siam is now producing that output using the least-cost combination of capital and labor.

All the long-run cost curves developed in Chapter 8 and used thereafter assume that the least-cost combination of inputs has been realized at each level of output. Any firm that combines resources in violation of the least-cost rule would have a higher-than-necessary average total cost at each level of output. That is, it would incur *X-inefficiency*, as discussed in Figure 10.7.

The producer's least-cost rule is analogous to the consumer's utility-maximizing rule described in Chapter 7. In achieving the utility-maximizing combination of goods, the consumer considers both his or her preferences as reflected in diminishing-marginal-utility data and the prices of the various products. Similarly, in achieving the cost-minimizing combination of resources, the producer considers both the marginal-product data and the price (costs) of the various resources.

The Profit-Maximizing Rule

Minimizing cost is not sufficient for maximizing profit. A firm can produce any level of output in the least costly way by applying equation 1. But only one unique level of output maximizes profit. Our earlier analysis of product markets showed that this profit-maximizing output occurs where marginal revenue equals marginal cost (MR = MC). Near the beginning of this chapter we determined that we could write this profit-maximizing condition as MRP = MRC as it relates to resource inputs.

In a purely competitive resource market the marginal resource cost (MRC) is equal to the resource price *P*. Thus, for any competitive resource market, we have as our profit-maximizing equation

$$\text{MRP (resource)} = P\text{ (resource)}$$

This condition must hold for every variable resource, and in the long run all resources are variable. In competitive markets, a firm will therefore achieve its **profit-maximizing combination of resources** when each resource is employed to the point at which its marginal revenue product equals its resource price. For two resources, labor and capital, we need both

$$P_L = \text{MRP}_L \qquad \text{and} \qquad P_C = \text{MRP}_C$$

We can combine these conditions by dividing both sides of each equation by their respective prices and equating the results to get

$$\frac{\text{MRP}_L}{P_L} = \frac{\text{MRP}_C}{P_C} = 1 \qquad (2)$$

Note in equation 2 that it is not sufficient that the MRPs of the two resources be *proportionate* to their prices; the MRPs must be *equal* to their prices and the ratios therefore equal to 1. For example, if $\text{MRP}_L = \$15$, $P_L = \$5$, $\text{MRP}_C = \$9$, and $P_C = \$3$, Siam is underemploying both capital and labor even though the ratios of MRP to resource price are identical for both resources. The firm can expand its profit by hiring additional amounts of both capital and labor until it moves down their downsloping MRP curves to the points at which $\text{MRP}_L = \$5$ and $\text{MRP}_C = \$3$. The ratios will then be 5/5 and 3/3 and equal to 1.

W 13.2
Optimal combination of resources

The profit-maximizing position in equation 2 includes the cost-minimizing condition of equation 1. That is, if a firm is maximizing profit according to equation 2, then it must be using the least-cost combination of inputs to do so. However, the converse is not true: A firm operating at least cost according to equation 1 may not be operating at the output that maximizes its profit.

Numerical Illustration

A numerical illustration will help you understand the least-cost and profit-maximizing rules. In columns 2, 3, 2′, and 3′ in Table 13.7 we show the total products and marginal products for various amounts of labor and capital that are assumed to be the only inputs Siam needs in producing its soup. Both inputs are subject to diminishing returns.

We also assume that labor and capital are supplied in competitive resource markets at \$8 and \$12, respectively, and that Siam soup sells competitively at \$2 per unit. For both labor and capital we can determine the total revenue associated with each input level by multiplying total product by the \$2 product price. These data are shown in columns 4 and 4′. They enable us to calculate the marginal revenue product of each successive input of labor and capital as shown in columns 5 and 5′, respectively.

Producing at Least Cost

What is the least-cost combination of labor and capital for Siam to use in producing, say, 50 units of output? The answer, which we can obtain by trial and error, is 3 units of labor and 2 units of capital. Columns 2 and 2′ indicate that this combination of labor and capital does, indeed, result in the required 50

TABLE 13.7 Data for Finding the Least-Cost and Profit-Maximizing Combination of Labor and Capital, Siam Soups*

Labor (Price = \$8)					Capital (Price = \$12)				
(1) Quantity	(2) Total Product (Output)	(3) Marginal Product	(4) Total Revenue	(5) Marginal Revenue Product	(1′) Quantity	(2′) Total Product (Output)	(3′) Marginal Product	(4′) Total Revenue	(5′) Marginal Revenue Product
0	0		\$ 0		0	0		\$ 0	
1	12	12	24	\$24	1	13	13	26	\$26
2	22	10	44	20	2	22	9	44	18
3	28	6	56	12	**3**	28	6	56	***12***
4	33	5	66	10	4	32	4	64	8
5	37	4	74	***8***	5	35	3	70	6
6	40	3	80	6	6	37	2	74	4
7	42	2	84	4	7	38	1	76	2

*To simplify, it is assumed in this table that the productivity of each resource is independent of the quantity of the other. For example, the total and marginal products of labor are assumed not to vary with the quantity of capital employed.

(= 28 + 22) units of output. Now, note from columns 3 and 3′ that hiring 3 units of labor gives us $MP_L/P_L = \frac{6}{8} = \frac{3}{4}$ and hiring 2 units of capital gives us $MP_C/P_C = \frac{9}{12} = \frac{3}{4}$. So equation (1) is fulfilled. How can we verify that costs are actually minimized? First, we see that the total cost of employing 3 units of labor and 2 of capital is \$48 [= (3 × \$8) + (2 × \$12)].

Other combinations of labor and capital will also yield 50 units of output, but at a higher cost than \$48. For example, 5 units of labor and 1 unit of capital will produce 50 (= 37 + 13) units, but total cost is higher, at \$52 [= (5 × \$8) + (1 × \$12)]. This comes as no surprise, because 5 units of labor and 1 unit of capital violate the least-cost rule—$MP_L/P_L = \frac{4}{8}$, $MP_C/P_C = \frac{13}{12}$. Only the combination (3 units of labor and 2 units of capital) that minimizes total cost will satisfy equation 1. All other combinations capable of producing 50 units of output violate the cost-minimizing rule, and therefore cost more than \$48.

Maximizing Profit Will 50 units of output maximize Siam's profit? No, because the profit-maximizing terms of equation 2 are not satisfied when the firm employs 3 units of labor and 2 of capital. To maximize profit, each input should be employed until its price equals its marginal revenue product. But for 3 units of labor, labor's MRP in column 5 is \$12 while its price is only \$8. This means the firm could increase its profit by hiring more labor. Similarly, for 2 units of capital, we see in column 5′ that capital's MRP is \$18 and its price is only \$12. This indicates that more capital should also be employed. By producing only 50 units of output (even though they are produced at least cost), labor and capital are being used in less-than-profit-maximizing amounts. The firm needs to expand its employment of labor and capital, thereby increasing its output.

Table 13.7 shows that the MRPs of labor and capital are equal to their prices, so equation 2 is fulfilled, when Siam is employing 5 units of labor and 3 units of capital. So this is the profit-maximizing combination of inputs.[2] The firm's total cost will be \$76, made up of \$40 (= 5 × \$8) of labor and \$36 (= 3 × \$12) of capital. Total revenue will be \$130, found either by multiplying the total output of 65 (= 37 + 28) by the \$2 product price or by summing the total revenues attributable to labor (\$74) and to capital (\$56). The difference between total revenue and total cost in this instance is \$54 (= \$130 − \$76). Experiment with other combinations of labor and capital to demonstrate that they yield an economic profit of less than \$54.

Note that the profit-maximizing combination of 5 units of labor and 3 units of capital is also a least-cost combination for this particular level of output. Using these resource amounts satisfies the least-cost requirement of equation 1 in that $MP_L/P_L = \frac{4}{8} = \frac{1}{2}$ and $MP_C/P_C = \frac{6}{12} = \frac{1}{2}$. **(Key Questions 6 and 7)**

Marginal Productivity Theory of Income Distribution

Our discussion of resource pricing is the cornerstone of the controversial view that fairness and economic justice are one of the outcomes of a competitive capitalist economy. Table 13.7 tells us, in effect, that workers receive income payments (wages) equal to the marginal contributions they make to their employers' outputs and revenues. In other words, workers are paid according to the value of the labor services that they contribute to production. Similarly, owners of the other resources receive income based on the value of the resources they supply in the production process.

In this **marginal productivity theory of income distribution,** income gets distributed according to contribution to society's output. So, if you are willing to accept the proposition "To each according to what he or she creates," income payments based on marginal revenue product seem to provide a fair and equitable distribution of society's income.

O 13.2
Marginal productivity theory of distribution

This sounds fair enough, but there are serious criticisms of this theory of income distribution:

- ***Inequality*** Critics argue that the distribution of income resulting from payment according to marginal productivity may be highly unequal because productive resources are very unequally distributed in the first place. Aside from their differences in mental and physical attributes, individuals encounter substantially different opportunities to enhance their productivity through education and training and the use of more and better equipment. Some people may not be able to participate in production at all because of mental or physical disabilities, and they would obtain no income under a system of distribution based solely on marginal productivity. Ownership of property resources is also highly unequal. Many landlords and capitalists obtain their property by inheritance rather than through their own productive effort. Hence, income from inherited property resources conflicts with the "To each according to what he or she

[2]Because we are dealing with discrete (nonfractional) units of the two outputs here, the use of 4 units of labor and 2 units of capital is equally profitable. The fifth unit of labor's MRP and its price (cost) are equal at \$8, so that the fifth labor unit neither adds to nor subtracts from the firm's profit; similarly, the third unit of capital has no effect on profit.

Last *Word*

Input Substitution: The Case of ATMs

Banks Are Using More Automatic Teller Machines (ATMs) and Employing Fewer Human Tellers.

As you have learned from this chapter, a firm achieves its least-cost combination of inputs when the last dollar it spends on each input makes the same contribution to total output. This raises an interesting real-world question: What happens when technological advance makes available a new, highly productive capital good for which *MP*/*P* is greater than it is for other inputs, say, a particular type of labor? The answer is that the least-cost mix of resources abruptly changes, and the firm responds accordingly. If the new capital is a substitute for labor (rather than a complement), the firm replaces the particular type of labor with the new capital. That is exactly what is happening in the banking industry, in which ATMs are replacing human bank tellers.

ATMs made their debut about 35 years ago when Diebold, a U.S. firm, introduced the product. Today, Diebold and NCR (also a U.S. firm) dominate global sales, with the Japanese firm Fujitsu being a distant third. The number of ATMs and their usage has exploded, and currently there are nearly 400,000 ATMs in the United States. In 1975, about 10 *million* ATM transactions occurred in the United States. Today there are about 11 *billion* U.S. ATM transactions each year.

ATMs are highly productive: A single machine can handle hundreds of transactions daily, thousands weekly, and millions over the course of several years. ATMs can not only handle cash withdrawals but also accept deposits and facilitate switches of funds between various accounts. Although ATMs are expensive for banks to buy and install, they are available 24 hours a day, and their cost per transaction is one-fourth the cost for human tellers. They rarely get "held up," and they do not quit their jobs (turnover among human tellers is nearly 50 percent per year). Moreover, ATMs are highly convenient; unlike human tellers, they are located not only at banks but also at busy street corners, workplaces, universities, and shopping malls. The same bank card that enables you to withdraw cash from your local ATM also enables you to withdraw pounds from an ATM in London, yen from an ATM in Tokyo, and even rubles from an ATM in Moscow. (All this, of course, assumes that you have money in your checking account.)

In the terminology of this chapter, the more productive, lower-priced ATMs have reduced the demand for a substitute in production—human tellers. Between 1990 and 2000, an estimated 80,000 human teller positions were eliminated, and more positions will disappear by 2010. Where will the people holding these jobs go? Most will eventually move to other occupations. Although the lives of individual tellers are disrupted, society clearly wins. Society obtains more convenient banking services as well as the other goods that these "freed-up" labor resources help produce.

Source: Based partly on Ben Craig, "Where Have All the Tellers Gone?" Federal Reserve Bank of Cleveland, *Economic Commentary*, Apr. 15, 1997; and statistics provided by the American Bankers Association.

creates" idea. This reasoning calls for government policies that modify the income distributions made strictly according to marginal productivity.

- ***Market imperfections*** The marginal productivity theory rests on the assumptions of competitive markets. Yet labor markets, for example, are riddled with imperfections, as you will see in Chapter 14. Some employers exert pricing power in hiring workers. And some workers, through labor unions, professional associations, and occupational licensing laws, wield monopoly power in selling their services. Even the process of collective bargaining over wages suggests a power struggle over the division of income. In this struggle, market forces—and income shares based on marginal productivity—may get pushed into the background. In addition, discrimination in the labor market can distort earnings patterns. In short, because of real-world market imperfections, wage rates and other resource prices frequently are not based solely on contributions to output.

Summary

1. Resource prices help determine money incomes, and they simultaneously ration resources to various industries and firms.
2. The demand for any resource is derived from the product it helps produce. That means the demand for a resource will depend on its productivity and on the market value (price) of the good it is producing.
3. Marginal revenue product is the extra revenue a firm obtains when it employs 1 more unit of a resource. The marginal revenue product curve for any resource is the demand curve for that resource, because the firm equates resource price and MRP in determining its profit-maximizing level of resource employment. Thus each point on the MRP curve indicates how many resource units the firm will hire at a specific resource price.
4. The firm's demand curve for a resource slopes downward, because the marginal product of additional units declines in accordance with the law of diminishing returns. When a firm is selling in an imperfectly competitive market, the resource demand curve falls for a second reason: Product price must be reduced for the firm to sell a larger output. The market demand curve for a resource is derived by summing horizontally the demand curves of all the firms hiring that resource.
5. The demand curve for a resource will shift as the result of (a) a change in the demand for, and therefore the price of, the product the resource is producing; (b) changes in the productivity of the resource; and (c) changes in the prices of other resources.
6. If resources A and B are substitutable for each other, a decline in the price of A will decrease the demand for B provided the substitution effect is greater than the output effect. But if the output effect *exceeds* the substitution effect, a decline in the price of A will increase the demand for B.
7. If resources C and D are complementary or jointly demanded, there is only an output effect; a change in the price of C will change the demand for D in the opposite direction.
8. The majority of the 10 fastest-growing occupations in the United States relate to health care or computers (review Table 13.5); the 10 most rapidly declining occupations, however, are more mixed (review Table 13.6).
9. The elasticity of demand for a resource measures the responsiveness of producers to a change in the resource's price. The coefficient of the elasticity of resource demand is

$$E_{rd} = \frac{\text{percentage change in resource quantity}}{\text{percentage change in resource price}}$$

When E_{rd} is greater than 1, resource demand is elastic; when E_{rd} is less than 1, resource demand is inelastic; and when E_{rd} equals 1, resource demand is unit-elastic.
10. The elasticity of demand for a resource will be greater (a) the greater the ease of substituting other resources for labor, (b) the greater the elasticity of demand for the product, and (c) the larger the proportion of total production costs attributable to the resource.
11. Any specific level of output will be produced with the least costly combination of variable resources when the marginal product per dollar's worth of each input is the same—that is, when

$$\frac{\text{MP of labor}}{\text{Price of labor}} = \frac{\text{MP of capital}}{\text{Price of capital}}$$

12. A firm is employing the profit-maximizing combination of resources when each resource is used to the point where its marginal revenue product equals its price. In terms of labor and capital, that occurs when the MRP of labor equals the price of labor and the MRP of capital equals the price of capital—that is, when

$$\frac{\text{MRP of labor}}{\text{Price of labor}} = \frac{\text{MRP of capital}}{\text{Price of capital}} = 1$$

13. The marginal productivity theory of income distribution holds that all resources are paid according to their marginal contribution to output. Critics say that such an income distribution is too unequal and that real-world market imperfections result in pay above and below marginal contributions to output.

Terms and Concepts

derived demand
marginal product (MP)
marginal revenue product (MRP)
marginal resource cost (MRC)
MRP = MRC rule
substitution effect
output effect
elasticity of resource demand
least-cost combination of resources
profit-maximizing combination of resources
marginal productivity theory of income distribution

Study Questions

1. What is the significance of resource pricing? Explain how the factors determining resource demand differ from those determining product demand. Explain the meaning and significance of the fact that the demand for a resource is a derived demand. Why do resource demand curves slope downward?

2. **KEY QUESTION** At the bottom of the page, complete the labor demand table for a firm that is hiring labor competitively and selling its product in a competitive market.
   a. How many workers will the firm hire if the market wage rate is $27.95? $19.95? Explain why the firm will not hire a larger or smaller number of units of labor at each of these wage rates.
   b. Show in schedule form and graphically the labor demand curve of this firm.
   c. Now again determine the firm's demand curve for labor, assuming that it is selling in an imperfectly competitive market and that, although it can sell 17 units at $2.20 per unit, it must lower product price by 5 cents in order to sell the marginal product of each successive labor unit. Compare this demand curve with that derived in question 2*b*. Which curve is more elastic? Explain.

3. Suppose that marginal product tripled while product price fell by one-half in Table 13.1. What would be the new MRP values in Table 13.1? What would be the net impact on the location of the resource demand curve in Figure 13.1?

4. In 2005 General Motors (GM) announced that it would reduce employment by 30,000 workers. What does this decision reveal about how it viewed its marginal revenue product (MRP) and marginal resource cost (MRC)? Why didn't GM reduce employment by more than 30,000 workers? By less than 30,000 workers?

5. **KEY QUESTION** What factors determine the elasticity of resource demand? What effect will each of the following have on the elasticity or the location of the demand for resource C, which is being used to produce commodity X? Where there is any uncertainty as to the outcome, specify the causes of that uncertainty.
   a. An increase in the demand for product X.
   b. An increase in the price of substitute resource D.
   c. An increase in the number of resources substitutable for C in producing X.
   d. A technological improvement in the capital equipment with which resource C is combined.
   e. A fall in the price of complementary resource E.
   f. A decline in the elasticity of demand for product X due to a decline in the competitiveness of product market X.

6. **KEY QUESTION** Suppose the productivity of capital and labor are as shown in the accompanying table. The output of these resources sells in a purely competitive market for $1 per unit. Both capital and labor are hired under purely competitive conditions at $3 and $1, respectively.

Units of Capital	MP of Capital	Units of Labor	MP of Labor
0		0	
	24		11
1		1	
	21		9
2		2	
	18		8
3		3	
	15		7
4		4	
	9		6
5		5	
	6		4
6		6	
	3		1
7		7	
	1		$\frac{1}{2}$
8		8	

   a. What is the least-cost combination of labor and capital the firm should employ in producing 80 units of output? Explain.
   b. What is the profit-maximizing combination of labor and capital the firm should use? Explain. What is the resulting level of output? What is the economic profit? Is this the least costly way of producing the profit-maximizing output?

7. **KEY QUESTION** In each of the following four cases, MRP_L and MRP_C refer to the marginal revenue products of labor and capital, respectively, and P_L and P_C refer to their prices. Indicate in each case whether the conditions are consistent with maximum profits for the firm. If not, state which

Units of Labor	Total Product	Marginal Product	Product Price	Total Revenue	Marginal Revenue Product
0	0	______	$2	$______	$______
1	17	______	2	______	______
2	31	______	2	______	______
3	43	______	2	______	______
4	53	______	2	______	______
5	60	______	2	______	______
6	65		2	______	

resource(s) should be used in larger amounts and which resource(s) should be used in smaller amounts.

a. MRP_L = \$8; P_L = \$4; MRP_C = \$8; P_C = \$4

b. MRP_L = \$10; P_L = \$12; MRP_C = \$14; P_C = \$9

c. MRP_L = \$6; P_L = \$6; MRP_C = \$12; P_C = \$12

d. MRP_L = \$22; P_L = \$26; MRP_C = \$16; P_C = \$19

8. Florida citrus growers say that the recent crackdown on illegal immigration is increasing the market wage rates necessary to get their oranges picked. Some are turning to \$100,000 to \$300,000 mechanical harvesters known as "trunk, shake, and catch" pickers, which vigorously shake oranges from the trees. If widely adopted, what will be the effect on the demand for human orange pickers? What does that imply about the relative strengths of the substitution and output effects?

9. **LAST WORD** Explain the economics of the substitution of ATMs for human tellers. Some banks are beginning to assess transaction fees when customers use human tellers rather than ATMs. What are these banks trying to accomplish?

Web-Based Questions

1. **SELECTED OCCUPATIONS—WHAT ARE THEIR EMPLOYMENT OUTLOOKS?** Use the A to Z index in the Bureau of Labor Statistics *Occupational Outlook*, at **www.bls.gov/oco/**, to determine the general and specific employment outlooks for (*a*) textile machinery operators, (*b*) financial managers, (*c*) computer operators, and (*d*) dental hygienists. Why do these job outlooks differ?

2. **THE OVERALL DEMAND FOR LABOR—IN WHICH COUNTRIES HAS IT INCREASED THE MOST?** In countries where real wages are steady or rising, increases in total employment reflect increases in labor demand. Go to the Bureau of Labor Statistics Web site, **www.bls.gov/fls/**, and select Comparative Civilian Labor Force Statistics. Find the percentage increases in civilian employment for the United States, Japan, Germany, France, Great Britain, Italy, and Canada for the most recent 10-year period. Which three countries have had the greatest growth of labor demand, as measured by the percentage change in employment? Which three the smallest?

IN THIS CHAPTER YOU WILL LEARN:

- Why labor productivity and real hourly compensation track so closely over time.
- How wage rates and employment levels are determined in competitive labor markets.
- How monopsony (a market with a single employer) can reduce wages below competitive levels.
- How unions can increase wage rates.
- The major causes of wage differentials.
- The types, benefits, and costs of "pay-for-performance" plans.

14

Wage Determination

Nearly 143 million Americans go to work each day. We work at an amazing variety of jobs for thousands of different firms and receive considerable differences in pay. What determines our hourly wage or annual salary? Why is the salary for, say, a topflight major-league baseball player $15 million or more a year, whereas the pay for a first-rate schoolteacher is $50,000? Why are starting salaries for college graduates who major in engineering and accounting so much higher than those for graduates majoring in journalism and sociology?

Having explored the major factors that underlie labor demand, we now bring *labor supply* into our analysis to help answer these questions. Generally speaking, labor supply and labor demand interact to determine the level of hourly wage rates or annual salaries in each occupation. Collectively, those wages and salaries make up 71 percent of all income paid to American resource suppliers.

Labor, Wages, and Earnings

Economists use the term "labor" broadly to apply to (1) blue- and white-collar workers of all varieties; (2) professional people such as lawyers, physicians, dentists, and teachers; and (3) owners of small businesses, including barbers, plumbers, and a host of retailers who provide labor as they carry on their own businesses.

Wages are the price that employers pay for labor. Wages not only take the form of direct money payments such as hourly pay, annual salaries, bonuses, commissions, and royalties but also fringe benefits such as paid vacations, health insurance, and pensions. Unless stated otherwise, we will use the term "wages" to mean all such payments and benefits converted to an hourly basis. That will remind us that the **wage rate** is the price paid per unit of labor services, in this case an hour of work. It will also let us distinguish between the wage rate and labor earnings, the latter determined by multiplying the number of hours worked by the hourly wage rate.

We must also distinguish between nominal wages and real wages. A **nominal wage** is the amount of money received per hour, day, or year. A **real wage** is the quantity of goods and services a worker can obtain with nominal wages; real wages reveal the "purchasing power" of nominal wages.

Your real wage depends on your nominal wage and the prices of the goods and services you purchase. Suppose you receive a 5 percent increase in your nominal wage during a certain year but in that same year the price level increases by 3 percent. Then your real wage has increased by 2 percent (= 5 percent − 3 percent). Unless otherwise indicated, we will assume that the overall level of prices remains constant. In other words, we will discuss only *real* wages.

General Level of Wages

Wages differ among nations, regions, occupations, and individuals. Wage rates are much higher in the United States than in China or India. They are slightly higher in the north and east of the United States than in the south. Plumbers are paid less than NFL punters. And one physician may earn twice as much as another physician for the same number of hours of work. Wage rates also differ by gender, race, and ethnic background.

The general, or average, level of wages, like the general level of prices, includes a wide range of different wage rates. It includes the wages of bakers, barbers, brick masons, and brain surgeons. By averaging such wages, we can more easily compare wages among regions and among nations.

As Global Perspective 14.1 suggests, the general level of real wages in the United States is relatively high—although not the highest in the world.

The simplest explanation for the high real wages in the United States and other industrially advanced economies (referred to hereafter as advanced economies) is that the demand for labor in those nations is relatively large compared to the supply of labor.

Role of Productivity

We know from the previous chapter that the demand for labor, or for any other resource, depends on its productivity. In general, the greater the productivity of labor, the greater is the demand for it. And if the total supply of labor is fixed, then the stronger the demand for labor, the higher is the average level of real wages. The demand for labor in the United States and the other major advanced economies is large because labor in those countries is

GLOBAL PERSPECTIVE 14.1

Hourly Wages of Production Workers, Selected Nations

Wage differences are pronounced worldwide. The data shown here indicate that hourly compensation in the United States is not as high as in some European nations. It is important to note, however, that the prices of goods and services vary greatly among nations and the process of converting foreign wages into dollars may not accurately reflect such variations.

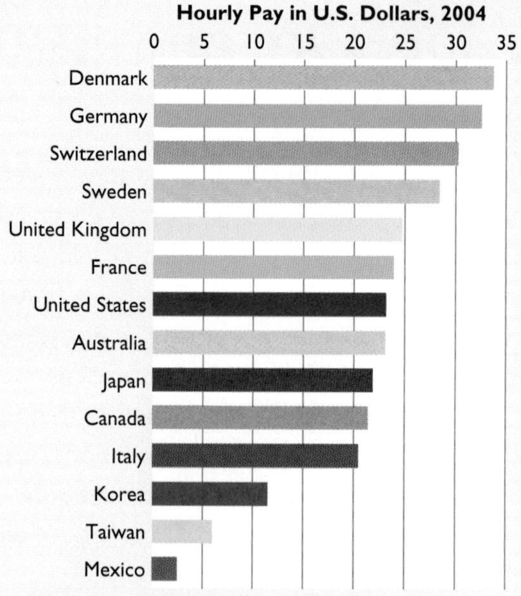

Source: U.S. Bureau of Labor Statistics, **www.bls.gov/**, 2006.

highly productive. There are several reasons for that high productivity:

- ***Plentiful capital*** Workers in the advanced economies have access to large amounts of physical capital equipment (machinery and buildings). In the United States $90,000 of physical capital is available, on average, for each worker.
- ***Access to abundant natural resources*** In advanced economies, natural resources tend to be abundant in relation to the size of the labor force. Some of those resources are available domestically and others are imported from abroad. The United States, for example, is richly endowed with arable land, mineral resources, and sources of energy for industry.
- ***Advanced technology*** The level of technological progress is generally high in advanced economies. Not only do workers in these economies have more capital equipment to work with, but that equipment is technologically superior to the equipment available to the vast majority of workers worldwide. Moreover, work methods in the advanced economies are steadily being improved through scientific study and research.
- ***Labor quality*** The health, vigor, education, and training of workers in advanced economies are generally superior to those in developing nations. This means that, even with the same quantity and quality of natural and capital resources, workers in advanced economies tend to be more efficient than many of their foreign counterparts.
- ***Other factors*** Less obvious factors also may underlie the high productivity in some of the advanced economies. In the United States, for example, such factors include (a) the efficiency and flexibility of management; (b) a business, social, and political environment that emphasizes production and productivity; (c) the vast size of the domestic market, which enables firms to engage in mass production; and (d) the increased specialization of production enabled by free-trade agreements with other nations.

Real Wages and Productivity

Figure 14.1 shows the close long-run relationship in the United States between output per hour of work and real hourly compensation (= wages and salaries + employers' contributions to social insurance and private benefit plans). Because real income and real output are two ways of viewing the same thing, real income (compensation) per worker can increase only at about the same rate as output per worker. When workers produce more real output per hour, more real income is available to distribute to them for each hour worked.

In the real world, however, suppliers of land, capital, and entrepreneurial talent also share in the income from production. Real wages therefore do not always rise in lockstep with gains in productivity over short spans of time. But over long periods, productivity and real wages tend to rise together.

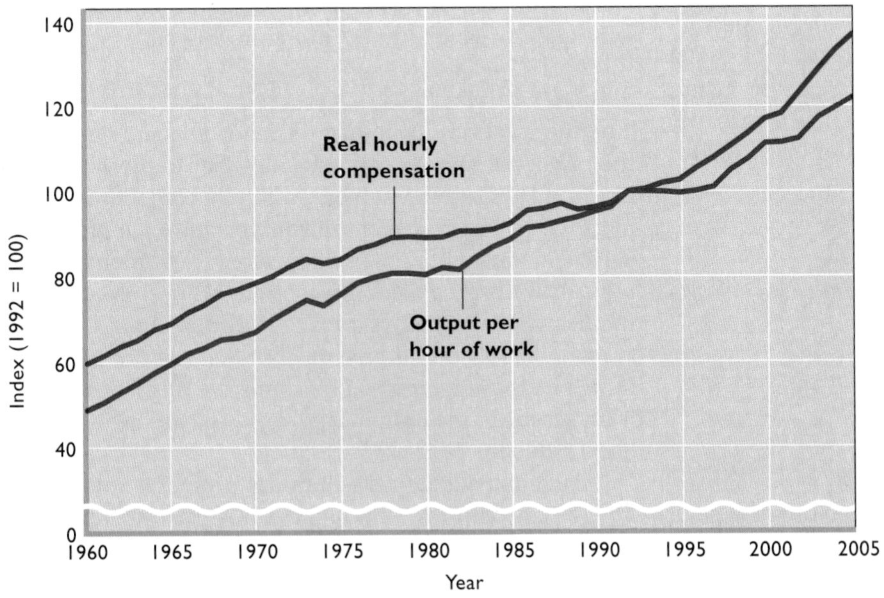

Source: Bureau of Labor Statistics, **stat.bls.gov.**

FIGURE 14.1 Output per hour and real hourly compensation in the United States. Over long periods of years, output per hour of work and real hourly compensation are closely related.

FIGURE 14.2 The long-run trend of real wages in the United States. The productivity of U.S. labor has increased substantially over the long run, causing the demand for labor *D* to shift rightward (that is, to increase) more rapidly than increases in the supply of labor *S*. The result has been increases in real wages.

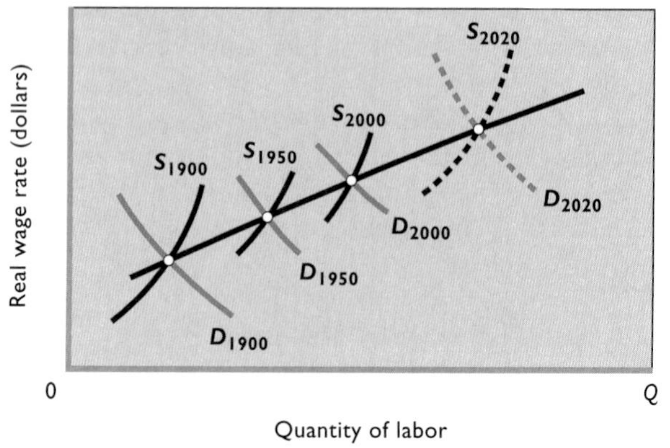

Secular Growth of Real Wages

Basic supply and demand analysis helps explain the long-term trend of real-wage growth in the United States. The nation's labor force has grown significantly over the decades. But, as a result of the productivity-increasing factors we have mentioned, labor demand has increased more rapidly than labor supply. Figure 14.2 shows several such increases in labor supply and labor demand. The result has been a long-run, or secular, increase in wage rates and employment.

A Purely Competitive Labor Market

We now turn from the average level of wages to specific wage rates. What determines the wage rate paid for some specific type of labor? Demand and supply analysis again is revealing. Let's begin by examining labor demand and labor supply in a **purely competitive labor market.** In this type of market:

- Numerous firms compete with one another in hiring a specific type of labor.
- Each of many qualified workers with identical skills supplies that type of labor.
- Individual firms and individual workers are "wage takers," since neither can exert any control over the market wage rate.

Market Demand for Labor

Suppose 200 firms demand a particular type of labor, say, carpenters. These firms need not be in the same industry; industries are defined according to the products they produce and not the resources they employ. Thus, firms producing wood-framed furniture, wood windows and doors, houses and apartment buildings, and wood cabinets will demand carpenters. To find the total, or market, labor demand curve for a particular labor service, we sum horizontally the labor demand curves (the marginal revenue product curves) of the individual firms, as indicated in **Figure 14.3 (Key Graph).** The horizontal summing of the 200 labor demand curves like *d* in Figure 14.3b yields the market labor demand curve *D* in Figure 14.3a.

Market Supply of Labor

On the supply side of a purely competitive labor market, we assume that there is no union and that workers individually compete for available jobs. The supply curve for each type of labor slopes upward, indicating that employers as a group must pay higher wage rates to obtain more workers. This is so because they must bid workers away from other industries, occupations, and localities. Within limits, workers have alternative job opportunities. For example, they may work in other industries in the same locality, or they may work in their present occupations in different cities or states, or they may work in other occupations.

Firms that want to hire these workers (here, carpenters) must pay higher wage rates to attract them away from the alternative job opportunities available to them. They must also pay higher wages to induce people who are not currently in the labor force—who are perhaps doing household activities or enjoying leisure—to seek employment. In short, assuming that wages are constant in other labor markets, higher wages in a particular labor market entice more workers to offer their labor services in that market—a fact confirmed by the upward-sloping market supply-of-labor curve *S* in Figure 14.3a.

Labor Market Equilibrium

The intersection of the market labor demand curve and the market supply curve determines the equilibrium wage rate and level of employment in purely competitive labor markets. In Figure 14.3a the equilibrium wage rate is W_c (\$10) and the number of workers hired is Q_c (1000). To the individual firm the market wage rate W_c is given. Each of the many firms employs such a small fraction of the total available supply of this type of labor that none of them can influence the wage rate. The supply of this labor is perfectly elastic to the individual firm, as shown by horizontal line *s* in Figure 14.3b.

Each individual firm will find it profitable to hire this type of labor up to the point at which marginal revenue product is equal to marginal resource cost. This is merely an application of the MRP = MRC rule we developed in Chapter 13.

FIGURE 14.3 Labor supply and labor demand in (a) a purely competitive labor market and (b) a single competitive firm. In a purely competitive labor market (a) the equilibrium wage rate W_c and the number of workers Q_c are determined by labor supply S and labor demand D. Because this market wage rate is given to the individual firm (b) hiring in this market, its labor supply curve s = MRC is perfectly elastic. Its labor demand curve, d, is its MRP curve (here labeled *mrp*). The firm maximizes its profit by hiring workers up to where MRP = MRC. Area 0*abc* represents both the firm's total revenue and its total cost. The green area is its total wage cost; the brown area is its nonlabor costs, including a normal profit—that is, the firm's payments to the suppliers of land, capital, and entrepreneurship.

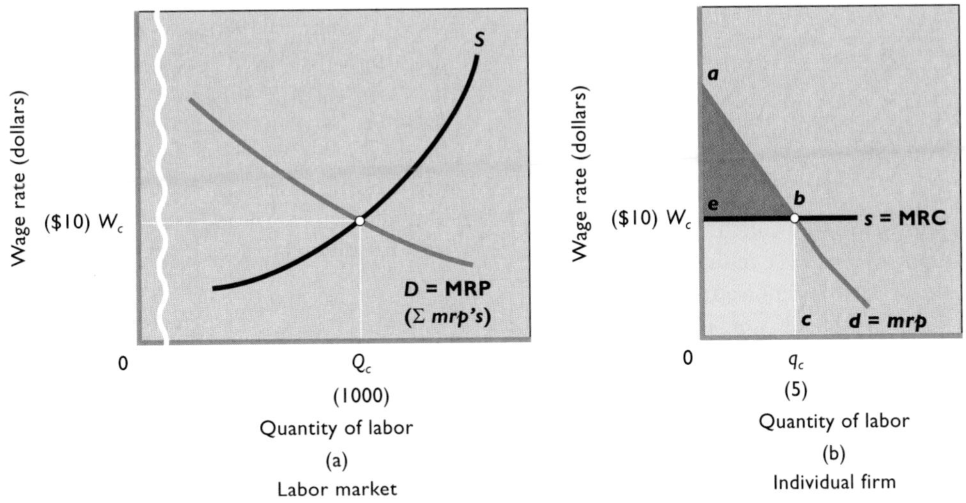

QUICK QUIZ 14.3

1. The supply-of-labor curve *S* slopes upward in graph (a) because:
   a. the law of diminishing marginal utility applies.
   b. the law of diminishing returns applies.
   c. workers can afford to "buy" more leisure when their wage rates rise.
   d. higher wages are needed to attract workers away from other labor markets, household activities, and leisure.
2. This firm's labor demand curve *d* in graph (b) slopes downward because:
   a. the law of diminishing marginal utility applies.
   b. the law of diminishing returns applies.
   c. the firm must lower its price to sell additional units of its product.
   d. the firm is a competitive employer, not a monopsonist.
3. In employing five workers, the firm represented in graph (b):
   a. has a total wage cost of $6000.
   b. is adhering to the general principle of undertaking all actions for which the marginal benefit exceeds the marginal cost.
   c. uses less labor than would be ideal from society's perspective.
   d. experiences increasing marginal returns.
4. A rightward shift of the labor supply curve in graph (a) would shift curve:
   a. *d* = *mrp* leftward in graph (b).
   b. *d* = *mrp* rightward in graph (b).
   c. *s* = MRC upward in graph (b).
   d. *s* = MRC downward in graph (b).

Answers: 1. d; 2. b; 3. b; 4. d

As Table 14.1 indicates, when the price of a resource is imposed on the individual competitive firm, the marginal cost of that resource (MRC) is constant and is equal to the resource price. Here, MRC is constant and is equal to the wage rate. Each additional worker hired adds precisely his or her own wage rate ($10 in this case) to the firm's total resource cost. So the firm in a purely competitive labor market maximizes its profit by hiring workers to the point at which its wage rate equals MRP. In Figure 14.3b this firm will hire q_c (5) workers, paying each of them the market wage rate W_c ($10). The other 199 firms (not shown) that are hiring workers in this labor market will do the same.

To determine a firm's total revenue from employing a particular number of labor units, we sum the MRPs of those units. For example, if a firm employs 3 labor units with marginal revenue products of $14, $13, and $12, respectively, then the firm's total revenue is $39 (= $14 + $13 + $12). In

TABLE 14.1 The Supply of Labor: Pure Competition in the Hire of Labor

(1) Units of Labor	(2) Wage Rate	(3) Total Labor Cost (Wage Bill)	(4) Marginal Resource (Labor) Cost
0	$10	$ 0	$10
1	10	10	10
2	10	20	10
3	10	30	10
4	10	40	10
5	10	50	10
6	10	60	

Figure 14.3b, where we are not restricted to whole units of labor, total revenue is represented by area $0abc$ under the MRP curve to the left of q_c. And what area represents the firm's total cost, including a normal profit? Answer: For q_c units, the same area—$0abc$. The green rectangle represents the firm's total wage cost ($0q_c \times 0W_c$). The brown triangle (total revenue minus total wage cost) represents the firm's nonlabor costs—its explicit and implicit payments to land, capital, and entrepreneurship. Thus, in this case, total cost (wages plus other income payments) equals total revenue. This firm and others like it are earning only a normal profit. Figure 14.3b represents a long-run equilibrium for a firm that is selling its product in a purely competitive product market and "buying" its labor in a purely competitive labor market. **(Key Questions 3 and 4)**

G 14.1
Competitive labor market

Monopsony Model

In the purely competitive labor market described in the preceding section, each employer hires too small an amount of labor to influence the wage rate. Each firm can hire as little or as much labor as it needs, but only at the market wage rate, as reflected in its horizontal labor supply curve. The situation is quite different in a **monopsony,** a market in which a single employer of labor has substantial buying (hiring) power. A labor market monopsony has the following characteristics:

- There is only a single buyer of a particular type of labor.
- This type of labor is relatively immobile, either geographically or because workers would have to acquire new skills.
- The firm is a "wage maker," because the wage rate it must pay varies directly with the number of workers it employs.

As is true of monopoly power, there are various degrees of monopsony power. In *pure* monopsony such power is at its maximum, because there is only a single employer in the labor market. The best real-world examples are probably the labor markets in some towns that depend almost entirely on one major firm. For example, a silver-mining company may be almost the only source of employment in a remote Idaho or Colorado town. A New England textile mill, a Wisconsin paper mill, or an Alaskan fish processor may provide most of the employment in its locale.

O 14.1
Monopsony

In other cases three or four firms may each hire a large portion of the supply of labor in a certain market and therefore have some monopsony power. Moreover, if they tacitly or openly act in concert in hiring labor, they greatly enhance their monopsony power.

Upward-Sloping Labor Supply to Firm

When a firm hires most of the available supply of a particular type of labor, its decision to employ more or fewer workers affects the wage rate it pays to those workers. Specifically, if a firm is large in relation to the size of the labor market, it will have to pay a higher wage rate to attract labor away from other employment or from leisure. Suppose there is only one employer of a particular type of labor in a certain geographic area. In that extreme case, the labor supply curve for that firm and the total supply curve for the labor market are identical. This supply curve is upward-sloping, indicating that the firm must pay a higher wage rate to attract more workers. The supply curve, S in Figure 14.4, is also the average-cost-of-labor curve for the firm; each point on it indicates the wage rate

FIGURE 14.4 The wage rate and level of employment in a monopsonistic labor market. In a monopsonistic labor market the employer's marginal resource (labor) cost curve (MRC) lies above the labor supply curve S. Equating MRC with MRP at point b, the monopsonist hires Q_m workers (compared with Q_c under competition). As indicated by point c on S, it pays only wage rate W_m (compared with the competitive wage W_c).

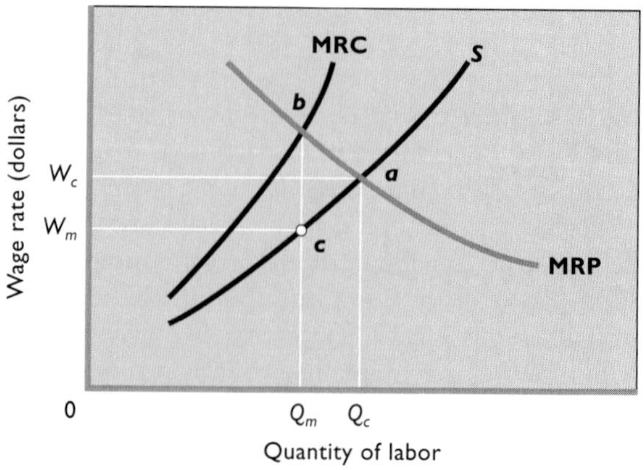

(cost) per worker that must be paid to attract the corresponding number of workers.

MRC Higher than the Wage Rate

When a monopsonist pays a higher wage to attract an additional worker, it must pay that higher wage to all the workers it is currently employing at a lower wage. If not, labor morale will deteriorate, and the employer will be plagued with labor unrest because of wage-rate differences existing for the same job. Paying a uniform wage to all workers means that the cost of an extra worker—the marginal resource (labor) cost (MRC)—is the sum of that worker's wage rate and the amount necessary to bring the wage rate of all current workers up to the new wage level.

Table 14.2 illustrates this point. One worker can be hired at a wage rate of \$6. But hiring a second worker forces the firm to pay a higher wage rate of \$7. The marginal resource (labor) cost of the second worker is \$8—the \$7 paid to the second worker plus a \$1 raise for the first worker. From another viewpoint, total labor cost is now \$14 (= 2 × \$7), up from \$6. So the MRC of the second worker is \$8 (= \$14 − \$6), not just the \$7 wage rate paid to that worker. Similarly, the marginal labor cost of the third worker is \$10—the \$8 that must be paid to attract this worker from alternative employment plus \$1 raises, from \$7 to \$8, for the first two workers.

The important point is that to the monopsonist, marginal resource (labor) cost exceeds the wage rate. Graphically, the MRC curve lies above the average-cost-of-labor curve, or labor supply curve *S*, as is clearly shown in Figure 14.4.

Equilibrium Wage and Employment

How many units of labor will the monopsonist hire, and what wage rate will it pay? To maximize profit, the monopsonist will employ the quantity of labor Q_m in Figure 14.4, because at that quantity MRC and MRP are equal (point *b*).[1] The monopsonist next determines how much it must pay to attract these Q_m workers. From the supply curve *S*, specifically point *c*, it sees that it must pay wage rate W_m. Clearly, it need not pay a wage equal to MRP; it can attract exactly the number of workers it wants (Q_m) with wage rate W_m. And that is what it will pay.

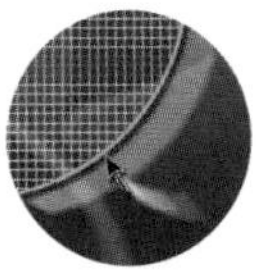

G 14.2
Monopsony

W 14.1
Labor markets: competition and monopsony

Contrast these results with those that would prevail in a competitive labor market. With competition in the hiring of labor, the level of employment would be greater (at Q_c) and the wage rate would be higher (at W_c). Other things equal, the monopsonist maximizes its profit by hiring a smaller number of workers and thereby paying a less-than-competitive wage rate. Society gets a smaller output, and workers get a wage rate that is less by *bc* than their marginal revenue product. Just as a monopolistic seller finds it profitable to restrict product output to realize an above-competitive price for its goods, the monopsonistic employer of resources finds it profitable to restrict employment in order to depress wage rates and therefore costs, that is, to realize wage rates below those that would occur under competitive conditions.

Examples of Monopsony Power

Monopsonistic labor markets are not common in the U.S. economy; typically, many potential employers compete for most workers, particularly for workers who are occupationally and geographically mobile. Also, where monopsony labor market outcomes might have otherwise occurred, unions have sprung up to counteract that power by forcing firms to negotiate wages. Nevertheless,

TABLE 14.2 The Supply of Labor: Monopsony in the Hire of Labor

(1) Units of Labor	(2) Wage Rate	(3) Total Labor Cost (Wage Bill)	(4) Marginal Resource (Labor) Cost
0	\$ 5	\$ 0	
1	6	6	\$ 6
2	7	14	8
3	8	24	10
4	9	36	12
5	10	50	14
6	11	66	16

[1] The fact that MRC exceeds resource price when resources are hired or purchased under imperfectly competitive (monopsonistic) conditions calls for adjustments in Chapter 13's least-cost and profit-maximizing rules for hiring resources. (See equations 1 and 2 in the "Optimal Combination of Resources" section of Chapter 13.) Specifically, we must substitute MRC for resource price in the denominators of our two equations. That is, with imperfect competition in the hiring of both labor and capital, equation 1 becomes

$$\frac{MP_L}{MRC_L} = \frac{MP_C}{MRC_C} \tag{1'}$$

and equation 2 is restated as

$$\frac{MRP_L}{MRC_L} = \frac{MRP_C}{MRC_C} = 1 \tag{2'}$$

In fact, equations 1 and 2 can be regarded as special cases of 1′ and 2′ in which firms happen to be hiring under purely competitive conditions and resource price is therefore equal to, and can be substituted for, marginal resource cost.

economists have found evidence of monopsony power in such diverse labor markets as the markets for nurses, professional athletes, public school teachers, newspaper employees, and some building-trade workers.

In the case of nurses, the major employers in most locales are a relatively small number of hospitals. Further, the highly specialized skills of nurses are not readily transferable to other occupations. It has been found, in accordance with the monopsony model, that, other things equal, the smaller the number of hospitals in a town or city (that is, the greater the degree of monopsony), the lower the beginning salaries of nurses.

Professional sports leagues also provide a good example of monopsony, particularly as it relates to the pay of first-year players. The National Football League, the National Basketball Association, and Major League Baseball assign first-year players to teams through "player drafts." That device prohibits other teams from competing for a player's services, at least for several years, until the player becomes a "free agent." In this way the league exercises monopsony power, which results in lower salaries than would occur under competitive conditions. **(Key Question 6)**

QUICK REVIEW 14.1

- Real wages have increased historically in the United States because labor demand has increased relative to labor supply.
- Over the long term, real wages per worker have increased at approximately the same rate as worker productivity.
- The competitive employer is a wage taker and employs workers at the point where the wage rate (= MRC) equals MRP.
- The labor supply curve to a monopsonist is upward-sloping, causing MRC to exceed the wage rate for each worker. Other things equal, the monopsonist, hiring where MRC = MRP, will employ fewer workers and pay a lower wage rate than would a purely competitive employer.

Three Union Models

We have assumed so far that workers compete with one another in selling their labor services. In some labor markets, however, workers sell their labor services collectively through unions. When a union is formed in an otherwise competitive labor market, it bargains with a relatively large number of employers. It has many goals, the most important of which is to raise wage rates. It can pursue that objective in several ways.

Demand-Enhancement Model

From the union's viewpoint, the most desirable technique for raising wage rates is to increase the demand for labor.

FIGURE 14.5 Unions and demand enhancement. When unions can increase the demand for labor (say, from D_1 to D_2), they can realize higher wage rates (W_c to W_u) and more jobs (Q_c to Q_u).

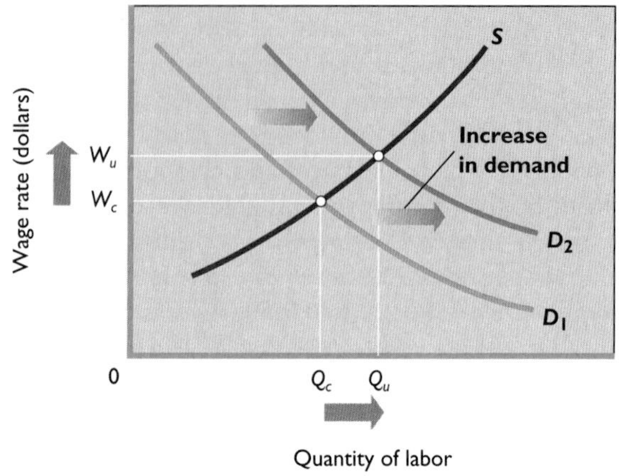

As Figure 14.5 shows, an increase in labor demand will create both higher wage rates and more jobs.

To increase labor demand, the union might alter one or more of the determinants of demand. For example, a union can attempt to increase the demand for the product or service it is producing, enhance the productivity of labor, or alter the prices of other inputs.

Increase Product Demand Unions can increase the demand for the products they help produce—and thus raise the demand for their own labor services — through advertising or political lobbying.

Occasionally, unions advertise union-produced goods or services. The long-running campaign urging consumers to "look for the union label" is an example. Less often, unions join with their employers to finance advertising campaigns designed to bolster product demand. The Communications Workers of America (CWA) once helped finance a large "Call or Buy Union" campaign to convince telephone users to choose the long-distance services and equipment of AT&T and Western Union, which together provided thousands of CWA jobs.

On the political front construction unions have lobbied for new highway, mass-transit, and stadium projects. Teachers' unions and associations have pushed for increased public spending on education. Unions in the aerospace industry have lobbied to increase spending on the military and on space exploration.

Increase Productivity Many decisions affecting labor productivity—for example, decisions concerning the quantity and quality of real capital used by workers—are made unilaterally by management. There is a growing tendency, however, to set up joint labor-management committees designed to increase labor productivity.

Alter the Price of Other Inputs Unions sometimes have tried to strengthen the demand for their labor by working to increase the price of substitute resources. For example, although union members are generally paid significantly more than the minimum wage, unions have strongly supported increases in the minimum wage. The purpose may be to raise the price of low-wage, nonunion labor, which in some cases is substitutable for union labor. A higher minimum wage for nonunion workers will discourage employers from substituting such workers for union workers and will thereby bolster the demand for union members.

Similarly, unions have sometimes sought to increase the demand for their labor by supporting public actions that will reduce the price of a complementary resource. For example, unions in industries that use large amounts of imported resources might urge reductions in tariffs on those imports. Where labor and the other resource are complementary, a price decrease for the other resource will increase the demand for labor through Chapter 13's output effect.

Unions recognize that their ability to influence the demand for labor is very limited. So it is not surprising that their efforts to raise wage rates have concentrated on the supply side of the labor market.

Exclusive or Craft Union Model

One way in which unions can boost wage rates is to reduce the supply of labor, and over the years organized labor has favored policies to do just that. For example, labor unions have supported legislation that has (1) restricted immigration, (2) reduced child labor, (3) encouraged compulsory retirement, and (4) enforced a shorter workweek.

Moreover, certain types of workers have adopted techniques designed to restrict the number of workers who can join their union. This is especially true of *craft unions*, whose members possess a particular skill, such as carpenters or brick masons or plumbers. Craft unions have frequently forced employers to agree to hire only union members, thereby gaining virtually complete control of the labor supply. Then, by following restrictive membership policies—for example, long apprenticeships, very high initiation fees, and limits on the number of new members admitted—they have artificially restricted labor supply. As indicated in Figure 14.6, such practices result in higher wage rates and constitute what is called **exclusive unionism.** By excluding workers from unions and therefore from the labor supply, craft unions succeed in elevating wage rates.

This craft union model is also applicable to many professional organizations, such as the American Medical Association, the National Education Association, the American Bar Association, and hundreds of others. Such groups seek to limit competition for their services from less qualified labor suppliers. One way to accomplish that is through **occupational licensing.** Here a group of workers in a given occupation pressure Federal, state, or municipal government to pass a law that says that some occupational group (for example, barbers, physicians, lawyers, plumbers, cosmetologists, egg graders, pest controllers) can practice their trade only if they meet certain requirements. Those requirements might include level of education, amount of work experience, the passing of an examination, and personal characteristics ("the practitioner must be of good moral character"). Members of the licensed occupation typically dominate the licensing board that administers such laws. The result is self-regulation, which often leads to policies that serve only to restrict entry to the occupation and reduce labor supply.

The purpose of licensing is supposedly to protect consumers from incompetent practitioners—surely a worthy goal. But such licensing, if abused, results in above-competitive wages and earnings for those in the licensed occupation (Figure 14.6). Moreover, licensing requirements often include a residency requirement, which inhibits the interstate movement of qualified workers. Some 600 occupations are now licensed in the United States.

FIGURE 14.6 Exclusive or craft unionism. By reducing the supply of labor (say, from S_1 to S_2) through the use of restrictive membership policies, exclusive unions achieve higher wage rates (W_c to W_u). However, restriction of the labor supply also reduces the number of workers employed (Q_c to Q_u).

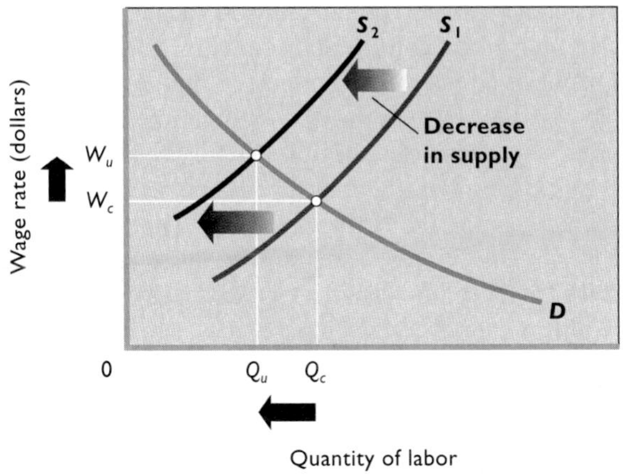

Inclusive or Industrial Union Model

Instead of trying to limit their membership, however, most unions seek to organize all available workers. This is especially true of the *industrial unions*, such as those of the automobile workers and steelworkers. Such unions seek as members all available unskilled, semiskilled, and skilled workers in an industry. A union can afford to be exclusive when its members are skilled craftspersons for whom there are few substitutes. But for a union composed of unskilled and semiskilled workers, a policy of limited membership would make available to the employers numerous nonunion workers who are highly substitutable for the union workers.

An industrial union that includes virtually all available workers in its membership can put firms under great pressure to agree to its wage demands. Because of its legal right to strike, such a union can threaten to deprive firms of their entire labor supply. And an actual strike can do just that.

We illustrate such **inclusive unionism** in Figure 14.7. Initially, the competitive equilibrium wage rate is W_c and the level of employment is Q_c. Now suppose an industrial union is formed that demands a higher, above-equilibrium wage rate of, say, W_u. That wage rate W_u would create a perfectly elastic labor supply over the range *ae* in Figure 14.7. If firms wanted to hire any workers in this range, they would have to pay the union-imposed wage rate. If they decide against meeting this wage demand, the union will supply no labor at all, and the firms will be faced with a strike. If firms decide it is better to pay the higher wage rate than to suffer a strike, they will cut back on employment from Q_c to Q_u.

By agreeing to the union's W_u wage demand, individual employers become wage takers. Because labor supply is perfectly elastic over range *ae*, the marginal resource (labor) cost is equal to the wage rate W_u over this range.

FIGURE 14.7 Inclusive or industrial unionism. By organizing virtually all available workers in order to control the supply of labor, inclusive industrial unions may impose a wage rate, such as W_u, which is above the competitive wage rate W_c. In effect, this changes the labor supply curve from S to aeS. At wage rate W_u, employers will cut employment from Q_c to Q_u.

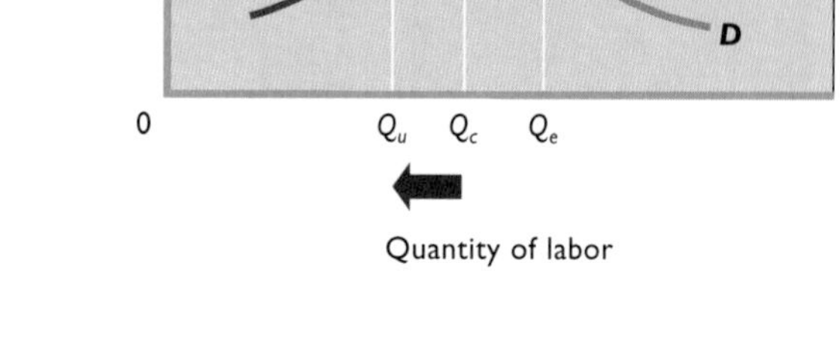

The Q_u level of employment is the result of employers' equating this MRC (now equal to the wage rate) with MRP, according to our profit-maximizing rule.

Note from point *e* on labor supply curve *S* that Q_e workers desire employment at wage W_u. But as indicated by point *b* on labor demand curve *D*, only Q_u workers are employed. The result is a surplus of labor of $Q_e - Q_u$ (also shown by distance *eb*). In a purely competitive labor market without the union, the effect of a surplus of unemployed workers would be lower wages. Specifically, the wage rate would fall to the equilibrium level W_c, where the quantity of labor supplied equals the quantity of labor demanded (each Q_c). But this drop in wages does not happen, because workers are acting collectively through their union. Individual workers cannot offer to work for less than W_u; nor can employers pay less than that.

Wage Increases and Unemployment

Have U.S. unions been successful in raising the wages of their members? Evidence suggests that union members on average achieve a 15 percent wage advantage over nonunion workers.

As Figures 14.6 and 14.7 suggest, the effect of wage-raising actions achieved by both exclusive and inclusive unionism is reduced employment. A union's success in achieving above-equilibrium wage rates thus tends to be accompanied by a decline in the number of workers employed. That result acts as a restraining influence on union wage demands. A union cannot expect to maintain solidarity within its ranks if it seeks a wage rate so high that joblessness will result for, say, 20 or 30 percent of its members.

The unemployment effect created by union-induced wage increases may be reduced in two ways:

- ***Growth*** The normal growth of the economy increases the demand for most kinds of labor over time. This continual rightward shift of the labor demand curves in Figures 14.6 and 14.7 might offset, or more than offset, the unemployment effect associated with the indicated wage increases. In that event, the increases in unemployment prompted by the unions would tend to *slow* the growth of job opportunities but would not reduce total employment by firms.
- ***Elasticity*** The size of the unemployment effect resulting from a union-induced wage increase depends on the elasticity of demand for labor. The more inelastic that demand, the smaller is the amount of unemployment that accompanies a given wage-rate increase. And if unions have sufficient bargaining strength, they

CPI -

may be able to win provisions in their collective bargaining agreements that reduce the elasticity of demand for union labor by reducing the substitutability of other inputs for that labor. For example, a union may bargain successfully for severance pay or layoff pay, which increases the cost to the firm of substituting capital for labor when wage rates are increased.

Bilateral Monopoly Model

Suppose a strong industrial union is formed in a labor market that is monopsonistic rather than competitive, creating a combination of the monopsony model and the inclusive unionism model. The result is called **bilateral monopoly** because in its pure form there is a single seller and a single buyer. The union is a monopolistic "seller" of labor that controls labor supply and can influence wage rates, but it faces a monopsonistic "buyer" of labor that can also affect wages by altering its employment. This is not an uncommon case, particularly in less pure forms in which a single union confronts two, three, or four large employers. Examples: steel, automobiles, construction equipment, professional sports, and commercial aircraft.

Indeterminate Outcome of Bilateral Monopoly

We show this situation in Figure 14.8, where we superimpose Figure 14.7 onto Figure 14.4. The monopsonistic employer will seek the below-competitive-equilibrium wage rate W_m, and the union presumably will press for some above-competitive-equilibrium wage rate such as W_u. Which will be the outcome? We cannot say with certainty.

FIGURE 14.8 Bilateral monopoly in the labor market. A monopsonist seeks to hire Q_m workers (where MRC = MRP) and pay wage rate W_m corresponding to quantity Q_m on labor supply curve S. The inclusive union it faces seeks the above-equilibrium wage rate W_u. The actual outcome cannot be predicted by economic theory. It will result from bargaining between the two parties.

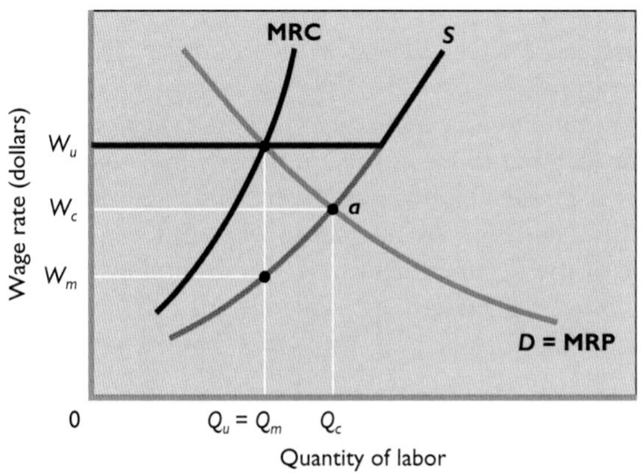

The outcome is "logically indeterminate" because the bilateral monopoly model does not explain what will happen at the collective bargaining table. We can expect the wage outcome to lie somewhere between W_m and W_u. Beyond that, about all we can say is that the party with the greater bargaining power and the more effective bargaining strategy will probably get a wage closer to the one it seeks.

Desirability of Bilateral Monopoly

The wage and employment outcomes in this situation might be more socially desirable than the term "bilateral monopoly" implies. The monopoly on one side of the market might in effect cancel out the monopoly on the other side, yielding competitive or near-competitive results. If either the union or management prevailed in this market—that is, if the actual wage rate were determined at either W_u or W_m—employment would be restricted to Q_m (where MRP = MRC), which is below the competitive level.

But now suppose the monopoly power of the union roughly offsets the monopsony power of management, and the union and management agree on wage rate W_c, which is the competitive wage. Once management accepts this wage rate, its incentive to restrict employment disappears; no longer can it depress wage rates by restricting employment. Instead, management hires at the most profitable resource quantity, where the bargained wage rate W_c (which is now the firm's MRC) is equal to the MRP. It hires Q_c workers. Thus, with monopoly on both sides of the labor market, the resulting wage rate and level of employment may be closer to competitive levels than would be the case if monopoly existed on only one side of the market. **(Key Question 7)**

QUICK REVIEW 14.2

- In the demand-enhancement union model, a union increases the wage rate by increasing labor demand through actions that increase product demand, raise labor productivity, or alter the prices of related inputs.
- In the exclusive (craft) union model, a union increases wage rates by artificially restricting labor supply, through, say, long apprenticeships or occupational licensing.
- In the inclusive (industrial) union model, a union raises the wage rate by gaining control over a firm's labor supply and threatening to withhold labor via a strike unless a negotiated wage is obtained.
- Bilateral monopoly occurs in a labor market where a monopsonist bargains with an inclusive, or industrial, union. Wage and employment outcomes are determined by collective bargaining in this situation.

The Minimum-Wage Controversy

Since the passage of the Fair Labor Standards Act in 1938, the United States has had a Federal **minimum wage.** That wage has ranged between 30 and 50 percent of the average wage paid to manufacturing workers and was $5.15 per hour in 2006. Sixteen states, however, have minimum wages that are higher than the Federal minimum wage. Some of these state minimum wages are relatively high. For example, in 2006 the minimum wage in the state of Washington was $7.63 an hour. The purpose of the minimum wage is to provide a "wage floor" that will help less skilled workers earn enough income to escape poverty.

Case against the Minimum Wage

Critics, reasoning in terms of Figure 14.7, contend that an above-equilibrium minimum wage (say, W_u) will simply push employers back up their labor demand curves, causing them to hire fewer workers. The higher labor costs may even force some firms out of business. Then some of the poor, low-wage workers whom the minimum wage was designed to help will find themselves out of work. Critics point out that a worker who is *unemployed* at a minimum wage of $5.15 per hour is clearly worse off than he or she would be if *employed* at a market wage rate of, say, $4.85 per hour.

A second criticism of the minimum wage is that it is "poorly targeted" to reduce household poverty. Critics point out that much of the benefit of the minimum wage accrues to workers, including many teenagers, who do not live in poverty households.

Case for the Minimum Wage

Advocates of the minimum wage say that critics analyze its impact in an unrealistic context. Figure 14.7, advocates claim, assumes a competitive, static market. But in a more real, low-pay labor market where there is some monopsony power (Figure 14.8), the minimum wage can increase wage rates without causing unemployment. Indeed, a higher minimum wage may even produce more jobs by eliminating the motive that monopsonistic firms have for restricting employment. For example, a minimum-wage floor of W_c in Figure 14.8 would change the firm's labor supply curve to $W_c aS$ and prompt the firm to increase its employment from Q_m workers to Q_c workers.

Moreover, a minimum wage may increase labor productivity, shifting the labor demand curve to the right and offsetting any reduced employment that the minimum wage might cause. For example, the higher wage rate might prompt firms to find more productive tasks for low-paid workers, thereby raising their productivity. Alternatively, the minimum wage may reduce *labor turnover* (the rate at which workers voluntarily quit). With fewer low-productive trainees, the *average* productivity of the firm's workers would rise. In either case, the higher labor productivity would justify paying the higher minimum wage. So the alleged negative employment effects of the minimum wage might not occur.

Evidence and Conclusions

Which view is correct? Unfortunately, there is no clear answer. All economists agree there is some minimum wage so high that it would severely reduce employment. Consider $20 an hour, as an absurd example. But no current consensus exists on the employment effects of the present level of the minimum wage. Evidence in the 1980s suggested that minimum-wage hikes reduced employment of minimum-wage workers, particularly teenagers (16- to 19-year-olds). The consensus then was that a 10 percent increase in the minimum wage would reduce teenage employment by about 1 to 3 percent. But the minimum-wage hikes in 1991, 1996, and 1997 seemed to produce smaller, and perhaps zero, employment declines among teenagers.[2]

The overall effect of the minimum wage is thus uncertain. On the one hand, the employment and unemployment effects of the minimum wage do not appear to be as great as many critics fear. On the other hand, because a large part of its effect is dissipated on nonpoverty families, the minimum wage is not as strong an antipoverty tool as many supporters contend.

It is clear, however, that the minimum wage has strong political support. Perhaps this stems from two realities: (1) More workers are helped by the minimum wage than are hurt, and (2) the minimum wage gives society some assurance that employers are not "taking undue advantage" of vulnerable, low-skilled workers.

Wage Differentials

Hourly wage rates and annual salaries differ greatly among occupations. In Table 14.3 we list average annual salaries for a number of occupations to illustrate such occupational **wage differentials.** For example, observe that surgeons on average earn eight times as much as retail salespersons. Not shown, there are also large wage differentials within some of the occupations listed. For example, some highly experienced surgeons earn several times as much income

[2]Alan Krueger, "Teaching the Minimum Wage in Econ 101 in Light of the New Economics of the Minimum Wage," *Journal of Economic Education*, Summer 2001.

TABLE 14.3 Average Annual Wages in Selected Occupations, 2005

Occupation	Average Annual Wages
1. Surgeons	$177,690
2. Aircraft pilots	135,040
3. Petroleum engineers	97,350
4. Financial managers	96,620
5. Law professors	95,570
6. Chemical engineers	79,230
7. Dental hygienists	60,620
8. Registered nurses	56,880
9. Police officers	47,270
10. Electricians	45,630
11. Travel agents	30,750
12. Barbers	24,700
13. Retail salespersons	23,170
14. Recreation workers	22,420
15. Teacher aides	21,100
16. Fast food cooks	15,500

Source: Bureau of Labor Statistics, **www.bls.gov/**, 2006.

as surgeons just starting their careers. And, although average wages for retail salespersons are relatively low, some top salespersons selling on commission make several times the average wages listed for their occupation.

What explains wage differentials such as these? Once again, the forces of demand and supply are revealing. As we demonstrate in Figure 14.9, wage differentials can arise on either the supply or the demand side of labor markets. Figure 14.9a and 14.9b represent labor markets for two occupational groups that have identical *labor supply curves*. Labor market (a) has a relatively high equilibrium wage (W_a) because labor demand is very strong. In labor market (b) the equilibrium wage is relatively low (W_b) because labor demand is weak. Clearly, the wage differential between occupations (a) and (b) results solely from differences in the magnitude of labor demand.

Contrast that situation with Figure 14.9c and 14.9d, where the *labor demand curves* are identical. In labor market (c) the equilibrium wage is relatively high (W_c) because labor supply is highly restricted. In labor market (d) labor supply is highly abundant, so the equilibrium wage (W_d) is

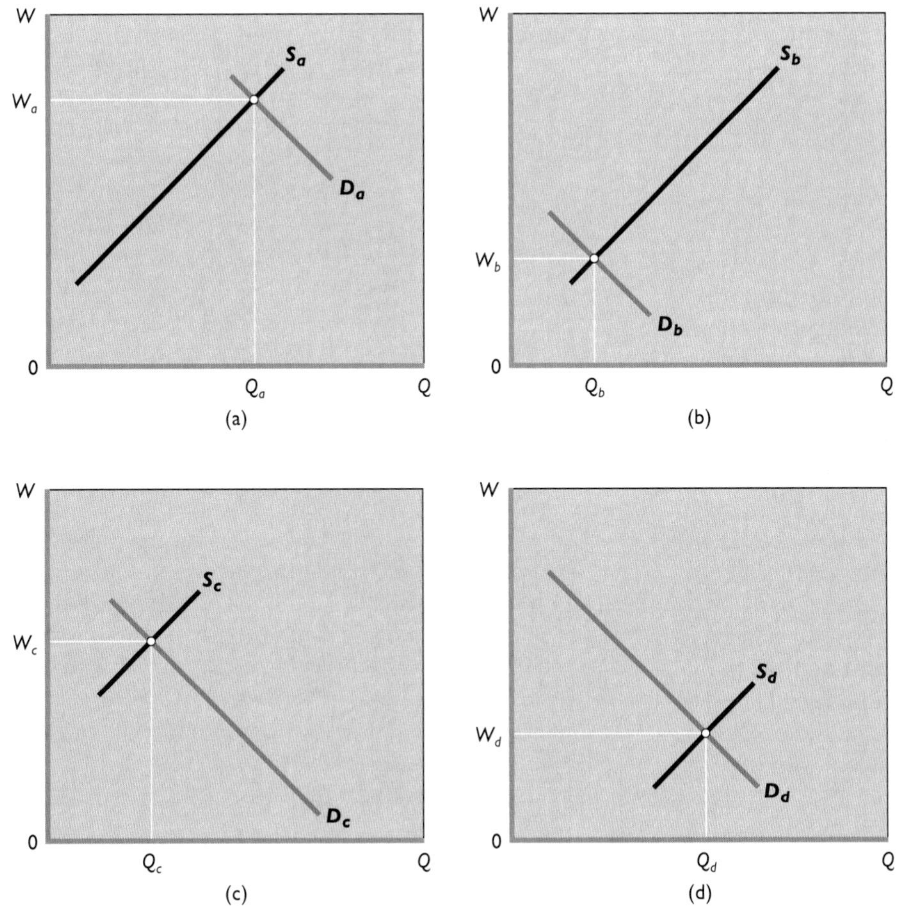

FIGURE 14.9 Labor demand, labor supply, and wage differentials. The wage differential between labor markets (a) and (b) results solely from differences in labor demand. In labor markets (c) and (d), differences in labor supply are the sole cause of the wage differential.

relatively low. The wage differential between (c) and (d) results solely from the differences in the magnitude of labor supply.

Although Figure 14.9 provides a good starting point for understanding wage differentials, we need to know *why* demand and supply conditions differ in various labor markets. There are several reasons.

Marginal Revenue Productivity

The strength of labor demand—how far rightward the labor demand curve is located—differs greatly among occupations due to differences in how much various occupational groups contribute to their employer's revenue. This revenue contribution, in turn, depends on the workers' productivity and the strength of the demand for the products they are helping to produce. Where labor is highly productive and product demand is strong, labor demand also is strong and, other things equal, pay is high. Top professional athletes, for example, are highly productive at producing sports entertainment, for which millions of people are willing to pay billions of dollars over the course of a season. So the **marginal revenue productivity** of these top players is exceptionally high, as are their salaries (as represented in Figure 14.9a). In contrast, in most occupations workers generate much more modest revenue for their employers, so their pay is lower (as in Figure 14.9b).

Noncompeting Groups

On the supply side of the labor market, workers are not homogeneous; they differ in their mental and physical capacities and in their education and training. At any given time the labor force is made up of many **noncompeting groups** of workers, each representing several occupations for which the members of a particular group qualify. In some groups qualified workers are relatively few, whereas in others they are highly abundant. And workers in one group do not qualify for the occupations of other groups.

Ability

Only a few workers have the ability or physical attributes to be brain surgeons, concert violinists, top fashion models, research chemists, or professional athletes. Because the supply of these particular types of labor is very small in relation to labor demand, their wages are high (as in Figure 14.9c). The members of these and similar groups do not compete with one another or with other skilled or semiskilled workers. The violinist does not compete with the surgeon, nor does the surgeon compete with the violinist or the fashion model.

The concept of noncompeting groups can be applied to various subgroups and even to specific individuals in a particular group. Some especially skilled violinists can command higher salaries than colleagues who play the same instrument. A handful of top corporate executives earn 10 to 20 times as much as the average chief executive officer. In each of these cases, the supply of top talent is highly limited, since less talented colleagues are only imperfect substitutes.

Education and Training

Another source of wage differentials is differing amounts of **human capital,** which is the personal stock of knowledge, know-how, and skills that enables a person to be productive and thus to earn income. Such stocks result from investments in human capital. Like expenditures on machinery and equipment, productivity-enhancing expenditures on education or training are investments. In both cases, people incur *present costs* with the intention that those expenditures will lead to a greater flow of *future earnings*.

O 14.2
Human capital

Figure 14.10 indicates that workers who have made greater investments in education achieve higher incomes during their careers. The reason is twofold: (1) There are

FIGURE 14.10 Education levels and individual annual earnings. Annual income by age is higher for workers with more education than less. Investment in education yields a return in the form of earnings differences enjoyed over one's work life.

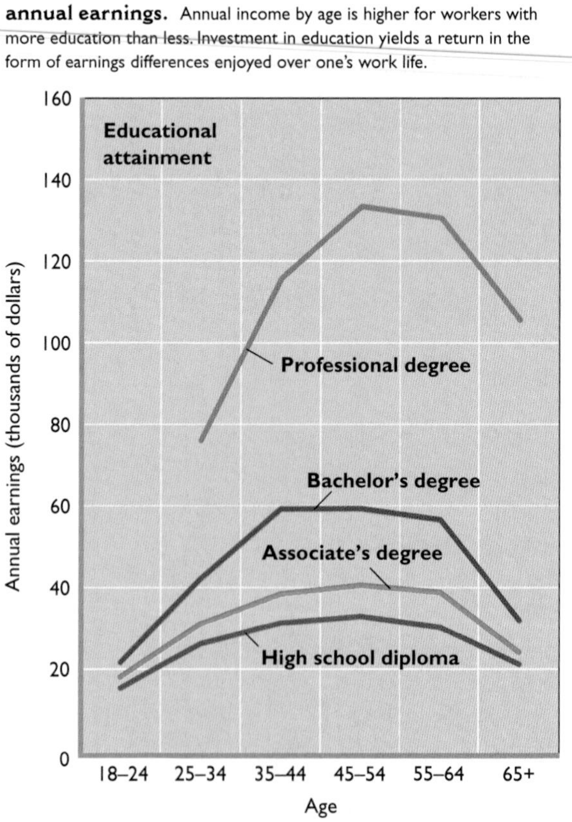

Source: U.S. Bureau of the Census. Data are for both sexes in 2004.

fewer such workers, so their supply is limited relative to less-educated workers, and (2) more-educated workers tend to be more productive and thus in greater demand. Figure 14.10 also indicates that the earnings of better-educated workers rise more rapidly than those of poorly educated workers. The primary reason is that employers provide more on-the-job training to the better-educated workers, boosting their marginal revenue productivity and therefore their earnings.

Although education yields higher incomes, it carries substantial costs. A college education involves not only direct costs (tuition, fees, books) but indirect or opportunity costs (forgone earnings) as well. Does the higher pay received by better-educated workers compensate for these costs? The answer is yes. Rates of return are estimated to be 10 to 13 percent for investments in secondary education and 8 to 12 percent for investments in college education. One generally accepted estimate is that each year of schooling raises a worker's wage by about 8 percent. Also, the pay gap between college graduates and high school graduates increased sharply between 1980 and 2003. Specifically, it rose from 28 percent to 46 percent for women and from 22 percent to 42 percent for men.

CONSIDER THIS ...

My Entire Life

Human capital is the accumulation of outcomes of prior investments in education, training, and other factors that increase productivity and earnings. It is the stock of knowledge, know-how, and skills that enables individuals to be productive and thus earn income. A valuable stock of human capital, together with a strong demand for one's services, can add up to a large capacity to earn income. For some people, high earnings have little to do with actual hours of work and much to do with their tremendous skill, which reflects their accumulated stock of human capital.

The point is demonstrated in the following story: It is said that a tourist once spotted the famous Spanish artist Pablo Picasso (1881–1973) in a Paris café. The tourist asked Picasso if he would do a sketch of his wife for pay. Picasso sketched the wife in a matter of minutes and said, "That will be 10,000 francs [roughly $2000]." Hearing the high price, the tourist became irritated, saying, "But that took you only a few minutes."

"No," replied Picasso, "it took me my entire life! "

Compensating Differences

If the workers in a particular noncompeting group are equally capable of performing several different jobs, you might expect the wage rates to be identical for all these jobs. Not so. A group of high school graduates may be equally capable of becoming salesclerks or general construction workers. But these jobs pay different wages. In virtually all locales, construction laborers receive much higher wages than salesclerks. These wage differentials are called **compensating differences,** because they must be paid to compensate for nonmonetary differences in various jobs.

The construction job involves dirty hands, a sore back, the hazard of accidents, and irregular employment, both seasonally and cyclically. The retail sales job means clean clothing, pleasant air-conditioned surroundings, and little fear of injury or layoff. Other things equal, it is easy to see why workers would rather pick up a credit card than a shovel. So labor supply is more limited to construction firms (as in Figure 14.9c) than to retail shops (as in Figure 14.9d). Construction firms must pay higher wages than retailers to compensate for the unattractive nonmonetary aspects of construction jobs.

Such compensating differences spring up throughout the economy. Other things equal, jobs having high risk of injury or death pay more than comparable, safer jobs. Jobs lacking employer-paid health insurance, pensions, and vacation time pay more than comparable jobs that provide these "fringe benefits." Jobs with more flexible hours pay less than jobs with rigid work-hour requirements. Jobs with greater risk of unemployment pay more than comparable jobs with little unemployment risk. Entry-level jobs in occupations that provide very poor prospects for pay advancement pay more than entry-level jobs that have clearly defined "job ladders."

These and other compensating differences play an important role in allocating society's scarce labor resources. If very few workers want to be garbage collectors, then society must pay high wages to garbage collectors to get the garbage collected. If many more people want to be salesclerks, then society need not pay them as much as it pays garbage collectors to get those services performed.

Market Imperfections

Differences in marginal revenue productivity, amounts of human capital, and nonmonetary aspects of jobs explain most of the wage differentials in the economy. But some persistent differentials result from various market imperfections that impede workers from moving from lower-paying jobs to higher-paying jobs.

Lack of Job Information Workers may simply be unaware of job opportunities and wage rates in other geographic areas and in other jobs for which they qualify. Consequently, the flow of qualified labor from lower-paying to higher-paying jobs—and thus the adjustments in labor supply—may not be sufficient to equalize wages within occupations.

Geographic Immobility Workers take root geographically. Many are reluctant to move to new places, to leave friends, relatives, and associates, to force their children to change schools, to sell their houses, or to incur the costs and inconveniences of adjusting to a new job and a new community. As Adam Smith noted over two centuries ago, "A [person] is of all sorts of luggage the most difficult to be transported." The reluctance or inability of workers to move enables geographic wage differentials within the same occupation to persist.

Unions and Government Restraints Wage differentials may be reinforced by artificial restrictions on mobility imposed by unions and government. We have noted that craft unions find it to their advantage to restrict membership. After all, if carpenters and bricklayers become too plentiful, the wages they can command will decline. Thus the low-paid nonunion carpenter of Brush, Colorado, may be willing to move to Chicago in the pursuit of higher wages. But her chances for succeeding are slim. She may be unable to get a union card, and no card means no job. Similarly, an optometrist or lawyer qualified to practice in one state may not meet licensing requirements of other states, so his or her ability to move is limited. Other artificial barriers involve pension plans, health insurance benefits, and seniority rights that might be jeopardized by moving from one job to another.

Discrimination Despite legislation to the contrary, discrimination sometimes results in lower wages being paid to women and minority workers than to white males doing virtually identical work. Also, women and minorities may be crowded into certain low-paying occupations, driving down wages there and raising them elsewhere. If this *occupational segregation* keeps qualified women and minorities from taking higher-paying jobs, then differences in pay will persist. (We discuss discrimination in Chapter 22.)

All four considerations—differences in marginal revenue productivity, noncompeting groups, nonmonetary differences, and market imperfections—come into play in explaining actual wage differentials. For example, the differential between the wages of a physician and those of a construction worker can be explained on the basis of marginal revenue productivity and noncompeting groups. Physicians generate considerable revenue because of their high productivity and the strong willingness of consumers (via insurance) to pay for health care. Physicians also fall into a noncompeting group where, because of stringent training requirements, only relatively few persons qualify. So the supply of labor is small in relation to demand.

In construction work, where training requirements are much less significant, the supply of labor is great relative to demand. So wages are much lower for construction workers than for physicians. However, if not for the unpleasantness of the construction worker's job and the fact that his or her craft union observes restrictive membership policies, the differential would be even greater than it is.

Pay for Performance

The models of wage determination we have described in this chapter assume that worker pay is always a standard amount for each hour's work, for example, $15 per hour. But pay schemes are often more complex than that both in composition and in purpose. For instance, many workers receive annual salaries rather than hourly pay. And workers receive differing proportions of fringe benefits (health insurance, life insurance, paid vacations, paid sick-leave days, pension contributions, and so on) as part of their pay. Finally, some pay plans are designed to elicit a desired level of performance from workers. This last aspect of pay plans requires further elaboration.

The Principal-Agent Problem Revisited

In Chapter 4 we identified the *principal-agent problem* as it relates to possible differences in the interests of corporate stockholders (principals) and the executives (agents) they hire. This problem extends to all workers. Firms hire workers because they are needed to help produce the goods and services the firms sell for a profit. Workers are the firms' agents; they are hired to advance the interest (profit) of the firms. The principals are the firms; they hire agents to advance their goals. Firms and workers have one interest in common: They both want the firm to survive and thrive. That will ensure profit for the firm and continued employment and wages for the workers.

O 14.3
Principal-agent problem

But the interests of the firm and of workers are not identical. A principal-agent problem arises when those interests diverge. Workers may seek to increase their utility by shirking on the job, that is, by providing less than the agreed-upon effort or by taking unauthorized breaks. They may improve their well-being by increasing their leisure during paid work hours, without forfeiting income. The night security guard in a warehouse may leave work early or spend time reading a novel rather than making the assigned rounds. A salaried manager may spend time away from the office visiting with friends rather than attending to company business.

Firms (principals) have a profit incentive to reduce or eliminate shirking. One option is to monitor workers, but monitoring is difficult and costly. Hiring another worker to supervise or monitor the security guard might double the cost of maintaining a secure warehouse. Another way of resolving a principal-agent problem is through some sort of **incentive pay plan** that ties worker compensation more closely to worker output or performance. Such incentive pay schemes include piece rates; commissions and royalties; bonuses, stock options, and profit sharing; and efficiency wages.

Piece Rates Piece rates consist of compensation paid according to the number of units of output a worker produces. If a principal pays fruit pickers by the bushel or typists by the page, it need not be concerned with shirking or with monitoring costs.

Commissions or Royalties Unlike piece rates, commissions and royalties tie compensation to the value of sales. Employees who sell products or services—including real estate agents, insurance agents, stockbrokers, and retail salespersons—commonly receive *commissions* that are computed as a percentage of the monetary value of their sales. Recording artists and authors are paid *royalties*, computed as a certain percentage of sales revenues from their works. Such types of compensation link the financial interests of the salespeople, artists, and authors to the profit interest of the firms.

Bonuses, Stock Options, and Profit Sharing *Bonuses* are payments in addition to one's annual salary that are based on some factor such as the performance of the individual worker, or of a group of workers, or of the firm itself. A professional baseball player may receive a bonus based on a high batting average, the number of home runs hit, or the number of runs batted in. A business manager may receive a bonus based on the profitability of her or his unit. *Stock options* allow workers to buy shares of their employer's stock at a fixed, lower price when the stock price rises. Such options are part of the compensation packages of top corporate officials, as well as many workers in relatively high-technology firms. *Profit-sharing plans* allocate a percentage of a firm's profit to its employees.

Efficiency Wages The rationale behind *efficiency wages* is that employers will enjoy greater effort from their workers by paying them above-equilibrium wage rates. Glance back at Figure 14.3, which shows a competitive labor market in which the equilibrium wage rate is \$10. What if an employer decides to pay an above-equilibrium wage of \$12 per hour? Rather than putting the firm at a cost disadvantage compared with rival firms paying only \$10, the higher wage might improve worker effort and productivity so that unit labor costs actually fall. For example, if each worker produces 10 units of output per hour at the \$12 wage rate compared with only 6 units at the \$10 wage rate, unit labor costs for the high-wage firm will be only \$1.20 (= \$12/10) compared to \$1.67 (= \$10/6) for firms paying the equilibrium wage.

O 14.4
Efficiency wages

An above-equilibrium wage may enhance worker efficiency in several ways. It enables the firm to attract higher-quality workers. It lifts worker morale. And it lowers turnover, resulting in a more experienced workforce, greater worker productivity, and lower recruitment and training costs. Because the opportunity cost of losing a higher-wage job is greater, workers are more likely to put forth their best efforts with less supervision and monitoring. In fact, efficiency wage payments have proved effective for many employers.

Addenda: Negative Side Effects of Pay for Performance

Although pay for performance may help overcome the principal-agent problem and enhance worker productivity, such plans may have negative side effects and require careful design. Here are a few examples:

- The rapid production pace that piece rates encourage may result in poor product quality and may compromise the safety of workers. Such outcomes can be costly to the firm over the long run.
- Commissions may cause some salespeople to engage in questionable or even fraudulent sales practices, such as making exaggerated claims about products or recommending unneeded repairs. Such practices may lead to private lawsuits or government legal action.

Last *Word*

Are Chief Executive Officers (CEOs) Overpaid?

The Multimillion-Dollar Pay of Major Corporate CEOs Has Drawn Considerable Criticism.

Top executives of U.S. corporations typically receive total annual pay (salary, bonuses, and stock options) in the millions of dollars. As shown in Table 1, each of the top five paid U.S. executives earned more than $120 million in 2005.

CEO pay in the United States is not only exceptionally high relative to the average pay of U.S. managers and workers but also high compared to the CEO pay in other industrial countries. For example, in 2005 the CEO pay at firms with about $500 million in annual sales averaged $2.2 million in the United States, compared to $1.2 million in France and Germany and less than $600,000 in South Korea and Japan.*

Is high CEO pay simply the outcome of labor supply and labor demand, as is the pay for star athletes and entertainers? Does it reflect marginal revenue productivity—that is, the contributions by CEOs to their company's output and revenue?

Observers who answer affirmatively point out that decisions made by the CEOs of large corporations affect the productivity of every employee in the organization. Good decisions enhance productivity throughout the organization and increase revenue; bad decisions reduce productivity and revenue. Only executives who have consistently made good business decisions attain the top positions in large corporations. Because the supply of these people is highly limited and their marginal revenue productivity is enormous, they command huge salaries and performance bonuses.

TABLE 1 The Five Highest-Paid U.S. CEOs, 2005

Name	Company	Total Pay, Millions
1. Richard D. Fairbank	Capital One Financial	$249
2. Terry S. Semel	Yahoo	231
3. Henry R. Silverman	Cendant	140
4. Bruce Karatz	KB Home	136
5. Richard S. Fuld, Jr.	Lehman Bros Holdings	123

Source: Forbes, May, 8, 2006, p. 138.

Also, some economists note that CEO pay in the United States may be like the prizes professional golfers and tennis players receive for winning tournaments. These high prizes are designed to promote the productivity of all those who aspire to achieve them. In corporations the top prizes go to the winners of the "contests" among managers to attain, at least eventually, the CEO positions. Thus high CEO pay does not derive solely from the CEO's direct productivity. Instead, it may exist because the high pay creates incentives that raise the productivity of scores of other corporate executives who seek to achieve the top position. In this view, high CEO pay remains grounded on high productivity.

Critics of existing CEO pay acknowledge that CEOs deserve substantially higher salaries than ordinary workers or typical managers, but they question pay packages that run into the millions of dollars. They reject the "tournament pay" idea on the grounds that corporations require cooperative team effort by managers and executives, not the type of high-stakes competition promoted by "winner-take-most" pay. They believe that corporations, although owned by their shareholders, are controlled by corporate boards and professional executives. Because many board members are present or past CEOs of other corporations, they often exaggerate CEO importance and, consequently, overpay their own CEOs. These overpayments are at the expense of the firm's stockholders.

In summary, defenders of CEO pay say that high pay is justified by the direct or indirect marginal-revenue contribution of CEOs. Like it or not, CEO pay is market-determined pay. In contrast, critics say that multimillion-dollar CEO pay bears little relationship to marginal revenue productivity and is unfair to ordinary stockholders. It is clear from our discussion that this issue remains unsettled.

**Worldwide Total Remuneration*, 2005–2006 (New York: Towers Perrin, Jan. 11, 2006, p. 20).

- Bonuses based on personal performance may disrupt the close cooperation needed for maximum team production. A professional basketball player who receives a bonus for points scored may be reluctant to pass the ball to teammates.
- Since profit sharing is usually tied to the performance of the entire firm, less energetic workers can "free ride" by obtaining their profit share on the basis of hard work by others.
- Stock options may prompt some unscrupulous executives to manipulate cost and revenue streams of their firms to create a false appearance of rapidly rising profit. When the firm's stock value rises, the executives exercise their stock options at inflated share prices and reap a personal fortune. In the early 2000s, some firms collapsed when the wrongdoings of their executives were exposed.
- There may be a downside to the reduced turnover resulting from above-market wages: Firms that pay efficiency wages have fewer opportunities to hire new workers and suffer the loss of the creative energy that they often bring to the workplace.

QUICK REVIEW 14.3

- Proponents of the minimum wage argue that it is needed to assist the working poor and to counter monopsony where it might exist; critics say that it is poorly targeted to reduce poverty and reduces employment.
- Wage differentials are attributable in general to the forces of supply and demand, influenced by differences in workers' marginal revenue productivity, education, and skills and by nonmonetary differences in jobs. But several labor market imperfections also play a role.
- As it applies to labor, the principal-agent problem is one of workers' pursuing their own interests to the detriment of the employer's profit objective.
- Pay-for-performance plans (piece rates, commissions, royalties, bonuses, stock options, profit sharing, and efficiency wages) are designed to improve worker productivity by overcoming the principal-agent problem.

Summary

1. The term "labor" encompasses all people who work for pay. The wage rate is the price paid per unit of time for labor. Labor earnings comprise total pay and are found by multiplying the number of hours worked by the hourly wage rate. The nominal wage rate is the amount of money received per unit of time; the real wage rate is the purchasing power of the nominal wage.
2. The long-run growth of real hourly compensation—the average real wage—roughly matches that of productivity, with both increasing over the long run.
3. Global comparisons suggest that real wages in the United States are relatively high, but not the highest, internationally. High real wages in the advanced industrial countries stem largely from high labor productivity.
4. Specific wage rates depend on the structure of the particular labor market. In a competitive labor market the equilibrium wage rate and level of employment are determined at the intersection of the labor supply curve and labor demand curve. For the individual firm, the market wage rate establishes a horizontal labor supply curve, meaning that the wage rate equals the firm's constant marginal resource cost. The firm hires workers to the point where its MRP equals its MRC.
5. Under monopsony the marginal resource cost curve lies above the resource supply curve because the monopsonist must bid up the wage rate to hire extra workers and must pay that higher wage rate to all workers. The monopsonist hires fewer workers than are hired under competitive conditions, pays less-than-competitive wage rates (has lower labor costs), and thus obtains greater profit.
6. A union may raise competitive wage rates by (a) increasing the derived demand for labor, (b) restricting the supply of labor through exclusive unionism, or (c) directly enforcing an above-equilibrium wage rate through inclusive unionism.
7. In many industries the labor market takes the form of bilateral monopoly, in which a strong union "sells" labor to a monopsonistic employer. The wage-rate outcome of this labor market model depends on union and employer bargaining power.
8. On average, unionized workers realize wage rates 15 percent higher than those of comparable nonunion workers.
9. Economists disagree about the desirability of the minimum wage as an antipoverty mechanism. While it causes unemployment for some low-income workers, it raises the incomes of those who retain their jobs.
10. Wage differentials are largely explainable in terms of (a) marginal revenue productivity of various groups of workers; (b) noncompeting groups arising from differences in the capacities and education of different groups of workers; (c) compensating wage differences, that is, wage differences

that must be paid to offset nonmonetary differences in jobs; and (d) market imperfections in the form of lack of job information, geographic immobility, union and government restraints, and discrimination.

11. The principal-agent problem arises when workers provide less-than-expected effort. Firms may combat this by monitoring workers or by creating incentive pay schemes that link worker compensation to performance.

Terms and Concepts

wage rate
nominal wage
real wage
purely competitive labor market
monopsony
exclusive unionism
occupational licensing
inclusive unionism
bilateral monopoly
minimum wage
wage differentials
marginal revenue productivity
noncompeting groups
human capital
compensating differences
incentive pay plan

Study Questions

1. Explain why the general level of wages is high in the United States and other industrially advanced countries. What is the single most important factor underlying the long-run increase in average real-wage rates in the United States?
2. Why is a firm in a purely competitive labor market a *wage taker?* What would happen if it decided to pay less than the going market wage rate?
3. **KEY QUESTION** Describe wage determination in a labor market in which workers are unorganized and many firms actively compete for the services of labor. Show this situation graphically, using W_1 to indicate the equilibrium wage rate and Q_1 to show the number of workers hired by the firms as a group. Show the labor supply curve of the individual firm, and compare it with that of the total market. Why the differences? In the diagram representing the firm, identify total revenue, total wage cost, and revenue available for the payment of nonlabor resources.
4. **KEY QUESTION** Complete the following labor supply table for a firm hiring labor competitively:

Units of Labor	Wage Rate	Total Labor Cost (Wage Bill)	Marginal Resource (Labor) Cost
0	$14	$ ______	
			$ ______
1	14	______	
			______
2	14	______	
			______
3	14	______	
			______
4	14	______	
			______
5	14	______	
			______
6	14	______	

a. Show graphically the labor supply and marginal resource (labor) cost curves for this firm. Explain the relationship of these curves to one another.

b. Plot the labor demand data of question 2 in Chapter 13 on the graph used in part *a* above. What are the equilibrium wage rate and level of employment? Explain.

5. Suppose the formerly competing firms in question 3 form an employers' association that hires labor as a monopsonist would. Describe verbally the effect on wage rates and employment. Adjust the graph you drew for question 3, showing the monopsonistic wage rate and employment level as W_2 and Q_2, respectively. Using this monopsony model, explain why hospital administrators sometimes complain about a "shortage" of nurses. How might such a shortage be corrected?
6. **KEY QUESTION** Assume a firm is a monopsonist that can hire its first worker for $6 but must increase the wage rate by $3 to attract each successive worker. Draw the firm's labor supply and marginal resource cost curves and explain their relationships to one another. On the same graph, plot the labor demand data of question 2 in Chapter 13. What are the equilibrium wage rate and level of employment? Why do these differ from your answer to question 4?
7. **KEY QUESTION** Assume a monopsonistic employer is paying a wage rate of W_m and hiring Q_m workers, as indicated in Figure 14.8. Now suppose an industrial union is formed that forces the employer to accept a wage rate of W_c. Explain verbally and graphically why in this instance the higher wage rate will be accompanied by an increase in the number of workers hired.
8. Have you ever worked for the minimum wage? If so, for how long? Would you favor increasing the minimum wage by a dollar? By two dollars? By five dollars? Explain your reasoning.
9. "Many of the lowest-paid people in society—for example, short-order cooks—also have relatively poor working conditions. Hence, the notion of compensating wage differentials is disproved." Do you agree? Explain.

10. What is meant by investment in human capital? Use this concept to explain (*a*) wage differentials, and (*b*) the long-run rise of real wage rates in the United States.

11. What is the principal-agent problem? Have you ever worked in a setting where this problem has arisen? If so, do you think increased monitoring would have eliminated the problem? Why don't firms simply hire more supervisors to eliminate shirking?

12. **LAST WORD** Do you think exceptionally high pay to CEOs is economically justified? Why or why not?

Web-Based Questions

1. **REAL WAGES AND PRODUCTIVITY—ARE WORKERS' PAYCHECKS KEEPING UP?** Over the long run, real wages grow at about the same pace as labor productivity. Go to the Bureau of Labor Statistics Web site, **www.bls.gov/lpc/**, and select Get Detailed Statistics and then Most Requested Statistics for current information on percentage changes in output per hour of all persons in the nonfarm business sector (labor productivity) and percentage changes in real compensation per hour. Has real compensation per hour kept up with output per hour over the latest 3 years shown?

2. **MEN'S AND WOMEN'S EARNINGS IN PROFESSIONAL GOLF—WHY THE DIFFERENCES?** Go to **espn.go.com** and select Golf and then Money Leaders. What are the annual earnings to date of the top 10 men golfers on the PGA tour? What are the earnings of the top 10 women golfers on the LPGA tour? Why the general differences in earnings between the men and the women golfers?

15

IN THIS CHAPTER YOU WILL LEARN:

- **The nature of economic rent and how it is determined.**
- **About the loanable funds theory of interest rates.**
- **How interest rates vary based on risk, maturity, loan size, and taxability.**
- **Why economic profits occur, and how profits, along with losses, allocate resources among alternative uses.**
- **The share of U.S. earnings received by each of the factors of production.**

Rent, Interest, and Profit

How do land prices (and land rents) get established, and why do they differ? For example, why do 20 acres of land in the middle of the Nevada desert sell for $5000 while 20 acres along the Las Vegas strip command $300 million or more?

What determines interest rates and causes them to change? For instance, why were interest rates on 3-month bank certificates of deposit 6.7 percent in July 2000, 1.3 percent in January 2003, and 5.4 percent in June 2006?

What are the sources of profits and losses and why do they vary? For example, why did Wal-Mart earn profits of $11 billion in 2005 whereas General Motors experienced losses of $11 billion?

In Chapter 14 we focused on resource payments in the forms of wages and salaries, which account for about 71 percent of all income paid to American resource suppliers. This chapter examines the other 29 percent of earnings, specifically rent, interest, and profit. We begin by looking at rent.

Economic rent

To most people, "rent" means the money paid for the use of an apartment or a dormitory room. To the business executive, "rent" is a payment made for the use of a factory building, machine, or warehouse facility. Such definitions of rent can be confusing and ambiguous, however. Residence hall room rent, for example, may include other payments as well: interest on money the university borrowed to finance the dormitory, wages for custodial services, utility payments, and so on.

Economists use "rent" in a much narrower sense. **Economic rent** is the price paid for the use of land and other natural resources that are completely fixed in total supply. As you will see, this fixed overall supply distinguishes rental payments from wage, interest, and profit payments.

Let's examine this idea and some of its implications through supply and demand analysis. We first assume that all land is of the same grade or quality, meaning that each arable (tillable) acre of land is as productive as every other acre. We assume, too, that all land has a single use, for example, producing wheat. And we suppose that land is rented or leased in a competitive market in which many producers are demanding land and many landowners are offering land in the market.

In Figure 15.1, curve *S* represents the supply of arable land available in the economy as a whole, and curve D_2 represents the demand of producers for use of that land. As with all economic resources, this demand is derived from the demand for the product being produced. The demand curve for land is downward-sloping because of diminishing returns and because, for producers as a group, product price must be reduced in order to sell additional units of output.

FIGURE 15.1 The determination of land rent. Because the supply *S* of land (and other natural resources) is perfectly inelastic, demand is the sole active determinant of land rent. An increase in demand from D_2 to D_1 or a decrease in demand from D_2 to D_3 will cause a considerable change in rent: from R_2 to R_1 in the first instance and from R_2 to R_3 in the second. But the amount of land supplied will remain at L_0. If demand is very weak (D_4) relative to supply, land will be a "free good," commanding no rent.

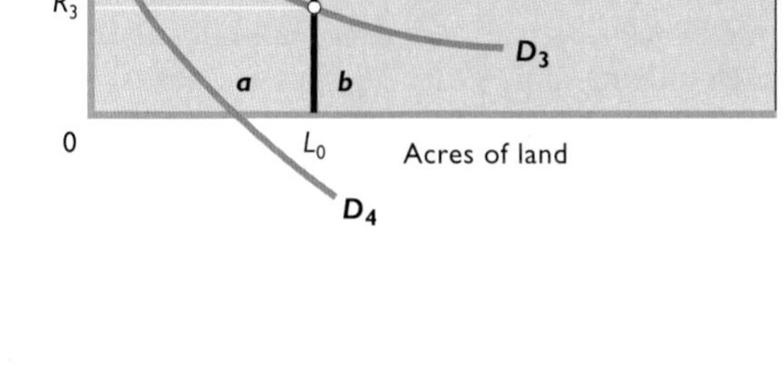

Perfectly Inelastic Supply

The unique feature of our analysis is on the supply side. For all practical purposes the supply of land is perfectly inelastic (in both the short run and the long run), as reflected in supply curve *S*. Land has no production cost; it is a "free and nonreproducible gift of nature." The economy has only so much land, and that's that. Of course, within limits any parcel of land can be made more usable by clearing, drainage, and irrigation. But these are capital improvements and not changes in the amount of land itself. Moreover, increases in the usability of land affect only a small fraction of the total amount of land and do not change the basic fact that land and other natural resources are fixed in supply.

Changes in Demand

Because the supply of land is fixed, demand is the only active determinant of land rent; supply is passive. And what determines the demand for land? The factors we discussed in Chapter 13: the price of the product produced on the land, the productivity of land (which depends in part on the quantity and quality of the resources with which land is combined), and the prices of the other resources that are combined with land.

If the demand for land in Figure 15.1 increased from D_2 to D_1, land rent would rise from R_2 to R_1. On the other hand, if the demand for land declined from D_2 to D_3, land rent would fall from R_2 to R_3. But, in either case, the amount of land supplied would remain the same at quantity L_0. Changes in economic rent have no effect on the amount of land available because the supply of land cannot be augmented. If the demand for land were only D_4, land rent would be zero. Land would be a *free good*—a good for which demand is so weak relative to supply that there is an excess supply of it even if the market price is zero. In Figure 15.1, we show this excess supply as distance $b - a$ at rent of zero. This essentially was the situation in the free-land era of U.S. history.

The ideas underlying Figure 15.1 help answer one of our chapter-opening questions. Land prices and rents are so high along the Las Vegas strip because the demand for that land is tremendous. It is capable of producing exceptionally high revenue from gambling, lodging, and entertainment. In contrast, the demand for isolated land in the middle of the desert is highly limited because very little revenue can be generated from its use. (It is an entirely different matter, of course, if gold can be mined from the land, as is true of some isolated lands in Nevada!)

Land Rent: A Surplus Payment

The perfectly inelastic supply of land must be contrasted with the relatively elastic supply of capital, such as apartment buildings, machinery, and warehouses. In the long run, capital is *not* fixed in total supply. A higher price gives entrepreneurs the incentive to construct and offer larger quantities of property resources. Conversely, a decline in price induces suppliers to allow existing facilities to depreciate and not be replaced. The supply curves of these nonland resources are upward-sloping, meaning that the prices paid to such resources provide an **incentive function.** A high price provides an incentive to offer more of the resource, whereas a low price prompts resource suppliers to offer less.

Not so with land. Rent serves no incentive function because the total supply of land is fixed. Whether rent is $10,000, $500, $1, or $0 per acre, the same amount of land is available to society for use in production. This is why economists consider rent a *surplus payment* not necessary to ensure that land is available to the economy as a whole.

Application: A Single Tax on Land

If land is a gift of nature, costs nothing to produce, and would be available even without rental payments, why should rent be paid to those who by historical accident, by inheritance, or by misdeed happen to be landowners? Socialists have long argued that all land rents are unearned incomes. They urge that land should be nationalized (owned by the state) so that any payments for its use can be used by the government to further the well-being of the entire population rather than being used by a landowning minority.

Henry George's Proposal

In the United States, criticism of rental payments has taken the form of a **single-tax movement,** which gained significant support in the late nineteenth century. Spearheaded by Henry George's provocative book *Progress and Poverty* (1879), supporters of this reform movement held that economic rent could be heavily taxed, or even taxed away, without diminishing the available supply of land or, therefore, the productive potential of the economy as a whole.

George observed that as population grew and the geographic frontier closed, landowners enjoyed larger and larger rents from their landholdings. That increase in rents was the result of a growing demand for a resource whose supply was perfectly inelastic. Some landlords were receiving fabulously high incomes, not through any productive effort but solely through their owning advantageously located land. George insisted that these increases in land rent belonged to the economy; he held that land rents should be heavily taxed and the revenue spent for public uses. In seeking popular support for his ideas on land taxation, George proposed that taxes on rental income be the *only* tax levied by government.

George's case for taxing land was based not only on equity or fairness but also on efficiency. That is, a tax on land is efficient because, unlike virtually every other tax, it does not alter the use of the resource being taxed. A tax on wages reduces after-tax wages and may weaken the incentive to work; an individual who decides to work for a $10 before-tax wage may decide to retire when an income tax reduces the wage to an after-tax $8. Similarly, a property tax on buildings lowers returns to investors in such property and might cause some to look for other investments. But no such reallocations of resources occur when land is taxed. The most profitable use of land before it is taxed remains the most profitable use after it is taxed. Of course, a landlord could withdraw land from production when a tax is imposed, but that would mean no rental income at all. And some rental income, no matter how small, is better than none.

Criticisms

The single tax on land has very few remaining advocates. Critics of the idea have pointed out that:

- Current levels of government spending are such that a land tax alone would not bring in enough revenue; it is unrealistic to consider it as a single tax.
- Most income payments consist of a mixture of such elements as interest, rent, wages, and profits. Land is typically improved in some way, and economic rent cannot be readily disentangled from payments for such improvements. So in practice it would be difficult to determine how much of any specific income payment actually amounted to economic rent.
- So-called unearned income accrues to many people other than landowners, especially when the economy is growing. For example, consider the capital-gains income received by someone who, some 20 or 25 years ago, chanced to purchase (or inherit) stock in a firm that has experienced rapid profit growth. Is such income more "earned" than the rental income of the landowner?
- Historically, a piece of land is likely to have changed ownership many times. Former owners may have

been the beneficiaries of past increases in the value of the land (and in land rent). It would hardly be fair to impose a heavy tax on current owners who paid the competitive market price for the land.

Productivity Differences and Rent Differences

So far we have assumed that all units of land are of the same grade. That is plainly not so. Different pieces of land vary greatly in productivity, depending on soil fertility and on such climatic factors as rainfall and temperature. Such factors explain, for example, why Kansas soil is excellently suited to wheat production, why the sagebrush plains of Wyoming are much less well suited, and why the desert of Arizona is nearly incapable of wheat production. Such productivity differences are reflected in resource demand and prices. Competitive bidding by producers will establish a high rent for highly productive Kansas land; less productive Wyoming land will command a much lower rent; and Arizona desert land may command no rent at all.

Location itself may be just as important in explaining differences in land rent. Other things equal, renters will pay more for a unit of land that is strategically located with respect to materials, transportation, labor, and customers than they will for a unit of land whose location is remote from these things. Examples include the enormously high land prices in major ski resorts and the high price of land that contains oil beneath it.

Figure 15.1, viewed from a slightly different perspective, reveals the rent differentials from quality differences in land. Assume, again, that only wheat can be produced on four grades of land, each of which is available in the fixed amount L_0. When combined with identical amounts of labor, capital, and entrepreneurial talent, the productivity or, more specifically, the marginal revenue product of each of the four grades of land is reflected in demand curves D_1, D_2, D_3, and D_4. Grade 1 land is the most productive, as shown by D_1, while grade 4 is the least productive, as shown by D_4. The resulting economic rents for grades 1, 2, and 3 land will be R_1, R_2, and R_3, respectively; the rent differential will mirror the differences in productivity of the three grades of land. Grade 4 land is so poor in quality that, given its supply S, farmers won't pay anything to use it. It will be a free good because it is not sufficiently scarce in relation to the demand for it to command a price or a rent.

Alternative Uses of Land

We have assumed that land has only one use. Actually, we know that land normally has alternative uses. An acre of Kansas farmland may be useful for raising not only wheat but corn, oats, barley, and cattle; or it may be useful for building a house or a highway or as a factory site. In other words, any particular use of land involves an opportunity cost—the forgone production from the next best use of the resource. Where there are alternative uses, individual firms must pay rent to cover those opportunity costs in order to secure the use of land for their particular purposes. To the individual firm, rent is a cost of production, just as are wages and interest.

Recall that, as viewed by society, economic rent is not a cost. Society would have the same amount of land with or without the payment of economic rent. From society's perspective, economic rent is a surplus payment above that needed to gain the use of a resource. But individual firms do need to pay rent to attract land resources away from alternative uses. For firms, rental payments *are* a cost. **(Key Question 2)**

QUICK REVIEW 15.1

- Economic rent is the price paid for resources such as land whose supply is perfectly inelastic.
- Land rent is a surplus payment, because land would be available to society even if this rent were not paid.
- The surplus nature of land rent served as the basis for Henry George's single-tax movement.
- Differential rents allocate land among alternative uses.

Interest

Interest is the price paid for the use of money. It is the price that borrowers need to pay lenders for transferring purchasing power from the present to the future. It can be thought of as the amount of money that must be paid for the use of $1 for 1 year.

- ***Interest is stated as a percentage.*** Interest is paid in kind; that is, money (interest) is paid for the loan of money. For that reason, interest is typically stated as a percentage of the amount of money borrowed rather than as a dollar amount. It is less clumsy to say that interest is "12 percent annually" than to say that interest is "$120 per year per $1000." Also, stating interest as a percentage makes comparison of the interest paid on loans of different amounts easier. By expressing interest as a percentage, we can immediately compare an interest payment of, say, $432 per year per $2880 with one of $1800 per year per $12,000. Both interest payments are 15 percent per year, which is not obvious from the actual dollar figures. This interest of 15 percent per year is referred to as a 15 percent interest rate.

- ***Money is not a resource.*** Money is *not* an economic resource. In the form of coins, paper currency, or checking accounts, money is not productive; it cannot produce goods and services. However, businesses "buy" the use of money because it can be used to acquire capital goods such as factories, machinery, warehouses, and so on. Such facilities clearly do contribute to production. Thus, in "hiring" the use of money capital, business executives are indirectly buying the use of real capital goods.

Loanable Funds Theory of Interest

In macroeconomics the interest rate is often viewed through the lens of the economy's total supply of and demand for money. But because our present focus is on microeconomics, it will be useful to consider a more micro-based theory of interest here. Specifically, the **loanable funds theory of interest** explains the interest rate not in terms of the total supply of and demand for *money* but, rather, in terms of the supply of and demand for *funds available for lending (and borrowing)*. As Figure 15.2 shows, the equilibrium interest rate (here, 8 percent) is the rate at which the quantities of loanable funds supplied and demanded are equal.

G 15.1
Loanable funds

FIGURE 15.2 The market for loanable funds. The upsloping supply curve *S* for loanable funds reflects the idea that at higher interest rates, households will defer more of their present consumption (save more), making more funds available for lending. The downsloping demand curve *D* for loanable funds indicates that businesses will borrow more at lower interest rates than at higher interest rates. At the equilibrium interest rate (here, 8 percent), the quantities of loanable funds lent and borrowed are equal (here, F_0 each).

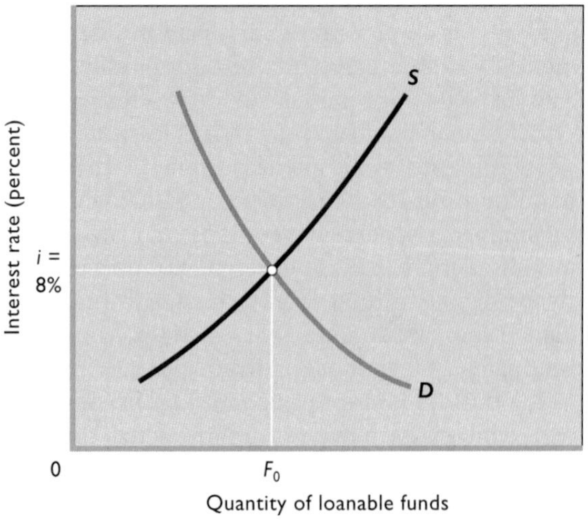

Let's first consider the loanable funds theory in simplified form. Specifically, assume households or consumers are the sole suppliers of loanable funds and businesses are the sole demanders. Also assume that lending occurs directly between households and businesses; no financial institutions are acting as intermediaries.

Supply of Loanable Funds

The supply of loanable funds is represented by curve *S* in Figure 15.2. Its upward slope indicates that households will make available a larger quantity of funds at high interest rates than at low interest rates. Most people prefer to use their incomes to purchase goods and services *today*, rather than delay purchases to sometime in the *future*. For people to delay consumption and increase their saving, they must be "bribed" or compensated by an interest payment. The larger the amount of that payment, the greater the deferral of household consumption and thus the greater the amount of money made available for loans.

There is disagreement among economists as to how much the quantity of loanable funds made available by suppliers changes in response to changes in the interest rate. Most economists view saving as being relatively insensitive to changes in the interest rate because people also save for reasons other than to secure interest payments. For example, they may save out of habit, or to have funds available for a "rainy day," or to accumulate funds for an expensive purchase. The supply curve of loanable funds may therefore be more inelastic than *S* in Figure 15.2 implies.

Demand for Loanable Funds

Businesses borrow loanable funds primarily to add to their stocks of capital goods, such as new plants or warehouses, machinery, and equipment. Assume that a firm wants to buy a machine that will increase output and sales such that the firm's total revenue will rise by \$110 for the year. Also assume that the machine costs \$100 and has a useful life of just 1 year. Comparing the \$10 earned with the \$100 cost of the machine, we find that the expected rate of return on this investment is 10 percent (= \$10/\$100) for the 1 year.

To determine whether the investment would be profitable and whether it should be made, the firm must compare the interest rate—the price of loanable funds—with the 10 percent expected rate of return. If funds can be borrowed at some rate less than the rate of return, say, at 8 percent, as in Figure 15.2, then the investment is profitable and should be made. But if funds can be borrowed only at an interest rate above the 10 percent rate of return, say, at 14 percent, the investment is unprofitable and should not be made.

Why is the demand for loanable funds downsloping, as in Figure 15.2? At higher interest rates fewer investment projects will be profitable and hence a smaller quantity of loanable funds will be demanded. At lower interest rates, more investment projects will be profitable and therefore more loanable funds will be demanded. Indeed, as we have just seen, purchasing the $100 machine is profitable if funds can be borrowed at 8 percent but not if the firm must borrow at 14 percent.

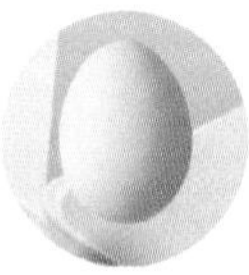

O 15.1
Interest rates

CONSIDER THIS . . .

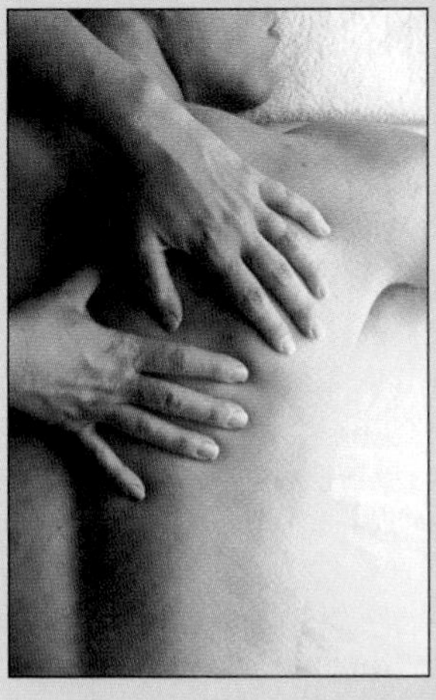

That Is Interest

Viewed from the supply side of the market for loanable funds, interest rates are the payments needed to entice individuals to sacrifice their present consumption, that is, to let someone else use their money for a period of time. The following story told by economist Irving Fisher (1867–1947) helps illustrate this "time-value of money."

In the process of a massage, a masseur informed Fisher that he was a socialist who believed that "interest is the basis of capitalism and is robbery." Following the massage, Fisher asked, "How much do I owe you?"

The masseur replied, "Thirty dollars."

"Very well," said Fisher, "I will give you a note payable a hundred years hence. I suppose you have no objections to taking this note without any interest. At the end of that time, you, or perhaps your grandchildren, can redeem it."

"But I cannot afford to wait that long," said the masseur.

"I thought you said that interest was robbery. If interest is robbery, you ought to be willing to wait indefinitely for the money. If you are willing to wait ten years, how much would you require?"

"Well, I would have to get more than thirty dollars."

His point now made, Fisher replied, "That is interest."*

*Irving Fisher, as quoted in Irving Norton Fisher, *My Father Irving Fisher* (New York: Comet, 1956), p. 77.

Extending the Model

We now make this simple model more realistic in several ways.

Financial Institutions Households rarely lend their savings directly to businesses that are borrowing funds for investment. Instead, they place their savings in banks (and other financial institutions). The banks pay interest to savers in order to attract loanable funds and in turn lend those funds to businesses. Businesses borrow the funds from the banks, paying them interest for the use of the money. Financial institutions profit by charging borrowers higher interest rates than the interest rates they pay savers. Both interest rates, however, are based on the supply of and demand for loanable funds.

Changes in Supply Anything that causes households to be thriftier will prompt them to save more at each interest rate, shifting the supply curve rightward. For example, if interest earned on savings were to be suddenly exempted from taxation, we would expect the supply of loanable funds to increase and the equilibrium interest rate to decrease.

Conversely, a decline in thriftiness would shift the supply-of-loanable-funds curve leftward and increase the equilibrium interest rate. Illustration: If the government expanded social insurance to cover the costs of hospitalization, prescription drugs, and retirement living more fully, the incentive of households to save might diminish.

Changes in Demand On the demand side, anything that increases the rate of return on potential investments will increase the demand for loanable funds. Let's return to our earlier example, where a firm would receive additional revenue of $110 by purchasing a $100 machine and, therefore, would realize a 10 percent return on investment. What factors might increase or decrease the rate of return? Suppose a technological advance raised the productivity of the machine such that the firm's total revenue increased by $120 rather than $110. The rate of return would then be 20 percent, not 10 percent. Before the technological advance, the firm would have demanded zero loanable funds at, say, an interest rate of 14 percent. But now it will demand $100 of loanable funds at that interest rate, meaning that the demand curve for loanable funds has been shifted to the right.

Similarly, an increase in consumer demand for the firm's product will increase the price of its product. So even though the productivity of the machine is unchanged, its potential revenue will rise from $110 to perhaps $120, increasing the firm's rate of return from 10 to 20 percent.

Again the firm will be willing to borrow more than previously at our presumed 8 or 14 percent interest rate, implying that the demand curve for loanable funds has shifted rightward. This shift in demand increases the equilibrium interest rate.

Conversely, a decline in productivity or in the price of the firm's product would shift the demand curve for loanable funds leftward, reducing the equilibrium interest rate.

Other Participants We must recognize that there are more participants on both the demand and the supply sides of the loanable funds market. For example, while households are suppliers of loanable funds, many are also demanders of such funds. Households borrow to finance expensive purchases such as housing, automobiles, furniture, and household appliances. Governments also are on the demand side of the loanable funds market when they borrow to finance budgetary deficits. And businesses that have revenues in excess of their current expenditures may offer some of those revenues in the market for loanable funds. Thus, like households, businesses operate on both the supply and the demand sides of the market.

Finally, in addition to gathering and making available the savings of households, banks and other financial institutions also increase funds through the lending process and decrease funds when loans are paid back and not lent back out. The Federal Reserve (the nation's central bank) controls the amount of this bank activity and thus influences interest rates.

This fact helps answer one of our chapter-opening questions: Why did the interest rate on 3-month certificates of deposit in the United States fall from 6.7 percent in 2000 to only 1.3 percent in early 2003? There are two reasons: (1) The demand for loanable funds sharply declined because businesses reduced their desire to purchase more capital goods, and (2) the Federal Reserve, fighting recession and sluggish recovery, took monetary actions that greatly increased the supply of loanable funds. In contrast, between 2003 and 2006 the Federal Reserve restricted the growth of loanable funds. Because the demand for loanable funds increased more rapidly than the supply of loanable funds, interest rates such as those on 3-month certificates of deposits rose. As indicated in the chapter opening, that rate increased from 1.3 percent in January 2003 to 5.4 percent in June 2006. **(Key Question 6)**

Range of Interest Rates

Although economists often speak in terms of a single interest rate, there are actually a number of interest rates. Table 15.1 lists several interest rates often referred to in the media. These rates range from 4.57 to 12.94 percent. Why the differences?

TABLE 15.1 Selected Interest Rates, April 2006

Type of Interest Rate	Annual Percentage
20-year Treasury bond rate (interest rate on Federal government security used to finance the public debt)	5.21%
90-day Treasury Bill rate (interest rate on Federal government security used to finance the public debt)	4.58
Prime interest rate (interest rate used as a reference point for a wide range of bank loans)	7.75
30-year mortgage rate (fixed-interest rate on loans for houses)	6.11
4-year automobile loan rate (interest rate for new autos by automobile finance companies)	6.72
Tax-exempt state and municipal bond rate (interest rate paid on a low-risk bond issued by a state or local government)	4.57
Federal funds rate (interest rate on overnight loans between banks)	4.78
Consumer credit card rate (interest rate charged for credit card purchases)	12.94

Sources: Federal Reserve, **www.federalreserve.gov,** and Bankrate.com, **www.bankrate.com.**

- ***Risk*** Loans to different borrowers for different purposes carry varying degrees of risk. The greater the chance that the borrower will not repay the loan, the higher the interest rate the lender will charge to compensate for that risk.
- ***Maturity*** The time length of a loan or its *maturity* (when it needs to be paid back) also affects the interest rate. Other things equal, longer-term loans usually command higher interest rates than shorter-term loans. The long-term lender suffers the inconvenience and possible financial sacrifice of forgoing alternative uses of his or her money for a greater period.
- ***Loan size*** If there are two loans of equal maturity and risk, the interest rate on the smaller of the two loans usually will be higher. The costs of issuing a large loan and a small loan are about the same in dollars, but the cost is greater *as a percentage* of the smaller loan.
- ***Taxability*** Interest on certain state and municipal bonds is exempt from Federal income taxation. Because lenders are interested in their after-tax rate of interest, borrowing by states and local governments can attract lenders even though the borrowers pay low interest rates. Consider a high-income lender who pays a 35 percent Federal income tax (2006) on marginal income. He or she may prefer a 5 percent

interest rate on a tax-exempt municipal bond to a 6 percent taxable interest rate on a corporate bond.

Pure Rate of Interest

Economists and financial specialists talk of "the" interest rate to simplify the cluster of rates (Table 15.1). When they do so, they usually have in mind the **pure rate of interest.** The pure rate is best approximated by the interest paid on long-term, virtually riskless securities such as long-term bonds of the U.S. government (20-year Treasury bonds). This interest payment can be thought of as being made solely for the use of money over an extended time period, because risk and administrative costs are negligible and the interest rate on these bonds is not distorted by market imperfections. In August 2006, the pure rate of interest in the United States was 5.1 percent.

Role of the Interest Rate

The interest rate is a critical price that affects the *level* and *composition* of investment goods production, as well as the *amount* of R&D spending.

Interest and Total Output

A lower equilibrium interest rate encourages businesses to borrow more for investment. As a result, total spending in the economy rises, and if the economy has unused resources, so does total output. Conversely, a higher equilibrium interest rate discourages business from borrowing for investment, thereby reducing investment and total spending. Such a decrease in spending may be desirable if an economy is experiencing inflation.

The Federal Reserve often manipulates the interest rate to try to expand investment and output, on the one hand, or to reduce investment and inflation, on the other. It affects the interest rate by changing the supply of money. Increases in the money supply increase the supply of loanable funds, causing the equilibrium interest rate to fall. This boosts investment spending and expands the economy. In contrast, decreases in the money supply decrease the supply of loanable funds, boosting the equilibrium interest rate. As a result, investment is constrained and so is the economy.

Interest and the Allocation of Capital

Prices are rationing devices. The price of money—the interest rate—is certainly no exception. The interest rate rations the available supply of loanable funds to investment projects that have expected rates of return at or above the interest rate cost of the borrowed funds.

If, say, the computer industry expects to earn a return of 12 percent on the money it invests in physical capital and it can secure the required funds at an interest rate of 8 percent, it can borrow and expand its physical capital. If the expected rate of return on additional capital in the steel industry is only 6 percent, that industry will find it unprofitable to expand its capital at 8 percent interest. The interest rate allocates money, and ultimately physical capital, to the industries in which it will be most productive and therefore most profitable. Such an allocation of capital goods benefits society.

But the interest rate does not perfectly ration capital to its most productive uses. Large oligopolistic borrowers may be better able than competitive borrowers to pass interest costs on to consumers because they can change prices by controlling output. Also, the size, prestige, and monopsony power of large corporations may help them obtain funds on more favorable terms than can smaller firms, even when the smaller firms have similar rates of profitability.

Interest and R&D Spending

Recall from Chapter 12 that, like the investment decision, the decision on how much to spend on R&D depends on the cost of borrowing funds in relationship to the expected rate of return. Other things equal, the lower the interest rate and thus the lower the cost of borrowing funds for R&D, the greater the amount of R&D spending that is profitable. The higher the interest rate, the less is the amount of R&D spending.

Also, the interest rate allocates R&D funds to firms and industries for which the expected rate of return on R&D is the greatest. Ace Microcircuits may have an expected rate of return of 16 percent on an R&D project, while Glow Paints has only a 2 percent expected rate of return on its R&D project. With the interest rate at 8 percent, loanable funds will flow to Ace, not to Glow. Society will benefit by having R&D spending allocated to projects that have high enough expected rates of return to justify using scarce resources for R&D rather than for other purposes.

Nominal and Real Interest Rates

This discussion of the role of interest in investment decisions and in R&D decisions assumes that there is no inflation. If inflation exists, we must distinguish between nominal and real interest rates, just like we needed to distinguish between nominal and real wages in Chapter 14. The **nominal interest rate** is the rate of interest expressed in dollars of current value. The **real interest rate** is the rate of interest expressed in purchasing power—dollars of inflation-adjusted value. (For a comparison of nominal interest rates on bank loans in selected countries, see Global Perspective 15.1.)

Example: Suppose the nominal interest rate and the rate of inflation are both 10 percent. If you borrow $100, you must pay back $110 a year from now. However, because of 10 percent inflation, each of these 110 dollars will be

GLOBAL PERSPECTIVE 15.1

Short-Term Nominal Interest Rates, Selected Nations

These data show the short-term nominal interest rates (percentage rates on 3-month loans) in various countries in 2005. Because these are nominal rates, much of the variation reflects differences in rates of inflation. But differences in central bank monetary policies and in risk of default also explain the variations.

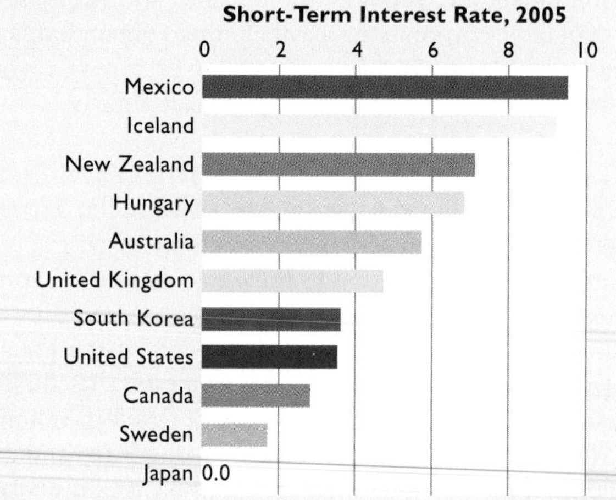

Source: Organization for Economic Cooperation and Development, **www.oecd.org/.**

worth 10 percent less. Thus, the real value or purchasing power of your $110 at the end of the year is only $100. In inflation-adjusted dollars you are borrowing $100 and at year's end you are paying back $100. While the nominal interest rate is 10 percent, the real interest rate is zero. We determine the real interest rate by subtracting the 10 percent inflation rate from the 10 percent nominal interest rate.

It is the real interest rate, not the nominal rate, that affects investment and R&D decisions. **(Key Question 8)**

Application: Usury Laws

O 15.2
Usury

A number of states have passed **usury laws,** which specify a maximum interest rate at which loans can be made. Such rates are a special case of *price ceilings,* discussed in Chapter 3. The purpose of usury laws is to hold down the interest cost of borrowing, particularly for low-income borrowers. ("Usury" simply means exorbitant interest.)

Figure 15.2 helps us assess the impact of such legislation. The equilibrium interest rate there is 8 percent, but suppose a usury law specifies that lenders cannot charge more than 6 percent. The effects are as follows:

- **Nonmarket rationing** At 6 percent, the quantity of loanable funds demanded exceeds the quantity supplied: There is a shortage of loanable funds. Because the market interest rate no longer can ration the available loanable funds to borrowers, lenders (banks) have to do the rationing. We can expect them to make loans only to the most creditworthy borrowers (mainly wealthy, high-income people), thus defeating the goal of the usury law. Low-income, riskier borrowers are excluded from the market and may be forced to turn to loan sharks who charge illegally high interest rates.
- **Gainers and losers** Creditworthy borrowers gain from usury laws, because they pay below-market interest rates. Lenders (ultimately bank shareholders) are losers, because they receive 6 percent rather than 8 percent on each dollar lent.
- **Inefficiency** We have just seen how the equilibrium interest rate allocates money to the investments and the R&D projects whose expected rates of return are greatest. Under usury laws, funds are much less likely to be allocated by banks to the most productive projects. Suppose Mendez has a project so promising she would pay 10 percent for funds to finance it. Chen has a less promising investment, and he would be willing to pay only 7 percent for financing. If the market were rationing funds, Mendez's highly productive project would be funded and Chen's would not. That allocation of funds would be in the interest of both Mendez and society. But with a 6 percent usury rate, Chen may get to the bank before Mendez and receive the loanable funds at 6 percent. So Mendez may not get funded. Legally controlled interest rates may thus inefficiently ration funds to less productive investments or R&D projects.

QUICK REVIEW 15.2

- Interest is the price paid for the use of money.
- In the loanable funds model, the equilibrium interest rate is determined by the demand for and supply of loanable funds.
- The range of interest rates is influenced by risk, maturity, loan size, taxability, and market imperfections.
- The equilibrium interest rate affects the total level of investment and therefore the levels of total spending and total output; it also allocates money and real capital to specific industries and firms. Similarly, the interest rate affects the level and composition of R&D spending.
- Usury laws that establish an interest-rate ceiling below the market interest rate may (a) deny credit to low-income people, (b) subsidize high-income borrowers and penalize lenders, and (c) diminish the efficiency with which loanable funds are allocated to investment and R&D projects.

Economic Profit

Recall from previous chapters that economists define profit narrowly. To accountants, "profit" is what remains of a firm's total revenue after it has paid individuals and other firms for the materials, capital, and labor they have supplied to the firm. To the economist, this definition overstates profit. The reason is that the accountant's view of profit considers only **explicit costs:** payments made by the firm to outsiders. It ignores **implicit costs:** the monetary income the firm sacrifices when it uses resources that it owns, rather than supplying those resources to the market. The economist considers implicit costs to be opportunity costs, and hence to be real costs that must be accounted for in determining profit. **Economic,** or **pure, profit** is what remains after all costs—both explicit and implicit costs, the latter including a normal profit—have been subtracted from a firm's total revenue. Economic profit may be either positive or negative (a loss).

Role of the Entrepreneur

The economist views profit as the return to a particular type of human resource: entrepreneurial ability. We know from earlier chapters that the entrepreneur (1) combines resources to produce a good or service, (2) makes basic, nonroutine policy decisions for the firm, (3) introduces innovations in the form of new products or new production processes, and (4) bears the economic risks associated with all those functions.

Part of the entrepreneur's return is a **normal profit.** This is the minimum payment necessary to retain the entrepreneur in his or her current line of production. We saw in Chapter 8 that normal profit is a cost—the cost of using entrepreneurial ability for a particular purpose. We saw also that a firm's total revenue may exceed its total cost; the excess revenue above all costs is its economic profit. This *residual profit* also goes to the entrepreneur. The entrepreneur is the *residual claimant:* the resource that receives what is left after all costs are paid.

Why should there be residual profit? There are three possible reasons, two relating to the risks involved in business and one based on monopoly power.

Sources of Economic Profit

Let's first construct an artificial economic environment in which economic profit would be zero. Then, by noting how the real world differs from such an environment, we will see where economic profit arises.

We begin with a purely competitive, static economy. A **static economy** is one in which the basic forces such as resource supplies, technological knowledge, and consumer tastes are constant and unchanging. As a result, all cost and supply data, on the one hand, and all demand and revenue data, on the other, are constant.

Given the nature of these data, the economic future is perfectly certain and foreseeable; there is no uncertainty. The outcome of any price or production policy can be accurately predicted. Furthermore, no product or production process is ever improved. Under pure competition any economic profit or loss that might have existed in an industry will disappear with the entry or exit of firms in the long run. All costs, explicit and implicit, are just covered in the long run, so there is no economic profit in this static economy.

The idea of zero economic profit in a static competitive economy suggests that profit is linked to the dynamic nature of real-world capitalism and its accompanying uncertainty. Moreover, it indicates that economic profit may arise from a source other than the directing, innovating, and risk-bearing functions of the entrepreneur. That source is the presence of some amount of monopoly power.

Risk and Profit

In a real, dynamic economy the future is not certain and predictable; there is uncertainty. This means that the entrepreneur must assume risks. Some or all of economic profit may be a reward for assuming risks.

In linking economic profit with uncertainty and risk bearing, we must distinguish between risks that are insurable and risks that are not. Some types of risk such as fire, floods, theft, and accidents to employees are measurable; that is, their frequency of occurrence can be estimated accurately. Firms can avoid losses due to **insurable risks** by paying an annual fee (an insurance premium) to an insurance company. The entrepreneur need not bear such risks.

However, the entrepreneur must bear the uninsurable risks of business, and those risks are a potential source of economic profit. **Uninsurable risks** are mainly the uncontrollable and unpredictable changes in the demand and supply conditions facing the firm (and hence its revenues and costs). Uninsurable risks stem from three general sources:

- **Changes in the general economic environment** A downturn in business (a recession), for example, can lead to greatly reduced demand, sales, and revenues, and thus to business losses. An otherwise-prosperous firm may experience such losses through no fault of its own.
- **Changes in the structure of the economy** Consumer tastes, technology, resource availability, and prices change constantly in the real world, bringing changes in production costs and revenues. For example, an airline earning economic profit one year may find its profit plunging the next year as the result of a significant increase in the price of jet fuel.

Last Word

Determining the Price of Credit

A Variety of Lending Practices May Cause the Effective Interest Rate to Be Quite Different from What It Appears to Be.

Borrowing and lending—receiving and granting credit—are a way of life. Individuals receive credit when they negotiate a mortgage loan and when they use their credit cards. Individuals make loans when they open a savings account in a commercial bank or buy a government bond.

It is sometimes difficult to determine exactly how much interest we pay and receive when we borrow and lend. Let's suppose that you borrow \$10,000 that you agree to repay plus \$1000 of interest at the end of 1 year. In this instance, the interest rate is 10 percent per year. To determine the interest rate i, we compare the interest paid with the amount borrowed:

$$i = \frac{\$1000}{\$10,000} = 10\%$$

But in some cases a lender—say, a bank—will discount the interest payment at the time the loan is made. Thus, instead of giving the borrower \$10,000, the bank discounts the \$1000 interest payment in advance, giving the borrower only \$9000. This increases the interest rate:

$$i = \frac{\$1000}{\$9000} = 11\%$$

While the absolute amount of interest paid is the same, in the second case the borrower has only \$9000 available for the year.

An even more subtle point is that, to simplify their calculations, many financial institutions assume a 360-day year (twelve 30-day months). This means the borrower has the use of the lender's funds for 5 days less than the normal year. This use of a "short year" also increases the actual interest rate paid by the borrower.

The interest rate paid may change dramatically if a loan is repaid in installments. Suppose a bank lends you \$10,000 and charges interest in the amount of \$1000 to be paid at the end of the year. But the loan contract requires that you repay the \$10,000 loan in 12 equal monthly installments. In effect, then, the average amount of the loan outstanding during the year is only \$5000. Therefore:

$$i = \frac{\$1000}{\$5000} = 20\%$$

Here interest is paid on the total amount of the loan (\$10,000) rather than on the outstanding balance (which averages \$5000 for the year), making for a much higher interest rate.

Another factor that influences the effective interest rate is whether or not interest is compounded. Suppose you deposit \$10,000 in a savings account that pays a 10 percent interest rate compounded semiannually. In other words, interest is paid on

- **Changes in government policy** A newly instituted regulation, the removal of a tariff, or a change in national defense policy may significantly alter the cost and revenue data of the affected industry and firms.

Regardless of how such revenue and cost changes come about, they are risks that the firm and entrepreneur must take in order to stay in business. Some or all of the economic profit in a real, dynamic economy may be compensation for taking risks.

Innovations and Profit Such uninsurable risks are beyond the control of the individual firm or industry and thus external to it. But one dynamic feature of capitalism—innovation—occurs at the initiative of the entrepreneur. Business firms deliberately introduce new methods of production to affect their costs favorably and new and improved products to affect their revenues favorably. The entrepreneur purposely undertakes to upset existing cost and revenue data in a way that promises to be profitable.

But again, uncertainty enters the picture. Despite exhaustive market surveys, new products or modifications of existing products may be economic failures. Similarly, of the many new novels, textbooks, movies, and compact discs that appear every year, only a handful garners large profits. Nor is it known with certainty whether new production machinery will actually yield projected cost economies. Thus, innovations undertaken by entrepreneurs entail uncertainty and the possibility of losses, not just the potential for increased profit. Some of the economic profit in an innovative economy may be compensation for dealing with the uncertainty of innovation.

Monopoly and Profit So far, we have linked economic profit with the uncertainties surrounding (1) the dynamic environment to which enterprises are exposed and (2) the dynamic business processes they initiate themselves. The existence of monopoly power is a final source of economic profit. Because a monopolist can restrict output and deter entry, it may persistently enjoy your "loan" to the bank twice a year. At the end of the first 6 months, $500 of interest (10 percent of $10,000 for half a year) is added to your account. At the end of the year, interest is calculated on $10,500 so that the second interest payment is $525 (10 percent of $10,500 for half a year). Thus:

$$i = \frac{\$1025}{\$10,000} = 10.25\%$$

This means that a bank advertising a 10 percent interest rate compounded semiannually is actually paying more interest to its customers than is a competitor paying a simple (noncompounded) interest rate of 10.2 percent.

Two pieces of legislation have attempted to clarify interest charges and payments. The Truth in Lending Act of 1968 requires that lenders state the costs and terms of consumer credit in concise and uniform language, in particular, as an annual percentage rate (APR). More recently, the Truth in Savings Act of 1991 requires that all advertisements of deposit accounts by banks and other financial institutions disclose all fees connected with such accounts and the interest rate and annual percentage return on each account. Nevertheless, some check-cashing firms that lend money to people in return for postdated personal checks have been found to receive interest equivalent to 261 to 913 percent a year. These interest rates prompted calls for state legislators to protect consumers from "predatory lenders."

More recently, many banks have established fee-based "bounce (overdraft) protection" for checking accounts. The bank agrees to pay each overdraft for a flat $20 to $35 fee. These fees are essentially interest on a loan for the amount of the overdraft. When the overdraft amount is small, the annual interest on the loan can easily exceed 1000 percent.

Similarly, late-payment fees on credit card accounts can boost the actual interest rate paid on credit card balances to extremely high levels. Furthermore, low "teaser" rates designed to attract new customers often contain "fine print" that raises the interest rate to 16 percent, or even 28 percent, if a payment on the account is late. "Let the borrower (or depositor) beware" remains a fitting motto in the world of credit.

above-competitive prices and economic profit if demand is strong relative to cost.

Economic uncertainty and monopoly are closely intertwined as sources of economic profit. A firm with some monopoly power can reduce business risk, or at least manipulate it enough to reduce its adverse effects, and thus increase and prolong economic profit. Furthermore, a firm can use innovation as a source of monopoly power and a means of sustaining itself and its economic profit.

An important distinction between profit stemming from uncertainty and profit resulting from monopoly has to do with the social desirability of these two sources of profit. Bearing business risk and undertaking innovation in an uncertain economic environment are socially desirable functions. Obtaining monopoly profit is not socially desirable, because it is typically founded on reduced output, above-competitive prices, and economic inefficiency. **(Key Question 10)**

Functions of Profit

Economic profit is the main energizer of the capitalistic economy. It influences both the level of economic output and the allocation of resources among alternative uses.

Profit and Total Output

The expectation of economic profit motivates firms to innovate. Innovation stimulates new investment, thereby increasing total output and employment. Thus, the pursuit of profit enhances economic growth by promoting innovation.

Profit and Resource Allocation

Profit also helps allocate resources among alternative lines of production, distribution, and sales. Entrepreneurs seek profit and shun losses. The occurrence of continuing profits in a firm or industry is a signal that society wants that particular firm or industry to expand. It attracts resources from firms and industries that are not profitable. But the rewards of profits are more than an inducement for a firm to expand; they also attract the financing needed for expansion. In contrast, continuing losses penalize firms or industries that fail to adjust their productive efforts to match consumer wants. Such losses signal society's desire for the afflicted entities to contract.

So, in terms of our chapter-opening question, Wal-Mart garnered large profits because it was locating its stores close to customers and delivering the mix of products many consumers wanted at exceptionally low prices. These profits signaled that society wanted more of its scarce resources allocated to Wal-Mart stores. General Motors (GM), in contrast, was not delivering products equivalent in value to the costs of the resources used to provide them—so the firm suffered losses. The losses signaled that society would benefit from a reallocation of all or a part of those resources to some other use. Indeed, GM announced in early 2006 that it was closing five assembly plants, phasing out seven other facilities, eliminating 30,000 jobs, and restructuring its pension plans.

QUICK REVIEW 15.3

- Pure or economic profit is what remains after all explicit and implicit costs (including a normal profit) are subtracted from a firm's total revenue.
- Economic profit has three sources: the bearing of uninsurable risk, the uncertainty of innovation, and monopoly power.
- Profit and profit expectations affect the levels of investment, total spending, and domestic output; profit and loss also allocate resources among alternative uses.

Income Shares

Our discussion in this and in the preceding chapter would not be complete without a brief reexamination of how U.S. income is distributed among wages, rent, interest, and profit.

It will be worth your while to look back at Figure 4.1, page 66. Although the income categories shown in that chart do not neatly fit the economic definitions of wages, rent, interest, and profits, they do provide insights about income shares in the United States. Note the dominant role of the labor resource and thus labor income in the U.S. economy. Even with labor income defined narrowly as "wages and salaries," labor receives about 71 percent of all income earned by Americans in a typical year. But some economists contend that the income of proprietors is largely composed of implicit wages and salaries and therefore should be added to the "wages and salaries" category to determine labor income. When we use this broad definition, labor's share rises to about 80 percent of national income, a percentage that has been remarkably stable in the United States since 1900. That leaves about 20 percent for capitalists in the form of rent, interest, and profit. Ironically, capitalist income is a relatively small share of the U.S. economy, which we call a capitalist system.

Summary

1. Economic rent is the price paid for the use of land and other natural resources whose total supplies are fixed.
2. Rent is a surplus payment that is socially unnecessary because land would be available to the economy even without rental payments. The idea of land rent as a surplus payment gave rise to the single-tax movement of the late 1800s.
3. Differences in land rent result from differences in the fertility and climatic features of the land and differences in location.
4. Although land rent is a surplus payment rather than a cost to the economy as a whole, to individual firms and industries, rental payments are correctly regarded as costs. These payments must be made to gain the use of land, which has alternative uses.
5. Interest is the price paid for the use of money. In the loanable funds theory, the equilibrium interest rate is determined by the demand for and supply of loanable funds. Other things equal, an increase in the supply of loanable funds reduces the equilibrium interest rate, whereas a decrease in supply increases it; increases in the demand for loanable funds raise the equilibrium interest rate, whereas decreases in demand reduce it.
6. Interest rates vary in size because loans differ as to risk, maturity, amount, and taxability. Market imperfections cause additional variations. The pure rate of interest is the interest rate on long-term, virtually riskless, 20-year U.S. Treasury bonds.
7. The equilibrium interest rate influences the level of investment and helps ration financial and physical capital to specific firms and industries. Similarly, this rate influences the size and composition of R&D spending. The real interest rate, not the nominal rate, is critical to investment and R&D decisions.

8. Although designed to make funds available to low-income borrowers, usury laws tend to allocate credit to high-income persons, subsidize high-income borrowers at the expense of lenders, and lessen the efficiency with which loanable funds are allocated.
9. Economic, or pure, profit is the difference between a firm's total revenue and the sum of its explicit and implicit costs, the latter including a normal profit. Profit accrues to entrepreneurs for assuming the uninsurable risks associated with organizing and directing economic resources and for innovating. Profit also results from monopoly power.
10. Profit expectations influence innovating and investment activities and therefore the economy's levels of employment and economic growth. The basic function of profits and losses, however, is to allocate resources in accord with consumers' preferences.
11. The largest share of all income earned by Americans—about 71 percent—goes to labor, a share narrowly defined as "wages and salaries." When labor's share is more broadly defined to include "proprietors' income," it rises to about 80 percent of national income, leaving about 20 percent as capital's share.

Terms and Concepts

economic rent	nominal interest rate	economic or pure profit
incentive function	real interest rate	normal profit
single-tax movement	usury laws	static economy
loanable funds theory of interest	explicit costs	insurable risks
pure rate of interest	implicit costs	uninsurable risks

Study Questions

1. How does the economist's use of the term "rent" differ from everyday usage? Explain: "Though rent need not be paid by society to make land available, rental payments are very useful in guiding land into the most productive uses."
2. **KEY QUESTION** Explain why economic rent is a surplus payment when viewed by the economy as a whole but a cost of production from the standpoint of individual firms and industries. Explain: "Land rent performs no 'incentive function' for the overall economy."
3. In the 1980s land prices in Japan surged upward in a "speculative bubble." Land prices then fell for 11 straight years between 1990 and 2001. What can we safely assume happened to *land rent* in Japan over those 11 years? Use graphical analysis to illustrate your answer.
4. How does Henry George's proposal for a single tax on land relate to the elasticity of supply of land? Why are there so few remaining advocates of George's proposal?
5. If money is not an economic resource, why is interest paid and received for its use? What considerations account for the fact that interest rates differ greatly on various types of loans? Use those considerations to explain the relative sizes of the interest rates on the following:
   a. A 10-year $1000 government bond.
   b. A $20 pawnshop loan.
   c. A 30-year mortgage loan on a $145,000 house.
   d. A 24-month $12,000 commercial bank loan to finance the purchase of an automobile.
   e. A 60-day $100 loan from a personal finance company.
6. **KEY QUESTION** Why is the supply of loanable funds upsloping? Why is the demand for loanable funds downsloping? Explain the equilibrium interest rate. List some factors that might cause it to change.
7. What are the major economic functions of the interest rate? How might the fact that many businesses finance their investment activities internally affect the efficiency with which the interest rate performs its functions?
8. **KEY QUESTION** Distinguish between nominal and real interest rates. Which is more relevant in making investment and R&D decisions? If the nominal interest rate is 12 percent and the inflation rate is 8 percent, what is the real rate of interest?
9. Historically, usury laws that put below-equilibrium ceilings on interest rates have been used by some states to make credit available to poor people who could not otherwise afford to borrow. Critics contend that poor people are those most likely to be hurt by such laws. Which view is correct?
10. **KEY QUESTION** How do the concepts of accounting profit and economic profit differ? Why is economic profit smaller than accounting profit? What are the three basic sources of economic profit? Classify each of the following according to those sources:
    a. A firm's profit from developing and patenting a new medication that greatly reduces cholesterol and thus diminishes the likelihood of heart disease and stroke.
    b. A restaurant's profit that results from the completion of a new highway past its door.
    c. The profit received by a firm due to an unanticipated change in consumer tastes.

11. Why is the distinction between insurable and uninsurable risks significant for the theory of profit? Carefully evaluate: "All economic profit can be traced to either uncertainty or the desire to avoid it." What are the major functions of economic profit?
12. Explain the absence of economic profit in a purely competitive, static economy. Realizing that the major function of profit is to allocate resources according to consumer preferences, describe the allocation of resources in such an economy.
13. What is the rent, interest, and profit share of the income earned by Americans in a typical year if proprietors' income is included within the labor (wage) share?
14. **LAST WORD** Assume that you borrow $5000 and pay back the $5000 plus $250 in interest at the end of the year. Assuming no inflation, what is the real interest rate? What would the interest rate be if the $250 of interest had been discounted at the time the loan was made? What would the interest rate be if you were required to repay the loan in 12 equal monthly installments?

Web-Based Questions

1. **WHAT ARE THE CURRENT NOMINAL AND REAL INTEREST RATES?** Go to **www.federalreserve.gov** (Research and Data; Statistics: Releases and Historical Data; Selected Interest Rates) and **www.bankrate.com** to update the interest rates in Table 15.1 to their latest recorded values. In what direction, if any, have the interest rates changed? Find the current annual rate of inflation at **www.bls.gov/cpi** (Latest Numbers; CPI-U, U.S. City Average, All Items, 12-months ending with the last month). Subtract this annual rate of inflation from your updated interest rates in the table to determine the real interest rates in each category.
2. **CORPORATE PROFITS—WHICH INDUSTRIES ARE MAKING THE MOST?** The Bureau of Economic Analysis provides profit data for various industries in the United States. Go to **www.bea.gov/** and find "National Income and Product Account Table 6.16D on Corporate Profits by Industry." Based on the most-recent figures, which of the following categories of industry classifications has the greatest profits: (*a*) financial or nonfinancial; (*b*) manufacturing, transportation, wholesale trade, or retail trade; (*c*) durable goods or nondurable goods? During the past year, which sectors had the largest and smallest percentage increases in profit? Which sectors, if any, experienced losses? What are the implications of the profit changes for expansion or contraction of the particular industries?

Bonus Web Chapter

15 WEB

www.mcconnell17.com

CHAPTER 15W CONTENTS

Resource Supplies: Boom or Doom?
Population Growth / Resource Consumption per Person
Energy Economics
Efficient Energy Use / Running out of Energy?
Natural Resource Economics
Using Present Values to Evaluate Future Possibilities
Nonrenewable Resources
Present Use versus Future Use / Market Failures Lead to Excessive Present Use / Applications
Renewable Resources
Forest Management / Optimal Forest Harvesting / Optimal Fisheries Management / Policies to Limit Catch Sizes
Last Word: *Is Economic Growth Bad for the Environment?*

Natural Resource and Energy Economics

Chapter 15 Web is a bonus chapter found at the book's Web site, **www.mcconnell17.com.** It extends the analysis of Part 3, "Microeconomics of Resource Markets," by examining issues relating to natural resource and energy use. Your instructor may (or may not) assign all or part of this chapter.

PART FOUR

Microeconomics of Government

16 GOVERNMENT AND MARKET FAILURE
17 PUBLIC CHOICE THEORY AND THE ECONOMICS OF TAXATION

IN THIS CHAPTER YOU WILL LEARN:

- How public goods are distinguished from private goods.
- The method for determining the optimal quantity of a public good.
- The basics of cost-benefit analysis.
- About externalities (spillover costs and benefits) and the methods to remedy them.
- How information failures can justify government interventions in some markets.

16

Government and Market Failure

The economic activities of government affect your well-being every day. If you drive to work or classes, you are using publicly provided highways and streets. If you attend a public college or university, taxpayers subsidize your education. When you receive a check from your part-time or summer job, you see deductions for income taxes and Social Security taxes. Government antipollution laws affect the air you breathe. Laws requiring seat belts, motorcycle helmets, and the sprinkler system in college residence halls are all government mandates.

This chapter examines government and *market failure*—a circumstance in which private markets do not bring about the allocation of resources that best satisfies society's wants. Where private markets fail, an economic role for government may arise. We want to examine that role as it relates to three kinds of market failure: public goods, externalities, and information asymmetries. Our discussion of externalities in turn facilitates a discussion of pollution and pollution policies.

In the next chapter—Chapter 17—we continue our discussion of the microeconomics of government by first analyzing potential government inefficiencies—called *government failure*—and then considering the economics of taxation.

Public Goods

To understand public goods, we first need to revisit the characteristics of private goods.

Private Goods Characteristics

We have seen that a full range of **private goods** is produced through the competitive market system. These are the goods offered for sale in stores, in shops, and on the Internet. Examples include automobiles, clothing, personal computers, household appliances, and sporting goods. Private goods have two characteristics: rivalry and excludability:

- ***Rivalry*** (in consumption) means that when one person buys and consumes a product, it is not available for another person to buy and consume. When Adams purchases and drinks a bottle of mineral water, it is not available for Benson to purchase and consume.
- ***Excludability*** means that sellers can keep people who do not pay for a product from obtaining its benefits. Only people who are willing and able to pay the market price for bottles of water can obtain these drinks and the benefits they confer.

Consumers fully express their personal demands for private goods in the market. If Adams likes bottled mineral water, that fact will be known by her desire to purchase the product. Other things equal, the higher the price of bottled water, the fewer bottles she will buy. So Adams' demand for bottled water will reflect an inverse relationship between the price of bottled water and the quantity of it demanded. This is simply *individual* demand, as described in Chapter 3.

The *market* demand for a private good is the horizontal summation of the individual demand schedules (review Figure 3.2). Suppose just two consumers comprise the market for bottled water and the price is \$1 per bottle. If Adams will purchase 3 bottles and Benson will buy 2, the market demand will reflect consumers' demand for 5 bottles at the \$1 price. Similar summations of quantities demanded at other prices will generate the market demand schedule and curve.

Suppose the equilibrium price of bottled water is \$1. Adams and Benson will buy a total of 5 bottles, and the sellers will obtain total revenue of \$5 (= \$1 × 5). If the sellers' cost per bottle is \$.80, their total cost will be \$4 (= \$.80 × 5). So sellers charging \$1 per bottle will obtain \$5 of total revenue, incur \$4 of total cost, and earn \$1 of profits for the 5 bottles sold.

Because firms can profitably "tap market demand" for private goods, they will produce and offer them for sale. Consumers demand private goods, and profit-seeking suppliers produce goods that satisfy the demand. Consumers willing to pay the market price obtain the goods; nonpayers go without. A competitive market not only makes private goods available to consumers but also allocates society's resources efficiently to the particular product. There is neither underproduction nor overproduction of the product.

Public Goods Characteristics

Recall from Chapter 4 that certain other goods and services—**public goods**—have the opposite characteristics of private goods. Public goods are distinguished by nonrivalry and nonexcludability.

- ***Nonrivalry*** (in consumption) means that one person's consumption of a good does not preclude consumption of the good by others. Everyone can simultaneously obtain the benefit from a public good such as national defense, street lighting, a global positioning system, or environmental protection.
- ***Nonexcludability*** means there is no effective way of excluding individuals from the benefit of the good once it comes into existence. Once in place, you cannot exclude someone from benefiting from national defense, street lighting, a global positioning system, or environmental protection.

These two characteristics create a **free-rider problem.** Once a producer has provided a public good, everyone including nonpayers can obtain the benefit. Most people do not voluntarily pay for something they can obtain for free!

With only free riders, the demand for a public good does not get expressed in the market. With no market demand, firms have no potential to "tap the demand" for revenues and profits. The free-rider problem makes it impossible for firms to gather together resources and profitably provide the good. If society wants a public good, society will have to direct government to provide it. Government can finance the provision of such goods through taxation.

CONSIDER THIS . . .

Art for Art's Sake

Suppose an enterprising sculptor creates a piece of art costing $600 and, with permission, places it in the town square. Also suppose that Jack gets $300 of enjoyment from the art and Diane gets $400. Sensing this enjoyment and hoping to make a profit, the sculptor approaches Jack for a donation equal to his satisfaction. Jack falsely says that, unfortunately, he does not particularly like the piece. The sculptor then tries Diane, hoping to get $400 or so. Same deal: Diane professes not to like the piece either. Jack and Diane have become free riders. Although feeling a bit guilty, both reason that it makes no sense to pay for something when anyone can receive the benefits without paying for them. The artist is a quick learner; he vows never to try anything like that again.

Optimal Quantity of a Public Good

If consumers need not reveal their true demand for a public good in the marketplace, how can society determine the optimal amount of that good? The answer is that the government has to try to estimate the demand for a public good through surveys or public votes. It can then compare the marginal benefit (MB) of an added unit of the good against the government's marginal cost (MC) of providing it. Adhering to the MB = MC rule, government can provide the "right," meaning "efficient," amount of the public good.

Demand for Public Goods

The demand for a public good is somewhat unusual. Suppose Adams and Benson are the only two people in the society, and their marginal willingness to pay for a public good, national defense, is as shown in columns 1 and 2 and columns 1 and 3 in Table 16.1. Economists might have discovered these schedules through a survey asking hypothetical questions about how much each citizen was willing to pay for various types and amounts of public goods rather than go without them.

Notice that the schedules in Table 16.1 are price-quantity schedules, implying that they are demand schedules. Rather than depicting demand in the usual way—the quantity of a product someone is willing to buy at each possible price—these schedules show the price someone is willing to pay for the extra unit of each possible quantity. That is, Adams is willing to pay $4 for the first unit of the public good, $3 for the second, $2 for the third, and so on.

TABLE 16.1 Demand for a Public Good, Two Individuals

(1) Quantity of Public Good	(2) Adams' Willingness to Pay (Price)		(3) Benson's Willingness to Pay (Price)		(4) Collective Willingness to Pay (Price)
1	$4	+	$5	=	$9
2	3	+	4	=	7
3	2	+	3	=	5
4	1	+	2	=	3
5	0	+	1	=	1

Suppose the government produces 1 unit of this public good. Because of nonrivalry, Adams' consumption of the good does not preclude Benson from also consuming it, and vice versa. So both consume the good, and neither volunteers to pay for it. But from Table 16.1 we can find the amount these two people would be willing to pay, together, rather than do without this 1 unit of the good. Columns 1 and 2 show that Adams would be willing to pay $4 for the first unit of the public good; columns 1 and 3 show that Benson would be willing to pay $5 for it. So the two people are jointly willing to pay $9 (= $4 + $5) for this first unit.

For the second unit of the public good, the collective price they are willing to pay is $7 (= $3 from Adams + $4 from Benson); for the third unit they will pay $5 (= $2 + $3); and so on. By finding the collective willingness to pay for each additional unit (column 4), we can construct a collective demand schedule (a willingness-to-pay schedule) for the public good. Here we are not adding the quantities demanded at each possible price, as we do when we determine the market demand for a private good. Instead, we are adding the prices that people are willing to pay for the last unit of the public good at each possible quantity demanded.

Figure 16.1 shows the same adding procedure graphically, using the data from Table 16.1. Note that we sum Adams' and Benson's willingness-to-pay curves *vertically* to derive the collective willingness-to-pay curve (demand curve). For example, the height of the collective demand curve D_c at 2 units of output is $7, the sum of the amounts that Adams and Benson are each willing to pay for the second unit (= $3 + $4). Likewise, the height of the collective demand curve at 4 units of the public good is $3 (= $1 + $2).

FIGURE 16.1 The optimal amount of a public good. The collective demand curve for a public good, as shown by D_c in (c), is found by summing vertically the individual willingness-to-pay curves D_1 in (a) and D_2 in (b) of Adams and Benson, the only two people in the economy. The supply curve of the public good represented in (c) slopes upward and to the right, reflecting rising marginal costs. The optimal amount of the public good is 3 units, determined by the intersection of D_c and S. At that output, marginal benefit (reflected in the collective demand curve D_c) equals marginal cost (reflected in the supply curve S).

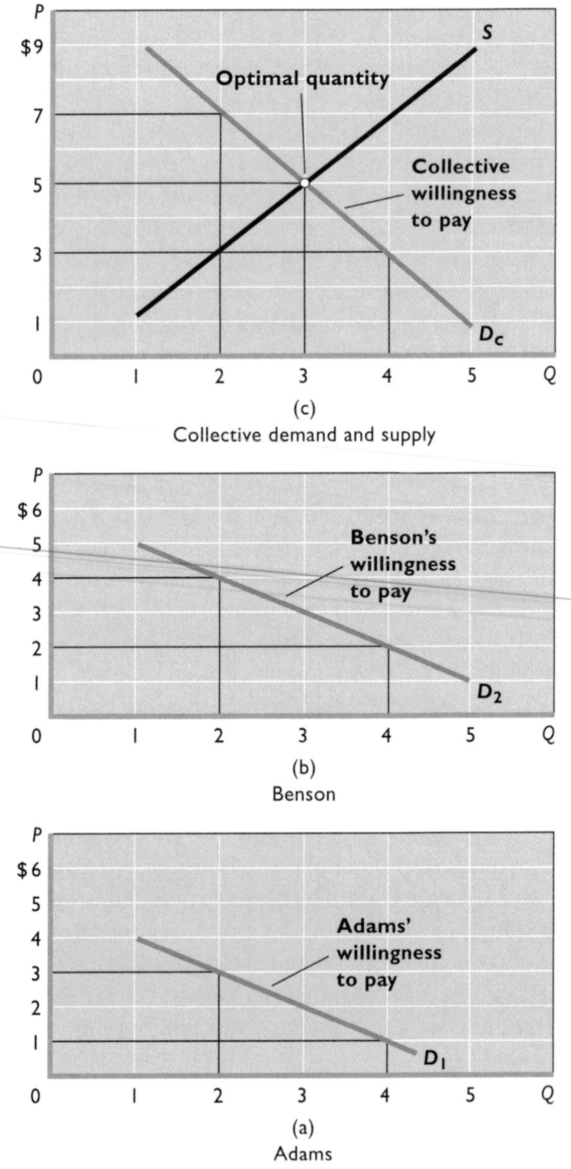

What does it mean in Figure 16.1a that, for example, Adams is willing to pay $3 for the second unit of the public good? It means that Adams expects to receive $3 of extra benefit or utility from that unit. And we know from the law of diminishing marginal utility that successive units of any good yield less and less added benefit. This is also true for public goods, explaining the downward slope of the willingness-to-pay curves of Adams, Benson, and society. These curves, in essence, are marginal-benefit (MB) curves. **(Key Question 1)**

Comparing MB and MC

The supply curve for any good, private or public, is its marginal-cost (MC) curve. Marginal cost rises as more of a good is produced. The reason is the law of diminishing returns, which applies whether a society is making missiles (a public good) or mufflers (a private good). In the short run, government has fixed resources (public capital) with which to "produce" public goods such as national defense. As it adds more units of a variable resource (labor) to these fixed resources, total product eventually rises at a diminishing rate. That means that marginal product falls and marginal cost rises, explaining why curve *S* in Figure 16.1c slopes upward.

We can now determine the optimal quantity of the public good. The collective demand curve D_c in Figure 16.1c measures society's marginal benefit of each unit of this particular good. The supply curve *S* in that figure measures society's marginal cost of each unit. The optimal quantity of this public good occurs where marginal benefit equals marginal cost, or where the two curves intersect. In Figure 16.1c that point is 3 units of the public good, where the collective willingness to pay for the last (third) unit—the marginal benefit—just matches that unit's marginal cost ($5 = $5). As we saw in Chapter 1, equating marginal benefit and marginal cost efficiently allocates society's scarce resources. **(Key Question 2)**

W 16.1
Optimal amount of a public good

Cost-Benefit Analysis

The above example suggests a practical means, called **cost-benefit analysis,** for deciding whether to provide a particular public good and how much of it to provide. Like our example, cost-benefit analysis (or marginal-benefit–marginal-cost analysis) involves a comparison of marginal costs and marginal benefits.

Concept Suppose the Federal government is contemplating a highway construction plan. Because the economy's resources are limited, any decision to use more resources in the public sector will mean fewer resources for the private sector. There will be an opportunity cost, as well as a benefit. The cost is the loss of satisfaction resulting from the accompanying decline in the production of private goods; the benefit is the extra satisfaction resulting from the output of more public goods. Should the needed resources be shifted from the private to the public sector? The answer is yes if the benefit from the extra public goods exceeds the cost that results from having fewer private goods. The answer is no if the cost of the forgone private goods is greater than the benefit associated with the extra public goods.

Cost-benefit analysis, however, can indicate more than whether a public program is worth doing. It can also help the government decide on the extent to which a project should be pursued. Real economic questions cannot usually be answered simply by "yes" or "no" but, rather, involve questions such as "how much" or "how little."

Illustration Although a few private toll roads exist, highways clearly have public goods characteristics because the benefits are widely diffused and highway use is difficult to price. Should the Federal government expand the Federal highway system? If so, what is the proper size or scope for the overall project?

Table 16.2 lists a series of increasingly ambitious and increasingly costly highway projects: widening existing two-lane highways; building new two-lane highways; building new four-lane highways; building new six-lane highways. The extent to which government should undertake highway construction depends on the costs and benefits. The costs are largely the costs of constructing and maintaining the highways; the benefits are improved flows of people and goods throughout the country.

The table shows that total annual benefit (column 4) exceeds total annual cost (column 2) for plans A, B, and C, indicating that some highway construction is economically justifiable. We see this directly in column 6, where total costs (column 2) are subtracted from total annual benefits (column 4). Net benefits are positive for plans A, B, and C. Plan D is not economically justifiable because net benefits are negative.

But the question of optimal size or scope for this project remains. Comparing the additional, or marginal, cost and the additional, or marginal, benefit relating to each plan determines the answer. The guideline is well known to you from previous discussions: Increase an activity, project, or output as long as the marginal benefit (column 5) exceeds the marginal cost (column 3). Stop the activity at, or as close as possible to, the point at which the marginal benefit equals the marginal cost. Do not undertake a project for which marginal cost exceeds marginal benefit.

In this case plan C (building new four-lane highways) is the best plan. Plans A and B are too modest; the marginal benefits exceed the marginal costs, and there is a better option. Plan D's marginal cost ($10 billion) exceeds the marginal benefit ($3 billion) and therefore cannot be justified; it overallocates resources to the project. Plan C is closest to the theoretical optimum because its marginal benefit ($10 billion) still exceeds marginal cost ($8 billion) but approaches the MB = MC (or MC = MB) ideal.

This **marginal-cost–marginal-benefit rule** actually tells us which plan provides the maximum excess of total benefits over total costs or, in other words, the plan that provides society with the maximum net benefit. You can confirm directly in column 6 that the maximum net benefit (= $5 billion) is associated with plan C.

Cost-benefit analysis shatters the myth that "economy in government" and "reduced government spending" are synonymous. "Economy" is concerned with using scarce resources efficiently. If the marginal cost of a proposed government program exceeds its marginal benefit, then the proposed public program should not be undertaken. But if the marginal benefit exceeds the marginal cost, then it would be uneconomical or "wasteful" not to spend on that government program. Economy in government does not mean minimization of public spending. It means allocating resources between the private and public sectors and among public goods to achieve maximum net benefit. **(Key Question 3)**

TABLE 16.2 Cost-Benefit Analysis for a National Highway Construction Project (in Billions)

(1) Plan	(2) Total Cost of Project	(3) Marginal Cost	(4) Total Benefit	(5) Marginal Benefit	(6) Net Benefit (4) − (2)
No new construction	$ 0		$ 0		$ 0
		$ 4		$ 5	
A: Widen existing highways	4		5		1
		6		8	
B: New 2-lane highways	10		13		3
		8		***10***	
C: New 4-lane highways	***18***		***23***		***5***
		10		3	
D: New 6-lane highways	28		26		−2

QUICK REVIEW 16.1

- Public goods are characterized by nonrivalry and nonexcludability.
- The demand (marginal-benefit) curve for a public good is found by vertically adding the prices that all the members of society are willing to pay for the last unit of output at various output levels.
- The socially optimal amount of a public good is the amount at which the marginal cost and marginal benefit of the good are equal.
- Cost-benefit analysis is the method of evaluating alternative projects or sizes of projects by comparing the marginal cost and marginal benefit and applying the MC = MB rule.

Externalities

In performing its allocation function, government not only produces public goods but also corrects for a market failure called **externalities,** or spillovers. Recall from Chapter 4 that an externality is a cost or a benefit accruing to an individual or group—a third party—that is *external* to a market transaction. An example of a negative externality is the cost of breathing polluted air; an example of a positive externality is the benefit of having everyone else inoculated against some disease. When there are negative externalities, an overproduction of the related product occurs and there is an overallocation of resources to this product. Conversely, underproduction and underallocation of resources result when positive externalities are present. We can demonstrate both graphically.

Negative Externalities

Figure 16.2a illustrates how negative externalities affect the allocation of resources. When producers shift some of their costs onto the community as external costs, producers' marginal costs are lower than otherwise. So their supply curves do not include or "capture" all the costs legitimately associated with the production of their goods. A polluting producer's supply curve such as *S* in Figure 16.2a therefore understates the total cost of production. The firm's supply curve lies to the right of (or below) the full-cost supply curve S_t, which would include the spillover cost. Through polluting and thus transferring cost to society, the firm enjoys lower production costs and has the supply curve *S*.

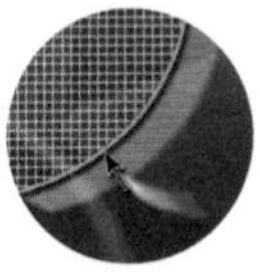

G 16.1

Externalities

The outcome is shown in Figure 16.2a, where equilibrium output Q_e is larger than the optimal output Q_o. This means that resources are overallocated to the production of this commodity; too many units of it are produced.

Positive Externalities

Figure 16.2b shows the impact of positive externalities on resource allocation. When external benefits occur, the market demand curve *D* lies to the left of (or below) the full-benefits demand curve. That is, *D* does not include the external benefits of the product, whereas D_t does. Consider inoculations against a communicable disease. Watson and Weinberg benefit when they get vaccinated, but so do their associates Alvarez and Anderson, who are less likely to contract the disease from them. The market demand curve reflects only the direct, private benefits to Watson and Weinberg. It does not reflect the external benefits—the positive externalities—to Alvarez and Anderson, which are included in D_t.

The outcome is that the equilibrium output Q_e is less than the optimal output Q_o. The market fails to produce enough vaccinations, and resources are underallocated to this product.

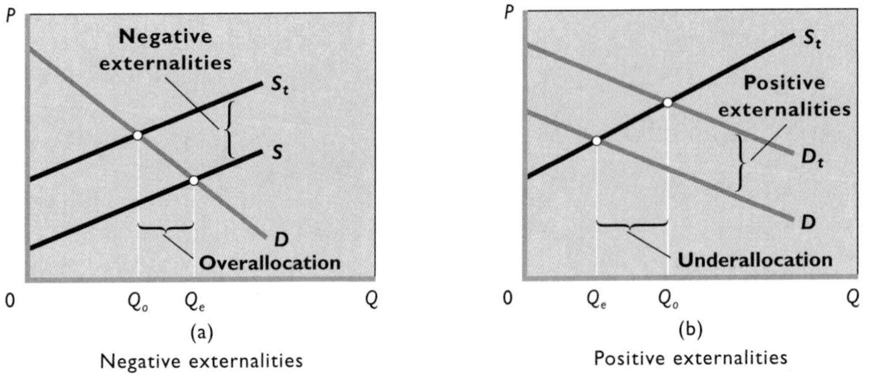

FIGURE 16.2 Negative externalities and positive externalities. (a) With negative externalities borne by society, the producers' supply curve S is to the right of (below) the full-cost curve S_t. Consequently, the equilibrium output Q_e is greater than the optimal output Q_o. (b) When positive externalities accrue to society, the market demand curve D is to the left of (below) the full-benefit demand curve D_t. As a result, the equilibrium output Q_e is less than the optimal output Q_o.

O 16.1
Externalities

Economists have explored several approaches to the problems of negative externalities and positive externalities. Let's first look at situations where government intervention is not needed and then at some possible government solutions.

Individual Bargaining: Coase Theorem

O 16.2
Coase theorem

In the **Coase theorem,** conceived decades ago by economist Ronald Coase at the University of Chicago, government is not needed to remedy external costs or benefits where (1) property ownership is clearly defined, (2) the number of people involved is small, and (3) bargaining costs are negligible. Under these circumstances the government should confine its role to encouraging bargaining between affected individuals or groups. Property rights place a price tag on an externality, creating opportunity costs for all parties. Because the economic self-interests of the parties are at stake, bargaining will enable them to find a mutually acceptable solution to the externality problem.

Example of the Coase Theorem

Suppose the owner of a large parcel of forestland is considering a plan to clear-cut (totally level) thousands of acres of mature fir trees. The complication is that the forest surrounds a lake with a popular resort on its shore. The resort is on land owned by the resort. The unspoiled beauty of the general area attracts vacationers from all over the nation to the resort, and the resort owner is against the clear-cutting. Should state or local government intervene to allow or prevent the tree cutting?

According to the Coase theorem, the forest owner and the resort owner can resolve this situation without government intervention. As long as one of the parties to the dispute has property rights to what is at issue, an incentive will exist for both parties to negotiate a solution acceptable to each. In our example, the owner of the timberland holds the property rights to the land to be logged and thus has the right to clear-cut it. The owner of the resort therefore has an economic incentive to negotiate with the forest owner to reduce the logging impact. Excessive logging of the forest surrounding the resort will reduce tourism and revenues to the resort owner.

But what is the economic incentive to the forest owner to negotiate with the resort owner? The answer draws directly on the idea of opportunity cost. One cost incurred in logging the forest is the forgone payment that the forest owner could obtain from the resort owner for agreeing not to clear-cut the fir trees. The resort owner might be willing to make a lump-sum or annual payment to the owner of the forest to avoid or minimize the negative externality. Or perhaps the resort owner might be willing to buy the forested land to prevent the logging. As viewed by the forest owner, a payment for not clear-cutting or a purchase price above the prior market value of the land is an opportunity cost of logging the land.

It is likely that both parties would regard a negotiated agreement as better than clear-cutting the firs.

Limitations

Unfortunately, many externalities involve large numbers of affected parties, high bargaining costs, and community property such as air and water. In such situations private bargaining cannot be used as a remedy. As an example, the global-warming problem affects millions of people in many nations. The vast number of affected parties could not individually negotiate an agreement to remedy this problem. Instead, they must rely on their governments to represent the millions of affected parties and find an acceptable solution.

Liability Rules and Lawsuits

Although private negotiation may not be a realistic solution to many externality problems, clearly established property rights may help in another way. The government has erected a framework of laws that define private property and protect it from damage done by other parties. Those laws, and the damage recovery system to which they give rise, permit parties suffering negative externalities to sue for compensation.

Suppose the Ajax Degreaser Company regularly dumps leaky barrels containing solvents into a nearby canyon owned by Bar Q Ranch. Bar Q eventually discovers this dump site and, after tracing the drums to Ajax, immediately contacts its lawyer. Soon after, Bar Q sues Ajax. If Ajax loses the case, it will have to pay for the cleanup, and may also have to pay Bar Q additional damages for ruining its property.

Clearly defined property rights and government liability laws thus help remedy some externality problems. They do so directly by forcing the perpetrator of the harmful externality to pay damages to those injured. They do so indirectly by discouraging firms and individuals from generating negative externalities for fear of being sued. It is not surprising, then, that many externalities do not involve private property but rather property held in common by society. It is the public bodies of water, the public lands, and the public air, where ownership is less clear, that often bear the brunt of negative externalities.

Caveat: Like private negotiations, private lawsuits to resolve externalities have their own limitations. Large legal fees and major time delays in the court system are commonplace. Also, the uncertainty associated with the court outcome reduces the effectiveness of this approach. Will the court accept your claim that your emphysema has resulted from the smoke emitted by the factory next door, or will it conclude that your ailment is unrelated to the plant's pollution? Can you prove that a specific firm in the area is the source of the contamination of your well? What happens to Bar Q's suit if Ajax Degreaser goes out of business during the litigation?

Government Intervention

Government intervention may be needed to achieve economic efficiency when externalities affect large numbers of people or when community interests are at stake. Government can use direct controls and taxes to counter negative externalities; it may provide subsidies or public goods to deal with positive externalities.

Direct Controls The direct way to reduce negative externalities from a certain activity is to pass legislation limiting that activity. Such direct controls force the offending firms to incur the actual costs of the offending activity. Historically, direct controls in the form of uniform emission standards—limits on allowable pollution—have dominated American air pollution policy. For example, the Clean Air Act of 1990 (1) forced factories and businesses to install "maximum achievable control technology" to reduce emissions of 189 toxic chemicals by 90 percent between 1990 and 2000; (2) required a 30 to 60 percent reduction in tailpipe emissions from automobiles by 2000; (3) mandated a 50 percent reduction in the use of chlorofluorocarbons (CFCs), which deplete the ozone layer (CFCs are used widely as a coolant in refrigeration, a blowing agent for foam, and a solvent in the electronics industry); and (4) forced coal-burning utilities to cut their emissions of sulfur dioxide by about 50 percent to reduce the acid-rain destruction of lakes and forests. Clean-water legislation limits the amount of heavy metals, detergents, and other pollutants firms can discharge into rivers and bays. Toxic-waste laws dictate special procedures and dump sites for disposing of contaminated soil and solvents. Violating these laws means fines and, in some cases, imprisonment.

Direct controls raise the marginal cost of production because the firms must operate and maintain pollution-control equipment. The supply curve S in Figure 16.3b, which does not reflect the external costs, shifts leftward to the full-cost supply curve, S_t. Product price increases, equilibrium output falls from Q_e to Q_o, and the initial overallocation of resources shown in Figure 16.3a is corrected.

Specific Taxes A second policy approach to negative externalities is for government to levy taxes or charges specifically on the related good. For example, the government has placed a manufacturing excise tax on CFCs, which deplete the stratospheric ozone layer protecting the earth from excessive solar ultraviolet radiation. Facing such an excise tax, manufacturers must decide whether to pay the tax or expend additional funds to purchase or

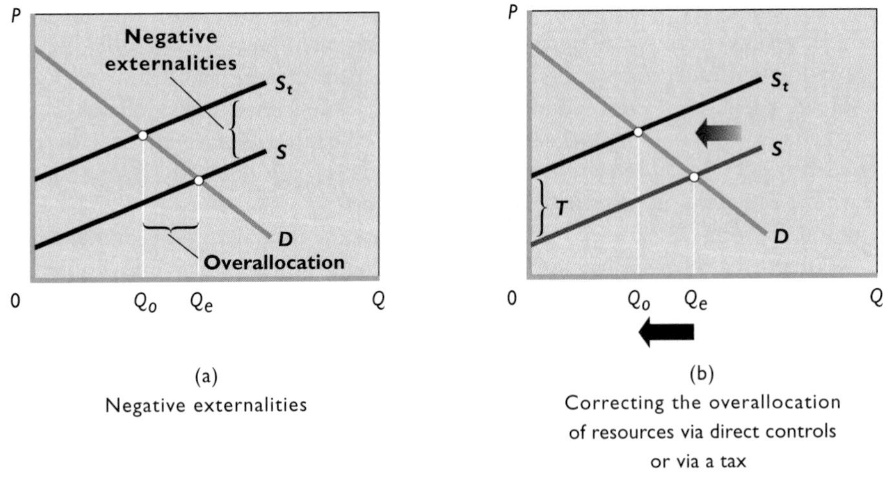

FIGURE 16.3 Correcting for negative externalities. (a) Negative externalities result in an overallocation of resources. (b) Government can correct this overallocation in two ways: (1) using direct controls, which would shift the supply curve from S to S_t and reduce output from Q_e to Q_o, or (2) imposing a specific tax T, which would also shift the supply curve from S to S_t, eliminating the overallocation of resources.

develop substitute products. In either case, the tax raises the marginal cost of producing CFCs, shifting the private supply curve for this product leftward (or upward).

In Figure 16.3b, a tax equal to *T* per unit increases the firm's marginal cost, shifting the supply curve from *S* to S_t. The equilibrium price rises, and the equilibrium output declines from Q_e to the economically efficient level Q_o. The tax thus eliminates the initial overallocation of resources.

Subsidies and Government Provision

Where spillover benefits are large and diffuse, as in our earlier example of inoculations, government has three options for correcting the underallocation of resources:

- ***Subsidies to buyers*** Figure 16.4a again shows the supply-demand situation for positive externalities. Government could correct the underallocation of resources, for example, to inoculations, by subsidizing consumers of the product. It could give each new mother in the United States a discount coupon to be used to obtain a series of inoculations for her child. The coupon would reduce the "price" to the mother by, say, 50 percent. As shown in Figure 16.4b, this program would shift the demand curve for inoculations from too low *D* to the appropriate D_t. The number of inoculations would rise from Q_e to the economically optimal Q_o, eliminating the underallocation of resources shown in Figure 16.4a.
- ***Subsidies to producers*** A subsidy to producers is a specific tax in reverse. Taxes are payments *to* the government that increase producers' costs. Subsidies are payments *from* the government that reduce producers' costs. As shown in Figure 16.4c, a subsidy of *U* per inoculation to physicians and medical clinics would reduce their marginal costs and shift their supply curve rightward from S_t to S'_t. The output of inoculations would increase from Q_e to the optimal level Q_o, correcting the underallocation of resources shown in Figure 16.4a.
- ***Government provision*** Finally, where positive externalities are extremely large, the government may decide to provide the product as a public good. The U.S. government largely eradicated the crippling disease polio by administering free vaccines to all children. India ended smallpox by paying people in rural areas to come to public clinics to have their children vaccinated. **(Key Question 4)**

A Market-Based Approach to Negative Externalities

One novel approach to negative externalities involves only limited government action. The idea is to create a market for externality rights. But before describing that approach, we first need to understand the idea called the **tragedy of the commons.**

The Tragedy of the Commons

The air, rivers, lakes, oceans, and public lands, such as parks and streets, are all objects for pollution because the rights to use those

FIGURE 16.4 Correcting for positive externalities. (a) Positive externalities result in an underallocation of resources. (b) This underallocation can be corrected through a subsidy to consumers, which shifts market demand from *D* to D_t and increases output from Q_e to Q_o. (c) Alternatively, the underallocation can be eliminated by providing producers with a subsidy of *U*, which shifts their supply curve from S_t to S_t', increasing output from Q_e to Q_o.

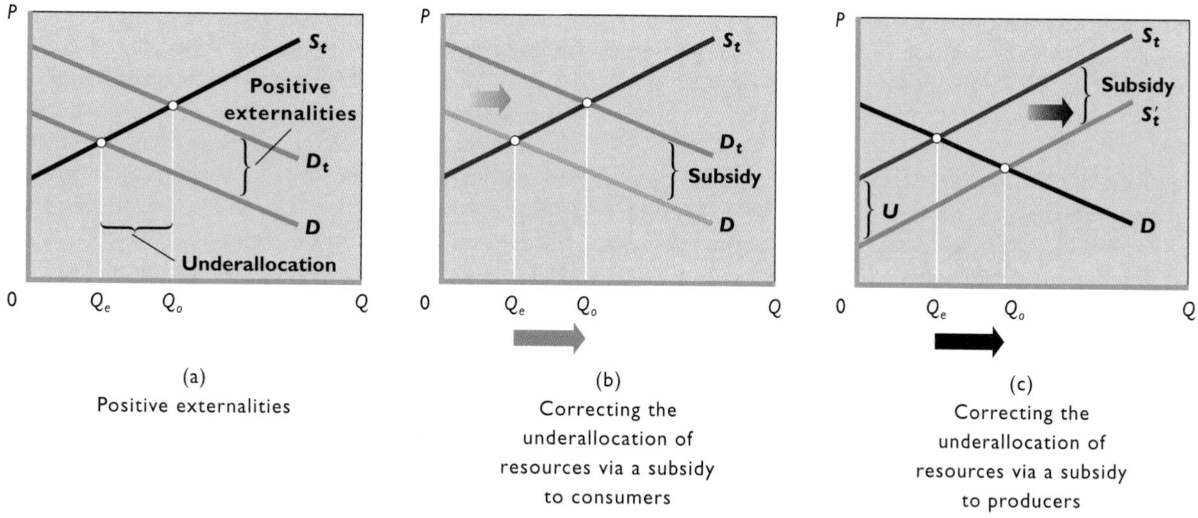

resources are held "in common" by society. No private individual or institution has a monetary incentive to maintain the purity or quality of such resources.

We maintain the property we own—for example, we paint and repair our homes periodically—in part because we will recoup the value of these improvements at the time of sale. But as long as "rights" to air, water, and certain land resources are commonly held and are freely available, there is no incentive to maintain them or use them carefully. As a result, these natural resources are overused and thereby degraded or polluted.

For example, a common pasture in which anyone can graze cattle will quickly be overgrazed because each rancher has an incentive to graze as many cattle as possible. Similarly, commonly owned resources such as rivers, lakes, oceans, and the air get used beyond their capacity to absorb pollution. Manufacturers will choose the least-cost combination of inputs and bear only unavoidable costs. If they can dump waste chemicals into rivers and lakes rather than pay for proper disposal, some businesses will be inclined to do so. Firms will discharge smoke into the air if they can, rather than purchase expensive abatement facilities. Even Federal, state, and local governments sometimes discharge inadequately treated waste into rivers, lakes, or oceans to avoid the expense of constructing expensive treatment facilities. Many individuals avoid the costs of proper refuse pickup and disposal by burning their garbage or dumping it in the woods.

The problem is mainly one of incentives. There is no incentive to incur internal costs associated with reducing or eliminating pollution when those costs can be transferred externally to society. The fallacy of composition (Last Word, Chapter 1) also comes into play. Each person and firm reasons their individual contribution to pollution is so small that it is of little or no overall consequence. But their actions, multiplied by hundreds, thousands, or millions, overwhelm the absorptive capacity of the common resources. Society ends up with a degradation or pollution problem.

A Market for Externality Rights

This outcome gives rise to a market-based approach to correcting negative externalities. The idea is that the government can create a **market for externality rights.** We confine our discussion to pollution, although the same approach might be used with other externalities.

Operation of the Market

In this market approach, an appropriate pollution-control agency determines the amount of pollutants that firms can discharge into the water or air of a specific region annually while maintaining the water or air quality at some acceptable level. Suppose the agency ascertains that 500 tons of pollutants can be discharged into Metropolitan Lake and "recycled" by nature each year. Then 500 pollution rights, each entitling the owner to dump 1 ton of pollutants into the lake in 1 year, are made available for sale to producers each year. The supply of these pollution rights is fixed and therefore perfectly inelastic, as shown in Figure 16.5.

FIGURE 16.5 A market for pollution rights. The supply of pollution rights S is set by the government, which determines that a specific body of water can safely recycle 500 tons of waste. In 2006, the demand for pollution rights is D_{2006} and the 1-ton price is $100. The quantity of pollution is 500 tons, not the 750 tons it would have been without the pollution rights. Over time, the demand for pollution rights increases to D_{2016} and the 1-ton price rises to $200. But the amount of pollution stays at 500 tons, rather than rising to 1000 tons.

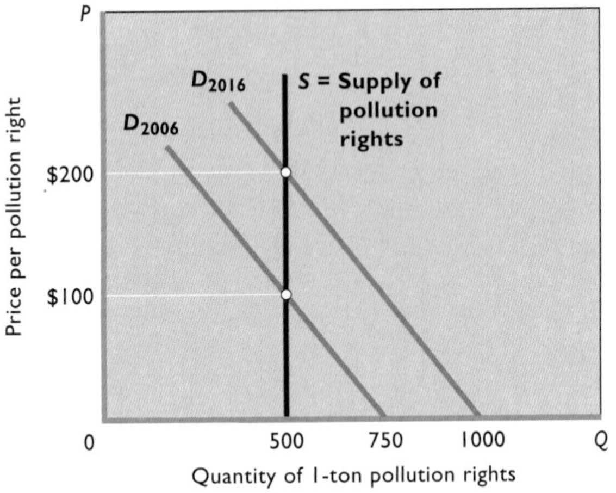

The demand for pollution rights, represented by D_{2006} in the figure, takes the same downsloping form as the demand for any other input. At higher prices there is less pollution, as polluters either stop polluting or pollute less by acquiring pollution-abatement equipment. An equilibrium market price for pollution rights, here $100, will be determined at which the environment-preserving quantity of pollution rights is rationed to polluters. Figure 16.5 shows that if the use of the lake as a dump site for pollutants were instead free, 750 tons of pollutants would be discharged into the lake; it would be "overconsumed," or polluted, in the amount of 250 tons.

Over time, as human and business populations expand, demand will increase, as from D_{2006} to D_{2016}. Without a market for pollution rights, pollution in 2016 would be 1000 tons, 500 tons beyond what can be assimilated by nature. With the market for pollution rights, the price would rise from $100 to $200, and the amount of pollutants would remain at 500 tons—the amount that the lake can recycle.

Advantages This scheme has several advantages over direct controls. Most important, it reduces society's costs by allowing pollution rights to be bought and sold. Suppose it costs Acme Pulp Mill $20 a year to reduce a specific noxious discharge by 1 ton while it costs Zemo Chemicals $8000 a year to accomplish the same 1-ton reduction. Also assume that Zemo wants to expand production, but doing so will increase its pollution discharge by 1 ton.

Without a market for pollution rights, Zemo would have to use $8000 of society's scarce resources to keep the 1-ton pollution discharge from occurring. But with a market for pollution rights, Zemo has a better option: It buys 1 ton of pollution rights for the $100 price shown in Figure 16.5. Acme is willing to sell Zemo 1 ton of pollution rights for $100 because that amount is more than Acme's $20 cost of reducing its pollution by 1 ton. Zemo increases its discharge by 1 ton; Acme reduces its discharge by 1 ton. Zemo benefits (by $8000 − $100), Acme benefits (by $100 − $20), and society benefits (by $8000 − $20). Rather than using $8000 of its scarce resources to hold the discharge at the specified level, society uses only $20 of those resources. Pollution rights thus decrease the cost of reducing pollution.

Market-based plans have other advantages. Potential polluters have a monetary incentive not to pollute, because they must pay for the right to discharge effluent. Conservation groups can fight pollution by buying up and withholding pollution rights, thereby reducing pollution below governmentally determined standards. As the demand for pollution rights increases over time, the growing revenue from the sale of a fixed quantity of pollution rights could be devoted to environmental improvement. At the same time, the rising price of pollution rights should stimulate the search for improved pollution-control techniques.

Real-World Examples Administrative and political problems have kept the government from replacing direct controls—such as uniform emission limits—with a full-scale market for pollution rights. But the Environmental Protection Agency (EPA) established a system of pollution rights, or "tradeable emission allowances," in the 1980s as part of a plan to reduce the sulfur dioxide emitted by coal-burning public utilities. Those emissions are the major source of acid rain. The market for such rights was greatly expanded by legislation in the 1990s.

The Clean Air Act of 1990 established a limited market for pollution rights, similar to that shown in Figure 16.5, by allowing utilities to trade emission credits provided by government. Utilities can obtain credits by reducing sulfur-dioxide emissions by more than the specified amount. They can then sell their emission credits to other utilities that find it less costly to buy the credits than to install additional pollution-control equipment.

This market for sulfur-dioxide-emission credits complements other air pollution policies that also permit the exchange of pollution rights. The EPA now allows firms to exchange pollution rights internally and externally. Polluters are allowed to transfer air pollution internally between individual sources within their plants. That is, as long as it meets the overall pollution standard assigned to it, a firm may increase one source of pollution by offsetting it with reduced pollution from another part of its operations.

The EPA also permits external trading of pollution rights. It has set targets for reducing air pollution in regions where the minimum standards are not being met. Previously, new pollution sources could not enter these regions unless existing polluters went out of business. But under the system of external trading rights, the EPA allows firms that reduce their pollution below set standards to sell their pollution rights to other firms. A new firm that wants to locate in the Los Angeles area, for example, might be able to buy rights to emit 20 tons of nitrous oxide annually from an existing firm that has reduced its emissions below its allowable limit. The price of emission rights depends on their supply and demand.

Finally, in 2003 the EPA extended the market-based approach to the Clean Water Act. Industry, agriculture, and municipalities within a defined watershed can meet their EPA-approved maximum daily discharge limits through trading "water quality credits." Entities that find reducing water pollution extremely expensive can buy credits from entities that can reduce pollution relatively inexpensively. Therefore, society incurs less total cost in improving water quality.

Table 16.3 reviews the major methods for correcting externalities.

Society's Optimal Amount of Externality Reduction

Negative externalities such as pollution reduce the utility of those affected, rather than increase it. These spillovers are not economic goods but economic "bads." If something is bad, shouldn't society eliminate it? Why should society allow firms or municipalities to discharge *any* impure waste into public waterways or to emit *any* pollution into the air?

Reducing a negative externality has a "price." Society must decide how much of a reduction it wants to "buy." Eliminating pollution might not be desirable, even if it

TABLE 16.3 Methods for Dealing with Externalities

Problem	Resource Allocation Outcome	Ways to Correct
Negative externalities (spillover costs)	Overallocation of resources	1. Individual bargaining 2. Liability rules and lawsuits 3. Tax on producers 4. Direct controls 5. Market for externality rights
Positive externalities (spillover benefits)	Underallocation of resources	1. Individual bargaining 2. Subsidy to consumers 3. Subsidy to producers 4. Government provision

were technologically feasible. Because of the law of diminishing returns, cleaning up the second 10 percent of pollutants from an industrial smokestack normally is more costly than cleaning up the first 10 percent. Eliminating the third 10 percent is more costly than cleaning up the second 10 percent, and so on. Therefore, cleaning up the last 10 percent of pollutants is the most costly reduction of all.

The marginal cost (MC) to the firm and hence to society—the opportunity cost of the extra resources used—rises as pollution is reduced more and more. At some point MC may rise so high that it exceeds society's marginal benefit (MB) of further pollution abatement (reduction). Additional actions to reduce pollution will therefore lower society's well-being; total cost will rise more than total benefit.

MC, MB, and Equilibrium Quantity

Figure 16.6 shows both the rising marginal-cost curve, MC, for pollution reduction and the downsloping marginal-benefit curve, MB, for this outcome. MB slopes downward because of the law of diminishing marginal utility: The more pollution reduction society accomplishes, the lower the utility (and benefit) of the next unit of pollution reduction.

The **optimal reduction of an externality** occurs when society's marginal cost and marginal benefit of reducing that externality are equal (MC = MB). In Figure 16.6 this optimal amount of pollution abatement is Q_1 units. When MB exceeds MC, additional abatement moves society toward economic efficiency; the added benefit of cleaner air or water exceeds the benefit of any alternative use of the required resources. When MC exceeds MB, additional abatement reduces economic efficiency; there would be greater benefits from using resources in some other way than to further reduce pollution.

In reality, it is difficult to measure the marginal costs and benefits of pollution control. Nevertheless, Figure 16.6 demonstrates that some pollution may be economically efficient. This is so not because pollution is desirable but because beyond some level of control, further abatement may reduce society's net well-being.

Shifts in Locations of Curves

The locations of the marginal-cost and marginal-benefit curves in Figure 16.6 are not forever fixed. They can, and probably do, shift over time. For example, suppose that the technology of pollution-control equipment improved noticeably. We would expect the cost of pollution abatement to fall, society's MC curve to shift rightward, and the optimal level of abatement to rise. Or suppose that society were to decide that it wanted cleaner air and water because of new

FIGURE 16.6 Society's optimal amount of pollution abatement. The optimal amount of externality reduction—in this case, pollution abatement—occurs at Q_1, where society's marginal cost MC and marginal benefit MB of reducing the spillover are equal.

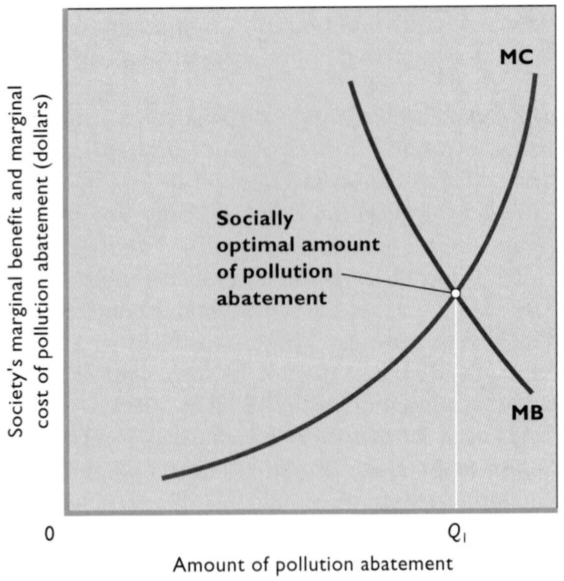

information about the adverse health effects of pollution. The MB curve in Figure 16.6 would shift rightward, and the optimal level of pollution control would increase beyond Q_1. Test your understanding of these statements by drawing the new MC and MB curves in Figure 16.6. **(Key Question 7)**

QUICK REVIEW 16.2

- Policies for coping with the overallocation of resources caused by negative externalities are (a) private bargaining, (b) liability rules and lawsuits, (c) direct controls, (d) specific taxes, and (e) markets for externality rights.
- Policies for correcting the underallocation of resources associated with positive externalities are (a) private bargaining, (b) subsidies to producers, (c) subsidies to consumers, and (d) government provision.
- The optimal amount of negative-externality reduction occurs where society's marginal cost and marginal benefit of reducing the externality are equal.

Global Warming

The United States has made significant progress in cleaning its air. According to the EPA, between 1990 and 2000 clean-air laws and antipollution efforts by businesses and local governments reduced concentrations of lead by 60 percent, carbon monoxide and sulfur dioxide by 36 percent each, particulate matter by 18 percent, nitrogen dioxide by 10 percent, and smog by 4 percent.

But significant air pollution problems remain, including the controversial problem of *global warming.* The earth's surface has warmed over the last century by about 1 degree Fahrenheit, with an acceleration of warming during the past two decades. Some of this surface warming may simply reflect natural fluctuations of warming and cooling, but the balance of scientific evidence suggests that human activity is a contributing factor. According to the EPA, carbon dioxide and other gas emissions from factories, power plants, automobiles, and other human sources are cumulating in the earth's atmosphere and creating a greenhouse effect.

Because of the greenhouse effect, average temperatures are predicted to rise by 1 to 4.5 degrees Fahrenheit over the next 50 years and 2.2 to 10 degrees by 3000. Although there will be significant regional variation, scientists say many parts of the world will experience noticeable climatic changes. Rainfall will increase, rainfall patterns will change, and ocean levels will gradually rise by as much as 2 feet. Snow accumulations may decline in some regions and rise in others. More violent storms such as tornadoes and hurricanes may occur in some regions. (Global Perspective 16.1 lists per capita carbon-dioxide emissions for selected nations.)

GLOBAL PERSPECTIVE 16.1

Carbon-Dioxide Emissions, Tons per Capita, Selected Nations

Carbon-dioxide emissions, the major type of greenhouse-gas emissions, vary per capita by nation primarily because of different degrees of industrialization and energy production from fossil fuels (coal, oil, and natural gas). The burning of such fuels is the major contributor to global warming.

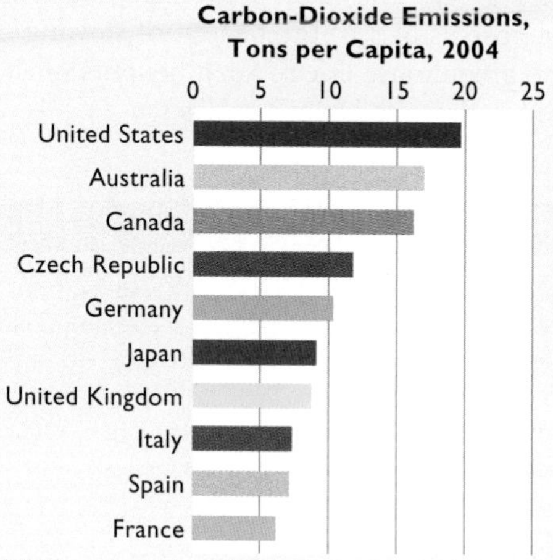

Source: OECD environmental data, **www.oecd.org.**

The world's nations have responded to the global-warming threat collectively and individually. In the Kyoto Protocol of 1997, representatives of the industrially advanced nations agreed to cut their greenhouse-gas emissions to 6 to 8 percent below their 1990 levels by 2012. Since 1997 all major nations except the United States have ratified the Kyoto agreement, although few are actually likely to meet the 2012 goals. In 2001 the United States opted out of the Kyoto agreement, concluding that the limitations on greenhouse gas would severely damage the U.S. economy. A year later the United States announced a "Global Climate Change" initiative designed to use clean-energy investments to reduce greenhouse gases per dollar of GDP by 18 percent by 2012.

Economists stress that global-warming policies that reduce greenhouse-gas emissions and thus slow or eliminate global warming create costs as well as benefits. Therefore it is imperative to consider the marginal costs and marginal benefits carefully in making policy decisions. Greenhouse-gas limits should not be so stringent that they end up costing society more than the value of the benefits they produce. But limits should not be so lenient that society forgoes substantial potential benefits that it would have otherwise achieved.

Economists also stress that the market mechanism, through its system of prices and profits and losses, will make appropriate adjustments based on new climatic realities. Air-conditioner sales may rise; snow shovel sales may fall. Some agricultural lands probably will be deserted; others farther north will be cultivated. The maple syrup industry in New England may shift to Canada. Nevertheless, the *transition costs*—the costs associated with making economic adjustments—of global warming will undoubtedly be very high if no actions are taken to reduce greenhouse gases. The reduction or elimination of these transition costs is part of the benefit of slowing or eliminating the greenhouse effect. Such benefits must be fully considered in the cost-benefit analysis.

QUICK REVIEW 16.3

- Society's pollution problem has largely resulted from increasing population, rising per capita consumption, certain changes in technology, and the so-called tragedy of the commons.
- The world's industrial nations are struggling to reduce emissions of greenhouse gases, which most scientists think are contributing to global warming.

Information Failures

Thus far we have added new details and insights concerning two types of market failure: public goods and externalities. There is another, subtler, market failure. This one results when either buyers or sellers have incomplete or inaccurate information and their cost of obtaining better information is prohibitive. Technically stated, this market failure occurs because of **asymmetric information**—unequal knowledge possessed by the parties to a market transaction. Buyers and sellers do not have identical information about price, quality, or some other aspect of the good or service.

Sufficient market information normally is available to ensure that goods and services are produced and purchased efficiently. But in some cases inadequate information makes it difficult to distinguish trustworthy from untrustworthy sellers or trustworthy from untrustworthy buyers. In these markets, society's scarce resources may not be used efficiently, thus implying that the government should intervene by increasing the information available to the market participants. Under rare circumstances the government may itself supply a good for which information problems have prohibited efficient production.

O 16.3
Information failures

CONSIDER THIS . . .

"Lemons"

Why does a new car lose substantial market value when it is purchased, even though the same car can sit on the dealer's lot for weeks, or even months, and still retain its market value? One plausible explanation for this paradox is based on the ideas of *asymmetric information* and *adverse selection*.[*]

Used-car owners (potential sellers) have much better information about the mechanical condition of their cars than do potential buyers. Because of this asymmetric information, an *adverse selection problem* occurs. Owners of defective used cars—so-called lemons—have an incentive to sell their cars to unsuspecting buyers, whereas owners of perfectly operating used cars have an incentive to retain their used cars. Although a mix of both good and bad used cars is offered for sale, the mix is tilted toward the poorer-quality used cars. So the average quality of the used cars is lower than that of the same makes and models that are not for sale.

The typical consumer finds it difficult to identify the higher-quality used cars from the average- (lower-) quality used cars simply by looking at them or taking them for a test drive. Anticipating repair costs, the customer is willing to pay only a price that reflects the lower quality.[†]

So we have a solution to the paradox: When purchased, the market values of new cars drop quickly to the value of the average-quality used cars of the same year, make, and model offered for sale in the market. This is true even though many individual used cars may be in perfect operating condition. Adverse selection, asymmetric information, and the resulting risk of "buying someone else's problem" drop the value of used cars relative to new cars still on the lot.

[*]This explanation is based on the work of economist George Akerlof.

[†]Transferable warrantees reduce, but do not eliminate, the potential repair costs of used cars. Consumers lose time in arranging repairs and forgo the use of their cars when the repairs are being done.

Inadequate Information Involving Sellers

Inadequate information about sellers and their products can cause market failure in the form of underallocation of resources. Examining the markets for gasoline and for the services of surgeons will show us how this comes about.

Example: Gasoline Market Assume an absurd situation: Suppose there is no system of weights and measures established by law, no government inspection of gasoline pumps, and no law against false advertising. Each gas station can use whatever measure it chooses; it can define a gallon of gas as it pleases. A station can advertise that its gas is 87 octane when in fact it is only 75. It can rig its pumps to indicate that it is providing more gas than the amount being delivered.

Obviously, the consumer's cost of obtaining reliable information under such chaotic conditions is exceptionally high, if not prohibitive. Customers or their representatives would have to buy samples of gas from various gas stations, have them tested for octane level, and test the accuracy of calibrations at the pump. And these activities would have to be repeated regularly, since a station owner could alter the product quality and the accuracy of the pump at will.

Because of the high costs of obtaining information about the seller, many customers would opt out of this chaotic market. One tankful of a 50 percent solution of gasoline and water would be enough to discourage most motorists from further driving. More realistically, the conditions in this market would encourage consumers to vote for political candidates who promise to provide a government solution. The oil companies and honest gasoline stations would not object to government intervention. They would realize that accurate information, by enabling this market to work, would expand their total sales and profit.

The government has in fact intervened in the market for gasoline and other markets with similar potential information difficulties. It has established a system of weights and measures, employed inspectors to check the accuracy of gasoline pumps, and passed laws against fraudulent claims and misleading advertising. There can be no doubt that these government activities have produced net benefits for society.

Example: Licensing of Surgeons Suppose now that anyone could hang out a shingle and claim to be a surgeon, much as anyone can become a house painter. The market would eventually sort out the true surgeons from those who are "learning by doing" or are fly-by-night operators who move into and out of an area. As people died from unsuccessful surgery, lawsuits for malpractice eventually would eliminate the medical impostors. People needing surgery for themselves or their loved ones could obtain information from newspaper reports, Internet sites, or from people who have undergone similar operations.

But this process of obtaining information for those needing surgery would take considerable time and would impose unacceptably high human and economic costs. There is a fundamental difference between getting an amateurish paint job on one's house and being on the receiving end of heart surgery by a bogus physician. The marginal cost of obtaining information about sellers in the surgery market would be excessively high. The risk of proceeding without good information would result in much less surgery than desirable—an underallocation of resources to surgery.

The government has remedied this market failure through a system of qualifying tests and licensing. The licensing provides consumers with inexpensive information about a service they only infrequently buy. The government has taken a similar role in several other areas of the economy. For example, it approves new medicines, regulates the securities industry, and requires warnings on containers of potentially hazardous substances. It also requires warning labels on cigarette packages and disseminates information about communicable diseases. And it issues warnings about unsafe toys and inspects restaurants for health-related violations.

Inadequate Information Involving Buyers

Just as inadequate information involving sellers can keep markets from achieving economic efficiency, so can inadequate information relating to buyers. The buyers may be consumers who buy products or firms that buy resources.

Moral Hazard Problem Private markets may underallocate resources to a particular good or service for which there is a severe **moral hazard problem.** The moral hazard problem is the tendency of one party to a contract or agreement to alter her or his behavior, after the contract is signed, in ways that could be costly to the other party.

Suppose a firm offers an insurance policy that pays a set amount of money per month to people who suffer divorces. The attractiveness of such insurance is that it would pool the economic risk of divorce among thousands of people and, in particular, would protect spouses and children from the economic hardship that divorce often brings. Unfortunately, the moral hazard problem reduces the likelihood that insurance companies can profitably provide this type of insurance.

After taking out such insurance, some people would alter their behavior in ways that impose heavy costs on the insurer. For example, married couples would have less of an incentive to get along and to iron out marital difficulties. At the extreme, some people might be motivated to obtain a divorce, collect the insurance, and then continue to live together. Such insurance could even promote more divorces, the very outcome it is intended to protect against. The moral hazard problem would force the insurer to charge such high premiums for this insurance that few policies would be bought. If the insurer could identify in advance those people most prone to alter their behavior, the firm could exclude them from buying it. But the firm's marginal cost of getting such information is too high compared with the marginal benefit. Thus, this market would fail.

Although divorce insurance is not available in the marketplace, society recognizes the benefits of insuring against the hardships of divorce. It has corrected for this underallocation of "hardship insurance" through child-support laws that dictate payments to the spouse who retains the children, when the economic circumstances warrant them. Alimony laws also play a role.

Since, unlike private firms, the government does not have to earn a profit when supplying services, it provides "divorce insurance" of sorts through the Temporary Assistance for Needy Families (TANF) program. If a divorce leaves a spouse with children destitute, the family is eligible for TANF payments for a period of time. Government intervention does not eliminate the moral hazard problem, but it does offset the problem's adverse effects.

The moral hazard problem is also illustrated in the following statements:

- Drivers may be less cautious because they have car insurance.
- Medical malpractice insurance may increase the amount of malpractice.
- Guaranteed contracts for professional athletes may reduce the quality of their performance.
- Unemployment compensation insurance may lead some workers to shirk.
- Government insurance on bank deposits may encourage banks to make risky loans.

Adverse Selection Problem

Another information problem resulting from inadequate information involving buyers is the **adverse selection problem.** This problem arises when information known by the first party to a contract or agreement is not known by the second and, as a result, the second party incurs major costs. Unlike the moral hazard problem, which arises after a person signs a contract, the adverse selection problem arises at the time a person signs a contract.

In insurance, the adverse selection problem is that people who are most likely to need insurance payouts are those who buy insurance. For example, those in poorest health will seek to buy the most generous health insurance policies. Or, at the extreme, a person planning to hire an arsonist to "torch" his failing business has an incentive to buy fire insurance.

Our hypothetical divorce insurance sheds further light on the adverse selection problem. If the insurance firm sets the premiums on the basis of the average divorce rate, many married couples who are about to obtain a divorce will buy insurance. An insurance premium based on average probabilities will make a great buy for those about to get divorced. Meanwhile, those in highly stable marriages will not buy it.

The adverse selection problem thus tends to eliminate the pooling of low and high risks, which is the basis of profitable insurance. Insurance rates then must be so high that few people would want to (or be able to) buy such insurance.

Where private firms underprovide insurance because of information problems, the government often establishes some type of social insurance. It can require that everyone in a particular group take the insurance and thereby can overcome the adverse selection problem. Example: Although the Social Security system in the United States is partly insurance and partly an income transfer program, in its broadest sense it is insurance against poverty during old age. The Social Security program requires nearly universal participation: People who are most likely to need the minimum benefits that Social Security provides are automatically participants in the program. So, too, are those not likely to need the benefits. There is, then, no adverse selection problem.

Workplace Safety

The labor market also provides an example of how inadequate information about buyers (employers) can produce market failures.

For several reasons employers have an economic incentive to provide safe workplaces. A safe workplace reduces the amount of disruption of the production process created by job accidents and lowers the costs of recruiting, screening, training, and retaining new workers. It also reduces a firm's worker compensation insurance premiums (legally required insurance against job injuries).

But a safe workplace is expensive: Safe equipment, protective gear, and a slower work pace all entail costs. The firm will decide how much safety to provide by comparing the marginal cost and marginal benefit of providing a safer workplace. Will this amount of job safety achieve economic efficiency, as well as maximize the firm's profit?

The answer is yes if the labor and product markets are competitive and if workers are fully aware of the job risks at various places of employment. With full information, workers will avoid employers having unsafe workplaces. The supply of labor to these establishments will be greatly restricted, forcing them to boost their wages to attract a workforce. The higher wages will then give these employers an incentive to provide increased workplace safety; safer workplaces will reduce wage expenses. Only firms that find it very costly to provide safer workplaces will choose to pay high compensating wage differentials rather than reduce workplace hazards.

But a serious problem arises when workers do not know that particular occupations or workplaces are unsafe. Because information involving the buyer—that is, about the employer and the workplace—is inadequate, the firm may not need to pay a wage premium to attract its workforce. Its incentive to remove safety hazards therefore will be diminished, and its profit-maximizing level of workplace safety will be less than economically desirable. In brief, the labor market will fail because of asymmetric information—in this case, sellers (workers) having less information than buyers (employers).

The government has several options for remedying this information problem:

- It can directly provide information to workers about the injury experience of various employers, much as it publishes the on-time performance of airlines.
- It can require that firms provide information to workers about known workplace hazards.
- It can establish standards of workplace safety and enforce them through inspections and penalties.

Although the Federal government has mainly employed the standards and enforcement approach to improve workplace safety, some critics contend that an information strategy might be less costly and more effective. **(Key Question 12)**

Qualification

People have found many ingenious ways to overcome information difficulties without government intervention. For example, many firms offer product warranties to overcome the lack of information about themselves and their products. Franchising also helps overcome this problem. When you visit a Wendy's or a Marriott, you know what you are going to get, as opposed to stopping at Slim's Hamburger Shop or the Triple Six Motel.

Also, some private firms and organizations specialize in providing information to buyers and sellers. *Consumer Reports*, *Mobil Travel Guide* and numerous Internet sites provide product information; labor unions collect and disseminate information about job safety; and credit bureaus provide information to insurance companies. Brokers, bonding agencies, and intermediaries also provide information to clients.

Economists agree, however, that the private sector cannot remedy all information problems. In some situations, government intervention is desirable to promote an efficient allocation of society's scarce resources.

QUICK REVIEW 16.4

- Asymmetric information is a source of potential market failure, causing society's scarce resources to be allocated inefficiently.
- Inadequate information about sellers and their products may lead to an underallocation of resources to those products.
- The moral hazard problem is the tendency of one party to a contract or agreement to alter its behavior in ways that are costly to the other party; for example, a person who buys insurance may willingly incur added risk.
- The adverse selection problem arises when one party to a contract or agreement has less information than the other party and incurs a cost because of that asymmetrical information. For example, an insurance company offering "no-medical-exam-required" life insurance policies may attract customers who have life-threatening diseases.

Last Word

Lojack: A Case of Positive Externalities

Economists Ian Ayres and Steven Levitt Find That an Auto Antitheft Device Called *Lojack* Produces Large Spillover Benefits.

Private expenditures to reduce crime are estimated to be $300 billion annually and are growing at a faster rate than is spending on public crime prevention. Unfortunately, some forms of private crime prevention simply redistribute crime rather than reduce it. For example, car alarm systems that have red blinking warning lights may simply divert professional auto thieves to vehicles that do not have such lights and alarms. The owner of a car with such an alarm system benefits through reduced likelihood of theft but imposes a cost on other car owners who do not have such alarms. Their cars are more likely to be targeted for theft by thieves because other cars have visible security systems.

Some private crime prevention measures, however, actually reduce crime, rather than simply redistribute it. One such measure is installation of a Lojack (or some similar) car retrieval system. Lojack is a tiny radio transmitter that is hidden in one of many possible places within the car. When an owner reports a stolen car, the police can remotely activate the transmitter. Police then can determine the car's precise location and track its subsequent movements.

The owner of the car benefits because the 95 percent retrieval rate on cars with the Lojack system is higher than the 60 percent retrieval rate for cars without the system. But, according to a study by Ayres and Levitt, the benefit to the car owner is only 10 percent of the total benefit. Ninety percent of the total benefit is external; it is a spillover benefit to other car owners in the community.

There are two sources of this positive externality. First, the presence of the Lojack device sometimes enables police to intercept the car while the thief is still driving it. For example, in California the arrest rate for cars with Lojack was three times greater than that for cars without it. The arrest puts the car thief out of commission for a time and thus reduces subsequent car thefts in the community. Second, and far more important, the device enables police to trace cars to "chop shops," where crooks disassemble cars for resale of the parts. When police raid the chop shop, they put the entire theft ring out of business. In Los Angeles alone, Lojack has eliminated 45 chop shops in just a few years. The purging of the chop shop and theft ring reduces auto theft in the community. So auto owners who do not have Lojack devices in their cars benefit from car owners who do. Ayres and Levitt estimate the *marginal social benefit* of Lojack—the marginal benefit to the Lojack car owner *plus* the spillover benefit to other car owners—is 15 times greater than the marginal cost of the device.

We saw in Figure 16.4a that the existence of positive externalities causes an insufficient quantity of a product and thus an underallocation of scarce resources to its production. The two general ways to correct the outcome are to subsidize the consumer, as shown in Figure 16.4b, or to subsidize the producer, as shown in Figure 16.4c. Currently, there is only one form of government intervention in place: state-mandated insurance discounts for people who install auto retrieval systems such as Lojack. In effect, those discounts on insurance premiums subsidize the consumer by lowering the "price" of the system to consumers. The lower price raises the number of systems installed. But, on the basis of their research, Ayres and Levitt contend that the current levels of insurance discounts are far too small to correct the underallocation that results from the positive externalities created by Lojack.

Source: Based on Ian Ayres and Steven D. Levitt, "Measuring Positive Externalities from Unobservable Victim Precaution: An Empirical Analysis of Lojack," *Quarterly Journal of Economics*, February 1998, pp. 43–77. The authors point out that Lojack did not fund their work in any way, nor do they have any financial stake in Lojack.

Summary

1. Public goods are distinguished from private goods. Private goods are characterized by rivalry (in consumption) and excludability. One person's purchase and consumption of a private good precludes others from also buying and consuming it. Producers can exclude nonpayers (free riders) from receiving the benefits. In contrast, public goods are characterized by nonrivalry (in consumption) and nonexcludability. Public goods are not profitable to private firms because nonpayers (free riders) can obtain and consume those goods. Only government is willing to provide desirable public goods, financing them through taxation.
2. The collective demand schedule for a particular public good is found by summing the prices that each individual is willing to pay for an additional unit. Graphically, that demand curve is therefore found by summing vertically the individual demand curves for that good. The resulting total demand curve indicates the collective willingness to pay for (or marginal benefit of) the last unit of any given amount of the public good.
3. The optimal quantity of a public good occurs where the society's willingness to pay for the last unit—the marginal benefit of the good—equals the marginal cost of the good.
4. Externalities, or spillovers, are costs or benefits that accrue to someone other than the immediate buyer or seller. Such costs or benefits are not captured in market demand or supply curves and therefore cause the output of certain goods to vary from society's optimal output. Negative externalities (or spillover costs or external costs) result in an overallocation of resources to a particular product. Positive externalities (or spillover benefits or external benefits) are accompanied by an underallocaton of resources to a particular product.
5. The Coase theorem suggests that private bargaining is capable of solving potential externality problems where (a) the property rights are clearly defined, (b) the number of people involved is small, and (c) bargaining costs are negligible.
6. Clearly established property rights and liability rules permit some negative externalities to be prevented or remedied through private lawsuits. Lawsuits, however, can be costly, time-consuming, and uncertain as to their results.
7. Direct controls and specific taxes can improve resource allocation in situations where negative externalities affect many people and community resources. Both direct controls (for example, smokestack emission standards) and specific taxes (for example, taxes on firms producing toxic chemicals) increase production costs and hence product price. As product price rises, the externality and overallocation of resources are reduced, since less of the output is bought and sold.
8. Government can correct the underallocation of resources that results from positive externalities in a particular market either by subsidizing consumers (which increases market demand) or by subsidizing producers (which increases market supply). Such subsidies increase the equilibrium output, reducing or eliminating the positive externality and consequent underallocation of resources.
9. Markets for pollution rights, where firms can buy and sell the right to discharge a fixed amount of pollution, put a price on pollution and encourage firms to reduce or eliminate it.
10. The socially optimal amount of externality abatement occurs where society's marginal cost and marginal benefit of reducing the externality are equal. This optimal amount of pollution abatement is likely to be less than a 100 percent reduction. Changes in technology or changes in society's attitudes toward pollution can affect the optimal amount of pollution abatement.
11. A growing body of scientific evidence suggests that accumulation of carbon dioxide and other greenhouse gases in the earth's atmosphere may be contributing to a global-warming problem. In the Kyoto Protocol of 1997 the world's industrial nations agreed to reduce their emissions of greenhouse gases to 6 to 8 percent below 1990 levels by 2012. The United States refused to ratify the Kyoto agreement, instead opting for a less aggressive policy of using clean-energy investments to reduce greenhouse emissions by 18 percent per dollar of GDP by 2012.
12. Asymmetric information between sellers and buyers can cause markets to fail. The moral hazard problem occurs when people alter their behavior after they sign a contract or reach an agreement, imposing costs on the other party. The adverse selection problem occurs when one party to a contract or agreement takes advantage of the other party's inadequate information, resulting in an unanticipated loss to the latter party.

Terms and Concepts

private goods
public goods
free-rider problem
cost-benefit analysis
marginal-cost–marginal-benefit rule
externalities
Coase theorem
tragedy of the commons
market for externality rights
optimal reduction of an externality
asymmetric information
moral hazard problem
adverse selection problem

Study Questions

1. **KEY QUESTION** On the basis of the three individual demand schedules below, and assuming these three people are the only ones in the society, determine (*a*) the market demand schedule on the assumption that the good is a private good and (*b*) the collective demand schedule on the assumption that the good is a public good. Explain the differences, if any, in your schedules.

Individual 1		Individual 2		Individual 3	
P	Q_d	P	Q_d	P	Q_d
$8	0	$8	1	$8	0
7	0	7	2	7	0
6	0	6	3	6	1
5	1	5	4	5	2
4	2	4	5	4	3
3	3	3	6	3	4
2	4	2	7	2	5
1	5	1	8	1	6

2. **KEY QUESTION** Use your demand schedule for a public good, determined in question 1, and the following supply schedule to ascertain the optimal quantity of this public good. Why is this the optimal quantity?

P	Q_s
$19	10
16	8
13	6
10	4
7	2
4	1

3. **KEY QUESTION** The following table shows the total costs and total benefits in billions for four different antipollution programs of increasing scope. Which program should be undertaken? Why?

Program	Total Cost	Total Benefit
A	$ 3	$ 7
B	7	12
C	12	16
D	18	19

4. **KEY QUESTION** Why are spillover costs and spillover benefits also called negative and positive externalities? Show graphically how a tax can correct for a negative externality and how a subsidy to producers can correct for a positive externality. How does a subsidy to consumers differ from a subsidy to producers in correcting for a positive externality?
5. An apple grower's orchard provides nectar to a neighbor's bees, while the beekeeper's bees help the apple grower by pollinating the apple blossoms. Use Figure 16.2b to explain why this situation might lead to an underallocation of resources to apple growing and to beekeeping. How might this underallocation get resolved via the means suggested by the Coase theorem?
6. Explain: "Without a market for pollution rights, dumping pollutants into the air or water is costless; in the presence of the right to buy and sell pollution rights, dumping pollutants creates an opportunity cost for the polluter." What is the significance of this opportunity cost to the search for better technology to reduce pollution?
7. **KEY QUESTION** Explain the following statement, using the MB curve in Figure 16.6 to illustrate: "The optimal amount of pollution abatement for some substances, say, water from storm drains, is very low; the optimal amount of abatement for other substances, say, cyanide poison, is close to 100 percent."
8. Explain the tragedy of the commons, as it relates to pollution.
9. What is the global-warming problem? How is it being addressed? Using an example other than one in the text, explain how global warming might hurt one industry, particular region, or country but help another.
10. Explain how marketable emission credits add to overall economic efficiency, compared to across-the-board limitations on maximum discharges of air pollutants by firms.
11. Why is it in the interest of new homebuyers and builders of new homes to have government building codes and building inspectors?
12. **KEY QUESTION** Place an "M" beside the items in the following list that describe a moral hazard problem and an "A" beside those that describe an adverse selection problem:
    a. A person with a terminal illness buys several life insurance policies through the mail.
    b. A person drives carelessly because he or she has automobile insurance.
    c. A person who intends to "torch" his warehouse takes out a large fire insurance policy.
    d. A professional athlete who has a guaranteed contract fails to stay in shape during the off-season.
    e. A woman who anticipates having a large family takes a job with a firm that offers exceptional child care benefits.
13. **LAST WORD** Explain how a global-positioning antitheft device installed by one car owner can produce a positive spillover to thousands of others in a city.

Web-Based Questions

1. **GLOBAL WARMING—THE EPA'S VIEW** Go to **www.epa.gov** and use the search feature to find the EPA's Global Warming site. What are the major greenhouse gases? How much greenhouse gas does the United States emit per person? What is the trend of emissions on a per-person basis? What is the trend of emissions per dollar of GDP in the United States? Use your own analysis to explain how total emissions can rise even though emissions per dollar of GDP substantially decline. Which of the two is most relevant for global warming?

2. **WORKPLACE SAFETY—OSHA'S ROLE** Visit **www.osha.gov** and first select Workers (under Audiences). How does a worker file a complaint or report a hazard? Where is the nearest OSHA office to you? Go back to the OSHA home page and select News Releases. In a sentence or two each, summarize three recent news releases that relate to fines or other penalties imposed by OSHA on employers for violations of workers' safety and health rules.

17

IN THIS CHAPTER YOU WILL LEARN:

- The difficulties of conveying economic preferences through majority voting.
- About "government failure" and why it occurs.
- The different tax philosophies and ways to distribute a nation's tax burden.
- The principles relating to tax shifting, tax incidence, and efficiency losses from taxes.

Public Choice Theory and the Economics of Taxation

In Chapter 16 we saw that private markets can occasionally produce *market failures,* which impede economic efficiency and justify government intervention in the economy. But the government's response to market failures is not without its own problems and pitfalls. Perhaps that is why government policies and decisions are the focus of hundreds of radio talk shows, television debates, and newspaper articles each day.

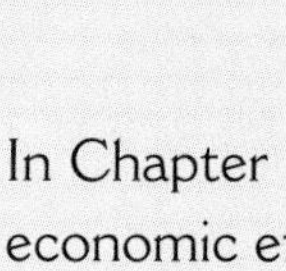

O 17.1
Public choice theory

In this chapter, we explore a number of *government failures* that impede economic efficiency in the public sector. Our spotlight is first on selected aspects of **public choice theory**—the economic analysis of government decision making, politics, and elections — and then on the economics of taxation.

Revealing Preferences through Majority Voting

Which public goods should government produce and in what amounts? To what extent should government intervene to correct externalities? How should the tax burden of financing government be apportioned?

Decisions like these are made collectively in the United States through a democratic process that relies heavily on majority voting. Candidates for office offer alternative policy packages, and citizens elect people who they think will make the best decisions on their collective behalf. Voters "retire" officials who do not adequately represent their collective wishes and elect persons they think do. Also, citizens periodically have opportunities at the state and local levels to vote directly on public expenditures or new legislation.

Although the democratic process does a reasonably good job of revealing society's preferences, it is imperfect. Public choice theory demonstrates that majority voting can produce inefficiencies and inconsistencies.

Inefficient Voting Outcomes

Society's well-being is enhanced when government provides a public good whose total benefit exceeds its total cost. Unfortunately, majority voting does not always produce that outcome.

Illustration: Inefficient "No" Vote Assume that the government can provide a public good, say, national defense, at a total expense of $900. Also assume that there are only three individuals—Adams, Benson, and Conrad—in the society and that they will share the $900 tax expense equally, each being taxed $300 if the proposed public good is provided. And assume, as Figure 17.1a illustrates, that Adams would receive $700 worth of benefits from having this public good; Benson, $250; and Conrad, $200.

What will be the result if a majority vote determines whether or not this public good is provided? Although people do not always vote strictly according to their own economic interest, it is likely Benson and Conrad will vote "no" because they will incur tax costs of $300 each while gaining benefits of only $250 and $200, respectively. Adams will vote "yes." So the majority vote will defeat the proposal even though the total benefit of $1150 (= $700 for Adams + $250 for Benson + $200 for Conrad) exceeds the total cost of $900. Resources should be devoted to this good, but they will not be. Too little of this public good will be produced.

Illustration: Inefficient "Yes" Vote Now consider a situation in which the majority favors a public good even though its total cost exceeds its total benefit. Figure 17.1b shows the details. Again, Adams, Benson, and Conrad will equally share the $900 cost of the public good; each will be taxed $300. But since Adams' benefit now is only $100 from the public good, she will vote against it. Meanwhile, Benson and Conrad will benefit by $350 each. They will vote for the public good because that benefit ($350) exceeds their tax payments ($300). The majority vote will provide a public good costing $900 that produces total benefits of only $800 (= $100 for Adams + $350 for Benson + $350 for Conrad). Society's resources will be inefficiently allocated to this public good. Too much of it will be produced.

Implications So an inefficient outcome may occur as either an overproduction or an underproduction of a specific public good, and therefore as an overallocation or underallocation of resources for that particular use. In

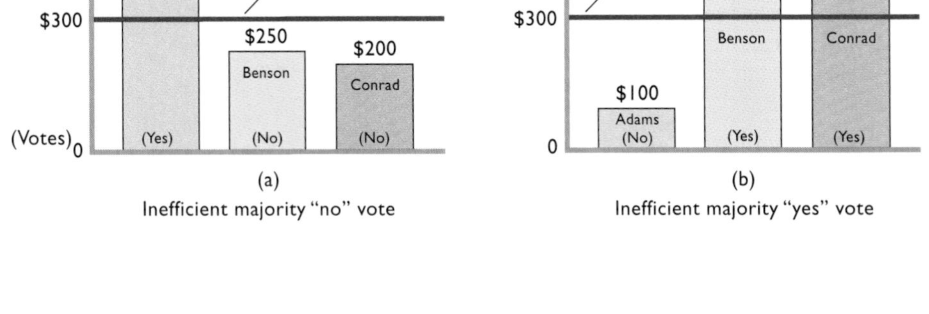

FIGURE 17.1 Inefficient voting outcomes. Majority voting can produce inefficient decisions. (a) Majority voting leads to rejection of a public good that would entail a greater total benefit than total cost. (b) Majority voting results in acceptance of a public good that has a higher total cost than total benefit.

Chapter 16 we saw that government can improve economic efficiency by providing public goods that the market system will not make available. Now we have extended that analysis to reveal that government might fail to provide some public goods whose production is economically justifiable while providing other goods that are not economically warranted.

In our examples, each person has only a single vote, no matter how much he or she might gain or lose from a public good. In the first example (inefficient "no" vote), Adams would be willing to purchase a vote from either Benson or Conrad if buying votes were legal. That way Adams could be assured of obtaining the national defense he so highly values. But since buying votes is illegal, many people with strong preferences for certain public goods may have to go without them.

When individual consumers have a strong preference for a specific *private good,* they usually can find that good in the marketplace even though it may be unpopular with the majority of consumers. A consumer can buy beef tongue or liver and squid in some supermarkets, although it is doubtful that these products would be available if majority voting stocked the shelves. But a person cannot easily "buy" a *public good* such as national defense once the majority has decided against it.

On the other hand, a consumer in the marketplace can decide not to buy a particular product, even a popular one. But although you may not want national defense, you must "buy" it through your tax payments when it is favored by the majority.

Conclusion: Because majority voting fails to incorporate the strength of the preferences of the individual voter, it may produce economically inefficient outcomes.

Interest Groups and Logrolling

There are avenues for resolving the inefficiencies associated with majority voting. Two examples follow.

Interest Groups Those who have a strong preference for a public good may band together into interest groups and use advertisements, mailings, and direct persuasion to convince others of the merits of that public good. Adams might try to persuade Benson and Conrad that it is in their best interest to vote for national defense—that national defense is much more valuable to them than their $250 and $200 valuations. Such appeals are common in democratic politics. Sometimes they are successful; sometimes they are not.

Political Logrolling **Logrolling**—the trading of votes to secure favorable outcomes—can also turn an inefficient outcome into an efficient one. In our first example (Figure 17.1a), perhaps Benson has a strong preference for a different public good, for example, a new road, which Adams and Conrad do not think is worth the tax expense. That would provide an opportunity for Adams and Benson to trade votes to ensure provision of both national defense and the new road. That is, Adams and Benson would each vote "yes" on both measures. Adams would get the national defense and Benson would get the road. Without the logrolling, both public goods would have been rejected. Moreover, the logrolling will add to society's well-being if, as was true for national defense, the road creates a greater overall benefit than cost.

But logrolling need not increase economic efficiency. Even if national defense and the road each cost more than the total benefit each produces, both might still be provided because of the vote trading. Adams and Benson might still engage in logrolling if each expects to secure a sufficient net gain from her or his favored public good, even though the gains would come at the clear expense of Conrad.

Logrolling is very common in state legislatures and Congress. It can either increase or diminish economic efficiency, depending on the circumstances.

Paradox of Voting

Another difficulty with majority voting is the **paradox of voting,** a situation in which society may not be able to rank its preferences consistently through paired-choice majority voting.

O 17.2
Paradox of voting

Preferences

Consider Table 17.1, in which we again assume a community of three voters: Adams, Benson, and Conrad.

TABLE 17.1 Paradox of Voting

	Preferences		
Public Good	**Adams**	**Benson**	**Conrad**
National defense	1st choice	3d choice	2d choice
Road	2d choice	1st choice	3d choice
Weather warning system	3d choice	2d choice	1st choice
Election		**Voting Outcomes: Winner**	
1. National defense vs. road		National defense (preferred by Adams and Conrad)	
2. Road vs. weather warning system		Road (preferred by Adams and Benson)	
3. National defense vs. weather warning system		Weather warning system (preferred by Benson and Conrad)	

Suppose the community has three alternative public goods from which to choose: national defense, a road, and a weather warning system. We expect that each member of the community prefers the three alternatives in a certain order. For example, one person might prefer national defense to a road and a road to a weather warning system. We can attempt to determine the preferences of the community through paired-choice majority voting. Specifically, a vote can be held between any two of the public goods, and the winner of that vote can then be matched against the third public good in another vote.

The three goods and the assumed individual preferences of the three voters are listed in the top part of Table 17.1. The data indicate that Adams prefers national defense to the road and the road to the weather warning system. This implies also that Adams prefers national defense to the weather warning system. Benson values the road more than the weather warning system and the warning system more than national defense. Conrad's order of preference is weather warning system, national defense, and road.

Voting Outcomes The lower part of Table 17.1 shows the outcomes of three hypothetical elections decided through majority vote. In the first, national defense wins against the road, because a majority of voters (Adams and Conrad) prefer national defense to the road. In the second election, to see whether this community wants a road or a weather warning system, a majority of voters (Adams and Benson) prefer the road.

We have determined that the majority of people in this community prefer national defense to a road and prefer a road to a weather warning system. It seems logical to conclude that the community prefers national defense to a weather warning system. But it does not!

To demonstrate this conclusion, we hold a direct election between national defense and the weather warning system. Row 3 shows that a majority of voters (Benson and Conrad) prefer the weather warning system to national defense. As listed in Table 17.1, then, the three paired-choice majority votes imply that this community is irrational: It seems to prefer national defense to a road and a road to a weather warning system, but would rather have a weather warning system than national defense.

The problem is not irrational community preferences but rather a flawed procedure for determining those preferences. We see that the outcome from paired-choice majority voting may depend on the order in which the votes are taken up. Under some circumstances majority voting fails to make consistent choices that reflect the community's underlying preferences. As a consequence, government may find it difficult to provide the "correct" public goods by acting in accordance with majority voting. Important note: This critique is not meant to suggest that there is some better procedure. Majority voting is much more likely to reflect community preferences than decisions by, say, a dictator or a group of self-appointed leaders. **(Key Question 2)**

Median-Voter Model

One final aspect of majority voting reveals insights into real-world phenomena. The **median-voter model** suggests that, under majority rule and consistent voting preferences, the median voter will in a sense determine the outcomes of elections. The median voter is the person holding the middle position on an issue: Half the other voters have stronger preferences for a public good, amount of taxation, or degree of government regulation, and half have weaker or negative preferences. The extreme voters on each side of an issue prefer the median choice rather than the other extreme position, so the median voter's choice predominates.

Example Suppose a society composed of Adams, Benson, and Conrad has reached agreement that as a society it needs a weather warning system. Each person independently is to submit a total dollar amount he or she thinks should be spent on the warning system, assuming each will be taxed one-third of that amount. An election will determine the size of the system. Because each person can be expected to vote for his or her own proposal, no majority will occur if all the proposals are placed on the ballot at the same time. Thus, the group decides on a paired-choice vote: They will first vote between two of the proposals and then match the winner of that vote against the remaining proposal.

The three proposals are as follows: Adams desires a \$400 system; Benson wants an \$800 system; Conrad opts for a \$300 system. Which proposal will win? The median-voter model suggests it will be the \$400 proposal submitted by the median voter, Adams. Half the other voters favor a more costly system; half favor a less costly system. To understand why the \$400 system will be the outcome, let's conduct the two elections.

First, suppose that the \$400 proposal is matched against the \$800 proposal. Adams naturally votes for her \$400 proposal, and Benson votes for his own \$800 proposal. Conrad, who proposed the \$300 expenditure for the warning system, votes for the \$400 proposal because it is closer to his own. So Adams' \$400 proposal is selected by a 2-to-1 majority vote.

Next, we match the \$400 proposal against the \$300 proposal. Again the \$400 proposal wins. It gets a vote from Adams and one from Benson, who proposed the \$800 expenditure and for that reason prefers a $400 expenditure to a $300 one. Adams, the median voter in this case, is in a sense the person who has decided the level of expenditure on a weather warning system for this society.

Real-World Applicability

Although our illustration is a simple one, it explains a great deal. We do note a tendency for public choices to match most closely the median view. Political candidates, for example, take one set of positions to win the nomination of their political parties; in so doing, they tend to appeal to the median voter within the party to get the nomination. They then shift their views more closely to the political center when they square off against opponents from the opposite political party. In effect, they redirect their appeal toward the median voter within the total population. They also try to label their opponents as being too liberal, or too conservative, and out of touch with "mainstream America." And they conduct polls and adjust their positions on issues accordingly.

Implications

The median-voter model has two important implications:

- Many people will be dissatisfied by the extent of government involvement in the economy. The size of government will largely be determined by the median preference, leaving many people desiring a much larger, or a much smaller, public sector. In the marketplace you can buy zero zucchinis, 2 zucchinis, or 200 zucchinis, depending on how much you enjoy them. In the public sector you get the number of Stealth bombers and interstate highways the median voter prefers.
- Some people may "vote with their feet" by moving into political jurisdictions where the median voter's preferences are closer to their own. They may move from the city to a suburb where the level of government services, and therefore taxes, is lower. Or they may move into an area known for its excellent, but expensive, school system.

For these reasons, and because our personal preferences for government activity are not static, the median preference shifts over time. Moreover, information about people's preferences is imperfect, leaving much room for politicians to misjudge the true median position. When they do, they may have a difficult time getting reelected. **(Key Question 3)**

Government Failure

As implied in our discussion of voting problems, government does not always perform its economic functions effectively and efficiently. In fact, public choice theory suggests that inherent shortcomings within the public sector can produce inefficient outcomes. Such shortcomings may result in **government failure**—inefficiency due to certain characteristics of the public sector. Let's consider some of these characteristics and outcomes.

Special Interests and Rent Seeking

Casual reflection suggests there may be a significant gap between "sound economics" and "good politics." Sound economics calls for the public sector to pursue various programs as long as marginal benefits exceed marginal costs. Good politics, however, suggests that politicians support programs and policies that will maximize their chance of getting elected and staying in office. The result may be that the government will promote the goals of groups of voters that have special interests to the detriment of the larger public. In the process, economic inefficiency may result.

Special-Interest Effect

Efficient public decision making is often impaired by the **special-interest effect.** This is any outcome of the political process whereby a small number of people obtain a government program or policy that gives them large gains at the expense of a much greater number of persons who individually suffer small losses.

The small group of potential beneficiaries is well informed and highly vocal on the issue in question, and they press politicians for approval. The large numbers facing very small individual losses, however, are generally uninformed on the issue. Politicians feel they will lose the campaign contributions and votes of the small special-interest group that backs the issue if they legislate against it but will not lose the support of the large group of uninformed voters, who are likely to evaluate the politicians on other issues of greater importance to them.

The special-interest effect is also evident in so-called *pork-barrel politics*, a means of securing a government project that yields benefits mainly to a single political district and its political representative. In this case, the special-interest group comprises local constituents, while the larger group consists of relatively uninformed taxpayers scattered across a much larger geographic area. Politicians clearly have a strong incentive to secure public goods ("pork") for their local constituents. Such goods win political favor because they are highly valued by constituents and the much larger group of relatively uninformed taxpayers bears the cost. Moreover, logrolling typically enters the picture. "Vote for my special local project and I will vote for yours" becomes part of the overall strategy for securing "pork" and remaining elected.

Finally, a politician's inclination to support the smaller group of special beneficiaries is enhanced because special-interest groups are often quite willing to help finance the campaigns of "right-minded" politicians and politicians who "bring home the pork." The result is that politicians may support special-interest programs and projects that cannot be justified on economic grounds.

Rent-Seeking Behavior The appeal to government for special benefits at taxpayers' or someone else's expense is called **rent seeking.** To economists, "rent" is a payment beyond what is necessary to keep a resource supplied in its current use. Corporations, trade associations, labor unions, and professional organizations employ vast resources to secure favorable government policies that result in rent—higher profit or income than would occur under competitive market conditions. The government is able to dispense such rent directly or indirectly through laws, rules, hiring, and purchases. Elected officials are willing to provide such rent because they want to be responsive to key constituents, who in turn help them remain in office.

Here are some examples of "rent-providing" legislation or policies: tariffs on foreign products that limit competition and raise prices to consumers; tax breaks that benefit specific corporations; government construction projects that create union jobs but cost more than the benefits they yield; occupational licensing that goes beyond what is needed to protect consumers; and large subsidies to farmers by taxpayers. None of these is justified by economic efficiency.

Clear Benefits, Hidden Costs

Some critics say that vote-seeking politicians will not weigh objectively all the costs and benefits of various programs, as economic rationality demands in deciding which to support and which to reject. Because political officeholders must seek voter support every few years, they favor programs that have immediate and clear-cut benefits and vague or deferred costs. Conversely, politicians will reject programs with immediate and easily identifiable costs but with less measurable but very high long-term benefits.

Such biases may lead politicians to reject economically justifiable programs and to accept programs that are economically irrational. Example: A proposal to construct or expand mass-transit systems in large metropolitan areas may be economically rational on the basis of cost-benefit analysis. But if (1) the program is to be financed by immediate increases in highly visible income or sales taxes and (2) benefits will occur only years from now when the project is completed, then the vote-seeking politician may oppose the program.

Assume, on the other hand, that a program of Federal aid to municipal police forces is not justifiable on the basis of cost-benefit analysis. But if the cost is paid for from budget surpluses, the program's modest benefits may seem so large that it will gain approval.

Limited and Bundled Choice

Public choice theorists point out that the political process forces citizens and their elected representatives to be less selective in choosing public goods and services than they are in choosing private goods and services.

In the marketplace, the citizen as a consumer can exactly satisfy personal preferences by buying certain goods and not buying others. However, in the public sector the citizen as a voter is confronted with, say, only two or three candidates for an office, each representing a different "bundle" of programs (public goods and services). None of these bundles of public goods is likely to fit exactly the preferences of any particular voter. Yet the voter must choose one of them. The candidate who comes closest to voter Smith's preference may endorse national health insurance, increases in Social Security benefits, subsidies to tobacco farmers, and tariffs on imported goods. Smith is likely to vote for that candidate even though Smith strongly opposes tobacco subsidies.

In other words, the voter must take the bad with the good. In the public sector, people are forced to "buy" goods and services they do not want. It is as if, in going to a sporting-goods store, you were forced to buy an unwanted pool cue to get a wanted pair of running shoes. This is a situation where resources are not being used efficiently to satisfy consumer wants. In this sense, the provision of public goods and services is inherently inefficient.

Congress is confronted with a similar limited-choice, bundled-goods problem. Appropriations legislation combines hundreds, even thousands, of spending items into a single bill. Many of these spending items may be completely unrelated to the main purpose of the legislation. Yet congressional representatives must vote the entire package—yea or nay. Unlike consumers in the marketplace, they cannot be selective. **(Key Question 4)**

Bureaucracy and Inefficiency

Some economists contend that public agencies are generally less efficient than private businesses. The reason is not that lazy and incompetent workers somehow end up in the public sector while ambitious and capable people gravitate to the private sector. Rather, it is that the market system creates incentives and pressures for internal efficiency that are absent from the public sector. Private enterprises have a clear goal—profit. Whether a private firm is in a competitive or monopolistic market, efficient management means lower costs and higher profit. The higher profit not only benefits the firm's owners but enhances the promotion prospects of managers. Moreover, part of the managers' pay may be tied to profit via profit-sharing plans, bonuses, and stock options. There is no similar gain to government agencies and their managers—no counterpart to profit—to create a strong incentive to achieve efficiency.

The market system imposes a very obvious test of performance on private firms: the test of profit and loss. An efficient firm is profitable and therefore successful; it survives, prospers, and grows. An inefficient firm is unprofitable and unsuccessful; it declines and in time goes out of business. But there is no similar, clear-cut test with which to assess the efficiency or inefficiency of public agencies. How can anyone determine whether a public hydroelectricity provider, a state university, a local fire department, the Department of Agriculture, or the Bureau of Indian Affairs is operating efficiently?

Cynics even argue that a public agency that inefficiently uses its resources is likely to survive and grow! In the private sector, inefficiency and monetary loss lead to the abandonment of certain activities or products or even firms. But the government, they say, does not like to abandon activities in which it has failed. Some suggest that the typical response of the government to a program's failure is to increase its budget and staff. This means that public sector inefficiency just continues on a larger scale.

Furthermore, economists assert that government employees, together with the special-interest groups they serve, often gain sufficient political clout to block attempts to pare down or eliminate their agencies. Politicians who attempt to reduce the size of huge Federal bureaucracies such as those relating to agriculture, education, health and welfare, and national defense incur sizable political risk because bureaucrats and special-interest groups will team up to defeat them.

Finally, critics point out that government bureaucrats tend to justify their continued employment by looking for and eventually finding new problems to solve. It is not surprising that social "problems," as defined by government, persist or even expand.

The Last Word at the end of this chapter highlights several recent media-reported examples of the special-interest effect, the problem of limited and bundled choices, and problems of government bureaucracy. You might want to read through these examples now, relating each to the section just completed.

Imperfect Institutions

It is possible to argue that such criticisms of public sector inefficiency are exaggerated and cynical. Perhaps they are. Nevertheless, they do tend to shatter the concept of a benevolent government that responds with precision and efficiency to the wants of its citizens. The market system of the private sector is far from perfectly efficient, and government's economic function is mainly to correct that system's shortcomings. But the public sector too is subject to deficiencies in fulfilling its economic function. "The relevant comparison is not between perfect markets and imperfect governments, nor between faulty markets and all-knowing, rational, benevolent governments, but between inevitably imperfect institutions."[1]

Because the market system and public agencies are both imperfect, it is sometimes difficult to determine whether a particular activity can be performed with greater success in the private sector or in the public sector. It is easy to reach agreement on opposite extremes: National defense must lie with the public sector, while computer production can best be accomplished by the private sector. But what about health insurance? Parks and recreation areas? Fire protection? Garbage collection? Housing? Education? It is hard to assess every good or service and to say absolutely that it should be assigned to either the public sector or the private sector. Evidence: All the goods and services just mentioned are provided in part by *both* private enterprises and public agencies.

QUICK REVIEW 17.1

- Majority voting can produce voting outcomes that are inefficient; projects having greater total benefits than total costs may be defeated, and projects having greater total costs than total benefits may be approved.
- The paradox of voting occurs when voting by majority rule does not provide a consistent ranking of society's preferences for public goods and services.
- The median-voter model suggests that under majority rule and consistent voting preferences, the voter who has the middle preference will determine the outcome of an election.
- Government failure allegedly occurs as a result of rent seeking, pressure by special-interest groups, shortsighted political behavior, limited and bundled choices, and bureaucratic inefficiency.

Apportioning the Tax Burden

We now turn from the difficulties of making collective decisions about public goods to the difficulties of deciding how those goods should be financed.

[1] Otto Eckstein, *Public Finance*, 3d ed. (Englewood Cliffs, N.J.: Prentice-Hall, 1973), p. 17.

It is difficult to measure precisely how the benefits of public goods are apportioned among individuals and institutions. We cannot accurately determine how much citizen Mildred Moore benefits from military installations, a network of highways, a public school system, the national weather bureau, and local police and fire protection.

The situation is different when it comes to paying for those benefits. Studies reveal with reasonable clarity how the overall tax burden is apportioned. (By "tax burden" we mean the total cost of taxes imposed on society.) This apportionment question affects each of us. The overall level of taxes is important, but the average citizen is much more concerned with his or her part of the overall tax burden.

Benefits Received versus Ability to Pay

There are two basic philosophies on how the economy's tax burden should be apportioned.

Benefits-Received Principle

The **benefits-received principle** of taxation asserts that households and businesses should purchase the goods and services of government in the same way they buy other commodities. Those who benefit most from government-supplied goods or services should pay the taxes necessary to finance them. A few public goods are now financed on this basis. For example, money collected as gasoline taxes is typically used to finance highway construction and repairs. Thus people who benefit from good roads pay the cost of those roads. Difficulties immediately arise, however, when we consider widespread application of the benefits-received principle:

- How will the government determine the benefits that individual households and businesses receive from national defense, education, the court system, and police and fire protection? Recall that public goods are characterized by nonrivalry and nonexcludability. So benefits from public goods are especially widespread and diffuse. Even in the seemingly straightforward case of highway financing it is difficult to measure benefits. Good roads benefit owners of cars in different degrees. But others also benefit. For example, businesses benefit because good roads bring them customers.
- The benefits-received principle cannot logically be applied to income redistribution programs. It would be absurd and self-defeating to ask poor families to pay the taxes needed to finance their welfare payments. It would be ridiculous to think of taxing only unemployed workers to finance the unemployment compensation payments they receive.

Ability-to-Pay Principle

The **ability-to-pay principle** of taxation asserts that the tax burden should be apportioned according to taxpayers' income and wealth. In the United States this means that individuals and businesses with larger incomes should pay more taxes in both absolute and relative terms than those with smaller incomes.

What is the rationale of ability-to-pay taxation? Proponents argue that each additional dollar of income received by a household yields a smaller amount of satisfaction or marginal utility when it is spent. Because consumers act rationally, the first dollars of income received in any time period will be spent on high-urgency goods that yield the greatest marginal utility. Successive dollars of income will go for less urgently needed goods and finally for trivial goods and services. This means that a dollar taken through taxes from a poor person who has few dollars represents a greater utility sacrifice than a dollar taken through taxes from a rich person who has many dollars. To balance the sacrifices that taxes impose on income receivers, taxes should be apportioned according to the amount of income a taxpayer receives.

This argument is appealing, but application problems arise here too. Although we might agree that the household earning $100,000 per year has a greater ability to pay taxes than a household receiving $10,000, we don't know exactly how much more ability to pay the first family has. Should the wealthier family pay the *same* percentage of its larger income, and hence a larger absolute amount, as taxes? Or should it be made to pay a *larger* fraction of its income as taxes? And how much larger should that fraction be?

There is no scientific way of making utility comparisons among individuals and thus of measuring someone's relative ability to pay taxes. That is the main problem. In practice, the solution hinges on guesswork, the tax views of the political party in power, expediency, and how urgently the government needs revenue.

Progressive, Proportional, and Regressive Taxes

Any discussion of taxation leads ultimately to the question of tax rates. Recall from Chapter 4 that an *average tax rate* is the total tax paid divided by some base against which the tax is compared.

Definitions

Taxes are classified as progressive, proportional, or regressive, depending on the relationship between average tax rates and taxpayer incomes. We focus on incomes because all taxes, whether on income or on a product or a building or a parcel of land, are ultimately paid out of someone's income.

- A tax is **progressive** if its average rate increases as income increases. Such a tax claims not only a larger absolute (dollar) amount but also a larger percentage of income as income increases.
- A tax is **regressive** if its average rate declines as income increases. Such a tax takes a smaller proportion of income as income increases. A regressive tax may or may not take a larger absolute amount of income as income increases. (You may want to derive an example to substantiate this conclusion.)
- A tax is **proportional** if its average rate *remains the same* regardless of the size of income.

We can illustrate these ideas with the personal income tax. Suppose tax rates are such that a household pays 10 percent of its income in taxes regardless of the size of its income. This is a *proportional* income tax. Now suppose the rate structure is such that a household with an annual taxable income of less than \$10,000 pays 5 percent in income taxes; a household with an income of \$10,000 to \$20,000 pays 10 percent; one with a \$20,000 to \$30,000 income pays 15 percent; and so forth. This is a *progressive* income tax. Finally, suppose the rate declines as taxable income rises: You pay 15 percent if you earn less than \$10,000; 10 percent if you earn \$10,000 to \$20,000; 5 percent if you earn \$20,000 to \$30,000; and so forth. This is a *regressive* income tax.

In general, progressive taxes are those that fall relatively more heavily on people with high incomes; regressive taxes are those that fall relatively more heavily on the poor. **(Key Question 7)**

Applications

Let's examine the progressivity, or regressivity, of several taxes.

Personal Income Tax

We noted in Chapter 4 that the Federal personal income tax is progressive, with marginal tax rates (those assessed on additional income) ranging from 10 to 35 percent in 2006. Rules that allow individuals to deduct from income interest on home mortgages and property taxes and that exempt interest on state and local bonds from taxation tend to make the tax less progressive than these marginal rates suggest. Nevertheless, average tax rates rise with income.

Sales Taxes

At first thought, a general sales tax with, for example, a 5 percent rate would seem to be proportional. But in fact it is regressive with respect to income. A larger portion of a low-income person's income is exposed to the tax than is the case for a high-income person; the rich pay no tax on the part of income that is saved, whereas the poor are unable to save. Example: "Low-income" Smith has an income of \$15,000 and spends it all. "High-income" Jones has an income of \$300,000 but spends only \$200,000 and saves the rest. Assuming a 5 percent sales tax applies to all expenditures of each individual, we find that Smith pays \$750 (5 percent of \$15,000) in sales taxes and Jones pays \$10,000 (5 percent of \$200,000). But Smith pays \$750/\$15,000, or 5 percent of income, as sales taxes, while Jones pays \$10,000/\$300,000, or 3.3 percent of income. The general sales tax therefore is regressive.

Corporate Income Tax

The Federal corporate income tax is essentially a proportional tax with a flat 35 percent tax rate. But this assumes that corporation owners (shareholders) bear the tax. Some tax experts argue that at least part of the tax is passed through to consumers in the form of higher product prices. To the extent that this occurs, the tax is like a sales tax and is thus regressive.

Payroll Taxes

Taxes levied on payrolls (Social Security and Medicare) are regressive because the Social Security tax applies to only a fixed amount of income. For example, in 2006 the Social Security tax rate was 6.2 percent, but only of the first \$94,200 of a person's wage income. The Medicare tax was 1.45 percent of all wage income. Someone earning exactly \$94,200 would pay \$7206, or 7.65 percent (= 6.2 percent + 1.45 percent) of his or her income. Someone with twice that wage income, or \$188,400, would pay \$8572 (= \$7206 on the first \$94,200 + \$1366 on the second \$94,200), which is only 4.55 percent of his or her wage income. So the average payroll tax falls as income rises, confirming that the payroll tax is regressive.

Moreover, government does not collect payroll taxes on nonwage income (such as interest, dividends, or rents). High-income persons tend to derive a higher percentage of total income from nonwage sources than do people who have incomes below the \$94,200 maximum on which social security taxes are paid. This makes payroll taxes even more regressive. If our individual with the \$188,400 of wage income also received \$188,400 of nonwage income, the \$8572 of payroll tax would be only 2.23 percent of his or her total income.

Property Taxes

Most economists conclude that property taxes on buildings are regressive for the same reasons as are sales taxes. First, property owners add the tax to the rents that tenants are charged. Second, property taxes, as a percentage of income, are higher for low-income families than for high-income families because the poor must spend a larger proportion of their incomes for housing. This alleged regressivity of property taxes may be increased by differences in property-tax rates from locality to locality. In general, property-tax rates are higher in poorer areas, to make up for lower property values.

Tax Incidence and Efficiency Loss

Determining whether a particular tax is progressive, proportional, or regressive is complicated, because those on whom taxes are levied do not always pay the taxes. We therefore need to try to locate the final resting place of a tax, or the **tax incidence.** The tools of elasticity of supply and demand will help. Let's focus on a hypothetical excise tax levied on wine producers. Do the producers really pay this tax, or do they shift it to wine consumers?

Elasticity and Tax Incidence

In Figure 17.2, *S* and *D* represent the pretax market for a certain domestic wine; the no-tax equilibrium price and quantity are $8 per bottle and 15 million bottles. Suppose that government levies an excise tax of $2 per bottle at the winery. Who will actually pay this tax?

FIGURE 17.2 **The incidence of an excise tax.** An excise tax of a specified amount, here $2 per unit, shifts the supply curve upward by the amount of the tax per unit: the vertical distance between S and S_t. This results in a higher price (here $9) to consumers and a lower after-tax price (here $7) to producers. Thus consumers and producers share the burden of the tax in some proportion (here equally at $1 per unit).

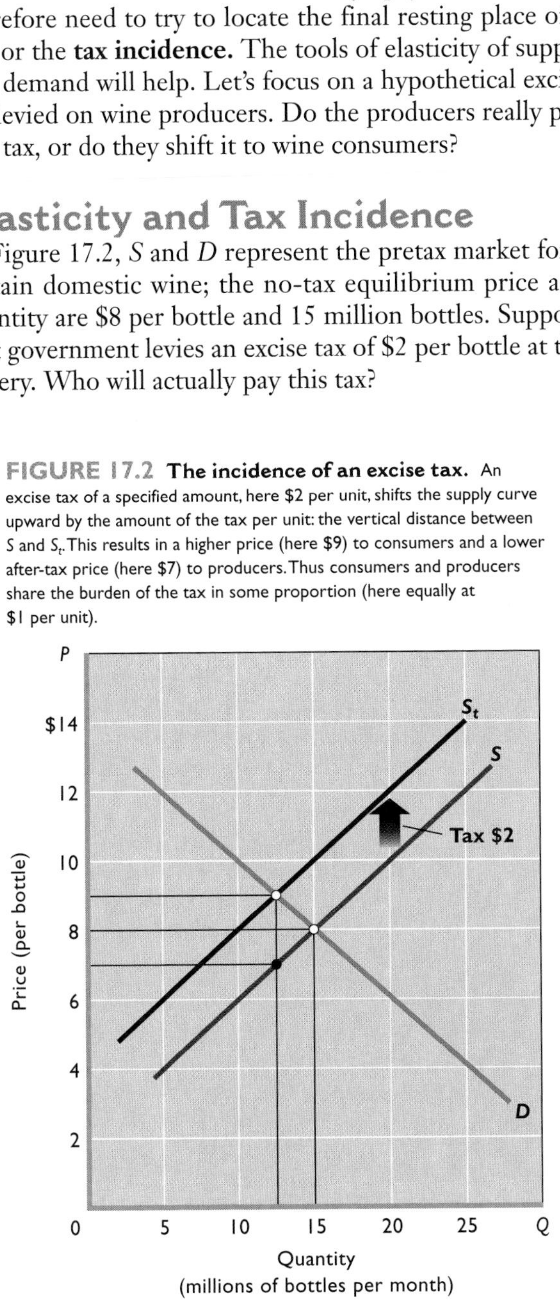

Division of Burden Since the government imposes the tax on the sellers (suppliers), we can view the tax as an addition to the marginal cost of the product. Now sellers must get $2 more for each bottle to receive the same per-unit profit they were getting before the tax. While sellers are willing to offer, for example, 5 million bottles of untaxed wine at $4 per bottle, they must now receive $6 per bottle (= $4 + $2 tax) to offer the same 5 million bottles. The tax shifts the supply curve upward (leftward) as shown in Figure 17.2, where S_t is the "after-tax" supply curve.

The after-tax equilibrium price is $9 per bottle, whereas the before-tax equilibrium price was $8. So, in this case, consumers pay half the $2 tax as a higher price; producers pay the other half in the form of a lower after-tax per-unit revenue. That is, after remitting the $2 tax per unit to government, producers receive $7, or $1 less than the $8 before-tax price. So, in this case, consumers and producers share the burden of the tax equally: Producers shift half the tax to consumers in the form of a higher price and bear the other half themselves.

G 17.1

Tax incidence

Note also that the equilibrium quantity declines because of the tax levy and the higher price that it imposes on consumers. In Figure 17.2 that decline in quantity is from 15 million bottles to 12.5 million bottles per month.

Elasticities If the elasticities of demand and supply were different from those shown in Figure 17.2, the incidence of tax would also be different. Two generalizations are relevant.

With a specific supply, the more inelastic the demand for the product, the larger is the portion of the tax shifted to consumers. To verify this, sketch graphically the extreme cases in which demand is perfectly elastic and perfectly inelastic. In the first case, the incidence of the tax is entirely on sellers; in the second, the tax is shifted entirely to consumers.

Figure 17.3 contrasts the more usual cases where demand is either relatively elastic or relatively inelastic in the relevant price range. With elastic demand (Figure 17.3a), a small portion of the tax ($P_e - P_1$) is shifted to consumers and most of the tax ($P_1 - P_a$) is borne by the producers. With inelastic demand (Figure 17.3b), most of the tax ($P_i - P_1$) is shifted to consumers and only a small amount ($P_1 - P_b$) is paid by producers. In both graphs the per-unit tax is represented by the vertical distance between S_t and S.

Note also that the decline in equilibrium quantity ($Q_1 - Q_2$) is smaller when demand is more inelastic. This

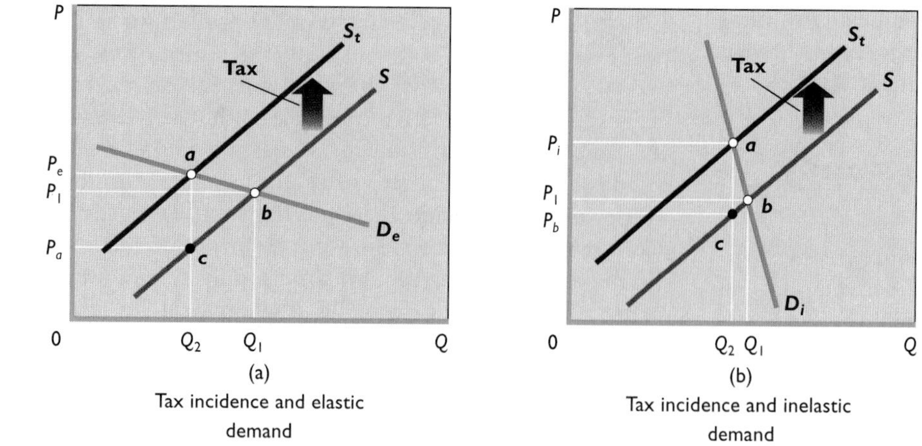

FIGURE 17.3 Demand elasticity and the incidence of an excise tax. (a) If demand is elastic in the relevant price range, price rises modestly (P_1 to P_e) when an excise tax is levied. Hence, the producer bears most of the tax burden. (b) If demand is inelastic, the price to the buyer increases substantially (P_1 to P_i) and most of the tax is shifted to consumers.

is the basis of our previous applications of the elasticity concept: Revenue-seeking legislatures place heavy excise taxes on liquor, cigarettes, automobile tires, telephone service, and other products whose demand is thought to be inelastic. Since demand for these products is relatively inelastic, the tax does not reduce sales by much, so the tax revenue stays high.

The second generalization is that, with a specific demand, the more inelastic the supply, the larger is the portion of the tax borne by producers. When supply is elastic (Figure 17.4a), the producers shift most of the tax ($P_e - P_1$) to consumers and bear only a small portion ($P_1 - P_a$) themselves. But where supply is inelastic (Figure 17.4b), the reverse is true: The major portion of the tax ($P_1 - P_b$) falls on sellers, and a relatively small amount ($P_i - P_1$) is shifted to buyers. The equilibrium quantity also declines less with an inelastic supply than it does with an elastic supply.

Gold is an example of a product with an inelastic supply and therefore one where the burden of an excise tax (such as an extraction tax) would mainly fall on producers. On the other hand, because the supply of baseballs is relatively elastic, producers would pass on to consumers much of an excise tax on baseballs.

Efficiency Loss of a Tax

We just observed that producers and consumers typically each bear part of an excise tax levied on producers. Let's now look more closely at the overall economic effect of the excise tax. Consider Figure 17.5, which is identical to Figure 17.2 but contains the additional detail we need for our discussion.

Tax Revenues In our example, a \$2 excise tax on wine increases its market price from \$8 to \$9 per bottle and reduces the equilibrium quantity from 15 million bottles to 12.5 million. Government tax revenue is \$25 million (= \$2 × 12.5 million bottles), an amount shown as the rectangle *efac* in Figure 17.5. The elasticities of supply and

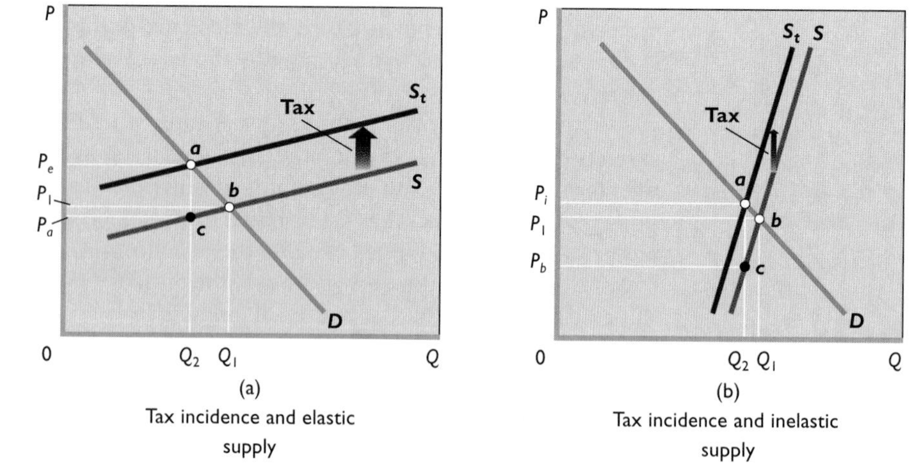

FIGURE 17.4 Supply elasticity and the incidence of an excise tax. (a) With elastic supply, an excise tax results in a large price increase (P_1 to P_e) and the tax is therefore paid mainly by consumers. (b) If supply is inelastic, the price rise is small (P_1 to P_i) and sellers bear most of the tax.

FIGURE 17.5 Efficiency loss (or deadweight loss) of a tax. The levy of a $2 tax per bottle of wine increases the price per bottle from $8 to $9 and reduces the equilibrium quantity from 15 million to 12.5 million. Tax revenue to the government is $25 million (area *efac*). The efficiency loss of the tax arises from the 2.5 million decline in output; the amount of that loss is shown as triangle *abc*.

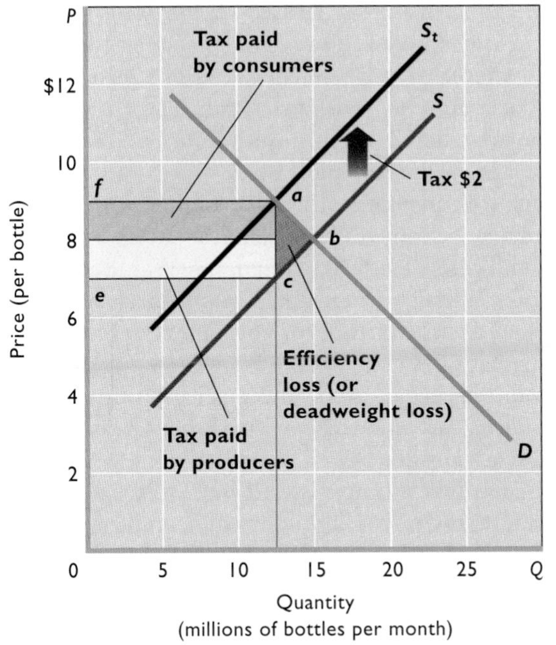

demand in this case are such that consumers and producers each pay half this total amount, or $12.5 million apiece (= $1 × 12.5 million bottles). The government uses this $25 million of tax revenue to provide public goods and services. So this transfer of dollars from consumers and producers to government involves no loss of well-being to society.

Efficiency Loss

The $2 tax on wine does more than require consumers and producers to pay $25 million of taxes; it also reduces the equilibrium amount of wine produced and consumed by 2.5 million bottles. The fact that consumers and producers demanded and supplied 2.5 million more bottles of wine before the tax means that those 2.5 million bottles provided benefits in excess of their production costs. This is clear from the following analysis.

Segment *ab* of demand curve *D* in Figure 17.5 indicates the willingness to pay—the marginal benefit—associated with each of the 2.5 million bottles consumed before (but not after) the tax. Segment *cb* of supply curve *S* reflects the marginal cost of each of the bottles of wine. For all but the very last one of these 2.5 million bottles, the marginal benefit (shown by a point on *ab*) exceeds the marginal cost (shown by a point on *cb*). Not producing all 2.5 million bottles of wine reduces well-being by an amount represented by the triangle *abc*. The area of this triangle identifies the **efficiency loss of the tax** (also called the *deadweight loss of the tax*). This loss is society's sacrifice of net benefit, because the tax reduces production and consumption of the product below their levels of economic efficiency, where marginal benefit and marginal cost are equal.

Role of Elasticities

Most taxes create some degree of efficiency loss, but just how much depends on the supply and demand elasticities. Glancing back at Figure 17.3, we see that the efficiency loss area *abc* is greater in Figure 17.3a, where demand is relatively elastic, than in Figure 17.3b, where demand is relatively inelastic. Similarly, area *abc* is greater in Figure 17.4a than in Figure 17.4b, indicating a larger efficiency loss where supply is more elastic. Other things equal, the greater the elasticities of supply and demand, the greater the efficiency loss of a particular tax.

Two taxes yielding equal revenues do not necessarily impose equal costs on society. The government must keep this fact in mind in designing a tax system to finance beneficial public goods and services. In general, it should minimize the efficiency loss of the tax system in raising any specific dollar amount of tax revenue.

Qualifications

We must acknowledge, however, that there may be other tax goals as important as, or even more important than, minimizing efficiency losses from taxes. Here are two examples:

- ***Redistributive goals*** Government may wish to impose progressive taxes as a way to redistribute income. The 10 percent excise tax the Federal government placed on selected luxuries in 1990 was an example. Because the demand for luxuries is elastic, substantial efficiency losses from this tax were to be expected. However, Congress apparently concluded that the benefits from the redistribution effects of the tax would exceed the efficiency losses.

  Ironically, in 1993 Congress repealed the luxury taxes on personal airplanes and yachts, mainly because the taxes had reduced quantity demanded so much that widespread layoffs of workers were occurring in those industries. But the 10 percent tax on luxury automobiles remained in place until it expired in 2003.
- ***Reducing negative externalities*** The government may have intended the $2 tax on wine in Figure 17.5 to reduce the consumption of wine by 2.5 million

bottles. It may have concluded that such consumption of alcoholic beverages produces certain negative externalities. Therefore, it might have purposely levied this tax to shift the market supply curve such that the price of wine increased and the amount of resources allocated to wine declined (as in Figure 17.3b). **(Key Question 9)**

Probable Incidence of U.S. Taxes

Let's look now at the probable incidence of each of the major sources of tax revenue in the United States.

Personal Income Tax

The incidence of the personal income tax generally is on the individual, because there is little chance for shifting it. But there might be exceptions. Individuals and groups who can control the price of their labor services may be able to shift a part of the tax. Doctors, dentists, lawyers, and other professional people who can readily increase their fees may do so because of the tax. Unions might regard personal income taxes as part of the cost of living and, as a result, strengthen their bargaining resolve for higher wages when personal income tax rates rise. If they are successful, they may shift part of the tax from workers to employers, who, by increasing prices, shift the wage increase to the public. Generally, however, the individual on whom the tax is initially levied bears the burden of the personal income tax. The same ordinarily holds true for payroll and inheritance taxes.

Corporate Income Tax

The incidence of the corporate income tax is much less certain. The traditional view is that a firm currently charging the profit-maximizing price and producing the profit-maximizing output will have no reason to change price or output when a tax on corporate income (profit) is imposed. The price and output combination yielding the greatest profit before the tax will still yield the greatest profit after a fixed percentage of the firm's profit is taken away via an income tax. In this view, the company's stockholders (owners) must bear the burden of the tax through lower dividends or a smaller amount of retained earnings.

However, economists recognize that where a small number of firms control a market, producers may be able to shift part of their corporate income tax to consumers through higher prices and to resource suppliers through lower prices and wages. That is, some firms may be able to use their monopoly power as sellers and monopsony power as buyers to reduce the actual amount of the tax paid by their corporate stockholders.

There simply is no consensus among experts on the overall incidence of the corporate income tax. Stockholders, customers, and resource suppliers may share the tax burden in some unknown proportions.

Sales and Excise Taxes

A *sales tax* is a general excise tax levied on a full range of consumer goods and services, whereas a *specific excise tax* is one levied only on a particular product. Sales taxes are usually transparent to the buyer, whereas excise taxes are often "hidden" in the price of the product. Sellers often shift both taxes partly or largely to consumers through higher product prices. There may be some difference in the extent to which sales taxes and excise taxes are shifted, however. Because a sales tax covers a much wider range of products than an excise tax, there is little chance for consumers to resist the price boosts that sales taxes entail. They cannot reallocate their expenditures to untaxed, lower-priced products. Therefore, sales taxes tend to be shifted from producers in their entirety to consumers.

Excise taxes, however, fall on a select list of goods. Therefore, the possibility of consumers turning to substitute goods and services is greater. An excise tax on theater tickets that does not apply to other types of entertainment might be difficult to pass on to consumers via price increases. Why? The answer is provided in Figure 17.3a, where demand is elastic. A price boost to cover the excise tax on theater tickets might cause consumers to substitute alternative types of entertainment. The higher price would reduce sales so much that a seller would be better off to bear all, or a large portion of, the excise tax.

With other products, modest price increases to cover taxes may have smaller effects on sales. The excise taxes on gasoline, cigarettes, and alcoholic beverages provide examples. Here consumers have few good substitute products to which they can turn as prices rise. For these goods, the seller is better able to shift nearly all the excise tax to consumers. Example: Prices of cigarettes have gone up nearly in lockstep with the recent, substantial increases in excise taxes on cigarettes.

As indicated in Global Perspective 17.1, the United States depends less on sales and excise taxes for tax revenue than do several other nations.

Property Taxes

Many property taxes are borne by the property owner, because there is no other party to whom they can be shifted. This is typically true for taxes on land, personal property, and owner-occupied residences. Even when land is sold, the property tax is not likely to be shifted. The buyer will understand that future taxes will have to be paid on it, and this expected taxation

TABLE 17.2 The Probable Incidence of Taxes

Type of Tax	Probable Incidence
Personal income tax	The household or individual on which it is levied.
Corporate income tax	Some economists conclude the firm on which it is levied bears the tax; others conclude the tax is shifted, wholly or in part, to consumers and resource suppliers.
Sales tax	Consumers who buy the taxed products.
Specific excise taxes	Consumers, producers, or both, depending on elasticities of demand and supply.
Property taxes	Owners in the case of land and owner-occupied residences; tenants in the case of rented property; consumers in the case of business property.

would be reflected in the price the buyer is willing to offer for the land.

Taxes on rented and business property are a different story. Taxes on rented property can be, and usually are, shifted wholly or in part from the owner to the tenant by the process of boosting the rent. Business property taxes are treated as a business cost and are taken into account in establishing product price; hence such taxes are ordinarily shifted to the firm's customers.

GLOBAL PERSPECTIVE 17.1

Taxes on Goods and Services as a Percentage of Total Tax Revenues, Selected Nations

A number of industrial nations rely more heavily on goods and services taxes—sales taxes, value-added taxes, and specific excise taxes—than does the United States. (A value-added tax applies only to the difference between the value of a firm's sales and the value of its purchases from other firms.)

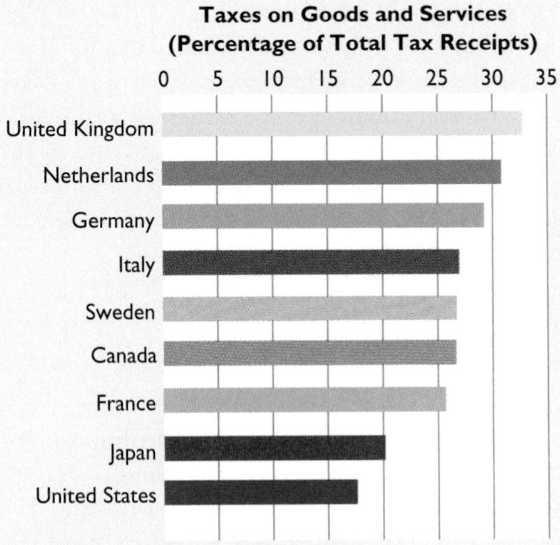

Source: Organization for Economic Cooperation and Development, **www.oecd.org/**. Data are for 2002.

Table 17.2 summarizes this discussion of the shifting and incidence of taxes.

The U.S. Tax Structure

Is the overall U.S. tax structure—Federal, state, and local taxes combined—progressive, proportional, or regressive? This question is difficult to answer. Estimates of the distribution of the total tax burden depend on the extent to which the various taxes are shifted to others, and who bears the ultimate burden is subject to dispute. But the majority view of economists is as follows:

- ***The Federal tax system is progressive.*** About one-third of filers of the Federal income tax owe no tax at all, and the average rates for the others rise with income. In contrast, Federal payroll taxes and excise taxes are regressive. But the overall Federal tax rate is progressive. This rate is found by dividing the total of Federal income taxes, payroll taxes, and excise taxes by income. In 2004, the 20 percent of families with the lowest income paid an average overall Federal tax rate of 5.2 percent. The 20 percent with the highest income paid a 23.8 percent rate; the top 10 percent paid 24.9 percent, and the top 1 percent paid 26.7 percent.[2]
- ***The state and local tax structures are largely regressive.*** As a percentage of income, property taxes and sales taxes fall as income rises. Also, state income taxes are generally less progressive than the Federal income tax.
- ***The overall U.S. tax system is slightly progressive.*** Higher-income people carry a slightly larger tax burden, as a percentage of their income, than do lower-income people.

Caution: While the U.S. tax system does not substantially alter the distribution of income, the system of

[2] *Effective Federal Tax Rates under Current Law, 2001–2014*, Congressional Budget Office, August 2004.

Last Word

"Government Failure" in the News

The Media Continually Report Government Actions That Illustrate Pork-Barrel Politics, Limited and Bundled Choices, or Bureaucratic Inefficiency.

Examples:

- As part of a radiation cleanup project in Pennsylvania in the late 1990s, the EPA spent an average of $651,700 to custom-build 10 new houses for homeowners. This was in addition to the cleanup costs. The old houses were worth an average of $147,000 each. (Gannett News Services)
- In 2001, Congress appropriated $350,000 for the Chicago Wilderness Program, $273,000 for the Blue Springs (Missouri) Youth Outreach Unit for educational training in combating the Goth culture, and $400,000 for the Montana Sheep Institute. (Citizens Against Waste, as reported in the *Lincoln Journal Star*)
- The 2001 Senate "economic stimulus" bill contained a $220 million subsidy for bison meat producers and eggplant, cauliflower, and pumpkin growers that experienced low prices during the 2000 and 2001 crop years. *(Los Angeles Times)*
- The disaster emergency relief section of the 2003 appropriations bill contained a provision to qualify catfish farmers for livestock compensation payments. Senator John McCain asked, "When did a catfish become analogous to a cow?" (Senator John McCain's Congressional "Pork" Web site, **www.mccain.senate.gov**)
- A 2003 spending bill contained 9300 special projects. Included were $3 million for a Florida-based nonprofit program than provides golf instruction to children and teens around the country, $50 million to build an indoor rainforest in Iowa, and $225 million to repair a 61-year-old municipal swimming pool in Nevada. (Knight Ridder Newspapers and the Associated Press)
- A 2004 spending bill set aside $1 million for the Norwegian American Foundation; $443,000 to develop salmon-fortified baby food; $350,000 for music education programs at the Rock and Roll Hall of Fame in Cleveland; and $250,000 for sidewalks, street furniture, and façade improvements in Boca Raton, Florida. (Associated Press)
- The corporate tax relief bill of 2004 contained 633 pages, with 276 special provisions. Included were provisions that benefited "restaurant owners and Hollywood producers; makers of bows, arrows, tackle boxes and sonar fish finders; NASCAR track owners; native Alaska whalers; and even importers of Chinese fans." **(www.Washington Post.com)**
- A 2005 spending bill provided $500,000 for Seattle's sculpture garden and $223,000 for a bridge from Ketchikan, Alaska, to an island populated by 50 people and having an airport. (*Seattle Post-Intelligencer*)
- Government investigations determined that millions of dollars of disaster relief for victims of hurricane Katrina were squandered. For example, investigators discovered that the Federal Emergency Management Agency (FEMA) made payouts on as many as 900,000 claims for disaster relief that contained invalid Social Security numbers or false names and addresses. (*Seattle Times*)

transfer payments does considerably reduce income inequality. Transfer payments to the poorest fifth of U.S. households almost quadruple their collective incomes. The combined tax-transfer system redistributes income by much more than does the tax system alone.

Summary

1. Public choice theory examines the economics of government decision making, politics, and elections.
2. Majority voting creates a possibility of (a) an underallocation or an overallocation of resources to a particular public good and (b) inconsistent voting outcomes. The median-voter model predicts that, under majority rule, the person holding the middle position on an issue will determine the outcome of an election involving that issue.
3. Public choice theorists cite reasons why government might be inefficient in providing public goods and services. (a) There are strong reasons for politicians to support special-interest legislation. (b) Politicians may be biased in favor of programs with immediate and clear-cut benefits and difficult-to-identify costs and against programs with immediate and easily identified costs and vague or deferred benefits. (c) Citizens as voters and congressional representatives face limited and bundled choices as to public goods and services, whereas consumers in the private sector can be highly selective in their choices. (d) Government bureaucracies have less incentive to operate efficiently than do private businesses.
4. The benefits-received principle of taxation states that those who receive the benefits of goods and services provided by government should pay the taxes required to finance them. The ability-to-pay principle states that those who have greater income should be taxed more, absolutely and relatively, than those who have less income.
5. The Federal personal income tax is progressive. The corporate income tax is roughly proportional. General sales, excise, payroll, and property taxes are regressive.
6. Excise taxes affect supply and therefore equilibrium price and quantity. The more inelastic the demand for a product, the greater is the portion of an excise tax that is shifted to consumers. The greater the inelasticity of supply, the larger is the portion of the tax that is borne by the seller.
7. Taxation involves the loss of some output whose marginal benefit exceeds its marginal cost. The more elastic the supply and demand curves, the greater is the efficiency loss (or deadweight loss) resulting from a particular tax.
8. Sales taxes normally are shifted to consumers; personal income taxes are not shifted. Specific excise taxes may or may not be shifted to consumers, depending on the elasticities of demand and supply. There is disagreement as to whether corporate income taxes are shifted. Property taxes on owner-occupied property are borne by the owner; those on rental property are borne by tenants.
9. The Federal tax structure is progressive; the state and local tax structure is regressive; and the overall tax structure is slightly progressive.

Terms and Concepts

public choice theory
logrolling
paradox of voting
median-voter model
government failure
special-interest effect
rent seeking
benefits-received principle
ability-to-pay principle
progressive tax
regressive tax
proportional tax
tax incidence
efficiency loss of a tax

Study Questions

1. Explain how affirmative and negative majority votes can sometimes lead to inefficient allocations of resources to public goods. Is this problem likely to be greater under a benefits-received or under an ability-to-pay tax system? Use the information in Figures 17.1a and 17.1b to show how society might be better off if Adams were allowed to buy votes.
2. **KEY QUESTION** Explain the paradox of voting through reference to the accompanying table, which shows the ranking of three public goods by voters Jay, Dave, and Conan:

	Rankings		
Public Good	**Jay**	**Dave**	**Conan**
Courthouse	2d choice	1st choice	3d choice
School	3d choice	2d choice	1st choice
Park	1st choice	3d choice	2d choice

3. **KEY QUESTION** Suppose there are only five people in a society and each favors one of the five highway construction options in Table 16.2 (include no highway construction as one of the options). Explain which of these highway options

will be selected using a majority paired-choice vote. Will this option be the optimal size of the project from an economic perspective?

4. **KEY QUESTION** How does the problem of limited and bundled choice in the public sector relate to economic efficiency? Why are public bureaucracies alleged to be less efficient than private enterprises?
5. Explain: "Politicians would make more rational economic decisions if they weren't running for reelection every few years."
6. Distinguish between the benefits-received and the ability-to-pay principles of taxation. Which philosophy is more evident in our present tax structure? Justify your answer. To which principle of taxation do you subscribe? Why?
7. **KEY QUESTION** Suppose a tax is such that an individual with an income of \$10,000 pays \$2000 of tax, a person with an income of \$20,000 pays \$3000 of tax, a person with an income of \$30,000 pays \$4000 of tax, and so forth. What is each person's average tax rate? Is this tax regressive, proportional, or progressive?
8. What is meant by a progressive tax? A regressive tax? A proportional tax? Comment on the progressivity or regressivity of each of the following taxes, indicating in each case where you think the tax incidence lies: (*a*) the Federal personal income tax; (*b*) a 4 percent state general sales tax; (*c*) a Federal excise tax on automobile tires; (*d*) a municipal property tax on real estate; (*e*) the Federal corporate income tax.
9. **KEY QUESTION** What is the incidence of an excise tax when demand is highly inelastic? Elastic? What effect does the elasticity of supply have on the incidence of an excise tax? What is the efficiency loss of a tax, and how does it relate to elasticity of demand and supply?
10. **ADVANCED ANALYSIS** Suppose the equation for the demand curve for some product X is $P = 8 - .6Q$ and the supply curve is $P = 2 + .4Q$. What are the equilibrium price and quantity? Now suppose an excise tax is imposed on X such that the new supply equation is $P = 4 + .4Q$. How much tax revenue will this excise tax yield the government? Graph the curves, and label the area of the graph that represents the tax collection "TC" and the area that represents the efficiency loss of the tax "EL." Briefly explain why area EL is the efficiency loss of the tax but TC is not.
11. **LAST WORD** How do the concepts of pork-barrel politics and logrolling relate to the items listed in the Last Word?

Web-Based Questions

1. **BUREAUCRACY AND INEFFICIENCY—THE POST OFFICE VERSUS UPS** Some economists contend that public agencies generally are less efficient than private businesses. United Parcel Service (UPS) competes directly with the U.S. Postal Service for express mail and packages. Assume you need to send an express letter and a 3-pound package from your address to either New York City or Los Angeles. On the basis of their interactive rate and options calculators at **www.ups.com** and **www.usps.com,** which service is more competitive as to price and delivery? Does a lower rate with greater delivery options mean greater efficiency? Why or why not?
2. **CALCULATING TAXES AND DETERMINING AVERAGE RATES** The Internal Revenue Service provides current tax-rate tables online at **www.irs.gov.** Enter "Tax Tables" in the search line for forms and publications and find "1040 Instructions (Tax Tables)" for the latest tax year. Find the tax payment you would owe if you were a single taxpayer with a taxable income of (1) \$23,360, (2) \$46,200, and (3) \$85,010 in the taxable year. Compare the average tax rates (taxable income/tax payment) for the three levels of income. Next, suppose that you live in a state with a 7 percent sales tax and that you spent 90 percent of your taxable income in the year. How much total sales tax would you pay at each income level? Add the total sales tax to the income tax for each income level and compute new average tax rates based on the combined income tax and sales tax as a percentage of taxable income. Compare the new percentages with the previous ones. What can you conclude from the comparison? (We are assuming that you take the standard deduction on your Federal income tax form and thus do not claim a sales tax deduction.)

PART FIVE

Microeconomic Issues and Policies

18 ANTITRUST POLICY AND REGULATION

19 AGRICULTURE: ECONOMICS AND POLICY

20 INCOME INEQUALITY AND POVERTY

21 THE ECONOMICS OF HEALTH CARE

22 LABOR MARKET INSTITUTIONS AND ISSUES: UNIONISM, DISCRIMINATION, IMMIGRATION

18

IN THIS CHAPTER YOU WILL LEARN:

- **The core elements of the major antitrust (antimonopoly) laws in the United States.**
- **Some of the key issues relating to the interpretation and application of antitrust laws.**
- **The economic principles and difficulties relating to the setting of prices (rates) charged by so-called natural monopolies.**
- **The nature of "social regulation," its benefits and costs, and its optimal level.**

Antitrust Policy and Regulation

We now can apply the economics of product markets (Part 2), resource markets (Part 3), and government (Part 4) to selected microeconomic issues and policies.

In this chapter we look at three sets of government policies toward business: antitrust policy, industrial regulation, and social regulation. **Antitrust policy** consists of the laws and government actions designed to prevent monopoly and promote competition. **Industrial regulation** consists of government regulation of firms' prices (or "rates") within selected industries. **Social regulation** is government regulation of the conditions under which goods are produced, the physical characteristics of goods, and the impact of the production and consumption of goods on society.

Then, in the remaining four chapters of Part 5, we discuss issues and policies relating to agriculture, income inequality, health care, and labor markets (unions, discrimination, and immigration).

The Antitrust Laws

The underlying purpose of antitrust policy (antimonopoly policy) is to prevent monopolization, promote competition, and achieve allocative efficiency. Although all economists would agree that these are meritorious goals, there is sharp conflict of opinion about the appropriateness and effectiveness of U.S. antitrust policy. As we will see, antitrust policy over the years has been neither clear-cut nor consistent.

Historical Background

Just after the U.S. Civil War (1861–1865), local markets widened into national markets because of improved transportation facilities, mechanized production methods, and sophisticated corporate structures. In the 1870s and 1880s, dominant firms formed in several industries, including petroleum, meatpacking, railroads, sugar, lead, coal, whiskey, and tobacco. Some of these oligopolists, near-monopolists, or monopolists were known as *trusts*—business combinations that assign control to a single decision group ("trustees"). Because these trusts "monopolized" industries, the word "trust" became synonymous with "monopoly" in common usage. The public, government, and historians began to define a business monopoly as a large-scale dominant seller, even though that seller was not always "a sole seller" as specified in the model of pure monopoly.

These dominant firms often used questionable tactics in consolidating their industries and then charged high prices to customers and extracted price concessions from resource suppliers. Farmers and owners of small businesses were particularly vulnerable to the power of large corporate monopolies and were among the first to oppose them. Consumers, labor unions, and economists were not far behind in their opposition.

The main economic case against monopoly is familiar to you from Chapter 10. Monopolists tend to produce less output and charge higher prices than would be the case if their industries were competitive. With pure competition, production occurs where $P = \text{MC}$. This equality represents an efficient allocation of resources because P measures the marginal benefit to society of an extra unit of output while marginal cost MC reflects the cost of an extra unit. When $P = \text{MC}$, society cannot gain by producing 1 more or 1 less unit of the product. In contrast, a monopolist maximizes profit by equating marginal revenue (not price) with marginal cost. At this $\text{MR} = \text{MC}$ point, price exceeds marginal cost, meaning that society would obtain more benefit than it would incur cost by producing extra units. There is an underallocation of resources to the monopolized product, and so the economic well-being of society is less than it would be with greater competition.

In the late 1800s and early 1900s, government concluded that market forces in monopolized industries did not provide sufficient control to protect consumers, achieve fair competition, and achieve allocative efficiency. So it instituted two alternative means of control as substitutes for, or supplements to, market forces:

- ***Regulatory agencies*** In the few markets where the nature of the product or technology creates a *natural monopoly*, the government established public regulatory agencies to control economic behavior.
- ***Antitrust laws*** In most other markets, social control took the form of antitrust (antimonopoly) legislation designed to inhibit or prevent the growth of monopoly.

Four particular pieces of Federal legislation, as refined and extended by various amendments, constitute the basic law relating to monopoly structure and conduct.

Sherman Act of 1890

The public resentment of trusts that emerged in the 1870s and 1880s culminated in the **Sherman Act** of 1890. This cornerstone of antitrust legislation is surprisingly brief and, at first glance, directly to the point. The core of the act resides in two provisions:

- ***Section 1*** "Every contract, combination in the form of a trust or otherwise, or conspiracy, in restraint of trade or commerce among the several States, or with foreign nations is declared to be illegal."
- ***Section 2*** "Every person who shall monopolize, or attempt to monopolize, or combine or conspire with any person or persons, to monopolize any part of the trade or commerce among the several states, or with foreign nations, shall be deemed guilty of a felony" (as later amended from "misdemeanor").

The Sherman Act thus outlawed *restraints of trade* (for example, collusive price fixing and dividing up markets) as well as *monopolization.* Today, the U.S. Department of Justice, the Federal Trade Commission, injured private parties, or state attorney generals can file antitrust suits against alleged violators of the act. The courts can issue injunctions to prohibit anticompetitive practices or, if necessary, break up monopolists into competing firms. Courts can also fine and imprison violators. Further, parties injured by illegal combinations and conspiracies can sue the perpetrators for *treble damages*—awards of three times the amount of the monetary injury done to them.

The Sherman Act seemed to provide a sound foundation for positive government action against business monopolies.

However, early court interpretations limited the scope of the act and created ambiguities of law. It became clear that a more explicit statement of the government's antitrust sentiments was needed. The business community itself sought a clearer statement of what was legal and what was illegal.

Clayton Act of 1914

The **Clayton Act** of 1914 contained the desired elaboration of the Sherman Act. Four sections of the act, in particular, were designed to strengthen and make explicit the intent of the Sherman Act:

- Section 2 outlaws *price discrimination* when such discrimination is not justified on the basis of cost differences and when it reduces competition.
- Section 3 prohibits **tying contracts,** in which a producer requires that a buyer purchase another (or others) of its products as a condition for obtaining a desired product.
- Section 7 prohibits the acquisition of stocks of competing corporations when the outcome would be less competition.
- Section 8 prohibits the formation of **interlocking directorates**—situations where a director of one firm is also a board member of a competing firm—in large corporations where the effect would be reduced competition.

The Clayton Act simply sharpened and clarified the general provisions of the Sherman Act. It also sought to outlaw the techniques that firms might use to develop monopoly power and, in that sense, was a preventive measure. Section 2 of the Sherman Act, by contrast, was aimed more at breaking up existing monopolies.

Federal Trade Commission Act of 1914

The **Federal Trade Commission Act** created the five-member Federal Trade Commission (FTC), which has joint Federal responsibility with the U.S. Justice Department for enforcing the antitrust laws. The act gave the FTC the power to investigate unfair competitive practices on its own initiative or at the request of injured firms. It can hold public hearings on such complaints and, if necessary, issue **cease-and-desist orders** in cases where it discovers "unfair methods of competition in commerce."

The **Wheeler-Lea Act** of 1938 gave the FTC the additional responsibility of policing "deceptive acts or practices in commerce." In so doing, the FTC tries to protect the public against false or misleading advertising and the misrepresentation of products. So the Federal Trade Commission Act, as modified by the Wheeler-Lea Act, (1) established the FTC as an independent antitrust agency and (2) made unfair and deceptive sales practices illegal.

Celler-Kefauver Act of 1950

The **Celler-Kefauver Act** amended the Clayton Act, Section 7, which prohibits a firm from merging with a competing firm (and thereby lessening competition) by acquiring its stock. Firms could evade Section 7, however, by instead acquiring the physical assets (plant and equipment) of competing firms. The Celler-Kefauver Act closed that loophole by prohibiting one firm from obtaining the physical assets of another firm when the effect would be reduced competition. Section 7 of the Clayton Act now prohibits anticompetitive mergers no matter how they are undertaken. **(Key Question 2)**

Antitrust Policy: Issues and Impacts

The effectiveness of any law depends on how the courts interpret it and on the vigor of government enforcement. The courts have been inconsistent in interpreting the antitrust laws. At times, they have applied them vigorously, adhering closely to their spirit and objectives. At other times, their interpretations have rendered certain laws nearly powerless. The Federal government itself has varied considerably in its willingness to apply the antitrust laws. Administrations holding a laissez-faire philosophy about monopoly have sometimes ignored them or have reduced the budgets of the enforcement agencies.

Issues of Interpretation

Differences in judicial interpretations have led to vastly different applications of the antitrust laws. Two questions, in particular, have arisen: (1) Should the focus of antitrust policy be on monopoly behavior or on monopoly structure? (2) How broadly should markets be defined in antitrust cases?

Monopoly Behavior versus Monopoly Structure

A comparison of three landmark Supreme Court decisions reveals two distinct interpretations of Section 2 of the Sherman Act as it relates to monopoly behavior and structure.

In the 1911 **Standard Oil case,** the Supreme Court found Standard Oil guilty of monopolizing the petroleum industry through a series of abusive and anticompetitive actions. The Court's remedy was to divide Standard Oil into several competing firms. But the Standard Oil case left open an important question: Is every monopoly in violation of Section 2 of the Sherman Act or just those created or maintained by anticompetitive actions?

In the 1920 **U.S. Steel case,** the courts established a **rule of reason,** saying that not every monopoly is illegal. Only monopolies that "unreasonably" restrain trade violate Section 2 of the Sherman Act and are subject to antitrust action. Size alone was not an offense. Although U.S. Steel clearly possessed monopoly power, it was innocent of "monopolizing" because it had not resorted to illegal acts against competitors in obtaining that power nor had it unreasonably used its monopoly power. Unlike Standard Oil, which was a so-called bad trust, U.S. Steel was a "good trust" and therefore not in violation of the law.

In the **Alcoa case** of 1945 the courts touched off a 20-year turnabout. The Supreme Court sent the case to the U.S. court of appeals in New York because four of the Supreme Court justices had been involved with litigation of the case before their appointments. Led by Judge Hand the court of appeals held that, even though a firm's behavior might be legal, the mere possession of monopoly power (Alcoa held 90 percent of the aluminum ingot market) violated the antitrust laws. So Alcoa was found guilty of violating the Sherman Act.

These two cases point to a controversy in antitrust policy. Should a firm be judged by its behavior (as in the U.S. Steel case) or by its structure or market share (as in the Alcoa case)?

"Structuralists" say that a firm with a very high market share will behave like a monopolist. Since the economic performance of such firms will be undesirable, they are legitimate targets for antitrust action. Changes in the structure of the industry, say, by splitting the monopolist into several smaller firms, will improve behavior and performance.

"Behavioralists" assert that the relationship among structure, behavior, and performance is tenuous and unclear. They feel a monopolized or highly concentrated industry may be technologically progressive and have a good record of providing products of increasing quality at reasonable prices. If a firm has served society well and has engaged in no anticompetitive practices, it should not be accused of antitrust violation just because it has an extraordinarily large market share. That share may be the product of superior technology, superior products, and economies of scale. "Why use antitrust laws to penalize efficient, technologically progressive, well-managed firms?" they ask.

Over the past 25 years, the courts have returned to the rule of reason, and most contemporary economists and antitrust enforcers reject strict structuralism. For instance, in 1982 the government dropped its 13-year-long monopolization case against IBM on the grounds that IBM had not unreasonably restrained trade. More recently, the government has made no attempt to break up Intel's monopoly in the sale of microcircuits for personal computers. And in prosecuting the Microsoft case (the subject of this chapter's Last Word), the Federal government made it clear that the behavior used by Microsoft to maintain and extend its monopoly, not the presence of its large market share, violated the Sherman Act. That is, the goverment in effect declared Microsoft "a bad monopoly."

The Relevant Market

Courts often decide whether or not market power exists by considering the share of the market held by the dominant firm. They have roughly adhered to a "90-60-30 rule" in defining monopoly: If a firm has a 90 percent market share, it is definitely a monopolist; if it has a 60 percent market share, it probably is a monopolist; if it has a 30 percent market share, it clearly is not a monopolist. The market share will depend on how the market is defined. If the market is defined broadly to include a wide range of somewhat similar products, the firm's market share will appear small. If the market is defined narrowly to exclude such products, the market share will seem large. The Supreme Court's task is to determine how broadly to define relevant markets, and it has not always been consistent.

In the Alcoa case, the Court used a narrow definition of the relevant market: the aluminum ingot market. But in the **DuPont cellophane case** of 1956 the Court defined the market very broadly. The government contended that DuPont, along with a licensee, controlled 100 percent of the cellophane market. But the Court accepted DuPont's contention that the relevant market included all "flexible packaging materials"—waxed paper, aluminum foil, and so forth, in addition to cellophane. Despite DuPont's monopoly in the "cellophane market," it controlled only 20 percent of the market for "flexible wrapping materials." The Court ruled that this did not constitute a monopoly.

Issues of Enforcement

Some U.S. presidential administrations have enforced the antitrust laws more strictly than others. The degree of Federal antitrust enforcement makes a difference in the overall degree of antitrust action in the economy. It is true that individual firms can sue other firms under the antitrust laws. For example, in 2005 AMD—a maker of microprocessors—filed an antitrust suit against Intel, claiming that Intel was a monopolist that used anticompetitive business practices to thwart the growth of AMD's market share.

But major antitrust suits often last years and are highly expensive. Injured parties therefore often look to the Federal government to initiate and litigate such cases. Once the Federal government gains a conviction, the injured parties no longer need to prove guilt and can simply sue the violator to obtain treble damages. In many cases, lack of Federal antitrust action therefore means diminished legal action by firms.

Why might one administration enforce the antitrust laws more or less strictly than another? The main reason is differences in political philosophies about the market economy and the wisdom of intervention by government. There are two contrasting general perspectives on antitrust policy.

The *active antitrust perspective* is that competition is insufficient in some circumstances to achieve allocative efficiency and ensure fairness to consumers and competing firms. Firms occasionally use illegal tactics against competitors to dominate markets. In other instances, competitors collude to fix prices or merge to enhance their monopoly power. Active, strict enforcement of the antitrust laws is needed to stop illegal business practices, prevent anticompetitive mergers, and remedy monopoly. This type of government intervention maintains the viability and vibrancy of the market system and thus allows society to reap its full benefits. In this view, the antitrust authorities need to act much like the officials in a football game. They must observe the players, spot infractions, and enforce the rules.

In contrast, the *laissez-faire perspective* holds that antitrust intervention is largely unnecessary, particularly as it relates to monopoly. Economists holding this position view competition as a long-run dynamic process in which firms battle against each other for dominance of markets. In some markets, a firm successfully monopolizes the market, usually because of its superior innovativeness or business skill. But in exploiting its monopoly power to raise prices, these firms inadvertently create profit incentives and profit opportunities for other entrepreneurs and firms to develop alternative technologies and new products to better serve consumers. A process of *creative destruction* (review Chapter 12) occurs, in which today's monopolies are eroded and eventually destroyed by tomorrow's technologies and products. The government therefore should not try to break up monopoly. It should stand aside and allow the long-run competitive process to work.

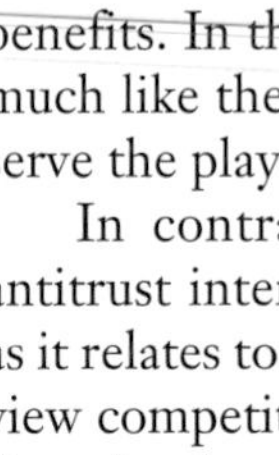

O 18.1
Creative destruction

The extent to which a particular administration adheres to—or leans toward—one of these contrasting antitrust perspectives usually gets reflected in the appointments to the agencies overseeing antitrust policy. Those appointees help determine the degree of strictness in enforcement of the laws.

Effectiveness of Antitrust Laws

Have the antitrust laws been effective? Although this question is difficult to answer, we can at least observe how the laws have been applied to monopoly, mergers, price fixing, price discrimination, and tying contracts.

Monopoly

On the basis of the rule of reason, the government has generally been lenient in applying antitrust laws to monopolies that have developed naturally. Generally, a firm will be sued by the Federal government only if it has a very high market share and there is evidence of abusive conduct in achieving, maintaining, or extending its market dominance.

Since the 1980s the issue of remedy arose in two particularly noteworthy monopoly cases. The first was the AT&T (American Telephone and Telegraph) case in which the government charged AT&T with violating the Sherman Act by engaging in anticompetitive practices designed to maintain its domestic telephone monopoly. As part of an out-of-court settlement between the government and AT&T, in 1982 AT&T agreed to divest itself of its 22 regional telephone-operating companies.

A second significant monopoly case was the **Microsoft case.** In 2000 Microsoft was found guilty of violating the Sherman Act by taking several unlawful actions designed to maintain its monopoly of operating systems for personal computers. A lower court ordered that Microsoft be split into two competing firms. A court of appeals upheld the lower-court finding of abusive monopoly but rescinded the breakup of Microsoft. Instead of the structural remedy, the eventual outcome was a behavioral remedy in which Microsoft was prohibited from engaging in a set of specific anticompetitive business practices.

Mergers

The treatment of mergers, or combinations of existing firms, varies with the type of merger and its effect on competition.

Merger Types

There are three basic types of mergers, as represented in Figure 18.1. This figure shows two stages of production (the input stage and the output, or final-product, stage) for two distinct final-goods industries (autos and blue jeans). Each rectangle (A, B, C, . . . X, Y, Z) represents a particular firm.

A **horizontal merger** is a merger between two competitors that sell similar products in the same geographic market. In Figure 18.1 this type of merger is shown as a combination of glass producers T and U. Actual examples

FIGURE 18.1 Types of mergers. Horizontal mergers (T + U) bring together firms selling the same product in the same geographic market; vertical mergers (F + Z) connect firms having a buyer-seller relationship; and conglomerate mergers (C + D) join firms in different industries or firms operating in different geographic areas.

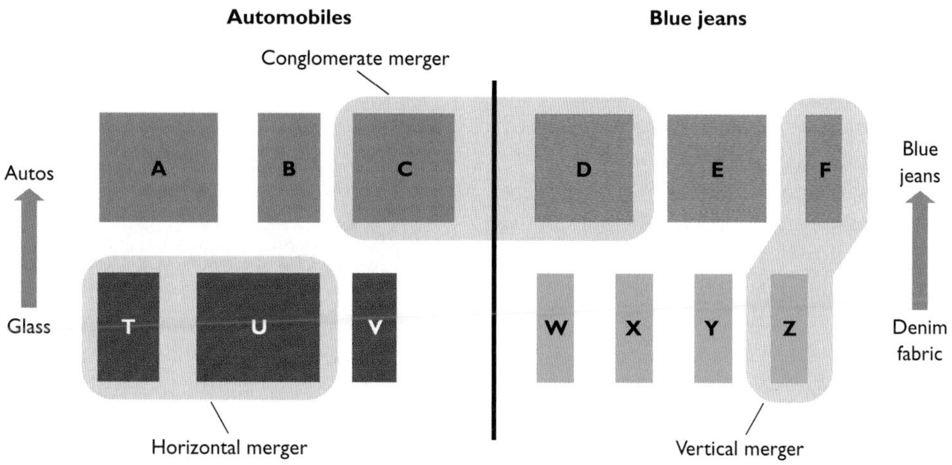

of such mergers include Chase Manhattan's merger with Chemical Bank, Boeing's merger with McDonnell Douglas, and Exxon's merger with Mobil.

A **vertical merger** is a merger between firms at different stages of the production process. In Figure 18.1, the merger between firm Z, a producer of denim fabric, and firm F, a producer of blue jeans, is a vertical merger. Vertical mergers are mergers between firms that have buyer-seller relationships. Actual examples of such mergers are PepsiCo's mergers with Pizza Hut, Taco Bell, and Kentucky Fried Chicken. PepsiCo supplies soft drinks to each of these fast-food outlets. (In 1997, PepsiCo spun off these entities into a separate company now called Yum! Brands.)

A **conglomerate merger** is officially defined as any merger that is not horizontal or vertical; in general, it is the combination of firms in different industries or firms operating in different geographic areas. Conglomerate mergers can extend the line of products sold, extend the territory in which products are sold, or combine totally unrelated companies. In Figure 18.1, the merger between firm C, an auto manufacturer, and firm D, a blue jeans producer, is a conglomerate merger. Real-world examples of conglomerate mergers include the merger between Walt Disney Company (movies) and the American Broadcasting Company (radio and television) and the merger between America Online (Internet service provider) and Time Warner (communications).

Merger Guidelines: The Herfindahl Index The Federal government has established very loose merger guidelines based on the Herfindahl index. Recall from Chapter 11 that this measure of concentration is the sum of the squared percentage market shares of the firms within an industry. An industry of only four firms, each with a 25 percent market share, has a Herfindahl index of 2500 ($= 25^2 + 25^2 + 25^2 + 25^2$). In pure competition, where each firm's market share is minuscule, the index approaches 0 ($= 0^2 + 0^2 + \ldots + 0^2$). In pure monopoly, the index for that single firm is 10,000 ($= 100^2$).

The U.S. government uses Section 7 of the Clayton Act to block horizontal mergers that will substantially lessen competition. It is likely to challenge a horizontal merger if the postmerger Herfindahl index would be high (above 1800) and if the merger has substantially increased the index (added 100 or more points). However, other factors, such as economies of scale, the degree of foreign competition, and the ease of entry of new firms, are also considered. Furthermore, horizontal mergers are usually allowed if one of the merging firms is suffering major and continuing losses. (This is one reason Boeing was allowed to acquire McDonnell Douglas in 1996: MD was losing money in producing its commercial airplanes.)

In recent years, the Federal government has blocked several proposed horizontal mergers. For example, it blocked the mergers between Staples and Office Depot, two major office-supply retailers; WorldCom and Sprint, two competing telecommunications firms; and Hughes (DirecTV) and Echostar (DISH), providers of direct broadcast satellite service.

Most *vertical mergers* escape antitrust prosecution because they do not substantially lessen competition in either of the two markets. (In Figure 18.1 neither the Herfindahl index in the industry producing denim fabric nor the index in the blue jeans industry changes when firms

Z and F merge vertically.) However, a vertical merger between large firms in highly concentrated industries may be challenged. For example, in 1999 the threat of FTC action spurred Barnes & Noble to abandon its merger with Ingram Book group, the nation's largest book wholesaler. The merger would have enabled Barnes & Noble to set the wholesale price of books charged to its direct retail competitors such as Borders and Amazon.com.

Conglomerate mergers are generally permitted. If an auto manufacturer acquires a blue jeans producer, no antitrust action is likely, since neither firm has increased its own market share as a result. That means the Herfindahl index remains unchanged in each industry. **(Key Question 5)**

Price Fixing Price fixing is treated strictly. Evidence of price fixing, even by small firms, will bring antitrust action, as will other collusive activities such as scheming to rig bids on government contracts or dividing up sales in a market. In antitrust law, these activities are known as **per se violations;** they are "in and of themselves" illegal, and therefore are *not* subject to the rule of reason. To gain a conviction, the government or other party making the charge need show only that there was a conspiracy to fix prices, rig bids, or divide up markets, not that the conspiracy succeeded or caused serious damage to other parties.

Price-fixing investigations and court actions are common. We list several relatively recent price-fixing cases in the Consider This box to the right.

Price Discrimination Price discrimination is a common business practice that rarely reduces competition and therefore is rarely challenged by government. The exception occurs when a firm engages in price discrimination as part of a strategy to block entry or drive out competitors.

Tying Contracts The Federal government strictly enforces the prohibition of tying contracts, particularly when practiced by dominant firms. For example, it stopped movie distributors from forcing theaters to buy the projection rights to a full package of films as a condition of showing a blockbuster movie. Also, it prevented Kodak—the dominant maker of photographic film—from requiring that consumers process their film only through Kodak.

What then can we conclude about the overall effectiveness of antitrust laws? Antitrust policy has not been very effective in restricting the rise of or in breaking up monopolies or oligopolies resulting from legally undertaken internal expansions of firms. But most economists do not deem that to be a flaw. The antitrust laws have been used more effectively against predatory or abusive monopoly, but that effectiveness has been diminished by the slow legal process and consequently long time between the filing of charges and the implementation of remedies. In contrast, antitrust policy *has* been effective in blocking blatantly anticompetitive mergers and in identifying and prosecuting price fixing and tying contracts.

Most economists conclude that, overall, U.S. antitrust policy has been moderately effective in achieving its goal of promoting competition and efficiency. Much of the success of antitrust policy arises from its deterrent effect on price fixing and anticompetitive mergers. Some economists,

CONSIDER THIS . . .

Of Catfish and Art (and Other Things in Common)

There are many recent examples of price fixing. Here are just a few:

- In 1996 ConAgra and Hormel agreed to pay more than $21 million to settle their roles in a nationwide price-fixing case involving catfish.
- In 1996 Archer Daniels Midland (ADM) and other agribusinesses admitted fixing the prices of citric acid and an additive to livestock feed. In the early 2000s ADM, Cargill, and Corn Products admitted fixing the price of high-fructose syrup, a sweetener made from corn. In 2004 ADM paid $430 million to resolve the government's antitrust action.
- The U.S. Justice Department fined UCAR International $110 million in 1998 for scheming with competitors to fix prices and divide the world market for graphite electrodes used in steel mills.
- In 2001 a court found the auction houses Sotheby's and Christie's guilty of conspiring over a 6-year period to set the same commission rates for sellers at auctions.
- In the early 2000s, Samsung (South Korea), Hynix Semiconductor (South Korea), Infineon (Germany), and Micron (United States) were found to have fixed the price of dynamic random access memory chips (DRAMs), which are used in personal computers, printers, cell phones, and other electronic devices. In 2004 and 2005, the companies paid fines totaling $645 million.
- In 2002 five major record companies and the three largest music retailers agreed to pay $143 million to settle a price-fixing case involving the setting of "minimum-advertised prices" on compact discs.

however, think that enforcement of antitrust laws has been too weak. Others believe that parts of U.S. antitrust policy are anachronistic in an era of rapidly changing technology that continuously undermines existing monopoly power.

QUICK REVIEW 18.1

- The Sherman Act of 1890 outlaws restraints of trade and monopolization; the Clayton Act of 1914 as amended by the Celler-Kefauver Act of 1950 outlaws price discrimination (when anticompetitive), tying contracts, anticompetitive mergers, and interlocking directorates.
- The Federal Trade Commission Act of 1914 as bolstered by the Wheeler-Lea Act of 1938 created the Federal Trade Commission (FTC) and gave it authority to investigate unfair methods of competition and deceptive acts or practices in commerce.
- "Structuralists" say highly concentrated industries will behave like monopolists; "behaviorists" hold that the relationship between industry structure and firm behavior is uncertain.
- The degree of strictness of enforcement of antitrust laws depends on the general antitrust philosophy of the U.S. administration and its appointees.
- Government treats existing monopoly relatively leniently, as long as it is not abusive; blocks most horizontal mergers between dominant, profitable firms in highly concentrated industries; and vigorously prosecutes price fixing and tying contracts.

Industrial Regulation

Antitrust policy assumes that society will benefit if monopoly is prevented from evolving or if it is dissolved where it already exists. We now return to a special situation in which there is an economic reason for an industry to be organized monopolistically.

Natural Monopoly

A **natural monopoly** exists when economies of scale are so extensive that a single firm can supply the entire market at a lower unit cost than could a number of competing firms. Clear-cut circumstances of natural monopoly are relatively rare, but such conditions exist for many *public utilities*, such as local electricity, water, natural gas, and telephone providers. As we discussed in Chapter 10, large-scale operations in some cases are necessary to obtain low unit costs and a low product price. Where there is natural monopoly, competition is uneconomical. If the market were divided among many producers, economies of scale would not be achieved and unit costs and prices would be higher than necessary.

TABLE 18.1 The Main Regulatory Commissions Providing Industrial Regulation

Commission (Year Established)	Jurisdiction
Federal Energy Regulatory Commission (1930)*	Electricity, gas, gas pipelines, oil pipelines, water-power sites
Federal Communications Commission (1934)	Telephones, television, cable television, radio, telegraph, CB radios, ham operators, etc.
State public utility commissions (50 states)	Electricity, gas, telephones

*Originally called the Federal Power Commission; renamed in 1977.

There are two possible alternatives for promoting better economic outcomes where natural monopoly exists. One is public ownership, and the other is public regulation.

Public ownership or some approximation of it has been established in a few instances. Examples: the Postal Service, the Tennessee Valley Authority, and Amtrak at the national level and mass transit, water supply systems, and garbage collection at the local level.

But *public regulation*, or what economists call *industrial regulation*, has been the preferred option in the United States. In this type of regulation, government commissions regulate the prices (usually called "rates") charged by natural monopolists. Table 18.1 lists the two major Federal regulatory commissions and their jurisdictions. It also notes that all 50 states have commissions that regulate the intrastate activities and "utility rates" of remaining natural monopolies.

The economic objective of industrial regulation is embodied in the **public interest theory of regulation.** In that theory, industrial regulation is necessary to keep a natural monopoly from charging monopoly prices and thus harming consumers and society. The goal of such regulation is to garner for society at least part of the cost reductions associated with natural monopoly while avoiding the restrictions of output and high prices associated with unregulated monopoly. If competition is inappropriate or impractical, society should allow or even encourage a monopoly but regulate its prices. Regulation should then be structured so that ratepayers benefit from the economies of scale—the lower per-unit costs—that natural monopolists are able to achieve.

In practice, regulators seek to establish rates that will cover production costs and yield a "fair" return to the enterprise. The goal is to set price equal to average total cost so that the regulated firm receives a normal profit, as described in the "Regulated Monopoly" section of Chapter 10. In particular, you should carefully review Figure 10.9.

Problems with Industrial Regulation

There is considerable disagreement on the effectiveness of industrial regulation. Let's examine two criticisms.

Costs and Inefficiency

An unregulated firm has a strong incentive to reduce its costs at each level of output because that will increase its profit. The regulatory commission, however, confines the regulated firm to a normal profit or a "fair return" on the value of its assets. If a regulated firm lowers its operating costs, the rising profit eventually will lead the regulatory commission to require that the firm lower its rates in order to return its profits to normal. The regulated firm therefore has little or no incentive to reduce its operating costs.

Worse yet, higher costs do not result in lower profit. Because the regulatory commission must allow the public utility a fair return, the regulated monopolist can simply pass through higher production costs to consumers by charging higher rates. A regulated firm may reason that it might as well have high salaries for its workers, opulent working conditions for management, and the like, since the "return" is the same in percentage terms whether costs are minimized or not. So, although a natural monopoly reduces cost through economies of scale, industrial regulation fosters considerable X-inefficiency (Figure 10.7). Due to the absence of competition, the potential cost savings from natural monopoly may never actually materialize.

Perpetuating Monopoly

A second general problem with industrial regulation is that it sometimes perpetuates monopoly long after the conditions of natural monopoly have ended.

Technological change often creates the potential for competition in some or even all portions of the regulated industry. Examples: Trucks began competing with railroads; transmission of voice and data by microwave and satellites began competing with transmission over telephone wires; satellite television began competing with cable television; and cell phones began competing with regular phones.

But spurred by the firms they regulate, commissions often protect the regulated firms from new competition by either blocking entry or extending regulation to competitors. Industrial regulation therefore may perpetuate a monopoly that is no longer a natural monopoly and would otherwise erode. Ordinary monopoly, protected by government, may supplant natural monopoly. If so, the regulated prices may exceed those that would occur with competition. The beneficiaries of outdated regulation are the regulated firms and their employees. The losers are consumers and the potential entrants.

Example: Regulation of the railroads by the Interstate Commerce Commission (ICC) was justified in the late 1800s and early 1900s. But by the 1930s, with the emergence of a network of highways, the trucking industry had seriously undermined the monopoly power of the railroads. That is, for the transport of many goods over many routes, railroad service was no longer a natural monopoly. At that time it would have been desirable to dismantle the ICC and let railroads and truckers, along with barges and airlines, compete with one another. Instead, in the 1930s the ICC extended regulation of rates to interstate truckers. The ICC remained in place until its elimination in 1996.

Second example: Until recently, unregulated long-distance telephone companies such as AT&T and MCI have been prohibited from offering local telephone services in competition with regulated local and regional telephone companies. But the very fact that these and other firms wanted to compete with regulated monopolies calls into question whether those local providers are in fact natural monopolies or, rather, are government-protected monopolies. **(Key Question 10)**

Legal Cartel Theory

The regulation of potentially competitive industries has produced the **legal cartel theory of regulation.** In place of having socially minded officials forcing regulation on natural monopolies to protect consumers, holders of this view see practical politicians "supplying" regulation to local, regional, and national firms that fear the impact of competition on their profits or even on their long-term survival. These firms desire regulation because it yields a legal monopoly that can virtually guarantee a profit. Specifically, the regulatory commission performs such functions as blocking entry (for example, in local telephone service). Or, where there are several firms, the commission divides up the market much like an illegal cartel (for example, prior to airline deregulation, the Civil Aeronautics Board assigned routes to specific airlines). The commission may also restrict potential competition by enlarging the "cartel" (for example, the ICC's addition of trucking to its regulatory domain).

While private cartels are illegal and unstable and often break down, the special attraction of a government-sponsored cartel under the guise of regulation is that it endures. The legal cartel theory of regulation suggests that regulation results from the rent-seeking activities of private firms and the desire of politicians to be responsive (Chapter 17).

Proponents of the legal cartel theory of regulation note that the Interstate Commerce Commission was welcomed by the railroads and that the trucking and airline industries both supported the extension of ICC regulation to their industries, arguing that unregulated competition was severe and destructive.

Occupational licensing is a labor market application of the legal cartel theory. Certain occupational groups—barbers, dentists, hairstylists, interior designers, dietitians, lawyers—demand stringent licensing on the grounds that it protects the public from charlatans and quacks. But skeptics say the real reason may be to limit entry into the occupational group so that practitioners can receive monopoly incomes. It is not surprising to these skeptics that a recent study found that, other things equal, dental fees were about 15 percent higher and dentists' income 10 percent higher in states with the most restrictive licensing laws compared to states with the least restricitive laws. The quality of dentistry apparently was not affected.[1]

Deregulation

Beginning in the 1970s, evidence of inefficiency in regulated industries and the contention that the government was regulating potentially competitive industries contributed to a wave of deregulation. Since then, Congress and many state legislatures have passed legislation that has deregulated in varying degrees the airline, trucking, banking, railroad, natural gas, television, and electricity industries. Deregulation has also occurred in the telecommunications industry, where antitrust authorities dismantled the regulated monopoly known as the Bell System (AT&T). Deregulation in the 1970s and 1980s was one of the most extensive experiments in economic policy to take place during the last 50 years.

While there are still some critics of deregulation, most economists believe that deregulation has clearly benefited consumers and the economy. Studies reveal that deregulation of formerly regulated industries is contributing more than $50 billion annually to society's well-being through lower prices, lower costs, and increased output.[2] Most of those gains are accruing in three industries: airlines, railroads, and trucking. Airfares (adjusted for inflation) have declined by about one-third, and airline safety has continued to improve. Trucking and railroad freight rates (again, adjusted for inflation) have dropped by about one-half.

Significant efficiency gains also have occurred in long-distance telecommunications, and there have been slight efficiency gains in cable television, stock brokerage services, and the natural gas industry. Moreover, deregulation has unleashed a wave of technological advances that have resulted in such new and improved products and services as fax machines, cellular phones, fiber-optic cable, microwave systems in communications, and the Internet.

The most recent and perhaps controversial industry to be deregulated is electricity. Deregulation is relatively advanced at the wholesale level, where firms can buy and sell electricity at market prices. They are also free to build generating facilities and sell electricity to local electricity providers at unregulated prices. In addition, several states have deregulated retail prices and encouraged households and businesses to choose among available electricity suppliers. This competition has generally lowered electricity rates for consumers and enhanced allocative efficiency.

But deregulation suffered a severe setback in California, where wholesale electricity prices, but not retail rates, were deregulated. Wholesale electricity prices surged in 2001 when California experienced electricity shortages. Because they could not pass on wholesale price increases to consumers, California electric utilities suffered large financial losses. California has recently filed lawsuits against several energy-trading companies that allegedly manipulated electricity supplies to boost the wholesale price of electricity during the California energy crisis. One multibillion-dollar energy trader—Enron—collapsed in 2002 when Federal investigators uncovered a pattern of questionable and fraudulent business and accounting practices.

The California deregulation debacle and the Enron collapse have muddied the overall assessment of electricity deregulation in the United States. It is simply far too soon to declare deregulation either a success or a failure.

QUICK REVIEW 18.2

- Natural monopoly occurs where economies of scale are so extensive that only a single firm can produce the product at minimum average total cost.
- The public interest theory of regulation says that government must regulate natural monopolies to prevent abuses arising from monopoly power. Regulated firms, however, have less incentive than competitive firms to reduce costs. That is, regulated firms tend to be X-inefficient.
- The legal cartel theory of regulation suggests that some firms seek government regulation to reduce price competition and ensure stable profits.
- Deregulation initiated by government in the past three decades has yielded large annual efficiency gains for society.

[1]Morris Kleiner and Robert Kudrle, "Does Regulation Affect Economic Outcomes? The Case of Dentistry," *Journal of Law and Economics*, October 2000, pp. 547–582.

[2]Clifford Winston, "Economic Deregulation: Days of Reckoning for Microeconomists," *Journal of Economic Literature*, September 1993, p. 1284; and Robert Crandall and Jerry Ellig, "Economic Deregulation and Consumer Choice," Center for Market Processes, Fairfax, Virginia.

Social Regulation

The industrial regulation discussed in the preceding section has focused on the regulation of prices (or rates) in natural monopolies. But in the early 1960s a new type of regulation began to emerge. This *social regulation* is concerned with the conditions under which goods and services are produced, the impact of production on society, and the physical qualities of the goods themselves.

The Federal government carries out most of the social regulation, although states also play a role. In Table 18.2 we list the main Federal regulatory commissions engaged in social regulation.

Distinguishing Features

Social regulation differs from industrial regulation in several ways.

First, social regulation applies to far more firms than does industrial regulation. Social regulation is often applied "across the board" to all industries and directly affects more producers than does industrial regulation. For instance, while the industrial regulation of the Federal Energy Regulatory Commission (FERC) applies to a relatively small number of firms, Occupational Safety and Health Administration (OSHA) rules and regulations apply to firms in all industries.

Second, social regulation intrudes into the day-to-day production process to a greater extent than industrial regulation. While industrial regulation focuses on rates, costs, and profits, social regulation often dictates the design of products, the conditions of employment, and the nature of the production process. As examples, the Consumer Product Safety Commission (CPSC) regulates the design of potentially unsafe products, and the Environmental Protection Agency (EPA) regulates the amount of pollution allowed during production.

TABLE 18.2 The Main Federal Regulatory Commissions Providing Social Regulation

Commission (Year Established)	Jurisdiction
Food and Drug Administration (1906)	Safety and effectiveness of food, drugs, and cosmetics
Equal Employment Opportunity Commission (1964)	Hiring, promotion, and discharge of workers
Occupational Safety and Health Administration (1971)	Industrial health and safety
Environmental Protection Agency (1972)	Air, water, and noise pollution
Consumer Product Safety Commission (1972)	Safety of consumer products

Finally, social regulation has expanded rapidly during the same period in which industrial regulation has waned. Between 1970 and 1980, the U.S. government created 20 new social regulatory agencies. More recently, Congress has established new social regulations to be enforced by existing regulatory agencies. For example, the Equal Employment Opportunity Commission, which is responsible for enforcing laws against workplace discrimination on the basis of race, gender, age, or religion, has been given the added duty of enforcing the Americans with Disabilities Act of 1990. Under this social regulation, firms must provide reasonable accommodations for qualified workers and job applicants with disabilities. Also, sellers must provide reasonable access for customers with disabilities.

The names of the regulatory agencies in Table 18.2 suggest the reasons for their creation and growth: As much of our society had achieved a fairly affluent standard of living by the 1960s, attention shifted to improvement in the nonmaterial quality of life. That focus called for safer products, less pollution, improved working conditions, and greater equality of economic opportunity.

The Optimal Level of Social Regulation

While economists agree on the need for social regulation, they disagree on whether or not the current level of such regulation is optimal. Recall that an activity should be expanded as long as its marginal benefit (MB) exceeds its marginal cost (MC). If the MB of social regulation exceeds its MC, then there is too little social regulation. But if MC exceeds MB, there is too much (review Figure 16.6). Unfortunately, the marginal costs and benefits of social regulation are not always easy to measure and therefore may be illusory. So ideology about the proper size and role of government often drives the debate over social regulation as much as, or perhaps more than, economic cost-benefit analysis.

In Support of Social Regulation Defenders of social regulation say that it has achieved notable successes and, overall, has greatly enhanced society's well-being. They point out that the problems that social regulation confronts are serious and substantial. According to the National Safety Council, about 5000 workers die annually in job-related accidents and 3.8 million workers suffer injuries that force them to miss a day or more of work. Air pollution continues to cloud major U.S. cities, imposing large costs in terms of reduced property values and increased health care expense. Numerous children and adults die each year because of poorly designed or manufactured products (for example, car tires) or tainted food (for example, *E. coli* in beef). Discrimination against some ethnic and racial minorities, persons with disabilities, and older workers reduces their earnings and imposes heavy costs on society.

Proponents of social regulation acknowledge that social regulation is costly. But they correctly point out that a high "price" for something does not necessarily mean that it should not be purchased. They say that the appropriate economic test should be not whether the costs of social regulation are high or low but, rather, whether the benefits of social regulation exceed the costs. After decades of neglect, they further assert, society cannot expect to cleanse the environment, enhance the safety of the workplace, and promote economic opportunity for all without incurring substantial costs. So statements about the huge costs of social regulation are irrelevant, say defenders, since the benefits are even greater. The public often underestimates those benefits, since they are more difficult to measure than costs and often become apparent only after some time has passed (for example, the benefits of reducing global warming).

Proponents of social regulation point to its many specific benefits. Here are just a few examples: It is estimated that highway fatalities would be 40 percent greater annually in the absence of auto safety features mandated through regulation. Compliance with child safety-seat and seat belt laws has significantly reduced the auto fatality rate for small children. The national air quality standards set by law have been reached in nearly all parts of the nation for sulfur dioxide, nitrogen dioxide, and lead. Moreover, recent studies clearly link cleaner air, other things equal, with increases in the values of homes. Affirmative action regulations have increased the labor demand for racial and ethnic minorities and females. The use of childproof lids has resulted in a 90 percent decline in child deaths caused by accidental swallowing of poisonous substances.

Some defenders of social regulation say there are many remaining areas in which greater regulation would generate net benefits to society. For instance, some call for greater regulation of the meat, poultry, and seafood industries to improve food safety. Others favor greater regulation of health care organizations and insurance companies to ensure "patients' rights" for consumers of health care services. Still others say that more regulation is needed to ensure that violent movies, CDs, and video games are not marketed to children.

Advocates of social regulation say that the benefits of such regulation are well worth the considerable costs. The costs are simply the price we must pay to create a hospitable, sustainable, and just society. **(Key Question 12)**

Criticisms of Social Regulation

Critics of social regulation contend that, in many instances, it has been expanded to the point where the marginal costs exceed the marginal benefits. In this view, society would achieve net benefits by cutting back on irritating social regulation. Critics say that many social regulation laws are poorly written, making regulatory objectives and standards difficult to understand. As a result, regulators pursue goals well beyond the original intent of the legislation. Businesses complain that regulators often press for additional increments of improvement, unmindful of costs.

Also, decisions must often be made and rules formed on the basis of inadequate information. Examples: Consumer Product Safety Commission (CPSC) officials may make decisions about certain cancer-causing ingredients in products on the basis of limited laboratory experiments with animals. Or government agencies may establish costly pollution standards to attack the global-warming problem without knowing for certain whether pollution is the main cause of the problem. These efforts, say critics, lead to excessive regulation of business.

Moreover, critics argue that social regulations produce many unintended and costly side effects. For instance, the Federal gas mileage standard for automobiles has been blamed for an estimated 2000 to 3900 traffic deaths a year because auto manufacturers have reduced the weight of vehicles to meet the higher miles-per-gallon standards. Other things equal, drivers of lighter cars have a higher fatality rate than drivers of heavier vehicles.

Finally, opponents of social regulation say that the regulatory agencies may attract overzealous workers who are hostile toward the market system and "believe" too fervently in regulation. For example, the EPA staff allegedly sees all pollution as bad and all polluters as "bad guys." They have been accused of avoiding the challenge of trying to identify the optimal amount of pollution based on a careful analysis of marginal costs and marginal benefits.

Two Reminders

The debate over the proper amount of social regulation will surely continue. We leave both proponents and opponents of social regulation with pertinent economic "reminders."

Last *Word*

United States v. Microsoft

The Recent Microsoft Antitrust Case Is the Most Significant Monopoly Case since the Breakup of AT&T in the Early 1980s.

The Charges In May 1998 the U.S. Justice Department (under President Clinton), 19 individual states, and the District of Columbia (hereafter, "the government") filed antitrust charges against Microsoft under the Sherman Antitrust Act. The government charged that Microsoft had violated Section 2 of the act through a series of unlawful actions designed to maintain its "Windows" monopoly. It also charged that some of that conduct violated Section 1 of the Sherman Act.

Microsoft denied the charges, arguing it had achieved its success through product innovation and lawful business practices. Microsoft contended it should not be penalized for its superior foresight, business acumen, and technological prowess. It also pointed out that its monopoly was highly transitory because of rapid technological advance.

The District Court Findings In June 2000 the district court ruled that the relevant market was software used to operate Intel-compatible personal computers (PCs). Microsoft's 95 percent share of that market clearly gave it monopoly power. The court pointed out, however, that being a monopoly is not illegal. The violation of the Sherman Act occurred because Microsoft used anticompetitive means to maintain its monopoly power.

According to the court, Microsoft feared that the success of Netscape's Navigator, which allowed people to browse the Internet, might allow Netscape to expand its software to include a competitive PC operating system—software that would threaten the Windows monopoly. It also feared that Sun's Internet applications of its Java programming language might eventually threaten Microsoft's Windows monopoly.

To counter these and similar threats, Microsoft illegally signed contracts with PC makers that required them to feature Internet Explorer on the PC desktop and penalized companies that promoted software products that competed with Microsoft products. Moreover, it gave friendly companies coding that linked Windows to software applications and withheld such coding from companies featuring Netscape. Finally, under license from Sun, Microsoft developed Windows-related Java software that made Sun's own software incompatible with Windows.

The District Court Remedy The district court ordered Microsoft to split into two competing companies, one initially selling the Windows operating system and the other initially selling Microsoft applications (such as Word, Hotmail, MSN, PowerPoint, and Internet Explorer). Both companies would be free to develop new products that compete with each other, and both could derive those products from the intellectual property embodied in the common products existing at the time of divestiture.

There Is No Free Lunch On the one hand, fervent supporters of social regulation need to remember that "there is no free lunch." Social regulation can produce higher prices, stifle innovation, and reduce competition.

Social regulation raises product prices in two ways. It does so directly because compliance costs normally get passed on to consumers, and it does so indirectly by reducing labor productivity. Resources invested in making workplaces accessible to disabled workers, for example, are not available for investment in new machinery designed to increase output per worker. Where the wage rate is fixed, a drop in labor productivity increases the marginal and average total costs of production. In effect, the supply curve for the product shifts leftward, causing the price of the product to rise.

Social regulation may have a negative impact on the rate of innovation. Technological advance may be stifled by, say, the fear that a new plant will not meet EPA guidelines or that a new medicine will require years of testing before being approved by the Food and Drug Administration (FDA).

Social regulation may weaken competition, since it usually places a relatively greater burden on small firms than on large ones. The costs of complying with social regulation are, in effect, fixed costs. Because smaller firms produce less output over which to distribute those costs, their compliance costs per unit of output put them at a competitive disadvantage with their larger rivals. Social regulation is more likely to force smaller firms out of business, thus contributing to the increased concentration of industry.

Less Government Is Not Always Better than More On the other hand, fervent opponents of social regulation need to remember that less government is not always better than more government. While the market system is a powerful engine of producing goods

The Appeals Court Ruling In late 2000 Microsoft appealed the district court decision to a U.S. court of appeals. In 2001 the higher court affirmed that Microsoft illegally maintained its monopoly, but tossed out the district court's decision to break up Microsoft. It agreed with Microsoft that the company was denied due process during the penalty phase of the trial and concluded that the district court judge had displayed an appearance of bias by holding extensive interviews with the press. The appeals court sent the remedial phase of the case to a new district court judge to determine appropriate remedies. The appeals court also raised issues relating to the wisdom of a structural remedy.

The Final Settlement At the urging of the new district court judge, the Federal government (now under President Bush) and Microsoft negotiated a proposed settlement. With minor modification, the settlement became the final court order in 2002. The breakup was rescinded and replaced with a behavioral remedy. It (1) prevents Microsoft from retaliating against any firm that is developing, selling, or using software that competes with Microsoft Windows or Internet Explorer or is shipping a personal computer that includes both Windows and a non-Microsoft operating system; (2) requires Microsoft to establish uniform royalty and licensing terms for computer manufacturers wanting to include Windows on their PCs; (3) requires that manufacturers be allowed to remove Microsoft icons and replace them with other icons on the Windows desktop; and (4) calls for Microsoft to provide technical information to other companies so that they can develop programs that work as well with Windows as Microsoft's own products.

The Microsoft actions and conviction have indirectly resulted in billions of dollars of fines and payouts by Microsoft. Main examples: To AOL Time Warner (Netscape), $750 million; to the European Commission, $600 million; to Sun Microsystems, $1.6 billion; to Novell, $536 million; to Burst.com, $60 million; to Gateway, $150 million, to InterTrust, $440 million; to RealNetworks, $761 million; and to IBM, $850 million.

Source: United States v. Microsoft (District Court Conclusions of Law), April 2000; *United States v. Microsoft* (Court of Appeals), June 2001; *U.S. v. Microsoft* (Final Judgment), November 2002; and Reuters and Associated Press News Services.

and services and generating income, it has its flaws. Through social regulation government can clearly increase economic efficiency and thus society's well-being. Ironically, by "taking the rough edges off of capitalism," social regulation may be a strong pro-capitalist force. Properly conceived and executed, social regulation helps maintain political support for the market system. Such support could quickly wane should there be a steady drumbeat of reports of unsafe workplaces, unsafe products, discriminatory hiring, choking pollution, ill-served medical patients, and the like. Social regulation helps the market system deliver not only goods and services but also a "good society."

QUICK REVIEW 18.3

- Social regulation is concerned with the conditions under which goods and services are produced, the effects of production on society, and the physical characteristics of the goods themselves.
- Defenders of social regulation point to the benefits arising from policies that keep dangerous products from the marketplace, reduce workplace injuries and deaths, contribute to clean air and water, and reduce employment discrimination.
- Critics of social regulation say uneconomical policy goals, inadequate information, unintended side effects, and overzealous personnel create excessive regulation, for which regulatory costs exceed regulatory benefits.

Summary

1. The cornerstones of antitrust policy are the Sherman Act of 1890 and the Clayton Act of 1914. The Sherman Act specifies that "every contract, combination . . . or conspiracy in the restraint of interstate trade . . . is . . . illegal" and that any person who monopolizes or attempts to monopolize interstate trade is guilty of a felony.
2. If a company is found guilty of violating the antimonopoly provisions of the Sherman Act, the government can either break up the monopoly into competing firms (a structural remedy) or prohibit it from engaging in specific anticompetitive business practices (a behavioral remedy).
3. The Clayton Act was designed to bolster and make more explicit the provisions of the Sherman Act. It declares that price discrimination, tying contracts, intercorporate stock acquisitions, and interlocking directorates are illegal when their effect is to reduce competition.
4. The Federal Trade Commission Act of 1914 created the Federal Trade Commission to investigate antitrust violations and to prevent the use of "unfair methods of competition." Empowered to issue cease-and-desist orders, the commission also serves as a watchdog agency over false and deceptive representation of products.
5. The Celler-Kefauver Act of 1950 prohibits one firm from acquiring the assets of another firm when the result will curtail competition.
6. Issues in applying antitrust laws include (a) determining whether an industry should be judged by its structure or by its behavior; (b) defining the scope and size of the dominant firm's market; and (c) deciding how strictly to enforce the antitrust laws.
7. Antitrust officials are more likely to challenge price fixing, tying contracts, and horizontal mergers than they are to break up existing monopolies. Nevertheless, antitrust suits by the Federal government led to the breakup of the AT&T monopoly in the early 1980s.
8. The objective of industrial regulation is to protect the public from the market power of natural monopolies by regulating prices and quality of service.
9. Critics of industrial regulation contend that it can lead to inefficiency and rising costs and that in many instances it constitutes a legal cartel for the regulated firms. Legislation passed in the late 1970s and the 1980s has brought about varying degrees of deregulation in the airline, trucking, banking, railroad, and television broadcasting industries.
10. Studies indicate that deregulation of airlines, railroads, trucking, and telecommunications is producing sizable annual gains to society through lower prices, lower costs, and increased output. Less certain is the effect of the more recent deregulation of the electricity industry.
11. Social regulation is concerned with product safety, working conditions, and the effects of production on society. Whereas industrial regulation is on the wane, social regulation continues to expand. The optimal amount of social regulation occurs where MB = MC.
12. Those who support social regulation point to its numerous specific successes and assert that it has greatly enhanced society's well-being. Critics of social regulation contend that businesses are excessively regulated to the point where marginal costs exceed marginal benefits. They also say that social regulation often produces unintended and costly side effects.

Terms and Concepts

antitrust policy
industrial regulation
social regulation
Sherman Act
Clayton Act
tying contracts
interlocking directorates
Federal Trade Commission Act
cease-and-desist order
Wheeler-Lea Act
Celler-Kefauver Act
Standard Oil case
U.S. Steel case
rule of reason
Alcoa case
DuPont cellophane case
Microsoft case
horizontal merger
vertical merger
conglomerate merger
per se violations
natural monopoly
public interest theory of regulation
legal cartel theory of regulation

Study Questions

1. Both antitrust policy and industrial regulation deal with monopoly. What distinguishes the two approaches? How does government decide to use one form of remedy rather than the other?
2. **KEY QUESTION** Describe the major provisions of the Sherman and Clayton acts. What government entities are responsible for enforcing those laws? Are firms permitted to initiate antitrust suits on their own against other firms?
3. Contrast the outcomes of the Standard Oil and U.S. Steel cases. What was the main antitrust issue in the DuPont cellophane case? In what major way do the Microsoft and Standard Oil cases differ?
4. Why might one administration interpret and enforce the antitrust laws more strictly than another? How might a change of administrations affect a major monopoly case in progress?
5. **KEY QUESTION** How would you expect antitrust authorities to react to:
   a. A proposed merger of Ford and General Motors.
   b. Evidence of secret meetings by contractors to rig bids for highway construction projects.
   c. A proposed merger of a large shoe manufacturer and a chain of retail shoe stores.
   d. A proposed merger of a small life-insurance company and a regional candy manufacturer.
   e. An automobile rental firm that charges higher rates for last-minute rentals than for rentals reserved weeks in advance.
6. Suppose a proposed merger of firms would simultaneously lessen competition and reduce unit costs through economies of scale. Do you think such a merger should be allowed?
7. In the 1980s, PepsiCo Inc., which then had 28 percent of the soft-drink market, proposed to acquire the Seven-Up Company. Shortly thereafter the Coca-Cola Company, with 39 percent of the market, indicated it wanted to acquire the Dr. Pepper Company. Seven-Up and Dr. Pepper each controlled about 7 percent of the market. In your judgment, was the government's decision to block these mergers appropriate?
8. Why might a firm charged with violating the Clayton Act, Section 7, try arguing that the products sold by the merged firms are in separate markets? Why might a firm charged with violating Section 2 of the Sherman Act try convincing the court that none of its behavior in achieving and maintaining its monopoly was illegal?
9. "The social desirability of any particular firm should be judged not on the basis of its market share but on the basis of its conduct and performance." Make a counterargument, referring to the monopoly model in your statement.
10. **KEY QUESTION** What types of industries, if any, should be subjected to industrial regulation? What specific problems does industrial regulation entail?
11. In view of the problems involved in regulating natural monopolies, compare socially optimal (marginal-cost) pricing and fair-return pricing by referring again to Figure 10.9. Assuming that a government subsidy might be used to cover any loss resulting from marginal-cost pricing, which pricing policy would you favor? Why? What problems might such a subsidy entail?
12. **KEY QUESTION** How does social regulation differ from industrial regulation? What types of benefits and costs are associated with social regulation?
13. Use economic analysis to explain why the optimal amount of product safety may be less than the amount that would totally eliminate risks of accidents and deaths. Use automobiles as an example.
14. **LAST WORD** Under what law and on what basis did the Federal district court find Microsoft guilty of violating the antitrust laws? What was the initial district court's remedy? How did Microsoft fare with its appeal to the court of appeals? Was the final remedy in the case a structural remedy or a behavioral remedy?

Web-Based Questions

1. **THE FTC AND THE ANTITRUST DIVISION—RECENT LEGAL ACTIONS** Go to the FTC Web site, **www.ftc.gov/ftc/antitrust.htm,** to find press releases in the Newsroom. Briefly summarize two antitrust (not false advertising) actions taken by the FTC over the past 12 months. Next, go to the Web site of the U.S. Department of Justice's Antitrust Division, **www.usdoj.gov/atr/index.html,** and select What's New and All Press Releases. Briefly summarize two antitrust actions taken by the Antitrust Division during the past 12 months.
2. **THE CONSUMER PRODUCT SAFETY COMMISSION—WHAT IS IT AND WHAT DOES IT DO?** What are the major functions of the Consumer Product Safety Commission, **www.cpsc.gov?** Name two products from the current Most Wanted list and explain why they are dangerous. From Recalls and Product Safety News, identify two product categories of interest to you. List three specific product recalls for each of your two product categories.

19

IN THIS CHAPTER YOU WILL LEARN:

- **Why agricultural prices and farm income are unstable.**
- **Why huge numbers of labor resources have exited U.S. agriculture during the past several decades.**
- **The rationale for farm subsidies and the economics and politics of price supports (price floors).**
- **Major criticisms of the price-support system in agriculture.**
- **The main elements of existing Federal farm policy.**

Agriculture: Economics and Policy

If you eat, you are part of agriculture! In the United States, agriculture is important for a number of reasons. It is one of the nation's largest industries and major segments of it provide real-world examples of the pure-competition model (Chapter 9). Also, agriculture clearly shows the effects of government policies that interfere with supply and demand. Further, the industry provides excellent illustrations of Chapter 17's special-interest effect and rent-seeking behavior. Finally, it demonstrates the globalization of markets for farm commodities.

This chapter examines the circumstances in agriculture that have resulted in government intervention, the types and outcomes of government intervention, and recent major changes in farm policy.

Economics of Agriculture

Although economists refer to "the agriculture industry," this segment of the economy is extremely diverse. Agriculture encompasses cattle ranches, fruit orchards, dairies, poultry plants, pig farms, grain farms, feed lots, vegetable plots, sugar-cane plantations, and much more. Some farm commodities (for example, soybeans and corn) are produced by thousands of individual farmers; other farm commodities (such as poultry) are produced by just a handful of large firms. Some farm products (for example, wheat, milk, and sugar) are heavily subsidized through Federal government programs; other farm products (such as fruits, nuts, and potatoes) receive little if any government support.

Moreover, agriculture includes both farm products, or **farm commodities** (for example, wheat, soybeans, cattle, and rice,) and also **food products** (items sold through restaurants or grocery stores). Generally, the number of competing firms in the market diminishes as farm products are refined into commercial food products. Although thousand of ranches and farms raise cattle, only four firms (Tyson, Smithfield, Swift, and Excel) account for 82 percent of red meat produced at cattle slaughtering/meat packing plants. And thousands of farms grow tomatoes, but only three companies (Heinz, Del-Monte, and Hunt) make the bulk of the catsup sold in the United States.

Our focus in this chapter will be on farm commodities (or farm products) and the farms and ranches that produce them. Farm commodities usually are sold in highly competitive markets, whereas food products tend to be sold in markets characterized by monopolistic competition or oligopoly.

Partly because of large government subsidies, farming remains a generally profitable industry. U.S. consumers allocate 14 percent of their spending to food and farmers and ranchers receive about $250 billion of revenue annually. Over the years, however, American farmers have experienced severely fluctuating prices and periodically low incomes. Further, they have had to adjust to the reality that agriculture is a declining industry. The farm share of GDP has declined from about 7 percent in 1950 to 1 percent today.

Let's take a close look at both the short-run and long-run economics of U.S. agriculture.

The Short Run: Price and Income Instability

Price and income instability in agriculture results from (1) an inelastic demand for agricultural products, combined with (2) fluctuations in farm output and (3) shifts of the demand curve for farm products.

Inelastic Demand for Agricultural Products

In industrially advanced economies, the price elasticity of demand for agricultural products is low. For agricultural products in the aggregate, the elasticity coefficient is between .20 and .25. These figures suggest that the prices of farm products would have to fall by 40 to 50 percent for consumers to increase their purchases by a mere 10 percent. Consumers apparently put a low value on additional farm output compared with the value they put on additional units of alternative goods.

Why is this so? Recall that the basic determinant of elasticity of demand is substitutability. When the price of one product falls, the consumer tends to substitute that product for other products whose prices have not fallen. But in relatively wealthy societies this "substitution effect" is very modest for food. Although people may eat more, they do not switch from three meals a day to, say, five or six meals a day in response to a decline in the relative prices of farm products. Real biological factors constrain an individual's capacity to substitute food for other products.

The inelasticity of agricultural demand is also related to diminishing marginal utility. In a high-income economy, the population is generally well fed and well clothed; it is relatively saturated with the food and fiber of agriculture. Additional farm products therefore are subject to rapidly diminishing marginal utility. So very large price cuts are needed to induce small increases in food and fiber consumption.

Fluctuations in Output Farm output tends to fluctuate from year to year, mainly because farmers have limited control over their output. Floods, droughts, unexpected frost, insect damage, and similar disasters can mean poor crops, while an excellent growing season means bumper crops (unusually large outputs). Such natural occurrences are beyond the control of farmers, yet they exert an important influence on output.

In addition to natural phenomena, the highly competitive nature of many parts of farming and ranching makes it difficult for those producers to form huge combinations to control production. If the thousands of widely scattered and independent producers happened to plant an unusually large or abnormally small portion of their land one year, an extra-large or a very small farm output would result even if the growing season were normal.

Curve *D* in Figure 19.1 suggests the inelastic demand for agricultural products. Combining that inelastic demand with the instability of farm production, we can see why agricultural prices and incomes are unstable. Even if the market demand for farm products remains fixed at *D*, its price inelasticity will magnify small changes in output into

FIGURE 19.1 The effects of changes in farm output on agricultural prices and income. Because of the inelasticity of demand for farm products, a relatively small change in farm output (from Q_n to Q_p or Q_b) will cause a relatively large change in agricultural prices (from P_n to P_p or P_b). Farm income will change from the orange area to the larger $0P_ppQ_p$ area or to the smaller $0P_bbQ_b$ area.

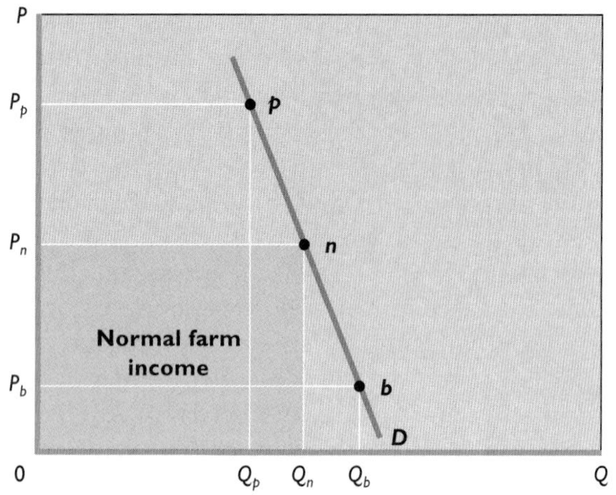

FIGURE 19.2 The effect of a demand shift on agricultural prices and income. Because of the highly inelastic demand for farm products, a small shift in demand (from D_1 to D_2) for farm products can drastically alter agricultural prices (P_1 to P_2) and farm income (area $0P_1aQ_n$ to area $0P_2bQ_n$), given a fixed level of production Q_n.

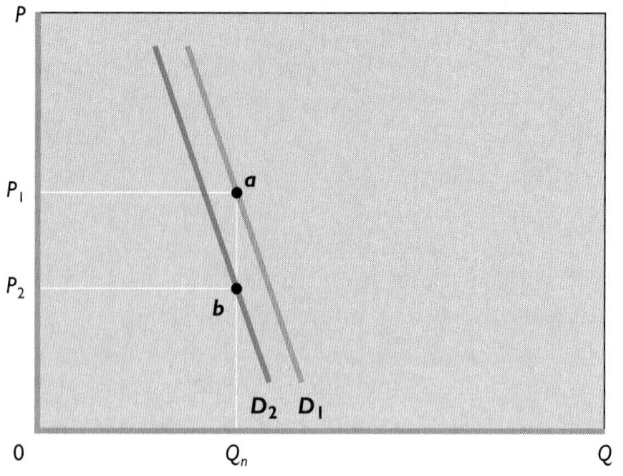

relatively large changes in agricultural prices and income. For example, suppose that a "normal" crop of Q_n results in a "normal" price of P_n and a "normal" farm income represented by the orange rectangle. A bumper crop or a poor crop will cause large deviations from these normal prices and incomes because of the inelasticity of demand.

If a good growing season occurs, the resulting large crop of Q_b will reduce farm income to that of area $0P_bbQ_b$. When demand is inelastic, an increase in the quantity sold will be accompanied by a more-than-proportionate decline in price. The net result is that total revenue, that is, total farm income, will decline disproportionately.

Similarly, a small crop caused by, say, drought will boost total farm income to that represented by area $0P_ppQ_p$. A decline in output will cause a more-than-proportionate increases in price and income when demand is inelastic. Ironically, for farmers as a group, a poor crop may be a blessing and a bumper crop a hardship.

Conclusion: With a stable market demand for farm products, the inelasticity of that demand will turn relatively small changes in output into relatively larger changes in agricultural prices and income.

Fluctuations in Demand

The third factor in the short-run instability of farm income results from shifts in the demand curve for agricultural products. Suppose that somehow farm output is stabilized at the "normal" level of Q_n in Figure 19.2. Now, because of the inelasticity of the demand for farm products, short-run changes in the demand for those products will cause markedly different prices and incomes to be associated with this fixed level of output.

A slight decline in demand from D_1 to D_2 will reduce farm income from area $0P_1aQ_n$ to $0P_2bQ_n$. So a relatively small decline in demand gives farmers significantly less income for the same amount of farm output. Conversely, a slight increase in demand—as from D_2 to D_1—provides a sizable increase in farm income for the same volume of output. Again, large price and income changes occur because demand is inelastic.

It is tempting to argue that the sharp declines in agricultural prices that accompany a decrease in demand will cause many farmers to close down in the short run, reducing total output and alleviating the price and income declines. But farm production is relatively insensitive to price changes in the short run because farmers' fixed costs are high compared with their variable costs.

Interest, rent, tax, and mortgage payments on land, buildings, and equipment are the major costs faced by the farmer. These are all fixed charges. Furthermore, the labor supply of farmers and their families can also be regarded as a fixed cost. As long as they stay on their farms, farmers cannot reduce their costs by firing themselves. Their variable costs are the costs of the small amounts of extra help they may employ, as well as expenditures for seed, fertilizer, and fuel. As a result of their high proportion of fixed costs, farmers are usually better off working their land even when they are losing money, since they would lose much more by shutting down their operations for the year. Only in the long run will exiting the industry make sense for them.

But why is agricultural demand unstable? The major source of demand volatility in U.S. agriculture springs from its dependence on world markets. As we show in

FIGURE 19.3 U.S. farm exports as a percentage of farm output, 1950–2005. Exports of farm output have increased as a percentage of total farm output in the United States. But this percentage has been quite variable, contributing greatly to the instability of the demand for U.S. farm output.

Source: U.S. Department of Agriculture and Federal Reserve Bank of St. Louis.

Figure 19.3, that dependency has increased since 1950. The figure also reveals that, as a percentage of total U.S. farm output, farm exports are highly unstable.

The incomes of U.S. farmers are sensitive to changes in weather and crop production in other countries: Better crops abroad mean less foreign demand for U.S. farm

FIGURE 19.4 Inflation-adjusted U.S. agricultural prices, selected commodities, 1950–1998. Inflation-adjusted U.S. prices (in 1998 dollars) for cattle, hogs, corn, and wheat during the second half of the twentieth century reflected both volatility and general decline.

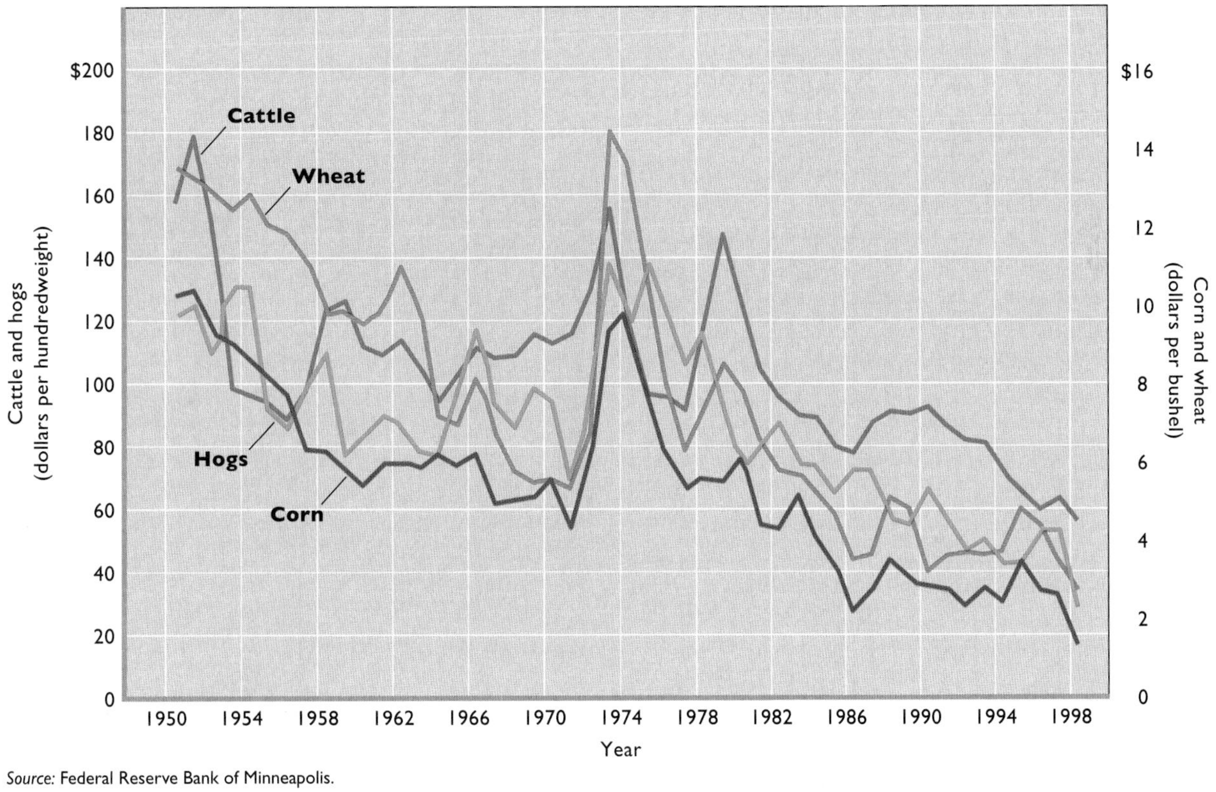

Source: Federal Reserve Bank of Minneapolis.

products. Similarly, cyclical fluctuations in incomes in Europe or Southeast Asia, for example, may shift the demand for U.S. farm products. Changes in foreign economic policies may also change demand. For instance, if the nations of western Europe decide to provide their farmers with greater protection from foreign competition, U.S. farmers will have less access to those markets and demand for U.S. farm exports will fall.

International politics also add to demand instability. Changing political relations between the United States and China and the United States and Russia have boosted exports to those countries in some periods and reduced them in others. Changes in the international value of the dollar may also be critical. Depreciation of the dollar increases the demand for U.S. farm products (which become cheaper to foreigners), whereas appreciation of the dollar diminishes foreign demand for U.S. farm products.

To summarize: The increasing importance of exports has amplified the short-run instability of the demand for U.S. farm products. Farm exports are affected not only by weather, income fluctuations, and economic policies abroad but also by international politics and changes in the international value of the dollar. **(Key Question 1)**

Figure 19.4 shows inflation-adjusted U.S. prices for cattle, hogs, corn, and wheat during the second half of the twentieth century. The short-run economics of price volatility is evident. So too are the general decline of real (inflation-adjusted) agricultural prices.

The Long Run: A Declining Industry

Two dynamic characteristics of agricultural markets explain why agriculture has been a declining industry:

- Over time, the supply of farm products has increased rapidly because of technological progress.
- The demand for farm products has increased slowly, because it is inelastic with respect to income.

Let's examine each of these supply and demand forces.

Technology and Supply Increases

A rapid rate of technological advance has significantly increased the supply of agricultural products. This technological progress has many roots: the mechanization of farms, improved techniques of land management, soil conservation, irrigation, development of hybrid crops, availability of improved fertilizers and insecticides, polymer-coated seeds, and improvements in the breeding and care of livestock. The amount of capital used per farmworker increased 15 times between 1930 and 1980, permitting a fivefold increase in the amount of land cultivated per farmer. The simplest measure of these advances is the increasing number of people a single farmer's output will support. In 1820 each farmworker produced enough food and fiber to

CONSIDER THIS . . .

Risky Business

The short-run instability of agricultural prices and farm income create considerable risk in agriculture. Later in this chapter we will find that farm programs (direct payments, countercyclical payments, and "repay-or-default" loans) reduce the risk of farming for many farmers. But these programs are limited to certain crops, such as grains and oilseeds.

Fortunately, several private techniques for managing risk have become commonplace in agriculture. The purpose of these measures is to "smooth" income over time, "hedging" against short-run output and price fluctuations. Hedging is an action by a buyer or seller to protect against a change in future prices prior to an anticipated purchase or sale.

Farm risk-management techniques include:

- ***Futures markets.*** In the futures market, farmers can buy or sell farm products at prices fixed now, for delivery at a specified date in the future. If the price falls, farmers will still obtain revenue based on the higher price fixed in the futures market. If the price rises, the buyer will benefit by getting the farm commodity at the lower fixed price in the future contract.
- ***Contracting with processors.*** In advance of planting, farmers can directly contract with food processors (firms such as sugar beet refiners, ethanol plants, and feed lots) to assure themselves of a fixed price per unit of their farm or ranch output.
- ***Crop revenue insurance.*** Farmers can buy crop revenue insurance, which insures them against gross revenue losses resulting from storm damage and other natural occurrences.
- ***Leasing land.*** Farm operators can reduce their risk by leasing some of their land to other operators who pay them cash rent. The rent payment is stable, regardless of the quality of the crop and crop prices.
- ***Nonfarm income.*** Many farm households derive substantial parts of their total income from off-farm income, such as spousal work and agricultural investments. These more-stable elements of income cushion the instability of farm income.

Although farming remains a risky business, farm operators have found creative ways to manage the inherent risk of price and income instability.

support 4 people; by 1948, about 13. By 2005 each farmer produced enough to support 105 people. Unquestionably, the physical volume of farm output per unit of farm labor in agriculture has risen spectacularly. Over the last 55 years, this physical productivity in agriculture has advanced twice as fast as that in the nonfarm economy.

Most of the technological advances in agriculture were not initiated by farmers. Rather, they are the result of government-sponsored programs of research and education and the initiative of the suppliers of farm inputs. Land-grant colleges, experiment stations, county agents of the Agricultural Extension Service, educational pamphlets issued by the United States Department of Agriculture (USDA), and the research departments of farm machinery, pesticide, and fertilizer producers have been the primary sources of technological advance in U.S. agriculture.

More recently, technological advance has been fueled by the incorporation of advanced information technologies into farming. Computers and the Internet give farmers instant access to information about soil conditions, estimated crop yields, farm-product prices, available land for purchase or lease, and much more. They also provide farmers with sophisticated business software to help track and manage their operations.

Lagging Demand Increases in the demand for agricultural products have failed to keep pace with these technologically created increases in the supply of the products. The reason lies in the two major determinants of agricultural demand: income and population.

In developing countries, consumers must devote most of their meager incomes to agricultural products—food and clothing—to sustain themselves. But as income expands beyond subsistence and the problem of hunger diminishes, consumers increase their outlays on food at ever-declining rates. Once consumers' stomachs are filled, they turn to the amenities of life that manufacturing and services, not agriculture, provide. Economic growth in the United States has boosted average per capita income far beyond the level of subsistence. As a result, increases in the incomes of U.S. consumers now produce less-than-proportionate increases in spending on farm products.

The demand for farm products in the United States is income-inelastic; it is quite insensitive to increases in income. Estimates indicate that a 10 percent increase in real per capita after-tax income produces about a 2 percent increase in consumption of farm products. That means a coefficient of income elasticity of .2 (= .02/.10). So as the incomes of Americans rise, the demand for farm products increases far less rapidly than the demand for goods and services in general.

The second reason for lagging demand relates to population growth. Once a certain income level has been reached, each consumer's intake of food and fiber becomes relatively fixed. Thus subsequent increases in demand depend directly on growth in the number of consumers. In most advanced nations, including the United States, the demand for farm products increases at a rate roughly equal to the rate of population growth. Because U.S. population growth has not been rapid, the increase in U.S. demand for farm products has not kept pace with the rapid growth of farm output.

Graphical Portrayal The combination of an inelastic and slowly increasing demand for agricultural products with a rapidly increasing supply puts strong downward pressure on agricultural prices and income. Figure 19.5 shows a large increase in agricultural supply accompanied by a very modest increase in demand. Because of the inelasticity of demand, those modest shifts result in a sharp decline in agricultural prices, accompanied by a relatively small increase in output. So farm income declines. On the graph, we see that farm income before the increases in demand and supply (measured by rectangle $0P_1aQ_1$) exceeds farm income after those increases ($0P_2bQ_2$). Because of an inelastic demand for farm products, an increase in supply of such products relative to demand creates persistent downward pressure on farm income.

FIGURE 19.5 The long-run decline of agricultural prices and farm income. In the long run, increases in the demand for U.S. farm products (from D_1 to D_2) have not kept pace with the increases in supply (from S_1 to S_2) resulting from technological advances. Because agricultural demand is inelastic, these shifts have tended to depress agricultural prices (from P_1 to P_2) and reduce farm income (from $0P_1aQ_1$ to $0P_2bQ_2$) while increasing output only modestly (from Q_1 to Q_2).

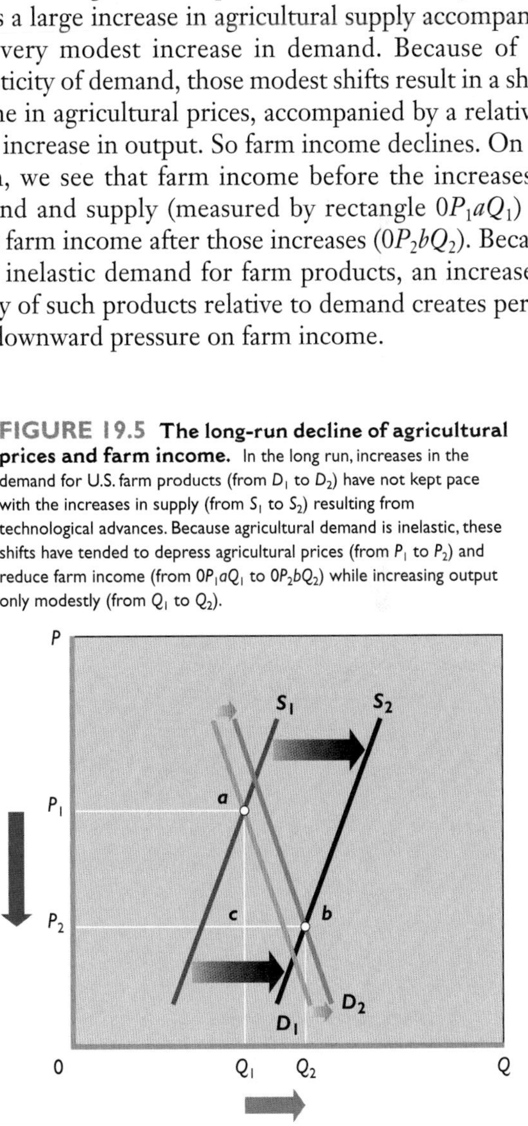

Consequences The actual consequences of the demand and supply changes over time have been those predicted by the pure-competition model. The supply and demand conditions just outlined have increased the minimum efficient scale (MES) in agriculture and reduced crop prices. Farms that are too small to realize productivity gains and take advantage of economies of scale have discovered that their average total costs exceed the (declining) prices for their crops. So they can no longer operate profitably. In the long run, financial losses in agriculture have triggered a massive exit of workers to other sectors of the economy, as shown by Table 19.1. They have also caused a major consolidation of smaller farms into larger ones. A person farming, say, 240 acres of corn three decades ago is today likely to be farming two or three times that number of acres. Large corporate firms, collectively called **agribusiness,** have emerged in some areas of farming such as potatoes, beef, fruits, vegetables, and poultry. Today, there are about 2 million farms compared to 4 million in 1960, and farm labor constitutes about 2 percent of the U.S. labor force compared to 11 percent in 1960. (Global Perspective 19.1 compares the most recent labor-force percentages for several nations.)

GLOBAL PERSPECTIVE 19.1

Percentage of Labor Force in Agriculture, Selected Nations

High-income nations devote a much smaller percentage of their labor forces to agriculture than do low-income nations. Because their workforces are so heavily committed to producing the food and fiber needed for their populations, low-income nations have relatively less labor available to produce housing, schools, autos, and the other goods and services that contribute to a high standard of living.

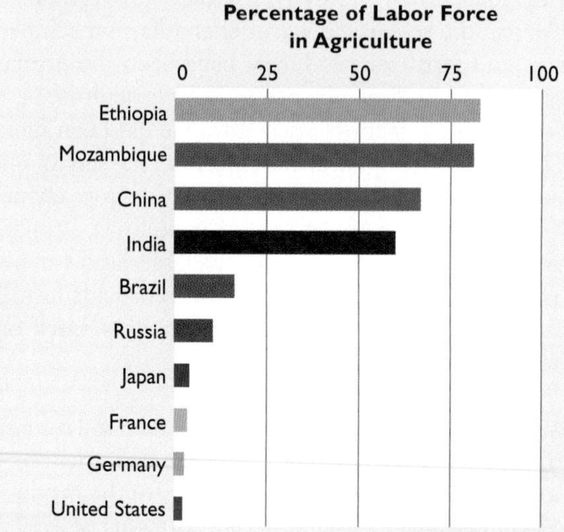

Source: World Resources Institute, **www.wri.org/.** Latest data for each country.

Farm-Household Income

Traditionally, the income of farm households was well below that of nonfarm households. But even with the lower real crop prices, that imbalance has reversed. In 2004—a particularly good year for agriculture—the average income of farm households was $81,480 compared to $60,528 for all U.S. households. Outmigration, consolidation, rising farm productivity, and significant government subsidies have boosted farm income *per farm household* (of which there are fewer than before).

Also, members of farm households operating smaller farms have increasingly taken jobs in nearby towns and cities. On average, only 17 percent of the income of farm households derives from farming activities. This average, however, is pulled downward by the many households living in rural areas and operating small "residential farms." For households operating "commercial farms"—farms with annual sales of $250,000 or more—a very high percentage of income derives from farming. In 2004 commercial-farm households on average earned about three times as much as did the average (farm + nonfarm) household in the United States. Although agriculture is a declining industry relative to the entire economy, the remaining, fewer operators of commercial farms in the United States are doing remarkably well, at least as a group. **(Key Question 3)**

TABLE 19.1 U.S. Farm Employment and Number of Farms, 1950–2004

	Farm Employment*		
Year	In Millions of People	As Percentage of Total Employment	Number of Farms, Thousands
1950	9.9	17	5388
1960	7.1	11	3962
1970	4.5	6	2954
1980	3.7	4	2440
1990	2.9	2	2146
2000	3.0	2	2172
2004	3.1	2	2113

*Includes self-employed farmers, unpaid farmworkers, and hired farmworkers. Authors' estimates for 2004 based on 2002 data.

Sources: U.S. Department of Agriculture, Economic Research Service, **www.nass.usda.gov/,** and U.S. Department of Commerce, Census Bureau, **www.census.gov/.**

QUICK REVIEW 19.1

- Agricultural prices and incomes are volatile in the short run because an inelastic demand converts small changes in farm output and demand into relatively larger changes in prices and income.
- Technological progress has generated large increases in the supply of farm products over time.
- Increases in demand for farm products have been modest in the United States, because demand is inelastic with respect to income and because population growth has been modest.
- The combination of large increases in supply and small increases in demand has made U.S. agriculture a declining industry (as measured by the value of agricultural output as a percentage of GDP).

GLOBAL PERSPECTIVE 19.2

Agricultural Subsidies, Selected Nations

Farmers in various countries receive large percentages of their incomes as government subsidies.

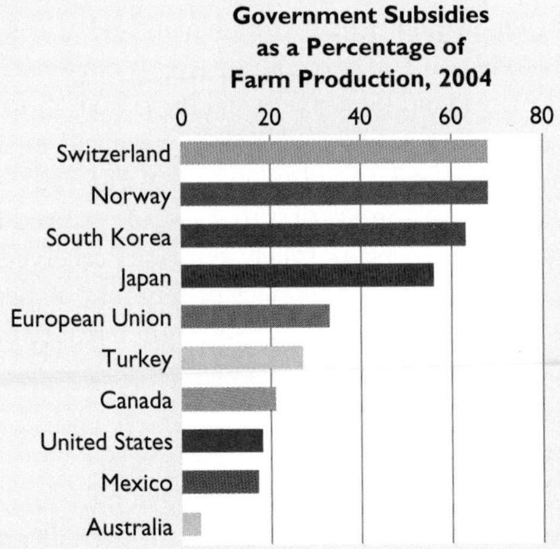

Source: Organization for Economic Cooperation and Development, **www.oecd.org.**

Economics of Farm Policy

The U.S. government has subsidized agriculture since the 1930s with a "farm program" that includes (1) support for agricultural prices, income, and output; (2) soil and water conservation; (3) agricultural research; (4) farm credit; (5) crop insurance; and (6) subsidized sale of farm products in world markets.

We will focus on the main element of farm policy: the programs designed to prop up prices and income. This topic is particularly timely because in recent years (specifically, 1996 and 2002) Congress passed new farm laws replacing traditional forms of farm subsidies with new forms. To understand these new policies, we need to understand the policies they replaced and the purposes and outcomes of farm subsidies. Between 2000 and 2005, American farmers received an average of $21.6 billion of direct government subsidies each year. (As indicated in Global Perspective 19.2, farm subsidies are common in many nations.)

Rationale for Farm Subsidies

A variety of arguments have been made to justify farm subsidies over the decades:

- Although farm products are necessities of life, many farmers have relatively low incomes, so they should receive higher prices and incomes through public help.
- The "family farm" is a fundamental U.S. institution and should be nurtured as a way of life.
- Farmers are subject to extraordinary hazards—floods, droughts, and insects—that most other industries do not face. Without government help, farmers cannot fully insure themselves against these disasters.
- While many farmers face purely competitive markets for their outputs, they buy inputs of fertilizer, farm machinery, and gasoline from industries that have considerable market power. Whereas those resource supplying industries are able to control their prices, farmers are at the "mercy of the market" in selling their output. The supporters of subsidies argue that agriculture warrants public aid to offset the disadvantageous terms of trade faced by farmers.

Background: The Parity Concept

The Agricultural Adjustment Act of 1933 established the **parity concept** as a cornerstone of agricultural policy. The rationale of the parity concept can be stated in both real and nominal terms. In real terms, parity says that year after year for a fixed output of farm products, a farmer should be able to acquire a specific total amount of other goods and services. A particular real output should always result in the same real income: "If a farmer could take a bushel of corn to town in 1912 and sell it for enough money to buy a shirt, he should be able to sell a bushel of corn today and buy a shirt." In nominal terms, the parity concept suggests that the relationship between the prices received by farmers for their output and the prices they must pay for goods and services should remain constant. The parity concept implies that if the price of shirts tripled over some time period, then the price of corn should have tripled too. Such a situation is said to represent 100 percent of parity.

The **parity ratio** is the ratio of prices received to prices paid, expressed as a percentage. That is:

$$\text{Parity ratio} = \frac{\text{prices received by farmers}}{\text{prices paid by farmers}}$$

Why farmers would benefit from having the prices of their products based on 100 percent of parity is obvious. By 2005 nominal prices paid by farmers had increased 16-fold since 1900–1914, whereas nominal prices received by farmers had increased only 7-fold. In 2005 the parity ratio stood at .40 (or 40 percent), indicating that prices received in 2005 could buy 40 percent as much as prices received in the 1910–1914 period. So farm policy calling for 100 percent of parity would require substantially higher prices for farm products.

Economics of Price Supports

The concept of parity provides the rationale for government price floors on farm products. In agriculture those minimum prices are called **price supports.** We have shown that, in the long run, the market prices received by farmers have not kept up with the prices paid by them. One way to achieve parity, or some percentage thereof, is to have the government establish above-equilibrium price supports for farm products.

Many different price-support programs have been tried, but they all tend to have similar effects, some of which are subtle and negative. Suppose in Figure 19.6 that the equilibrium price is P_e and the price support is P_s. Then the major effects would be as follows.

FIGURE 19.6 Price supports, agricultural surpluses, and transfers to farmers. The market demand *D* and supply *S* of a farm product yield equilibrium price P_e and quantity Q_e. An above-equilibrium price support P_s results in consumption of quantity Q_c, production of quantity Q_s, and a surplus of quantity Q_sQ_c. The orange rectangle represents a transfer of money from taxpayers to farmers.

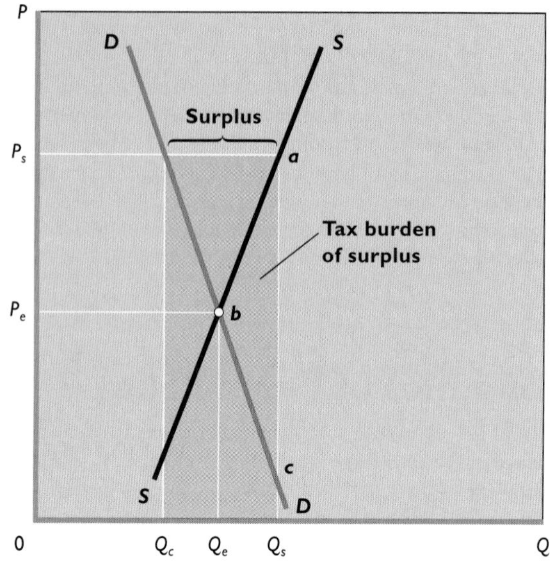

Surplus Output

The most obvious result is a product surplus. Consumers are willing to purchase only Q_c units at the supported price, while farmers supply Q_s units. What about the Q_sQ_c surplus that results? The government must buy it to make the above-equilibrium price support effective. As you will see, this surplus farm output means that agriculture receives an overallocation of resources.

Gain to Farmers

Farmers benefit from price supports. In Figure 19.6, gross farm revenue rises from the free-market level represented by area $0P_ebQ_e$ to the larger, supported level shown by area $0P_saQ_s$.

Loss to Consumers

Consumers lose; they pay a higher price (P_s rather than P_e) and consume less (Q_c rather than Q_e) of the product. In some instances differences between the market price and the supported price are substantial. For example, the U.S.-supported price of a pound of sugar is about two times the world market price, and a quart of fluid milk is estimated to cost consumers twice as much as it would without government programs. Moreover, the burden of higher food prices falls disproportionately on the poor because they spend a larger part of their incomes on food.

Efficiency Losses

Society loses because price supports create allocative inefficiency by encouraging an overallocation of resources to agriculture. A price floor (P_s) attracts more resources to the agricultural sector than would the free-market price (P_e). Viewed through the pure-competition model, the market supply curve in Figure 19.6 represents the marginal costs of all farmers producing this product at the various output levels. An efficient allocation of resources occurs at point *b*, where the market price P_e is equal to marginal cost. So the output Q_e reflects that efficient allocation of resources.

In contrast, the output Q_s associated with the price support P_s represents an overallocation of resources; for all units of output between Q_e and Q_s, marginal costs (measured on curve *S*) exceed the prices people are willing to pay for those units (measured on curve *D*). Simply stated, the marginal cost of the extra production exceeds its marginal benefit to society. Society incurs an efficiency loss (or a deadweight loss) from the price-support system.

Other Social Losses

Society at large loses in other ways.

Taxpayers pay higher taxes to finance the government's purchase of the surplus. This added tax burden is equal to the surplus output Q_sQ_c multiplied by its price P_s, as shown by the orange area in Figure 19.6. Recall, too, that the mere collection of taxes imposes an efficiency loss (Figure 17.5). Also, the cost of storing surplus farm output adds to this tax burden.

Government's intervention in agriculture also entails administrative costs. Thousands of government workers are needed to administer U.S. price supports and other farm programs.

Finally, the rent-seeking activity involved—the pursuit of political support to maintain price supports—is costly and socially wasteful. Farm groups spend considerable sums to sustain political support for price floors and other programs that enhance farm incomes.

Environmental Costs

We know from Figure 19.6 that price supports encourage additional production. Although some of that extra output may come from the use of additional land, much of it comes from heavier use of fertilizer and pesticides. Those pesticides and fertilizers may pollute the environment (for example, groundwater) and create residues in food that pose health risks to farmworkers and consumers. Research shows a positive relationship between the level of price-support subsidies and the use of agrochemicals.

Farm policy also may cause environmental problems in less obvious ways. Farmers benefit from price supports only when they use their land consistently for a specific crop such as corn or wheat. That creates a disincentive to practice crop rotation, which is a nonchemical technique for controlling pests. Farm policy thus encourages the substitution of chemicals for other forms of pest control.

Also, we know from the concept of derived demand that an increase in the price of a product will increase the demand for relevant inputs. In particular, price supports for farm products increase the demand for land. And the land that farmers bring into farm production is often environmentally sensitive "marginal" land, such as steeply sloped, erosion-prone land, or wetlands that provide wildlife habitat. Similarly, price supports result in the use of more water for irrigation, and the resulting runoff may contribute to soil erosion.

International Costs

Actually, the costs of farm price supports go beyond those indicated by Figure 19.6. Price supports generate economic distortions that cross national boundaries. For example, price supports make the U.S. agricultural market attractive to foreign producers. But inflows of foreign agricultural products would serve to increase supplies in the United States, aggravating the problem of U.S. surpluses. To prevent that from happening, the United States is likely to impose import barriers in the form of tariffs or quotas. Those barriers tend to restrict the output of more efficient foreign producers while encouraging more output from less efficient U.S. producers. The result is a less efficient use of world agricultural resources. This chapter's Last Word suggests that this is indeed the case for sugar.

Similarly, as the United States and other industrially advanced countries with similar agricultural programs dump surplus farm products on world markets, the prices of such products are depressed. Developing countries are often heavily dependent on world commodity markets for their incomes. So they are particularly hurt because their export earnings are reduced. Thus, U.S. subsidies for rice production have imposed significant costs on Thailand, a major rice exporter. Similarly, U.S. cotton programs have adversely affected Egypt, Mexico, and other cotton-exporting nations. **(Key Question 8)**

Reduction of Surpluses

Figure 19.6 suggests that programs designed to reduce market supply (shift *S* leftward) or increase market demand (shift *D* rightward) would help boost the market price toward the supported price P_s. Further, such programs would reduce or eliminate farm surpluses. The U.S. government has tried both supply and demand approaches to reduce or eliminate surpluses.

Restricting Supply

Until recently, public policy focused mainly on restricting farm output. In particular, **acreage allotments** accompanied price supports. In return for guaranteed prices for their crops, farmers had to agree to limit the number of acres they planted in that crop. The U.S. Department of Agriculture first set the price support and then estimated the amount of the product consumers would buy at the supported price. It then translated that amount into the total number of planted acres necessary to provide it. The total acreage was apportioned among states, counties, and ultimately individual farmers.

These supply-restricting programs were only partially successful. They did not eliminate surpluses, mainly because acreage reduction did not result in a proportionate decline in production. Some farmers retired their worst land and kept their best land in production. They also cultivated their tilled acres more intensively. Superior seed, more and better fertilizer and insecticides, and improved farm equipment were used to enhance output per acre. And nonparticipating farmers expanded their planted acreage in anticipation of overall higher prices. Nevertheless, the net effect of acreage allotment undoubtedly was a reduction of farm surpluses and their associated costs to taxpayers.

Bolstering Demand Government has tried several ways to increase demand for U.S. agricultural products. For example, both government and private industry have spent large sums on research to create new uses for agricultural goods. The production of "gasohol," which is a blend of gasoline and alcohol (ethanol) made from grain, is one such successful attempt to increase the demand for farm output. Recent attempts to promote "biodiesel," a fuel made from soybean oil and other natural vegetable oils, also fit the demand-enhancement approach. Thus far, such endeavors—even though heavily subsidized—have been only modestly successful in bolstering the overall demand for farm products.

The government has also created a variety of programs to stimulate domestic consumption of farm products. For example, the objective of the food-stamp program is not only to reduce hunger but also to bolster the demand for food. Similarly, the Food for Peace program has enabled developing countries to buy U.S. surplus farm products with their own currencies, rather than having to use dollars. The Federal government spends millions of dollars each year to advertise and promote global sales of U.S. farm products. Furthermore, U.S. negotiators have pressed hard in international trade negotiations to persuade foreign nations to reduce trade barriers to the importing of farm products.

During the era of price supports, the government's supply-restricting and demand-increasing efforts boosted agricultural prices and reduced surplus production, but they did not succeed in eliminating the sizable surpluses.

QUICK REVIEW 19.2

- The parity concept suggests that farmers should obtain a constant ratio of the prices they receive for their farm products and the prices they pay for goods and services in general.
- Price supports are government-imposed price floors (minimum prices) on selected farm products.
- Price supports cause surplus production (which the government must buy and store); raise farm income; increase food prices to consumers; and overallocate resources to agriculture.
- Domestic price supports encourage nations to erect trade barriers against imported farm products and to dump surplus farm products on world markets.

Criticisms and Politics

After decades of experience with government price-support programs, it became apparent in the 1990s that farm policy was not working well. Major criticisms of farm subsidies emerged, as did more skeptical analysis of the politics of those subsidies.

Criticisms of the Parity Concept

Economists uniformly rejected the rationale of the parity concept. They found no economic logic in the proposition that if a bushel of wheat could buy a shirt in 1900, it should still be able to buy a shirt several decades later. The relative values of goods and services are established by supply and demand, and those relative values change over time as technology changes, resource prices change, tastes change, and substitute resources and new products emerge. A fully equipped personal computer, monitor, and printer could buy an inexpensive new automobile in 1985. That was not true just a decade later, because the price of computer equipment had dropped so dramatically. Based on the parity concept, one could argue that price supports and subsidies were justified for computer manufacturers!

Criticisms of the Price-Support System

Criticisms of the price-support system were equally severe.

Symptoms, Not Causes The price-support strategy in agriculture was designed to treat the symptoms, not the causes of the farm problem. The root cause of the long-run farm problem was misallocation of resources between agriculture and the rest of the economy. Historically, the problem had been one of too many farmers. The effect of that misallocation was relatively low agricultural prices and low farm income. But the price and income supports encouraged people to stay in farming rather than move to nonfarm occupations. That is, the price and income orientation of the farm program slowed the reallocation of resources necessary to resolve the long-run farm problem.

Misguided Subsidies Because price supports were on a per-bushel basis, the subsidy system benefited those farmers who needed subsidies the least. If the goal of farm policy was to raise low farm incomes, it followed that any program of Federal aid should have been aimed at farmers with the lowest incomes. But the poor, low-output farmer did not produce and sell enough in the market to get much aid from price supports. Instead, the large, prosperous farmer reaped the benefits because of sizable output. On equity grounds, direct income payments to struggling farmers are highly preferable to indirect price-support subsidies that go primarily to large-scale, prosperous farmers. Better yet, say many economists, would be transition and retraining support for farmers willing to move out of farming and into other occupations and businesses in greater demand.

A related point concerns land values. The price and income benefits that the price-support system provided increased the value of farmland. By making crops more valuable, price supports made the land itself more valuable. That was helpful to farmers who owned the land they farmed but not to farmers who rented land. Farmers rented about 40 percent of their farmland, mostly from well-to-do nonfarm landlords. So, price supports became a subsidy to people who were not actively engaged in farming.

Policy Contradictions

Because farm policy had many objectives, it often led to contradictions. Whereas most subsidized research was aimed at increasing farm productivity and the supply of farm products, acreage-allotment programs required that farmers take land out of production in order to reduce supply. Price supports for crops meant increased feed costs for ranchers and farmers and high consumer prices for animal products. Tobacco farmers were subsidized even though tobacco consumption was causing serious health problems. The U.S. sugar program raised prices for domestic producers by imposing import quotas that conflicted with free-trade policies. Conservation programs called for setting aside land for wildlife habitat, while price supports provided incentives to bring such acreage into production.

All these criticisms helped spawn policy reform. Nevertheless, as we will see, those reforms turned out to be less substantive than originally conceived. Nearly all these criticisms are as valid for current farm policy as they were for the price-support program.

The Politics of Farm Policy

In view of these criticisms, why did the United States continue its price-support program for 60 years and why does it still continue that program for sugar, milk, and tobacco? Why do farm subsidies in the billions of dollars still occur?

Public Choice Theory Revisited

Public choice theory (Chapter 17) helps answer these questions. Recall that rent-seeking behavior occurs when a group (a labor union, firms in a specific industry, or farmers producing a particular crop) uses political means to transfer income or wealth to itself at the expense of another group or of society as a whole. And recall that the special-interest effect involves a program or policy from which a small group receives large benefits at the expense of a much larger group whose members individually suffer small losses. Both rent-seeking behavior and the special-interest effect help explain the politics of farm subsidies.

Suppose a certain group of farmers, say, peanut or sugar producers, organize and establish a well-financed political action committee (PAC). The PAC's job is to promote government programs that will transfer income to the group (this is rent-seeking behavior). The PAC vigorously lobbies U.S. senators and representatives to enact or to continue price supports, production quotas, or import quotas for peanuts or sugar. The PAC does this in part by making political contributions to sympathetic legislators. Although peanut production is heavily concentrated in a few states such as Georgia, Alabama, and Texas, the peanut PAC will also make contributions to legislators from other states in order to gain support.

But how can a small interest group like peanut or sugar growers successfully lobby to increase its own income at the expense of society as a whole? Because, even though the total cost of the group's programs might be considerable, the cost imposed on each individual taxpayer is small (this is the special-interest effect). Taxpayers are likely to be uninformed about and indifferent to such programs, since they have little at stake. Unless you grow sugar beets or peanuts, you probably have no idea how much these programs cost you as an individual taxpayer and consumer and therefore do not object when your legislator votes for, say, a sugar-support program. Thus, the PAC encounters little or no lobbying against its efforts.

Political logrolling—the trading of votes on policies and programs—also works to perpetuate certain programs: Senator Foghorn agrees to vote for a program that benefits Senator Moribund's constituents, and Moribund returns the favor. Example: Many members of Congress who represent low-income urban areas vote in favor of farm subsidies. In return, representatives of agricultural areas support such programs as food stamps, which subsidize food for the poor. The result is a rural-urban coalition through which representatives from both areas provide benefits for their constituents and enhance their reelection chances. Such coalitions help explain why farm subsidies persist and why the food-stamp program was, until recently, regularly expanded over the years.

Large agribusinesses that supply inputs to agriculture also lend political support to farm subsidies because subsidies increase the amounts of agrochemicals and farm machinery that farmers are able to buy. And most of the thousands of government employees whose jobs depend on farm programs are highly supportive. So, too, are owners of farmland.

Last Word

The Sugar Program: A Sweet Deal

The Sugar Program Is a Sweet Deal for Domestic Sugar Producers, but It Imposes Heavy Costs on Domestic Consumers, Domestic Candy Manufacturers, Foreign Producers, and the American Economy.

The continuing U.S. sugar program uses price supports and import quotas to guarantee a minimum price of sugar for domestic sugar producers. The program has significant effects, both domestically and internationally.

Domestic Costs Price supports and import quotas have boosted the domestic price of sugar to twice the world price (for 2004, $.23 per pound compared to the international price of $.11 per pound). The estimated aggregate cost to domestic consumers is between $1.5 billion and $1.9 billion per year. In contrast, each sugar producer receives from subsidies alone an amount estimated to be twice the nation's average family income. In one recent year, a single producer received an estimated $30 million in benefits. Many sugar producers obtain more than $1 million each year in benefits.

Import Quotas As a consequence of high U.S. domestic price supports, foreign sugar producers have a strong incentive to sell their output in the United States. But an influx of lower-priced foreign sugar into the U.S. domestic market would undermine U.S. price supports. The government therefore has imposed import quotas on foreign sugar. It decides how much sugar can be imported at a zero or very low tariff rate, and then it charges a prohibitively high tariff for any quantities above that amount. As the gap between U.S.-supported prices and world prices has widened, imports have declined as a percentage of sugar consumed in the United States. In 1975, about 30 percent of the sugar consumed in the United States was imported; currently about 16 percent comes from abroad. Domestic policy regarding the U.S. sugar industry largely dictates the nation's international trade policy with respect to sugar.

Developing Countries The loss of the U.S. market has had several harmful effects on sugar-exporting developing countries such as the Philippines, Brazil, and several Central American countries.

First, exclusion from the U.S. market has significantly reduced their export revenues—by an amount estimated to be many billions of dollars per year. That decline in export revenues is important, because many of the sugar-producing countries depend on such revenues to pay interest and principal on large debts owed to the United States and other industrially advanced nations.

Public choice theory also tells us that politicians are likely to favor programs that have hidden costs. As we have seen, that is often true of farm programs. Our discussion of Figure 19.6 indicated that price supports involve not simply a transfer of money from taxpayer to farmer but costs that are hidden as higher food prices, storage costs for surplus output, costs of administering farm programs, and costs associated with both domestic and international misallocations of resources. Because those costs are largely indirect and hidden, farm programs are much more acceptable to politicians and the public than they would be if all costs were explicit.

Changing Politics

In spite of rent seeking, special interests, and logrolling, a combination of factors has somewhat altered the politics of farm subsidies.

Declining Political Support As the farm population declines, agriculture's political power weakens. The farm population was about 25 percent of the general population in the 1930s, when many U.S. farm programs were established; now it is less than 2 percent. Urban congressional representatives now constitute a 10-to-1 majority over their rural colleagues. An increasing number of legislators are critically examining farm programs for their effects on consumers' grocery bills as well as on farm incomes. Also, more farmers themselves are coming to resent the intrusion of the Federal government into their farming decisions. Many rural-state congressional members now support free-market agriculture.

World Trade Considerations The United States has taken the lead to reduce barriers to world trade in agricultural products. This has also contributed to the more critical attitude toward farm subsidies, particularly price supports. The nations of the European Union (EU) and many other nations support agricultural prices. And, to maintain their high domestic prices, they restrict imports of foreign farm products by imposing tariffs and quotas. They then try to rid themselves of their domestic

Second, barred by quotas from sale in the U.S. market, the sugar produced by the developing countries has been added to world markets, where the increased supply has depressed the world price of sugar.

Third, domestic price supports have caused U.S. sugar production to expand to the extent that the United States may soon change from a sugar-importing to a sugar-exporting nation. That is, the U.S. sugar program may soon be a source of new competition for the sugar producers of the developing countries. Sugar price supports in the European Union have already turned that group of nations into sugar exporters.

U.S. Efficiency Loss The sugar program benefits sugar producers by about $1 billion annually but costs U.S. consumers about $1.5 billion to $1.9 billion each year. The excess of losses over gains is therefore $500 million to $900 million annually. This efficiency loss (or deadweight loss) results from the overallocation of U.S. resources to growing and processing sugar beets and sugar cane.

As a secondary effect, the higher domestic sugar prices have encouraged several U.S. confectionery firms (candy manufacturers) to relocate their domestic operations to Canada or Mexico. According to the U.S. Commerce Department, for every American job that has been added by the price supports in the cane sugar and sugar beet industries, three American jobs have been lost in the industries buying sugar. The total job loss in the confectionery industry is estimated at 10,000 workers since 1997.

Global Resource Misallocation Both domestically and globally, the sugar price-support programs of the United States and other industrially advanced economies have distorted the worldwide allocation of agricultural resources. Price supports have caused a shift of resources to sugar production by less efficient U.S. producers, and U.S. import quotas and consequent low world sugar prices have caused more efficient foreign producers to restrict their production. Thus high-cost producers are producing more sugar and low-cost producers are producing less, resulting in the inefficient use of the world's agricultural resources.

Adding to the inefficient use of world resources, the relocation of candy manufacturers—to avoid artificially sweetened U.S. sugar prices—is moving capital and labor resources away from their place of comparative advantage.

surpluses by subsidizing exports into world markets. The effects on the United States are that (1) trade barriers hinder U.S. farmers from selling to EU nations and (2) subsidized exports from those nations depress world prices for agricultural products, making world markets less attractive to U.S. farmers.

Perhaps most important, farm programs such as those maintained by the EU and the United States distort both world agricultural trade and the international allocation of agricultural resources. Encouraged by artificially high prices, farmers in industrially advanced nations produce more food and fiber than they would otherwise. The resulting surpluses flow into world markets, where they depress prices. This means that farmers in countries with no farm programs—many of them developing countries—face artificially low prices for their exports, which signals them to produce less. Overall, the result is a shift in production away from what would occur on the basis of comparative advantage. As an example, price supports cause U.S. agricultural resources to be used for sugar production, even though sugar can be produced at perhaps half the cost in the Caribbean countries and Australia.

Recognizing these distortions, in 1994 the 128 nations then belonging to the World Trade Organization (WTO) agreed to reduce farm price-support programs by 20 percent by the year 2000 and to reduce tariffs and quotas on imported farm products by 15 percent. Larger, more significant, reductions of farm subsidies and agricultural tariffs are part of the agenda of the most recent round of trade negotiations (the Doha Round). But reaching agreement on those reductions has proved difficult. As of mid-2006, negotiations over these issues were stalled.

Recent Reform

In the mid-1990s economists and political leaders shared the feeling that the goals and techniques of farm policy needed to be reexamined and revised. Moreover, crop prices were relatively high at the time and Congress wanted to reduce large Federal budget deficits.

Freedom to Farm Act of 1996

In 1996 Congress radically revamped 60 years of U.S. farm policy by passing the **Freedom to Farm Act.** The law ended price supports and acreage allotments for wheat, corn, barley, oats, sorghum, rye, cotton, and rice. Farmers were allowed to respond to changing crop prices by planting as much or as little of these crops as they chose. Also, they were free to plant crops of their choice. If the price of, say, oats increased, farmers could plant more oats and less barley. Markets, not government programs, were to determine the kinds and amounts of crops grown.

To ease the transition away from price supports, the Freedom to Farm Act granted declining annual transition payments through 2002. The $37 billion of total scheduled payments through 2002 was based on the production levels of the crops each farmer previously had grown under the price-support system. So a previous wheat farmer, for example, would receive cash payments for 7 years regardless of the current price of wheat or amount of wheat presently grown.

But this ambitious plan to wean American agriculture from subsidies unraveled in 1998 and 1999, when sharply reduced export demand and strong crop production in the United States depressed the prices of many farm products. Congress responded by supplementing the direct payments with large "emergency aid" payments to farmers. Agricultural subsidies for 1999–2002 averaged $20 billion annually—even more than they were before passage of the Freedom to Farm Act.

The Farm Act of 2002

In 2002 Congress passed the **Farm Act of 2002,** which continues the "freedom to plant" and "direct-payment" approaches of the 1996 farm law but incorporates an automatic system of "emergency aid." This 6-year $118 billion farm bill also extends the direct-payment system of the 1996 law to peanuts, soybeans, and other oilseeds. The law represents a substantial retreat from the free-market intent of the 1996 law. It provides three basic forms of commodity subsidies.

Direct Payments

The **direct payments** are similar to the transition payments paid under the Freedom to Farm Act. The cash payments are fixed for each crop based on a farmer's past production and are unaffected by current crop prices or current production. Farmers are free to plant as much or as little of any particular crop as they want and still receive these payments. Unlike the 1996 law, direct payments do not decline from year to year. They are a permanent part of the subsidy program.

Countercyclical Payments

A new component of farm policy ties a separate set of subsidies to the difference between market prices of specified farm products and a target price set for each crop. Like direct payments, these **countercyclical payments (CCPs)** are based on previous crops grown and are received regardless of the current crop planted. For example, the target price for corn in the years 2004–2007 is $2.63 per bushel. If corn is at or exceeds $2.63 in one of those years, the farmer who qualifies will receive no CCP. But if the price is below $2.63, the farmer will receive CCP payments geared to the size of the price gap. The CCP system returns a form of price supports to a prominent role in farm policy, but it bases those supports on past crops grown, not current crops planted.

Marketing Loans

Finally, the 2002 Farm Act contains a **marketing loan program** under which farmers can receive a loan (on a per-unit-of-output basis) from a government lender. If the crop price at harvest is higher than the price specified in the loan (the loan price), farmers can repay their loans, with interest. If the crop price is lower than the loan price, farmers can forfeit their harvested crops to the lender and be free of their loans. In this second case, farmers receive a subsidy because the proceeds from the loan exceed the revenues from the sale of the crop in the market.

The Farm Act of 2002 establishes that the political clout of the farm lobby, although weaker than in earlier periods, remains very strong. All three components of the 2002 Farm Act help reduce the risk of price and income variability for farmers and raise farm incomes. But the act does not address the fundamental problem of subsidies. However structured, large subsidies slow the exodus of resources from agriculture and maintain high production levels. That means low crop prices and low market incomes for farmers. Those low prices and incomes, in turn, provide the rationale for continued government subsidies!

QUICK REVIEW 19.3

- Farm policy in the United States has been heavily criticized for delaying the shift of resources away from farming, directing most subsidies to wealthier farmers, and being fraught with policy contradictions.
- The persistence of farm subsidies can largely be explained in terms of rent-seeking behavior, the special-interest effect, political logrolling, and other aspects of public choice theory.
- The Freedom to Farm Act of 1996 eliminated price supports and acreage allotments for many of the nation's crops, while continuing direct subsidies to farmers for 7 years.
- The 2002 Farm Act runs through 2007 and provides three types of farm subsidies: direct payments, countercyclical payments, and marketing loans.

Summary

1. In the short run, the highly inelastic demand for farm products transforms small changes in output and small shifts in demand into large changes in prices and income.
2. Over the long run, rapid technological advance, together with a highly inelastic and relatively slow-growing demand for agricultural output, has made agriculture a declining industry in the United States and dictated that resources exit the industry.
3. Historically, farm policy has been centered on price and based on the parity concept, which suggests that the relationship between prices received and paid by farmers should be constant over time.
4. The use of price floors or price supports has a number of economic effects: It (a) causes surplus production; (b) increases the incomes of farmers; (c) causes higher consumer prices for farm products; (d) creates an overallocation of resources to agriculture; (e) obliges society to pay higher taxes to finance the purchase and storage of surplus output; (f) increases pollution because of the greater use of agrochemicals and vulnerable land; and (g) forces other nations to bear the costs associated with import barriers and depressed world agricultural prices.
5. With only limited success, the Federal government has pursued programs to reduce agricultural supply and increase agricultural demand as a way to reduce the surpluses associated with price supports.
6. Economists have criticized U.S. farm policy for (a) confusing symptoms (low farm incomes) with causes (excess capacity), (b) providing the largest subsidies to high-income farmers, and (c) creating contradictions among specific farm programs.
7. The persistence of agricultural subsidies can be explained by public choice theory and, in particular, as rent-seeking behavior; the special-interest effect; and political logrolling.
8. Political backing for price supports and acreage allotments has eroded for several reasons: (a) The number of U.S. farmers, and thus their political clout, has declined relative to the number of urban consumers of farm products; and (b) successful efforts by the United States to get other nations to reduce their farm subsidies have altered the domestic debate on the desirability of U.S. subsidies.
9. The Freedom to Farm Act of 1996 ended price supports and acreage allotments for wheat, corn, barley, oats, sorghum, rye, cotton, and rice. The law established declining annual transition payments through the year 2002, but those payments were no longer tied to crop prices or the current crop produced.
10. When crop prices plummeted in 1998 and 1999, Congress supplemented the transition payments of the Freedom to Farm Act with large amounts of emergency aid. Total subsidies to agriculture averaged $20 billion annually in the years 1999–2002.
11. The Farm Act of 2002, which extends through 2007, retreated from the free-market goal of the Freedom to Farm Act. The 2002 law provides farmers with direct payments (based on previous crops planted), countercyclical payments (based on the differences between market prices and targeted prices), and marketing loans (based on a specified crop price and an option to either pay back the loan or forfeit the crop to the government lender).

Terms and Concepts

farm commodities	parity ratio	Farm Act of 2002
food products	price supports	direct payments
agribusiness	acreage allotments	countercyclical payments (CCPs)
parity concept	Freedom to Farm Act	marketing loan program

Study Questions

1. **KEY QUESTION** Carefully evaluate: "The supply and demand for agricultural products are such that small changes in agricultural supply result in drastic changes in prices. However, large changes in agricultural prices have modest effects on agricultural output." (Hint: A brief review of the distinction between supply and quantity supplied may be helpful.) Do exports increase or reduce the instability of demand for farm products? Explain.
2. What relationship, if any, can you detect between the facts that farmers' fixed costs of production are large and the supply of most agricultural products is generally inelastic? Be specific in your answer.
3. **KEY QUESTION** Explain how each of the following contributes to the farm problem:
   a. The inelasticity of demand for farm products.
   b. The rapid technological progress in farming.
   c. The modest long-run growth in demand for farm commodities.
   d. The volatility of export demand.

4. The key to efficient resource allocation is shifting resources from low-productivity to high-productivity uses. In view of the high and expanding physical productivity of agricultural resources, explain why many economists want to divert additional resources from farming to achieve allocative efficiency.
5. Explain and evaluate: "Industry complains of the higher taxes it must pay to finance subsidies to agriculture. Yet the trend of agricultural prices has been downward while industrial prices have been moving upward, suggesting that on balance agriculture is actually subsidizing industry."
6. "Because consumers as a group must ultimately pay the total income received by farmers, it makes no real difference whether the income is paid through free farm markets or through price supports supplemented by subsidies financed out of tax revenue." Do you agree?
7. If in a given year the indexes of prices received and paid by farmers were 120 and 165, respectively, what would the parity ratio be? Explain the meaning of that ratio.
8. **KEY QUESTION** Explain the economic effects of price supports. Explicitly include environmental and global impacts in your answer. On what grounds do economists contend that price supports cause a misallocation of resources?
9. Use supply and demand curves to depict equilibrium price and output in a competitive market for some farm product. Then show how an above-equilibrium price floor (price support) would cause a surplus in this market. Demonstrate in your graph how government could reduce the surplus through a policy that (*a*) changes supply or (*b*) changes demand. Identify each of the following actual government policies as primarily affecting the supply of or the demand for a particular farm product: acreage allotments; food-stamp program; Food for Peace program; a government buyout of dairy herds; export promotion.
10. Do you agree with each of the following statements? Explain why or why not.
    a. The problem with U.S. agriculture is that there are too many farmers. That is not the fault of farmers but the fault of government programs.
    b. The Federal government ought to buy up all U.S. farm surpluses and give them away to developing nations.
    c. All industries would like government price supports if they could get them; agriculture obtained price supports only because of its strong political clout.
11. What are the effects of farm subsidies such as those of the United States and the European Union on (*a*) domestic agricultural prices, (*b*) world agricultural prices, and (*c*) the international allocation of agricultural resources?
12. Use public choice theory to explain the persistence of farm subsidies in the face of major criticisms of those subsidies. If the special-interest effect is so strong, what factors made it possible in 1996 for the government to end price supports and acreage allotments for several crops?
13. What was the major intent of the Freedom to Farm Act of 1996? Do you agree with the intent? Why or why not? Did the law succeed in reducing overall farm subsidies? Why or why not?
14. How do direct subsidies, countercyclical payments, and marketing loan subsidies differ under the Farm Act of 2002? In what way do countercyclical payments and marketing loans help reduce the volatility of farm income? In what way do direct subsidies perpetuate the long-run farm problem of too many resources in agriculture?
15. **LAST WORD** What groups benefit and what groups lose from the U.S. sugar subsidy program?

Web-Based Questions

1. **AGRICULTURAL PRICES—WHAT'S UP, WHAT'S DOWN?** The USDA, at **www.nass.usda.gov/**, provides up-to-date color charts of current data for agricultural prices received by farmers. Find Charts and Maps on the right side of the home page and navigate to Agricultural Prices and Prices Received. Check the prices received for cattle, corn, cotton, hogs, milk, soybeans, and wheat and describe in general terms the price trend for each over the period shown in the chart. Why is knowing output levels, as well as prices, essential in evaluating how individual farmers have fared in the market over that period?
2. **FARM SIZE AND FARM SALES REVENUE** Go to **www.nass.usda.gov/** and find Charts and Maps. Under Economics, find information on farm size and farm revenue. Which of these three states had the smallest and largest average farm sizes: California, Florida, or Texas? What was the national average size of farms with sales revenue of less than $10,000 in the latest year? More than $100,000? What percentage of farms had $100,000 or more of sales? What percentage of land was in farms earning $100,000 or more?

IN THIS CHAPTER YOU WILL LEARN:

- **How income inequality in the United States is measured and described.**
- **The extent and sources of income inequality.**
- **How income inequality has changed since 1970.**
- **The economic arguments for and against income inequality.**
- **How poverty is measured and its incidence by age, gender, ethnicity, and other characteristics.**
- **The major components of the income-maintenance program in the United States.**

20

Income Inequality and Poverty

Evidence that suggests wide income disparity in the United States is easy to find. In 2005 movie producer George Lucas (of *Star Wars*) earned $235 million, talk-show host Oprah Winfrey earned $225 million, and golfer Tiger Woods earned $90 million. In contrast, the salary of the president of the United States is $400,000, and the typical schoolteacher earns $45,000. A full-time minimum-wage worker at a fast-food restaurant makes about $10,000. Cash welfare payments to a mother with two children average $5000.

In 2004 about 37 million Americans—or 12.7 percent of the population—lived in poverty. An estimated 500,000 people were homeless in that year. The richest fifth of American households received about 50.1 percent of total income, while the poorest fifth received 3.4 percent.

What are the sources of income inequality? Is income inequality rising or falling? Is the United States making progress against poverty? What are the major income-maintenance programs in the United States? Has welfare reform succeeded? These are some of the questions we will answer in this chapter.

Facts about Income Inequality

Average household income in the United States is among the highest in the world; in 2004, it was $60,528 per household (one or more persons occupying a housing unit). But that average tells us nothing about income inequality. To learn about that, we must examine how income is distributed around the average.

Distribution by Income Category

One way to measure **income inequality** is to look at the percentages of households in a series of income categories. Table 20.1 shows that 15.4 percent of all households had annual before-tax incomes of less than $15,000 in 2004, while another 15.7 percent had annual incomes of $100,000 or more. The data in the table suggest considerable inequality of household income in the United States.

Distribution by Quintiles (Fifths)

A second way to measure income inequality is to divide the total number of individuals, households, or families (two or more persons related by birth) into five numerically equal groups, or *quintiles*, and examine the percentage of total personal (before-tax) income received by each quintile. We do this for households in the table in Figure 20.1, where we also provide the upper income limit for each quintile. Any amount of income greater than that listed in each row of column 3 would place a household into the next-higher quintile.

TABLE 20.1 The Distribution of U.S. Income by Households, 2004

(1) Personal Income Category	(2) Percentage of All Households in This Category
Under $10,000	8.7
$10,000–$14,999	6.7
$15,000–$24,999	12.9
$25,000–$34,999	11.9
$35,000–$49,999	14.8
$50,000–$74,999	18.3
$75,000–$99,999	11.0
$100,000 and above	15.7
	100.0

Source: Bureau of the Census, **www.census.gov/.**

The Lorenz Curve and Gini Ratio

We can display the quintile distribution of personal income through a **Lorenz curve.** In Figure 20.1, we plot the cumulative percentage of households on the horizontal axis and the percentage of income they obtain on the vertical axis. The diagonal line 0*e* represents a *perfectly equal distribution of income* because each point along that line indicates that a particular percentage of households receive the same percentage of income. In other words, points representing 20 percent of all households receiving 20 percent of total income, 40 percent receiving 40 percent, 60 percent receiving 60 percent, and so on, all lie on the diagonal line.

FIGURE 20.1 The Lorenz curve and Gini ratio. The Lorenz curve is a convenient way to show the degree of income inequality (here, household income by quintile in 2004). The area between the diagonal (the line of perfect equality) and the Lorenz curve represents the degree of inequality in the distribution of total income. This inequality is measured numerically by the Gini ratio—area *A* (shown in brown) divided by area *A* + *B* (the brown + green area). The Gini ratio for the distribution shown is 0.466.

(1) Quintile (2004)	(2) Percentage of Total Income	(3) Upper Income Limit
Lowest 20 percent	3.4	$ 18,500
Second 20 percent	8.7	34,738
Third 20 percent	14.7	55,331
Fourth 20 percent	22.2	88,029
Highest 20 percent	50.1	No limit
Total	100.0	

Source: Bureau of the Census, **www.census.gov/.** Numbers do not add to 100 percent due to rounding.

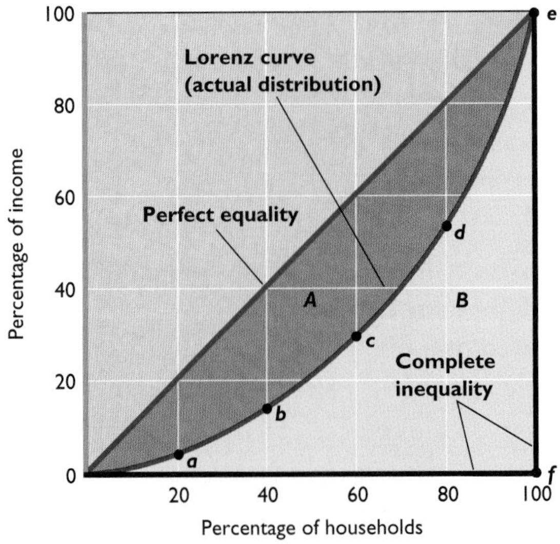

By plotting the quintile data from the table in Figure 20.1, we obtain the Lorenz curve for 2004. The bottom 20 percent of all households received 3.4 percent of the income, as shown by point *a*; the bottom 40 percent received 12.1 percent (= 3.4 + 8.7), as shown by point *b*; and so forth. The brown area between the diagonal line and the Lorenz curve is determined by the extent that the Lorenz curve sags away from the diagonal and indicates the degree of income inequality. If the actual income distribution were perfectly equal, the Lorenz curve and the diagonal would coincide and the brown area would disappear.

W 20.1
Lorenz curve

At the opposite extreme is complete inequality, where all households but one have zero income. In that case the Lorenz curve would coincide with the horizontal axis from 0 to point *f* (at 0 percent of income) and then would move immediately up from *f* to point *e* along the vertical axis (indicating that a single household has 100 percent of the total income). The entire area below the diagonal line (triangle 0*ef*) would indicate this extreme degree of inequality. So the farther the Lorenz curve sags away from the diagonal, the greater is the degree of income inequality.

The income inequality described by the Lorenz curve can be transformed into a **Gini ratio**—a numerical measure of the overall dispersion of income:

$$\text{Gini ratio} = \frac{\text{area between Lorenz curve and diagonal}}{\text{total area below the diagonal}} = \frac{A \text{ (brown area)}}{A + B \text{ (brown + green area)}}$$

The Gini ratio is 0.466 for the distribution of household income shown in Figure 20.1. As the area between the Lorenz curve and the diagonal gets larger, the Gini ratio rises to reflect greater inequality. Lower Gini ratios denote less inequality; higher ratios indicate more inequality. The Gini coefficient for complete income equality is zero and for complete inequality is 1.

Because Gini ratios are numerical, they are easier to use than Lorenz curves for comparing the income distributions of different ethnic groups and countries. For example, in 2004 the Gini ratio of U.S. household income for Hispanics was 0.450; for Asians and whites, 0.460 each; and for African-Americans, 0.476.[1] Gini ratios for various nations range from 0.025 (Japan) to 0.707 (Namibia). Examples within this range include Sweden, 0.250; Italy, 0.360; Mexico, 0.546; Chile, 0.571; and South Africa, 0.578.[2] **(Key Question 2)**

G 20.1
Lorenz curve

Income Mobility: The Time Dimension

The income data used so far have a major limitation: The income accounting period of 1 year is too short to be very meaningful. Because the Census Bureau data portray the distribution of income in only a single year, they may conceal a more equal distribution over a few years, a decade, or even a lifetime. If Brad earns $1000 in year 1 and $100,000 in year 2, while Jenny earns $100,000 in year 1 and only $1000 in year 2, do we have income inequality? The answer depends on the period of measurement. Annual data would reveal great income inequality, but there would be complete equality over the 2-year period.

This point is important because evidence suggests considerable "churning around" in the distribution of income over time. Such movement of individuals or households from one income quintile to another over time is called **income mobility.** For most income receivers, income starts at a relatively low level, reaches a peak during middle age, and then declines. It follows that if all people receive exactly the same stream of income over their lifetimes, considerable income inequality would still exist in any specific year because of age differences. In any single year, the young and the old would receive low incomes while the middle-aged receive high incomes.

If we change from a "snapshot" view of income distribution in a single year to a "time exposure" portraying incomes over much longer periods, we find considerable movement of income receivers among income classes. For example, many relatively low-income students in professional programs in one year eventually graduate to become high-income doctors, lawyers, and accountants in subsequent years. Professional athletes and entertainers may have high incomes in one year and much lower incomes several years later. All this correctly suggests that income is more equally distributed over a 5-, 10-, or 20-year period than in a single year.

In short, individual and family income mobility over time is significant; for many people, "low income" and "high income" are not permanent conditions. Also, the longer the time period considered, the more equal the distribution of income becomes.

[1] U.S. Census Bureau, *Historical Income Tables*, **www.census.gov.**

[2] World Bank, *World Development Indicators, 2005*, **www.worldbank.org.**

FIGURE 20.2 The impact of taxes and transfers on U.S. income inequality. The distribution of household income is significantly more equal after taxes and transfers are taken into account than before. Transfers account for most of the lessening of inequality and provide most of the income received by the lowest quintile of households.

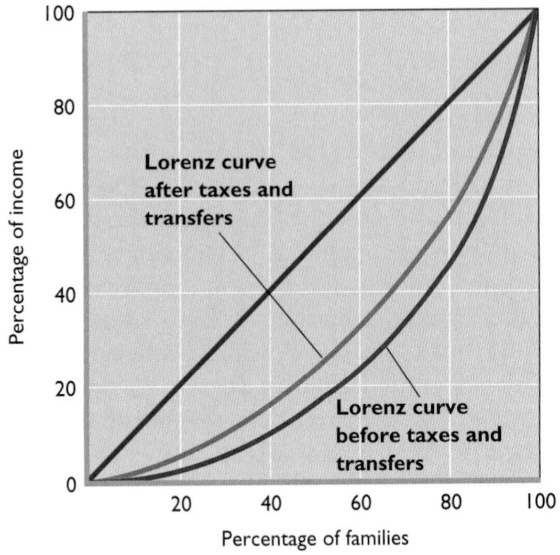

	Percentage of Total Income Received, 2003	
Quintile	**(1) Before Taxes and Transfers**	**(2) After Taxes and Transfers**
Lowest 20 percent	0.8	4.5
Second 20 percent	7.2	10.7
Third 20 percent	14.8	16.4
Fourth 20 percent	24.0	24.0
Highest 20 percent	53.1	44.4

Source: Bureau of the Census, **www.census.gov/.** The data include all money income from private sources, including realized capital gains and employer provided health insurance. The "after taxes and transfers" data include the value of noncash transfers as well as cash transfers. Numbers do not add to 100 percent due to rounding. *Source:* Bureau of the Census; **www.census.gov/.**

Effect of Government Redistribution

The income data in Table 20.1 and Figure 20.1 include wages, salaries, dividends, and interest. They also include all cash transfer payments such as Social Security, unemployment compensation benefits, and welfare assistance to needy families. The data are before-tax data and therefore do not take into account the effects of personal income and payroll (Social Security) taxes that are levied directly on income receivers. Nor do they include in-kind or **noncash transfers,** which provide specific goods or services rather than cash. Noncash transfers include such things as Medicare, Medicaid, housing subsidies, subsidized school lunches, and food stamps. Such transfers are "incomelike," since they enable recipients to "purchase" goods and services.

One economic function of government is to redistribute income, if society so desires. Figure 20.2 and its table[3] reveal that government significantly redistributes income from higher- to lower-income households through taxes and transfers. Note that the U.S. distribution of household income before taxes and transfers are taken into account (dark red Lorenz curve) is substantially less equal than the distribution after taxes and transfers (light red Lorenz curve). Without government redistribution, the lowest 20 percent of households in 2003 would have received only 0.9 percent of total income. *With* redistribution, they received 4.5 percent, or five times as much.

Which contributes more to redistribution, government taxes or government transfers? The answer is transfers. Because the U.S. tax system is only modestly progressive, after-tax data would reveal only about 20 percent less inequality. Roughly 80 percent of the reduction in income inequality is attributable to transfer payments, which account for more than 75 percent of the income of the lowest quintile. Together with growth of job opportunities, transfer payments have been the most important means of alleviating poverty in the United States.

Causes of Income Inequality

There are several causes of income inequality in the United States. In general, the market system is an impersonal mechanism that embodies no conscience concerning what is an "equitable" or "just" distribution of income. It is permissive of a high degree of income inequality because it rewards individuals based on the contribution their resources make in producing society's output.

More specifically, the factors that contribute to income inequality are the following.

Ability

People have different mental, physical, and aesthetic talents. Some have inherited the exceptional mental qualities

[3]The "before" data in this table differ from the data in the table in Figure 20.1 because the latter include cash transfers. Also, the data in Figure 20.2 are based on a broader concept of income than are the data in Figure 20.1.

that are essential to such high-paying occupations as medicine, corporate leadership, and law. Others are blessed with the physical capacity and coordination to become highly paid professional athletes. A few have the talent to become great artists or musicians or have the beauty to become top fashion models. Others have very weak mental endowments and may work in low-paying occupations or may be incapable of earning any income at all. The intelligence and skills of most people fall somewhere in between.

Education and Training

Native ability alone rarely produces high income; people must develop and refine their capabilities through education and training. Individuals differ significantly in the amount of education and training they obtain and thus in their capacity to earn income. Such differences may be a matter of choice: Nguyen enters the labor force after graduating from high school, while Nyberg takes a job only after earning a college degree. Other differences may be involuntary: Nguyen and her parents may simply be unable to finance a college education.

People also receive varying degrees of on-the-job training, which contributes to income inequality. Some workers learn valuable new skills each year on the job and therefore experience significant income growth over time; others receive little or no on-the-job training and earn no more at age 50 than they did at age 30. Moreover, firms tend to select for advanced on-the-job training the workers who have the most formal education. That added training magnifies the education-based income differences between less educated and better-educated individuals.

Discrimination

Discrimination in education, hiring, training, and promotion undoubtedly contributes to income inequality in the United States, although the degree is uncertain. If discrimination restricts racial and ethnic minorities (or women) to low-paying occupations, the supply of labor will be great relative to demand in those occupations. So wages and incomes will be low. Conversely, discrimination reduces the competition that whites (or men) face in the occupations in which they are predominant. Thus, labor supply is artificially limited relative to demand in those occupations, with the result that wages and incomes are high.

Preferences and Risks

Incomes also differ because of differences in preferences for market work relative to leisure, market work relative to work in the household, and types of market work. People who choose to stay home with children, work part-time, or retire early usually have less income than those who make the opposite choices. Those who are willing to take arduous, unpleasant jobs (for example, underground mining or heavy construction), to work long hours with great intensity, or to "moonlight" will tend to earn more.

Individuals also differ in their willingness to assume risk. We refer here not only to the race driver or the professional boxer but also to the entrepreneur. Although many entrepreneurs fail, many of those who develop successful new products or services realize very substantial incomes. That contributes to income inequality.

Unequal Distribution of Wealth

Income is a *flow;* it represents a stream of wage and salary earnings, along with rent, interest, and profits, as depicted in Chapter 2's circular flow diagram. In contrast, wealth is a *stock*, reflecting at a particular moment the financial and real assets an individual has accumulated over time. A retired person may have very little income and yet own a home, mutual fund shares, and a pension plan that add up to considerable wealth. A new college graduate may be earning a substantial income as an accountant, middle manager, or engineer but has yet to accumulate significant wealth.

As you will discover in this chapter's Last Word, the ownership of wealth in the United States is more unequal than the distribution of income. This inequality of wealth leads to inequality in rent, interest, and dividends, which in turn contributes to income inequality. Those who own more machinery, real estate, farmland, stocks and bonds, and savings accounts obviously receive greater income from that ownership than people with less or no such wealth.

Market Power

The ability to "rig the market" on one's own behalf also contributes to income inequality. For example, in *resource* markets certain unions and professional groups have adopted policies that limit the supply of their services, thereby boosting the incomes of those "on the inside." Also, legislation that requires occupational licensing for, say, doctors, dentists, and lawyers can bestow market power that favors the licensed groups. In *product* markets, "rigging the market" means gaining or enhancing monopoly power, which results in greater profit and thus greater income to the firms' owners.

Luck, Connections, and Misfortune

Other forces also play a role in producing income inequality. Luck and "being in the right place at the right time" have helped individuals stumble into fortunes. Discovering oil on a ranch, owning land along a proposed freeway interchange, and hiring the right press agent have accounted for some high incomes. Personal contacts and political connections are other potential routes to attaining high income.

In contrast, economic misfortunes such as prolonged illness, serious accident, death of the family breadwinner, or unemployment may plunge a family into the low range of income. The burden of such misfortune is borne very unevenly by the population and thus contributes to income inequality. **(Key Question 5)**

Income inequality of the magnitude we have described is not exclusively an American phenomenon. Global Perspective 20.1 compares income inequality (here by individuals, not by households) in the United States with that in several other nations. Income inequality tends to be greatest in South American nations, where land and capital resources are highly concentrated in the hands of a relatively small number of wealthy families.

GLOBAL PERSPECTIVE 20.1

Percentage of Total Income Received by the Top One-Tenth of Income Receivers, Selected Nations

The share of income going to the highest 10 percent of income receivers varies among nations.

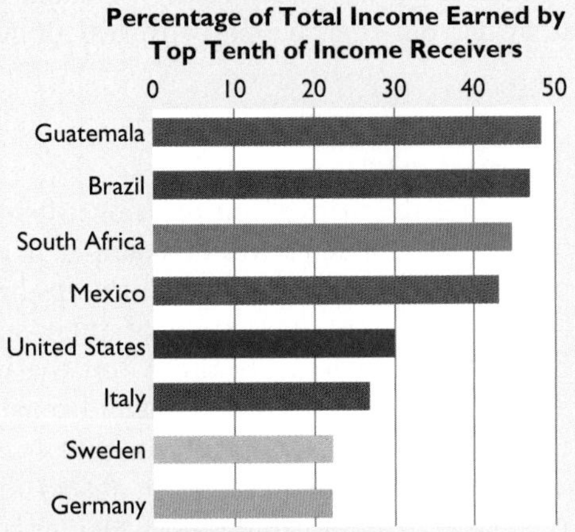

Source: World Bank, *World Development Indicators, 2005*, **www.worldbank.org/.**

QUICK REVIEW 20.1

- Data reveal considerable income inequality in the United States; in 2004 the richest fifth of all households received 50.1 percent of before-tax income, and the poorest fifth received 3.4 percent.
- The Lorenz curve depicts income inequality graphically by comparing percentages of total families and percentages of total income. The Gini ratio is a measure of the overall dispersion of income and is found by dividing the area between the diagonal and the Lorenz curve by the total area below the diagonal.
- The distribution of income is less unequal over longer time periods.
- Government taxes and transfers significantly reduce income inequality by redistributing income from higher-income groups to lower-income groups; the bulk of this redistribution results from transfer payments.
- Differences in ability, education and training, tastes for market work versus nonmarket activities, property ownership, and market power—along with discrimination and luck—help explain income inequality.

Income Inequality over Time

Over a period of years economic growth has raised incomes in the United States: In *absolute* dollar amounts, the entire distribution of income has been moving upward. But incomes may move up in *absolute* terms while leaving the *relative* distribution of income less equal, more equal, or unchanged. Table 20.2 shows how the distribution of household income has changed since 1970. This income is "before tax" and includes cash transfers but not noncash transfers.

Rising Income Inequality since 1970

It is clear from Table 20.2 that the distribution of income by quintiles has become more unequal since 1970. In 2004 the lowest 20 percent of households received 3.4 percent of total before-tax income, compared with 4.1 in 1970. Meanwhile, the income share received by the highest 20 percent rose from 43.3 in 1970 to 50.1 percent in 2004. Also, the percentage of income received by the top 5 percent of households rose significantly over the 1970–2004 period.

Causes of Growing Inequality

Economists suggest several major explanations for the growing U.S. income inequality since 1970.

Greater Demand for Highly Skilled Workers Perhaps the most significant contributor to the growing income inequality has been an increasing

TABLE 20.2 Percentage of Total Before-Tax Income Received by Each One-Fifth, and by the Top 5 Percent, of Households, Selected Years

Quintile	1970	1975	1980	1985	1990	1995	2000	2004
Lowest 20 percent	4.1	4.4	4.3	4.0	3.9	3.7	3.6	3.4
Second 20 percent	10.8	10.5	10.3	9.7	9.6	9.1	8.9	8.7
Third 20 percent	17.4	17.1	16.9	16.3	15.9	15.2	14.8	14.7
Fourth 20 percent	24.5	24.8	24.9	24.6	24.0	23.3	23.0	23.2
Highest 20 percent	43.3	43.2	43.7	45.3	46.6	48.7	49.8	50.1
Total	100.0	100.0	100.0	100.0	100.0	100.0	100.0	100.0
Top 5 percent	16.6	15.9	15.8	17.0	18.6	21.0	22.1	21.8

Source: Bureau of the Census, **www.census.gov/**. Numbers may not add to 100 percent due to rounding.

demand by many firms for workers who are highly skilled and well-educated. Moreover, several industries requiring highly skilled workers have either recently emerged or expanded greatly, such as the computer software, business consulting, biotechnology, health care, and Internet industries. Because highly skilled workers remain relatively scarce, their wages have been bid up. Consequently, the wage differences between them and less skilled workers have increased.

Between 1980 and 2003 the wage difference between college graduates and high school graduates rose from 28 to 46 percent for women and from 22 to 42 percent for men. And the so-called *90-10 ratio*—earnings at the 90th percentile of the wage and salary distribution compared to earnings at the 10th percentile—rose from 3.6 in 1980 to 4.4 in 2003.[4]

The rising demand for skill has also shown up in rapidly rising pay for chief executive officers (CEOs), sizable increases in income from stock options, substantial increases in income for professional athletes and entertainers, and huge fortunes for successful entrepreneurs. This growth of "superstar" pay has also contributed to rising income inequality.

Demographic Changes The entrance of large numbers of less experienced and less skilled "baby boomers" into the labor force during the 1970s and 1980s may have contributed to greater income inequality in those two decades. Because younger workers tend to earn less income than older workers, their growing numbers contributed to income inequality. There has also been a growing tendency for men and women with high earnings potential to marry each other, thus increasing household income among the highest income quintiles. Finally, the number of households headed by single or divorced women has increased greatly. That trend has increased income inequality because such households lack a second major wage earner and also because the poverty rate for female-headed households is very high.

International Trade, Immigration, and Decline in Unionism Other factors are probably at work as well. Stronger international competition from imports has reduced the demand for and employment of less skilled (but highly paid) workers in such industries as the automobile and steel industries. The decline in such jobs has reduced the average wage for less skilled workers. It also has swelled the ranks of workers in already low-paying industries, placing further downward pressure on wages there.

Similarly, the transfer of jobs to lower-wage workers in developing countries has exerted downward wage pressure on less skilled workers in the United States. Also, an upsurge in the immigration of unskilled workers has increased the number of low-income households in the United States. Finally, the decline in unionism in the United States has undoubtedly contributed to wage inequality, since unions tend to equalize pay within firms and industries.

Two cautions: First, when we note growing income inequality, we are not saying that the "rich are getting richer and the poor are getting poorer" in terms of absolute income. Both the rich and the poor are experiencing rises in real income. Rather, what has happened is that, while incomes have risen in all quintiles, income growth has been fastest in the top quintile. Second, increased income inequality is not solely a U.S. phenomenon. The recent rise of inequality has also occurred in several other industrially advanced nations.

The Lorenz curve can be used to contrast the distribution of income at different points in time. If we plotted Table 20.2's data as Lorenz curves, we would find that the curves shifted farther away from the diagonal between 1970 and 2004. The Gini ratio rose from 0.394 in 1970 to 0.466 in 2004.

[4]Economic Policy Institute, **www.epinet.org.** The college wage premiums are adjusted for differences in earnings based on race, ethnicity, marital status, and region.

Equality versus Efficiency

The main policy issue concerning income inequality is how much is necessary and justified. While there is no general agreement on the justifiable amount, we can gain insight by exploring the cases for and against greater equality.

The Case for Equality: Maximizing Total Utility

The basic argument for an equal distribution of income is that income equality maximizes total consumer satisfaction (utility) from any particular level of output and income. The rationale for this argument is shown in Figure 20.3, in which we assume that the money incomes of two individuals, Anderson and Brooks, are subject to diminishing marginal utility. In any time period, income receivers spend the first dollars received on the products they value most—products whose marginal utility is high. As their most pressing wants become satisfied, consumers then spend additional dollars of income on less important, lower-marginal-utility goods. The identical diminishing-marginal-utility-from-income curves (MU_A and MU_B in the figure) reflect the assumption that Anderson and Brooks have the same capacity to derive utility from income.

Now suppose that there is \$10,000 worth of income (output) to be distributed between Anderson and Brooks. According to proponents of income equality, the optimal distribution is an equal distribution, which causes the marginal utility of the last dollar spent to be the same for both persons. We can prove this by demonstrating that if the income distribution is initially unequal, then distributing income more equally can increase the combined utility of the two individuals.

Suppose that the \$10,000 of income initially is distributed unequally, with Anderson getting \$2500 and Brooks \$7500. The marginal utility, *a*, from the last dollar received by Anderson is high, and the marginal utility, *b*, from Brooks' last dollar of income is low. If a single dollar of income is shifted from Brooks to Anderson—that is, toward greater equality—then Anderson's utility increases by *a* and Brooks' utility decreases by *b*. The combined utility then increases by *a* minus *b* (Anderson's large gain minus Brooks' small loss). The transfer of another dollar from Brooks to Anderson again increases their combined utility, this time by a slightly smaller amount. Continued transfer of dollars from Brooks to Anderson increases their combined utility until the income is evenly distributed and both receive \$5000. At that time their marginal utilities from the last dollar of income are equal (at a' and b'), and any further income redistribution beyond the \$2500 already transferred would begin to create inequality and decrease their combined utility.

FIGURE 20.3 The utility-maximizing distribution of income. With identical marginal-utility-of-income curves MU_A and MU_B, Anderson and Brooks will maximize their combined utility when any amount of income (say, \$10,000) is equally distributed. If income is unequally distributed (say, \$2500 to Anderson and \$7500 to Brooks), the marginal utility derived from the last dollar will be greater for Anderson than for Brooks, and a redistribution of income toward equality will result in a net increase in total utility. The utility gained by equalizing income at \$5000 each, shown by the blue area below curve MU_A in panel (a), exceeds the utility lost, indicated by the red area below curve MU_B in (b).

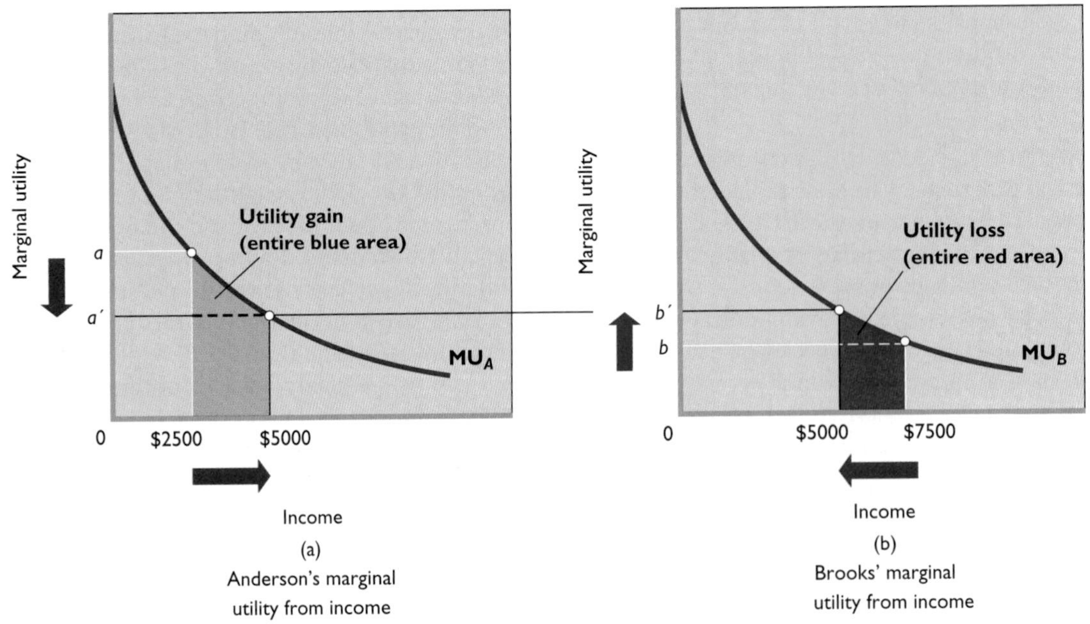

The area under the MU curve and to the left of the individual's particular level of income represents the total utility of that income. Therefore, as a result of the transfer of the $2500, Anderson has gained utility represented by the blue area below curve MU_A, and Brooks has lost utility represented by the red area below curve MU_B. The blue area is obviously greater than the red area, so income equality yields greater combined total utility than income inequality does.

The Case for Inequality: Incentives and Efficiency

Although the logic of the argument for equality is sound, critics attack its fundamental assumption that there is some fixed amount of output produced and therefore income to be distributed. Critics of income equality argue that the way in which income is distributed is an important determinant of the amount of output or income that is produced and is available for distribution.

Suppose once again in Figure 20.3 that Anderson earns $2500 and Brooks earns $7500. In moving toward equality, society (the government) must tax away some of Brooks' income and transfer it to Anderson. This tax and transfer process diminishes the income rewards of high-income Brooks and raises the income rewards of low-income Anderson; in so doing, it reduces the incentives of both to earn high incomes. Why should high-income Brooks work hard, save and invest, or undertake entrepreneurial risks when the rewards from such activities will be reduced by taxation? And why should low-income Anderson be motivated to increase his income through market activities when the government stands ready to transfer income to him? Taxes are a reduction in the rewards from increased productive effort; redistribution through transfers is a reward for diminished effort.

In the extreme, imagine a situation in which the government levies a 100 percent tax on income and distributes the tax revenue equally to its citizenry. Why would anyone work hard? Why would anyone work at all? Why would anyone assume business risk? Or why would anyone save (forgo current consumption) in order to invest? The economic incentives to "get ahead" will have been removed, greatly reducing society's total production and income. That is, the way income is distributed affects the size of that income. The basic argument for income inequality is that inequality is essential to maintain incentives to produce output and income—to get the output produced and income generated year after year.

CONSIDER THIS . . .

Slicing the Pizza

The equality-efficiency tradeoff might better be understood through an analogy. Assume that society's income is a huge pizza, baked year after year, *with the sizes of the pieces going to people on the basis of their contribution to making it.* Now suppose that for fairness reasons, society decides some people are getting pieces that are too large and others are getting pieces too small. But when society redistributes the pizza to make the sizes more equal, they discover the result is a smaller pizza than before. Why participate in making the pizza if you get a decent-size piece without contributing? The shrinkage of the pizza represents the efficiency loss—the loss of output and income—caused by the harmful effects of the redistribution on incentives to work, to save and invest, and to accept entrepreneurial risk. The shrinkage also reflects the resources that society must divert to the bureaucracies that administer the redistribution system.

How much pizza shrinkage will society accept while continuing to agree to the redistribution? If redistributing pizza to make it less unequal reduces the size of the pizza, what amount of pizza loss will society tolerate? Is a loss of 10 percent acceptable? 25 percent? 75 percent? This is the basic question in any debate over the ideal size of a nation's income redistribution program.

The Equality-Efficiency Tradeoff

At the essence of the income equality-inequality debate is a fundamental tradeoff between equality and efficiency. In this **equality-efficiency tradeoff,** greater income equality (achieved through redistribution of income) comes at the opportunity cost of reduced production and income. And greater production and income (through reduced redistribution) comes at the expense of less equality of income. The tradeoff obligates society to choose how much redistribution it wants, in view of the costs. If society decides it wants to redistribute income, it needs to determine methods that minimize the adverse effects on economic efficiency.

The Economics of Poverty

We now turn from the larger issue of income distribution to the more specific issue of very low income, or "poverty." A society with a high degree of income inequality can have a high, moderate, or low amount of poverty. We need to learn about the extent of poverty in the United States, the characteristics of the poor, and the programs designed to reduce poverty.

Definition of Poverty

Poverty is a condition in which a person or a family does not have the means to satisfy basic needs for food, clothing, shelter, and transportation. The means include currently earned income, transfer payments, past savings, and property owned. The basic needs have many determinants, including family size and the health and age of its members.

The Federal government has established minimum income thresholds below which a person or a family is "in poverty." In 2004 an unattached individual receiving less than $9645 per year was said to be living in poverty. For a family of four, the poverty line was $19,307; for a family of six, it was $25,785. Using these thresholds, we find for 2004 that about 37 million Americans lived in poverty. In 2004 the **poverty rate**—the percentage of the population living in poverty—was 12.7 percent.

Incidence of Poverty

The poor are heterogeneous: They can be found in all parts of the nation; they are of all races and ethnicities, rural and urban, young and old. But as Figure 20.4 indicates, poverty is far from randomly distributed. For example, the poverty rate for African-Americans is above the national average, as is the rate for Hispanics, while the rate for whites and Asians is below the average. In 2004, the poverty rates for African-Americans and Hispanics were 24.7 and 21.9 percent, respectively; the rate for whites and Asians, 9.8 and 10.8 percent.

Figure 20.4 shows that female-headed households (no husband present), foreign-born noncitizens, and children under 18 years of age have very high incidences of poverty. Marriage and full-time, year-round work are associated with low poverty rates, and, because of the Social Security system, the incidence of poverty among the elderly is less than that for the population as a whole.

The high poverty rate for children is especially disturbing because poverty tends to breed poverty. Poor children are at greater risk for a range of long-term problems, including poor health and inadequate education, crime, drug use, and teenage pregnancy. Many of today's impoverished children will reach adulthood unhealthy and illiterate and unable to earn above-poverty incomes.

As many as half of people in poverty are poor for only 1 or 2 years before climbing out of poverty. But poverty is much more long-lasting among some groups than among others. In particular, African-American and Hispanic families, families headed by women, persons with little education and few labor market skills, and people who are dysfunctional because of drug use, alcoholism, or mental illness are more likely than others to remain in poverty. Also, long-lasting poverty is heavily present in depressed areas of cities, parts of the Deep South, and some Indian reservations. **(Key Question 10)**

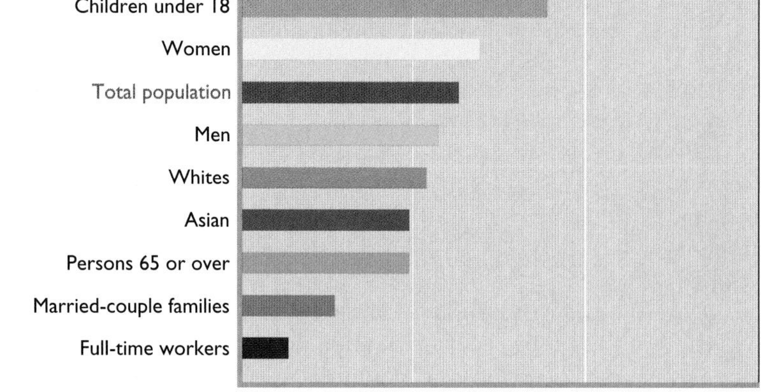

Source: Bureau of the Census, **www.census.gov/.**

FIGURE 20.4 Poverty rates among selected population groups, 2004. Poverty is disproportionately borne by African-Americans, Hispanics, children, foreign-born residents who are not citizens, and families headed by women. People who are employed full-time, have a college degree, or are married tend to have low poverty rates.

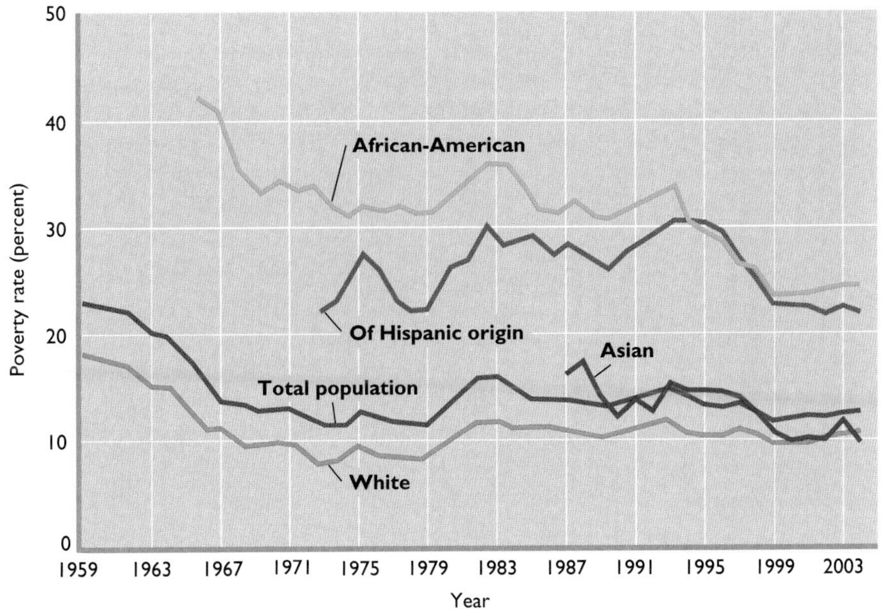

Source: Bureau of the Census, **www.census.gov/**.

FIGURE 20.5 Poverty-rate trends, 1959–2004. Although the national poverty rate declined sharply between 1959 and 1969, it stabilized in the 1970s only to increase significantly in the early 1980s. Between 1993 and 2000 it substantially declined, before rising slightly again in the immediate years following the 2001 recession. Although poverty rates for African-Americans and Hispanics are much higher than the average, they significantly declined during the 1990s.

Poverty Trends

As Figure 20.5 shows, the total poverty rate fell significantly between 1959 and 1969, stabilized at 11 to 13 percent over the next decade, and then rose in the early 1980s. In 1993 the rate was 15.1 percent, the highest since 1983. Between 1993 and 2000 the rate turned downward, falling to 11.3 percent in 2000. Because of recession, slow employment growth, and relatively slow wage growth, the poverty rate rose from 11.7 percent in 2001 to 12.7 percent in 2004. During the second half of the 1990s, poverty rates plunged for African-Americans, Hispanics, and Asians, and they have remained historically low.

Measurement Issues

The poverty rates and trends in Figures 20.4 and 20.5 should be interpreted cautiously. The official income thresholds for defining poverty are necessarily arbitrary and therefore may inadequately measure the true extent of poverty in the United States.

Some observers say that the high cost of living in major metropolitan areas means that the official poverty thresholds exclude millions of families whose income is slightly above the poverty level but clearly inadequate to meet basic needs for food, housing, and medical care. These observers use city-by-city studies on "minimal income needs" to show that poverty in the United States is much more widespread than officially measured and reported.

In contrast, some economists point out that using income to measure poverty understates the standard of living of many of the people who are officially poor. When individual, household, or family *consumption* is considered rather than family *income*, some of the poverty in the United States disappears. Some low-income families maintain their consumption by drawing down past savings, borrowing against future income, or selling homes. Moreover, many poverty families receive substantial noncash benefits such as food stamps and rent subsidies that boost their living standards. Such "in-kind" benefits are not included in determining a family's official poverty status.

The U.S. Income-Maintenance System

Regardless of how poverty is measured, economists agree that considerable poverty exists in the United States. Helping those who have very low income is a widely accepted goal of public policy. A wide array of antipoverty programs, including education and training programs, subsidized employment, minimum-wage laws, and antidiscrimination policies, are designed to increase the earnings of the poor. In addition, a number of income-maintenance programs were devised to reduce poverty; the most important are listed in Table 20.3. These programs involve large expenditures and have numerous beneficiaries.

The U.S. income-maintenance system consists of two kinds of programs: (1) social insurance and (2) public assistance, or "welfare." Both are known as **entitlement programs,** because all eligible persons are ensured (entitled to) the benefits set forth in the programs.

TABLE 20.3 Characteristics of Major Income-Maintenance Programs

Program	Basis of Eligibility	Source of Funds	Form of Aid	Expenditures,* Billions	Beneficiaries, Millions
Social Insurance Programs					
Social Security	Age, disability, or death of parent or spouse; individual earnings	Federal payroll taxes on employers and employees	Cash	$493	48
Medicare	Age or disability	Federal payroll tax on employers and employees	Subsidized health insurance	303	42
Unemployment compensation	Unemployment	State and Federal payroll taxes on employers	Cash	34	8
Public Assistance Programs					
Supplemental Security Income (SSI)	Age or disability; income	Federal revenues	Cash	37	7
Temporary Assistance for Needy Families (TANF)	Certain families with children; income	Federal-state-local revenues	Cash and services	9	5
Food stamps	Income	Federal revenues	Vouchers	25	24
Medicaid	Persons eligible for TANF or SSI and medically indigent	Federal-state-local revenues	Subsidized medical services	213	50
Earned-income tax credit (EITC)	Low-wage working families	Federal revenues	Refundable tax credit, cash	55	26

*Expenditures by Federal, state, and local governments; excludes administrative expenses.

Source: Social Security Administration, *Annual Statistical Supplement, 2005*, **www.socialsecurity.gov/,** and other government sources. Latest data.

Social Insurance Programs

Social insurance programs partially replace earnings that have been lost due to retirement, disability, or temporary unemployment; they also provide health insurance for the elderly. The main social insurance programs are Social Security, unemployment compensation, and Medicare. Benefits are viewed as earned rights and do not carry the stigma of public charity. These programs are financed primarily out of Federal payroll taxes. In these programs the entire population shares the risk of an individual's losing income because of retirement, unemployment, disability, or illness. Workers (and employers) pay a part of wages into a government fund while they are working. The workers are then entitled to benefits when they retire or when a specified misfortune occurs.

Social Security and Medicare

The major social insurance program is known as **Social Security.** It is a Federal pension program that replaces part of the earnings lost when workers retire, become disabled, or die. This gigantic program ($493 billion in 2005) is financed by compulsory payroll taxes levied on both employers and employees. Workers currently may retire at age 65 and receive full retirement benefits or retire early at age 62 with reduced benefits. When a worker dies, benefits accrue to his or her family survivors. Special provisions provide benefits for disabled workers.

Social Security covers over 90 percent of the workforce; some 48 million people receive Social Security benefits averaging about $995 per month. In 2006, those benefits were financed with a combined Social Security and Medicare payroll tax of 15.3 percent, with both the worker and the employer paying 7.65 percent on their first $94,200 of earnings. The 7.65 percent tax comprises 6.2 percent for Social Security and 1.45 percent for Medicare. Self-employed workers pay a tax of 15.3 percent.

Medicare is a Federal insurance program that provides health insurance benefits to those 65 or older and people who are disabled. It is financed by payroll taxes on employers and employees. This overall 2.9 percent tax is paid on all work income, not just on the first $94,200. Medicare also makes available supplementary low-cost insurance programs that help pay for doctor visits and, beginning in 2006, prescription drug expenses. In 2005, some 42 million people received Medicare benefits. The benefits paid totaled $303 billion.

The number of retirees drawing Social Security and Medicare benefits is rapidly rising relative to the number of workers paying payroll taxes. As a result, Social Security and Medicare face serious long-term funding problems. These fiscal imbalances have spawned calls to reform the programs.

Unemployment Compensation

All 50 states sponsor unemployment insurance programs called **unemployment compensation,** a Federal–state social insurance program that makes income available to workers who are unemployed. This insurance is financed by a relatively small payroll tax, paid by employers, which varies by state and by the size of the firm's payroll. Any insured worker who becomes unemployed can, after a short waiting period, become eligible for benefit payments. The program covers almost all wage and salary workers. The size of payments and the number of weeks they are made available vary considerably from state to state. Generally, benefits approximate 33 percent of a worker's wages up to a certain maximum payment. In 2005 benefits averaged about $262 weekly. The number of beneficiaries and the level of total disbursements vary with economic conditions.

Public Assistance Programs

Public assistance programs (welfare) provide benefits to people who are unable to earn income because of permanent handicaps or who have no or very low income and also have dependent children. These programs are financed out of general tax revenues and are regarded as public charity. They include "means tests" which require that individuals and families demonstrate low incomes in order to qualify for aid. The Federal government finances about two-thirds of the welfare program expenditures, and the rest is paid for by the states.

Many needy persons who do not qualify for social insurance programs are assisted through the Federal government's **Supplemental Security Income (SSI)** program. This is a Federal program (financed by general tax revenues) that provides a uniform nationwide minimum income for the aged, blind, and disabled who do not qualify for benefits under the Social Security program in the United States. The purpose of SSI is to establish a uniform, nationwide minimum income for the aged, blind, and disabled who are unable to work and who do not qualify for Social Security aid. In 2005 the average monthly payment was $579 for individuals and $869 for couples with both people eligible. More than half the states provide additional income supplements to the aged, blind, and disabled.

The **Temporary Assistance for Needy Families (TANF)** program is the basic welfare program (financed through general tax revenues) for low-income families in the United States. It is state-administered but is financed partly with Federal grants. The program provides cash assistance to families with children and also seeks to reduce welfare dependency by promoting job preparation and work. TANF's predecessor was the Aid to Families with Dependent Children (AFDC) program. But unlike that program, TANF has work requirements and limits on the length of time a family can receive welfare payments. In 2004 about 5 million people (including children) received TANF assistance. The average monthly payment was $397.

The **food-stamp program** is a Federal program (financed through general tax revenues) that permits eligible low-income persons to obtain vouchers which can be used to buy food. It is designed to provide all low-income Americans with a "nutritionally adequate diet." Under the program, eligible households receive monthly allotments of coupons that are redeemable for food. The amount of food stamps received varies inversely with a family's earned income.

Medicaid is a Federal program (financed by general tax revenues) that provides medical benefits to people covered by the Supplemental Security Income (SSI) and TANF (basic welfare) programs. It helps finance the medical expenses of individuals participating in those programs.

The **earned-income tax credit (EITC)** is a refundable Federal tax credit provided to low-income wage earners to supplement their families' incomes and encourage work. It is available for low-income working families, with or without children. The credit reduces the Federal income taxes that such families owe or provides them with cash payments if the credit exceeds their tax liabilities. The purpose of the credit is to offset Social Security taxes paid by low-wage earners and thus keep the Federal government from "taxing families into poverty." In essence, EITC is a wage subsidy from the Federal government that works out to be as much as $2 per hour for the lowest-paid workers with families. Under the program many people owe no income tax and receive direct checks from the Federal government once a year. According to the Internal Revenue Service, 21 million taxpayers received $36 billion in payments from the EITC in 2003.

Several other welfare programs are not listed in Table 20.3. Some provide help in the form of noncash transfers. Head Start provides education, nutrition, and social services to economically disadvantaged 3- and 4-year-olds. Housing assistance in the form of rent subsidies and funds for construction is available to low-income families. Pell grants provide assistance to undergraduate students from low-income families. Low-income home energy assistance provides help with home heating bills. Other programs—such as veteran's assistance and black lung benefits—provide cash assistance to those eligible.

QUICK REVIEW 20.2

- The basic argument for income equality is that it maximizes total utility by equalizing the marginal utility of the last dollar of income received by all people.
- The basic argument for income inequality is that it is necessary as an economic incentive for production.
- By government standards, 37 million people in the United States, or 12.7 percent of the population, lived in poverty in 2004.
- The U.S. income-maintenance system includes both social insurance programs and public assistance (welfare) programs.

Welfare: Goals and Conflicts

An ideal public assistance (welfare) program should achieve three goals. First, the program should be effective in getting individuals and families out of poverty. Second, it should provide adequate incentives for able-bodied, nonretired people to work. Third, its cost should be "reasonable." Unfortunately, these three goals conflict with one another, causing tradeoffs and necessitating compromises. To understand why, consider the three hypothetical welfare plans shown in Table 20.4.

Common Features

We first examine the two common elements in these three plans (and in real-world public assistance plans). First, there is a *minimum annual income* that the government will provide if the family has no earned income. Second, there is a *benefit-reduction rate,* which is the rate at which benefits are reduced or "lost" as a result of earned income.

Consider plan 1. The minimum annual income provided by the government is $8000, and the benefit-reduction rate is 50 percent. If a family earns no income, it will receive cash transfer payments totaling $8000. If it earns $4000, it will lose $2000 of transfer payments ($4000 of earnings × 50 percent benefit-reduction rate); its total income will then be $10,000 (= $4000 of earnings + $6000 of transfer payments). If it earns $8000, its transfer payments will fall to $4000, and so on. Note that at an income of $16,000, transfer payments are zero. The level of earned income at which the transfer payments disappear is called the *break-even income.*

We might criticize plan 1 on the grounds that a 50 percent benefit-reduction rate is too high and therefore does not provide sufficient incentives to work. As earned income increases, the loss of transfer payments constitutes a "tax" on earnings. Some people may choose not to work when they lose 50 cents of each extra dollar earned. Thus in plan 2 the $8000 minimum income is retained, but the benefit-reduction rate is reduced to 25 percent. But note that the break-even level of income increases to $32,000, so many more families would now qualify for transfer payments. Furthermore, a family with any earned income under $32,000 will receive a larger total transfer payment. For both reasons, a reduction of the benefit-loss rate to enhance work incentives will raise the cost of the income-maintenance plan.

After examining plans 1 and 2, we might argue that the $8000 minimum annual income is too low—it does not get families out of poverty. Plan 3 raises the minimum income to $12,000 and retains the 50 percent benefit-reduction rate of plan 1. While plan 3 does a better job of raising the incomes of the poor, it too yields a higher break-even income than plan 1 and therefore will be more costly. Also, if the $12,000 income guarantee of plan 3 were coupled with plan 2's 25 percent benefit-reduction rate to strengthen work incentives, the break-even income level would shoot up to $48,000 and add even more to the costs of the public assistance program.

TABLE 20.4 Tradeoffs among Goals: Three Public Assistance Plans

Plan 1 ($8000 Minimum Income and 50% Benefit-Reduction Rate)			Plan 2 ($8000 Minimum Income and 25% Benefit-Reduction Rate)			Plan 3 ($12,000 Minimum Income and 50% Benefit-Reduction Rate)		
Earned Income	Transfer Payment	Total Income	Earned Income	Transfer Payment	Total Income	Earned Income	Transfer Payment	Total Income
$ 0	$8000	$ 8000	$ 0	$8000	$ 8000	$ 0	$12,000	$12,000
4000	6000	10,000	8000	6000	14,000	8000	8000	16,000
8000	4000	12,000	16,000	4000	20,000	16,000	4000	20,000
12,000	2000	14,000	24,000	2000	26,000	24,000*	0	24,000
16,000*	0	16,000	32,000*	0	32,000			

*Indicates break-even income. Determined by dividing the minimum income by the benefit-reduction rate.

Conflicts among Goals

Clearly, then, the goals of eliminating poverty, maintaining work incentives, and holding down program costs are in conflict.

Plan 1, with a low minimum income and a high benefit-reduction rate, keeps cost down. But the low minimum income means that this plan is not very effective in eliminating poverty, and the high benefit-reduction rate weakens work incentives.

In comparison, plan 2 has a lower benefit-reduction rate and therefore stronger work incentives. But it is more costly, because it sets a higher break-even income and therefore pays benefits to more families.

W 20.2

Public assistance plans

Compared with plan 1, plan 3 has a higher minimum income and is more effective in eliminating poverty. While work incentives are the same as those in plan 1, the higher guaranteed income in plan 3 makes the plan more costly. **(Key Question 12)**

Welfare Reform

The tradeoffs just mentioned shed light on the nation's relatively recent reform of the welfare system. In 1996 the public assistance or welfare part of the U.S. income-maintenance program underwent major reform. The reform grew out of the reality that welfare spending was not ending poverty. While the number of people receiving welfare benefits under the Aid to Families with Dependent Children (AFDC) program rose substantially in the 1980s and early 1990s, the number of people in poverty went up, instead of down. The AFDC program appeared to create dependency on the government, thereby robbing individuals and family members of motivation and dignity.

The Personal Responsibility Act of 1996 replaced AFDC with the *Temporary Assistance for Needy Families (TANF)* program, which ended the Federal government's six-decade-old welfare program based on cash assistance for poor families. Under the new law, the Federal government instead pays each state a lump-sum of Federal money each year to operate its own welfare and work programs. These lump-sum payments are called TANF funds. But the TANF reform did much more. It:

- Set a lifetime limit of 5 years on receiving TANF benefits and required able-bodied adults to work after receiving assistance for 2 years.
- Ended food-stamp eligibility for able-bodied persons age 18 to 50 (with no dependents) who are not working or engaged in job-training programs.
- Tightened the definition of "disabled children" as it applies for eligibility of low-income families for Supplemental Security Income (SSI) assistance.
- Established a 5-year waiting period on public assistance for new legal immigrants who have not become citizens.

Supporters of TANF believe that it already has played a key role in helping to end a "culture of welfare" in which dropping out of school, having a child, and going on welfare were allegedly becoming a normal way of life for part of the welfare population. They cite large declines in the welfare rolls as evidence of the law's effectiveness. In 1996 there were 12.6 million welfare recipients, including children, or 4.8 percent of the U.S. population. By the middle of 2005 those totals had declined to 4.5 million and 2 percent of the population. Economists attribute about half the decline to welfare reform and the other half to the strong demand for labor and the low unemployment accompanying the economic expansion in the last half of the 1990s. Many more single mothers with children under age 6—a group particularly prone to welfare dependency—are working than prior to TANF. The employment rate (= employment/population) for this group is a striking 13 percentage points higher today than in 1996.

The recession of 2001 and the slack labor market in 2002 slowed the decline of welfare recipients but did not reverse the downward trend. Economists judge the positive results of the 1996 welfare reform as strong confirmation of two economic principles: Economic growth and high levels of employment are powerful antipoverty forces, and welfare program incentives (and disincentives) clearly matter.

Last Word

U.S. Family Wealth and Its Distribution

In 2006 the Federal Reserve Reported Its Latest Findings on Family Wealth (= Net Worth = Assets *Minus* Liabilities) in the United States. Between 1995 and 2004 Family Wealth Rose Rapidly and Became More Unequal.

The Federal Reserve conducts a Survey of Consumer Finances in the United States every 3 years, through which it determines median family wealth, average family wealth, and the distribution of wealth. *Median family wealth* is the wealth received by the family at the midpoint of the distribution; *average family wealth* is simply total wealth divided by the number of families. As shown in Table 1, median and average family wealth, adjusted for inflation, was considerably higher in 2004 than in 1995. That is, the value of family assets rose more rapidly than the value of liabilities, increasing net worth—or wealth. Between 1995 and 2004, median and average wealth rose by 31 percent and 72 percent, respectively. In general, American families are wealthier than they were before.

Table 2 looks at the distribution of family wealth for various percentile groups and reveals that the distribution of wealth is highly unequal. In 2004 the wealthiest 10 percent of families owned almost 70 percent of the total wealth and the top 1 percent owned 33 percent. The bottom 90 percent held only about 30 percent of the total wealth.

Moreover, the general trend is toward greater inequality of wealth. The lowest 90 percent of the families owned about 32 percent of total U.S. wealth in 1995, but that percentage fell to about 30 percent in 2004.

So from a normative standpoint, Tables 1 and 2 present a "mixed-news" combination. The welcome news is that median and average wealth in the United States rose substantially between 1995 and 2004. The discouraging news is that such wealth grew less rapidly for the typical American family than for the top 10 percent of American families over the entire period.

Tables 1 and 2 raise many interesting questions: Will the inequality of wealth continue to grow in the future? If so, what are the implications for the future character of the American society? Should government do more, or less, in the future to try to redistribute wealth? Would new government policies to redistribute wealth endanger or slow the creation of wealth and the growth of income for average Americans? The Federal estate tax is currently scheduled to phase out in 2012 and then return to very high levels. Should the phase-out be made permanent or replaced with a new estate tax at a lower rate?

Sources: Brian K. Bucks, Arthur B. Kennickell, and Kevin B. Moore, "Recent Changes in U.S. Family Finances: Evidence from the 2001 and 2004 Survey of Consumer Finances," *Federal Reserve Bulletin*, January 2006, p. 8; Arthur B. Kennickell, "Currents and Undercurrents: Changes in the Distribution of Wealth, 1989–2004," Survey of Consumer Finances working paper, January 2006, p. 11.

TABLE 1 Median and Average Family Wealth, Survey Years, 1995–2004 (in 2004 Dollars)

Year	Median	Average*
1995	70,800	260,800
1998	83,100	327,500
2001	91,700	421,500
2004	93,100	448,200

*The averages greatly exceed the medians because the averages are boosted by the multibillion-dollar wealth of a relatively few families.

TABLE 2 Percentage of Total Family Wealth Held by Different Percentile Groups, Survey Years, 1995–2004

	Percentile of Wealth Distribution		
Year	Bottom 90%	Top 10%	Top 1%
1995	32.2%	67.8%	34.6%
1998	31.4	68.6	33.9
2001	30.2	69.8	32.7
2004	30.5	69.5	33.4

Summary

1. The distribution of income in the United States reflects considerable inequality. The richest 20 percent of households receive 50.1 percent of total income, while the poorest 20 percent receive 3.4 percent.
2. The Lorenz curve shows the percentage of total income received by each percentage of families. The extent of the gap between the Lorenz curve and a line of total equality illustrates the degree of income inequality.
3. The Gini ratio measures the overall dispersion of the income distribution and is found by dividing the area between the diagonal and the Lorenz curve by the entire area below the diagonal. Higher Gini ratios signify greater degrees of income inequality.
4. Recognizing that the positions of individual families in the distribution of income change over time and incorporating the effects of noncash transfers and taxes would reveal less income inequality than do standard census data. Government transfers (cash and noncash) greatly lessen the degree of income inequality; taxes also reduce inequality, but not nearly as much as transfers.
5. Causes of income inequality include differences in abilities, in education and training, and in job tastes, along with discrimination, inequality in the distribution of wealth, and an unequal distribution of market power.
6. Census data show that income inequality has increased since 1970. The major cause of the recent increases in income inequality is a rising demand for highly skilled workers, which has boosted their earnings significantly.
7. The basic argument for income equality is that it maximizes consumer satisfaction (total utility) from a particular level of total income. The main argument for income inequality is that it provides the incentives to work, invest, and assume risk and is necessary for the production of output, which, in turn, creates income that is then available for distribution.
8. Current statistics reveal that 12.7 percent of the U.S. population lives in poverty. Poverty rates are particularly high for female-headed families, young children, blacks, and Hispanics.
9. The present income-maintenance program in the United States consists of social insurance programs (Social Security, Medicare, and unemployment compensation) and public assistance programs (SSI, TANF, food stamps, Medicaid, and earned-income tax credit).
10. Public assistance programs (welfare) are difficult to design because their goals of reducing poverty, maintaining work incentives, and holding down program costs are often in conflict with one another.
11. In 1996 Congress established the Temporary Assistance for Needy Families (TANF) program, which shifted responsibility for welfare from the Federal government to the states. Among its provisions are work requirements for adults receiving welfare and a 5-year lifelong limit on welfare benefits.
12. A strong economy and TANF reduced the U.S. welfare rolls by more than one-half between 1996 and 2005.

Terms and Concepts

income inequality
Lorenz curve
Gini ratio
income mobility
noncash transfers
equality-efficiency tradeoff
poverty rate
entitlement programs
social insurance programs
Social Security
Medicare
unemployment compensation
public assistance programs
Supplemental Security Income (SSI)
Temporary Assistance for Needy Families (TANF)
food-stamp program
Medicaid
earned-income tax credit (EITC)

Study Questions

1. Use quintiles to briefly summarize the degree of income inequality in the United States. How and to what extent does government reduce income inequality?
2. **KEY QUESTION** Assume that Al, Beth, Carol, David, and Ed receive incomes of \$500, \$250, \$125, \$75, and \$50, respectively. Construct and interpret a Lorenz curve for this five-person economy. What percentage of total income is received by the richest quintile and by the poorest quintile?
3. How does the Gini ratio relate to the Lorenz curve? Why can't the Gini ratio exceed 1? What is implied about the direction of income inequality if the Gini ratio declines from 0.42 to 0.35? How would one show that change of inequality in the Lorenz diagram?

4. Why is the lifetime distribution of income more equal than the distribution in any specific year?
5. **KEY QUESTION** Briefly discuss the major causes of income inequality. With respect to income inequality, is there any difference between inheriting property and inheriting a high IQ? Explain.
6. What factors have contributed to increased income inequality since 1970?
7. Should a nation's income be distributed to its members according to their contributions to the production of that total income or according to the members' needs? Should society attempt to equalize income or economic opportunities? Are the issues of equity and equality in the distribution of income synonymous? To what degree, if any, is income inequality equitable?
8. Do you agree? Or disagree? Explain your reasoning. "There need be no tradeoff between equality and efficiency. An 'efficient' economy that yields an income distribution that many regard as unfair may cause those with meager incomes to become discouraged and stop trying. So efficiency may be undermined. A fairer distribution of rewards may generate a higher average productive effort on the part of the population, thereby enhancing efficiency. If people think they are playing a fair economic game and this belief causes them to try harder, an economy with an equitable income distribution may be efficient as well."[5]
9. Comment on or explain:
   a. Endowing everyone with equal income will make for very unequal enjoyment and satisfaction.
   b. Equality is a "superior good"; the richer we become, the more of it we can afford.
   c. The mob goes in search of bread, and the means it employs is generally to wreck the bakeries.
   d. Some freedoms may be more important in the long run than freedom from want on the part of every individual.
   e. Capitalism and democracy are really a most improbable mixture. Maybe that is why they need each other—to put some rationality into equality and some humanity into efficiency.
   f. The incentives created by the attempt to bring about a more equal distribution of income are in conflict with the incentives needed to generate increased income.
10. **KEY QUESTION** How do government statisticians determine the poverty rate? How could the poverty rate fall while the number of people in poverty rises? Which group in each of the following pairs has the highest poverty rate: (*a*) children or people age 65 or over? (*b*) African-Americans or foreign-born noncitizens? (*c*) Asians or Hispanics?
11. What are the essential differences between social insurance and public assistance programs? Why is Medicare a social insurance program whereas Medicaid is a public assistance program? Why is the earned-income tax credit considered to be a public assistance program?
12. **KEY QUESTION** The following table contains three hypothetical public assistance plans:

Plan 1		
Earned Income	Transfer Payment	Total Income
$ 0	$4000	$ 4000
2000	3000	5000
4000	2000	6000
6000	1000	7000

Plan 2		
Earned Income	Transfer Payment	Total Income
$ 0	$4000	$ 4000
4000	3000	7000
8000	2000	10,000
12,000	1000	13,000

Plan 3		
Earned Income	Transfer Payment	Total Income
$ 0	$8000	$ 8000
4000	6000	10,000
8000	4000	12,000
12,000	2000	14,000

   a. Determine the minimum income, the benefit-reduction rate, and the break-even income for each plan.
   b. Which plan is the most costly? The least costly? Which plan is the most effective in reducing poverty? The least effective? Which plan contains the strongest disincentive to work? The strongest incentive to work?
   c. Use your answers in part *b* to explain the following statement: "The dilemma of public assistance is that you cannot bring families up to the poverty level and simultaneously preserve work incentives (without work requirements) and minimize program costs."
13. What major criticisms of the U.S. welfare system led to its reform in 1996 (via the Personal Responsibility Act)? How did this reform try to address those criticisms? Do you agree with the general thrust of the reform and with its emphasis on work requirements and time limits on welfare benefits? Has the reform reduced U.S. welfare rolls or increased them?
14. **LAST WORD** Go to Table 1 in the Last Word and compute the ratio of average wealth to median wealth for each of the 4 years. What trend do you find? What is your explanation for the trend? The Federal estate tax redistributes wealth in two ways: by encouraging charitable giving, which reduces the taxable estate, and by heavily taxing extraordinarily large estates and using the proceeds to fund government programs. Do you favor repealing the estate tax? Explain.

[5]Paraphrased from Andrew Schotter, *Free Market Economics* (New York: St. Martin's Press, 1985), pp. 30–31.

Web-Based Questions

1. **HOW MUCH FAMILY INCOME DOES IT TAKE TO BE IN THE RICHEST 5 PERCENT?** Go to the U.S. Census Bureau Web site, **www.census.gov,** and select Income (under People), Historical Income Tables (CPS), and Income Inequality. What is the lower limit of household income for the richest 5 percent of families in the most recent year listed? Do the historical data in the table suggest the poor are getting poorer and the rich are getting richer in absolute terms? Return to the tables on inequality and determine what has happened to the relative income share of the richest 5 percent of households over the last 10 years listed.
2. **IS POVERTY ON THE RISE OR ON THE DECLINE?** Go to the U.S. Census Bureau Web site, **www.census.gov,** and select Poverty (under People). Use the data provided to answer the following questions:
   - **a.** Is the number of people living below the official government poverty level higher or lower than it was in the preceding year? Than it was a decade earlier?
   - **b.** Is the poverty rate (in percent) higher or lower than it was in the preceding year for the general population, children under 18, blacks, Asians, Pacific Islanders, and whites?
   - **c.** How many states had increases in the poverty rate compared to the preceding year?

21

IN THIS CHAPTER YOU WILL LEARN:

- Important facts about rising health care costs in the United States.
- The economic implications of rising health care costs.
- The problem of limited access to health care for those without insurance.
- The demand and supply factors explaining rising health care costs.
- The types of potential reforms of the U.S. health care system.
- How recent legislation has altered the U.S. health care system.

The Economics of Health Care

Rarely can you read a newspaper or look at a television news program without encountering a story about the high costs of health care in the United States, seriously ill people who have no health insurance, or government health insurance programs that threaten to drain Federal and state budgets. Some news stories document disputes between employers and workers over sharing the cost of health insurance or cite instances of insurance companies dictating the medical care that doctors can provide. We even learn of companies that break their promises to provide health insurance to retirees and of lawsuits challenging such actions. Moreover, difficult ethical questions concerning "extreme care" for the acutely or terminally ill arise from time to time.

Health care accounts for 15 percent of U.S. GDP and 10 percent of total employment, making it worthy of specific study. Further, the tools of microeconomic analysis are particularly helpful in understanding the U.S. health care system, major health care issues, and actual and proposed reforms.

The Health Care Industry

Because the boundaries of the health care industry are not precise, defining the industry is difficult. In general, it includes services provided in hospitals, nursing homes, laboratories, and physicians' and dentists' offices. It also includes prescription and nonprescription drugs, artificial limbs, and eyeglasses. Note, however, that many goods and services that may affect health are not included, for example, low-fat foods, vitamins, and health club services.

Health care is one of the largest U.S. industries, employing about 9 million people, including about 736,000 practicing physicians, or 267 doctors per 100,000 of population. There are about 5800 hospitals containing 965,000 beds. Americans make more than 1 billion visits to office-based physicians each year.

Twin Problems: Costs and Access

Two highly publicized problems are related to the U.S. health care system:

- The cost of health care has risen rapidly in response to higher prices and an increase in the quantity of services provided. (Spending on health care involves both "prices" and "quantities" and is often loosely referred to as "health care costs.") The price of medical care has increased faster than the overall price level. For example, the December-to-December index of medical care prices rose by 5.0 percent in 2002, 3.7 percent in 2003, 4.2 percent in 2004, and 4.3 percent in 2005. (The overall price index increased by an annual average of 2.8 percent for those four years.) Health care spending (price × quantity) grew by 6.4 percent in 2002, 8.2 percent in 2003, and 7.9 percent in 2004. It is projected to grow at an annual rate of 7.3 percent over the next 10 years.
- Some 46 million Americans do not have health insurance coverage, and many Americans have limited, or no, access to health care.

Efforts to reform health care have focused on controlling costs and making it accessible to everyone. Those two goals are related, since high and rising prices make health care services unaffordable to a significant portion of the U.S. population. In fact, a dual system of health care may be evolving in the United States. Those with insurance or other financial means receive the world's highest quality medical treatment, but many people, because of their inability to pay, do not obtain the most basic treatment. When they do seek treatment, they may receive poorer care than those who have insurance.

High and Rising Health Care Costs

We need to examine several aspects of health care spending and health care costs.

Health Care Spending

Health care spending in the United States is high and rising in both absolute terms and as a percentage of domestic output.

Total Spending on Health Care

Figure 21.1a gives an overview of the major types of U.S. health care spending ($1.88 trillion in 2004). It shows that 30 cents of each health care dollar is spent on hospitals, while 21 cents goes to physicians and 24 cents for other health care services (dental, vision, and home care).

Figure 21.1b shows the sources of funds for health care spending. It reveals that four-fifths of health care spending is financed by insurance. Public insurance (Medicaid, Medicare, and insurance for veterans, current military personnel, and government employees) is the source of 45 cents of each dollar spent. Private insurance accounts for 35 cents. So public and private insurance combined provide 80 cents of each dollar spent. The remaining 20 cents comes directly out of the health care consumer's pocket. It is paid mainly as insurance **deductibles** (that is, the insured pays the first $250 or $500 of each year's health care costs before the insurer begins paying) or **copayments** (that is, the insured pays, say, 20 percent of all health care costs and the insurance company pays 80 percent).

Recall that Medicare is a nationwide Federal health care program available to Social Security beneficiaries and persons with disabilities. One part of Medicare is a hospital insurance program that, after a deductible of $952 (in 2006), covers all reasonable costs for the first 60 days of inpatient care per "benefit period" and lesser amounts (on a cost-sharing basis) for additional days. Coverage is also provided for posthospital nursing services, home health care, and hospice care for the terminally ill. The second part of Medicare, a medical insurance program (for physicians' services, laboratory and other diagnostic tests, and outpatient hospital services), is voluntary but is heavily subsidized by government. The $88.50 monthly premiums (in 2006) that participants pay cover about one-fourth of the cost of the benefits provided.

Medicaid provides payment for medical benefits to certain low-income people, including the elderly, the blind, persons with disabilities, children, and adults with dependent children. Those who qualify for Temporary

FIGURE 21.1 Health care expenditures and finance. (a) Most health care expenditures are for hospitals and the services of physicians and other skilled professionals. (b) Public and private insurance pay for four-fifths of health care.

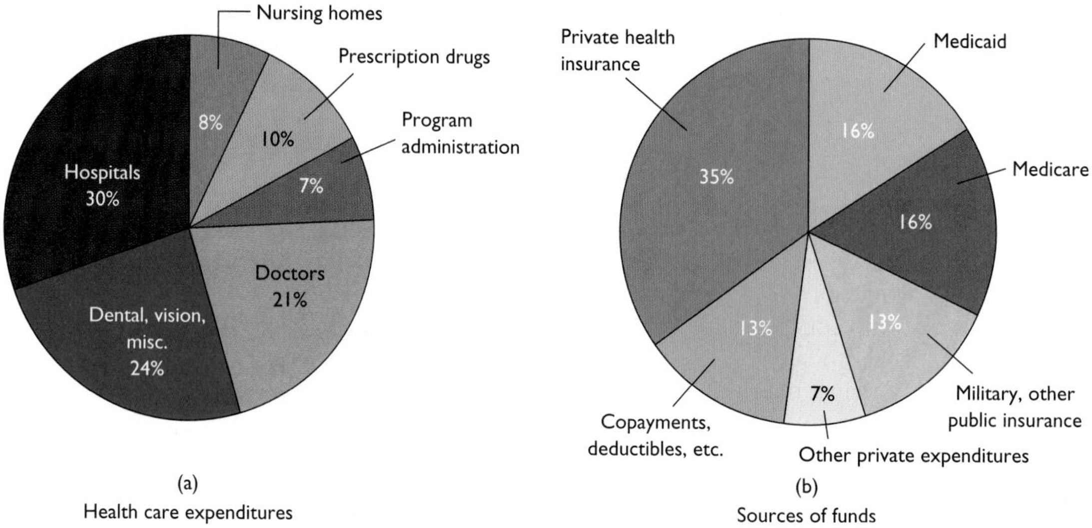

Source: Centers for Medicare and Medicaid Services, **cms.hhs.gov/.** Data are for 2004 and are compiled by the authors.

Aid for Needy Families (TANF) and the Supplemental Security Income (SSI) program are automatically eligible for Medicaid. Nevertheless, Medicaid covers less than half of those living in poverty. The Federal government and the states share the cost of Medicaid. On average, the states fund 43 percent and the Federal government 57 percent of each Medicaid dollar spent.

Overall, about 20 percent of each dollar spent on health care is financed by direct out-of-pocket payments by individuals. The fact that most U.S. health care is paid for by private insurance companies or the government is an important contributor to rising health care costs.

Percentage of GDP Figure 21.2 shows how U.S. health care spending has been increasing as a percentage of GDP. Health care spending absorbed 5.2 percent of GDP in 1960 but rose to 16 percent by 2004. Government agencies project that national health care expenditures will reach 18 percent of GDP by 2010.

International Comparisons Global Perspective 21.1 reveals that among the industrialized nations, health care spending as a percentage of GDP is highest in the United States. It is reasonable to assume that health care spending varies positively with output and incomes, but that doesn't account for the higher U.S. health expenditures as a percentage of GDP. For whatever reason, the United States is "in a league of its own" as to its proportion of output devoted to health care.

Quality of Care: Are We Healthier?

To compare the quality of health care from country to country is difficult. Yet there is general agreement that medical care (although not health and not "preventive

FIGURE 21.2 U.S. health care expenditures as a percentage of GDP. U.S. health care spending as a percentage of GDP has greatly increased since 1960 and is projected to rise still more.

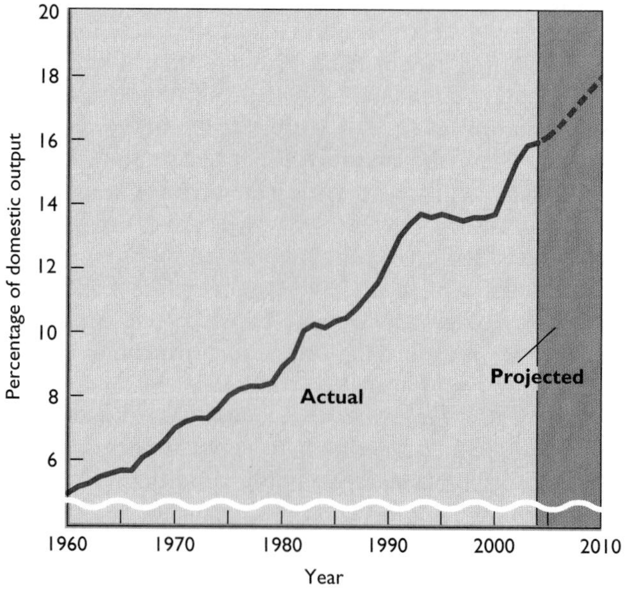

Source: Centers for Medicare and Medicaid Services, **cms.hhs.gov/.**

GLOBAL PERSPECTIVE 21.1

Health Care Spending as a Percentage of GDP, Selected Nations

The United States tops the chart when it comes to health care expenditures as a percentage of GDP.

Health Care Spending as a Percentage of GDP, 2003

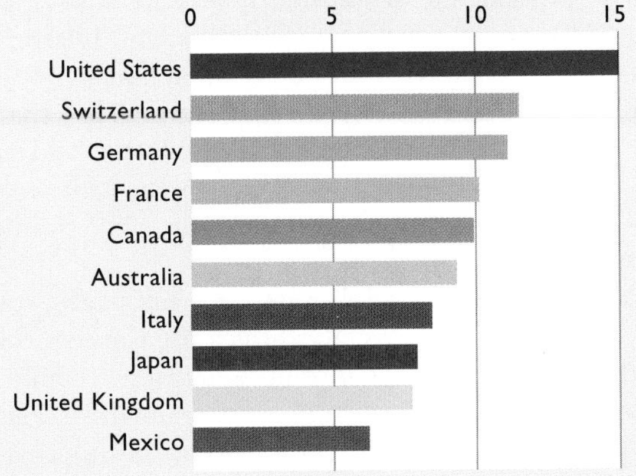

Source: Organization for Economic Cooperation and Development, **www.oecd.org/.**

treatment") in the United States is probably the best in the world. Average life expectancy in the United States has increased by 6 years since 1970, and U.S. physicians and hospitals employ the most advanced medical equipment and technologies. Also, more than half the world's medical research funding is done in the United States. As a result, the incidence of disease has been declining and the quality of treatment has been improving. Polio has been virtually eliminated, ulcers are successfully treated without surgery, angioplasty and coronary bypass surgery greatly benefit those with heart disease, sophisticated body scanners are increasingly available diagnostic tools, and organ transplants and prosthetic joint replacements are more and more common.

That is the good news. But there is other news as well. Despite new screening and treatment technologies, the breast cancer mortality rate has shown little change. Tuberculosis, a virtually forgotten disease, has reappeared. The AIDS epidemic has claimed more than 530,000 American lives. More generally, some experts say that high levels of health care spending have not produced significantly better health and well-being. U.S. health care expenditures are the highest in the world absolutely, as a proportion of GDP, and on a per capita basis. Yet many other nations rank higher than the United States in fixed life expectancy, maternal mortality, and infant mortality.

Economic Implications of Rising Costs

The most visible economic effects of rising health care costs are higher health insurance premiums to employers and higher out-of-pocket costs to workers. But rising health care costs have other economic effects as well.

Reduced Access to Care

Higher health care costs and insurance premiums reduce access to health care. Some employers reduce or eliminate health insurance as part of their pay packages and some uninsured workers go without private health insurance. Consequently, the number of uninsured grows. We will consider this issue in detail momentarily.

Labor Market Effects

Surging health care costs have three main effects on labor markets:

- ***Slower wage growth*** First, gains in workers' total compensation (wage plus fringe benefits, including health insurance paid for by employers) generally match gains in productivity. When health care costs (and thus insurance prices) rise more rapidly than productivity, firms wanting to maintain the existing level of health care benefits for their workers must reduce the growth of the wage portion of the total compensation package. Thus, in the long run, workers bear the burden of rising health care costs in the form of slower-growing wages.
- ***Use of part-time and temporary workers*** The high cost of employer-provided health insurance has led some employers to restructure their workforces: Full-time workers with health insurance benefits are employed in smaller numbers, and uninsured part-time or temporary workers are employed in greater numbers. Similarly, a large, prosperous employer with a generous health care plan might reduce its health insurance expense by discharging its insured lower-wage workers—janitors, gardeners, and cafeteria staff—and replacing them with outside independent contractors who provide no health insurance to their employees.
- ***Outsourcing (and Offshoring)*** Burdened by rising insurance costs, some firms may find that shifting part of their work to domestic or international suppliers is profitable. This outsourcing may lower labor costs in situations where the outside suppliers provide lesser medical benefits to their workers.

Offshoring (international outsourcing) has shifted jobs to developing economies such as Mexico, India, and China. Although labor productivity in these countries is considerably lower than that in the United States, lower wages and employer-provided medical benefits may be sufficient to make offshoring profitable. Rising domestic medical expenses therefore may join a host of other factors, including shifts in comparative advantage, in encouraging this practice.

Personal Bankruptcies Large, uninsured medical bills are one of the major causes of personal bankruptcy. Health care experts point out that medical bills are often the last to be paid because unlike other bills there is nothing to repossess, shut off, or foreclose. So medical bills sometimes build up beyond the point of a realistic means for full repayment. Even individuals who pay all bills in a timely fashion can find themselves in tremendous financial difficulty when they face large, uncompensated medical bills for major operations (such as open-heart surgery) and expensive medical procedures (such as cancer treatment).

Impact on Government Budgets The budgets of Federal, state, and local governments are negatively affected by spiraling and sometimes unpredictable health care expenditures. In the past two decades, spending for health care through Medicare and Medicaid has been by far the fastest-growing segment of the Federal budget. To cover those rising expenditures, the government must either raise taxes or reduce the portion of the budget used for national defense, education, environmental programs, scientific research, and other spending categories.

The states are also finding it difficult to cover their share of the Medicaid bill. Most of them have been forced to raise their tax rates and search for new sources of revenue, and many of them have had to reduce spending on nonhealth programs such as infrastructure maintenance, welfare, and education. Local governments face similar budget strains in trying to finance public health services, hospitals, and clinics.

Too Much Spending?

Increased spending on computers or houses would be a sign of prosperity, not a cause for alarm, because society is obtaining more of each. What is different about increased spending on health care? Maybe nothing, say some economists. William Nordhaus of Yale, for example, recently estimated that the economic value of increases in longevity over the last 100 years nearly equals the total value of the additional GDP during that period. According to Kevin Murphy and Robert Topel, economists at the University of Chicago, reduced mortality from heart disease alone contributes \$1.5 trillion of benefits a year in the United States. That amount exceeds the entire annual GDP of Canada.

While all economists agree that improved health care has greatly contributed to society's GDP and well-being, many economists think that health care expenditures in the United States are inefficiently large. The production of health care requires scarce resources such as capital in the form of hospitals and diagnostic equipment and the highly skilled labor of physicians, technicians, and nurses. The total output of health care in the United States may be so large that health care, at the margin, is worth less than the alternative goods and services these resources could otherwise have produced. The United States therefore may be consuming health care beyond the $MB = MC$ point that defines efficiency.

If resources are overallocated to health care, society incurs an efficiency loss. Resources used excessively in health care could be used more productively to build new factories, support research and development, construct new bridges and roads, support education, improve the environment, or provide more consumer goods.

The suggested "too much of a good thing" results from peculiarities in the market for health care. We will see that the possibility of overspending arises from the way health care is financed, the asymmetry of information between consumers and providers, and the interaction of health insurance with technological progress in the industry.

Limited Access

The other health care problem is limited access. Even though there may be an overallocation of resources to health care, not all Americans can obtain the health care they need. In 2004 about 46 million Americans, or roughly 16 percent of the population, had no health insurance for the entire year. As health care costs (and therefore health care insurance premiums) continue to rise, the number of uninsured could grow.

Who are the medically uninsured? As incomes rise, so does the probability of being insured. So it is no surprise that the uninsured are concentrated among the poor. Medicaid is designed to provide health care for the poor who are on welfare. But many poor people work at low or minimum-wage jobs without health care benefits, earning "too much" to qualify for Medicaid yet not enough to afford private health insurance. About half of the uninsured have a family head who works full-time. Many single-parent families, African Americans, and Hispanics are uninsured simply because they are more likely to be poor.

Curiously, those with excellent health and those with the poorest health also tend to be uninsured. Many young people with excellent health simply choose not to buy health insurance. The chronically ill find it very difficult and too costly to obtain insurance because of the likelihood that they will incur substantial health care costs in the future. Because private health insurance is most frequently obtained through an employer, the unemployed are also likely to lack insurance.

Workers for smaller firms are also less likely to have health insurance. The main reason is that administrative expenses for a small firm may be 30 to 40 percent of insurance premiums, as opposed to only 10 percent for a large firm. Also, corporations can deduct health insurance premiums from income to obtain substantial tax savings. Small unincorporated businesses can deduct only part of their health insurance expenses.

Low-wage workers are also less likely to be insured. Earlier we noted that in the long run employers pass on the increasing expense of health care insurance to workers as lower wages. This option is not available to employers who are paying the minimum wage. Thus as health care insurance premiums rise, employers cut or eliminate this benefit from the compensation package for their minimum- and low-wage workers. As a result, these workers are typically uninsured.

Although many of the uninsured forgo health care, some do not. A few are able to pay for it out of pocket. Others may wait until their illness reaches a critical stage and then go to a hospital for admittance or to be treated in the emergency room. These methods of treatment are inappropriate and unnecessarily costly. It is estimated that hospitals provide $25 billion to $30 billion of uncompensated ("free") health care per year. The hospitals then try to shift these costs to those who have insurance or who can pay out of pocket. **(Key Question 2)**

QUICK REVIEW 21.1

- Health care spending in the United States has been increasing absolutely and as a percentage of gross domestic output.
- Rising health care costs have caused (a) more people to find health insurance unaffordable; (b) adverse labor market effects, including slower real-wage growth and increased use of part-time and temporary workers; and (c) restriction of nonhealth spending by governments.
- Rising health care spending may reflect an overallocation of resources to the health care industry.
- Approximately 16 percent of all Americans have no health insurance and, hence, no (or limited) access to health care.

Why the Rapid Rise in Costs?

The rising prices, quantities, and costs of health care services are the result of the demand for health care increasing much more rapidly than supply. We will examine the reasons for this in some detail. But first it will be helpful to understand certain characteristics of the health care market.

Peculiarities of the Health Care Market

We know that purely competitive markets achieve both allocative and productive efficiency: The most desired products are produced in the least costly way. We also have found that many imperfectly competitive markets, perhaps aided by regulation or the threat of antitrust action, provide outcomes generally accepted as efficient. What, then, are the special features of the health care market that have contributed to rising prices and thus escalating costs to buyers?

- ***Ethical and equity considerations*** Ethical questions inevitably intervene in markets when decisions involve the quality of life, or literally life or death. Although we might not consider it immoral or unfair if a person cannot buy a Mercedes or a personal computer, society regards it as unjust for people to be denied access to basic health care or even to the best available health care. In general, society regards health care as an "entitlement" or a "right" and is reluctant to ration it solely by price and income.
- ***Asymmetric information*** Health care buyers typically have little or no understanding of complex diagnostic and treatment procedures, while the physicians who are the health care sellers of those procedures possess detailed information. This creates the unusual situation in which the doctor (supplier) as the agent of the patient (consumer) tells the patient what health care services he or she should consume. We will say more about this shortly.
- ***Positive externalities*** The medical care market often generates positive externalities (spillover benefits). For example, an immunization against polio, smallpox, or measles benefits the immediate purchaser, but it also benefits society because it reduces the risk that other members of society will be infected with a highly contagious disease. Similarly, a healthy labor force is more productive, contributing to the general prosperity and well-being of society.
- ***Third-party payments: insurance*** Because nearly four-fifths of all health care expenses are paid

through public or private insurance, health care consumers pay much lower out-of-pocket "prices" than they would otherwise. Those lower prices are a distortion that results in "excess" consumption of health care services.

The Increasing Demand for Health Care

With these four features in mind, let's consider some factors that have increased the demand for health care over time.

Rising Incomes: The Role of Elasticities

Because health care is a normal good, increases in domestic income have caused increases in the demand for health care. While there is some disagreement as to the exact income elasticity of demand for health care, several studies for industrially advanced countries suggest that the income elasticity coefficient is about 1. This means that per capita health care spending rises approximately in proportion to increases in per capita income. For example, a 3 percent increase in income will generate a 3 percent increase in health care expenditures. There is some evidence that income elasticity may be higher in the United States, perhaps as high as 1.5.

Estimates of the price elasticity of demand for health care imply that it is quite inelastic, with this coefficient being as low as .2. This means that the quantity of health care consumed declines relatively little as price increases. For example, a 10 percent increase in price would reduce quantity demanded by only 2 percent. An important consequence is that total health care spending will increase as the price of health care rises.

The relative insensitivity of health care spending to price changes results from four factors. First, people consider health care a necessity, not a luxury. There are few, if any, good substitutes for medical care in treating injuries and infections and alleviating various ailments. Second, medical treatment is often provided in an emergency situation in which price considerations are secondary or irrelevant. Third, most consumers prefer a long-term relationship with their doctors and therefore do not "shop around" when health care prices rise. Fourth, most patients have insurance and are therefore not directly affected by the price of health care. If insured patients pay, for example, only 20 percent of their health care expenses, they are less concerned with price increases or price differences between hospitals and between doctors than they would be if they paid 100 percent themselves. **(Key Question 7)**

An Aging Population The U.S. population is aging. People 65 years of age and older constituted approximately 9 percent of the population in 1960 but 12.4 percent by 2000. Projections for the year 2030 indicate 20 percent of the population will be 65 or over.

This aging of the population affects the demand for health care because older people encounter more frequent and more prolonged spells of illness. Specifically, those 65 and older consume about three and one-half times as much health care as those between 19 and 64. In turn, people over 84 consume almost two and one-half times as much health care as those in the 65 to 69 age group. Health care expenditures are often extraordinarily high in the last year of one's life.

Looking ahead, in 2011 the 76 million people born between 1946 and 1964 will begin turning 65. We can expect that fact to create a substantial surge in the demand for health care.

Unhealthy Lifestyles Substance abuse helps drive up health care costs. The abuse of alcohol, tobacco, and illicit drugs damages health and is therefore an important component of the demand for health care services. Alcohol is a major cause of injury-producing traffic accidents and liver disease. Tobacco use markedly increases the probability of cancer, heart disease, bronchitis, and emphysema. Illicit drugs are a major contributor to violent crime, health problems in infants, and the spread of AIDS. In addition, illicit-drug users make hundreds of thousands of costly visits to hospital emergency rooms each year. And overeating and lack of exercise contribute to heart disease, diabetes, and many other ailments. Obesity-related medical costs are estimated to be about $75 billion per year, with taxpayers picking up more than half the tab through Medicare and Medicaid.

The Role of Doctors Physicians may increase the demand for health care in several ways.

Supplier-Induced Demand As we mentioned before, doctors, the suppliers of medical services, have much more information about those services than consumers, who are the demanders. While a patient might be well informed about food products or more complex products such as cameras, he or she is not likely to be well informed about diagnostic tests such as magnetic resonance imaging or medical procedures such as joint replacements. Because of this asymmetric information (informational imbalance), a principal-agent problem emerges: The supplier, not the demander, decides what types and amounts of health care are to be consumed. This situation creates a possibility of "supplier-induced demand."

This possibility becomes especially relevant when doctors are paid on a **fee-for-service** basis, that is, paid separately for each service they perform. In light of the asymmetric information and fee-for-service arrangement, doctors have an opportunity and an incentive to suggest more health care services than are absolutely necessary (just as an auto repair shop has an opportunity and an incentive to recommend replacement of parts that are worn but still working).

More surgery is performed in the United States, where many doctors are paid a fee for each operation, than in foreign countries, where doctors are often paid annual salaries unrelated to the number of operations they perform. Furthermore, doctors who own X-ray or ultrasound machines do four times as many tests as doctors who refer their patients to radiologists. More generally, studies suggest that up to one-third of common medical tests and procedures are either inappropriate or of questionable value.

The seller's control over consumption decisions has another result: It eliminates much of the power buyers might have in controlling the growth of health care prices and spending.

Defensive Medicine "Become a doctor and support a lawyer," says a bumper sticker. The number of medical malpractice lawsuits admittedly is high. Today, every patient represents not only a need for medical care but also a possible malpractice suit. As a result, physicians tend to practice **defensive medicine.** That is, they recommend more tests and procedures than are warranted medically or economically in order to protect themselves against malpractice suits.

Medical Ethics Medical ethics may drive up the demand for health care in two ways. First, doctors are ethically committed to use "best-practice" techniques in serving their patients. This often means the use of costly medical procedures that may be of only slight benefit to patients.

Second, public values seem to support the medical ethic that human life should be sustained as long as possible. This makes it difficult to confront the notion that health care is provided with scarce resources and therefore must be rationed like any other good. Can society afford to provide $5000-per-day intensive care to a comatose patient unlikely to be restored to reasonable health? Public priorities seem to indicate that such care should be provided, and those values again increase the demand for health care.

Role of Health Insurance

As we noted in Figure 21.1, 80 percent of health care spending is done not by health care consumers through direct out-of-pocket payments but by private health insurance companies or by the government through Medicare and Medicaid.

Individuals and families face potentially devastating monetary losses from a variety of hazards. Your house may burn down; you may be in an auto accident; or you may suffer a serious illness. An insurance program is a means of protection against the huge monetary losses that can result from such hazards. A number of people agree to pay certain amounts (premiums) periodically in return for the guarantee that they will be compensated if they should incur a particular misfortune. Insurance is a means of paying a relatively small known cost for protection against an uncertain and much larger cost. While health insurance is therefore highly beneficial, it also contributes to rising costs and possible overconsumption of health care.

The Moral Hazard Problem

The moral hazard problem is the tendency of one party to an agreement to alter her or his behavior in a way that is costly to the other party. Health care insurance can change behavior in two ways. First, some insured people may be less careful about their health, taking fewer steps to prevent accident or illness. Second, insured individuals have greater incentives to use health care more intensively than they would if they did not have insurance. Let's consider both aspects of moral hazard.

Less Prevention Health insurance may increase the demand for health care by encouraging behaviors that require more health care. Although most people with health care insurance are probably as careful about their health as are those without insurance, some may be more inclined to smoke, avoid exercise, and eat unhealthful foods, knowing they have insurance. Similarly, some individuals may take up ski jumping or rodeo bull riding if they have insurance covering the costs of orthopedic surgeons. And if their insurance covers rehabilitation programs, some people may be more inclined to experiment with alcohol or drugs.

Overconsumption Insured people go to doctors more often and request more diagnostic tests and more complex treatments than they would if they were uninsured because, with health insurance, the price or opportunity cost of consuming health care is minimal. For example, many individuals with private insurance pay a fixed premium for coverage, and beyond that, aside from a modest deductible, their health care is "free." This situation differs from most markets, in which the price to the consumer reflects the full opportunity cost of each unit of the good or service. In all markets, price provides a direct economic incentive to restrict use of the product. The minimal direct price to the insured consumer of health care, in contrast, creates an incentive to overuse the health care system. Of course, the penalty for overuse will ultimately show up in higher insurance premiums, but all policyholders will share those premiums. The cost increase for the individual health consumer will be relatively small.

Also, the availability of insurance removes the consumer's budget constraint (spending limitation) when he or she decides to consume health care. Recall from Chapter 7 that budget constraints limit the purchases of most products. But insured patients face minimal or no out-of-pocket expenditures at the time they purchase health care. Because affordability is not the issue, health care may be overconsumed.

Government Tax Subsidy Federal tax policy toward employer-financed health insurance works as a **tax subsidy** that strengthens the demand for health care services. Specifically, employees do not pay Federal income or payroll tax (Social Security) on the value of the health insurance they receive as an employee benefit. Employees thus request and receive more of their total compensation as nontaxed health care benefits and less in taxed wages and salaries.

The government rationale for this tax treatment is that positive spillover benefits are associated with having a healthy, productive workforce. So it is appropriate to encourage health insurance for workers. The tax break does enable more of the population to have health insurance, but it also contributes to greater consumption of health care. Combined with other factors, the tax break may result in an overconsumption of health care.

To illustrate: If the marginal tax rate is, say, 28 percent, $1 worth of health insurance is equivalent to 72 cents in after-tax pay. Because the worker can get more insurance for $1 than for 72 cents, the exclusion of health insurance from taxation increases purchases of health insurance, thus increasing the demand for health care. In essence, the 28-cent difference acts as a government subsidy to health care. A recent estimate suggests that this subsidy costs the Federal government $120 billion per year in forgone tax revenue and boosts private health insurance spending by about one-third. Actual health care spending may be 10 to 20 percent higher than otherwise because of the subsidy.

Graphical Portrayal A simple demand and supply model illustrates the effect of health insurance on the health care market. Figure 21.3a depicts a competitive market for health care services; curve *D* shows the demand for health care services if all consumers are uninsured, and *S* represents the supply of health care. At market price P_u the equilibrium quantity of health care is Q_u.

Recall from the theory of competitive markets that output Q_u results in allocative efficiency, which means there is no better alternative use for the resources allocated to producing that level of health care. To see what we mean by "no better use," we must realize that:

- As we move down along demand curve *D*, each succeeding point indicates, via the price it represents, the marginal benefit that consumers receive from that unit.
- The supply curve is the producers' marginal-cost curve. As we move up along the supply curve, each succeeding point indicates the marginal cost of that unit of health care.
- For each unit produced up to the equilibrium quantity Q_u, marginal benefit exceeds marginal cost (because points on *D* are above those on *S*). At Q_u marginal benefit equals marginal cost, designating allocative efficiency. No matter what else those

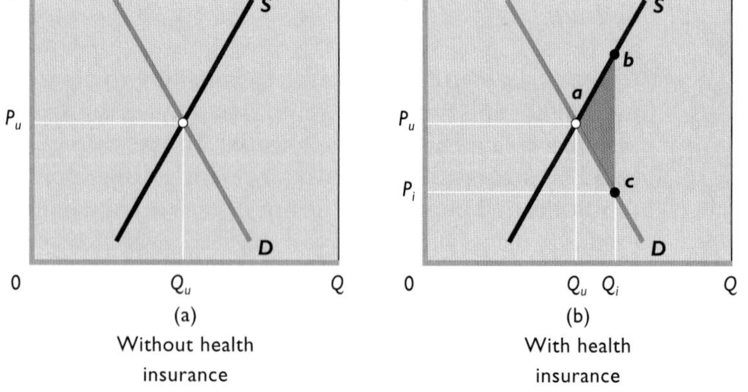

FIGURE 21.3 Insurance and the overallocation of resources to health care. (a) Without health insurance, the optimal amount of health care consumed is Q_u, where the marginal benefit and marginal cost of health care are equal. (b) The availability of private and public insurance reduces the direct price of health care from P_u to P_i, resulting in its overconsumption (Q_i rather than Q_u) and an overallocation of resources to the health care industry. Area *abc* represents the efficiency loss from that overallocation.

resources could have produced, the greatest net benefit to society is obtained by using those resources to produce Q_u units of health care.

But allocative efficiency occurs only when we pay in full for a product, as is assumed in Figure 21.3a. What happens when we introduce health insurance that covers, say, one-half of all health care costs? In Figure 21.3b, with health insurance paying half the price, the consumer in effect is confronted with price P_i ($= \frac{1}{2} P_u$). The health care consumer reacts by purchasing Q_i units rather than just Q_u. This is economically inefficient because between Q_u and Q_i each unit's marginal cost to society (on curve *S*) exceeds its marginal benefit (on curve *D*). Each unit of health care between Q_u and Q_i reflects an overallocation of resources to health care. The total efficiency loss is represented by area *abc*. Because health insurance typically covers 80, not just 50, percent of health care costs, the efficiency loss in Figure 21.3b understates the actual efficiency loss to society. On the other hand, this loss may not be as large as the 80 percent figure would imply, because of the positive spillovers associated with health care.[1]

Figure 21.3b implies that there is a tradeoff between efficiency and equity. Standards of fairness or equity in the United States lead people to believe that all citizens should have access to basic health care, which is why government created social insurance in the form of Medicare and Medicaid. Also, it helps explain the Federal tax subsidy to private health insurance, which again makes health care more accessible. The problem, as Figure 21.3b shows, is that the greater the availability of insurance (and thus the more equitable society makes access to health care), the greater the overallocation of resources to the health care industry. This overallocation would be even greater if health care were provided completely "free" under a program of national health insurance. Consumers would purchase health care as long as the marginal benefit to themselves as individuals was positive, regardless of the true cost to society. **(Key Question 10)**

Supply Factors in Rising Health Care Prices

Supply factors have also played a role in rising health care prices. Specifically, the supply of health care services has increased, but more slowly than demand. A combination of factors has produced this relatively slow growth of supply.

[1]Technical footnote: There is no shortage at price P_i in Figure 21.3b. Insurance reduces the direct cost of health care to the insured, so in effect the supply curve shifts rightward (not shown) and intersects demand at point *c*.

Supply of Physicians The supply of physicians in the United States has increased over the years; in 1975 there were 169 physicians per 100,000 people; by 2004 there were 267. But this increase in supply has not kept up with the increase in the demand for physicians' services. As a result, physicians' fees and incomes have increased more rapidly than average prices and incomes for the economy as a whole.

Conventional wisdom has been that physician groups, for example, the American Medical Association, have purposely kept admissions to medical schools, and therefore the supply of doctors, artificially low. But that is too simplistic. A rapidly rising cost of medical education seems to be the main cause of the relatively slow growth of doctor supply. Medical training requires 4 years of college, 4 years of medical school, an internship, and perhaps 3 or 4 years of training in a medical specialty. The opportunity cost of this education has increased, because the salaries of similarly capable people have soared in other professions. The direct expenses have also increased, largely due to the increasingly sophisticated levels of medical care and therefore of medical training.

High and rising education and training costs have necessitated high and rising doctors' fees to ensure an adequate return on this sort of investment in human capital. Physicians' incomes are indeed high, averaging about $220,000 in 2004, but so too are the costs of obtaining the skills necessary to become a physician. Data show that while doctors have high rates of return on their educational expenses, those returns are below the returns for lawyers and holders of masters of business administration degrees.

Slow Productivity Growth Productivity growth in an industry tends to reduce costs and increase supply. In the health care industry, such productivity growth has been modest. One reason is that health care is a service, and it is generally more difficult to increase productivity for services than for goods. It is relatively easy to increase productivity in manufacturing by mechanizing the production process. With more and better machinery, the same number of workers can produce greater output. But services often are a different matter. It is not easy, for example, to mechanize haircuts, child care, and pizza delivery. How do you significantly increase the productivity of physicians, nurses, and home care providers?

Also, competition for patients among many providers of health care has not been sufficiently brisk to force them to look for ways to reduce cost by increasing productivity. When buying most goods, customers typically shop around for the lowest price. This shopping requires that sellers keep their prices low and look to productivity increases to maintain or expand their profits. But patients rarely shop for the lowest prices when seeking medical care. In fact, a patient may feel uncomfortable about being operated on by a physician who charges the lowest price. Moreover, if insurance pays for the surgery, there is no reason to consider price at all. The point is that unusual features of the market for health care limit competitive pricing and thus reduce incentives to achieve cost saving via advances in productivity.

Changes in Medical Technology Some technological advances in medicine have lowered costs. For example, the development of vaccines for polio, smallpox, and measles has greatly reduced health care expenditures for the treatment of those diseases. And reduced lengths of stays in hospitals have lowered the costs of medical care.

But many medical technologies developed since the Second World War have significantly increased the cost of medical care either by increasing prices or by extending procedures to a greater number of people. For example, because they give more accurate information, advanced body scanners costing up to $1000 per scan are often used in place of X rays that cost less than $100 for each scan. Desiring to offer the highest quality of service, hospitals want to use the very latest equipment and procedures. These newer, more expensive treatments are surely more effective than older ones. But doctors and hospital administrators both realize that the fixed high cost of such equipment means it must be used extensively to lower the cost per patient.

As another example, organ transplants are extremely costly. Before the development of this technology, a person with a serious liver malfunction died. Now a liver transplant can cost $200,000 or more, with subsequent medical attention costing $10,000 to $20,000 per year for the rest of the patient's life.

Finally, consider new prescription medications. Pharmaceutical companies have developed very expensive drugs that often replace less expensive ones and are prescribed for a much wider range of physical and mental illnesses. Although these remarkable new medications greatly improve health care, they also contribute to rising health care costs.

The historical willingness of private and public insurance to pay for new treatments without regard to price and number of patients has contributed to the incentive to develop and use new technologies. Insurers, in effect, have encouraged research into and development of health care technologies, regardless of their cost. Recently, when insurance companies resisted paying for new expensive treatments such as bone marrow transplants, public outcries led them to change their minds. So expanding insurance coverage leads to new, often more expensive medical technologies, which in turn lead to a demand for a wider definition of what should be covered by insurance.

Relative Importance

According to most analysts, the demand and supply factors we have discussed vary in their impact on escalating health care costs. As we noted, the income elasticity of demand for health care is estimated to be +1 to +1.5, meaning that increased income brings with it proportionate or more-than-proportionate increases in health care spending. But rising income does not alone explain the rocketing increase in health care spending as a percentage of total domestic output (income). Furthermore, government studies estimate that the aging population accounts for less than 10 percent of the current increase in per capita health care spending.

Most experts attribute the relative rise in health care spending to (1) advances in medical technology, combined with (2) the medical ethic of providing the best treatment available, (3) private and public health insurance, and (4) fee-for-service physicians' payments by health insurance firms. Through technological progress, great strides have been made in the diagnosis, treatment, and prevention of

CONSIDER THIS . . .

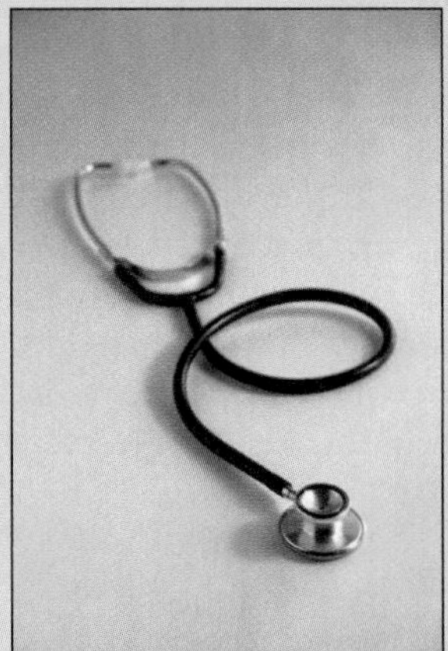

What's Cold, Clammy, and Possibly Endangered?

Medical technology often improves health care but adds to its cost. *The Wall Street Journal* reports that the stethoscope may eventually give way to a new hand-held ultrasound machine that enables the physician to visibly check a patient's heart and lungs. The new devices—produced by SonoSite and General Electric—capture images of the vital organs and thus allow for enhanced, albeit more expensive, physical exams. Stethoscopes cost between $50 and $200. Portable ultrasound machines range in price from $12,500 to $55,000. Physical exams, of course, are usually fully covered by private and government health insurance. Welcome to the world of modern technology, improved health care, and rising health care costs!

Source: Based on Amy Dockser Marcus, "What's Cold, Clammy, and Out of Date?" *The Wall Street Journal (On-Line)*, Dec. 4, 2002.

illness. But the third-party (insurance) payment system provides little incentive to limit the development or use of such technologies, because it has no mechanism to force an equating of marginal costs and marginal benefits. And the "best treatment available" ethic, together with the fee-for-service payment system, ensures that any new technology with a positive marginal benefit will get used and be billed for, regardless of the marginal cost to society.

QUICK REVIEW 21.2

- Characteristics of the health care market are (a) the widespread view of health care as a "right," (b) asymmetric information between consumers and suppliers, (c) the presence of positive externalities, and (d) payment mostly by insurance.
- The demand for health care has increased for many reasons, including rising incomes, an aging population, unhealthy lifestyles, the role of doctors as advisers to patients, the practice of defensive medicine, and a fee-for-service payment system via health insurance.
- The supply of health care has grown slowly, primarily because of (a) relatively slow productivity growth in the health care industry, (b) rising costs of medical education and training, and (c) greater use of very high cost health care technologies.

Reform of the Health Care System

What, if anything, can be done to ensure access for more Americans to the health care system? And how might health care costs be contained? Reform of the health care system to achieve these two goals will be difficult. First, there is a tradeoff between the two objectives: Greater access to the system will mean rising costs. Second, health care reform is complex because expectations (for example, access to the "best" medical care), tradition (the "right" to choose one's doctor), and the goals of self-interest groups (private insurers, health maintenance organizations, drug companies, physicians, and hospitals) all come into play.

This latter point is especially significant. The numerous affected interest groups will not passively accept rearrangement of costs and benefits in an industry that accounts for one-seventh of total U.S. spending. Physicians, hospitals, health insurers, health maintenance organizations, and drug companies seek to prevent price controls on their services and products. Older people—represented by AARP—want government to pay a larger portion of long-term (nursing-home) health care. Health insurance companies hope their business will not be curtailed by reforms. Labor unions advocate a generous basic-benefits package and oppose taxation of employer-financed health insurance. Drug companies want prescription drugs covered under Medicare. Psychiatrists, physical therapists, acupuncturists, and chiropractors want their services included in any new proposal. Trial lawyers want existing malpractice laws left alone. Small businesses strongly oppose any law requiring all companies to provide health insurance for their employees. The beer, liquor, and tobacco industries do not want additional "sin" taxes levied on them to help finance any reform proposal.

Universal Access

How can health care insurance, and thus health care, be made available to all U.S. citizens? Let's briefly consider three reform concepts.

"Play or Pay" Because much of the nation's health insurance is paid by employers, one way is to expand that coverage using a **play-or-pay** approach. All employers would be required to either provide a basic health insurance program for their workers and their dependents ("play") or pay a special payroll tax to finance health insurance for uninsured workers ("pay"). Some form of publicly sponsored health care plan would cover people who are not in the labor force and thus uninsured.

Such plans, however, probably would lead to lower real wages. Also, unemployment might increase in firms currently paying wages at or near the minimum wage.

Tax Credits and Vouchers Another approach, using tax credits and vouchers, would help the poor pay for health insurance. The Federal government would provide a tax credit, for example, of $1500 for a single person and $4000 for a family of four, to low-income individuals and families for use in purchasing health insurance. The size of the tax credit would diminish as the recipient's income rises. Those whose incomes are so low as to be exempt from the income tax would be issued a voucher for purchasing health insurance. This proposal is essentially a tax subsidy designed to make insurance more affordable to low-income people.

National Health Insurance The most far-reaching and controversial reform concept is to establish a system of **national health insurance (NHI)** along the lines of the present Canadian system. The Federal government would provide a basic package of health care to every citizen at no direct charge or at a low cost-sharing level. The system would be financed out of tax revenues rather than out of insurance premiums.

NHI is not the same as socialized medicine. Under NHI the government would not own health care facilities such as hospitals, clinics, and nursing homes. Nor would health care practitioners such as doctors, nurses, and technicians be government employees. Under NHI the government would simply sponsor and finance basic health care for all citizens. Although the role of private health insurers would be reduced under NHI, they could provide health insurance for any medical procedures that were not covered in the basic NHI health care package.

Arguments for NHI Proponents say that NHI is the simplest and most direct way of providing universal access to health care:

- It allows patients to choose their own physicians.
- It would reduce administrative costs. The present system, it is argued, is administratively chaotic and expensive because hundreds of private health care insurers are involved, each with its own procedures and claim forms. Administration costs in the Canadian system are less than 5 percent of total health care costs compared with almost 17 percent in the United States.
- It would separate health care availability from employment and therefore would eliminate the hiring of part-time and temporary workers as a way to avoid providing health care insurance.
- It would allow the government to use its single-insurer market power to contain costs. The government could apply its buying power to mandate fees for various medical procedures and thus control physician and hospital costs. Hospitals would operate on budgets set by the government.

Arguments against NHI Opponents of NHI provide weighty counterarguments:

- Government-determined price ceilings on physicians' services are not likely to control costs. Doctors can protect their incomes from fixed fees by manipulating the amount of care they provide a patient. Suppose the maximum fee for an office visit is $30. Doctors might spread a given number of diagnostic tests over three or four office visits, although all the tests could be done in one visit. Or a doctor might require an office visit to explain test results instead of phoning the patient. Similar arguments apply to government regulation of hospital charges.
- In the Canadian system patients often have waits of weeks, months, or even years for certain diagnostic procedures and surgeries. This is the result of the Canadian government's effort to control expenditures by restricting hospitals' capital spending. To illustrate, there are only one-fifth as many magnetic resonance imaging machines per million people in Canada as in the United States. This results in a waiting list for use of MRIs in Canada. NHI might strongly conflict with U.S. expectations of medical care "on demand."
- Doctors can mount "strikes" against low payments from the government, as they have done is several areas of Canada. Such disruptions in medical care rarely happen in the United States.
- The Federal government has a very poor record of containing costs. Despite its considerable buying power, the Department of Defense, for example, has a long history of cost overruns and mismanagement. And, as you have seen, spending has spiraled upward under the government's Medicare and Medicaid programs. Also recall (Figure 21.3b) that insurance is a critical factor in the overconsumption of health care. Under NHI a completely "free" basic health care package would prompt consumers to "purchase" health care as long as marginal benefits were positive, regardless of the true cost to society.
- Subtle and perhaps undesirable redistribution effects would result under NHI. Under private health insurance, a particular health care insurance package costs the same regardless of the insured's income. This makes the cost of insurance resemble a regressive tax, since low-income workers pay a larger percentage of their incomes for the insurance than do high-income insurees. If NHI were financed out of personal income tax revenues, this financing would be progressive. Under NHI those with low incomes would receive health insurance and pay little or none of the cost. While some might view this as desirable, others believe that income redistribution in the United States has been overdone and that further redistribution through NHI would be unfair. Depending on the type of tax and its size, employers and workers in industries such as automobile and steel might receive windfalls in the form of higher profits and wages when NHI replaced their health insurance programs. Employers and workers in small retail establishments and fast-food restaurants, where health insurance is typically absent, might not realize such gains.

Cost Containment: Altering Incentives

Can the United States control the growth of health care costs, prices, and spending by reducing incentives to overconsume health care?

Deductibles and Copayments Insurance companies have reacted to rising health care costs by imposing sizable deductibles and copayments on those they insure. Instead of covering all of an insuree's medical costs, a policy might now specify that the insuree pay the first $250 or $500 of each year's health care costs (the deductible) and 15 or 20 percent of all additional costs (the copayment). The deductible and copayment are intended to alleviate the overuse problem by creating a direct payment and therefore an opportunity cost to the health care consumer. The deductible has the added advantage of reducing the administrative costs of insurance companies in processing many small claims.

Managed Care Managed-care organizations (or systems) are those in which medical services are controlled or coordinated by insurance companies or health care organizations in order to reduce health care expenditures. In 2005 about 88 percent of all U.S. workers received health care through such "managed care." These organizations are of two main types.

Some insurance companies have set up **preferred provider organizations (PPOs),** which require that hospitals and physicians accept discounted prices for their services as a condition for being included in the insurance plan. The policyholder receives a list of participating hospitals and doctors and is given, say, 80 to 100 percent reimbursement of health care costs when treated by PPO physicians and hospitals. If a patient chooses a doctor or hospital outside the PPO, the insurance company reimburses only 60 to 70 percent. In return for being included as a PPO provider, doctors and hospitals agree to rates set by the insurance company for each service. Because these fees are less than those usually charged, PPOs reduce health insurance premiums and health care expenditures.

Many Americans now receive their medical care from **health maintenance organizations (HMOs),** which provide health care services to a specific group of enrollees in exchange for a set annual fee per enrollee. HMOs employ their own physicians and contract for specialized services with outside providers and hospitals. They then contract with firms or government units to provide medical care for their workers, who thereby become HMO members. Because HMOs have fixed annual revenue, they may lose money if they provide "too much" care. So they have an incentive to hold down costs. They also have an incentive to provide preventive care in order to reduce the far larger expense of corrective care.

Both PPOs and HMOs are managed-care organizations because medical use and spending are "managed" by close monitoring of physicians' and hospitals' behavior; the purpose is to eliminate unnecessary diagnostic tests and remedial treatments. Doctors in managed-care organizations might not order an MRI scan or an ultrasound test or suggest surgery because their work is monitored and because they may have a fixed budget. In contrast, an independent fee-for-service physician may face little or no control and have a financial incentive to order the test or do the surgery. Doctors and hospitals in a managed-care organization often share in an "incentive pool" of funds when they meet their cost-control goals.

The advantages of managed-care plans are that they provide health care at lower prices than traditional insurance and emphasize preventive medicine. The disadvantages are that the patient usually is restricted to physicians employed by or under contract with the managed-care plan. Also, some say that the focus on reducing costs has gone too far, resulting in denial of highly expensive, but effective, treatment. This "too far" criticism was mainly leveled at HMOs, where incentives to reduce costs were the greatest. Perhaps because of a backlash against HMOs, firms have increasingly shifted managed care toward PPOs. In 2005, about 67 percent of workers obtained health care through PPOs, up from 42 percent in 2000. Only 21 percent of workers now belong to HMOs.

Medicare and DRG In 1983 the Federal government altered the way it makes payments for hospital services received by Medicare patients. Rather than automatically paying all costs related to a patient's treatment and length of hospital stay, Medicare submitted payments based on a **diagnosis-related-group (DRG) system.** Under DRG a hospital receives a fixed payment for treating each patient; that payment is an amount associated with the one of several hundred carefully detailed diagnostic categories that best characterize the patient's condition and needs.

DRG-system payments obviously give hospitals the incentive to restrict the amount of resources used in treating patients. It is no surprise that under DRG the length of hospital stays has fallen sharply and more patients are treated on an outpatient basis. Critics, however, argue that this is evidence of diminished quality of medical care.

Recent Laws and Proposals

Although Congress has rejected major reforms of the health care system, it recently made some noteworthy changes.

Prescription Drug Coverage Until recently, Medicare paid for doctor visits, hospitalization, and short-term nursing care, but not for prescription drugs. But these medications have become an integral part of modern health care, and their expense has claimed a growing part of the income of older Americans. Moreover, the number of older Americans and their adult children has greatly increased among the voting citizenry. Prompted by these medical, financial, and political realities, in late 2003 the Bush administration and Congress added prescription drug coverage to Medicare.

The Medicare Prescription Drug, Improvement, and Modernization Act of 2003 established **Medicare Part D,** beginning in 2006. Medicare enrollees can shop among private health insurance companies to buy highly subsidized insurance for prescription drugs. Under the standard plan, individual enrollees paid a monthly premium averaging about \$24 (in 2006), a \$250 annual deductible, 25 percent of annual prescription costs up to \$2250, then 100 percent of costs between \$2250 and \$3600, and 5 percent of costs above \$3600. The gap in coverage between \$2250 and \$3600—the so-called donut hole—is designed to hold down program costs and thus enable the 95 percent coverage for annual prescription expenses above \$3600 a year. Such high expenses are "catastrophic" for many retirees, and particularly for those receiving only Social Security income.

The law also bars the Federal government from establishing a formulary—a list of drugs that are covered by the insurance policies—although the private insurers may do so. Additionally, the law prohibits the Federal government from using its monopsony power (price-setting power as a large buyer) to negotiate prices with the pharmaceutical industry. Finally, it provides subsidies to large employers to encourage them to maintain existing prescription drug coverage in their retirees' health insurance plans.

Some 38 million people had signed up for the Medicare prescription drug plan by mid-2006. The projected cost of the prescription drug coverage is \$746 million over its first 10 years. Proponents say prescription drug coverage will ease the burden of personal medical costs for millions of older Americans and greatly improve their health care. Critics point out that the huge added expense of Medicare Part D will exacerbate the gigantic underfunding problem facing Medicare in the coming decades. Other observers predict the new law will drive up already escalating drug prices by increasing the demand for prescription drugs without controlling their costs.

Health Savings Accounts

The 2003 Medicare law also established **health savings accounts (HSAs).** These accounts are available to all workers who are covered by health insurance plans with annual deductibles of \$1000 or more and do not have other first-dollar insurance coverage. Individuals can make tax-deductible contributions into their HSAs, even if they do not itemize deductions on their tax forms. Employers can also make tax-free contributions to workers' accounts if they choose. Earnings on the funds in HSAs are not taxable and the owners of these accounts can use them to pay for qualified medical expenses. Unused funds in HSAs accumulate from year to year and remain available for later out-of-pocket medical expenses. Account holders can add money to the accounts in each year between age 55 and the year they become eligible for Medicare.

HSAs are designed to promote personal saving out of which workers can pay routine health care expenses while working and can pay for Medicare copayments and deductibles later, during retirement. HSAs are also designed to reduce escalating medical expenses by interjecting an element of competition into health care delivery. Because individuals are using some of their own HSA money to pay for health care, they presumably will assess their personal marginal costs and marginal benefits in choosing how much and what type of health care to obtain. They will also have a strong incentive to inquire about and compare prices charged by various qualified medical providers. Holders of HSAs never lose their accumulated funds. The can remove money for nonmedical purchases but must pay income taxes and a 10 percent penalty on such withdrawals.

Limits on Malpractice Awards

Congress has recently attempted to cap (at, say, \$250,000 or \$500,000) the "pain and suffering" awards on medical malpractice lawsuits against physicians. Those who support malpractice caps say that patients should receive full compensation for economic losses but not be made wealthy through huge jury awards. They contend that capping the awards will reduce medical malpractice premiums and therefore lower health care costs. Opponents of caps counter that large "pain and suffering" awards deter medical malpractice. If so, such awards improve the overall quality of the health care system. Opponents also point out that malpractice awards are a negligible percentage of total health care costs. Twenty-seven states now (2006) have placed caps on the "pain and suffering" portion of malpractice awards.

The economic challenges facing health care will only get stronger. The combination of an aging population and advances in medical technology seem to be on a collision course with the reality of economic scarcity. Individuals and society will face increasingly difficult choices about how much health care to consume and how to pay for it.

Last *Word*

Mandatory Health Insurance: Play to Stay

In 2006 the state of Massachusetts passed legislation that will require everyone in the state to have health care insurance, just as many states require all car owners to have auto insurance. Is this reform a viable model for the United States?

Recall from this chapter that one of the suggested options for health care reform in the United States is called "play or pay," because *employers* would have to provide basic health insurance ("play") or pay a special payroll taxes to finance health insurance for the uninsured ("pay"). The state of Massachusetts has added a bold twist to "play or pay." This novel plan might be called "play to stay!"

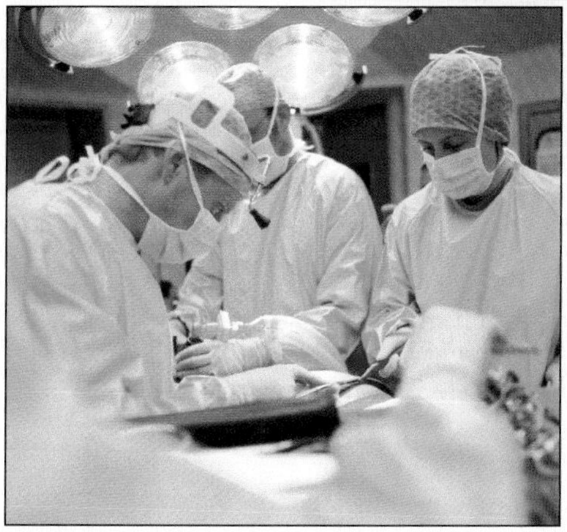

Beginning on July 1, 2007, all *residents* of the state will be required to have health insurance, much like owners of autos are required to have car insurance. In 2008, everyone will have to provide proof of health insurance on their state income tax forms. Those without insurance coverage will face penalties ranging up to $1200 a year.

The purpose of the law is to create universal health insurance coverage for all state residents and eliminate free riders who do not have health insurance but use medical facilities for expensive "free" emergency care. That behavior simply transfers health care costs to other residents who must pay higher deductibles and coinsurance, larger insurance premiums (and thus receive less take-home pay), or greater state taxes to cover the costs.

The law is expected to reduce the cost of health insurance to those who are already insured by removing the current hidden surcharge for "uninsured patients." It also is expected to increase the demand for employer-provided health insurance by workers, even if the added benefits mean lower cash pay. If people must "play to stay," it will be important for them to seek out the least-expensive way to obtaining health insurance coverage. Traditionally, that has been through group health insurance provided by employers as part of their compensation packages. Moreover, the law charges employers who do not offer health insurance $295 per worker per year to help subsidize those without employer-provided insurance. Employers can eliminate that expense by providing insurance.

But how will the poorest among the estimated 550,000 uninsured residents of Massachusetts obtain insurance? Here the subsidy and income redistribution side of the law comes into play. The state would spend as much as $1 billion annually to subsidize private insurance companies that provide new policies for basic health insurance. Because of the state subsidies, the price of these policies would range from about $250 per month to as little as nothing. Uninsured people who earn less than the Federal poverty line would pay no premiums but would pay small copayments when they obtain medical care. People above the poverty line but earning less than three times that amount would pay highly subsidized premiums based on their income levels.

Is this plan a potential model for the United States? Some observers think that it may be, because it combines popular concepts such as personal responsibility and compassion for those in need. It also does not disrupt the current system of private health insurance, personal physicians, and established hospitals.

But critics point out that the health care problem is a problem not only of access but of high and rising costs. The cost-containment features of the plan are indirect and relatively weak. Universal coverage could simply drive up the demand for health care, placing additional upward pressure on the prices of medical services. Another problem for transferring the plan nationally is that the percentage of residents currently uninsured in Massachusetts is considerably lower than that of the nation as a whole. The overall cost of the plan to taxpayers at the Federal level might be prohibitive.

Will the Massachusetts plan create an adverse selection problem for nearby states? That is, will some low-income residents of Massachusetts move across the border to avoid paying for health insurance, no matter how small the premiums? If so, that problem could be overcome by a national plan, since the only escape from the mandate would be to move to another country!

Obviously, many questions about the Massachusetts law are still unanswered. In terms of health care reform, this is an experimental medicine. Economists will be very interested in assessing its costs, benefits, and side-effects.

Summary

1. The U.S. health care industry comprises 9 million workers (including about 736,000 practicing physicians) and 5800 hospitals.
2. U.S. health care spending has increased both absolutely and as a percentage of GDP.
3. Rising health care costs and prices have (a) reduced access to the health care system, (b) contributed to slower real wage growth and expanded the employment of part-time and temporary workers, and (c) caused governments to restrict spending on nonhealth programs and to raise taxes.
4. The core of the health care problem is an alleged overallocation of resources to the health care industry.
5. About 46 million Americans, or 16 percent of the population, do not have health insurance. The uninsured are concentrated among the poor, the chronically ill, the unemployed, the young, those employed by small firms, and low-wage workers.
6. Special characteristics of the health care market include (a) the belief that health care is a "right," (b) an imbalance of information between consumers and suppliers, (c) the presence of positive externalities, and (d) the payment of most health care expenses by private or public insurance.
7. While rising incomes, an aging population, and substance abuse have all contributed to an increasing demand for health care, the role of doctors is also significant. Because of asymmetric information, physicians influence the demand for their own services. The fee-for-service payment system, combined with defensive medicine to protect against malpractice suits, also increases demand for health care.
8. The moral hazard problem arising from health insurance takes two forms: (a) People may be less careful of their health, and (b) there is an incentive to overconsume health care.
9. The exemption of employer-paid health insurance from the Federal income tax subsidizes health care.
10. Slow productivity growth in the health care industry and, more important, cost-increasing advances in health care technology have restricted the expansion of the supply of medical care and have boosted prices.
11. Reforms designed to increase access to the health care system include (a) "play-or-pay" proposals designed to increase employer-sponsored health insurance, (b) tax credits and vouchers to help low-income families afford health care, and (c) national health insurance.
12. Insurance companies have introduced deductibles and copayments in an attempt to contain health care prices and spending.
13. Managed-care organizations—preferred provider organizations (PPOs) and health maintenance organizations (HMOs)—attempt to control their enrolled members' use of health care in order to contain health care costs.
14. The Medicare Prescription Drug, Improvement, and Modernization Act of 2003 added prescription drug benefits to the Medicare program for the first time. Under Medicare Part D, individuals pay small monthly premiums (about $24 in 2006) for subsidized private insurance coverage. The supplementary Medicare insurance requires a $250 annual deductible and pays 75 percent of the costs of prescription drugs up to $2250, zero from $2250 to $3600, and 95 percent above $3600.
15. The 2003 Medicare law also established health savings accounts (HSAs), which enable individuals who have high-deductible private insurance to place tax-free dollars into special accounts. Account holders can then withdraw funds to pay for routine medical expenses. Unused funds accumulate tax free and eventually become available to pay for the deductibles and copayments required under supplemental Medicare insurance plans. Funds withdrawn for nonmedical purposes require payment of income tax on the amount withdrawn, plus a 10 percent penalty.

Terms and Concepts

deductibles
copayments
fee for service
defensive medicine
tax subsidy
"play or pay"
national health insurance (NHI)
preferred provider organizations (PPOs)
health maintenance organizations (HMOs)
diagnosis-related-group (DRG) system
Medicare Part D
health savings accounts (HSAs)

Study Questions

1. Why would increased spending as a percentage of GDP on, say, household appliances or education in a particular economy be regarded as economically desirable? Why, then, is there so much concern about rising expenditures as a percentage of GDP on health care?
2. **KEY QUESTION** What are the "twin problems" of the health care industry as viewed by society? How are they related?
3. Briefly describe the main features of Medicare and Medicaid, indicating how each is financed.
4. What are the implications of rapidly rising health care prices and spending for (*a*) the growth of real-wage rates, (*b*) government budgets, and (*c*) off shoring of U.S. jobs? Explain.
5. Who are the main groups without health insurance?
6. List the special characteristics of the U.S. health care market and specify how each affects health care problems.
7. **KEY QUESTION** What are the estimated income and price elasticities of demand for health care? How does each relate to rising health care costs?
8. Briefly discuss the demand and supply factors that contribute to rising health costs. Specify how (*a*) asymmetric information, (*b*) fee-for-service payments, (*c*) defensive medicine, and (*d*) medical ethics might cause health care costs to rise.
9. How do advances in medical technology and health insurance interact to drive up the costs of medical care?
10. **KEY QUESTION** Using the concepts in Chapter 7's discussion of consumer behavior, explain how health care insurance results in an overallocation of resources to the health care industry. Use a demand and supply diagram to specify the resulting efficiency loss.
11. How is the moral hazard problem relevant to the health care market?
12. What is the rationale for exempting a firm's contribution to its workers' health insurance from taxation as worker income? What is the impact of this exemption on allocative efficiency in the health care industry?
13. Comment on or explain:
    a. Providing health insurance to achieve equity goals creates a tradeoff with the efficient allocation of resources to the health care industry.
    b. If the government were to require employer-sponsored health insurance for all workers, the likely result would be an increase in the unemployment of low-wage workers.
14. Briefly describe (*a*) "play or pay," (*b*) tax credits and vouchers, and (*c*) national health insurance as means of increasing access to health care. What are the major criticisms of national health insurance?
15. What are (*a*) preferred provider organizations and (*b*) health maintenance organizations? In your answer, explain how each is designed to alleviate the overconsumption of health care.
16. What major factors led to the inclusion of prescription drug coverage under Medicare? Is the insurance purchased directly from the Federal government or from private insurers? What is the annual deductible under the coverage? In percentage terms, what is the copayment for prescription drug expenses below $2250 annually? What percentage of expenses is covered above $3600 annually? Why might the new coverage boost the price of prescription drugs?
17. What are health savings accounts (HSAs)? How might they reduce the overconsumption of health care resulting from traditional insurance? How might they introduce an element of price competition into the health care system?
18. **LAST WORD** Compare and contrast the general policy approach of the Massachusetts health care reform of 2006 and the Federal law that created health savings accounts. Are the two laws compatible with one another? Which of the two approaches do you think has the best chance of reducing the percentage of people without medical insurance? Which of the two approaches do you think has the best chance of reducing health care costs?

Web-Based Question

1. **HEALTH EXPENDITURES PER CAPITA—GOING UP OR DOWN?** Go to the Web site of the Centers for Medicare and Medicaid, **www.cms.hhs.gov**, and use the search box to find information on *health expenditures per capita* for the United States. What was the level of such expenditures in 1990? In 2000? For the most recent year shown? Is the level of expenditures per capita projected to rise or to fall over the next 5 years? Find information on *health expenditures as a percentage of GDP.* Contrast the percentage for the latest year shown with the percentage projected for the most distant future year shown. Is the health care problem going away?

22

IN THIS CHAPTER YOU WILL LEARN:

- **Who belongs to U.S. unions; the basics of collective bargaining; why unions are in decline; and the effects of unions on wages, efficiency, and productivity.**
- **The types and costs of discrimination, economic theories of discrimination, and current antidiscrimination issues.**
- **The extent and effects of U.S. immigration.**

Labor Market Institutions and Issues: Unionism, Discrimination, Immigration

Experts on etiquette agree that in social conversations with new acquaintances, bringing up certain topics—politics and religion, for example—is unwise. Such topics often evoke strong emotions, different opinions, and the potential for unwanted debate. "Unionism," "discrimination," and "immigration" belong in this category as well. A strongly expressed opinion on these subjects stated in a social setting may well set off verbal fireworks.

Opinion, of course, is not fact, and opinion is not always based on sound analysis. In this chapter, we will approach these three topics factually and analytically. This chapter will provide useful information that should help you develop informed opinions on these important aspects of the U.S. labor market.

2 Things
Negotiations
- Contracts

AFSCME

American Federation
State County Municipal
Employees

Unionism in America

In 2005 about 16 million U.S. workers—12.5 percent of employed wage and salary workers—belonged to unions. (Global Perspective 22.1 compares this percentage with those of several other nations.) Some 9 million of the 16 million U.S. union members belong to one of many unions that are loosely and voluntarily affiliated with the **American Federation of Labor and the Congress of Industrial Organizations (AFL-CIO).** Examples of AFL-CIO unions are the United Autoworkers, Communications Workers, and United Steelworkers. Another 7 million union members belong to **independent unions** that are not affiliated with the AFL-CIO. Among those unions are the Teamsters, Service Employees Union, and Nurses' Union.

Business Unionism

In the United States, unions generally have adhered to a philosophy of **business unionism:** unionism that is concerned with the short-run economic objectives of higher pay, better benefits, shorter hours, and improved working conditions. These unions have not pushed for long-run idealistic objectives aimed at significantly modifying or overthrowing the capitalistic system. Nor have union members organized into a distinct political party, such as the "labor parties" of several European nations. Unionism's political philosophy has been to reward its friends and punish its enemies at the polls, regardless of political party.

Union Membership

The likelihood that any particular worker will be a union member depends mainly on the industry in which the worker works and his or her occupation. Figure 22.1a shows that the rate of unionization (percentage of workers unionized) is high in government, transportation, telecommunications, construction, and manufacturing. The rate of unionization is very low in finance, agriculture, and retail trade. Figure 22.1b shows that unionism also varies greatly by occupation. Teachers, protective service

GLOBAL PERSPECTIVE 22.1

Union Membership as a Percentage of the Employed Labor Force, Selected Nations

Compared with the percentages unionized in most other industrialized nations, union membership in the United States is small.

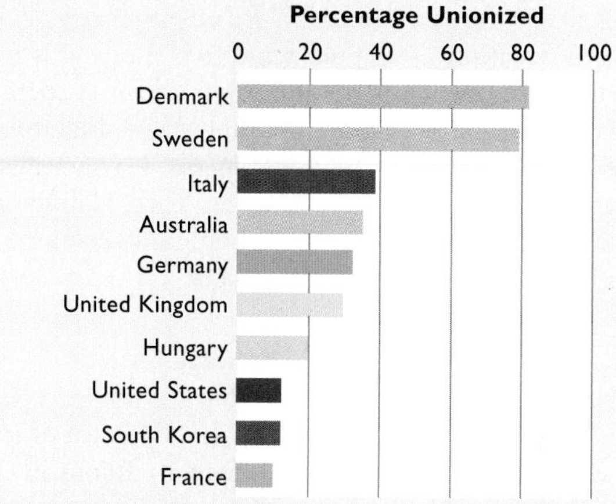

Source: Statistical agencies in individual countries. Latest data.

FIGURE 22.1 Union membership as a percentage of employed wage and salary workers, selected industries and occupations, 2005. In percentage terms, union membership varies greatly by (a) industry and (b) occupation.

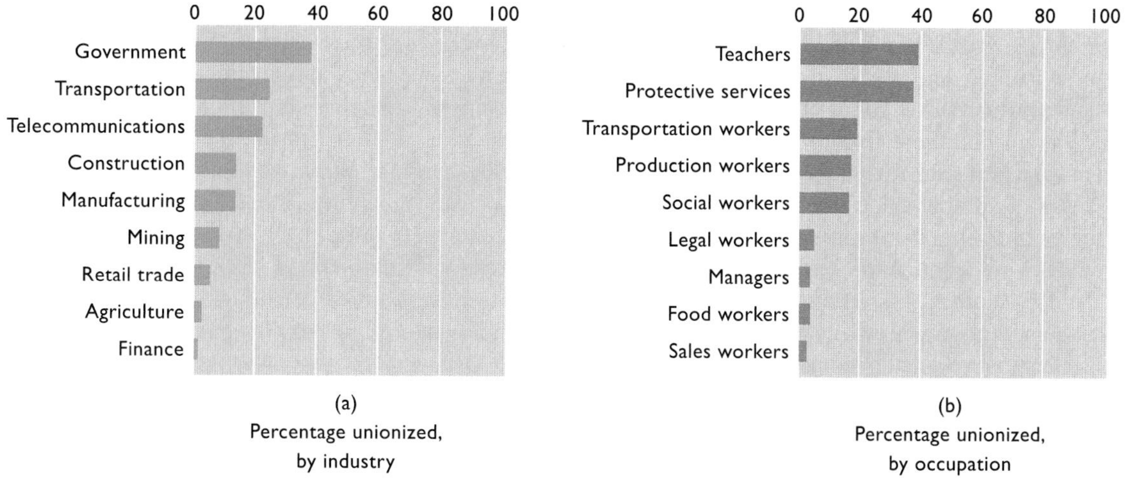

Source: Bureau of Labor Statistics, **www.bls.gov.**

workers, transportation workers, production workers, and social workers have high rates of unionization; sales workers, food workers and managers have very low rates.

Because disproportionately more men than women work in the industries and occupations with high unionization rates, men are more likely to be union members than women. Specifically, 14 percent of male wage and salary workers belong to unions compared with 11 percent of women. For the same reason, African-Americans have higher unionization rates than whites: 17 percent compared with 12 percent. The unionization rate for Hispanics is 10 percent; Asians, 11 percent. Unionism in the United States is largely an urban phenomenon. Six heavily urbanized, heavily industrialized states (New York, California, Pennsylvania, Illinois, Ohio, and Michigan) account for approximately half of all union members.

The Decline of Unionism

Since the mid-1950s, union membership has not kept pace with the growth of the labor force. While 25 percent of employed wage and salary workers belonged to unions in the mid-1950s, today only 12.5 percent are union members. Over recent years, even the absolute number of union members has declined significantly. More than 22 million workers were unionized in 1980 but only about 16 million in 2005.

What explains the decline in unionization, relatively and absolutely?

Structural Changes According to the **structural-change hypothesis,** changes unfavorable to the expansion of union membership have occurred in both the economy and the labor force.

Employment has shifted away from traditionally unionized industries. For example, U.S. domestic employment has moved away from manufactured goods (where unions have been strong) and toward services (where unions have been weak). Also, consumer demand in some cases has shifted toward foreign manufactured goods and away from goods produced by union labor in the United States. Increased foreign competition in several highly unionized manufacturing industries such as automobile and steel has reduced unionized workforces and, therefore, union membership. And within manufacturing, production has shifted from highly unionized "old-economy" firms to software production, computer manufacturing, and other "high-tech" industries in which unionization is virtually nonexistent.

Another factor in the decline in unionism is that an unusually high proportion of the increase in employment in recent decades has been concentrated among women, youths, and part-time workers. These groups are allegedly difficult to organize into unions, because they are less strongly attached to the labor force. Furthermore, the long-term trend of industry to shift from the northeast and midwest, where unionism is "a way of life," to "hard-to-organize" areas of the south and southwest has reduced the growth of union membership.

An ironic possibility is that the relative decline of unionism may in part reflect the success that unions have achieved in gaining a sizable wage advantage over nonunion workers in the United States. Confronted with high union wages, employers may have substituted machinery for workers, subcontracted more work to nonunion suppliers, opened nonunion plants in less industrialized areas, or shifted production of components to low-wage nations. All these actions reduce the employment of union workers and thus the level of union membership.

The success of unions in raising wages may have also raised the prices of union-produced goods relative to the prices of goods produced by nonunion workers. If so, we would expect output and employment in lower-cost nonunion firms and industries to increase at the expense of output and employment in higher-cost union firms and industries.

Managerial Opposition Another view of the decline of unionism is that intensified managerial opposition to unions has deterred union growth. According to this **managerial-opposition hypothesis,** the wage advantage that union workers enjoy causes union firms to be less profitable than nonunion firms. The managements of both nonunionized and unionized firms have therefore undertaken policies to oppose or dissuade unionization. One managerial strategy has been to employ labor-management consultants who specialize in mounting aggressive anti-union drives to dissuade workers from unionizing or, alternatively, to persuade union workers to decertify (officially vote out) their union. Also, confronted with strikes by union workers, management has increasingly hired permanent strikebreakers to take the place of striking workers, in the expectation that these nonunion workers will later vote to eliminate the union. A conciliatory strategy by management has been to improve working conditions and personnel policies. When management treats workers with dignity and respect, workers feel less need to join unions. So the demand for unionism declines.

Collective Bargaining

Despite the decline of unionism, **collective bargaining** (the negotiation of labor contracts) remains an important feature of labor-management relations. The goal of

American, grew up in a public housing development; Becky, who is white, grew up in a wealthy suburb. You can admit only one of the two. Which would you admit and why? Now suppose that Ann is white and Becky is African-American, all else equal. Does that change your selection? Why or why not?

12. **KEY QUESTION** Use graphical analysis to show the gains and losses resulting from the migration of population from a low-income country to a high-income country. Explain how your conclusions are affected by (*a*) unemployment, (*b*) remittances to the home country, (*c*) backflows of migrants to their home country, and (*d*) the personal characteristics of the migrants. If the migrants are highly skilled workers, is there any justification for the sending country to levy a "brain drain" tax on emigrants?

13. If a person favors the free movement of labor within the United States, is it then inconsistent to also favor restrictions on the international movement of labor? Why or why not?

14. Evaluate: "If the United States deported, say, 1 million unauthorized immigrants, the number of unemployed workers in the United States would decline by 1 million."

15. **LAST WORD** What two types of discrimination are represented by the discrimination evidenced in this chapter's Last Word?

Web-Based Questions

1. **UNION MEMBERSHIP—FALLING OR RISING?** Go to the Bureau of Labor Statistics Web site, **www.bls.gov**, and select A-Z Index and then Workstoppages for historical data on strikes. What has been the trend concerning the number of strikes involving more than 1000 workers over the past 20 years? Use the A-Z Index to update the text's data on union membership. For the latest year, determine (*a*) the overall unionization rate for wage and salary workers, (*b*) the unionization rates for men and women wage and salary workers, and (*c*) the unionization rates for black, white, and Hispanic wage and salary workers. Have the unionization rates gone up, down, or stayed constant compared to the data reported in this chapter?

2. **ILLEGAL IMMIGRANTS—A NEW LAW?** In the spring of 2006, the U.S. Congress was debating legislation pertaining to illegal immigration to the United States and the disposition of the some 12 million unauthorized immigrants already here. Use a standard Internet search engine such as Google, **www.google.com,** to determine the progress and outcome, if any, of that legislative debate. Did a new immigration law emerge? If so, what are its main features? If not, what is the current status of the legislative debate relating to unauthorized immigrants?

PART SIX

International Economics

23 INTERNATIONAL TRADE
24 EXCHANGE RATES, THE BALANCE OF PAYMENTS, AND TRADE DEFICITS

IN THIS CHAPTER YOU WILL LEARN:

- **The graphical model of comparative advantage, specialization, and the gains from trade.**
- **How differences between world prices and domestic prices prompt exports and imports.**
- **How economists analyze the economic effects of tariffs and quotas.**
- **The rebuttals to the most frequently presented arguments for protectionism.**
- **About the assistance provided workers under the Trade Adjustment Act of 2002.**
- **How the offshoring of U.S. jobs relates to the growing international trade in services.**

23

International Trade

The WTO, trade deficits, dumping. Exchange rates, the current account, the G8 nations. The IMF, official reserves, currency interventions. This is some of the language of international economics, the subject of Part 6. To understand the increasingly integrated world economy, we need to learn more about this language and the ideas that it conveys.

In this chapter we build on Chapter 5 by providing both a deeper analysis of the benefits of international trade and a fuller appraisal of the arguments for protectionism. Then in Chapter 24 we examine exchange rates and the U.S. balance of payments.

Some Key Facts

In Chapter 5, we provided an abundance of statistical information about U.S. international trade. The following "executive summary" reviews the most important of those facts:

- A *trade deficit* occurs when imports exceed exports. The United States has a trade deficit in goods. In 2005, U.S. imports of goods exceeded U.S. exports of goods by $782 billion.
- A *trade surplus* occurs when exports exceed imports. The United States has a trade surplus in services (such as air transportation services and financial services). In 2005, U.S. exports of services exceeded U.S. imports of services by $58 billion.
- Principal U.S. exports include chemicals, consumer durables, agricultural products, semiconductors, and computers; principal imports include petroleum, automobiles, household appliances, computers, and metals.
- Like other advanced industrial nations, the United States imports some of the same categories of goods that it exports. Examples: automobiles, computers, chemicals, semiconductors, and telecommunications equipment.
- Canada is the United States' most important trading partner quantitatively. In 2005, some 24 percent of U.S. exported goods were sold to Canadians, who in turn provided 17 percent of the U.S. imports of goods.
- The United States has a sizable trade deficit with China. In 2005, it was $202 billion.
- The U.S. dependence on foreign oil is reflected in its trade with members of OPEC. In 2005, the United States imported $125 billion of goods (mainly oil) from OPEC members, while exporting $31 billion of goods to those countries.
- The United States leads the world in the combined volume of exports and imports, as measured in dollars. Germany, the United States, China, Japan, and France are the top five exporters by dollar volume (see Global Perspective 5.1, p. 88). Currently, the United States provides about 9 percent of the world's exports (see Global Perspective 23.1).
- Exports of goods and services (on a national income account basis) make up about 11 percent of total U.S. output. That percentage is much lower than the percentage in many other nations, including Canada, Italy, France, and the United Kingdom (see Table 5.1, p. 86).
- China has become a major international trader, with an estimated $762 billion of exports in 2005. Other Asian economies—including South Korea, Taiwan, and Singapore—are also active in international trade. Their combined exports exceed those of France, Britain, or Italy.
- International trade (and finance) links world economies (review Figure 5.1, page 85). Through trade, changes in economic conditions in one place on the globe can quickly affect other places.
- International trade is often at the center of debates over economic policy, both within the United States and internationally.

With this information in mind, let's look more closely at the economics of international trade.

GLOBAL PERSPECTIVE 23.1

Shares of World Exports, Selected Nations

Germany has the largest share of world exports, followed by the United States and China. The eight largest export nations account for nearly 50 percent of world exports.

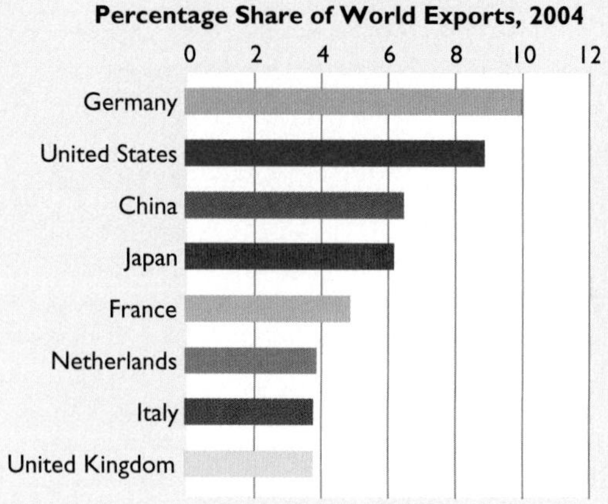

Source: World Trade Organization, **www.wto.org.**

The Economic Basis for Trade

Chapter 5 revealed that international trade enables nations to specialize their production, enhance their resource productivity, and acquire more goods and services. Sovereign nations, like individuals and the regions of a nation, can gain by specializing in the products they can produce with greatest relative efficiency and by trading for the goods they cannot produce as efficiently. A more complete answer to the question "Why do nations trade?" hinges on three facts:

- The distribution of natural, human, and capital resources among nations is uneven; nations differ in their endowments of economic resources.

- Efficient production of various goods requires different technologies or combinations of resources.
- Products are differentiated as to quality and other nonprice attributes. A few or many people may prefer certain imported goods to similar goods made domestically.

To recognize the character and interaction of these three facts, think of Japan, for example, which has a large, well-educated labor force and abundant, and therefore inexpensive, skilled labor. As a result, Japan can produce efficiently (at low cost) a variety of **labor-intensive goods** such as digital cameras, video game players, and DVD players whose design and production require much skilled labor.

In contrast, Australia has vast amounts of land and can inexpensively produce such **land-intensive goods** as wheat, wool, and meat. Brazil has the soil, tropical climate, rainfall, and ready supply of unskilled labor that are needed for the efficient, low-cost production of coffee.

Industrially advanced economies with relatively large amounts of capital can inexpensively produce goods whose production requires much capital, including such **capital-intensive goods** as automobiles, agricultural equipment, machinery, and chemicals.

All nations, regardless of their labor, land, or capital intensity, can find special niches for individual products that are in demand worldwide because of their special qualities. Examples: fashions from Italy, luxury automobiles from Germany, software from the United States, and watches from Switzerland.

The distribution of resources, technology, and product distinctiveness among nations, however, is not forever fixed. When that distribution changes, the relative efficiency and success with which nations produce and sell goods also changes. For example, in the past few decades South Korea has upgraded the quality of its labor force and has greatly expanded its stock of capital. Although South Korea was primarily an exporter of agricultural products and raw materials a half-century ago, it now exports large quantities of manufactured goods. Similarly, the new technologies that gave us synthetic fibers and synthetic rubber drastically altered the resource mix needed to produce these goods and changed the relative efficiency of nations in manufacturing them.

As national economies evolve, the size and quality of their labor forces may change, the volume and composition of their capital stocks may shift, new technologies may develop, and even the quality of land and the quantity of natural resources may be altered. As such changes occur, the relative efficiency with which a nation can produce specific goods will also change.

Comparative Advantage: Graphical Analysis

Implicit in what we have been saying is the principle of comparative advantage, described through production possibilities tables in Chapter 5. Let's look again at that idea, now using graphical analysis.

Two Isolated Nations

Suppose the world economy is composed of just two nations: the United States and Brazil. Also for simplicity, suppose that the labor forces in the United States and Brazil are of equal size. Each nation can produce both wheat and coffee, but at different levels of economic efficiency. Suppose the U.S. and Brazilian domestic production possibilities curves for coffee and wheat are as shown in Figure 23.1a and 23.1b. Note especially three realities relating to these production possibilities curves:

- ***Constant costs*** The "curves" are drawn as straight lines, in contrast to the bowed-outward production possibilities frontiers we examined in Chapter 1. This means that we have replaced the law of increasing opportunity costs with the assumption of constant costs. This substitution simplifies our discussion but does not impair the validity of our analysis and conclusions. Later we will consider the effects of increasing opportunity costs.
- ***Different costs*** The production possibilities curves of the United States and Brazil reflect different resource mixes and differing levels of technological progress. Specifically, the differing slopes of the two curves tell us that the opportunity costs of producing wheat and coffee differ between the two nations.
- ***U.S. absolute advantage in both*** In view of our assumption that the U.S. and Brazilian labor forces are of equal size, the two production possibilities curves show that the United States has an *absolute advantage* in producing both products. If the United States and Brazil use their entire (equal-size) labor forces to produce either coffee or wheat, the United States can produce more of either than Brazil. The United States, using the same number of workers as Brazil, has greater production possibilities. So output per worker—labor productivity—in the United States exceeds that in Brazil in producing both products.

United States In Figure 23.1a, with full employment, the United States will operate on its production possibilities curve. On that curve, it can increase its output of wheat from 0 tons to 30 tons by forgoing 30 tons of coffee output. This

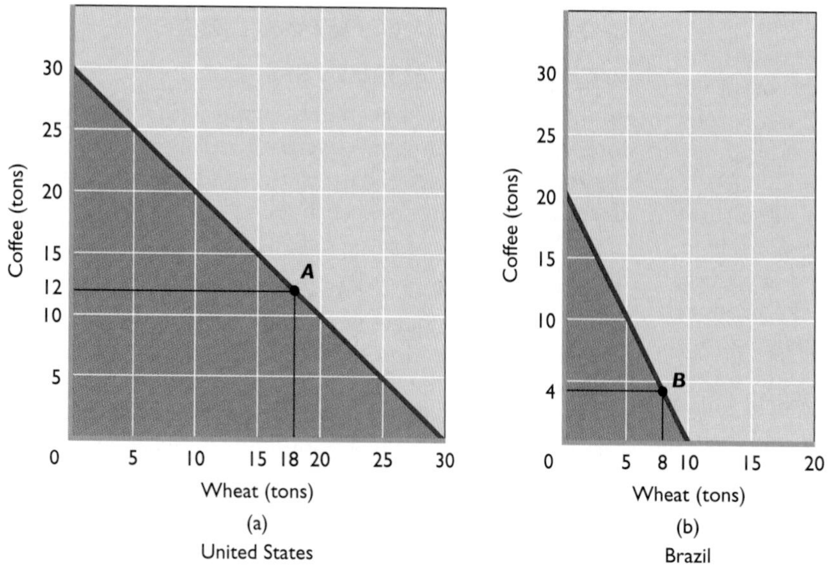

FIGURE 23.1 Production possibilities for the United States and Brazil. The two production possibilities curves show the combinations of coffee and wheat that (a) the United States and (b) Brazil can produce domestically. The curves for both countries are straight lines because we are assuming constant opportunity costs. The different cost ratios, 1 coffee ≡ 1 wheat for the United States, and 2 coffee ≡ 1 wheat for Brazil, are reflected in the different slopes of the two lines.

means that the slope of the production possibilities curve is -1 ($= -30$ coffee/$+30$ wheat), implying that 1 ton of coffee must be sacrificed for each extra ton of wheat. In the United States the domestic exchange ratio or **opportunity-cost ratio** for the two products is 1 ton of coffee for 1 ton of wheat, or $1C \equiv 1W$. (As in Chapter 5, the "≡" sign simply means "equivalent to.") Said differently, the United States can "exchange" a ton of coffee for a ton of wheat. Our constant-cost assumption means that this exchange or opportunity-cost equation prevails for all possible moves from one point to another along the U.S. production possibilities curve.

Brazil Brazil's production possibilities curve in Figure 23.1b represents a different full-employment opportunity-cost ratio. In Brazil, 20 tons of coffee must be given up to get 10 tons of wheat. The slope of the production possibilities curve is -2 ($= -20$ coffee/$+10$ wheat). This means that in Brazil the opportunity-cost ratio for the two goods is 2 tons of coffee for 1 ton of wheat, or $2C \equiv 1W$.

Self-Sufficiency Output Mix If the United States and Brazil are isolated and are to be self-sufficient, then each country must choose some output mix on its production possibilities curve. It will choose the mix that provides the greatest total utility, or satisfaction. Assume that point *A* in Figure 23.1a is the optimal mix in the United States; that is, society deems the combination of 18 tons of wheat and 12 tons of coffee preferable to any other combination of the goods available along the production possibilities curve. Suppose Brazil's optimal product mix is 8 tons of wheat and 4 tons of coffee, indicated by point *B* in Figure 23.1b. These choices are reflected in column 1 of Table 23.1.

Specializing Based on Comparative Advantage

Although the United States has an absolute advantage in producing both goods, gains from specialization and trade are possible. Specialization and trade are mutually

TABLE 23.1 International Specialization According to Comparative Advantage and the Gains from Trade

Country	(1) Outputs before Specialization	(2) Outputs after Specialization	(3) Amounts Exported (−) and Imported (+)	(4) Outputs Available after Trade	(5) Gains from Specialization and Trade (4) − (1)
United States	18 wheat 12 coffee	30 wheat 0 coffee	−10 wheat +15 coffee	20 wheat 15 coffee	2 wheat 3 coffee
Brazil	8 wheat 4 coffee	0 wheat 20 coffee	+10 wheat −15 coffee	10 wheat 5 coffee	2 wheat 1 coffee

beneficial, or profitable, to the two nations if the *comparative* opportunity costs of producing the two products within the two nations differ, as they do in this example. The **principle of comparative advantage** says that total output will be greatest when each good is produced by the nation that has the lowest domestic opportunity cost for that good. In our two-nation illustration, the United States has the lower domestic opportunity cost for wheat; the United States need forgo only 1 ton of coffee to produce 1 ton of wheat, whereas Brazil must forgo 2 tons of coffee for 1 ton of wheat. The United States has a comparative (cost) advantage in wheat and should specialize in wheat production. The "world" (that is, the United States and Brazil) in our example would clearly not be economizing in the use of its resources if a high-cost producer (Brazil) produced a specific product (wheat) when a low-cost producer (the United States) could have produced it. Having Brazil produce wheat would mean that the world economy would have to give up more coffee than is necessary to obtain a ton of wheat.

G 23.1
Comparative advantage

Brazil has the lower domestic opportunity cost for coffee; it must sacrifice only $\frac{1}{2}$ ton of wheat in producing 1 ton of coffee, while the United States must forgo 1 ton of wheat in producing a ton of coffee. Brazil has a comparative advantage in coffee and should specialize in coffee production. Again, the world would not be employing its resources economically if coffee were produced by a high-cost producer (the United States) rather than by a low-cost producer (Brazil). If the United States produced coffee, the world would be giving up more wheat than necessary to obtain each ton of coffee. Economizing requires that any particular good be produced by the nation having the lowest domestic opportunity cost, or the comparative advantage for that good. The United States should produce wheat, and Brazil should produce coffee.

In column 2 of Table 23.1 we verify that specialized production enables the world to get more output from its fixed amount of resources. By specializing completely in wheat, the United States can produce 30 tons of wheat and no coffee. Brazil, by specializing completely in coffee, can produce 20 tons of coffee and no wheat. The world ends up with 4 more tons of wheat (30 tons compared with 26) *and* 4 more tons of coffee (20 tons compared with 16) than it would if there were self-sufficiency or unspecialized production.

Terms of Trade

But consumers of each nation want both wheat *and* coffee. They can have both if the two nations trade the two products. But what will be the **terms of trade?** At what exchange ratio will the United States and Brazil trade wheat and coffee?

Because $1W \equiv 1C$ in the United States, the United States must get *more than* 1 ton of coffee for each ton of wheat exported; otherwise, it will not benefit from exporting wheat in exchange for Brazilian coffee. The United States must get a better "price" (more coffee) for its wheat in the world market than it can get domestically; otherwise, there is no gain from trade and it will not occur.

Similarly, because $1W \equiv 2C$ in Brazil, Brazil must get 1 ton of wheat by exporting some amount *less than* 2 tons of coffee. Brazil must be able to pay a lower "price" for wheat in the world market than it must pay domestically, or else it will not want to trade. The international exchange ratio or terms of trade must lie somewhere between

$$1W \equiv 1C \text{ (United States' cost conditions)}$$

and

$$1W \equiv 2C \text{ (Brazil's cost conditions)}$$

But where between these limits will the world exchange ratio fall? The United States will prefer a rate close to $1W \equiv 2C$, say, $1W \equiv 1\frac{3}{4}C$. The United States wants to get as much coffee as possible for each ton of wheat it exports. Similarly, Brazil wants a rate near $1W \equiv 1C$, say, $1W \equiv 1\frac{1}{4}C$. Brazil wants to export as little coffee as possible for each ton of wheat it receives in exchange. The exchange ratio or terms of trade determine how the gains from international specialization and trade are divided between the two nations.

The actual exchange ratio depends on world supply and demand for the two products. If overall world demand for coffee is weak relative to its supply and if the demand for wheat is strong relative to its supply, the price of coffee will be lower and the price of wheat higher. The exchange ratio will settle nearer the $1W \equiv 2C$ figure the United States prefers. If overall world demand for coffee is great relative to its supply and if the demand for wheat is weak relative to its supply, the ratio will settle nearer the $1W \equiv 1C$ level favorable to Brazil. (We discuss equilibrium world prices later in this chapter.)

Gains from Trade

Suppose the international terms of trade are $1W \equiv 1\frac{1}{2}C$. The possibility of trading on these terms permits each nation to supplement its domestic production possibilities curve with a **trading possibilities line** (or curve), as shown in **Figure 23.2 (Key Graph).** Just as a production possibilities curve shows the amounts of these products a full-employment economy can obtain by shifting resources from one to the other, a trading possibilities line shows the amounts of two products a nation can obtain by specializing

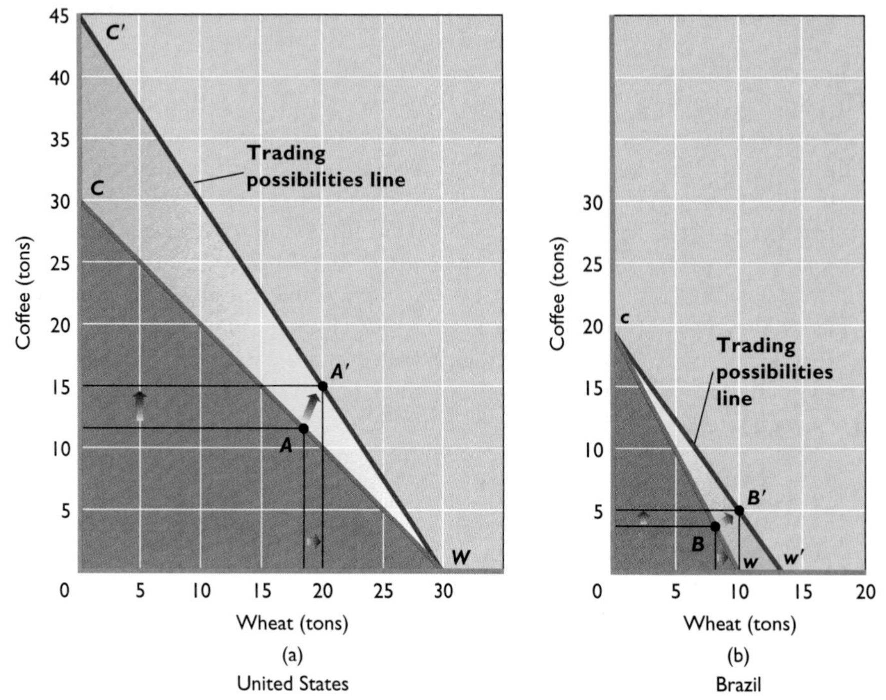

FIGURE 23.2 Trading possibility lines and the gains from trade. As a result of specialization and trade, both the United States and Brazil can have higher levels of output than the levels attainable on their domestic production possibilities curves. (a) The United States can move from point *A* on its domestic production possibilities curve to, say, *A′* on its trading possibilities line. (b) Brazil can move from *B* to *B′*.

QUICK QUIZ 23.2

1. The production possibilities curves in graphs (a) and (b) imply:
   a. increasing domestic opportunity costs.
   b. decreasing domestic opportunity costs.
   c. constant domestic opportunity costs.
   d. first decreasing, then increasing, domestic opportunity costs.
2. Before specialization, the domestic opportunity cost of producing 1 unit of wheat is:
   a. 1 unit of coffee in both the United States and Brazil.
   b. 1 unit of coffee in the United States and 2 units of coffee in Brazil.
   c. 2 units of coffee in the United States and 1 unit of coffee in Brazil.
   d. 1 unit of coffee in the United States and $\frac{1}{2}$ unit of coffee in Brazil.
3. After specialization and international trade, the world output of wheat and coffee is:
   a. 20 tons of wheat and 20 tons of coffee.
   b. 45 tons of wheat and 15 tons of coffee.
   c. 30 tons of wheat and 20 tons of coffee.
   d. 10 tons of wheat and 30 tons of coffee.
4. After specialization and international trade:
   a. the United States can obtain units of coffee at less cost than it could before trade.
   b. Brazil can obtain more than 20 tons of coffee, if it so chooses.
   c. the United States no longer has a comparative advantage in producing wheat.
   d. Brazil can benefit by prohibiting coffee imports from the United States.

Answers: 1. c; 2. b; 3. c; 4. a

in one product and trading for the other. The trading possibilities lines in Figure 23.2 reflect the assumption that both nations specialize on the basis of comparative advantage: The United States specializes completely in wheat (at point *W* in Figure 23.2a), and Brazil specializes completely in coffee (at point *c* in Figure 23.2b).

Improved Options Now the United States is not constrained by its domestic production possibilities line, which requires it to give up 1 ton of wheat for every ton of coffee it wants as it moves up its domestic production possibilities line from, say, point *W*. Instead, the United States, through trade with Brazil, can get $1\frac{1}{2}$ tons of coffee for every ton of wheat it exports to Brazil, as long as Brazil has coffee to export. Trading possibilities line *WC′* thus represents the $1W \equiv 1\frac{1}{2}C$ trading ratio.

Similarly, Brazil, starting at, say, point *c*, no longer has to move down its domestic production possibilities curve, giving up 2 tons of coffee for each ton of wheat it wants. It can now export just $1\frac{1}{2}$ tons of coffee for each ton of wheat it wants by moving down its trading possibilities line cw'.

Specialization and trade create a new exchange ratio between wheat and coffee, reflected in each nation's trading possibilities line. This exchange ratio is superior for both nations to the unspecialized exchange ratio embodied in their production possibilities curves. By specializing in wheat and trading for Brazil's coffee, the United States can obtain more than 1 ton of coffee for 1 ton of wheat. By specializing in coffee and trading for U.S. wheat, Brazil can get 1 ton of wheat for less than 2 tons of coffee. In both cases, self-sufficiency is undesirable.

Added Output By specializing on the basis of comparative advantage and by trading for goods that are produced in the nation with greater domestic efficiency, the United States and Brazil can realize combinations of wheat and coffee beyond their production possibilities curves. Specialization according to comparative advantage results in a more efficient allocation of world resources, and larger outputs of both products are therefore available to both nations.

Suppose that at the $1W \equiv 1\frac{1}{2}C$ terms of trade, the United States exports 10 tons of wheat to Brazil and in return Brazil exports 15 tons of coffee to the United States. How do the new quantities of wheat and coffee available to the two nations compare with the optimal product mixes that existed before specialization and trade? Point A in Figure 23.2a reminds us that the United States chose 18 tons of wheat and 12 tons of coffee originally. But by producing 30 tons of wheat and no coffee and by trading 10 tons of wheat for 15 tons of coffee, the United States can obtain 20 tons of wheat and 15 tons of coffee. This new, superior combination of wheat and coffee is indicated by point A' in Figure 23.2a. Compared with the no-trade amounts of 18 tons of wheat and 12 tons of coffee, the United States' **gains from trade** are 2 tons of wheat and 3 tons of coffee.

Similarly, recall that Brazil's optimal product mix was 4 tons of coffee and 8 tons of wheat (point B) before specialization and trade. Now, after specializing in coffee and trading, Brazil can have 5 tons of coffee and 10 tons of wheat. It accomplishes that by producing 20 tons of coffee and no wheat and exporting 15 tons of its coffee in exchange for 10 tons of American wheat. This new position is indicated by point B' in Figure 23.2b. Brazil's gains from trade are 1 ton of coffee and 2 tons of wheat.

As a result of specialization and trade, both countries have more of both products. Table 23.1, which summarizes the transactions and outcomes, merits careful study.

The fact that points A' and B' are economic positions superior to A and B is enormously important. We know that a nation can expand its production possibilities boundary by (1) expanding the quantity and improving the quality of its resources or (2) realizing technological progress. We have now established that international trade can enable a nation to circumvent the output constraint illustrated by its production possibilities curve. The outcome of international specialization and trade is equivalent to having more and better resources or discovering improved production techniques.

W 23.1
Gains from trade

Trade with Increasing Costs

To explain the basic principles underlying international trade, we simplified our analysis in several ways. For example, we limited discussion to two products and two nations. But multiproduct and multinational analysis yields the same conclusions. We also assumed constant opportunity costs (linear production possibilities curves), which is a more substantive simplification. Let's consider the effect of allowing increasing opportunity costs (concave-to-the-origin production possibilities curves) to enter the picture.

Suppose that the United States and Brazil initially are at positions on their concave production possibilities curves where their domestic cost ratios are $1W \equiv 1C$ and $1W \equiv 2C$, as they were in our constant-cost analysis. As before, comparative advantage indicates that the United States should specialize in wheat and Brazil in coffee. But now, as the United States begins to expand wheat production, its cost of wheat will rise; it will have to sacrifice more than 1 ton of coffee to get 1 additional ton of wheat. Resources are no longer perfectly substitutable between alternative uses, as the constant-cost assumption implied. Resources less and less suitable to wheat production must be allocated to the U.S. wheat industry in expanding wheat output, and that means increasing costs—the sacrifice of larger and larger amounts of coffee for each additional ton of wheat.

Similarly, Brazil, starting from its $1W \equiv 2C$ cost ratio position, expands coffee production. But as it does, it will find that its $1W \equiv 2C$ cost ratio begins to rise. Sacrificing a ton of wheat will free resources that are capable of producing only something less than 2 tons of coffee, because those transferred resources are less suitable to coffee production.

As the U.S. cost ratio falls from $1W \equiv 1C$ and the Brazilian ratio rises from $1W \equiv 2C$, a point will be reached where the cost ratios are equal in the two nations, perhaps at $1W \equiv 1\frac{3}{4}C$. At this point the underlying basis for further specialization and trade—differing cost ratios—has disappeared, and further specialization is therefore uneconomical. And, most important, this point of equal cost ratios may be reached while the United States is still producing some coffee along with its wheat and Brazil is producing some wheat along with its coffee. The primary effect of increasing opportunity costs is less-than-complete specialization. For this reason we often find domestically produced products competing directly against identical or similar imported products within a particular economy. **(Key Question 4)**

QUICK REVIEW 23.1

- International trade enables nations to specialize, increase productivity, and increase output available for consumption.
- Comparative advantage means total world output will be greatest when each good is produced by the nation that has the lowest domestic opportunity cost.
- Specialization is less than complete among nations because opportunity costs normally rise as any given nation produces more of a particular good.

The Case for Free Trade

The case for free trade reduces to one compelling argument: Through free trade based on the principle of comparative advantage, the world economy can achieve a more efficient allocation of resources and a higher level of material well-being than it can without free trade.

Since the resource mixes and technological knowledge of the world's nations are all somewhat different, each nation can produce particular commodities at different real costs. Each nation should produce goods for which its domestic opportunity costs are lower than the domestic opportunity costs of other nations and exchange those goods for products for which its domestic opportunity costs are high relative to those of other nations. If each nation does this, the world will realize the advantages of geographic and human specialization. The world and each free-trading nation can obtain a larger real income from the fixed supplies of resources available to it. Government trade barriers lessen or eliminate gains from specialization. If nations cannot trade freely, they must shift resources from efficient (low-cost) to inefficient (high-cost) uses in order to satisfy their diverse wants.

One side benefit of free trade is that it promotes competition and deters monopoly. The increased competition from foreign firms forces domestic firms to find and use the lowest-cost production techniques. It also compels them to be innovative with respect to both product quality and production methods, thereby contributing to economic growth. And free trade gives consumers a wider range of product choices. The reasons to favor free trade are the same as the reasons to endorse competition.

A second side benefit of free trade is that it links national interests and breaks down national animosities. Confronted with political disagreements, trading partners tend to negotiate rather than make war.

Supply and Demand Analysis of Exports and Imports

Supply and demand analysis reveals how equilibrium prices and quantities of exports and imports are determined. The amount of a good or a service a nation will export or import depends on differences between the equilibrium world price and the equilibrium domestic price. The interaction of *world* supply and demand determines the equilibrium **world price**—the price that equates the quantities supplied and demanded globally. *Domestic* supply and demand determine the equilibrium **domestic price**—the price that would prevail in a closed economy that does not engage in international trade. The domestic price equates quantity supplied and quantity demanded domestically.

In the absence of trade, the domestic prices in a closed economy may or may not equal the world equilibrium prices. When economies are opened for international trade, differences between world and domestic prices encourage exports or imports. To see how, consider the international effects of such price differences in a simple two-nation world, consisting of the United States and Canada, that are both producing aluminum. We assume there are no trade barriers, such as tariffs and quotas, and no international transportation costs.

Supply and Demand in the United States

Figure 23.3a shows the domestic supply curve S_d and the domestic demand curve D_d for aluminum in the United States, which for now is a closed economy. The intersection of S_d and D_d determines the equilibrium domestic price of \$1 per pound and the equilibrium domestic quantity of 100 million pounds. Domestic suppliers produce 100 million pounds and sell them all at \$1 a pound. So there are no domestic surpluses or shortages of aluminum.

FIGURE 23.3 U.S. export supply and import demand. (a) Domestic supply S_d and demand D_d set the domestic equilibrium price of aluminum at $1 per pound. At world prices above $1 there are domestic surpluses of aluminum. At prices below $1 there are domestic shortages. (b) Surpluses are exported (top curve), and shortages are met by importing aluminum (lower curve). The export supply curve shows the direct relationship between world prices and U.S. exports; the import demand curve portrays the inverse relationship between world prices and U.S. imports.

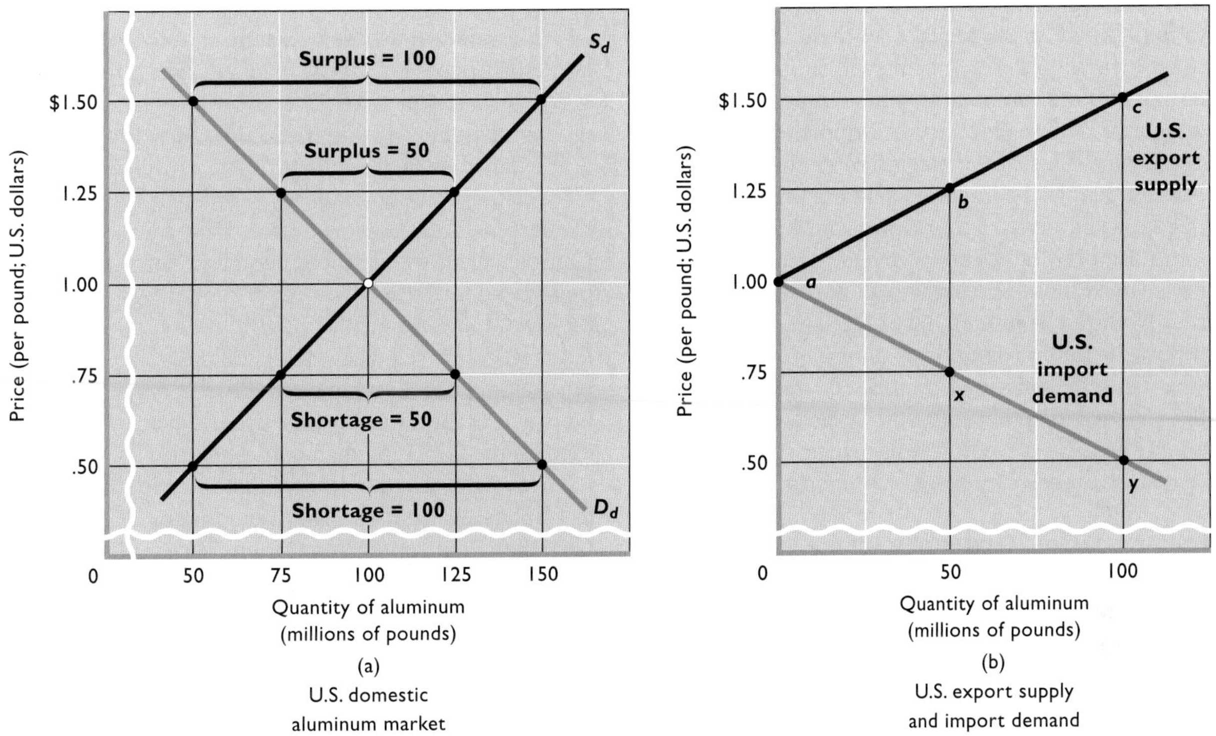

But what if the U.S. economy were opened to trade and the world price of aluminum were above or below this $1 domestic price?

U.S. Export Supply If the aluminum price in the rest of the world (that is, Canada) exceeds $1, U.S. firms will produce more than 100 million pounds and will export the excess domestic output. First, consider a world price of $1.25. We see from the supply curve S_d that U.S. aluminum firms will produce 125 million pounds of aluminum at that price. The demand curve D_d tells us that the United States will purchase only 75 million pounds at $1.25. The outcome is a domestic surplus of 50 million pounds of aluminum. U.S. producers will export those 50 million pounds at the $1.25 world price.

What if the world price were $1.50? The supply curve shows that U.S. firms will produce 150 million pounds of aluminum, while the demand curve tells us that U.S. consumers will buy only 50 million pounds. So U.S. producers will export the domestic surplus of 100 million pounds.

Toward the top of Figure 23.3b we plot the domestic surpluses—the U.S. exports—that occur at world prices above the $1 domestic equilibrium price. When the world and domestic prices are equal (= $1), the quantity of exports supplied is zero (point *a*). There is no surplus of domestic output to export. But when the world price is $1.25, U.S. firms export 50 million pounds of surplus aluminum (point *b*). At a $1.50 world price, the domestic surplus of 100 million pounds is exported (point *c*).

The U.S. **export supply curve,** found by connecting points *a*, *b*, and *c*, shows the amount of aluminum U.S. producers will export at each world price above $1. This curve *slopes upward*, indicating a direct or positive relationship between the world price and the amount of U.S. exports. As world prices increase relative to domestic prices, U.S. exports rise.

U.S. Import Demand If the world price is below the domestic $1 price, the United States will import aluminum. Consider a $.75 world price. The supply curve in Figure 23.3a reveals that at that price U.S. firms produce only 75 million pounds of aluminum. But the demand curve shows that the United States wants to buy 125 million pounds at that price. The result is a domestic shortage of 50 million pounds. To satisfy that shortage, the United States will import 50 million pounds of aluminum.

At an even lower world price, \$.50, U.S. producers will supply only 50 million pounds. Because U.S. consumers want to buy 150 million pounds at that price, there is a domestic shortage of 100 million pounds. Imports will flow to the United States to make up the difference. That is, at a \$.50 world price U.S. firms will supply 50 million pounds and 100 million pounds will be imported.

In Figure 23.3b we plot the U.S. **import demand curve** from these data. This *downsloping curve* shows the amounts of aluminum that will be imported at world prices below the \$1 U.S. domestic price. The relationship between world prices and imported amounts is inverse or negative. At a world price of \$1, domestic output will satisfy U.S. demand; imports will be zero (point *a*). But at \$.75 the United States will import 50 million pounds of aluminum (point *x*); at \$.50, the United States will import 100 million pounds (point *y*). Connecting points *a*, *x*, and *y* yields the *downsloping* U.S. import demand curve. It reveals that as world prices fall relative to U.S. domestic prices, U.S. imports increase.

Supply and Demand in Canada

We repeat our analysis in Figure 23.4, this time from the viewpoint of Canada. (We have converted Canadian dollar prices to U.S. dollar prices via the exchange rate.) Note that the domestic supply curve S_d and the domestic demand curve D_d for aluminum in Canada yield a domestic price of \$.75, which is \$.25 lower than the \$1 U.S. domestic price.

The analysis proceeds exactly as above except that the domestic price is now the Canadian price. If the world price is \$.75, Canadians will neither export nor import aluminum (giving us point *q* in Figure 23.4b). At world prices above \$.75, Canadian firms will produce more aluminum than Canadian consumers will buy. Canadian firms will export the surplus. At a \$1 world price, Figure 23.4b tells us that Canada will have and export a domestic surplus of 50 million pounds (yielding point *r*). At \$1.25, it will have and will export a domestic surplus of 100 million pounds (point *s*). Connecting these points yields the upsloping Canadian export supply curve, which reflects the domestic surpluses (and hence the exports) that occur when the world price exceeds the \$.75 Canadian domestic price.

At world prices below \$.75, domestic shortages occur in Canada. At a \$.50 world price, Figure 23.4a shows that Canadian consumers want to buy 125 million pounds of aluminum but Canadian firms will produce only 75 million pounds. The shortage will bring 50 million pounds of

FIGURE 23.4 Canadian export supply and import demand. (a) At world prices above the \$.75 domestic price, production in Canada exceeds domestic consumption. At world prices below \$.75, domestic shortages occur. (b) Surpluses result in exports, and shortages result in imports. The Canadian export supply curve and import demand curve depict the relationships between world prices and exports or imports.

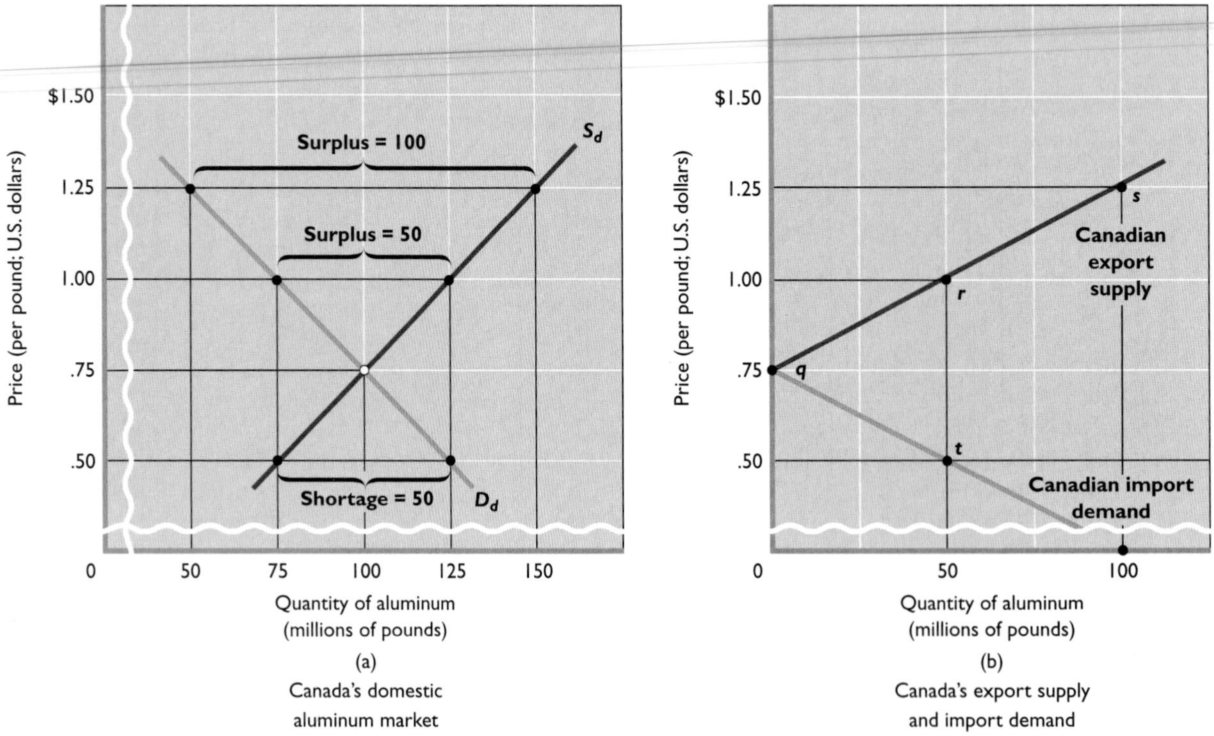

imports to Canada (point *t* in Figure 23.4b). The Canadian import demand curve in that figure shows the Canadian imports that will occur at all world aluminum prices below the $.75 Canadian domestic price.

Equilibrium World Price, Exports, and Imports

We now have the tools for determining the **equilibrium world price** of aluminum and the equilibrium world levels of exports and imports when the world is opened to trade. Figure 23.5 combines the U.S. export supply curve and import demand curve in Figure 23.3b and the Canadian export supply curve and import demand curve in Figure 23.4b. The two U.S. curves proceed rightward from the $1 U.S. domestic price; the two Canadian curves proceed rightward from the $.75 Canadian domestic price.

W 23.2
Equilibrium world price, exports, and imports

International equilibrium occurs in this two-nation model where one nation's import demand curve intersects another nation's export supply curve. In this case the U.S. import demand curve intersects Canada's export supply curve at *e*. There, the world price of aluminum is $.88. The Canadian export supply curve indicates that Canada will export 25 million pounds of aluminum at this price. Also at this price the United States will import 25 million pounds from Canada, indicated by the U.S. import demand curve. The $.88 world price equates the quantity of imports demanded and the quantity of exports supplied (25 million pounds). Thus there will be world trade of 25 million pounds of aluminum at $.88 per pound.

FIGURE 23.5 Equilibrium world price and quantity of exports and imports. In a two-nation world, the equilibrium world price (= $.88) is determined by the intersection of one nation's export supply curve and the other nation's import demand curve. This intersection also decides the equilibrium volume of exports and imports. Here, Canada exports 25 million pounds of aluminum to the United States.

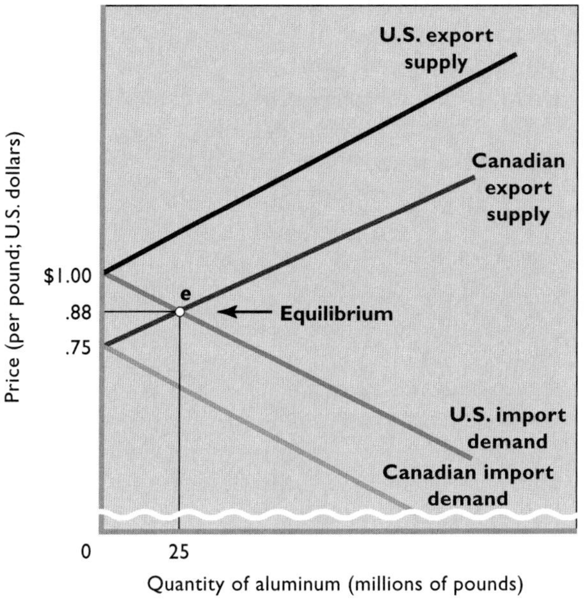

Note that after trade, the single $.88 world price will prevail in both Canada and the United States. Only one price for a standardized commodity can persist in a highly competitive world market. With trade, all consumers can buy a pound of aluminum for $.88, and all producers can sell it for that price. This world price means that Canadians will pay more for aluminum with trade ($.88) than without it ($.75). The increased Canadian output caused by trade raises Canadian per-unit production costs and therefore raises the price of aluminum in Canada. The United States, however, pays less for aluminum with trade ($.88) than without it ($1). The U.S. gain comes from Canada's comparative cost advantage in producing aluminum.

Why would Canada willingly send 25 million pounds of its aluminum output to the United States for U.S. consumption? After all, producing this output uses up scarce Canadian resources and drives up the price of aluminum for Canadians. Canadians are willing to export aluminum to the United States because Canadians gain the means—the U.S. dollars—to import other goods, say, computer software, from the United States. Canadian exports enable Canadians to acquire imports that have greater value to Canadians than the exported aluminum. Canadian exports to the United States finance Canadian imports from the United States. **(Key Question 6)**

QUICK REVIEW 23.2

- A nation will export a particular product if the world price exceeds the domestic price; it will import the product if the world price is less than the domestic price.
- In a two-country world model, equilibrium world prices and equilibrium quantities of exports and imports occur where one nation's export supply curve intersects the other nation's import demand curve.

Trade Barriers

No matter how compelling the case for free trade, barriers to free trade *do* exist. Let's expand Chapter 5's discussion of trade barriers.

Excise taxes on imported goods are called **tariffs;** they may be imposed to obtain revenue or to protect domestic firms. A **revenue tariff** is usually applied to a product that is not being produced domestically, for example, tin, coffee, or bananas in the case of the United States. Rates on revenue tariffs are modest; their purpose is to provide the Federal government with revenue. A **protective tariff** is designed to shield domestic producers from foreign competition. Although protective tariffs are usually not high enough to stop the importation of foreign goods, they put foreign producers at a competitive disadvantage in selling in domestic markets.

An **import quota** specifies the maximum amount of a commodity that may be imported in any period. Import quotas can more effectively retard international commerce than tariffs. A product might be imported in large quantities despite high tariffs; low import quotas completely prohibit imports once quotas have been filled.

A **nontariff barrier (NTB)** is a licensing requirement that specifies unreasonable standards pertaining to product quality and safety, or unnecessary bureaucratic red tape that is used to restrict imports. Japan and the European countries frequently require that their domestic importers of foreign goods obtain licenses. By restricting the issuance of licenses, imports can be restricted. The United Kingdom uses this barrier to bar the importation of coal.

A **voluntary export restriction (VER)** is a trade barrier by which foreign firms "voluntarily" limit the amount of their exports to a particular country. VERs, which have the effect of import quotas, are agreed to by exporters in the hope of avoiding more stringent trade barriers. In the late 1990s, for example, Canadian producers of softwood lumber (fir, spruce, cedar, pine) agreed to a VER on exports to the United States under the threat of a permanently higher U.S. tariff. Later in this chapter we will consider the arguments and appeals that are made to justify protection.

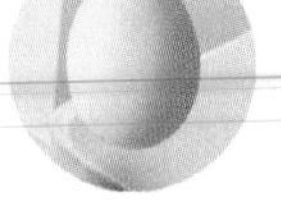

O 23.1
Mercantilism

Economic Impact of Tariffs

Once again we turn to supply and demand analysis—now to examine the economic effects of protective tariffs. Curves D_d and S_d in Figure 23.6 show domestic demand and supply for a product in which a nation, say, the United States, has a comparative disadvantage—for example, digital versatile disk (DVD) players. (Disregard curve $S_d + Q$ for now.) Without world trade, the domestic price and output would be P_d and q, respectively.

Assume now that the domestic economy is opened to world trade and that the Japanese, who have a comparative advantage in DVD players, begin to sell their players in the United States. We assume that with free trade the domestic price cannot differ from the world price, which here is P_w. At P_w domestic consumption is d and domestic production is a. The horizontal distance between the domestic supply and demand curves at P_w represents imports of ad. Thus far, our analysis is similar to the analysis of world prices in Figure 23.3.

FIGURE 23.6 The economic effects of a protective tariff or an import quota. A tariff that increases the price of a good from P_w to P_t will reduce domestic consumption from d to c. Domestic producers will be able to sell more output (b rather than a) at a higher price (P_t rather than P_w). Foreign exporters are injured because they sell less output (bc rather than ad). The brown area indicates the amount of tariff paid by domestic consumers. An import quota of bc units has the same effect as the tariff, with one exception: The amount represented by the brown area will go to foreign producers rather than to the domestic government.

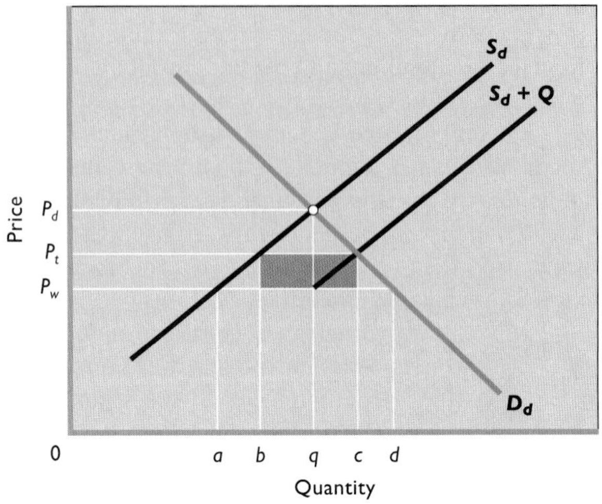

Direct Effects Suppose now that the United States imposes a tariff on each imported DVD player. The tariff, which raises the price of imported players from P_w to P_t, has four effects:

- ***Decline in consumption*** Consumption of DVD players in the United States declines from d to c as the higher price moves buyers up and to the left along their demand curve. The tariff prompts consumers to buy fewer players, and reallocate a portion of their expenditures to less desired substitute products. U.S. consumers are clearly injured by the tariff, since they pay P_wP_t more for each of the c units they buy at price P_t.
- ***Increased domestic production*** U.S. producers—who are not subject to the tariff—receive the higher price P_t per unit. Because this new price is higher than the pretariff world price P_w, the domestic DVD-player industry moves up and to the right along its supply curve S_d, increasing domestic output from a to b. Domestic producers thus enjoy both a higher price

and expanded sales; this explains why domestic producers lobby for protective tariffs. But from a social point of view, the greater domestic production from *a* to *b* means that the tariff permits domestic producers of players to bid resources away from other, more efficient, U.S. industries.

- ***Decline in imports*** Japanese producers are hurt. Although the sales price of each player is higher by P_wP_t, that amount accrues to the U.S. government, not to Japanese producers. The after-tariff world price, or the per-unit revenue to Japanese producers, remains at P_w, but the volume of U.S. imports (Japanese exports) falls from *ad* to *bc*.
- ***Tariff revenue*** The brown rectangle represents the amount of revenue the tariff yields. Total revenue from the tariff is determined by multiplying the tariff, P_wP_t per unit, by the number of players imported, *bc*. This tariff revenue is a transfer of income from consumers to government and does not represent any net change in the nation's economic well-being. The result is that government gains this portion of what consumers lose by paying more for DVD players.

Indirect Effect Tariffs have a subtle effect beyond what our supply and demand diagram can show. Because Japan sells fewer DVD players in the United States, it earns fewer dollars and so must buy fewer U.S. exports. U.S. export industries must then cut production and release resources. These are highly efficient industries, as we know from their comparative advantage and their ability to sell goods in world markets.

Tariffs directly promote the expansion of inefficient industries that do not have a comparative advantage; they also indirectly cause the contraction of relatively efficient industries that do have a comparative advantage. Put bluntly, tariffs cause resources to be shifted in the wrong direction—and that is not surprising. We know that specialization and world trade lead to more efficient use of world resources and greater world output. But protective tariffs reduce world trade. Therefore, tariffs also reduce efficiency and the world's real output.

Economic Impact of Quotas

We noted earlier that an import quota is a legal limit placed on the amount of some product that can be imported in a given year. Quotas have the same economic impact as a tariff, with one big difference: While tariffs generate revenue for the domestic government, a quota transfers that revenue to foreign producers.

Suppose in Figure 23.6 that, instead of imposing a tariff, the United States prohibits any imports of Japanese DVD players in excess of *bc* units. In other words, an import quota of *bc* players is imposed on Japan. We deliberately chose the size of this quota to be the same amount as imports would be under a P_wP_t tariff so that we can compare "equivalent" situations. As a consequence of the quota, the supply of players is $S_d + Q$ in the United States. This supply consists of the domestic supply plus the fixed amount *bc* (= *Q*) that importers will provide at each domestic price. The supply curve $S_d + Q$ does not extend below price P_w, because Japanese producers would not export players to the United States at any price below P_w; instead, they would sell them to other countries at the world market price of P_w.

Most of the economic results are the same as those with a tariff. Prices of DVD players are higher (P_t instead of P_w) because imports have been reduced from *ad* to *bc*. Domestic consumption of DVD players is down from *d* to *c*. U.S. producers enjoy both a higher price (P_t rather than P_w) and increased sales (*b* rather than *a*).

The difference is that the price increase of P_wP_t paid by U.S. consumers on imports of *bc*—the brown area—no longer goes to the U.S. Treasury as tariff (tax) revenue but flows to the Japanese firms that have acquired the rights to sell DVD players in the United States. For consumers in the United States, a tariff produces a better economic outcome than a quota, other things being the same. A tariff generates government revenue that can be used to cut other taxes or to finance public goods and services that benefit the United States. In contrast, the higher price created by quotas results in additional revenue for foreign producers. **(Key Question 7)**

Net Costs of Tariffs and Quotas

Figure 23.6 shows that tariffs and quotas impose costs on domestic consumers but provide gains to domestic producers and, in the case of tariffs, revenue to the Federal government. The consumer costs of trade restrictions are calculated by determining the effect the restrictions have on consumer prices. Protection raises the price of a product in three ways: (1) The price of the imported product goes up; (2) the higher price of imports causes some consumers to shift their purchases to higher-priced domestically produced goods; and (3) the prices of domestically produced goods rise because import competition has declined.

Study after study finds that the costs to consumers substantially exceed the gains to producers and government. A sizable net cost or efficiency loss to society arises from trade protection. Furthermore, industries employ large amounts of economic resources to influence Congress to pass and retain protectionist laws. Because these rent-seeking efforts divert resources away from more socially desirable purposes, trade restrictions impose that cost on society.

Conclusion: The gains that U.S. trade barriers create for protected industries and their workers come at the expense of much greater losses for the entire economy. The result is economic inefficiency.

The Case for Protection: A Critical Review

Despite the logic of specialization and trade, there are still protectionists in some union halls, corporate boardrooms, and the halls of Congress. What arguments do protectionists make to justify trade barriers? How valid are those arguments?

Military Self-Sufficiency Argument

The argument here is not economic but political-military: Protective tariffs are needed to preserve or strengthen industries that produce the materials essential for national defense. In an uncertain world, the political-military objectives (self-sufficiency) sometimes must take precedence over economic goals (efficiency in the use of world resources).

Unfortunately, it is difficult to measure and compare the benefit of increased national security against the cost of economic inefficiency when protective tariffs are imposed. The economist can only point out that when a nation levies tariffs to increase military self-sufficiency it incurs economic costs.

All people in the United States would agree that relying on hostile nations for necessary military equipment is not a good idea, yet the self-sufficiency argument is open to serious abuse. Nearly every industry can claim that it makes direct or indirect contributions to national security and hence deserves protection from imports.

Are there not better ways than tariffs to provide needed strength in strategic industries? When it is achieved through tariffs, this self-sufficiency increases the domestic prices of the products of the protected industry. Thus only those consumers who buy the industry's products shoulder the cost of greater military security. A direct subsidy to strategic industries, financed out of general tax revenues, would distribute those costs more equitably.

Diversification-for-Stability Argument

Highly specialized economies such as Saudi Arabia (based on oil) and Cuba (based on sugar) are dependent on international markets for their income. In these economies, wars, international political developments, recessions abroad, and random fluctuations in world supply and demand for one or two particular goods can cause deep declines in export revenues and therefore in domestic income. Tariff and quota protection are allegedly needed in such nations to enable greater industrial diversification. That way, these economies will not be so dependent on exporting one or two products to obtain the other goods they need. Such goods will be available domestically, thereby providing greater domestic stability.

CONSIDER THIS . . .

Shooting Yourself in the Foot

In the lore of the Wild West, a gunslinger on occasion would accidentally pull the trigger on his pistol while retrieving it from its holster, shooting himself in the foot. Since then, the phrase "shooting yourself in the foot" implies doing damage to yourself rather than the intended party.

That is precisely how economist Paul Krugman sees a trade war:

> A trade war in which countries restrict each other's exports in pursuit of some illusory advantage is not much like a real war. On the one hand, nobody gets killed. On the other, unlike real wars, it is almost impossible for anyone to win, since the main losers when a country imposes barriers to trade are not foreign exporters but domestic residents. In effect, a trade war is a conflict in which each country uses most of its ammunition to shoot itself in the foot.*

The same analysis is applicable to trade boycotts between major trading partners. Such a boycott was encouraged by some American commentators against French imports because of the opposition of France to the U.S.- and British-led war in Iraq. But the decline of exports to the United States would leave the French with fewer U.S. dollars to buy American exports. So the unintended effect would be a decline in U.S. exports to France and reduced employment in U.S. export industries. Moreover, such a trade boycott, if effective, might lead French consumers to retaliate against American imports. As with a "tariff war," a "boycott war" typically harms oneself as much as the other party.

*Paul Krugman, *Peddling Prosperity* (New York: Norton, 1994), p. 287.

There is some truth in this diversification-for-stability argument. But the argument has little or no relevance to the United States and other advanced economies. Also, the economic costs of diversification may be great; for example, one-crop economies may be highly inefficient at manufacturing.

Infant Industry Argument

The infant industry argument contends that protective tariffs are needed to allow new domestic industries to establish themselves. Temporarily shielding young domestic firms from the severe competition of more mature and more efficient foreign firms will give infant industries a chance to develop and become efficient producers.

This argument for protection rests on an alleged exception to the case for free trade. The exception is that young industries have not had, and if they face mature foreign competition will never have, the chance to make the long-run adjustments needed for larger scale and greater efficiency in production. In this view, tariff protection for such infant industries will correct a misallocation of world resources perpetuated by historically different levels of economic development between domestic and foreign industries.

Counterarguments

There are some logical problems with the infant industry argument. In the developing nations it is difficult to determine which industries are the infants that are capable of achieving economic maturity and therefore deserving protection. Also, protective tariffs may persist even after industrial maturity has been realized.

Most economists feel that if infant industries are to be subsidized, there are better means than tariffs for doing so. Direct subsidies, for example, have the advantage of making explicit which industries are being aided and to what degree.

Strategic Trade Policy

In recent years the infant industry argument has taken a modified form in advanced economies. Now proponents contend that government should use trade barriers to reduce the risk of investing in product development by domestic firms, particularly where advanced technology is involved. Firms protected from foreign competition can grow more rapidly and achieve greater economies of scale than unprotected foreign competitors. The protected firms can eventually dominate world markets because of their lower costs. Supposedly, dominance of world markets will enable the domestic firms to return high profits to the home nation. These profits will exceed the domestic sacrifices caused by trade barriers. Also, advances in high-technology industries are deemed beneficial, because the advances achieved in one domestic industry often can be transferred to other domestic industries.

Japan and South Korea, in particular, have been accused of using this form of **strategic trade policy.** The problem with this strategy and therefore with this argument for tariffs is that the nations put at a disadvantage by strategic trade policies tend to retaliate with tariffs of their own. The outcome may be higher tariffs worldwide, reduction of world trade, and the loss of potential gains from technological advances.

Protection-against-Dumping Argument

The protection-against dumping argument contends that tariffs are needed to protect domestic firms from "dumping" by foreign producers. **Dumping** is the selling of excess goods in a foreign market at a price below cost. Economists cite two plausible reasons for this behavior. First, firms may use dumping abroad to drive out domestic competitors there, thus obtaining monopoly power and monopoly prices and profits for the importing firm. The long-term economic profits resulting from this strategy may more than offset the earlier losses that accompany the below-cost sales.

Second, dumping may be a form of price discrimination, which is charging different prices to different customers even though costs are the same. The foreign seller may find it can maximize its profit by charging a high price in its monopolized domestic market while unloading its surplus output at a lower price in the United States. The surplus output may be needed so that the firm can obtain the overall per-unit cost saving associated with large-scale production. The higher profit in the home market more than makes up for the losses incurred on sales abroad.

Because dumping is an "unfair trade practice," most nations prohibit it. For example, where dumping is shown to injure U.S. firms, the Federal government imposes tariffs called *antidumping duties* on the specific goods. But relatively few documented cases of dumping occur each year, and specific instances of unfair trade do not justify widespread, permanent tariffs. Moreover, antidumping duties can be abused. Often, what appears to be dumping is simply comparative advantage at work.

Increased Domestic Employment Argument

Arguing for a tariff to "save U.S. jobs" becomes fashionable when the economy encounters a recession or experiences slow job growth during a recovery (as in the early

2000s in the United States). In an economy that engages in international trade, exports involve spending on domestic output and imports reflect spending to obtain part of another nation's output. So, in this argument, reducing imports will divert spending on another nation's output to spending on domestic output. Thus domestic output and employment will rise. But this argument has several shortcomings.

While imports may eliminate some U.S. jobs, they create others. Imports may have eliminated the jobs of some U.S. steel and textile workers in recent years, but other workers have gained jobs unloading ships, flying imported aircraft, and selling imported electronic equipment. Import restrictions alter the composition of employment, but they may have little or no effect on the volume of employment.

The *fallacy of composition*—the false idea that what is true for the part is necessarily true for the whole—is also present in this rationale for tariffs. All nations cannot simultaneously succeed in restricting imports while maintaining their exports; what is true for one nation is not true for all nations. The exports of one nation must be the imports of another nation. To the extent that one country is able to expand its economy through an excess of exports over imports, the resulting excess of imports over exports worsens another economy's unemployment problem. It is no wonder that tariffs and import quotas meant to achieve domestic full employment are called "beggar my neighbor" policies: They achieve short-run domestic goals by making trading partners poorer.

Moreover, nations adversely affected by tariffs and quotas are likely to retaliate, causing a "trade-barrier war" that will choke off trade and make all nations worse off. The **Smoot-Hawley Tariff Act** of 1930 is a classic example. Although that act was meant to reduce imports and stimulate U.S. production, the high tariffs it authorized prompted adversely affected nations to retaliate with tariffs equally high. International trade fell, lowering the output and income of all nations. Economic historians generally agree that the Smoot-Hawley Tariff Act was a contributing cause of the Great Depression.

Finally, forcing an excess of exports over imports cannot succeed in raising domestic employment over the long run. It is through U.S. imports that foreign nations earn dollars for buying U.S. exports. In the long run a nation must import in order to export. The long-run impact of tariffs is not an increase in domestic employment but, at best, a reallocation of workers away from export industries and to protected domestic industries. This shift implies a less efficient allocation of resources.

Cheap Foreign Labor Argument

The cheap foreign labor argument says that domestic firms and workers must be shielded from the ruinous competition of countries where wages are low. If protection is not provided, cheap imports will flood U.S. markets and the prices of U.S. goods—along with the wages of U.S. workers—will be pulled down. That is, the domestic living standards in the United States will be reduced.

This argument can be rebutted at several levels. The logic of the argument suggests that it is not mutually beneficial for rich and poor persons to trade with one another. However, that is not the case. A low-income farmworker may pick lettuce or tomatoes for a rich landowner, and both may benefit from the transaction. And both U.S. consumers and Chinese workers gain when they "trade" a pair of athletic shoes priced at $30 as opposed to a similar shoe made in the United States for $60.

Also, recall that gains from trade are based on comparative advantage, not on absolute advantage. Look back at Figure 23.1, where we supposed that the United States and Brazil had labor forces of exactly the same size. Noting the positions of the production possibilities curves, observe that U.S. labor can produce more of either good. Thus, it is more productive. Because of this greater productivity, we can expect wages and living standards to be higher for U.S. labor. Brazil's less productive labor will receive lower wages.

The cheap foreign labor argument suggests that, to maintain its standard of living, the United States should not trade with low-wage Brazil. What if it does not trade with Brazil. Will wages and living standards rise in the United States as a result? No. To obtain coffee, the United States will have to reallocate a portion of its labor from its efficient wheat industry to its inefficient coffee industry. As a result, the average productivity of U.S. labor will fall, as will real wages and living standards. The labor forces of both countries will have diminished standards of living because without specialization and trade they will have less output available to them. Compare column 4 with column 1 in Table 23.1 or points A' and B' with A and B in Figure 23.2 to confirm this point.

Trade Adjustment Assistance

A nation's comparative advantage in the production of a certain product is not forever fixed. As national economies evolve, the size and quality of their labor forces may change, the volume and composition of their capital stocks may shift, new technologies may develop, and even the quality of land and the quantity of natural resources may be altered. As these changes take place, the relative efficiency with which a nation can produce specific goods will also change. Also, new trade agreements can suddenly leave formerly protected industries highly vulnerable to major disruption or even collapse.

Shifts in patterns of comparative advantage and removal of trade protection can hurt specific groups of workers. For example, the erosion of the United States' once strong comparative advantage in steel has caused production plant shutdowns and layoffs in the U.S. steel industry. The textile and apparel industries in the United States face similar difficulties. Clearly, not everyone wins from free trade (or freer trade). Some workers lose.

The **Trade Adjustment Assistance Act** of 2002 introduced some new, novel elements to help those hurt by shifts in international trade patterns. The law provides cash assistance (beyond unemployment insurance) for up to 78 weeks for workers displaced by imports or plant relocations abroad. To obtain the assistance, workers must participate in job searches, training programs, or remedial education. Also provided are relocation allowances to help displaced workers move geographically to new jobs within the United States. Refundable tax credits for health insurance serve as payments to help workers maintain their insurance coverage during the retraining and job search period. Workers who are 50 years of age or older are eligible for "wage insurance," which replaces some of the difference in pay (if any) between their old and new jobs. Trade adjustment assistance not only helps workers hurt by international trade but also helps create the political support necessary to reduce trade barriers and export subsidies. For both reasons, many economists support it.

But not all observers are fans of trade adjustment assistance. Loss of jobs from imports or plant relocations abroad is only a small fraction (about 3 percent in recent years) of total job loss in the economy each year. Many workers also lose their jobs because of changing patterns of demand, changing technology, bad management, and other dynamic aspects of a market economy. Some critics ask, "What makes losing one's job to international trade worthy of such special treatment, compared to losing one's job to, say, technological change?" Economists can find no totally satisfying answer.

Offshoring

Not only are some U.S. jobs lost because of international trade, but some are lost because of globalization of resource markets. In recent years U.S. firms have found the outsourcing of work abroad increasingly profitable. Economists call this business activity **offshoring:** shifting work previously done by American workers to workers located in other nations. Offshoring is not a new practice but traditionally has involved components for U.S. manufacturing goods. For example, Boeing has long offshored the production of major airplane parts for its "American" aircraft.

Recent advances in computer and communications technology have enabled U.S. firms to offshore service jobs such as data entry, book composition, software coding, call-center operations, medical transcription, and claims processing to countries such as India. Where offshoring occurs, some of the value added in the production process accrues to foreign countries rather than the United States. So part of the income generated from the production of U.S. goods is paid to foreigners, not to American workers.

Offshoring is a major burden on Americans who lose their jobs, but it is not necessarily bad for the overall economy. Offshoring simply reflects a growing specialization and international trade in services. That trade has been made possible by recent trade agreements and new information and communication technologies. Like trade in goods, trade in services reflects comparative advantage and is beneficial to both trading parties. Moreover, the United States has a sizable trade surplus with other nations in services. The U.S. gains by specializing in high-valued services such as transportation services, accounting services, legal services, and advertising services, where it still has a comparative advantage. It then "trades" to obtain lower-valued services such as call-center and data entry work, for which comparative advantage has gone abroad.

Offshoring also increases the demand for complementary jobs in the United States. Jobs that are close substitutes for existing U.S. jobs are lost, but complementary jobs in the United States are expanded. For example, the lower price of writing software code in India may mean a lower cost of software sold in the United States and abroad. That, in turn, may create more jobs for U.S.-based workers such as software designers, marketers, and distributors. Moreover, the offshoring may encourage domestic investment and expansion of firms in the United States by reducing their production costs and keeping them competitive worldwide. In some instances, "offshoring jobs" may equate to "importing competitiveness." Entire firms that might otherwise disappear abroad may remain profitable in the United States only because they can offshore some of their work.

Last Word

The WTO Protests

Various Protest Groups Have Angrily Targeted the World Trade Organization (WTO). What Is the Source of All the Noise and Commotion?

The WTO became known to the general public in November 1999, when tens of thousands of people took part in sometimes violent demonstrations in Seattle. Since then, international WTO meetings have drawn large numbers of angry demonstrators. The groups involved include some labor unions (which fear loss of jobs and labor protections), environmental groups (which oppose environmental degradation), socialists (who dislike capitalism and multinational corporations), and a few anarchists (who detest government authority of any kind). Dispersed within the crowds are other, smaller groups such as European farmers who fear the WTO will threaten their livelihoods by reducing agricultural tariffs and farm subsidies.

The most substantive WTO issues involve labor protections and environmental standards. Labor unions in industrially advanced countries (hereafter, "advanced countries") would like the international trade rules to include such labor standards as collective bargaining rights, minimum wages, workplace safety standards, and prohibitions of child labor. Such rules are fully consistent with the long-standing values and objectives of unions. But there is a hitch. Imposing labor standards on low-income developing countries (hereafter, "developing countries") would raise labor and production costs in those nations. The higher costs in the developing countries would raise the relative price of their goods and make them less competitive with goods produced in the advanced countries (which already meet the labor standards). So the trade rules would increase the demands for products and workers in the advanced countries and reduce them in the developing countries. Union workers in the advanced countries would benefit; consumers in the advanced countries and workers in the developing countries would be harmed. The trade standards would contribute to poverty in the world's poorest nations.

Not surprisingly, the developing countries say "thanks, but no thanks" to the protesters' pleas for labor standards. Instead, they want the advanced countries to reduce or eliminate tariffs on goods imported from the developing countries. That would expand the demand for developing countries' products and workers, boosting developing countries' wages. As living standards in the developing countries rise, those countries then can afford to devote more of their annual productivity advances to improved working conditions.

The 149-nation WTO points out that its mandate is to liberalize trade through multilateral negotiation, not to set labor standards for each nation. That should be left to the countries themselves.

QUICK REVIEW 23.3

- A tariff on a product increases its price, reduces its consumption, increases its domestic production, reduces its imports, and generates tariff revenue for government; an import quota does the same, except a quota generates revenue for foreign producers rather than for the government imposing the quota.
- Most rationales for trade protections are special-interest requests that, if followed, would create gains for protected industries and their workers at the expense of greater losses for the economy.
- The Trade Adjustment Assistance Act of 2002 is designed to help some of the workers hurt by shifts in international trade patterns.
- Offshoring is a major burden on American workers who lose their jobs, but not necessarily negative for the overall American economy.

The World Trade Organization

As indicated in Chapter 5, the Uruguay Round of 1993 established the **World Trade Organization (WTO).** In 2006, the WTO, which oversees trade agreements and rules on disputes relating to them, had 149 member nations. It also provides forums for further rounds of trade negotiations. The ninth and latest round of negotiations—the **Doha Round**—was launched in Doha, Qatar, in late 2001. (The trade rounds occur over several years in several geographic venues and are named after the city or country of origination.) The negotiations are aimed at further reducing tariffs and quotas, as well as agricultural subsidies that distort trade. One of this chapter's questions asks you to update the progress of the Doha Round (or, alternatively, the Doha Development Agenda) via an Internet search.

As a symbol of trade liberalization and global capitalism, the WTO has become a target of a variety of protest groups. This chapter's Last Word examines some of the reason for the protests, and we strongly suggest that you read it.

Economists suggest that protesters channel their efforts to supporting activities of the International Labour Organization (ILO), which strives to improve wages and working conditions worldwide. Demonstrators might also help local groups bring political pressure on individual nations to improve their labor protections as their standards of living rise.

Environmental standards are the second substantive WTO issue. Critics are concerned that trade liberalization will encourage more activities that degrade sensitive forests, fisheries, and mining lands and contribute to air, water, and solid-waste pollution. Critics would like the WTO to establish trade rules that set minimum environmental standards for the member nations. The WTO nations respond that environmental standards are outside the mandate of the WTO and must be established by the individual nations via their own political processes.

Moreover, imposing such standards on developing countries may simply provide competitive cost advantages to companies in the advanced countries. As with labor standards, that will simply slow economic growth and prolong poverty in the developing countries. Studies show that economic growth and rising living standards are strongly associated with greater environmental protections. In the early phases of their development, low-income developing nations typically choose to trade off some environmental damage to achieve higher real wages. But studies show that the tradeoff is usually reversed once standards of living rise beyond threshold levels.

Labor standards and environmental protections are worthy objectives. But impeding efforts to liberalize trade may be an ineffective—even detrimental—way to achieve them. Reductions in tariffs and impediments to investment increase productivity, output, and incomes worldwide. The higher living standards enable developing and developed nations alike to "buy" more protections for labor and the environment. Strong, sustained economic growth typically results not only in more goods and services but also in more socially desirable and environmentally sensitive production methods.

Summary

1. The United States leads the world in the combined volume of exports and imports. Other major trading nations are Germany, Japan, the western European nations, and the Asian economies of China, South Korea, Taiwan, and Singapore.
2. World trade is based on three considerations: the uneven distribution of economic resources among nations, the fact that efficient production of various goods requires particular techniques or combinations of resources, and the differentiated products produced among nations.
3. Mutually advantageous specialization and trade are possible between any two nations if they have different domestic opportunity-cost ratios for any two products. By specializing on the basis of comparative advantage, nations can obtain larger real incomes with fixed amounts of resources. The terms of trade determine how this increase in world output is shared by the trading nations. Increasing (rather than constant) opportunity costs limit specialization and trade.
4. A nation's export supply curve shows the quantities of a product the nation will export at world prices that exceed the domestic price (the price in a closed, no-international-trade economy). A nation's import demand curve reveals the quantities of a product it will import at world prices below the domestic price.
5. In a two-nation model, the equilibrium world price and the equilibrium quantities of exports and imports occur where one nation's export supply curve intersects the other nation's import demand curve.
6. Trade barriers take the form of protective tariffs, quotas, nontariff barriers, and "voluntary" export restrictions. Supply and demand analysis reveals that protective tariffs and quotas increase the prices and reduce the quantities demanded of the affected goods. Sales by foreign exporters diminish; domestic producers, however, gain higher prices and enlarged sales. Consumer losses from trade restrictions greatly exceed producer and government gains, creating an efficiency loss to society.
7. The strongest arguments for protection are the infant industry and military self-sufficiency arguments. Most other arguments for protection are interest-group appeals or reasoning fallacies that emphasize producer interests over consumer interests or stress the immediate effects of trade barriers while ignoring long-run consequences.

8. The Trade Adjustment Assistance Act of 2002 provides cash assistance, education and training benefits, health care subsidies, and wage subsidies (for persons age 50 or older) to qualified workers displaced by imports or plant relocations abroad.
9. Offshoring is the practice of shifting work previously done by Americans to workers located in other nations. While offshoring reduces some U.S. jobs, it lowers production costs, expands sales, and therefore may create other U.S. jobs. Less than 3 percent of all job losses in the United States each year result from imports, offshoring, and plant relocations to abroad.
10. In 2006 the World Trade Organization (WTO) consisted of 149 member nations. The WTO oversees trade agreements among the members, resolves disputes over the rules, and periodically meets to discuss and negotiate further trade liberalization. In 2001 the WTO initiated a new round of trade negotiations in Doha, Qatar. By 2006 the Doha Round (or Doha Development Agenda) was still in progress.
11. As a symbol of global capitalism, the WTO has become a target of considerable protest. The controversy surrounding the WTO is the subject of this chapter's Last Word. Most economists are concerned that tying trade liberalization to a host of other issues such as environmental and labor standards will greatly delay or block further trade liberalization. Such liberalization is one of the main sources of higher living standards worldwide.

Terms and Concepts

labor-intensive goods
land-intensive goods
capital-intensive goods
opportunity-cost ratio
principle of comparative advantage
terms of trade
trading possibilities line
gains from trade
world price
domestic price
export supply curve
import demand curve
equilibrium world price
tariffs
revenue tariff
protective tariff
import quota
nontariff barrier (NTB)
voluntary export restriction (VER)
strategic trade policy
dumping
Smoot-Hawley Tariff Act
Trade Adjustment Assistance Act
offshoring
World Trade Organization (WTO)
Doha Round

Study Questions

1. Quantitatively, how important is international trade to the United States relative to other nations?
2. Distinguish among land-, labor-, and capital-intensive commodities, citing one nontextbook example of each. What role do these distinctions play in explaining international trade? What role do distinctive products, unrelated to cost advantages, play in international trade?
3. Suppose nation A can produce 80 units of X by using all its resources to produce X or 60 units of Y by devoting all its resources to Y. Comparable figures for nation B are 60 units of X and 60 units of Y. Assuming constant costs, in which product should each nation specialize? Why? What are the limits of the terms of trade?
4. **KEY QUESTION** To the right are hypothetical production possibilities tables for New Zealand and Spain. Each country can produce apples and plums.

Plot the production possibilities data for each of the two countries separately. Referring to your graphs, answer the following:

a. What is each country's cost ratio of producing plums and apples.
b. Which nation should specialize in which product?

New Zealand's Production Possibilities Table (Millions of Bushels)

	Production Alternatives			
Product	**A**	**B**	**C**	**D**
Apples	0	20	40	60
Plums	15	10	5	0

Spain's Production Possibilities Table (Millions of Bushels)

	Production Alternatives			
Product	**R**	**S**	**T**	**U**
Apples	0	20	40	60
Plums	60	40	20	0

c. Show the trading possibilities lines for each nation if the actual terms of trade are 1 plum for 2 apples. (Plot these lines on your graph.)
d. Suppose the optimum product mixes before specialization and trade were alternative B in New Zealand and

alternative S in Spain. What would be the gains from specialization and trade?

5. "The United States can produce X more efficiently than can Great Britain. Yet we import X from Great Britain." Explain.
6. **KEY QUESTION** Refer to Figure 3.6, page 54. Assume that the graph depicts the U.S. domestic market for corn. How many bushels of corn, if any, will the United States export or import at a world price of \$1, \$2, \$3, \$4, and \$5? Use this information to construct the U.S. export supply curve and import demand curve for corn. Suppose the only other corn-producing nation is France, where the domestic price is \$4. Which country will export corn; which will import it?
7. **KEY QUESTION** Draw a domestic supply and demand diagram for a product in which the United States does not have a comparative advantage. What impact do foreign imports have on domestic price and quantity? On your diagram show a protective tariff that eliminates approximately one-half of the assumed imports. What are the price-quantity effects of this tariff on (*a*) domestic consumers, (*b*) domestic producers, and (*c*) foreign exporters? How would the effects of a quota that creates the same amount of imports differ?
8. "The potentially valid arguments for tariff protection are also the most easily abused." What are those arguments? Why are they susceptible to abuse? Evaluate the use of artificial trade barriers, such as tariffs and import quotas, as a means of achieving and maintaining full employment.
9. Evaluate the following statements:
   a. Protective tariffs reduce both the imports and the exports of the nation that levies tariffs.
   b. The extensive application of protective tariffs destroys the ability of the international market system to allocate resources efficiently.
   c. Unemployment in some industries can often be reduced through tariff protection, but by the same token inefficiency typically increases.
   d. Foreign firms that "dump" their products onto the U.S. market are in effect providing bargains to the country's citizens.
   e. In view of the rapidity with which technological advance is dispersed around the world, free trade will inevitably yield structural maladjustments, unemployment, and balance-of-payments problems for industrially advanced nations.
   f. Free trade can improve the composition and efficiency of domestic output. Competition from Volkswagen, Toyota, and Honda forced Detroit to make a compact car, and foreign imports of bottled water forced American firms to offer that product.
   g. In the long run, foreign trade is neutral with respect to total employment.
10. Suppose Japan agreed to a voluntary export restriction (VER) that reduced U.S. imports of Japanese steel by 10 percent. What would be the likely short-run effects of that VER on the U.S. and Japanese steel industries? If this restriction were permanent, what would be its long-run effects in the two nations on (*a*) the allocation of resources, (*b*) the volume of employment, (*c*) the price level, and (*d*) the standard of living?
11. What forms do trade adjustment assistance take in the United States? How does such assistance promote support for free trade agreements? Do you think workers who lose their jobs because of changes in trade laws deserve special treatment relative to workers who lose their jobs because of other changes in the economy, say, changes in patterns of government spending?
12. What is offshoring of white-collar service jobs, and how does it relate to international trade? Why has it recently increased? Why do you think more than half of all the offshored jobs have gone to India? Give an example (other than that in the textbook) of how offshoring can eliminate some U.S. jobs while creating other U.S. jobs.
13. What is the WTO and how does it relate to international trade? How many nations belong to the WTO? (Update the number given in this book at **www.wto.org.**) What did the Uruguay Round (1994) of WTO trade negotiations accomplish? What is the name of the current WTO round of trade negotiations?
14. **LAST WORD** What are the main concerns of the WTO protesters? What problems, if any, arise when too many extraneous issues are tied to efforts to liberalize trade?

Web-Based Questions

1. **TRADE LIBERALIZATION—THE WTO** Go to the Web site of the World Trade Organization **(www.wto.org)** to retrieve the latest news from the WTO. List and summarize three recent news items relating to the WTO.
2. **THE U.S. INTERNATIONAL TRADE COMMISSION—WHAT IS IT AND WHAT DOES IT DO?** Go to **www.usitc.gov** to determine the duties of the U.S. International Trade Commission (USITC). How does this organization differ from the World Trade Organization (question 13)? Go to the "Information Center" and find News Releases. Identify and briefly describe three USITC "determinations" relating to charges of unfair international trade practices that harm U.S. producers.

24

IN THIS CHAPTER YOU WILL LEARN:

- **How currencies of different nations are exchanged when international transactions take place.**
- **About the balance sheet the United States uses to account for the international payments it makes and receives.**
- **How exchange rates are determined in currency markets.**
- **The difference between flexible exchange rates and fixed exchange rates.**
- **The causes and consequences of recent record-high U.S. trade deficits.**

Exchange Rates, the Balance of Payments, and Trade Deficits

If you take a U.S. dollar to the bank and ask to exchange it for U.S. currency, you will get a puzzled look. If you persist, you may get a dollar's worth of change: One U.S. dollar can buy exactly one U.S. dollar. But on April 25, 2006, for example, 1 U.S. dollar could buy 2353 Colombian pesos, 1.34 Australian dollars, .56 British pounds, 1.13 Canadian dollars, .80 European euros, 114.82 Japanese yen, or 11.15 Mexican pesos. What explains this seemingly haphazard array of exchange rates?

In Chapter 23 we examined comparative advantage as the underlying economic basis of world trade and discussed the effects of barriers to free trade. Now we introduce the highly important monetary or financial aspects of international trade.

Financing International Trade

One factor that makes international trade different from domestic trade is the involvement of different national currencies. When a U.S. firm exports goods to a Mexican firm, the U.S. exporter wants to be paid in dollars. But the Mexican importer possesses pesos. The importer must exchange pesos for dollars before the U.S. export transaction can occur.

This problem is resolved in foreign exchange markets (or currency markets), in which dollars can purchase Mexican pesos, European euros, South Korean won, British pounds, Japanese yen, or any other currency, and vice versa. Sponsored by major banks in New York, London, Zurich, Tokyo, and elsewhere, foreign exchange markets facilitate exports and imports.

U.S. Export Transaction

Suppose a U.S. exporter agrees to sell $300,000 of computers to a British firm. Assume, for simplicity, that the rate of exchange—the rate at which pounds can be exchanged for, or converted into, dollars, and vice versa—is $2 for £1 (the actual exchange rate is about $1.80 = 1 pound). This means the British importer must pay the equivalent of £150,000 to the U.S. exporter to obtain the $300,000 worth of computers. Also assume that all buyers of pounds and dollars are in the United States and Great Britain. Let's follow the steps in the transaction:

- To pay for the computers, the British buyer draws a check for £150,000 on its checking account in a London bank and sends it to the U.S. exporter.
- But the U.S. exporting firm must pay its bills in dollars, not pounds. So the exporter sells the £150,000 check on the London bank to its bank in, say, New York City, which is a dealer in foreign exchange. The bank adds $300,000 to the U.S. exporter's checking account for the £150,000 check.
- The New York bank deposits the £150,000 in a correspondent London bank for future sale to some U.S. buyer who needs pounds.

Note this important point: U.S. exports create a foreign demand for dollars, and the fulfillment of that demand increases the supply of foreign currencies (pounds, in this case) owned by U.S. banks and available to U.S. buyers.

Why would the New York bank be willing to buy pounds for dollars? As just indicated, the New York bank is a dealer in foreign exchange; it is in the business of buying (for a fee) and selling (also for a fee) one currency for another.

U.S. Import Transaction

Let's now examine how the New York bank would sell pounds for dollars to finance a U.S. import (British export) transaction. Suppose a U.S. retail firm wants to import £150,000 of compact discs produced in Britain by a hot new musical group. Again, let's track the steps in the transaction:

- The U.S. importer purchases £150,000 at the $2 = £1 exchange rate by writing a check for $300,000 on its New York bank. Because the British exporting firm wants to be paid in pounds rather than dollars, the U.S. importer must exchange dollars for pounds, which it does by going to the New York bank and purchasing £150,000 for $300,000. (Perhaps the U.S. importer purchases the same £150,000 that the New York bank acquired from the U.S. exporter.)
- The U.S. importer sends its newly purchased check for £150,000 to the British firm, which deposits it in the London bank.

Here we see that U.S. imports create a domestic demand for foreign currencies (pounds, in this case), and the fulfillment of that demand reduces the supplies of foreign currencies (again, pounds) held by U.S. banks and available to U.S. consumers.

The combined export and import transactions bring one more point into focus. U.S. exports (the computers) make available, or "earn," a supply of foreign currencies for U.S. banks, and U.S. imports (the compact discs) create a demand for those currencies. In a broad sense, any nation's exports finance or "pay for" its imports. Exports provide the foreign currencies needed to pay for imports.

Postscript: Although our examples are confined to exporting and importing goods, demand for and supplies of pounds also arise from transactions involving services and the payment of interest and dividends on foreign investments. The United States demands pounds not only to buy imports but also to buy insurance and transportation services from the British, to vacation in London, to pay dividends and interest on British investments in the United States, and to make new financial and real investments in Britain. **(Key Question 2)**

The Balance of Payments

A nation's **balance of payments** is the sum of all the transactions that take place between its residents and the residents of all foreign nations. Those transactions include exports and imports of goods, exports and imports of services, tourist expenditures, interest and dividends received or paid abroad, and purchases and sales of financial or real assets abroad. The U.S. Commerce Department's

Bureau of Economic Analysis compiles the balance-of-payments statement each year. The statement shows all the payments a nation receives from foreign countries and all the payments it makes to them. It shows "flows" of inpayments to and outpayments from the United States.

Table 24.1 is a simplified balance-of-payments statement for the United States in 2005. Let's take a close look at this accounting statement to see what it reveals about U.S. international trade and finance. To help our explanation, we divide the single balance-of-payments account into two components: the *current account* and the *capital and financial account.*

Current Account

The top portion of Table 24.1 summarizes U.S. trade in currently produced goods and services and is called the **current account.** Items 1 and 2 show U.S. exports and imports of goods (merchandise) in 2005. U.S. exports have a *plus* (+) sign because they are a *credit;* they earn and make available foreign exchange in the United States. As you saw in the preceding section, any export-type transaction that obligates foreigners to make "inpayments" to the United States generates supplies of foreign currencies in the U.S. banks.

U.S. imports have a *minus* (−) sign because they are a *debit;* they reduce the stock of foreign currencies in the United States. Our earlier discussion of trade financing indicated that U.S. imports obligate the United States to make "outpayments" to the rest of the world that reduce available supplies of foreign currencies held by U.S. banks.

Balance on Goods Items 1 and 2 in Table 24.1 reveal that in 2005 U.S. goods exports of $893 billion did not earn enough foreign currencies to finance U.S. goods imports of $1675 billion. A country's *balance of trade on goods* is the difference between its exports and its imports of goods. If exports exceed imports, the result is a surplus on the balance of goods. If imports exceed exports, there is a trade deficit on the balance of goods. We note in item 3 that in 2005 the United States incurred a trade deficit on goods of $782 billion.

Balance on Services The United States exports not only goods, such as airplanes and computer software, but also services, such as insurance, consulting, travel, and brokerage services, to residents of foreign nations. Item 4 in Table 24.1 shows that these service "exports" totaled

TABLE 24.1 The U.S. Balance of Payments, 2005 (in Billions)

Current account		
(1) U.S. goods exports	$+893	
(2) U.S. goods imports	−1675	
(3) *Balance on goods*		$−782
(4) U.S. exports of services	+380	
(5) U.S. imports of services	−322	
(6) *Balance on services*		+58
(7) *Balance on goods and services*		−724
(8) Net investment income	+2	
(9) Net transfers	−83	
(10) **Balance on current account**		**−805**
Capital and financial account		
Capital account		
(11) *Balance on capital account*		−6
Financial account		
(12) Foreign purchases of assets in the United States	+1298*	
(13) U.S. purchases of assets abroad	−487*	
(14) *Balance on financial account*		+811
(15) **Balance on capital and financial account**		**+ 805**
		$ 0

*Includes one-half of a $10 billion statistical discrepancy that is listed in the capital account.

Source: U.S. Department of Commerce, Bureau of Economic Analysis, **www.bea.gov/.** Preliminary 2005 data. The export and import data are on a "balance-of-payment basis," and usually vary from the data on export and imports reported in the National Income and Product Accounts.

\$380 billion in 2005 and are a credit (thus the + sign). Item 5 indicates that the United States "imports" similar services from foreigners; those service imports were \$322 billion in 2005 and are a debit (thus the − sign). So the balance on services (item 6) in 2005 was \$58 billion.

The **balance on goods and services** shown as item 7 is the difference between U.S. exports of goods and services (items 1 and 4) and U.S. imports of goods and services (items 2 and 5). In 2005, U.S. imports of goods and services exceeded U.S. exports of goods and services by \$724 billion. So a **trade deficit** (or "unfavorable balance of trade") occurred. In contrast, a **trade surplus** (or "favorable balance of trade") occurs when exports of goods and services exceed imports of goods and services. (Global Perspective 24.1 shows U.S. trade deficits and surpluses with selected nations.)

Balance on Current Account Item 8, *net investment income*, represents the difference between (1) the interest and dividend payments foreigners paid the United States for the use of exported U.S. capital and (2) the interest and dividends the United States paid for the use of foreign capital invested in the United States. Observe that in 2005 U.S. net investment income was a positive \$2 billion worth of foreign currencies.

Item 9 shows net transfers, both public and private, between the United States and the rest of the world. Included here is foreign aid, pensions paid to U.S. citizens living abroad, and remittances by immigrants to relatives abroad. These \$83 billion of transfers are net U.S. outpayments that decrease available supplies of foreign exchange. They are, in a sense, the exporting of goodwill and the importing of "thank-you notes."

By adding all transactions in the current account, we obtain the **balance on current account** shown in item 10. In 2005 the United States had a current account deficit of \$805 billion. This means that the U.S. current account transactions (items 2, 5, 8, and 9) created outpayments of foreign currencies from the United States greater than the inpayments of foreign currencies to the United States.

GLOBAL PERSPECTIVE 24.1

U.S. Trade Balances in Goods and Services, Selected Nations, 2004

The United States has large trade deficits in goods and services with several nations, in particular, China, Japan, and Canada.

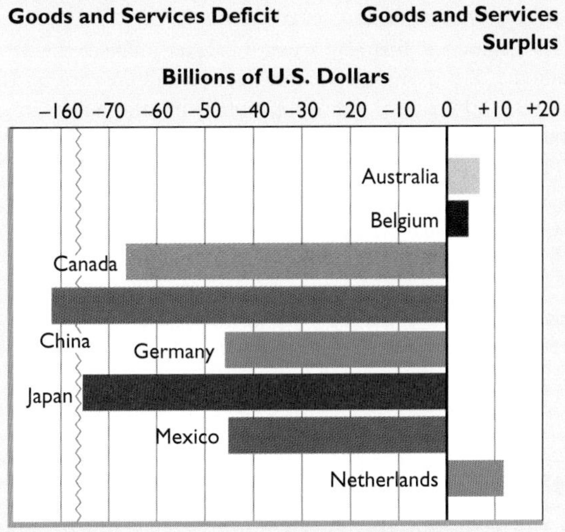

Source: Department of Commerce, Bureau of Economic Analysis, **www.bea.gov/.**

Capital and Financial Account

The second account within the overall balance-of-payments account is the **capital and financial account,** which consists of two separate accounts: the *capital account* and the *financial account.*

Capital Account The capital account is a "net" account (one that can be either + or −) that mainly measures debt forgiveness. Line 11 tells us that in 2005 Americans forgave \$6 billion more of debt owed to them by foreigners than foreigners forgave debt owed to them by Americans. The − sign indicates a debit; it is an "on-paper" outpayment by the net amount of debt forgiven.

Financial Account The financial account summarizes the purchase or sale of real or financial assets and the corresponding flows of monetary payments that accompany them. For example, a foreign firm may buy a real asset, say, an office building in the United States, or a financial asset, for instance, a U.S. government security. Both kinds of transaction involve the "export" of the ownership of U.S. assets from the United States in return for inpayments of foreign currency. As indicated in line 12, these "exports" of ownership of assets are designated foreign purchases of assets in the United States. They have a + sign because, like exports of U.S. goods and services, they represent inpayments of foreign currencies.

Conversely, a U.S. firm may buy, say, a hotel chain (real asset) in a foreign country or some of the common stock (financial asset) of a foreign firm. Both transactions involve the "import" of the ownership of the real or financial assets to the United States and are paid for by outpayments of foreign currencies. These "imports" are designated U.S. purchases of assets abroad and, as shown in line 13, have a − sign; like U.S. imports of goods and services, they represent outpayments of foreign currencies from the United States.

Items 11 and 12 combined yielded an $811 billion balance on the financial account for 2005 (line 14). In 2005 the United States "exported" $1298 billion of ownership of its real and financial assets and "imported" $487 billion. Thought of differently, this capital account surplus brought in inpayments of $811 billion of foreign currencies to the United States.

The **balance on the capital and financial account** (line 15) is $805 billion. It is the sum of the $6 billion deficit on the capital account and the $811 billion surplus on the financial account. Observe that this $805 billion surplus in the capital and financial account equals the $805 billion deficit in the current account. The various components of the balance of payments (the current account, the capital account, and the financial account) must together equal zero. Every unit of foreign exchange used (as reflected in a minus outpayment or debit transaction) must have a source (a plus inpayment or credit transaction).

Payments, Deficits, and Surpluses

Although the balance of payments must always sum to zero, as in Table 24.1, economists and policymakers sometimes speak of **balance-of-payments deficits and surpluses.** The central banks of nations hold quantities of **official reserves,** consisting of foreign currencies, reserves held in the International Monetary Fund, and stocks of gold. These reserves are drawn on—or replenished— to make up any net deficit or surplus that otherwise would occur in the balance-of-payment account. (This is much as you would draw on your savings or add to your savings as a way to balance your annual income and spending.) In some years, a nation must make an inpayment of official reserves to its capital and financial account in order to balance it with the current account. In these years, a *balance-of- payments deficit* is said to occur.

In other years, an outpayment of official reserves from the capital and financial account must occur to balance that account with the current account. The outpayment adds to the stock of official reserves. A *balance-of payments-surplus* is said to exist in these years.

A balance-of-payments deficit is not necessarily bad, just as a balance-of-payments surplus is not necessarily good. Both simply happen. However, any nation's official reserves are limited. Persistent payments deficits, which must be financed by drawing down those reserves, would ultimately deplete the reserves. That nation would have to adopt policies to correct its balance of payments. Such policies might require painful macroeconomic adjustments, trade barriers and similar restrictions, or a major depreciation of its currency. For this reason, nations strive for payments balance, at least over several-year periods.

The United States held $75 billion of official reserves in 2005. The typical annual depletion or addition of official reserves is not of major concern, particularly because withdrawals and deposits roughly balance over time. For example, the stock of official U.S. reserves rose from $79 billion in 2003 to $86 billion in 2004. It fell to $75 billion in 2005.

The historically large current account deficits that the United States has been running over the past several years are of more concern than annual balance-of-payment deficits or surpluses. The current account deficits need to be financed by equally large surpluses in the capital and financial account. Thus far, that has not been a problem. Later in this chapter, we will examine the causes and potential consequences of large current account deficits. **(Key Question 3)**

W 24.1
Balance of payments

QUICK REVIEW 24.1

- U.S. exports create a foreign demand for dollars, and fulfillment of that demand increases the domestic supply of foreign currencies; U.S. imports create a domestic demand for foreign currencies, and fulfillment of that demand reduces the supplies of foreign currency held by U.S. banks.
- The current account balance is a nation's exports of goods and services less its imports of goods and services plus its net investment income and net transfers.
- The capital and financial account balance includes the net amount of the nation's debt forgiveness and the nation's sale of real and financial assets to people living abroad less its purchases of real and financial assets from foreigners.
- The current account balance and the capital and financial account balance always sum to zero.
- A balance-of-payments deficit occurs when a nation must draw down its official reserves to balance the capital and financial account with the current account; a balance-of-payments surplus occurs when a nation adds to its official reserves in order to balance the two accounts.

Flexible Exchange Rates

Both the size and the persistence of a nation's balance-of-payments deficits and surpluses and the adjustments it must make to correct those imbalances depend on the system of exchange rates being used. There are two "pure" types of exchange-rate systems:

- A **flexible- or floating-exchange-rate system** through which demand and supply determine exchange rates and in which no government intervention occurs.
- A **fixed-exchange-rate system** through which governments determine exchange rates and make necessary adjustments in their economies to maintain those rates.

We begin by looking at flexible exchange rates. Let's examine the rate, or price, at which U.S. dollars might be exchanged for British pounds. In **Figure 24.1 (Key Graph)** we show demand D_1 and supply S_1 of pounds in the currency market.

G 24.1
Flexible exchange rates

The *demand-for-pounds curve* is downward-sloping because all British goods and services will be cheaper to the United States if pounds become less expensive to the United States. That is, at lower dollar prices for pounds, the United States can obtain more pounds and therefore more British goods and services per dollar. To buy those cheaper British goods, U.S. consumers will increase the quantity of pounds they demand.

The *supply-of-pounds curve* is upward-sloping because the British will purchase more U.S. goods when the dollar price of pounds rises (that is, as the pound price of dollars falls). When the British buy more U.S. goods, they supply a greater quantity of pounds to the foreign exchange market. In other words, they must exchange pounds for dollars to purchase U.S. goods. So, when the dollar price of pounds rises, the quantity of pounds supplied goes up.

The intersection of the supply curve and the demand curve will determine the dollar price of pounds. Here, that price (exchange rate) is \$2 for £1.

Depreciation and Appreciation

An exchange rate determined by market forces can, and often does, change daily like stock and bond prices. When the dollar price of pounds *rises*, for example, from \$2 = £1 to \$3 = £1, the dollar has *depreciated* relative to the pound (and the pound has appreciated relative to the dollar). When a currency depreciates, more units of it (dollars) are needed to buy a single unit of some other currency (a pound).

When the dollar price of pounds *falls*, for example, from \$2 = £1 to \$1 = £1, the dollar has *appreciated* relative to the pound. When a currency appreciates, fewer units of it (dollars) are needed to buy a single unit of some other currency (pounds).

In our U.S.-Britain illustrations, depreciation of the dollar means an appreciation of the pound, and vice versa. When the dollar price of a pound jumps from \$2 = £1 to \$3 = £1, the pound has appreciated relative to the dollar because it takes fewer pounds to buy \$1. At \$2 = £1, it took £$\frac{1}{2}$ to buy \$1; at \$3 = £1, it takes only £$\frac{1}{3}$ to buy \$1. Conversely, when the dollar appreciated relative to the pound, the pound depreciated relative to the dollar. More pounds were needed to buy a dollar.

Determinants of Exchange Rates

What factors would cause a nation's currency to appreciate or depreciate in the market for foreign exchange? Here are three generalizations:

- If the demand for a nation's currency increases (all else equal), that currency will appreciate; if the demand declines, that currency will depreciate.
- If the supply of a nation's currency increases, that currency will depreciate; if the supply decreases, that currency will appreciate.
- If a nation's currency appreciates, some foreign currency depreciates relative to it.

With these generalizations in mind, let's examine the determinants of exchange rates—the factors that shift the demand or supply curve for a certain currency.

Changes in Tastes

Any change in consumer tastes or preferences for the products of a foreign country may alter the demand for that nation's currency and change its exchange rate. If technological advances in U.S. wireless phones make them more attractive to British consumers and businesses, then the British will supply more pounds in the exchange market in order to purchase more U.S. wireless phones. The supply-of-pounds curve will shift to the right, causing the pound to depreciate and the dollar to appreciate.

In contrast, the U.S. demand-for-pounds curve will shift to the right if British woolen apparel becomes more fashionable in the United States. So the pound will appreciate and the dollar will depreciate.

Relative Income Changes

A nation's currency is likely to depreciate if its growth of national income is more rapid than that of other countries. Here's why: A country's imports vary directly with its income level. As total income rises in the United States, people there buy both more domestic goods and more foreign goods. If the U.S. economy is expanding rapidly and the British economy is stagnant, U.S. imports of British goods, and therefore U.S. demands for pounds, will increase. The dollar price of pounds will rise, so the dollar will depreciate.

keygraph

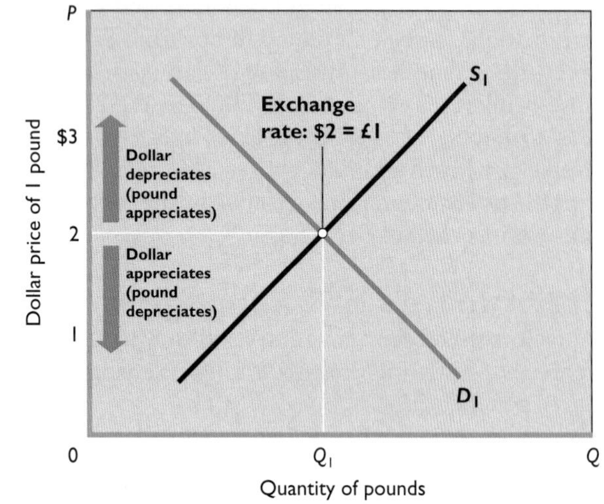

FIGURE 24.1 The market for foreign currency (pounds). The intersection of the demand-for-pounds curve D_1 and the supply-of-pounds curve S_1 determines the equilibrium dollar price of pounds, here, $2. That means that the exchange rate is $2 = £1. The upward green arrow is a reminder that a higher dollar price of pounds (say, $3 = £1, caused by a shift in either the demand or the supply curve) means that the dollar has depreciated (the pound has appreciated). The downward green arrow tells us that a lower dollar price of pounds (say, $1 = £1, again caused by a shift in either the demand or the supply curve) means that the dollar has appreciated (the pound has depreciated).

QUICK QUIZ 24.1

1. Which of the following statements is true?
   a. The quantity of pounds demanded falls when the dollar appreciates.
   b. The quantity of pounds supplied declines as the dollar price of the pound rises.
   c. At the equilibrium exchange rate, the pound price of $1 is £$\frac{1}{2}$.
   d. The dollar appreciates if the demand for pounds increases.
2. At the price of $2 for £1 in this figure:
   a. the dollar-pound exchange rate is unstable.
   b. the quantity of pounds supplied equals the quantity demanded.
   c. the dollar price of £1 equals the pound price of $1.
   d. U.S. goods exports to Britain must equal U.S. goods imports from Britain.
3. Other things equal, a leftward shift of the demand curve in this figure:
   a. would depreciate the dollar.
   b. would create a shortage of pounds at the previous price of $2 for £1.
   c. might be caused by a major recession in the United States.
   d. might be caused by a significant rise of real interest rates in Britain.
4. Other things equal, a rightward shift of the supply curve in this figure would:
   a. depreciate the dollar and might be caused by a significant rise of real interest rates in Britain.
   b. depreciate the dollar and might be caused by a significant fall of real interest rates in Britain.
   c. appreciate the dollar and might be caused by a significant rise of real interest rates in the United States.
   d. appreciate the dollar and might be caused by a significant fall of interest rates in the United States.

Answers: 1. c; 2. b; 3. c; 4. c

Relative Price-Level Changes Changes in the relative price levels of two nations may change the demand and supply of currencies and alter the exchange rate between the two nations' currencies.

The **purchasing-power-parity theory** holds that exchange rates equate the purchasing power of various currencies. That is, the exchange rates among national currencies adjust to match the ratios of the nations' price levels: If a certain market basket of goods costs $10,000 in the United States and £5,000 in Great Britain, according to this theory the exchange rate will be $2 = £1. That way, a dollar spent on goods sold in Britain, Japan, Turkey, and other nations will have equal purchasing power.

In practice, however, exchange rates depart from purchasing power parity, even over long periods. Nevertheless, changes in relative price levels are a determinant of exchange rates. If, for example, the domestic price level rises rapidly in the United States and remains constant in Great Britain, U.S. consumers will seek out low-priced British goods, increasing the demand for pounds. The British will purchase fewer U.S. goods, reducing the supply of pounds. This combination of demand and supply

CONSIDER THIS . . .

The Big Mac Index

The purchasing-power-parity (PPP) theory says that exchange rates will adjust such that a given broad market basket of goods and services will cost the same in all countries. If the market basket costs $1000 in the United States and 100,000 yen in Japan, then the exchange rate will be $1 = ¥100 (= 1000/100,000). If instead the exchange rate is $1 = ¥110, we can expect the dollar to depreciate and the yen to appreciate such that the exchange rate moves to the purchasing-power-parity rate of $1 = ¥100. Similarly, if the exchange rate is $1 = ¥90, we can expect the dollar to appreciate and the yen to depreciate.

Instead of using a market basket of goods and services, *The Economist* magazine has offered a light-hearted test of the purchasing-power-parity theory through its *Big Mac index.* It uses the exchange rates of 100 countries to convert the domestic currency price of a Big Mac into U.S. dollar prices. If the converted dollar price in, say, Britain exceeds the dollar price in the United States, the *Economist* concludes (with a wink) that the pound is overvalued relative to the dollar. On the other hand, if the adjusted dollar price of a Big Mac in Britain is less than the dollar price in the United States, then the pound is undervalued relative to the dollar.

The *Economist* finds wide divergences in actual dollar prices across the globe and thus little support for the purchasing-power-parity theory. Yet it humorously trumpets any predictive success it can muster (or is that "mustard"?):

> Some readers find our Big Mac index hard to swallow. This year (1999), however, has been one to relish. When the euro was launched at the start of the year most forecasters expected it to rise. The Big Mac index, however, suggested the euro was overvalued against the dollar—and indeed it has fallen [13 percent]. . . . Our correspondents have once again been munching their way around the globe . . . [and] experience suggests that investors ignore burgernomics at their peril.*

Maybe so—bad puns and all. Economist Robert Cumby examined the Big Mac index for 14 countries for 10 years.† Among his findings:

- A 10 percent undervaluation, according to the Big Mac standard, in one year is associated with a 3.5 percent appreciation of that currency over the following year.
- When the U.S. dollar price of a Big Mac is high in a country, the relative local currency price of a Big Mac in that country generally declines during the following year.

Hmm. Not bad.

*"Big MacCurrencies," *The Economist*, Apr. 3, 1999; "Mcparity," *The Economist*, Dec. 11, 1999.

†Robert Cumby, "Forecasting Exchange Rates and Relative Prices with the Hamburger Standard: Is What You Want What You Get with Mcparity?" National Bureau of Economic Research, January 1997.

changes will cause the pound to appreciate and the dollar to depreciate.

Relative Interest Rates Changes in relative interest rates between two countries may alter their exchange rate. Suppose that real interest rates rise in the United States but stay constant in Great Britain. British citizens will then find the United States an attractive place in which to make financial investments. To undertake these investments, they will have to supply pounds in the foreign exchange market to obtain dollars. The increase in the supply of pounds results in depreciation of the pound and appreciation of the dollar.

Speculation Currency speculators are people who buy and sell currencies with an eye toward reselling or repurchasing them at a profit. Suppose speculators expect the U.S. economy to (1) grow more rapidly than the British economy and (2) experience a more rapid rise in its price level than will Britain. These expectations translate into an anticipation that the pound will appreciate and the dollar will depreciate. Speculators who are holding dollars will therefore try to convert them into pounds. This effort will increase the demand for pounds and cause the dollar price of pounds to rise (that is, cause the dollar to depreciate). A self-fulfilling prophecy occurs: The pound appreciates and the dollar depreciates because speculators act on the belief that these changes will in fact take place. In this way, speculation can cause changes in exchange rates. (We deal with currency speculation in more detail in this chapter's Last Word.)

Table 24.2 has more illustrations of the determinants of exchange rates; the table is worth careful study.

Flexible Rates and the Balance of Payments

Proponents of flexible exchange rates say they have an important feature: They automatically adjust and eventually eliminate balance-of-payments deficits or surpluses.

TABLE 24.2 Determinants of Exchange Rates: Factors That Change the Demand for or the Supply of a Particular Currency and Thus Alter the Exchange Rate

Determinant	Examples
Change in tastes	Japanese electronic equipment declines in popularity in the United States (Japanese yen depreciates; U.S. dollar appreciates).
	European tourists reduce visits to the United States (U.S. dollar depreciates; European euro appreciates).
Change in relative incomes	England encounters a recession, reducing its imports, while U.S. real output and real income surge, increasing U.S. imports (British pound appreciates; U.S. dollar depreciates).
Change in relative prices	Switzerland experiences a 3% inflation rate compared to Canada's 10% rate (Swiss franc appreciates; Canadian dollar depreciates).
Change in relative real interest rates	The Federal Reserve drives up interest rates in the United States, while the Bank of England takes no such action (U.S. dollar appreciates; British pound depreciates).
Speculation	Currency traders believe South Korea will have much greater inflation than Taiwan (South Korean won depreciates; Taiwan dollar appreciates).
	Currency traders think Norway's interest rates will plummet relative to Denmark's rates (Norway's kroner depreciates; Denmark's krone appreciates).

We can explain this idea through Figure 24.2, in which S_1 and D_1 are the supply and demand curves for pounds from Figure 24.1. The equilibrium exchange rate of \$2 = £1 means that there is no balance-of-payments deficit or surplus between the United States and Britain. At that exchange rate, the quantity of pounds demanded by U.S. consumers to import British goods, buy British transportation and insurance services, and pay interest and dividends on British investments in the United States equals the amount of pounds supplied by the British in buying U.S. exports, purchasing services from the United States, and making interest and dividend payments on U. S. investments in Britain. The United States would have no need to either draw down or build up its official reserves to balance its payments.

Suppose tastes change and U.S. consumers buy more British automobiles; the U.S. price level increases relative to Britain's; or interest rates fall in the United States compared to those in Britain. Any or all of these changes will increase the U.S. demand for British pounds, for example, from D_1 to D_2 in Figure 24.2.

If the exchange rate remains at the initial \$2 = £1, a U.S. balance-of-payments deficit will occur in the amount of *ab*. At the \$2 = £1 rate, U.S. consumers will demand the quantity of pounds shown by point *b* but Britain will supply only the amount shown by *a*. There will be a shortage of pounds. But this shortage will not last because this is a competitive market. Instead, the dollar price of pounds will rise (the dollar will depreciate) until the balance-of-payments deficit is eliminated. That occurs at the new equilibrium exchange rate of \$3 = £1, where the quantities of pounds demanded and supplied are again equal.

To explain why this occurred, we reemphasize that the exchange rate links all domestic (U.S.) prices with all foreign (British) prices. The dollar price of a foreign good is found by multiplying the foreign price by the exchange rate (in dollars per unit of the foreign currency). At an exchange rate of \$2 = £1, a British automobile priced at £15,000 will cost a U.S. consumer \$30,000 (= 15,000 × \$2).

FIGURE 24.2 Adjustments under flexible exchange rates and fixed exchange rates. Under flexible exchange rates, a shift in the demand for pounds from D_1 to D_2, other things equal, would cause a U.S. balance-of-payments deficit *ab*. That deficit would be corrected by a change in the exchange rate from \$2 = £1 to \$3 = £1. Under fixed exchange rates, the United States would cover the shortage of pounds *ab* by using international monetary reserves, restricting trade, implementing exchange controls, or enacting a contractionary stabilization policy.

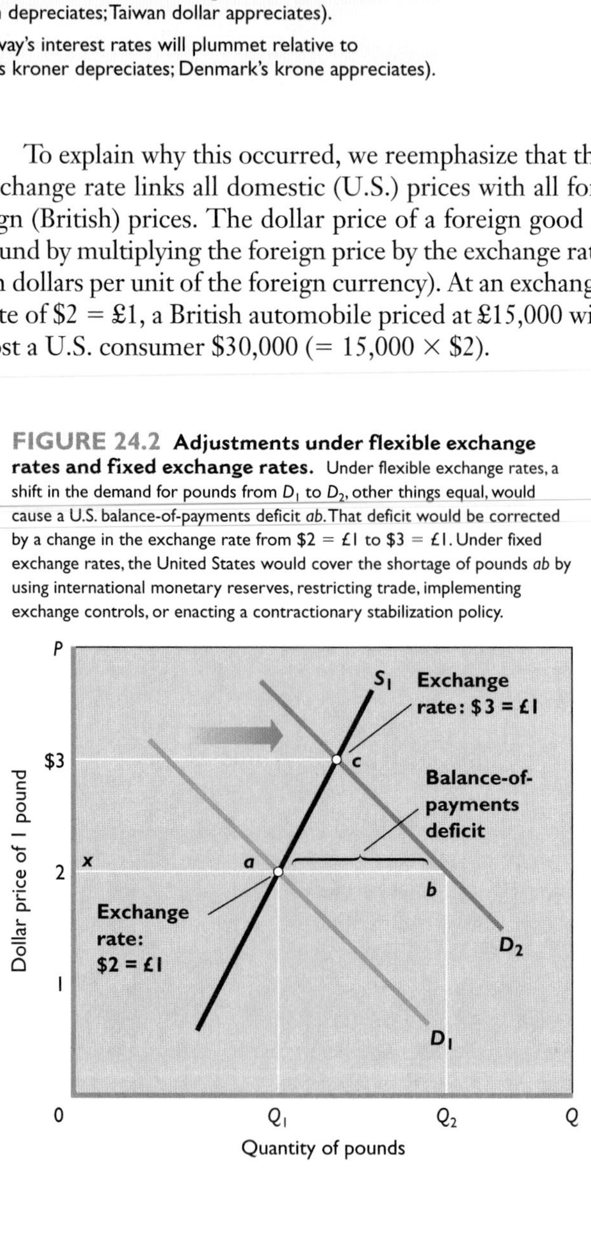

A change in the exchange rate alters the prices of all British goods to U.S. consumers and all U.S. goods to British buyers. The shift in the exchange rate (here from $2 = £1 to $3 = £1) changes the relative attractiveness of U.S. imports and exports and restores equilibrium in the U.S. (and British) balance of payments. From the U.S. view, as the dollar price of pounds changes from $2 to $3, the British auto priced at £15,000, which formerly cost a U.S. consumer $30,000, now costs $45,000 (= 15,000 × $3). Other British goods will also cost U.S. consumers more, and U.S. imports of British goods will decline. A movement from point *b* toward point *c* in Figure 24.2 graphically illustrates this concept.

From Britain's standpoint, the exchange rate (the pound price of dollars) has fallen (from £$\frac{1}{2}$ to £$\frac{1}{3}$ for $1). The international value of the pound has appreciated. The British previously got only $2 for £1; now they get $3 for £1. U.S. goods are therefore cheaper to the British, and U.S. exports to Britain will rise. In Figure 24.2, this is shown by a movement from point *a* toward point *c*.

The two adjustments—a decrease in U.S. imports from Britain and an increase in U.S. exports to Britain—are just what are needed to correct the U.S. balance-of-payments deficit. These changes end when, at point *c*, the quantities of British pounds demanded and supplied are equal. **(Key Questions 7 and 10)**

Disadvantages of Flexible Exchange Rates

Even though flexible exchange rates automatically work to eliminate payment imbalances, they may cause several significant problems.

Uncertainty and Diminished Trade

The risks and uncertainties associated with flexible exchange rates may discourage the flow of trade. Suppose a U.S. automobile dealer contracts to purchase 10 British cars for £150,000. At the current exchange rate of, say, $2 for £1, the U.S. importer expects to pay $300,000 for these automobiles. But if during the 3-month delivery period the rate of exchange shifts to $3 for £1, the £150,000 payment contracted by the U.S. importer will be $450,000.

That increase in the dollar price of pounds may thus turn the U.S. importer's anticipated profit into substantial loss. Aware of the possibility of an adverse change in the exchange rate, the U.S. importer may not be willing to assume the risks involved. The U.S. firm may confine its operations to domestic automobiles, so international trade in this product will not occur.

The same thing can happen with investments. Assume that when the exchange rate is $3 to £1, a U.S. firm invests $30,000 (or £10,000) in a British enterprise. It estimates a return of 10 percent; that is, it anticipates annual earnings of $3000 or £1000. Suppose these expectations prove correct in that the British firm earns £1000 in the first year on the £10,000 investment. But suppose that during the year, the value of the dollar appreciates to $2 = £1. The absolute return is now only $2000 (rather than $3000), and the rate of return falls from the anticipated 10 percent to only 6$\frac{2}{3}$ percent (= $2000/$30,000). Investment is risky in any case. The added risk of changing exchange rates may persuade the U.S. investor not to venture overseas.[1]

Terms-of-Trade Changes

A decline in the international value of its currency will worsen a nation's terms of trade. For example, an increase in the dollar price of a pound will mean that the United States must export more goods and services to finance a specific level of imports from Britain.

Instability

Flexible exchange rates may destabilize the domestic economy because wide fluctuations stimulate and then depress industries producing exported goods. If the U.S. economy is operating at full employment and its currency depreciates, as in our illustration, the results will be inflationary, for two reasons. (1) Foreign demand for U.S. goods may rise, increasing total spending and pulling up U.S. prices. Also, the prices of all U.S. imports will increase. (2) Conversely, appreciation of the dollar will lower U.S. exports and increase imports, possibly causing unemployment.

Flexible or floating exchange rates may also complicate the use of domestic stabilization policies in seeking full employment and price stability. This is especially true for nations whose exports and imports are large relative to their total domestic output.

Fixed Exchange Rates

To circumvent the disadvantages of flexible exchange rates, at times nations have fixed or "pegged" their exchange rates. For our analysis of fixed exchange rates, we assume that the United States and Britain agree to maintain a $2 = £1 exchange rate.

The problem is that such a government agreement cannot keep from changing the demand for and the supply of pounds. With the rate fixed, a shift in demand or supply will threaten the fixed-exchange-rate system, and government must intervene to ensure that the exchange rate is maintained.

[1]You will see in this chapter's Last Word, however, that a trader can circumvent part of the risk of unfavorable exchange-rate fluctuations by "hedging" in the "futures market" or "forward market" for foreign exchange.

In Figure 24.2, suppose the U.S. demand for pounds increases from D_1 to D_2 and a U.S. payment deficit *ab* arises. Now, the new equilibrium exchange rate ($3 = £1) is above the fixed exchange rate ($2 = £1). How can the United States prevent the shortage of pounds from driving the exchange rate up to the new equilibrium level? How can it maintain the fixed exchange rate? The answer is by altering market demand or market supply or both so that they will intersect at the $2 = £1 rate. There are several ways to do this.

Use of Reserves

One way to maintain a fixed exchange rate is to manipulate the market through the use of official reserves. Such manipulations are called **currency interventions.** By selling part of its reserves of pounds, the U.S. government could increase the supply of pounds, shifting supply curve S_1 to the right so that it intersects D_2 at *b* in Figure 24.2 and thereby maintains the exchange rate at $2 = £1.

How do official reserves originate? Perhaps a balance-of-payments surplus occurred in the past. The U.S. government would have purchased that surplus. That is, at some earlier time the U.S. government may have spent dollars to buy the surplus pounds that were threatening to reduce the exchange rate to below the $2 = £1 fixed rate. Those purchases would have bolstered the U.S. official reserves of pounds.

Nations have also used gold as "international money" to obtain official reserves. In our example, the U.S. government could sell some of its gold to Britain to obtain pounds. It could then sell pounds for dollars. That would shift the supply-of-pounds curve to the right, and the $2 = £1 exchange rate could be maintained.

It is critical that the amount of reserves and gold be enough to accomplish the required increase in the supply of pounds. There is no problem if deficits and surpluses occur more or less randomly and are of similar size. Then, last year's balance-of-payments surplus with Britain will increase the U.S. reserve of pounds, and that reserve can be used to "finance" this year's deficit. But if the United States encounters persistent and sizable deficits for an extended period, it may exhaust its reserves, and thus be forced to abandon fixed exchange rates. Or, at the least, a nation whose reserves are inadequate must use less appealing options to maintain exchange rates. Let's consider some of those options.

Trade Policies

To maintain fixed exchange rates, a nation can try to control the flow of trade and finance directly. The United States could try to maintain the $2 = £1 exchange rate in the face of a shortage of pounds by discouraging imports (thereby reducing the demand for pounds) and encouraging exports (thus increasing the supply of pounds). Imports could be reduced by means of new tariffs or import quotas; special taxes could be levied on the interest and dividends U.S. financial investors receive from foreign investments. Also, the U.S. government could subsidize certain U.S. exports to increase the supply of pounds.

The fundamental problem is that these policies reduce the volume of world trade and change its makeup from what is economically desirable. When nations impose tariffs, quotas, and the like, they lose some of the economic benefits of a free flow of world trade. That loss should not be underestimated: Trade barriers by one nation lead to retaliatory responses from other nations, multiplying the loss.

Exchange Controls and Rationing

Another option is to adopt exchange controls and rationing. Under **exchange controls** the U.S. government could handle the problem of a pound shortage by requiring that all pounds obtained by U.S. exporters be sold to the Federal government. Then the government would allocate or ration this short supply of pounds (represented by *xa* in Figure 24.2) among various U.S. importers, who demand the quantity *xb*. This policy would restrict the value of U.S. imports to the amount of foreign exchange earned by U.S. exports. Assuming balance in the capital and financial account, there would then be no balance-of-payments deficit. U.S. demand for British imports with the value *ab* would simply not be fulfilled.

There are major objections to exchange controls:

- ***Distorted trade*** Like tariffs, quotas, and export subsidies (trade controls), exchange controls would distort the pattern of international trade away from the pattern suggested by comparative advantage.
- ***Favoritism*** The process of rationing scarce foreign exchange might lead to government favoritism toward selected importers (big contributors to reelection campaigns, for example).
- ***Restricted choice*** Controls would limit freedom of consumer choice. The U.S. consumers who prefer Volkswagens might have to buy Chevrolets. The business opportunities for some U.S. importers might be impaired if the government were to limit imports.
- ***Black markets*** Enforcement problems are likely under exchange controls. U.S. importers might want foreign exchange badly enough to pay more than the $2 = £1 official rate, setting the stage for black-market dealings between importers and illegal sellers of foreign exchange.

Domestic Macroeconomic Adjustments

A final way to maintain a fixed exchange rate would be to use domestic stabilization policies (monetary policy and fiscal policy) to eliminate the shortage of foreign currency. Tax hikes, reductions in government spending, and a high-interest-rate policy would reduce total spending in the U.S. economy and, consequently, domestic income. Because the volume of imports varies directly with domestic income, demand for British goods, and therefore for pounds, would be restrained.

If these "contractionary" policies served to reduce the domestic price level relative to Britain's, U.S. buyers of consumer and capital goods would divert their demands from British goods to U.S. goods, reducing the demand for pounds. Moreover, the high-interest-rate policy would lift U.S. interest rates relative to those in Britain.

Lower prices on U.S. goods and higher U.S. interest rates would increase British imports of U.S. goods and would increase British financial investment in the United States. Both developments would increase the supply of pounds. The combination of a decrease in the demand for and an increase in the supply of pounds would reduce or eliminate the original U.S. balance-of-payments deficit. In Figure 24.2 the new supply and demand curves would intersect at some new equilibrium point on line *ab*, where the exchange rate remains at $2 = £1.

Maintaining fixed exchange rates by such means is hardly appealing. The "price" of exchange-rate stability for the United States would be a decline in output, employment, and price levels—in other words, a recession. Eliminating a balance-of-payments deficit and achieving domestic stability are both important national economic goals, but to sacrifice stability to balance payments would be to let the tail wag the dog.

QUICK REVIEW 24.2

- In a system in which exchange rates are flexible (meaning that they are free to float), the rates are determined by the demand for and supply of individual national currencies in the foreign exchange market.
- Determinants of flexible exchange rates (factors that shift currency supply and demand curves) include changes in (a) tastes, (b) relative national incomes, (c) relative price levels, (d) real interest rates, and (e) speculation.
- Under a system of fixed exchange rates, nations set their exchange rates and then maintain them by buying or selling reserves of currencies, establishing trade barriers, employing exchange controls, or incurring inflation or recession.

International Exchange-Rate Systems

In recent times the world's nations have used three different exchange-rate systems: a fixed-rate system, a modified fixed-rate system, and a modified flexible-rate system.

The Gold Standard: Fixed Exchange Rates

Between 1879 and 1934 the major nations of the world adhered to a fixed-rate system called the **gold standard.** Under this system, each nation must:

- Define its currency in terms of a quantity of gold.
- Maintain a fixed relationship between its stock of gold and its money supply.
- Allow gold to be freely exported and imported.

If each nation defines its currency in terms of gold, the various national currencies will have fixed relationships to one another. For example, if the United States defines $1 as worth 25 grains of gold, and Britain defines £1 as worth 50 grains of gold, then a British pound is worth 2 × 25 grains, or $2. This exchange rate was fixed under the gold standard. The exchange rate did not change in response to changes in currency demand and supply.

Gold Flows If we ignore the costs of packing, insuring, and shipping gold between countries, under the gold standard the rate of exchange would not vary from this $2 = £1 rate. No one in the United States would pay more than $2 = £1 because 50 grains of gold could always be bought for $2 in the United States and sold for £1 in Britain. Nor would the British pay more than £1 for $2. Why should they when they could buy 50 grains of gold in Britain for £1 and sell it in the United States for $2?

Under the gold standard, the potential free flow of gold between nations resulted in fixed exchange rates.

Domestic Macroeconomic Adjustments When currency demand or supply changes, the gold standard requires domestic macroeconomic adjustments to maintain the fixed exchange rate. To see why, suppose that U.S. tastes change such that U.S. consumers want to buy more British goods. The resulting increase in the demand for pounds creates a shortage of pounds in the United States (recall Figure 24.2), implying a U.S. balance-of-payments deficit.

What will happen? Remember that the rules of the gold standard prohibit the exchange rate from moving from the fixed $2 = £1 rate. The rate cannot move to, say, a new equilibrium at \$3 = £1 to correct the imbalance. Instead, gold will flow from the United States to Britain to correct the payments imbalance.

But recall that the gold standard requires that participants maintain a fixed relationship between their domestic money supplies and their quantities of gold. The flow of gold from the United States to Britain will require a reduction of the money supply in the United States. Other things equal, that will reduce total spending in the United States and lower U.S. real domestic output, employment, income, and, perhaps, prices. Also, the decline in the money supply will boost U.S. interest rates.

The opposite will occur in Britain. The inflow of gold will increase the money supply, and this will increase total spending in Britain. Domestic output, employment, income, and, perhaps, prices will rise. The British interest rate will fall.

Declining U.S. incomes and prices will reduce the U.S. demand for British goods and therefore reduce the U.S. demand for pounds. Lower interest rates in Britain will make it less attractive for U.S. investors to make financial investments there, also lessening the demand for pounds. For all these reasons, the demand for pounds in the United States will decline. In Britain, higher incomes, prices, and interest rates will make U.S. imports and U.S. financial investments more attractive. In buying these imports and making these financial investments, British citizens will supply more pounds in the exchange market.

In short, domestic macroeconomic adjustments in the United States and Britain, triggered by the international flow of gold, will produce new demand and supply conditions for pounds such that the \$2 = £1 exchange rate is maintained. After all the adjustments are made, the United States will not have a payments deficit and Britain will not have a payments surplus.

So the gold standard has the advantage of maintaining stable exchange rates and correcting balance-of-payments deficits and surpluses automatically. However, its critical drawback is that nations must accept domestic adjustments in such distasteful forms as unemployment and falling incomes, on the one hand, or inflation, on the other hand. Under the gold standard, a nation's money supply is altered by changes in supply and demand in currency markets, and nations cannot establish their own monetary policy in their own national interest. If the United States, for example, were to experience declining output and income, the loss of gold under the gold standard would reduce the U.S. money supply. That would increase interest rates, retard borrowing and spending, and produce further declines in output and income.

Collapse of the Gold Standard

The gold standard collapsed under the weight of the worldwide Depression of the 1930s. As domestic output and employment fell worldwide, the restoration of prosperity became the primary goal of afflicted nations. They responded by enacting protectionist measures to reduce imports. The idea was to get their economies moving again by promoting consumption of domestically produced goods. To make their exports less expensive abroad, many nations redefined their currencies at lower levels in terms of gold. For example, a country that had previously defined the value of its currency at 1 unit = 25 ounces of gold might redefine it as 1 unit = 10 ounces of gold. Such redefining is an example of **devaluation**—a deliberate action by government to reduce the international value of its currency. A series of such devaluations in the 1930s meant that exchange rates were no longer fixed. That violated a major tenet of the gold standard, and the system broke down.

The Bretton Woods System

The Great Depression and the Second World War left world trade and the world monetary system in shambles. To lay the groundwork for a new international monetary system, in 1944 major nations held an international conference at Bretton Woods, New Hampshire. The conference produced a commitment to a modified fixed-exchange-rate system called an *adjustable-peg system*, or, simply, the **Bretton Woods system.** The new system sought to capture the advantages of the old gold standard (fixed exchange rate) while avoiding its disadvantages (painful domestic macroeconomic adjustments).

Furthermore, the conference created the **International Monetary Fund (IMF)** to make the new exchange-rate system feasible and workable. The new international monetary system managed through the IMF prevailed with modifications until 1971. (The IMF still plays a basic role in international finance; in recent years it has performed a major role in providing loans to developing countries, nations experiencing financial crises, and nations making the transition from communism to capitalism.)

IMF and Pegged Exchange Rates

How did the adjustable-peg system of exchange rates work? First, as with the gold standard, each IMF member had to define its currency in terms of gold (or dollars), thus establishing rates of exchange between its currency and the currencies of all other members. In addition, each nation was obligated to keep its exchange rate stable with respect to every other currency. To do so, nations would have to use their official currency reserves to intervene in foreign exchange markets.

Assume again that the U.S. dollar and the British pound were "pegged" to each other at \$2 = £1. And suppose again that the demand for pounds temporarily increases so that a shortage of pounds occurs in the United States (the United States has a balance-of-payments deficit). How can the United States keep its pledge to maintain a \$2 = £1 exchange rate when the new equilibrium rate is, say, \$3 = £1? As we noted previously, the United States can supply additional pounds to the exchange market, increasing the supply of pounds such that the equilibrium exchange rate falls back to \$2 = £1.

Under the Bretton Woods system there were three main sources of the needed pounds:

- ***Official reserves*** The United States might currently possess pounds in its official reserves as the result of past actions against a payments surplus.
- ***Gold sales*** The U.S. government might sell some of its gold to Britain for pounds. The proceeds would then be offered in the exchange market to augment the supply of pounds.
- ***IMF borrowing*** The needed pounds might be borrowed from the IMF. Nations participating in the Bretton Woods system were required to make contributions to the IMF based on the size of their national income, population, and volume of trade. If necessary, the United States could borrow pounds on a short-term basis from the IMF by supplying its own currency as collateral.

Fundamental Imbalances: Adjusting the Peg

The Bretton Woods system recognized that from time to time a nation may be confronted with persistent and sizable balance-of-payments problems that cannot be corrected through the means listed above. In such cases, the nation would eventually run out of official reserves and be unable to maintain its fixed-exchange-rate system. The Bretton Woods remedy was correction by devaluation, that is, by an "orderly" reduction of the nation's pegged exchange rate. Also, the IMF allowed each member nation to alter the value of its currency by 10 percent, on its own, to correct a so-called fundamental (persistent and continuing) balance-of-payments deficit. Larger exchange-rate changes required the permission of the Fund's board of directors.

By requiring approval of significant rate changes, the Fund guarded against arbitrary and competitive currency devaluations by nations seeking only to boost output in their own countries at the expense of other countries. In our example, devaluation of the dollar would increase U.S. exports and lower U.S. imports, correcting its persistent payments deficit.

Demise of the Bretton Woods System

Under this adjustable-peg system, nations came to accept gold and the dollar as international reserves. The acceptability of gold as an international medium of exchange derived from its earlier use under the gold standard. Other nations accepted the dollar as international money because the United States had accumulated large quantities of gold, and between 1934 and 1971 it maintained a policy of buying gold from, and selling gold to, foreign governments at a fixed price of \$35 per ounce. The dollar was convertible into gold on demand, so the dollar came to be regarded as a substitute for gold, or "as good as gold." And since the discovery of new gold was limited, the growing volume of dollars helped provide a medium of exchange for the expanding world trade.

But a major problem arose. The United States had persistent payments deficits throughout the 1950s and 1960s. Those deficits were financed in part by U.S. gold reserves but mostly by payment of U.S. dollars. As the amount of dollars held by foreigners soared and the U.S. gold reserves dwindled, other nations began to question whether the dollar was really "as good as gold." The ability of the United States to continue to convert dollars into gold at \$35 per ounce became increasingly doubtful, as did the role of dollars as international monetary reserves. Thus the dilemma was: To maintain the dollar as a reserve medium, the U.S. payments deficit had to be eliminated. But elimination of the payments deficit would remove the source of additional dollar reserves and thus limit the growth of international trade and finance.

The problem culminated in 1971 when the United States ended its 37-year-old policy of exchanging gold for dollars at \$35 per ounce. It severed the link between gold and the international value of the dollar, thereby "floating" the dollar and letting market forces determine its value. The floating of the dollar withdrew U.S. support from the Bretton Woods system of fixed exchange rates and, in effect, ended the system.

The Current System: The Managed Float

The current international exchange-rate system (1971–present) is an "almost" flexible system called **managed floating exchange rates.** Exchange rates among major currencies are free to float to their equilibrium market levels, but nations occasionally use currency interventions in the foreign exchange market to stabilize or alter market exchange rates.

Normally, the major trading nations allow their exchange rates to float up or down to equilibrium levels based on supply and demand in the foreign exchange market. They recognize that changing economic conditions among nations require continuing changes in equilibrium exchange rates to avoid persistent payments deficits or surpluses. They rely on freely operating foreign exchange markets to accomplish the necessary adjustments. The result has been considerably more volatile exchange rates than those during the Bretton Woods era.

But nations also recognize that certain trends in the movement of equilibrium exchange rates may be at odds with national or international objectives. On occasion, nations therefore intervene in the foreign exchange market by buying or selling large amounts of specific currencies. This way, they can "manage" or stabilize exchange rates by influencing currency demand and supply.

The leaders of the *G8 nations* (Canada, France, Germany, Italy, Japan, Russia, United Kingdom, and United States) meet regularly to discuss economic issues and try to coordinate economic policies. At times they have collectively intervened to try to stabilize currencies. For example, in 2000 they sold dollars and bought euros in an effort to stabilize the falling value of the euro relative to the dollar. In the previous year the euro (€) had depreciated from €1 = \$1.17 to €1 = \$.87.

The current exchange-rate system is thus an "almost" flexible exchange-rate system. The "almost" refers mainly to the periodic currency interventions by governments; it also refers to the fact that the actual system is more complicated than described. While the major currencies such as dollars, euros, pounds, and yen fluctuate in response to changing supply and demand, some developing nations peg their currencies to the dollar and allow their currencies to fluctuate with it against other currencies. Also, some nations peg the value of their currencies to a "basket" or group of other currencies.

How well has the managed float worked? It has both proponents and critics.

In Support of the Managed Float

Proponents of the managed-float system argue that is has functioned far better than many experts anticipated. Skeptics had predicted that fluctuating exchange rates would reduce world trade and finance. But in real terms world trade under the managed float has grown tremendously over the past several decades. Moreover, as supporters are quick to point out, currency crises such as those in Mexico and southeast Asia in the last half of the 1990s were not the result of the floating-exchange-rate system itself. Rather, the abrupt currency devaluations and depreciations resulted from internal problems in those nations, in conjunction with the nations' tendency to peg their currencies to the dollar or to a basket of currencies. In some cases, flexible exchange rates would have made these adjustments far more gradual.

Proponents also point out that the managed float has weathered severe economic turbulence that might have caused a fixed-rate system to break down. Such events as extraordinary oil price increases in 1973–1974 and again in 1981–1983, inflationary recessions in several nations in the mid-1970s, major national recessions in the early 1980s, and large U.S. budget deficits in the 1980s and the first half of the 1990s all caused substantial imbalances in international trade and finance, as did the large U.S. budget deficits and soaring world oil prices that occurred in the middle of the first decade of the 2000s. Flexible rates enabled the system to adjust to all these events, whereas the same events would have put unbearable pressures on a fixed-rate system.

Concerns with the Managed Float

There is still much sentiment in favor of greater exchange-rate stability. Those favoring more stable exchange rates see problems with the current system. They argue that the excessive volatility of exchange rates under the managed float threatens the prosperity of economies that rely heavily on exports. Several financial crises in individual nations (for example, Mexico, South Korea, Indonesia, Thailand, Russia, and Brazil) have resulted from abrupt changes in exchange rates. These crises have led to massive "bailouts" of those economies via IMF loans. The IMF bailouts, in turn, may encourage nations to undertake risky and inappropriate economic policies since they know that, if need be, the IMF will come to the rescue. Moreover, some exchange-rate volatility has occurred even when underlying economic and financial conditions were relatively stable, suggesting that speculation plays too large a role in determining exchange rates.

Perhaps more important, assert the critics, the managed float has not eliminated trade imbalances, as flexible rates are supposed to do. Thus, the United States has run persistent trade deficits for many years, while Japan has run persistent surpluses. Changes in exchange rates between dollars and yen have not yet corrected these imbalances, as is supposed to be the case under flexible exchange rates.

Skeptics say the managed float is basically a "nonsystem"; the guidelines concerning what each nation may or may not do with its exchange rates are not specific enough to keep the system working in the long run. Nations inevitably will be tempted to intervene in the foreign exchange market, not merely to smooth out short-term fluctuations in exchange rates but to prop up their currency if it is chronically weak or to manipulate the exchange rate to achieve domestic stabilization goals.

So what are we to conclude? Flexible exchange rates have not worked perfectly, but they have not failed miserably. Thus far they have survived, and no doubt have eased, several major shocks to the international trading system. Meanwhile, the "managed" part of the float has given nations some sense of control over their collective economic destinies. On balance, most economists favor continuation of the present system of "almost" flexible exchange rates.

QUICK REVIEW 24.3

- Under the gold standard (1879–1934), nations fixed exchange rates by valuing their currencies in terms of gold, by tying their stocks of money to gold, and by allowing gold to flow between nations when balance-of-payments deficits and surpluses occurred.
- The Bretton Woods exchange-rate system (1944–1971) fixed or pegged exchange rates but permitted orderly adjustments of the pegs under special circumstances.
- The managed floating system of exchange rates (1971–present) relies on foreign exchange markets to establish equilibrium exchange rates. The system permits nations to buy and sell foreign currency to stabilize short-term changes in exchange rates or to correct exchange-rate imbalances that are negatively affecting the world economy.

FIGURE 24.3 U.S. trade deficits, 1994–2005. (a) The United States experienced large deficits in *goods* and in *goods and services* between 1997 and 2005. (b) The U.S. current account, generally reflecting the goods and services deficit, was also in substantial deficit. These trade deficits are expected to continue throughout the current decade.

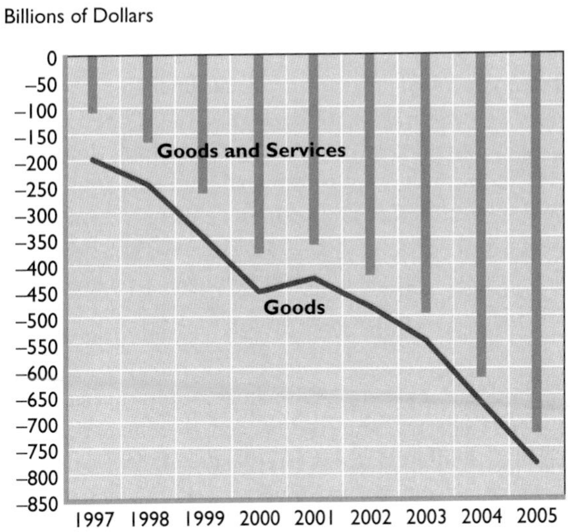

(a)
Balance of trade

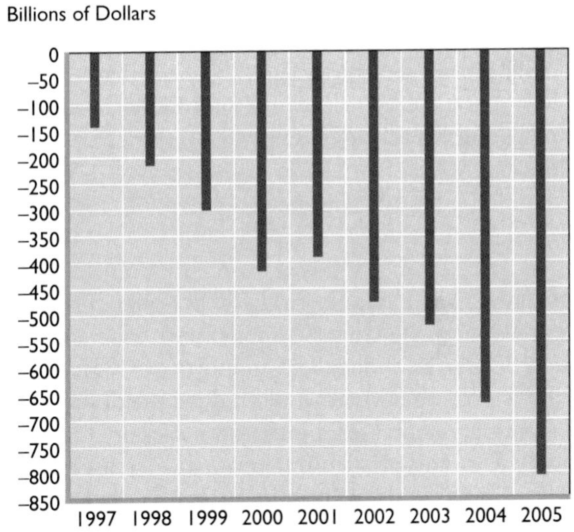

(b)
Balance on current account

Recent U.S. Trade Deficits

As indicated in Figure 24.3a, the United States has experienced large and persistent trade deficits over the past several years. These deficits climbed steadily between 1997 and 2000, fell slightly in the recessionary year 2001, and rose sharply between 2002 and 2005. In 2005 the trade deficit on goods was $782 billion and the trade deficit on goods and services was $724 billion. The current account deficit (Figure 24.3b) reached a record $805 billion in 2005. It rose from 5.7 percent of GDP in 2004 to 6.4 percent of GDP in 2005. Large trade deficits are expected to continue for many years, both in absolute and relative terms.

Causes of the Trade Deficits

Several reasons account for these large trade deficits. First, between 1997 and 2000, and again between 2003 and 2005, the U.S. economy grew more rapidly than the economies of several of its major trading partners. That strong growth of U.S. income enabled Americans to buy more imported goods. In contrast, Japan and some European nations either suffered recession or experienced slower income growth. So their purchases of U.S. exports did not keep pace with the growing U.S. imports.

Also, large trade deficits with China have emerged, reaching $202 billion in 2005. This amount is even greater than the U.S. trade imbalance with Japan ($83 billion in 2005). The United States is China's largest export market, and although China has increased its imports from the United States, its standard of living has not yet increased enough for its citizens to afford large quantities of U.S. goods and services. Adding to the problem, China has fixed the exchange rate of it currency, the yuan, to a basket of currencies that includes the dollar. Therefore its large trade surplus with the United States has not caused the yuan to

Last Word

Speculation in Currency Markets

Are Speculators a Negative or a Positive Influence in Currency Markets and International Trade?

Most people buy foreign currency to facilitate the purchase of goods or services from another country. A U.S. importer buys Japanese yen to purchase Japanese autos. A Hong Kong financial investor purchases Australian dollars to invest in the Australian stock market. But there is another group of participants in the currency market—speculators—that buys and sells foreign currencies in the hope of reselling or rebuying them later at a profit.

Contributing to Exchange-Rate Fluctuations Speculators were much in the news in late 1997 and 1998 when they were widely accused of driving down the values of the South Korean won, Thailand baht, Malaysian ringgit, and Indonesian rupiah. The value of these currencies fell by as much as 50 percent within 1 month, and speculators undoubtedly contributed to the swiftness of those declines. The expectation of currency depreciation (or appreciation) can be self-fulfilling. If speculators, for example, expect the Indonesian rupiah to be devalued or to depreciate, they quickly sell rupiah and buy currencies that they think will increase in relative value. The sharp increase in the supply of rupiah indeed reduces its value; this reduction then may trigger further selling of rupiah in expectation of further declines in its value.

But changed economic realities, not speculation, are normally the underlying causes of changes in currency values. That was largely the case with the southeast Asian countries in which actual and threatened bankruptcies in the financial and manufacturing sectors undermined confidence in the strength of the currencies. Anticipating the eventual declines in currency values, speculators simply hastened those declines. That is, the declines in value probably would have occurred with or without speculators.

Moreover, on a daily basis, speculation clearly has positive effects in foreign exchange markets.

Smoothing Out Short-Term Fluctuations in Currency Prices When temporarily weak demand or strong supply reduces a currency's value, speculators quickly buy the currency, adding to its demand and strengthening its value. When temporarily strong demand or weak supply increases a currency's value, speculators sell the currency. That selling increases the supply of the currency and reduces its value. In this way speculators smooth out supply and demand, and thus exchange rates, over short time periods. This day-to-day exchange-rate stabilization aids international trade.

Absorbing Risk Speculators also absorb risk that others do not want to bear. Because of potential adverse changes in exchange rates, international transactions are riskier than domestic trans-

appreciate in value relative to the U.S. dollar. That appreciation would make Chinese goods more expensive in the United States and reduce U.S. imports of Chinese goods. In China a stronger yuan would reduce the dollar price of U.S. goods and increase Chinese purchases of U.S. exports. Reduced U.S. imports from China and increased U.S. exports to China would reduce the large U.S. trade deficit.

Another factor causing the large U.S. trade deficits has been the rapid rise of the price of oil. Because the United States imports a large percentage of its oil, rising prices tend to aggravate trade deficits. For example, in 2005 the United States had a $94 billion trade deficit with the OPEC countries.

Finally, a declining U.S. saving rate (= saving/total income) has also contributed to U.S. trade deficits. In recent years, the saving rate has declined while the investment rate (= investment/total income) has remained stable or even increased. The gap has been met through foreign purchases of U.S. real and financial assets, creating a large capital and financial account surplus. Because foreign savers are willingly financing a larger part of U.S. investment, Americans are able to save less than otherwise and consume more. Part of that added consumption spending is on imported goods. Also, many foreigners view U.S. real assets favorably because of the relatively high risk-adjusted rates of return they generate. The purchase of those assets provides foreign currency to Americans to finance their strong appetite for imported goods.

The point is that the capital account surplus may be a partial cause of the trade deficits, not just a result of those deficits.

Implications of U.S. Trade Deficits

The recent U.S. trade deficits are the largest ever run by a major industrial nation. Whether the large trade deficits should be of significant concern to the United States and actions. Suppose AnyTime, a hypothetical retailer, signs a contract with a Swiss manufacturer to buy 10,000 Swatch watches to be delivered in 3 months. The stipulated price is 75 Swiss francs per watch, which in dollars is \$50 per watch at the present exchange rate of, say, \$1 = 1.5 francs. AnyTime's total bill for the 10,000 watches will be \$500,000 (= 750,000 francs).

But if the Swiss franc were to appreciate, say, to \$1 = 1 franc, the dollar price per watch would rise from \$50 to \$75 and AnyTime would owe \$750,000 for the watches (= 750,000 francs). AnyTime may reduce the risk of such an unfavorable exchange-rate fluctuation by hedging in the futures market. Hedging is an action by a buyer or a seller to protect against a change in future prices. The futures market is a market in which currencies are bought and sold at prices fixed now, for delivery at a specified date in the future.

AnyTime can purchase the needed 750,000 francs at the current \$1 = 1.5 francs exchange rate, but with delivery in 3 months when the Swiss watches are delivered. And here is where speculators come in. For a price determined in the futures market, they agree to deliver the 750,000 francs to AnyTime in 3 months at the \$1 = 1.5 francs exchange rate, regardless of the exchange rate then. The speculators need not own francs when the agreement is made. If the Swiss franc depreciates to, say, \$1 = 2 francs in this period, the speculators profit. They can buy the 750,000 francs stipulated in the contract for \$375,000, pocketing the difference between that amount and the \$500,000 AnyTime has agreed to pay for the 750,000 francs. If the Swiss franc appreciates, the speculators, but not AnyTime, suffer a loss.

The amount AnyTime must pay for this "exchange-rate insurance" will depend on how the market views the likelihood of the franc depreciating, appreciating, or staying constant over the 3-month period. As in all competitive markets, supply and demand determine the price of the futures contract.

The futures market thus eliminates much of the exchange-rate risk associated with buying foreign goods for future delivery. Without it, AnyTime might have decided against importing Swiss watches. But the futures market and currency speculators greatly increase the likelihood that the transaction will occur. Operating through the futures market, speculation promotes international trade.

In short, although speculators in currency markets occasionally contribute to swings in exchange rates, on a day-to-day basis they play a positive role in currency markets.

the rest of the world is debatable. Most economists see both benefits and costs to trade deficits.

Increased Current Consumption At the time a trade deficit or a current account deficit is occurring, American consumers benefit. A trade deficit means that the United States is receiving more goods and services as imports from abroad than it is sending out as exports. Taken alone, a trade deficit allows the United States to consume outside its production possibilities curve. It augments the domestic standard of living. But here is a catch: The gain in present consumption may come at the expense of reduced future consumption. When and if the current account deficit declines, Americans may have to consume less than before and perhaps even less than they produce.

Increased U.S. Indebtedness A trade deficit is considered unfavorable because it must be financed by borrowing from the rest of the world, selling off assets, or dipping into official reserves. Recall that current account deficits are financed primarily by net inpayments of foreign currencies to the United States. When U.S. exports are insufficient to finance U.S. imports, the United States increases both its debt to people abroad and the value of foreign claims against assets in the United States. Financing of the U.S. trade deficit has resulted in a larger foreign accumulation of claims against U.S. financial and real assets than the U.S. claim against foreign assets. Today, the United States is the world's largest debtor nation. In 2004 foreigners owned \$2.5 billion more of U.S. assets (corporations, land, stocks, bonds, loan notes) than U.S. citizens and institutions owned in foreign assets.

If the United States wants to regain ownership of these domestic assets, at some future time it will have to export more than it imports. At that time, domestic consumption will be lower because the United States will need to send more of its output abroad than it receives as imports. Therefore, the current consumption gains delivered by U.S. current account deficits may mean permanent debt, permanent foreign ownership, or large sacrifices of future consumption.

We say "may mean" above because the foreign lending to U.S. firms and foreign investment in the United States increases the U.S. capital stock. U.S. production capacity therefore might increase more rapidly than otherwise because of a large surplus on the capital and financial account. Faster increases in production capacity and real GDP enhance the economy's ability to service foreign debt and buy back real capital, if that is desired.

In short, trade deficits are a mixed blessing. The long-term impacts of the record-high U.S. trade deficits are largely unknown. That "unknown" worries some economists, who are concerned that foreigners will lose financial confidence in the United States. If that happens, they would restrict their lending to American households and businesses and also reduce their purchases of U.S. assets. Both actions would decrease the demand for U.S. dollars in the foreign exchange market and cause the U.S. dollar to depreciate. A sudden, large depreciation of the U.S. dollar might disrupt world trade and negatively affect economic growth worldwide. Other economists, however, downplay this scenario. Because any decline in the U.S. capital and financial account surplus is automatically met with a decline in the current account deficit, the overall impact on the American economy would be slight.

Summary

1. U.S. exports create a foreign demand for dollars and make a supply of foreign exchange available to the United States. Conversely, U.S. imports create a demand for foreign exchange and make a supply of dollars available to foreigners. Generally, a nation's exports earn the foreign currencies needed to pay for its imports.
2. The balance of payments records all international trade and financial transactions taking place between a given nation and the rest of the world. The balance on goods and services (the trade balance) compares exports and imports of both goods and services. The current account balance includes not only goods and services transactions but also net investment income and net transfers.
3. The capital and financial account includes (a) the net amount of the nation's debt forgiveness and (b) the nation's sale of real and financial assets to people living abroad less its purchases of real and financial assets from foreigners.
4. The current account and the capital and financial account always sum to zero. A deficit in the current account is always offset by a surplus in the capital and financial account. Conversely, a surplus in the current account is always offset by a deficit in the capital and financial account.
5. A balance-of-payments deficit is said to occur when a nation must draw down its official reserves, making inpayments to its balance of payments, in order to balance the capital and financial account with the current account. A balance-of-payments surplus occurs when a nation must increase its official reserves, making outpayments from its balance of payments, to balance the two accounts. The desirability of a balance-of-payments deficit or surplus depends on its size and its persistence.
6. Flexible or floating exchange rates between international currencies are determined by the demand for and supply of those currencies. Under flexible rates a currency will depreciate or appreciate as a result of changes in tastes, relative income changes, relative price changes, relative changes in real interest rates, and speculation.
7. The maintenance of fixed exchange rates requires adequate reserves to accommodate periodic payments deficits. If reserves are inadequate, nations must invoke protectionist trade policies, engage in exchange controls, or endure undesirable domestic macroeconomic adjustments.
8. The gold standard, a fixed-rate system, provided exchange-rate stability until its disintegration during the 1930s. Under this system, gold flows between nations precipitated sometimes painful changes in price, income, and employment levels in bringing about international equilibrium.
9. Under the Bretton Woods system, exchange rates were pegged to one another and were stable. Participating nations were obligated to maintain these rates by using stabilization funds, gold, or loans from the IMF. Persistent or "fundamental" payments deficits could be resolved by IMF-sanctioned currency devaluations.
10. Since 1971 the world's major nations have used a system of managed floating exchange rates. Market forces generally set rates, although governments intervene with varying frequency to alter their exchange rates.
11. Between 1997 and 2005, the United States had large and rising trade deficits, which are projected to last well into the future. Causes of the trade deficits include (a) more rapid income growth in the United States than in Japan and some European nations, resulting in expanding U.S. imports relative to exports, (b) the emergence of a large trade deficit

with China, (c) rising prices of imported oil, and (d) a large surplus in the capital and financial account, which enabled Americans to reduce their saving and buy more imports.

12. U.S. trade deficits have produced current increases in the living standards of U.S. consumers. The accompanying surpluses on the capital and financial account have increased U.S. debt to the rest of the world and increased foreign ownership of assets in the United States. This greater foreign investment in the United States, however, has undoubtedly increased U.S. production possibilities.

Terms and Concepts

balance of payments
current account
balance on goods and services
trade deficit
trade surplus
balance on current account
capital and financial account
balance on capital and financial account
balance-of-payments deficits and surpluses
official reserves
flexible- or floating-exchange-rate system
fixed-exchange-rate system
purchasing-power-parity theory
currency interventions
exchange controls
gold standard
devaluation
Bretton Woods system
International Monetary Fund (IMF)
managed floating exchange rates

Study Questions

1. Explain how a U.S. automobile importer might finance a shipment of Toyotas from Japan. Trace the steps as to how a U.S. export of machinery to Italy might be financed. Explain: "U.S. exports earn supplies of foreign currencies that Americans can use to finance imports."

2. **KEY QUESTION** Indicate whether each of the following creates a demand for or a supply of European euros in foreign exchange markets:
   a. A U.S. airline firm purchases several Airbus planes assembled in France.
   b. A German automobile firm decides to build an assembly plant in South Carolina.
   c. A U.S. college student decides to spend a year studying at the Sorbonne in Paris.
   d. An Italian manufacturer ships machinery from one Italian port to another on a Liberian freighter.
   e. The U.S. economy grows faster than the French economy.
   f. A U.S. government bond held by a Spanish citizen matures, and the loan amount is paid back to that person.
   g. It is widely believed that the euro will depreciate in the near future.

3. **KEY QUESTION** Alpha's balance-of-payments data for 2006 are shown below. All figures are in billions of dollars. What are the (*a*) balance on goods, (*b*) balance on goods and services, (*c*) balance on current account, and (*d*) balance on capital and financial account? Suppose Alpha needed to deposit $10 billion of official reserves into the capital and financial account to balance it against the current account. Does Alpha have a balance-of-payments deficit or surplus? Explain.

Goods exports	+$40
Goods imports	−30
Service exports	+15
Service imports	−10
Net investment income	−5
Net transfers	+10
Balance on capital account	0
Foreign purchases of Alpha assets	+20
Alpha purchases of assets abroad	−40

4. China had a $150 billion overall current account surplus in 2005. Assuming that China's net debt forgiveness was zero in 2005 (its capital account balance was zero), what can you specifically conclude about the relationship of Chinese purchases of financial and real assets abroad versus foreign purchases of Chinese financial and real assets? Explain.

5. "A rise in the dollar price of yen necessarily means a fall in the yen price of dollars." Do you agree? Illustrate and elaborate: "The critical thing about exchange rates is that they provide a direct link between the prices of goods and services produced in all trading nations of the world." Explain the purchasing-power-parity theory of exchange rates.

6. Suppose that a Swiss watchmaker imports watch components from Sweden and exports watches to the United States. Also suppose the dollar depreciates, and the Swedish krona appreciates, relative to the Swiss franc. Speculate as to how each would hurt the Swiss watchmaker.

7. **KEY QUESTION** Explain why the U.S. demand for Mexican pesos is downward-sloping and the supply of pesos to

Americans is upward-sloping. Assuming a system of flexible exchange rates between Mexico and the United States, indicate whether each of the following would cause the Mexican peso to appreciate or depreciate:

a. The United States unilaterally reduces tariffs on Mexican products.

b. Mexico encounters severe inflation.

c. Deteriorating political relations reduce American tourism in Mexico.

d. The U.S. economy moves into a severe recession.

e. The United States engages in a high-interest-rate monetary policy.

f. Mexican products become more fashionable to U.S. consumers.

g. The Mexican government encourages U.S. firms to invest in Mexican oil fields.

h. The rate of productivity growth in the United States diminishes sharply.

8. Explain why you agree or disagree with the following statements:

a. A country that grows faster than its major trading partners can expect the international value of its currency to depreciate.

b. A nation whose interest rate is rising more rapidly than interest rates in other nations can expect the international value of its currency to appreciate.

c. A country's currency will appreciate if its inflation rate is less than that of the rest of the world.

9. "Exports pay for imports. Yet in 2005 the nations of the world exported about $724 billion more worth of goods and services to the United States than they imported from the United States." Resolve the apparent inconsistency of these two statements.

10. **KEY QUESTION** Diagram a market in which the equilibrium dollar price of 1 unit of fictitious currency zee (Z) is $5 (the exchange rate is $5 = Z1). Then show on your diagram a decline in the demand for zee.

a. Referring to your diagram, discuss the adjustment options the United States would have in maintaining the exchange rate at $5 = Z1 under a fixed-exchange-rate system.

b. How would the U.S. balance-of-payments surplus that is created (by the decline in demand) get resolved under a system of flexible exchange rates?

11. Compare and contrast the Bretton Woods system of exchange rates with that of the gold standard. What caused the collapse of the gold standard? What caused the demise of the Bretton Woods system?

12. Describe what is meant by the term "managed float." Did the managed-float system precede or follow the adjustable-peg system? Explain.

13. What have been the major causes of the large U.S. trade deficits since 1997? What are the major benefits and costs associated with trade deficits? Explain: "A trade deficit means that a nation is receiving more goods and services from abroad than it is sending abroad." How can that be called "unfavorable"?

14. **LAST WORD** Suppose Winter Sports—a hypothetical French retailer of snowboards—wants to order 5000 snowboards made in the United States. The price per board is $200, the present exchange rate is 1 euro = $1, and payment is due in dollars when the boards are delivered in 3 months. Use a numerical example to explain why exchange-rate risk might make the French retailer hesitant to place the order. How might speculators absorb some of Winter Sports' risk?

Web-Based Questions

1. **THE U.S. BALANCE ON GOODS AND SERVICES—WHAT ARE THE LATEST FIGURES?** The U.S. Census Bureau reports the latest data on U.S. trade in goods and services at its Web site, **www.census.gov/indicator/www/ustrade.html.** In the latest month, did the trade balance in goods and services improve (that is, yield a smaller deficit or a larger surplus) or deteriorate? Was the relative trade strength of the United States compared to the rest of the world in goods or in services? Which product groups had the largest increases in exports? Which had the largest increases in imports?

2. **THE YEN-DOLLAR EXCHANGE RATE** The Federal Reserve Board of Governors provides exchange rates for various currencies for the last decade at **www.federalreserve.gov/releases** (Foreign Exchange Rates; Historical bilateral rates). Has the dollar appreciated, depreciated, or remained constant relative to the Canadian dollar, the European euro, the Japanese yen, the Swedish krona, and the Swiss franc since 2000?

Glossary

Note: Terms set in *italic* type are defined separately in this glossary.

ability-to-pay principle The idea that those who have greater *income* (or *wealth*) should pay a greater proportion of it as taxes than those who have less income (or wealth).

acreage allotment program A pre-1996 government program that determined the total number of acres to be used in producing (reduced amounts of) various food and fiber products and allocated these acres among individual farmers. These farmers had to limit their plantings to the allotted number of acres to obtain *price supports* for their crops.

adjustable pegs The device used in the *Bretton Woods system* to alter *exchange rates* in an orderly way to eliminate persistent payments deficits and surpluses. Each nation defined its monetary unit in terms of (pegged it to) gold or the dollar, kept the *rate of exchange* for its money stable in the short run, and adjusted its rate in the long run when faced with international payments disequilibrium.

adverse selection problem A problem arising when information known to one party to a contract or agreement is not known to the other party, causing the latter to incur major costs. Example: Individuals who have the poorest health are most likely to buy health insurance.

advertising A seller's activities in communicating its message about its product to potential buyers.

affirmative action Policies and programs that establish targets of increased employment and promotion for women and minorities.

AFL-CIO An acronym for the American Federation of Labor–Congress of Industrial Organizations; the largest federation of *labor unions* in the United States.

agency shop A place of employment where the employer may hire either *labor union* members or nonmembers but where those who do not join the union must either pay union dues or donate an equivalent amount of money to a charity.

aggregate A collection of specific economic units treated as if they were one. For example, all prices of individual goods and services are combined into a *price level*, or all units of output are aggregated into *gross domestic product*.

Alcoa case A 1945 case in which the courts ruled that the possession of monopoly power, no matter how reasonably that power had been used, was a violation of the antitrust laws; temporarily overturned the *rule of reason* applied in the *U.S. Steel case*.

allocative efficiency The apportionment of resources among firms and industries to obtain the production of the products most wanted by society (consumers); the output of each product at which its *marginal cost* and *price* or *marginal benefit* are equal.

antitrust laws Legislation (including the *Sherman Act* and *Clayton Act*) that prohibits anticompetitive business activities such as *price fixing*, bid rigging, monopolization, and *tying contracts*.

antitrust policy The use of the *antitrust laws* to promote *competition* and economic efficiency.

appreciation (of the dollar) An increase in the value of the dollar relative to the currency of another nation, so a dollar buys a larger amount of the foreign currency and thus of foreign goods.

asset Anything of monetary value owned by a firm or individual.

asymmetric information A situation where one party to a market transaction has much more information about a product or service than the other. The result may be an under- or overallocation of resources.

average fixed cost (AFC) A firm's total *fixed cost* divided by output (the quantity of product produced).

average product (AP) The total output produced per unit of a *resource* employed (*total product* divided by the quantity of that employed resource).

average revenue Total revenue from the sale of a product divided by the quantity of the product sold (demanded); equal to the price at which the product is sold when all units of the product are sold at the same price.

average tax rate Total tax paid divided by total (taxable) income, as a percentage.

average total cost (ATC) A firm's *total cost* divided by output (the quantity of product produced); equal to *average fixed cost* plus *average variable cost*.

average variable cost (AVC) A firm's total *variable cost* divided by output (the quantity of product produced).

backflows The return of workers to the countries from which they originally migrated.

balance of payments (See *international balance of payments*.)

balance-of-payments deficit The amount by which *inpayments* from a nation's stock of *official reserves* are required to balance that nation's *capital and financial account* with its *current account* (in its *balance of payments*).

balance-of-payments surplus The amount by which *outpayments* to a nation's stock of *official reserves* are required to balance that nation's *capital and financial account* with its *current account* (in its *international balance of payments*).

balance on current account The exports of goods and services of a nation less its imports of goods and services plus its *net investment income* and *net transfers* in a year.

balance on goods and services The exports of goods and services of a nation less its imports of goods and services in a year.

barrier to entry Anything that artificially prevents the entry of firms into an industry.

barter The exchange of one good or service for another good or service.

benefit-reduction rate The percentage by which subsidy benefits in a *public assistance program* are reduced as earned income rises.

benefits-received principle The idea that those who receive the benefits of goods and services provided by government should pay the taxes required to finance them.

bilateral monopoly A market in which there is a single seller *(monopoly)* and a single buyer *(monopsony)*.

bond A financial device through which a borrower (a firm or government) is obligated to pay the principal and interest on a loan at a specific date in the future.

break-even income The level of *disposable income* at which *households* plan to consume (spend) all their income and to save none of it; also, in an income transfer program, the level of earned income at which subsidy payments become zero.

break-even output Any output at which a (competitive) firm's *total cost* and *total revenue* are equal; an output at which a firm has neither an *economic profit* nor a loss, at which it earns only a *normal profit*.

break-even point An output at which a firm makes a *normal profit* (*total revenue* = *total cost*) but not an *economic profit*.

Bretton Woods system The international monetary system developed after the Second World War in which *adjustable pegs* were employed, the *International Monetary Fund* helped stabilize foreign exchange rates, and gold and the dollar were used as *international monetary reserves*.

budget constraint The limit that the size of a consumer's income (and the prices that must be paid for goods and services) imposes on the ability of that consumer to obtain goods and services.

budget line A line that shows the different combinations of two products a consumer can purchase with a specific money income, given the products' prices.

business firm (See *firm*.)

business unionism Labor unionism that concerns itself with such practical and short-run objectives as higher wages, shorter hours, and improved working conditions.

capital Human-made resources (buildings, machinery, and equipment) used to produce goods and services; goods that do not directly satisfy human wants; also called capital goods.

capital and financial account The section of a nation's *international balance of payments* that records (1) debt forgiveness by and to foreigners and (2) foreign purchases of assets in the United States and U.S. purchases of assets abroad.

capital and financial account deficit A negative balance on its *capital and financial account* in a country's *international balance of payments*.

capital and financial account surplus A positive balance on its *capital and financial account* in a country's *international balance of payments*.

capital gain The gain realized when securities or properties are sold for a price greater than the price paid for them.

capital goods (See *capital*.)

capital-intensive commodity A product that requires a relatively large amount of *capital* to be produced.

capitalism An economic system in which property resources are privately owned and markets and prices are used to direct and coordinate economic activities.

capital stock The total available *capital* in a nation.

cartel A formal agreement among firms (or countries) in an industry to set the price of a product and establish the outputs of the individual firms (or countries) or to divide the market for the product geographically.

causation A relationship in which the occurrence of one or more events brings about another event.

cease-and-desist order An order from a court or government agency to a corporation or individual to stop engaging in a specified practice.

ceiling price (See *price ceiling*.)

Celler-Kefauver Act The Federal act of 1950 that amended the *Clayton Act* by prohibiting the acquisition of the assets of one firm by another firm when the effect would be less competition.

central economic planning Government determination of the objectives of the economy and how resources will be directed to attain those goals.

***ceteris paribus* assumption** (See *other-things-equal assumption*.)

change in demand A change in the *quantity demanded* of a good or service at every price; a shift of the *demand curve* to the left or right.

change in quantity demanded A change in the amount of a product that consumers are willing and able to purchase because of a change in the product's price.

change in quantity supplied A change in the amount of a product that producers offer for sale because of a change in the product's price.

change in supply A change in the *quantity supplied* of a good or service at every price; a shift of the *supply curve* to the left or right.

circular flow diagram An illustration showing the flow of resources from *households* to *firms* and of products from firms to households. These flows are accompanied by reverse flows of money from firms to households and from households to firms.

Civil Rights Act of 1964 Federal law that, in Title VII, outlaws *discrimination* based on race, color, religion, gender, or national origin in hiring, promoting, and compensating workers.

Clayton Act The Federal antitrust act of 1914 that strengthened the *Sherman Act* by making it illegal for firms to engage in certain specified practices.

closed economy An economy that neither exports nor imports goods and services.

closed shop A place of employment where only workers who are already members of a labor union may be hired.

Coase theorem The idea, first stated by economist Ronald Coase, that *externalities* can be resolved through private negotiations of the affected parties.

coincidence of wants A situation in which the good or service that one trader desires to obtain is the same as that which another trader desires to give up and an item that the second trader wishes to acquire is the same as that which the first trader desires to surrender.

COLA (See *cost-of-living adjustment.*)

collective bargaining The negotiation of labor contracts between *labor unions* and *firms* or government entities.

collective voice The function a *labor union* performs for its members as a group when it communicates their problems and grievances to management and presses management for a satisfactory resolution.

collusion A situation in which firms act together and in agreement (collude) to fix prices, divide a market, or otherwise restrict competition.

command system A method of organizing an economy in which property resources are publicly owned and government uses *central economic planning* to direct and coordinate economic activities; command economy; communism.

communism (See *command system.*)

comparative advantage A lower relative opportunity cost than that of another producer or country.

compensating differences Differences in the *wages* received by workers in different jobs to compensate for nonmonetary differences in the jobs.

compensation to employees *Wages* and salaries plus wage and salary supplements paid by employers to workers.

competition The presence in a market of independent buyers and sellers competing with one another along with the freedom of buyers and sellers to enter and leave the market.

competitive industry's short-run supply curve The horizontal summation of the short-run supply curves of the *firms* in a purely competitive industry (see *pure competition*); a curve that shows the total quantities offered for sale at various prices by the firms in an industry in the short run.

competitive labor market A resource market in which a large number of (noncolluding) employers demand a particular type of labor supplied by a large number of nonunion workers.

complementary goods Products and services that are used together. When the price of one falls, the demand for the other increases (and conversely).

concentration ratio The percentage of the total sales of an industry made by the four (or some other number) largest sellers in the industry.

conglomerate merger The merger of a *firm* in one *industry* with a firm in another industry (with a firm that is not a supplier, customer, or competitor).

conglomerates Firms that produce goods and services in two or more separate industries.

constant-cost industry An industry in which expansion by the entry of new firms has no effect on the prices firms in the industry must pay for resources and thus no effect on production costs.

constant opportunity cost An *opportunity cost* that remains the same for each additional unit as a consumer (or society) shifts purchases (production) from one product to another along a straight-line *budget line* (*production possibilities curve*).

constant returns to scale Unchanging *average total cost* of producing a product as the firm expands the size of its plant (its output) in the *long run.*

consumer goods Products and services that satisfy human wants directly.

consumer sovereignty Determination by consumers of the types and quantities of goods and services that will be produced with the scarce resources of the economy; consumers' direction of production through their dollar votes.

consumer surplus The difference between the maximum price a consumer is (or consumers are) willing to pay for an additional unit of a product and its market price; the triangular area below the demand curve and above the market price.

copayment The percentage of (say, health care) costs that an insured individual pays while the insurer pays the remainder.

copyright A legal protection provided to developers and publishers of books, computer software, videos, and musical compositions against the copying of their works by others.

corporate income tax A tax levied on the net income (accounting profit) of corporations.

corporation A legal entity ("person") chartered by a state or the Federal government that is distinct and separate from the individuals who own it.

correlation A systematic and dependable association between two sets of data (two kinds of events); does not necessarily indicate causation.

cost-benefit analysis A comparison of the *marginal costs* of a government project or program with the *marginal benefits* to decide whether or not to employ resources in that project or program and to what extent.

cost-of-living adjustment (COLA) An automatic increase in the incomes (wages) of workers when inflation occurs; guaranteed by a collective bargaining contract between firms and workers.

craft union A labor union that limits its membership to workers with a particular skill (craft).

creative destruction The hypothesis that the creation of new products and production methods simultaneously destroys the market power of existing monopolies.

credit An accounting item that increases the value of an asset (such as the foreign money owned by the residents of a nation).

cross elasticity of demand The ratio of the percentage change in *quantity demanded* of one good to the percentage change in the price of some other good. A positive coefficient indicates the two products are *substitute goods;* a negative coefficient indicates they are *complementary goods.*

crowding model of occupational discrimination A model of labor markets suggesting that *occupational discrimination* has kept many women and minorities out of high-paying occupations and forced them into a limited number of low-paying occupations.

currency appreciation (See *exchange-rate appreciation.*)

currency depreciation (See *exchange-rate depreciation.*)

currency intervention A government's buying and selling of its own currency or foreign currencies to alter international exchange rates.

current account The section in a nation's *international balance of payments* that records its exports and imports of goods and services, its net *investment income*, and its *net transfers*.

deadweight loss (See *efficiency loss.*)

debit An accounting item that decreases the value of an asset (such as the foreign money owned by the residents of a nation).

declining industry An industry in which *economic profits* are negative (losses are incurred) and that will, therefore, decrease its output as firms leave it.

decreasing-cost industry An industry in which expansion through the entry of firms lowers the prices that firms in the industry must pay for resources and therefore decreases their production costs.

deductible The dollar sum of (for example, health care) costs that an insured individual must pay before the insurer begins to pay.

defensive medicine The recommendation by physicians of more tests and procedures than are warranted medically or economically as a way of protecting themselves against later malpractice suits.

demand A schedule showing the amounts of a good or service that buyers (or a buyer) wish to purchase at various prices during some time period.

demand curve A curve illustrating *demand.*

demand schedule (See *demand.*)

dependent variable A variable that changes as a consequence of a change in some other (independent) variable; the "effect" or outcome.

depository institutions Firms that accept deposits of *money* from the public (businesses and persons); *commercial banks, savings and loan associations, mutual savings banks,* and *credit unions.*

depreciation (See *consumption of fixed capital.*)

depreciation (of the dollar) A decrease in the value of the dollar relative to another currency, so a dollar buys a smaller amount of the foreign currency and therefore of foreign goods.

derived demand The demand for a resource that depends on the demand for the products it helps to produce.

determinants of demand Factors other than price that determine the quantities demanded of a good or service.

determinants of supply Factors other than price that determine the quantities supplied of a good or service.

devaluation A decrease in the governmentally defined value of a currency.

developing countries Many countries of Africa, Asia, and Latin America that are characterized by lack of capital goods, use of nonadvanced technologies, low literacy rates, high unemployment, rapid population growth, and labor forces heavily committed to agriculture.

diagnosis-related group (DRG) system Payments to doctors and hospitals under *Medicare* based on which of hundreds of carefully detailed diagnostic categories best characterize the patient's condition and needs.

differentiated oligopoly An *oligopoly* in which the firms produce a *differentiated product.*

differentiated product A product that differs physically or in some other way from the similar products produced by other firms; a product such that buyers are not indifferent to the seller when the price charged by all sellers is the same.

diffusion The spread of an *innovation* through its widespread imitation.

dilemma of regulation The tradeoff faced by a *regulatory agency* in setting the maximum legal price a monopolist may charge: The *socially optimal price* is below *average total cost* (and either bankrupts the *firm* or requires that it be subsidized), while the higher, *fair-return price* does not produce *allocative efficiency.*

diminishing marginal returns (See *law of diminishing returns.*)

direct foreign investment The building of new factories (or the purchase of existing capital) in a particular nation by corporations of other nations.

direct payments Cash subsidies paid to farmers based on past production levels; unaffected by current crop prices and current production.

direct relationship The relationship between two variables that change in the same direction, for example, product price and quantity supplied; positive relationship.

discrimination The practice of according individuals or groups inferior treatment in hiring, occupational access, education and training, promotion, wage rates, or working conditions even though they have the same abilities, education, skills, and work experience as other workers.

discrimination coefficient A measure of the cost or disutility of prejudice; the monetary amount an employer is willing to pay to hire a preferred worker rather than a nonpreferred worker.

diseconomies of scale Increases in the *average total cost* of producing a product as the *firm* expands the size of its *plant* (its output) in the *long run.*

disposable income (DI) *Personal income* less personal taxes; income available for *personal consumption expenditures* and *personal saving.*

dividends Payments by a corporation of all or part of its profit to its stockholders (the corporate owners).

division of labor The separation of the work required to produce a product into a number of different tasks that are performed by different workers; *specialization* of workers.

Doha Round The latest, uncompleted (as of fall 2006) sequence of trade negotiations by members of the *World Trade Organization;*

named after Doha, Qatar, where the set of negotiations began.

dollar votes The "votes" that consumers and entrepreneurs cast for the production of consumer and capital goods, respectively, when they purchase those goods in product and resource markets.

domestic capital formation The process of adding to a nation's stock of *capital* by saving and investing part of its own domestic output.

domestic price The price of a good or service within a country, determined by domestic demand and supply.

dumping The sale of a product in a foreign country at prices either below cost or below the prices commonly charged at home.

DuPont cellophane case The antitrust case brought against DuPont in which the U.S. Supreme Court ruled (in 1956) that while DuPont had a monopoly in the narrowly defined market for cellophane, it did not monopolize the more broadly defined market for flexible packaging materials. It was thus not guilty of violating the *Sherman Act*.

durable good A consumer good with an expected life (use) of 3 or more years.

earned-income tax credit (EITC) A refundable Federal tax credit for low-income working people designed to reduce poverty and encourage labor-force participation.

earnings The money income received by a worker; equal to the *wage* (rate) multiplied by the amount of time worked.

economic concentration A description or measure of the degree to which an industry is dominated by one or a handful of firms or is characterized by many firms. (See *concentration ratio*.)

economic cost A payment that must be made to obtain and retain the services of a *resource;* the income a firm must provide to a resource supplier to attract the resource away from an alternative use; equal to the quantity of other products that cannot be produced when resources are instead used to make a particular product.

economic efficiency The use of the minimum necessary resources to obtain the socially optimal amounts of goods and services; entails both *productive efficiency* and *allocative efficiency*.

economic growth (1) An outward shift in the *production possibilities curve* that results from an increase in resource supplies or quality or an improvement in *technology;* (2) an increase of real output *(gross domestic product)* or real output per capita.

economic law An *economic principle* that has been tested and retested and has stood the test of time.

economic model A simplified picture of economic reality; an abstract generalization.

economic perspective A viewpoint that envisions individuals and institutions making rational decisions by comparing the marginal benefits and marginal costs associated with their actions.

economic policy A course of action intended to correct or avoid a problem.

economic principle A widely accepted generalization about the economic behavior of individuals or institutions.

economic profit The *total revenue* of a firm less its *economic costs* (which include both *explicit costs* and *implicit costs*); also called "pure profit" and "above-normal profit."

economic regulation (See *industrial regulation* and *social regulation*.)

economic rent The price paid for the use of land and other natural resources, the supply of which is fixed *(perfectly inelastic)*.

economic resources The *land*, *labor*, *capital*, and *entrepreneurial ability* that are used in the production of goods and services; productive agents; factors of production.

economics The social science concerned with how individuals, institutions, and society make optimal (best) choices under conditions of scarcity.

economic system A particular set of institutional arrangements and a coordinating mechanism for solving the economizing problem; a method of organizing an economy, of which the *market system* and the *command system* are the two general types.

economic theory A statement of a cause-effect relationship; when accepted by all or nearly all economists, an *economic principle*.

economies of scale Reductions in the *average total cost* of producing a product as the firm expands the size of plant (its output) in the *long run;* the economies of mass production.

economizing problem The choices necessitated because society's economic wants for goods and services are unlimited but the resources available to satisfy these wants are limited (scarce).

efficiency loss Reductions in combined consumer and producer surplus caused by an underallocation or overallocation of resources to the production of a good or service. Also called deadweight loss.

efficiency loss of a tax The loss of net benefits to society because a tax reduces the production and consumption of a taxed good below the level of allocative efficiency. Also called the deadweight loss of the tax.

efficiency wage A wage that minimizes wage costs per unit of output by encouraging greater effort or reducing turnover.

efficient allocation of resources That allocation of an economy's resources among the production of different products that leads to the maximum satisfaction of consumers' wants, thus producing the socially optimal mix of output with society's scarce resources.

elastic demand Product or resource demand whose *price elasticity* is greater than 1. This means the resulting change in *quantity demanded* is greater than the percentage change in *price*.

elasticity coefficient The number obtained when the percentage change in *quantity demanded* (or supplied) is divided by the percentage change in the *price* of the commodity.

elasticity formula (See *price elasticity of demand*.)

elasticity of resource demand A measure of the responsiveness of firms to a change in the price of a particular *resource* they employ or use; the percentage change in the quantity of the resource demanded divided by the percentage change in its price.

elastic supply Product or resource supply whose price elasticity is greater than 1. This means the resulting change in quantity supplied is greater than the percentage change in price.

employment discrimination Inferior treatment in hiring, promotions, work assignments, and such for a particular group of employees.

entitlement programs Government programs such as *social insurance, food stamps, Medicare,* and *Medicaid* that guarantee particular levels of transfer payments or noncash benefits to all who fit the programs' criteria.

entrepreneurial ability The human resource that combines the other resources to produce a product, makes nonroutine decisions, innovates, and bears risks.

equality-efficiency tradeoff The decrease in *economic efficiency* that may accompany a decrease in *income inequality;* the presumption that some income inequality is required to achieve economic efficiency.

Equal Pay Act of 1963 Federal government legislation making it illegal to pay men and women different wage rates if they do equal work on jobs that require equal skill, effort, and responsibility and that are performed under similar working conditions.

equilibrium position In the indifference curve model, the combination of two goods at which a consumer maximizes his or her *utility* (reaches the highest attainable *indifference curve*), given a limited amount to spend (a *budget constraint*).

equilibrium price The *price* in a competitive market at which the *quantity demanded* and the *attainable supplied* are equal, there is neither a shortage nor a surplus, and there is no tendency for price to rise or fall.

equilibrium quantity (1) The quantity demanded and supplied at the equilibrium price in a competitive market; (2) the profit-maximizing output of a firm.

euro The common currency unit used by 12 European nations (as of 2006) in the Euro zone, which consists of Austria, Belgium, Finland, France, Germany, Greece, Ireland, Italy, Luxembourg, the Netherlands, Portugal, and Spain.

European Union (EU) An association of 25 European nations that has eliminated tariffs and quotas among them, established common tariffs for imported goods from outside the member nations, eliminated barriers to the free movement of capital, and created other common economic policies.

excess capacity Plant resources that are underused when imperfectly competitive firms produce less output than that associated with achieving minimum average total cost.

exchange control (See *foreign exchange control.*)

exchange rate The *rate of exchange* of one nation's currency for another nation's currency.

exchange-rate appreciation An increase in the value of a nation's currency in foreign exchange markets; an increase in the *rate of exchange* for foreign currencies.

exchange-rate depreciation A decrease in the value of a nation's currency in foreign exchange markets; a decrease in the *rate of exchange* for foreign currencies.

exchange-rate determinant Any factor other than the *rate of exchange* that determines a currency's demand and supply in the *foreign exchange market.*

excise tax A tax levied on the production of a specific product or on the quantity of the product purchased.

exclusive unionism The practice of a *labor union* of restricting the supply of skilled union labor to increase the wages received by union members; the policies typically employed by a *craft union.*

exhaustive expenditure An expenditure by government resulting directly in the employment of *economic resources* and in the absorption by government of the goods and services those resources produce; a *government purchase.*

exit mechanism The process of leaving a job and searching for another one as a means of improving one's working conditions.

expanding industry An industry whose firms earn *economic profits* and for which an increase in output occurs as new firms enter the industry.

expectations The anticipations of consumers, firms, and others about future economic conditions.

expected rate of return The increase in profit a firm anticipates it will obtain by purchasing capital (or engaging in research and development); expressed as a percentage of the total cost of the investment (or R&D) activity.

expected-rate-of-return curve As it relates to research and development (*R&D*), a curve showing the anticipated gain in *profit,* as a percentage of R&D expenditure, from an additional dollar spent on R&D.

explicit cost The monetary payment a *firm* must make to an outsider to obtain a *resource.*

exports Goods and services produced in a nation and sold to buyers in other nations.

export subsidies Government payments to domestic producers to enable them to reduce the *price* of a good or service to foreign buyers.

export supply curve An upward-sloping curve that shows the amount of a product that domestic firms will export at each *world price* that is above the *domestic price.*

export transaction A sale of a good or service that increases the amount of foreign currency flowing to a nation's citizens, firms, and government.

external benefit (See *positive externality.*)

external cost (See *negative externality.*)

external debt Private or public debt owed to foreign citizens, firms, and institutions.

externality A cost or benefit from production or consumption, accruing without compensation to someone other than the buyers and sellers of the product (see *negative externality* and *positive externality*) .

external public debt The portion of the public debt owed to foreign citizens, firms, and institutions.

factors of production *Economic resources: land, capital, labor,* and *entrepreneurial ability.*

fair-return price The price of a product that enables its producer to obtain a *normal profit* and that is equal to the *average total cost* of producing it.

fallacy of composition The false notion that what is true for the individual (or part) is necessarily true for the group (or whole).

Farm Act of 2002 Farm legislation that continued the "freedom to plant" and direct subsidies of the *Freedom to Farm Act* of 1996 but added an automatic, countercyclical system of emergency farm aid.

farm commodities Agricultural products such as grains, milk, cattle, fruits, and vegetables that are usually sold to processors, who use the products as inputs in creating *food products.*

fast-second strategy An approach by a dominant firm in which it allows other firms in its industry to bear the risk of innovation and then quickly becomes the second firm to offer any successful new product or adopt any improved production process.

Federal government The government of the United States, as distinct from the state and local governments.

Federal Trade Commission (FTC) The commission of five members established by the *Federal Trade Commission Act* of 1914 to investigate unfair competitive practices of firms, to hold hearings on the complaints of such practices, and to issue *cease-and-desist orders* when firms were found to engage in such practices.

Federal Trade Commission Act The Federal act of 1914 that established the *Federal Trade Commission.*

fee for service In the health care industry, payment to physicians for each visit made or procedure performed rather than payment as an annual salary.

financial capital (See *money capital.*)

firm An organization that employs resources to produce a good or service for profit and owns and operates one or more *plants.*

fiscal policy Changes in government spending and tax collections designed to achieve a full-employment and noninflationary domestic output; also called *discretionary fiscal policy.*

fixed cost Any cost that in total does not change when the *firm* changes its output; the cost of *fixed resources.*

fixed exchange rate A *rate of exchange* that is set in some way and therefore prevented from rising or falling with changes in currency supply and demand.

fixed resource Any resource whose quantity cannot be changed by a firm in the *short run.*

flexible exchange rate A *rate of exchange* determined by the international demand for and supply of a nation's money; a rate free to rise or fall (to float).

floating exchange rate (See *flexible exchange rate.*)

food products Processed agricultural commodities sold through grocery stores and restaurants. Examples: bread, meat, fish, chicken, pork, lettuce, peanut butter, and breakfast cereal.

food-stamp program A program permitting low-income persons to purchase for less than their retail value, or to obtain without cost, coupons that can be exchanged for food items at retail stores.

foreign competition (See *import competition.*)

foreign exchange control The control a government may exercise over the quantity of foreign currency demanded by its citizens and firms and over the *rates of exchange* in order to limit its *outpayments* to its *inpayments* (to eliminate a *payments deficit*).

foreign exchange market A market in which the money (currency) of one nation can be used to purchase (can be exchanged for) the money of another nation; currency market.

foreign exchange rate (See *rate of exchange.*)

freedom of choice The freedom of owners of property resources to employ or dispose of them as they see fit, of workers to enter any line of work for which they are qualified, and of consumers to spend their incomes in a manner that they think is appropriate.

freedom of enterprise The freedom of *firms* to obtain economic resources, to use those resources to produce products of the firm's own choosing, and to sell their products in markets of their choice.

Freedom to Farm Act A law passed in 1996 that revamped 60 years of U.S. farm policy by ending *price supports* and *acreage allotments* for wheat, corn, barley, oats, sorghum, rye, cotton, and rice.

free-rider problem The inability of potential providers of an economically desirable good or service to obtain payment from those who benefit, because of *nonexcludability.*

free trade The absence of artificial (government-imposed) barriers to trade among individuals and firms in different nations.

fringe benefits The rewards other than *wages* that employees receive from their employers and that include pensions, medical and dental insurance, paid vacations, and sick leaves.

functional distribution of income The manner in which *national income* is divided among the functions performed to earn it (or the kinds of resources provided to earn it); the division of national income into wages and salaries, proprietors' income, corporate profits, interest, and rent.

gains from trade The extra output that trading partners obtain through specialization of production and exchange of goods and services.

game theory A means of analyzing the pricing behavior of oligopolists that uses the theory of strategy associated with games such as chess and bridge.

GDP (See *gross domestic product.*)

G8 nations A group of eight major nations (Canada, France, Germany, Italy, Japan, Russia, United Kingdom, and United States) whose leaders meet regularly to discuss common economic problems and try to coordinate economic policies.

General Agreement on Tariffs and Trade (GATT) The international agreement reached in 1947 in which 23 nations agreed to give equal and nondiscriminatory treatment to one another, to reduce tariff rates by multinational negotiations, and to eliminate *import quotas*. It now includes most nations and has become the *World Trade Organization*.

generalization Statement of the nature of the relationship between two or more sets of facts.

Gini ratio A numerical measure of the overall dispersion of income among households, families, or individuals; found graphically by dividing the area between the diagonal line and the *Lorenz curve* by the entire area below the diagonal line.

gold standard A historical system of fixed exchange rates in which nations defined their currencies in terms of gold, maintained a fixed relationship between their stocks of gold and their money supplies, and allowed gold to be freely exported and imported.

government failure Inefficiencies in resource allocation caused by problems in the operation of the public sector (government), specifically, rent-seeking pressure by special-interest groups, shortsighted political behavior, limited and bundled choices, and bureaucratic inefficiencies.

government purchases (*G*) Expenditures by government for goods and services that government consumes in providing public goods and for public (or social) capital that has a long lifetime; the expenditures of all governments in the economy for those *final goods and services*.

government transfer payment The disbursement of money (or goods and services) by government for which government receives no currently produced good or service in return.

grievance procedure The method used by a *labor union* and a *firm* to settle disputes that arise during the life of the collective bargaining agreement between them.

gross domestic product (GDP) The total market value of all *final goods and services* produced annually within the boundaries of the United States, whether by U.S.- or foreign-supplied resources.

guiding function of prices The ability of price changes to bring about changes in the quantities of products and resources demanded and supplied.

health maintenance organizations (HMOs) Health care providers that contract with employers, insurance companies, labor unions, or government units to provide health care for their workers or others who are insured.

health savings accounts (HSAs) Accounts into which people with high-deductible health insurance plans can place tax-free funds each year and then draw on these funds to pay out-of-pocket medical expenses such as *deductibles* and *copayments*. Unused funds accumulate from year to year and later can be used to supplement *Medicare*.

Herfindahl index A measure of the concentration and competitiveness of an industry; calculated as the sum of the squared percentage market shares of the individual firms in the industry.

homogeneous oligopoly An *oligopoly* in which the firms produce a *standardized product*.

horizontal axis The "left-right" or "west-east" measurement line on graph or grid.

horizontal merger The merger into a single *firm* of two firms producing the same product and selling it in the same geographic market.

household An economic unit (of one or more persons) that provides the economy with resources and uses the income received to purchase goods and services that satisfy economic wants.

human capital The knowledge and skills that make a person productive.

human capital discrimination The denial of equal access to productivity-enhancing education and training to members of particular groups.

human capital investment Any expenditure undertaken to improve the education, skills, health, or mobility of workers, with an expectation of greater productivity and thus a positive return on the investment.

hypothesis A tentative explanation of cause and effect that requires testing.

illegal immigrant (See *unauthorized immigrant*.)

IMF (See *International Monetary Fund*.)

imitation problem The potential for a firm's rivals to produce a close variation of (imitate) a firm's new product or process, greatly reducing the originator's profit from *R&D* and *innovation*.

immobility The inability or unwillingness of a worker to move from one geographic area or occupation to another or from a lower-paying job to a higher-paying job.

imperfect competition All market structures except *pure competition;* includes *monopoly*, *monopolistic competition*, and *oligopoly*.

implicit cost The monetary income a *firm* sacrifices when it uses a resource it owns rather than supplying the resource in the market; equal to what the resource could have earned in the best-paying alternative employment; includes a *normal profit*.

import competition The competition that domestic firms encounter from the products and services of foreign producers.

import demand curve A downsloping curve showing the amount of a product that an economy will import at each *world price* below the *domestic price*.

import quota A limit imposed by a nation on the quantity (or total value) of a good that may be imported during some period of time.

imports Spending by individuals, *firms*, and governments for goods and services produced in foreign nations.

import transaction The purchase of a good or service that decreases the amount of foreign money held by citizens, firms, and governments of a nation.

incentive function of price The inducement that an increase in the price of a commodity gives to sellers to make more of it available (and conversely for a decrease in price), and the inducement that an increase in price offers to buyers to purchase smaller quantities (and conversely for a decrease in price).

incentive pay plan A compensation structure that ties worker pay directly to performance. Such plans include piece rates, bonuses, *stock options*, commissions, and *profit sharing*.

inclusive unionism The practice of a labor union of including as members all workers employed in an industry.

income A flow of dollars (or purchasing power) per unit of time derived from the use of human or property resources.

income effect A change in the quantity demanded of a product that results from the change in *real income (purchasing power)* caused by a change in the product's price.

income elasticity of demand The ratio of the percentage change in the *quantity demanded* of a good to a percentage change in consumer income; measures the responsiveness of consumer purchases to income changes.

income inequality The unequal distribution of an economy's total income among households or families.

income-maintenance system A group of government programs designed to eliminate poverty and reduce inequality in the distribution of income.

income mobility The extent to which income receivers move from one part of the income distribution to another over some period of time.

increase in demand An increase in the *quantity demanded* of a good or service at every price; a shift of the *demand curve* to the right.

increase in supply An increase in the *quantity supplied* of a good or service at every price; a shift of the *supply curve* to the right.

increasing-cost industry An *industry* in which expansion through the entry of new firms raises the prices *firms* in the industry must pay for resources and therefore increases their production costs.

increasing marginal returns An increase in the *marginal product* of a resource as successive units of the resource are employed.

increasing returns An increase in a firm's output by a larger percentage than the percentage increase in its inputs.

independent goods Products or services for which there is little or no relationship between the price of one and the demand for the other. When the price of one rises or falls, the demand for the other tends to remain constant.

independent unions U.S. unions that are not affiliated with the *AFL-CIO*.

independent variable The variable causing a change in some other (dependent) variable.

indifference curve A curve showing the different combinations of two products that yield the same satisfaction or *utility* to a consumer.

indifference map A set of *indifference curves*, each representing a different level of *utility*, that together show the preferences of a consumer.

individual demand The demand schedule or *demand curve* of a single buyer.

individual supply The supply schedule or *supply curve* of a single seller.

industrially advanced countries High-income countries such as the United States, Canada, Japan, and the nations of western Europe that have highly developed *market economies* based on large stocks of technologically advanced capital goods and skilled labor forces.

industrial regulation The older and more traditional type of regulation in which government is concerned with the prices charged and the services provided to the public in specific industries, in contrast to *social regulation*.

industrial union A *labor union* that accepts as members all workers employed in a particular industry (or by a particular firm).

industry A group of (one or more) *firms* that produce identical or similar products.

inelastic demand Product or resource demand for which the *elasticity coefficient* for price is less than 1. This means the resulting percentage change in *quantity demanded* is less than the percentage change in *price*.

inelastic supply Product or resource supply for which the price elasticity coefficient is less than 1. The percentage change in *quantity supplied* is less than the percentage change in *price*.

inferior good A good or service whose consumption declines as income rises (and conversely), price remaining constant.

inflation A rise in the general level of prices in an economy.

information technology New and more efficient methods of delivering and receiving information through use of computers, fax machines, wireless phones, and the Internet.

infrastructure The capital goods usually provided by the *public sector* for the use of its citizens and firms (for example, highways, bridges, transit systems, wastewater treatment facilities, municipal water systems, and airports).

injunction A court order directing a person or organization not to perform a certain act because the act would do irreparable damage to some other person or persons; a restraining order.

in-kind transfer The distribution by government of goods and services to individuals for which the government receives no currently produced good or service in return; a *government transfer payment* made in goods or services rather than in money; also called a noncash transfer.

innovation The first commercially successful introduction of a new product, the use of a new method of production, or the creation of a new form of business organization.

insurable risk An event that would result in a loss but whose frequency of occurrence can be estimated with considerable accuracy. Insurance companies are willing to sell insurance against such losses.

interest The payment made for the use of money (of borrowed funds).

interest income Payments of income to those who supply the economy with *capital.*

interest rate The annual rate at which interest is paid; a percentage of the borrowed amount.

interest-rate-cost-of-funds curve As it relates to research and development (*R&D*), a curve showing the *interest rate* the firm must pay to obtain any particular amount of funds to finance R&D.

interindustry competition The competition for sales between the products of one industry and the products of another industry.

interlocking directorate A situation where one or more members of the board of directors of a *corporation* are also on the board of directors of a competing corporation; illegal under the *Clayton Act.*

international balance of payments A summary of all the transactions that took place between the individuals, firms, and government units of one nation and those of all other nations during a year.

international balance-of-payments deficit (See *balance-of-payments deficit.*)

international balance-of-payments surplus (See *balance-of-payments surplus.*)

international gold standard (See *gold standard.*)

International Monetary Fund (IMF) The international association of nations that was formed after the Second World War to make loans of foreign monies to nations with temporary *payments deficits* and, until the early 1970s, to administer the *adjustable pegs.* It now mainly makes loans to nations facing possible defaults on private and government loans.

international monetary reserves The foreign currencies and other assets such as gold that a nation can use to settle a *balance-of-payments deficit.*

international value of the dollar The price that must be paid in foreign currency (money) to obtain one U.S. dollar.

invention The first discovery of a product or process through the use of imagination, ingenious thinking, and experimentation and the first proof that it will work.

inverse relationship The relationship between two variables that change in opposite directions, for example, product price and quantity demanded; negative relationship.

inverted-U theory A theory saying that, other things equal, *R&D* expenditures as a percentage of sales rise with industry concentration, reach a peak at a four-firm *concentration ratio* of about 50 percent, and then fall as concentration further increases.

investment Spending for the production and accumulation of *capital* and additions to inventories.

investment goods Same as *capital* or capital goods.

investment in human capital (See *human capital investment.*)

"invisible hand" The tendency of firms and resource suppliers that seek to further their own self-interests in competitive markets to also promote the interest of society.

kinked-demand curve The demand curve for a noncollusive oligopolist, which is based on the assumption that rivals will match a price decrease and will ignore a price increase.

labor People's physical and mental talents and efforts that are used to help produce goods and services.

labor force Persons 16 years of age and older who are not in institutions and who are employed or are unemployed and seeking work.

labor-force participation rate The percentage of the working-age population that is actually in the *labor force.*

labor-intensive commodity A product requiring a relatively large amount of *labor* to be produced.

labor market discrimination (See *discrimination.*)

labor productivity Total output divided by the quantity of labor employed to produce it; the *average product* of labor or output per hour of work.

labor union A group of workers organized to advance the interests of the group (to increase wages, shorten the hours worked, improve working conditions, and so on).

laissez-faire capitalism (See *capitalism.*)

land Natural resources ("free gifts of nature") used to produce goods and services.

land-intensive commodity A product requiring a relatively large amount of *land* to be produced.

law of demand The principle that, other things equal, an increase in a product's price will reduce the quantity of it demanded, and conversely for a decrease in price.

law of diminishing marginal utility The principle that as a consumer increases the consumption of a good or service, the *marginal utility* obtained from each additional unit of the good or service decreases.

law of diminishing returns The principle that as successive increments of a variable resource are added to a fixed resource, the *marginal product* of the variable resource will eventually decrease.

law of increasing opportunity costs The principle that as the production of a good increases, the *opportunity cost* of producing an additional unit rises.

law of supply The principle that, other things equal, an increase in the price of a product will increase the quantity of it supplied, and conversely for a price decrease.

learning by doing Achieving greater *productivity* and lower *average total cost* through gains in knowledge and skill that accompany repetition of a task; a source of *economies of scale.*

least-cost combination of resources The quantity of each resource a firm must employ in order to produce a particular output at the lowest total cost; the combination at which the ratio of the *marginal product* of a resource to its *marginal resource cost* (to its *price* if the resource is employed in a competitive market) is the same for the last dollar spent on each of the resources employed.

legal cartel theory of regulation The hypothesis that some industries seek regulation or want to maintain regulation so that they may form or maintain a legal *cartel.*

legal immigrant A person who lawfully enters a country for the purpose of residing there.

liability A debt with a monetary value; an amount owed by a firm or an individual.

limited liability Restriction of the maximum loss to a predetermined amount for the owners (stockholders) of a *corporation.* The maximum loss is the amount they paid for their shares of stock.

loanable funds *Money* available for lending and borrowing.

loanable funds theory of interest The concept that the supply of and demand for *loanable funds* determine the equilibrium rate of interest.

lockout An action by a firm that forbids workers to return to work until a new collective bargaining contract is signed; a means of imposing costs (lost wages) on union workers in a collective bargaining dispute.

logrolling The trading of votes by legislators to secure favorable outcomes on decisions concerning the provision of *public goods* and *quasi-public goods.*

long run (1) In *microeconomics,* a period of time long enough to enable producers of a product to change the quantities of all the resources they employ; period in which all resources and costs are variable and no resources or costs are fixed. (2) In *macroeconomics,* a period sufficiently long for *nominal wages* and other input prices to change in response to a change in the nation's *price level.*

long-run aggregate supply curve The aggregate supply curve associated with a time period in which input prices (especially *nominal wages*) are fully responsive to changes in the *price level.*

long-run competitive equilibrium The price at which firms in *pure competition* neither obtain *economic profit* nor suffer losses in the *long run* and the total quantity demanded and supplied are equal; a price equal to the *marginal cost* and the minimum long-run *average total cost* of producing the product.

long-run supply A schedule or curve showing the prices at which a purely competitive industry will make various quantities of the product available in the *long run.*

Lorenz curve A curve showing the distribution of income in an economy. The cumulated percentage of families (income receivers) is measured along the horizontal axis and cumulated percentage of income is measured along the vertical axis.

macroeconomics The part of economics concerned with the economy as a whole; with such major aggregates as the household, business, and government sectors; and with measures of the total economy.

managed floating exchange rate An *exchange rate* that is allowed to change (float) as a result of changes in currency supply and demand but at times is altered (managed) by governments via their buying and selling of particular currencies.

managerial-opposition hypothesis An explanation that attributes the relative decline of unionism in the United States to the increased and more aggressive opposition of management to unions.

managerial prerogatives The decisions that management of the firm has the sole right to make; often enumerated in the labor contract (work agreement) between a *labor union* and a *firm.*

marginal analysis The comparison of marginal ("extra" or "additional") benefits and marginal costs, usually for decision making.

marginal benefit The extra (additional) benefit of consuming 1 more unit of some good or service; the change in total benefit when 1 more unit is consumed.

marginal cost (MC) The extra (additional) cost of producing 1 more unit of output; equal to the change in *total cost* divided by the change in output (and, in the short run, to the change in total *variable cost* divided by the change in output).

marginal cost-marginal benefit rule As it applies to *cost-benefit analysis,* the tenet that a government project or program should be expanded to the point where the *marginal cost* and *marginal benefit* of additional expenditures are equal.

marginal product (MP) The additional output produced when 1 additional unit of a resource is employed (the quantity of all other resources employed remaining constant); equal to the change in total product divided by the change in the quantity of a resource employed.

marginal productivity theory of income distribution The contention that the distribution of income is equitable when each unit of each resource receives a money payment equal to its marginal contribution to the firm's revenue (its *marginal revenue product*).

marginal rate of substitution (MRS) The rate at which a consumer is willing to substitute one good for another (from a given combination of goods) and remain equally satisfied (have the same *total utility*); equal to the slope of a consumer's *indifference curve* at each point on the curve.

marginal resource cost (MRC) The amount the total cost of employing a *resource* increases when a firm employs 1 additional unit of the resource (the quantity of all other resources employed remaining constant); equal to the change in the *total cost* of the resource divided by the change in the quantity of the resource employed.

marginal revenue The change in *total revenue* that results from the sale of 1 additional unit of a firm's product; equal to the change in total revenue divided by the change in the quantity of the product sold.

marginal-revenue–marginal-cost approach A method of determining the total output where *economic profit* is a maximum (or losses are a minimum) by comparing the *marginal revenue* and the *marginal cost* of each additional unit of output.

marginal revenue product (MRP) The change in a firm's *total revenue* when it employs 1 additional unit of a resource (the quantity of all other resources employed remaining constant);

equal to the change in total revenue divided by the change in the quantity of the resource employed.

marginal tax rate The tax rate paid on each additional dollar of income.

marginal utility The extra *utility* a consumer obtains from the consumption of 1 additional unit of a good or service; equal to the change in total utility divided by the change in the quantity consumed.

market Any institution or mechanism that brings together buyers (demanders) and sellers (suppliers) of a particular good or service.

market demand (See *total demand*.)

market economy An economy in which the private decisions of consumers, resource suppliers, and firms determine how resources are allocated; the *market system*.

market failure The inability of a market to bring about the allocation of resources that best satisfies the wants of society; in particular, the overallocation or underallocation of resources to the production of a particular good or service because of *externalities* or informational problems or because markets do not provide desired *public goods*.

market for externality rights A market in which firms can buy rights to discharge pollutants. The price of such rights is determined by the demand for the right to discharge pollutants and a *perfectly inelastic supply* of such rights (the latter determined by the quantity of discharges that the environment can assimilate).

market period A period in which producers of a product are unable to change the quantity produced in response to a change in its price and in which there is a *perfectly inelastic supply*.

market system All the product and resource markets of a *market economy* and the relationships among them; a method that allows the prices determined in those markets to allocate the economy's scarce resources and to communicate and coordinate the decisions made by consumers, firms, and resource suppliers.

marketing loan program A Federal farm subsidy under which certain farmers can receive a loan (on a per-unit-of-output basis) from a government lender and then, depending on the price of the crop, either pay back the loan with interest or keep the loan proceeds while forfeiting their harvested crop to the lender.

median-voter model The theory that under majority rule the median (middle) voter will be in the dominant position to determine the outcome of an election.

Medicaid A Federal program that helps finance the medical expenses of individuals covered by the *Supplemental Security Income (SSI)* and *Temporary Assistance for Needy Families (TANF)* programs.

Medicare A Federal program that is financed by *payroll taxes* and provides for (1) compulsory hospital insurance for senior citizens, (2) low-cost voluntary insurance to help older Americans pay physicians' fees, and (3) subsidized insurance to buy prescription drugs.

Medicare Part D The newly enacted (2006) portion of Medicare that enables enrollees to shop among private health insurance companies to buy highly subsidized insurance to help reduce the out-of-pocket expense of prescription drugs.

medium of exchange Any item sellers generally accept and buyers generally use to pay for a good or service; *money;* a convenient means of exchanging goods and services without engaging in *barter*.

merger The combination of two (or more) firms into a single firm.

microeconomics The part of economics concerned with decision making by individual units such as a *household*, a *firm*, or an *industry* and with individual markets, specific goods and services, and product and resource prices.

Microsoft case A 2002 antitrust case in which Microsoft was found guilty of violating the *Sherman Act* by engaging in a series of unlawful activities designed to maintain its monopoly in operating systems for personal computers; as a remedy the company was prohibited from engaging in a set of specific anticompetitive business practices.

midpoint formula A method for calculating *price elasticity of demand* or *price elasticity of supply* that averages the two prices and two quantities as the reference points for computing percentages.

minimum efficient scale (MES) The lowest level of output at which a firm can minimize long-run *average total cost*.

minimum wage The lowest *wage* that employers may legally pay for an hour of work.

monetary policy A central bank's changing of the *money supply* to influence interest rates and assist the economy in achieving price stability, full employment, and economic growth.

money Any item that is generally acceptable to sellers in exchange for goods and services.

money capital Money available to purchase *capital;* simply *money*, as defined by economists.

money income (See *nominal income*.)

monopolistic competition A market structure in which many firms sell a *differentiated product*, into which entry is relatively easy, in which the firm has some control over its product price, and in which there is considerable *nonprice competition*.

monopoly A market structure in which the number of sellers is so small that each seller is able to influence the total supply and the price of the good or service. (Also see *pure monopoly*.)

monopsony A market structure in which there is only a single buyer of a good, service, or resource.

moral hazard problem The possibility that individuals or institutions will change their behavior as the result of a contract or agreement. Example: A bank whose deposits are insured against loss may make riskier loans and investments.

most-favored-nation (MFN) status An agreement by the United States to allow some other nation's *exports* into the United States at the lowest tariff level levied by the United States, then or at any later time.

MR = MC rule The principle that a firm will maximize its profit (or minimize its losses) by producing the output at which *marginal revenue* and *marginal cost* are equal, provided product price is equal to or greater than *average variable cost*.

MRP = MRC rule The principle that to maximize profit (or minimize losses), a firm should employ the quantity of a resource at which its *marginal revenue product* (MRP) is equal to its *marginal resource cost* (MRC), the latter being the wage rate in pure competition.

multinational corporations Firms that own production facilities in two or more countries and produce and sell their products globally.

mutual interdependence A situation in which a change in price strategy (or in some other strategy) by one firm will affect the sales and profits of another firm (or other firms). Any firm that makes such a change can expect the other rivals to react to the change.

national health insurance (NHI) A proposed program in which the Federal government would provide a basic package of health care to all citizens at no direct charge or at a low cost-sharing level. Financing would be out of general tax revenues.

National Labor Relations Act (Wagner Act of 1935) As amended, the basic labor-relations law in the United States; defines the legal rights of unions and management and identifies unfair union and management labor practices; established the *National Labor Relations Board*.

National Labor Relations Board (NLRB) The board established by the *National Labor Relations Act* of 1935 to investigate unfair labor practices, issue *cease-and-desist orders*, and conduct elections among employees to determine if they wish to be represented by a *labor union*.

natural monopoly An industry in which *economies of scale* are so great that a single firm can produce the product at a lower average total cost than would be possible if more than one firm produced the product.

negative externality A cost imposed without compensation on third parties by the production or consumption of sellers or buyers. Example: A manufacturer dumps toxic chemicals into a river, killing the fish sought by sports fishers; an external cost or a spillover cost.

negative relationship (See *inverse relationship*.)

net exports (X_n) *Exports* minus *imports*.

net foreign factor income Receipts of resource income from the rest of the world minus payments of resource income to the rest of the world.

net investment income The interest and dividend income received by the residents of a nation from residents of other nations less the interest and dividend payments made by the residents of that nation to the residents of other nations.

net transfers The personal and government transfer payments made by one nation to residents of foreign nations less the personal and government transfer payments received from residents of foreign nations.

network effects Increases in the value of a product to each user, including existing users, as the total number of users rises.

net worth The total *assets* less the total *liabilities* of a firm or an individual; for a firm, the claims of the owners against the firm's total assets; for an individual, his or her wealth.

New Economy The label attached by some economists and the popular press to the U.S. economy since 1995. The main characteristics are accelerated *productivity growth* and *economic growth*, caused by rapid technological advance and the emergence of the global economy.

NLRB (See *National Labor Relations Board*.)

nominal wage The amount of money received by a worker per unit of time (hour, day, etc.); money wage.

noncash transfer A *government transfer payment* in the form of goods and services rather than money, for example, food stamps, housing assistance, and job training; also called in-kind transfers.

noncollusive oligopoly An *oligopoly* in which the firms do not act together and in agreement to determine the price of the product and the output that each firm will produce.

noncompeting groups Collections of workers in the economy who do not compete with each other for employment because the skill and training of the workers in one group are substantially different from those of the workers in other groups.

nondurable good A *consumer good* with an expected life (use) of less than 3 years.

nonexcludability The inability to keep nonpayers (free riders) from obtaining benefits from a certain good; a *public good* characteristic.

nonexhaustive expenditure An expenditure by government that does not result directly in the employment of economic resources or the production of goods and services; see *government transfer payment*.

nonprice competition Competition based on distinguishing one's product by means of *product differentiation* and then *advertising* the distinguished product to consumers.

nonrivalry The idea that one person's benefit from a certain good does not reduce the benefit available to others; a *public good* characteristic.

nontariff barriers (NTBs) All barriers other than *protective tariffs* that nations erect to impede international trade, including *import quotas*, licensing requirements, unreasonable product-quality standards, unnecessary bureaucratic detail in customs procedures, and so on.

normal good A good or service whose consumption increases when income increases and falls when income decreases, price remaining constant.

normal profit The payment made by a firm to obtain and retain *entrepreneurial ability;* the minimum income entrepreneurial ability must receive to induce it to perform entrepreneurial functions for a firm.

normative economics The part of economics involving value judgments about what the economy should be like; focused on which economic goals and policies should be implemented; policy economics.

North American Free Trade Agreement (NAFTA) A 1993 agreement establishing, over a 15-year period, a free-trade zone composed of Canada, Mexico, and the United States.

occupation A category of activities or tasks performed by a set of workers for pay, independent of employer or industry. Examples are managers, nurses, farmers, and cooks.

occupational discrimination The arbitrary restriction of particular groups from entering the more desirable, higher-paying occupations.

occupational licensure The laws of state or local governments that require that a worker satisfy certain specified requirements and obtain a license from a licensing board before engaging in a particular occupation.

occupational segregation The crowding of women or minorities into less desirable, lower-paying occupations.

official reserves Foreign currencies owned by the central bank of a nation.

offshoring The practice of shifting work previously done by American workers to workers located abroad.

oligopoly A market structure in which a few firms sell either a *standardized* or *differentiated product,* into which entry is difficult, in which the firm has limited control over product price because of *mutual interdependence* (except when there is collusion among firms), and in which there is typically *nonprice competition.*

OPEC (See *Organization of Petroleum Exporting Countries.*)

open economy An economy that exports and imports goods and services.

open-market operations The buying and selling of U.S. government securities by the *Federal Reserve Banks* for purposes of carrying out *monetary policy.*

open shop A place of employment in which the employer may hire nonunion workers and the workers need not become members of a *labor union.*

opportunity cost The amount of other products that must be forgone or sacrificed to produce a unit of a product.

opportunity-cost ratio An equivalency showing the number of units of two products that can be produced with the same resources; the cost 1 corn ≡ 3 olives show that the resources required to produce 3 units of olives must be shifted to corn production to produce 1 unit of corn.

optimal amount of R&D The level of *R&D* at which the *marginal benefit* and *marginal cost* of R&D expenditures are equal.

optimal reduction of an externality The reduction of a *negative externality* such as pollution to the level at which the *marginal benefit* and *marginal cost* of reduction are equal.

Organization of Petroleum Exporting Countries (OPEC) A cartel of 11 oil-producing countries (Algeria, Indonesia, Iran, Iraq, Kuwait, Libya, Nigeria, Qatar, Saudi Arabia, Venezuela, and the UAE) that controls the quantity and price of crude oil exported by its members and that accounts for a large percentage of the world's export of oil.

other-things-equal assumption The assumption that factors other than those being considered are held constant; *ceteris paribus* assumption.

outpayments The expenditures of domestic or foreign currency that the individuals, firms, and governments of one nation make to purchase goods and services, for remittances, to pay investment income, and for purchases of foreign assets.

output effect The situation in which an increase in the price of one input will increase a firm's production costs and reduce its level of output, thus reducing the demand for other inputs; conversely for a decrease in the price of the input.

paradox of voting A situation where paired-choice voting by majority rule fails to provide a consistent ranking of society's preferences for *public goods* or services.

parity concept The idea that year after year a specific output of a farm product should enable a farmer to acquire a constant amount of nonagricultural goods and services.

parity ratio The ratio of the price received by farmers from the sale of an agricultural commodity to the prices of other goods paid by them; usually expressed as a percentage; used as a rationale for *price supports.*

partnership An unincorporated firm owned and operated by two or more persons.

patent An exclusive right given to inventors to produce and sell a new product or machine for 20 years from the time of patent application.

payments deficit (See *balance-of-payments deficit.*)

payments surplus (See *balance-of-payments surplus.*)

payroll tax A tax levied on employers of labor equal to a percentage of all or part of the wages and salaries paid by them and on employees equal to a percentage of all or part of the wages and salaries received by them.

P = MC rule The principle that a purely competitive firm will maximize its profit or minimize its loss by producing that output at which the *price* of the product is equal to *marginal cost,* provided that price is equal to or greater than *average variable cost* in the short run and equal to or greater than *average total cost* in the long run.

per capita GDP *Gross domestic product* (GDP) per person; the average GDP of a population.

per capita income A nation's total income per person; the average income of a population.

perfectly elastic demand Product or resource demand in which *quantity demanded* can be of any amount at a particular product *price;* graphs as a horizontal *demand curve.*

perfectly elastic supply Product or resource supply in which *quantity supplied* can be of any amount at a particular product or resource *price;* graphs as a horizontal *supply curve.*

perfectly inelastic demand Product or resource demand in which *price* can be of any amount at a particular quantity of the product or resource demanded; *quantity demanded* does not respond to a change in price; graphs as a vertical *demand curve.*

perfectly inelastic supply Product or resource supply in which *price* can be of any amount at a particular quantity of the product or resource demanded; *quantity supplied* does not respond to a change in price; graphs as a vertical *supply curve*.

per se violations Collusive actions, such as attempts by firms to fix prices or divide a market, that are violations of the *antitrust laws*, even if the actions themselves are unsuccessful.

personal consumption expenditures The expenditures of *households* for *durable* and *nondurable consumer goods* and *services*.

personal distribution of income The manner in which the economy's *personal* or *disposable income* is divided among different income classes or different households or families.

personal income (PI) The earned and unearned income available to resource suppliers and others before the payment of personal taxes.

personal income tax A tax levied on the taxable income of individuals, households, and unincorporated firms.

Personal Responsibility Act A 1996 law that eliminated the Federal government's six-decade-long guarantee of cash assistance for poor families, whether adults in the family work or not; sets a limit of 5 years on receiving *Temporary Assistance for Needy Families (TANF)* benefits and requires that able-bodied adults work after 2 years to continue to receive public assistance.

personal saving The *personal income* of households less personal taxes and *personal consumption expenditures; disposable income* not spent for *consumer goods*.

per-unit production cost The average production cost of a particular level of output; total input cost divided by units of output.

plant A physical establishment that performs one or more functions in the production, fabrication, and distribution of goods and services.

"play or pay" A means of expanding health insurance coverage by requiring that employers either provide insurance for their workers or pay a special *payroll tax* to finance insurance for noncovered workers.

policy economics The formulation of courses of action to bring about desired economic outcomes or to prevent undesired occurrences.

positive economics The analysis of facts or data to establish scientific generalizations about economic behavior.

positive externality A benefit obtained without compensation by third parties from the production or consumption of sellers or buyers. Example: A beekeeper benefits when a neighboring farmer plants clover. An *external benefit* or a spillover benefit.

positive relationship (See *direct relationship*.)

***post hoc, ergo propter hoc* fallacy** The false belief that when one event precedes another, the first event must have caused the second event.

potential competition The new competitors that may be induced to enter an industry if firms now in that industry are receiving large *economic profits*.

poverty A situation in which the basic needs of an individual or family exceed the means to satisfy them.

poverty rate The percentage of the population with incomes below the official poverty income levels that are established by the Federal government.

preferred provider organization (PPO) An arrangement in which doctors and hospitals agree to provide health care to insured individuals at rates negotiated with an insurer.

price The amount of money needed to buy a particular good, service, or resource.

price ceiling A legally established maximum price for a good or service.

price discrimination The selling of a product to different buyers at different prices when the price differences are not justified by differences in cost.

price elasticity of demand The ratio of the percentage change in *quantity demanded* of a product or resource to the percentage change in its *price;* a measure of the responsiveness of buyers to a change in the price of a product or resource.

price elasticity of supply The ratio of the percentage change in *quantity supplied* of a product or resource to the percentage change in its *price;* a measure of the responsiveness of producers to a change in the price of a product or resource.

price fixing The conspiring by two or more firms to set the price of their products; an illegal practice under the *Sherman Act*.

price floor A legally determined minimum price above the *equilibrium price*.

price leadership An informal method that firms in an *oligopoly* may employ to set the price of their product: One firm (the leader) is the first to announce a change in price, and the other firms (the followers) soon announce identical or similar changes.

price-level stability A steadiness of the price level from one period to the next; zero or low annual inflation; also called "price stability."

price maker A seller (or buyer) of a product or resource that is able to affect the product or resource price by changing the amount it sells (or buys).

price support A minimum price that government allows sellers to receive for a good or service; a legally established or maintained minimum price.

price taker A seller (or buyer) of a product or resource that is unable to affect the price at which a product or resource sells by changing the amount it sells (or buys).

price war Successive and continued decreases in the prices charged by firms in an oligopolistic industry. Each firm lowers its price below rivals' prices, hoping to increase its sales and revenues at its rivals' expense.

principal-agent problem A conflict of interest that occurs when agents (workers or managers) pursue their own objectives to the detriment of the principals' (stockholders') goals.

private good A good or service that is individually consumed and that can be profitably provided by privately owned firms because they can exclude nonpayers from receiving the benefits.

private property The right of private persons and firms to obtain, own, control, employ, dispose of, and bequeath *land, capital,* and other property.

private sector The *households* and business *firms* of the economy.

process innovation The development and use of new or improved production or distribution methods.

producer surplus The difference between the actual price a producer receives (or producers receive) and the minimum acceptable price; the triangular area above the supply curve and below the market price.

product differentiation A strategy in which one firm's product is distinguished from competing products by means of its design, related services, quality, location, or other attributes (except price).

product innovation The development and sale of a new or improved product (or service).

production possibilities curve A curve showing the different combinations of two goods or services that can be produced in a *full-employment, full-production* economy where the available supplies of resources and technology are fixed.

productive efficiency The production of a good in the least costly way; occurs when production takes place at the output at which *average total cost* is a minimum and *marginal product* per dollar's worth of input is the same for all inputs.

productivity A measure of average output or real output per unit of input. For example, the productivity of labor is determined by dividing real output by hours of work.

productivity growth The percentage increase in *productivity* from one period to another.

product market A market in which products are sold by *firms* and bought by *households.*

profit The return to the resource *entrepreneurial ability* (see *normal profit*); *total revenue* minus *total cost* (see *economic profit*).

profit-maximizing combination of resources The quantity of each resource a firm must employ to maximize its profit or minimize its loss; the combination in which the *marginal revenue product* of each resource is equal to its *marginal resource cost* (to its *price* if the resource is employed in a competitive market).

profit-sharing plan A compensation device through which workers receive part of their pay in the form of a share of their employer's profit (if any).

progressive tax A tax whose *average tax rate* increases as the taxpayer's income increases and decreases as the taxpayer's income decreases.

property tax A tax on the value of property (*capital, land, stocks* and *bonds,* and other *assets*) owned by *firms* and *households.*

proportional tax A tax whose *average tax rate* remains constant as the taxpayer's income increases or decreases.

proprietor's income The net income of the owners of unincorporated firms (proprietorships and partnerships).

protective tariff A *tariff* designed to shield domestic producers of a good or service from the competition of foreign producers.

public assistance programs Government programs that pay benefits to those who are unable to earn income (because of permanent disabilities or because they have very low income and dependent children); financed by general tax revenues and viewed as public charity (rather than earned rights).

public choice theory The economic analysis of government decision making, politics, and elections.

public good A good or service that is characterized by *nonrivalry* and *nonexcludability;* a good or service with these characteristics provided by government.

public interest theory of regulation The presumption that the purpose of the regulation of an *industry* is to protect the public (consumers) from abuse of the power possessed by *natural monopolies.*

public sector The part of the economy that contains all government entities; government.

public utility A firm that produces an essential good or service, has obtained from a government the right to be the sole supplier of the good or service in the area, and is regulated by that government to prevent the abuse of its monopoly power.

purchasing power The amount of goods and services that a monetary unit of income can buy.

purchasing power parity The idea that exchange rates between nations equate the purchasing power of various currencies. Exchange rates between any two nations adjust to reflect the price-level differences between the countries.

pure competition A market structure in which a very large number of firms sells a *standardized product,* into which entry is very easy, in which the individual seller has no control over the product price, and in which there is no nonprice competition; a market characterized by a very large number of buyers and sellers.

purely competitive labor market A *resource market* in which many firms compete with one another in hiring a specific kind of labor, numerous equally qualified workers supply that labor, and no one controls the market wage rate.

pure monopoly A market structure in which one firm sells a unique product, into which entry is blocked, in which the single firm has considerable control over product price, and in which *nonprice competition* may or may not be found.

pure profit (See *economic profit.*)

pure rate of interest An essentially risk-free, long-term interest rate that is free of the influence of market imperfections.

quantity demanded The amount of a good or service that buyers (or a buyer) desire to purchase at a particular price during some period.

quantity supplied The amount of a good or service that producers (or a producer) offer to sell at a particular price during some period.

quasi-public good A good or service to which excludability could apply but that has such a large *positive externality* that government sponsors its production to prevent an underallocation of resources.

R&D Research and development activities undertaken to bring about *technological advance.*

rate of exchange The price paid in one's own money to acquire 1 unit of a foreign currency; the rate at which the money of one nation is exchanged for the money of another nation.

rate of return The gain in net revenue divided by the cost of an investment or an *R&D* expenditure; expressed as a percentage.

rational behavior Human behavior based on comparison of marginal costs and marginal benefits; behavior designed to maximize total utility.

rationing function of prices The ability of market forces in competitive markets to equalize *quantity demanded* and *quantity supplied* and to eliminate shortages and surpluses via changes in prices.

real capital (See *capital.*)

real GDP (See *real gross domestic product.*)

real gross domestic product (GDP) *Gross domestic product* adjusted for inflation; gross domestic product in a year divided by the GDP *price index* for that year, the index expressed as a decimal.

real income The amount of goods and services that can be purchased with *nominal income* during some period of time; nominal income adjusted for inflation.

real interest rate The interest rate expressed in dollars of constant value (adjusted for *inflation*) and equal to the *nominal interest rate* less the expected rate of inflation.

real wage The amount of goods and services a worker can purchase with his or her *nominal wage;* the purchasing power of the nominal wage.

recession A period of declining real GDP, accompanied by lower real income and higher unemployment.

Reciprocal Trade Agreements Act A 1934 Federal law that authorized the president to negotiate up to 50 percent lower tariffs with foreign nations that agreed to reduce their tariffs on U.S. goods. (Such agreements incorporated the *most-favored-nation* clause.)

regressive tax A tax whose *average tax rate* decreases as the taxpayer's income increases and increases as the taxpayer's income decreases.

regulatory agency An agency, commission, or board established by the Federal government or a state government to control the prices charged and the services offered by a *natural monopoly.*

rental income The payments (income) received by those who supply *land* to the economy.

rent-seeking behavior The actions by persons, firms, or unions to gain special benefits from government at the taxpayers' or someone else's expense.

resource A natural, human, or manufactured item that helps produce goods and services; a productive agent or factor of production.

resource market A market in which *households* sell and *firms* buy resources or the services of resources.

revenue tariff A *tariff* designed to produce income for the Federal government.

reverse discrimination The view that the preferential treatment associated with *affirmative action* efforts constitutes discrimination against other groups.

right-to-work law A state law (in about 22 states) that makes it illegal to require that a worker join a *labor union* in order to retain his or her job; laws that make *union shops* and *agency shops* illegal.

rule of reason The rule stated and applied in the *U.S. Steel case* that only combinations and contracts unreasonably restraining trade are subject to actions under the antitrust laws and that size and possession of monopoly power are not illegal.

rule of 70 A method for determining the number of years it will take for some measure to double, given its annual percentage increase. Example: To determine the number of years it will take for the *price level* to double, divide 70 by the annual rate of *inflation.*

sales tax A tax levied on the cost (at retail) of a broad group of products.

saving Disposable income not spent for consumer goods; equal to *disposable income* minus *personal consumption expenditures.*

scarce resources The limited quantities of *land, capital, labor,* and *entrepreneurial ability* that are never sufficient to satisfy people's virtually unlimited economic wants.

scientific method The procedure for the systematic pursuit of knowledge involving the observation of facts and the formulation and testing of hypotheses to obtain theories, principles, and laws.

seasonal variations Increases and decreases in the level of economic activity within a single year, caused by a change in the season.

self-interest That which each firm, property owner, worker, and consumer believes is best for itself and seeks to obtain.

seniority The length of time a worker has been employed absolutely or relative to other workers; may be used to determine which workers will be laid off when there is insufficient work for them all and who will be rehired when more work becomes available.

separation of ownership and control The fact that different groups of people own a *corporation* (the stockholders) and manage it (the directors and officers).

service An (intangible) act or use for which a consumer, firm, or government is willing to pay.

Sherman Act The Federal antitrust act of 1890 that makes monopoly and conspiracies to restrain trade criminal offenses.

shirking Workers' neglecting or evading work to increase their *utility* or well-being.

shortage The amount by which the *quantity demanded* of a product exceeds the *quantity supplied* at a particular (below-equilibrium) price.

short run (1) In microeconomics, a period of time in which producers are able to change the quantities of some but not all of the resources they employ; a period in which some resources (usually plant) are fixed and some are variable. (2) In macroeconomics, a period in which nominal wages and other input prices do not change in response to a change in the price level.

short-run competitive equilibrium The price at which the total quantity of a product supplied in the *short run* in a purely competitive industry equals the total quantity of the product demanded and that is equal to or greater than *average variable cost*.

short-run supply curve A supply curve that shows the quantity of a product a firm in a purely competitive industry will offer to sell at various prices in the *short run;* the portion of the firm's short-run marginal cost curve that lies above its *average-variable-cost* curve.

shutdown case The circumstance in which a firm would experience a loss greater than its total *fixed cost* if it were to produce any output greater than zero; alternatively, a situation in which a firm would cease to operate when the *price* at which it can sell its product is less than its *average variable cost*.

simultaneous consumption The same-time derivation of *utility* from some product by a large number of consumers.

slope of a line The ratio of the vertical change (the rise or fall) to the horizontal change (the run) between any two points on a line. The slope of an upward-sloping line is positive, reflecting a direct relationship between two variables; the slope of a downward-sloping line is negative, reflecting an inverse relationship between two variables.

Smoot-Hawley Tariff Act Legislation passed in 1930 that established very high tariffs. Its objective was to reduce imports and stimulate the domestic economy, but it resulted only in retaliatory tariffs by other nations.

social insurance programs Programs that replace the earnings lost when people retire or are temporarily unemployed, that are financed by payroll taxes, and that are viewed as earned rights (rather than charity).

socially optimal price The price of a product that results in the most efficient allocation of an economy's resources and that is equal to the *marginal cost* of the product.

social regulation Regulation in which government is concerned with the conditions under which goods and services are produced, their physical characteristics, and the impact of their production on society; in contrast to *industrial regulation*.

Social Security The social insurance program in the United States financed by Federal payroll taxes on employers and employees and designed to replace a portion of the earnings lost when workers become disabled, retire, or die.

sole proprietorship An unincorporated *firm* owned and operated by one person.

special-interest effect Any result of government promotion of the interests (goals) of a small group at the expense of a much larger group.

specialization The use of the resources of an individual, a firm, a region, or a nation to concentrate production on one or a small number of goods and services.

speculation The activity of buying or selling with the motive of later reselling or rebuying for profit.

SSI (See *Supplemental Security Income*.)

standardized product A product whose buyers are indifferent to the seller from whom they purchase it as long as the price charged by all sellers is the same; a product all units of which are identical and thus are perfect substitutes for each other.

Standard Oil case A 1911 antitrust case in which Standard Oil was found guilty of violating the *Sherman Act* by illegally monopolizing the petroleum industry. As a remedy the company was divided into several competing firms.

start-up (firm) A new firm focused on creating and introducing a particular new product or employing a specific new production or distribution method.

static economy A hypothetical economy in which the basic forces such as resource supplies, technological knowledge, and consumer tastes are constant and unchanging.

statistical discrimination The practice of judging an individual on the basis of the average characteristic of the group to which he or she belongs rather than on his or her own personal characteristics.

stock (corporate) An ownership share in a corporation.

stock options Contracts that enable executives or other key employees to buy shares of their employers' stock at fixed, lower prices when the stock prices rise.

strategic behavior Self-interested economic actions that take into account the expected reactions of others.

strategic trade policy The use of trade barriers to reduce the risk inherent in product development by domestic firms, particularly that involving advanced technology.

strike The withholding of labor services by an organized group of workers (a *labor union*).

structural-change hypothesis The explanation that ascribes the decline of unionism in the United States to changes in the structure of the economy and of the labor force.

subsidy A payment of funds (or goods and services) by a government, firm, or household for which it receives no good or service in return. When made by a government, it is a *government transfer payment*.

substitute goods Products or services that can be used in place of each other. When the price of one falls, the demand for the other product falls; conversely, when the price of one product rises, the demand for the other product rises.

substitution effect (1) A change in the quantity demanded of a *consumer good* that results from a change in its relative expensiveness caused by a change in the product's price; (2) the effect of a change in the price of a *resource* on the quantity of the resource employed by a firm, assuming no change in its output.

sunk cost A cost that has been incurred and cannot be recovered.

Supplemental Security Income (SSI) A federally financed and administered program that provides a uniform nationwide minimum income for the aged, blind, and disabled who do not qualify for benefits under *Social Security* in the United States.

supply A schedule showing the amounts of a good or service that sellers (or a seller) will offer at various prices during some period.

supply curve A curve illustrating *supply*.

supply schedule (See *supply*.)

surplus The amount by which the *quantity supplied* of a product exceeds the *quantity demanded* at a specific (above-equilibrium) price.

surplus payment A payment to a resource that is not required to ensure its availability in the production process; for example, land rent.

tacit understanding Any method used by an oligopolist to set prices and outputs that does not involve outright (or overt) *collusion. Price leadership* is a frequent example.

TANF (See *Temporary Assistance for Needy Families.*)

tariff A tax imposed by a nation on an imported good.

taste-for-discrimination model A theory that views discrimination as a preference for which an employer is willing to pay.

tax An involuntary payment of money (or goods and services) to a government by a *household* or *firm* for which the household or firm receives no good or service directly in return.

tax incidence The person or group that ends up paying a tax.

tax subsidy A grant in the form of reduced taxes through favorable tax treatment. For example, employer-paid health insurance is exempt from Federal income and payroll taxes.

technological advance New and better goods and services and new and better ways of producing or distributing them.

technology The body of knowledge and techniques that can be used to combine *economic resources* to produce goods and services.

Temporary Assistance for Needy Families (TANF) A state-administered and partly federally funded program in the United States that provides financial aid to poor families; the basic welfare program for low-income families in the United States; contains time limits and work requirements.

terms of trade The rate at which units of one product can be exchanged for units of another product; the price of a good or service; the amount of one good or service that must be given up to obtain 1 unit of another good or service.

theoretical economics The process of deriving and applying economic theories and principles.

theory of human capital The generalization that *wage differentials* are the result of differences in the amount of *human capital investment* and that the incomes of lower-paid workers are raised by increasing the amount of such investment.

total cost The sum of *fixed cost* and *variable cost*.

total demand The demand schedule or the *demand curve* of all buyers of a good or service; also called market demand.

total product (TP) The total output of a particular good or service produced by a firm (or a group of firms or the entire economy).

total revenue (TR) The total number of dollars received by a firm (or firms) from the sale of a product; equal to the total expenditures for the product produced by the firm (or firms); equal to the quantity sold (demanded) multiplied by the price at which it is sold.

total-revenue test A test to determine elasticity of *demand* between any two prices: Demand is elastic if *total revenue* moves in the opposite direction from price; it is inelastic when it moves in the same direction as price; and it is of unitary elasticity when it does not change when price changes.

total spending The total amount that buyers of goods and services spend or plan to spend; also called *aggregate expenditures*.

total supply The supply schedule or the *supply curve* of all sellers of a good or service; also called market supply.

total utility The total amount of satisfaction derived from the consumption of a single product or a combination of products.

Trade Adjustment Assistance Act A U.S. law passed in 2002 that provides cash assistance, education and training benefits, health care subsidies, and wage subsidies (for persons age 50 or older) to workers displaced by imports or relocations of U.S. plants to other countries.

trade balance The export of goods (or goods and services) of a nation less its imports of goods (or goods and services).

trade bloc A group of nations that lower or abolish trade barriers among members. Examples include the *European Union* and the nations of the *North American Free Trade Agreement*.

trade controls *Tariffs, export subsidies, import quotas,* and other means a nation may employ to reduce *imports* and expand *exports*.

trade deficit The amount by which a nation's *imports* of goods (or goods and services) exceed its *exports* of goods (or goods and services).

trademark A legal protection that gives the originators of a product an exclusive right to use the brand name.

tradeoff The sacrifice of some or all of one economic goal, good, or service to achieve some other goal, good, or service.

trade surplus The amount by which a nation's *exports* of goods (or goods and services) exceed its *imports* of goods (or goods and services).

trading possibilities line A line that shows the different combinations of two products that an economy is able to obtain (consume) when it specializes in the production of one product and trades (exports) it to obtain the other product.

tragedy of the commons The tendency for commonly owned *natural resources* to be overused, neglected, or degraded because their common ownership gives nobody an incentive to maintain or improve them.

transfer payment A payment of *money* (or goods and services) by a government to a *household* or *firm* for which the payer receives no good or service directly in return.

tying contract A requirement imposed by a seller that a buyer purchase another (or other) of its products as a condition for buying a desired product; a practice forbidden by the *Clayton Act*.

unauthorized immigrant A person who enters a country unlawfully for the purposes of residing there.

underemployment A situation in which workers are employed in positions requiring less education and skill than they have.

undistributed corporate profits After-tax corporate profits not distributed as dividends to stockholders; corporate or business saving; also called retained earnings.

unemployment The failure to use all available *economic resources* to produce desired goods and services; the failure of the economy to fully employ its *labor force*.

unemployment compensation (See *unemployment insurance*).

unemployment insurance The social insurance program that in the United States is financed by state *payroll taxes* on employers and makes income available to workers who become unemployed and are unable to find jobs.

unemployment rate The percentage of the *labor force* unemployed at any time.

uninsurable risk An event that would result in a loss and whose occurrence is uncontrollable and unpredictable. Insurance companies are not willing to sell insurance against such a loss.

union shop A place of employment where the employer may hire either *labor union* members or nonmembers but where nonmembers must become members within a specified period of time or lose their jobs.

unit elasticity Demand or supply for which the *elasticity coefficient* is equal to 1; means that the percentage change in the quantity demanded or supplied is equal to the percentage change in price.

unit labor cost Labor cost per unit of output; total labor cost divided by total output; also equal to the *nominal wage* rate divided by the *average product* of labor.

unlimited liability Absence of any limits on the maximum amount that an individual (usually a business owner) may become legally required to pay.

unlimited wants The insatiable desire of consumers for goods and services that will give them satisfaction or *utility*.

Uruguay Round A 1995 trade agreement (fully implemented in 2005) that established the *World Trade Organization (WTO)*, liberalized trade in goods and services, provided added protection to intellectual property (for example, *patents* and *copyrights*), and reduced farm subsidies.

U.S. Steel case The antitrust action brought by the Federal government against the U.S. Steel Corporation in which the courts ruled (in 1920) that only unreasonable restraints of trade were illegal and that size and the possession of monopoly power were not violations of the antitrust laws.

usury laws State laws that specify the maximum legal interest rate at which loans can be made.

utility The want-satisfying power of a good or service; the satisfaction or pleasure a consumer obtains from the consumption of a good or service (or from the consumption of a collection of goods and services).

utility-maximizing rule The principle that to obtain the greatest *utility*, the consumer should allocate *money income* so that the last dollar spent on each good or service yields the same marginal utility.

value-added tax A tax imposed on the difference between the value of the product sold by a firm and the value of the goods purchased from other firms to produce the product; used in several European countries.

value judgment Opinion of what is desirable or undesirable; belief regarding what ought or ought not to be (regarding what is right or just and wrong or unjust).

variable cost A cost that in total increases when the firm increases its output and decreases when the firm reduces its output.

VAT (See *value-added tax*.)

venture capital That part of household saving used to finance high-risk business enterprises in exchange for shares of the profit if the enterprise succeeds.

vertical axis The "up-down" or "north-south" measurement line on a graph or grid.

vertical integration A group of *plants* engaged in different stages of the production of a final product and owned by a single *firm*.

vertical intercept The point at which a line meets the vertical axis of a graph.

vertical merger The merger of one or more *firms* engaged in different stages of the production of a final product.

very long run A period in which *technology* can change and in which *firms* can introduce new products.

voice mechanism Communication by workers through their union to resolve grievances with an employer.

voluntary export restrictions (VER) Voluntary limitations by countries or firms of their exports to a particular foreign nation to avoid enactment of formal trade barriers by that nation.

wage The price paid for the use or services of *labor* per unit of time (per hour, per day, and so on).

wage differential The difference between the *wage* received by one worker or group of workers and that received by another worker or group of workers.

wage discrimination The payment of a lower wage to members of a less preferred group than that paid to members of a more preferred group for the same work.

wage rate (See *wage*.)

wages The income of those who supply the economy with *labor*.

wealth Anything that has value because it produces income or could produce income. Wealth is a stock; income is a flow. Assets less liabilities; net worth.

welfare programs (See *public assistance programs*.)

Wheeler-Lea Act The Federal act of 1938 that amended the *Federal Trade Commission Act* by prohibiting and giving the commission power to investigate unfair and deceptive acts or practices of commerce (such as false and misleading advertising and the misrepresentation of products).

world price The international market price of a good or service, determined by world demand and supply.

World Trade Organization (WTO) An organization of 149 nations (as of fall 2006) that oversees the provisions of the current world trade agreement, resolves trade disputes stemming from it, and holds forums for further rounds of trade negotiations.

WTO (See *World Trade Organization*.)

X-inefficiency The production of output, whatever it level, at a higher average (and total) cost than is necessary for producing that level of output.

Credits

Page 4 Courtesy of Robbins Recreation, www.4americanrecreation.com, and artist Katherine Robbins.

Page 5 © Syracuse Newspapers/The Image Works

Page 9 © Mike Theiler/Reuters/Corbis

Page 14 © Royalty-Free/Corbis

Page 16 © James Leynse/Corbis

Page 33 © Robert W. Ginn/PhotoEdit

Page 34 © The McGraw-Hill Companies, Inc./John Flournoy, photographer

Page 40 © Royalty-Free/Corbis

Page 55 © Robert W. Ginn/PhotoEdit

Page 58 © Nancy R. Cohen/Getty Images

Page 61 © Olivier Matthys/epa/Corbis

Page 70 © Reuters/Corbis

Page 74 © Colin Young-Wolff/PhotoEdit

Page 79 © Royalty-Free/Corbis

Page 90 © David Frazier/PhotoEdit

Page 93 © Getty Images

Page 100 © J. Luke/PhotoLink/Getty Images

Page 108 © Nancy R. Cohen/Getty Images

Page 121 © Tom Prettyman/PhotoEdit

Page 126 © Kim Kulish/Corbis

Page 134 © Digital Vision/Getty Images

Page 141 Courtesy of Maps a la carte, Inc.

Page 147 © Comstock Images/JupiterImages

Page 161 © Jonnie Miles/Getty Images

Page 174 © Getty Images

Page 185 © Tannen Maury/epa/Corbis

Page 203 © Richard Gross/Corbis

Page 206 © PhotoLink/Getty Images

Page 211 © Richard Cummins/Corbis

Page 229 © Burke/Triolo Productions/Getty Images

Page 244 © Don Farrall/Getty Images

Page 249 Courtesy of Hewlett-Packard Company.

Page 259 © Adriane Jaeckle/Getty Images

Page 267 © age fotostock/SuperStock

Page 285 Reunion des Musees Nationaux/Art Resource, NY. © 2007 Estate of Pablo Picasso/Artist Rights Society (ARS), New York

Page 288 © Peter Weber/Getty Images

Page 297 © Matthew Borkoski/Index Stock Imagery, Inc.

Page 303 © Royalty-Free/Corbis

Page 311 © David Frazier/PhotoEdit

Page 322 © Bruce Ayres/Getty Images

Page 326 © Brownie Harris/Corbis

Page 344 © Royalty-Free/Corbis

Page 354 © AP Photo/Stephen Lance Dennee

Page 361 © Ted Soqui/Corbis

Page 368 © Digital Vision/PunchStock

Page 377 © Envision/Corbis

Page 389 © Royalty-Free/Corbis

Page 396 © Rick Gomez/Corbis

Page 410 © Nancy R. Cohen/Getty Images

Page 415 © Stockbyte/Punchstock

Page 436 © Robert Newald/epa/Corbis

Page 454 © Grant V. Faint/Getty Images

Page 459 © Steve Allen/Getty Images

Page 469 © The McGraw-Hill Companies, Inc./John Flournoy, photographer

Page 479 © PhotoLink/Getty Images

Photos on the Web site:

Page 15W-3 © Digital Vision/Getty Images

Page 15W-9 © T. O'Keefe/PhotoLink/Getty Images

Page 15W-19 © PhotoLink/Getty Images

Index

Page numbers followed by n indicate notes.

Ability
  entrepreneurial, 10
  and income inequality, 384–385
  and specialization, 32
  of workers, 284
Ability-to-pay principle, 337
Above-equilibrium wage rate, 280, 287
Absolute advantage, 90, 443
Access to health care, 401, 404–405
Accounting costs, 145
Accounting profit, 301
  versus economic profit, 146
  and implicit costs, 145
Accounting scandals, 70
Acreage allotments, 373
Active antitrust perspective, 352
Acura, 234
Adams, Walter, 229, 249
Adidas, 46
Adjustable-peg system, 474–475
Advanced Micro Devices, 351
Adverse selection problem, 322, 324
Advertising
  determination of, 227
  misleading, 228
  in monopolistic competition, 212
  negative effects, 228–229
  in oligopoly, 227–229
  positive effects, 227–228
  and product attributes, 216
  self-canceling, 229
  ten largest in U.S., 227
  by unions, 278
Advertising Age, 232
Affirmative action
  court rulings, 432
  definition, 431
  ended in California, 432
  executive orders, 431
  opposition to, 432
  and reverse discrimination, 432
  support for, 431–432
Affordable R&D, 239–240
Afghanistan war, 14
AFL-CIO, 419
African Americans
  and affirmative action, 431–432
  and labor market discrimination, 425–427
  in labor unions, 420
  medically uninsured, 404
  occupational segregation, 429–430
  in poverty, 390
  and taste-for-discrimination model, 427–428
African American–white wage ratio, 428
After-tax income, 67
Agency shop, 421
Agents, 70
Aggregate, 6
Aging population, 406
Agribusiness, 370, 375
Agricultural Adjustment Act of 1933, 371
Agricultural subsidies, 365
  criticisms of, 374–375
  and farm profitability, 365
  global perspective, 371
  kinds of, 371
  misguided policy, 374–375
  rationale for, 371
  in U.S. 1999–2002, 378
Agriculture, 365–371; *see also* Farm policy
  agribusiness, 370
  commercial farms, 370
  consequences of changes, 370
  economics of, 365–371
  farm commodities, 365
  farm-household income, 370
  farm population, 376
  fixed costs, 366
  fluctuations in demand, 366–368
  food products, 365
  gain from price supports, 372
  graphical portrayal, 369
  inelastic demand, 365
  inflation-adjusted prices, 367
  labor force in, 370
  lagging demand, 369
  long-run decline, 368–370
  output fluctuations, 365–366
  political action committees, 375
  price and income instability, 365–368
  and price elasticity of demand, 112–113
  range of businesses, 365
  residential farms, 370
  risk management, 368
  short-run problems, 365–368
  technology and supply increases, 368–369
  variable costs, 366
  in world markets, 366–368
Agriculture Extension Service, 369
AIDS epidemic, 403
Aid to Families with Dependent Children, 393
  repealed, 395
Airbus Industrie, 85, 95
Aircraft plants, 162
Airline industry
  deregulation, 357
  price elasticity of demand, 121
Air pollution, 72
Akerlof, George, 322
Alamo Rent-a-Car, 234
Alcoa case, 351
Algebraic restatement utility-maximizing rule, 130–131
Allen, Paul, 236, 248
Allocative efficiency, 55–56, 120
  competition vs. monopoly, 199
  disrupted by price floors, 60
  in health care, 408–409
  of international trade, 447
  and invisible hand theory, 186
  lacking in monopolistic competition, 215
  lacking in oligopoly, 229–230
  in pure competition, 184
  and technological advance, 247
Allocative inefficiency
  of price supports, 372
  of sugar program, 377
Amazon.com, 232
American Association of Retired Persons, 411
American Bar Association, 279
American Broadcasting Company, 353
American Federation of Labor, 419
American Medical Association, 279, 409
Americans with Disabilities Act, 358
America Online, 249, 353
Amgen, 236
Amtrak, 355
Anacin, 211
Andreessen, Marc, 249
Anheuser-Busch Companies, 228–229
Annual percentage rate, 303
Antidiscrimination policies
  affirmative action, 431–432
  Civil Rights Act, 431
  court rulings, 432
  Equal Pay Act, 431
  and reverse discrimination, 432
Antidumping argument, 455
Antidumping duties, 455
Anti-globalization protests, 458–459
Antipoverty programs, 391
Antiques Roadshow, 115–116
Antitrust, 71
Antitrust laws
  cease-and-desist orders, 350
  Celler-Kefauver Act, 350
  Clayton Act, 350
  and cross elasticity of demand, 117
  degree of enforcement, 351–352
  effectiveness
    conclusions on, 354–355
    on mergers, 352–354
    on monopoly, 352
    on price discrimination, 354
    on price fixing, 354
    on tying contracts, 354
  Federal Trade Commission Act, 350
  historical background, 349
  on interlocking directorates, 350
  loose enforcement, 352
  obstacle to collusion, 226
  option against monopoly, 202
  per se violations, 351
  rule of reason, 352
  Sherman Act, 349–350
  strict enforcement, 352
  on tying contracts, 350
  Wheeler-Lea Act, 350
Antitrust policy, 348
  Alcoa case, 351
  AMD vs. Intel, 351
  AT&T case, 352
  behavioralists, 351
  DuPont case, 351
  IBM case, 351
  issues of enforcement, 351–352
    activist perspective, 352
    laissez-faire perspective, 352
    litigation costs, 352

Antitrust policy—*Cont.*
issues of interpretation
monopoly behavior vs. structure, 350–351
relevant market, 351
Microsoft case, 192, 202, 209, 249, 351, 352, 360–361
90-60-30 rule, 351
rule of reason, 351, 352
Standard Oil case, 202, 349–351
structuralists, 351
United States steel case, 351
AOL Time Warner, 361
Apple Computer, 236, 242, 248
Appreciation, 94, 467, 468
Archer Daniels Midland, 225, 354
ARPANET, 248
Arthur Andersen, 70
Asian currency crises, 476, 478
Asymmetric information, 322
in health care market, 405, 406
Atari, 236
A.T.Kearney, 99
AT&T, 227, 236, 243, 248, 278, 356
antitrust case, 352
breakup of, 357
Attainable combinations, 8–9
Auctioneers, 45
Australia, land-intensive goods, 443
Auto antitheft devices, 326
Automatic teller machines, 267
Automobile industry, 158
cost of strikes, 424
Auto theft, 326
Average cost curves, 151–152
Average family wealth, 396
Average fixed cost, 151–152
for pure competition, 171–178
Average fixed cost curve, 154–155
Average product, 147
and law of diminishing returns, 148–150
Average revenue, 167–168
Average tax rate, 78–79, 337–338
Average total cost, 152
competitive firm and market, 183
constant returns to scale, 159
daily newspapers, 160–162
in information technology, 200
and marginal cost, 153–154
in monopolistic competition, 215–216
for monopoly, 191
in natural monopoly, 159, 205–207
and plant size, 155
and price discrimination, 204
process innovation, 241–242
with productive efficiency, 183–184
for pure competition, 171–178
start-up firms, 160
Average total cost curve
competitive firm and market, 183
in constant-cost industry, 181
in increasing-cost industry, 181–182
insurance premiums, 160
long run, 156
in monopolistic competition, 213, 215
of monopoly, 191
shifts in, 154–155
X-inefficiency, 200–201
Average variable cost, 152
and marginal cost, 153–154
for pure competition, 171–178
Average variable cost curve, 152
shifts in, 154–155
Avis, 234
Ayres, Ian, 326

Baby boomers
incomes of, 387
and Social Security shortfall, 78–79
Backflow of migrants, 434
Balance of payments
Bretton Woods system, 474–475
capital account, 465
current account, 464–465
definition, 463–464
financial account, 465–466
with flexible exchange rates, 469–471
global perspective, 465
with gold standard, 473–474
official reserves account, 466
of United States in 2005, 464
Balance-of-payments deficits and surpluses, 466
Balance of trade
on goods, 464
and managed float, 476
on services, 464–465
Balance on current account, 465
Balance on goods and services, 465
Balance on the capital and financial accounts, 466
Bankruptcy, 404
Banks and banking
automatic teller machines, 267
bounce protection, 303
loanable funds, 297
loans for R&D, 237
Barnes & Noble, 8, 232, 354
Barriers to entry
lacking in monopolistic competition, 212
limit pricing, 226
under monopoly, 190–192
control of resources, 192
definition, 190
economies of scale, 191
entry deterrence strategies, 192
licensing, 192
patents, 191–192
plant size, 191
pricing strategies, 192
research and development, 201
occupational licensing, 279
in oligopoly, 217
time lags, 243
Barter, 32, 43
Bastiat, Frédéric, 100
Bayer AG, 202
Bayer aspirin, 211
Bayer Chemicals, 89
Beck Beer, 229
Beer industry oligopoly, 228–229
Beggar-my-neighbor policy, 456
Behavioralists, 351
Bell System, 357
Benefit-reduction rate, 394
Benefits-received principle, 337
Biases, 16
Big Mac index, 469
Bilateral monopoly model
desirability, 281
indeterminate outcomes, 281
Biodiesel fuel, 374
Biotechnology, 16
Black market for foreign exchange, 472
Black markets, 59
Blind auditions, 436
Blockbuster Video, 245
Blocked entry, 190
Blue Springs Youth Outreach Unit, 344
Boeing Company, 85, 95, 99, 146, 162, 353, 457
Bonds, 69
for R&D, 237
tax-exempt, 298–299
Bonuses, 287
for CEOs, 288
negative side effects, 287–289
Borden's, 224
Borders, 8
Borrowing from IMF, 475
Boston rent controls, 59
Boudreaux, Donald, 40
Bounce protection, 303
Boycott war, 454
Boyd, L., 244
BP Amoco, 202
Brand-name loyalty, 228
Brand-name recognition, 243
Brand names
global perspective, 227
in monopolistic competition, 211
Brannock Device Company, 190
Brazil, comparative advantage, 443–448
Break-even income, 394
Break-even point, 169–170
Breast cancer, 403
Bretton Woods system
creation of IMF, 474
demise of, 475
fundamental imbalances, 475
gold sales, 475
IMF borrowing, 475
official reserves, 475
origin of, 474
pegged exchange rates, 474–475
British Petroleum, 70
British pounds, 463, 467–471
Brock, James, 229, 249
Buck, Brian K., 396
Budget, effect of health care costs, 404
Budget constraints; *see* Budget line
Budget line, 128–129, 138
attainable/unattainable combinations, 8–9
and choice, 9
definition, 8, 138
and demand curve, 142
global perspective, 8
and health insurance, 408
income change and, 10
income changes and, 138–139
opportunity cost, 9
price changes and, 138–139
tradeoffs, 9
Budget Rent-a-Car, 234
Bufferin, 211
Bureaucracy, 335–336
Bureau of Economic Analysis, 464
Bureau of Labor Statistics
Labor Force Statistics, 20
Occupational Outlook, 270
occupational trends, 261–262
Burger King, 217, 226

Bush, George W., 361
Business population
  advantages of corporations, 68–69
  and competition, 71
  corporations, 68–70
  demand for loanable funds, 296
  firms, 68
  industry, 68
  legal forms of business, 68
  legal structure, 71
  partnerships, 68
  plants, 68
  principal-agent problem, 69–70
  producers, 144
  R&D expenditures, 235
  shares of domestic output, 69
  sole proprietorships, 68
Business sector
  in circular flow model, 39
  in product market, 41
  as resource market, 39–41
Business unionism, 419
Buy American campaign, 33
Buyers, number of, 48

California
  end of affirmative action, 432
  energy crisis, 357
Canada
  export supply curve, 450–451
  health care system, 411–412
  import demand curve, 450–451
  U.S. trade with, 87
  U.S. trading partner, 442
  voluntary export restrictions, 452
Canon, 234, 236
Capital
  complementary resources, 260–261
  efficient, 158
  elastic supply, 294
  as factor of production, 10
  fixed proportion of, 260
  least-cost combination of resources, 264
  private ownership of, 29–30
  and productivity, 273
  and substitution effect, 260
Capital account, 465
Capital account surplus, 478
Capital accumulation, 37
Capital allocation, 299
Capital expenditures, 217
Capital flows, 85
Capital goods, 10
  capital accumulation, 37
  in command systems, 29
  versus current consumption, 11
  definition, 11
  in market system, 31–32
Capital-intensive goods, 443
Capitalism, 29, 235–236
Capital rationing, 299
Carbon-dioxide emissions, 321
Carleton, Dennis W., 244
Carnegie, Andrew, 236
Carrel, 354
Cartels; *see also* Game theory model
  covert collusion, 224–225
  definition, 224
  legal cartel theory of regulation, 356
  obstacles to collusion
    antitrust law, 226
    cheating, 225
    demand/cost differences, 225
    number of firms, 225
    potential entry, 226
    recession, 225
  from occupational licensing, 357
  overt collusion, 224
  price-output collusion, 223–224
  tacit understandings, 225
Cash gifts, 134
Caterpillar, Inc., 99
Causation versus correlation, 17
CBS, 248
CBS Sports Line, 137
Cease-and-desist orders, 350
Celler-Kefauver Act, 350
Cellular phones, 16
Census Bureau, 64, 83, 383
Central banks
  currency interventions, 472
  official reserves, 466
Central planning, 29
Ceteris paribus; see Other-things-equal assumption
Chaloupka, Frank, 113n
Change, in market system, 36
Change in demand
  versus change in quantity demanded, 49
  complements, 49
  complex cases, 56–57
  consumer expectations, 49
  consumer tastes, 47–48
  definition, 47
  and equilibrium price/quantity, 56
  graphs, 57
  income, 48–49
  number of buyers, 48
  price of unrelated goods, 49
Change in quantity demanded, 49–50
Change in quantity supplied, 52–53
Change in supply, 177
  versus change in quantity supplied, 52–53
  complex cases, 56–57
  definition, 51, 53
  and equilibrium price/quantity, 56
  graphs, 57
  number of sellers, 52
  prices of other goods, 52
  producer expectations, 52
  resource prices, 51
  taxes and subsidies, 52
  technology, 52
Chase Manhattan Bank, 353
Cheap foreign labor argument, 456
Cheating
  by cartels, 225
  by oligopolists, 220–221
Checking accounts, bounce protection, 303
Chef America, 243
Chemical Bank, 353
Chevron, 70
Chicago Board of Trade, 45
Chicago Wilderness Protection Program, 344
Chief executive officer pay, 288
Children, poverty rate, 390
China, 29, 38
  in international trade, 89
  U.S. trade deficit with, 442, 477–478
  U.S. trade with, 87–88
  volume of trade, 442
Chlorofluorocarbons, 316
Choice
  and budget line, 8
  freedom of, 30
  restricted, 472
  and scarcity, 4
Chop shops, 326
Christie's, 354
Chrysler Corporation, 85
Circular flow model, 38–41
  households, 39
  including government, 75–76
  product market, 41
  resource markets, 39–41
Cisco Systems, 160
Citizens Against Waste, 344
Civil Aeronautics Board, 356
Civilian goods, 14
Clayton Act
  amendments, 350
  on mergers, 353
  provisions, 350
Clean Air Act, 316, 319
Clean Water Act, 319
Clinton, Bill, 360
Closed economy, 95
Closed shop, 421
CNN/Sports Illustrated, 137
Coase, Ronald, 315
Coase theorem, 315
Coca-Cola Company, 6, 68, 89, 99, 117, 161, 227, 243, 244
Coefficient of cross elasticity of demand, 116
Coefficient of income elasticity of demand, 117
Coefficient of price elasticity of demand
  definition, 106
  elimination of minus sign, 107
  examples, 113
  formula, 106
  interpretations
    elastic demand, 107
    inelastic demand, 107
    perfectly elastic/inelastic demand, 107–108
    unit elasticity, 107
  midpoint formula, 106
  using percentages, 106–107
Coefficient of price elasticity of supply
  degree of elasticity, 114
  formula, 114
  midpoint formula, 114
Coffee prices, 58
Coincidence of wants, 32
Colgate-Palmolive, 243
Collective bargaining, 281
  company counteroffer, 421
  deadline, 421–422
  goal of, 420–421
  process, 421–422
  union demands, 421
  work agreement, 421
College education
  earnings of graduates, 9
  tuition, 121
  and wage differentials, 285
Collusion
  covert, 224–225
  lacking in monopolistic competition, 211
  obstacles to, 225–226
    antitrust law, 226
    cheating, 225
    cost differences, 225
    demand differences, 225
    number of firms, 225

Collusion—*Cont.*
potential entry, 226
recession, 225
by oligopolists, 220
in output, 224–225
overt, 224
in pricing, 224–225
tacit understandings, 225
Command system
characteristics, 29
coordination problems, 38
demise of, 38
incentive problem, 38
Commercial farms, 370
Commissions, 287
Commodore, 246
Communicating price changes, 226
Communications technology, 88
Communications Workers of America, 278, 419
Communism, collapse of, 89
Communist party, 38
Compaq Computer, 248
Comparative advantage
based on specialization, 444–445
Brazil, 443–448
constant-cost assumption, 443
definition, 91
different costs, 443
graphical analysis, 443–447
and offshoring, 457
opportunity-cost ratio, 444
production possibilities analysis
assumptions and comparative costs, 90–91
gains from specialization, 91–92
gains from trade, 91–92
terms of trade, 91
self-sufficiency output mix, 444
shifts in patterns, 457
and specialization, 89–92
two isolated nations, 443–444
United States, 443–448
Comparative costs, 90–91
Comparative exports, 88
Compensating differences, 285
Compensation; *see also* Wage *entries*
bonuses, 287
of CEOs, 288
commissions, 287
pay for performance, 286–287
of physicians, 398
piece rate system, 287
profit sharing, 287, 289
royalties, 287
stock options, 287, 289
Competition; *see also* Imperfect competition; Market structure; Pure competition
in agriculture, 365
and allocative efficiency, 55–56
from cheap foreign labor, 456
and cross elasticity of demand, 117
and discrimination, 428–429
and equilibrium price, 53–54
foreign, 420
from foreign multinational corporations, 202
in free trade, 448
global, 99
in health care, 409–410
impact of social regulation, 360
imperfect, 166
and invisible hand, 37
in least-cost production, 35
maintained by government, 71
in market system, 31
nonprice, 166, 190
prevented by regulation, 356
and productive efficiency, 55
by real-world industries, 210
Complementary goods
and cross elasticity of demand, 117
DVDs and DVD players, 132
Complementary resources, 260–261
Complements, 49
and change in demand, 49
Compliance costs, 360
Compounded interest, 302–303
Computers
and fast-growing occupations, 262
history of, 248–249
ConAgra, 354
Concentration ratio
definition, 218
versus Herfindahl index, 219
import competition, 218–219
interindustry competition, 218
localized markets, 218
low, 246
Concrete plants, 162
Conglomerate mergers, 353, 354
Conglomerates, 68
Congress of Industrial Organizations, 419
Connections, 386
Conoco Phillips, 70
Constant cost assumption, 443
Constant-cost industry, 179, 181
Constant returns to scale, 158, 159
Constraints in production possibilities curve, 11–12
Consumer behavior
applications and extensions
cash vs. noncash gifts, 134
diamond-water paradox, 132–133
DVD's and DVD players, 132
medical care purchases, 133–134
value of time, 133
choice and budget constraint, 128–129
and criminal behavior, 134–135
and cross elasticity of demand, 116–117
decision-making process, 129–130
and income elasticity of demand, 117
indifference curve analysis, 138–142
and law of diminishing marginal utility, 126
preferences, 128
and price elasticity of demand, 106–114
and price elasticity of supply, 114–116
and prices, 128–129
purposeful, 4–5
rational, 128
sensitivity to price changes, 106
theories of, 6
utility-maximizing rule, 129–132
Consumer choice, 128–129
Consumer demand
for foreign goods, 420
in pure competition, 180–181
Consumer expectations, 49
Consumer goods, 10; *see also* Goods
in command systems, 29
definition, 11
Consumer Product Safety Commission, 358, 359, 363
Consumer Reports, 228, 325
Consumers
budget line, 8–10
costs of trade barriers, 453–454
equilibrium position, 140–141, 142
gains from deregulation, 357
inadequate information
adverse selection problem, 324
moral hazard problem, 323–324
income transfer from, 199
limited income, 7
losses from price supports, 372
losses to sugar program, 376
prices and demand, 106
restricted choice, 472
subsidies for, 73
Consumer sovereignty, 34
Consumer surplus
definition, 118–119
effect of monopoly on, 199
and efficiency, 120
efficiency losses, 120–122
in pure competition, 184
Consumer tastes
and change in demand, 47–48
changes in, 36
and exchange rates, 467
time span, 126
Consumption
diminishing marginal utility, 46
effect of tariffs, 452
versus income in poverty, 391
versus saving, 67
and trade deficits, 479
Consumption expenditures, 67–68
Contracting with processors, 368
Convexity of indifference curves, 139–140
Coordination problem, 38
Coors Brewery, 228–229
Copayments, 401, 413
Copyrights, 243
Corn Products, 354
Corona beer, 229
Corporate income tax, 80, 338
incidence of, 342
Corporate securities, 68–69
Corporations
advantages, 68–69
definition, 68
financing of, 68–69
limited liability, 69
principal-agent problem, 69–70
world's ten largest, 70
Correlation versus causality, 17
Cost-benefit analysis
Coase theorem, 315
concept, 312–313
of government failure, 335
health care spending, 404
illustration, 313
of immigration, 435
MB=MC rule, 313
of pollution reduction, 320–321
social regulation, 358

Cost-benefit decision, 5
Costco, 247
Cost containment, health care
copayments, 413
deductibles, 413
diagnosis-related-group system, 413
federal government failures, 412
management health care, 413
Cost curves
average total cost, 156
in monopolistic competition, 213, 215
and productivity curves, 155
pure competition, 179
shifts in, 154–155
short-run, 160
Cost minimization, 255
Cost-of-living adjustments, 421
Costs
of health care, 401
of industrial regulation, 356
of labor market discrimination, 426–427
of migration, 434
of strikes, 423
of sugar program, 376
Costs of production, 144
aircraft industry, 162
allocative efficiency, 184
complications in monopoly
economies of scale, 199–200
rent-seeking behavior, 201
technological advance, 201
X-inefficiency, 200–201
concrete plants, 162
constant-cost industry, 181
decreasing-cost industry, 181
economic cost, 145
and economic profit, 145–146
explicit, 145
implicit, 145
increasing-cost industry, 181–182
insurance premiums in, 160
law of diminishing returns, 147–150
least-cost combination of resources, 264, 265–266
least cost production, 184
long-run, 146
diseconomies of scale, 159
economies of scale, 156–159
firm size and costs, 155
long-run cost curve, 155
minimum efficient scale, 159–160
in monopoly, 195–196
newspapers, 160–162
normal profit in, 145
obstacle to collusion, 225
opportunity cost, 145
productive efficiency, 183–184
profit-maximizing combination of resources, 264–266
in pure competition, 171–178
raised by direct controls, 316
reasons for, 145
security costs, 160
short-run, 146, 147–150
average fixed cost, 151–152
average total cost, 152
average variable cost, 152
fixed costs, 150
marginal cost, 152–154
per-unit costs, 151–152
shifts of cost curves, 154–155
total cost, 151
variable costs, 150
start-up costs, 158
start-up firms, 160
sunk costs, 161
Verson stamping machines, 160
Countercyclical payments, 378
Covert collusion, 224–225
Cox, W. Michael, 33
Craft union model
exclusive unionism, 279
occupational licensing, 279
Craig, Ben, 267
Crandall, Robert, 357n
Creative destruction, 36–37, 247–249, 352
Creative Technology, 242
Credit, determining price of, 302–303
Credits, 464
Crime prevention, 326
Criminal behavior, 134–135
Crop revenue insurance, 368
Crop rotation, 373
Crop yields, 112–113
Cross elasticity of demand
application of, 117
coefficient, 116
complementary goods, 116
definition, 116
independent goods, 116
substitute goods, 116
Crowding, occupational, 429–430
Cuba, 29
Culture of welfare, 395
Cumby, Robert, 469
Currency, 33, 93
appreciation, 94
depreciation, 94
devaluation, 474
rationing of, 472
Currency crises, 476, 478
Currency interventions, 472
Currency markets, 463
Currency prices, 478
Currency speculators, 469
absorbing risk, 478–479
and exchange rate fluctuations, 478
Current account
balance on, 465
balance on goods, 464
balance on services, 464–465
credits and debits, 464
definition, 464
Current account deficit, 466, 477, 479

Daily newspapers, 160–162
DaimlerChrysler, 70, 227, 234
Deadweight loss
consumer/producer surplus, 120–122
of monopoly, 199
of taxes, 340–341
Dean Foods, 224
De Beers diamond syndicate, 190, 206
Debits, 464
Decreasing-cost industry, 182
Decriminalization of illegal drugs, 113–114
Deductibles, 401, 413
Defense goods, 14
Defensive medicine, 407
Dell, Michael, 248
Dell Computer, 160, 200, 248
Del Monte, 365
Demand; *see also* Income elasticity of demand; Labor demand; Price elasticity of demand; Resource demand
in beer industry, 228
bolstering, 374
causes of change in, 47–49
changes in, 56–57
loanable funds, 297–298
and rent, 293–294
cross elasticity of, 116–117
decrease and supply decrease, 56
decrease and supply increase, 56
decrease in, 47
definition, 45
derived, 255
determinants of, 47–49
elastic, 106, 107, 108–109
excess, 54–55
fluctuations in farm products, 366–367
for foreign goods, 420
income effect and, 46
income elasticity of, 117
increase and supply decrease, 56
increase and supply increase, 56
increase in, 47
inelastic, 106, 107, 109–110
lagging for farm products, 369
law of demand, 46
for loanable funds, 296–297
and marginal utility, 128
market demand, 46–47
of monopolist, 199
in monopoly
assumptions, 192
marginal revenue less than cost, 193–194
price elasticity, 195
price makers, 194
perfectly elastic, 107–108, 167–168
perfectly inelastic, 107–108
for private goods, 310
for public goods, 311–312
in pure competition, 167–168
pure competition vs. monopoly, 192
substitution effect and, 46
supplier-induced, 406–407
unit elasticity, 107, 110
Demand curve, 46
for agriculture, 366–367
and consumer surplus, 119, 120
derivation of, 142
factors that shift, 47–49
in imperfect competition, 256
imports, 449–451
kinked, 223
and law of diminishing marginal utility, 128
for monopolist, 192–195
in monopolistic competition, 212–214
monopoly vs. pure competition, 192–193
of natural monopoly, 205
obstacle to collusion, 225
and positive externalities, 72
and price elasticity, 107
price elasticity along, 110–111
of price makers, 194
and producer surplus, 120
for resources, 258
and utility maximization
deriving demand curve, 131
income effect, 131–132
substitution effect, 131–132
Demand elasticities
efficiency loss of taxes, 341

Demand elasticities—*Cont.*
for labor, 263
in monopolistic competition, 212–214
for products, 263
and tax incidence, 339–340
Demand-enhancement union model
increased product demand, 278
increased productivity, 278–279
price of other inputs, 279
Demand-for-pounds curve, 467, 468
Demand schedule, 45
in pure competition, 167–168
Demand shifters, 47
Democrats, 20
Demographics
of income inequality, 387
of poverty, 390
Dentsply, 192
Department of Agriculture, 64, 369, 373
Department of Commerce, 377, 463–464
Department of Justice, 349, 350, 354, 360
Dependent variables
definition, 22–23
and vertical axis, 21
Depreciation (currency), 94
of United States dollar, 467, 468
Deregulation, 357
Derived demand, 255
and price supports, 373
and productivity, 255–256
and product price, 256
Determinants of demand, 47
complements, 49
consumer expectations, 49
consumer tastes, 47–48
income, 48–49
individual demand, 131
for labor, 261
new products, 247
number of buyers, 48
price of unrelated goods, 49
substitutes, 49
unrelated goods, 49
Determinants of price elasticity of demand
luxuries vs. necessities, 112
proportion of income, 112
substitutability, 111–112
time, 112
Determinants of resource demand
changes in resource prices, 260–261
occupational trends, 261–262
product demand changes, 259
productivity changes, 259–260
Determinants of supply, 51
number of sellers, 52
prices of other goods, 52
producer expectations, 52
resource prices, 51
subsidies, 52
table, 53
taxes, 52
technology, 52
Devaluation, 474, 475
Developing countries
costs of food, 369
and environmental standards, 459
labor standards issue, 458
and sugar program, 376–377
transfer of jobs to, 387
Diagnosis-related-group system, 413
Diamond market, 206
Diamond-water paradox, 132–133
Diebold, 267
Diet Coke, 242
Different costs, 443
Differentiated oligopoly, 217
Diffusion
of economic power, 31
of innovation, 234–235
Digital Equipment Corporation, 248
Dilemma of regulation, 207
Diminishing marginal rate of substitution, 139–140
Diminishing marginal utility, 46, 126–128
pollution reduction, 320
of public goods, 312
Diminishing-marginal-utility-from-income curves, 388–389
Diminishing returns, 147–150
and marginal cost, 177
Direct controls, 316
Direct costs of crime, 135
Direct payments, 378
Direct relationship, 22
DirecTV, 353
Discrimination
and income inequality, 385
in labor market, 286, 425–432
in orchestra hiring, 436
Discrimination coefficient, 427–428
Diseconomies of scale, 159
and minimum efficient scale, 159–160
Dissave, 67
Distorted trade, 472
Diversification-for-stability argument, 454–455
Division of labor, 32
Divorce, 324
Doha Round, 97, 377, 458
Dollar votes, 34
Dollar-yen market, 93–94
Domestic employment argument, 455–456
Domestic exchange ratio, 444
Dual health care system, 401
Dual pricing, 121
Duetsch, Larry, 229
Dumping
definition and purpose, 455
of farm products, 373
DuPont Corporation, 191
antitrust case, 351
Durable goods, 68, 126
DVDs and DVD players, 132

Earned-income tax credit, 393
Earnings
of college graduates, 9
professional golfers, 291
Eastern Europe, 89
Eastman Kodak, 116, 117, 243, 354
eBay, 43
Echostar, 353
Eckstein, Otto, 336n
Economic costs, 145
economic profit and, 145–146
explicit costs, 146
implicit costs, 146
long-run, 146
normal profit in, 146
short-run, 146
Economic efficiency, 35
Economic growth
definition, 15
increase in resource supplies, 15
and labor demand, 280
promotion of, 36–37
technological advance, 15–16
and trade deficits, 477
Economic models; *see* Models
Economic perspective
marginal analysis, 5
opportunity cost, 4
pitfalls in reasoning, 16–17
purposeful behavior, 4–5
scarcity and choice, 4
utility, 4
Economic policy
farm policy, 371–378
government difficulties, 74–75
for inflation, 74
to maintain exchange rates, 473
and normative economics, 7
for unemployment, 74
Economic power, 31
Economic principles
definition, 6
generalizations, 6
graphical expression, 6
other-things-equal assumption, 6
Economic problem
resource categories, 10–11
scarce resources, 10
Economic profit, 34, 145–146
in constant-cost industry, 181
definition, 301
eliminated in long-run equilibrium, 180
functions
promoting innovation, 303
resource allocation, 303–304
in increasing-cost industry, 181–182
from innovation, 245
from licensing, 192
of monopolist, 195–196
in monopolistic competition, 213
in pure competition, 172, 177–178
and risk, 302–303
role of entrepreneur, 301
sources of, 301–303
Economic reasoning
biases, 16
correlation vs. causation, 17
fallacy of composition, 16
loaded terminology, 16
post hoc fallacy, 17
Economic rent
ad productivity, 295
and changes in demand, 293–294
definition, 293
and perfectly inelastic supply, 293
single-tax movement, 294–295
as surplus payment, 294, 295
Economic resources
categories of, 10–11
definition, 10
Economics
of agriculture, 365–370
definition, 4
farm policy, 371–374
of immigration, 433–435
of international trade, 441–448
of labor market discrimination, 427–430
of labor unions, 423–425
macroeconomics, 6

microeconomics, 6–7
of monopoly
assessment and policy options, 201–202
cost complications, 199–201
income transfer, 199
price, output, and efficiency, 198–199
normative, 7
no-free-lunch theory, 360
of poverty, 389–391
positive, 7
scientific method, 5–6
of technological advance, 235–236
Economics of war, 14
Economic stability, 74
Economic systems
command system, 29
communism, 29
definition, 29
demise of command systems, 38
differences in, 29
Index of Economic Freedom, 30
market system, 29
socialism, 29
Economies of scale
aircraft industry, 162
and average total cost curve, 156
concrete plants, 162
daily newspapers, 160–162
efficient capital, 158
labor specialization, 156–157
learning by doing, 158
managerial specialization, 157
and minimum efficient scale, 159–160
in monopoly, 191, 199–200
in natural monopoly, 205
network effects, 200
in oligopoly, 217
significance of, 159
and simultaneous consumption, 200
start-up costs, 158
start-up firms, 160
Verson stamping machines, 160
Economist, 469
Economists
on antitrust policy, 354–355
on global warming, 321
on health care spending, 404
on technological advance, 235–236
Economizing problem
definition, 7
of individuals
budget line, 9–10
limited income, 7
unlimited wants, 7–8
of society
resource categories, 10–11
scarce resources, 10
Economy
circular flow model, 38–41
closed, 95
effect of offshoring, 457
and income elasticity of demand, 117
and international specialization, 18
open, 89
present choices and future possibilities, 16–18
role of government
and circular flow model, 75–76
dealing with market failure, 72–74
income redistribution, 71–72
maintaining competition, 71
promoting stability, 74–75
providing legal structure, 71
qualification on, 74–75
resource reallocation, 72–74
static, 301
Education
and income inequality, 385
and labor market discrimination, 426
medical school, 409
as positive externality, 72
state and local expenditures, 80
and wage differentials, 284–285
Efficiency
allocative, 120
and consumer/producer surplus, 120
effect of monopoly, 198–199
from freedom of migration, 434
gains from deregulation, 357
versus income inequality
case for equality, 388–389
case for inequality, 389
efficiency-equality tradeoff, 389
and logrolling, 332
of market system, 37
mixed research findings on unions, 425
in monopolistic competition
allocative efficiency, 215
excess capacity, 215–216
productive efficiency, 215
negative effect of unions, 422–424
featherbedding, 423
labor misallocation, 423–424
strikes, 423
work rules, 423
in oligopoly
allocative efficiency, 229–230
productive efficiency, 229–230
qualifications on, 230
positive effect of unions
informal training, 425
longer-run impact, 314
reduced turnover, 424–425
productive, 120
and pure competition
allocative efficiency, 184
dynamic adjustments, 184–186
gains from, 185
and invisible hand, 186
productive efficiency, 183–184
of tax on land, 294
and technological advance
allocative efficiency, 247
creative destruction, 247–249
productive efficiency, 247
Efficiency loss, 120–122
in health care, 409
in health care spending, 404
of monopoly, 199
from price supports, 372–373
from sugar program, 377
from tariffs and quotas, 453–454
Efficiency loss of a tax
loss, 341
qualification, 341–342
tax revenues, 340–341
Efficiency wages, 287
Efficient allocation, 55–56
Efficient capital, 158
Elastic demand, 106
definition, 107
for luxuries, 341
in monopolistic competition, 212–214
and tax incidence, 339–340
and total revenue test, 108–109
Elasticities
of labor demand, 280–281
pricing power, 121
of product demand, 263
role in health care, 406
and tax burden, 339–340
Elasticity of resource demand, 262–263
coefficient, 263
ease of substitutability, 263
product demand, 263
ratio of cost to total cost, 263
Elasticity of supply, 341
Electric utilities
deregulation, 357
price discrimination by, 203
Elleg, Jerry, 357n
Elzinga, Kenneth G., 229
Emission standards, 316
Employers
statistical discrimination by, 429
taste-for-discrimination model, 427–429
Employment
in bilateral monopoly, 281
discrimination in, 426
equilibrium, 277
in farming, 370
in health care, 401
increased by North American Free Trade Agreement, 98
and labor market discrimination, 426
number of Americans, 271
occupational trends, 261–262
shit away from unions, 420
Engelbart, Douglas, 246
ENIAC, 248
Enron Corporation, 70, 357
Entitlement programs, 391–392
Entrepreneurial ability, 10
Entrepreneurial teams, 236
Entrepreneurs
anticipating the future, 236
and capital accumulation, 37
examples of, 236
exploiting research, 237
forming start-ups, 236
freedom of enterprise, 30
functions, 10
innovating in existing firms, 236
normal profit, 301
Entry; *see also* Barriers to entry
blocked by monopoly, 190
in constant-cost industry, 181
in decreasing-cost industry, 182
efficiency gains from, 185
free in pure competition, 167
in increasing-cost industry, 181–182
and long-run profit maximization, 179
in monopolistic competition, 212, 214
obstacle to collusion, 225
Entry deterrence strategies, 192
Environmental issues
and globalization, 458–459
price supports, 373

Environmental Protection Agency, 319, 322–323, 329, 344, 358, 359, 360
Equal Employment Opportunity Commission, 358
Equality-efficiency tradeoff, 389
Equation
  linear relationship, 24
  marginal revenue cost, 256
  marginal revenue product, 256
Equilibrium domestic price, 448
Equilibrium employment, 277
Equilibrium in pure competition, 179–181
Equilibrium interest rate
  and total output, 299
  and usury laws, 300
Equilibrium position, 140–141, 142
Equilibrium price, 53–54
  after and before taxes, 339
  in competitive markets, 56
  complex supply and demand cases, 56–57
  and consumer surplus, 118–119
  effect of change in demand, 56
  effect of change in supply, 56
  and efficiency, 120
  exports and imports, 448–451
  and price ceilings, 58
  and price floors, 59
  and producer surplus, 119
  in pure competition
    determination of, 177
    firm vs. industry, 178
    market price and profit, 177–178
Equilibrium quantity, 53–54
  in competitive markets, 56
  complex supply and demand cases, 56–57
  effect of change in demand, 56
  effect of change in supply, 56
  and efficiency, 120
  and tax burden, 339
Equilibrium quantity of pollution, 320
Equilibrium wage, 277, 283–284
Equilibrium wage rate, 274
Equilibrium world price, 448
  determining, 451
Equity in health care, 405, 409
Erasmo, 244
ESPN Sportszone, 137
Ethanol production, 374
Ethics
  in health care market, 405
  medical, 407
Euro, 89
Europe, in international trade, 89
European Commission, 361
European Union
  drawbacks, 89
  EuroZone, 98
  farm policy, 376–377
  import licenses, 452
  membership, 98
  as trade bloc, 98
EuroZone, 98
Excel, 365
Excess capacity, 215–216
Excess demand, 54–55
Excess supply, 54
Exchange
  by barter, 32, 43
  facilitated by money, 32–33
  facilitated by private property, 30
Exchange controls
  objections to, 472
  operation of, 472
Exchange rate fluctuations, 478
Exchange-rate risk, 478–479
Exchange rates
  adjustable-peg system, 474–475
  appreciation, 467
  Big Mac index, 469
  in Bretton Woods system, 474–475
  changes in, 94
  definition, 92
  depreciation, 467
  determinants
    changes in taste, 467
    generalizations on, 467
    income changes, 467
    interest rates, 469
    price-level changes, 468–469
    speculation, 469
  and devaluation, 474
  dollar-yen market, 93–94
  exchange controls, 472
  in export transaction, 463
  fixed, 471–473
  flexible, 466–471
  function of, 92–93
  global perspective, 92
  with gold standard, 473–474
  in import transaction, 463
  managed float, 475–477
  and purchasing power parity theory, 468–469
  systems, 467
  for United States dollar, 462
Exchange-rate stability, 473
Exchange-rate volatility, 476
Exchange ratio
  domestic, 444
  and specialization, 447
  world, 445
Excise taxes, 80
  incidence of, 342
  on luxuries, 341
  and price elasticity of demand, 113
  protective tariffs, 95
  specific targets, 342
  tariffs, 451–452
Excludability, 310
  of private goods, 73
Exclusive unionism, 279
Executive pay, 70
Exit
  free in pure competition, 167
  and long-run profit maximization, 179
  in monopolistic competition, 212, 214
Exit mechanism, 424
Expected rate of return
  and interest rate, 299
  from R&D, 238–239
  for R&D in pure competition, 245
Expected-rate-of-return ratio, 238–239
Explicit costs, 145, 301
Exports
  equilibrium world price, 451
  global perspective, 442
  national comparisons, 86, 88
  percentage of GDP, 85, 86
  of services, 88
  supply and demand analysis
    Canada, 450–451
    equilibrium world price, 451
    United States, 448–450
  of U.S. trade, 87
  voluntary export restrictions, 452
Export subsidies, 95
Export supply curve
  Canada, 450–451
  United States, 449
Export transaction, 463
Externalities
  and Coase theorem, 315
  correcting for negative externalities, 72
  correcting for positive externalities, 73
  definition, 72, 314
  global warming, 321–322
  government intervention
    direct controls, 316
    government provision, 317
    specific taxes, 316–317
    subsidies, 317
  liability rules and lawsuits, 315–316
  market for externality rights, 318–319
  negative, 72, 314
  optimal amount of reduction, 319–321
  positive, 72, 314–315
  taxation to reduce, 341–342
  tragedy of the commons, 317–318
Exxon, 353
ExxonMobil, 68, 69, 70

Factors of production
  categories of, 10
  changes in, 443
  definition, 11
  income from production, 273
  marginal cost, 50
Fairbank, Richard D., 288
Fair Labor Standards Act, 282
Fair return, 356
Fair-return price, 205–207
Fallacy of composition, 16–17, 178, 318, 456
Family wealth, 396
Farm Act of 2002
  countercyclical payments, 378
  direct payments, 378
  marketing loan program, 378
Farm commodities, 365
  dumping, 373
  prices of, 64
Farm exports, 367–368
Farm-household income, 370
Farm lobby, 378
Farm policy
  acreage allotments, 373
  criticisms of
    parity concept, 374
    price supports, 374–375
  economics of, 371–374
  in European Union, 376–377
  hidden costs, 376
  parity concept, 371–372
  parity ratio, 372
  politics of
    declining support, 376
    public choice theory, 375–376
    and world trade, 376–377
  price supports
    efficiency loss, 372–373
    environmental costs, 373
    gains to farmers, 372
    international costs, 373
    loss to consumers, 372
    social losses, 373
    surplus output, 372
  rationale for subsidies, 371
  recent reforms, 377–378
    Farm Act of 2002, 378

Freedom to Farm Act, 378
marketing loan program, 378
reduction of surpluses
by bolstering demand, 374
by supply restrictions, 373–374
subsidies, 365
sugar program, 376–377
Farm population, 376
Fast-food lines, 5
Favoritism, 472
Featherbedding, 423
Federal Communications Commission, 192, 355
Federal Emergency Management Agency, 344
Federal Energy Regulatory Commission, 355, 358
Federal Express, 227
Federal finance
expenditures, 77
intergovernmental grants, 80
tax revenues, 77–80
Federal Reserve System, 74
control of interest rates, 298
Survey of Consumer Finances, 396
Federal tax revenues
corporate income tax, 80
excise taxes, 80
payroll taxes, 80
personal income tax, 78–79
sources, 77
Federal tax system, 343–344
Federal Trade Commission, 349, 353, 363
Federal Trade Commission Act, 350
Fee-for-service basis, 406–407
Filo, David, 249
Financial account, 465–466
Financial flows, 85
Financial institutions, 297
Financing
of corporations, 68–69
venture capital, 237–238
Firms, 68
collusion and number of, 225
interests of workers, 287
old vs. high-tech, 420
optimal amount of R&D, 237–240
in pure competition, 177–178
shock effect of union wages, 424
start-up, 160, 236
sunk costs, 161
supply curve, 178
use of dumping, 455
wage takers, 256–257
First Data Corporation, 190
First-mover benefits
brand-name recognition, 243
copyrights, 243
learning by doing, 143
patents, 242–243
profitable buyouts, 243–244
time lags, 143
trademarks, 243
trade secrets, 243, 244
Fiscal policy, to maintain exchange rates, 473
Fisher, Irving, 297
Fisher, Irving Norton, 297
Fixed costs
in agriculture, 366
definition, 150, 151
insurance premiums, 160
Fixed exchange rates, 467, 471–473
currency interventions, 472
exchange controls, 472
with gold standard, 473–474
and rationing, 472
stabilization policies for, 473
trade policies, 472
Fixed plant capacity, 146
Fixed resources assumption, 11
Fixed technology assumption, 11
Flexible exchange rates, 466–471
appreciation, 468
and balance of payments, 469–471
Big Mac index and, 469
depreciation, 468
determinants
changes in tastes, 467
income changes, 467
interest rates, 469
price-level changes, 468–469
purchasing power parity theory, 468–469
speculation, 469
disadvantages
diminished trade, 471
instability, 471
terms-of-trade-changes, 471
uncertainty, 471
and managed float, 476
Floating exchange rate system, 467
Flow of income, 385
Food and Drug Administration, 285, 358, 360
Food for Peace, 374
Food products, 365
Food-stamp program, 393
Ford, Henry, 236
Ford Focus, 8
Ford Motor Company, 70, 94, 227, 423
Foreign competition, 230
Foreign exchange market, 92–94, 463
and changing rates, 94
dollar-yen market, 93–94
manipulation of, 472
speculation in, 478–479
For whom to produce, 35–36
Frank, Robert, 259
Free agent, 278
Freedom of choice, 30
basis of competition, 31
Freedom of enterprise, 30
Freedom of market system, 37
Freedom to Farm Act of 1996, 378
Free entry and exit, 167
Free good, 293
Free products, 4
Free-rider problem, 310, 311
for public goods, 73
and street entertainers, 74
Free trade
case for, 448
versus infant industry argument, 455
Free trade zones
European Union, 98
NAFTA, 98
Frisbees, 190
Fuji film, 116
Fujitsu, 267
Fuld, Richard S., Jr., 288
Full employment
assumption, 11
and immigration, 435
Full employment policy, 74
Functional distribution of income, 66
Future, anticipating, 236
Future and Its Enemies (Postrel), 40
Futures market, 368, 479

Gains from speculation, 91–92
Gains from trade, 91–92, 445–447
added output, 447
government misunderstanding of, 95
improved options, 446–447
trading possibilities line, 445–446
Game theory model
cheating by cartels, 225
collusion, 220
incentives to cheat, 220–221
mutual interdependence, 219–220
payoff matrix, 219
strategy combinations, 219–220
Gas mileage standards, 359
Gasohol, 374
Gasoline market, 322–323
Gasoline prices, 224
price ceilings on, 58–59
Gates, Bill, 8, 9, 236, 248, 361
Gateway 2000, 249, 361
G8 nations, 441, 476
General Agreement on Tariffs and Trade, 97
General Electric, 191, 227, 410
Generalizations, 6
General Mills, 226
General Motors, 70, 227, 292, 304, 423
Generic drugs, 185
Gentlemen's agreement, 225
Geographic immobility, 286
Geographic markets, 162
Geographic monopolies, 190
Geographic specialization, 32
George, Henry, 294
Gerber baby food, 85
Gifts, cash vs. noncash, 134
Gillette Company, 242
Gini ratio, 382–383, 387
GlaxoSmithKline, 227
Global Climate Change initiative, 321
Global competition, 99
Global economy, 84–85
Globalization, 99
Global perspective
agricultural subsidies, 371
average income, 8
balance of payments, 465
carbon-dioxide emissions, 321
comparative exports, 88
distribution of U.S. patents, 243
exchange rates, 92
foreign multinational corporations, 202
health care spending, 403
hourly wages, 272
index of economic freedom, 30
labor force in agriculture, 370
nominal interest rate, 300
OPEC, 225
R&D expenditures, 235
taxation, 343
tax revenues as percentage of output, 77
top ten brand names, 227
top tenth of income receivers, 386
top 12 globalized nations, 99
union membership, 419
U.S. immigration, 433
world exports, 442

Global warming, 322–323
Gold
in Bretton Woods system, 475
as international money, 472
price volatility, 116
sales of, 475
Goldin, Claudia, 436
Gold standard
collapse of, 474
domestic stabilization policies, 473–474
gold flows, 473
operation of, 473
Goods; *see also* Consumer goods
attainable/unattainable, 8–9
capital-intensive, 443
complementary, 49
defense vs. civilian, 14
durable, 68, 126
independent, 49
inferior, 49, 117, 130
labor-intensive, 443
land-intensive, 443
luxuries, 7–8, 112
in market system, 29
necessities, 7–8, 112
nondurable, 68
normal, 48, 117
private, 73
private vs. public, 310–313
public, 73
quasi-public, 73
substitutes, 49
superior, 48
unrelated, 49
Goods and services flows, 85
Google, Inc., 160, 249
Government
antitrust perspectives, 352
in circular flow model, 75–76
in command economy, 29
and cross elasticity of demand, 117
demand for loanable funds, 298
dilemma of regulation, 207
economic activities, 309
effect of health care costs, 404
less vs. more, 360–361
market for externality rights, 318–319
policy options for monopoly, 201–202
poverty rate, 390
public goods, 310–313
R&D expenditures, 235
redistributive goals, 341
reducing negative externalities, 341–342
regulated monopolies, 204–207
role in economy
in circular flow model, 75–76
dealing with market failure, 72–74
income redistribution, 71–72
maintaining competition, 71
promoting stability, 74
providing legal structure, 71
qualification on, 74–75
resource reallocation, 72–74
role in market system, 29, 33
size of, 334
subsidies to agriculture, 365
tax subsidy, 408
workplace safety, 325
Government decision making
inefficient voting outcomes, 331–332
interest group influence, 332
by logrolling, 332
median-voter model, 333–334
and paradox of voting, 332–333
preferences and voting, 331–334
special interest effect, 333–334, 334–335
Government employees, 336
Government failure
benefits vs. hidden costs, 335
bureaucracy and inefficiency, 335–336
definition, 334
examples, 344
imperfect institutions, 336
limited bundle choice, 335
versus market failure, 330
pork-barrel politics, 334–335
reluctance to abandon, 336
rent-seeking behavior, 335
special interest effect, 334–335
Government favoritism, 472
Government finance
federal level, 76–80
local level, 80
purchases and transfers, 75–76
state level, 80
Government intervention, 71
antitrust laws, 349–355
for correct externalities
direct controls, 316
provision of public goods, 317
specific taxes, 316–317
subsidies to buyers, 317
subsidies to producers, 317
currency devaluation, 474
deregulation, 357
farm policy, 371–378
in gasoline market, 323
income-maintenance system, 391–395
industrial regulation, 355–357
licensing, 323
minimum wage, 282
social regulation, 358–361
strategic trade policy, 454
in trade
costs to society, 96
export subsidies, 95
impediments and subsidies, 95
import quotas, 95
misunderstanding gains from trade, 95
nontariff barriers, 95, 452
political considerations, 95–96
reasons for, 95–96
tariffs, 95, 451–453
trade adjustment assistance, 456–457
usury laws, 300
and wage differentials, 286
Government purchases, 75–76
Government research, 237
Government securities, 299
Government-set prices, 57–61
price ceilings, 58–59
price floors, 59–61
rent controls, 59
Government spending
areas of, 77
federal level, 77
impact of immigration, 435
intergovernmental grants, 80
by local government, 80
local level, 80
on Medicare, 392–393
on public assistance programs, 393–394
size of, 76
on Social Security, 392–393
Social Security problems, 78–79
state level, 80
by states, 80
on unemployment compensation, 393
Graphical expression, 6
Graphs
circular flow model, 39
construction of, 21–22
definition, 21
dependent variables, 22–23
direct relationships, 22
equation of a linear relationship, 24
equilibrium price/quantity, 54
gains from trade, 446
horizontal axis, 21
independent variables, 22–23
inverse relationships, 22
kinked demand curve, 222
labor demand, 275
labor supply, 275
law of diminishing returns, 148–150
long-run decline of agriculture, 369
long-run equilibrium in pure competition, 183
marginal cost, 153, 154
market for foreign currency, 468
monopolistic competition, 213
monopoly profit maximization, 196
other-things-equal assumption, 23
P=MC rule, 176
price discrimination, 204
production possibilities curve, 12
R&D expenditures, 239
short-run loss minimization, 173
short-run profit maximization, 173
slope of a line, 23–24
slope of a nonlinear curve, 24–25
total and marginal utility, 127
trading possibilities line, 446
vertical axis, 21
vertical intercept, 24
Great Depression, 17
end of gold standard, 474
Smoot-Hawley Tariff, 96, 456
Greenhouse effect, 322
Greer, Douglas F., 229, 246n
Grievance procedures, 421
Gross Domestic Product
exports as percentage of, 85, 86
health care spending, 400, 402
R&D expenditures in., 235
Social Security percentage of, 78
U.S. trade as percentage of, 86
Guilt costs, 135
Guinness, 229

H. J. Heinz Company, 365
Hand, Learned, 351
Handspring, 234
Hardship insurance, 324
Head Start, 393
Health care
demand for
aging population, 406
defensive medicine, 407

medical ethics and, 407
moral hazard problem, 407–408
rising incomes, 406
supplier-induced, 406–407
unhealthy lifestyles, 406
implications of rising costs, 403–404
limited access, 404–405
quality of, 402–403
Health care costs, 401
implications of increase
impact on budget, 404
labor market effects, 403–404
personal bankruptcy, 404
reduced access, 403
and limited access, 404–405
reasons for increase
market peculiarities, 405–406
rising demand, 406–407
role of insurance, 407–409
supply factors, 409–410
technological advance, 410–411
supply factors, 409–410
and technological advance, 410–411
Health care industry
adequacy of spending, 404
competition in, 409–410
costs and access, 401
dual system, 401
implications of rising costs, 403–404
increasing demand, 406–407
limited access, 404–405
mandatory insurance, 415
market peculiarities, 405–406
number of workers in, 401
quality of care, 402–403
reasons for rising costs, 405–411
reform proposals, 411–412
role of health insurance, 407–409
supply factors, 409–411
Health care market
asymmetric information, 405
ethics and equity, 405
positive externalities, 405
third-party payments, 405–406
Health care reform
cost containment, 413–414
health savings accounts, 414
interest groups, 411
malpractice award limits, 414
by national health insurance, 412
prescription drug program, 413–414
universal access, 411–412
Health care spending, 77
components, 401
copayments, 401
deductibles, 401
international comparisons, 402–403
Medicaid, 401–402
Medicare, 401
percentage of GDP, 400, 402
total, 401–402
Health insurance
and budget line, 408
copayments, 401, 413
deductibles, 401, 413
expanding coverage, 410
function, 407
Massachusetts law, 415
and medically uninsured, 404–405
moral hazard problem
less prevention, 407
overconsumption, 407–408
national, 411–412
private, 401
public, 401
third-party payments, 405–406
Health maintenance organizations, 413
Health savings accounts, 414
Hedging, 368, 479
Heileman's, 228
Henderson, Diedtra, 249
Herfindahl index
merger guidelines, 353–354
for oligopoly, 219
top fifty manufacturing firms, 212
Hertz, 234
Hewlett-Packard, 234, 236
High-concentration manufacturing, 218
High-tech firms, 420
Hispanics
labor market discrimination, 425–427
in labor unions, 420
medically uninsured, 404
occupational segregation, 429–430
in poverty, 390
Homogeneous oligopoly, 217
Honda Accord, 242
Honda Civic, 8
Honda Motors, 94, 227, 423
Hopper, Grace Murray, 248
Horizontal axis, 21
Horizontal mergers
and antitrust law, 353
definition, 352–353
Hormel, 354
Hours of work, 421
Households
demand for loanable funds, 297–298
family wealth, 396
in farming, 370
income distribution, 382
income quintiles 1970–2004, 387
as income receivers
functional distribution of income, 66
kinds of income, 66
personal distribution of income, 66–67
in product market, 41
quintiles of income, 66, 382–383
as resource market, 39–41
richest vs. poorest, 381
as spenders
consumption expenditures, 67–68
personal saving, 67
personal taxes, 67
suppliers of loanable funds, 296
Housing assistance, 393
How to produce, 35
Hughes Corporation, 353
Human capital
components, 284
wage differentials, 284–285
Human capital discrimination, 426
Hunt Company, 365
Hurricane Katrina, 344
Hynix Semiconductor, 354
Hypothesis, 5–6
Hypothesis testing, 6

IBM, 191, 227, 234, 247, 248, 361
antitrust case, 351
IBM System/360 computer, 248
Illegal behavior, 134–135
Illegal drugs, decriminalization of, 113–114
Illegal immigrants, 433
Imation, 236
IMF; *see* International Monetary Fund
Imitation
diffusion through, 234–235
R&D incentives, 242–244
Imitation problem, 242
Immigrants
backflow of, 434
remittances by, 434
statistics 1950–2004, 433
Immigration, 433–435
changing mix of, 435
costs of, 434
by country of origin, 433
economics of, 433–435
backflows, 434
costs of migration, 434
fiscal impact, 435
full employment vs. unemployment, 435
income shares, 434
remittances, 434
wage rates and output, 434
elimination of barriers, 434
and income inequality, 387
legal, 433
opposing views on, 435
unauthorized, 433
Imperfect competition
kinds of, 166
price makers, 194
resource demand, 257–258
Implicit costs, 145, 301
Import competition, 218–219
Import demand curve
Canada, 450–451
United States, 449–450
Import licenses, 452
Import quotas, 95, 452; *see also* Protectionism
costs to society, 96
economic impact, 453
net costs of, 453–454
and sugar program, 376
Imports
effect of tariffs, 453
equilibrium world price, 451
job creation from, 456
supply and demand analysis
Canada, 450–451
equilibrium world price, 451
United States, 448–450
of U.S. trade, 87
Import transaction, 463
Incentive function, 294
Incentive pay plan, 287
Incentives
for cheating, 220–221
and income inequality, 389
of market system, 37
as problem in command systems, 38
Incidence of poverty, 390–391
Inco, 192
Income
break-even, 394
budget constraint, 128
and budget line, 138–139
and change in demand, 48–49
change in expectations about, 49
versus consumption, 391
exchange rates and changes in, 467

Income—*Cont.*
of farm households, 370
as flow, 385
functional distribution, 66
global perspective, 8, 386
and labor market discrimination, 426
limited, 7
minimum annual, 394
minimum threshold, 390
nonfarm, 368
personal distribution, 66
and price elasticity of demand, 112
quintiles, 66, 382–383
sources of, 36
unearned, 294
Income changes, 10
Income distribution
case for equality, 388–389
case for inequality, 389
churning around, 383
effect of, 384
equality-efficiency tradeoff, 389
and income mobility, 383
inequality, 266–267
marginal productivity theory of, 266–267
and market imperfections, 267
of U.S. households, 382
utility-maximizing, 388
Income effect, 46
and utility maximization, 131–132
Income elasticity of demand
and business fluctuations, 117
coefficient, 117
for farm products, 369
for health care, 406
inferior goods, 117
normal goods, 117
Income inequality, 66, 266–267
case for equality, 388–389
case for inequality, 389
causes
ability, 384–385
discrimination, 385
education and training, 385
luck and connections, 386
market power, 386
misfortune, 386
preferences and risks, 385
unequal wealth distribution, 385
effect of redistribution, 384
equality-efficiency tradeoff, 389
Gini ratio, 384, 387
impact of taxes and transfers, 384
income distribution, 382
and income mobility, 383
Lorenz curve, 382–383, 387
measuring, 382
over time
decline of unions, 387
demand for skilled workers, 386–387
demographic changes, 387
immigration, 387
increase since 1970, 386
international trade, 387
quintiles of income, 382–383
Income instability, 365–368
Income-maintenance system, 77
characteristics, 392
earned-income tax credit, 393
entitlement programs, 391–392
food-stamp program, 393
Head Start program, 393
home energy assistance, 393–394
kinds of programs, 391–392
means tests, 393
Medicaid, 393
Medicare, 392–393
Pell grants, 393
public assistance programs, 393–394
social insurance, 392
Social Security, 392–393
Supplemental Security Income, 393
Temporary Assistance for Needy Families, 393
unemployment compensation, 393
welfare
common features, 394
conflicts among goals, 395
for immigrants, 435
reform of, 395
Income mobility, 383
Income quintiles, 382–383, 387
Income redistribution
case against, 389
by government, 71–72
by market intervention, 71
by progressive taxation, 341
by taxation, 71
transfer payments, 71
Income shares, 304
and immigration, 434
Income smoothing, 368
Income tax
corporate, 80
personal, 78–79
of U.S. households, 67
Income transfer
by monopoly, 199
by rent-seeking behavior, 201
Increasing-cost industry, 181–182
Independent action, 211
Independent goods, 49
and cross elasticity of demand, 116
Independent unions, 419
Independent variables
definition, 22–23
and horizontal axis, 21
Index of Economic Freedom, 30
Indifference curve analysis
budget line, 138–139
derivation of demand curve, 142
equilibrium at tangency, 140–141
indifference curves, 139–140
indifference map, 140
measurement of utility, 141–142
Indifference curves
convex, 139–140
definition, 139
downsloping, 139
and marginal rate of substitution, 139–140
Indifference map, 140
and topographical map, 141
Individual demand, 46
cause of changes in, 47–49
determinants, 131
versus market demand, 47
for private goods, 310
in pure competition, 167
Industrial regulation, 348
compared to social regulation, 358
legal cartel theory, 356–357
of natural monopoly, 355
problems with
costs and inefficiency, 356
perpetuating monopoly, 356
public interest theory, 355
versus public ownership, 355
regulatory commissions, 358
X-inefficiency, 356
Industrial union model
employers as wage takers, 280
inclusive unionism, 279–280
Industry, 68
constant-cost, 181
decreasing-cost, 182
increasing-cost, 181–182
low-concentration, 212
monopolistically competitive, 212
in pure competition, 177–178
real-world, 210
Industry concentration, 353–354
Industry long-run supply curve
horizontal, 181
upsloping, 182
Industry structure
diseconomies of scale, 159
economies of scale, 155–159
factors influencing, 160
high-concentration, 218
minimum efficient scale, 159–160
optimal for R&D, 246
in pure competition, 166–167
Industry supply curve, 178
Inefficiency
of bureaucracy, 335–336
of industrial regulation, 356
of monopolistic competition, 215
of pure monopoly, 198
of usury laws, 300
of voting outcomes, 331–332
Inelastic demand, 106
definition, 107
for farm products, 365
and tax incidence, 339–340
and total revenue test, 109–110
Inelastic supply of land, 293
Infant industry argument
counterarguments, 455
strategic trade policy, 455
Inferior goods, 49, 130
and income elasticity of demand, 117
Infineon, 354
Infinite slope, 24
Inflation
government policies for, 74
and real interest rate, 299–300
Information failures
asymmetric information, 322
involving buyers
adverse selection problem, 324
moral hazard problem, 323–324
involving sellers
gasoline market, 322–323
licensing surgeons, 323
overcoming, 325
used car market, 322
workplace safety, 324–325
Information technology, 200
in farming, 369
Information technology flows, 85
Ingram Book Group, 354
Injunctions, 349
Innovation
anticipating the future, 236
causing creative destruction, 247–249

definition and types, 234
diffusion of, 234–235
and economic profit, 302
within existing firms, 236
fast-second strategy, 242
first-mover benefits, 242–244
imitation problem, 242
impact of social regulation, 360
increased profit from
process innovation, 241–242
product innovation, 240–241
and monopoly power, 247, 249
and profit expectations, 303
time lags, 243
Innovators, 236
Input prices
and short-run supply curve, 175–177
and unions, 279
Inputs, in command systems, 38
Input substitution, 263, 267
Instability, 471
Installment payments, 302
Insurable risks, 301
Insurance; *see also* Health insurance
adverse selection problem, 324
crop revenue, 368
moral hazard problem, 323–324
Insurance premiums, 160
Intel Corporation, 99, 160, 191, 227, 233–234, 234, 248, 249, 351
Intellectual property, 30
Interest, 66
compounded, 302–303
definition, 295
loanable funds theory, 296–298
stated as percentage, 295
Interest groups, 332
farm lobby, 378
government employees, 336
in health care reform, 411
Interest on public debt, 77
Interest rate cost of funds
bank loans, 237
bonds, 237
personal savings, 238
retained earnings, 237
venture capital, 237–238
Interest-rate-cost-of-funds curve, 238
Interest rates, 292
annual percentage rate, 303
and capital allocation, 299
determining, 302–303
effect of usury laws, 300
and exchange rates, 469
Fed control of, 298
loanable funds theory, 296–298
nominal, 299–300
pure, 299
range of, 298–299
and R&D spending, 299
real, 299–300
selected securities, 298
teaser rates, 303
and total output, 299
Intergovernmental grants, 80
Interindustry competition, 218
Interlocking directorates, 350
Internal Revenue Service, 346
and barter exchange, 43
International costs of price supports, 373
International equilibrium, 451
International Labor Organization, 459
International linkages, 84
International Monetary Fund, 466
bailouts by, 476
borrowing from, 475
creation of, 474
current role, 474
devaluation under, 475
pegged exchange rates, 474–475
International money
gold, 472
United States dollar, 475
International Nickel Company, 192
International specialization, 18
International trade, 84–85, 441–460; *see also* Trade barriers
absolute advantage, 90, 443
aided by specialization, 32
balance of payments, 463–466
beggar-my-neighbor policy, 456
in Bretton Woods system, 474–475
case for free trade, 448
case for protection, 454–457
and changes in factors of production, 443
and communications technology, 88
comparative advantage, 90–92, 443–445
constant cost assumption, 443
costs of intervention, 96
decline in tariffs, 88
dependence of U.S., 86–87
distorted, 472
economic basis, 442–443
equilibrium world price, 451
and exchange controls, 472
and farm policy, 376–377
financial impact, 88
financing of, 463
with fixed exchange rates, 471–473
with flexible exchange rates, 466–471
and foreign exchange market, 92–94
free trade zones, 98
gains from trade, 445–447
global competition, 99
with gold standard, 473–474
government intervention, 95–96
impediments and subsidies, 95
import competition, 218–219
and income inequality, 387
with increasing costs, 447–448
key facts on, 442
with managed float, 475–477
most-favored-nation clauses, 97
multilateral agreements, 96–98
offshoring, 457
participants
recent additions, 89
U.S., Japan, and Europe, 88–89
patterns, 87–88
and production possibilities curve, 443–448
and production possibilities model, 18
rapid growth in U.S., 88
reasons for, 442–443
reasons for intervention, 95–96
and resource distribution, 443
shifting patterns of, 457
specialization, 89–90, 444–445
specialty niches, 443
and stabilization policies, 473
supply and demand analysis, 448–451
terms of trade, 445
and trade policies, 472
trade wars, 454
trading possibilities line, 445–446
and transportation technology, 88
U.S. volume, 85–86
and World Trade Organization, 458
Internet, 16
and fast-growing occupations, 262
history of, 248–249
Internet Explorer, 192, 249, 360
Interstate Commerce Commission, 356
InterTrust, 361
Intrapreneurs, 236
Intuit, 243–244
Invention, 234
Inventory control systems, 241–242
Inverse relationship, 22
Inverted-U theory of R&D, 246
Investment
as factor of production, 10
with flexible exchange rates, 471
role of interest rates, 299–300
Investment rate, 478
Investors, 69
Invisible hand theory, 37
and pure competition, 186
iPod, 242
Iraq war, 14

Japan
import licenses, 452
in international trade, 89
labor-intensive goods, 443
strategic trade policy, 455
Japanese yen, 93–94
Jeep Grand Cherokee, 234
Job information, 286
Job loss, 262
and international trade, 457
from offshoring, 457
Job protection, 421
Jobs
compensating differences, 285
increased by offshoring, 457
protectionist argument, 455–456
transfer to developing countries, 387
John Deere and company, 255
Johnson & Johnson, 227, 234, 243
Just-in-time systems, 242

Karatz, Bruce, 288
Kellogg's, 226, 243
Kennickell, Arthur B., 396
Kentucky Fried Chicken, 353
Kilby, Jack, 246
Kinked demand curve, 223
Kinked demand theory, 221–223
Kleenex, 243
Kleiner, Morris, 357n
Krueger, Alan, 282n
Krugman, Paul, 454
Kudrle, Robert, 357n
Kyoto Protocol, 322

Labor
  definition, 272
  as factor of production, 10
  fixed proportion of, 260
  income shares, 304
  international flow of, 434
  least-cost combination of resources, 264
  and marginal cost, 50
Labor costs
  and outsourcing, 403–404
  per-unit, 152
Labor demand
  in advanced nations, 260
  and decline in welfare, 395
  in demand-enhancement model, 278
  determinants, 261
  and economic growth, 280
  effect of union wage advantage, 423–424
  elasticity of, 263, 280–281
  and immigration, 433
  in imperfect competition, 257–258
  increased by unions, 279
  market demand, 274
  and minimum wage, 282
  MRP=MRC rule, 256
  occupational trends, 261–262
  and output effect, 260
  and productivity, 272–274
  and productivity changes, 259–260
  in pure competition, 256
  in purely competitive market, 274–276
  and resource price changes, 260–261
  for skilled workers, 386–387
  and substitution effect, 260
  and wage differentials, 282–286
Labor demand curve, 283–284
  shift in, 261
Labor flows, 85
Labor force
  in agriculture, 370
  demographic changes, 387
  noncompeting groups, 284–285
  and occupational segregation, 429
Labor force participation, 426
Labor Force Statistics, 20
Labor-intensive goods, 443
Labor law
  on closed shop, 421
  Landrum-Griffin Act, 422
  National Labor Relations Act, 422
  Taft-Hartley Act, 422
  Wagner Act, 422
Labor-management consultants, 420
Labor market
  bilateral monopoly, 281
  demand for skilled workers, 386–387
  discrimination in, 286
  effect of health care costs
    outsourcing, 403–404
    part-time workers, 403
    slower wage growth, 403
    temporary workers, 403
  equilibrium wage, 283–284
  minimum wage controversy, 282
  monopsony model
    characteristics, 276
    equilibrium employment, 277
    equilibrium wage, 277
    examples, 277–278
    labor supply curve, 276–277
    monopsony power, 276
    MRC higher than wages, 277
  occupational segregation, 286
  statistical discrimination, 429
  union models, 278–280
  union wage increases, 280–281
  wage differentials, 282–286
    compensating differences, 285
    marginal revenue productivity, 284
    market imperfections, 285–286
    noncompeting groups, 284–285
  and workplace safety, 324–325
Labor market discrimination
  antidiscrimination policies, 431–432
  costs of, 426–427
  definition, 425
  economic analysis, 427–430
  economic disparities from, 426
  employment discrimination, 426
  human capital, 426
  occupational, 426
  occupational segregation, 429–430
  in orchestra hiring, 436
  and production possibilities curve, 427
  statistical discrimination, 429
  taste-for-discrimination model, 427–429
  wage discrimination, 425–426
Labor market equilibrium, 274–276
Labor market imperfections, 285–286
  discrimination, 286
  geographic immobility, 286
  government restraints, 286
  lack of job information, 286
  unions, 286
Labor misallocation, 423–424
Labor-output relationship
  law of diminishing returns, 148–150
  marginal cost, 152–154
  per-unit production costs, 151–152
  short-run production costs, 150–154
Labor parties, 329
Labor productivity; *see also* Productivity
  and minimum wage, 282
  reasons for, 272–273
  and unions, 278–279
Labor quality, 273
Labor specialization, 156–157
Labor standards issue, 458
Labor supply
  market supply, 274
  nonunion labor market, 422
  and productivity, 272–274
  in purely competitive market, 274–276
  and wage differentials, 282–286
  and wage rate, 271
Labor supply curve, 283
  in monopsony model, 276–277
Labor turnover, 282
Labor unions; *see also* Collective bargaining; Unionism
  advertising by, 278
  agency shop, 421
  anti-globalization protests, 458–459
  bilateral monopoly model, 281
  closed shop, 421
  collective voice of members, 424–425
  craft unions, 279
  demand-enhancement model, 278–279
  economic effects, 423–425
  and income inequality, 385
  income inequality and decline of, 387
  independent, 419
  industrial unions, 279–280
  international membership, 419
  job-conscious, 421
  lobbying by, 278
  male vs. female membership, 420
  membership decline, 420
  open shop, 421
  and right-to-work laws, 421
  short-run objectives, 419
  union shop, 421
  U.S. membership, 419
  and wage differentials, 286
  wage increases and unemployment, 280–281
Laissez-faire, 29
Laissez-faire antitrust perspective, 352
Land
  alternative uses, 295
  as factor of production, 10
  impact of price supports, 373
  leasing, 368
  oligopoly ownership, 217
  perfectly inelastic supply, 293
  price changes over time, 294–295
  price of, 292
  supply and demand analysis, 293–295
Land-grant colleges, 369
Land-intensive goods, 443
Land rent
  and demand, 293–294
  determination of, 293
  and location, 295
  productivity differences, 295
  single-tax movement, 294–295
  surplus payment, 294
Landrum-Griffin Act of 1949, 422
Land values, 375
Las Vegas, Nevada, 292
Law of demand, 46, 142
  apparent violations of, 58
  income effect, 46
  on prices, 106
  substitution effect, 46
Law of diminishing marginal utility
  definition, 126
  and demand curve, 128
  and pollution reduction, 320
  of public goods, 312
Law of diminishing returns
  and average variable cost, 152
  graphical example, 148–150
  in long run, 156
  and marginal cost curve, 153
  in pure competition, 177
  rationale, 147–148
  tabular example, 148
Law of increasing opportunity costs
  definition, 12–13

economic rationale, 13
slope of curve, 13
Law of supply, 50
apparent violations of, 58
Learning by doing, 32, 158, 243
Leases of land, 368
Least-cost combination of resources, 264, 265–266
Least-cost production, 35, 184
Least-cost rule, 267
Legal barriers to entry
licensing, 192
patents, 191–192
Legal cartel theory of regulation, 356
Legal immigrants, 433
Legal structure, 71
Legislation to correct for negative externalities, 72
Lemons, 322
Lenders, and usury laws, 300
Levi's, 243
Levitt, Steven D., 326
Lexus, 8, 234
Liability rules, 315–316
Licensing, 192
occupational, 279, 357
of surgeons, 323
Life expectancy, 403
Limited income, 7
Limited liability, 68–69
Limit pricing, 226, 230
Linear demand curve, 110–111
Linear relationship, 22
Linear relationship equation, 24
Linux operating system, 190, 247
Litigation
expense of, 352
malpractice award limits, 414
over externalities, 315–316
Loaded terminology, 16
Loanable funds
demand changes, 297–298
demand for, 296–297
and nonmarket rationing, 300
supply changes, 297
supply of, 296
Loanable funds theory of interest rates
definition, 296
financial institutions, 297
other participants
businesses, 298
government, 298
households, 298
Loans
and interest rate range, 298
maturity, 298
price of credit, 302–303
risk, 298
Lobbying
by farmers, 378
by unions, 278
Local government
finances, 80
health care costs, 404
regressive taxes, 343
Localized markets, 218
Location, 211
and land rent, 295
Lockouts, 422
Logitech, 246
Logrolling, 332, 375
Lojack, 326
Lonestar Beer, 228
Long run
costs of production in, 146
decline in agriculture, 368–370
and law of diminishing returns, 156
in monopolistic competition
complications, 214–215
losses, 214
profits, 214
price elasticity of supply, 115
very long run, 234
Long-run adjustment, 146
Long-run average total-cost curve, 156
determination of shape, 160
diseconomies of scale, 159
economies of scale, 156–159
natural monopoly, 191
in pure competition, 181
Long-run equilibrium
competitive firm and market, 183
for monopolistic competition, 215
pure competition, 179–181
consumer surplus, 184
efficiency characteristics, 182
losses eliminated by exit, 180–181
producer surplus, 184
profit eliminated by entry, 180
Long-run production costs
constant returns to scale, 159
diseconomies of scale, 159
economies of scale, 156–159
firm size and costs, 155
long-run cost curve, 156
minimum efficient scale, 159–160
Long-run supply curve
constant-cost industry, 181
decreasing-cost industry, 182
increasing-cost industry, 181–182
Lorenz curve, 382–383, 384, 387
Losses, 34
due to work rules, 423
eliminated in long-run equilibrium, 180–181
from featherbedding, 423
from labor misallocation, 423–424
in monopolistic competition, 213, 214
possible for monopolist, 197–198
from strikes, 423
Loss-minimizing position
of monopolist, 198
in pure competition, 172–174
Lotteries, 80
Lowest-unit-cost advantage, 191
Low-income home energy assistance, 393–394
Low-wage workers, 405
Lucent Technologies, 236
Luck, 386
Luxuries, 7–8
elastic demand for, 341
and price elasticity of demand, 112
Luxury tax repeal, 341

Macroeconomics, 6
Majority voting; *see* Voting
Major League Baseball, 278
Malaysia, 89
Malpractice award limits, 414
Managed floating exchange rates
concerns with, 476–477
definition, 475
and flexible exchange rates, 476
and G8 nations, 476
support for, 720
Managerial-opposition hypothesis of union decline, 420
Managerial prerogatives, 421
Managerial specialization, 157
Mandatory health insurance, 415
Manufacturing costs, 50
Marcus, Amy Dockser, 410
Marginal analysis, 5
Marginal benefit, 5; *see also* MB=MC rule
of R&D, 237
social regulation, 358
Marginal benefit curve, 320–321
Marginal cost, 5, 50; *see also* MB=MC analysis
and average total cost, 153–154
and average variable cost, 153–154
calculations, 152–153
competitive firm and market, 183
defining, 154
of extra production, 372–373
graphical portrayal, 153, 154
law of diminishing returns, 177
marginal decisions, 153
and marginal product, 153
and opportunity cost, 184
public goods, 312
for pure competition, 171–178
of R&D, 237
social regulation, 358
Marginal cost curve
and average total cost, 153–154
and average variable cost, 153–154
and law of diminishing returns, 153
of monopolist, 199
in monopolistic competition, 213, 215
public goods, 312
of reducing pollution, 320–321
shift in, 154–155
Marginal product, 147, 256
and law of diminishing returns, 148–150
and marginal cost, 153
Marginal product curve, 153
variable costs, 150
Marginal productivity theory
of income distribution, 266–267
of resource demand
demand schedule, 256–257
derived demand, 255
imperfect competition, 257–258
marginal revenue product, 255–256
market demand, 258
rule for, 256
Marginal product of capital, 264
Marginal product of labor, 264
Marginal rate of substitution, 139–140, 141
Marginal resource cost, 277
Marginal revenue; *see also* MR=MC rule
in monopoly, 193–194
in pure competition, 167–168

Marginal revenue cost, 256; *see also* MRP=MRC rule
Marginal revenue curve
  of monopolist, 194
  in monopolistic competition, 213, 215
  in pure competition, 178
Marginal-revenue–marginal-cost approach, 170–171
Marginal revenue product; *see also* MRP=MRC rule
  definition, 256
  in imperfect competition, 257–258
  and resource demand, 255–256
  as resource demand schedule, 256–257
  and union wages, 423–424
Marginal revenue productivity, 284
Marginal social benefit, 326
Marginal tax rate, 78–79
  and health care, 408
Marginal utility
  cash vs. noncash gifts, 134
  definition, 126
  and demand, 128
  diamond-water paradox, 132–133
  diminishing, 46
  and indifference curve theory, 141–142
  per dollar, 129
  and total utility, 126–128
  in utility-maximizing rule, 129–131
  and value of time, 133
  and vending machines, 126
Marginal utility/price ratio, 240–241
Market(s), 29
  definition, 31
  functions of, 45
  geographic, 162
  for human organs, 60–61
  localized, 218
  winner-take-all, 259
Market-clearing price, 53
Market demand, 46–47, 47–49
  constant-cost industry, 181
  decreasing-cost industry, 182
  increasing-cost industry, 181–182
  for labor, 274
  lacking for public goods, 310
  for private goods, 310
  in pure competition, 167, 177–178
  for resources, 258
Market demand curve
  for monopolist, 192–195
  natural monopoly, 191, 205
Market equilibrium
  and changes in supply and demand, 56–57
  efficient allocation, 55–56
  equilibrium price, 53–55
  equilibrium quantity, 53–55
  and price controls, 57–61
  rationing function of prices, 55
Market failure, 33
  definition, 309
  externalities, 72–73, 314–322, 326
  versus government failure, 330
  information failure, 322–325
  to provide public goods, 73
  public goods, 310–313
  quasi-public goods, 73
Market for externality rights, 318–319
Marketing loan program, 378
Market intervention, 71
Market period, 114–115
Market power, 121
  and income inequality, 385
  of monopoly, 199
Market price, 180
Market segregation, 203
Market share
  and antitrust policy, 351
  defining, 351
  Herfindahl index, 219, 353
  in monopolistic competition, 211
Market structure
  characteristics of models, 166
  monopolistic competition, 166, 210–216
  monopoly, 166, 189–204
  monopsony, 276–278
  natural monopoly, 204–207
  oligopoly, 166, 210, 217–229
  pure competition, 166–186
  and technological advance, 245–247
Market supply, 50–51
  constant-cost industry, 181
  decreasing-cost industry, 182
  increasing-cost industry, 181–182
  of labor, 274
  in long-run equilibrium, 180
  in pure competition, 177–178
  reduction in farm surpluses, 373–374
Market supply curves, 181
Market system
  accommodating change, 36
  arrangement of world's resources, 40
  versus bureaucracy, 335–336
  capital accumulation, 37
  capital goods, 31–32
  characteristics, 29–33
  circular flow model, 38–41
  as communications system, 35
  compared to public sector, 336
  competition in, 31, 71
  consumer sovereignty, 34
  creative destruction, 36–37
  definition, 29
  disposition of output, 35–36
  division of labor, 32
  efficiency of, 37
  five fundamental questions, 34–37
  freedom in, 37
  freedom of choice, 30
  freedom of enterprise, 30
  how will goods be produced, 35
  imperfections, 267
  incentives in, 37
  and income inequality, 384
  invisible hand thesis, 37
  legal structure, 71
  limited government, 33
  markets and prices, 31
  private property, 29–30
  promotion of progress, 36–37
  provision of private goods, 310
  self-interest in, 30–31
  specialization, 32
  technological advance, 36–37
  technology, 31–32
  use of money, 32–33
  what will be produced, 34–35
Marriott Hotels, 325
Massachusetts health insurance law, 415
Matsushita, 234
Maturity, and interest rate range, 298
MB=MC rule
  and economics of war, 14
  and immigration, 435
  for optimal resource allocation, 13–14
McCain, John, 344
McCaw Communications, 243
McDonald's Corporation, 34, 99, 161, 217, 226, 227, 245
McDonnell Douglas, 353
MCI Communications, 356
Means tests, 393
Median family wealth, 396
Median-voter model
  example, 333–334
  implications, 334
  real-world applicability, 334
Medicaid, 401–402
Medical care purchases, 133–134
Medical education, 409
Medical ethics, 407
Medically uninsured, 404–405
Medical research funding, 403
Medical technology, 410
Medicare, 401
  description, 392–393
  diagnosis-related-group system, 413
Medicare Part D, 414
Medicare Prescription Drug, Improvement, and Modernization Act of 2003, 414
Medicare tax, 78, 80, 338
Medium of exchange, 32
Meister-Brau, 242
Mercedes, 8, 234
Mercedes-Benz, 227
Mergers and acquisitions
  beer industry, 228–229
  conglomerate mergers, 353
  and cross elasticity of demand, 117
  effectiveness of antitrust, 352–354
  Herfindahl index, 353–354
  horizontal merger, 352–353
  in oligopoly, 217–218
  profitable buyouts, 243–244
  vertical merger, 353
Mexico
  chronic unemployment, 435
  labor demand, 433
  loss of cheap labor, 434
  production possibilities analysis, 90–91
  wage rates, 434
Michelin, 202
Microeconomics, 6–7
Micron Technology, 234, 354
Microsoft Corporation, 9, 99, 160, 189, 200, 227, 234, 236, 243–244, 247, 249
  antitrust case, 71, 192, 202, 209, 249, 351, 352, 360–361
  founding of, 248
Midpoint formula, 106
Military self-sufficiency argument, 454
Miller Brewing Company, 85, 228–229, 242
Minimum annual income, 394
Minimum efficient scale, 159–160
  in aircraft and concrete plants, 162
  start-up firms, 160

Minimum wage
case against, 282
case for, 282
evidence and conclusions, 282
origin of, 282
Minnetonka, 243
Minorities
and affirmative action, 431–432
labor-force discrimination, 286
medically uninsured, 404
occupational segregation, 286
in poverty, 390
Misallocation of resources, 374, 377
Misfortune, 386
Mitsubishi, 89
Mobil Oil, 353
Mobil Travel Guide, 325
Models, 6
graphs for illustrating, 21–25
Monetary policy
and gold standard, 474
to maintain exchange rates, 473
Money
versus barter, 32
definition, 32
medium of exchange, 32
paper, 33
uses of, 32–33
Money flows, 41
Money-income determination, 255
Money supply, 474
Monopolistic competition; *see also* Oligopoly
advertising, 212
brand names, 211
characteristics, 166, 211
control over prices, 211–212
definition, 166
and efficiency
allocative efficiency, 215
excess capacity, 215–216
productive efficiency, 215
entry and exit, 212
independent action, 211
kinds of industries, 212
large number of sellers, 211
no collusion, 211
packaging, 211
price and output
demand curve, 212–214
long run, 213–215
short run, 214
product attributes, 211
product differentiation, 211–212
product variety, 216
small market share, 211
and technological advance, 245
Monopolization, 349
Monopoly, 71, 189–208; *see also* Antitrust *entries;* Natural monopoly
assessment and policy options, 201–202
barriers to entry
control of resources, 192
definition, 190
deterrence strategies, 192
economies of scale, 191
licensing, 191–192
patents, 191–192
plant size, 191
pricing strategies, 192
research and development, 201
behavior vs. structure, 350–351
characteristics, 166
compared to monopolistic competition, 214
conditions for
blocked entry, 190
no close substitutes, 190
nonprice competition, 190
price maker, 190
single seller, 190
De Beers diamond syndicate, 206
definition, 166
demand in, 192–195
deterred by free trade, 448
dual objectives, 190
economic effects
cost complications, 199–201
income transfer, 199
price, output, and efficiency, 198–199
and economic profit, 302–303
economies of scale, 199–200
effectiveness of antitrust, 352
examples of, 190
marginal revenue less than price, 193–194
market demand curve, 192–193
90-60-30 rule, 351
by occupational licensing, 279
output and price determination
cost data, 195
MR=MC rule, 195–196
no supply curve, 196–197
perpetuated by regulation, 356
price discrimination, 202–204
at baseball park, 203
conditions for, 203
examples, 203–204
graphical analysis, 204
as price maker, 194
pricing misconceptions
not highest price, 197
possibility of losses, 197–198
total, not unit, profit, 197
pricing policy, 192, 195
rent-seeking behavior, 201
and technological advance, 201, 246
trusts, 349
X-inefficiency, 200–201
Monopoly marketing, 206
Monopoly power
creating profit incentives, 352
from innovation, 247, 249
and price discrimination, 203
of unions vs. monopsony power, 281
Monopsony, 276
Monopsony model
characteristics, 276
equilibrium wage/ employment, 277
examples, 277–278
interest costs, 299
monopsony power, 276
MRC higher than wages, 277
professional sports, 278
upward-sloping labor supply curve, 276–277
Monopsony power
examples, 277–278
pure, 276
versus union monopoly power, 281
Monsanto, 99
Montana Sheep Institute, 344
Moore, Kevin B., 396
Moral hazard problem
in health insurance
less prevention, 407
overconsumption, 407–408
as inadequate information, 323–324
Most-favored-nation clauses, 97
Motel business, 174
Movie business
price discrimination by, 203
price elasticity of demand, 110–111
MP3 player, 242
MRC; *see* Marginal resource cost
MR=MC rule
and antitrust policy, 349
applications
loss minimizing case, 172–174
profit-maximizing case, 171–172
shutdown case, 174–175
and change in supply, 177
and criminal behavior, 134–135
and efficiency, 120
and equilibrium price, 177–178
features of, 171
generalized depiction, 175–177
health care spending, 404
and law of diminishing returns, 177
and long-run equilibrium, 179–180
of monopolist, 199
in monopolistic competition, 213, 214
in monopoly, 195–197
for natural monopoly, 205
and normal profit, 182
and price discrimination, 204
for public goods, 311, 313
for R&D, 237
and sunk costs, 161
MRP=MRC rule, 256, 265
labor market equilibrium, 274–276
in pure competition, 257
MS-DOS, 248, 249
Multilateral trade agreements
General Agreement on Tariffs and Trade, 97
most-favored-nation clauses, 97
Reciprocal Trade Agreements Act, 97
World Trade Organization, 97–98
Multinational corporations
foreign competitors, 202
in international trade, 89
Multiplant firms, 68
Multiple pricing, 121
Municipal bonds, 298–299
Murphy, Kevin, 404
Mutual interdependence
complications, 221
in oligopoly, 217, 220

National Aeronautics and Space Administration, 252
National Basketball Association, 278
National Bureau of Economic Research, 124
National defense spending, 77
National Education Association, 279
National Football League, 278
National health insurance, 411–412
arguments against, 412
arguments for, 412

National Labor Relations Act, 422
National Labor Relations Board, 422
National Safety Council, 358
National Science Foundation, 252
Native American Arts and Crafts store, 220
Natural monopoly, 71, 159
conditions for, 355
creation of, 349
dilemma of regulation, 207
fair-return price, 205–207
and industrial regulation, 355
long-run-average total-cost curve, 191
lowest-unit-cost advantage, 191
policy options for, 202
public ownership option, 355
rate regulation, 204–205
socially optimal price, 205
supplanted by monopoly, 356
NCR, 267
Near-monopolies, 190
NEC, 202
Necessities, 7–8
and price elasticity of demand, 112
Negative externalities
characteristics, 314
and Coase theorem, 315
correcting for, 72
definition, 72
global warming, 321–322
government intervention
direct controls, 316
specific taxes, 316–317
subsidies, 317
liability rules and lawsuits, 315–316
market for externality rights, 318–319
optimal amount of reduction, 319–321
price of reducing, 319–320
taxes to reduce, 341–342
and tragedy of the commons, 317–318
Negative slope, 23
Nestlé, 89, 202, 243
Net investment income, 465
Netscape Communications, 249
Netscape Navigator, 192, 360
Network effects, 200
Net worth, 396
New Balance, 46
New products
determinant of demand, 247
gaining acceptance, 240–241
importance of price, 241
unsuccessful, 241
Newspapers, 160–162
New York City rent controls, 59
New York Stock Exchange, 45
Nike, Inc., 46, 233–234
Nikon, 94
90-60-30 rule for monopoly, 351
90-10 ratio wage differentials, 387
Nissan Motors, 94
No-free-lunch theory, 4, 360
Nokia, 202, 227
Nominal interest rate, 299–300
global perspective, 300
Nominal wage, 272
Noncash gifts, 134
Noncash transfers, 384
Noncollusive oligopoly, 221–223
combined strategy, 223
criticisms of model, 223
ignore price change, 221–222
kinked demand curve, 223
match price changes, 221
price inflexibility, 223
price war, 223
Noncompeting groups
ability, 284
education and training, 284–285
Nondurable goods, 68
Nonexcludability, 310
of public goods, 73
Nonfarm income, 368
Nonlinear curve, 24–25
Nonmarket rationing, 300
Nonprice competition, 166, 190
in monopolistic competition, 212
Nonrivalry
in consumption, 200, 310
of public goods, 73
Nontariff trade barriers, 95, 452
Nordhaus, William, 404
No resale, 203
Normal goods, 48
and income elasticity of demand, 117
Normal profit, 145, 301, 356
break-even point, 169–170
in monopolistic competition, 214–215
MR=MC rule, 182
Normative economics, 7
North Korea, 29
Noyce, Robert, 246
Number of buyers, 48
Number of sellers, 52
Nurses' Union, 419
Occupational discrimination, 426
Occupational licensing, 279, 357
Occupational Outlook, 270
Occupational Safety and Health Administration, 329, 358
Occupational segregation, 286
assumptions, 429
effects of crowding, 429–430
elimination of, 430
Occupations
fastest-growing, 261–262
rapidly declining, 262
Office Depot, 353
Official reserves
in Bretton Woods system, 475
of central banks, 466
to maintain exchange rates, 472
U.S. dollars, 475
Offshoring, 403–404, 457
Oil imports, 442
cause of trade deficits, 478
Old-economy firms, 420
Oligopoly; *see also* Game theory model
advertising by, 227–229
barriers to entry, 217
in beer industry, 228–229
cartels, 223–226
characteristics, 166, 210
complications of interdependence, 221
concentration ratios, 218–219
control over prices, 217
definition, 166, 217
differentiated, 217
diversity of, 221
and efficiency
allocative efficiency, 229–230
foreign competition and, 230
limit pricing, 230
productive efficiency, 229–230
technological advance, 230
few large producers, 217
in game theory model, 219–221
Herfindahl index, 219
homogeneous, 217
interest costs, 299
market share, 227
mergers, 217–218
mutual interdependence, 217
noncollusive, 221–223
price leadership model, 226
reasons for models, 221
strategic behavior, 217
and technological advance, 245
OmniSky, 234
Open economy, 89
Open shop, 421
Opportunity cost, 12, 145
and budget line, 9
in Coase theorem, 315
of college attendance, 9
definition, 4
in free trade, 448
implicit cost, 301
in international trade, 445
law of increasing opportunity costs, 12–13
in marginal analysis, 5
and marginal cost, 184
of medical education, 398
Opportunity-cost ratio, 444
Optimal allocation, 13–14
Optimal amount of R&D
adjustments, 240
versus affordable amount, 239–240
determination of, 239
expected returns, 240
Optimal reduction of negative externalities, 320–321
Organization of Petroleum Exporting Countries, 87, 88
as cartel, 224
daily oil production, 225
oil imports from, 442
Organ transplants, 60–61, 410
Osborne Computer, 246
Other-things-equal assumption, 6
demand and prices, 45
in graphs, 23
and law of demand, 46
for R&D, 246–247
Output
collusion in, 223–224
in command systems, 29, 38
constant-cost industry, 181
decreasing-cost industry, 182
effect of monopoly, 198–199
farm surplus, 372
fixed costs, 150–151
fluctuations in agriculture, 365–366
and hourly pay, 273
and immigration, 434
and income inequality, 389
increasing-cost industry, 181–182
and interest rates, 299
least-cost combination of resources, 264
in least-cost production, 35
losses due to work rules, 423
losses from strikes, 423

low-concentration manufacturing, 212
in monopolistic competition, 212–215
in monopoly
cost data, 195
lack of supply curve, 196–197
misconceptions, 197
MR=MC rule, 195–196
possibility of losses, 197–198
of price makers, 194
in pure competition
marginal-revenue–marginal-cost approach, 170–171
total-revenue–total-cost approach, 168–170
total cost, 151
of U.S. businesses, 69
value of in U.S., 65
variable costs, 150–151
X-inefficiency, 200–201
Output-determining rule, 171
Output effect, 260
Outsourcing, 457
and health care costs, 403–404
Overallocation of resources, 372, 408–409
Overconsumption of health insurance
supply and demand model, 408–409
tax subsidy for care, 407–408
Overt collusion, 224
Ozone layer, 316

Pabst Brewery, 228–229
Packaging, 211
Palm Company, 236
Palm Pilot, 234
Paper money, 33
Paradox of voting
preferences, 332–333
voting outcomes, 333
Parity concept
criticisms of, 374
definition, 371–372
and price supports, 372–373
Parity ratio, 372
Partnerships, 68
Part-time workers, 403
Patent protection, 185
Patents, 191–192, 234
expiration of, 201–202
first-mover strategies, 242–243
global perspective, 243
Pay for performance, 74
bonuses, stock options, and profit sharing, 287
commissions, 287
efficiency wages, 287
negative side effects, 287–289
piece rates, 287
principal-agent problem, 287–289
royalties, 287
Payoff matrix, 220
Payroll taxes, 80, 338
for unemployment compensation, 393
Pegged exchange rates, 471–473, 474–475
Pell grants, 393
Pensions and income security spending, 77
PepsiCo, 6, 117, 242, 353
Per capita income, 8
Perfectly elastic demand, 107–108
in pure competition, 167–168
Perfectly inelastic demand, 107–108
Perloff, Jeffrey, 244
Per se violations, 354
Personal bankruptcy, 404
Personal computer, 248–249
Personal consumption expenditures, 67–68
Personal distribution of income, 66–67
Personal income tax, 338
federal, 78–79
incidence of, 342
of states, 80
Personal Responsibility Act of 1996, 395
Personal saving, 67
for R&D, 238
Personal taxes, 67
Per-unit costs
average fixed cost, 151–152
average total cost, 152
average variable cost, 152
marginal cost, 152–154
and plant size, 156
Per-unit profit, 172, 241
Petition of the Candlemakers (Bastiat), 100
Pet Milk, 224
Pfizer, Inc., 68, 191
Pharmaceutical industry, 185
and health care costs, 410
patents, 192
Philip Morris Company, 229
Philips Electronics, 202
Physicians
and demand for health care
defensive medicine, 407
ethics, 407
fee-for-service basis, 406–407
supplier-induced, 406–407
number of, 409
salaries, 409
Picasso, Pablo, 126, 285
Piece rates, 287
Pizza Hut, 353
Planning curve, 156
Plant, 68
Plant capacity
fixed, 146
for long run, 155–156
variable, 146
Plant size
aircraft industry, 162
and average total cost, 155
as barrier to entry, 191
concrete plants, 162
constant returns to scale, 158, 159
diseconomies of scale, 159
economies of scale, 156–159
efficient capital, 158
and labor specialization, 156–157
and managerial specialization, 157
Play or pay approach, 411
P=MC rule, 171, 349
allocative efficiency, 184
generalized depiction, 175–177
and normal profit, 182
Polaroid, 242–243
Policy contradictions, 375
Policy issues for resource market, 255
Policy options for monopoly, 201–202
Polio, 403
Political action committees, 375
Politics
and agriculture demand, 368
of farm policy
declining support, 376
public choice theory, 375–376
trade considerations, 376–377
of government failure, 334–336
pork-barrel politics, 334–335
of protectionism, 95–96
of rent-seeking, 335
special interests, 334–335
Pollution, 72
carbon-dioxide emissions, 321
equilibrium quantity, 320
Pollution rights market, 318–319
Pollution rights trading, 319
Pong, 236
Popular Mechanics, 236
Population
aging of, 406
percentage in farming, 376
poverty rates, 390
Population growth
and demand for food products, 369
from immigration, 433
Pork-barrel politics
characteristics, 334–335
examples, 344
Positive economics, 7
Positive externalities
auto antitheft devices, 326
characteristics, 314–315
Coase theorem, 315
correcting for, 73
definition, 72
government provision, 317
in health care market, 405
Positive slope, 23
Post Cereals, 226
Post hoc fallacy, 17
Postrel, Virginia, 40
Poverty
consumption vs. income, 391
definition, 390
economics of, 389–391
extent of, 381
incidence of, 390–391
measurement issues, 391
medically uninsured, 404–405
trends, 391
Poverty line, 390
Poverty rate, 390
children, 390
minorities, 390
trends 1959–2004, 391
Preferences, 128
and income inequality, 385
indifference curves, 139–140
median-voter model, 333–334
and paradox of voting, 332–333
pork-barrel politics, 334–335
for private goods, 332
and rest-seeking behavior, 335
revealed by voting, 331–334
and size of government, 334
of special interests, 334–335
Preferred provider organizations, 413
Prejudice, 428
Prescription drug coverage, 413–414
Price(s); *see also* Equilibrium price; Price elasticity of demand; Price elasticity of supply
constant-cost industry, 181

Price—*Cont.*
and consumer behavior, 128
and consumer surplus, 118–119, 184
and consumer tastes, 35
of credit, 302–303
decreasing-cost industry, 182
and demand, 45–46
on demand curve, 46
and distribution of output, 35–36
DVDs and DVD players, 132
effect of monopoly, 198–199
effect of shortage, 54–55
effect of surplus, 54
effect of tariffs/quotas, 452–453
fair-return, 205–207
of gold, 116
incentive functions, 294
income effect, 46
increasing-cost industry, 181–182
and inflation, 74
law of demand on, 106
in law of supply, 50
in market system, 31
in monopolistic competition, 211–212, 212–215
in monopoly, 193–194
of new products, 241
in oligopoly, 217
parity concept, 371–372
and producer surplus, 119, 184
of products, 184
in pure competition
long run, 178–182
short run, 175–178
and quantity demanded, 46
raised by social regulation, 360
rationing function, 55
regulation of, 355
and resource demand, 256
set by government, 57–61
socially optimal, 205
substitution effect, 46
terms of trade, 445
and ticket scalping, 55
for union-produced goods, 420
Price ceilings
black market result, 59
definition, 58
on gasoline, 58–59
graphical analysis, 58
rationing problem, 58–59
rent controls, 59
usury laws, 300
Price changes
and budget line, 138–139
communicating, 226
consumer sensitivity to, 106
and health care, 406
ignoring, 221–222
infrequent, 226
matching, 221
Price discrimination, 121
at baseball games, 204
in Clayton Act, 350
conditions for
market segregation, 203
monopoly power, 203
no resale, 203
definition, 202
dumping as, 455
effectiveness of antitrust, 354
examples, 203–204
forms of, 202–203
graphical analysis, 204
successful, 203
Price elasticity of demand
in airline industry, 121
applications
decriminalization of illegal drugs, 113–114
excise taxes, 113
large crop yields, 112–113
coefficient
elastic demand, 107
elimination of minus sign, 107
formula, 106
inelastic demand, 107
midpoint formula, 106
perfectly elastic/inelastic demand, 107–108
unit elasticity, 107
using averages, 106
using percentages, 106–107
definition, 106
determinants
luxuries vs. necessities, 112
proportion of income, 112
substitutability, 112
time, 112
examples, 113
for farm products, 365
for health care, 406
in monopolistic competition, 212–214
and monopoly, 195
for movie tickets, 110–111
summary of, 112
total revenue test
definition, 108
elastic demand, 108–109
elasticity along linear demand curve, 110–111
inelastic demand, 109–110
and total revenue curve, 111
unit elasticity, 110
Price elasticity of supply
applications
antiques and reproductions, 115–116
volatile gold prices, 116
coefficient, 114
degree of, 114
long run, 115
market period, 114–115
short run, 115
Price fixing
effectiveness of antitrust, 354
recent cases, 354
Price floors
additional consequences, 60–61
definition, 59
graphical analysis, 59–60
minimum wage, 282
surpluses from, 59–60
Price inflexibility, 223
Price instability, 365–368
Price leadership, 226
Price leadership model
breakdowns, 226
communicating price changes, 226
infrequent changes, 226
limit pricing, 226
Price level; *see* Price elasticity of demand; Price elasticity of supply
Price-level changes, 468–469
Price makers
monopolists as, 190, 194
oligopoly, 217
resource demand, 257–258
Price–marginal cost gap, 215
Price of unrelated goods, 49
Price-quantity combination
of cartels, 224
constant-cost industry, 181
decreasing-cost industry, 181
increasing-cost industry, 181–182
of monopolist, 193–194, 195, 198–199
natural monopoly, 205
and taxes, 342
Price-quantity principle, 6
Prices of other goods, 52
Price supports
administrative costs, 373
criticisms of
misallocation of resources, 374
misguided subsidies, 374–375
policy contradictions, 375
economics of, 372–373
efficiency loss, 372–373
environmental costs, 373
gains to farmers, 372
international costs, 373
and land values, 375
losses to consumers, 372
rent-seeking behavior, 373
social losses, 373
sugar program, 375, 376–377
and surplus output, 372
tax burden, 372, 373
Price taker, 167, 255
Price wars, 223, 226
Pricing policy
as barrier to entry, 192
cheating, 225
collusion in, 223–224
dual pricing, 121
game theory model, 219–221
collusion, 220
incentives to cheat, 220–221
mutual interdependence, 220
payoff matrix, 219
strategy combinations, 219–220
limit pricing, 226
and market power, 121
in monopoly
cost data, 195
lack of supply curve, 196–197
misconceptions, 197
MR=MC rule, 195–196
possibility of losses, 197–198
multiple pricing, 121
noncollusive oligopoly, 222–223
by oligopolists, 226
for resources, 255
Pricing power, 121
Principal-agent problem, 69–70
and pay for performance, 286–287
Principals, 70
Principle of comparative advantage, 445
Private goods, 73
characteristics, 310
excludability, 310
market demand for, 310
preferences for, 332
in public choice theory, 335
rivalry in consumption, 310
Private property
definition, 30
and freedom of choice, 30
in market system, 29–30
Private sector
business population, 68–70
households, 66–68
Process innovation, 234
average total cost, 241–242

reduced cost from, 241–242
total cost, 242
Procter & Gamble, 227
Prodigy Services, 248
Producer expectations, 52
Producers, in oligopoly, 217
Producer surplus
definition, 119
effect of monopoly on, 199
and efficiency, 120
efficiency losses, 120–122
in pure competition, 184
Product attributes
and advertising, 216
in monopolistic competition, 211
Product demand
change in, 259
in demand-enhancement model, 278
elasticity, 263
Product development, 227
Product differentiation, 166
in monopolistic competition, 211–212, 245
and productive efficiency, 216
Product durability, 112
Product improvements, 241
Product innovation, 234
increased revenue from, 240–241
Production
average product, 147
in command systems, 29
defense vs. civilian goods, 14
effect of tariffs, 452–453
efficiency losses, 120–122
least-cost, 35
marginal cost, 50
marginal product, 147
problems in command systems, 38
substitution in, 52
total product, 147
Production costs; *see* Costs of production
Production decisions, 34–35
Production possibilities curve
comparative advantage, 90–92, 443–448
definition, 11–12
and economic growth, 15–16
effects of discrimination, 427
law of increasing opportunity costs, 12–13
optimal resource allocation, 13–14
present choices and future possibilities, 16–18
slope of, 13
unemployment in, 14–15
United States and Brazil, 444–448
Production possibilities model
assumptions, 11
economics of war, 14
and international trade, 18
law of increasing opportunity costs, 12–13
optimal allocation, 13–14
with two goods, 11–14
Production possibilities table, 11
Mexico, 90
United States, 90
Production targets, 38
Productive efficiency, 55, 120
competition vs. monopoly, 198–199
lacking in monopolistic competition, 215
lacking in oligopoly, 229–230
versus product differentiation, 216
in pure competition, 183–184
and technological advance, 247
Productivity; *see also* Labor productivity
access to resources, 273
advanced technology, 273
labor quality, 273
of land, 295
mixed research findings on unions, 425
negative effect of unions, 422–424
featherbedding, 423
labor misallocation, 423–424
strikes, 423
work rules, 423
plentiful capital, 273
positive effect of unions
informal training, 425
longer-run impact, 424
reduced turnover, 424–425
and real wage, 272–274
and resource demand, 255–256, 259–260
slow growth in health care, 409–410
Product market, 41
and income inequality, 385
Product price, 51
meaning of, 184
and resource demand, 256
Products
free, 4
network effects, 200
simultaneous consumption, 200
standardized, 166–167
Product supply, 177
Product variety, 216
Professional baseball teams, 203
Professional golf, 291
Professional sports
free agents, 278
monopsony model, 278
teams, 190
Profit, 34, 66; *see also* Economic profit; Normal profit
and consumer tastes, 35
economic/pure, 145–146
increased by innovation, 240–242
in monopolistic competition, 214
normal, 145
in pure competition, 177–178
and X-inefficiency, 201
Profitable buyouts, 243–244
Profit maximization
by cartels, 224
long-run, 178–182
assumptions, 179
constant-cost industry, 181
decreasing-cost industry, 182
goal of analysis, 179
increasing-cost industry, 181–182
long-run equilibrium, 179–181
of monopolist, 195–196
MRP=MRC rule, 256
and price discrimination, 204
for pure competition
long-run approaches, 178–182
short-run approaches, 168–172
in pure competition
MR=MC rule, 171
Profit-maximizing combination of resources, 264–266
Profit-maximizing output
of monopolist, 195–196, 199
in monopolistic competition, 215
of natural monopoly, 205
for pure competition, 171–172
marginal-revenue–marginal cost approach, 170–171
total-revenue–total-cost approach, 168–170
Profit sharing plans, 287
negative side effects, 289
Progress
capital accumulation, 37
technological advance, 36–37
Progress and Poverty (George), 294
Progressive taxes, 78, 338
federal system, 343
for income redistribution, 341
Property rights
and Coase theorem, 315
and tragedy of the commons, 317–318
Property taxes, 338–339
incidence of, 342–343
Proportional tax, 338
Protectionism; *see also* Trade barriers
antidumping argument, 455
Bastiat's critique, 100
cheap foreign labor argument, 456
diversification-for-stability argument, 454–455
domestic employment argument, 455–456
and end of gold standard, 474
infant industry argument, 455
military self-sufficiency argument, 454
politics of, 95–96
rising prices from, 453–454
Smoot-Hawley Tariff, 96
trade adjustment assistance, 456–457
Protective tariffs, 95, 452
Prototypes, 234
Public assistance programs, 393–394
Public choice theory
definition, 330
on farm policy, 375–376
on government failure, 334–336
public vs. private goods, 335
revealing preferences by voting, 331–334
Public debt, interest on, 77
Public goods, 75
benefits-received principle, 337
characteristics, 310
cost-benefit analysis, 312–313
definition, 73
demand for, 311–312
examples, 73
free-rider problem, 73, 310
and interest groups, 332
and majority voting, 332
marginal cost/benefit, 312
median-voter model, 333–334
nonexcludability, 310
nonrivalry, 310
optimal quantity, 311, 312
and paradox of voting, 332–333
paying for, 337

Public goods—*Cont.*
and positive externalities, 317
in public choice theory, 335
Public interest theory of regulation, 355
Public ownership, 355
Public regulation, 355
Public sector
and circular flow model, 75–76
government failure, 334–336
government finance, 75–80
federal level, 77–80
global perspective, 76
local level, 80
purchases and transfers, 75–76
state level, 80
government role in economy, 71–75
and circular flow model, 75
promoting stability, 74
qualification on, 74–75
resource reallocation, 72–74
imperfect institutions, 336
Public utilities; *see* Natural monopoly
Purchasing power
income effect, 46
substitution effect, 46
Purchasing power parity theory, 468–469
and Big Mac index, 469
Pure capitalism, 29
Pure competition
allocative efficiency, 199
average revenue, 167–168
break-even point, 169–170
characteristics
free entry and exit, 167
price takers, 167
standardized product, 166–167
very large numbers, 166
compared to monopolistic competition, 214
compared to monopoly, 192
definition, 166
and efficiency, 182–186
allocative efficiency, 184
consumer surplus, 184
dynamic adjustments, 184–186
invisible hand theory, 186
producer surplus, 184
productive efficiency, 183–184
efficiency gains from entry, 285
long-run profit maximization, 178–182
assumptions, 179
constant-cost industry, 181
decreasing-cost industry, 182
equilibrium, 179–181
goal of analysis, 179
increasing-cost industry, 181–182
long-run supply curve, 181
loss-minimization case, 172–174
marginal cost, 175–178
marginal revenue, 167–168
MRP=MRC rule, 257
occurrence, 166
perfectly elastic demand, 167
and price supports, 372
productive efficiency, 198–199
profit-maximization, 171–172
short-run profit maximization
marginal-revenue–marginal-cost approach, 170–171
total-revenue–total cost approach, 168–170
short-run supply curve, 177
shutdown case, 173–175
and technological advance, 245
total revenue, 167–168
Purely competitive labor market
demand for labor, 274
equilibrium, 274–276
supply of labor, 274
Pure monopoly; *see also* Monopoly
rarity of, 190
Pure profit, 145–146
Pure rate of interest, 299
Purposeful behavior, 4–5
Pyramid, 229

Quantity demanded, 46
change in, 49–50
and equilibrium price, 54–55, 177–178
income effect and, 131–132
and price, 46
substitution effect and, 131–132
Quantity supplied
changes in, 52–53
and equilibrium price, 54–55, 177–178
and price, 50
Quasi-public goods, 73
Quintiles of income, 66, 382–383
U.S. households 1970–2004, 387
Quit rate, 425

Railroads
price discrimination by, 203
regulation errors, 356
Rainer, 228
Rational behavior, 128
Rational self-interest, 4–5
Rationing
of currency, 472
function of prices, 55
problems of price ceilings, 58–59
Rawlings sports equipment, 217
R&D; *see* Research and development
Real flow of economic resources, 41
Real interest rate, 299–300
RealNetworks, 361
Real wage
definition, 272
developed vs. developing countries, 260
long-run trends, 274
and productivity, 272–274
secular growth, 274
Recession
and income elasticity of demand, 117
obstacle to collusion, 225
Reciprocal Trade Agreements Act of 1934, 97
Reebok International, 46, 112
Regressive taxes, 338, 343
Regulated monopoly, 71; *see also* Natural monopoly
Regulation
control of monopolies, 71
dilemma of, 207
optimal amount, 71
Regulatory agencies/commissions
for antitrust policy, 349
industrial regulation, 355
social regulation, 358
Related goods, 49
Relevant market, 351
Remittances, 434
Rent, 293; *see also* Economic rent
Rent controls, 59
Rent-providing legislation, 335
Rent-seeking behavior, 201
of dominant firms, 249
in government, 335
in price supports, 373, 375
from tariffs and quotas, 453–454
Reproductions, 115–116
Republicans, 20
Resale, 203
Research, exploitation of, 237
Research and development
and advertising, 227
as barrier to entry, 201
evidence on, 246–247
expected vs. guaranteed returns, 240
firm's optima amount
conclusions, 239–240
expected rate of return, 238–239
interest rate cost of funds, 237–238
first-mover benefits, 242–244
imitation problem, 242
increased profit from
process innovation, 241–242
product innovation, 240–241
for innovation, 234
for invention, 234
inverted-U theory, 246
and market structure, 245–247
monopolistic competition, 245
monopoly, 246
by oligopolists, 230
oligopoly, 245
and patents, 191–192
pharmaceutical industry, 285
pure competition, 245
as sunk cost, 161
by universities and government, 237
Research and development expenditures
adjustments, 240
by business, 235
expected rate of return, 238–239
by government, 235
growth in U.S. 1980–2005, 244
interest rate cost of funds, 237–238
and interest rates, 299
MB=MC rule, 237–238
optimal, 239–240
on scientific research, 237
Residential farms, 370
Residual claimant, 301
Residual profit, 301
Resource allocation, 255
and economic profit, 303–304
by government, 72–74
and market failure, 72–73
process, 73–74
quasi-public goods, 73
Resource demand
cost minimization, 255
determinants
occupational trends, 261–262
product demand changes, 259
productivity changes, 259–260

resource price changes, 260–261
elasticity
ease of substitutability, 262–263
product demand elasticity, 263
ratio of cost to total cost, 263
least-cost rule, 263
marginal productivity theory of
derived demand, 255
imperfect competition, 257–258
marginal revenue product, 255–256
marginal revenue product/ demand schedule, 256–257
market demand, 258
rule for employing resources, 256
money-income determination, 255
numerical illustration, 264–265
policy issues, 255
profit-maximizing rule, 263–264
resource allocation, 255
X-inefficiency, 264
Resource demand schedule, 256–257
Resource flows, 85
Resource markets, 39–41
and income inequality, 385
Resource prices
and changes in supply, 51
constant-cost industry, 181
decreasing-cost industry, 182
increasing-cost industry, 181–182
ratio to total cost, 263
Resource pricing
complementary resources, 260–261
in imperfect competition, 257–258
in pure competition, 256–257
substitute resources, 260
and unions, 279
Resource reallocation
free-rider problem, 73
public goods and services, 73
Resources, 3–4
allocative efficiency, 55–56, 184
capital, 10
in command systems, 29
complementary, 260–261
and consumer tastes, 36
dynamic adjustments, 184–186
employment of, 34–35
entrepreneurial ability, 10–11
increase in supply, 15
investment, 10
labor, 10
land, 10
limits on use of, 13
in market system, 29
misallocation of, 374, 377
monopoly control of, 192
oligopoly control of, 217
optimal allocation, 13–14
optimal combination of, 264–266
origin of, 254
overallocated in health care, 408–409
overallocation, 72, 372
productivity and abundance of, 273
quality of, 259–260
quantities of other, 259
scarcity of, 4, 10
substitutes, 260
underallocation, 72–73
Restraint of trade, 349
Retained earnings, 237
Revenue, 50
from tariffs, 453
of ten largest corporations, 70
Revenue tariff, 452
Reynolds Aluminum, 234
Ricardo, David, 90
Rigging the market, 385
Right-to-work laws, 421
Risk
of currency speculation, 478–479
and income inequality, 385
insurable, 301
and interest rate range, 298
and profit, 301–302
uninsurable, 301–302
Risk management techniques, 368
Rivalry
in consumption, 310
of private goods, 73
Rock and Roll Hall of Fame, 344
Rodriguez, Alex, 9
Ross, David, 201n
Rouse, Cecilia, 436
Royal Crown Cola, 242
Royal Dutch/Shell, 202
Royalties, 287
Rule of reason, 351, 352
Russia, 29
economic reforms, 89
SAB Miller, 228–229
Saffer, Henry, 113n
St. Louis Cardinals, 190
Sales tax, 80, 338
incidence of, 342
Salsa manufacturers, 58
Samsung, 234, 354
Samuel Adams, 229
Sanders, Harlan, 244
San Francisco rent controls, 59
Saving
by households, 67
for R&D, 238
and trade deficits, 478
Scalping tickets, 55
Scarcity
and budget line, 10–11
and choice, 4
and marginal benefit, 5
and production possibilities table, 11
of resources, 10
Schaefer, 228
Scherer, F. M., 201n
Schmidts, 228
Schotter, Andrew, 398
Schumpeter, Joseph A., 247–248
Scientific method, 5–6
Sears Roebuck, 248
Seattle anti-globalization protests, 458
Seattle Mariners, 190
Security, 67
Security costs, 160
Self-canceling advertising, 229
Self-interest
and invisible hand, 37
in market system, 30–31
Self-sufficiency output mix, 444
Sellers
inadequate information, 322–323
in monopolistic competition, 211
number of, 52
in pure competition, 166–167
Semel, Terry S., 288
Seniority, 421, 425
Service
in monopolistic competition, 211
Service Employees Union, 419
Service-oriented economy, 68
Services, 8
U.S. exports, 88
Shell Oil, 68, 70, 117, 146
Shepherd, William G., 201n
Sherman Antitrust Act, 71
Alcoa case, 351
and Microsoft case, 352, 360
provisions, 349–350
Standard Oil case, 351
United States Steel case, 351
Shock effect of union wages, 424
Shortages, 54–55
of human organs for transplants, 60
from price ceilings, 58–59
from rent controls, 59
Short run
costs of production in, 146
in monopolistic competition, 214
price elasticity of supply, 115
problems in agriculture, 365–368
Short-run adjustment, 146
Short-run cost curves, 160
Short-run profit maximization
marginal-revenue-marginal-cost approach, 170–171
total-revenue-total-cost approach, 168–170
Short-run supply curve, 177
Shutdown case, 174–175
Silverman, Henry R., 288
Simultaneous consumption, 200
Singapore, 89
Single-channel marketing, 206
Single seller, 190
Single-tax movement
criticisms of, 294–295
proposal, 294
Skilled workers, 386–387
Slope
infinite vs. zero, 24
and marginal analysis, 23
and measurement units, 23
negative, 23
of a nonlinear curve, 24–25
positive, 23
of a straight line, 23
Smith, Adam, 37, 89–90, 132, 286
Smithfield, 365
Smoot-Hawley Tariff of 1930, 96, 456
Social insurance
health care coverage, 401–402
programs, 392
Socialists, 294
Socially optimal price, 205
Social regulation, 348
compliance costs, 360
criticisms of, 359
definition, 358
features of, 358
less vs. more government, 360–361
no-free-lunch theory, 360
optimal level of, 358–359

Social regulation—*Cont.*
  regulatory commissions, 358
  support for, 358–359
Social Security, 324
  description, 392–393
  in government spending, 77
  long-run shortfall, 78–79
  pay-as-you-go program, 78
  payroll tax, 338
  payroll taxes, 80
  reform proposals, 79
Social Security Administration, 78–79
Social Security trust fund, 78
Sole proprietorships, 68
Sony Corporation, 94, 202
Sony Walkman, 243
Sotheby's, 354
South African Breweries, 229
South Korea, 89
  strategic trade policy, 455
Soviet Union, 29, 38
Special interest effect, 334–335
  and price supports, 375
Specialization
  Adam Smith on, 89–90
  and allocative efficiency, 448
  based on comparative advantage, 444–445
  and comparative advantage, 89–92
  and different cost ratios, 448
  division of labor, 32
  exchange ratios, 448
  and free trade, 448
  gains from, 91–92
  gains from trade, 445–446
  geographic, 32
  in market system, 32
  terms of trade, 445
  and trade, 18
  and trading possibilities line, 445–446
Specific tax
  to correct externalities, 316–317
  to deal with pollution, 72
  excise tax, 342
Speculation, 469
  reason for saving, 67
Spillovers, 72
Spreading the overhead, 152
Sprint PLC, 353
Sprite, 117
Stabilization policies
  and flexible exchange rates, 471
  and gold standard, 473–474
  for inflation, 74
  for unemployment, 74
Standardized product, 166–167
Standard of living, 456
Standard Oil case, 202, 350–351
Staples, 353
Starbucks Coffee Company, 160, 236, 245
Start-up costs, 158
Start-up firms, 160, 236
State finances, 80
State government
  Medicaid payments, 404
  minimum wage laws, 282
  public utility commissions, 355
  regressive taxes, 343
  usury laws, 300
State-run lotteries, 80
Static economy, 301
Statistical discrimination, 429
Stock, 69
Stock market
  bubble of 1990s, 70
  crash of 1929, 17
Stock of wealth, 385
Stock options, 70, 287
  for CEOs, 288
  negative side effects, 289
Strategic behavior, 217
Strategic trade policy, 455
Strauss, Levi, 236
Street entertainers, 74
Strikebreakers, 420
Strikes, 422
  losses due to, 423
Structural-change hypothesis of union decline, 420
Structuralists, 351
Subsidies, 75; *see also* Agricultural subsidies
  and changes in supply, 51
  to correct externalities, 317
  to correct for positive externalities, 73
  to exports, 95
  for health care, 408
Substitutability
  and cross elasticity of demand, 116
  of farm products, 365
  importance of, 117
  and price elasticity of demand, 112
  of resources, 263
Substitute resources
  net effect, 260
  output effect, 260
  substitution effect, 260
Substitutes, 49
  and change in demand, 49
  DVDs and videocassettes, 132
  lacking for monopoly, 190
Substitution effect, 46, 365
  and labor demand, 260
  and utility maximization, 131–132
Substitution in production, 52
Sugar program, 375, 376–377
Sulfur-dioxide emission credits, 319
Sunk costs, irrelevance of, 161
Sun Microsystems, 360
Superior goods, 48
Supplemental Security Income, 393, 402
  for immigrants, 435
Supplier-induced demand, 406–407
Suppliers, subsidies for, 73
Supply; *see also* Price elasticity of supply
  in beer industry, 228
  changes
    in loanable funds, 297
    in pure competition, 177
  changes in, 51–52, 56–57
  decrease and demand increase, 56
  definition, 50
  determinants of, 51
  excess, 54
  factors in health care costs
    medical technology, 410
    number of physicians, 409
    slow productivity growth, 409–410
  increase and demand decrease, 56
  increase and demand increase, 56
  of land inelastic, 293
  law of supply, 50
  of loanable funds, 296
  long-run
    constant-cost industry, 181
    decreasing-cost industry, 182
    increasing-cost industry, 181–182
  market supply, 50–51
  in pure competition, 177–178
  restrictions on, 373–374
  short-run, 175–178
Supply and demand analysis
  complexities, 56–57
  diamond-water paradox, 132–133
  dollar-yen market, 93–94
  efficiency loss of taxes, 340–342
  of exports and imports, 448–451
  foreign exchange market, 94
  government-set prices, 55–61
  health insurance, 408–409
  labor market, 274–276
  land, 293–295
  market equilibrium, 53–57
  organ transplants, 60–61
  of price controls, 57–61
  of real wage, 272–274
  of tax incidence, 339–340
  ticket scalping, 55
  of wage differentials, 283–286
Supply curve, 50
  and consumer/producer surplus, 120
  exports, 449–451
  lacking for monopolist, 196–197
  on negative externalities, 72
  public goods, 312
Supply elasticities, 341
Supply of pounds curve, 467, 468
Supply schedule, 50
  competitive firms, 175–177
Supply shifters, 51
Surgeons, licensing of, 323
Surgery, 407
Surpluses, 54
  from price floors, 59
  reduction
    by bolstering demand, 374
    by restricting supply, 373–374
Surplus output, 372
Surplus payment, 294, 295
Survey of Consumer Finances, 396
Swift Meatpackers, 365
Symphony orchestras, 436

Tacit understandings, 225
Taco Bell, 128, 353
Taft-Hartley Act of 1947, 422
Taiwan, 89
Tandy Radio Shack, 246
Tangent, 25
Tariffs
  abolished in European Union, 89
  antidumping duties, 455
  costs to society, 96
  definition, 451–452
  direct effects
    decline in consumption, 452
    decline in imports, 453
    domestic production increased, 452–453
    revenue, 453
  economic impact, 452–453
  under GATT, 97–98
  general decline in, 88
  indirect effects, 453
  legislation 1860–2001, 96
  net costs of, 453–454

protective, 452
rates in U.S. 1860–2005, 96
reduced in 1934, 97
revenue, 452
Smoot-Hawley Tariff Act, 456
under World Trade Organization, 97–98
Taste-for-discrimination model
competition and, 428–429
definition, 427
discrimination coefficient, 427–428
by musical directors, 436
prejudice, 428
Tastes; *see* Consumer tastes
Taxable income, 78
Taxation, 336–344
ability-to-pay principle, 337
benefits-received principle, 337
and changes in supply, 51
corporate income tax, 80, 338
to correct externalities, 316–317
to correct for negative externalities, 72
earned-income tax credit, 393
effect on income inequality, 384
effect on price floors, 60
efficiency loss, 340–342
excise taxes, 80
federal revenues, 77–80
global perspective, 77, 343
impact of immigration, 435
for income redistribution, 71
and interest rate range, 298–299
by local government, 80
payroll taxes, 80, 338
personal income tax, 78–79, 338
personal taxes, 67
progressive, 337–338
property tax, 80, 338–339
proportional, 337–338
for public goods, 75
redistributive goals, 341
to reduce externalities, 341–342
regressive, 337–338
repeal of luxury tax, 341
sales tax, 338
by states, 80
U.S. structure, 343–344
Tax brackets, 78
Tax burden, 337, 339
and demand elasticities, 339–340
division of, 339
of price supports, 372, 373
Tax credits, 411
Tax Freedom Day, 76–77
Taxicab licensing, 192
Tax incidence
corporate income tax, 342
definition, 339
elasticities, 339–340
excise tax, 342
personal income tax, 342
property taxes, 342–343
sales tax, 342
Tax rates, 78–79, 338
Tax rate tables, 346
Tax shifting, 342
Tax subsidy for health care, 408
Teams, entrepreneurial, 236
Teamsters Union, 419
Teaser rates, 303
Technological advance, 15–16
allocative efficiency, 247
creative destruction, 247–248
definition, 233–234
from deregulation, 357
determinant of supply, 52
diffusion of, 234–235
evidence on, 246–247
and farm supply increases, 368–369
fast-second strategy, 242
first-mover benefits
brand-name recognition, 243
copyrights, 243
learning by doing, 243
patents, 242–243
profitable buyouts, 243–244
time lags, 243
trademarks, 243
trade secrets, 243, 244
and health care costs, 410–411
imitation problem, 242
by innovation, 234
Internet, 248–249
by invention, 234
inverted-U theory, 246
and least-cost rule, 267
in market system, 36–37
modern view of, 235–236
monopolistic competition, 245
and monopoly, 201, 246
by oligopolists, 230
oligopoly, 245
optimal amount of R&D, 237–240
personal computer, 248–249
productive efficiency, 247
profit from product innovation, 240–241
pure competition, 245
R&D expenditures, 235
reduced cost from process innovation, 241–242
and resource demand, 259
role of entrepreneurs, 236–237
role of market structure, 244–247
very long run, 234
Technology
and changes in supply, 51
in market system, 31–32
medical, 410
and productivity, 273
Technology flows, 85
Teenage unemployment, 282
Telecommunications industry deregulation, 357
Telephone industry
deregulation, 357
regulation, 356
Temporary Assistance for Needy Families, 324, 393, 395, 401–402
Temporary workers, 403
Tennessee Valley Authority, 355
Terms of trade, 91, 445
and flexible exchange rates, 471
Terrorist attack of 2001, 14, 160
Theories of behavior, 6
Third-party payments, 405–406
3Com Corporation, 236
3M Corporation, 236
Ticket scalping, 55
Time
and costs of production, 146
and elasticity of supply, 115
and input substitution, 263
market period, 114–115
and price elasticity of demand, 112
saved by specialization, 32
value to consumers, 133
Time lags, 243
Time Warner, 227, 353
Title VII of the Civil Rights Act, 428
Topel, Robert, 404
Topographical map, 141
Total cost, 34
definition, 151
ratio of resource cost to, 263
Total output, 303
Total product, 147
and law of diminishing returns, 148–150
Total profit
monopoly goal, 197
from new products, 241
versus per-unit profit, 172
Total revenue, 34, 108
in pure competition, 167–168
Total revenue curve, 111
of monopolist, 194
Total revenue test
and elastic demand, 108–109
and inelastic demand, 109–110
lacking for elasticity of supply, 115
and monopoly, 195
price elasticity along a linear demand curve, 110–111
and unit elasticity, 110
Total-revenue–total-cost approach, 168–170
Total utility
definition, 126
diamond-water paradox, 133
and income distribution, 388–389
indifference curves, 139
and marginal utility, 126–128
for new products, 241
Toxic waste laws, 316
Toyota Motor Company, 70, 202, 227, 423
Tradable emission allowances, 319
Trade adjustment assistance, 456–457
Trade Adjustment Assistance Act, 457
Trade barriers; *see also* Protectionism
export subsidies, 95
on farm products, 373
impact of quotas, 453
impact of tariffs, 452–453
import quotas, 95, 452
net costs of, 453–454
nontariff barriers, 95, 452
protectionism, 95–96
protectionist arguments, 455–457
protective tariffs, 95
strategic trade policy, 455
tariffs, 451–452
trade war, 96
voluntary export restrictions, 452
Trade blocs, 89
Trade deficit, 87–88, 442
causes
capital account surplus, 478
low saving rate, 478
oil prices, 478
with China, 478–479
definition, 465
implications
increased consumption, 479
increased indebtedness, 479–480
of U.S. 1994–2005, 477–480

Trade deficit—*Cont.*
unknown long-term impact, 480
Trade flows, 84
Trademarks, 243
Tradeoffs, and budget line, 9
Trade patterns, 87–88
Trade policies, 472
Trade secrets, 243, 244
Trade surplus, 87–88, 442, 465
Trade war, 96, 454
Trading possibilities line, 445–446
Tragedy of the commons, 317–318
Training
costs in medicine, 398
and income inequality, 385
informal, 425
and wage differentials, 284–285
Transferable warranties, 322
Transfer payments, 71; *see also* Income-maintenance system
effect on income inequality, 384
percentage of output, 75–76
under welfare, 394–395
Transistor, 248
Transportation technology, 88
Treble damages, 349
Trump, Donald, 7
Trusts, 349
good vs. bad, 351
Truth in Lending Act, 303
Truth in Saving Act, 303
Turnover, 424–425
Twain, Shania, 259
Tying contracts
definition, 350
effectiveness of antitrust, 354
Tyson Foods, 365

UCAR International, 354
Ultrasound machines, 410
Unattainable combinations, 8–9
Unauthorized immigrants, 433
Uncertainty
and economic profit, 301–302
of flexible exchange rates, 471
and monopoly, 303
new products, 302
Unearned income, 294
Unemployment
effect of minimum wage, 282
government policies for, 74
in Great Depression, 14
and immigration, 435
in production possibilities curve, 14–15
teenage, 282
from union-induced wages, 280–281
Unemployment compensation, 393
Unfair trade practices, 455
Unhealthy lifestyles, 406
Unilever, 89, 202
Uninsurable risks, 301–302
Unionism; *see also* Labor unions
business unionism, 419
decline of
managerial-opposition hypothesis, 420
structural-change hypothesis, 420
independent unions, 419
in United States, 419–420
urban phenomenon, 420
Unions; *see* Labor unions
Union shop, 421
Union status, 421
United Auto Workers, 419
United Parcel Service, 227, 346
United States
debtor nation, 479
number of immigrants 1950–2004, 433
sources of immigrants, 433
United States dollar
and Big Mac index, 469
and British pounds, 463, 467–471
depreciation, 467, 468
exchange rates for, 462
as international money, 475
international value of, 94
marginal utility per, 129
with pegged exchange rates, 475
United States economy
advantages of corporations, 68–69
annual sales of corporations, 69
before antitrust policy, 349
balance of payments deficits, 475
balance of payments in 2005, 464
business population, 68
causes of trade deficits, 477–478
CEO pay, 288
comparative advantage, 443–448
current account deficits, 466
dependence on foreign oil, 442
export supply curve, 449
export transaction, 463
family wealth, 396
farm employment, 370
farm exports, 367–368
fastest-growing occupations, 261–262
functional distribution of income, 66
and government purchases, 75–76
growth in R&D expenditures, 244
health care spending, 401–402
implications of trade deficits, 478–480
import demand curve, 449–450
imports, 442
import transaction, 463
income inequality, 381
income shares, 304
international linkages, 84
legal forms of business, 68
long-run wage trends, 274
number of households, 66
number of workers, 271
official reserves in 2005, 466
as open economy, 89
output and hourly pay, 273
personal consumption spending, 67–68
personal distribution of income, 66–67
personal saving, 67
personal taxes, 67
poverty line, 390
principal-agent problem, 69–70
principal exports, 442
production possibilities analysis, 90–91
rapidly declining occupations, 262
R&D expenditures, 235
service-oriented, 68
tariff rates 1860–2005, 96
ten largest advertisers, 227
ten largest corporations, 70
trade deficits, 442, 477–480
trade surplus, 442
and transfer payments, 75–76
unionism in, 419–420
value of output, 65
in world trade
dependence on other countries, 86–87
exports and imports by area, 87
exports of services, 88
foreign oil, 88
and new participants, 89
principal exports and imports, 87
prominence in, 89
rapid growth, 88
trade deficit, 87–88
trade patterns, 87–88
trade surplus, 87–88
trade with Canada, 87
trade with China, 87–88
volume of trade, 85–86
United States International Trade Commission, 461
United States Postal Service, 201, 346, 355
United States Steel case, 351
United States Supreme Court
affirmative action rulings, 432
antitrust rulings, 350–351
defining relevant market, 351
on fair-price return, 207
United States tax structure, 343–344
United Steelworkers, 419
Unit elasticity
definition, 107
and total revenue test, 110
Universal access to health care, 411–412
University research, 237
Unlimited wants, 7–8
Unrelated goods, 49
Uruguay Round, 97
Used car market, 322
U-shaped long-run average-total-cost curve, 156
Usury laws
gainers and losers, 300
inefficiency of, 300
nonmarket rationing, 300
Utility, 4
and consumer surplus, 118
definition, 126
law of diminishing marginal utility, 126
marginal utility, 126–128
measurement of, 141–142
total utility, 126–128
Utility maximization
income distribution, 388
for new products, 240
Utility-maximizing rule
algebraic restatement, 130–131
definition, 129
and demand curve, 131–132
diamond-water paradox, 132–133
income effect, 131–132
numerical example
decision-making process, 129–130
inferior goods, 130
marginal utility per dollar, 129

substitution effect, 131–132
Utils, 126

Variable costs
in agriculture, 366
definition, 150, 151
security workers, 160
Variable plant capacity, 146
Vending machines, 126
Venture capital for R&D, 237–238
Verizon Communications, 227
Verson stamping machines, 160
Vertical axis, 21
Vertical intercept, 24
Vertically integrated firms, 68
Vertical mergers
and antitrust law, 353–354
definition, 353
Very long run, 234
Videocassette players, 132
Voice mechanism, 424–425
Voluntary export restrictions, 452
Voting
inefficiency outcomes, 331–332
and logrolling, 332
median-voter model, 333–334
paradox of, 332–333
revealing preferences, 331–333
Voting with their feet, 334
Vouchers for health care, 411

Wage(s), 66; *see also* Compensation
in bilateral monopoly, 281
in collective bargaining, 421
definition, 272
efficiency wages, 287
equilibrium, 277
global perspective, 272
and health care costs, 403
incentive pay plan, 287
income shares, 304
increased by unions, 280–281
nominal, 272
and output, 273
pay for performance, 286–287
real, 272
real wage and productivity, 273
role of productivity, 272–273
secular growth of real wage, 274
in selected occupations, 283
shock effect for firms, 424
union-produced goods and, 420
unions and labor misallocation, 423–424
and workplaces safety, 325
Wage differentials, 282–286
compensating differences, 285
and costs of migration, 434
marginal revenue productivity, 284
market imperfections, 285–286
discrimination, 286
geographic immobility, 286
government restraints, 286
lack of job information, 286
unions, 286
noncompeting groups
by ability, 284
by education and training, 284–285
reasons for, 283–284
Wage discrimination, 425–426
Wage insurance, 457
Wage maker, 256–257
Wage rates, 272
above-equilibrium, 280
in craft unions, 279
in demand-enhancement model, 278
equilibrium, 274
and immigration, 434
industrial unions, 280
marginal revenue cost of labor, 257
minimum wage, 282
in monopsony model, 277
national differences, 272
and taste-for-discrimination model, 427–428
union advantage, 420, 422
Wage taker, 255, 256–257
Wagner Act of 1935, 422
Waitt, Ted, 249
Wall Street Journal, 410
Wal-Mart Stores, 68, 70, 137, 233–234, 241–242, 247, 304
Walt Disney Company, 227, 353
Wants, 3–4
coincidence of, 32
unlimited, 7–8
War, economics of, 14
War on terrorism, 73
Water pollution, 72
Water quality credits, 319
Wealth
as stock, 385
unequal distribution, 385
of U.S. families, 396
Wealth of Nations (Smith), 37
Welfare
common features, 394
conflicts among goals, 395
culture of, 395
immigrants on, 435
reform of, 395
Wendy's, 325
Western Union, 190, 278
Wham-O, 190
What to produce, 34–35
Wheat price floors, 59–61
Wheeler-Lea Act, 350
Wilkinson blades, 242
Wilson sporting goods, 85, 217
Windows operating system, 190
Windows 95 operating system, 249
Winfrey, Oprah, 9, 381
Winner-take-all markets, 259
Winston, Clifford, 357n
Women
and affirmative action, 431–432
and labor market discrimination, 425–427
in labor unions, 420
occupational segregation, 286, 429–430
orchestra hiring, 436
Woods, Tiger, 381
Work agreement
cost-of-living adjustments, 421
grievance procedures, 421
managerial prerogatives, 421
seniority and job protection, 421
union status, 421
wages and hours, 421
Worker alienation, 159
Workers
in advanced nations, 260
and antiunion efforts, 420
exit mechanism, 424
in health care, 401
income of, 266
and interests of firm, 287
international movement of, 434
job-conscious, 421
low-wage, 405
part-time, 403
quit rate, 425
reduced turnover, 424–425
skilled vs. unskilled, 435
temporary, 403
voice mechanism, 424–425
Workplace safety, 325
Work rules, 423
Work stoppages, 422
WorldCom, 70, 353
World exchange ratio, 445
World Trade Organization
critics of, 97
establishment of, 458
and farm price supports, 377
origin and functions, 97–98
proponents of, 97–98
protests against, 458–459
World Wide Web, 249

Xerox Corporation, 191, 248
X-inefficiency, 200–201, 264
industrial regulation, 356

Yahoo!, 249
Yang, Jerry, 249
Yum! Brands, 353

Zero slope, 24

Relevant economic statistics, selected years, 1983–2005

	1983	1984	1985	1986	1987	1988	1989	1990	1991	1992
1 Sales by manufacturers (billions of dollars)*	2,114.3	2,335.0	2,331.4	2,220.9	2,378.2	2,596.2	2,745.1	2,810.7	2,761.1	2,890.2
2 Profits by manufacturers (billions of dollars)*	133.1	165.6	137.0	129.3	173.0	215.3	187.6	158.1	98.7	31.4
3 After-tax manufacturing profits per dollar of sales (cents)*	4.1	4.6	3.8	3.7	4.9	5.9	4.9	3.9	2.4	0.8
4 Index of business sector productivity (1992 = 100)	83.0	85.2	87.1	89.7	90.1	91.5	92.4	94.4	95.9	100.0
5 Annual change in business sector productivity (%)	3.6	2.7	2.2	2.9	0.5	1.5	1.0	2.1	1.6	4.3
6 Nonagricultural employees in goods-producing industries (millions)	22.1	23.4	23.6	23.3	23.5	23.9	24.0	23.7	22.6	22.1
7 Nonagricultural employees in service-producing industries (millions)	68.2	71.1	73.9	76.2	78.6	81.4	84.0	85.8	85.8	86.6
8 Compensation of employees (billions of dollars)	2,042.6	2,255.6	2,424.7	2,570.1	2,750.2	2,967.3	3,145.2	3,338.2	3,445.2	3,635.4
9 Average weekly hours in private nonagricultural industries**	40.1	40.7	40.5	40.7	40.9	41.0	40.9	40.5	40.4	40.7
10 Average hourly earnings in private nonagricultural industries (dollars)	8.19	8.48	8.73	8.92	9.13	9.43	9.80	10.19	10.50	10.76
11 Average weekly earnings in private nonagricultural industries (dollars)	285.83	297.65	304.68	309.52	316.81	326.28	338.10	349.25	358.06	367.83
12 Federal minimum wage rate (dollars per hour)	3.35	3.35	3.35	3.35	3.35	3.35	3.35	3.80	4.25	4.25
13 Prime interest rate (%)	10.79	12.04	9.93	8.33	8.21	9.32	10.87	10.01	8.46	6.25
14 Ten-year Treasury bond interest rate (%)	11.10	12.44	10.62	7.68	8.39	8.85	8.49	8.55	7.86	7.01
15 Net farm income (billions of dollars)	14.3	26.0	28.6	31.1	38.0	39.6	46.5	46.3	40.2	50.7
16 Index of prices received by farmers (1990–1992 = 100)	98	101	91	87	89	99	104	104	100	98
17 Index of prices paid by farmers (1990–1992 = 100)	86	89	86	85	87	91	96	99	100	101
18 Persons below poverty level (millions)	35.3	33.7	33.1	32.4	32.2	31.7	31.5	33.6	35.7	38.0
19 Poverty rate (% of population)	15.2	14.4	14.0	13.6	13.4	13.0	12.8	13.5	14.2	14.8
20 Gini ratios for household income distribution (range = 0–1)	0.414	0.415	0.419	0.425	0.426	0.427	0.431	0.428	0.428	0.434
21 U.S. goods exports (billions of dollars)	201.8	219.9	215.9	223.3	250.2	320.2	359.9	387.4	414.1	439.6
22 U.S. goods imports (billions of dollars)	268.9	332.4	338.1	368.4	409.8	447.7	477.2	498.4	491.0	536.5
23 Trade balance on current account (billions of dollars)	−38.7	−94.3	−118.2	−147.2	−160.7	−121.2	−99.5	−79.0	2.9	−50.1
24 Industry R&D expenditures (billions of dollars)	63.7	73.1	82.4	85.9	90.2	94.9	99.9	107.4	114.7	116.7
25 Price of crude oil (U.S. average, dollars per barrel)	29.08	28.75	26.92	14.44	17.75	14.87	18.33	23.19	20.20	19.25

*Revised definition for this series beginning in 1973.

**Includes overtime.

***Revised data that might not exactly match text data.